Kingdom of Sicily
1130-1266

Also by Louis Mendola and Jacqueline Alio

The Peoples of Sicily
A Multicultural Legacy

Sicilian Studies
A Guide and Syllabus for Educators

Norman-Arab-Byzantine
Palermo, Monreale and Cefalù

Sicilian Court Culture 1061-1266

Kingdom of Sicily 1130-1266
Study Guide

By Jacqueline Alio

Queens of Sicily 1061-1266

Sicilian Queenship
Power and Identity in the Kingdom of Sicily 1061-1266

The Ferraris Chronicle
(translation and notes)

Margaret, Queen of Sicily

Women of Sicily
Saints, Queens and Rebels

Notes on Norman-Swabian Sicily
New Research in Old Sources

By Louis Mendola

The Kingdom of Sicily 1130-1860

Sicilian Genealogy and Heraldry

The Kingdom of the Two Sicilies 1734-1861

Sicily's Rebellion against King Charles
The Story of the Sicilian Vespers by John of Procida
(translation and notes)

Frederick, Conrad and Manfred of Hohenstaufen, Kings of Sicily
The Chronicle of Nicholas of Jamsilla
(translation and notes)

The Battle of Benevento according to Andrew of Hungary and Saba Malaspina
(translation and notes)

SICILIAN MEDIEVAL STUDIES

Kingdom of Sicily
1130-1266

The Norman-Swabian Age and the Identity of a People

Louis Mendola · Jacqueline Alio

Copyright © 2021 Louis A.M. Mendola. All rights reserved.

Published by Trinacria Editions, New York.

This book may not be reproduced by any means whatsoever, in whole or in part, including illustrations, photographs and maps, in any form beyond the fair-use copying permitted by the United States Copyright Law and the Berne Convention, except by reviewers for the public press (magazines, newspapers and their websites), without written permission from the copyright holder.

The right of Louis André Mendola and Calogera Jacqueline Alio to be identified as the authors of this work has been asserted by them in accordance with the Copyright, Design and Patents Act, 1988 (UK).

Legal Deposit: Library of Congress, British Library (and Bodleian Libraries, Cambridge University Library, Trinity College Library, National Libraries of Scotland and Wales), Italian National Libraries (Rome, Florence).

This book, of which the text was completed in September 2021, was assigned a Library of Congress Control Number on 14 September 2021 with the title *Kingdom of Sicily 1130-1266: The Norman-Swabian Age and the Identity of a People*. Identifying information was registered by the British Library through Bibliographic Data Services on 15 September 2021 under ALDL number 1.4214609 (Acq 5137878.1). Pre-registration was effected with the United States Copyright Office on 14 January 2023 under number PRE000012713 (as a literary work in book form). Some material contained herein previously appeared in other books by these authors for which they hold the copyrights and is used by permission.

Except where otherwise indicated, all translations contained herein are by the authors. Illustrations, photographs, maps, tables, image editing and cover design by Louis Mendola. Additional credits in acknowledgments. The text of this monograph was peer-reviewed.

ORCID identifiers: Louis André Mendola 0000-0002-1965-6072, Calogera Jacqueline Alio 0000-0003-1134-1217

Printed in the United States of America on acid-free paper.

10 9 8 7 6 5 4 3

ISBN 9781943639397 (softcover)
ISBN 9781943639403 (hardcover)
ISBN 9781943639410 (ebook)

Library of Congress Control Number 2021947177

A CIP catalogue record for this book is available from the British Library.

I, Gregory, invest you, Robert, as the Duke of those lands bequeathed upon you by my predecessors Nicholas and Alexander, of saintly memory.

— Pope Gregory VII to Robert Hauteville at Ceprano, June 1080

Adelaide, as *Malaka* of Sicily, commands the nobles and *caïds* of our city of Kasr'Janni, owing fealty to us, to heed this order to refrain from disturbing the monks of the Monastery of Saint Philip, and to be faithful to them and give them protection.

— Adelaide, Countess of Sicily, in Messina, March 1109

The Queen, being a wise and prudent woman, and knowing well the spirit of the populace, which was very disturbed for the mistreatment the subjects had endured under the late William I, undertook through copious concessions to instill their love and fealty toward her son. Acting on sage counsel, she opened the jails and released many prisoners, restoring their lands and forgiving their debts.

— Hugh Falcandus writing about Queen Margaret in Palermo, May 1166

Do not forget what I am saying to you now, Tancred. Before long, your rising star shall turn against you, just as my star has fallen upon me. Destiny cannot be changed. I do not seek "your" kingdom but that of my father, which is mine by right. Are you Roger's son? Not by any means. I am the king's universal heiress because I am his legitimate child by my mother. The legal rights of both my parents bequeath me the realm you presently hold as a usurper.

— Queen Constance, speaking to King Tancred in Messina, September 1191

Know all of you here with me today, that I can not help but be content. Here I will either live or die. If I emerge victorious, no greater joy awaits me, for I will no longer fear any other mortal. If I die, I will die as a king who gloriously ended his reign fighting for his kingdom. Let nobody think that there exists the third possibility of being taken alive.

— King Manfred at the Battle of Benevento, February 1266

Creation of the Kingdom: Roger II crowned by Christ in an engraving based on a mosaic in Palermo's Martorana

FOREWORD

It is a pleasure to write a brief preface to this weighty book – weighty in both senses of the term, since it is not just substantial in length but based on careful reading of masses of primary and secondary literature.

The study of the Norman Kingdom of Sicily and of the reign of Frederick II has advanced in leaps and bounds over the roughly fifty years that have passed since the death of the founder of Norman Sicilian studies in the English-speaking world, Evelyn Jamison, who spent her academic career at Lady Margaret Hall in the University of Oxford. Anglo-American fascination with the Sicilian kingdom can be traced further, for instance to the rather general comments of Charles Homer Haskins, of Harvard University, an American historian of considerable influence. But Miss Jamison was the first scholar in the Anglosphere to delve deeply into the archives of the *Regno,* beginning her research before the First World War.

The explosion in Norman Sicilian studies has not, however, been accompanied by an explosion in the number of reliable and readable general books about the period, and the same is true of Frederick II, who has been the subject of many new studies in Italian, French and German, while my own biography of the emperor dates back an incredible (to me) thirty-five years, and is much more widely read in its Italian translation, still in print, than in the original English text.

Therefore, it is right to welcome this account of the *Regno* during the twelfth and early thirteenth centuries, which is accompanied by fascinating material on the legacy of south Italian and Sicilian culture in modern Italy.

I have always fought keenly against the idea that the history of Italy is the history of the north and centre and that the south and the islands are of negligible importance.

The history of Italy also needs to be written from a southern perspective, and Louis Mendola and Jacqueline Alio have been able to exploit their deep familiarity with the region to produce this innovative book. Their enthusiasm for the subject matter is visible on every page.

— David Abulafia

Professor Emeritus of Mediterranean History, University of Cambridge
Commendatore dell'Ordine della Stella d'Italia

Cambridge
March 2023

EXORDIUM

The moment has arrived to break the silence of seven centuries.

Can a thing of the medieval past be resurrected so long after its presumed demise? Can significant facts and truths about it still be unearthed and shared? The authors of this work know of at least one place in Europe where such things can still be discovered, interpreted and cherished.

Welcome to the Kingdom of Sicily, where facts, realities and traditions are ubiquitous long after the disappearance of the state whose history is the subject of the following pages.

This is not just a book of history. It is a journey to a time and place about which many have written but few have made a sufficient effort to understand. There are historians aplenty, but the best among them are more than scholars and educators. The most effective historians are inspirers, guides to lead you, the curious reader, along a route that most of the other scholars have overlooked.

"Disseminating sound knowledge is one of the most virtuous acts of righteousness," said Malik ibn Anas, whose ideas shaped jurisprudence in Muslim Sicily.

Important as they are, the names, dates and commentary typical of published histories are only the beginning of the experience of discovery. This work presents myriad historical details of that kind, but it offers much more, such as insights into the ethnic origins of the people of a kingdom that existed in some form until 1861. It does not, strictly speaking, propose a novel paradigm so much as what some may view as a rather fresh approach, with new ways to see old facts.

Accurate, genuine history was never meant to be a secret reserved to a few specialized researchers. Here two scholars take a great many pages to scratch into the patina of the centuries to reveal the immutable essence of the Kingdom of Sicily. This is history told from the point of view of those who encounter its living legacy every day. In that respect, it differs from most of the texts written about this subject in English in the original.

"Any fool can know," declared Albert Einstein. "The point is to understand."

Be it agreed that a knowledge of the collective past is important, its presentation reflects an eclectic range of approaches. Many general histories and specialized academic monographs authored by scholars outside the place about which they write are efficacious for essential facts, documentary research and perhaps analysis. Yet no researcher, however diligent, can begin to grasp the implications and effects of history without a personal, firsthand knowledge of the place and its people. That place is southern Italy, and the authors of this volume are two of those people.

In most cases, a historian chooses a subject; in rarer instances, such as this one, the subject chooses the historian. For the authors of this work, being historians dedicated to southern Italy is not simply *what* they are, it's *who* they are. While it is part of the authors' métier, the effort leading to this volume is far more than that. As autohistory, it reflects the duty of Anglophone scholars in southern Italy to make their medieval heritage known to a wider global readership.

"I definitely think one's background helps to determine how to approach one's subject," noted David Abulafia. "In my case the Sephardim and the Mediterranean."

In academic parlance, autohistory is defined as a work of history written by scholars having multigenerational roots in the nation, territory or ethnic group to which the work refers. This reflects the principle that people have an inherent, God-given right to write their own history, which gave birth to their identity, instead of having others write it for them. History, by its very nature, is an essential element in defining who we are. For that reason and others, the vital work of writing the history of the Kingdom of Sicily, or any region, must be undertaken by those whose ancestors forged the story of that place so many centuries ago. They are its guardians, charged with the duty of preserving its tangible legacy, but also much that is intangible.

"Those who tell the stories," said Plato, "rule society." At the very least, they are the masters of their own identities.

EXORDIUM

This work differs from most others in another important way. It is the first general history of its subject written collaboratively, chapter by chapter, by a woman and a man, as an authorial couple, thus reflecting both female and male perspectives about a great many topics. The authors could be said to have initiated the trend of couples writing the history of southern Italy in English with *The Peoples of Sicily* in 2013.

This book is but the first step in a voyage of discovery, to be realized in its fullness with your visit to the former realm, beginning, perhaps, with its remarkable royal capital. In this singular city, you can follow the paths of kings, queens, bishops, knights and the millions of ordinary people of the kingdom's complex chessboard.

Here you can touch history. And history will touch you.

Buon viaggio!

— Louis Mendola and Jacqueline Alio

Panormus, Regnum Siciliae
Septembris MMXXI, Safar 1443, Tishrei 5782

Rogerian Legend: This engraving from the 1675 edition of Summonte's history depicts Roger II in a quasi-mystical manner, yet very little is known about his named sword (see note 366) and he did not use a coat of arms (see note 401).

PREFACE

Complexity. Diversity. Particularity. There are moments that define a people and their society, rendering them unlike what came before or after. Moments disappear into the long shadows of the centuries. Stories live forever, transporting us back in time to discover something about our ancestors, our heroes and ourselves.

History is time's immemorial gift to us. We seek to learn something about the past because, in the words of Cicero: "Those who are ignorant of what happened before their own births will always be children."

Learning about history should be more than a purely academic exercise. History can inspire us. It lives and breathes as an integral part of the heritage of a people. It cannot be appreciated, or even studied very closely, without a profound knowledge about the society and culture it represents. This interconnectivity is key to understanding the past and how it shaped the present.

The formal telling of history begins with the stories told by those witnessing its unfolding development and evolution. No less a figure than Diodorus Siculus could have written the foundational history of ancient Sicily, the place of his birth. Later, the tradition established by historians of his era was propagated during the Middle Ages by local chroniclers such as Godfrey Malaterra, and then, during the age of printing, by Thomas Fazello, Angelo Di Costanzo, Giovanni Summonte and others we shall meet.

The epoch that is the subject of this work was a singular moment in time nurtured by the aspirations of singular monarchs, and it is worthy of our attention, indeed our reverence, for here, wrapped in the wrinkled fabric of ten centuries, is to be found the eternal lesson of strength and unity in diversitude. Much in the medieval cultures of the Kingdom of Sicily has survived in some way, an eternal flame that sometimes flickers but is never extinguished.

KINGDOM OF SICILY

This book is about an unusual – even unique – era in European and Mediterranean medieval history, a long moment that has much to bequeath us. In our story, the place and its people are at least as significant as the leaders and their politics. They are the beating heart of a timeless spirit.

Our journey is part of a millennial memory. The year 2016 marked ten centuries since the known arrival of the Normans in southern Italy.

We find in the Kingdom of Sicily that flourished under Hauteville and Hohenstaufen rule the roots of the social culture of southern Italy that we know today. Before their tolerant, polycultural society gave way, in 1266, to the rise of an overwhelmingly Latin monoculture overseen by dynasties from France and Spain, the peoples of this region could claim a kind of equilibrium under the watchful eye of enlightened monarchs raised in the kingdom they ruled.

The multicultural Kingdom of Sicily exemplified what in our times is occasionally called *exceptionalism*.

This is the story of how several cultures merged to become one. Not that the kingdom's society was ever perfect, either in its final manifestation or at any of the steps along the way. In some respects, however, it reflected the principle, expressed by Aristotle when his Greeks ruled southern Italy, of *Kalós kai agathós,* "the beautiful with the good."

Owing to its geographic position and cultural lineage, the kingdom found itself in several important spheres, shaped by them even as it was influencing them. There was the Byzantine Empire, the Dar al-Islam, the Jewish diaspora, an evolving Christianity, the feudalism of northern and central Europe, and more.

The first wave of Normans arrived in southern Italy early in the eleventh century, and over the course of the next six or seven decades they gradually supplanted the influence of the Italianized Lombards, the Byzantine Greeks and, finally, the Muslim Arabs who had arrived long before them. They adopted much from these peoples, and in 1130 Roger II, the scion of his dynasty, brought several Norman dominions together to form the *Regnum Siciliae,* as the polyglot Kingdom of Sicily was called in one of its official languages.

A decade later, he promulgated the kingdom's first unifying legal code, consolidating his power whilst protecting the rights of all his subjects even though the Normans themselves were Latinizers. That this code refers to "the diversity of our peoples" confirms the concept of multiculturalism as a medieval one known to our kings.

The Swabian era began at the very end of the twelfth century, with the death of Roger's daughter, Constance, his universal heiress as his only surviving legitimate child, who had ruled in her own right as queen regnant for a few years. This was a reasonably smooth transition and Constance's son and heir, Frederick II, emulated his Norman grandfather as a great thinker of his time, earning the epithet *Stupor Mundi,* "Wonder of the World." His father's father was formidable Frederick I "Barbarossa," a Holy Roman Emperor who knew a thing or two about the effective use of power.

Some salient milestones are the fruit of the kingdom's golden age. Divorce was legal and women could inherit property. Rape was not only outlawed but severely punished. Unfortunately, some personal rights of this kind, guaranteed in the reign of Frederick II, were eventually abandoned; divorce was not legalized again in Italy until 1970, and only in 1996 was rape outlawed as a felonious form of violent assault.

Although the more imaginative among us might discern in the complex medieval society of southern Italy a few seeds of the Renaissance, its High Middle Ages were not "modern" as we understand that word today. In fact, the kingdom was a confluence of medieval cultures, a social synergy. Literacy, and with it a certain diversitude of thought, was fostered by such practical developments as the widespread use of paper first introduced in China, along with the use of Hindu-Arabic numerals from India, both brought to Sicily by the Muslims. The audacious rulers were Normans whose Norse kin had ventured to places as far from Europe as North America.

Our *Regnum* wasn't the only European realm to boast this kind of cultural diversity in everything from its languages to its administration to its cuisine. To the west, several Iberian kingdoms, places like Aragon and Navarre, stimulated the emergence of a multicultural environment, and even a touch of pluralistic tolerance. To the east, the population of the Kingdom of Jerusalem, essentially a European feudal state perched tenuously on the edge of Asia, was polycultural. The same could be said of Constantinople, that glittering gateway between continents. But by the end of the medieval era none of these societies could claim anything like a true spirit of diversity or equality.

Whereas northern and central Italy see in the Renaissance their cultural apogee, the regions to the south of Rome look to the High Middle Ages for their sense of identity.

Besides the Normans and Swabians, who were the peoples that gave us the pieces of the multicolored mosaic that forms this identity?

Four distinct groups made up the population.

Lombards: These were descendants of the Longobards who arrived in Italy in the wake of the Ostrogoths and Vandals following the fall of the Roman Empire. At the dawn of the eleventh century, just before the arrival of the Normans, the Lombard rulers of Salerno, Capua and Benevento were at best princes; the last Lombard kings of Italy, based in Pavia, had been subjugated by Charlemagne as his vassals, their lands integrated into his Holy Roman Empire. By 1000, the Lombards of southern Italy were highly Italianized, and by 1200 they were amalgamated with the general population.

Byzantine Greeks: More often than not, the Greeks of Bari and Brindisi answered to Constantinople, or Byzantium, even when Apulia and Calabria were only nominally part of that "other" Roman Empire, the one ruled in the east. There was also a large Byzantine Greek population in the Kalbids' Emirate of Sicily, especially on the eastern half of the island, with its Greek Orthodox monasteries. Few of these "Greeks" were part of an immigrant population; most were descendants of the people already present in southern Italy when the Byzantines defeated the Ostrogoths and Vandals in the sixth century.

Muslim Arabs: The Kalbid emirs in Sicily were subject to the authority of Fatimid caliphs based in Cairo. About half the population of Sicily was Muslim, though there were three sects of Islam on the island. Eventually, most speakers of Arabic came to be identified generically as "Arabs." In fact, the greater number of Sicily's Muslims were Berber, which is to say Amazigh. By the eleventh century, they were integrated into the larger Arabo-Berber society ruled by the Kalbids, the island's government being distinctly Islamic, marked by influences such as Maliki Law. The Muslims fostered a renaissance in science and technology.

Jews: There had been Jews in southern Italy since the days of the Roman Empire. In Sicily they had close contact with their brethren in Tunisia and spoke Judeo-Arabic. The Jews came to dominate certain professions, and efforts were made to protect this small population.

These are just a few *strata* of the historic civilization of southern Italy.

The lands of the *Regnum* were bordered on their north by the Duchy of Spoleto, itself an imperial fief, and the Papal State ruled by the popes.

When it was founded, the state erected by Roger II was the only kingdom in what is now Italy. A duke might be invested in a formal ceremony, but kings and queens were, and are, anointed and crowned; kingship and queenship are somewhat different from what is entailed in ruling a duchy, even one as important as Tuscany, Spoleto or Savoy, for a king is a sovereign in every respect, answering to but one Master.

While it could be argued that the Italianate *ethnie,* or "ethnic" social culture, of southern Italy seen today began to emerge long before the defeat of Manfred, a son of Frederick II, at Benevento in February 1266, the Normans and Swabians ensured that the Muslims, Jews and Greek Orthodox Christians of the kingdom were accorded essentially the same rights as those who practiced the Roman Catholic faith of its sovereigns and barons. This changed with the Angevin rule that supplanted that of the last Hohenstaufens.

In a process that culminated in 1300 with the destruction of the Muslim city of Lucera in Puglia, Islam vanished in southern Italy. Although a few tiny communities of Greek Orthodox monks remained at Stilo in Calabria and in isolated monasteries in Sicily's Nebrodian Mountains, the thirteenth century had already found them gradually brought under Rome's yoke. The number and size of the Jewish communities diminished, generation by generation, to finally disappear from Sicily in 1493 as part of a general suppression that eventually enveloped southern peninsular Italy as well.

An obvious effect of this ethnogenesis is that visitors to southern Italy, like the Italians themselves, see a society that superficially appears to be as "Italian" as those of Lazio, Tuscany, Piedmont and Veneto, with rather few obvious reminders of the multicultural past. As we shall see, however, there are traces of the cultures of the Norman-Swabian era in everything from the "regional" languages to the cuisine, along with much art, architecture and written history. Arab and Byzantine culture are part of this.

One conspicuous example among many is Palermo's cathedral, historically the largest church of the *Regnum* and its primatial see, with its raucous cacophony of architectural styles. At the entrance to the fifteenth-century portico designed in the Catalonian Gothic style is a supporting column taken from a local mosque; it bears an ornate Arabic inscription citing the first verse of the Koran. In the wall protected by the portico, gazing down upon us from a niche above an arched Gothic portal, is a Byzantine mosaic of the *Theotokos,* the Mother of God. The exterior of the apse is wholly Fatimid. These vestiges of the Middle Ages are more than reminders of the past; they are part of a precious patrimony, complemented by like examples throughout southern Italy, in Bari, Salerno and other cities.

As we shall see, there have been a few deliberate efforts to subsume or misrepresent certain aspects of this heritage, some hatched in Guelph circles as early as the thirteenth century, leading to divisive views about some of our kings and queens amongst Italians. The focus of our journey will be factual history, not retrospective opinions and theories.

This work doesn't present a "thesis" of statehood, government or ethnic identity. It is a *res ipsa loquitur* presentation of "facts that speak for themselves." It is meant to be useful to general readers as well as scholars. The lengthy Introduction is presented in such a way that a reader may easily focus on those sections of greatest personal or academic interest, or begin with the Prologue that introduces the chronological history.

Our perspective shall be a cosmopolitan one, albeit colored by a slightly Siculo-Neapolitan orientation. Any history completely lacking an authorial voice is likely to be left with no voice at all. It is appropriate that this one, though expressed in English, emanates from deep within the social, cultural and geographic heart of the former kingdom.

The approach taken in this work is humanistic yet scientific. This volume will not thrust upon the reader a great deal of flowery prose or cryptic academese. Its purpose is to inform, not to confuse. Esoteric academic studies, and some of the people who present them, occasionally, and perhaps unintentionally, foster the misplaced notion that any examination of the Middle Ages is merely "ornamental," lacking true purpose in a technological age. This is not a work of "dead" history.

Many books that seek to explain the relevance of the Middle Ages to today's society are unconvincing. The authors of *this* one begin with the presupposition that southern Italy and its people are in some way special, and that the signs of our medieval heritage are enduring and ubiquitous, readily evident to those of us who are fortunate enough to be part of this society, and to visitors willing to discover it. This book was written by knowledgeable insiders for those seeking "inside" knowledge, be they curious *cognoscenti,* serious scholars, or readers having ancestral roots in southern Italy.

Sicilianistics, or *sicilianistica,* is the study of the language, culture and literature of Sicily, including the state that during our Norman-Swabian era extended northward almost to Rome. One who studies this field is a Sicilianist, or *sicilianista.* That describes the authors of this work.

While most general histories about the Kingdom of Sicily accomplish their essential tasks, this one is different. It's more than an ingress and egress framing a few reigns. Besides covering both the Hauteville and Hohenstaufen periods, it considers what came in the centuries immediately before the *Regnum* and what we have inherited from it, forming a historical, cultural and social bridge to us from the Middle Ages. In that respect, it is *living* history, perhaps even "engaged" or "public" scholarship of the kind that touches a few issues confronting our world today.

To the extent that such things are possible, this book provides a glimpse of what life was like in the kingdom. While a fair amount has been published about medieval life in other parts of Europe and other parts of Italy, particularly for periods after 1300, this one, with its focus on the people of southern Italy and their civilization before that time, covers some oft-neglected territory.

Along the way, we hope to give a voice to important figures, and even the common folk, who are no longer among us to speak for themselves, for their story is our inheritance.

As epic history, the story of the kingdom under the Hautevilles and Hohenstaufens demands ample attention and dignified treatment.

The footsteps of the past mark the path toward the present. We can learn from history as long as we remember it.

Viva lu Regnu!

Acknowledgments

Some of the research that led to this work was effected decades ago. For unrestricted access to the Vatican Apostolic Library and the Vatican Secret Archive, gratitude is expressed posthumously to Cardinal Jacques Martin, Prefect of the Pontifical Household, and Cardinal Alfons Stickler, Archivist and Librarian of the Holy Roman Church. This facilitated the examination of, amongst other sources, an unedited contemporary diplomatic reference to the legal statutes identified with King Roger II and Ariano in a poorly-conserved charter. Many thanks to the late Frà Matthew Festing, Prince Grand Master of the Sovereign Military Order of Malta, and to the late Desmond Seward, an expert on the crusading orders.

The authors thank the cooperative staffs of the British Library and other libraries and archives where charters, letters and chronicles mentioned in this volume are kept, including repositories at Palermo, Naples, Bari, Cava de' Tirreni, Montecassino, Munich, Pamplona, Zaragoza, Toledo, Barcelona and Kew (London), which permitted consultation of these precious documents, of which rather few are available on the internet. Special thanks to the Hawthorne-Longfellow Library at Bawdoin College (Maine, United States) for access to the papers of Thomas Curtis Van Cleve regarding Frederick II.

Thanks to the Archdiocese of Palermo for permission to photograph the crown of Constance of Aragon shown on this book's cover, and to the Metropolitan Museum of Art, New York, for permission to publish the photograph of the pendant of Queen Margaret through the OASC program. The royal anointing spoon of England in the Tower of London appears by gracious courtesy of the Royal Collection Trust, and the "coronation mantle" of Roger II by courtesy of the Kaiserliche Schatzkammer in Vienna. The names of the archives that granted the use of photographs of charters are indicated on the pages reproducing these documents.

It was a privilege for the authors to see the painted muqarnas ceiling of the Palatine Chapel (Palermo) up close, from the scaffolding, during its restoration in 2008.

Sincerest gratitude is expressed to the colleagues who read the manuscript of this monograph prior to publication. Heartfelt thanks to the authors' fans, thousands of readers who constitute a "tribe" that enthusiastically welcomes publication of each of their books. Such a following is a rare phenomenon in the world of academic publishing, where a printing of more than a few hundred copies of a work like this one is the exception rather than the rule.

The authors wish to thank Professor Leonard Chiarelli, a leading Arabist, for his invaluable suggestions regarding the history of the Muslims in southern Italy. Monsignor Lorenzo Casati, Orthodox Archbishop of Palermo and the Archdiocese of Italy, offered useful suggestions regarding the historiography and theology of the Great Schism and Eastern Orthodoxy in general. Many thanks to Antonino Costantino for his input on certain details regarding the Palatine Chapel and other topics that are ignored in most of the literature, and to professors Patrick O'Boyle, Salvatore Giardina, Virginia Agostinelli and Beniamino Inserra. Special thanks to Karen La Rosa, John Keahey, Stephanie Longo and Mary Ann Kuchera for their highly valuable views, observations and input. Thanks to Doctor Gabrielle Storey and Professor Matthew King for sharing information about their very recent monographs going to press.

His Royal Highness Prince Carlo di Borbone of the Two Sicilies, Duke of Castro, kindly provided access to his family's private archive, which confirmed the provenance and possession of the pendant of Queen Margaret described in Appendix 2.

Many thanks to the publisher, and particularly Salvatore Insenga, for making this volume available in softcover at a price affordable to students and underfunded libraries in a market where academic monographs of this length typically sell for two or three times the price of this one and include but a tiny fraction of the number of figures, maps and tables seen in the following pages, and for publishing a series dedicated to the medieval history and culture of southern Italy.

Last, but by no means least, much gratitude is conveyed to Professor David Abulafia, whose many accomplishments include a stint as Chairman of the History Faculty of the University of Cambridge, for taking time from his overburdened schedule to cast an eye over the manuscript and write the foreword. Academics working in our field will need no introduction to this singular scholar, known for *Frederick II: A Medieval Emperor* (1988). He has also written bestsellers such as *The Great Sea: A Human History of the Mediterranean* (2011) and *The Boundless Sea: A Human History of the Oceans* (2019). Professor Abulafia was one of the first recipients of the British Academy Medal, and in 2020 he was awarded the Wolfson History Prize. His life's work shines the light of knowledge into the dark crevices of history to reveal more about the past than we thought we knew.

Commendable efforts have been made to introduce material about the Kingdom of Sicily in undergraduate courses at universities outside Italy, particularly in Britain and the United States. Several books by the authors of this volume have been used in such courses, particularly at American universities. While *The Peoples of Sicily* is the most popular of these, the memoir of John of Procida was a required text in a 300-level course on medieval history at a university in Pennsylvania, where the students enjoyed its contemporaneous narrative of the War of the Vespers emphasizing the behavior of kings, knights, prelates and the common folk.

The book you are reading might well have seen the light of day a decade or two earlier than it did. However, the authors thought it necessary, before bringing this project to fruition, to make available to scholars several essential reference works on subjects of this era which had not yet been published, such as the translations of certain chronicles and poems, and the biographies of the queens of this period, to which the reader might refer while reading this one, in the *Sicilian Medieval Studies* series. A few of these are listed on the reverse of the very first page of this volume. The books on queens and queenship ran to, respectively, more than seven hundred and four hundred pages, while the memoir of John of Procida is the longest translation of a medieval work from the original Sicilian to be published in English.

Academic freedom is occasionally endangered and always precious. One of the sober realities motivating the writing of this book was a heartfelt desire to present accurate information about our medieval forebears in a publishing environment that sometimes produces misleading suppositions, particularly by non-Italians writing the history of southern Italy.

Each of this book's authors has a profound, direct, personal, lifelong, ancestral, cultural, intellectual connection to this history, as well as an academic and professional one.

When the Sicilian author of a book titled *Women of Sicily* gives a lecture on that topic, you are hearing a Sicilian woman's informed point of view. A lecture by the Sicilian author of a book called *The Kingdom of the Two Sicilies,* whose ancestors played a part in that monarchy, is likely to reflect the lessons of a few familial anecdotes. While outsiders may be knowledgeable of essential facts, they cannot express such ideas as, for example, the influence of medieval history and culture on the people living here in southern Italy today as credibly as somebody who witnesses those things for decades.

A number of blunt realities — not all pleasant — prompted the writing of this book, the most salient being that there was nothing quite like it available in English. Most other works of any substantial length are either insufficiently-footnoted, hyper-specialized, excessively "theoretical," or arcanely thematic, perhaps emphasizing a certain reign, religion, city or social phenomenon. Some academic monographs are tainted by banal errors or surreal points of view, while certain foreign authors openly disparage the people of southern Italy.

Much that has been published elsewhere about the topics addressed in these pages is incorrect; in the interest of civility, and to avoid what might be interpreted as *ad hominem* attacks, we shall not negatively critique recent secondary works written after 1970, because that would necessitate identifying some living authors.

History is intertwined with identity. To write the history of a people, and certainly an *ethnie,* presupposes an ethical, indeed moral, responsibility on the part of the author. This is one reason, among others, for essential history, work that forms the foundation for further study, to be authored by somebody in the group about which it is written, such as a Fazello, Di Costanzo or Summonte, for such a responsibility can never be assumed by somebody outside the group. This is as true today as it ever was. Those *within* an ethnic culture are its natural "representatives," charged with presenting its history in a way that is consistent with the unique ethnic identity of its people. "Exogenous" views have their place, but historians *outside* the ethnic society about which they write are prone to errors that result from the lack of a thorough, "native" understanding of myriad social realities beyond what may be inferred from written sources, hence an Englishman's bizarre notion that the Mafia originated among Palermo's Muslims during the twelfth century.

To grasp the impact of the kingdom's multiconfessionality in a personal way, beyond traditions, language and cuisine, one need only consider that some ancestors of this book's authors were Jews who lived in Cammarata, in the Sicanian Mountains, until 1493, when that minority population was forcibly converted to Catholicism. The Torah finials from the town's synagogue are now in a museum in Mallorca. Into the twentieth century, our families held land in this locality, the Kamrat of the Kalbids, overlooking the Platani Valley, known to the court geographer Idrisi and the royal kinswoman Lucy Hauteville.

As the only historians based in Palermo, once the capital of the kingdom, writing this history in English, the authors have assumed a special responsibility as "public scholars" in promoting it; this involves tasks such as assisting in the production of documentary films about our kings and queens, something one does not expect of scholars working outside Italy.

History is not catechesis. Its dogmas are few, its "truths" elusive. We shall seek its facts.

In consulting a reference work such as this one, the reader is entitled to know something of the authors' backgrounds, which may inform views. It was stated in the Preface that while the point of view of this book is international, it reflects a discreetly Siculo-Neapolitan orientation, just as a book about English medieval history written by somebody having English roots and living in England will have a certain English outlook. Although the authors reside in southern Italy, where this book was written, they are not affiliated with any Italian political party or movement. They do not represent any governmental, religious, ethnic or academic institution, organization or group, nor speak on behalf of any.

The authors alone are responsible for the positions, conclusions, and any errors, present in the pages that follow.

Buona lettura!

HISTORIA HV-
GONIS FALCANDI SICVLI DE
rebus gestis in Siciliæ regno, iam primùm typis
excusa, studio & beneficio Reuerendi D. Domini
Matthæi Longogçi Suessionũ pontificis & regni
Galliæ ab interiore ac penitiore consilio.

Huc accefsit in librum præfatio, & hiftoricæ le&ionis Encomi
um per Geruasium Tornacæum Sucfsionensem.

PARISIIS

Apud Mathurinum Dupuys via Iacobea,
sub insigni Hominis sylueſtris, & Frobenij.
M. D. L.

CVM PRIVILEGIO REGIS.

First edition of the chronicle of Hugh Falcandus, a witness to events at court during the reigns of William I and William II, and the reign of Margaret of Navarre as queen regent.

ABBREVIATIONS

From the seventeenth century into the twentieth, a general European preservation movement saw many important chronicles, annals and charters transcribed and published, generally obviating the need for scholars to consult original (parchment) copies of these precious documents. Several well-known compilations of such records are cited rather frequently in these pages; full titles are given in the Sources. Though certain information cited in the notes appears in more than one of these publications, in most instances a sole work is indicated.

BAS
Biblioteca Arabo-Sicula (1880 edition)

BRP
Bullarum Diplomatum et Privilegiorum Sanctorum Romanorum Pontificum

DGA
I Diplomi Greci ed Arabi di Sicilia

DNS
I Documenti Inediti dell'Epoca Normanna in Sicilia

HDF
Historia Diplomatica Friderici Secundi

ITP
Italia Pontificia

ITS
Italia Sacra (1721 edition)

MGH
Monumenta Germaniae Historica

PCC
Patrologiae Cursus Completus

RHC
Recueil des Historiens des Croisades

RIS
Rerum Italicarum Scriptores

RPR
Regesta Pontificum Romanorum (1 volume 1851, 2 volumes 1874)

SIS
Sicilia Sacra (editions indicated)

CHRONICON
ROMUALDI II.
ARCHIEPISCOPI SALERNITANI.
In Christi nomine incipit Chronica.

DE ÆTATIBUS.

Rima mundi ætas est ab Adam usque ad diluvium, côtinens annos, juxtaHebraicam veritatem mille sexcentos quinquaginta sex, juxta septuaginta verò Interpretes duo millia ducentos quadraginta duos ; generationes verò juxta utramque editionem numero decem, quæ universali est deleta diluvio, sicut primam cujusque hominis oblivio demergere consuevit ætatem. Fuerunt Noë filii tres, ex quibus ita. sunt ortæ gentes. De Japhet quindecim. De Cham triginta. De Sem XXVII. Sem annos duos post diluvium genuit Salem : à quo Samaritæ & Indi. Sale genuit Heber : à quo Hebræi. Heber genuit Falech, cujus tempore turris ædificatur, & linguarum divisio sit. In solo Heber prisca remansit lingua, quia in ea conspiratione non fuit. Turris verò duo millia CLXXIV. dicitur passuum. Hanc Nembroth gigas construxit. Hac ætate Scitharum regnum oritur, ubi primus regnavit Ihannus. Tunc & regnum Ægyptiorum ubi primus regnavit Thoës. Dehinc regnum Assiriorum, ubi primus regnavit Belus, quem dicunt Saturnum quidam : deinde Ninus, qui condidit Ninivem. Hoc tempore Abraham nascitur: & post mortem Nini à Semiramide Regina reædificata est Babylonia, ubi regnavit annos quadraginta.

Secunda ætas à Noë usque ad Abraham generationes juxta Hebraicam veritatem complexa decem, annos autem ducentos nonaginta duos ; porrò juxta septuaginta Interpretes anni MLXXII. Generationes verò XI. hæc verò quasi pueritia fuit generationis populi Dei, & ideo in lingua inventa est Hebræa, à pueritia namque homo incipit noscere loqui, quæ ideirco appellata est, quòd fari non potest. Ab Adam itaque usque ad Abraham juxta Hebraicam veritatem computantur anni mille nongenti quadraginta octo, secundùm septuaginta Interpretes fiunt anni tria millia trecenti quatuordecim.

Tertia ab Abraham usque ad David generationes juxta utramque auctoritatem XIV. annos verò, secundùm Hebræorum auctoritatem nongentos quadraginta duos complectens; juxta septuaginta verò Interpretes anni tria millia CXXXVII. hæc velut quædam adolescentia fuit populi Dei, à qua ætate incipit homo posse generare, propterea Matthæus Evangelista generationum ab Abraham sumpsit exordium, qui etiam pater multarum gentium constitutus est, quando mutatum nomen accepit. Ab Adam verò juxta Hebræorum auctoritatem usque ad David fiunt anni duo millia octingenti nonaginta, secundùm septuaginta Interpretes tria millia CV. Cur autem annorum hæc diversitas sit, in sequentibus ostendetur.

Quarta à David usque ad transmigrationem

CONTENTS

Foreword	vii
Exordium	ix
Preface	xiii
Abbreviations	xxiii
Introduction: Discovering the Kingdom	1
Maps and Charts	47
Prologue	71
1. Before the Normans	75
2. The Normans	91
3. Trial by Fire	117
4. Christians East and West	127
5. Apulia and Calabria	139
6. Sicily	143
7. Polycultural Cities	151
8. Consolidation	161
9. Rites of Passage	179
10. Geopolitics	197
11. Regnum Siciliae	211
12. Normanization	235
13. Power	269
14. Continuum	277
15. Inheritance	287
16. Parenti Serpenti	297
17. Regency	307
18. Leadership	351

19. Multicultural Monastery	369
20. Reign	381
21. Dynasticism	395
22. Regnancy	407
23. Regnum Vivum	417
24. Lingua dellu Regnu	429
25. Hegemony	443
26. Society and Law	461
27. Culinary Culture	473
28. Permanency	497
29. European Kingdom	513
30. Catholic Kingdom	527
31. Hereditament	539
32. Kingship	547
Epilogue	563
Conclusion: The Living Kingdom	567
Afterword	577
Genealogical Tables	581
Timeline	609
Appendix 1: Assizes of Ariano	619
Appendix 2: Margaret's Pendant	633
Appendix 3: Constance's Crown	635
Appendix 4: The Contrasto	637
Appendix 5: Coronation Rite	643
Appendix 6: Historiography	651
Appendix 7: Twin Kingdoms	665
Glossary	669
Notes	677
Sources and Bibliography	789
Index	831

Introduction
DISCOVERING THE KINGDOM

"Our purpose is to present the facts as we find them," wrote Frederick II in his treatise on falconry.

Facts are only the beginning, for just as a temple is more than stone, the story of a people consists of more than facts. There is a living history that dwells within the people of southern Italy, reflected in many moments of everyday life. Its lasting legacy is at least as important as the names, dates and places that uninspired historians ponder. Unconcealed yet unspoken, this inheritance is slightly elusive, sometimes standing just beyond view, but readily revealed to those visitors who wish to see it.

Historians — academics and popularizers alike — have only rarely captured its substance. Few even try.

The story of southern Italy during the "High Middle Ages" is anything but pedestrian.[1] Distinguished for its time, it is noteworthy, perhaps even instructive. Though its story has been told, one way or another, this is the first general survey of length dedicated to the Kingdom of Sicily during its Hauteville and Hohenstaufen reigns to be published in English that is supplemented by notes and other information, with ample attention paid to queens as well as kings, and commoners as well as rulers, obviating the need for the reader to consult several volumes to find these essential facts. Specialized works have their place, and original research by this book's authors is reported here, but in its essence this book is a road map, a framework to put theories and minutiae in their proper context.

Its publication is long overdue. Filling a void, this reference work should have been written decades ago, ideally by somebody here in southern Italy familiar with the place and its people.

This is one of the lengthiest volumes in English on the monarchies of southern Italy for the period from around 1000 to 1266, and it has far more citations (notes) than most of the monographic histories covering the Kingdom of Sicily during the Norman-Swabian era in this language. Indeed, there was a very real risk of the "back matter" of appendices, notes, bibliography and index being longer than the main text.

We live in an age of challenges, some novel, ranging from calamitous climate change to lethal global pandemics to the emergence of artificial intelligence and the erosion of personal privacy and individuality. The Middle Ages, by comparison, were simpler, if no less harsh, with tyranny, bigotry, plague and sickness the norm in most places and at most times.

Like many historical topics, a great deal about the Kingdom of Sicily, thanks to the numerous publications about it in Italy and elsewhere, and a fair amount on the internet, has been pushed into the realm of "public knowledge." In fact, most of the foundational information ultimately comes to us from a number of medieval chroniclers, frequently cited here, while some of what is encountered in recent publications is less than accurate. In repeating this misinformation, travel writers and other authors still propagate erroneous clichés.[2]

In history, as in other studies, known facts evolve based on research and discovery. Historians, like scientists, are willing to revise opinions when the facts, and hence our potential for understanding, change.

Certain historians — generalists as well as specialists — writing in English present opinion and theory shrouded as fact, some of it based on a foreigner's suppositions about the place and its people. Errors rooted in outsiders' lack of knowledge of the society of southern Italy, both medieval and modern, are legion.

Yet there can be no dispositively "canonical" history of the Kingdom of Sicily. What is presented in these pages is not intended to be explicitly analytical, anthropological, revisionist, positivist, deconstructionist, nativist or even monarchist. It is, first and foremost, factual, historical and cultural. So much the better if the story makes for an interesting narrative.

Granted that all history is, to some degree, a "construct," this work reflects what is essentially an "unmediated" historicism consisting of facts supplemented by explanations of background and context. Unlike some historical writing that has been published in recent times, even in academic circles, it is not based on a certain thesis or ideology, with discursive facts selected to support a particular theory or belief. Analysis has its place, of course, but historical works should be fundamentally descriptive rather than prescriptive, not "inventing" history but reporting it. In the sage words of Barbara Tuchman, "the material must precede the thesis."[3] This work is "originalist," relying on the medieval sources themselves, without the embellishment or theorizing that came later.

Whilst a historical work may have "entertainment value," most of us read history out of curiosity, to learn something from it. Ideally, it should be informative, often revealing, and perhaps inspiring. Above all, it must be accurate.

INTRODUCTION

Unlike most general histories written in English about the medieval Kingdom of Sicily, this one, though essentially a chronology complemented by a few topical excursions (such as those in chapters 2 and 12), gives due consideration to the process of ethnogenesis, the formation and emergence of an *ethnie,* the ethnic identity of a people.

These prefatory pages, rather than those in the numbered chapters, succinctly address a few concepts germane to this work, and others about the same subject, either as integral components of the medieval history of southern Italy or our means of examining it. The nexus of these otherwise disparate topics is their relevance to the study of the Kingdom of Sicily and its people. This exposition shall be informative and direct, candid and blunt; enlightening for most, unsettling for a few.

Objectives and Scope

This volume is part of a journey. For some, it marks the beginning, an introduction to whet the curious reader's appetite for further knowledge about a complicated era in the history of southern Italy that made an impact beyond its own borders. For others, it will be a destination unto itself, more than sufficient to slake their present curiosity. For many, it may serve as a useful reference to consult, even if piecemeal, in the quest for accurate information. Those wishing to embark upon further study will find this to be a useful guide to methods and sources.

A few readers will find these pages to be an edifying stop along the route of a personal journey, for while this history has a general relevance to Europe, the Mediterranean, and indeed the world, it holds special pertinence in defining, if only partially, the identity of those of us descended from ancestors in southern Italy. It was the Norman-Swabian era that formed the foundation for the identity of the people of southern Italy that existed by the middle of the thirteenth century and still exists today.

Today, the "culture of authenticity," an idea expressed eloquently during the last century by the philosopher Charles Taylor, reflects a sense of individual identity based on influences of this kind, permitting each of us to be unique, and true to ourselves, whilst being part of a group. This is related to the idea of *positionality* formulated more recently by social scientists. Colin Morris, a historian, suggested that our concept of the individual originates in the Middle Ages, and not, as was long presumed, during the Renaissance. Those are deeper waters than we need wade into, but identity, in one form or another, is a significant part of what is presented here. The culture of southern Italy is one metaphor among many for what are now ethnic groups and diasporas around the world.

The value placed by a people on the free expression of its ethno-cultural identity is sometimes dismissed, usually by outsiders, as something of a benign anachronism, as if it were irrelevant to our times.

That, indeed, is one of the most important reasons for learning about the past, because history teaches us something about ourselves, whether its focus is our own forebears or, more generally, our predecessors in the entire human family.

KINGDOM OF SICILY

Its multicultural society makes the Kingdom of Sicily ruled by the Hautevilles and Hohenstaufens an unusual object of study compared to most other European realms. For that fact alone it merits our attention.

Whatever motivates one's interest, the following narrative, though supported by rigorous academic research, does not presume much prior knowledge about the subject on the part of the reader, who may be encountering the Kingdom of Sicily, the *Regnum Siciliae,* for the first time.

In emphasizing historicity over theory, this work is not highly "philosophical" or excessively analytical. It does not seek to infer more than what is presented by evidence, social context and comparative history.

In purely epistemological terms, knowledge may be viewed as a "subset" of belief, being the fraction of beliefs that meet the scientific standard of valid evidence, hence *justified true belief*. What is accepted as historical fact should be free from fallacies in logic (fundamental errors in reasoning). Sophistry and confirmation bias must be avoided. The facts should not be presented "selectively," or out of context, to support a preconceived theory. (The sound epistemological approach to the study of history employs such principles as simple positivism and methodological naturalism, which permit the examination of evidence from a scientific perspective that is not excessively hypothetical, speculative or ideological.)

Until now, it was rare to find much information about both the Hauteville and Hohenstaufen reigns, in English, in one book dedicated to the topic. Naturally, no single volume on this subject can be all things to all people. The orientation of this one straddles the needs of two readerships, namely the general and the academic. (Otherwise, it would have been necessary to write *two* books: one for scholars and another for everybody else.)

Although ruling personages are key to this study, this is not, by any means, a dynastic history or collection of royal biographies, much less an attempt to apply the principles of behavioral theory to the lives of medieval personages. Rather, it is a *general* history that presents, in addition to a chronological account of events and political developments, something about the society and culture that defined, and still define, the people of southern Italy.

Most general histories and academic monographs written about the High Middle Ages are wanting for an overarching, multi-century "world view" to clearly and accurately connect the medieval past to our present. A modern view holds that the history of the Kingdom of Sicily is a metaphor for Mediterranean and global history.[4]

We'll discover how, in the course of a few centuries, the *Regnum* became *lu Regnu* and then *il Regno.*

Relevant as they are to our study, the papacy, the medieval Roman empires of Byzantium and Germany, and the societies of Norman England and Fatimid Africa, despite their substantive influences on the *Regnum,* will necessarily receive less emphasis in a one-volume work dedicated to southern Italy than they would in a topical monograph. In viewing the long reign of Frederick II, our focus is his rule of the Kingdom of Sicily rather than his dominions in central Europe, northern Italy and the Holy Land.

INTRODUCTION

There is an instinctive temptation to dismiss the impact of monarchy in a country, like Italy, where one has been lacking for a few generations. Leaving aside the rational reasons behind Italians' general lack of nostalgia for the cacotopia that was the modern Kingdom of Italy from 1861 until 1946, institutional (governmental) vestiges of the Norman-Swabian era were part of life until quite recently. Feudalism, as a system of land ownership, was abolished in Sicily by the ephemeral constitution of 1812, which is itself rather recent in historical terms, but the island's last *latifondi,* the large, formerly-feudal estates, were finally dissolved only in 1949.

Normans and Swabians

Outside Italy, our Norman and Swabian eras are usually considered separately. Here in southern Italy, however, both periods are often regarded as two sides of the same coin, one being an extension, or continuation, of the other.

That makes sense not only for dynastic reasons but because the initial influx of Germans into the *Regnum* at the end of the twelfth century was not large enough to constitute anything quite like a "migration." Very little in administration immediately changed; despite what one might expect, there were rather few specific policies introduced from the Holy Roman Empire. The legal code of 1231, though clearly innovative and superior in highly significant ways, could not be said to differ entirely from that of 1140, from which certain statutes were adopted. Historians debate the nuances of distinction between Hauteville and Hohenstaufen rule, yet the kings of each house were born and raised in southern Italy, as were most of their counsellors, clergy, barons and justiciars.

In 1994, your authors attended a major academic conference in Palermo, *L'Età Normanna e Sveva in Sicilia,* held in conjunction with an exhibit that occasioned publication of a book of the same title, reflecting the Italian approach to addressing the two dynastic periods together.[5]

Several academic institutions use the term, most notably the University of Bari, where we find the Centro Studi Normanno-Svevi, which publishes collections such as *Strumenti, Tempi e Luoghi di Comunicazione nel Mezzogiorno Normanno-Svevo* (1995). Papers delivered at conferences held at Ariano Irpino have been published in the *Archivio Normanno-Svevo.*

The Basilicata University Press, at Potenza, published an edited collection, *Il Regno di Sicilia in Età Normanna e Sveva: Forme e organizzazioni della cultura e della politica* (2021), consistent with this "inter-dynastic" concept of the history of this era. At the same time, Richard Barber's *Magnificence: Princely Splendour in the Middle Ages,* which features the mantle of Roger II on its cover, dedicated the first part of its third chapter, "The Culture of Kingship," to our Norman-Swabian regnal period. In contrast to the term *Norman-Swabian,* which is typically used in a dynastic or political context, the phrase *Norman-Arab* is usually heard in a cultural setting, often referring to a certain style of architecture.

Charles Homer Haskins was inclined to view the royal patronage of intellectual pursuits seen in the kingdom's Swabian era during the long reign of Frederick II as a continuation of the environment cultivated in Norman times under Roger II, an idea reflected in his *Studies in the History of Mediaeval Science,* published in 1924.

Long before printing arrived, the *Ferraris Chronicle,* arguably the first "history," rather than an annal or chronicle, of the Kingdom of Sicily, considered the Normans and Swabians together. Building upon the work of Falco of Benevento and other precursors, this was completed near Naples in 1228 by a monk who met Frederick II. Even if, as chroniclers were wont to do, its author was merely striving for completeness by mentioning events that occurred before his time, it is clear that he saw no chasm of distinction separating the reign he knew from those that had existed immediately prior to it.

It could be argued that the fundamental nature of the kingdom changed more in 1266, with the inception of Angevin rule, leading to the realm's separation into two distinct polities, than it did with the hereditary transition from the Hautevilles to the Hohenstaufens in the waning years of the twelfth century. In 1282, the *Regnum* was divided into what became the kingdoms of Naples and Sicily, and by 1300 memory had become history.

In biography, as opposed to general history, much more has been written in recent decades about Frederick II than Roger II. One obvious reason for this distinction is that Roger's story, in contrast to Frederick's, is interwoven so intricately into the foundation and early history of the kingdom that few writers see fit to approach it separately, as a biography.

This work reflects an international view. It may be noted, at all events, that in the past British historians often looked to the history of the Normans of southern Italy for insight into the Norman and "Plantagenet" eras in England. German scholars were sometimes inclined to cast a long glance toward the Staufen, or Hohenstaufen, kings of Sicily as a case of their imperial sovereigns ruling Mediterranean lands. Those approaches, though perfectly valid, have generally been eclipsed by more cosmopolitan ones that are less Eurocentric and perhaps more Mediterraneocentric. Specifically, the Kingdom of Sicily is placed into a wider European-Mediterranean, even global, context than it was in the past.

However, it must be borne in mind that a knowledge of Normandy, Swabia and other regions from whence our dynasties came is highly relevant to our understanding of these families and those that accompanied them to southern Italy.

This volume may well become the catalyst for a trend among Anglophone historians to address the Norman and Swabian eras of the Kingdom of Sicily together, just as *Margaret, Queen of Sicily* inspired interest among scholars, as well as casual readers, in that oft-ignored regent. In part, it is a response to professors who requested a text on this subject for undergraduate history courses (a study guide is published as a supplement to this book).

Authorial Voices

Transcending mere stewardship, writing a general history is a monumental responsibility. Accuracy is of paramount importance, but so is the tone, for there are innumerable ways to write history, some more informative, enlightening and understandable than others. In our times, the eloquence of clarity is an elusive virtue.

History is not religion. The field of medieval history has learned experts but no immutable authorities. At best, it may bring us a broad scholarly consensus about the most rudimentary facts concerning developments such as the Norman invasions of Sicily and England.

Our guide is the sound epistemology that facilitates reliable research methodology and valid findings, without the excessive deconstructionism, postmodernism or nationalism that color certain historical niches. In these pages, revisionism, or purported revisionism, is not advanced for its own sake, simply to make certain ideas appear "originative" or "corrective."

Nevertheless, social context, comparative history and modern approaches at discovery were rigorously integrated into the efforts that led to this volume.

Only a few generalist works have been published in English about the medieval history of the Kingdom of Sicily, most with an emphasis on a specific dynastic era: Norman, Swabian, Angevin, Aragonese. Conversely, histories of the Roman Empire, the Renaissance, the papacy, Italian unification and organized crime have been published to death.

The majority of work on the medieval Kingdom of Sicily and also (for the period after 1282) the Kingdom of Naples has been published in Italian, French, German and English. Only in the second half of the twentieth century, following the end of the Second World War, did English emerge as the most important publishing language globally in certain humanistic fields, and its instruction for students in Italian schools is now mandatory beginning at the age of six. Italians in certain regions speak languages other than Italian as their mother tongue, for example German in South Tyrol and French in Aosta.

In the academic sphere, contrary to what certain Anglophone and Francophone scholars would have a general readership believe, much fine work has been published in Italian about the medieval history of southern Italy. During the nineteenth century we find, for example, excellent scholarship by the Arabists Salvadore Morso, Michele Amari and Salvatore Cusa, and numerous charters of King Roger II transcribed and summarized by historians such as Antonino Mongitore and Carlo Alberto Garufi. At the same time there was publication of the most important charters conserved at Cava, Montecassino, the Vatican and other archives in collections such as the multi-volume *Codex Diplomaticus Cavensis* (beginning in 1873). There are useful timelines like the *Annali Critico-Diplomatici* (1805) of Alessandro Di Meo. Giovanni Battista Siragusa's *Il Regno di Guglielmo I di Sicilia Illustrato con Nuovi Documenti* (1885) offers us an excellent narrative and historiography.

More recently, scholars such as the late Salvatore Tramontana and Enrico Pispisa have contributed much to the field, even if very little of their work was translated into English.

Before 1990, the major "modern" works published about the Normans of Italy in English in the original were the two volumes about them by John Julius Norwich, *The Normans in the South 1016-1130* (1967) and *The Kingdom in the Sun 1130-1194* (1970). For the Swabian era, Thomas Kington's two-volume *History of Frederick II* (1862) was a useful work, while *The Emperor Frederick II of Hohenstaufen, Immutator Mundi* (1972), by Thomas Curtis Van Cleve, and *Frederick II: A Medieval Emperor* (1988), by David Abulafia, were both in print and available in many public and university libraries. James Powell had written a volume dedicated to Frederick's Constitutions of Melfi. Steven Runciman's book, *The Sicilian Vespers* (1958), considered the reign of Frederick's son, Manfred, and its aftermath. There were insightful academic articles about the Siculo-Normans by Charles Homer Haskins, whose landmark works, *The Normans in European History* (1915) and *The Renaissance of the Twelfth Century* (1927), prominently mention our Sicilian kings, and Evelyn Jamison, whose rigorous research led to *Admiral Eugenius of Sicily* (1957), amongst other important contributions. Lynn Townsend White, a student of Haskins, produced a fine study, *Latin Monasticism in Norman Sicily* (1938).

It is not true, as some imagine, that "nothing" had ever been published about most of these topics, just that very little had been written *in English*. In retrospect, the greatest criticism one could make about works of this kind is that some were occasionally, very obviously, Anglocentric in orientation and tone, a characteristic likewise present in certain monographs and papers published since 1990.

Most of the English-language monographs and papers written by scholars raised and educated in Italy are works in translation. Others are, in truth, excessively "edited" or "proofread" by native speakers of English, even in instances where that fact is concealed from the reader.

There were a few notable works in languages besides Italian and English, most importantly Ferdinand Chalandon's two-volume *magnum opus* on the Normans of Sicily, published in 1907, and Erich Caspar's monumental tome on the reign of Roger II, published in 1904, both still useful today. Ernst Kantorowicz wrote a biography and source supplement of Frederick II.

Writing in 1913, Evelyn Jamison, whose studies led the way among Anglophone scholars, expressed herself with her characteristic eloquence when she wrote that, "Some fifteen years ago, when this wave of interest was as yet hardly suspected, I was attracted, as all students of the Middle Ages must be, not only by the dramatic story of the Norman adventure in the South, but by the extreme importance of the constitutional and administrative system which grew up in the conquered regions."[6]

Two years later, Charles Homer Haskins recognized the multicultural complexity of the Normans' Kingdom of Sicily when he observed that, "Then, masters of southern Italy and Sicily, they put to work their powers of assimilation and organization and created a strong, well-governed state and a rich, composite civilization which were the wonder of Europe."[7]

These are all solid works. Except for a handful of details "corrected," or developed further, by subsequent scholarship, they generally stand the test of time despite a few linguistic artefacts typical of their era.[8] What is more, the "literary" writing styles of Norwich, Runciman and others in this cohort are far superior to what often passes for historical narrative in today's publishing environment, be it general or academic.

INTRODUCTION

Despite this competence among some historians, one is struck by the information overlooked in reasonably detailed publications. Greater Palermo boasts more surviving churches and chapels of the twelfth century than any other city in Europe, yet that fact is rarely noted by otherwise astute authors writing about such things.

If, however, a single, underlying criticism is to be made regarding the majority of general histories, as opposed to specialized academic monographs, published in English about the Kingdom of Sicily, it is that their footnotes (or endnotes) often fail to provide the more curious reader, or aspiring scholar, with information sufficient to facilitate the ready consultation of original sources. It would be useful, for example, to inform the reader that the *Gesta Tancredi* setting forth the story of Tancred Hauteville "of Galilee" can be found in the third volume of *Recueil des Historiens des Croisades, Historiens Occidentaux*, published in Paris in 1866.

Nowadays, very few publishers produce volumes containing more than a handful of useful maps and charts. The original hardcover edition of *The Sicilian Vespers* rewarded the reader's attention with three concertina fold-out pages of genealogical tables measuring up to sixty-two centimeters (twenty-four inches) in width, but *Frederick II: A Medieval Emperor* lacked pedigree charts altogether. Most editors are equally parsimonious with book length, leaving us with very few "major" works consisting of more than six hundred pages (Erich Caspar's history of the reign of Roger II ran to nearly seven hundred), though some academic presses compensate for this by using rather small, barely-legible type sizes that elicit complaints from readers.

Because very few of the native speakers of English writing such books have lived for very long in southern Italy or been raised in families from this region, their knowledge of certain traditions and languages is not always sufficient to facilitate keen comparisons between the past and present. This is especially important when one seeks to determine how certain elements of culture have been preserved over time, perhaps using surviving artistic or linguistic clues to learn something about medieval history. In these pages, the chapters on language and cuisine benefitted greatly from this, but so did the sections on religion and iconography.

Until quite recently, Italian women were grossly underrepresented in this field, as in others.[9] Of the twenty-four papers presented in December 1972, a few months after Evelyn Jamison's death during the apex of the women's movement, an international conference held in Palermo on the Normans of medieval Italy saw exactly one presented by a woman; the lone *professoressa* was the late Marina Scarlata.

While the Kingdom of Sicily is a natural subject of interest for those of us who, like Professor Scarlata, have roots in it, its appeal to foreign scholars has increased exponentially since around 1990, largely because it is something about which comparatively little has been written in English vis-à-vis the exhaustively-studied Kingdom of England.

Until the present century, just a few dozen medievalists published much about the Lombard, Arab, Byzantine and Norman eras of southern Italy. Now there are many hundreds publishing in this broad field, and the proliferation of work is uneven in quality and tone, written by old historicists, new historicists, revisionists, deconstructionists, Siculophiles, Italophiles, Italophobes, and others. Where there were formerly just a few detailed papers published about, for example, the invaluable chronicles of Godfrey Malaterra, Hugh Falcandus and Peter of Eboli, there is now a plethora of journal articles, book chapters and scholarly monographs, each seeking, in academic parlance, to "add something to the conversation," as if every thought were legitimate merely by virtue of it being expressed in the public sphere. Yet the writing in some of the more recent work is strikingly uniform, even imitative, in style, with little to distinguish the thoughts of one scholar from those of another, despite the introduction of a few bizarre ideas (see note 34).

With this stampede of neophilia comes a protean mass of ideas, many seeking to be original, and some are rather contentious. As one might imagine, a competitive field where every affirmation is greeted with a contrarian view is not lacking in polemical personalities, with acrimonious rivalries between academics sometimes spawning *ad hominem* attacks; certain historians thus define themselves "dialectically," in a Hegelian manner, by the very colleagues whose work they are so vehemently censuring, much as the early Protestants defined themselves by Catholicism. That this is sometimes motivated by factors other than the work itself is hardly a novel phenomenon.[10] At all events, more important work is more likely to elicit noise from rivals than less consequential study, which may well be ignored, and peer review is not always as ethical or efficacious as it should be.[11]

This is not the venue for a detailed exposé of the complexities of academe's battlegrounds and their influence on scholarly study. Here it shall suffice to say that in these quasi-feudal turf wars there are no true winners because, unlike a proven theorem in calculus, medieval history rarely presents us with definitive "proof" of this or that thesis but an entropy of facts, events and details. So-called "truths" must be approached with caution. Where a novel theory is based on an earlier one, which itself may not be very tenable, the result is a fragile "house of cards" built upon a weak foundation.

Too frequently in journal articles, monographs, edited collections (anthologies) and exhibition catalogues, even where there is peer review, does one encounter errors such as the misidentification of the location of sites (churches and castles) that no longer exist and even figures, such as those in the painted muqarnas ceiling of Palermo's Palatine Chapel and the carved capitals of Monreale's cloister. As just one example, Palermo's jousting ground (see note 396) is rarely even mentioned by Anglophone scholars writing about the medieval history of this singular city.

There are many schools of thought, some supported by their own cliques, about the reigns of Roger II and Frederick II, but there is no universal law governing these studies, nor can there be one. Diverse opinions abound, as they should in any society where there is freedom of thought and expression.

In these pages, however, facts are the foundation; historians may well formulate varying theories about *why* the Aghlabids conquered Sicily or the

INTRODUCTION

Hautevilles repeatedly invaded Greece, but nobody debates the fact that they did it.

As we have observed, most of the lengthier books published in English about the medieval Kingdom of Sicily have been written xenocentrically by "foreigners" based outside southern Italy, typically by Siculophile authors lacking a native's familiarity with this region.

Commendable as those "exogenous" efforts are, it is usually more efficacious for foundational work about important medieval subjects to be authored, in the first instance, by scholars in the place where the history occurred, is most evident, and has had a direct impact. By way of example, one expects the first biography of English-born Elizabeth I of England to be written by somebody in the country of her birth and death, like William Camden, not by a biographer in Russia or Italy. Naturally, the first biographies of Joanna I of Naples were written by Neapolitans.

While many foreign scholars are fine Latinists and Italianists, very few are Sicilianists truly conversant with studies involving the emergence of the native culture of southern Italy during the Norman-Swabian era. Even those who have written something about, for example, the Sicilian language, are unlikely to attempt actually speaking it to Palermitans or Catanians in Sicily. It is pure folly to presume the familiarity of a foreigner with the labyrinth of medieval streets in the capital known to our kings and queens. Yet it is a first-hand familiarity with the place and its people that fosters an accurate reading of what was written by medieval chroniclers and expressed through art, architecture, language, music and cuisine. A historian sufficiently acquainted with old Palermo, one of Europe's largest surviving medieval districts, can more readily grasp the significance of the narrative of Hugh Falcandus about the events that transpired here (where these words are being written) than one who has spent only a few months in this unique city. This is where Sicilianistics are important.

History is part of a broader "horizon of significance" (Charles Taylor's term) against which an individual's sense of identity can be gauged and defined. Here we see the abstract but real principle of people being part of something greater than themselves. It is history's close connection to personal identity that makes its writing by scholars within its *ethnie* appropriate, even necessary. Frederick Douglass and William Edward Du Bois wrote about the history of African-Americans with insight that would have been lacking in the mind of somebody outside that group.

To best understand the foundations and effects of our Middle Ages, one needs to study our history as it unfolded over the course of three millennia, from *Megale Hellas* into the modern era. One doesn't presume that everybody raised outside Italy will know the difference between the *fritella* and *frittola* of Sicily, compared to the *frittoli* of Calabria and the *fritola* of Veneto, much less the distinction between a *salma* and a *tomolo,* or the meanings of *baccalà* and *babbaluci.*

An Arabist proficient in Sicilian, a language not taught in many schools even here in Sicily, can tell you which modern words in that tongue derive from Arabic. An equally competent philologist unfamiliar with Sicilian cannot be expected to know that.

"No non-Sicilian, I suspect, will ever be able to penetrate the island's mysteries altogether," noted the late John Julius Norwich in his history of Sicily published in 2015.

Just as Italian literature is, by definition, written by people in Italy, we expect Italian history, in the first instance, to be written by Italians. Otherwise, it runs the risk of lacking verisimilitude, genuine Italianness, or *Italianità,* by depicting Italians as if we were people who just happened to live in Italy and speak Italian, lacking any personal connection to our past. More explicitly, there exist *Napoletanità* and *Sicilianità.*

In its most essential form, history is a factual story. Xenocentric historical narratives run the risk of the reader sensing that the human element in a story is missing. Standpoint theory, which typically deals with the study of women's history, is a modern manifestation of the idea that scholars must look to people to tell their own story rather than attempting to contrive a narrative for them through an outsider's impressions or even serendipity. In the collection *Women in the Medieval Islamic World* (1998), only three chapters, out of a total of twenty-three, were written by identifiably Muslim women.

Autohistory reflects the modern "post-colonialist" notion that a people, an *ethnie,* has the right, nay the duty, to write its own history, without a civilization being defined almost entirely by outsiders. It necessitates the perspective of an author intimately familiar with the people and the place about which the history is being written.[12] This is broadly consistent with the view of Edward Carr, who believed the historical facts and the historian to be so closely linked that one would be useless without the other.

Ethnography is the anthropological study of peoples and cultures, with a focus on their distinctive customs and habits, sometimes with a view to comparing one society or *ethnie* to another. This is where we encounter the *emic* and the *etic,* the former emanating chiefly from the view of the people themselves and the latter resulting from observations about their relationship to society at large. This principle is mirrored in the use of autonyms such as *Amazigh* over exonyms like *Berber.*

Ethnohistory typically relates more specifically to the use of non-textual sources of artistic, linguistic and cultural information characteristic of an *ethnie,* especially where written records are few. While this approach is not usually applied to the study of European and Mediterranean societies, it could be used here to complement more "conventional" academic research methods. Certain longstanding oral traditions, religious practices and folk customs might be said to fall into the category of ethnohistory.

Autoethnography usually deals with lived experiences considered in a wider societal context. In medieval studies, this might be construed to include such sources as travel diaries, but in most cases the term relates to modern genres such as memoir.

"Race memory" may be defined as the collective body of experiences, beliefs and general recollections transmitted from one generation of humanity to another. This is linked to the concept of living history. It is highly relevant to our study where certain traditions and customs of our Norman-Swabian era are still propagated in southern Italy today, seven centuries after the demise of the Hohenstaufen dynasty.

Decade by decade, xenocentrism in the academy is becoming increasingly normalized as ever more scholars take an interest in places with which they have no personal association and where they have never actually lived, and this includes medievalist studies of southern Italy. It is a natural, inevitable result of life in an ever shrinking, globalized, amalgamated world where cultures, religions, and even ethnic identities, can be adopted, or appropriated, at will. Yet a foundational work, though full of facts that may well be evaluated with some competence by outsiders, relates to the identity of the people it describes. It would be illogical for the people of southern Italy, or any place, to have their autochthonous identity defined for them by those from outside their society.

On a more prosaic note, to be a competent medievalist requires far more than a knowledge of a place during its Middle Ages. For southern Italy, this embraces the panoply of thirty centuries, from the ancient Greek and Punic era to the Kingdom of the Two Sicilies. Arguably, non-Italians may be more prone to "medievalist's myopia," and the flawed perceptions that accompany it, than historians raised here in southern Italy.[13]

Major surveys written in Italian only rarely make their way into English, but most of the "natives" are at least reasonably familiar with the culture of the former kingdom, which casts a long shadow into the modern era (see "Living Legacy" below). This is likely to prevent gross errors based on misperceptions (see note 34). The legacy of the Kingdom of Sicily is far more distinct here in southern Italy than it could ever be elsewhere.

The first published histories to include substantial sections on the medieval Kingdom of Sicily were written, in Latin and Italian, by native historians like Thomas Fazello and his rival, Francesco Maurolico, as post-incunables in the middle of the sixteenth century, which is when the *editio princeps* of the chronicle of Hugh Falcandus, an important source work, saw the light of day. The early decades of the twentieth century witnessed the publication of "modern" histories. Owing to the political situation in Italy during that era, however, the first lengthy modern works about the Normans of Italy and the reign of Frederick II were published abroad, respectively in France and Germany.[14]

In the following pages, the place and its culture are not mere backdrops but omnipresent "characters" in the dramatic story of our golden age.

Identity and Ethos

It is the past that shapes present concepts of group identity. From a sociocultural perspective, southern Italy is not very different from any other European region that had, or has, kings and queens, though the closest medieval comparisons would be Navarre and Aragon, polycultural Mediterranean regions from which princesses became queens of Sicily (the term *princess* wasn't yet in wide use).

One is reluctant to refer to a medieval European polity such as a kingdom or duchy as anything more than a "state" because *nation,* as that word is normally used, is usually regarded as a modern concept. However, we encounter occasional medieval usage. In letters, Llywelyn ap Gruffudd, Prince of Wales, the penultimate independent ruler of the Welsh people and a contemporary of Frederick II, referred to *nostra nacio*.[15]

It can be postulated that ethnogenesis and state-building (sometimes "nation-building"), though not identical to each other, often coincide or overlap.

Literary historians tend to think of the birth of a language as a development coinciding with the emergence of an ethnic identity, or at least reflecting one. That was certainly the case in the Kingdom of Sicily.

A kingdom may well be associated with an *ethnie* or, in the case of Roger's realm in 1130, several distinct ethnic cultures. Even so, by the end of Frederick's reign, in 1250, the ethnogenesis of the southern Italians was well under way; some would say that most of this identity was already formed by then, and that it may even have been teleological, the inevitable natural consequence of the Latinization begun by the Normans, almost as if it were an intentional result.

The Normans arrived in Palermo in 1071, when scarcely anybody living here spoke a Romance language, yet the city was thoroughly "Sicilianized" by the time the *Regnum* fell in 1266.

The history of southern Italy would be much the lesser without our first few kings and queens, who epitomize a collective historical experience. Could we present a complete view of history without them?

Even if a citizen living today did not consciously recognize the significance of our first kings and queens, they are an integral part of the foundations, the very underpinnings, of a collective identity. If only because monarchy survived in Italy for so long, and until so recently, this early royalty could be said to be more immediately significant and meaningful than, for example, certain figures of the classical age, such as the tyrants of Greek Syracuse.

Like forms of government, practices connected to monarchy evolve over time. That the symbolic or cultural importance of our medieval kings and queens has outlived monarchy itself is not atypical.

Many European republics embrace the past as an important element in the formation of their heritage. Even the revolutions of France and Russia could not cancel the "race memory" of the medieval era, since it was that very past, with its monarchies and complexities, that established solid cultural foundations for the modern era. Whatever one thinks about them, the Norman and Swabian kings of Sicily are untainted by the ills of modern politics.

Whether through migration, imperialism, commerce or publishing, and now globalization, we see cultures exported and propagated far beyond their places of origin. Beginning late in the nineteenth century, the culture of southern Italy was introduced by a sea of emigrés to nations around the world, where it thrived on its own, as a "diaspora," with no help or hindrance from the Italian state. This brings to mind "stateless" ethnic groups like the Hmong and Kurds flourishing without their own sovereignty.

Today, Italy has twenty "political regions," some characterized by very distinct cultures rooted in the Middle Ages. By no means is this situation unique

INTRODUCTION

to Italy. The experiences of Catalonia and Scotland are not unlike those of the former Kingdom of the Two Sicilies (see Appendix 7), whose territory at Italian unification in 1860 was coterminous to that of the *Regnum Siciliae* of the Hautevilles and Hohenstaufens. That Sicily, geographically the largest of these political regions, is today an "autonomous region" with its own mini-parliament recognizes its historical sovereignty from the days of Kalbid emirs and Norman counts.

Just as a people or *ethnie* has the right to write its own history, it has the right to determine which parts of that history, however eclectic or complex, it considers most representative of its identity and which personages are, for lack of a more precise term, its heroes. While these choices may at first be determined by the politics of the moment, over time certain medieval figures, especially prominent monarchs, are seen to be emblematic of the people they ruled. They are joined by a handful of knights remembered for their noble spirit. Their very names evoke awe: Charlemagne, Leif Erikson, William the Conqueror, Alfred the Great, Hugh Capet, Frederick Barbarossa, William Wallace, El Cid. These iconic leaders have become quasi-mythological figures.

Here in the former Kingdom of Sicily, Roger II and Frederick II enjoy a place of honor. Most obviously, this manifests itself in school history curricula, street names, monuments, museum exhibits, and activities such as tourism promotion, but all of this is much more than idealizing. Roger and Frederick are part of the warp and woof of our *social identity,* defined as an individual's self-concept derived from membership in a relevant social group, almost as if identifying with their legacy were part of what it means to be Sicilian, Neapolitan or Calabrian.

Just as Anglo-Norman chivalry brings us figures such as William Marshal, the world of Siculo-Norman knighthood presents Richard of Mandra, Hervé the Florid and William Borrello, knights mentioned by chroniclers who lived here in southern Italy.

More generally, in Italy as a whole, we think of Julius Caesar being emblematic of antiquity and Leonardo da Vinci epitomizing the Renaissance; to call them "archetypes" or "heroes" is to minimize their significance.

Fundamentally, the choice of specific personages exemplifying part of a people's historical patrimony is a question of prerogative. Heritage, by definition, is the part of the past that a society chooses to preserve. This is a right recognized in international law. For example, the *Convention for the Safeguarding of Intangible Heritage* of UNESCO (to which Italy is a signatory) mentions "practices, representations, expressions, knowledge, skills, as well as the instruments, objects, artefacts and cultural spaces therewith, that communities, groups and, in some cases, individuals recognize as part of their cultural heritage." This includes, among other things, languages; Sicilian and Neapolitan are recognized as part of a cultural heritage.

It makes sense that the English, for example, should decide for themselves which of their kings to celebrate. Were the people of a foreign country to question this, perhaps electing a comparatively obscure king as a "better" representation of England's medieval history or culture than, for example, Henry II, the English themselves might well ridicule the very notion that foreign interlocutors would presume to act as interlopers by arrogating such a decision to their alien instincts (see note 13). Like the people of southern Italy, those of Great Britain are perfectly cognizant of their own history, without the need for instruction from outlanders.

Is this to suggest that scholars should refrain from studying societies that are not their own, or that foreign visitors should suppress their personal opinions about the medieval personages encountered in the history of a country or region they are visiting? Of course not. It merely means that the choice of whether a particular historical figure merits special stature, even respect, as a symbolic representative of part of a certain society's past rests with the members of that society. It would be ridiculous for any outsider to try to tell the people of southern Italy how to study or express our history, or which parts of it to appreciate, as if Neapolitans were being instructed in how to be Neapolitan.

Here we are not referring to the medieval concept, or status, of the monarch or knight as a quasi-mystical figure, or even as a personification of the state, but as a symbol of a proud past. Nevertheless, the sense of a certain cultural continuity from the past to the present defines a society to some degree. This clearly exists, and the phenomenon is hardly unique to just one place (see note 15).

Therefore, while the prerogative to study history is not an exclusive right reserved to those descended from the civilization being studied, the culture derived from that history has often been recognized, socially and even legally, as an incorporeal form of hereditary "property" appertaining to a certain *ethnie,* sometimes over the course of many centuries. Here southern Italy differs somewhat from certain other parts of Europe, such as Britain, for the great diversity of constituent cultures from which it historically derives, considered in Chapter 1, a fact that necessitates a rather wide scope in our examination of it.

Be it agreed that the legacy bequeathed upon us from the *Regnum* ruled by Hautevilles and Hohenstaufens is integral to the identity of southern Italians, it is necessary to note that many of the "mainlanders" have a greater affinity for the Angevins, who defeated Manfred Hohenstaufen at Benevento in 1266 and transferred his capital to Naples, while the Sicilians revere the legacy of the earlier monarchs. This is reasonable, and it reflects the socio-political concept of a *Nazione Napoletana,* the "Neapolitan Nation," cultivated during the fifteenth century and revived in the eighteenth.

Nevertheless, amongst the statues of the kings displayed in the niches of the façade of the royal palace in Naples we find, firstly (on the left as the observer faces the building), Roger II, followed by Frederick II and then Charles I.

Most of the kings, and a few queens, of the Norman-Swabian era are prominently entombed in Palermo and Monreale: Roger II, William I, William II, Henry VI, Frederick II, Margaret of Navarre, Constance of Sicily, Constance of Aragon. Roger's mother, Adelaide, who in widowhood was crowned Queen of Jerusalem, rests in the cathedral of Patti near Messina, where the effigy on her tomb is a modern creation.

INTRODUCTION

The theological aspect of this reverence cannot be overlooked. There are still occasions when masses are celebrated for our kings and queens, and for Louis IX of France, whose heart reposes in serene dignity in Monreale, placed there by his brother, Charles I of Sicily (see note 31). The veneration of Louis as his country's heavenly patron is unambiguous, but no medieval king or queen of Sicily has been canonized.

If the Kingdom of Sicily has anything like a "founding myth," it is the story of the Hautevilles in southern Italy. Certain elements of the Hauteville mythos are apocryphal, or at least remain unconfirmed by evidence that is currently known. The family name is a feudal toponym typical of its time, yet its use in Italy was discarded in favor of local ones, leaving us with "Roger of Sicily," never "Roger of Hauteville." The dynasty does not seem to have used a coat of arms, its representation at Monreale being added long after the completion of the other mosaics seen there, and Mikalis, the "mystical" sword of Roger II, has yet to be found. The Mikalis legend may be rooted in the claim that Richard I "Lionheart" of England, while in Sicily *en route* to the Third Crusade, gave King Tancred a sword named "Excalibur," a detail, or tale, recounted by the English chronicler Roger of Howden, who witnessed the exchange of gifts (see note 366). The historicity of the shipwreck of Roger II at Cefalù in 1131 has been called into question (see note 320).

Despite what is stated in books published early in the print era, no contemporary evidence is known to suggest that Roger II founded a knightly order along the lines of the Templars or Hospitallers. The story of his so-called "Golden Knights" constituting an actual order of chivalry is likely as apocryphal as Mikalis. The anachronistic term *torquati aurati* ("wearers of a golden chain") seems to refer, perhaps colloquially, to those enfeoffed knights loyal to him during the first decade of his reign when there was much baronial dissension in the kingdom.

Truth be told, the greatness of the Hohenstaufen, or Staufer, dynasty in Swabia wasn't much more venerable than that of the Hautevilles in Normandy and then Italy. Germany is a land of many historical kings and emperors, amongst whom the Hohenstaufens of the eleventh century might well be viewed as upstarts.

It would be all too convenient for lazy scholars to regard the interest in our medieval monarchs as a revival, perhaps even a novelty, much like foreign scholars' curiosity about the *Regnum*. Yet it is clear, looking at works such as the history of Sicily penned by Thomas Fazello (mentioned above), that this interest, even reverence, has existed for centuries, even if it was suppressed to some degree for a few decades after 1860.

We find, for example, Saint Rosalie, about whom very little is known with certainty, made the principal patroness of Palermo in the seventeenth century and thenceforth taking precedence over Saint Oliva and Saint Ninfa, ascribed a Norman pedigree as if she were a kinswoman of the Hautevilles like Lucy of Cammarata. (Although Rosalie is considered perfunctorily in Chapter 12, the authors deemed it inappropriate to dedicate much space to debunking her legend.)

Aside from strictly religious traditions, rather few exclusively medieval monarchical institutions remain in southern Italy from the Middle Ages; the University of Naples, a secular center of learning founded by Frederick II (and now named for him), need not have been established in a monarchy to be significant. Titles of nobility, which in recent centuries represented little more than unearned privilege, have not been recognized in Italy since 1948, and the state does not grant or recognize personal coats of arms in the manner of the national heraldic authorities in London and Dublin. The head of the Royal House of Bourbon of the Two Sicilies, whose family ruled southern Italy until 1860, bestows honors in several dynastic orders of chivalry recognized by the Italian government, but none of these are medieval in origin (see Appendix 7). Although the crusading Knights Hospitaller and Teutonic Knights were present in the Kingdom of Sicily, both orders surviving in a modern form under the authority of the Holy See in Rome, these distinct entities were not part of the monarchy.

Italy has no more coronations. More than "formal" royal traditions from the Middle Ages, what we find here in the south of the country are the *symbols* of the Norman-Swabian monarchy.

Symbols

Only the most recondite mental gymnastics would permit any historian to give much credit to the Normans and Swabians, earnest as they were, for governing their Italian realms according to a longterm policy, one reflecting anything more than the vague outlines of monarchical government endowed with an efficient system of administration and law. While every monarchy encountered its occasional obstacles, such as The Anarchy in England, even Frederick's long reign saw the Kingdom of Sicily too neoteric to have established itself as firmly in its politics as some contemporaries might have wished. There was chronic strife among the baronage during the Hauteville era and endless discord between the crown and the papacy during that of the Hohenstaufens. Manfred, our last Swabian king, spent the better part of his reign fighting just to survive. Yet the economy and the arts flourished despite these vicissitudes, endowing us with a great legacy.

The principle that kings and queens were, themselves, the embodiment of the population and state they ruled is considered at the end of Chapter 2.

For the most part, the chief surviving symbols of the kingdom and its culture are either artistic, architectural or literary.

Although poetry was composed in Arabic, Greek and even Norman French, that written in Sicilian after 1200 has come to be most closely linked to the people (see Chapter 24). This is a language which, in a slightly more modern form, can still be heard today. Neapolitan, like Tuscan, emerged in its fullness around 1300 when the Kingdom of Naples was already separated from the Kingdom of Sicily.

The Sicilian poetry taught in Sicily's secondary schools is not usually that of Giacomo of Lentini or even Frederick II but the *Contrasto* of Cielo of Alcamo, known in Sicily as *Ciullo d'Alcamo.* (See Appendix 4.) This is more significant for its language and form than its originality, since it was closely inspired by a popular French work. However, it is the lengthiest poem composed in an Italian language during this early era. Sicilians usually identify it by its first line, *Rosa fresca aulentissima.*

The cuisine of southern Italy, as we shall see (in Chapter 27), is a legacy of the past. Spaghetti was known at the court of Roger II and lasagna was served at Frederick's traveling court.

The oldest royal crown to survive as more than a fragment is that of Constance of Aragon, the first consort of Frederick II. (See Appendix 3.)

The Byzantine crown worn by Roger II is shown in the mosaic icon of him in the Martorana, crowned directly by Christ (see Chapter 11). The same crown appears on the ducat and elsewhere, including the mosaics of William II in Monreale. The image of Roger in the Martorana has become very popular for the covers of books about the kingdom, to the point of overuse.

The oldest surviving regalia of the kingdom is Roger's mantle, preserved in a museum in Vienna.

The pendant of Queen Margaret (see Appendix 2) is conserved in New York. This is not, strictly speaking, regalia but royal jewelry.

The imperial eagle, the heraldic symbol of the Hohenstaufens, can be seen carved above the entrances to churches and palaces throughout the former kingdom. Known in ancient Rome, this was long associated with both successive Roman empires, the one in the eastern Mediterranean and the other in what are now Germany, Austria and other parts of central Europe. It is no longer used as an official symbol for Sicily, though a classical variation of it represents the city of Palermo.

Less evident is the lion of the Hautevilles, which appears in Palermo's cathedral and Monreale's *duomo,* in the throne room and chapel of the royal palace, and on a mantle worn by Roger II, but never seems to have been an "official" heraldic symbol of the dynasty.

Several places stand out as sites and sights emblematic of the kingdom. The Palatine Chapel is in the Norman Palace in Palermo. This was the principal royal residence. Palermo Cathedral, much altered since medieval times, and Monreale Abbey, as we have seen, are important churches but also the sites of royal tombs. Castel del Monte is a castle of Frederick II set in what was once a royal hunting ground near Andria in Puglia.

Less tangible but equally important in the public mind is the status of Roger, Frederick and the other royal figures. Our kings embodied the medieval image of sovereigns as conquering knights, defenders, rulers and lawgivers, and there is a certain affection for our queens.

Here in the south, the public attention paid to these historical monarchs diminished somewhat after southern Italy was annexed to the nascent Kingdom of Italy in 1861 (see Appendix 6). In the aftermath of that state's demise, in 1946, expressly anti-monarchical attitudes lingered in Italy for a number of years because of the close association of the dystopic Italian monarchy with Fascism, along with the death and destruction of the Second World War. This had a subtle impact on attitudes about kings and queens generally. At all events, it is noteworthy that the referendum establishing the republic, which marked the first time Italian women could vote nationally, saw the south of the country, in stark contrast to the north, voting to retain the monarchy, and in our century there are "Neo-Bourbon" movements that recognize the heritage of the south under the dynasty that ruled from Naples until 1860.

It is not very unusual to see German visitors placing flowers at the tomb of their emperor, Frederick II, in Palermo. Frederick is something of a cultural icon north of the Alps.

Cultural Evolution

That cultures and societies evolve over time is obvious enough, witness the rapid emergence of a loosely-defined, international "global" culture during the present century. It is accurate to say that cultures are born, thrive and disappear; they may even interact with other cultures to form new "composite" cultures which, during the course of time, can come to be seen as "homogeneous" despite their heterogeneous origins. The society of ancient Rome never made the slightest pretense to deny that its predominant cultural precursor was Greece, embellished by some contributions from a few other civilizations, such as those of the Etruscans and even the Phoenicians. The only way to avoid "external" influences altogether would be through complete isolation.

Most often, a "people," an *ethnie,* consists of a single dominant culture, perhaps with localized subcultures linked to it, and one language, but there is no universal model. Like the countries of the Americas, the Kingdom of Sicily was a society born of several distinct cultures. Much of what was present at its foundation did not, by the end of the Swabian era, disappear from the global stage, only from the south of Italy. Islam continued to flourish elsewhere and the Byzantine Empire survived in Greece and the Balkans. Even the Norman and Swabian cultures did not vanish completely from continental Europe following the end of the Middle Ages. The true casualty of the *Regnum Siciliae* was the Lombard culture of southern Italy, whose living legacy consists of little more than a few words that have come down to us in the Sicilian, Neapolitan and Italian tongues.

The exact point at which the medieval inhabitants of southern Italy became an identifiable, monocultural "Latin" or "Italianate" group is fodder for debate because, like human evolution, it was a gradual process marked by starts and stops. Certainly, the suppression of the last Muslim communities in 1300 was a tangible sign of it. By then, a "Catholic" monoculture enveloped most of what is now Italy, leaving only the diminishing population of Jews unconverted.

Although this type of social evolution did occur elsewhere in medieval Europe during the same period, especially in the Iberian lands where there were at first pronounced differences between Christians and Muslims, it was accomplished in southern Italy with less overt conflict. That is not to suggest that it was always pleasant, or devoid of violence. Frederick II established Lucera, in Apulia, by transplanting Muslims there from towns such as Jato (Iato) in the mountains to the south of Monreale, ostensibly because of civil unrest. Parts of fortified Lucera's impressive walls still stand watch over the surrounding country.

The essential mechanisms of social integration are well known and are still seen in many societies today, particularly in countries having large immigrant populations. The models (or "theories") recognized traditionally by anthropologists and sociologists are accommodation, assimilation and amalgamation. In accommodation, individuals from one culture or society tolerate those of another by accepting them without imposing more than minimal change upon them. This occurred when the Normans reached the large Muslim Arab city of Balharm (Palermo) in 1071 and advocated co-existence with the people living here. Assimilation occurs when those of one group assume the language, religion or social practices of another in a process sometimes called acculturation. This is what happened as the Palermitan Muslims converted to Christianity during the twelfth century. Amalgamation refers to intermarriage between people of different groups, perhaps with some married couples choosing to raise their children in one culture (or religion) or the other. In the Kingdom of Sicily we see accommodation become assimilation, with eventual amalgamation. The loss of alterity on one hand was part of a developing ethnogenesis on the other.

Another reality is the phenomenon of social "change blindness," the inability to recognize subtle changes over time, year by year. The Muslim conversions to Christianity were incremental, like the Latinization of the church. The development of the Sicilian vernacular language must have begun decades before the reign of Frederick II.

In Sicily, the conversion of Greek Orthodox Christians to Roman Catholicism (described in Chapter 4) was a subtle process accomplished by the gradual introduction of Latin liturgy, clergy and monasteries. On the mainland, in Byzantine cities like Bari and Brindisi, it was achieved through more sudden measures such as papal policies implemented by Norman forces. (The Byzantine Catholic communities that dot southern Italy today were founded by Albanians fleeing the fall of their homeland to the Ottomans in the fifteenth century.)

"We are the Normans, Arabs, Greeks and Jews." That is the response one is likely to hear after querying Sicilians (including your authors) about what became of our island's medieval peoples. This reply referring to a fact of ancestry, now confirmed through genetic haplotyping and phylogeography (considered below), is not a novel claim. It was commonplace decades before DNA testing became popular whenever, in explanation, Sicilians would point to the diversity of complexions, along with eye and hair colors, in the population. While this kind of view is more widespread in Sicily, arguably the world's most conquered island, than in most of peninsular Italy, it is not unknown in regions like Puglia and Calabria.

In our age, the relationship between identity and culture is conditioned by modern factors, many facilitated by faster communication than what was possible in the past.

Some forms of cultural assimilation are more direct. In southern Italy, one sees the sale of orange pumpkins in October for the feast of Halloween, a holiday imported from North America. There are American fast-food restaurants here that sell hamburgers and fried chicken. However, compared to Rome and the regions north of it, southern Italy has experienced less of this "invasive" foreign culinary culture, probably for the fact of its own cuisine being considered superior. Likewise, Protestant sects have not made significant inroads into southern Italy, for while the locals may not all be practicing Catholics they are unlikely to embrace a Christian denomination viewed as "foreign."

The anthropological concept of cultural appropriation, as it is usually explicated today, is a modern one, fraught with complexity; typically, it concerns the illicit (or inappropriate) use of the culture of a disadvantaged ethnic group or "less developed" country by persons from an advantaged or privileged group. There is a clear distinction between appreciating a foreign culture in a normal way by enjoying its literature, art, music and cuisine, and, conversely, trying to "usurp" it as if it were one's own. One may well admire, or even acquire, a castle, but to thereby presume to be a king or queen would be whimsical. There's a difference between observing and participating.

Xenocentrism, mentioned earlier in reference to certain foreign scholars interested in the history that is the subject of this book, is the phenomenon of individuals being highly attracted to the culture or society of a foreign country, perhaps to the point of identifying with it personally or even preferring it to their own; this may lead to self-motivated changes in self-identity, perhaps entailing cultural appropriation. There are, of course, varying degrees of cultural appropriation and xenocentrism; it is especially entertaining when foreigners repackage something Italian and attempt to sell it to Italians (see note 1284).

Cultural syncretism often occurs consciously and voluntarily; a modern example is found in cookery, where recipes are invented that draw their inspiration simultaneously from two or three ethnic cuisines. The syncretic Norman-Arab style of art and architecture seen in Sicily was developed by people from distinct cultures working together to create something new. The same could be said of the Normans' adoption and adaptation of some of the existing institutions they found in Sicily, such as the *diwan*, the treasury, which utilized Arab accounting methods, and the *tiraz*, the royal workshop that produced jewelry and silk based on Byzantine and Fatimid traditions. It is nearly impossible to formulate any new art form without some influences from earlier movements.

The Sicilian language, with its numerous borrowings from several tongues, and Sicilian cuisine, with its fusion of eclectic influences, exemplify the process of cultural syncretism.

Living Legacy

Much of the tangible patrimony passed down to us from the Norman-Swabian era, such as its art and architecture, is still with us, and a few symbols of the monarchy itself have already been mentioned. Yet the patina of time has left us with sundry cultural complexities.

The Latin monoculture that prevailed in southern Italy by 1300 was far from monolithic. Within it, two major subcultures eventually emerged: Neapolitan and Sicilian. More precisely, each evolved from the common ancestor born in 1130.

The divergence of the cultures of the kingdom that divided into two states in 1282 was at first rather subtle, and even today the foreign visitor crossing the Strait of Messina to explore the regions on either side of it would be forgiven for failing to recognize the nuances that differentiate the society of Calabria from that of Sicily. While regional differences among Italians certainly exist and can be discerned, the political effort to create a united "Italy," along with an attendant national identity, has attenuated the outward appearance of much that once distinguished each region, be it Tuscany, Piedmont, Umbria or Sardinia.

Beginning in 1282, many of the superficial differences between the royal capitals, Angevin Naples and Aragonese Palermo, concerned such things as architectural styles, with each regnant dynasty looking to its cultural origins abroad for inspiration. A variation of the French Gothic was introduced in the churches erected in Naples (Santa Chiara) while the Catalonian Gothic found its way to Palermo (Santa Maria della Catena). Despite their nomenclature, the interpretation of these movements in southern Italy reflected Romanesque models; the pure Gothic seen in much of western Europe made very few inroads in the "twin kingdoms" of Naples and Sicily.

Turning to philology, late-medieval Neapolitan was influenced more by French while Sicilian bears the marks of Catalan. Sicilian, which during the reign of Frederick II was spoken not only in Sicily but in parts of Apulia and Calabria, boasts more "foreign" influences, notably those from Arabic, than we encounter in Neapolitan and Tuscan. This is not very evident in the surviving poetry of the Sicilian School because the texts in most of the manuscripts known to us, such as those conserved in the Vatican, were Tuscanized, an adulteration that renders more facile translation by Anglophone scholars unlikely to understand much of the Sicilian spoken in the streets of Palermo or Catania. John of Procida, onetime counsellor to Frederick II, brings us these words from his chronicle, or memoir, written about the War of the Vespers:

Or prisu l'unu conviatu di l'altru et dissi lu modu chi avissi a tinirj di quistu factu per fina a la mia tornata, imperò kj ipsu havia ad ordinarj cum lu Plagalogu et cum li sichilianj et cum lu Sanctu Patri Papa Nicola terzu. Et cussì si partiu l'unu da l'altru et andausindj per marj et lu Re di Aragona rumasi in Barsilona.

Then King Peter of Aragon and John of Procida took leave of each other, agreeing to keep the proposed plan to themselves until John could return to Catalonia after meeting with Pope Nicholas III, Emperor Michael of Constantinople and the Sicilian barons. For now, each departed by sea, with King Peter returning to Barcelona.

John of Procida was eloquent for his time.

These words from the thirteenth century are strikingly similar to the Sicilian heard today, though, like Neapolitan, it is rarely spoken in its purest form and includes modern words such as *computer*. Like Welsh, which should not be confused with "Wenglish," the Sicilian sometimes encountered nowadays has been influenced, or corrupted, by Italian. That is also true of Neapolitan and Calabrian.

Despite some recent efforts to bring a knowledge of the Sicilian tongue to the wider world, it remains arcane, but its importance as the first of the Italian vernacular languages to find acceptability in writing, as well as speech, cannot be underestimated.

The disappearance of a language is a significant phenomenon usually related, in some way, to the evolution of a culture. Neapolitan, Calabrian and Sicilian are still with us, if spoken by an ever diminishing segment of the population.

Besides language, certain foods trace their roots to the Middle Ages. In some cases, precise recipes are known. In others, medieval origins are presumed from historical context. The Arabs introduced the rice used in rice balls, and the sugar that sweetens cannoli and other pastries. The transmission of recipes from one generation to the next is an excellent example of the kind of tradition that can thrive, virtually unchanged, over many centuries.

Mosaicry and certain other art forms come to us from the distant past. Even the design of traditional Neapolitan and Sicilian playing cards is medieval in origin. However, the ubiquitous *living* legacies that touch the everyday lives of most people in the south of Italy are the eternal triumvirate of faith, language and cuisine. Not everybody is an art aficionado, but southern Italy's Catholic culture is omnipresent, while communicating and dining are indispensable to living.

Pleasures of the tongue — eating and speaking — offer us at least some insight into the culture of the common folk to complement our knowledge of the medieval social triad of the nobility, clergy and commonalty. That is because, except for legal codes and the occasional mention of such details as popular uprisings or the jurisdiction over serfs, this largest of social classes is conspicuously underrepresented in the written record relied upon by medievalists.

Medieval medicine also merits our consideration. A few medieval medical practices and remedies survived in modern witchcraft.

Apart from obvious cultural manifestations like language, literature, artistic traditions, cuisine and liturgical rites, significant as these legacies are, it is all but impossible to trace the precise path of particular social practices along a straight line from the Middle Ages to the present. It has long been conjectured, however, that certain modern practices are indeed rooted in medieval institutions. An oft-cited example, part of a theory that has become something of a trope, concerns government.

Collectively, the Neapolitans and Palermitans, as the inhabitants of long-extant kingdoms into the middle of the nineteenth century, seem to display less civic consciousness than the Florentines and Milanese, whose cities were historically communes ("city-states") where the ruling dukes answered to strong local councils composed of "citizens." This is not easily quantified, much less proven (at best it is based on observation and inference), but most northerners appear to view their cities with overt pride, as extensions of themselves, while most southerners seem to regard local government as something imposed upon them, as if by a king.[16] This reflects broad theoretical distinctions between the essentially "vertical" administration of the Kingdom of Sicily and the more "horizontal" administrations of the northern communes.

The greatest living legacy is to be found in the people themselves, and here a few explanatory, if perfunctory, remarks about phylogeography are in order.

Genes, Populations and Cultures

Phylogeography is properly defined as the process of mapping the geographic distribution of genetic lineages to certain places, and a map in this book shows these origins for the inhabitants of the Kingdom of Sicily and their descendants (page 53).

In their essence, genetic lineages reflect the presence of haplotypes, and hence haplogroups, that are identified with remote ancestors. A haplogroup, at its simplest, indicates common descent of many people (actually very distant cousins) from a single common ancestor who lived long ago, and it is possible to estimate, in a very general way, approximately when and where that ancestor lived. For our purposes, this profile reaches down across millennia along one line of descent from a remote ancestor through a person's father (the Y haplotype via the father's father) or mother (mtDNA via the mother's mother), two ancestral lines out of millions. The lineages of most people living today have around thirty generations of ancestry since around 1100; of course, not every ancestor in the thirtieth generation of ascent is unique.

Haplotypes are associated with certain historical populations and their migrations. Historical facts complement our genetic knowledge.

The J2 haplotype, for example, originated in the Fertile Crescent thousands of years ago, being successively transmitted in the male line over many generations that migrated in all directions. One path was through Greece and into southern Italy, implying that many Italians in this haplogroup descend from the ancient Greeks. If genetic testing on an Englishman whose known patrilineal ancestors have been in England for a number of generations results in J2, it is highly likely that he is descended, through his father's father's father, and so forth, from a Roman man, perhaps a soldier, present in Britannia in the time of Julius Caesar.

Only the most isolated ethnic populations in the world are associated with just one haplotype. Conversely, the Kingdom of Sicily is the quintessential example of genetic diversity; haplotype sampling of the population of southern Italy is an object lesson in the way that DNA research can confirm a documentary record of historical ethnic diversity resulting from successive waves of immigration.[17]

History, however, is much more than the story of gene distribution, because culture is not based on haplogroups but on social practices and ideas. Although many Normans had red hair, it wasn't red hair that made them Norman; it was their culture that made them Norman. A Sicilian having black hair and brown eyes could very well be descended from medieval Normans in the paternal line, while one having red hair and blue eyes might descend patrilineally from Berbers. To reiterate, each of us has millions of ancestral lines, and current haplotyping methods permit the complete identification of only two, so even those lacking proof of Norman ancestry probably have it.

The people of southern Italy have inherited more from their medieval forebears than red hair (about four percent of those in southern Italy) and blue eyes (around twenty-two percent). Medical conditions such as multiple sclerosis and rosacea are a genetic legacy of the presence of northern peoples like the Goths, Vandals, Longobards, Vikings and Normans (see note 17). Thalassemia is identified with the Phoenicians and Greeks. Genetics may be a factor in the rather low level of alcoholism seen in southern Italy.

Interestingly, the people of southern Italy have always linked physical traits to certain civilizations. Thus a red-haired boy is called a *Normanno* while a girl having black hair is a *Mora* (Moor).

As we shall see in Chapter 1, historians have sometimes taken to identifying the historical peoples of southern Italy rather broadly, overlooking the fact that, for example, the descendants of the Longobards who arrived in Italy during the sixth century were very "Italianized" by the time they encountered the Normans early in the eleventh (the *Placet of Capua* considered in Chapter 24 was written in an early Neapolitan that is far more Italian than Longobardic). This was the result of the assimilation and amalgamation described earlier.

The vast majority of Normans who came to southern Italy were men, such as knights and their retainers. Most of them necessarily wed women who were already present in this region.

Palimpsest

Because, as we have said, history has no authorities, and therefore no "dogma," it is characterized by views that reflect varied perceptions. In our story, the personage about whom the greatest range of interpretations has been published is Frederick II. Be that as it may, we shall concentrate on the essential, viewing Frederick as neither a messianic figure nor a demonic one.

It falls to the historian to separate likely fact from likely fiction. Even the simplest facts and their implications might be viewed differently by two or three authors writing about the same people, places and events. In interpreting essential facts, the historian should consider such factors as historical context with an eye to making presentation of the subject clear, understandable, readable. But nothing must ever be enhanced or "interpreted" to the point that it becomes historical fiction. Jumping to conclusions means springing into an abyss.

Like *multiculturalism* (sometimes "ethnic pluralism"), the term *revisionism* is

INTRODUCTION

often viewed negatively by the population at large. Yet *corrective* revisionism is sometimes necessary if we are to arrive at an accurate account and perception of history instead of tired tropes (see note 2).

Only a few perspectives presented in this work could be described as significantly "revisionist." For example, the view that the accomplishments of Margaret of Navarre might be considered more noteworthy than those of our other queens was rarely expressed in print until the publication of her biography a few years ago. Yet so little was ever published about Margaret that there was little to revise (see note 551).

While history (the chronology of events) itself does not change, our knowledge and perceptions of it certainly do. Some corrective revisionism is rooted in social, scientific and intellectual evolution. Often, it simply broadens and deepens our view about things like bastardy (illegitimacy of birth).[18] Steven Runciman's work was distinguished in its time because it explored the experiences of the vanquished as well as the victors, a novel concept in a predominantly Eurocentric era.

Since around 1960, historiography and the historical method have been shaped by a number of evolving if occasionally conflicting ideas, some quite complex, about what history should be and how it should be written.

Into the early decades of the twentieth century, phenomena such as mental health, spousal abuse and sexual orientation were relegated to the realm of the unspoken and unwritten, particularly when these deviated from the perceived, accepted norm. This was especially the case for women, and these three topics may be relevant to, respectively, Isabella of England, third wife of Frederick II, Matilda Hauteville, sister of Roger II, and Constance of Sicily, Roger's daughter. At all events, the known details are too sparse to facilitate definitive conclusions.

It is logical to expect medieval history written in 2020 to be somewhat different in sociological perspective from what was written in 1920. In the past, before computers and instant communication, several centuries might pass before historians recognized that certain details about medieval royalty should be reconsidered, perhaps revised, in biography.

Into the twentieth century, historians were still referring to William I "the Bad" and his son, William II "the Good," yet these were anachronistic epithets popularized during the modern era.

The new paradigm has spawned the concept of the "modern" history of medieval times. This development is generally beneficial so long as we do not seek to ascribe modern views to medieval people. The "new" approach to biography is consistent with multidisciplinary (or interdisciplinary) research and such ideas as intersectionality and feminism. In general, it is to be applauded (this is considered in Appendix 6).

The revision of ideas involves more than prominent individuals. It concerns our views of events, trends, attitudes, social development, law, education and the arts.

Some concepts, as they are presented, are implicitly rhetorical, or at least more nuanced than they appear. While one might refer, accurately, to the Norman conquest of the island of Sicily, beginning with the Battle of Messina against Kalbid forces in 1061, use of the term "conquest" is less accurate in describing the prior Norman presence on the Italian mainland, where there was a tenuous but real co-existence with the Lombards and Byzantines by the middle of the eleventh century. Indeed, Robert "Guiscard" Hauteville married Sichelgaita of Salerno, a Lombard maiden. What we see are different means to the introduction of Norman power.

Historians in southern Italy were aware of this distinction, but after the Italian unification of 1861 it became commonplace, in order to bolster the new (Savoyard) regime, to paint nearly all the civilizations of southern Italy, from the Punics to the Bourbons, as "invaders" or "foreigners."

That was the biased view advocated by historians like Michele Amari, a rabid supporter of the unification movement. Paradoxically, Amari, a competent Arabist, regarded the Aghlabids, who literally invaded Byzantine Sicily, as benevolent colonizers, while depicting the Neapolitan Angevins cast out of Palermo during the thirteenth century as malevolent occupiers. That simplistically deceptive stance facilitated his inappropriate comparison of the Vespers uprising of 1282 to the ouster of the Neapolitan Bourbons in 1860. It was one of many surreal narratives that collapsed following the arrival of democracy in 1945. Steven Runciman, among others, recognized that Amari's perspective of the Vespers was tainted by the politics of its time.

While a broad consideration of the failure of the Italian unification movement to bring about a true sense of national identity among today's Italians, divided socially by immense chasms separating north from south and left from right, lies beyond the scope of this work, a few facts are noted in appendices 6 and 7.

Amongst medievalist academics seeking to save their own professions as universities outside Europe reduce courses of study in specialized aspects of European history and literature while most students shun the hyper-esoteric, one reads self-centered essays full of pathos about how to attract interest to the field or how medieval culture is somehow "misunderstood."

Recent efforts to identify "Mediterranean" studies are sometimes misdirected. In these pages one recognizes a synchronicity between the Mediterranean and the European, without the excessive need for defining one or the other. Likewise, the contact of the cosmopolitan Kingdom of Sicily with three continents linked by the Mediterranean Sea is obvious enough. In other words, the study of the kingdom, from its prelude and inception until around 1270, transcends either a strictly Mediterranean or European focus. More aptly, it might be described as "Euro-Mediterranean." In this work, however, simplistic characterizations of that kind are generally avoided.

Outside southern Italy, very few courses are dedicated exclusively to the topic(s) addressed in this large volume. We find scholars attempting to make specialized medieval studies, as opposed to introductory or generalist approaches, more "relevant" or "interesting" to people living today. Yet the authors of this book introduce many thousands of curious visitors to the Middle Ages during a typical year (far more than most university professors) through lectures and tours in Sicily, while *The Peoples of Sicily* has sold more copies than the typical academic monograph, and is used in undergraduate courses. Small cities like Monreale and Canterbury have built their tourism economy around an interest in the Middle Ages.

Here in southern Italy there is no risk of our history being forgotten. Everything from the marionette tradition to Neapolitan and Sicilian playing cards to traditional weights and measures to folk customs to religious practices to the cuisine recalls our medieval past. Some of it is explored in these pages, whose authors suggest that a greater interest in the Middle Ages (if indeed this is truly lacking) can be encouraged, not only in universities but in secondary schools, through a presentation of medieval culture as *living* history. A related concept, "lived experience," is more obvious in southern Italy than in the Italian "diaspora" outside Italy, but even abroad it is more often present, and certainly more authentic, among Italian descendants than among "transethnic" Italophiles (see note 1307).

One way that historical studies have evolved for the better in recent times is the importance now ascribed to medieval women.

Women's History

Women's history and the integration of the modern principles of feminist (and gender) theory into the writing of general history bring us certain complexities and challenges. This is usually regarded as the kind of social (rather than political) history mentioned below, but the role of certain women, particularly Adelaide del Vasto, Margaret of Navarre and Constance Hauteville, as regents for future kings placed them in decisive positions.

We may view women's history, as it is approached today, to encompass several main principles. The historical (social, political, economic) roles of women should be identified, whereas in the past these were often overlooked or minimized by the men who wrote history. This presupposes an examination of how women influenced events beyond what may have been noted by their contemporaries, such as chroniclers.

Queenhood itself has religious connections, not only to archetypes but to theology. In Roman Catholicism, perhaps more overtly than in Eastern Orthodoxy, Mary, the mother of Jesus, is revered as the Queen of Heaven. This is one subtle way in which the existence of queens facilitated Catholic belief as the Latinization of Sicily, Calabria and Apulia was slowly achieved during the twelfth and thirteenth centuries. More relevant to our current social culture is the fact that queenhood is perfectly consistent with the concept of Heaven long espoused by the Catholic Church. Not surprisingly, many of the statues of Mary displayed in religious processions are adorned with crowns.

Our countesses and queens were the first female leaders, or consorts of leaders, resident in southern Italy during the Middle Ages about whom much is known. The emperor Constans II was in Syracuse in 663, but we do not know for certain that his wife, Fausta, was with him. Lombard ladies like Gaitelgrima, the wife of Atenulf I "the Great" of Capua who controlled much of southern Italy by 900, are little more than names recorded in the annals of history. Virtually nothing is known about the specific wives of Sicily's emirs.

According to its simplest definition, feminism is an essential paradigm of equality between men and women. That, however, doesn't mean that women were accorded nearly as much attention as men in the medieval record, which was essentially androcentric (rather than gynocentric).

Other connotations, influenced by specific schools of feminist thought, have led some scholars to question whether, for example, certain medieval queens' biographies are sufficiently feminist.[19] Some scholars expect reginal biographies to focus on queenship and feminism from a postmodernist perspective, and criticize those that do not, yet Hubert Houben's fine biography of Roger II is not criticized for its conventional format as the chronology of a king's life rather than a deconstructionist tome.

Arguably, we may be arriving at a place where nearly all female historians, and most of their male colleagues, are implicitly feminist. It could be argued further that most reginal biographies written in our times are intrinsically feminist by their very nature, perhaps for the simple fact of their being written.

The term, and the phenomenon it represents, may be more necessary in some countries than others; a certain lack of feminism (or female equality) in Italy partly accounts for the dearth of reginal biographies in this country until quite recently.[20] It is still the case that women's studies is occasionally considered something of a "niche" in medieval studies, certainly in Italy. However, it receives more attention than it has in the past.[21]

Each woman's story is dictated to some extent by what can be known about her from the historical record. Amongst our Sicilian queens, for example, we find a vast difference in the available sources between Margaret of Navarre and Beatrice of Savoy.

No single solution is suitable to every medieval woman's story.[22]

With the exceptions of Adelaide, the mother of Roger II, and especially Constance, the mother of Frederick II, the queens of our Norman-Swabian era have generally been ignored in Anglophone circles.[23] Until recently, there was no biography of Margaret of Navarre, probably the greatest Queen of Sicily during that period.

There was long a "double standard," articulating one norm for men and another for women. Hugh Falcandus tells us that rumor mongers dared to "slut shame" Margaret for an imagined sexual liaison simply because she smiled at a certain man, who was her cousin. No contemporary Sicilian chronicler criticized Sicily's kings in this manner, despite their harems.

Women are accorded only scant attention in Fazello's *De Rebus Siculis,* published in 1558 as the first major work of secondary literature on Sicilian history to be printed. Here Margaret is mentioned perfunctorily, in such fleeting passages as *Margaritam Reginam eius uxorem voluit totius regni administratricem,* in this case stating simply that she undertook royal administration. A few lines later the source is revealed. *Quod aliquot post annos sub nomine Hugonis Falcandi dum pararem haec edere.* Tellingly, Fazello does not grant Margaret so much as the dignity of an entry in his book's index.

INTRODUCTION

More recent centuries have seen a fair amount written about certain medieval women of southern Italy; we find a multitude of biographies of Joanna I of Naples, who died in 1382. Figures such as Sichelgaita, and also Trota, another woman who studied at Salerno's medical school, are mentioned in Salvatore De Renzi's lengthy *Storia Documentata della Scuola Medica di Salerno,* published in a second edition in 1857, amongst other works. Sichelgaita was much praised beyond Italy by contemporaries such as Orderic Vitalis in England and Anna Comnena in Greece.

The conscious injection of feminist tenets into the writing of history prompts occasional revision as we consider, or reconsider, the importance of certain women based on modern insight and prosopography.

Sources and Methods

This work relies upon original, contemporary ("primary") sources, chiefly chronicles, annals, charters (the diplomatic record), letters (the epistolary record), papal bulls, and such social evidence (art, architecture, coinage, various linguistic and culinary traditions, and so forth) that survives or can be identified.

There are other forms of written records contemporary to the facts they describe, some highly important in the Kingdom of Sicily. We find geographies, most notably that composed by Idrisi for Roger II, and travel diaries like those of Benjamin of Tudela and Ibn Jubayr, who visited the kingdom. There are, of course, the records of the *diwan,* the royal treasury overseen by the kingdom's Arabs. The chronicle of Alexander of Telese, commissioned by Roger's sister, Matilda, reads like a laudatory biography of the king. That of John of Procida, a counsellor to Frederick II and then his son, was written in Sicilian about the War of the Vespers almost as if it were a memoir, albeit in the third-person; intended for a general audience rather than one that could read Latin, it might even be thought of as a very early precursor of what is now called "narrative journalism," or "creative nonfiction." The legal codes are highly informative; apart from those issued at Ariano and Melfi governing law in the entire realm, there were several localized codes.

Besides what, in the work of Alexander and John, might be viewed as a specific literary form, there is poetry, which can be highly informative. By the thirteenth century this was being composed in the kingdom in Sicilian, whereas earlier it was written in the other tongues spoken here: Arabic, Greek, Latin, Norman French. The lengthiest poem of the Sicilian School is the *Contrasto* of Cielo of Alcamo, which appears here, though the body of work of Giacomo of Lentini, by profession a court notary, is more voluminous. The known poems composed by Frederick II are included; this is the entire "Frederican Canon."

Chronicles can be poetic. A stylistic distinction is drawn between prose chronicles, narratives such as that of Hugh Falcandus, compared to those such as that of Peter of Eboli which is composed in verse.

Speaking generally, chronicles provide the fundamental record of events, and some read like histories; many chroniclers were "clerks" (clergy), usually monks. Annals are essentially timelines. Charters are typically decrees formulated by notaries or clerks in the service of the personages issuing them. Like letters, these offer us many useful details, often on a localized or "micro" level.

Chronicles, in particular, must be read critically. For example, the numerical strength of the Norman and Arab armies as reported by Godfrey Malaterra is in some cases quite obviously exaggerated. Falco of Benevento, whose ancestry was probably Lombard, entertained certain biases against the Normans. Naturally, some details reported in chronicles are more easily verified than others; if one of our kings is said to have visited a certain town on a specified date, a decree recorded in a surviving charter that he issued on that day confirms the fact. Some of the contemporary unsealed charters identified by skeptical scholars as "forgeries" are simply copies for which the originals have been lost at some time during the last seven or eight centuries. A few chronicles are hoaxes; here that of Matthew Spinelli of Giovinazzo comes to mind.

The "Norman" chronicles of Amato of Montecassino, Godfrey Malaterra and William of Apulia cover the eleventh century. Godfrey's text takes us through the longest period, to 1098. After that, Falco of Benevento, writing after 1112, picks up the story. Thenceforth, our "on-site" information comes from the chronicles of Hugh Falcandus, Romuald of Salerno and others.

While a chronicler like Matthew Paris, who famously described Frederick II as *stupor mundi,* "the wonder of the world," might well mention details acquired from distant lands, chronicles were necessarily written in or near the places where most of the events recounted actually occurred (see note 1207).

Some stories and quotations have made their way into the modern historical record despite the lack of confirmation in known original sources. The monarch to whom non-contemporaneous writers have attributed the greatest number of myths, libels and statements is Frederick II.[24]

Roger of Howden could write reliably about certain incidents in the Kingdom of Sicily because he passed through it with his king, Richard Lionheart, and probably knew other writers who lived there; he mentioned that the royal tombs of King Tancred and his son in Palermo's Magione church were destroyed as part of an effort by Constance Hauteville to erase every trace of them from the public mind.[25]

Robert of Torigni, a Norman, was the abbot of Mont Saint-Michel; significant as his chronicles are, his statement about Joanna of England giving birth to a son, Bohemond, by her husband William II is probably inaccurate.[26]

Where it regards Italy, rather than his native Normandy, Robert's chronicle was "epiphenomenal." Similarly, some chroniclers are "continuators" whose work is at least partly based on that of their predecessors; examples relevant to our study are the author of the *Ferraris Chronicle,* whose text is drawn partly from that of Falco of Benevento, and Ali ibn al-Athir al-Jazari, whose chronicle is based largely on that of the Zirid scholar Abd al-Aziz ibn Shaddad.

Our Adelaide was derided by Orderic Vitalis, who never even saw her, as "old and wrinkled" when she died aged about forty. Hugh Falcandus, characterized by the Sicilian historian Santi Correnti as "the Tacitus of Sicily," was infamously biased and perhaps a bit nasty, yet his chronicle is overwhelmingly accurate in its essential chronology and details.

The words of Queen Margaret quoted by Hugh Falcandus are probably accurate as he was likely present in Palermo to hear them. Conversely, the speeches attributed by Andrew of Hungary to Manfred Hohenstaufen and Charles of Anjou before the Battle of Benevento may owe something to conjecture.

Like the synoptic gospels, different chronicles sometimes offer us divergent accounts of the same events; this is the case of the descriptions of the adventurous deeds of Richard I of England and Philip II of France during the Third Crusade and at Messina, in 1190, when Richard's sister, Joanna was released from captivity.

It is important to bear in mind that the great majority of decrees and letters, and perhaps even a few minor chronicles, of the Kingdom of Sicily during the Norman era no longer exist. In considering, for example, the letter of Thomas Becket to Queen Margaret quoted in these pages, preserved in the chancery draft kept by the archbishop himself, it must be remembered that we do not, at present, have much of the queen's correspondence beyond that, though some of it is inferred from other sources.

Amongst documentary records of the greatest significance, the known extant manuscripts of the Assizes of Ariano (copies of the laws promulgated around 1140) and the *Ferraris Chronicle* (mentioned above) were rediscovered in Italy during the nineteenth century, and some coronation rites early in the twentieth. A series of letters between Frederick II and his heir, Conrad, was rediscovered in a library during the present century and published in 2017.

Even these sources, noteworthy as they are, did not alter our fundamental knowledge about the kingdom. Rather, they validated the conclusions resulting from prior study. Italian historians had long referred, in a generic way, to "the laws of King Roger" without, so far as we know, having seen the full text of either version of the Assizes published in an appendix of this book, and some of the information in the *Ferraris Chronicle* was adapted from the earlier work of Falco of Benevento, while most of the details from the reign of Frederick II can be found in other sources of that era.

The extant copies of the Assizes of Ariano were copied long after the laws were codified, hence a few historians have questioned the dating of the original act because Falco's chronicle mentions Roger II instituting the controversial ducat at Ariano in 1140 but not the legal code.[27]

The lost chronicle of the Zirid historian Abd al-Aziz ibn Shaddad is the basis for much of what is found in the subsequent work of Ali ibn al-Athir al-Jazari, and the later writing of Wali al Din ibn Khaldun and Abu Abd Allah al Tijani.

Although it may at first glance seem insignificant in the history of the unitary kingdom before 1266, a study of the kingdoms of Naples and Sicily into the first half of the fourteenth century is relevant because some of the developments of that period, reflected in royal charters and other records, are based on events, policies and legislation of the Norman-Swabian era. By way of example, a useful work, though it comprises but a fraction of the relevant material that must be consulted, is the *Codice Diplomatico dei Re Aragonesi di Sicilia 1282-1355* of Giuseppe La Mantia, published in 1918.

While the potential problem has, for the most part, been obviated by the publishing of important records and the redundant availability of work in libraries and on the internet, the loss of significant source information can be a hindrance to the writing of history. Yet "absence of evidence is not evidence of absence." Sometimes an "older" reference work, such as a compilation transcribed and published before 1800, mentions, or even publishes, an original ("primary") source that no longer exists. An oft-cited case that comes to mind was the intentional destruction, by burning, of some parts of the *Catalogus Baronum,* the kingdom's earliest surviving feudal roll, and chancery registers of the reign of Frederick II for 1239 and 1240, by German troops in Naples in September 1943; fortunately, some of this invaluable source material had been transcribed or even photographed before the Second World War, in works such as La Mantia's *Codice Diplomatico* mentioned above.[28]

Some losses are less obvious. The original charters of a number of decrees transcribed by historians such as Thomas Fazello, who died in 1570, no longer exist. Thus we find Jean Huillard-Bréholles, in his *Historia Diplomatica Friderici Secundi* published in the middle of the nineteenth century, citing Fazello, rather than a manuscript, as a source for a decree issued by Frederick II in 1237.

Beyond documentary evidence, another example relates to the church marking the location of the home of the nephews of Thomas Becket in Palermo, personages mentioned in a letter sent by the archbishop to Queen Margaret whilst she was regent for William II. This structure has escaped the notice of most historians because no foundation charter or other contemporaneous record seems to survive that mentions its location precisely; it was later reconstructed as a Baroque chapel (see note 572).

Still another architectural example is the faded, illegible Arabic inscription around the exterior of the cupola of the Martorana church in Palermo. Fortunately for posterity, Michele Amari transcribed it around 1849, before it all but vanished with the incessant weathering of time.

In the same vein, we are fortunate that the funerary epitaph of Joanna of England, the widow of our William II, was recorded before its destruction at Fontevrault Abbey during the French Revolution.

It is equally fortunate that a fragile charter issued by Adelaide del Vasto in Greek and Arabic, being one of the earliest surviving paper documents in Europe, though not the oldest as some scholars claim, was transcribed by Salvatore Cusa in 1868 before it deteriorated further (see note 195).

An interesting example is a charter of Roger I issued in June 1090 which exists only as a translation into Sicilian in the fourteenth century, the original diploma, written in Latin, no longer being in existence. During the nineteenth century, historians actually reconstructed a Latin text from the Sicilian.

A few of Roger's charters were destroyed in the fire at Naples in 1943 (mentioned above) but most of these had already been transcribed and even

INTRODUCTION

published. Unfortunately, some later Angevin records of the Kingdom of Naples which had not been transcribed were burned.

In some instances a record exists in contemporary inscriptions rather than charters. Our proof of the foundation of a church in Palermo dedicated to Saint Peter in 1081 under the patronage of Robert Hauteville and his consort, Sichelgaita of Salerno, is not a charter but the Greek inscription long preserved in that church, razed in 1834, now retained in a museum in Palermo (see note 176). Our evidence for the year of death of Nicodemus, Archbishop of Palermo when the Normans breached the city's walls in 1072, is not a necrology or the prelate's tomb, as his sarcophagus lacks an inscription, but a contemporaneous reference that no longer exists (see note 175).

Thomas Fazello and his contemporaries did not always cite their sources very clearly. Indeed, some were not cited at all. Into the nineteenth century, such works might have marginalia and footnotes, and perhaps generalized bibliographies, without offering the reader much detail beyond that. Such was the spirit of the age, and we should not infer from it that every "unsupported" statement made in a secondary work is inaccurate. Nevertheless, we must seek to confirm the affirmations whenever possible.

Some secondary literature is hardly worth citing, much less relying upon, in a work that seeks accuracy. For example, Isidoro La Lumia, a politician, whose biography of William II presents a narrative about the regency of Margaret of Navarre that merely parrots the chronicles of Hugh Falcandus and Romuald of Salerno, described the queen's physical condition at the age of thirty-eight (she was actually about thirty-one) as "still beautiful, slender and proud." The problem is that La Lumia had no way of knowing anything about Margaret's physical condition or appearance, unmentioned by local chroniclers. Margaret was around forty-eight when she died. The remains in her tomb had been destroyed during a fire in 1811, before La Lumia was born, and by the time he wrote his book, in 1867, the gold reliquary pendant bearing what may (or may not) be an accurate likeness of Margaret was in the possession of Maria Sophia, the exiled Queen of the Two Sicilies (see Appendix 7). Repeating one of La Lumia's errors, John Julius Norwich likewise reports Margaret's birth date inaccurately, at around 1128, something unlikely considering the probable date of her parents' marriage, whereas Charles Homer Haskins thought the book required revision (see note 33). The date of her death has also been reported inaccurately on occasion (see note 754).

The informed history of the following pages, with its slightly Siculo-Neapolitan orientation, is implicitly, necessarily corrective of certain histories written in English during the last few decades by those lacking personal connections to the former kingdom. Rather than a history of the Kingdom of Sicily "seen through the eyes of foreign historians," or a (male) foreigner's narrative that "rethinks" the topic, this one is seen through the eyes of Sicilian historians, both female and male, something rare in major monographs published in English. Though this approach does not necessarily reflect a highly complex "philosophy," it is informed by an authenticity lacking in some works.

While some native Sicilianists might occasionally err, the importance of local knowledge is not to be underestimated. A potential problem arises when a historian is not sufficiently familiar with the social culture of the place being studied. For our purposes, this is southern Italy, hence our chapters on the language and cuisine of our region during the Norman-Swabian era. Among the many other significant topics are medicine, law and religion, along with local feudal practices, both Frankish and Longobard.

Contradictory information is rarely addressed adequately in the broader academic community. What conclusion is to be drawn when a chronicle or charter implies that a certain town in Lucania (Basilicata) is Lombard, yet we find a Byzantine icon that was written (sic) there, on a church wall, when the document was written? At the very least, the artistic evidence suggests that there may have been some Byzantine Greeks in the town at the same time as there were Lombards.

Recent secondary literature (papers and monographs) must be considered, of course, and a fair amount is cited in these pages, but it cannot constitute the nucleus of this history; rather, it is important for historians to evaluate the primary sources themselves instead of relying on their peers to do it for them, to avoid repeating any errors present in that work.

"The facts in a secondary source have already been pre-selected, so that in using them one misses the opportunity of selecting one's own," said Barbara Tuchman.[29]

Some studies blatantly violate the heuristic principle of *lex parsimoniae* advocated by William of Ockham that the simplest explanation of an event about which little is known is usually the most likely one.

Many papers and monographs published today, even when peer-reviewed, focus on what is sometimes called "microhistory," resulting in the verbose study of a single charter, icon, object, chattel, church or localized event. They may explain methodology and sources in their main texts. In this volume such topics, however interesting, are relegated to the appendices and notes. An example in these pages is the discussion of the Kyriaca church and Archbishop Nicodemus, which was initially published in an edited collection of papers (see note 164).

That treacherous Pandulf IV found refuge in his feudal town of Sant'Agata de' Goti when, confronted by a formidable Norman force, he fled Capua in 1038, is less important than the fact that he was expelled from Capua. Do we need a detailed, deconstructionist analysis of his psychological state, reasoning and tactics to understand the immediate, practical effects of his retreat? Is it necessary, or even possible, to discover a semiotic "truth" in his motivations?

At their worst, secondary works advancing extensive analyses or theses, which may reflect a pretense at originality where there is none, perhaps claiming to uncover theretofore "unknown" facts or to reveal new "truths," can be so whimsical that they lead the reader into the pastures of ambiguity. A few descend, quite literally, into the realm of fantasy.[30]

Certain approaches to research and analysis reflect rather recent models. Prosopography, broadly defined as research into the history or characteristics of people for whom specific biographical details are not very complete, is relevant not only for individuals but for the general population. Ethnography is important.

In some cases, the genuinely "new" information is what has been discovered through the application of recent science, such as the genetic haplotyping of the general population or the genetic forensic analysis of bodily remains like the heart of King Louis IX of France at Monreale, efforts which confirm what was already presumed based on contemporary written records.[31] Phylogeography, the most frequent use for haplotyping in historical studies, was mentioned in a previous section.

Climatology is at least peripherally relevant to our studies, useful for making comparisons between past and present. Southern Italy, like many parts of the world, is much warmer now than it was in the Middle Ages. Avocados, mangoes and coffee beans are now grown in Sicily, where wild green parrots fly around Palermo (as they now do in Barcelona, Lisbon and Malaga). The rainfall has diminished and the red palm weevil is decimating the population of stately date palms.

The Kingdom of Sicily has no Geoffrey of Monmouth to muddy the waters of history by mingling them with legend, but the Guelphic biases of authors such as Dante and Boccaccio have shaped perceptions of the Hohenstaufens, and especially Frederick II, here in Italy for centuries, their iconoclasm occasionally becoming predominant to the exclusion of accurate history. The opinion of Dante, who was born fifteen years after Frederick's death, isn't even contemporary.

At the other extreme, the panegyric biography of Frederick II written by Ernst Kantorowicz is a fawning hagiography. It was widely criticized by traditionalists for being more philosophical than strictly historical, requiring a subsequent supplemental volume full of notes and sources to support what it presented.[32]

Italy's historians, like Italians generally, are perpetually divided. Yet this fact of life in Italy is not the scholar's greatest obstacle. Today, the gravest blemish tainting the perspectives of many Italian-educated medievalists, compared to most of their foreign counterparts, is rooted in stagnant pedagogy. Italy's schools, and even its universities, still teach humanities and social science by rote memorization rather than the modern inquiry approach, based on an updated application of the Socratic method, that encourages critical thinking. The serious implications of this retrograde approach on the study of history are far too numerous to encapsulate here, but they have occasionally been noted by historians.[33]

Some weeds blossom into wildflowers, but others remain mere weeds, serving no greater purpose than to occupy space in an otherwise virtuous flower bed. The authors have sought to bring you an orderly garden, not an untamed jungle. Let us leave the weeds to thrive someplace else.

There are various approaches to history. Viewed in its most general, albeit laconic, terms, the major distinction is to be found between *political* history, essentially the chronology of great events, with a focus on prominent figures, compared to *social* history, which tends to focus on myriad details beyond that to encompass specialized topics and the stories of ordinary people. Social history may be said to include women's history, ethnic history, family history, art history and culinary history, as well as studies of the history of music, religion, philosophy, literature, economics and sexuality, usually through an analytical approach. By way of example, a "traditional" history of the French Revolution, emphasizing major events and essential facts, would be mostly political in nature, while one considering heretofore less-studied French women of that era could be said to be chiefly social.

Today, many historical works, including this one, are *both* political and social, overlapping several fields and disciplines. Traditionally, however, most of the histories and biographies written for the general public were broadly political and presented chronologically, while those reflecting esoteric academic studies were essentially social and arranged topically. Political history affords us the framework for social history because underlying facts must be known before they can be evaluated and their relevance ascertained.

There exist many varied, often contentious, ideas about how the writing of history should be undertaken (Appendix 6 lists a number of works in this area). We are concerned with facts and affirmations, not clichés and rebuttals.

In these pages, it is not the authors' intent to respond to every thesis, however creative, that has ever been published, nor to critique the work of peers.[34] It would be ridiculous to engage in a running debate about, for example, the precise number of Norman knights who participated in the Maniakes expedition of 1038, or whether that military operation was a "crusade." Historians even disagree about many names, dates and translations (topics considered in the following sections).

At Ariano, did the Drengot family found the first Norman fief in southern Italy? This is another point, among thousands, debated by scholars (see note 76).

An equally esoteric example regards Bishop Cosmas of Mahdia. Despite what is stated by historians who repeat the errors of their predecessors and peers, the prelate is not mentioned in the Latin chronicle usually cited. The *prima facie* evidence for his presence in Palermo is the sarcophagus in the cathedral's crypt and a related charter, both overlooked by most scholars (see note 411).

In the following chapters, no partisanship shall be expressed in the bitter rivalries that plague the field.

Terms, Definitions, Usage

This work seeks to avoid the semantic and the pedantic.

The usage of certain terms brings us medieval connotations, some unique to the Kingdom of Sicily, and an effort has been made to bring clarity to a lexicon characterized by academic jargon and potentially confusing phrases. This is sometimes complicated further by usage that varied from one place to the other. Apart from the concise glossary, a few terms and phrases are explained here and in the relevant notes.

INTRODUCTION

Recent usage in academic circles has found the word *queenship* referring to the exercise of reginal power, while *queenhood* might be a more general term for the state of being a queen. Traditional references to concepts such as the Queenship of Mary (as Queen of Heaven) make more general use of *queenship,* the Italian *reginalità*. Yet the word *kingship* usually refers simply to a king's reign, without attaching other meanings to it.

A *monastery* was a community of monks, while an *abbey* was any monastery overseen by an abbot or (for nuns) an abbess, though some religious orders use the term *prior*. A *cathedral,* for which Italians sometimes prefer the word *duomo,* was the seat of a bishop, while a *basilica* was a church (though not necessarily a large cathedral) having a certain status in canon law; Palermo's Magione is a basilica even though it is not very large.

Under Roger I the island of Sicily was a "great county," but by the middle of the twelfth century a *county* was nothing more than a non-sovereign feudal territory larger than a *barony*.

In theory, a *principality* or *duchy* encompassed numerous *counties* consisting of *baronies* composed of *manors*. In fact, certain principalities and duchies established by the Byzantines, and especially the Lombards, before the Norman era (Amalfi, Capua, Gaeta), though smaller than the Normans' Duchy of Apulia, were prosperous and at times sovereign. By the twelfth century, some counties were larger than certain duchies. *Duke* finds its origin in the Latin *dux,* but the Longobards introduced the title of *gastald,* which had several meanings.

The holder of a *manor* (or "fief") within a *barony* was typically an enfeoffed knight; in the Kingdom of Sicily the chief feudal roll was the *Catalogus Baronum,* of which only a portion is known. The military (crusading) knightly orders were also present, having *preceptories* and *commanderies* where knights lived like monks.

A distinction is drawn between *serfs,* who were tied to the land, and other members of the peasantry; not every peasant was a serf. The Italian for *manor* is *feudo* (fief), but this book generally uses *manorial* rather than *feudal* to describe such an estate, manorialism being associated with the wider feudal system (as explained in Chapter 2). In this volume *baronage* usually refers to landed nobles collectively, regardless of their rank as counts, barons or enfeoffed knights. Following traditional Italian nomenclature, a *demesnial* estate was royal property owned directly by the crown, compared to the *manorial* lands held "in fee" by barons.

Titles like *familiaris* (royal counsellor), for which Sicily's Greeks preferred *archon,* as well as the Arabic *caïd* (chiefly a title of respect), had specific meanings which, it could be argued, changed slightly over time. For *familiaris* the authors use the Anglice *familiare*. Though it may share the same root, an *amiratus* was much more than an *admiral*.

The contextual connotations of terms such as *constable* and *justiciar* are explained in the text and notes.

At times the kings and queens of Sicily found themselves involved with dominions having other customs and therefore different titles and ranks. We shall use the local nomenclature so that Greek *despots* and Arab *emirs* retain their native dignity. The Holy Roman Empire also had its own hierarchy and ranks.

A *dower* was land given to a bride by her husband (for our queens this was Mount Sant'Angelo in Apulia), whereas a *dowry* was land or gold held by the bride as a gift from her father and perhaps given to her husband at marriage.

Ecclesiastical terms such as *archimandrite* have specific meanings in the Orthodox Church (the eastern church after 1054). By tradition, the Archbishop of Messina bears this title, just as the Archbishop of Venice is a "patriarch."

For clarity, the mainland part of the kingdom after 1282 is referred to as the Kingdom of *Naples,* even though its kings claimed Sicily into the fourteenth century. In some cases, the ethnonym *Sicilian* refers not only to the islanders but to *all* the inhabitants of the Kingdom of Sicily before 1282, though this potentially confusing usage has generally been avoided. *Sicily,* rather than terms like *Regnum Siciliae,* usually denotes the island alone.

Constance of Sicily, the daughter of Roger II, is usually referred to as *Constance Hauteville* to avoid confusion with her daughter-in-law, Constance of Aragon, who, as a queen consort, could be called "Constance of Sicily."

The *tarì* was a small gold coin introduced by the Arabs. The *ducat* was a silver coin introduced by Roger II at Ariano in 1140. The *augustale* was a gold coin inaugurated by Frederick II with the Constitutions of Melfi in 1231. The various weights of the *follaris,* or *follis,* were copper, though it seems that a few were struck in bronze.

The use of certain proper nouns depends on context. In general, *Syracuse* refers to the ancient and medieval city, *Siracusa* the modern one; we find the Arabs' *Balharm* becoming the Normans' *Palermo,* which was *Panormos/Panormus* to the ancients. The proper nouns *Apulia* and *Lucania* are the ancient and medieval names for *Puglia* and *Basilicata,* but the *Apulia* known to the Normans included part of *Basilicata,* while the *Duchy of Apulia* eventually encompassed most of peninsular Italy south of Rome, even Campania (the region that includes Naples and Salerno). In general, unless reference is made explicitly to the dukedom, *Puglia* is used to indicate the geographical region (excluding Basilicata) from the end of the Norman era. In order to minimize confusion, the use of political names of small regions such as *Terra di Lavoro* and *Principato* is generally avoided. *Camera Reginale* (see note 404) and *Monarchia Sicula* (note 227) are not used as those terms were popularized after 1300.

Swabia (see the map) was much larger in 1200 than it is today. The use of such terms as *Spain* and *Spanish,* likewise *Italy* and *Italians,* is rather general, not necessarily descriptive of actual states or their inhabitants. Depending on context, *Germans* are speakers of German, and *Arabs* speakers of Arabic, even though most of Sicily's "Arabs" were of Berber (Amazigh) ancestry. *Fatimid* refers to a dynasty, to which the Kalbids owed fealty, and its culture, though *Arabo-Berber* is sometimes more accurate in reference to the Sicilian Muslim population ethnically.

In certain contexts modern names are preferred, so the Italian *Garigliano,* rather than the Neapolitan *Gagliano,* is used for the river near Minturno, *Agrigento* over *Girgenti,* and *Enna* rather than *Castrogiovanni.*

To avoid confusion in references to the two "Roman Empires" that existed during the period under study and had an impact on the Kingdom of Sicily, the authors use *Holy Roman Empire* for the German lands ruled by the Hohenstaufens and *Byzantine Empire* for the predominantly Greek lands of the Balkans, Greece and Asia Minor ruled from Constantinople. For clarity, the "King of the Romans" is usually "King of the Germans" and the "Emperor of Constantinople" is usually the "Byzantine Emperor." Terms such as "imperial" may refer to either, depending on context.

The Greeks sometimes referred to Puglia, Calabria, Basilicata and other parts of southern Italy collectively as *Longobardia,* while peoples in what is now Italy often identified the Byzantine Empire as *Romania.* To avoid confusion, such terms are not generally used here.

There was no state called *Italy* during our Norman-Swabian era, when that term appears in charters only occasionally, usually because of its etymology from an ancient proper noun for *Calabria* (see note 279). In modern usage, it is grossly incorrect, and offensive to Italians, to refer to "Italy *and* Sicily" because (since 1861) *Italy* denotes the *entire* Apennine Peninsula, plus some Alpine territories, Sicily and Sardinia. Much preferred is the more accurate "peninsular" or "mainland" Italy; conferatur "continental" United States, which excludes Alaska and Hawaii.

Orthodox and *Orthodoxy* refer to the Grecophone "eastern" church in southern Italy in the ecclesiastical jurisdiction of Constantinople or (occasionally) Cyprus. This reference is not restricted to the "Byzantine" churches after 1054 but even those present centuries earlier, the obvious exceptions being Latin monasteries, such as those of the Benedictines, as well as certain "secular" (diocesan) clergy in Lombard territories (Salerno, Capua, Benevento) into the eleventh century. Terms such as *Catholic* and *Roman Catholic* refer to "western" or "Latin" dioceses and clergy under the papal jurisdiction of Rome, whether before or after 1054.

The term "Basilian" is not used for clergy and churches that were Byzantine Greek and subsequently Orthodox. "Byzantine" is often used as shorthand for "Byzantine Greek" or "Italo-Greek." Whether the Grecophone population of medieval Italy should be regarded as ethnically Greek is a matter of debate.

Although, as we shall see, the Great Schism of 1054 was merely the first step in the division of Christianity, the terms *Orthodox* (for Eastern or Greek) and *Catholic* (for Western or Latin) are generally used beginning with that year.

The term *medieval* is preferred to *pre-modern.*

Regardless of any doubts about his origin and identity, there was no convincing reason to refer to *Hugh Falcandus* by anything other than his traditional name. Here in Italy, the mother of Roger II is usually *Adelaide del Vasto,* not "Adelaide of Saronno." In some records, such as those referring to a daughter of Roger II, we find *Adelisa* or *Adelina.*

Heraldry has its own terminology, which in English records is derived from Norman French, with words like *gules* (red) and *sable* (black). This art is incidentally relevant to battles, tournaments, seals and coinage after 1200.

In these pages, the terms *multicultural* and *diversity* are descriptive, not used in the sense of certain political connotations or any political "agenda," ditto *polycultural.*

Translations, Spellings, Legibility

Except where it is otherwise stated, all of the translations in this volume are the work of its two authors. In some instances, these were the first translations of certain passages ever published in English; in other cases, however, the authors simply preferred to render their own translations, effected without reference to those of others.

For the benefit of specialist scholars, some notes, as well as the first appendix, include the original Latin texts.

Almost all of our contemporaneous sources are to be found in Latin, Arabic or Greek, those in Norman French or Middle Sicilian being rarer. Certain Latin terms are open to interpretation depending upon context, where *castrum* may be a remote castle or a fortified town. We find the term *comes* (count) more often than *baronis* (baron), with the latter sometimes inferred from context (though *seigneur* is used in French) when it refers to a landed noble who had several knights under his feudal authority. The word *miles*, sometimes *milites*, refers to a knight.

Certain names are rendered in a way that preserves their Siculo-Neapolitan character, so *Godfrey* Malaterra, recalling *Goffredo*, instead of the more common *Geoffrey*. For the Swabian dynasty, *Hohenstaufen* is generally preferred to *Staufer* and *Staufen*.

While *Gregory* and *Gerard* are different names, there is confusion between them in some sources. Even in Latin, *Isabella* of England, the wife of Frederick II, seems to have been known by that name, sometimes written *Ysabella*, rather than *Elizabeth*. Certain names are not translated very simply despite conventional practice (see note 1001).

For some places medieval spellings are preferred, hence *Manopello* instead of *Manoppello*.

In some cases Italian is preferred to Latin, so *Amato of Montecassino* and *Leo Marsicano*. The *Annales Ceccanenses* is also known as the *Fossanova Chronicle*.

The Albanian *Durrës*, Italian *Durazzo*, Latin *Dyrrachium* and Greek *Dyrracheion* all refer to the same city, with the last preferred during the era of the Byzantine Empire.

Transcriptions from the Arabic depend mostly on the more common usages in English, with *Koran* rather than *Quran*, and *Hasan* as-Samsam but *Hassan* al-Kalbi.

Most spellings are American rather than British, and abbreviations are generally eschewed, even in the notes. *Rome* is sometimes a metonym for the papacy.

Garamond, which was popular in the Kingdom of the Two Sicilies and remains in wide use in Italy, is a forgiving typeface in relatively small print sizes. Were it much larger than what is used here, this work would have run to two volumes.

Dating

Although the exact days of certain events are given, some are indicated more generally, by month or season. This is not for lack of accuracy in Latin or Greek charters, where kalends and indictions are precise enough, or even the differences in local calendars. Rather, chronicles, letters and charters do not always indicate days but only months. Chronicles and necrologies are infamous for their lack of concordance, while a Muslim year can straddle two Gregorian years.

Despite what some authors would have you believe, the exact days of many events are unknown or even debated.

Discovery

A few remarks about the structure of this work are appropriate.

As a general work on a major subject, this book is very different from the monographs of perhaps three hundred pages that typically focus on a very specific topic and era. Unlike a thematic work on, let's say, urban development in medieval Puglia or the iconography in the mosaics of Monreale, this one has a unifying, chronological narrative.

For convenience, and to avoid the publication of a volume consisting of thousands of pages of excessively arcane explanations, tangents and digressions, the text is sprinkled with citations of works by various scholars supported by detailed endnotes. (Nowadays, the main narrative texts of many monographs in the humanities are tainted by authorial speculation and reflection that should be relegated to notes or appendices.)

For the purpose of convenient reference to a public-domain work, some of Michele Amari's Italian translations of Arabic chronicles are cited even though English versions (listed in the Sources) have been published.

In this volume, esoteric topics, or those that are only peripheral to the Kingdom of Sicily itself, are largely avoided in the main text without, one hopes, rendering the narrative too reductive. To avoid redundancy, works by the authors are occasionally cited which, in turn, give original sources that are not listed here; most of the chapter on the regency of Margaret of Navarre was adapted from *Margaret, Queen of Sicily*.

The appendices bring to the reader something of the "tangible" legacy of the Norman-Swabian era, obviating the need to consult several books or articles to find this information. Appendix 7 presents a few details about the "revival" of the kingdom in the nineteenth century.

Compared to most academic monographs, which, for the sake of brevity, rely upon simple citations and notes, this reference work includes a fair number of original texts, such as Robert Guiscard's oath of fealty to the pope and the papacy's subsequent declarations of the apostolic legateship to Roger I and Roger II, likewise the Treaty of Benevento during the reign of William I. A letter of Thomas Becket to Queen Margaret is also included, in both Latin and English.

The authors found it necessary to include the Assizes of Ariano because of the code's significance in establishing the framework of the kingdom as its fundament, and for the benefit of scholars and aficionados the original text has been retained. It is surprisingly difficult to find the texts of both codices published together.

This book is the first publication to include the Sicilian royal coronation rite (Appendix 5) with rubrics and notes in English.

Not only is the *Contrasto* the lengthiest poem of the Sicilian School, in Sicily it is generally considered the most important one. Here the English translation accompanies the Sicilian text.

Because the genealogical tables are intended to show ancestry, kinship and marriage as simply as possible, such details as birth order are not always indicated. For visual clarity (and to avoid drawing lines that confusingly cross over other lines), an elder sibling may occasionally be placed where the reader would normally expect to find a younger one, or a first spouse positioned where the reader might reasonably presume to see a second one.

Some of the genealogical tables of royal women include coats of arms even where these were assumed after the lifetime of the countess or queen indicated. Since the use of armorial heraldry in most of western Europe arrived in the third quarter of the twelfth century, it is clear that Elvira of Castile and Sibylla of Burgundy never saw the coats of arms later associated with their dynasties. As we stated earlier, the Hautevilles did not make use of a coat of arms or heraldic insignia as we understand the term; the design depicted in mosaic in Monreale, representing the blazon *azure a bend checky argent and gules,* is apocryphal.

Original sources are most often cited where there is direct relevance to the medieval Kingdom of Sicily, while secondary literature sometimes suffices for events elsewhere or during other historical periods. For the convenience of most readers, there was a preference for books in English where generalist works are suggested for very broad topics such as the crusades.

Citations of information drawn from chronicles may not indicate the location in the text very precisely because not all of these narratives are divided into chapters and some lack identifying rubrics altogether. For that reason, certain citations in this book's narrative are general or quote the original Latin, while others (Falco of Benevento, Romuald of Salerno, Richard of San Germano) cite the year of the entry. The chapters in the chronicle of Hugh Falcandus are based on those formulated by Giovanni Battista Siragusa in 1897. An imperfect alternative, for a few sources, is to cite transcriptions or translations in specific publications by page number. By necessity, the numeration of the statutes (articles) in one of the codices of the Assizes of Ariano in Appendix 1 was added by the authors. Likewise, the authors had to divide the *Ferraris Chronicle* (Alio 2017) and the *Jamsilla Chronicle* (Mendola 2016) into chapters as neither was yet published with the text divided into chapters or otherwise (by years or events).

For convenience in consultation, citations from charters usually refer to published transcriptions rather than manuscripts conserved in archives or libraries even when the authors consulted the original documents. Sometimes more than one compendium is indicated for the same charter.

A few statements regarding the results of original scientific research are "unsourced" because the authors, though informed of certain details, are not at liberty to identify every source of data to which they are privy. The precise location of Sicily's few surviving Kalamata olive cultivars (in the southeastern part of the island) is based on a genetic testing report provided to the regional

INTRODUCTION

agriculture ministry which prefers, in order to protect the trees from potential vandalism, not to make it public. A DNA study commissioned by the Archdiocese of Palermo on a sample of the bones of Saint Rosalie, now the chief patroness of this city, is likewise unpublished and remains so in order to preserve the dignity of her cult. Only one instance of an uncatalogued charter is mentioned (see note 27) in these pages.

This volume is not an exercise in modern historiography or retrospective commentary. That Friedrich Nietzsche regarded Frederick II as "the first European" is not very relevant to this reference work. At best, it might be noteworthy in a study of the monarch as an inspiration for modern movements. Shakespeare's use of a "Kingdom of Sicily" as the setting in a play has no connection to actual history.

The section of the bibliography dedicated to secondary literature lists works consulted which were found informative or at least somewhat relevant, and therefore worthy of mention even if sometimes contradictory to the facts presented in this book. A number of works are listed that were not cited in the notes, with an effort made to recognize recent studies (post-2000) by scholars having various academic interests and backgrounds.

The bibliography does *not* reflect an attempt to list *every* monograph or paper ever published, whether useful or not, nor is the listing of any work an indication of your authors' agreement with every idea presented in it. Indeed, certain works are listed for the purpose of offering the reader alternative perspectives, although (as stated in note 34) it is not the purpose of this book to debunk various theses advanced by fellow scholars. While several monographs, articles and dissertations listed in the bibliography cite our work, that certainly was not a criterion for consideration (book reviewers often criticize books in which their own monographs or papers are not cited). Works related to peripheral topics mentioned in this Introduction are not listed in the bibliography.

The typical "academic" monograph burdens its main text, and hence its readers, with details about theories and research, utilizing concise footnotes.

In this work, endnotes were chosen over footnotes because the former allow for quoting passages of original text at greater length (for the benefit of scholars) and tend to distract less from readability of the narrative (for casual readers). Observed the Italophile historian Sir Harold Acton, "The cult of the footnote, involving, at its apogee, a page crammed with encyclopaedic detail in small type to a solitary line of text, is no doubt a proof of diligence, but it may also be a tedious form of exhibitionism."

Very few websites are cited. In the few instances where internet content is cited in an endnote, the most relevant passage(s) are quoted verbatim.

A few passages of text, and some of the photographs, charts, tables and maps, published in the following pages previously appeared in books or articles the authors wrote and for which they hold the exclusive copyrights. While one seeks to publish completely original work at every turn, in certain instances there is no need to "reinvent the wheel." As this work is the result of years of research by the authors into the history of medieval Sicily, it is logical that a few parts of it have already been published elsewhere in some form, or delivered by them as papers at lectures.

The crown shown on the title page is an adaptation of those in the illuminated chronicle of Peter of Eboli completed early in the reign of Frederick II. Most of the photographs that appear in this book were taken by the authors. Except for scholarly citations of secondary works, the opinions and positions expressed in these pages are those of the authors.

Most books published in English (in the original) about the Kingdom of Sicily are written by non-Italian authors outside the territory of the former kingdom, hence the use of words such as *they, their* and *there* rather than *we, our* and *here*. This book was written by Sicilians in Palermo, hence the latter forms, as in "our" kings and "here" in the capital.

One never knows the precise extent to which a book will be distributed, especially in an age that finds electronic editions supplanting paper volumes. Public and university libraries are by no means "obligated" to purchase works such as this one, and the publisher made an effort to keep the softcover edition's price affordable.

Let's begin our journey.
Buon proseguimento.

MAPS and CHARTS

KINGDOM OF SICILY

Europe in the 10th Century

Before the Normans: Lands and Peoples in 1000

KINGDOM OF SICILY

Regnum Siciliae: The Norman-Swabian Kingdom of Sicily

MAPS

KINGDOM OF SICILY

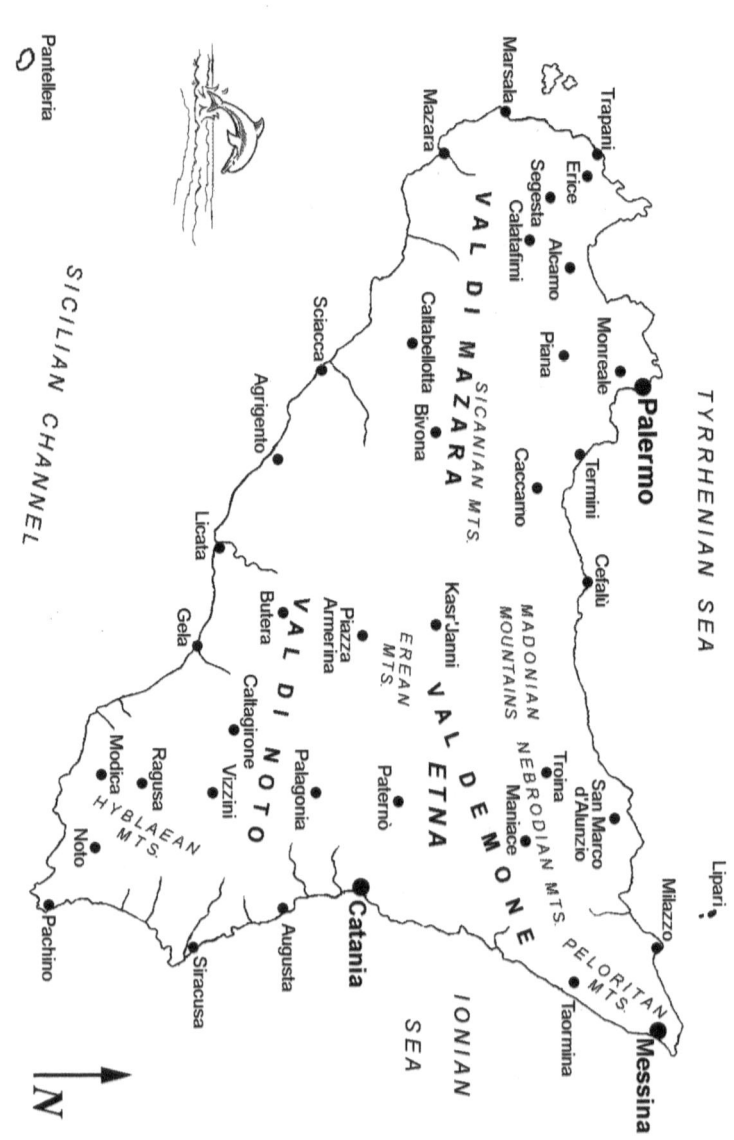

MAPS

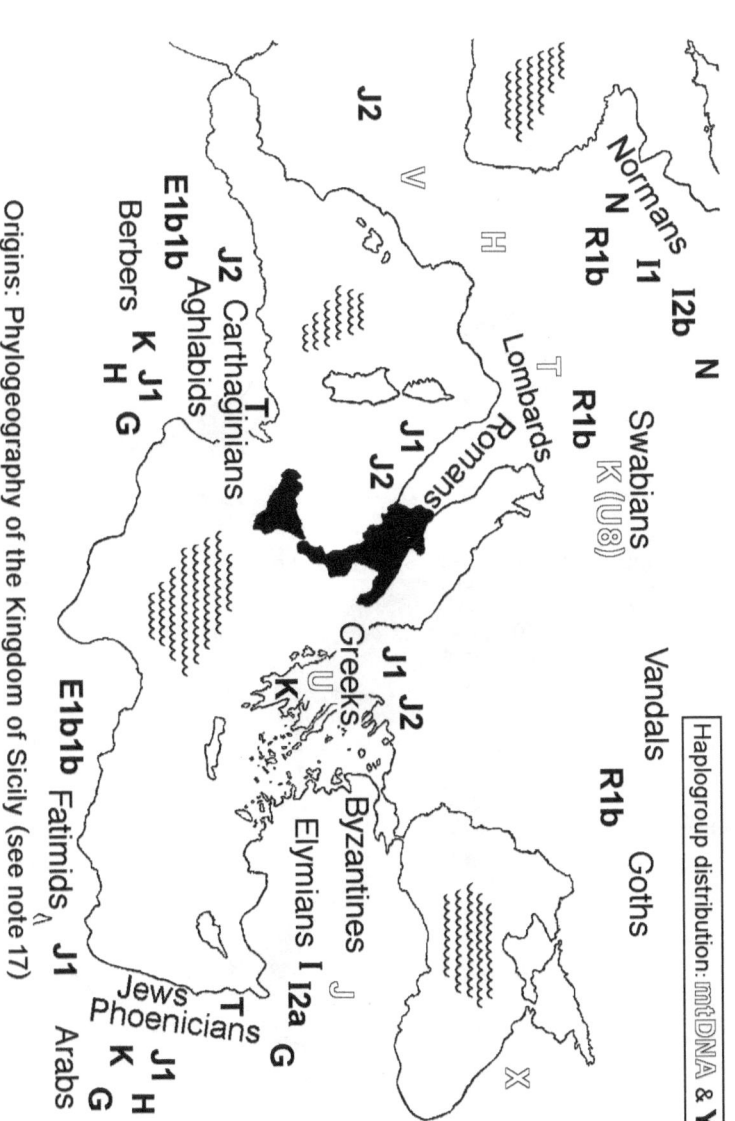

Origins: Phylogeography of the Kingdom of Sicily (see note 17)

53

KINGDOM OF SICILY

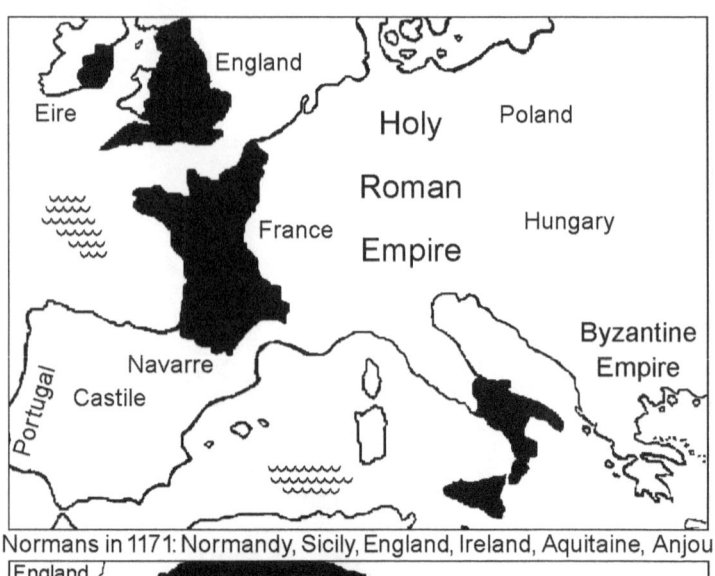

Normans in 1171: Normandy, Sicily, England, Ireland, Aquitaine, Anjou

Hohenstaufen dominions under Frederick II in 1229

MAPS

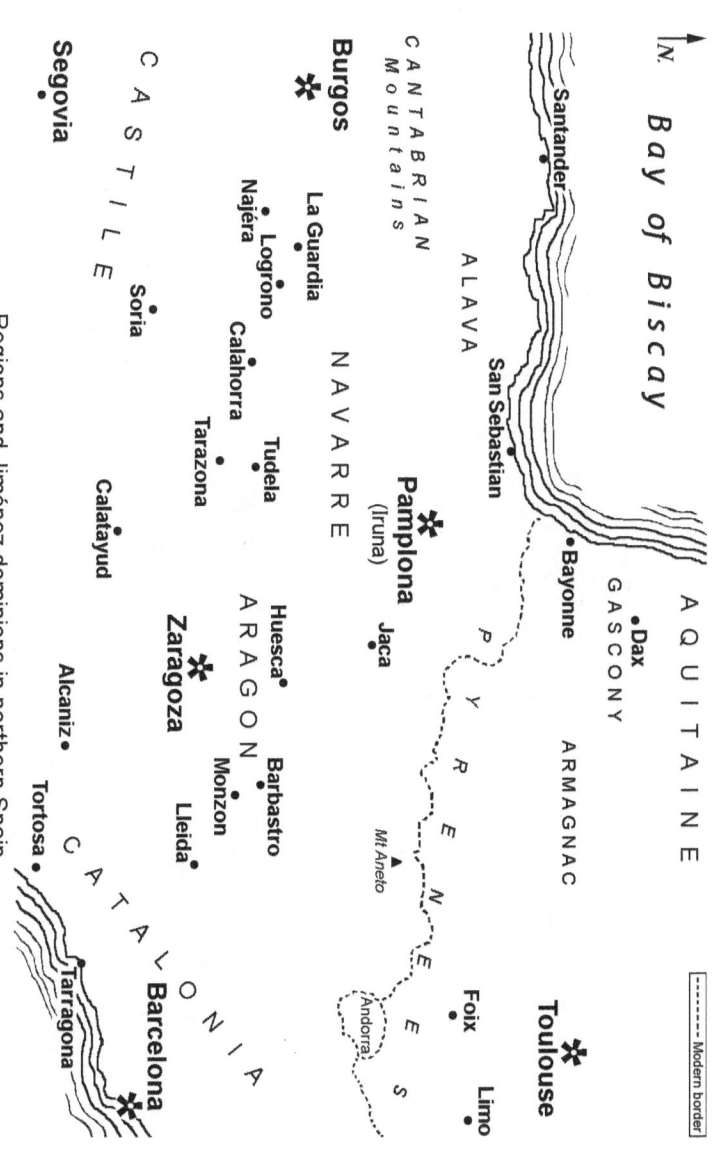

Regions and Jiménez dominions in northern Spain

55

KINGDOM OF SICILY

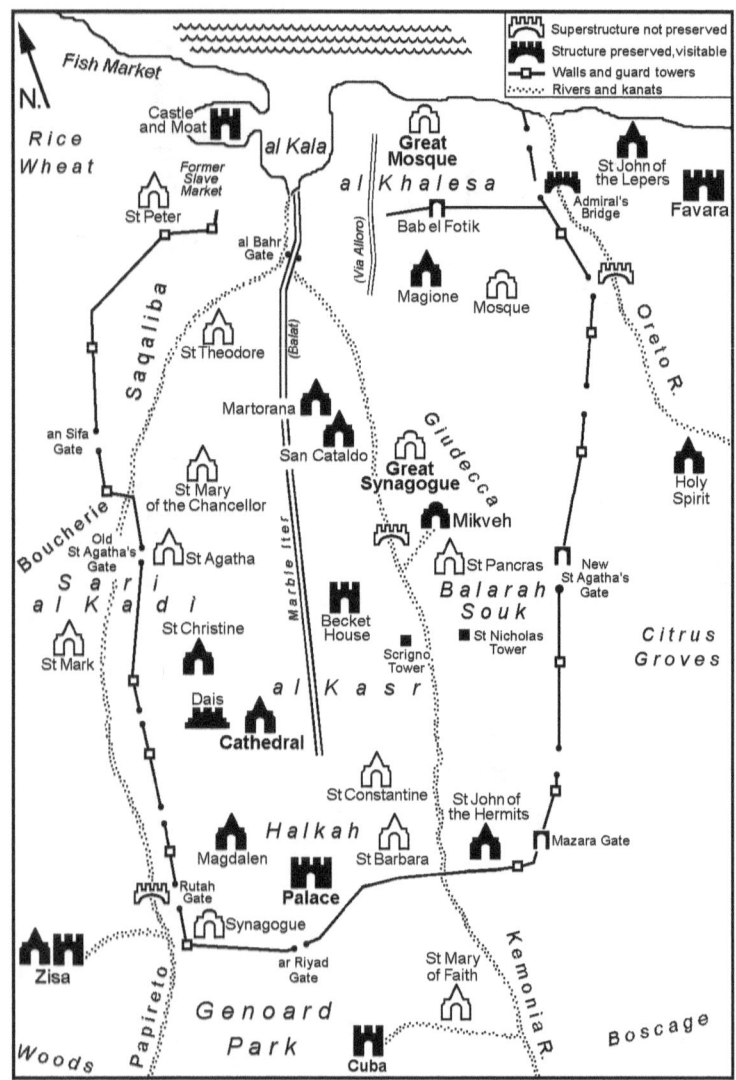

Palermo around 1180

MAPS

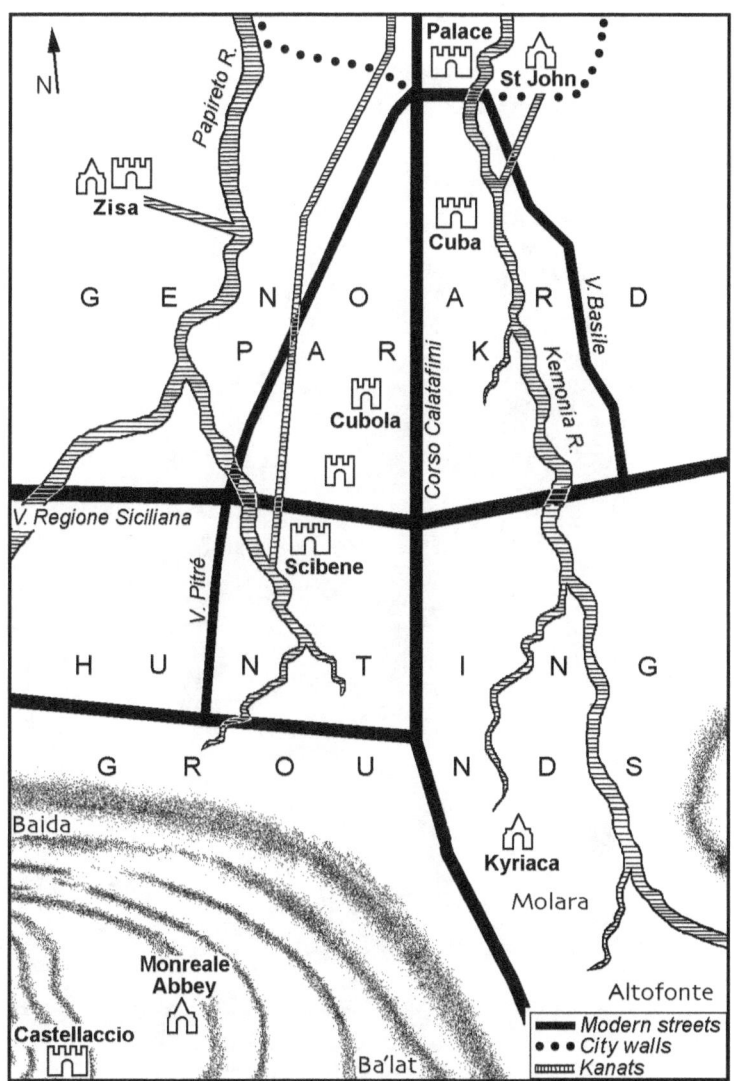

The Genoard Park south of Palermo

KINGDOM OF SICILY

This map dated 1570 shows some streets that existed in medieval Palermo. The city wall shown was erected in 1536.

MAPS

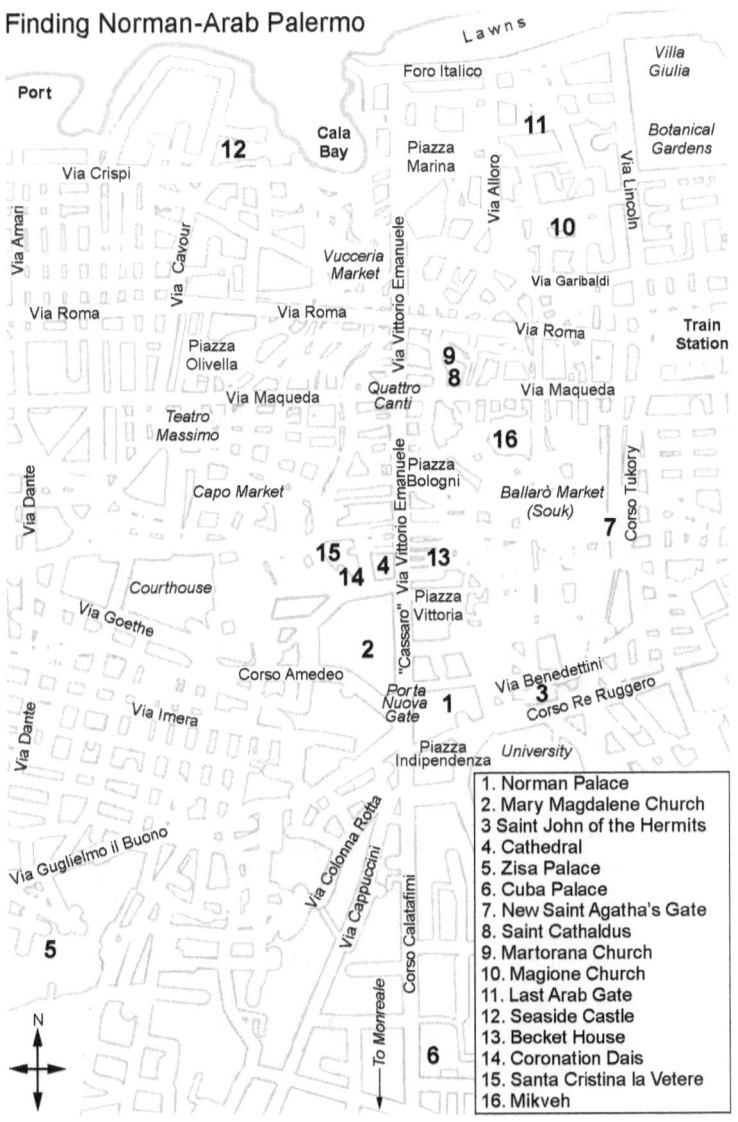

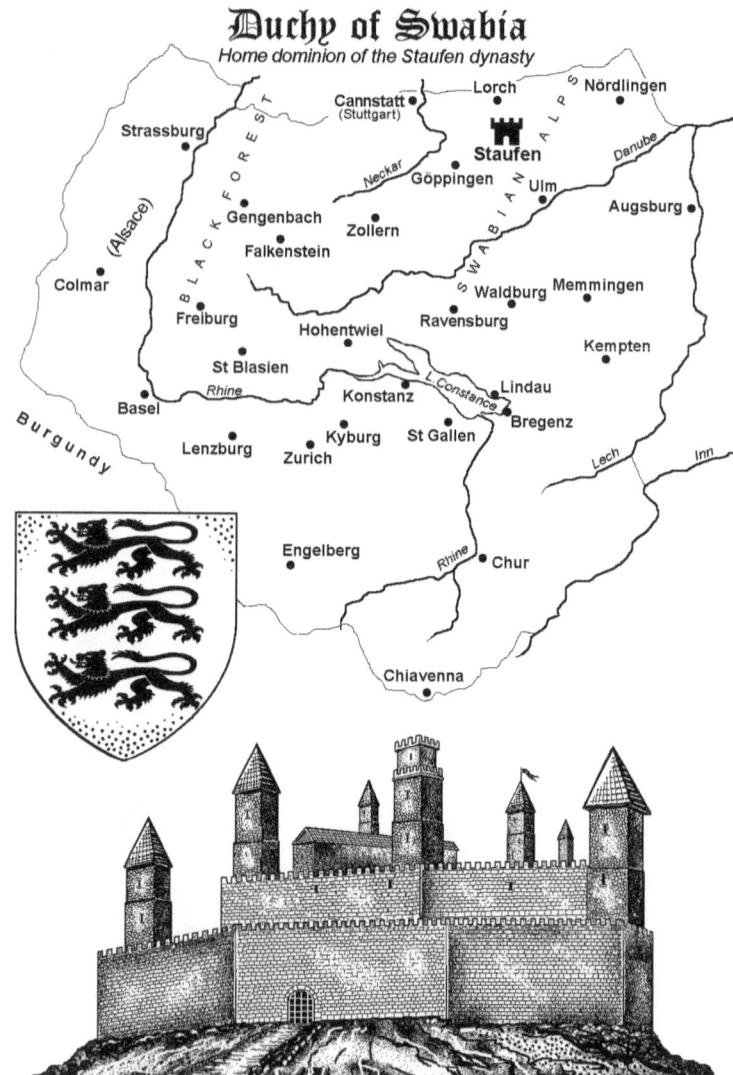

Hohenstaufen Castle in the 13th century

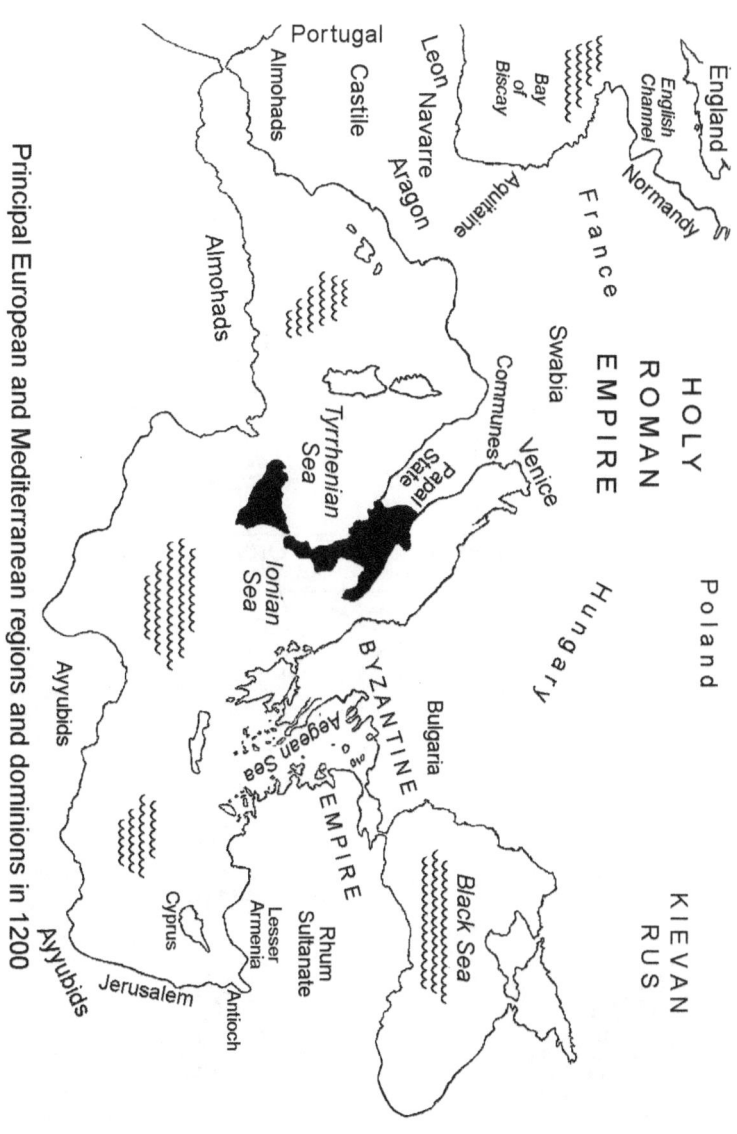

Principal European and Mediterranean regions and dominions in 1200

Jewish Districts of Siracusa and Palermo

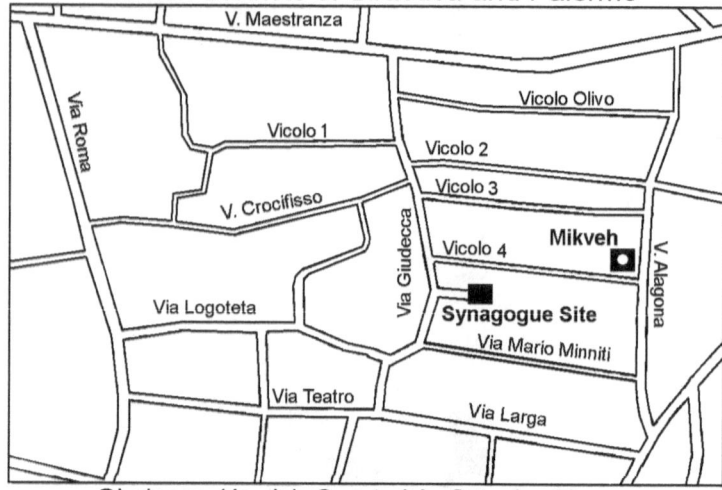

Giudecca (Jewish Quarter) in Ortygia, Siracusa
Great synagogue site is St John's Church. Mikveh at Via Alagona 52.

Jewish Quarter and souk (Ballarò Market) in Palermo
Great synagogue site is San Nicolò da Tolentino Church. Mikveh under Jesuit cloister.

MAPS

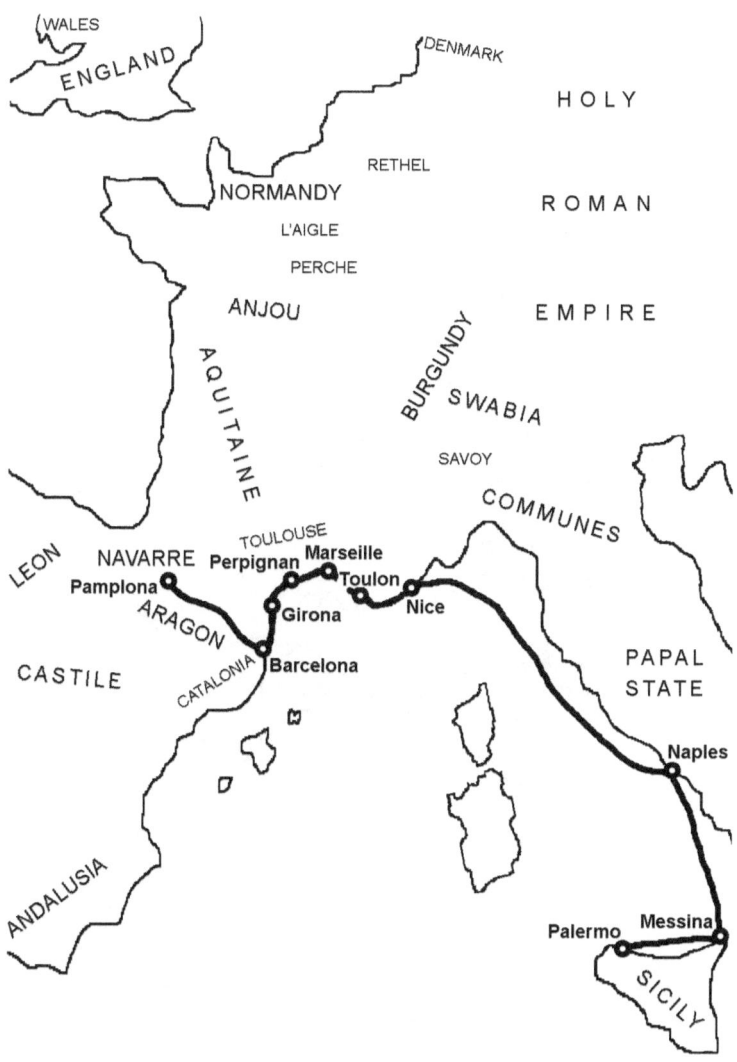

Journey of Margaret of Navarre to Palermo to wed William I

KINGDOM OF SICILY

Journey of Joanna of England to Palermo to wed William II

Principal Mosaics in the Palatine Chapel

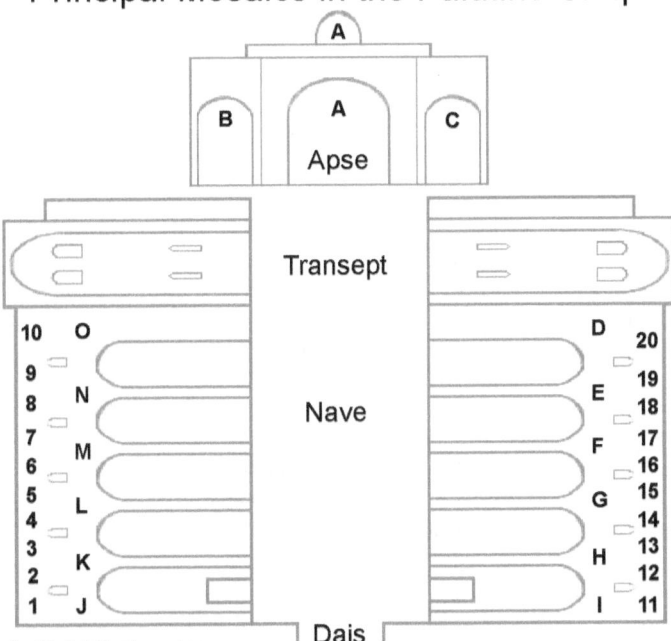

A. Christ Pantocrator
B. Saint Andrew
C. Saint Paul
D. Dove appears
E. Noah leaves ark
F. Noah plants vines
G. Construction of Babel
H. Abraham greets angels
I. Lot confronts Sodomites
J. Lot leaves Sodom
K. Abraham sacrifices Isaac
L. Rebecca at well
M. Jacob blessed by Isaac
N. Jacob dreams
O. Jacob confronts angel
1. Adam and Eve sin
2. Knowledge of sin
3. Expulsion from Paradise
4. Adam and Eve in Paradise
5. Cain and Abel
6. Cain murders Abel
7. Lamech and his wives
8. Enoch ascends into Heaven
9. Noah and his family
10. Noah builds ark
11. God creates Eve
12. God shows Adam the tree
13. God rests
14. God creates Adam
15. God creates beasts
16. God creates birds and fish
17. God creates the heavens
18. God creates trees
19. God separates land from sea
20. God creates light and seas

Monreale Duomo and Abbey

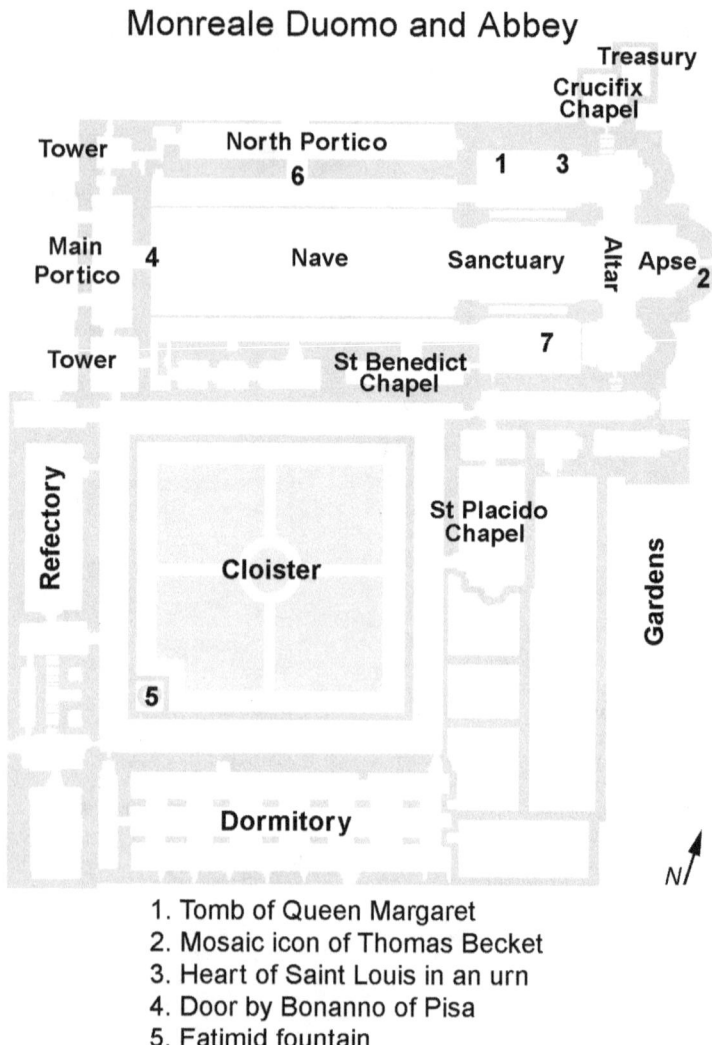

1. Tomb of Queen Margaret
2. Mosaic icon of Thomas Becket
3. Heart of Saint Louis in an urn
4. Door by Bonanno of Pisa
5. Fatimid fountain
6. Door by Barisano of Trani
7. Tombs of William I and William II

MAPS

Carved Capitals in Monreale's Cloister

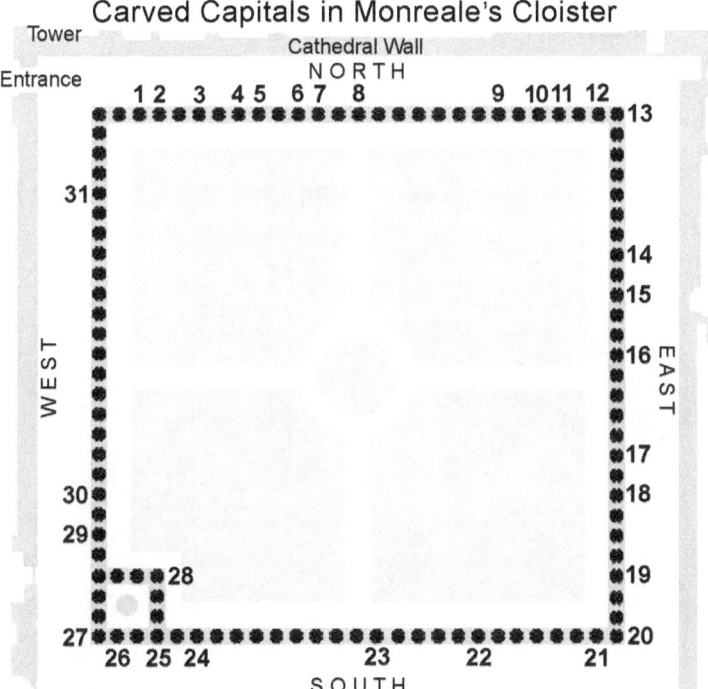

1. Arab archer and swordsman
2. Lions and other beasts
3. Merman (triton) and knights
4. Parable of Lazarus
5. Knights and Saracens
6. Windswept leaves
7. Men killing beasts
8. Life of John the Baptist
9. Story of Samson
10. Norman knights
11. Massacre of the Innocents
12. Evangelists and mermaids
13. Magi, Annunciation, etc.
14. Men supporting capitals
15. Vigilant owls, harpies
16. Men, beasts, lizards
17. Joseph of Old Testament
18. Abraham sacrifices Isaac
19. Resurrection of Jesus
20. Willam and Margaret (?)
21. Lions devour men and stags
22. Acrobats
23. Eagles supporting capital
24. Arab killing sheep or goat
25. Mounted Norman knights
26. Harvesting of grapes
27. Apostles, Flight into Egypt
28. Wine barrels, seasons
29. Prophets and angels
30. William II offers cathedral to Virgin
31. Lion slaughters pig as Norman knight and Saracen warrior watch

Selected Mosaics at Monreale

```
                    1
              48  U  49
          X   50 □VW51  Y
                Apse

        ┌─28─┐          ┌─29─┐
        │ 26 │ Transept │ 27 │
        └────┘          └────┘

   23 T  ┌47┐                    ┌30┐  A  2
   22    └──┘                    └──┘     3
   21 S  ┌46┐                    ┌31┐  B  4
   20 R  ┌45┐          Nave      ┌32┐  C  5
   19 Q  ┌44┐                    ┌33┐  D  6
   18 P  ┌43┐                    ┌34┐  E  7
   17 O  ┌42┐                    ┌35┐  F  8
   16 N  ┌41┐                    ┌36┐  G  9
   15 M  ┌40┐                    ┌37┐  H 10
   14 L  ┌39┐                    ┌38┐  I 11

            25  K  Z  J  24
                13  □ 12
```

Squares indicate mosaics behind pillars

Key to Numeration of Selected Mosaics

1. Christ Pantocrator (ruler of all)
2. God creates Heaven and Earth
3. God divides light from dark
4. God divides waters
5. God separates lands from seas
6. Creation of sun, moon, stars
7. Creation of birds and fish
8. Creation of Adam and animals
9. God rests
10. Adam placed in Garden of Eden
11. Adam dwells in Eden alone
12. God creates Eve
13. Eve presented to Adam
14. Eve tempted by serpent
15. Forbidden fruit consumed
16. God confronts Adam and Eve
17. Expulsion from Eden
18. Adam and Eve toiling
19. Sacrifice of Cain and Abel
20. Cain kills Abel
21. God confronts Cain
22. Lamech kills Cain
23. Noah commanded to build ark
24. Miracle of loaves and fishes
25. Healing of crooked woman
26. Events from life of Jesus
27. Miracles of Jesus
28. William crowned by Christ
29. William dedicates church to Mary
30. Possessed woman healed
31. Healing of leper
32. Healing of lame man
33. Peter rescued from water
34. Raising of widow's son
35. Healing of woman's hemorrhage
36. Raising of Jairus' daughter
37. Peter's mother-in-law healed
38. Loaves and fishes (also 24)
39. Crooked woman healed (also 25)
40. Man suffering edema healed
41. Healing of ten lepers
42. Healing of two blind men
43. Money changers expelled
44. Jesus saves adulteress
45. Paralyzed man healed
46. Healing of lame and blind
47. Magdalene washes Jesus' feet
A. Noah constructs ark
B. Animals board Noah's ark
C. Dove arrives
D. Animals exit ark
E. Rainbow signifies God's covenant
F. Drunken Noah in vineyard
G. Tower of Babel constructed
H. Abraham meets angels at Sodom
I. Abraham's hospitality
J. Lot protects angels
K. Lot flees destruction of Sodom
L. God commands sacrifice of Isaac
M. Angel stops sacrifice of Isaac
N. Rebecca offers water to servant
O. Rebecca journeys to meet Isaac
P. Isaac with sons Esau and Jacob
Q. Isaac blesses Jacob
R. Jacob flees Esau
S. Jacob dreams of ladder
T. Jacob wrestles with angel
U. Theotokos and Jesus enthroned
V. Saint Sylvester
W. Saint Thomas Becket
X. Saint Paul enthroned
Y. Saint Peter enthroned
Z. Theotokos and Infant Jesus

48. John, Philip, Bartholomew, Luke, James, Peter, Archangel Michael
49. Angel Gabriel, Paul, Andrew, Mark, Thomas, Simon, Matthew
50. Martin, Agatha, Anthony, Blaise, Stephen, Peter of Alexandria, Clement
51. Lawrence, Hilarion, Benedict, Mary Magdalene, Nicholas

Principal Mosaics in the Martorana

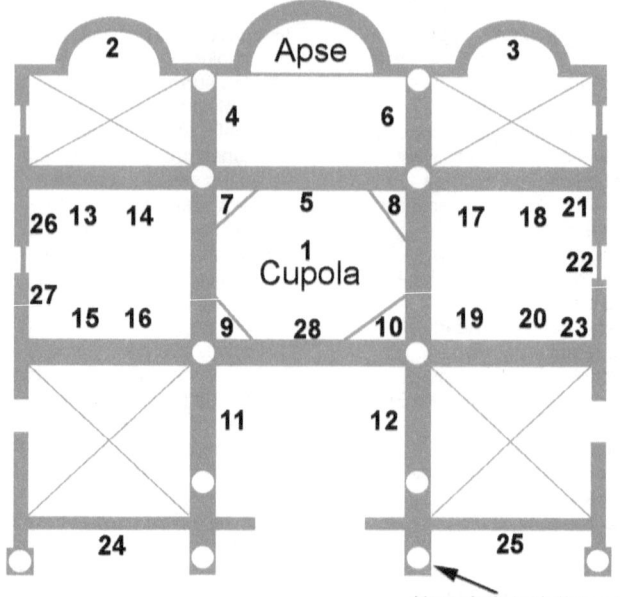

Koranic inscription on pillar

1. Christ (in cupola)
2. Joachim
3. Ann
4. Angel Michael
5. Annunciation
6. Angel Gabriel
7. Matthew
8. John
9. Mark
10. Luke
11. The Nativity
12. The Dormition
13. Andrew
14. Peter
15. Philip
16. Thomas
17. Paul
18. James
19. Bartholomew
20. Simon
21. Cyrus
22. Hermes
23. Timothy, Titus or Tarasios
24. George of Antioch and Mary
25. Roger II crowned by Christ
26. Damian (defaced)
27. Cosmas (defaced)
28. Presentation in the Temple

PROLOGUE

The Kingdom of Sicily was built, very literally, upon the ancient civilizations of southern Italy.

Some of Europe's oldest Paleolithic cave art will be found in Sicily and its coastal island, Levanzo, while the earliest "European" megalithic temples, erected around 3600 BC (BCE), stand on Malta, long associated with southern Italy. On Sicily there are vestiges of similar structures and a few dolmens, and on the mainland Matera may be nearly as old.

The first identifiable civilizations of southern Italy are those of the Sikanians in Sicily and parallel societies such as those of the Samnites in what are now Abruzzi and Campania, the Oenotrians of Calabria, and the Mesapian cultures in Puglia and other regions. Sicily was eventually contested by Greek and Punic peoples, with the former finally dominating most of the large island, along with nearly all of the Apennine Peninsula south of Rome.

This was what became known as *Megale Hellas,* "Greater Greece," the Romans' *Magna Graecia.* The Greeks left us much more than a few temples, statues and theatres. Their mythology, literature, philosophy and science form the basis of the civilizations of Europe and the Mediterranean. Here the writing of history is an ancient art perfected by natives like Diodorus Siculus. Later, Paul of Tarsus, the author of much of the New Testament, preached in Sicily.

Megale Hellas, once home to more Greeks than Greece itself, was a loose conglomeration of sovereign states, with Syracuse, the home of Archimedes, as its cultural cornerstone but independent cities occasionally siding with foreigners, such as the Carthaginians, against fellow Greeks. Under Rome, the Greek language so esteemed by the Romans, its alphabet sharing the same Phoenician origins, was still spoken in isolated pockets of the former *Magna Graecia,* and it was taught to children of the patrician class. Greek civilization, of course, left its indelible mark on Rome and the world, and its medieval incarnation would figure in the culture of the Kingdom of Sicily, the *Regnum Siciliae*.

Palermo, the capital of the *Regnum Siciliae*, was founded as a Phoenician city around 740 BC. Unlike Rome, where one must dig to find something that boasts comparable antiquity, Palermo, the Greek *Panormos* and Arabic *Balharm*, has standing Punic walls even along those narrow urban streets ignored by most tourists. The fortified palace of our Norman kings was erected upon such walls of what was once a Phoenician or Carthaginian citadel, where an archway of that era is preserved.

The construction of churches on the sites of Greek temples is not unusual. In southern Italy the cathedral of Syracuse is one of the most magnificent examples. Many of the saints traditionally venerated in southern Italy are local martyrs of antiquity: Januarius in Naples, Agatha in Catania, Lucy in Syracuse. They are associated with feasts and even foods.

Most medievalists who specialize in the subject that is the chief focus of this volume are at least vaguely aware of the influence of antiquity on the society and culture of the Kingdom of Sicily. Not for nothing is the chronicler Hugh Falcandus, with his allusions to an earlier age, compared to Tacitus, while the roots of the Assizes of Ariano are readily found in the Code of Justinian.

The place itself merits our consideration.

Most of the former *Magna Graecia* was ruggedly mountainous, certainly more so than regions like Tuscany and Umbria, with their graceful, rolling hills. Even where the peaks were not very high, they were rocky and imposing. It was never easy to tame such a defiant landscape, despite its seductive beauty. Agriculture was a perpetual challenge, and so was travel.

The *Regnum Siciliae* covered around 112,000 square kilometers (43,243 square miles) which, as a point of reference, was slightly smaller than England's 130,000. The peninsular part of the kingdom extended over an area of approximately 85,000 square kilometers; for comparison, Scotland encompasses around 80,000. At 26,711 square kilometers, the island of Sicily is larger than Wales and slightly smaller than Massachusetts.

The most northern point of the mainland territory was just north of Pescara on the Adriatic side and Terracina, in what is now Lazio (essentially the ancient Latium) on the peninsula's Tyrrhenian side.

There are a number of impressive mountain chains, like the Sila of Calabria and the Gran Sasso of western Abruzzi, that are part of the Apennine range for which Italy is famous. The highest peak in the peninsular part of the kingdom is Corno Grande near Teramo in Abruzzi, at 2912 meters (9553 feet). Of course, the most famous mountain in the southern part of the peninsula is Vesuvius, the ominous volcano that casts its shadow over Naples. It is 1281 meters high. Like Etna, Vesuvius boasts a very long recorded history useful to geologists.

Majestic Mount Etna, Europe's largest active volcano and greatest natural wonder, rises to a variable 3329 meters above sea level. Sicily's next highest peak is rocky Pizzo Carbonara at 1979 meters, in the Madonian Mountains.

PROLOGUE

Much of the medieval flora and fauna are extinct. The native deer and boar have been supplanted by foreign species. The Nebrodian fir, whose resinous timber provided the wood for the ceilings of Palermo's palace chapel and Monreale's *duomo,* is endangered and the Abruzzo bear is rare. Storks, similar to those of northern Spain, have been reintroduced. There are still a few wild cats, which resemble the grey tabby. The Norman deerhound, the Sicilians' *cerveru,* is long gone, but breeds such as the *cirneco* (Sicilian Hound), Neapolitan Mastiff, Abruzzo Sheepdog (the white *maremmano* related to the Pyrenean) and *cane corso* (similar to the Bull Mastiff) were known in the Middle Ages. The greyhound is mentioned in the falconry treatise of Frederick II.

Some of the places and edifices mentioned in the following pages are not readily identified. In certain cases, the descriptions by chroniclers and other writers are, by today's standards, imprecise. Woods have vanished and the courses of rivers have been diverted. Certain churches, such as Saint Barbara in Palermo, were destroyed during the Middle Ages, with nothing attesting to their quondam existence except a few lines of text in a charter. Little remains of Saint Cyriacus (see note 164), near Monreale. The locality identified by Idrisi, the court geographer of Roger II, as "Platani" could be any of several towns overlooking Sicily's Platani Valley, where the king's cousin, Lucy of Cammarata, had a castle.

If certain sights, sounds and creatures are gone, they are hardly forgotten. Indeed, they are integral to our story.

Greek temple at Segesta (top), and the Norman castle built upon the Temple of Venus at Erice, the medieval Mount Saint Julian

Chapter 1
BEFORE THE NORMANS

The beginning of the "Middle Ages," from the Latin *medium aevum,* is traditionally, and conveniently, dated to the deposition of the last Roman emperor in 476. This nomenclature appeared during the Renaissance in the fifteenth century; every age is touched by the chronocentrism that leads those living in it to think of themselves as time's brightest light.

The End of an Empire

The fall of the empire in the west was, in truth, a slow, complex process that coincided with the rise of other peoples and the emergence, indeed the dominance, of Christianity, a fact now recognized by historians. It was a murky morass that found the western part of the empire, in its waning years, ruled not from Rome but from the city of Ravenna, on the Adriatic coast to the east of Bologna, while the eastern half was ruled from Constantinople, a vast metropolis straddling Europe and Asia. Masters of the Mediterranean and a large chunk of Europe, the Romans were the first to unite southern Italy under a centralized administration. In 285, the great Roman Empire was divided into its western (Latin) and eastern (Greek) halves, and in 330 the Emperor Constantine, who legalized the practice of Christianity, chose to rule all of it from Byzantium, or Constantinople, his "New Rome." Despite its continued power and prosperity, however, Rome, both east and west, was to face many challenges during the fourth century.

In 378, a Roman army was defeated at the Battle of Adrianople, now Edirne in European Turkey, by the ravenous Goths, a Germanic people forced into imperial territory by the migrating Huns. Despite a widespread belief, there is little evidence that the stirrup was used by the victorious Goth cavalry at this battle; their success was owed to superior infantry tactics and the philosophical will to win, things they probably learned from their Roman foes.[35]

The Goths' foundational history, the *Getica,* was completed in 551 by a certain Jordanes, himself a Goth educated by Romans. Based partly on the work of Cassiodorus, his text is significant for its clues about men who might be considered the first medieval European "kings."

Although the exact origins of European kingship are much debated, a popular theory posits that it was an outgrowth of tribal customs known in such societies even before they were conquered by the Romans. Descriptions of this "Germanic kingship" owe much to the secondhand account of Tacitus, but a fruition of these social practices likely occurred before most tribes were Christianized. The Germanic kings were at once judges and military leaders, and in some cases kingship became hereditary. Women also seem to have had a role in tribal leadership. Though our knowledge of these societies during this early period is too sparse to draw firm conclusions, one is tempted to make certain comparisons with the Celtic cultures, where similar customs may have been known.

We know much more about millennial Rome, and so did her adversaries. Jordanes was hardly unique; men like him had been familiarizing themselves with Rome's culture for centuries. Some of the greatest Germanic military leaders were trained by the Romans, who permitted people on the fringe of the empire to obtain citizenship. In an earlier time, such a man was Arminius, or Hermann, who won a decisive battle against the Romans in the Teutoburg Forest in AD 9 using what today would be called guerrilla tactics. In the fourth century, the Germanic ranks were full of aspiring Hermanns.

By the time the Vandals, Suevians, Burgundians, Alans and other tribes crossed the Rhine in 406, the "Great Invasion" had well and truly begun. Alaric's Visigoths, or "Western Goths," sacked Rome four years later, but the great leader died of malaria at Cosenza, in Calabria, before he could invade Sicily.

In 429, the Vandals under Gaiseric (Genseric) occupied the Roman province of Africa, within striking distance of Sicily. Their arrival in his city the next year was one of the last events witnessed by a dying Augustine of Hippo, who would not have approved of the invaders' Arianism.

An invasion of Sicily in 440 was followed by a series of mass raids, but the sporadic Vandalic incursions were halted by the island's Byzantine Greeks over the next few years.

What followed was a series of migrations and invasions throughout the moribund empire. Attila's wandering Huns invaded northern Italy in 452, though they never made it to Sicily.

Following the pattern established by the Visigoths, the Vandals sacked Rome in 455, returning to Sicily in a long series of raids in 461. By 468 they were masters of the island. Compared to much of their African domain, Sicily was a verdant jewel, more lushly forested than it is today, a precious emerald in a sapphire sea. Syracuse was the wealthiest city under their direct rule.

The Vandals left most of the existing administration in place but, true to their eponym, they vandalized the synagogue of Syracuse, leaving it little more than a pile of rubble.

The Dark Ages

In 476, Odoacer deposed the last Western Roman Emperor, the eleven year-old usurper Romulus Augustulus, and, as stated earlier, the beginning of the Middle Ages is usually dated from this time. The Vandal king Gaiseric, meanwhile, concluded a "perpetual" peace with Constantinople's "Romanized Greeks" shortly before his death.[36]

In 491 the Ostrogoths, or "Eastern Goths," achieved complete control of Sicily, ousting the Vandals and Alans, who retreated to their kingdom in Tunisia. In imitation of the last western Roman rulers, the Goths made Ravenna their Italian capital.

Like the Phoenicians and Carthaginians before them, the Vandals and Goths suffered the fate of having most of their history written for them, in Latin, in a disparaging tone, by detractors. This has colored modern perceptions of these civilizations which are only now being corrected by historians based on sources such as the *Getica*.[37]

Where the Greeks and Romans of southern Italy left something of cultural value behind, the legacy of the Vandals and Ostrogoths is more difficult to quantify, apart from some genes for blondish hair and blue eyes. However, the Germanic languages are their lasting legacy. Their rule defined a brief *entr'acte*, bridging the gap between what are now identified as the ancient and medieval epochs, even if nobody living in the year 500 was likely to have made such a distinction.

For the moment, their success seemed assured, but Sicily was a coveted gem. Only with the assiduous effort might the Vandals and Ostrogoths keep the precious possession in their grip. Peninsular Italy would be still more difficult to hold.

The Ostrogoth leader Theodoric the Great managed to keep his people unified against the Byzantine Greeks. His death in 526 brought an end to decades of peace.

Beginning in 535, the Byzantine Greek general Belisarius defeated the Vandalic and Gothic "Barbarians" during the Gothic War, a conflict as cultural as it was political. This left the island of Sicily and most of the peninsula south of Rome under the control of the Byzantine Empire ruled from Constantinople. At its greatest extent, this "Eastern Roman Empire" encompassed Greece, Asia Minor, the southern Balkans, some lands around the Black Sea, parts of Arabia and Egypt, and the Holy Land, but its history after the sixth century is largely a story of the gradual loss of territory, wealth and influence.

With a few exceptions (notably some monasteries in Ireland), it was the Byzantine Greeks who conserved much of the cultural legacy of Rome and the early church while a great part of western Europe was obscured by the shadow of the "Dark Ages," the first few medieval centuries, until the reign of Charlemagne beginning in 768.

For now, the Byzantine Empire could afford campaigns such as those prosecuted against the Vandals and Goths. A vestige of its prosperity is the grand basilica dedicated to Saint Sophia, erected in Constantinople in 537. The world's largest church epitomized Byzantine wealth and culture.

Back in Italy, however, the tenacious Goths did not succumb easily. The Ostrogoth leader Totila raided Sicily in 550 in an attempt to reclaim it for his people. In reality, this was little more than a lengthy incursion. Totila's defeat by Byzantine forces at the Battle of Taginae, in Umbria, two years later signalled the end of Ostrogothic influence in Italy, but their Visigothic cousins continued to rule part of what is now Spain.

The Lombards

Following the Byzantine victories over the Ostrogoths in the bloody Gothic War, another Germanic people, the Longobards, invaded Italy *en masse* in 568, establishing a base at Pavia and eventually reaching the south of the peninsula.

In crossing the Alps into Italy, the Longobards acquired a defined identity as an *ethnie,* where previously they were just one of many tribes that the Romans associated with the Suevians known to Julius Caesar, lacking a known history beyond some sparse outlines of an oral tradition. Yet some of their early art has been preserved.[38]

Coming to be called *Lombards,* and lending their name to a region of northern Italy, they handily conquered rural areas of the peninsula's south, where they introduced something vaguely resembling rudimentary manorialism, inspired, perhaps, by certain aspects of the "Roman villa economy" of the fourth century associated with the emperors Diocletian and Constantine. The Byzantines, for their part, were generally content to rule the more important urban and monastic centers, leaving the rest for the Lombards, but over the next few centuries there were occasional conflicts. A decisive factor in Byzantine military campaigns at this time had little to do with strategy itself. For a generation or two, the problem was raising troops. An epidemic of bubonic plague in 541 decimated the population of the Byzantine Empire, rendering a reconquest of Italy all but impossible.

What soon emerged in southern peninsular Italy was a complex checkerboard of manorial and ecclesiastical dominions. Bari remained essentially Byzantine, while Salerno became the seat of the most important Lombard principality. Rome was held by the popes as the cornerstone of a pontifical state. The Greek influence was greatest in Apulia and Calabria; major Latin abbeys like Cassino and (later) Cava answered to Rome.

Christianity was soon to lose its monopoly on the western world. Muhammad, the founder of Islam as its Prophet, was born in Mecca in 570.

In 603, Pope Gregory I "the Great" made a peace with the Lombards which encouraged the conversion of more of them to Christianity, and four decades later the Edict of Rothari formalized their legal code, which seems to have differed significantly from those of the Vandals, Goths and other Germanic peoples. With the Donation of Sutri, in 728, Liutprand, a Lombard king, ceded the sovereignty of Rome and its environs to Pope Gregory II. This territory was the cornerstone of what became the Papal State.[39]

By this time, cracks were forming in the façade of Lombard influence. Spoleto and Benevento, though Lombard, challenged Liutprand's authority. Nevertheless, he is generally regarded as the greatest Lombard monarch, distinguished for his legislation and sagacity. Liutprand died in 744 and was entombed in Pavia, his capital. Successful as he was, he had failed to unite the entire Italian peninsula under his rule.

At the greatest geographic extent of Lombard power in the middle years of the eighth century, their dominions included most of what is today Italy except for Sicily, Sardinia, Apulia, Calabria, and the area around Rome that they had given to the papacy. However, with Charlemagne's subjugation of the Lombards' "Kingdom of Italy" following the Battle of Pavia in 774, all that remained under their complete control were their principalities in the central and southern parts of the peninsula.

Thenceforth, the Carolingians claimed juridical sovereignty over all the Lombards of Italy, even in Campania and Apulia, into the eleventh century, and we find Conrad II, Holy Roman Emperor, confirming the first formal Norman infeudation, at Aversa, in 1038. Yet the true extent of imperial control over the princes of Salerno during the eleventh century is much debated, while the Duchy of Spoleto, following some complex vicissitudes, often found itself under direct imperial control.

Paul the Deacon, a Benedictine at Mount Cassino, wrote his detailed, if occasionally imaginative, history of the Lombards at some time after 787. This became a popular work of which there are more than a hundred surviving codices.[40]

Significantly, Paul was one of first native chroniclers of the Lombard society of southern peninsular Italy to express overt resentment of the Byzantines and their civilization, a sentiment that would fester for centuries. Underlying this theme was the political reality of the Byzantine control of Calabria, most of Apulia and part of Lucania (Basilicata).

In considering the history of the Lombards up to this era, it is important to bear in mind that almost all of the surviving accounts were written by the Byzantines, the Franks or papal proponents, most obviously Gregory the Great himself. Paul, a Friulian of Lombard ancestry who knew Charlemagne, sought to rectify the negative impressions of the Lombards as a vanquished people, losers, recently deprived of their sovereignty of Lombardy by the Franks. Despite some efforts over the next few decades, however, Lombardy would never again rise to the level of a kingdom, and Milan eventually eclipsed Pavia in importance.

In Paul's time, the Lombards south of Rome were no longer viewed as rustic invaders. Their dominions were ruled from three great cities. Salerno became known for its medical school, originally the "Salernitan School" as a collective of teachers in and near that city rather than an edifice where they taught. Capua and Benevento also emerged as important centers of administration and learning. Although they might occasionally join forces out of necessity, these distinct polities could not be said to constitute anything like a unitary Lombard state.

Despite their endonym, *Longobardus,* several centuries of life in southern Italy found the Lombards of this region thoroughly amalgamated with the people they ruled, the general population speaking a language derived chiefly from vulgar Latin, albeit with Lombardic influences; this is identified with early Neapolitan (see notes 132 and 908). The Lombardic tongue has left us more nouns than verbs, and precious few traces of written material, mostly inscriptions, because, like Paul's history, the Lombards' usual written language was Latin.[41] Hence there is no later Lombardic literature quite comparable to the Norman French *Chanson d'Aspremont,* a story set in Calabria as part of the Charlemagne Cycle.

Yet it seems that at least a few Lombards, mostly in northern Italy, were still speaking a form of Lombardic as recently as 1000, and there are traces of a later form of their language in a few Nebrodian dialects of Sicilian.[42]

Significantly, the Lombards of the Italian south, despite their localized administration, still identified themselves collectively as a people. In 982, a joint Lombard army supported by imperial German forces was routed by the Arabs of Sicily near the Byzantine stronghold of Stilo, in Calabria (see note 68). This was a harbinger of things to come. A generation later, the Arabs may have been extorting tribute from the Salernitans in exchange for protecting their trading vessels from pirates operating out of Messina, though the Sicilian emirs themselves probably sanctioned these acts of piracy.

Writing in the twelfth century, the chronicler Hugh Falcandus distinguished between what he referred to as the "Longobards" of northern Italy, such as the knights of Adelaide, the wife of Roger I, compared to the more Latinized "Lombards" of the south, from cities such as Salerno and Benevento, who arrived in Sicily with the Normans.

The Lombard society of southern Italy identifiable when the Normans arrived early in the eleventh century had disappeared by 1200, absorbed into the vaguely "Italianate" environment that would predominate by the end of the Swabian era. Indeed, much of its alterity had largely vanished by 1100, either through assimilation, amalgamation or conquest, even though many people still identified themselves as "Lombards." The last ruler who was obviously identifiable as Lombard, Lando IV of Capua, was deposed in 1098.

Fortunately, some of the Lombards' documented history concerning the church, land and families into the Norman period is preserved in the records retained at the Cava monastery near Salerno, founded early in the eleventh century.

About that time, another group from northern Europe set foot in southern Italy.

The Norse

Little is known of the Norse (Viking) visits during the ninth and tenth centuries, noted by chroniclers of varying reliability. Their presence, if perhaps fleeting, would be consistent with their other travels around the central

Mediterranean, resulting in coastal visits rather than incursions into the hinterland. Some of them ended up in Constantinople, others in Russia. The Norse voyage to Newfoundland, possibly their Vinland, was described in the Nordic sagas.[43]

Meanwhile, their residual civilization in northwestern France became Norman.

Led by Harald Sigurdsson Hardrada, later King of Norway, some Vikings were present in Sicily with the Byzantine and Norman forces that tried to wrest control of the emirate from the reigning Kalbids in 1038.

Over time, Norse society morphed into the modern Scandinavian cultures.

Most of the Norse lineages among the Italians are traced through their medieval descendants, the Normans, whom we shall meet in the next chapter.

The Byzantine Greeks

The term "Byzantine" refers to a region as well as a culture. The medieval Byzantine Greeks of southern Italy were descended not only from Mycenaean and Minoan traders present in remote antiquity but from the Greeks who arrived as colonists beginning around 700 BC. They also had descent from various "indigenous" peoples present long before that era.

In the complex ethnogenesis of the High Middle Ages, we might even think of them as "Greek Italians" or "Italianized Greeks." Compared to the Lombards of southern Italy, who were far more Latinized, the Byzantine Greeks of Apulia (Puglia), Calabria, Lucania (Basilicata) and Sicily spoke Greek and worshipped in a Greek rite of Christianity.

What made them Greek following the fall of the Roman Empire was chiefly their language and liturgy, and the fact that they generally looked to the east, beyond the Adriatic and Ionian, for their social culture.[44]

In 660, the Byzantine Emperor, Constans II, established his court at Syracuse with an eye to crossing into Calabria and invading the Lombard lands. This plan never materialized, and by the end of his reign, by assassination, eight years later Constantinople had, for the time being, given up any hope for such a conquest.[45]

Significantly, the bishops in the Byzantine territories, and even in a few of the Lombard ones, were under the ecclesiastical jurisdiction of the Patriarch of Constantinople, not the Pope of Rome. Equally important, the Byzantine cities implemented a variance of the Code of Justinian while in the Longobardic lands, at least initially, a form of Germanic law was enforced (see note 39).

After 975, the Byzantine lands of the Greeks' *Longobardia,* a *thema* or province rather than a state, were governed by a catepan recommended by the authorities in Constantinople and approved by the emperor. Though, like the Byzantine Empire itself, this catepanate, which included Apulia, Lucania and Calabria, was part of a monarchy, it was not itself sovereign and the office of catepan was not hereditary.

Like many of the inhabitants of southern Italy generically identified as

"Lombards," those described as "Byzantine Greeks," though mostly Greek-speaking, were, in fact, the descendants, through most lines, of people who had been present for many centuries, whether Samnite, Sicanian, Carthaginian, Greek or Roman. That is to say, most of them were descended from ancestors in several of these groups. Just as there were no "pure" Lombards, there were no pure "Greeks."

With the fall of the Roman Empire, Latin, which appears not to have always been the chief spoken language in every community in southern Italy during the Roman era, was almost completely eclipsed by Greek, initially the chief language of Christian scripture and liturgy. Christianity would openly split only much later, but by the seventh century, with the distinctions between Greek east and Latin west little more than an arcane nuance, subtle differences were already growing between the two spheres of influence, namely Rome and Constantinople. Typical of the debates within the universal church was the Iconoclast Controversy.[46] For the present, however, there were greater differences between Christians, on the one hand, and Muslims on the other.

One thinks of scribes as monks, but the clergy, the "clerks," were not the only ones to perform this role. A number of manuscripts recording the work of great thinkers were preserved (in Greek) in the Byzantine Empire. Some were later translated into Arabic. Euclid's *Division of Figures* is an oft-cited example. In a few cases, the Arabic editions were the sources of later (Latin) translations when the Greek copies were lost or destroyed.

The Byzantine Empire, which was the medieval Greeks' continuation of the Eastern Roman Empire, survived in some form until 1453, when the Ottoman Turks finally took Constantinople. While there were inspired pockets of learning in Europe's monasteries as far afield as Ireland, until the eleventh century the greatest flowering of Christian culture was to be found in the Byzantine world.

Unlike the Lombards, whose system of landholding by the eleventh century was essentially feudal (and manorial), the Greek system, like that of the Arabs, was based on smallholding despite the presence of a few large land owners. It was not feudal.[47]

Although we have no reliable figures, such evidence as can be gathered suggests that general literacy in southern Italy under the Byzantine Greeks was higher than in most of western Europe, and in Sicily it was augmented further under the Arabs.

The Jews

Although they never populated an entire city or region of the Italian south, the Jews of southern Italy were ever present during this era, and generally tolerated by those who ruled them. Estimates vary widely, but it is quite possible that they comprised as much as six or seven percent of the population in 1000, with particular concentrations in the larger cities and towns. Their congregation in Rome is the oldest religious community in Europe, but many localities in southern Italy had Jewish districts.

It was under Byzantine rule that what are thought to be the oldest surviving mikvehs in Europe, at Palermo and Siracusa, were built by the Jews of these cities. Each is a hypogeum fed by a subterranean spring.[48]

The Jews of Sicily were closely connected with those of Tunisia and spoke an Arabic dialect, Judeo-Arabic, which has made its way into documents and inscriptions. Those in localities such as Salerno and Bari had a close affinity with their brethren in Rome.[49]

Halakah law formed the basis for their legal system.

The Arabs

Muhammad's death in 632 signalled a new onslaught, bringing with it a social culture quite distinct from those of the Lombards and Byzantines present in Italy for centuries. It was inextricably linked to religion.

The concept now referred to as *Dar al-Islam* was born of the idea that Muslims should be ruled by Muslims in societies that were predominantly Muslim. This may be compared, if only in the abstract, to the concept of *Christendom*. However, it would be less than accurate to refer to the Norman conquest of Sicily, in a literal sense, as a "crusade."

Though the Normans' experience in southern peninsular Italy cannot be divorced from questions of religion, particularly in Apulia and Calabria, the Islamic ethos that dominated Sicily probably seemed somewhat more alien to them. Nevertheless, the Muslim Arabs had a fair amount of contact with the Lombards, and of course the Byzantines, long before the arrival of the Normans in Italy. If the *Dar al-Islam* was the home of Islam, this land of Christians was the *Dar al-Kufr*, the home of unbelief.

Islam was the impetus for the spread of Arab power from east to west across northern Africa. The most popular modern definition of the gentilic "Arab," which places any native speaker of Arabic in the same vague ethnic category, rings slightly simplistic to the ears of the medievalist. But Arabic is the language of the Koran, and in its nascent years Islam was inextricably linked to Arab culture. It was also a case of the Arabs having their own written language, whereas some of the peoples they conquered did not make use of one.

Despite divisive differences within Islam between what came to be known as the Shia and Sunni sects, amongst others, the Koran and hadiths came to form the foundation of Muslim law, such as the Maliki school.

In 652 a small Arab force landed in Sicily but soon departed. Other raids followed, yet the greatest assault on the island was still to come. For now, the few Muslims in southern Italy were traders.[50]

Around 670, the Muslim Arabs founded Kairouan (Qayrawan), considered the first Muslim city of northern Africa, conquering Carthage in 698, and by 700 Ifriqiya, consisting of regions such as the place we now call Tunisia, was almost entirely under their influence. Before long, the great majority of Ifriqiyans had converted to Islam and Arabic was the language that united them, but they were the descendants of Berbers, Carthaginians, Romans and even Vandals. For this reason, identifying the medieval Tunisians, or even the

Moroccans, generically as "Arabs" is something of a simplification. Whatever one chooses to call them, there is no doubt that these peoples flourished as part of a larger Muslim society whose influence eventually ranged from Portugal to Pakistan.

Working their way westward, the Muslims invaded Iberia in 711, seizing islands like Malta and Pantelleria along the way. An Arab force was defeated by Charles Martel at Tours in 732, but this did not impede the general expansion of Islam. Syracuse, still Sicily's largest city, was attacked in 740 and again in 752.

Internecine disputes characterized the expansion. The Berbers, properly Amazigh (plural Imazighen), in particular, sometimes resented the Arabian leadership. By 800 there were Berber traders in Sicily, particularly at Sciacca, Marsala and Mazara.

The Bedouins, who were normally nomadic, traced their remote origins to the Arabian Peninsula and typically lived in the desert, their society based on a tribal model. The Berbers, by comparison, usually dwelled in sedentary communities and coastal cities, being indigenous to northern Africa, though descended in some lines from Carthaginians and other peoples of this region.

In 826, Euphemius, a Sicilian general disgruntled with the Byzantine Emperor Michael II, offered control of Sicily to the Aghlabids, the regnant dynasty of Ifriqiya, to whom he would render tribute. In the event Euphemius, who lent military support to the Aghlabids, was killed by Byzantine loyalists.

In July of the following year, Asad ibn al-Furat sailed from Tunisia with over ten thousand Arab and Berber troops, along with some Persians, landing at Mazara in the western part of Sicily.

The facile first stage of the conquest belied difficulties to come. In September 831 Balharm (Palermo) was finally conquered by the Aghlabids following a year-long siege. Informally called *al-Madinah*, this city was destined to become the capital of the Emirate of Sicily, but it took the better part of seventy years for the Aghlabids to bring all of the island, including the Greek areas of the east, under their control.

There were several reasons for the preference of Palermo as the island's capital. It was closer than Syracuse to the Aghlabids' Tunisian capital, and farther away from the potentially troublesome Byzantines. Coming from the east, a Byzantine attack on the Syracuse region would leave time to notify Palermo of an attempted invasion.

In this magnificent city one of the largest souks became what is today Ballarò, the oldest street market in Europe. Its Sicilian name is thought to derive from the Arabic *Suk al Balari*. This may refer to much of the produce coming from *Bahlara*, a farming village near Monreale, or to *Balat*, the name of Palermo's principal stone street.

In 836, the Aghlabids, using the island of Ponza as their base, helped the rulers of Naples to repel an attempted Lombard invasion of the city.

Supported by Sergio I of Naples, whose roots may have been Byzantine, the Aghlabid attack on Bari in 841 led to that city falling under Aghlabid control, with its own emirate, which was suppressed in 881. Meanwhile, some Muslims established a community at Naples. The papacy, naturally, disapproved of this. Sergio II of Naples, who ruled the duchy beginning in 870, was excommunicated for his tolerance of Islam.

Elsewhere, the Aghlabids were more successful. By 903 they controlled all of Sicily, and Islam was the official religion. They tolerated Christianity and Judaism on the island, without encouraging either. In Sicily, the Arabs were rulers more than colonizers, masters more than leaders. Because Islamic law could be harsh to non-believers, many Christians converted, though precise numbers are not known and in the northeastern part of the island there were Greek monasteries throughout the thirteenth century. However, it must be said that Islamic society and culture were advanced; under the Muslims Palermo emerged as one of Europe's richest cities.

In truth, the great majority of Sicily's Muslims were of Berber ancestry, even if their language and culture was Arabized. There were occasional conflicts between the predominantly Arab leadership of Palermo, Marsala and Trapani, cities that controlled the island, and the Berbers who had settled in Agrigento, Sciacca and elsewhere. To a great extent, these violent Berber revolts mirrored the situation in Tunisia, and worsened with the arrival of Fatimid rule after 909. They were, in effect, anti-Fatimid riots tantamount to a localized civil war that ended only following a siege at Agrigento, or *Kerkent,* in 938.

Even though the Fatimids and their successors, the Kalbids, were Shiites, a fact that fostered the image of Sicily as a "Shia emirate," they retained many laws established by the Aghlabids, who were Hanafi and then Maliki. Most of Sicily's Muslims, being Sunni, seem to have viewed the Shia as a ruling elite. The Aghlabids advocated Maliki law, whose roots are to be found in the Sunni tradition. It has been suggested that this may have influenced English common law in the twelfth century when contact between Palermo and London was frequent.[51]

Peninsular Italy was not overlooked, and by 900 there was a small Arab trading settlement at the mouth of the Garigliano River on the Tyrrhenian near the town of Minturno. Among their number may have been a few Aghlabids expelled from Naples some years earlier. Lying near the papal domain, this was, arguably, Lombard territory, but Rome took an interest in it as the Muslim community grew in size over the next decade.

Meanwhile, since the Fatimids had succeeded the Aghlabids in Tunisia and Sicily, it was to this new dynasty that the settlers on the Garigliano answered. In the spirit of Fatimid zeal, the settlers began to raid small towns in the immediate vicinity. At first they did so with impunity, exploiting the fact that the Lombards' dominion was, for the most part, a rather loose federation of baronial estates lacking a large standing army. By 915, the papacy could no longer tolerate this nuisance. In that year, in a rare expression of unity, a joint army of Papal, Lombard and Byzantine troops attacked the Muslims and expelled them.

In Sicily, however, the arrival of the Arabs portended great changes. They instituted a period of religious tolerance, though giving precedence to Islam and converting a number of churches, including the cathedrals of Syracuse and Palermo, to mosques.

The Arabs were prolific. They founded or resettled numerous fortified towns around Sicily. Most obviously, places whose names begin with *cal* or *calta* bear the mark of Arabic: Caltagirone, Caltabellotta, Caltanissetta, Calascibetta, Calamonaci, Caltavuturo, Calatafimi. Also in this category are places whose names begin with derivatives of *gebal* (Gibilmanna, Gibellina) and *rahal* (Regalbuto, Racalmuto). This expansion, and the fact that wealthier Muslims could take more than one wife, explains how Sicily's population doubled or trebled during the few centuries of Arab rule. There were also many conversions to Islam, especially of young Byzantine women marrying comparatively affluent Muslim men. These facile conversions reflect the fact that in the Mediterranean many of the social differences between Muslims, Christians and Jews were fairly subtle well into the Middle Ages. Twelfth-century visitors such as Abdullah al Idrisi and Ibn Jubayr observed that the vast majority of Sicilian women dressed in a similar style which both chroniclers described as the "Muslim" fashion; in fact some kind of veil or scarf was traditional among Sicily's Jews and Christians as well as its Arabs.

By the middle of the eleventh century the island's populace was divided about equally between Muslims and Christians, with Jews constituting the remaining population, less than a tenth of the total.

Kalbite society had its strictures for non-Muslims. As *dhimmi,* Christians and Jews were taxed more heavily than Muslims, and there were restrictions on the number of new churches and synagogues that could be built. Church bells could not be rung, and Christians could not read aloud from the scriptures within earshot of Muslims or display large crosses in public. Christians and Jews could not drink wine in public, though Muslims sometimes did so in private. Jews and Christians had to stand when Muslims entered a room and make way for them in the souks, streets and other public places. In Arab Sicily there was harmony and tolerance if not absolute equality.

The Arabs introduced mulberries (for silk making), cotton, oranges, watermelons, aubergines (eggplant), spinach, rice and sugar cane. They are thought to have introduced the markhor, from which the Girgentan goat, with its distinctive corkscrewing horns, is descended. The basis of much of Sicilian cuisine was formed during this era. Halal and kosher dietary observances made their influence felt, a fact which may account for the dearth of traditional pork recipes.

The process of distillation, important in chemistry and in the making of spirits, was developed by the Arabs.

They built water passages, *kanats,* under Palermo. Besides the *kanats,* feats of engineering left to us by the Arabs include some well-constructed bridges outside Corleone, Adrano and Roccamena. They introduced anti-seismic features. They constructed passive cooling systems in their palaces; one can be seen in a wall tower erected in the thirteenth century near Palermo's Ballarò street market. There were also *hammams* (baths); one survives at Cefala Diana in Sicily (see note 53).

Of Asian origin, chess was a popular game introduced by the Arabs. The Europeans eventually altered its pieces to reflect their own society of kings, queens, bishops, knights, foot soldiers and, of course, castles.

Although some of these developments originated in India and China, it was the Arabs who brought them to Europe and the Mediterranean. Europe's first paper was made in Sicily and in Spain, where the continent's oldest surviving paper documents are preserved. Hindu-Arabic numerals were introduced.

Advances in mathematics were facilitated by the use of the new numerals, which trace their origin to Brahmi and Sanskrit. In Baghdad, the ninth-century Persian mathematician Abdallah Muhammad al Khwarizmi made use of this numeration system to simplify the algebra of Diophantus of Alexandria; its modern name comes to us from the Arabic *al-jabr wa'l muqabalah* (see note 962). Hindu-Arabic numerals are not merely a simpler writing system than Roman numerals; they more clearly isolate concepts such as fractions and *zero,* whose Medieval Latin form, *zephirum,* derives from the Arabic *sifr,* "cipher," from a Sanskrit word.

These concepts were useful in accounting. The treasury, or *diwan,* was highly efficient.[52] Khwarizmi's studies also encompassed trigonometry, astronomy and geography.

Schools were established for girls as well as boys, and literacy became the norm. Paper made it that much easier for the young students to master writing.

The Fatimids migrated their center of power to Egypt in 948, delegating the administration of Sicily to the local Kalbids. Before long, Mahdia (in Tunisia) was eclipsed by Balharm.

There were isolated pockets of resistance from time to time. The Battle of Rometta, a town on high ground to the west of Messina, may have begun as little more than a rare Byzantine revolt, but the arrival of thousands of troops from Constantinople in 964 suggests, instead, that this was the last city in Sicily to fall to the Arabs. Its very name means "fortress," from the Greek *erymata.* Emir Hassan al-Kalbi was killed during the fighting, but the Kalbids prevailed.

Abu al-Hasan Jawhar al-Siqilli, who may have been born in Sicily and was probably of Sicilian ancestry, founded the Fatimid city of Al-Qahira (Cairo) in 969. Significantly, the Fatimids brought Sicily into a wide orbit of trade and prosperity. By now, Palermo was a metropolis whose opulence was said by visitors to rival that of Baghdad. For such descriptions we look to Muhammad ibn Hawqal in the tenth century and Abu Hussain Muhammad bin Ahmad ibn Jubayr in the twelfth.[53]

Ibn Hawqal famously observed that some of the Muslims he encountered in Sicily married Christians. For the most part, these were Muslim men whose non-Muslim wives converted to Islam. Where that did not occur, there were cases of Christian women raising their daughters as Christian and their sons as Muslim.

Great Muslim thinkers were never missing from the Sicilian landscape. The polymath Ibn Zafar al Siqilli and court geographer Idrisi are just two names that come to mind.

Like Sicily's Christians, who by the twelfth century found themselves divided between Byzantines and Latins, the Muslims were a diverse population. Not only were there Sunnis and Shia, but an Ibadi community flourished at Kasr'Janni (Enna) and perhaps in other localities on the island.[54]

The Arabs of Sicily have left us a significant body of literature and poetry, and much more.[55] Amongst the surviving vestiges of Arab civilization in language and cookery is the *mattanza,* a medieval method for capturing large tuna. The leader of the fishing team is called a *rais,* from the Arabic. (The last Sicilian *mattanza* took place at Favignana in 2007.)

The Normans of Italy cannot be said to have had a monolithic or unifying view of Islam or Arab culture, and we find their policies changing over time based on expedience, depending on the needs of the moment. While the Muslims of southern Italy were generally tolerated, and their rights respected, by the Hauteville dynasty, the papacy and the baronage often took contrarian positions. Foreign affairs (crusading) and commercial interests (trade) with the Muslims of northern Africa and western Asia were the two greatest influences on the more general policies.

We the Peoples

We shall frequently revisit these peoples, their cultures and faiths in future chapters.

This is merely an introduction to the civilizations present in southern Italy before the arrival of the Normans, their presence attested not only by the documentary and artistic records but by the plethora of genetic lineages they left behind (see note 17). If the written record offers us a fair degree of evidence of marriages between persons of differing ethnic or religious backgrounds, and the conversions of Muslims to Christianity, the genetic record is the key.

Although they cannot be said to have completely "disappeared" during the Norman era, the Lombard, Byzantine and Arab populations were largely amalgamated into a general "Siculo-Neapolitan" population by the definitive end of the Swabian period. This occurred through widespread Latinization and assimilation as well as amalgamation. It was most insidious for the Lombards, least so for the Arabs.

None of the distinct populations that existed in southern Italy at the dawn of the eleventh century can be defined exclusively by comparison to any other. Despite their differences, however, they shared some underlying similarities. They worshipped in the Abrahamic religions. Their cultures, like many, owed much to what they inherited from those that had flourished around the Mediterranean in antiquity. Together, these faith traditions came to form an integral part of what was later, if perhaps misleadingly, called "western civilization."[56]

Geographically, this extended across most of the territory identified by Herodotus, including Europe, along with Africa north of the Sahara and Asia to the west of India. The ancient Romans knew about most of these lands even if many were beyond their rule and influence.

Of course, the Romans, like the Phoenicians and Greeks before them, viewed the world in the context of the Mediterranean, and it could be argued that the Norman kings of Sicily, whether by choice or necessity, came to think of it from this perspective despite the trend toward Latinizing the Byzantines and Arabs. If nothing else, it was a reality imposed by geography.[57]

It was during the Middle Ages that the term "European" came to refer, in common parlance, to more than geography, becoming a vague gentilic for the people of a place regarded as a continent (with use of the term *Eurasia* popularized later). Interestingly, it was coined, in its current usage, by the Iberian author of the *Chronicle of 754* to contrast Christians and Muslims at the Battle of Tours.[58]

While we look to a cohesive identity of the people of southern Italy emerging at some point in the thirteenth century, Charlemagne, who died in 814, is considered "the Father of Europe" for having united much of the western part of the continent under his Frankish dynasty, at least for as long as he ruled.[59]

Most of the knights led by Charlemagne's grandfather, Charles Martel, at Tours were Franks, but that ethnonym was destined to be abused.[60] During the crusades it referred to virtually any European Christian from a predominantly Catholic country of western and central Europe.

Even where ethnic identity was comparatively unaffected by amalgamation and other social phenomena, it evolved over time, if only as a result of the modernization of languages, customs and traditions. In our century this occurs rather rapidly due to instant communication, and with it cultural exchange. It could be argued that ethnic groups, as they exist today, are not quite as distinct as they once were, for global commonalities have influenced many social practices, even in timeless Italy, leaving us with certain international norms that dominate our lives.

As we shall see, medieval ethnogenesis could be hastened by the conquests that brought people of one society into contact with those of another. Here a quintessential example is the case of the Normans.

Who, exactly, were these oft-mentioned people?

Palermo's great mosque had at least seven mihrabs like this one in Cordoba, a city to which it was sometimes compared.

Chapter 2
THE NORMANS

The European society with which the High Middle Ages are most strongly identified in southern Italy is that of the Normans, and while they did not immediately displace the cultures they found here, such as that of the Lombards, their efforts led to the foundation of a unitary kingdom and the wider Latinization evident by the thirteenth century. The ethnogenesis of the Normans themselves was, in fact, quite recent.

Origins

As an *ethnie,* the Normans were the "result" of the recent amalgamation of two European cultures which, though distinct, were familiar to each other, sometimes competing for control of the same territory. These were the Frankish and Nordic peoples.

The *Franks* known to the ancient Romans were a Germanic population. By the middle of the sixth century, their unifying dynasty, the Merovingians, had consolidated most of France and part of Germany under their aegis, seizing power from various tribes, such as the Goths led by Theodoric the Great. Following two centuries of prosperity, the end of the Merovingian dynasty saw the rise of families headed by other leaders. Chief among them was Charles Martel, the hero of the Battle of Tours, whose son, Pepin the Short, became king in 751.[61] Pepin's son, Charlemagne, generally considered the greatest Frankish monarch, further extended the Franks' territory, adding such regions as Carinthia and, as we have seen, Lombardy, to the orbit of a Carolingian empire that, in 800, became the Holy Roman Empire.

The only part of what is now France that remained outside Charlemagne's control was Brittany, a peninsula where the culture was almost exclusively Celtic and Breton was the spoken language. Elsewhere in France, the vernacular was an evolving form of what became French, though the Occitan tongues, amongst others, are actually distinct languages. Naturally, the German regions to the east had their own languages. Charlemagne had to speak several languages to communicate with his own people. His death resulted in the territorial division of these lands amongst his three jealous sons and, arguably, an increasing cultural division between the Frankish and Germanic peoples.

By then, the *Norse,* or "Vikings," whom we met in the previous chapter, ruled several dominions in Scandinavia. In precise parlance, the exonym *Viking* referred specifically to Norse raiders, not to the Norse population generally.[62] Whatever one calls them, by the ninth century the Norsemen were making incursions into the Frankish territories running along the Atlantic coast north of Brittany, and even into what are now Russia and Ukraine. They raided Ireland, where they founded Dublin.

Some of these Norsemen were Christianized but most were not, and they became known for pillaging monasteries, hence the understandable antipathy toward them expressed in chronicles, typically written by monks. Despite the looting of precious metal objects, and the theft of as many gold and silver coins as they could carry, the Vikings eventually established trade, and English clergy fell into the habit of remitting tribute money, *danegeld,* to encourage them to leave churches and monasteries undisturbed. Their mass invasion of northern England in 865 led to settlements that became mini-monarchies. Alfred the Great curtailed their ambitions, in the process uniting much of the country under his Saxons, hence English historians have traditionally dated the creation of the Kingdom of England to his reign even though the Norse territories known as the *Danelaw* remained outside his control.

A Norse military expedition along the Seine to Paris in 845 infamously degenerated into a bloody siege. Following his inadequate military response to this attack, Charles the Bald, Charlemagne's grandson who ruled West Francia, purchased a tenuous peace by bribing the invaders, who retreated to their towns in a coastal area in the region once known to the Franks as *Neustria.* Most of these communities were in the Cotentin Peninsula or the hinterland to its immediate east.

In 867, Charles sought to rein in these Vikings by naming the Breton king Salomon as this region's ruler, effective his proxy, but the *Nortmanni,* or Men of the North, were there to stay. Conflicts followed, culminating in a Frankish victory by Charles the Simple over Rollo, or Hrolf, the leader of the Vikings in France, in 911. Rollo was baptized and pledged fealty to Charles as his vassal, making Rouen, the Romans' *Rotomagus,* the Norman capital. Based on the Vikings' Latin ethnonym, the region became known as *Normaundie,* its people *Normands,* and gradually expanded over the next few generations; amongst its dominions were several islands in the English Channel.

Most of the Norsemen took local Frankish women as their brides. Immersed in the local culture, they assimilated in almost every way. This led, by the middle of the tenth century, to the ethnogenesis of an identifiable people, the Normans, who spoke their own dialect of French influenced by Old Norse. The impact of Norman French may not have been very great in southern Italy, but it was overwhelming in England, which was conquered by the regnant dynasty of Normandy in the eleventh century. In English, many words of Latin origin were introduced via Norman French.[63]

Distinctive Norman styles of art and architecture emerged, along with social practices influenced by the Franks. This was the *Normanitas* described by historians. It came to be linked to the *Gens Normannorum,* the Normans as a people. Through their conquests, the Normans eventually introduced their manorial system, based on Frankish traditions, in their acquired dominions, gradually supplanting those of the Saxons in England and the Lombards in Italy.[64]

Meanwhile, the early decades of the eleventh century found the kings of Sweden, Denmark and Norway discouraging the kind of marauding for which the Vikings were known.

Normandy's dukes were kings of England from 1066, and Normandy became part of France in 1204.

Arrival

By tradition, the first band of Normans to make their way to southern Italy is said to have arrived in 999, either as mercenaries or pilgrims, or, in the spirit of the times, both.[65] The group consisted of knights, probably accompanied by the usual retainers. Naturally, this would have included a few monks. The clergy were dutiful beyond their religious vocation, for they wrote most of the correspondence, hence our word *clerk* comes to us from *cleric.*

There would not have been any women in the group. The knights might seek the company of young maidens they encountered in their travels, but only if protective fathers, and a certain proficiency in the local languages, permitted it.

The more popular of two accounts of the Normans' arrival in the south of Italy, the description by Amato of Montecassino, tells us that a group of forty knights traveling through Italy from the pilgrimage site of the Holy Sepulchre, in Jerusalem, was astonished to see that Salerno's Lombard prince, young Guaimar III, was paying tribute, extortion money, to Muslim pirates from Sicily. For the prince's failure to effect the most recent payment due the pirates, a force arrived by sea to attack the coastal city.

The locals had long accepted this kind of treatment. The Normans could not. With the help of some Salernitans who they convinced to fight to defend the city, the visitors routed the invaders as soon as they disembarked. In view of this generous assistance, Guaimar, perhaps speaking an early form of Neapolitan, invited the knights to stay in Salerno as his guests, and it is reasonable to surmise that the brave warriors would have been offered wives as an incentive. To the prince's disappointment, the men explained that they could not remain, but others in Normandy might be encouraged to come. There is evidence to suggest that a few eventually did.[66]

This story, replete with the symbolism of an impending, apocalyptic millennial year and the Biblical number forty, may well be apocryphal, at least in certain details, yet it was repeated by contemporary writers.[67] It is, of course, quite possible that a company of Norman knights had sailed from the Holy Land to Brindisi or Messina, perhaps on a merchant ship, and then made their way up the peninsula, stopping at Salerno about this time and encountering some Arabs. Amato may have intended to show that, although Guaimar was noted for taking control of other Lombard cities in southern Italy, his military power was insufficient to effectively fend off pirates, much less an invading army. Considering that Amato wrote his account after the Normans had faced the Arabs in other engagements, the Salerno story could have been meant to foreshadow events such as the conquest of Sicily.

Nevertheless, the account is broadly consistent with the general pattern of Arab incursions and what became part of the established history of southern Italy. Writing early in the thirteenth century, the author of the *Ferraris Chronicle,* following the lead of his predecessors, states that: "The Arabs oppressed and greatly devastated Apulia, Calabria and the coast of Campania. Otto III, King of the Germans, visited Benevento in 999. In August of the following year, the Arabs reached Benevento and occupied Capua, Naples and the surrounding lands."[68]

The other account comes to us chiefly from the chronicler William of Apulia.[69] Here too a veneer of religious devotion makes the violent warrior instinct palatable.

Describing events of a slightly later time, it doesn't entirely negate or contradict the outlines of Amato's narrative. We are told that in 1016 some Normans were in Apulia visiting the shrine of Saint Michael the Archangel, a patron of knights, on Mount Sant'Angelo along a slope of Mount Gargano. The monks of this shrine had connections to their confreres at Mont Saint-Michel in Normandy. Whilst in Apulia, the knights were introduced to Melus (or Melo), a Lombard friend of Guaimar born in Bari.

Melus told the Normans his story. Overthrowing Bari's Byzantine government in 1009, he had governed the city for two years until he was expelled by the catepan Basil Mesardonites, who exiled his family to Constantinople. Melus now enlisted these Normans, and others they summoned, to serve as mercenaries, or something very similar to mercenaries, in his effort to take back Bari. By 1017, knights were arriving from Normandy to assist Melus and claim their own fortunes.

Bari was the capital of the Byzantine Greek catepanate in southern Italy, and Melus would be the last Lombard activist of stature to attempt to topple it. Like the chronicle of Amato, that of William was cited by contemporary writers.[70]

This leaves posterity with two historical traditions of the arrival of the Normans in southern Italy.[71]

Most were knights in search of better opportunities than what awaited them in Normandy, where only the eldest son in a large family like the Hautevilles would inherit his father's property. At least a few were renegades, even criminals; the Drengot brothers fit this mold, having been banished from Normandy.[72]

First Families

The Drengots are the first securely identified family of knightly Norman siblings to arrive in southern Italy. It was these brothers who met Melus, though perhaps not at Mount Sant'Angelo or even in Apulia, and organized what became the first army of Norman knights in Italy.

To the extent that Melus and his combined force of Lombards and Normans enjoyed papal support, it was because Rome could no longer tolerate the Greek liturgy in Apulia and Calabria, or the Italian policy of the Macedonian dynasty reigning in Constantinople. Cassino and other abbeys, including the one recently established at Cava near Salerno, were full of monks best described as Italianized Lombards or, if one prefers, Lombardic Italians. The chasm between the eastern and western churches, if not their people, was growing wider and deeper with every passing year, and schism seemed imminent.

Yet Melus was merely the most recent Lombard leader to attempt to remove a Bariot catepan. Over the centuries, the Salernitans and other Lombards had succeeded, at best, to control the Byzantine territories tenuously, for a decade or two at a time. In reality, the papacy had long been ambivalent about the Lombards' political power. It seems unlikely that many in Rome ever lamented the taking of Lombardy by the Franks and the subsequent crowning of Charlemagne by Pope Leo III. After all, this broke the Lombards' stranglehold on Italy.

For his part, Melus wanted to rule Bari just as Guaimar ruled Salerno, and the recent death of the troublesome catepan Basil Mesardonites only encouraged his fervor. Now a major campaign was planned.

The first engagements were nothing like pitched battles. Yet the new catepan, Kontoleon Tornikios, was unprepared for the Normans, who won a battle near Arenula on the Fortore River in May of 1017. This was followed by a Norman victory at Civitate (San Paolo di Civitate), and still another at Vaccarizza, near Troia, upon which Kontoleon was replaced by the more competent Basil Boiannes.

Basil brought with him a massive army, including a contingent of the Varangian Guard, Vikings in the service of the Byzantine Emperor. In October 1018 this Byzantine force met the Normans and Lombards near Cannae (now Canne della Battaglia), on the Ofanto River near Barletta, and won the day, killing two Drengot brothers, namely Gilbert and Osmond, and many other Norman knights.[73] Melus fled his native Apulia, though, it seems, not before ensuring that the surviving Drengots were rewarded for their sacrifices (see note 76).

The surviving Normans were enlisted by the catepan, though the service of most knights seems to have lasted for just a few years.

In 1018, this commitment reflected economic expediency rather than an intrinsically natural affinity, for the Normans, in every social and cultural sense, had far more in common with the Latinized Lombards than they had with the Byzantine Greeks.

In a very real sense, their alliance with the catepan placed them at odds with the pope, Benedict VIII, a man descended from the Lombard dukes of Spoleto. During the previous century, the Lombards of the Italian south had successfully negotiated for their metropolitan bishops of Salerno, Capua and Benevento the authority to assume "Latin" jurisdiction over parishes in remote territories confiscated from the Byzantines, this despite the fact that both Latins and Greeks were still part of the same universal church. Thus the jurisdictions of these major bishoprics included a patchwork of isolated parishes dotting regions, such as Lucania (Basilicata), set amidst areas that were still largely Byzantine. Consequently, one town in the mountains might have a Latin church while the next one had a Greek parish, its liturgy reflecting the rite of the ruler.

The chief effect of Lombard rule was the expropriation of Byzantine lands. These confiscated estates were given to Lombard knights as part of the feudal system. This might force Greek farmers, smallholders, into serfdom.

Mercenaries were long a fact of life, but knighthood, as it existed by the eleventh century, was not a customary part of the Byzantine Greek military tradition despite the presence of quasi-knightly units such as the Varangian Guard. The ultimate objective of the Normans who first arrived in southern Italy was enfeoffment, feudal tenure. This was part of a wider institution known in central and western Europe by this time, and it conditioned Norman attitudes and policy over the next few decades.

Enfeoffed Knighthood

The knight of the eleventh century was more than a mounted warrior, but that was the origin of his vocation.

Owning and maintaining horses was always a significant expense, even a luxury, and in ancient Roman society one spoke of the equestrian class. Though this "equestrian order" was indeed a distinct social *stratum,* ranking immediately below the patricians and senators, into which one was born, it came into being largely because the military leaders rode horses while the greater number of fighting men traveled on foot. The cavalry was led by these *equites.*

Yet the true strength of Rome's armies was its infantry. Under most conditions, the Roman cavalry was effective for very simple attacks, but without stirrups to hold himself in place a rider was easily dismounted, and without reasonably heavy armor covering more than his chest and back he was just as vulnerable to an arrow as any soldier. At best, a rider could reach a point near the enemy, throw a spear, and retreat. In the heat of battle, he might ride into the fray and attack with his sword, but the typical gladius was too short to be of great use to a man on a horse, and without special protection the animal itself could fall prey to injury.

The stirrup, which arrived from Asia by the seventh century, changed this.

So did the development of true chain mail armor, rather than small rings of metal sewn onto a leather garment. But the arrival of these innovations came too late to save Rome.

As recently as the Battle of Tours in 732, the Franks led by Charles Martel were chiefly armies of infantry, even if some elite units traveled to the battlefield on horseback. A few decades were to pass before European mounted warriors came to resemble the Norman knights depicted in the Bayeux Tapestry.

Simple as it seems, the stirrup permitted the mounted man-at-arms to fight without being unseated, or even, in the worst scenario, thrown from his horse. It meant that he could launch a direct, frontal attack using a long lance without a great risk of falling. He might even make use of a long sword. In effect, horse and rider became a single fighting unit that some modern commentators have compared to a tank. A suit of chain mail protected the rider from many forms of blow with a sword. There was even armor for horses.

Providing a man with armor, weapons and several horses sturdy enough to carry the extra weight was an expensive undertaking. Training such men in combat skills required years of effort. These were costs that few rulers incurred very willingly. The solution was to devise a way for the mounted man-at-arms himself to assume this responsibility.

Rulers might occasionally lack much money, but most had an abundance of land. It was, after all, the control of extensive territory that defined sovereignty, and even kingship itself. By the eleventh century, the Lombard rulers in southern Italy were not kings but sovereign princes and dukes, effectively crowned monarchs in everything but name despite nominal imperial ties.

Known in written records by the Latin term *miles*, denoting their military status, the first knights served their lord, be he a king, duke or count, in exchange for feudal tenure, the right to hold landed estates. This obviated the need for the monarch to directly assume the cost of outfitting knights.

The essential estate was a manor, or fief; the usual Italian terms are *feudo* (fief) and *signoria* (lordship). A fraction of a fief was a moiety. Several contiguous manors held by the same knight, or by several knights loyal to the same minor lord, constituted a larger unit of property that came to be known as a barony.

It is imprecise to compare this arrangement to the "proto-manorialism" of the "Roman villa system" and its "serfdom" introduced in the fourth century by Diocletian and Constantine, even if that Roman concept may have influenced the Lombards' early approach to land administration in Italy.

In modern usage, the term *feudalism* usually refers principally to the relationship of vassals, such as barons, to their lord, typically a king, in a general hierarchy based on fealty and homage to the ruler, whereas *manorialism* encompasses the relationship of a baron (or enfeoffed knight) to his manor and its people, some of whom might be serfs. Feudalism was chiefly socio-political and military, while manorialism was more directly economic. Manorialism, sometimes *seignorialism,* became a basic component of Europe's "feudal system," a phrase that in common parlance is often construed to embrace feudalism and manorialism jointly.

Speaking generally, but with special reference to southern Italy by the Norman era, manorial rights included direct baronial authority over a delineated area. This governed most hunting rights, especially for deer and boar, but sometimes for hare and edible birds. There were still bears in some forests of southern Italy; the rare Marsican brown bear survives in Abruzzi.

Some pasturage might be made available to peasants to graze their sheep and goats. Feudal tenure included most water and mineral rights, and the right to timber, but not the right to dam a stream that flowed through the estates of several holders. It occasionally permitted some local taxation, typically paid in the form of agricultural produce. Territories and towns that were not manorial (feudal) were demesnial (royal), belonging directly to the crown, and religious orders such as the Benedictines also held land. A knight or baron might occasionally be permitted to hunt on demesnial land but this was rigorously regulated.

As early as the time of Charlemagne, knights constituted a specific social class which eventually became hereditary as part of a martial tradition in certain families. Charlemagne may not have invented knighthood, but he was one of the first monarchs to put it into practice as part of a wider military and economic arrangement. The manors, or *benefices,* given to Carolingian knights in exchange for military service were not originally hereditary, but they became so by the tenth century, hence the manors associated with particular families. This was a rudimentary step in the evolution of vassalage and an important development in what became the feudal system.

This trend incidentally led to the earliest hereditary European surnames, toponyms like *de Hauteville* and *de Mowbray* (to cite two Norman examples) based on the name of the estate held by the enfeoffed knight, his son and grandson.

Historians have long speculated about the remote origins of such practices as the elevation of young men to knighthood as a rite of passage into an elite caste of warriors. Tacitus described the public ceremony of arming a candidate with a lance and shield, but his *Germania* was a secondhand account. We know that Charlemagne girded his son, Louis, with a sword. The dubbing ceremony that saw the Drengot brothers raised to knighthood was certainly a simple one. Here our focus is feudal knighthood; the orders of chivalry associated with crusading during the twelfth century shall be considered later.[74]

The training of a boy destined for knighthood began early, before the age of thirteen. Typically, but not necessarily, he would be sent to live in a household in a neighboring manor, perhaps in the castle of one of his father's knightly friends or kinsmen, where he would master the martial skills required of the fighting man. His intellectual teachers were tutors and monks. A man might be born to be king, but this didn't automatically make him a knight. Knighthood was not merely an honor; it was a status that reflected years of rigorous training, and the assumption of a commitment to service in a society where, quite often, might made right. Nevertheless, there were cases of young kings being knighted immediately prior to their coronations because it was unthinkable that a king would not be a knight; thus Frederick II was knighted whilst still a child.

Knighthood itself was not hereditary, but the right to become a knight was often predicated on nobility of birth. In its broadest terms, this meant being born within marriage to parents in the landed or knightly class, though there were so many exceptions to this norm that the first King of Sicily had to legislate it, while the bastard sons of kings were sometimes permitted to be knighted.

Before there were noblemen, says an old Oxfordian adage, there were noble men. The English *nobility*, like the Italian *nobiltà*, comes to us from the Latin *nobilitas*, "known," but while knights and other tenured landholders were certainly known and respected, the mysticism with which knighthood became imbued was a later development.

Nonetheless, knights were accorded great respect even in the eleventh century, for they were an essential, often decisive, part of the ultimate military force. Yet knights were not always beloved by the general populace; they could be condescending, even cruel, to the common folk. What we now call "chivalry," a notion of civilized knightly behavior, arrived later.

Society came to be rigidly stratified based on the "three estates" of the nobility, the clergy and the commonalty. Knights were part of the nobility.

The feudal system constituted a hierarchy that effectively determined the social order, with nobles and bishops at its apex and serfs and monks near its base. Peasants were not only serfs but persons of the lower classes generally. A freeman, though lacking high social status, enjoyed freedom of movement. A serf (or villein), who in southern Italy was sometimes called a *villico*, was a rural peasant tied to the land and sometimes "sold" with it in the purchase of a manor or barony, as if he were part of the property itself. Actual slavery was rare in southern Italy; in medieval times it was seen more often in cities of the Italian north.

There were subtle gradations of social status even within the aristocracy. Among barons and knights, a certain distinction was drawn between the importance of a castellan, who might be quite affluent, compared to the holder of a humble bailey, the Italian *baglio*, a solitary tower guarding low buildings that were erected around a courtyard. As we have seen, the first Norman knights to arrive in Italy were actually landless.

Fiefs varied greatly in size and wealth. As Lombard power waned during the eleventh century, their feudal title of *gastald*, an official charged with control of royal lands, gave way to Norman titles such as *seigneur*. These survive in surnames like *Castaldi* and the Italian *signore* and *signora*. Into the twentieth century, one still encountered forms of address such as *Vostra Signoria* ("Your Lordship"), which Sicilians shortened to *Vossìa*.

The church was omnipresent, but the earliest form of knighthood lacked a specifically spiritual or Catholic character. Only later did dubbing come to be a religious rite performed in a church or chapel. A Norman or Lombard man was elevated to knighthood around the age of nineteen in a very simple public ceremony conducted by the senior knight who had trained the young man during squirehood.

In truth, the manorial system was rather complex, assuming slightly differing forms depending upon where one lived. Our focus is its development in what became the Kingdom of Sicily.

Here a simple form of feudalism was introduced by the Lombards. Under Longobardic feudal law, a fief (or manor), the basic unit of hereditary property, might be divided among a knight's several sons.

According to the Frankish feudal law introduced by the Normans, only the eldest son inherited a manor. This male primogeniture left younger sons the choice of becoming non-feudal knights, effectively soldiers of fortune such as the Drengot brothers, or choosing a life in the church (see note 64).

Many knights were reasonably well-educated beyond combat tactics. At the least, most could read Latin passably well and comprehend it when recited in liturgy. Enfeoffed knights had to have a rudimentary understanding of agriculture and geography, and competence in falconry and hunting.

The destriers favored by the knights of southern Italy were sturdy Arabian horses whose bloodlines live in the Sanfratellan breed of northeastern Sicily. The author of the informative *Jamsilla Chronicle* gives this account about the knights of Manfred Hohenstaufen, son of Frederick II and future King of Sicily, confronting a rebel baron in 1254:

Not wishing to risk endangering his men through imprudence, Manfred sought to avoid riding through a potentially dangerous valley. Not wearing armor, he asked only for a helmet, which he placed upon his head. Some in the royal suite, who were often annoyed by Borrello's arrogance in offending Manfred's name and honor, saw this as the right time and place to vindicate a grave offense. They dismounted the palfreys they were riding and mounted their destriers. Sighting Borrello and his companions, they immediately gave chase to them on the heavy steeds at full gallop. A few knights in Manfred's company were especially belligerent not by their lord's command but out of personal resentment for the verbal barbs the insolent Borrello had launched at somebody they respected. Manfred's knights drew their swords as they pursued Borrello and his knights. Borrello's flight alone was sufficient to satisfy Manfred's sense of honor. It was only out of respect for the pope that the regent [Manfred] wished to avoid slaying Borrello. With that in mind, he called back the knights and squires who were pursuing his nemesis.

Alas, William Borrello of Agnone, who had illicitly occupied a royal fief that constituted the traditional dower of the queens of Sicily, was killed during the encounter despite Manfred's efforts to spare him (see note 1237).

Most mounted men-at-arms were knights, but an army was composed of hundreds or thousands of men. There were footmen, squires, pages, grooms, pikemen, halbardiers, archers and sundry specialists, such as those who constructed catapults. Also present were armorers, cutlers, cooks and clergy.

Except for the archers and clergy, very few of these figures are ever mentioned explicitly by the earliest chroniclers of Norman Italy. It is likely that the three hundred Norman knights in the Byzantine expedition to Sicily in 1038 were accompanied by some of these other military men, such as squires. Consequently, there could have been twice or thrice the number of Normans reported.

A knight's manor might include forests and pastures but in its essence it was agricultural. Though there were certainly exceptions, the typical enfeoffed knight and his family lived in some kind of fortified dwelling.

Castles and Other Fortifications

One of the many cultural differences between southern and northern Europe during the Middle Ages involved the very placement and construction of most rural residences, including those of knights. There were small hamlets and monasteries outside towns, of course, and many of these were manors. However, in keeping with longstanding traditions inherited from the ancient Greeks, most people in southern Italy lived in towns even if this meant that their farms or orchards were some distance away from their homes. Here there were stone "row houses" along winding streets similar to what one encountered in Jerusalem and Cairo.

Most feudal castles of southern Italy were erected atop mountains or hills. Here it was extremely rare to find a moat around a castle except for the seaside fortresses guarding major port cities like Bari and Syracuse.

It is formulaic to state that castle building became generalized in Europe during the ninth century, but in the Kingdom of Sicily many castles were erected from edifices that had existed long before that time. Sites such as Kasr'Janni (Enna), Caccamo, and of course Palermo's royal palace, had been fortified since antiquity. During the Greek era, the site of the castle at Mount Saint Julian (Erice) housed a temple dedicated to Aphrodite, the goddess of love, where sacred prostitution was practiced.

Contrary to popular belief, not every medieval barony was the site of a large castle, though many were. Some castles were erected in or near existing towns, which in southern Italy might be quite ancient. The Hauteville castle at San Marco d'Alunzio, in northeastern Sicily, overlooks a town mentioned by Cicero. Sicignano degli Alburni, in what is now the province of Salerno, was built at the site of a settlement founded by a Roman named Lucius Sicinius Dentatus.

Broadly speaking, there were three types of fortified dwelling in the Kingdom of Sicily (and these are merely general descriptions rather than precise definitions).

The bailey, or *baglio,* described earlier was essentially several connected buildings made of stone, including a barn, living quarters and armory, and perhaps even a *palmento* (winemaking house), protected by a tower of three or four levels where the knight and his family lived. Many of those seen today are, in fact, post-medieval. This was the simplest kind of knightly or baronial dwelling. One might also encounter a feudal residence consisting of a single, isolated tower.

The castle could take many forms. In general, however, manorial castles had at least two towers and usually lacked large central courtyards. A few castles were squarish, quasi-monolithic structures that, from a distance, resembled crude blocks set upon high ground. The term *fortress* is more generic, but certain demesnial (royal) castles built around courtyards might be described in this way (see note 541). Castel del Monte in Puglia and Ursino Castle in Catania, both erected by Frederick II, are considered castles, not fortresses or palaces. Architectural typology is sometimes imprecise because many "Norman" or "Swabian" castles in southern Italy began their lives as Byzantine or Arab structures which were modified during the twelfth or thirteenth centuries. The erection of "private" (feudal) castles was regulated by royal legislation (see note 1137).

It has occasionally been suggested that the architecture of the first Norman fortifications in southern peninsular Italy, at places like Mileto in Calabria, may have been influenced somewhat by what existed in Normandy, but it is more likely that they simply conformed to a general European norm. However, some of the structures erected on the orders of Frederick II later in his reign reflect certain characteristics of what he saw during his crusade to Palestine.

By definition, a palace was the residence of a king or other sovereign. Some medieval palaces, such as Palermo's Norman Palace (see note 352), were actually fortified, resembling fortresses, complete with high towers. Others, such as the Zisa, though not heavily fortified, might withstand a superficial assault.

Some monasteries, particularly large abbeys such as that of the Benedictines at Monreale (Chapter 19), were fortified. Not only does Monreale's cathedral have two stout towers for defense, the abbey's walls were protected by a number of towers, of which several survive.

With the exception of just a few churches erected during the Hauteville and Hohenstaufen periods, the true Gothic arrived in southern Italy late in the thirteenth century with the Angevins and Aragonese. The castles and other structures mentioned here might best be described architecturally as "Romanesque" (see note 731).

In Latin records, we find the term *castrum* sometimes used to describe not only castles but fortified towns, those having defensive walls and towers. In Naples, Palermo and many other localities some segments of such walls are still standing, along with a few gates and towers.

A demesnial castle might house a garrison, but in southern Italy most of the commanderies of knightly orders such as the Hospitallers and Templars were more akin to monasteries than fortresses. Here a seeming exception was Margana Castle, near Prizzi in Sicily, held by the Teutonic Order. However, this was, in reality, a feudal castle overlooking a manorial estate belonging to that order's principal Sicilian commandery, the Magione in Palermo, not a military outpost.

As the great majority of people did not live in castles, palaces or even monasteries, it is worth considering where and how they did live.

Hearth and Home

Compared to what was more common in parts of northern Europe, the "typical" house in the kingdom had stone walls. It had a ground floor (pavement) of stone and a second storey. The actual floor of the second storey (the ceiling of the ground floor), was constructed of timber. Likewise, the roof was made of wood; this was usually covered with terra cotta tiles in a method still seen in Italy today, but in Puglia we find the *trullo,* a small house having a conical roof made of layered stone (scholars debate whether the first *trulli* were built in medieval times or in later centuries). Though a thatched roof might be seen atop a humble rural hut, that was highly unusual.

While houses in the country outside towns and hamlets existed, chiefly for seasonal use by hunters or farmers, most of these structures were built along streets within cities or towns, which offered greater protection for the common folk from bandits, armies and wolves. A comparatively wealthy man might build a slightly larger house in a *piazza* (square) next to a church, though only with permission from the local baron or council. Most houses were not rented but owned outright.

One hears stories of shepherds keeping some of their livestock on the ground floor, as if it were a barn, while the family lived upstairs, but this kind of arrangement was exceptional. Most often, a separate structure served as a barn, forge or workshop. Cities and towns had specific districts for the shops of tailors, blacksmiths and those of other professions.

Privacy was precious. Parents might have their own sleeping quarters while children would most usually share a room or two.

Courtship, such as it was, tended to be very "proper" (conservative), almost public. A young maiden would not normally be left alone in the company of a young man other than her brother. A nubile girl's virginity was considered a virtue. Romantic trysts, when they occurred, usually took place in the countryside beyond the view of prying eyes. Love was sometimes taken into account in betrothals. Although Catholic canon law eventually permitted the marriage of girls as young as twelve, that was highly unusual outside the aristocracy. By the age of fifteen or sixteen, most girls were ready to embrace conjugal life, perhaps as an escape from the strictures of childhood (betrothal and marriage are considered further in Chapter 12).

Much has been written about royal bastardy, the social status of children fathered outside wedlock by kings and princes (see note 18). However, the child born to an unwed peasant girl was destined to face more challenges than the illegitimate son or daughter of a king. The unwed mother herself might be exposed to scorn. The papacy promulgated laws banning men born outside marriage from ordination, particularly as "secular" (diocesan) clergy outside the monastic orders, largely out of principle but partly because some were the sons of priests and might, as heirs, try to claim ecclesiastical property. More lenient were the laws regarding girls born outside wedlock taking vows as nuns and entering convents. Legally, the man married to a baby's mother was considered the child's father, but this might be contested if circumstances argued against paternity, as when a woman's husband was not present locally at the time of conception.

Infant mortality (of newborns) aside, even babies who lived to four or five months faced gargantuan risks. By some estimates, about fifty percent of all children died by the age of two years. It is believed that at least ten percent of births resulted in the death of the mother, either during delivery or shortly thereafter.

Estimates vary considerably, but during the twelfth century those in the kingdom who survived to adulthood had a life expectancy of almost sixty years on average (see note 1158).

The population of Europe was probably around thirty-five million in 1000, doubling by the middle of the fourteenth century. As a reasonable estimate, the population of the *Regnum* was likely something over two million in 1170 (see note 625), and at least twice that number by 1250 (see note 1157).

During this period of the kingdom's history we do not encounter "major" wars or epidemics of a magnitude sufficient to decimate the population of a city the size of Palermo. There were, of course, outbreaks of bubonic plague and localized epidemics spawned by various contagions. The "Black Death" that infamously ravaged Europe during the middle of the fourteenth century was a pandemic.

In common parlance, one might refer to the medieval inhabitants of large cities such as Palermo, Bari, Naples and Rome as "citizens." However, the modern use of the terms *citizen* and *citizenship* relate to a later phenomenon (see note 77).

Although manorialism governed the possession and administration of most land, some common men (peasants), and a few women, owned at least a plot of their own, such as a large garden or small orchard. Until the fourteenth century this was nothing like the smallholding that had existed in Sicily under the Fatimids and Kalbids, or on the mainland under the Byzantine Greeks, but it contrasts with the stereotype of the "landless peasant."

Records such as the *rivelo,* a tax roll based on the *collecta* and later the *donativo* levied occasionally on property, refer to *fuochi* (hearths) and *anime* (souls). The first comprehensive *riveli* were instituted only in the fifteenth century (in Sicily rather than the mainland), indicating the ages of men and boys, to identify those old enough to work or offer military service, but not women and girls.

From what little information is available, or can be inferred, literacy was still fairly high among the eighty percent of people who constituted the general lay population, the commonalty. This excluded the aristocratic and religious classes which were predominantly literate. Yet literacy among the majority of people declined following the Hohenstaufen era.

Most women occupied themselves chiefly as wives and mothers. This, of course, entailed cooking, weaving (and sewing) and much more. A woman's social status was based principally on that of her father and then her husband. Except for privileged women such as baronesses and abbesses, very few females were ever permitted much public freedom to express their opinions or beliefs, or to assert themselves socially in a very overt way. Though females were generally subordinate to males, a wealthy widow with several children might emerge as an unusually strong woman.

While most girls were trained to become wives and mothers, many boys, beginning around the age of twelve, were apprenticed, sometimes to practice the same trades as their fathers. Apprenticeship among commoners may be compared to squireship among the baronial or knightly class. For the most part, the manner in which apprenticeships were conducted followed the guidelines established by guilds (described in Chapter 12).

Religious confession — Christian, Muslim, Judaic — conditioned much in family life, with striking social similarities between those of differing faiths living in Mediterranean regions such as southern Italy.

The use of terms such as "patriarchy" is not always very precise or universal, but society was clearly androcentric, even for women in the highest social class.

Ladies

The three "feminine estates" were virgin, wife and widow, defining women by their relationship to men. Medieval society distinguished between the privileged aristocratic *lady,* or noblewoman, and the ordinary "common" *woman.*

Aristocratic girls were educated, for the most part, in convents. Living with the nuns, they learned piety and devotion.

Even the castle of a petty baron might assume the character of a royal court in miniature, as if the lady of the house were a queen. Except for the care of strictly male concerns, such as arms and horses, the lady was responsible for almost everything.

Many noblewomen were better-educated than their brothers.

Lessons included languages, especially Latin, and simple arithmetic, along with penmanship. The rudiments of botany and agriculture were studied. Poetry and theology were important. Parts of the Bible were studied, perhaps memorized. Some sense of canon law was inculcated into the children's minds. There might be a touch of music, and such studies as alchemy.

Aristocratic children learned how to play chess, and the girls were taught to let the boys win. This singular game mirrored feudal society. Queens were inevitably sacrificed to kings, but there was a healthy respect for unpredictable knights, avaricious bishops and ambitious pawns. The children were taught to appreciate the complexities of human nature as these were perceived in the medieval mind.[75]

Horsemanship was important, even for a girl. This began with docile ponies and ended with palfreys. A knowledge of history, geography, genealogy, architecture, iconography and coinage was part of a young aristocrat's education.

The girls were taught how to recognize good fruit and luxurious fabric, and how to cook and weave. Even if a noble lady never had to butcher a goat or shear a sheep, her place as the directress of an important household, which included servants and others as well as her family, made it necessary for her to be able to oversee those who did.

In many aristocratic families the mother, rather than the father, was the intellectual compass for the children.

An unspoken but very real part of the education of a young noblewoman involved learning about morality and responsibility. As she became an adult, she came to understand what was expected of her, something she must accept without question or complaint. The most important part of her adult role, which might commence as early as the age of fifteen, was marriage and motherhood, but intrepid wives like Sichelgaita of Salerno and Judith of Evreux, whom we shall meet shortly, were capable of leading knights, even into combat if needs be.

Although the right of a brotherless noblewoman to succeed to her father's manorial estate, which might be a barony, was codified in law during the thirteenth century, this occasionally occurred in Norman and Lombard families even before 1200. It was undertaken through the use of testaments (wills), and assent either by the ruler or by the lord who was suzerain of the woman's father.

In a society overwhelmingly dominated by men, some women were respected more than others.

Treatment of Women

Like an aristocratic lady, a woman outside the nobility could, in the absence of brothers, inherit land from her father. This property was typically an orchard, a small farm or an exceptionally large garden, and perhaps part of a manorial estate. There were also dowries. A young, childless widow might also come into possession of land that had belonged to her late husband.

A married woman's status was defined chiefly by her role as wife and mother.

At what point in history did it become normal to accord ordinary women the same courtesy usually (but not always) rendered to aristocratic ladies? Medieval realities differed somewhat from what one sometimes encounters in literature and various genres of fiction written in recent centuries.

In the Kingdom of Sicily, we find some evidence of "courtliness," chivalrous behavior toward noblewomen, during the reign of William II, whose wife brought such ideals from the court of her mother, Eleanor of Aquitaine. Yet in his treatise, or parody, about "love" André the Chaplain, a Frenchman familiar with Eleanor's court, implies that the sexual assault of a peasant woman was at least thinkable (see note 74).

Though the rape of maidens was expressly outlawed in the *Regnum,* prosecuting a knight for such a crime anyplace in Europe was difficult, thus we read about a member of the Drengot family killing William Repostel for raping his sister (see note 72).

Later, during the reign of Frederick II, another dose of French influence conditioned the poetry of the Sicilian School, the *Contrasto* of Cielo of Alcamo being the supreme example of this, but there the emphasis was courtliness among aristocrats, not the common folk.

It is obvious that noblewomen and nuns generally fared better than ordinary women in their treatment at the hands of men, even if there were exceptions. The case of Matilda Hauteville (described in Chapter 11) may have involved her husband's marital infidelity rather than him assaulting her physically.

The moral "double standard" for men and women generally permitted extramarital adventures by husbands, particularly aristocrats, that would never be tolerated for wives. Rodrigo of Navarre, the half-brother of Queen Margaret of Sicily, whom we shall meet, was the result of adultery by a woman who betrayed her husband in this way and thus he was excluded from the line of succession (see Chapter 17).

Juridical cases of adultery in the Kingdom of Sicily were rather rare, and in practice usually referred to the church for judgment, but Margaret was asked to preside over one brought to her as regent. Involving a nobleman and his wife, this resulted in divorce, or annulment (see note 405).

Peasants were hardly ever afforded such justice. A certain number of children born outside marriage to common women were "adulterine bastards" whose fathers, being wed to other women, were not free to marry the mother of the illegitimate (extramarital) child. Giving birth to a child conceived outside wedlock was not, in itself, a crime, but the adultery that might lead to such a pregnancy certainly was. Apart from grave offenses such as murder, adultery was seen as the worst crime a woman could commit.

Misogyny was rife, yet a man of any rank who publicly accused a woman of being sexually promiscuous, a "slut," ran the risk of social judgment, perhaps even violence against his person, especially if the woman were married, and certainly if she were an aristocrat.

Impugning the honor or virtue of a royal woman was downright dangerous. Even the chronicler Hugh Falcandus, vituperative as he was, prudently equivocated about "rumors" regarding Margaret's chastity during her regency for William II.

Most women instinctively exercised care to avoid even the appearance of marital infidelity, libertine promiscuity, or sexual impropriety. Even prostitutes, and the concubines of the harem of a king or emir, were reasonably discreet in their outward behavior.

By modern standards, this emphasis on women's sexuality may seem excessive. Alas, gender differences, and female sexuality, were the keys to the dominance and control of women by men. Not for nothing do we encounter simplistic social tropes such as the Virgin, the Mother, the Witch, the Harlot and the Trickster, amongst others, popularized during our Norman era.

These stereotypes were the products of a patriarchal society that represented women in a way that would not threaten androcentric perceptions. This was reflected in literature.

Naturally, the poetry of love flourished in southern Italy long before the arrival of the Normans, continuing into the Hauteville and Hohenstaufen eras. That of the Muslims and Jews was particularly noteworthy (see note 55).

However, it was not until the reign of Frederick II, with the emergence of the Sicilian vernacular as a written language, that poetry of this kind truly blossomed, influenced by sophisticated models in what is now France and oriented toward the aristocracy. In romantic literature, troubadours sang the praises of virginal maidens who might make faithful wives, the epitome of this in southern Italy being the *Contrasto* (translated in Appendix 4). The introduction of this genre in the Kingdom of Sicily has sometimes been credited to Joanna of England, whose mother, Eleanor of Aquitaine, supported poets at her court. That is a reasonable presumption consistent with the arrival of certain artistic movements with Joanna, but very little poetry of this kind is known to have been composed in the Kingdom of Sicily that can be attributed directly to her influence or patronage. For that we look to the Sicilian School during the next century (see Chapter 24).

The outright sexualization of women in the visual arts is comparatively rare beyond, for example, such images as the depiction of the mermaid Melusina carved into a capital of Monreale's famed cloister. Here, through Joanna, may be a French influence, since the story of Melusina is associated with Poitou, where Eleanor had her court, and linked to her Angevin ancestors (see note 723).

The troubadours of Norman-Swabian Sicily are elusive. For the most part, the poets of the Sicilian School were court officials, and here we find no figure comparable to Bernard of Ventadour, whose work flattered Eleanor.

Even outside the nobility, women were expected to comport themselves in a way that would not suggest anything other than virtue. Flirtation could be risky. Much in romantic poetry represented ideals rather than realities.

A less popular genre dealt with female perceptions. Composed late in the thirteenth century, *Der Rosendorn* expresses a woman's thoughts about her own body and its appeal to men. This may be seen as the antithesis of romantic literature.

Feminine beauty standards in southern Italy, as elsewhere, were dictated largely by the preferences of men. Throughout the period considered here, there was not a prevalent norm based on height, complexion, eye color or hair color, which were quite diverse. Most artistic representations of famous persons, such as those in illuminations depicting Constance Hauteville having red hair, seem to have been accurate. There is nothing to suggest societal standards favoring women having hair of a specific color, which is the kind of physical detail mentioned by chroniclers without biased commentary. Herbal formulas existed for coloring gray hair; the Arabs, in particular, sometimes made use of henna as a hair coloring agent. Women usually wore their hair long, sometimes braided, and normally concealed by a scarf in public. Icons, illuminations and other works of art show women's bodies adhering to an "average" form, neither very voluptuous nor excessively slender; the depiction of women having long limbs was a later trend. The cosmetics section in the *Trotula,* a medical treatise written in Salerno, considers the removal of body hair (see note 374), which in Sicily had long been advocated by the Muslims.

Most women, regardless of religion or rank, wore their hair long, usually covered by a light scarf or veil in public (see note 381). Only nuns, or very old women, might cut their hair shorter, perhaps to shoulder length. Young, unmarried women outside the aristocracy might occasionally appear in public without scarves covering their hair, but this freedom was not generally encouraged, nor was it permitted in a place of worship. Tressing (braiding) was commonplace, particularly among aristocrats, and at the end of the twelfth century, during the reign of Constance Hauteville, there was even a distinctive "Palermitan" hairstyle popular among noblewomen in the capital. Modesty prevailed, with the shoulder and the upper portion of the arm covered and most dresses ending around the ankles. Reports of married women, especially those under the age of about thirty, deviating slightly from these norms are extremely rare; usually these rebels were noble ladies whose rank protected them from public censure. For fabrics, linen, cotton and wool were the norm, but in more affluent cities even many comparatively humble women owned a few items of silk, which was woven in Sicily.

If true obesity was rare, voluptuous figures were appreciated as a sign of health and even privilege, reflecting good nutrition despite the occasional scarcity of food. Not only were full breasts, substantial thighs and rounded derrières aesthetically desirable, they were regarded as a further indication that a girl of fifteen or sixteen was nubile and strong.

There was a cruel tendency to ascribe sympathetic or virtuous traits, such as kindness and even intelligence, to women perceived as being more beautiful than others, leaving less attractive women to be considered in unflattering terms.

For the most part, questions of sex and gender were addressed only in the most conventional ways.

Heteronormativity

It is impossible to know with certainty the number of people in the kingdom who were not heteronormative or cisgendered. By the twelfth century, none of the Abrahamic faiths condoned the practice of homosexuality even if, at times, efforts were made to pretend that the phenomenon simply didn't exist.

In Catholic circles, we find the belief that homosexual activity was "immoral" reflected in penitentials, lists setting forth the penances to be imposed by confessors upon penitents for specific sins.

The abbess Hildegard of Bingen, who died in 1179 and was known in the Kingdom of Sicily, wrote rather extensively about sexuality, often in a sympathetic way, but she claimed to have learned during a mystical vision that God saw sexual relations between women as evil. Bolstered by papal sanction, this became a prevalent belief in most of Europe even if, in earlier times, female homosexuality (lesbianism) was usually tolerated more than that between men. The French theologian Peter Cantor, who died in 1197, condemned male homosexuality. It was later that Thomas Aquinas, who was born near the kingdom's jagged northern border during the reign of Frederick II, characterized homosexuality, though chiefly that of men, as a violation of natural law. Like Peter, Thomas advocated scholasticism.

Eunuchs were usually treated as a "third gender," as if they were asexual (see Chapter 12).

Among Catholics, who were overwhelmingly predominant in the kingdom by the thirteenth century, the religious orders were havens for those, both male and female, who, for whatever reason, did not wish to seek conjugal life. Given their religious vocations, Hildegard and Thomas knew of the presence of homosexuality in monasteries and abbeys.

Outside the monastic environment, there were known instances of prominent personages who did not "seem" to conform to the norms of the heterosexual majority, but we know too little of their intimate lives to infer very much about them.

An example was Constance Hauteville, who became queen regnant and gave birth to Frederick II. Constance, who was betrothed rather "late" as she neared the age of thirty, does not seem to have enjoyed the company of men. Her marriage does not appear to have been very blissful, and indeed she may have had no pregnancies before the one culminating in the birth of her only known son (see note 758).

This, however, is modern speculation based on purely circumstantial evidence. Nothing in contemporary chronicles, even what might be inferred from "reading between the lines," transparently implies Constance to be anything other than heteronormative, dutiful in her role as wife and queen.

Such was the need for children to be born to become the workers, caregivers, warriors and monarchs of the future that, regardless of intrinsic sexual orientation, most people who did not choose religious life were strongly encouraged to marry and raise families. During the reign of Frederick II, Pope Gregory IX declared that those rare marriages contracted by couples unwilling to have children were not to be considered valid.

The avoidance of childbirth was not only a social or spiritual matter but a physical one.

Abortion and Contraception

Like many other practices, abortion was condemned by Thomas Aquinas and his contemporaries based on what was already the long-established position of the church. Aquinas viewed it as being contrary to the fundamental principles of natural law. In fact, abortion was proscribed explicitly as early as the ecumenical church councils of the fourth century, condoned only in extreme cases, such as a particularly difficult pregnancy or delivery that found the mother's life imminently, obviously endangered. Such a predicament was not the motivation for what, in modern times, is sometimes called an "elective" abortion, one performed at the pregnant woman's discretion.

Aquinas, whose view gained currency in Catholic circles, embraced the traditional Aristotelian idea that the ensoulment of a male embryo occurred at forty days of gestation, while a female fetus attained a soul at eighty days. This, however, was not construed as a sanction for early-term abortions.

Like Christian teachings, those of Islam and Judaism opposed abortion under most circumstances. Scripturally, Jewish scholars relied upon passages in Numbers and Exodus, which were also cited by Christians. Among Muslims, several hadiths were quoted, and the Maliki principles known in Sicily were unequivocal in condemning abortion.

In Christianity, abortion was considered a sin, but juridical punishment was the exception rather than the rule. Indeed, abortion was addressed only rarely in a direct or punitive way by civil statutes.

It is mentioned in the *Digest,* or "Pandects," of Justinian compiled in the sixth century. This complements his famous code, upon which the Assizes of Ariano of 1140 were partly based. It appears that Justinian's wife, Theodora, advocated abortion and contraception (see note 589). Sources suggest that the *Littera Florentina,* formerly the *Littera Pisana,* the earliest known copy of Justinian's *Digest,* was discovered, or rediscovered, at Amalfi by Pisan invaders just five years before Roger II promulgated his Assizes. It seems clear that the first King of Sicily and his successors had no interest in legislating abortion. Instead, they left it to the jurisdiction of the church, just as they usually recognized the right to grant divorces, or marital annulments, as an ecclesiastical prerogative (see note 405).

Particularly where an "early" abortion was performed, and given that the apparel worn by most women was not very revealing, the elective termination of a pregnancy was a rather private matter. To avoid becoming the focus of local gossip, a woman seeking an abortion might travel to a neighboring town for it.

The reasons for elective abortion varied widely, but certain situations, such as a nun's pregnancy, are not hard to imagine. Nor is it difficult to envisage medieval surgical procedures being fraught with risk.

Some of the same midwives who delivered babies performed abortions. For the most part, these women were the obstetricians of their time, but the Kingdom of Sicily had a fine medical school at Salerno where gynecology was taught.

Contraception was discouraged by the church. Like fertility treatment, it was sometimes addressed by the medical literature of the day. Avicenna's *Canon of Medicine,* completed around 1025 and widely consulted around the Mediterranean, described contraception methods explicitly. The *Trotula* (see Chapter 12), the medical treatise mentioned earlier, does not refer to contraception directly.

There is no evidence to suggest the practice of the infanticide of females to favor survival of a greater number of males in families in the Kingdom of Sicily, either during or after the Middle Ages. Baptisms were recorded regularly in the modern period, with some early registers in Sicily dating from around 1490. Nothing in these records suggests infanticide, nor do the *riveli* (tax rolls) recording the names of both sons and daughters in the kingdom's households imply anything of this kind (see note 1288).

Except for the cases of births to unwed mothers, most children were born into identifiable families, their paternity and legitimacy recognized in law.

Identification of Families

As we have seen, aristocratic families were usually identified by toponyms based on their principal feudal territories, thus the family of Thomas Aquinas was "of Aquino" and to Italians the saint is *Tommaso d'Aquino*. The Hautevilles in Italy were normally distinguished as being "of Apulia" or "of Sicily," and not identified as "de Hauteville" or even the more Italianate "Altavilla," though their Norman surname was itself thought to be a toponym (see note 85). Robert "Guiscard" was usually known by his nickname. The Lombard rulers of Salerno were, most often, simply "of Salerno." Except for the most prominent families, toponymic names of this kind usually lasted only so long as those in a line of descent held the territory by which they were known; the medieval Conversano clan vanished into obscurity with the loss of their lands. Toponymic appellations could change with the loss or acquisition of important estates, so Richard of Mandra was eventually known as "Richard of Molise," while Rodrigo of Navarre was given a new identity as "Henry of Montescaglioso."

Among the common folk, surnames became hereditary for all families only in the fifteenth century, when the church made the recording of baptisms and marriages mandatory. Onomastic origins varied greatly, but most surnames referred either to an occupation, a locality of origin or a personal characteristic, and some were patronymic.

Professions were sometimes practiced in families over generations, so a family of shepherds might come to be known as *Pastore* or *Pecoraro*. A family of blacksmiths would be identified as *Ferraro* or *Ferro* for the iron they forged and worked; *Maniscalco* usually referred to a maker of horse shoes. *Russo* and *Rosso* identified people with red hair or reddish, sun-burnt complexions. Some names were merely symbolic, perhaps representing characters in folk plays performed by ordinary people, hence *Principe* (prince) and the Sicilian *Parrinu* and *Presti* (priest). *Aspromonte* and *Madonia* refer to mountain ranges, while the names *Salerno* and *Messina* obviously owe their origin to cities.

The great majority of surnames used in southern Italy reflect Neapolitan or Sicilian linguistic influences, though in many cases they sound quite similar to those of Tuscany and other regions. *Rinaldi* and *Castaldi* are clearly Salernitan Lombardic.

When hereditary surnames became universal in southern Italy, the medieval practice continued of a maid using the same surname she had used as a maiden. Today, Italian women use their "maiden" (natal) names after marriage, a practice that differs markedly from what exists in certain other countries.

While non-aristocratic medieval families might be identified for two or three generations that mattered very little to the general populace, kings and queens, whose public status was firmly tied to birthright, necessarily viewed themselves as part of a longer tradition.

In a monarchy, the family that was identified most prominently was the royal family.

Kings and Queens

Hereditary monarchy has existed, in one form or another, since antiquity. In medieval Christian Europe its origins and patterns, like those of knighthood, were essentially Frankish and Germanic, though the Byzantine Greek concept of monarchy expressed in Constantinople emulated certain imperial Roman principles. Monarchy itself was a system of government which, in Europe, came to include an entire hereditary class, the nobility. Its Christianity, legal codes and feudalism distinguished medieval monarchy from the "tribal," if sometimes monarchical, societies of ancient Europe described by Julius Caesar and even Tacitus.

By definition, a monarch is the head of a state for life or until abdication. Contrary to popular belief, not all medieval monarchs were kings. In the eleventh century the princes of Salerno, dukes of Apulia and counts of Sicily were legitimate, if uncrowned, monarchs even though they were not, strictly speaking, "royalty."

Most monarchs were sovereigns, but we find certain lesser rulers submitting to higher civil authorities. Here the most obvious European examples are "minor" German monarchs, such as the dukes of Saxony and Bavaria, under the Kings of the Germans and Holy Roman Emperors.

In Europe, succession to monarchical power was most often based on fundamental requirements embodied in certain aspects of Salic Law (see note 770) formulated early in the sixth century following the fall of the Roman Empire in the west. The norm was male agnatic primogeniture. While a line of succession might, in an exceptional case, be transmitted through a female, most European monarchs were males. Typically, a woman who inherited a monarchy would see her dominion ruled by her husband, in her name, *jure uxoris,* and then transmitted to her son as her lawful dynastic heir. As we shall see, this occurred in the Kingdom of Sicily at the end of the twelfth century.

A fundamental difference between a king or queen on the one hand, and a ruling prince or duke on the other, was that kings and queens were anointed and crowned, while these lower-ranking monarchs were merely invested, almost as if they were glorified barons. The coronation ritual was much more than a mere "ceremony." It was a religious rite corollary to the belief that the prerogative to rule emanated from God. In medieval eyes, coronation was tantamount to a sacrament.

The coronation was public by its very nature. Kings and queens were crowned in cathedrals by bishops and normal usage presumed the collective support, or acclamation, of the high nobility present to witness the religious rites. Individual kings were known to be crowned more than once in the same kingdom.

The prerogative to crown a king was usually reserved to the highest prelate of the realm. In the Kingdom of Sicily this was the Archbishop of Palermo as primate. In England it was traditionally the Archbishop of Canterbury (see note 228).

Dynasties were familial in nature. Belonging to a dynasty was based on agnate (patrilineal) ascent and descent. That is to say, children were presumed to belong to the dynasties of their fathers rather than those of their mothers. Legitimacy of birth was the rule. In general, bastards (mentioned earlier) were not dynasts entitled to succeed to the throne. Whether a king could lawfully legitimize a son born outside marriage depended on practices and laws that varied over time, from one kingdom to another. Frederick II is believed to have "legitimized" Manfred by marrying the boy's mother, but this principle was far from universal. In general, paternal recognition of such a child was not equivalent to full legitimization that would place him in the line of succession, and we find Frederick issuing a testament to clarify which of his sons would succeed to which realm or office (see notes 1208 and 1209).

Rulers like Roger I, Roger II and Frederick II might father numerous children outside marriage, to the point that a precise number, including daughters, cannot be known with certainty. However, being part of a "family" presupposed being born to a woman wed to one of these men. In middle age, we find all of them, as widowers, marrying women young enough to be their daughters in order to give birth to sons.

A king's daughter succeeded to the throne as queen regnant only when there were no male heirs left. For the kingdom and period considered here, Constance Hauteville, daughter of Roger II, is the only example of this.

Monarchy was "corporate" in the sense that there was usually an extended royal family at its summit, consisting of the sovereign's spouse, siblings and cousins. There were, of course, court officers, counsellors, law experts, military leaders and clergy. The perception of rule by one person is thus rather illusory.

Various paradigms of medieval monarchical "theory" have been advanced over the centuries. If only in the abstract, it could be argued that the three essential, overlapping elements of monarchy are (firstly) law and religion, (secondly) familial and national identity, and (thirdly) rites, traditions and symbols confirming claims to sovereignty. These elements are common to most hereditary monarchies, including those in predominantly Muslim societies.

Law and religion govern the exercise of power by kings, whose rule is based on legislation and even religious belief, while monarchs themselves can make law. Familial and national identity are what validate the right to rule and to represent the people of a kingdom, the family being the most basic unit in society. Rites and symbols, such as coronations and crowns, provide an obvious way to distinguish monarchs from the general population.

From these rudimentary elements flow many precepts, such as the principle that the person of a crowned monarch, having been anointed by a bishop, and therefore elevated in the eyes of God, is "sacred" and inviolable. This "royal sacrality," expressed in the rites of coronation for both kings and queens, represented the elevation of the sovereign to something greater than the physical nature of a human being. For that reason, one sometimes speaks of the "dual nature" of a crowned monarch (see note 1038).

Here we are reminded of the "supernatural" (or "spiritual") in the state of royalty and, to a lesser degree, nobility. To the modern mind, this may seem arcane, even quaint, but to people living in the Middle Ages it was one of the things that defined their world, explaining, if not always justifying, destiny and the stratification of society.

There was no "secular" (non-religious) rite of coronation in the Kingdom of Sicily. Yet the idea, particularly in Catholic kingdoms, that there could be a "papal monarchy" reflected more general perceptions advocated by the popes (see note 1005). This was linked to the more obvious concept of hierocracy (see note 1126).

Although knightly and feudal investiture eventually came to be ascribed a "religious" character (with the former sometimes regarded almost as a sacrament), the only rite in medieval European society comparable in significance to the coronation of a king or queen was the crowning of a pope.

In contrast to their comrades and kinsmen in Normandy and England, the Normans who migrated to southern Italy during the eleventh century necessarily encountered civilizations, such as those of the Muslim Arabs and Byzantine Greeks, that were obviously somewhat different from their own. Here only the society of the Lombards would have seemed reasonably familiar.

Despite some localized practices mirrored in custom and law, medieval European notions about royalty and monarchy were strikingly uniform. This facilitated marriages between royal spouses from rather distant, unconnected lands. Royal betrothals could be complicated, and in the Kingdom of Sicily that of an English princess, Joanna, to William II, boasts a more detailed record than the others. This was our youngest queen.

A queen's body was a "sacred vessel" destined, or at least suitable, to give birth to kings. This was one of the most obvious ways in which royal women differed from ordinary "common" women. To the general public, queens were expected to be seen as paragons of loyalty and piety.

Our Norman and Swabian periods witnessed the emergence of several theoretical "models" of Catholic kingship written by scholars familiar with the Kingdom of Sicily. These advice-filled tomes continued the genre called the "mirror for princes."

Around 1159, John of Salisbury completed his *Policraticus* (see note 427). Here he identified, among many other things, the four chief duties of kings. These were described as a reverence for God, a respect for subjects, discipline and restraint for himself, and respect for the advice of his counsellors. According to John, kings who failed to obey the laws established by themselves or their royal predecessors risked becoming tyrants.

A mode of rule sometimes, perhaps inaccurately, attributed to our Hohenstaufens may have inspired *De Regno ad Regem Cypri,* a treatise completed around 1271 by Thomas Aquinas, who was no apologist for Frederick's dynasty. In the tradition of similar works written over the centuries, it was intended as advice for a monarch, in this case probably Hugh III, King of Cyprus and Jerusalem.

Such writings doubtless aided the evolution of kingship and even monarchy. In practice, however, kings relied chiefly on their own counsellors, not outsiders, for recommendations and guidance.

Beyond debate was the belief that a medieval king or emperor was presumed to be, or become, a social and cultural symbol of the people he ruled.

The "parasocial interaction" of a population with its royal family is generally viewed as a modern phenomenon more evident in some places (Great Britain) than others (Japan), reliant on the kind of communication and media that emerged during the twentieth century, spawning a certain conflation of royalty with celebrity (fame).

However, the pragmatic concept of the royal family as "the nation's family" certainly existed, in some form, in the Middle Ages, and it was especially obvious when there was a queen consort raising several children at court. In the Kingdom of Sicily, this paradigm was most evident when Elvira of Castile and Margaret of Navarre, both of northern Spain's Jiménez dynasty, were queens.

Although the queens' husbands were not always present, it is likely that the people of Palermo, one of Europe's most highly populated royal capitals, frequently caught a glimpse of these women and their children. Casual interactions of the royal family with the common folk are rarely documented except in instances of particular events, such as coronations, feasts or uprisings, but they are not difficult to imagine. Not only was Palermo's royal palace located in the city itself, it was not far from the main souk, now the Ballarò street market, where the queens shopped for silk and other products. These souks were the Palermitan equivalent of the fairs of other regions.

The ubiquitous rebellions that plagued the Kingdom of Sicily only rarely touched Palermo, and those that did were usually instigated by feudal renegades such as Matthew Bonello, whom we shall meet. More, perhaps, than subjects in most of the realm's other cities, the Palermitans seem to have regarded the king and his family as protectors and allies, especially during the Hauteville reigns.

Visibility itself was an impetus for such loyalty, and it was one of the many things that preserved the power of a dynasty. First, of course, a knightly family had to become royal, and that transition could be a slow one, realized principally through successful military exploits and expedient politics.

A key objective was the control of territory.

Chapter 3
TRIAL BY FIRE

That the Normans wanted land is beyond doubt, and it is possible that the Drengot family occupied the town of Ariano, in the Irpinian Mountains, long enough to have their claim to it noticed by the Lombards. If actual, formal enfeoffment occurred, it likely would have been a reward for their service to Melus. At all events, it proved ephemeral. Ariano was eventually ceded to another family while the Drengots were destined to obtain other, more important, localities.[76]

Upward Nobility

Melus died at the court of Henry II, Holy Roman Emperor, in Bamberg, in April 1021, having sought the intervention of the latter against the Byzantine Greeks of Apulia. Pope Benedict VIII was also present, and supported an invasion.

Meanwhile, in June, the Byzantines, assisted by the collaboration of wily Pandulf IV of Capua, himself a Lombard, prosecuted a successful campaign around that city, deep in Lombard territory, against Dattus, the brother-in-law of Melus. Many Lombards were killed but, following a siege, most of the Normans were spared. Dattus was taken prisoner, and summarily executed at Bari in June in the *mazzeratura,* or *poena cullei,* which entailed being sewn into a sack that was then tossed into the sea. In July, the Diet of Nijmegen approved Henry's plan to invade Apulia.

Henry entered Italy late in 1021. By May of the following year he had attacked Troia, where there were Normans among both the besiegers and the besieged, without taking the city, though, as a condition of peace, its citizens accepted a bishop of the Latin rite.[77] He soon returned to Germany, stopping at Mount Cassino along the way. Both Benedict and Henry were dead by the end of 1024.

At this moment, a large army sent from Constantinople was amassed in southern Italy as the result of a planned, but aborted, attack on Muslim Sicily. Aided by this impressive force, the Bariots sought nothing less than the erosion of Lombard power, and with it Latin ecclesiastical influence, in the regions south of Rome.

The next few years saw various bands of Normans involved in isolated engagements, some little more than skirmishes. The knights usually acquitted themselves well and suffered minimal losses.[78] A great number committed themselves to the service of Guaimar III in response to the Byzantine attacks.[79]

Without support from the Holy Roman Emperor, the Lombard princes stood little chance against a major army. An anomaly in this milieu was that Sergio IV of Naples was a vassal of Constantinople, at least in name; his family's origins were not Lombard.

A long succession of battles was fought between Lombards and Byzantines in the Campania region, especially the areas around Salerno, Naples and Capua. Like the siege at Troia, these engagements sometimes pitted one Norman against another, though the greater number fought on the Lombard side. There were even instances of Lombards fighting each other.

In these complex times, the Drengots were still supporting the Lombard cause, sometimes changing their alliances. Perfidious Pandulf IV of Capua, whom Ranulf Drengot, a surviving brother of Gilbert and Osmond, had once served, deposed the Duke of Naples, Sergio IV, in 1027. Two years later Ranulf defeated the usurper, restoring the duke to power. In recognition of this, Sergio enfeoffed Ranulf with Aversa, formerly a Byzantine town, in 1030.[80] Conrad II, the Holy Roman Emperor, eventually confirmed him as a count.[81]

Even before Ranulf's investiture, Aversa was on its way to becoming the focal point of Norman culture in southern Italy.[82] Now it was a Norman city.

That the emperor of the west supported the papacy and the Lombards against the emperor of the east was to be expected, but Conrad's responsibilities north of the Alps severely restricted his efforts in southern Italy, where Byzantine power remained formidable. Even so, the Normans had shown their mettle.

If the landed Drengots were now firmly in the Lombard camp, a few Normans were still willing to work for the Byzantines. This was especially true of new arrivals who lacked pre-existing loyalties, except perhaps to the pursuit of lucre.

The Hautevilles

In the spring of 1038, with the support of Emperor Conrad II, Ranulf Drengot led a successful attack on Capua, ruled by duplicitous Pandulf IV, his onetime ally, who had fled the city to avoid capture.[83] Not only was Pandulf, whom we met earlier, fundamentally disloyal, he was an arrogant opportunist.

Many of his actions were patently criminal. Most recently, he had raided the abbey of Mount Cassino, installed his own young son as Capua's bishop, and blatantly attempted to rape a young noblewoman.

Among Ranulf's knights were three brothers from Normandy who had already been in his service for three years. William "Iron Arm," Drogo and Humphrey were the eldest sons of a certain Tancred, the prolific, if not very wealthy, lord of Hauteville.[84] The twice-married Tancred had twelve sons and at least two daughters.[85]

The Hauteville brothers, like many other Norman knights who had fought for Pandulf, were now fighting against him. Joining them were fellow Normans already in the service of Guaimar IV of Salerno. Pandulf, who made his way to the Byzantine court in Constantinople, would eventually return, but for now Capua belonged to Guaimar, who happened to be his nephew.[86]

Michael IV, the Byzantine Emperor, was planning an invasion of Sicily, where he hoped to exploit the dissension growing among the island's factions to facilitate a reconquest of what had been lost in the ninth century. For this he needed the support of the Lombards, however odious they may have seemed to him. As a gesture of solidarity with his potential allies, he jailed Pandulf, who had so often betrayed them. This gesture cost him nothing and gained him some trust from those who, until now, had been his adversaries. In fact, the Lombards had solicited the cooperation of the Byzantines against the Muslim pirates over the years, most recently in 1036.

It is unlikely that the Lombards viewed the Sicilian campaign as anything like a conquest of their own. At best, its success would eliminate the nuisance of Arab piracy along the Campanian and Calabrian coasts, while cooperation with the Byzantines might foster a better rapport with these fellow Christians following many years of conflict. At the same time, Guaimar found this an expedient way to send some three hundred Norman knights, whose power in his dominions was clearly increasing, to fight elsewhere.[87] This meant less competition with Guaimar's Lombard knights for land, money and women.

For the Sicilian mission, the Norman knights were placed under the command of William Hauteville. Accompanying them was a smaller Lombard contingent under its own commander, Arduin.[88]

The Normans seem to have welcomed the Sicilian expedition as something of an opportunity.

Sicily

About half the Sicilian population was Byzantine Greek, but except for clergy and traders Constantinople had boasted no significant presence on the island since the fall of Rometta in 965 (see Chapter 1), and an invasion under consideration as recently as 1025 never came to pass.

George Maniakes had prior experience fighting the Muslims, having wrested Edessa from their control in 1031. Now, in 1038, he sought a reprise.

Besides the Normans and Lombards, and some Byzantine Greeks from southern Italy, the army mustered by Maniakes included troops from Greece and elsewhere. Among them was the Varangian Guard led by Harald Hardrada Sigurdsson of Norway.

The pirates who had been raiding the Calabrian coasts were based somewhere near Messina in the northeastern part of the island.[89] This is the first area Maniakes attacked.

The initial assaults were successful since the Kalbid defenders were generally unprepared for an invasion. Yet the larger coastal cities were fortified, while smaller localities like Taormina had castles set atop rocky summits.

During the battle at Syracuse, William Hauteville defeated the city's Arab leader during a sword fight in single combat, earning the nickname "Iron Arm."[90] For all we know, this encounter may have been little more than a popular tale, but it brought William great fame.

While at Syracuse, Maniakes expanded the fortifications of the seaside fortress that bears his name. One of the citizens, an aged man, offered the victors the relics of Saint Lucy, the town's patron, kept in a local church.[91] There is nothing to suggest that William and his brothers were great ideologues, or even more religiously devout than their peers. They were still mercenaries, strictly speaking, and this was not a crusade, though some Christians may have painted it as one. Nevertheless, they respected religious tradition.

At Troina, a town high in the Nebrodian Mountains, the audacious Normans, again led by William, distinguished themselves against a numerically superior Kalbid force.

With continued effort, the incursion might well have penetrated the lands farther west. Unfortunately, internal problems intervened. In an incident about which the exact details are not very clear, Maniakes publicly humiliated the Lombard leader after the latter complained about receiving far less booty than that to which he felt entitled. It seems that Arduin was cheated out of a fine Arabian steed that he fancied, having slain its owner. Reacting to this protest, Maniakes is said to have ordered him stripped to the waist and publicly flogged, though it seems rather improbable that a Lombard knight would have readily submitted to a physical punishment of this kind. Whatever actually occurred, it provoked a skirmish, a rebellion in the ranks, with Lombards and Normans pitted against Byzantines.

This gross lack of respect toward a knight wasn't the only matter of concern to the Normans; they had been poorly compensated with the spoils confiscated during the campaign. Disgusted by the events that had transpired, Arduin and William, accompanied by the men they commanded, returned to the mainland. Harald and his Varangian Guard also departed.[92]

This ended the imperial Byzantine occupation of about a fifth of the island, including those regions where the greatest number of Greek speakers and their clergy lived. Maniakes lacked the men and other resources to leave garrisons to defend the territories he had taken. Messina, Catania and Syracuse returned to Arab control. Yet the Sicilians themselves had seen how vulnerable the island could be to a concerted attack, and the military failures provoked further political turmoil amongst the ruling class.

If the invasion of Sicily ended in a debacle, it at least afforded the

Hautevilles and their companions an opportunity to see the island and its people for themselves. Here was an alluring gem to behold.

Melfi

The loss of a chunk of Sicily wasn't the only result of Byzantine Greek arrogance. The Normans and Lombards were not inclined to forget their poor treatment at the hands of a pompous general, and the consequences would be dire.

Nikephoros Dokeianos, the catepan, was assassinated in Ascoli in January 1040 at the instigation of Lombard knights disgruntled by the treatment of Arduin in Sicily, to be replaced by another Dokeianos, Michael.[93]

Seeking a new Lombard sponsor, the Normans elected one of Guaimar's kinsmen, Atenulf of Benevento, as their protector. By this time, however, the Normans were already acting independently, having taken matters into their own hands. Atenulf's patronage was little more than nominal, perhaps intended, more than anything else, to indicate a Norman break from Guaimar.[94]

Still desiring recompense for the indignities he had suffered in Sicily, Arduin, assisted by William "Iron Arm," seized the town of Melfi.[95] This occurred without a siege because Arduin convinced the people, with whom he had a good rapport, to accept his leadership over that of the Byzantines, who offered the Melfitans less independence and even less military protection. The catepan eventually recognized Arduin as the city's governor, but Melfi was to become the Norman base for operations against the Byzantines. For now, the knights raided and pillaged the surrounding countryside, but they also began to conquer and administer towns.

In March 1041, Michael Dokeianos, supported by the Varangian Guard and other troops, did battle against the Normans, including the army of Ranulf Drengot, on the Olivento River near Venosa; this was a defeat for the Byzantines but enough of them survived to fight another day. In May, the Normans routed a Byzantine force at Montemaggiore, near Cannae; many Byzantines drowned in the waters of the Ofanto River as they retreated.[96]

At Montepeloso in September, the Normans defeated the troops sent by a new catepan, Exaugustus Boiannes, who they took captive and consigned to the custody of Atenulf.

The Normans' pact with Atenulf was dissolved when he fled with the money remitted by the Greeks to ransom Exaugustus.

There was another unsavory ingredient in this cauldron of chaos. Shortly before gasping his last earthly breath in December 1041, Michael IV, the emperor Maniakes served, freed Pandulf IV, who immediately returned to Italy to harass his foes. Guaimar IV could not have relished the reappearance of this duplicitous uncle.[97] More immediately, however, Guaimar had to address the actions of his allies.

In the wake of his misadventure in Sicily, George Maniakes found himself and his undisciplined army in Apulia early in the spring of 1042. Before long, he had to hasten to Constantinople, where, Zoë, the widow of Michael IV, wed a man who would be crowned as Emperor Constantine IX. The new emperor was manipulated into opposing Maniakes and confiscating his land. Maniakes could not leave a large force to put down the Normans in Italy that he might well require to suppress the ambitions of Constantine in Greece. This mooted any prospect of a major Byzantine campaign to subdue the Normans and reclaim lost territories in Apulia.[98]

At a meeting held in Melfi in September 1042 following the death of Arduin the previous year, Guaimar IV of Salerno recognized the feudal right of William "Iron Arm" Hauteville to Melfi and the mountainous territories surrounding it, erecting this dominion as the County of Apulia. William's authority also extended to the Norman garrison at Troia. Present to witness this act was Ranulf Drengot of Aversa, whose title of count was reconfirmed. William wed Guida, a niece of Guaimar as the daughter of Guy of Sorrento.[99]

A number of knights were enfeoffed under William. This included his brothers and other men who formed the nucleus of what became the Norman nobility of southern Italy.

By elevating William, Guaimar, in reality, renounced very little, for most of these lands were in areas that were long contested, and still claimed, by the catepan. Melfi was far enough from Salerno and Aversa that neither Guaimar or Ranulf need be concerned about Norman attacks on their own dominions in the immediate future.

Nevertheless, the Normans led by the Hautevilles now had a firm foothold in Italy. The next few years saw them prosecuting sundry campaigns in Apulia, Lucania (Basilicata) and Calabria to curtail Byzantine influence whilst accruing more lands for themselves.

From Heel to Toe

William "Iron Arm" died in 1046, leaving Drogo as the senior Hauteville in Italy.[100]

The same year, Drogo defeated the catepan Eustathios Palatinos near Taranto, and his brother, Humphrey Hauteville, convinced the Bariots to agree to a treaty. The next year, Drogo won lands around Cosenza, in Calabria, which he gave to his younger brother, Robert "Guiscard," who had arrived from Normandy.

Month by month, the Hautevilles were making their presence felt increasingly in Apulia, the heel of the Apennine peninsula, and in Calabria, its outstretched toe.

The Byzantine Greeks could no longer presume to have free rein in these regions. Apulia, their *Longobardia,* was a province of the Byzantine Empire, effectively one of the last vestiges of the catepanate that once included everything to the south and east of a jagged line drawn from Mount Gargano to a point near Salerno.

In recent centuries, Calabria had become a "wild west" peopled by Greeks, visited by Arabs, coveted by Lombards. In its varied, and generally unguarded, landscape the Normans could discern not only the mountainous barriers to entry but the green valleys of opportunity.

By now, no action could be undertaken south of Rome without reckoning with the Normans, and specifically with the House of Hauteville.

They may not have advocated any ideology beyond a vague European feudalism, but the Normans were ever Latin in their language, culture and faith. Like the Lombards, they favored the pope's Christianity over that of the patriarch in Constantinople. The emperor, to whom they pledged at least nominal fealty, was not Greek but German.

Under Norman influence, a Greek church in a Calabrian town could easily segue to the use of unleavened bread and the Latin liturgy, complete with its creed. What were generally missing in the Byzantine lands were major abbeys like those of the Benedictines.

These sundry realities were reflected in the formal policies implemented in the localities the Normans seized from Byzantine control but also in daily life amongst the common folk. Edging toward the middle of the eleventh century, bilingualism, or even trilingualism, was the norm. One might encounter people who spoke both Greek and a "Longobardic" Latin.[101] The Normans spoke their own brand of French among themselves, and it became a common vernacular in Norman localities such as Melfi, Aversa and Mileto.

The Normans' impact greatly transcended their numbers. That alone could have intimidated their detractors. The Apulian and Calabrian towns that fell under the Normans simply adhered to general feudal norms. There was no need to garrison every locality in the Norman orbit, or to make special provisions for its administration. The feudal system, bolstered by the church, was more than sufficient. Naturally, certain aspects of the transition to manorialism were highly evident in Byzantine towns because they brought something clearly different from what had formerly existed. In towns that were formerly Lombard, and already feudal, the juridical changes, though real, were minimal, and minimally perceived.

With territorial domination came the kind of covert envy that spawns overt resentment. Many Lombards and Byzantines loathed the Normans even in times of relative peace. The Normans were hardly heretics, nor was their rule, even at this early date, excessively repressive, despite what a few outspoken critics abroad may have believed based on reports they received.

Yet the Normans' harshness struck some as overzealous, even indiscriminate, prompting Amato of Montecassino, usually an apologist, to write that in the spring of 1050, following visits to Salerno and Capua, Pope Leo IX, a dogmatic German aristocrat who harbored grave doubts about the Hautevilles' legitimacy in Italy, "made his way to Melfi to protest the recent incidents perpetrated by the powerful Normans, imploring them to cease their cruelty and abuse of the poor. He explained to them that an offense against the poor is an offense to God, and that, conversely, it pleases God when the poor are treated humanely. He implored them to faithfully defend the clergy and property of the church, and urged them to perform good works, offer their wealth to God through His church, and behave honorably toward their neighbors and the others they met."[102]

Meanwhile, the papacy was attempting to convince the Byzantine Emperor and the Patriarch of Constantinople to renounce their interests in southern Italy. To that end, Pope Leo IX appointed the zealous French cardinal Humbert of Silva Candida as his advisor. It is reasonable to believe that much of Leo's "Norman policy" was formulated by Humbert.

In 1051, Drogo was assassinated in an ambush after returning from a meeting with Leo IX at Benevento at which he had promised to restrain his knights from raiding and looting that city.[103] This left Humphrey as the oldest member of the Hauteville family. At the same time, it provoked a certain degree of instability amongst the Normans.

At the root of papal antipathy were popular discontent and Lombard machinations, laments emanating from both the Greek and Latin elements of what, for now, was the universal church.

However, two things stood out in the minds of contemporaries, and both were emblematic of a wider acrimony.

For their part, the Normans' subjects in areas taken from the Byzantines complained, in particular, about incidents such as reprisals taken by Humphrey following the assassination of Drogo.[104] Needless to say, these punishments were overzealous, conducted without so much as the semblance of fair trials. Italy's Normans, compared to those back in Normandy, were not yet very accustomed to formulating effective legislation and appointing competent judges. Their law was the sword.

For the Lombards, the series of Norman raids on Benevento was especially disturbing. The citizens had recently expelled the two Lombard co-princes, and they feared that the Normans now wanted to make the city a principality of their own. Desperate for relief, the Beneventans asked Leo to take their prosperous city under his protection, a decision that led to it becoming an extraterritorial papal possession, with future princes ruling as vassals of the pope.

These factors provoked papal intervention in the form of an invasion spearheaded by the forces of the Holy Roman Emperor Henry III. This would be the last major military engagement of its numerical size against the Normans and their allies in southern Italy involving the Lombards as participants. More than a turning point, it was the swan song of Lombard power in Italy and the most salient milestone along the path toward papal recognition of the Normans and their dominions as a bona fide polity. The name of this battle dominates the annals of Italy's Norman age: Civitate.[105]

Civitate

The town of Civitate, not far from the newer locality of San Paolo di Civitate, was a fortified site on generally flat land near the Fortore River and the Gargano Peninsula, northwest of Foggia, in the northern part of Apulia called *Capitanata,* which may be a corruption of *catepan.* Little identifies the medieval site today except for part of a solitary tower. Although a Roman settlement stood nearby, Civitate was founded as a Byzantine town. At the council held at Melfi in 1042, it was given to a Norman knight named Walter.

Here, in June of 1053, a joint imperial army of Swabians, Lombards and papal troops challenged the Normans led by the Hautevilles for military, and therefore, feudal supremacy in southern Italy. At the head of the invading force were Gerard, Duke of Lorraine, and Rudolf, a Swabian who was now governing Benevento on behalf of the papacy.

The Normans were forewarned by their scouts and messengers of the large army wending its way through Campania and Apulia into their home territory, the lands around Melfi. They had probably heard that most of the Swabian knights were more adept at fighting on the ground than on their mounts. Every knowable detail argued for an engagement in flat country. That meant the valleys and plains to the east of Melfi.

Whereas most of the Normans' previous campaigns were offensive, this one was decidedly defensive. What is more, the Hautevilles and their followers may still have been in some disarray following the deaths of William and then Drogo, who were known for their leadership. Humphrey's leadership was largely untested. For many knights, the mental challenge alone would be great.[106]

There were physical challenges as well. Thus far, poor harvests had left the Normans and their subjects less nourished than they might have been otherwise. The flat terrain made the prospects of either side seem about equal, except for the numbers.

Here the disparity was daunting. Precise figures are unknown, but it appears that the Normans had some three thousand men at their disposal, of which perhaps a tenth of that number were knights or squires. Pope Leo's polyglot force boasted at least twice that number, including seven hundred Swabian knights.

"The enemy of my enemy is my friend," says an old adage. Leo's overtures to Argyros, son of the fabled Melus and now catepan of Bari, to join the coalition against the Normans resulted in some military posturing but little more.

The Norman force consisted mostly of archers and foot soldiers from the regions they ruled. These were Byzantine Greeks who, whatever they thought about the Normans, lacked much affinity for the Lombards, much less a zealous pontiff from the "alien" lands beyond the Alps. Whereas they had endured Norman misbehavior for a few years, they had been at odds with the Lombards for centuries. On the Norman side there were also some Slavs, whose perceptions of the Germans and their emperor were never very flattering.

True, the Normans were Latinizers, and their rule could be harsh, but thus far they had tolerated the Greek practice of Christianity, leaving the Byzantine monasteries largely undisturbed, and they built new towns.[107] From the Byzantine point of view, rule by Rome and her Lombard surrogates might be far worse.

This was the time for the Hautevilles and their loyal knights, now vassals, to show their adversaries, and indeed all of Europe, their true mettle. It was do or die, the supreme existential challenge.

Humphrey was joined by his brother Robert "Guiscard," whom we met earlier and whose very nickname meant "crafty," and the men enfeoffed under him. There were knights from the lands of Aversa and Capua, led by Richard Drengot.

And so the invaders arrived, pitching camp along the Fortore River the day before they planned to strike at Civitate. Except for the expected papal offer of a truce, and the promise of decent treatment of the Normans if they surrendered now, before the fighting began, there seems to have been none of the usual taunting. Both sides knew why they were here and what was at stake. The mere presence of so many men-at-arms was antagonizing enough for those unbaptized in the gritty reality of warfare.

The next morning, as they neared each other, the two armies were separated by a very low hill. The Normans were divided into three mounted units led by Humphrey in the middle, with Robert and Richard on either side. The infantry was arrayed behind them.

Following a volley of arrows loosed by the skilled Byzantine bowmen, and a return volley from the less-skilled archers on the other side, the battle began. Richard led the initial charge of mounted knights, veering slightly toward one of the enemy's flanks where most of the Lombard footmen were marching. Unprepared for such audacity, most of the Lombard troops, following a token effort at fighting, dispersed in fear. They retreated in all directions except that of the Norman attack. Many fled to the countryside, never to return.

Having sown such thorough chaos, Richard rounded back to assist Humphrey and Robert against the Swabian knights in an arduous mêlée. This fighting was difficult, but it painted the green fields red with the blood of Pope Leo's sorely vanquished compatriots, a fallen army. Receiving news of this, Leo, who was waiting in Civitate, may have intervened to put an end to further slaughter.

Once again, the Normans had snatched victory from the jaws of defeat. They had won the day, and perhaps even the century.

Most of the German commanders, people like Gerard of Lorraine, lived to fight another day.

The pope was taken prisoner, returning to Rome only many months later. His wings had been clipped, his ego bruised, but he still exercised power in the spiritual realm.

If Leo's long campaign against the Normans had ended in abject failure, accomplishing little more than the deaths of Swabian knights, he might still achieve victory over the Greeks. He would excommunicate them. In no part of western Europe would his decision be felt more, and more immediately, than in southern Italy.

Chapter 4

CHRISTIANS EAST AND WEST

By the time the Normans arrived in Italy, people spoke quite openly of the Latin "Western" bishops and their Greek "Eastern" counterparts.

In southern Italy, this usually, though by no means always, correlated to the ethnic identities of the Italianized Lombard Christians under Rome and the Byzantine Greek Christians under Constantinople. However, it may be remembered that Melus, though presumably Lombard through his father, was raised among Byzantines in Bari, where his son, Argyros, eventually became catepan. Clearly, the ethnic lines could be blurred, whether through marriage or as a result of the simple assimilation resulting from living in a place dominated by people of a certain religion and language.

In 1054, a move initiated by Pope Leo IX led the twin factions of Christianity to become identified as what are now known as the *Catholic* and *Orthodox* churches.[108] The impact of this formal division was felt in southern Italy long after that signal year.

Greeks and Latins

Let us imagine a trip southward along the rocky Tyrrhenian coast in 1002, the year that the future Pope Leo was born as Bruno of Egisheim. To the immediate south of Rome, most of the territories find themselves firmly in the Latin camp. Farther south, Gaeta, on a promontory north of Naples, is ruled by a family whose authority is confirmed by Constantinople; here the duke, Marino II, has prevailed upon the ecclesiastical hierarchy to consecrate his son, Bernard, as bishop, an appointment that reflects the local church's links to his Docibilian dynasty, which probably originated in this region of Italy. In Naples one encounters a dynasty historically subordinate to Constantinople; here the Greek liturgy is accepted even though the diocese itself is under Rome. Salerno, ruled by Lombards, is thoroughly Latin, but Calabria, the region to its immediate south, is overwhelmingly Greek.

Some of the liturgical practices, and even the Greek language, of the Byzantine Christians of Apulia, Lucania and Calabria may have annoyed the popes in Rome, but the greater offense, viewed from the Tiber, was the fact of these brethren being under the ecclesiastical jurisdiction of the Patriarch of Constantinople, a status coinciding with the political jurisdiction of the Eastern Roman (Byzantine) emperor who ruled from that city. That once-imperial Rome found herself counterpoised in Italy by ever-imperial Constantinople was unpalatable to many in the Eternal City.

North of the Alps, an invisible longitudinal line separated the churches of the Latin tradition to the west from those of the Greek and Slavic traditions to the east, with isolated pockets of non-conformity on each side.

Over the centuries, the mentality that dominated Roman thought was impressed upon the Franks, Germans and Lombards of the Apennine Peninsula, who came to view the Byzantine Greeks not as the direct heirs of the eastern part of the Roman Empire but as usurpers of territory that belonged, as if by divine right, to these "western" peoples of Italy.

The Latin-versus-Greek ecclesiological paradigm cannot be dismissed *a priori,* since it was based on well-founded beliefs, but its detrimental side-effects would have been easier to contain were it merely cultural rather than political. Unlike some of his predecessors, Pope Leo IX was not predisposed to ignoring Constantinopolitan episcopal sees in his own unkempt backyard where, many of his confederates felt, the only patriarchal jurisdiction should be that of papal Rome.

Whatever the Greeks and Latins of the universal church thought of each other prior to 1054, Christianity was the defining faith of medieval Europe. It might even unite disparate Christians against a common foe, such as the Muslims, as it did at Garigliano in 915 and, less successfully, in eastern Sicily in 1038. This was consistent with the evolving concept of "Christendom." The deterioration of the Maniakes invasion of Sicily was the result not of religious differences among the Christians but social conflicts based chiefly on their personalities.

Byzantine Legacy

The church in central Palermo now known as the *Martorana* is perennially popular among visitors, and the more curious among them may even visit the more austere Church of San Cataldo next door. Few realize what this pairing represents, for the churches, each dating from the middle of the twelfth century, were built for different communities.

The walls of the Martorana are covered in mosaic icons, its original floor plan a simple "cross-in-square" (or Greek cross) beneath a single dome, around the exterior of which is an inscription in Arabic. The Martorana was, in fact, built as a Greek Orthodox church dedicated to the *Theotokos* (most literally "God-Bearer"), its charter of 1143 written in Greek and Arabic. It was completed in 1151.

Constructed in the same Norman-Arab style, San Cataldo has a long nave and very simple Romanesque arches. Resembling a mosque, it was consecrated as a Catholic church around 1160, possibly as the chapel of a courtier who lived nearby, and dedicated to Catald, Bishop of Taranto, an Irish-born saint who died in 685.

Elsewhere in the former *Regnum Siciliae* there are churches reflecting eclectic architectural influences. Monreale's abbey, as we shall see, is at once Norman, Arab and Byzantine, but while it initially had an iconostasis, and though its mosaics cover an area larger than those of Saint Mark's in Venice, it was founded as a Benedictine church. There are a few churches remaining in southern Italy that were constructed explicitly for the diminishing Orthodox communities following what has come to be known as the *Great Schism*.

Fomented for several centuries, the Great Schism of 1054 separated the "Latin" church from "Greek" or "Byzantine" Christianity, and it was a historic development used by the papacy to justify the Normans' confiscation of southern Italy.

It wasn't until the invention of the printing press, shortly before the fall of Constantinople, that the Catholic and Orthodox churches came to be referred to very widely in casual parlance as much more than "western" and "eastern," or "Roman" and "Greek."

Iconography

Icons, though often associated with the Byzantine tradition, were once commonplace in much of Europe, if more so in the east. The art of iconography has ancient roots, but the traditional form most widely seen dates from the earliest years of the Middle Ages. Icons were Christianity's earliest holy images, objects of veneration but not, as some imagine, worship. Icons are not idols, although the Iconoclast Controversy (see note 46) sought to suppress their display.

Iconography is one of the forms of art on which subsequent European painting was based. To believers, the painting of an icon is almost a spiritual experience and the icon, once blessed by a priest, becomes a religious symbol. In English, it is often said in the Orthodox Church that the iconographer does not "paint" an icon; rather, he or she "writes" it. This may be based on a misinterpretation of the Slavonic words for "painting" and "writing," but it is a reminder that creating an icon is unlike creating any other work of art. Iconography is Christianity's oldest art form.

It is not extreme realism. The figures in an icon are represented as they are believed to exist in Heaven. Dimensionalism is limited. Religious icons, while resembling stylized portraits, actually represent their subjects rather than depict them literally. This is intentional. Physical proportions are distorted, while perspective is treated in a surreal manner even as details such as clothing and landscapes are often strikingly natural.

In viewing an icon, one almost imagines that the Renaissance, with its scientific and humanistic influences, never took place. Iconography is one of the few visual arts that has not changed significantly since the earliest centuries of Christianity. Spirituality, not science, is its focus.

Orthodox Christians regard icons as windows to Heaven.

Mosaic, an ancient art much favored by the Greeks and Romans, lends a certain permanence to icons. However, some of the icons created in southern Italy during the Norman era, such as those that once graced the walls of the church of Saint John of the Hermits, in Palermo, were painted in fresco.

The icon of Thomas Becket in Monreale is exceptional if viewed through the lens of religious tradition because, though canonized by Rome, Thomas of Canterbury was not venerated by the Orthodox. Apart from this, not every mosaic in Sicily showing a human image is, strictly speaking, an icon. Icons depict saints, and saints have halos.

In the mosaic of Roger II, vested in a Byzantine *loros,* in the Martorana, only the portion of the image that depicts Christ is actually an icon (see Chapter 11).

Differences

Before the vast Roman Empire split in two (see Chapter 1), Latin was its official tongue, but even in Italy Greek enjoyed prestige as the second language of learned people, while it was the popular vernacular in the Balkans, Sicily and the eastern Mediterranean. With the Empire divided, and the western part descending into chaos and even ignorance, language became divisive. Misunderstandings grew more frequent because many in Italy spoke no Greek, while few Greeks bothered to learn Latin. At the dawn of the Middle Ages, the distance between Rome and Constantinople wasn't only linguistic; geography itself imposed a definite obstacle, especially now that a central imperial government no longer controlled the entire Mediterranean. The church found itself no more monolithic than the factionalized Roman world itself.

The early church was collegial; patriarchs, including the one in Constantinople, recognized the Patriarch of "the West" (in Rome) as "the first among equals." (Contrary to popular belief outside Orthodox circles, the Patriarch of Constantinople is not an "Orthodox pope.")

In the early centuries of the church, matters such as the definition of doctrine and canon law were decided by groups of bishops rather than a single patriarch, and that is how ecumenical councils, beginning at Nicaea in 325, determined fundamental theological beliefs and questions such as which gospels were to be included in the canon of the New Testament. The *Codex Sinaiticus,* the earliest complete record of the canonical gospels known to us, was written in Koine Greek between 330 and 360 (the contemporaneous *Codex Vaticanus* includes Old Testament books as well).

It is noteworthy that Christianity became the official faith in Armenia in 301 before the Edict of Milan even made it legal elsewhere in 313; the Armenian Apostolic Church separated itself from the other churches in 554 based on theological differences expressed at an ecumenical council. Eventually, most

Orthodox jurisdictions became national or ethnic, making use of vernacular languages such as Slavonic.

Nevertheless, despite exceptions such as Armenia, Egypt and Ethiopia, the early church was essentially united until 1054. In much of western Europe the liturgy was celebrated not in Greek but in Latin, often in the Gallican Rite. In Spain we find the Mozarabic Rite and in Britain the Sarum Rite.

By the Middle Ages, Christians in regions from the German-speaking lands and those to their west, such as France, had very little exposure to the influence of Constantinople even though the Byzantine Empire fostered and preserved the greatest learning in Christendom during this period.

In general, the papacy wanted ecclesiastical control of the Latin-speaking territories, but the Christians in Sicily, Calabria and Apulia were mostly Greek-speaking into the eleventh century.

Beyond questions of territorial jurisdiction (in the middle of the ninth century Rome contested a Byzantine episcopal appointment in Syracuse even though Sicily was outside papal authority), there were conflicts over certain theological teachings and liturgical usages. In Greece, for example, the theology of Augustine of Hippo was little appreciated, while Rome's use of unleavened bread in the Eucharist differed from the Greeks' leavened bread. An indicatory difference was the infamous debate over the *filioque,* Rome's use of a phrase in the Creed which seemed to alter the traditional dogma of the Trinity.

In a portent of potential trouble, John II, bishop of the Apulian diocese of Trani, elicited an adamant response from Leo IX for drawing the pontiff's attention to some of these matters. The pope thought John insolent.[109]

Ecclesiastical forces in Rome's jurisdiction, particularly under Charlemagne and his immediate successors, advocated for papal authority over Constantinople, something unlikely to be approved by the various patriarchates of the East (Constantinople, Antioch, Alexandria, Jerusalem). This "Latin" view was unsurprising considering that, in the secular realm, the pope was viewed as a kingmaker who could crown the likes of Charlemagne and other monarchs.

Except for a few lengthy intervals, the patriarchs of the East commemorated (and prayed for) the Patriarch of the West and vice versa. These *diptychs,* lists of bishops commemorated during the liturgy, were seen as a sign that communion existed, however tenuously.

Finally, in 1054, papal emissaries sent by Leo IX to Michael I, Patriarch of Constantinople, presented a letter of excommunication to him.[110]

Leo himself had died during the eastward trek of the papal embassy led by his advisor Humbert of Silva Candida.[111] In reality, the Patriarch of Rome lacked the authority to excommunicate or even command his brother in Constantinople.[112]

Significant for Italy's Greek community was the Council of Bari convened by Pope Urban II in the same year as the First Crusade. This formally established that the Orthodox Church in Apulia would be integrated into the Catholic Church, something mostly achieved by the middle of the twelfth century, though the papal effort was backed up by Norman force.

Despite the acrimony, bilateral efforts to mend the torn fabric of a divided

Christianity continued, but by the Second Crusade, in 1147, some Roman Catholics were becoming highly suspicious of Orthodox Christianity's co-existence with Islam in certain regions, such as Palestine.

In 1143 Nilos Doxopatrios, an Orthodox cleric of Palermo who had formerly served in Constantinople, authored a theological treatise supporting Greek Orthodox traditions over the Roman Catholic influences that were taking root under the Normans.[113] This alone tells us that the gradual Latinizing was effective despite some lingering resistance, if not overt antipathy. King Roger II flirted with Orthodoxy without embracing it.

Among popes, Adrian IV was particularly amenable to a cordial rapport with the Orthodox patriarchs, but his pontificate was a short one.

Yet the Hauteville era witnessed several serious attempts to reunite Christianity. In 1166, for example, the *sebastos* Jordan Drengot (see note 487), acting on behalf of the Patriarch of Constantinople and the Byzantine Emperor, sought the cooperation of Pope Alexander III for a reconciliation. Jordan, the son of Robert II of Capua, was raised Catholic but had embraced Orthodoxy. Though the papacy appreciated the gesture, nothing of substance was concluded.

In Constantinople, the "Massacre of the Latins" of 1182 was ostensibly targeted at Italian mercantile power epitomized by the maritime republics' encroaching activities in that city, but the Italians' Roman Catholic ecclesiastical hegemony itself provoked a certain degree of Greek hostility. The bloody sack of Constantinople perpetrated by Catholics in the Fourth Crusade, in 1204, did little to foster hopes of a reconciliation (see note 863). The following year a Latin army was defeated at Adrianople (Edirne in Turkey) and in the next few decades the Teutonic Knights attempted to conquer predominantly Orthodox republics such as Novgorod in Russia. Enmity had come to define a political, if not theological, relationship lost in a deep chasm of perpetual misunderstanding.

Identities

The fundamental doctrines of Catholicism and Orthodoxy didn't change during the Norman-Swabian era, when efforts at reunification continued. Over the centuries, however, Catholic theology came to be perceived as comparatively more "legalistic" and, inspired by theologians such as Thomas Aquinas, with their scholasticism, rather more "philosophical" than it was before the Schism. Even today, Catholicism appears, in certain respects, to emphasize the letter of the law, whereas Orthodoxy seems to focus more on its intent.

An obvious social example seen in modern times concerns divorce. Although the procedure itself has been streamlined and made more accessible, the annulment of a Catholic marriage remains a complex process. Even its terminology is quasi-juridical in tone, with references to institutions such as a "tribunal," as if the spouses themselves were being tried (for an example of a case at the Sicilian court see note 405). The Orthodox approach to spousal separation was, and remains, pastoral in its essence and comparatively simple in its procedure.

Even though many cultural aspects of the parallel yet distinct paths taken by Latin and Greek Christians after 1054 were not entirely theological, it could be argued that most of these were indicative of underlying religious views.

Artistic and architectural movements such as the Gothic and the Baroque reflected, or at least complemented, theological ideas, while Orthodox churches, devoid of statues and stained-glass, exemplified the ascetic tradition of Saint Basil and his contemporaries.

With the passing of time after 1054, Catholic teachings regarding Original Sin, Papal Authority, Purgatory and, still later, the Immaculate Conception, came to differ from those of Orthodoxy. In practice, the Orthodox administer the sacraments according to the ancient usages: triple immersion for baptism followed immediately by chrismation (confirmation), and then the reception of the Eucharist (always given in both kinds). Married men may be ordained to the priesthood, something tacitly tolerated in the Catholic sphere until the Lateran Councils of the twelfth century. Nevertheless, the Catholic magisterium recognizes Orthodox orders (sacraments) and apostolic succession.

Today, specific Orthodox views regarding certain aspects of the sacraments differ slightly from those of Catholicism. Orthodox canon law (based on the determinations of early Ecumenical Councils) is essentially unchanged since the Middle Ages while the more complex Catholic code of canon law was revised most recently in the twentieth century.

As a generality, the Orthodox do not venerate Catholic saints canonized after 1054. In southern Italy, Saint Louis, Saint Francis of Assisi and Saint Thomas Becket are obvious examples. For their part, the Catholics do not venerate saints canonized by the Orthodox after that year.

Over time, monasticism in the two churches came to differ in obvious ways. Orthodoxy had distinct monastic communities but no large "international" monastic orders such as the Benedictines, Dominicans or Franciscans. Orthodox monks follow the Basilian Rule. Monks, whether Orthodox or Catholic, live in monasteries, while the monastery headed by an abbot is, by definition, an abbey, and usually larger than the typical monastery. Hermit monks, now rare in Catholicism, live alone or in very small, isolated *kellia* (hermitages). Most medieval Orthodox monasteries were outside cities or towns. A convent, or nunnery, under the direction of an abbess is an abbey. Under the Normans, there was a tendency to encourage Orthodox monks to live in larger monasteries rather than hermitages.

The divergence of Catholicism and Orthodoxy after 1054 coincided with an increase in the number of religious orders in the Catholic sphere.

Even after the onslaught of the Renaissance, people in Italy could readily see the vestiges of Byzantine culture in the magnificent medieval churches of Venice, Ravenna and Palermo. There are also Byzantine Catholic ("Eastern Rite") dioceses and monasteries in Italy.[114]

Conversion

The conversion of the Orthodox population of southern Italy to Catholicism took several essential forms, and for most people is was not the rigid process that modern minds tend to envision. Indeed, it was often quite insidious, working in tandem with the cultural Latinization introduced by the Normans in the regions they ruled.

In many cases, Byzantine Greek clergy simply accepted Rome's jurisdiction over them while continuing, sometimes for generations, to use Greek in liturgy for the benefit of the Grecophone faithful; an example of this is Theophanes Kerameus, who preached and recorded his homilies in Greek into the middle of the twelfth century (see note 118). Unlike some Byzantine clerics, Theophanes found himself in a comparatively "remote" region. By the time he died, in 1152, the large metropolis of Palermo had just a few Orthodox churches, such as the Martorana, which was founded by George of Antioch, a Bariot of a Byzantine family, and Nilos Doxopatrios, whom we met earlier. The Byzantine clergy in cities like Palermo, Bari and Messina encountered ever more pressure to embrace Latin liturgy than their counterparts in rural areas; the obvious exceptions were tiny urban communities of Orthodox monks such as those serving the Martorana under royal protection.

However, it was their allegiance to the papacy, not the use of Latin, that made clergy Catholic. Theophanes, though a speaker of Greek attached to Byzantine tradition, was not actually Orthodox.

By 1054, the monastery founded by Nilo of Rossano at Grottaferrata a half-century earlier was one of the larger Byzantine monastic communities in Italy, with over two hundred monks. It retained its Greek character into the twelfth century. Yet Grottaferrata, which had a number of dependencies in Norman territory, quickly fell under papal control following the Schism even as it retained the use of Greek for another century.

After 1054, most of the junior clergy installed in diocesan and parochial ("secular") churches to replace Grecophone clerics were encouraged, even coerced, to use Latin in liturgy. This was one of the factors in the general evolution of language amongst the population. Although Neapolitan and Sicilian bear the mark of Greek, they are Romance languages; some Byzantines in Apulia and Lucania were already conversant in the Latin-influenced tongue of the Lombards.

Latinized or not, Italy's Byzantine churches were canonically "Catholic" from the moment that their clergy accepted Rome's jurisdiction over that of Constantinople at any time after 1054.

The holdouts were those, such as Nicodemus, the Archbishop of Palermo when the Normans conquered it in 1072, who, being in a Muslim territory beyond Rome's political grasp in the years immediately after the Schism, were not "converted." Aghlabid (and then Fatimid) rule sometimes found at least some of Sicily's clergy under the direct canonical jurisdiction not of Constantinople but of Cyprus. Only much later, as Latin supplanted Greek, did the archbishop's church, the Kyriaca outside Palermo, become known as *Santa Ciriaca* and then *Santa Domenica*.

As a Greek, Nicodemus was marginalized despite the pope's confirmation of his status as Palermo's archbishop. With a papal bull issued in 1083, Pope Gregory VII named Alcherio, a Latin, the Archbishop of Palermo (see note 164).

Unlike his predecessor, Alcherio made use of Latin in liturgy and was Roman Catholic in every sense. Grecophone Catholics were not the only ones affected by church policy regarding liturgy. Alcherio's consecration coincided with the papal suppression of the use of various traditional rites known for centuries, such as those popular in northern Spain (see note 195).

The first major wave of Latinization was helped along, in decisive measure, by the introduction of Catholic monastic orders in areas that fell under Norman control. The immediate effect of this on the general population is difficult to gauge. In Sicily, the Benedictines, the oldest religious order, had a presence before the arrival of the Aghlabids; the monastery of Saint John of the Hermits, mentioned above, may have been one of their early foundations in the sixth century, to be refounded during the reign of Roger II.

It was the efforts of Roger II that facilitated the integration of the Christians in the conquered Tunisian territory of Ifriqiya into the Catholic environment. Like Nicodemus, Cosmas, bishop of the Greek diocese of Mahdia, is entombed in Palermo's cathedral (see note 411).

Naturally, the Normans and Lombards controlling formerly Byzantine lands and pre-existing Orthodox parishes in these districts favored the use of Latin in liturgy. Yet, in society at large, there may have been some degree of linguistic compromise, at least for a time, in the (many) cases of Norman knights marrying Grecophone women. The chronicler Hugh Falcandus tells us that Norman French was still spoken at court in the middle of the twelfth century, but this is not the principal root language of Sicilian or Neapolitan (see Chapter 24).

It would take more than the surviving charters to determine, with much accuracy, the true extent of cultural change in specific localities over time, year by year. Leaving aside the strict question of religion, it is interesting that even the jurats at Enna (Kasr'Janni), members of a civic council better educated than the general population, were still using Greek and Arabic in 1109 when Adelaide, as regent for her young son, sent them a letter (shown in these pages) in those languages. That this communication ordered them to cease infringing upon the rights of what, by then, was a Catholic monastery, Saint Philip (near Frazzanò), to a salt mine implies that the ecclesiastical Latinizing was taking root in the most Grecophone region of Sicily even if the linguistic Latinization was, for the moment, laggard. While Greek and Arabic were widely-spoken vernacular languages in that part of Sicily, Latin was not. Another century would pass before Latin-based tongues like Sicilian and Neapolitan had evolved into anything like the languages we know today.

Amongst Arabs and Berbers, the greatest number of conversions from Islam to Christianity occurred during the twelfth century, not to Orthodoxy but to Catholicism. These were literal conversions entailing baptism, something very different from the gradual, nearly unseen, manner in which Catholicity prevailed over Orthodoxy through changes in liturgy and language, eventually becoming part of the collective identity of the people of southern Italy.

Institutions such as knighthood were more Latin than Greek. Like crusading itself, the knightly (crusading) orders, such as the Hospitallers and Templars, founded in the twelfth century were a product of Catholicism, not Orthodoxy.

Ultimately, the division between the Christians of east and west was a slow, if continuous, process that may be said to have culminated with the crusaders' sack of Constantinople in 1204.

Nevertheless, a number of Orthodox practices were preserved in southern Italy beyond that date. We find, for example, triple immersion used in baptisms at Bari long afterward. In Altamura, in Puglia, the Greek church of Saint Nicholas was built at the same time as the Catholic cathedral erected on the orders of Frederick II.

A certain accommodation of the kingdom's dwindling minority of Orthodox Christians was maintained throughout the Norman and Swabian eras.

Martorana tower and church with San Cataldo (at right)

Icons in mosaic decorating the ceiling of the Martorana

Chapter 5
APULIA AND CALABRIA

The Normans were not destined to be papal foes forever. Their victory at Civitate left them generally unopposed and perhaps a bit emboldened, though simple observation leaves the impression that raw courage was an intrinsic element in their character. Troublesome Pope Leo IX died in April 1054, not surviving even long enough to witness the early effects of the ecclesiastical schism for which he had acted as the catalyst.

Destiny

The next pope, Victor II, a Swabian aristocrat related to the Holy Roman Emperor Henry III then reigning, spent most of his brief pontificate addressing legal matters such as clerical marriage and simony. He undertook to reclaim lost papal lands, mostly in and around Tuscany. Victor's death in 1057 marked the end of a period of close cooperation between the Holy See and the Holy Roman Empire, a change that would make it somewhat easier for popes to sanction the growing Norman power in Italy, which was already perceived by some as a force that might eventually challenge German ambitions for control of the peninsula. Presently, however, Norman objectives were more localized.

From his headquarters at Aversa, Richard Drengot, one of the heroes of Civitate, eyed Capua, which he would soon win. For now, he gradually occupied lands in that region, encroaching on many of those belonging to the princes of Salerno.[115] Within a few years, Salerno's ruling family controlled very little territory beyond their own city.

The Hautevilles, meanwhile, appropriated most of Calabria. In Apulia, they extended their territory almost to the gates of Brindisi and Bari, and occupied Taranto.[116]

In 1057, following Humphrey's death, Robert "Guiscard," his younger half-brother, succeeded him as the recognized head of the family, who might speak for the others in the ongoing negotiations with the papacy for recognition of their claims. The Hautevilles were now arguably a nascent "dynasty," not unlike their compatriots the Drengots. That Geoffrey, who was Humphrey's full brother, was passed over, need not have been of inordinate concern as he already had his own lands. Guiscard promised to protect the inheritance due Humphrey's young sons; in the end he usurped it for himself.[117]

This wasn't Guiscard's only dubious behavior toward his own siblings. He also had a brief feud with his younger brother, Roger, over some lands in Calabria. This was resolved amicably when the junior Hauteville was enfeoffed with territories in that region to the south of Catanzaro, along with the island of Sicily.

The Hauteville and Drengot conquests continued unabated. As they acquired feudal lands, or Byzantine lands they made feudal, both families awarded these to their loyal followers. In this way, many Norman knights were enfeoffed, becoming barons, though at this early date that title was rarely used, the toponym being sufficient to identify a man and his manor. The sprawling area controlled by the Hautevilles was much larger than the districts ruled by the Drengots.

The Hautevilles' government was no longer as harsh as it had been in the past, and Humbert of Silva Candida did not seem so blatantly opposed to it as he may have been during the pontificate of Leo IX. After all, the Normans were gradually opening up the lands confiscated from the Byzantines to ecclesiastical Latinization. This included not only diocesan ("secular") communities but monasteries. In practice, the Latinization took longer in some areas, such as Calabria, than in others.[118]

The Benedictines, ever the most powerful religious order in southern Italy, would not overlook this opportunity.[119]

The wholesale Latinization was rendered easier than ever by the "othering" of the Byzantine clergy and faithful since 1054. There was no immediate sign of a serious papal effort at rapprochement with the Orthodox, even if this would be attempted in the future.

The Hautevilles' domination was becoming a *fait accompli,* whether, for the moment, it was recognized formally by the pope or not.

Pope Victor II had little time in his busy schedule to look southward, and he expired in 1057. His successor, Stephen IX, died in March of the following year, to be succeeded in January 1059 by Gerard of Burgundy, Bishop of Florence, elected as Nicholas II.[120]

This transition was not a smooth one. The new pontiff's advisors were concerned because certain elements in Italy were still supporting John Mincio who, immediately following Stephen's death, had managed to get himself elected illegally as Benedict X with the aid of some Roman aristocrats. On Easter, Nicholas issued a bull banning the influence of the nobility in papal elections and establishing that thenceforth all electors must be cardinals.[121]

Seeking reliable military support to suppress Mincio, Nicholas had Hildebrand of Sovana, a confidant, advisor and future pontiff, negotiate with the Norman families for military support.[122] This marked the first time that a pope looked to the Normans of southern Italy as actual military allies in a specific campaign against a sworn enemy of the papacy.

In the summer of 1059, Nicholas II was in Melfi for a series of decisive meetings. Sichelgaita, the new wife of Robert Guiscard and daughter of Guaimar IV of Salerno, acted as hostess of this momentous event.[123]

The synod itself dealt with numerous ecclesiastical matters, resulting in a number of pronouncements, such as the umpteenth papal condemnation of the practice of clergy taking wives and concubines. It made Melfi's diocese subject to Rome, reflecting what had become the papal policy of expropriating Byzantine (now Orthodox) bishoprics, monasteries and parishes throughout the Italian south, unequivocally Latinizing the lands conquered by the Normans. Nicholas deposed Bishop John II of Trani, who had protested Rome's liturgical practices (see note 109). Of course, new episcopal appointments reflected obedience to Rome even when the nominees themselves were Grecophones ordained or consecrated during the Byzantine era.[124]

The popes were still kingmakers. Desiderio of Benevento, the Abbot of Mount Cassino, had labored long and hard to ensure that the diplomatic and jurisdictional relationship between the Normans and the popes might be placed on a solid footing.[125]

At Melfi, Nicholas gave form to the status of the Normans in Italy. This agreement, which has come to be called the "Treaty of Melfi," officially recognized their jurisdictions and conquests.[126]

Its effect was to establish the sovereignty of the Duchy of Apulia and Calabria under Robert, who also pledged fealty to the Holy See, which recognized him as the future ruler of Sicily.[127] It is clear that Nicholas was encouraging further conquests; indeed, he had already consecrated Humbert of Silva Candida, who attended the synod at Melfi, as Archbishop of Sicily.[128]

While the focus of this diplomatic milestone was southern Italy, the very fact of official papal recognition led to the Normans south of Rome being taken seriously as a rising European power.

If the papal motives were obvious enough, the Normans, for their part, were equally earnest in their ambitions, as hungry for Sicily's territory as the papacy was covetous of its souls. Both would triumph in the end, firmly planting their banners in Sicilian soil.

Richard Drengot was confirmed as Prince of Capua, the city he took the previous year. The papacy no longer seemed excessively concerned about the Norman confiscation of Lombard lands.

Later in 1059, Hildebrand accompanied a small Norman army led by Richard Drengot of Aversa to Galera Antica, north of Rome, to confront the antipope Mincio and his supporters.

In the same eventful year, Nicholas consecrated, or reconsecrated, the Benedictine abbey at Venosa, in Lucania, where Robert buried his brothers and his first wife. This was an early attempt to link the Hautevilles, as a dynasty, to a specific familial church.

Most of the Normans arriving in southern Italy in good numbers were men and most took Lombard brides like Robert's Salernitan wife Sichelgaita, or her sister, Gaitelgrima, who wed his nephew. Except for some initial reticence on the part of the Lombards, who sometimes viewed the Normans as crude, there does not seem to have been great opposition to these unions; indeed they were encouraged, for they united Lombard tradition with Norman power.[129]

Identity

Chroniclers, when speaking generally, had long referred to "the people of Italy," but at this date, despite the loss of most of their lands, the Lombards of the Italian south still had a distinct ethnic identity.[130] Now, however, part of the place once called *Longobardia* was beginning to assume an identity of its own that was not purely Lombard, Byzantine or even Norman.[131]

In truth, very little is known about the Lombards' language as it was spoken in the south of Italy during the eleventh century except from scant written vestiges such as the *Placet of Capua* recorded in 960, but as a Romance tongue it was perhaps more susceptible than Greek to influences from vernacular languages such as Norman French.[132] However, while the Byzantine Greeks were "the others," the Italianized Lombards became brothers.

With a few strokes of the pen, Apulia and Calabria, along with most of Lucania, had become something different from what they were before the arrival of the Normans. Like so many small dominions in Europe, they were evolving into the kind of elements that, with effort, could be forged into larger polities.

For the moment, the Normans were forging steel into swords. The greater political strategies would have to wait. Despite the pope's encouragement, it is unlikely that even the most ambitious among the Norman knights could see what lay beyond the next year or two, even if a few were old enough to remember the bittersweet Maniakes expedition to the other side of the Strait of Messina.

Chapter 6
SICILY

Preparing for the invasion of Sicily approved by the pope at Melfi in 1059 would take time. Ships had to be built, weapons manufactured and men recruited. The incursion would have to be launched from a point where transportation and supply lines could be managed efficiently. Roger, the younger brother of Robert Guiscard, had established a center of Norman administration at the Calabrian town of Mileto, but the Hautevilles needed a base nearer the port city of Reggio to the south.

The Sicilians — Arab and Greek alike — expected an invasion sooner or later. Events on the mainland were hardly a secret. There was plenty of communication. Small communities of Arab traders were present in cities like Reggio, and there was a free flow of traffic between that locality and Messina across the strait.[133]

In recent years, Sicily, the Arabs' Siqiliya, though still nominally an emirate under the Kalbids in Balharm (Palermo), had experienced the kind of internecine strife that can divide a populace bitterly. The discontent stemming from the poor response to the Maniakes invasion two decades earlier was but one element in this miserable mix. In 1044, the ruling emir, Hasan as-Samsam al-Dawla, divided Sicily into four *qadits,* each having its own administration under a *caïd,* who might be regarded locally as an *emir.*[134] Since then, the island had been governed in this way, sacrificing centralized control to what was thought to be the efficiency of localized administration in one of the many dominions of the vast Fatimid Empire ruled from Cairo. Though they officially answered to the greater Sicilian emir's authority, these caïds, or lesser emirs, often acted independently of him, as if they were governing *taifas,* small sovereign principalities such as those in Muslim Spain.

Matters worsened with the deposition of Hasan as-Samsam al-Dawla in 1053. By 1060, there were four principal emirs present, each ruling part of the island, where there were fulsome poets to sing his praises in the form of a *qasida*.[135]

Muhammad ibn al-Thumna (Timnah), the emir who ruled a qadit from Catania, was especially dissatisfied with the state of affairs, and his vantage point on the Ionian Sea afforded him close contact with Norman Calabria. The Byzantine Greeks of Calabria, like those who populated Sicily, had long been willing to treat with the Arabs, whether for commerce or to maintain a tenuous peace.[136]

Attempting to maintain a fragile peace of his own, Robert Guiscard, now Duke of Apulia and Calabria, spent part of 1060 besieging Troia, ostensibly one of his own cities. It was also necessary to take full control of the city of Reggio, in Calabria. With this accomplished, he and his brothers could focus their attention on Sicily.

It wasn't too difficult for al-Thumna to contact the Hautevilles, though details of this are sparse.[137]

The emir sought the Hautevilles' protection from intrigues against him in Sicily and encouraged them to invade the island. Robert met in council to discuss this with his leading barons. Presently, something less than a major assault would be undertaken. Unfortunately, the Normans' experience in Italy had not facilitated the development of keen navigation skills or even very good vessels.

Incursions

The first "incursion" into Sicily was tenuous at best, not executed very efficiently, and bearing all the hallmarks of an impromptu pirate raid. Accompanied by al-Thumna, some one hundred sixty knights led by Roger Hauteville and his faithful vassal Geoffrey Ridel sailed across the strait early in 1061, in a season when the weather is capricious. They went to the town of Rometta, which they raided, and then to an area along the Tyrrhenian coast.[138]

Near Messina they were attacked by Arab troops and had to retreat to safety in the mountains for two days. They waited in the cold winter weather for the storm to pass, fearing that their ships might not survive the crossing back to Calabria in the rough waters. In the event, it was the enemy forces, not the tempest, that placed them in the gravest danger. The Normans barely made it back alive, but on the Calabrian side they were defended by the citizens of Reggio, Muslim as well as Christian, against a few Messinians who had pursued them across the strait.

If, however, the Arabs of Sicily inferred from this experience that the Hautevilles were merely a nuisance, they were sorely mistaken. Unaccustomed to the taste of defeat, the Normans set about preparing for a real invasion of the island they desired.

Finally, on a clear night in May of 1061, the sleek galleys, vessels reminiscent of the long ships of their Norse forebears, began transporting men, horses and arms to a place six miles south of Messina, disembarking along Sicily's

Ionian coast. Each ship arrived silently, landing in Sicily and then going back across the strait to Calabria to bring more knights and foot men to the island.[139]

True, Sicily's Arabs expected an attack sooner or later, but from a more northern point directly across the strait at its narrowest, hence their concentration of ships patrolling Tyrrhenian waters on the other side of Cape Faro, where they had last encountered the Normans.

In the event, the undermanned garrison guarding Messina's seaside fortress was taken unawares, being unprepared for a ground assault from the south. By dawn, the Messinians, most of whom were Greek speakers, awoke to find their city, a springboard for trade as an important port, in Norman hands. Indeed, the fighting itself was brief and decisive. Most of the defenders were killed but only a few attackers were injured.

Although the invading force of some three hundred knights, along with squires, foot soldiers and archers, consisted of thousands, the fortifications were taken by an initial wave of a few hundred under the command of Roger, who advanced and attacked without waiting for additional men to arrive from Calabria with his elder brother, the equally audacious Robert.

The battle was followed by the typical pillaging, along with the occasional rape. At least one Muslim decided to kill his own sister rather than risk her falling into the invaders' hands.

The victory gave the Hauteville brothers a toehold in Sicily and absolute control over ships traversing the Strait of Messina and most of the Ionian Sea. As it happened, the response from the emirs of the other Sicilian cities was underwhelming. Those jealous rulers were too busy nurturing their petty grudges against each other to respond in a serious way to the threat posed by the Normans. Yet their failure to send a large army to take back Messina did not mean they would give up their taifas without a fight.

Although Pope Nicholas II wanted Sicily's Muslims ousted, or at least converted to Catholicism, he also made it known that the island's Greek-speaking Orthodox Christians would be expected to recognize Rome's ecclesiastical authority over them. This presupposed, even in the initial stages of the conquest, that these Byzantines would accept the Normans as liberators. Such a hypothesis presumed, in the most optimistic scenario, a Christian rebellion against Muslim rule. Nothing like that occurred.

The Byzantines had long co-existed with the Arabs. Although the two communities were distinguished by their faiths and mother tongues, they lived in the same localities, where intermarriage was not unknown. Many Sicilians were bilingual, and Siculo-Arabic was full of Greek words.[140] In the eleventh century there existed a pragmatic accommodation.

By the summer of 1061, Byzantine political power had been purged throughout most of Robert Guiscard's peninsular dominions. Use of the Greek language subsisted, along with some religious practices inherited from Orthodoxy, but defiant Bari was now the only major Byzantine city left and henceforth the only new monastic foundations in Norman Italy would be those of the Catholic orders.

Sicily's Greeks adopted a posture rooted in these realities. Under Arab rule they were at least permitted to worship as they wished despite certain restrictions on public observances and the construction of new churches. The Normans were fellow Christians but they were also foreigners, Latinizers generally unreceptive to Orthodoxy beyond its superficial cultural elements, such as its Byzantine art and architecture.

Typical of their Latinizing was the introduction of Catholic clergy from as far afield as their native Normandy. One of these clerics was Robert of Grandmesnil who, before choosing ordination, had been a knight in the service of William, Duke of Normandy.[141] In Calabria he was given an abbey, while his half-sister, Judith of Evreux wed Roger Hauteville.

The wedding afforded Roger a respite from his campaigning in Sicily, where he was occupying town after town in the island's northeastern regions.

The extended campaign was to be a cumbersome enterprise not unlike the one prosecuted by the Arabs two centuries earlier. Pursuing their objectives without delay, the Hautevilles, supported by a force of Normans and Lombards hungry for land, began a bold series of incursions into the Nebrodian and Peloritan mountains. These were complemented by excursions into the heartland, as far as Kasr'Janni (Enna), a mountaintop stronghold that proved impregnable.

They set about erecting their first fortress in Sicily atop a rocky mountain overlooking the Tyrrhenian at San Marco d'Alunzio, once the site of an ancient Greek settlement and by this time an Orthodox monastery.[142]

At the outset, the Norman occupiers seemed tolerant of the people they encountered in the hinterland, whether Greek or Arab.[143] For now, conquest was the priority. Conversions would have to wait. Nevertheless, they brought with them some Catholic clerics, especially Benedictines.

Back in Calabria, Roger's elder brother, Robert, was encroaching on some towns and revenues that, by prior agreement, belonged to Roger. Following a series of skirmishes in the important Hauteville strongholds of Mileto and Gerace, the two brothers made peace. Unaware of this, Robert's wife, Sichelgaita, thinking herself to have been widowed during the fighting, fled to Tropea on the Tyrrhenian coast.[144] Although Judith may have been with her sister-in-law, who was a year or two her senior, it seems more likely that she was staying at her brother's abbey.

Sichelgaita was a remarkable figure in her own right, a physician who later became famous for leading troops on her husband's behalf.[145] Now, however, she was in her early twenties and the busy mother of two young children.

Instead of dividing their family, the Hauteville brothers divided Calabria. This seemed like a practical solution to their longstanding dispute over land. Anyway, Roger hoped to claim a few chunks of Sicily.

Returning to the island, he took Judith with him. Sichelgaita joined her husband in Apulia.

Troina

Finding himself again in the Nebrodian Mountains early in 1062, Roger set out to take control of several large towns, having already seized many, including Rometta, whose caïd paid homage to him. At Troina, the Greeks, so we are told by Malaterra, were especially annoyed by the knights' presence, perhaps more than they were during Roger's prior visit. Considering this, he left his bride there with a small garrison that resumed work on the fortifications of the existing castle.[146]

Despite Judith's presence, the Greeks feared for their wives and daughters, with whom some of the knights flirted. Had he been present, Roger might have made an effort to discourage the young knights' more zealous attempts at seduction.

One day, while Roger was off besieging Nicosia, another Byzantine town, the people of Troina decided to attack the Norman knights in their locality and take Judith hostage.

The few knights acquitted themselves well enough against the mob, retreating with Judith and her ladies-in-waiting to some narrow streets. Fortunately, the Normans were able to send a messenger to Roger. At nightfall, they were still cornered but held their ground.

By the next morning, when Roger arrived with his contingent, the Greeks had been joined by some Arabs from nearby towns and erected barricades to restrict the Normans to one part of Troina.

The Normans' adversaries were well supplied with food and arms.[147] What soon confronted the knights was a force of nature, the coldest, snowiest winter of the last few decades.

In the frigid temperatures, Roger and Judith shared a mantle they used as a blanket, but there was not much to eat.

In Malaterra's words, "The young countess slaked her thirst by drinking water, but sated her hunger only with her tears and her slumber, having nothing to eat." It seems that the Normans eventually butchered their own horses and roasted the meat.

A few engagements were fought against the enemy. In one skirmish, Roger slew several men with his sword despite his horse being felled by arrows. Then, showing no fear or urgency, he leisurely removed its saddle and strolled back to the Normans' secure quarter. The local people opposed to the Normans could not avoid noting the invaders' tenacity and courage.

The bitter stalemate dragged on for weeks that became months. Finally, snow accumulated on the narrow streets. As the temperatures grew ever colder, the Greek and Arab guards charged with watching the Normans' position at night began to consume wine in an effort to keep warm.[148]

This gave birth to a strategy. Day by day, night after long night, the knights kept as quiet as possible, hoping to lull the guards into a false sense of security.

The ploy worked. One night, the knights left their position behind the timber barricades. A freshly-fallen layer of powdery snow muffled their footsteps into the part of town where the drunken guards were sleeping. It didn't take much to surprise them. Next, having overpowered the guards with minimal effort, the Normans took control of Troina in the violent confrontation that ensued.

With the city secured, its populace subdued, Roger ordered the execution of the ringleaders. Others were punished less harshly.

He then returned to Calabria to procure for his men, who had lost (or eaten) their mounts, some of the sturdy horses he favored. Judith, meanwhile, stayed at Troina and very diligently inspected the continuing work on the fortifications. She reassured the men that their efforts would be rewarded upon her husband's return.[149]

When he got back to Sicily, Roger continued to occupy lands, both Arab and Byzantine, in the Nebrodian and Peloritan regions.

Judith spent the next few years at San Marco along with the wives of some of the knights in her husband's army. Here there was a small garrison, a monastery and a large crew of architects and builders working to ensure the castle's rapid completion.

Two avid supporters of the Norman conquest of Sicily had died, Pope Nicholas II in 1061 and Muhammad ibn al-Thumna the following year, the latter killed in an ambush orchestrated by Ibn al-Hawas, the emir who ruled Kasr'Janni and other lands in central Sicily.

Cerami

The next Norman objective was Kasr'Janni, sometimes *Kasr'Yanna,* "Fortress of Enna." Founded in antiquity by the Sikels and then ruled by the ancient Greeks, who called it *Enna,* this city, protected by steep slopes and a large citadel, boasted commanding views that would have facilitated Roger's unhindered dominance of east-central Sicily. Although Roger had not yet been to Kasr'Janni, he had visited tiny Calascibetta nearby; reached across a narrow valley, this town afforded him the opportunity to view the fortified city's topography and walls.[150]

By 1063, Sicily's Arabs, unable to impede the Norman advance on their own, were receiving reinforcements from the Zirids of Tunisia, who were allied not with the Fatimids in Cairo but the Abbasids in Baghdad. Greatly outnumbered, the Normans suffered a humiliating defeat at Kasr'Janni, though the number of casualties on their side was not very high. Discouraging as this was, it was not the result of a defensive campaign on their own territory but rather their attempt to assault a well-fortified city on high ground.[151]

The next major battle would be decisive.

In June 1063, the Normans met a large, combined Arab force in a valley near Cerami, to the immediate northwest of Troina.[152] There were many thousands on each side, with the exact numbers unknown, but the Normans were very clearly outmanned. Though they could recruit foot men, they seemed to have had only about four hundred knights. Notwithstanding prominent exceptions like Civitate, the Hautevilles usually chose the place and day of their battles. In this case, the enemy came to them, indeed almost to their door.

Unlike Civitate, however, this was rugged country characterized by steep, rocky slopes. The Normans were adept at fighting in this kind of treacherous terrain. The same could not be said of the great majority of troops in the opposing army led by Ibn al-Hawas of Kasr'Janni, with the assistance of two Zirid princes leading numerous Berbers.

Ibn al-Hawas did not attack for two days. One morning, an advance party under the Zirid command assaulted Cerami, attempting to besiege it. This was unsuccessful. With his nephew, Serlo, attacking its flank, Roger then led a charge against the main part of the army.

The fighting was intense, lasting until nightfall at the end of one of the longest days of the year. After an initial effort, most of the Arabs and Berbers broke into disarray and scattered into the valleys. It seems that a good number escaped. Those taken prisoner were sold into slavery according to what was then a common practice.

This debacle provoked accusations and recriminations among the Arab leadership. While Kasr'Janni might still be safe, the Norman victory left much of central and eastern Sicily vulnerable to attack and occupation. The Zirid generals would think twice before sending another army.

As a gesture of solidarity and support, and a sign of the Normans' success, Roger sent to the new pontiff, Alexander II, four fine camels confiscated from the defeated army.

Though the Pisans had long traded with the emir at Palermo, some recent conflicts had caused them to view the Arabs as a nuisance. Considering this an opportune time to raid the city, they solicited Roger's support to lead an assault on the ground while the Pisan vessels attacked Palermo's commercial port. He refused, citing other obligations, but stated that he might be amenable to such a campaign in the future. In early August, a Pisan flotilla attacked Palermo at the mouth of the Oreto River, breaking the large protective chain that restricted traffic into the harbor, a gesture full of symbolism since it represented a violation of the emir's sovereignty, as if emasculating him.[153] This netted them six ships and much booty, including some prized white marble used in the construction of Pisa's cathedral, where an inscription commemorates the source.[154]

This revealed Pisa to be a potential ally.

Stalemate

By 1064, while Roger was occupying parts of Sicily, Robert was bringing some Apulian cities under Norman control, but Bari was free of Norman domination. At Cosenza early in the year, Roger met his elder brother, who brought with him five hundred knights and at least twice as many foot soldiers to continue the conquest of Sicily.

What followed was a series of sieges in Sicily and Calabria. In the former, the Normans made it to Cefalù, historically a Greek town, though they did not remain there, and they also scouted the area around Palermo.[155]

Robert had to return to Calabria to suppress some localized revolts there, while Roger remained in Sicily. At Petralia, in the Madonian Mountains, Roger erected a castle.

So stagnant was the progress that a few of Robert's knights went to Normandy to join William the Conqueror in his conquest of England, which began with the Battle of Hastings in October 1066. Shortly before William's invasion,

Harald Hardrada, who led the Varangian Guard in the ill-fated Maniakes expedition, was killed at the Battle of Stamford Bridge while attempting to seize the English crown for himself.[156]

Back in Sicily, Ibn al-Hawas was killed at Agrigento in 1068 during a battle waged against him by his recent allies, the Zirids, after he had challenged their claim on Sicily.

During the same year, the next Norman thrust westward took Roger and his knights to Misilmeri, within striking distance of Palermo.[157] This unforeseen engagement achieved little in material terms for the Normans despite their decisive victory. Yet it signalled to Palermo's governor, who had a castle above the town, that he could no longer ignore the imposing power of the Hautevilles.

Continued unrest in the Arab camp again worked to the Normans' advantage, for what ultimately unseated the Zirids, prompting them to abandon Sicily and return to Africa in 1069, was a mass rebellion against their pretensions. By then, Robert Guiscard was in southern Apulia and required Roger's assistance.

Chapter 7
POLYCULTURAL CITIES

Sooner or later, the Normans would have to conquer Palermo. In 1068 most of the knights were being employed to enforce Robert's authority on the mainland. The most effective solution to this problem was to finally and utterly subdue Bari, a chronic distraction as the last major pocket of resistance in Robert's peninsular dominions, thus making men and resources available for the conquest of Sicily.

Bari

Bari was one of the wealthiest cities in Italy. Her connection to Greece across the Adriatic made this thriving metropolis on the coast part of a great empire. Everything about Bari was strikingly Byzantine. The Church of Saint Mark of the Venetians still stands, along with some other structures of the eleventh century.

With the loss of most of Apulia to the Normans, the catepanate was little more than a mirage, at best a shadow of its former self. Bari could not long survive without the military support of Constantinople.

Although the Byzantine Empire was still strong, its frayed edges were showing signs of wear. In its eastern regions, the Seljuk Turks were making inroads into areas along the frontier and in neighboring Armenia. The new emperor, Romanos IV, decided to prepare a military response to this threat. That, however, would require all the resources he could muster, leaving very little aid for the Bariots and other peoples who looked to Constantinople for protection and prosperity.

The Hautevilles were probably aware of the predicament in which their antagonist, the Byzantine Empire, found itself.[158]

While Roger was in Sicily, Robert undertook to conquer Bari. This would necessitate organizing the greatest siege of his career.

Until this point, most of the Normans' sieges in Apulia, Calabria and Sicily had been improvised with whatever men and matériel were available. The term *castrum* refers to a fortified town, meaning that it had protective walls of some kind and perhaps a tower or two; not all of the fortified localities had castles.

Although the Hautevilles and Drengots usually prevailed, they had never besieged a very large city. Messina, for example, fell without a siege, and the chroniclers make no mention of the Normans transporting, or even attempting to transport, the necessary equipment across the strait. In fact, the forces led by Robert and Roger were fortunate because the attack, in the form it took, coming from an unexpected direction in the darkness of night, was not predicted by Messina's defenders.

By August 1068, when Robert began the siege, the Bariots were divided between those citizens who supported the Byzantine Empire and those willing to accept Norman rule.

He would seek to exploit this dissension. Initially, however, the citizens closed the city gates and refused to negotiate terms. The city was surrounded and the assaults began.[159]

Expecting a long resistance at Bari, the Normans took Otranto, which could no longer rely upon the larger city for succor and began a siege of Brindisi. Apulia was far from entirely subdued, and there were still engagements in the field.

Many Norman tactics were thwarted. The blockade of Bari's port was broken, permitting ships to depart for Constantinople to seek help. Since Norman maritime capabilities were somewhat limited, there was no fleet to prevent such actions, and Constantinople sent ships laden with grain.

Early in 1070, Robert went to Brindisi to lead a siege that was already underway; the city finally surrendered in December, but not without great losses. Some forty Normans who breached the city walls were beheaded, along with as many of their companions, probably footmen.[160]

At the beginning of 1071, Roger arrived from Sicily with hundreds of knights to support Robert's efforts.

Meanwhile, Emperor Romanos IV had dispatched a small fleet under the command of Joscelin of Molfetta, a Norman in the service of Constantinople.[161] With him came Stephen Pateran, the newly-appointed catepan. The Normans had enough naval power to defeat this fleet, and did so.

Finding the situation hopeless, the Bariots capitulated in April and Robert entered the city. He chose rapprochement over reprisal.

This Norman victory did not squelch the dissent amongst many of the citizens in the years to come, and Bari remained factionalized, but for now it did not oppose Robert's rule. The loss of the city to the Normans discouraged open rebellion elsewhere in the region.

At all events, the siege occasioned a serious consideration of the strategy and tactics that might be employed in conquering another large coastal city.

Palermo

With Bari conquered and placated, at least for the moment, Robert made preparations to assist his brother in the conquest of Palermo. The last few years had found the Norman advance in Sicily sluggish, though, before going to Bari late in 1070, Roger made use of this time by consolidating his position. Even if his Norman forces were sparse, they were augmented by a number of Lombards. There were also Byzantines in his ranks, mostly footmen and archers enlisted from the populations of Calabria and eastern Sicily, where the Norman successes of the last few years offered convincing evidence that the knights were here to stay.

The siege at Bari marked Robert's first significant use of naval power. Now he was having some sixty ships built by his Byzantine subjects in Apulia, keen navigators who met him at Otranto before sailing the vessels to Messina, where their duke would join them after putting down the dissent that arose sporadically in Calabria.

The Arabs' Balharm was the largest, wealthiest city in what is now Italy, its populace numbering perhaps two hundred thousand.[162] It was predominantly Muslim. Perhaps a quarter of the population was Byzantine Greek, and a thriving Jewish community was present.[163]

The Byzantine cathedral had long ago been converted to a mosque that could house seven thousand worshippers. The archbishop, Nicodemus, resided about four miles away, in a valley near the mountain crowned by what is now the town of Monreale, where he had a small church called the Kyriaka.[164]

The departure of the pompous Zirids left the bustling metropolis underprotected. Its governor, Ibn al-Ba'ba, does not seem to have been a paragon of duty.[165] He spent most of his time not at the Kasr, the fortress overlooking the city from high ground, or even the Khalesa, the administrative district near the port, but at the emir's private palace, the Favara, surrounded by lakes, springs and gardens, to the east of the walled city.[166]

Whatever privileges he arrogated to himself, Ibn al-Ba'ba was not an emir in the traditional sense, and Sicily itself was no longer an emirate.

Before attacking Sicily's largest city, Robert and Roger thought it expedient to seize Catania, its third or fourth largest, once the domain of their murdered friend Muhammad ibn al-Thumna. This may have been an attempt to mislead the Arabs of Palermo into thinking that their own city was safe.[167]

Still the siege continued, with no sign of the Arabs.

With the occupation of Catania accomplished, the brothers put the finishing touches on the fleet needed to attack Palermo. Indeed, that campaign would be a concerted assault by both land and sea.

A years-long siege was unthinkable. Palermo was not Bari. It was infinitely larger and better fortified.[168] Ibn al-Ba'ba might easily obtain assistance from the cities to the south and west that the Normans had not yet captured: Trapani, Marsala, Mazara, Agrigento.

The Hautevilles began their approach to Palermo in the heat of early August 1071. As a prelude to the major battle, Roger fought some skirmishes as he neared the city from the east, before arriving at the Oreto River.[169]

The large fleet led by Robert shadowed the progress of the land forces led by Roger. Fearing a major invasion based on early reports, Ibn al-Ba'ba sent for help from the Zirids in Africa, but the city's defense would be left to its governor.[170]

The defenders were fairly audacious, initiating some fighting on the ground in the flat areas before the city walls. It continued inexorably, day after day, into the autumn. The city was besieged, but not yet desperate. Nevertheless, the invaders couldn't be put down.

Little use was made of the ships in the first assaults except, perhaps, for a round of attacks on the Kala port near the sea castle. Robert ordered the fleet to remain, for the most part, in the harbor at the mouth of the Oreto, where the Pisans had conducted their raid years earlier.

Finally, in early autumn, an Arab fleet arrived. This consisted of ships from cities to the west, such as Marsala, but also from Zirid Tunisia.[171] Robert was expecting them and a fierce battle ensued in the waters near Palermo, with the Normans emerging victorious.

Still the siege continued, with no sign of the city capitulating despite the looming shortage of food.

In December, Robert received word that some vassals on the mainland were rebelling, something that had occurred in the recent past. Faced with the choice between disciplining the rebels in his old house or conquering a new one, he chose the latter and remained in Sicily. With the cold winter rains approaching, and feeling the pressure of time now that several mainland cities were in open rebellion, he decided upon a bold maneuver.

In early January the steadfast Duke of Apulia and Calabria launched an assault on the Kasr district, which was protected by its own stout walls. After this ambitious move failed, he aggressively attacked the Khalesa district on lower ground near the shore. Here his troops made it over the walls and through a gate onto a main street.[172] This gave them access to much of the city, including its treasury, prison and administrative offices, as well as one of the emir's main palaces. The fighting was intense, but as the sun set beyond the conical, snow-covered peak of Mount Cuccio to the south it was clear that the day belonged to the Normans.

Following two days of negotiations, Palermo officially surrendered. On January tenth, Robert, Roger and their knights entered the city ceremonially. The mosque, which had begun its life as a church, was reconsecrated as a cathedral by Archbishop Nicodemus, who celebrated mass in the presence of the new ruler.

Acculturation

Robert decreed that the people would retain their existing freedoms, institutions and houses of worship. They might even enjoy some local self-government, though he would leave Roger and others here to ensure that his orders were followed and taxes collected. Commerce would continue. There would be no punishments or reprisals.

The emir's citadel in the Halkah, the highest point of the Kasr, would be largely reconstructed, and a chapel built within it. Other churches would also be erected.

The Hautevilles had seized Sicily's most important city, but half the island had yet to be conquered. Some time would pass before Roger, who for now acted as Robert's surrogate in Sicily, could take up residence in Palermo. This meant that Judith and his children remained at San Marco d'Alunzio and Messina for the next few years, with occasional visits to Palermo or Mileto.

In the wake of the conquest of Palermo, most Muslims remained, for this was the only home they had ever known. It was theirs. A few, like the poet Abd al Gabbar ibn Muhammad ibn Hamdis al-Azdi al-Siqilli (most commonly simply Ibn Hamdis), who was born and raised in southeastern Sicily, eventually chose to emigrate rather than be ruled by Christians. "Oh blond tribe," he wrote in his *Siqilliyyat,* "my blood is on your hands."[173]

Many shared his concerns, unable to see how this polyglot city could be governed.

At the time, anybody who might have suggested that an unruly band of brigands from Normandy could establish a truly functional, multicultural society would have been dismissed as a lunatic. It was the beginning of medieval Europe's greatest, unplanned social experiment.

While the conquest of Palermo was itself a pivotal point, the Normans and Lombards under Roger, who henceforth would spend most of his time in Sicily, still had much work to do.

In terms of social Latinization, as opposed to the ecclesiastical variety, time would pass before the Greek language, or even Arabic, fell into general disuse (see Chapter 4). Except in its vulgar, colloquial, evolving form, Latin itself was not a spoken tongue outside the liturgical and literary spheres. The emergence of the fullness of Sicilian and Neapolitan was a century in the future.

It would take more than a French-speaking baron, in a town of hundreds or thousands, for the citizens to learn his language.

Whereas the Apulians, Lucanians and Calabrians had long had social contact with the Lombards, very few of the Arabs and Byzantines of Sicily ever had, the rare exceptions being traders and pirates.

To the Sicilians, therefore, the spoken languages of the Normans and Lombards were essentially alien. There is no evidence that they were ever spoken very widely in Sicily.

In the Normans' Italian dominions, Norman French was spoken by the Normans amongst themselves. It became a spoken (though not written) language of officialdom. Indeed, the chronicler Hugh Falcandus tells us that it was "necessary for those at court to know."[174] Yet in Italy, compared to England, which witnessed a veritable wave of Norman immigration after 1066, its general influence was minimal.

Madinah

To the Arabs, the metropolis was still simply *al-Madinah,* "the city." To visitors, it probably seemed as if very little in Palermo was noticeably different by the middle of 1072 from what it was immediately before the invasion. In the years to come it would undergo monumental changes, but most of these arrived after 1100.

As a mosque, the cathedral was greatly altered under Muslim rule. The present structure, while it conserves a few Islamic elements such as the muqarnas in a corner of its oldest section near the apse, is more than a reconstruction. The Byzantine basilica which became the mosque in the ninth century was oriented to a position generally perpendicular to the cathedral seen today, and its layout was essentially square, extending into what is now the large open space running along the nave and the portico on the eastern façade. The Aghlabids enlarged the basilica, and as a mosque it is thought to have had as many as seven mihrabs, though its size was nothing like that of Cordoba's Mezquita.

From the time the Normans ordered the basilica reconsecrated in January 1072 until its reconstruction over a century later, the modifications were minimal. Archbishop Nicodemus seems to have been marginalized after the arrival of the Normans, and he may have soon died. His successor wasn't appointed until 1083.[175] At all events, the cultural-social-ecclesiastical orientation embodied by Nicodemus was essentially that of a Byzantine Greek, not a cleric from the Latin sphere.

This might suggest that Robert and Roger, whose other duties kept them away from the city for long periods, wished to avoid the possibility of an archbishop closely aligned with Rome occupying a local position of power in their absence, possibly repressing Palermo's Arabs, Greeks and Jews.

Nevertheless, churches such as Saint Peter "of the Bagnara" were built in the city. This church was dedicated by Robert Guiscard and his wife, Sichelgaita, in 1081, before the consecration of Palermo's new archbishop, Alcherio.[176]

The churches of Saint Barbara, in the Halkah district near the Kasr citadel, and Saint Pancras, near the souk, were also erected during this era (both are long gone). Saint John of the Lepers, at the site of the palace or fort occupied by Roger *en route* to Palermo, seems to have been built somewhat later, in the twelfth century.[177]

There were, of course, old churches besides the cathedral which may have been used as mosques and reconsecrated, but few traces of these remain. Standing near a gate bordering the meat market in the Sari al Kadi district was a Paleo-Christian church dedicated to Saint Agatha.[178]

Like the Messinians, the Palermitans, as a group, embraced Norman rule without too many undo conflicts. Certainly, there would be occasional protests in the decades to come, indeed into the middle of the twelfth century, but few of these riots resembled anything like a general social upheaval. While many realities explain this, a few stand out from the others.

Firstly, the Normans protected the Muslim population, which survived, albeit in a diminished form, into the reign of Frederick II. This was protection not only from Catholic conversion but from the bigotry of some of the Norman and Lombard barons, whose attitudes toward the Arabs were usually conditioned by local politics and the lust for the Muslims' wealth more than genuine questions of faith.

Secondly, it was less than certain that the Zirids across the Sicilian Channel would render military assistance in the event of a major Muslim rebellion in Palermo. Although they raided the Calabrian and Sicilian coasts over the next few years, an actual invasion was unrealistic. Moreover, Zirid domination wasn't necessarily more appealing than Norman rule.

Thirdly, the Normans did not impose particularly harsh social or religious strictures on the Muslims and Greeks. If his means permitted it, a man faithful to Islam could still have four wives. Except where they were housed in former churches, most mosques remained standing so long as they had congregations, one in the Khalesa district was enlarged to become the largest mosque in the city. The Greeks, for their part, still celebrated their own liturgy in their own language despite the gradual, albeit constant, introduction of Latin.

Fourthly, existing institutions survived besides religion. The *diwan*, or treasury, which made use of Arab accounting principles, functioned throughout the Norman period. Fatimid artistic traditions were cultivated, to the point of enhancing those of the Normans. The schools were undisturbed. A mastery of Latin might be encouraged, but not to the exclusion of Arabic or Greek. Except for clergy, there was not a great influx of Normans and Lombards into the city.

Social Change

There seems to have been tolerance in casual social encounters. A Norman's wife might roast a pig, but she wouldn't prevail upon her Muslim or Jewish neighbors to feast on the forbidden meat. Indeed, the greater number of her neighbors in a city like Palermo might be Christians. For some time, city people lived, for the most part, in their own ethnic neighborhoods.

However, the Normans introduced certain practices which, though acceptable in the Middle Ages, were never very just. These changes were most felt outside the major cities, in the hinterland, where the great majority of people lived.

The Lombards had already implemented feudalism (manorialism) in parts of southern Italy, but now the Normans brought it to Arab and Greek lands where it was previously unknown, in Apulia, Lucania and Calabria but, perhaps most conspicuously, in Sicily.

Feudalism, though not an intrinsically Roman Catholic institution, found a convenient co-existence with the church. As Archbishop of Palermo, Alcherio wasn't just one of the most important prelates in southern Italy, he was coincidentally a feudal vassal of the Hautevilles. A charter of Roger "Borsa," son of Robert Guiscard and Sichelgaita, ceded to Alcherio's direct authority several manors, along with nearly a hundred serfs living on these. This was repeated a few years later when the other Roger, who had helped Robert conquer Palermo, issued a similar charter to the same archbishop.[179]

Until the arrival of the Normans, the common folk, though living under the ordered, even paternalistic, society of the Fatimids, held small farms which were, in effect, their own property. Under feudalism, many farmers became serfs tied to the land, which was controlled by a recently-arrived ruling class.

The Arabs and Greeks weren't the only ones to find their lives altered for the worse. In a charter of 1089, Sichelgaita, by then a widow, granted Alcherio authority over the Jews of Palermo.[180] This became a longstanding status of the city's Jews, and while the arrangement was framed to imply that the archbishop was their "protector," he had the right to tax them.

Sichelgaita was an unusual woman in exceptional circumstances. Outside the aristocracy, in the general population, the lives of most "ordinary" women in southern Italy were essentially similar whether they were Norman, Lombard, Arab, Jewish or Greek. Their rights were rather limited compared to those of men. Unless she were a widow, a female was unlikely to be the head of a family, and a woman widowed at a young age would be encouraged to remarry.

At this early date, the Normans permitted each population to be judged, for the most part, by its own laws. This imperfect system of justice certainly created complexities, yet the surviving records tell us very little except about prominent cases involving Christians, and most of those mentioned are aristocrats. A local caïd might rule on a case concerning his own people. Often, however, a baron or churchman would decide cases in his own territorial jurisdiction, meting out justice as he saw fit; this was part of feudalism.

Besides baronies, the Normans founded new bishoprics in Sicily. Like a pre-existing diocese, such as Palermo or Messina, a new one, such as Troina (the first episcopal foundation in Norman Sicily), would be given land confiscated from the Arabs. In rarer instances, these were estates "inherited" from the Greeks, an example being the monastery of San Filippo of Fragalà (mentioned in Chapter 4). The bishop might adjudicate legal cases in his feudal lands, and an abbot would do likewise on lands owned by his abbey, as if these clerics were dukes or barons.

In Apulia and Calabria, some Byzantine (and subsequently Orthodox) monasteries had held fairly large estates under the jurisdiction of the catepans. In Sicily, conversely, most holdings of that kind had long been subject, ultimately, to the civil (non-ecclesiastical) authority of the island's emirs, which sometimes entailed taxation, and by the eleventh century many had disappeared altogether.[181]

Disappointingly little is known of the Byzantine presence in the metropolis of Palermo during the Kalbid era, and any estimate of the number of the city's Greek Orthodox churches would be dubious at best. Except for the Kyriaca of Archbishop Nicodemus, very few churches or parishes in the Arabs' prosperous Balharm are named in contemporaneous records, and some of those mentioned were long inactive by 1072.[182]

Through its bishoprics and abbeys, the Catholic church soon became the largest landholder in the Norman dominions.[183] In conjunction with this, there was an incremental increase in the number of religious vocations, for women as well as men. Over time, it became ever more likely for those in the laity to encounter monks and nuns, and this socialization doubtless facilitated the conversions of many Muslims.

Most charters granting lands to the church also included the peasants, who now became serfs, living on it, with the comparative number of Arabs and

Greeks dependent on the locality's ethnic composition.[184] Implicit in this development was a feudal (and temporal) authority that many Muslim Arabs, understandably, were reluctant to accept.[185]

If the most blatant "official" discrimination shown toward Sicily's Jews by the island's Catholic hierarchy may be said to have begun with Sichelgaita's charter, the Muslims, for their part, could expect less than equitable treatment as serfs living on lands held by bishops and abbots antipathetic to Islam.

Arguably, the Normans erred in ceding so much authority to the church, but this trend finds contemporary parallels in Spain, where land held by Muslims was confiscated without so much as a second thought, even in cities known for their historical tolerance of polycultural populations.[186]

This, indeed, was inevitable in medieval times, when the church was the greatest feudal landholder of western and central Europe. It was through their material generosity to the church that the Normans achieved their most effective Latinizing.

In the event, what the Normans did in southern Italy cannot be precisely compared to the efforts of Rotrou of Perche as part of the reconquest of northern Spain or, as we shall see, Bohemond Hauteville during the First Crusade.[187]

Apart from lands given to the church, the surviving documentary record abounds with early examples of the enfeoffment (infeudation) of Normans and Lombards by Robert and Roger as the rulers of Apulia, Calabria and Sicily. This was continued by their heirs.[188]

Standing beside ecclesiastical authority was "civil" law. The Lombards and Greeks had their own historic legal codes, while the Muslims of Sicily had Koranic law and Maliki influences. This jurisprudence was broadly adequate for most situations.

Two European practices have come to evoke the spirit of medieval justice in the public mind. Both were known in southern Italy.

In trial by ordeal, the accused was subjected to a physical test, with innocence proven by survival, as if God willed the suspect to escape unscathed. Not every ordeal was lethal, but most, such as reaching into a cauldron of boiling water to retrieve a stone placed in it, were intrinsically dangerous. The papacy abolished these judicial ordeals in the thirteenth century. By then, trials by judges were considered a more pragmatic solution.

Trial by combat, the duel, survived papal proscription. This, however, was reserved almost exclusively to knights; commoners were only rarely granted a request to duel an opponent, or a "champion" representing the crown, to prove their innocence.[189]

Charter of 1089 issued by Sichelgaita of Salerno granting the Archbishop of Palermo the right to taxation of the local Jews

Chapter 8

CONSOLIDATION

Palermo was the jewel in the crown, but the crown itself was still elusive in 1072. Robert had to return to the mainland to quell dissent and Roger still had to conquer more than half of Sicily, one city at a time.

At Kasr'Janni, where the mountainous region around the unconquered city was to be defended by Serlo, Roger's nephew, based at Cerami, the Arabs feigned peace. A certain Ibrahim, a prominent man of this town, exchanged gifts with Serlo. Having gained his confidence, he subsequently ordered an ambush upon Serlo while the young Hauteville knight was hunting near Nicosia. Serlo and his small company were not wearing armor, yet they fought the numerous ambushers upon a site later called the "Rock of Serlo." Overwhelmed by the attackers, Serlo was killed. Malaterra tells us that his head was sent to Tamim, the Zirid sultan in Tunisia.

Robert

Encouraged by Sichelgaita, Robert sought to expand his reach beyond Apulia, Calabria and Lucania into historically Lombard territories. In this feat he was largely successful. Initially, he set his sights on Salerno and Capua, but he didn't overlook the regions of Abruzzi and Molise to the north of his present dominions. He achieved his objectives over the next few years, sometimes through attrition or acquiescence. In some instances internal squabbling paved the way for an external force, the Hautevilles, to subvert local power.

In the dominions that were already his by law as duke, these campaigns were part of a military enterprise that only provoked further embitterment among the rebel barons, who didn't seem to respect Robert's title or the rights that went with it. He suppressed rebellion in one city only to see it erupt in another, sometimes instigated by his own nephews.[190]

Intrigues involving the papacy were not altogether absent from this complex scenario. While Pope Alexander II, who died in 1073, generally supported the Normans, in Italy as well as England, his loyalty to the Hautevilles was tested when imperial German interests entered the mix. His successor, Hildebrand of Sovana, whom we met in Chapter 5, elected as Gregory VII, more firmly opposed the German hegemony embodied by the Holy Roman Emperor Henry IV (see Table 3). For the moment, the newly-elected pontiff was perhaps indifferent about the Hautevilles, yet compelled to excommunicate Robert Guiscard for perceived offenses against the interests of the church. The greatest of these misdeeds was attacking, and finally occupying, papal Benevento and other papal territories. It was not beneath Gregory to plot against the Normans.[191]

A treaty was signed with Michael VII, the Byzantine Emperor, in 1074. As part of this détente, Robert's very young daughter, Olympia, whom the Greeks called *Helena,* was betrothed to Michael's even younger son, Constantine Doukas, and sent to the imperial court at Constantinople in 1076. Michael's deposition in 1078 ended this arrangement, with Olympia sent to a convent and subsequently returned to her father in Italy.[192]

The Hautevilles' relations with their southern neighbors were not quite so friendly. Some Zirid flotillas were sent by the sultan, Tamim ibn al-Mu'izz, to attack the Norman dominions. They assaulted Nicotera, in Calabria, in June 1074. Here they took hostages who were released following payment of a ransom, in what bore the marks of a pirate raid.[193]

Encouraged by their success at Nicotera, the Zirids attempted to repeat this exploit at Mazara, in western Sicily, the following year. Roger was in the neighborhood, and his forces rushed to the town to confront the invaders. Very few survived to escape.[194] If anything, Roger's courage of conviction was made obvious to Tamim. That Mazara was a predominantly Muslim city did not seem to dissuade the Zirid attack, a fact that could not have been lost on the local population.

Back on the mainland, Salerno was taken by Robert in 1077. Here Sichelgaita, after much effort to negotiate a compromise, took a position against her brother, Gisulf II. This represented the definitive end of the Lombard rule of Salerno. Sichelgaita herself was painted by later historians as a lawful heiress of the principality, as if Robert ruled it *jure uxoris,* by right of his wife. In the event, her children were as Lombard as they were Norman.

Robert ensured that Sergio VI of Naples, despite a largely symbolic alliance with the Byzantine Emperor and what seemed like merely nominal fealty to the Holy Roman Emperor, had at least one foot in the Hauteville camp. He bolstered the position of his nephew, Jordan Drengot, in Capua.

For the present, Robert held Benevento, much to Pope Gregory's chronic consternation, but far worse, in the papal view, was the fall of the eastern reaches of Christendom, in Asia Minor, to the Seljuk Turks. Day by day, the pontiff, despite being a consummate politician, and notwithstanding his continuing problems with Henry IV, was more immediately occupied by matters such as enforcing clerical celibacy and liturgical reform, not only in Italy but throughout Catholic Europe.[195] He strongly advocated the doctrine of the transubstantiation of the Eucharist.

Whatever misgivings Pope Gregory entertained about Robert, his rapport with Henry IV, who, like his imperial predecessors, wanted to control papal elections, was far less auspicious. In 1077, Henry submitted himself to Gregory at Canossa (in what is now Emilia-Romagna) in an episode that has become a historical metonym for humiliation. Henry could not long endure life as a supplicant, and the conflict between the empire and the papacy was reignited shortly thereafter. With his excommunication and its restrictions lifted, the Holy Roman Emperor could more easily recruit baronial support in the German lands.[196]

Roger

The conquest of Sicily continued unabated but its progress was painfully slow.

On the mainland, Robert had a growing cadre of loyal barons and knights upon whom he could call. Forming an army was not usually a great challenge. In Sicily, conversely, Roger still lacked the manpower he needed. While most of his knights were Norman or Lombard, he was, of necessity, recruiting foot men, archers and engineers from the Sicilian populace of Arabs and Greeks.

The Arab archers, in particular, were an effective tactical asset. Killing fellow Muslims with the sword on behalf of a Christian ruler might be considered less than acceptable, but loosing an arrow upon the ruler's armed foes from a distance was viewed as a matter of duty for a man-at-arms, and a comparatively impersonal way of dispatching an adversary.[197]

Sicily's independent, local emirs may not have desired Kalbid or Zirid rule, but neither would they embrace the Hautevilles' feudalism and the serfdom that came with it.

A trade treaty was negotiated with the Zirids in 1075 or shortly thereafter. Even the pirates who had attempted to raid Mazara must have appreciated the benefits of legitimate commerce. Eventually, the Sicilians imported cotton cloth and beeswax (though both were also produced locally), as well as gold sent by camel caravan across the Sahara to Kairouan and Mahdia, while exporting hard wheat and dried meats. This treaty was to govern their relationship with the Zirids for the next sixty years. It was one of several factors that would inform the position taken by Roger and his son, also Roger, regarding the first two crusades.

Judith, the wife of Roger, died of natural causes around 1076. She was entombed in her brother's monastery at Saint Euphemia, in Calabria. Very little of this remains standing today.[198]

Though Roger soon remarried, his most immediate task was not building a family but building the foundation of a monarchy, even if the two objectives overlapped. Unlike Sichelgaita, who almost always traveled with Robert and even besieged a rebel city while he was doing so elsewhere, Eremburga of Mortain, Roger's second wife, did not accompany her husband on every campaign.[199]

The campaigns were many. In 1076, Roger subdued the city of Caltagirone in a battle against Ibn al Wardi (Bernavert), the Emir of Syracuse, who remained in control of a chunk of southeastern Sicily. As prisoners, some of the widows were sent in servitude to Calabria. The Arab cities of Trapani and nearby Mount Saint Julian (Erice) fell to the Normans in 1077 in a campaign during which Roger's audacious son, Serlo, distinguished himself as a leader. Taormina was taken two years later.[200] However, Catania was eventually reoccupied by forces supported by Ibn al Wardi.

Papal Knights

Just as a Bariot might be described, in modern terms, as "Greek-Lombard," perhaps being the child of a Lombard father and a Byzantine mother, this ethnic amalgamation was known in Sicily, but here the differences between Christianity and Islam were clearly more pronounced than those between the eastern and western Christians of Apulia and Calabria. This compelled a Sicilian married couple, in which one spouse was Byzantine and another Arab, to choose between religions (Islam or Christianity) rather than a liturgical rite (Latin or Greek). Most often, this was Islam.

More generally, in Sicily there existed a longstanding societal accommodation, a compromise of sorts, seen in the Byzantine Greek acceptance of Muslim Arab rule. This began as a pragmatic recognition of reality, but after two centuries it was a fact of life.

From the beginning of the Norman conquest of Sicily, in places like Troina, the Byzantines, as Orthodox Christians of the Greek tradition, and likely antipathetic toward the Norman feudalism that would make many of them serfs, stood with the Muslims against the invaders. This nurtured a resistance that was not easily overcome.

It was unsurprising, therefore, that in the Sicilian cities east of Muslim Kasr'Janni many Christians opposed Norman rule. At Catania, the population rebelled against the Normans and installed an emir. Neither Syracuse or Noto showed any sign of surrendering to Roger. Kerkent (Agrigento), with its large Arab and Berber citizenry, was equally resistant.

Robert met Pope Gregory VII at Ceprano in June of 1080 to swear fealty to the papacy and have his excommunication lifted. This treaty, for such it was in every effect, confirmed papal recognition of the Hauteville conquests in Italy which, over the last few years, saw Robert taking control of Salerno while suppressing dissent amongst his own barons. Although the agreement at Melfi stipulated twenty-one years earlier had spelled out the essential terms for the foundation of an Apulian-Calabrian-Sicilian "state" under the Hautevilles, the accord of Ceprano effectively legitimized most of Robert's recent actions even as it curtailed a few. Among other effects, it could be said to recognize the reality that Lombard rule no longer existed, even if Gregory lamented the Norman occupation of Salerno and Robert, in his oath, recognized that the city was not his by right. Amalfi, which had long been a mercantile port city not unlike Pisa and Genoa, still retained a degree of independence and is also mentioned. For his part, Robert recognized the papal sovereignty of the city of Benevento. Never mind that zealous Gregory claimed a few lands that had never been papal in the first place, and demanded monies that Robert agreed to remit.[201]

The entropy of Lombard power in southern Italy, begun decades earlier, was thus essentially complete, its realization recognized by the papacy. This was not the only shift in power.

Further afield, the Seljuk Turks had taken Jerusalem from the Fatimids in 1171; the same year, these invaders won a victory against the Byzantine Greeks at the Battle of Manzikert. By 1080, Anatolia was under Turkish control as a cornerstone of the Rum Sultanate. Pope Gregory was already contemplating a "crusade" against the Turks even before he agreed to the Treaty of Ceprano with Robert. Some historians have discerned in his efforts the seeds of the earliest crusades to the Holy Land.[202] At the very least, Gregory's ideas reflected what would become a prevailing papal view.

Importantly, the agreement with Robert Guiscard established a firm Norman bond with the papacy that, in principle, transcended other political relationships. This meant that the rapport of Guiscard, along with Roger as his vassal, with papal Rome took precedence over the Normans' relationships with both "Roman" emperors, the one in Germany and the other in Constantinople. In the past, the Normans had fought against the forces of both emperors. In future conflicts, for these were inevitable, they would do so as the rulers of a bona fide monarchy.

In a time before there were standing armies, the potential military strength of southern Italy under the Hautevilles was formidable and growing more so. The Byzantine Empire, hardly the monolithic behemoth that its more adamant proponents might imagine it to be, was showing its weakness due to internal factionalization and external threats. The Holy Roman Empire, with its tenuous unity, was not quite so powerful as it had once been. Each empire had its vulnerabilities.

To the north, Gregory's long-running enmity with Emperor Henry IV had only worsened since Canossa. For the moment, the Hautevilles, occupied with such challenges as the conquest of Sicily, saw no role for themselves in such a conflict.

Watching distant events on the other side of the Adriatic through Rome's blurry lens, Gregory knew that Nikephoros III had usurped the Byzantine throne. The pope wanted the Normans to assert the rights of young Constantine Doukas, son of the recently-deposed Michael VII, and then perhaps squelch some Turkish ambitions. Here there was at least a quasi-legitimate involvement since one of Robert's daughters had been affianced to the boy.[203]

The penultimate decade of the eleventh century found the Hautevilles recognized diplomatically by the three powers nearest their dominions: Zirid Ifriqiya to the south, the Byzantine Empire to the east, the Papal State to the north. It was crystal clear that the Duchy of Apulia, Calabria and Sicily could not exist in isolation. Whether they wished to or not, the Hautevilles had to formulate certain policies toward these neighboring powers, and also for their own people. While Guiscard was at heart a knight, Roger was usually more inclined to confront the rigors and complexities of government.

Around 1080, Roger erected a diocese at Troina. This was the first bishopric founded by the Normans in a Sicilian city where there was not an existing, even if presently vacant, episcopal see, such as Cefalù. Here was a supreme example of Latinization. Troina was destined to be a family affair. Its first bishop was a certain Robert, one of Roger's cousins. One of Roger's sons, Mauger (Malgerio), was eventually enfeoffed with the town; this was probably one of Eremburga's children and his name figures in many of his father's charters. The diocese itself was suppressed within twenty years, and Bishop Robert installed as the first Latin (Catholic) Archbishop of Messina. In 1080, Roger's eldest daughter, Matilda, wed Raymond IV of Toulouse, who visited Sicily for the nuptials and to sign a treaty.[204]

Despite its polyculturalism, Robert Guiscard's duchy made no pretense at being anything other than a Catholic monarchy founded on the western model. Yet, notwithstanding his oath of fealty to the pope, something expected from many rulers, Guiscard's dominion was independent, effectively sovereign, compared to what had come before it.

The Lombard princes of southern Italy, who were at least nominal vassals of the Holy Roman Emperor, were the "diaspora" of a society based at Pavia. Through the catepan of Bari, the Byzantine Greeks were subject to rule from Constantinople. The Kalbid emirs ruled Sicily as part of the Fatimid Empire. Unlike these other civilizations, the Normans answered only to themselves and, so far as it was necessary, the pope.

Within the complex scheme of southern Italy during the ninth and tenth centuries, the Salernitans undertook no great conquest of Sicily and the Bariots only rarely considered the prospect of an outright occupation of Salerno. By grand strategy or warrior instinct, and largely the latter, the brash Normans were changing the game.

That Robert Guiscard, now "Robert of Apulia," could betroth one of his daughters to an emperor and another to the ruler of affluent Catalonia reflected the tacit recognition by monarchs, from the east to the west of the Mediterranean, that his duchy in southern Italy was a political reality in the center of this timeless sea. Amongst the enterprising "Italian" peoples of the eleventh century, the mercantile Pisans and Venetians, and even the ambitious Amalfitans, might establish coastal "colonies" to facilitate trade, but the Normans were prosecuting an extended campaign to make Sicily their own.

In 1081, Roger took back Catania. He received from his brother what can only be described as token military support, for Guiscard, firmly ensconced in peninsular Italy, was planning conquests farther away.

Battling Two Emperors

While Roger was confronting tangible realities in Sicily, Robert Guiscard was receiving information, accurate or not, that led him to become concerned about the potential threat posed by forces gathered across the Adriatic by

Nikephoros III, the general who had deposed Michael VII to become Byzantine Emperor. Robert may well have been contemplating an invasion of the Greek lands as early as Michael's dethronement in 1078. As we have seen, Michael had sought Guiscard's help against the Seljuk Turks, and to that end signed a treaty.

In 1080, Robert, who was presently at Salerno with Sichelgaita, began building his fleet and readying the invasion, apparently motivated partly by a belief, or feigned belief, in the pretensions of a Greek impostor who arrived in Italy claiming to be the exiled Michael.[205]

The invasion was thus predicated on the objective of restoring "Michael" to the throne, which presumably would lead to the restoration of the treaty and the return of young Olympia to Constantinople to be married. Whether the annulment of the betrothal of Robert's daughter to Michael's son constituted sufficient grounds for an invasion may well be debated, but it made a convenient pretext even after the pseudo-Michael was exposed as a charlatan.

In 1081, Nikephoros himself was deposed by Alexios I Comnenus, who was crowned emperor. Alexios, like his predecessor, was unwilling to honor the terms of Michael's treaty with Robert.

By then, the Hautevilles' preparations for an invasion were well under way, and it is quite possible that Robert's motives were influenced not only by this momentum but by perceptions about the new leadership in Constantinople.[206]

Rooted in realpolitik or opportunism — or both — the invasion was expected by the Byzantines, who were already soliciting Venetian naval support. Yet Alexios may not have been prepared for such a large force consisting of some twenty thousand troops, including many Arab foot men and archers from Sicily.[207] The first overseas campaign prosecuted by the Normans of Italy was an impressive enterprise despite some initial setbacks during sea battles against the Venetians, who loathed the very thought of the Hautevilles controlling the Strait of Otranto, separating Apulia and Albania by just forty-five miles and guarding entry to the Adriatic.

In June of 1081, a large fleet carrying the Norman army departed from Otranto and landed at Corfu, the island secured in advance by a flotilla led by Robert's eldest son, Bohemond. They were soon at Durrës, or Durazzo, the ancient Dyrracheion (in what is now Albania), where the main battle described so eloquently by Anna Comnena ensued on October eighteenth. It was here that Sichelgaita revealed her greatest valor in encouraging the troops. The city finally capitulated months later in freezing February.

Amongst the Hautevilles' adversaries on the ground were familiar faces, namely the Varangian Guard, some Franks, and even a few Normans. Alexios had recruited a contingent of Seljuk mercenaries, proof that both sides were willing to employ Muslims in such campaigns.

The Venetians were formidable, and while their naval intervention ultimately did little to hinder the Normans' advance from Durrës into Greece, their treaty with the Byzantines granted them many trade privileges and even the use of a district in Constantinople. Indeed, with the golden bull, or *chrysobull*, of Alexios I in 1082 the maritime republic obtained rights along the Adriatic coast of Albania, Dalmatia, and even Greece, that would lead to centuries of control of certain cities as part of a thalassocracy. With this came further Venetian prominence in the central and eastern Mediterranean, since the Byzantines no longer possessed a large navy.

The spring of 1082 found Robert Guiscard and Bohemond advancing eastward, initially following a segment of the Via Egnatia, thence across Thessaly, to Kastoria, deep in Greek territory. Here a messenger reached Robert with the news that Henry IV, disgruntled by another excommunication, was marching into Italy to assail the pope. Leaving Bohemond in charge of the Greek campaign, Robert took only a small company of the army westward, presuming he could raise additional troops in southern Italy to respond to this other imperial threat.

Bohemond, meanwhile, besieged the walled city of Larissa but could not take it. Considering further efforts useless, he was soon *en route* to Italy with the rest of the army to support his father against Henry, who was now allied with Alexios.

While the campaign against Alexios might not have been justified, that against Henry rested on the solid foundation of Robert's treaty with Pope Gregory VII. Protesting his most recent excommunication as purely political, and therefore illegal, Henry convinced a church council to depose Gregory. Before long, a number of cardinals supported Henry's choice of Guibert, Archbishop of Ravenna, to replace the defiant pontiff.

With the Hautevilles in southern Italy preparing their knights, archers and foot soldiers for a campaign against him, Henry was virtually unopposed until he reached the dominion of Matilda of Tuscany, a papal ally. Despite a lengthy detour, the German army eventually arrived in Rome in June 1083.

While Gregory took refuge in Castel Sant'Angelo, Robert was getting ready to attack Henry. By the spring of 1084, the Norman force was finally marching toward the Eternal City.

Robert's army, which by some accounts boasted over thirty thousand men despite the recent attrition in Greece, may have outnumbered Henry's. It certainly out-muscled his force, which retired without a fight.

This precipitated a riot by the citizens. In suppressing the revolt, Robert's overzealous Normans and Arabs ended up pillaging the city. A Roman response to this then led to the Normans setting fire to some districts.

The invaders eventually withdrew from the undefended city, whose overwhelmingly Catholic populace, their homes destroyed, was hardly sympathetic to an assault of any kind by non-Christians.

The same year, Robert dedicated the new cathedral of Salerno, a gesture that signalled the Norman domination of this Lombard city. Whether the tomb of Saint Matthew in the crypt truly contains any remains of this apostle is a matter of debate. Very little of the superstructure survives from the Norman era.

In 1085, Robert returned to Greece with a large force, capturing Corfu, Cephalonia and a small part of the coast despite Venetian opposition. Here he died of fever in July, succeeded by Sichelgaita and several children. He is interred in the family mausoleum in the Holy Trinity Abbey at Venosa.

Sichelgaita ensured that her son, Roger Borsa, aged about twenty-four, succeeded to most of Robert's lands, setting aside Bohemond, Robert's son by his first wife (see Table 26). Since she had convinced her husband to accept this arrangement, it was not immediately challenged by most of the baronage after his death.[208]

Nevertheless, it was contested by Bohemond. Roger Borsa and Sichelgaita were supported by the late Guiscard's loyal brother, Roger, as early as September 1085, but Bohemond, a more-than-competent military leader, soon took Taranto, Oria and Otranto, aided by the Hautevilles' kinsman Jordan I of Capua (see Table 4), though opposed by another, Rudolph of Catanzaro.

This led to a compromise that resulted in the feuding half-brothers being co-rulers. Then, in the summer of 1087, Bohemond attacked and defeated his younger brother at Fragneto, re-occupying the important port city of Taranto for himself. A civil war followed. Only the mediation of the new pope, Urban II (Odo of Châtillon), ended it, in 1089, with Bohemond permitted to have Taranto, Cosenza and other lands while his half-brother was invested by the pontiff as Duke of Apulia. As part of this agreement, Bohemond recognized the right of his half-brother to succeed him as the eventual heir to these territories.[209]

Many of the Hauteville estates in southern Calabria were still held by Sichelgaita's brother-in-law, Roger, who also came to be called "Count of Sicily" and, later, "Roger I."

Transitions

Robert Guiscard is remembered as one of the most distinguished warriors of his age, valorous but no more or less cruel than his contemporaries. Even amongst his brothers, he stands out as the leader who united the disparate elements of southern Italy into something resembling a cohesive monarchy.

Roger had little time to mourn his beloved elder brother or to console his sister-in-law, for he was occupied with challenges in Sicily.

Under the ancient Greeks, Syracuse was the most important city in southern Italy before the emergence of Rome. It remained Sicily's wealthiest, most populous city until the Aghlabids established Balharm, at the site of the Romans' Panormus, as the capital of an emirate. Yet Syracuse prospered under the Arabs.

A few years before he married Judith, Roger fathered a son outside wedlock named Jordan, who fought at some of the battles in Sicily, most prominently at Taormina. In 1083, with his father away helping Robert Guiscard, Jordan openly rebelled against him, though he later returned to the fold.

In 1085, Bin al Wardi (Bernavert) of Syracuse raided the Calabrian coastal towns of Nicotera and Reggio. This served to remind Roger of the risk posed by this local emir, who still controlled several towns in southeastern Sicily. Syracuse finally fell in October 1086 after Jordan attacked it by land and Roger by sea. Bin al Wardi was killed during the fighting, but his wife and son fled to Noto.[210]

Noto, which wavered back and forth between Arab and Norman control, would have to be repossessed later. In most localities, however, the populations resigned themselves to Norman rule. Daily administration did not immediately change.

Efficiency was the norm. Initially, as the Normans were few in number, they left most existing organs of government undisturbed. The precise extent to which Roger's administration in Sicily was Byzantine or Arab is not known; clearly, it was a combination of both, with Norman feudalism outside the cities. For now, the manorial system was introduced slowly, one estate at a time, with monasteries established along feudal lines. Roger's standing army and royal Saracen bodyguard obviated the need for more than an elite cadre of knights, at least for the present, but many were enfeoffed.

As we have seen, the Kalbid "treasury," the *diwan,* was preserved. Its name survives in the French *douane* and Italian *dogana,* referring simply to a customs duty, but in Sicily the *diwan* was a key institution organized along Fatimid lines. Like other essential agencies, it was maintained in Palermo's Khalesa, which had been Balharm's administrative center. The *diwan* oversaw the wealth of the Kalbid emirate and then the Norman monarchy, its responsibilities ranging from the accounting of monies to landed estates to serfs. The *diwan* may have been more sophisticated than analogous financial institutions such as England's exchequer, but Sicily's exceptional wealth meant there was more to manage.[211]

Officially, Roger was Robert's surrogate in Sicily, but over time his personal influence on the island increased, and never more than in the years following Guiscard's death, when he came to be identified, invariably and unequivocally, as its count.[212]

Whereas Roger was willing to embrace the tedium of administration as a necessary task, Robert seemed destined by nature to be a swashbuckling knight. This may explain the tendency of the latter to delegate duties whenever he could. That these generalities about the two brothers have become clichés says little about their true personalities, about which we can only speculate, but both were decisive, even audacious, in their actions.

We find distinctions in the next generation as well. Robert's eldest son, Bohemond, clearly inherited his father's taste for adventure and conquest. Roger Borsa, conversely, seems to have preferred life as a governor. Indeed, his nickname derives from the word for "purse," supposedly inspired by his penchant for counting money.

With Robert's death, his widow, Sichelgaita, the mother of at least eight children, willingly inherited some of his duties. Devoutly Catholic, she placed the Jews of Palermo and Bari under the authority of the archbishops of those cities (see note 180). She does not seem to have attempted to infringe greatly upon Roger's authority in Sicily and Calabria.

In 1086, Adelaide, one of Roger's daughters by Judith, wed Henry of Mount Sant'Angelo. Through his mother, this Henry was a grandson of Guaimar IV of Salerno and a nephew of Sichelgaita. With other vassals, he had rebelled against Robert Guiscard, effectively siding against him with Alexios I of Constantinople. Presently, Henry was one of the major feudatories in the duchy and loyal to Roger Borsa.

In Sicily, the cities of Kerkent (Agrigento) and Kasr'Janni (Enna), and the towns in the path between them, fell to the control of the elder Roger in 1087 when Ibn Hammud, emir of both, agreed to a negotiated surrender in order to save face.[213]

In the same year, some Bariot merchants expropriated the bodily relics of Saint Nicholas, a bishop of the fourth century, from coastal Myra, near the mouth of the Andriacus River in Asia Minor, on the pretext that since the city had fallen to control of the Seljuk Turks the holy remains were in danger of desecration by these Muslims.[214] The bones were eventually translated to a basilica in Bari dedicated to the saint, who became the city's patron. Devotion to Saint Nicholas became popular among the Normans. In the next decade, he was venerated by crusaders, who disseminated his cult across western Europe.

The Normans may have established a healthy commercial relationship with the Zirids, but in 1087 the Pisans and Genoans, with the consent of Pope Victor III, attacked Ifriqiya, raiding and pillaging Mahdia in reprisal for some piracy and other attacks to their shipping that seemed to be instigated by the sultan. They offered this territory to Roger, who refused it because he had a treaty with the Zirids.[215] These maritime cities challenged the Venetians for trade in the central Mediterranean, especially to the south and west of Italy.

Roger had his own challenges. In 1088 or 1089, not long after the death of Eremburga, he wed his third wife, Adelaide of Incisa "del Vasto" of Savona, a younger woman from northern Italy, where her Aleramid family was influential.[216]

Adelaide brought with her some knights from her region, where the language still had many strong traces of Lombardic. A few were enfeoffed in the Nebrodian Mountains around San Marco d'Alunzio, establishing towns such as San Fratello, introducing elements of their language that became part of the local dialect of Sicilian.[217]

Sichelgaita of Salerno died in April 1090, at about fifty-three years of age. She was entombed, based on her wishes, at the Abbey of Mount Cassino. This singular princess, learned in the study of medicine and willing to lead knights into combat, is remembered as one of the most distinguished Italian women of her century.

Gisulf II, the brother Sichelgaita had displaced from Salerno, was already dead. In March 1088, he had been chosen by the Amalfitans to be their duke and lead them against attacks by the Normans, but this tenure lasted for only a year.

Meanwhile, the new pontiff, Urban II, visited Roger at Troina to encourage the continued Latinization of Sicily's bishoprics.

Noto and Butera finally surrendered in 1091. Both cities had resisted under the command of the widow of Ibn al Wardi of Syracuse. She departed for Africa with her son following their capitulation. Little is known about this stalwart woman, the last defender of Muslim temporal power in Sicily. Roger gave the town of Butera to his son, Jordan.

Some of Butera's Muslims were sent to live in Calabria so that there might be less dissent among the Arabs in this part of Sicily. No such discord existed in Palermo, though there was occasional discontent in rural areas even around the capital.

Despite an ostensible peace with the Zirids, Roger I, as the ruler of Sicily, considered it expedient to occupy Malta, annexing it to his dominion, as a strategic position. This he achieved in 1091, freeing the Christian prisoners but leaving Malta and Gozo under the administration of its Muslim caïds as his delegates, who would render tribute.[218] Whilst on his expedition to Malta, Roger left his son, Jordan, in charge of Sicily.

Upon returning from Malta, Roger I answered the request of his nephew, Roger Borsa, to suppress a revolt in Cosenza, one of the towns ostensibly belonging to Bohemond.

What followed was a period of relative calm, with Roger I, Bohemond of Taranto and Roger Borsa ruling a kind of Hauteville "federation" in southern Italy, bordered on the north by the Papal State and a few smaller polities like the County of Mount Sant'Angelo (in the Gargano region) and Capua. The senior Roger seems to have been respected by his two feuding nephews.

Sadly, his son, Jordan, to whom he had given the town of Butera, died in September 1092. Malaterra states that, at the time, he was "Roger's last living son," but this may not have been accurate (see note 232). Jordan was survived by his wife, a younger sister of Adelaide del Vasto.

In the same year, Roger Borsa wed Adele of Flanders, daughter of Robert I of Flanders and widow of King Canute IV of Denmark. This may be seen as the most important Hauteville union to date. About four years later, Adele gave birth to the son, William, who became Roger Borsa's heir to the Duchy of Apulia. Her other known children by Roger Borsa were Louis and Guiscard, who died young, and perhaps a daughter. Roger Borsa had another son, William of Gesualdo, born outside marriage. If one tangible merit may be attributed to Roger Borsa, it is his development of various towns in an early form of urban planning.

His uncle was planning alliances. In 1095, one of Roger's daughters by Eremburga, probably Maximilla, married Conrad II, the second son of the Holy Roman Emperor Henry IV. As the ruler of Lombardy and Piedmont, Conrad was styled "King of Italy," a largely symbolic title that recalled much of northern Italy, an imperial dominion since the time of Charlemagne, once being a Lombard monarchy. The wedding was celebrated in Pisa. Malaterra mentions the union but not Maximilla's name. Sadly, the marriage was short-lived, as Conrad died six years later, aged just twenty-eight.

First Crusade

Alexios I Comnenus, the Byzantine Emperor, had recruited Seljuk mercenaries to fight Robert Guiscard, but these same Muslim Turks were encroaching ever more on his dominions in Asia Minor. By now, they occupied Anatolia and other areas. Whatever religious differences he might have with the Christians of the west, Alexios solicited their support at the Council of Piacenza in 1095. The next year, at the Council of Clermont, Pope Urban II publicly answered this request by preaching the First Crusade.[219]

Geographically, the chief objective of this paradoxical cross between war and pilgrimage was not the reconquest of Anatolia but Jerusalem, a city holy to all three Abrahamic faiths. What linked the two regions politically in 1096 was the Seljuk rule of both, with administration of Jerusalem itself left to the Artuqid dynasty. It was reasonable to presume, therefore, that a campaign against these Muslims in either place might spill into the other. This would soon change when the Fatimids took back Jerusalem and its environs shortly before the arrival of the crusaders.

Rivers of ink flowing into a sea of words have chronicled the causes and effects of this crusade, rendering conclusions about it slightly muddled. Ultimately, however, the pope's admonition to the people of western Christendom addressed Byzantine concerns only indirectly. Just as the papacy wanted a Latin Sicily, it desired a Latin Palestine. If there were a comparable precedent, it was the ongoing effort in Iberia that came to be known as the *Reconquista* (see note 284).

There is very little to suggest that Urban harbored sincere sympathy toward Byzantine theology or Orthodoxy in the wake of the Great Schism. In October of 1098, he convened the Council of Bari to address various matters, including the lingering Byzantine ecclesiology still held by some bishops in the Duchy of Apulia. The "Greek" bishops who attended were not those from the Byzantine Empire but prelates of southern peninsular Italy who formerly had been under the jurisdiction of the Patriarch of Constantinople and, in some cases, still clung to liturgical traditions associated with the east. Anselm, Archbishop of Canterbury, presently exiled by William II of England, was there to rant against his king and defend the *filioque* retained by Rome in the face of protests by Constantinople (see Chapter 4).[220]

At least a few leaders eyed the Greek lands for themselves. For his part, Bohemond of Taranto, Robert Guiscard's son, had never forgotten the lost conquest of the Byzantine Empire. Neither of the two Rogers, his uncle and half-brother, would offer much material support for the enterprise, even though many crusaders from France, Germany, England and elsewhere would depart for the east from Messina or Brindisi.

Once part of the Byzantine Empire, the Holy Land might well become Christian again. For some Christians, the conquest of Palestine from Islam reflected a sincere belief rooted in faith. For others, it was a pretext, a springboard to other things, some yet unknown.

This was to be Bohemond's war, his conquest, his glory.

Whilst besieging Amalfi in 1097 with his uncle, Roger of Sicily, Bohemond encountered crusaders passing through Italy *en route* to the Holy Land. Whether or not this was the catalyst for his participation, he soon departed himself. He was, arguably, the most experienced military leader of the crusade.

Each faction took its own route, with Bohemond leading his Apulian-Calabrian contingent as part of the so-called "Princes' Crusade" through Greece to Constantinople. Accompanying him was his nephew, Emma's son, Tancred (see Table 26), along with some five hundred knights and their companies, and perhaps ten times as many foot soldiers. Bohemond may have wanted to sack Constantinople, perhaps soliciting Godfrey of Bouillon to support this plan, which never materialized. He made it to Antioch, where he continued the siege begun under Stephen of Blois. Following a dispute with Raymond IV of Toulouse, who sought to persuade him to keep his oath to Alexios to restore formerly Byzantine lands, such as Antioch, to Constantinople, he gained complete control of the city early in 1099 and became its prince. Later, at Christmas of that year, he went south to Jerusalem following its capitulation to fulfill his vow as a crusader.

Bohemond and his nephew thus became sovereigns in their own right, rulers in the general orbit of the incipient Kingdom of Jerusalem, where Godfrey of Bouillon was the first monarch, though he reigned only briefly and did not use the title of king. Despite the presence of the Sunni Seljuks to the north and east, and the Shia Fatimids to the south, the various "crusader states" occupied the Mediterranean coast or areas very near it, from Armenian Cilicia and the County of Edessa in Asia Minor to the Principality of Antioch, the County of Tripoli (part of what is now Lebanon) and the Kingdom of Jerusalem (essentially Israel).

Whereas the Christian presence in this region had formerly been predominantly Greek, it now became Latin, and despite their promises none of these "Franks" was willing to relinquish the conquered lands to the Byzantine Emperor.

Bohemond eventually married Constance, a daughter of King Philip I of France. His nephew, Tancred, became Prince of Galilee and wed Constance's half-sister, Cecile of France.

Neither of the two Rogers became very involved in the events taking place on the eastern edge of the Mediterranean except for trade, though there was contact with the crusaders and pilgrims. Brindisi and Messina remained the maritime gateways to the crusader states, lending a certain geopolitical significance to Norman Italy.[221]

For the elder Roger, the presence of a large Sicilian Muslim population, from which he drew his archers and many of his foot men, probably argued against direct participation in a "holy war" against Islam. According to the chronicler Ali ibn al-Athir, Roger intimated this as early as 1087, when he refused the request of the Pisans and Genoans to attack Zirid Ifriqiya in response to some raids on Italian territory and shipping (see note 215).

Nevertheless, Roger's daughter, Matilda, who died in 1094, was wed to Raymond IV of Toulouse, the crusader who became Count of Tripoli. Odo of Bayeux, half-brother of William the Conqueror, visited Roger *en route* to the Holy Land; he died in Sicily in February 1097 and is interred in the crypt of Palermo's cathedral.[222]

There were, of course, many other connections to the First Crusade and its crusaders. After he returned home to Europe, Robert II of Flanders, the brother-in-law of Roger Borsa, came to be known among his people as "Robert of Jerusalem."

The well-chronicled adventures of Bohemond of Antioch, who still held Taranto, and Tancred of Galilee are nothing if not interesting.[223] Nevertheless, a few years were to pass before the other Hautevilles of Italy became involved very closely with the Kingdom of Jerusalem and its second monarch, King Baldwin I, the younger brother of Godfrey of Bouillon.

The Papal Legateship

One of the territories on the political and geographic fringe of the Duchy of Apulia and Calabria was Capua, long ruled by the Drengot dynasty, which by now was related to the Hautevilles (see Table 2). The *de jure* Prince of Capua was Richard II, who had been exiled from the city since his youth by a usurper, Lando IV, being left only with Aversa. He now solicited the help of his cousin, Roger Borsa, to reclaim his Capuan patrimony.

In June 1098, with the support of Roger of Sicily and an imposing army consisting largely of Arabs, Richard was restored his rightful inheritance and swore fealty to Roger Borsa.[224] In connection with this campaign, which resulted in the end of Lombard rule over any major locality in southern Italy, Roger of Sicily obtained Naples and claimed Amalfi, which had not historically been ruled by the Hautevilles except for very brief periods. This meant that, in addition to Sicily and Calabria, the elder Roger now controlled many of the Italian territories along the Tyrrhenian northward to Naples, even though Amalfi resisted.

Roger exploited this occasion to host Pope Urban II in Salerno to discuss a matter involving ecclesiastical jurisdiction in Sicily. Urban recognized Roger's civil authority as Count of Sicily, and he had been instrumental in arranging the marriage of his daughter to a son of Henry IV who ruled part of northern Italy, but a jurisdictional dispute arose when the pontiff decided to grant a bishop authority as his papal legate on the island. Now Roger was able to negotiate a unique agreement that allowed him, and henceforth his heirs, to nominate Sicily's bishops or, at the very least, to approve (or veto) the papacy's episcopal appointments. This *apostolic legateship* was to become the envy of other Catholic sovereigns, such as England's monarchs.[225] However, it did not extend to Roger's mainland dominions.

Historians have long debated the scope and duration of this authority, which was eventually confirmed by Urban's successor, Paschal II, to Roger's son and successor, Roger II.[226] It seems to have been renounced a century later by Constance, the daughter of Roger II, as queen regnant, shortly before her death.[227] That the legateship later came to be called the *Monarchia Sicula,* or "Sicilian Monarchy," was a sign of its perceived importance over the centuries as a prerogative at the very heart of royal power.

Although this legatine privilege was only rarely exercised, even when Rome appointed notoriously ornery bishops who sought to meddle in affairs of state, it reflected the increasing prestige of the Hautevilles in papal eyes.

Urban's decision to concede to the ruler of Sicily specific rights of refusal or approval over the appointment of certain prelates may be viewed in the contemporary context of the dispute of Anselm of Canterbury with William II "Rufus" of England, which began with the king's request for monies but soon embroiled both archbishop and sovereign in broader questions of ecclesiastical jurisdiction and royal authority. This was an early example of what, in modern times, would be regarded as a contention between the power of the church on one side and that of the state on the other in the temporal realm.

However, while England had a longstanding primatial see, namely Canterbury, no archdiocese in Sicily was yet accorded such privileged status. In the same year as the Council of Bari and establishment of the legateship, Urban made Alfano II, Archbishop of Salerno, a primate, albeit not of the entirety of Apulia but over just a few suffragan archbishops in Campania and Lucania.[228]

In practice, the chief effect of the legateship was that important prelates sent to Sicily by the papacy, or answering directly to the pope, and particularly those having special powers or duties, were expected, even required, to advise the ruler of their activities on the island. Nothing involving ecclesiastical administration in a diocese in Sicilian territory could be hidden from the eyes of the monarch, who for now was a count but would eventually be a king.

The spirit, and perhaps even the letter, of the legateship facilitated the appointment of bishops, but Roger had already done this for Messina, Syracuse and Agrigento (Kerkent).

It is difficult to assess in objective terms the degree to which the church in Sicily, compared to most other European regions, may have seemed to assume something of a "political" character, as if it were rather closely associated with the secular realm. Yet a few historians have suggested this as one possible result of the legateship despite its general lack of application in specific cases that are known to us.

Viewed another way, the obvious foundation of the monarchy under papal auspices in 1059, something confirmed in 1080, ensured its close identification with the papacy, a fact recognized by historians over the centuries. It was accentuated by the large number of Latin (Catholic) diocesan, parochial and monastic foundations supported by the Hautevilles in what were formerly Byzantine or Muslim areas. Among the many examples is the abbey of Bruno of Cologne, founder of the Carthusians, in Calabria.[229]

Yet Latinization of the Byzantine Greeks and Christianization of the Muslim Arabs proceeded far more slowly than the Hautevilles may have wished. At this date, the Normans' efforts were anything but overtly coercive.

It is not possible to point to a specific moment in time when Roger I, as Count of Sicily, came to be regarded as a monarch invested with a form of sovereignty. He was identified as a count in charters at least five years before Robert Guiscard's death, while contemporary chroniclers referred to him in this way. The very fact that Pope Urban accorded the legateship to him, and not to his nephew, Roger Borsa, implies that the papacy now recognized him as the lawful ruler of Sicily and no longer the delegate of the Duke of Apulia. We find Roger I styled by Urban II as *Rogerio Comiti Calabriae et Siciliae,* and Roger II by Paschal II as *Rogerio Comiti Siciliae.* By 1090 we encounter phrases such as "the Servant of Jesus Christ and Defender of Christians."[230] Appellations such as "Defender of the Faith" had long been used for Christian rulers.

Apart from the usual nuances found in Latin records, titles written in Greek and Arabic vary somewhat depending on when a phrase was written and by whom. However, while phraseology may well reflect perceptions and is important in that respect, sometimes it is simply the result of local usage.

The Latin titles, *dux* and *comes,* gave rise to their modern cognates in Italian and English. In Greek we find *doukas* and *komes*. The Greek for *countess* was *komessa*. The translations of *rex* and *regina* are equally clear.

In Arabic, the words *malik* and *malikah* were connoted to mean "great leader" but also "king" and "queen." Nevertheless, the use of such terms in the Hauteville dominions before there was a kingdom reflects the limitations of language rather than the premature elevation of our rulers to the status of royalty by their Muslim subjects. There was no universal Arabic word for *count,* as the medieval European ranks of nobility differed from those in the Arab world. As we have seen, the term *emir,* for a leader or commander, was sometimes used rather loosely. With Norman rule achieved, we find the continued use of words such as *caïd.*

By 1098, Roger I seems to have enjoyed as much prestige, more wealth, and almost certainly more territorial power, than his nephew, Roger Borsa, who now resided mostly at Salerno but was frequently at Melfi and elsewhere, necessarily traveling most of the time.

Like his nephew, Roger I also had to travel around his dominions frequently, indeed almost continuously.[231] He crossed the Strait of Messina many times. Roger and his large family of daughters and sons only occasionally resided in the castle, or fortified palace, hastily erected on high ground in the *Halkah* section of Palermo's *Kasr* district at the site of the Arab fortress. The original royal chapel, a quaint structure beneath the present palatine chapel, for which it is now the "crypt," can still be seen there.

The castle at San Marco d'Alunzio was maintained as a safe haven for Roger's children, and that seems to be where most were raised, speaking several languages, including Norman French. However, Roger spent much time at Mileto and Messina as well. His vantage points in southern Calabria and northeastern Sicily permitted him to monitor the activity of his people in both dominions. For example, he populated Focerò, a region in the Nebrodian mountains, with Christian subjects from Oliveri and coastal Milazzo, originally administered by a group of archons rather than a baron.

Consistent with their traditions, the Byzantines and Arabs seem to have accorded the ruler of Sicily more obeisance and authority than that to which the typical European Christian ruler was accustomed, something suggested by the observations of the theologian Eadmer of Canterbury (see note 224).

San Marco d'Alunzio: Norman church at the site of an ancient temple (top) and last standing wall of the Hauteville family castle

Chapter 9
RITES OF PASSAGE

Roger I, Count of Sicily and Calabria, the last of the large family of Hauteville brothers, and the last ruler of his dynasty, as we must now define it, to be born in Normandy, died on the twenty-second of June of 1101 in Mileto, aged about seventy. For this era, he seems to have been quite active for a man his age.

Comital Regency

Roger's third wife, Adelaide, was now around twenty-seven years old and the mother of four children, including two sons. The elder son, Simon, born in 1093, was Roger's heir.[232]

The extent to which Adelaide was directly involved in her husband's administrative duties in the years immediately before his death is not known, although her name appears with his in several charters.[233] The chroniclers imply nothing like the active roles of Sichelgaita, Robert Guiscard's second wife, or even Judith, Roger's first consort. With her brothers, however, Adelaide seems to have overseen the recently enfeoffed "Lombard" lands in the Nebrodian Mountains. Considering that he had fathered some eighteen children by his three wives and sundry mistresses, Roger survived most of his sons.

Now, with her husband's death, Adelaide became the effective governor of his dominions on both sides of the Strait of Messina, the "regent" for her own young son, confirming the rights of many bishoprics and monasteries.

Anomously for the Norman-Swabian era, the years of Adelaide's regency for her sons, coinciding with the last decade of the reign of Roger Borsa on the mainland, are not addressed by any local chroniclers who were writing at that time and therefore privy to contemporaneous events; annalists report such details as a famine in Apulia at the end of 1102, which seems to have been the result of a drought throughout Europe that affected some regions more than others.

For this period, we know more about the Hautevilles in the Holy Land than we do of their kinsmen in southern Italy. Nevertheless, except for some baronial dissent in Calabria at the beginning of her regency, there do not seem to have been many major upheavals of the kind that might make their way into chronicles.[234]

Even so, in the absence of contemporary local chronicles, the surviving evidence suggests that both Adelaide del Vasto and Roger Borsa had to respond to occasional unrest by barons and others in the populace, if nothing so severe as a general insurrection. Writing a few years after the fact, the chronicler and archbishop Romuald of Salerno tells us that in 1105 Roger Borsa had to rein in his kinsman Robert, Count of Mount Sant'Angelo, who had refused to pledge fealty to him as Duke of Apulia. This was to become a familiar pattern.

Adelaide and Roger both undertook to insediate Catholic pastors and abbots in what had been Orthodox localities even as Greek remained the popular liturgical and vernacular language for many people. A certain harmony prevailed. There was peaceful trade with the Zirids and a tenuous peace with both emperors.[235]

In Sicily and Calabria, Adelaide was assisted by her knightly uncles, brothers and cousins, but hers is the name that appears in charters and it was in Simon's name that authority was exercised. So far as we know, there were no overt contestations, no open conflicts arising from a half-brother's pretensions.

Young Roger suffered an ear infection in 1101, and one of Adelaide's first decrees is a charter issued in Greek in October of that year, four months after her husband's death, making a donation of four serfs, along with their families and property (including land) to the Byzantine monastery of San Filippo di Fragalà, near Frazzanò in the Nebrodian Mountains, in gratitude for the boy's "miraculous recovery." Here we see the unabashed, sometimes ruthless, application of feudalism, as the same charter also grants the abbot additional lands, including vineyards confiscated from some serfs, presumably Arabs or Greeks, who had fled and were forcibly repatriated, yet the preservation of the monastery's Greek faith tradition. It is the earliest known statement by a woman charged with acting as a ruler in Norman Italy.[236]

Her son's illness, whatever it was, seems to have been rather severe, probably *otisis media* if not something worse. At the very least, it left a lasting impression on Adelaide, for she later made another donation to this monastery to commemorate Roger being cured. Undertaken eleven years later (in November 1112), and perhaps to mark Roger reaching the age of majority, this involved five named serfs ceded from the territory of the Hauteville demesne of San Marco d'Alunzio, with the proviso that henceforth all rights of justice and taxation over these men and their families was to remain exclusively under royal authority, exempt from any other civil jurisdiction. Until then, the serfs may have enjoyed Adelaide's personal patronage and protection.

RITES OF PASSAGE

There was no firm rule about the exact age at which a young heir reached the age of majority. Normally, he would be considered an adult at around fifteen. There were rites of passage. For example, the son of a baron or other feudal lord would be knighted at nineteen or twenty following several years as a squire, though the son of a king, duke or count might be knighted sooner.

The realms Adelaide ruled in the name of her young son had to be governed well if his inheritance was to be preserved. Here there were political complexities.

Adelaide — in Simon's name — enjoyed the apostolic legateship in Sicily but she lacked the same privilege in mainland territories like Calabria. Therefore, her relations with the papacy were subtly different in Sicily and Calabria.

While most of her counsellors in Calabria and northeastern Sicily were "Latins" (Normans and Lombards), Palermo and other important cities were administered by Greeks and Arabs. This included the treasury, the *diwan*. Most abbots were Greek Orthodox.

Contrary to what one might imagine, such a culturally eclectic environment did not pose a great threat to Adelaide's rule, for much had changed since the Normans' ordeal during that frigid winter at Troina four decades earlier. In practice, these non-Latin urban populations looked to their ruler to defend their interests against the zealous feudal baronage being introduced in rural areas. The comital bodyguard consisted of famously loyal Muslims.

The regent had few female peers to advise her. Adelaide doubtless looked to her own siblings and cousins for advice, but she eventually made a certain Christodoulos, a Greek, her chief counsellor, entrusting him with day-to-day administration as *amiratus*. (see note 255).

One of Adelaide's stepdaughters, who may have been named Yolanda, married Robert of Burgundy, who seems to have become an advisor.[237] Whatever his status, he died a few years following his arrival in Sicily.

Initially, Adelaide chose to live with her children at San Marco d'Alunzio. Besides Matilda, Simon, Roger and Maximilla, there may have been a girl who did not live to see adulthood.

The town and castle of San Marco were about a hundred twenty kilometers (seventy-five miles) east of Palermo, and five hundred fifty meters above sea level. Cicero famously observed that the corrupt Roman governor Verres refused to ascend these heights to extort payments from the town's citizens, the Aluntians, choosing instead to wait on the coast a few miles away whilst minions collected the money for him. The castle stood on the summit overlooking the town, with Greek churches nearby. A Catholic chapel was erected by the Normans upon the stylobate of the Temple of Hercules. In addition to its Greeks, San Marco had a thriving community of Jews engaged in silk making, and they probably produced fabric for the Hautevilles.

However, Adelaide's geographical power base was at Messina, from which she could keep an eye on her sons' Calabrian dominions across the strait, and it was in that city that most of her few extant decrees were issued. Preserved for centuries in monastic archives, a smattering of these charters were spared the fate of Messina's Arab-Norman castle, of which the last vestiges were destroyed by a catastrophic earthquake in 1908. (This was not a unique event. Over time, seismic activity has taken its toll across eastern Sicily and much of Calabria; only a single wall remains of the Hauteville castle at San Marco d'Alunzio.)

Adelaide made a serious effort to continue her husband's work to establish and endow Latin abbeys in Sicily and Calabria whilst assisting the efforts of the Greek communities to preserve their language and rite.[238] Her charters to the monasteries in the Nebrodian region were written in Greek.

Norman French was the chief vernacular of the Hautevilles and their feudatories. Simon and Roger also learned Latin, as well as some Greek and Arabic.

The next few years were remarkably — and fortunately — uneventful in the dominions Adelaide governed. The only major incident we know of is her suppression of an impromptu rebellion by some barons, to which chroniclers abroad make only vague references. This trial of nerves, which does not seem to have been part of a wider conspiracy, revealed who was loyal and who was not. Unfortunately, the fealty of the restless Norman baronage would frequently be called into question during the new century.

Further afield, Bohemond of Taranto was ensconced at Antioch, while his half-brother, Roger Borsa, comfortably ruled Apulia and other parts of the Italian mainland.

Alexander of Telese would describe Adelaide as "a very prudent woman."[239]

In his chronicle later commissioned by Matilda, Adelaide's daughter, Alexander alludes to a sibling rivalry, noting that Roger once taunted his elder brother, Simon, following a fight that ensued while playing a game of chance (flipping coins), stating that he, Roger, should rule Sicily and that Simon should instead become pope.[240]

In his next chapter, Alexander praises young Roger's piety, and also his generosity, explaining how the boy would give alms to poor men and pilgrims, and seek out his mother for additional coin when his funds were exhausted.[241] Were these the coins he won from his elder, pious brother?

Most of the charters of Adelaide that survive, beginning shortly after her husband's death in 1101, deal with the grant, confirmation or protection of the rights, privileges or estates of churches and monasteries. The earliest ones, as we have seen, refer to the regent and her young sons with appellations such as "Adelaide and her sons Simon and Roger."

In the early months of 1105, southern Italy seems to have had much more snow than usual. This may have been one of the climatic effects of a major eruption of Hekla, a volcano in Iceland.

Adelaide's catastrophes were nearer home. Sadly, Simon died in September of 1105 at the age of twelve. He was buried next to his father at Mileto.

This left Roger, born in 1095, as his father's recognized heir. Nonetheless, a few years would pass before the boy reached the age of majority.

One of the reasons why rather few of Adelaide's charters survive is because some were written on paper rather than more durable parchment or vellum.[242]

The Arabs' introduction of paper facilitated correspondence, accounting and learning; the Sicilian population in Adelaide's time enjoyed a high rate of literacy, among women as well as men. That Adelaide was present at San Marco d'Alunzio in the autumn of 1109 is attested by a decree issued at the Hauteville castle to recapitulate the extent of the lands long held by a nearby abbey dedicated to Saint Barbarus, the original charter having been destroyed.

In August 1106, Henry IV, Holy Roman Emperor, died. His son, Henry V, wed Matilda (Maude), daughter, and eventual heiress, of Henry I of England. He would be the last ruler of his Salian dynasty (see Table 3).

From 1106 to 1108, Bohemond of Antioch was in his Italian dominions. A papal bull of November 1106 mentions him and his half-brother, Roger Borsa, in connection with the relics of Nicholas of Myra officially being placed in the basilica under construction in Bari, and the recent death of Elias, the city's archbishop, who had ensured the translation of the bones to a great church to be erected in the saint's name rather than a chapel that his predecessor, Urso, wanted to construct in the catepan's palace. Archbishop Elias was esteemed by both brothers, but especially by Roger Borsa.

Bohemond's main reason for being in Italy was to gather men and build ships for an assault on Durrës. This last episode in his long feud with Emperor Alexios I of Constantinople was unsuccessful and the two made peace in the autumn of 1108. Early the next year Bohemond returned to Italy.

As her son neared the age of majority, it became obvious that Adelaide would have to spend more time in Palermo. By now, the fortified palace built around four stout towers had been erected on high ground, replacing the Kalbid castle. Overlooking a labyrinth of urban streets to the north and an extensive hunting ground to the south, it would be a secure residence, if not a home, for Adelaide and her children. Her late husband had left a garrison there, and another at the seaside fortress erected by the Fatimids less than a mile away. The Christians were still a minority in the bustling metropolis, but several Catholic churches, besides the palace chapel, were being built for the city's growing Norman population.[243]

Most of this construction was quite rapid. The simple Romanesque architecture facilitated erection of the typical church, in the Norman-Arab style of Saint John of the Hermits or Saint John of the Lepers, in a year or two. The Arab architects and their artisans were masters of such projects, and large work crews of hundreds permitted uncommon alacrity while the general uniformity in design obviated the need for unduly creative solutions. They had been building edifices of this kind around the Mediterranean for centuries, with rather little distinction between the structure of a mosque, church or synagogue.

This move to the west was more significant in the twelfth century than it might seem today; over time, the rivalry between Palermo and Messina took on a life of its own. The former, mostly Arab, was the richer and more populous; the latter, still mostly Byzantine, was an important springboard to the Italian peninsula and the eastern Mediterranean.

Neither Latin Salerno nor Greek Bari, important and impressive as they were, could compete with the two largest cities of Sicily. Indeed, Palermo was the most populated city in what is now Italy. Messina, a key port for transit between southern Italy and points south and east, eventually developed a reputation for its jovial ambience and gambling houses, a fact mentioned by the chronicler Hugh Falcandus.

Adelaide's rapport with the papacy was good. In March 1110, we find her convening a meeting of barons and prelates at Messina's cathedral to confirm the privileges granted by her husband to a church in Squillace, in Calabria. This was approved by Pope Paschal II the following month.[244]

About the same time, perhaps a few months earlier, Sigurd I Magnusson, King of Norway, nicknamed "the Crusader," visited Roger II and Adelaide in Palermo *en route* to Jerusalem. The record of this visit describes Roger in flattering terms as a count worthy of kingship.[245]

Multicultural Matronage

Adelaide's outright patronage, or matronage, of what was still a Byzantine monastery, Saint Philip, seems to fly in the face of the tide of Latinization that was engulfing the Hauteville dominions in southern Italy. Although there is no indication of this monastery being placed outside papal authority, this was something of an aberration even if, as we saw in Chapter 4, a Catholic diocese in Calabria had a Grecophone bishop into the middle of the twelfth century. Significantly, Adelaide was supporting an existing foundation, not establishing a new one, and it was in a remote, mountainous, predominantly Byzantine area not unlike some parts of Calabria.

Even so, if she wished, the countess could well have ceded the monastery to an order such as Bruno's Carthusians, who cared for her late husband shortly before his death from an acute illness, and of course there were always the Benedictines.

To the west, Adelaide founded the abbey dedicated to the Holy Spirit, outside Caltanissetta, as a Latin benefice in a territory that was overwhelmingly Muslim, conversions being an implicit motivation. The demesnial castle and Catholic church in Calascibetta, gazing at Muslim Enna (Kasr'Janni) across a chasm, reflected part of the general effort at Latinization. That Adelaide issued a charter (shown in these pages) to the bailiffs around Enna in Arabic and Greek suggests a heterogeneous population in that region at that time. Any true Sicilian knows that an invisible line divides the island, east and west, into vaguely Catanian and Palermitan spheres. This may have been inevitable, and there is no evidence of it being rooted exclusively in medieval perceptions, but the "boundary" corresponds to a zone between Enna and Caltanissetta. Adelaide's time found the island divided into three districts identified by the Arabs: Val Demone (the northeast), Val di Noto (the southeast), Val di Mazara (the west). These did not correspond precisely to the Kalbid qadits, and the Normans often chose to ignore them, identifying their subjects by faith, language and culture rather than geography.

While there can be no talk of Adelaide and her children being anything but Roman Catholic, the influence upon them by Byzantine clergy, and even advisors like Christodoulos, lent a certain Greek sympathy to their government that seems to have transcended mere tolerance. Indeed, Alexios I of Constantinople recognized the advocacy of Byzantine culture by Christodoulos. For all their cooperation with the papacy and its ecclesiastical objectives, and even bearing in mind the reality that such changes were unlikely to occur in the course of just two or three generations, the Hautevilles never suppressed Greek liturgy or culture as much as one might expect of dynasts seeking to Latinize a monarchy. On the contrary, they actually adopted a few Byzantine customs, as we can see in their regalia and their affinity for icons and mosaicry.

Recent years had found both Bohemond of Antioch (and Taranto) and Roger Borsa in southern Italy, but despite an undercurrent of tension there was no actual war between them during this period.

In their peninsular dominions, compared to Adelaide's Sicily, there were few Muslims to malign, harass or convert. Bohemond, compared to the half-brother he found so annoying, seems to have exerted rather little overt effort to bring the Greeks to the pope, whether in Antioch or in his piece of southern Italy, except for founding Catholic monasteries.

Complexities were ubiquitous. Too much importance should not be ascribed to the intrinsic prejudices of chroniclers such as the Hauteville apologists and Catholic clerics Godfrey Malaterra and Romuald of Salerno, counterposing the devoutly Muslim Abd al-Aziz ibn Shaddad and his continuator Ali ibn al-Athir al-Jazari, Arabs who were understandably critical of such exploits as the dynasty's invasive activities in Ifriqiya during the reign of Roger II. Beyond strictly "situational" realities based on the politics of the moment, this was an era of strong religious biases, whether between Christians and Muslims, Orthodox and Catholics, or Sunnis and Shia. Indeed, it was such differences that often shaped politics. Conquests, crusades and jihads were merely their most obvious manifestations.

Infidels, schismatics, heretics. There was no dearth of derogatory nouns to identify "the other," and little incentive to refrain from spewing the venom of derision, either in conversation or on parchment. This alone made any collective effort at tolerance and co-existence worthy of note.

Both Bohemond and Roger died in 1111, leaving young sons as their successors. This meant that their wives, respectively Constance of France and Adele of Flanders, became regents for boys who were not yet old enough to rule on their own. In this sense, Adelaide was no longer alone as the regent of a young Norman heir, even if her regency was nearing its end.

Bohemond was succeeded by his son, Bohemond II of Antioch, and Roger Borsa by his own son, William II of Apulia. Fulfilling the earlier agreement reached by the antagonistic half-brothers following the death of their father, Robert Guiscard, this left William as the heir of some of the elder Bohemond's lands in Apulia and Calabria. Though this did not include Taranto and certain important towns inherited by Bohemond II, William became the ruler of much of peninsular Italy south of Rome.

Nevertheless, Adelaide's son held southern Calabria, with some lands and cities along the Tyrrhenian coast north of Salerno. We know of no open hostilities instigated by Bohemond or Roger Borsa against Adelaide.

However, as regent she was called upon to mediate at least a few disputes involving barons, notably a conflict between the enfeoffed knight who held Agira and the prelate who held Regalbuto.[246] This kind of intervention by her, through her advisor and uncle, Robert Avenel, was not altogether unusual, and there is a hint of it in her decree of October 1101 (see note 236). Indeed, such interventions by rulers were normal, almost routine, as monarchs, be they kings, dukes or counts, were, in effect, the court of last appeal in matters for which there was no higher authority. This even occurred after a system of justiciars (circuit judges) was instituted. Despite the apostolic legateship, however, Sicily's monarchs rarely became embroiled in cases concerning the church except where a dispute involved lay (secular) concerns such as a dispute over the land claimed by a baron or, more rarely, even a peasant, or a contestation between two monasteries for the same manor. Although the chroniclers mention some of these cases, many are indicated by specific charters known to us.

Elsewhere in the Norman sphere of influence, in 1111, Robert I of Capua, who had succeeded his brother, Richard II (see Table 4), sought to assist Pope Paschal II, now held hostage by Henry V of Germany for having refused to crown him Holy Roman Emperor. Robert's army was repulsed before it could engage in a pitched battle, and Henry was crowned in Rome in April of that year. Had Roger Borsa lived even a year longer, he probably would have supported the pope militarily, having pledged to do so. It is likely that, together, the combined armies of Roger and Robert could have defeated Henry's imperial force.

Paschal and Henry renewed the feud of their predecessors when the former excommunicated the latter.

Robert's defiance was more subtle. He refused to maintain the pledge of vassalage his late brother had made to Roger Borsa, but he did not wage open war against young William II, the present Duke of Apulia. It may be noted that William's ordinal is based on his uncle, "Iron Arm," the elder brother of Robert Guiscard, being William I.

That three women — Constance, Adele, Adelaide — found themselves governing the Hauteville dominions during the same year or two has drawn little attention from historians. Certain it is that they each faced unique realities in their separate domains, yet there were commonalities in these essentially Christian and feudal societies. Among the similarities, all three mothers were responsible for territories in southern peninsular Italy peopled by a certain number of Byzantine Greeks, and each woman was raising a son destined to rule. All three women were born into ruling families, and thus familiar with this social environment and its potential perils. Each would assume responsibilities normally destined for a father rather than a mother. One of these involved the very act of leading a son from boyhood to manhood.

Majority

To Constance and Adelaide fell the duty of raising a son to knighthood. As we have seen (in Chapter 2), a man might be born to rule, succeeding his father as a duke, count or even king without a formal ceremony, but no man was born a knight. This status was bestowed in a prescribed, if simple, ceremony held before witnesses, followed by festivities as a significant rite of passage. It seems that both Simon and Roger II had been knighted years earlier, as children, but now a public event was deemed necessary for the latter.

Varied though they were, the knightings of the sons of kings, dukes and counts shared a few universal characteristics. The ceremonies were public and they were usually held on recurring feasts, with at least a few other knights present as witnesses. An older person, usually the king or duke himself, dubbed a younger one. Some kind of arming was involved, be it placing a helm upon the new knight's head, girding him with a sword belt or placing a sword in his hand. Knighting signalled, or coincided with, the young man coming of age, typically at around twenty for the son of a baron or *seigneur* (manorial lord) but usually a few years earlier for the son of a sovereign leader. Whether in Italy, France or England, the knightings of the twelfth century were simple and frequent enough, and their formal procedure known so well, that chroniclers rarely thought it necessary to describe the actual ceremonies in great detail.

In the beginning of the twelfth century, despite the first knightly orders being founded in the Holy Land, dubbing knights was still usually a secular affair. Some Catholic abbots controlling large estates were, in effect, feudal lords required to provide their sovereign a certain number of knights, just as a baron or other vassal would have to do. Yet the seventeenth canon issued at the Council of London of 1102 forbade such abbots to dub knights, and it would not be unreasonable to presume the application of a similar principle in southern Italy during this era. Indeed, in view of the apostolic legateship granted to Roger I in 1098, Adelaide may well have exercised more control over the church in Sicily than King Henry I enjoyed in England.

Where royalty or "quasi-royalty" was concerned, the latter referring to sovereign ruling families such as the Hautevilles before their foundation of a kingdom, it was normally presumed that a young prince (though that term was not yet in common use), as his father's heir, would be knighted before succeeding him. A king's son might thus be knighted at around the age of fifteen or sixteen.

Instructive examples will be found in the other great Norman dominion. In 1086, William the Conqueror knighted his son, the future Henry I of England, who was then seventeen or eighteen years old.[247]

It must be remembered that all western European monarchs except women and popes were assumed to be knighted. This was not merely a formality. It was presumed that a king or duke might be called upon to lead troops into combat to defend his rights and his people. He need not be the most capable warrior in the realm, but at the very least he had to be marginally competent as a battlefield commander. The Arabs' *furusiyya* was somewhat similar to knighthood in its warrior code.

Until now, the Hautevilles had held few ceremonies in Palermo besides such events as the funeral of Odo of Bayeux in 1097. Except for a few walls that remain, the cathedral was not the present structure but the older edifice described earlier. The royal palace was still under construction in the Halkah district nearby, overlooking the Kasr, but it is quite possible that Roger II was knighted there or even at one of the other Arab palaces, such as the Kalbids' Favara to the east of the city in what is now the Brancaccio district. There is, however, another possibility, and it seems more likely in view of its geographic centrality.

Next to the cathedral stands a chapel erected in Byzantine times at the corner of what are now Via Incoronazione and Via Bonello. For a time, this edifice too had been used as a mosque, but the Normans had restored it as a church. Attached to it is a stone dais.

The longstanding belief that the small church itself was the site of coronations may be dismissed as mere supposition. However, the dais could well have been a convenient place to present the newly-crowned queens and kings to the people. Though much altered over time, its height and dimensions are essentially unchanged since the eleventh century.

It is highly possible that Adelaide knighted Roger on this spot, and she was not the only Hauteville consort of her era to raise her own son to knighthood.[248] Even inclement weather would not have dissuaded the people from witnessing such an event, and the dais could easily have been covered by a canopy if necessary.

We know little of the ceremony. It was performed late in 1111 or early in 1112, for we find Roger referred to as a both count and knight by the middle of the latter year.

While it was not yet a religious rite, its significance might be enhanced by the presence of a prelate and its proximity to a great church. In 1111, a certain Walter, possibly of Norman extraction, was consecrated Archbishop of Palermo, succeeding Alcherio who had died the previous year.

It may be that one of Roger's uncles girded him with a sword belt, removed the sword from its scabbard and handed it to him, with Adelaide then clutching his arm to raise it so that the sword's point was directed upward toward the heavens as she announced that her son was now a knight. Most of the people witnessing the event were Arabs who would have hailed Adelaide as *Malikah Adelida*.

Having reached the age of majority, Roger II was now old enough to rule in his own name as Great Count of Sicily.[249]

In 1112, not long after Adelaide had ceded the effective rule of Sicily and Calabria to Roger, envoys arrived from Baldwin I, King of Jerusalem, seeking her hand in marriage for their sovereign. That the proposal was endorsed by Arnulf of Chocques, the Latin Patriarch of Jerusalem, lent it legitimacy.[250]

The widowed Adelaide crossed the Mediterranean to marry King Baldwin of Jerusalem, who was desperately in need of Norman funds and soldiers. Since she was not yet forty and might still bear another child, she stipulated that a hypothetical son born of this union should inherit the Hierosolymitan crown, and that otherwise it would pass to Roger. Unbeknownst to Adelaide, the wily Baldwin, though lacking sons, was already married to an estranged spouse, Arda of Edessa, whom he had confined to a convent. This bigamy resulted in an annulment of his union with Adelaide, but not the restitution of her entire dowry, of which Baldwin kept the gold. The queen dowager returned to Sicily humiliated, if not broken-hearted, in 1117.[251]

Knightly Orders

While Roger was being knighted by Adelaide in Sicily, a novel form of knighthood was emerging in Palestine. In 1113, Pope Paschal II granted papal protection to the Knights Hospitaller, the Order of Saint John, who cared for sick pilgrims in the Holy Land and were establishing hospices around Europe along routes such as the *Via Francigena*.[252] This order of chivalry was a large company of knights which, though drawn from the nobility, formed a crusade-oriented corps that existed apart from any secular authority, even the King of Jerusalem.

Although many of its knights, clergy, serving brothers and nurses were from France and other parts of western Europe, the earliest roots of the Order of the Hospital of Saint John were to be found in the essentially Lombard culture around Salerno. Christian pilgrims and merchants were present in Jerusalem long before the First Crusade, and some Amalfitan traders helped to rebuild the city's chief hospice following its destruction by the zealous Fatimid caliph Abu Ali Mansur in 1005. Around 1080, a Benedictine named Gerard, who was born in the Duchy of Amalfi, became the head of the chief hospital, which the crusaders greatly enlarged during the first years of the twelfth century with financial support from Baldwin I, Roger Borsa and others.

By 1113, there were hospices of the order along the pilgrim route in Italy at Asti, Pisa, Bari, Otranto, Taranto and Messina. Some hospices of this kind eventually became conventual commanderies of the order similar to monasteries.

The same era saw the foundation of the Poor Soldiers of Christ of the Temple of Solomon. Like the Hospitallers, these Templars were based in Jerusalem but established a network of quasi-monastic commanderies, or preceptories, around Catholic Europe. They became known for their financial activities, introducing an Arab instrument, the *saqq*, from which the French *cheque* may derive, as a written promise of payment honored at any preceptory almost as if it were a branch of a bank. Although it seems that the *saqq* already existed amongst the Arabs of Sicily and Spain, it was a novelty in other regions of Europe.

The Order of Saint Lazarus was founded in Jerusalem around this time to care for lepers. Although it seems to have existed in an earlier form before assuming the nature of a knightly order, little of its history before the twelfth century is known with much certainty. It appears that some brethren of this order arrived in Sicily *circa* 1119 with Adelaide's support and were given the church and monastic complex of Saint John of the Lepers near Palermo, one of several leprosaria they eventually operated in Europe.[253]

Various disfiguring illnesses were certainly known, and it has long been believed that many conditions thought to be leprosy were misdiagnosed by medieval physicians. Godfrey, a son of Roger I, probably suffered from leprosy (see note 198), and Henry, the firstborn son of Frederick II, almost certainly did (see note 1101).

The Teutonic Order would be founded in the Holy Land later in the twelfth century, with commanderies in southern Italy and in the German lands. In the same vein, the Order of Santiago was founded as part of the *Re-*

conquista and to protect pilgrims traversing northern Spain to the shrine of Saint James (see note 284).

Apart their combat duties, each of these "military-religious" knightly orders shared a few characteristics. They were a natural outgrowth of the crusades, which brought European armies together in a common purpose. Destined to assume a significant role in Europe, they complemented the power of Christendom's monarchs but occasionally challenged it.

The knights and serving brothers of an order answered to an elected leader, a grand master, whose authority came from the pope rather than a king, duke or other monarch. The grand master dubbed knights of the order in a rite of investiture that was more religious than that of their enfeoffed "secular" counterparts, who were knighted by a monarch or even a baron and rendered military service in exchange for feudal tenure.

The papacy approved knightly orders as if, despite their military function, they were religious orders like the Franciscans or Dominicans. The knights followed a religious rule and took vows, hence the oxymoronic phrase "monks of war." The serving brothers and (eventually) serving sisters undertook the day-to-day work of the order, which might necessitate caring for the sick.

In the Holy Land, the Hospitallers and Templars had their own sovereign estates. It was in such a territory that the Hospitallers erected Krak des Chevaliers, their greatest castle, on the site of an older Kurdish fortress in what is now Syria.

Most of these knights were recruited from among the ranks of the landed nobility. In many cases, they were the younger sons of barons or enfeoffed knights. Under the Frankish system of feudal succession in force in most countries, younger sons, being "cadets," were excluded from inheriting familial property. Trained as knights but lacking land, they sought their fortunes farther afield. In the twelfth century, the eastern Mediterranean was about as far afield as a man from western Europe, even southern Italy, could get.

In addition to the knights, an order of this kind had serving brothers, clergy and others in its large organization. It also had a distinctly Christian, quasi-monastic character. Few saw what, to the modern mind, was the obvious contradiction in men whose Christianity formed the basis for their vocation prosecuting wars against "infidels," but such were the Middle Ages.

Compared to enfeoffed knights, who might not be rigidly dogmatic, the social orientation of knights in the orders reflected the Catholic principles and papal policies of the time. In that respect, and despite their military duties, they were monks in almost everything but name. Religious devotion, even to the point of zealotry, was not unusual. Indeed, it was a fundamental part of their *raison d'être*.[254]

To this day, the historical legacy of the medieval crusading orders, though significant, is complex, and not universally revered. The very idea of a devout Christian "monk" willing to kill "infidels" lends itself to contradictions. It has been suggested, however, that by the time the crusading era faded and the Kingdom of Jerusalem was dissolved toward the end of the thirteenth century many knights of the orders long resident in predominantly Arab lands, particularly the Templars, had grown culturally and socially sympathetic to the local populations.

In the rare case of an open conflict between order and crown, it was extremely unusual for a pope to take the position of an order's grand master against the authority of a king in his own realm.

Maturity

Roger was exercising his own authority as a true leader in Palermo, his principal residence as what was coming to be regarded as the "capital" of the County of Sicily.

Advised by the trusted *amiratus* Christodoulos, in effect a chancellor, Roger's first official acts would prove bold enough. Derived from the Arabic, the title of *amiratus* assumed a life of its own.[255]

Another advisor, slightly younger than Christodoulos, was George of Antioch, a man of Byzantine Greek ancestry born around 1090 in the city from which he took his name. After Antioch was conquered by Bohemond during the First Crusade, young George fled with his parents, Michael and Ninfa, to Ifriqiya. There Michael found himself a place in the service of the Zirid sultan, Tamim ibn al-Mu'izz. When the sultan's less accommodating son, Abu Ali Yahya ibn Tamim, succeeded in 1108, George and his family fell into disfavor at court and sought better fortunes in Sicily, where they were welcomed by Adelaide. George's knowledge of the Zirids would prove useful.

That Roger's cousin, William II of Apulia, likely lacked the benefit of advisors as competent as Christodoulos and George would partly explain why most chroniclers, as well as later historians, posit him to be a less able administrator. More so than Roger, William was plagued by baronial unrest. The first major incident was provoked by Jordan of Buonalbergo in 1112.

Jordan, who held the town of Ariano, was a grand-nephew of Alberarda, the first wife of Robert Guiscard.[256] As a cousin of the late Bohemond I of Antioch, with whom William's father, Roger Borsa, had feuded following the death of Guiscard, Jordan had long harbored a hereditary grudge against the branch of the Hauteville family he probably viewed as usurping that to which he was related by blood.

Ever since succeeding his father, Eribert, a decade earlier, Jordan had refused to formally submit to the authority of the Duke of Apulia, of whom he was a vassal. By 1112, he was in open rebellion, and encouraging other barons in his region to follow him. With his sometime ally, Robert of Alife, he also attacked Benevento.[257]

At about seventeen, William was approximately the same age as Roger. Like his cousin, he relied upon older, experienced counsellors for advice. They suggested that he solicit Roger for help. This would come at a price.

For the moment, Jordan thought better of openly defying the joint Hauteville forces arrayed against him, but he would continue to prove troublesome, interfering in the affairs of Capua, itself now defiant of William's authority and desiring to be ruled by the Holy Roman Emperor. He also harassed some towns around Ariano.

For inspiration, William need only have looked to the west, where his cousin, Raymond Berenguer III of Barcelona (see Table 26), took the Balearic Islands from their Muslim masters in 1114 with the assistance of the Pisans. Unfortunately, an Almoravid force repossessed them two years later.

To the south, Roger was learning how to use power. In 1114, he deposed the Archbishop of Cosenza even though this diocese, being in Calabria, was beyond his jurisdiction as apostolic legate of Sicily.[258]

William, meanwhile, had to suppress a revolt in the city of Bari, whose Byzantines, led by a local man named Grimoald Alferanites, son of a certain Guaranca, were beginning to rebel against him.[259] Like Jordan, Grimoald was a problem that would not be eliminated easily. Whereas Jordan was a disgruntled feudal lord in search of land, Grimoald was a charismatic manipulator capable of persuading the populace of a major city to accept an ideology of independence.

In the same year, just before his twentieth birthday, William wed Gaitelgrima, the daughter of Robert of Alife (see Table 4). This union may have been part of an attempt at an alliance with Robert who, despite being William's vassal, sometimes affiliated himself with his nemesis, Jordan of Buonalbergo, who was still in rebellion. Robert died the following year. His son, and hence William's brother-in-law, Ranulf II, who, for now, opposed Jordan, wed Matilda Hauteville, Roger's sister.

Roger's Norman counsellors were also making an effort to find him a suitable spouse, not that he lacked for female companionship, since the palace had a harem.[260]

On the mainland, William endowed the abbey at Cava with lands while Roger continued to support monasteries in Sicily.

There was no obvious role awaiting Adelaide in Sicily, where she retired to one of the nunneries under her patronage, the Holy Savior Convent, which her husband, Roger, had founded. This was located outside the town of Patti. It was a tranquil environment nestled between the coast and the foothills of the Nebrodian Mountains. Here Adelaide had her own small castle.

The dowager Queen of Jerusalem found time to attend her son's wedding in Palermo during the autumn of 1117.[261] Arguably, Adelaide's presence made this the first major "royal" event to be held in the Sicilian capital.

The woman Roger married would have an impact on her husband and her adopted country. Elvira Jiménez of Castile (see Table 11) wed Roger when she was around seventeen and he was twenty-two. Born in Toledo, she was the daughter of Alfonso VI "the Brave," King of Castile and León, by his fourth wife, Isabel, the former Zaida of Seville, a Muslim widow who was previously the monarch's mistress.[262]

Isabel died while Elvira was still a child, leaving her to be raised amongst half-siblings. One of them, Elvira's elder half-sister Urraca "the Reckless," succeeded as queen regnant (and generally regarded as the first woman in Europe to attain this status) upon Alfonso's death in 1109, being his heiress.[263]

Urraca wasn't too reckless to oversee Elvira's betrothal to Roger, although she probably left the details to her courtiers. Thus began a connection between Sicily and Spain that would last for centuries, bringing the island nearer the Iberian orbit than the Italian one.

In many ways, twelfth-century Palermo was not too different from the Spanish cities known to Elvira. It had much in common with the dominions of northern Spain, everything from the climate to the cuisine to the diversity of her peoples.

By the time Elvira was born at the dawn of the twelfth century, several branches of her father's Jiménez dynasty ruled much of northern Spain, the greenest part of the Iberian peninsula, vying for power with rival dynasties, both Christian and Muslim.[264] The family's roots were Navarrese, and the Jiménez were closely connected to polycultural Pamplona, a city of Christians, Muslims and Jews.

The population of Toledo, Elvira's birthplace, boasted a comparable diversitude. By now, however, Iberian *convivencia* was becoming ever more fragile. The Christians were beginning to embrace the idea of the crusade, while the Moors were adopting a form of jihad. Important cities like Zaragoza, in Aragon, were under Christian control one moment and Muslim domination the next. Despite occasional truces, the ruling Jiménez cousins sometimes found themselves at odds with each other.

Elvira barely knew her mother-in-law. Adelaide died peacefully at Patti on the sixteenth of April in 1118. She is entombed in the medieval church dedicated to Saint Bartholomew which became the cathedral.[265]

The end of Adelaide's life saw Elvira giving birth to a new one, a son christened Roger. For now, matrimony and fatherhood would prove to be the most reliable things that Elvira's husband faced.

We don't know know what killed Adelaide, but her sorrow would have been sufficient for the task. His mother's disgrace doubtless formed Roger's opinion about the Kingdom of Jerusalem and its administration, and whether he would ever assist Baldwin or his successors. Nor did the episode endear him to the ecclesiastical hierarchy that permitted an uncanonical, indeed unlawful, marriage to take place in a kingdom founded on Christian, nay Roman Catholic, principles. Presently, however, Roger had more immediate concerns nearer to home.

This charter issued by Adelaide in 1109 in Greek and Arabic is the oldest surviving paper document in Italy and one of the oldest in Europe (Spain has earlier exemplars). The damaged seal may be Adelaide's.

Ἀδελάσια χομητήσσα καλαβριας χαὶ σιχελίας
Διορξζωμεν χαὶ τοῖς πᾶσιν ἐξονσιασταῖς βεοχομίτοις
πᾶσι τε χαὶ χάϊτες τῆς ἡμετέρας χώρας χαςτροιωάν
νου τοῖς νῦν οὖσι χαὶ τοῖς μέλλουσι ταύτην ἔγχειρ
ξζεσε εἰς τὴν ἐμὴν δουλείαν
ἀναχολύτως ἰ ἀρεστὸν μὴ ἐνοχλούμενοι παρά τινων
ἐρχόμενοι ἀλλὰ μᾶλλον βοήφειαν παρέχειν αὐτοῖς
ἀιτήσεως χαὶ τῆς ταύτης περιλείψεως τοῦ δὲ
ἐστερξα
τὸ παρὸν
ἔνταλμα βουλλωθὲν χαὶ σφραγισθὲν τῇ συνήθεν
ἡμῶν διαχηρῶ βούλλη μηνὶ μαρτίω εἰς τὰς ινδιχτιῶνι
β'οὖσης μου εἰς μεσίνην.

بسم الله الرحمن الرحيم

هذا كتاب من السيدة الجليلة ملكة صقلية وقلاورية الناصرة
لدين النصرانية

قد امرنا الى كل من قرى كتابنا هذا او قرى عليه
العمال والقواد الذين هم فى خدمتنا والمصرفين فى اوامرنا
و فيما يعد بقصريانة الى   الرهبان المقيمين
يدينى القديس فيلب الذى بدمنش بخندق السنهارشى

فقد امرنا فى ستة خلون من
مرطيوس الذى من الحول الثانى
المخبرتون بالشمع ح

Adelaide's charter of 1109 transcribed by Salvatore Cusa in 1868

Polycultural Palermo: Tombstone of 1148 inscribed in Greek, Arabic, Latin, and a form of Hebrew bearing Judeo-Arabic elements.

Chapter 10
GEOPOLITICS

The long absence of his mother, and her death shortly after returning from Jerusalem, left no doubt that Roger was making his own decisions about how to govern his dominions, though he certainly had help. Advisors such as the two Greeks, Christodoulos and George, complemented by some Sicilian Arabs at court, would plot a course through the treacherous political waters to the south, east and west of Sicily, and even its north. There were likely also a few of Elvira's countrymen present who were familiar with the Almoravids to the immediate south of Castile.

Flexing Muscles

Whilst his cousin, William II of Apulia, was a duke, Roger was still a count, technically a lower rank despite his exercise of *de facto* sovereignty over most of Sicily. The size and importance of a domain was more significant, in real terms, than the title associated with it. The County of Ariano, held by William's vassal Jordan of Buonalbergo, could not be compared to Roger's County of Sicily.

During this period, we find William generally using Salerno as his administrative base for the Duchy of Apulia, with Roger usually at Palermo, the "capital" of the County of Sicily. Since the time of Robert Guiscard, William's branch of the family had enjoyed certain rights in both Palermo and Messina, and possession of the *duchy* of Calabria, the northern part of that region, while Roger had inherited the *county*, or southern part.

Vestiges of the past, these territorial jurisdictions, if far from perfect, were reasonably efficient for the moment. Yet their nomenclature was slightly misleading. Salerno was not in the geographic Apulia (Puglia) region, and Roger's rule of Sicily did not include the areas belonging to William.

The Arabs referred to Roger as *malik,* the same word they usually used for a king; the phrase "emir of emirs," as we have seen, came to be used for the *amiratus,* Roger's chief counsellor. Sigurd I of Norway, whom we met earlier, probably learned the Arabic word during his stay in Palermo, and is said to have recognized Roger as a king (see note 245). This certainly reflected the count's importance, and in some minds kingship may have been lurking around a corner. Yet Roger was already exercising the duties of a monarch, albeit without a royal title, and his Sicilian dominion, more so than Calabria, was beginning to resemble a kingdom or principality in its government and social culture, largely because of the Arabs' esteem for a ruler who, though a Christian, respected them and even mastered their language. Nowhere was this more the case than in Palermo which, after all, had been the seat of the Kalbid emirate, from which Roger inherited institutions such as the *diwan*.[266]

The Favara palace was a tangible reminder of this legacy, just as William had inherited the Lombards' Arechi Castle overlooking Salerno and the catepan's palace in Bari. Little could compete with the luxury of Roger's chief palace in Palermo. Not only did he live like a king, Roger was soon acting like one, a reality that could not have escaped the notice of the people who visited him in his prosperous capital. Roger and his advisors had little time to cultivate a close relationship with William's camp. That the two cousins were never very close, either socially or geographically, would strain their rapport. For the moment, Roger was not looking north but south.

In 1116, Abu Ali Yahya ibn Tamim, the Sultan of Ifriqiya, was assassinated, possibly by two or three of the brothers he had exiled; the murderers have never been identified with certainty. Yahya had made many enemies during his sixteen-year reign, waging war against Berbers and Europeans alike. In the event, he was succeeded as sultan by his son, Ali ibn Yahya. Present to eulogize the deceased Zirid leader was the self-exiled Sicilian poet, Abd al Gabbar ibn Muhammad ibn Hamdis al-Azdi al-Siqilli.[267]

Until now, Roger II of Sicily and his cousin, the Duke of Apulia, may have been on reasonably good terms with their Tunisian neighbors, if only for the sake of commerce. There were Sicilian commercial agents in Mahdia to ensure the efficient movement of the ships arriving and departing the busy port and to collect fees. Despite the smooth transition from one Zirid generation to another, however, dissent was brewing within Ifriqiya's ruling class. Some of this was born of complexities in their relations with other Muslims, notably the Almoravids and Hammadids to their west, but certain controversies reflected longstanding grievances against Christian mercantile powers such as Genoa and, more recently, Norman Sicily. There were also internal rivalries, some provoked by economic realities and the growth of certain cities.

Rafi ibn Makken al Dahmani, the incumbent governor of coastal Gabés, an inveterate rival of Ali ibn Yahya and his late father, was not kindly disposed to the trade agreement that had existed for decades between the Zirids and the Hautevilles. Specifically, it was Rafi's desire to develop his city into a "free" port somewhat independent of the sultan, whose trade monopoly he clearly resented. To that end, he built merchant ships and expanded the harbor. Even before this audacious initiative, while raffish Rafi was viewed as something of a rogue, little action was taken against him. One of the new vessels he constructed was especially ostentatious, gigantic compared to the others. This drew a response from Ali despite his late father having supported the enterprise.[268]

What is more, Rafi was making overtures to Roger for a separate trade treaty, competing with, and perhaps even undermining, the existing one. By 1117, despite negotiations with Ali, Sicily was effectively banished from the lucrative Tunisian market for her grain pending a new arrangement which Rafi was only too happy to provide. The economic consequences of this development may also have been felt in Calabria and the Duchy of Apulia.

Until this point, it does not seem to have been the intention of Roger's government to involve itself in the politics of Ifriqiya. Whether Roger himself was inclined by nature to sponsor a policy of expansionism beyond his own dominions cannot be known, but the loss of Sicily's chief agricultural trade market forced his hand. Rebuffed by Ali, he would treat with Rafi.[269]

For the moment, however, he was busy issuing charters establishing Catholic churches and monasteries across Sicily and Calabria, tasks he could perform at his palace in Palermo.[270]

Papal Rome was in one of its frequent periods of controlled chaos. Following the death of Pope Paschal II in January 1118, the papacy was contested by two men. Gelasius II (John Caetani), a monk of Mount Cassino and longtime assistant to the late Paschal, was generally accepted as the lawful pope, but he was challenged by the antipope, Gregory VIII (Maurice Bourdin), whose partisans favored the Holy Roman Emperor, Henry V, in the seemingly endless Investiture Controversy.

The Hautevilles, of course, supported Gelasius, who fled southward to Gaeta, his birthplace, in March 1118. Under Norman protection, he returned to Rome in July. Unfortunately, he was soon forced to escape again when the city's powerful Frangipani family tried to kill him. This time he went to France, where he died early the next year, and Guy of Burgundy, a member of one of Europe's most important families, was elected as Callixtus II. Here was a fortuitous connection, for Guy's elder brother, Raymond, now deceased, had been married to Urraca of Castile (see Table 11), the older half-sister of Elvira, Roger's wife. This made Roger the pope's brother-in-law, but by now Urraca, Queen of Castile in her own right, was wed to her second husband, a Jiménez cousin.[271]

Callixtus proved to be a competent pontiff. At the Concordat of Worms in 1122, he ended the Investiture Controversy. The next year he convened the First Lateran Council. It proscribed concubinage and marriage among the clergy, and simony, but in this effort Callixtus would prove no more successful than his predecessors. The council also tried to enforce the "Truce of God" proposed during the previous century; this prohibited warfare on holy days, Saturdays and Sundays. An allied concept was the "Peace of God."[272]

Trouble in Apulia

Jordan of Buonalbergo, who had his own private feud with William's brother-in-law, Ranulf II of Alife, was hardly the only thorn in William's side. Much of his ducal dominion was in chaos and he lacked the manpower to bring it under control.

In theory, there should have been enough enfeoffed knights in the extended Duchy of Apulia, which included Basilicata and much of Campania as well as Puglia and a piece of northern Calabria, to constitute a strong army for William. Unfortunately, much of his territory had fallen into disarray, and some of the barons who should have been loyal to him were apathetic about his rule.

In August 1115, in view of William's failure to pacify his dominions, the pope had to impose the fragile "Truce of God" upon the unruly city of Troia and all of Apulia for a term of three years.[273] The effects of this effort would prove minimal, as if feral dogs fighting over a piece of meat could be moved by stern words to desist.

Seditious Grimoald Alferanites may have been behind the assassination of Risone, the Archbishop of Bari, in 1117, by a certain Argiro who led a band of rebels. The next year, Grimoald proclaimed himself prince of the city.[274] The *soi-disant* "prince" then began negotiating with the Venetians for diplomatic recognition, as if Bari were a sovereign power.

In August 1119, Grimoald's rebels even kidnapped Constance, the widow of Bohemond I of Antioch, imprisoning her in the fortress at coastal Giovinazzo north of Bari, probably in reprisal for having taken unlawful possession of some towns in the region, and perhaps even part of the city itself (see note 285). The small force William sent to rescue her was unsuccessful and perhaps not highly motivated to defend the duchy. Only papal intervention, and Constance's renunciation of her regency over the Principality of Taranto for her young son, Bohemond II, secured her release. However, the pope used this opportunity to constrain William to restore some lands to the monastery of Saint Nicholas at Troia.

There was a grave risk of these uprisings spreading to Roger's Calabrian lands. In 1121, he crossed over to the peninsula to suppress a revolt at San Marco (now San Marco Argentano). Located in northern Calabria, this fortified town, where a Norman tower still stands, was the birthplace, and later a fief, of the late Bohemond I of Antioch. It was claimed by both Roger and William. The rebels at San Marco were merely taking advantage of the chaos that was growing in southern peninsular Italy.

This conflict over the town of San Marco was resolved by the mediation of Pope Callixtus.[275] Other problems were not so easily remedied. In seven years of marriage, William's wife had not conceived a child.

There were greater threats to William's authority than the rebellion of a Calabrian locality. In 1121, Jordan of Buonalbergo, who had agreed to the pope's "Truce of God" but, like most of the barons, soon reneged on his promise, razed the town of Nusco, near his own fief of Ariano, and was now threatening to attack William directly.

In theory, there should have been enough enfeoffed knights in the extended Duchy of Apulia to constitute a sufficiently strong army for William. Unfortunately, much of his dominion had fallen into disarray. There simply weren't enough loyal knights to form an effective fighting force. So grave was the lack of confidence in William among the baronage that some of his vassals wanted to transfer their feudal allegiance to the pope, effectively crumbling the duchy into pieces as if it were a stale *biscotto*.

Most — but by no means all — of the grievances against the Hautevilles by vassals and other subjects fell into one of three broad categories.

Firstly, and most notably, there was a widespread, underlying resentment of the ruling family amongst the senior ranks of the baronage. True, there were personal, localized motives for particular complaints, but some Norman barons seem to have been envious of a family which, like their own, had begun as simple knights and mercenaries, only to emerge as a ruling dynasty. Certain other barons, particularly those descended chiefly from Lombards, may have been instilled by their fathers and grandfathers with a discreet nostalgia for the princes of Salerno, and in some instances this provoked a subtle antipathy toward the Normans even if, by around 1120, this kind of "ethnic" bias was rarely very blatant amongst the amalgamated population of Catholics in southern Italy outside the Byzantine sphere.

Secondly, there were disgruntled segments of the Grecophone population, especially in Bari and its environs, if less so in Calabria and Sicily, that desired a closer link to Constantinople. Many of these Byzantine Greeks clung stubbornly to their faith traditions and language while rebelling against feudalism, taxation and other strictures imposed by the Norman administration. A few wanted to restore the catepanate. By contrast, the Latinization of Sicily's Christians, though constant, was altogether more nuanced; Roger could afford to be more accommodating than William by permitting the Grecophone abbey of Saint Philip, in the Nebrodian Mountains, to retain much of its Byzantine character. Southern Calabria also enjoyed a certain latitude in this regard, hence the case of Theophanes Kerameus (whom we met in Chapter 4).

Thirdly, there were large cities like Capua, and wealthy baronies in regions such as Molise, particularly (but not exclusively) on the fringes of the Hauteville dominions, that were not firmly integrated into the evolving Norman state and had no wish to be part of a centralized monarchy. Troia and Brindisi, and certainly Naples and Amalfi, were governed almost as if they were communes like Genoa and Pisa. The acceptance of Hauteville rule in these places was long in coming. Many barons, especially those related to the Hautevilles, acted independently simply because they could. This was little more than opportunism in areas where the power structure had been fragmented, with William controlling some regions and Constance, as the regent for Bohemond II, more influential in others. The "fluid" frontiers, with borders between counties and baronies delineated only imprecisely in many charters, only worsened matters, as we saw in the quarrel over San Marco Argentano.[276] Yet some areas enjoyed a certain stability. With the San Marco dispute resolved, Calabria was quite serene. The environs of Salerno, William's city, were generally free of violence.

These are merely generalities. The reasons that might explain certain cases of resentment or dissent by specific barons, perhaps leading to open hostility, have been lost to time; there may well have been localized incidents that were unknown to the chroniclers and unreported in extant charters. Nevertheless, baronial rebellion, in one form or another, would plague the essential foundations of Hauteville rule for some years to come, particularly in the mainland dominions, and it cannot be said to be a rare phenomenon anywhere in western Europe.[277]

Compared to the revolts among the Christian population, protests by Muslims in Sicily were far less frequent during this period. Despite some occasional dissent, the Muslims rarely contested the Hautevilles' right to rule so much as specific policies. This may be explained, in part, by the fact that the Hautevilles' most vocal critics among Sicily's Muslims, viewing their political prospects as hopeless, had left the island, residing in self-imposed exile in the Islamic monarchies of northern Africa, with a few ending up as far away as Iberia or Asia.

The Jews of southern Italy, being a tiny minority of the population, rarely staged mass protests. They were, in a sense, "protected" by the archbishops in larger cities such as Palermo and Bari, even if this arrangement masked a form of exploitation (see note 180).

Obviously enough, the Bariot riots were a backlash against the imposition of Latin culture, particularly that expressed through Catholicism. In this respect, the unrest was rooted chiefly in religious differences. Politically and socially, the situation in Apulia, once a province of the Byzantine Empire, was fundamentally different from that of Sicily, where the Grecophone population had been part of a Fatimid emirate, its bishops sometimes under the jurisdiction of Cyprus rather than Constantinople. Indeed, as we have seen, Adelaide and Roger II made greater efforts to accommodate the Byzantine Greeks in Sicily than Roger Borsa and William II, subjected to more rigorous papal scrutiny, seem to have attempted in Apulia.

Beyond Bari and its neighboring cities, this opposition was somewhat factionalized. Only rarely did one group of William's detractors make common cause with another, even if their interests and objectives sometimes overlapped. Dissent was part of a disturbing trend nurtured by what seems to have been a baronial perception of William as an ineffective leader, but it was not a highly organized "movement." Except for Grimoald, none of the renegades publicly proclaimed himself a prince or duke, and only a major city like Bari offered the setting that might facilitate such a gesture.

Elsewhere, dissent was precipitated by circumstances that, arguably, may be seen as more legitimately "political" or juridical, and less subjective. This was the case in the Italian regions north of the Papal State ruled by the Holy Roman Emperor, Henry V, whose wife, Matilda of England (whom we met earlier), sometimes served as his regent for the imperial communes. In November 1120, Matilda became heiress to the English throne when the "White Ship" transporting over two hundred across the English Channel sunk, leaving her brother, William Adelin, the heir apparent of Henry I of England, among the dead. In the wake of this disaster, Matilda was designated her father's successor, effectively a "crown princess" (though that term was not used) destined to become queen regnant. Many nobles and prelates opposed the very idea of a woman ruling the country in her own right.[278]

Clearly, southern Italy was not unique in being unsettled. The first decades of Europe's twelfth century were rife with conflict, which was something of a zeitgeist of its era. By any measure, the Hautevilles' unification of southern Italy was a tortuous process.

In February of 1122, William and Roger met in Messina to discuss a strategy for bringing peace to the duchy. In exchange for military support from Roger, William ceded to him northern Calabria, along with the full right to that territorial title, and his manors in Sicily. This also included the half of the city of Palermo, with its tax revenue, that William had inherited from his grandfather, Robert Guiscard, through Roger Borsa.[279]

In law, William had been Duke of Apulia and Calabria, while Roger was Count of Sicily and Calabria. Henceforth, William was Duke of Apulia while Roger was Duke of Calabria and Count of Sicily.

The childless William also made Roger his heir. By now, Elvira had given birth to two more sons: Tancred in 1119, Alfonso in 1121. She eventually had at least one daughter, Adelisa (or Adelaide).

Part of Roger's recently-assembled army was already in Calabria and therefore prepared to attack. Making their way northward, his forces, led by William, consisted of some seven hundred knights, accompanied by hundreds of lethal Arab archers. This army assaulted and reclaimed towns held by Jordan and his allies: Roseto, Montegiove, Apice. Ariano, Montecorvino and others followed. Confronted by such a force, Jordan finally submitted to William's authority. At Montevico, the Duke of Apulia punished the people who had killed Warren of Ollia, a Norman baron. These actions pacified Campania and Lucania but not Apulia proper, where the Bariots and a few barons continued to resist. Parts of Molise and Abruzzo were also acting independently.

While the Capuans, who were supposed to be loyal to William, failed to support him, the Beneventans, with papal encouragement, did so. Whatever challenges the Hautevilles faced, the papacy was not prepared to let them fall to the vagaries of odium and factionalism.

Roger's Campaigns

Sicily and Calabria were now consolidated into what, in modern terms, would be considered a prosperous unitary state. The same could not be said of William's Duchy of Apulia where, in 1122, the "principality" of Bari was formally recognized by the Venetians as a sovereignty, even if, across the Adriatic, the Byzantine Emperor John II Comnenus (see Table 6), son of the late Alexios II, was reluctant to legitimize the schismatic state by following suit.

By most accounts, John was a sage monarch. The Comnenus dynasty, like the Hautevilles, had seen its share of contestations and intrigues amongst its kin. If actions speak more loudly than words, the fact that neither John nor

Roger named people in their families to the most important administrative posts suggests a certain pragmatism.

John, like Roger, had his own challenges to confront in the form of an ambitious Muslim power to his immediate south; he would prove largely successful in restoring part of the empire that had been lost to the Seljuk Sultanate of Rum, which was Turkic in origin but essentially Persian culturally.

Whereas John's foes were entrenched chiefly in Asia Minor and would be fought mostly in land battles, Roger's adversaries controlled northern coastal Africa and boasted naval power capable of harassing, even attacking, Sicily and Calabria.

As we have seen, when the Zirids of Ifriqiya abruptly withdrew from a trade agreement with Sicily in 1117 in search of more favorable terms, Rafi ibn Makken al Dahmani, the governor of Gabés, sought to establish a separate treaty of his own with Roger. Ifriqiya's growing population and occasional famines had long made Sicily's hard wheat a product worth acquiring. Nevertheless, the political winds were changing.

It was likely Roger's shipping agents in Ifriqiya who sent news to Palermo that the sultan, Ali ibn Yahya, was stifling Rafi's plans, and so interrupting shipments between Gabés and Sicily. As a display of force, and to show his support for Rafi, Roger sent a flotilla to Ifriqiya early in 1118, ostentatiously sailing past Mahdia *en route* to Gabés to ensure that Ali learned of the trade agreement his rival had signed with Sicily.

With this, Ali immediately attacked Gabés, but the Sicilians, choosing to avoid direct involvement in a domestic dispute, refrained from defending Rafi militarily and returned to the port of Mazara in Sicily.

Despite Zirid attempts to enlist the Fatimid Caliphate in Cairo, with which the County of Sicily had a good relationship, to intervene diplomatically on behalf of Ifriqiya, an angry exchange of letters followed between Roger and Ali ibn Yahya. This resolved nothing. Indeed, the sultan found Roger's tone arrogant and insulting. The damage may have been more moral than material, but it prompted Ali to solicit the aid of the Almoravids of Morocco. Roger's rapport with the Fatimid Caliphate, which received George of Antioch as his emissary, precluded any attacks from Egyptian quarters, but in the spring of 1122 an Almoravid fleet raided the Calabrian coast. At Nicotera, the killing, raping and enslaving of many residents was an eerie reprise of the assaults of the previous century.

This action was not instigated by Ali ibn Yahya, who had recently died, or his young son and successor, Abul-Hasan al-Hasan ibn Ali. It was the work of the new leadership in Ifriqiya, in collaboration with the more powerful Almoravids. Nevertheless, it was not beneath the Zirids of Ifriqiya to use piracy as a source of revenue when legitimate trade was lacking.

Retaliation was inevitable. Although Roger had never undertaken a coastal attack, his advisors were encouraged by the successful Venetian assault on the Fatimids in May 1123 at Ascalon, where they acquired a number of galleys.[280]

Led by Christodoulos and George, a large Sicilian fleet set sail from Marsala, whose name means "Port of Allah," and attacked the coast of Ifriqiya in the summer of 1123. As if by an act of Allah, an unseasonal storm blew many of the ships off course, and those that reached the shore were largely ineffectual. A battle that followed at fortified al-Dimas, near Mahdia, left the Sicilian force defeated.

The only beneficial impact of this debacle was to show the Zirids and others that Roger was willing to respond to Arab piracy by attacking Ifriqiya itself. Despite the losses, the island of Pantelleria was seized, becoming a Sicilian dominion.[281]

Trouncing a Siculo-Norman force near Ifriqiya's highly-populated capital may have boosted morale amongst the local people who witnessed it, but the gradual decline of the Zirid sultanate's political power was inexorable. Whether Roger and Christodoulos envisaged this attack as a territorial invasion is a matter of debate, but they set about fortifying windy Pantelleria (see note 171). Like Malta, this was a useful outpost.

An isolated element of Ifriqiya's leadership seems to have maintained discreet contact with the Sicilian court in the hopes of healing the diplomatic rift.[282] Trade eventually resumed, though, for the moment, without the major wheat shipments from Sicily. Sicilian commerce also existed with the Fatimids to the east. The Jews of Sicily and Calabria continued to facilitate what was, in practice, their own Mediterranean trading network. Certain Maliki legal principles governed trade between the Europeans and the Muslim states of northern Africa, the most significant writings of the time being those of the Sicilian jurist Muhammad al-Maziri, who is entombed in Monastir on the Tunisian coast and commemorated in Mazara, presumed to be his birthplace.[283]

Roger II wasn't the only Christian ruler to contend with the Almoravids. In Spain, his sister-in-law, Urraca of Castile and León, was enjoined by Diego Gelmírez, the Archbishop of Santiago de Compostela, to support a crusade preached by the zealous prelate, who was the guardian of the queen's son, as part of the revived *Reconquista* of Al-Andalus, Muslim Iberia.[284]

The ill-fated African campaign wasn't the only action that Roger was called upon to take against those who doubted his strength of will. Another conflict was spawned by the usual fickle alliances and avaricious barons.

Montescaglioso was an inland city in southeastern Lucania, not far from Taranto, seized from the Byzantines during the previous century and long held by a certain Rudolf "Maccabeo," who was wed to Roger's elder half-sister, Emma (see Table 8). Following her husband's death without heirs, Emma herself governed this manor and other territories until her own death. In 1124, Roger's claim to this inheritance was challenged by three of his distant cousins, the brothers Alexander, Tancred and Robert of Conversano, who had been rewarded with manors by Constance, the widow of Bohemond I, for defending the rights of her young son, Bohemond II, in the region around Taranto. It is likely that Constance had usurped several towns that did not belong to the boy by right. This irritated the Bariots, who sought to control the localities around their city, and they took the mother of the three Conversano brothers hostage, releasing the woman when her sons arrived to rescue her.[285] (As we have seen, Grimoald's co-conspirators had even kidnapped Constance herself.)

The threat of military action by an army led by Christodoulos was sufficient to enforce Roger's claim to Montescaglioso. However, in gaining possession of the town, Roger was not infringing on William's ducal prerogatives. This was simply a familial feudal inheritance from Emma.[286] Yet the bitterness lingered, with the names of the Conversano brothers added to a growing list of Roger's detractors.

Pope Callixtus II died in December 1124. Amongst his other accomplishments, he issued the bull *Sicut Judaeis* to defend Jews in Europe in view of attacks against them connected with the First Crusade against "infidels." This protected the Jews themselves, as well as their property, synagogues, mikvehs and cemeteries, and affirmed their rights to practice their religion. It proscribed Catholics, on pain of excommunication, from committing such acts or forcing conversions. Papal directives of this kind had been issued over the centuries.[287]

The next pontiff, the learned Honorius II, born Lamberto Scannabecchi, would prove to be rigid in his opinions and politics. He showed no reluctance to intervene in ecclesiastical affairs in France, England and Spain. In Italy, he was willing to lead troops against his own papal vassals when he deemed it necessary.

Although the Investiture Controversy had been resolved, the death of the Holy Roman Emperor, Henry V, without a generally-accepted successor, in May 1125, led to a struggle for the imperial crown that lasted for years. Henry, the last of his Salian dynasty to rule, was survived by his wife, Matilda of England. Lacking a son, he had named his nephew, Frederick "the One-Eyed" Hohenstaufen, Duke of Swabia, as his heir (see Table 3). Instead, Lothair III of Supplinburg, Duke of Saxony, was elected, becoming King of the Germans and then emperor.[288] It wasn't long before a vocal faction in Germany began to support Frederick's younger brother, Conrad III, to be king.

The same year found Honorius using military force to subdue Ceccano and some other towns to the south of Rome near Frosinone based on reports of their lords mistreating the local people. Unrest continued in this region for the next few years as the vassals resisted papal authority.[289]

Certain disturbances had a particularly unforgiving effect on the common folk. In October 1125, a major earthquake shook the Benevento area, with weeks of aftershocks. Some may have viewed this as divine punishment for one sin or another. That Benevento was a papal city made it easy to blame the new pontiff.[290]

Constance of France had died in September, leaving her son, Bohemond II, who was about seventeen, to begin planning to finally return to Antioch, a journey he would make a year later. He did not renounce Taranto, which the Bariots coveted.

Not every papal rival in southern Italy was a prince, duke or bishop. Sometimes it was the abbot of Mount Cassino, the largest abbey in Italy and certainly the most powerful, who challenged a pope. While the Normans supported Mount Cassino and endowed its monastic foundations, the abbey was in papal territory. The Hautevilles and their vassals made a very obvious effort to introduce orders besides the Benedictines in their dominions, partly to avoid facilitating undue influence by granting a monopoly over monastic life to a single community. Pope Honorius had a longstanding feud with Oderisio of Sangro, the abbot of Mount Cassino, rooted in a number of personal differences. Most recently, he resented the refusal of the abbot to assist with the costs entailed in the military campaigns around Ceccano. After deposing Oderisio, the pontiff excommunicated him.[291]

In September 1126, Bohemond II departed for the Holy Land, where he wed Alice, the daughter of Baldwin II of Jerusalem, leaving Taranto, Otranto and Brindisi to the care of Alexander of Conversano.[292]

In July 1127, William II, Duke of Apulia, died in Salerno of natural causes. His widow cut her hair short as a sign of mourning and the pope claimed the duchy as a sign of victory. It may well be that William II bequeathed the duchy to different parties at different times (but see note 279). Whatever the case, this was the catalyst for a chain of unpleasant events.

The "usual suspects" in the baronage of Puglia, Molise, Abruzzi and Basilicata rebelled, almost instinctively, against Roger's succession, which was rooted in feudal practice and Salic Law as well as William's public declaration five years earlier. William's widow is not known to have contested Roger's right, nor do many elements in the populace of Salerno seem to have done so. However, the city's archbishop, Romuald I, was reluctant to endorse Roger, who was invested as duke by a suffragan, Alfano, the Bishop of Capaccio, despite papal approbation.[293] As an expedient shortcut to ensure that he would obtain the baronial support he needed in the region, Roger entrusted his brother-in-law, Ranulf of Alife, with the exercise of a kind of lordship over Roger Buonalbergo of Ariano and several other vassals who might otherwise be tempted to oppose him.

As one might expect, Grimoald Alferanites, the "Prince of Bari," joined the dissenting barons. Predictably, the Capuans, who had often opposed Hauteville rule in recent times, chose not to support Roger. This attitude was reinforced by Honorius actively instigating Capua's resistance. At least a few barons supported the papacy out of fear of Roger, who was known to use military force more frequently than William. Deprived of prosperous Montescaglioso a few years earlier, the Conversano clan exemplified this antipathy.

However, the two most influential feudal vassals to oppose Roger were Robert II of Capua, his distant cousin, and Ranulf II of Alife, his brother-in-law (see Table 4 for both), who justified their stance by citing the "crusade" preached against him by Pope Honorius in November 1127, which was followed by excommunication the next month. These facts made a convenient pretext, even a justification, for disloyalty because, according to the strictest interpretation of canon law, vassals were not obligated to respect their pledge of fealty to an excommunicated suzerain.

There were other motivations. Ranulf may have been irritated at not having received Ariano, which Roger seems to have promised him. This county was now held by the son of the late Jordan of Buonalbergo, Ranulf's onetime ally. Ranulf was in a unique position, being the brother-in-law of both Roger II and William II.

Robert, for his part, had been promised the Duchy of Apulia by Pope Honorius, who may even have invested him with it. This was a seductive prize. The kinship between Ranulf and Robert as part of the same Drengot family, though likely less important to the two men than these material considerations, was still another factor in the mix.

Sergio VII of Naples, being accustomed to William's *laissez-faire* approach to overlordship of that growing port city, wavered at first, reluctant to embrace Roger's rule, but he was not as intransigent as some of the others.[294]

The papal rantings were afforded a flimsy veneer of ecclesiastical legitimacy because after the pontiff announced his opposition to Roger's succession to the duchy, the latter banned the Sicilian bishops from going to him. This allowed Honorius, with a morsel of credibility, to accuse Roger of undermining papal authority over the episcopal hierarchy.

Given that the whole of the duchy was in rebellion except for the area around Salerno, where he was recognized as prince and duke, Roger left some troops in that city while he returned to Sicily to raise an army sufficient for a major campaign. The pope, meanwhile, raised an army which gathered with him in Benevento early in 1128.

Domestic matters were not Roger's only concern. He was cultivating alliances with other rulers. To that end, he sent his kinsman Raymond Berenguer III, Count of Barcelona, fifteen ships to fight the Muslims along the Iberian coast.[295]

Having raised a formidable force in Sicily, Roger led his army into Puglia and Basilicata in the spring of 1128. Though he undertook to subdue the rebels, whose armies may not have been as large as his own, he sought to avoid pitched battles, especially against the papal forces.[296]

In May or June, he took Taranto, Otranto and Brindisi despite these important cities belonging to the absent Bohemond II. Only at Brindisi, effectively the domain of Tancred of Conversano, does there seem to have been much fighting. In July, the forces of Roger and Honorius met in a standoff at the Bradano River, to the west of Taranto and south of Matera. Here Roger refused to initiate a battle despite having a superior army.[297] Indeed, some of the knights in the papal army defected from Honorius to join Roger. Troia and Melfi soon fell to Roger.

Seeing the failure of the coalition he had assembled, Honorius invested Roger as duke at Benevento in August.[298] This led to recognition by Robert II of Capua and Sergio VII of Naples. In reality, some Apulian barons were disappointed by the pope's "compromise" with their foe.[299]

The rebellion at Bari was somewhat more complex and protracted, reflecting deeply-held grievances against Norman rule. Supporting the Conversano family, Grimoald Alferanites attacked and conquered Brindisi in the autumn of 1128.[300] Yet even Grimoald was eventually persuaded to accept Roger's nominal overlordship, at least for the moment. In 1129, Roger, reciprocally recognized Grimoald's control of what was supposed to be a demesnial city of the Hautevilles. That he similarly granted special privileges to the demesnial city of Messina is dubious at best (see the last note in Appendix 6).

GEOPOLITICS

This moment was the first time since the fall of the Roman Empire that one man ruled almost all of Italy south of Rome, including Sicily, without facing overt contestation. Nevertheless, Honorius opposed the formal unification of all of Roger's dominions as a single polity, a unitary state. For now, this conglomeration of domains constituted a "personal union" of territories united politically by their common rule by the same monarch.

It had proven fortunate for Roger that his adversaries lacked standing armies such as the orders of knighthood being established in Jerusalem. Further afield, early in 1129, Bernard of Clairvaux, an adamant supporter of Honorius, convened the Council of Troyes. Here he introduced the rule he had recently formulated for the Order of the Temple founded a decade earlier, which until now had very few knights.[301] The rule of the Templars, who were initially reluctant to embrace the novel concept of warriors-as-monks, differed somewhat from that of the Hospitallers. Arguably, as an early, idealized "code of chivalry" (though its precepts were rarely put into practice), it represented a step in the evolution of the crusading, or military-religious, orders of knighthood.[302] Like the Hospitallers, the Templars soon began to establish a presence in southern Italy, but more immediately relevant to Roger II would be Bernard's presence and interference here.[303]

Pope Honorius II died in February 1130, succeeded by Innocent II (Gregory Papereschi), whose election was challenged by Peter Pierleoni, who took the name Anacletus II and has come to be regarded as an antipope.[304] Anacletus, whose family had long been a major force in and around Rome, imposed his control over the walled Leonine City, which consisted of most of what is now the Vatican and, at its eastern edge, the fortress of Castel Sant'Angelo overlooking the Tiber. He made his influence felt in central and southern Italy. Innocent left Italy to garner support from potential allies in the Holy Roman Empire and France.

During the same month, Bohemond II was killed in an ambush by Danishmend Turks abetted by Leo, the ruler of Armenian Cilicia, a state to the immediate north of the Principality of Antioch.[305]

In Antioch, Bohemond had fathered a daughter, Constance, but no surviving sons. By now, in early 1130, Roger II had five legitimate sons entitled to succeed him, and at least one son born outside marriage; he also had at least one daughter. At this time, therefore, the only legitimately-born Hauteville males were Roger and his sons by Elvira. It is rather improbable that Bohemond, informed that Taranto and his other Italian estates had been expropriated by Roger, thought of this kinsman as his potential heir to Antioch.

Closer to home, Roger needed baronial support. To that end, in September he summoned a *curiae generales,* an assembly of barons and prelates. The first meeting was held at Salerno, with a larger one following in Palermo.[306] In the same month, Anacletus II consented to Roger being crowned king by the Archbishop of Palermo.[307]

Though the support of the church and baronage, coupled with the hereditary possession of his dominions, may have argued for Roger's right to wear a crown, it seems unlikely that he or his counsellors initially had a very precise idea about the form this kingship would assume. There was no legal code; the existing body of law had been cobbled together from several disparate traditions. The Principality of Salerno offered the nearest, most recent, historical precedent for a hereditary European monarchy based in southern Italy, yet Roger's most trusted lay advisors were Byzantine Greeks and Muslim Arabs who looked to very different models for inspiration. Given Elvira's origins in northern Spain, kingdoms such as Castile or Navarre may have been viewed as something comparable to what was envisaged for southern Italy. It is even possible that Normans familiar with England suggested a government along the lines of what existed under English law. In the end, Roger's kingdom would be characterized by elements which, if not drawn directly from these models, were similar in certain respects. There were, after all, fundamental principles common to most of the kingdoms of Catholic Europe.[308]

Though it was created later in his reign, and while too much should not be inferred from it, the mosaic in Palermo's Martorana church depicting Roger crowned directly by Christ reflects the concept of the king reigning by the grace of God, sovereignty depending on divine right rather than papal prerogative (see Chapter 11). An image similar to this, carved into wood, that represents the emperor Constantine VII is conserved in Russia (see the notes of Appendix 5).

The retrospect of nine centuries has given rise to endless theories about the political and social strategies reflected in the decision of Roger and his advisors to found a kingdom, effectively a new state, at this moment. The "nature" of the king's intentions is much discussed, sometimes based on comparisons with other monarchies extant in 1130, analyses of Hauteville hegemony, or examinations of philosophical (or theological) considerations. Although definite motivations rooted in those realities doubtless existed, the most fundamental reasoning was likely quite simple. The unification of southern Italy under the Hauteville family occurred at an opportune moment, and under favorable conditions, for establishing a new European polity of Christian orientation in a geographical position suitable to embracing Mediterranean wealth, commerce and culture. This facilitated more effective competition with other powers in Europe, northern Africa and western Asia.

It was time for the conquerors and colonizers to become kings, and for the people they ruled to become part of something greater than themselves.

Chapter 11
REGNUM SICILIAE

With the assent of the baronage and clergy, Roger II was anointed and crowned King of Sicily on Christmas Day in 1130 in Palermo's cathedral by Peter, the archbishop, who was assisted by the bishops of Syracuse, Agrigento, Mazara and Catania. The witnesses were legion. Following the ceremony, the king was acclaimed by the city's multiconfessional populace, probably standing on the same dais where he was knighted by his mother less than twenty years earlier. The rite of coronation conformed to those used elsewhere in Europe (see Appendix 5), and his consort, Elvira, the daughter of a king, was crowned queen.

Some reorganization was effected.[309] Most notably, Roger appointed a chancellor, a certain Guarino (Warren), to manage day-to-day administration. There were other new arrivals at court; from England came Robert of Selby and Thomas le Brun.

As king, we find Roger styled variously in royal charters, everything from "King of Sicily, Apulia and Calabria" to "King of Sicily and Italy," but the commonality is that Sicily always comes first in the titulature. Reflecting the kingdom's institutional structure and administration, this usage is characterized by both sound reasoning and obvious contradictions, with modern opinions about it ranging from the superficial to the existential. Apulia and Calabria were hardly forgotten, but the realm was to be known simply as the *Regnum Siciliae,* the Kingdom of Sicily.

With a few grains of imagination, the papal bull, or treaty, issued by Pope Anacletus II in September 1130 could be seen as the "foundation charter" of the kingdom. It was also an act of annexation, for it added both Capua, historically ruled by the Drengots as a papal fief, and Naples, long ruled by the independent Docibilian dynasty as a nominally Byzantine territory (with occasional vassalage to the Holy Roman Emperor), to a "composite" realm consisting of the lands the Normans had acquired over the course of a century from Greeks, Arabs and Lombards. Lands in Abruzzi and Molise once belonging to the erstwhile dukes of Benevento had long been in the hands of Norman barons who no longer answered to that city, and didn't usually want to answer to the Hautevilles.

As part of the agreement with Anacletus, Roger had rendered a payment of six hundred gold *schifati follari* (described in the next chapter), not a very unusual practice. In the bull itself we read the name of Roger's eldest son as heir, *et filio tuo Rogerio,* with the "other sons," *et aliis filiit tuis,* following, leaving no doubt about the kingdom's hereditary nature and immediate succession. Apulia became a dukedom vested in the person of the eldest son as heir apparent.

Sicily had been a Roman province, then a Byzantine one, and then an emirate and recently a county, but never a kingdom. Here was the novelty, and it was Roger's conflict with Pope Innocent II that made the new kingdom a contentious element in a European conflict.

Palermo, as we have seen, was always a natural capital for the emirate and county, the last redoubt in the event of an invasion by land or even by sea. Protected by a ring of mountains, it was accessible by roads so difficult that Trapani and Messina were more easily reached by ship.

Kingship was not for the faint of heart. Fate was to dictate that Roger would not spend much time in his capital during the next decade. The first years of his reign as king were to be characterized by the alternating defiance and compliance of barons and citizens, with the social situation in the countryside at least as complex as what existed in the cities.

The Face of the Kingdom

Significantly, Roger II felt called upon to represent *all* the people of his newborn kingdom, regardless of language, ethnicity or creed. Clichéd it may be, but that fact, so timeless and timely, can never be overemphasized.

The mythos that Roger was crowned directly by Christ found its way into visual imagery a few years after his coronation, being represented in an enameled panel in Bari's cathedral. This idea is best exemplified in a mosaic in the Church of Saint Mary of the Admiral, or Martorana, erected specifically by and for the ever diminishing Grecophone community of Palermo (a drawing appears at the beginning of this volume and a photo follows this chapter).

The very thought of the display of a stylistically Byzantine image, the juxtaposition of a sacred icon and a royal portrait, seems to contradict the popular perception and connotation of a "papal monarchy." However, it is to be remembered that one of the parish's founders was none other than Nilos Doxopatrios, who, while at court, advanced his thesis about the ecclesiastical position of the Orthodox Christians and the rights of Constantinople with respect to Rome (see Chapter 4). Moreover, as an image rendered by Greeks in a Greek church, it is reasonable that it would reflect Byzantine imagery and usage.

The Martorana mosaic was created near the end of Roger's reign or shortly after his death. Little about it can be known with certainty, and no extant records contemporary to its era of creation describe it in great detail. As if such explanation were needed, the Greek text identifying both Christ and king is clear enough.

The work may have been meant to represent the independence of thought and deeds of the first King of Sicily as the ruler of a multiconfessional society. Perhaps the king himself, or somebody at court, thought of him as something more than that.

Here, to be seen by all and sundry, was the crowned monarch as leader, lawgiver, protector of peoples, surrogate high priest and even, lest one dare utter the words, intermediary of the Divine, for kings rule by the grace of God. The act of Roger receiving his crown directly from Christ recalls Peter being called personally by Jesus.

That a great quantity of words in ink and bytes, whether insightfully accurate or sorely flawed, has been dedicated to an image now regarded by many as the epitome of the visual representation of the kingdom necessitates some exposition in the interest of clarity.

The mosaic's original position is not known with precision. Although it seems to have been moved when the church was expanded in the seventeenth century, the possibility of an earlier date cannot be excluded from consideration.

Its design is typical of its time. Whether the Greeks in Constantinople favored a *loros* (the ceremonial stole) of this type at this moment is not entirely useful in dating the work. The year of Nilos' death is not known with certainty; he may have suggested that the *loros* be rendered in this manner.

It has been suggested that a gold repeating motif on the blue robe may be a fleur-de-lis, and thus a proto-heraldic emblem later popularized elsewhere in Europe (see note 401). This heraldic charge now associated with France was not yet used by the Angevins (Capetians) as an identifying symbol, nor was armorial heraldry (Chapter 12) in wide use until around 1180, and probably later in the Kingdom of Sicily (note 399).

Therefore, if the motif, usually thought to be a cross, is indeed a fleur-de-lis, it was inspired by symbols in the Holy Land and elsewhere, not in Capetian dominions. A similar robe worn by William II, as rendered in mosaic in Monreale, clearly depicts crosses.

The crown is similar to that of a Byzantine basileus. Its display in various other contexts, such as the obverse of the ducat coin instituted in 1140, likely reflects the fact that the king actually wore such a crown. In the event, precious little survives of what is believed to be Roger's crown.

Roger's hair is shown to be brownish, perhaps with a tinge of red, and his eyes appear to be brown. Local execution of the work argues for the accuracy of these details.

This image clearly inspired that of William II, Roger's grandson, created in Monreale some four decades later.

Palatine Glory

King Roger II immediately undertook to give Palermo the ambience of a royal capital. One of his first acts was the construction of a new Palatine Chapel, in what was now a royal palace, work that had begun above the existing chapel a year earlier. Designed in the syncretic Norman-Arab style, the splendid chapel was consecrated a decade later.[310] Of this effort the chronicler Romuald of Salerno wrote that:

He had the chapel decorated with marvelous images in mosaic, embellished by precious stones, its walls covered in various types of marble. He had it appointed in gold and silver, with lush tapestries. The chapel was served by numerous clerics, endowed by as many ecclesiastical benefices. The monarch ensured every reverence toward God in the divine office celebrated there.[311]

Although Michael the Archangel and Nicholas of Bari, amongst others, were venerated by them, the Hautevilles lacked an exclusive familial patron saint. The chapel was dedicated to Peter the Apostle. Peter was the first bishop of Rome according to Catholic belief, and also the first bishop of Antioch in Orthodox tradition, being the founder of two great patriarchal sees.

Following Byzantine tradition, the chapel's apse, like that of Monreale, is oriented generally toward the east. At a modest thirty-two meters (one hundred and five feet) long, the Romanesque chapel conforms to the typical Latin "basilica" plan. The main part of its nave is divided into three aisles by ten columns preserved from antiquity. At the end of the nave opposite the three apses is a dais for the thrones of the king and queen; on this wall are mosaics of two lions passant guardant reminiscent of the heraldic felines in the coat of arms of the kings of England, this being the closest thing to a royal symbol of the Norman kings of Sicily.

Fashioned of local Nebrodian fir and painted in tempera by Arab artists, the muqarnas ceiling over the central nave, which is somewhat similar to the Abbasid style then in vogue in Baghdad, is the largest surviving Fatimid work of its kind. It was constructed and painted as a unit, and then lowered into position onto the chapel. Here one sees depicted flora and fauna typical of the Mediterranean and Africa, along with such figures as men playing chess, which was introduced in Sicily by the Aghlabids. The king is depicted wearing Arab garb, and Kufic inscriptions abound. The ceilings over the lateral aisles of the nave portray the Koranic virgins of Islamic Paradise, each woman holding a cup. Asian fables are represented, such as a story recounted by the court scholar Ibn Zafar (see Appendix 6).

The walls are covered entirely by polychrome mosaics on a gold background or, in the lower sections, by marble and porphyry inlay.

As befits such a church, the dominant mosaic figures, the focal point, are impressive icons of Christ Pantocrator in the cupola and central apse. Flanking the Pantocrator of the cupola are eight angels, Old Testament prophets and kings, and the four evangelists. Represented among the figures in the sanctuary are the fathers of the Orthodox Church: Basil, Nicholas, John Chrysostom, Gregory of Nissa, Gregory the Theologian. The icons are accompanied by Greek or Latin inscriptions. On the lateral walls of the nave is a cycle of Biblical scenes. (These mosaics are identified in the diagram in this book's map section.)

The motifs of the pavement are based on Fatimid geometry and Byzantine circle groups.

The elevated pulpit was constructed during the twelfth century, though perhaps after Roger's reign. Its design is consistent with the style of the chapel; the zigzag pattern of its pillars is not unlike that of the Arab fountain, and some columns, in the cloister of Monreale Abbey. The carved design of the Paschal candle stand recalls the Provençal motifs of the capitals of the columns in the cloisters at Monreale and Cefalù, although its base is slightly more classical. The baptismal font is contemporaneous to the pulpit.

Realizing such a project, which transcends any single work of art, was a supreme challenge met by numerous artists and architects.

Some projects were simpler. Among those of George of Antioch was a bridge across the Oreto, though the course of this river has been diverted. Erected in 1131, the sturdy structure is still known as the *Ponte dell'Ammiraglio*, the "Admiral's Bridge."

Constructing the kingdom would prove more difficult.

Popes, Barons, Emperors, Kings

That Pope Innocent II objected to his rival, Anacletus II, sanctioning the creation of a kingdom came as no great revelation. The "exiled" Innocent sought and obtained the agreement of the rulers of France, Germany and England that Roger II should not be recognized as King of Sicily. While the degree to which Innocent's initial resentment of Roger merely reflected his antipathy toward Anacletus may well be debated, there is little doubt that a kingdom in southern Italy represented still another power center that might challenge a pope, and even other monarchs. In the event, while the barons enfeoffed in Sicily, Calabria and the environs of Salerno were generally supportive of the new king, it wasn't long before some of the truculent vassals in the other regions expressed their displeasure. After a brief hiatus, rebellion was back in fashion.

Amidst this furor, Roger was constantly occupied with more mundane tasks. We find him, for example, confirming grants of lands to the church in 1131 while at Messina during one of his frequent crossings between Sicily and the mainland.[312]

It may well be that Roger's counsellors ensured the presence of a great part of the baronage at what was now a royal court not only to acclaim him as king but to plan a military response to the uprisings that were doubtless predicted.

Innocent had already begun to conspire against Roger and Anacletus. He sought to form a military coalition of Pisans, Venetians, Capuans and possibly Amalfitans, along with Lothair III, who needed the pope to crown him Holy Roman Emperor, and perhaps even John II Comnenus of Constantinople. Except for reluctance of the Capuans, who initially resisted his overtures, Innocent's efforts proved largely successful. At Liège, in March 1131, he convinced the aspiring emperor to take part in the action against Roger. With Bernard of Clairvaux present, Innocent crowned compliant Lothair as King of the Germans (King of the Romans), a dilatory gesture as the Archbishop of Milan had already crowned his rival, Conrad Hohenstaufen, with this right and dignity three years earlier. Just as there was an antipope, there was an "anti-emperor" or, more precisely, an anti-king, pitted against Lothair.

For now, most of Lothair's knights were busy keeping the Hohenstaufen supporters in check in the German lands. In 1132, he attempted to take Milan, the only city in northern Italy whose archbishop still refused to recognize Innocent as the legitimate pope. That Lothair failed in this effort reflected the fact that his military forces were thin on the ground. Yet he was able to muster a small company of knights to escort the pope and himself safely to Rome, where the Leonine City was held by Anacletus, for an imperial coronation.

Whilst these pontifical machinations were beyond Roger's control, the loss of at least two important vassals to Innocent's camp was the king's own fault.

Matilda Hauteville

Matilda Hauteville, whom we met earlier, was Roger's elder sister wed to Ranulf of Alife and Caiazzo (see Table 4), holder of a number of large estates in and around the Volturno Valley near Naples.[313] This marriage may have seemed like hypergamy on Ranulf's part, but it is worth recalling that his Drengot ancestors had ruled Capua until they were expelled by the city's Lombards, and under other circumstances this Norman house might have seriously challenged the Hautevilles for power.

Matilda is known to posterity as the patron of Alexander of Telese, whom she commissioned to write about her younger brother, the king. Alexander's chronicle, effectively a biography, has little to say about Matilda except for her unhappy marriage. Clearly, the work is intended for the edification of her brother, not for her.

Nevertheless, it is remarkable that Matilda thought her unfortunate marital experience worth noting in a project over which she had some control. She thus exercised a degree of female "editorial" agency rare in her times. Matilda does not appear to have been excessively worried about her experience with Ranulf becoming known to posterity or even to contemporaries, nor it being held against her; here there was no "victim shaming." It may be that, sensing her story would be mentioned by any chronicler who became privy to it, she felt the need (through Alexander) to write her own narrative rather than have somebody else write it for her. Admittedly, the situation was likely to become known through gossip in court circles, where other women, and perhaps a few men, even not knowing any details, might speculate that there were only so many reasons for a noblewoman to leave her husband. This was Matilda's chance to "set the record straight." It is highly unlikely that she would have had such an opportunity were she not the king's sister.

Ranulf initially supported Roger as king. Early in 1131, at the king's command, he and his Drengot kinsman, Robert of Capua, led an expedition to Rome in a show of Norman force to impress Roger's strength upon the supporters of Pope Innocent II.

Meanwhile, Amalfi, which had rebelled, was suppressed following a coordinated attack by land and sea. Sergio of Naples, hearing of this, remained loyal for now. Matilda soon learned that her brother was at Salerno.

In the late spring of that year, in Ranulf's absence, Matilda fled to her brother, leaving the castle of Alife for Salerno, taking her young son (and possibly her daughter) with her and explaining to Roger that she had been abused by her husband. Despite the growing baronial unrest in the region, Matilda and her suite traveled to Salerno without incident because most of the lands they passed through were those of her husband.

Roger responded to his sister's lament by divesting Ranulf of some of these feudal lands, including manors held by his younger brother, Richard, notably the prosperous town of Avellino. Learning of this, and that Matilda had received protection and refuge from the king, Ranulf and Robert, along with their two hundred knights, left Rome to discuss matters with the sovereign. Initially at least, there was a serious effort at negotiation. When this deteriorated, both men came to oppose the king's rule. This was not insignificant, for what followed was protracted warfare over the next eight years. Without ignoring the gravity of this situation, which came to involve other players, let us consider Matilda's predicament.

Matilda declared that she would not return to live with her husband unless her dower, the Caudine Valley, was returned to her. This territory included several towns and straddles what are now the provinces of Benevento and Avellino.

Three chroniclers state that Matilda was mistreated by her husband. Alexander of Telese mentions it in passing. Falco of Benevento notes it, and the anonymous monk at the monastery of Santa Maria della Ferraria, whose chronicle, based partly on Falco's work, was completed a century later, refers to it.

According to Alexander of Telese, Roger found his sister's complaints justified and permitted her to stay at court as long as she wished, seeing no way to obtain justice for her except through royal intervention.

When Ranulf demanded, through messengers, that his wife, his son and his lands be returned to him, Roger responded that he, the king, was not forcing Matilda to stay with the traveling court. She was free to return to Ranulf, to whom Roger had arranged her betrothal years earlier, if and when she wished. However, the monarch chastised Ranulf for remaining silent when his brother, Richard, had refused to pay homage to the king at the recent coronation in Palermo. Now Ranulf himself refused to go to Salerno to pay homage and fealty to Roger.[314]

The historical record does not state or very convincingly imply that Ranulf assaulted his wife. Only with caution might we compare Matilda's predicament to that of her contemporary, Urraca "the Reckless" of Castile, elder half-sister of Queen Elvira. Urraca accused her husband, Alfonso I "the Battler" of

Aragon (who was also King of Pamplona), of physically abusing her. Elvira may well have heard of Urraca's treatment at the hands of Alfonso.[315]

Falco of Benevento states simply, and concisely, that Roger, who loved his sister, learned that Ranulf had humiliated Matilda in many ways. The king honorably received her, consoled her and sent her to Sicily. Being something of a critic of Roger, Falco goes on to explain Ranulf's grief, and his effort at intervention by Pope Anacletus.[316] Clearly, this chronicler pitied Ranulf, whom he saw as a victim.

Only the monk at Santa Maria della Ferraria states that Ranulf's chief affront to Matilda was adultery, writing much later that:

Roger's sister, Matilda, was the wife of Ranulf of Alife, who had taken a concubine. Matilda much lamented her husband's comportment. Learning of this situation, Roger rescued his sister, along with her son by Ranulf, from the unfaithful husband. For this reason, Ranulf was ever more indignant about the king and grew ever nearer Roger's adversaries. Robert of Capua, who Pope Anacletus had sent to Roger's coronation, was fearful that the king might use the same tactics with him that he used with Ranulf. With this in mind, and seeking allies, Robert solicited the Pisans and Genoans, offering them gifts. The citizens of these important mercantile cities then sent a large fleet of galleys to Naples against the King of Sicily.[317]

The significance of Matilda's impact on the events leading to a *de facto* civil war in the peninsular regions of Roger's kingdom has generally been overlooked by historians. As there were other factors in play, we cannot know for certain that her leaving her husband, to whom she returned after three years, was a significant catalyst for what ensued in the region. Clearly, however, it provoked reactions that would not have occurred otherwise, depriving Roger of useful knights and requiring him to fight extra battles.

As events unfolded, Ranulf and his allies, supported by Pope Innocent and the emperors of east and west, prosecuted a largely successful campaign against Roger's forces across southern Italy over the next few years. Innocent and the two emperors might well have invaded anyway, but the Drengots and certain other families of the realm probably would have supported the king had the incident with Matilda never transpired.

After Ranulf died in 1139, Roger ordered his corpse exhumed from its tomb at Troia so that, according to Falco, he could drag it from his horse as he rode around the city. Ranulf was survived by his two children, Robert and Adelisa. By then Matilda may already have been deceased.

Alexander's chronicle ends in 1136, about two years after Matilda returned to Ranulf, although the biographer lived on. This has suggested to some historians that Matilda died in that year. Falco of Benevento does not mention her reacting to her husband's death in 1139.

The accounts differ slightly, yet all three allude to the mistreatment of Matilda by her husband, implying offense taken by Roger that his sister did not receive the respect she deserved.

It is tempting to speculate about why Matilda returned to her husband, apart from the question of her dower being restored to her. If Ranulf's only misdeed were conjugal betrayal, he may have promised not to repeat it. Much remains unknown, and neither Matilda or Ranulf lived very long after their separation.

Marital infidelity, particularly by men, was not terribly unusual; Roger himself fathered children outside wedlock. Perhaps Matilda felt especially humiliated because her husband took up with a woman of low birth. On the other hand, it may have been a woman she knew, such as a lady-in-waiting. There could have been other affronts she was forced to endure. The surviving reports are rather vague about what Ranulf actually did. In the twelfth century, it was rare for any woman to leave her husband, and the "scandal" was arguably magnified when the woman was an aristocrat.

Few woman of lower birth than Matilda Hauteville would have been afforded the possibility of leaving an abusive spouse, for they would have been dependent on him socially and financially. This includes not only common women but most countesses and baronesses. Matilda's success in fleeing Ranulf was based on her exalted social status and her geographical proximity to her protective brother at a certain moment, as well as that brother's willingness to defend her.

Significantly, Roger's attention to Matilda's complaints is the first case of a King of Sicily using his authority to "arbitrate" a personal matter concerning a member of the royal family.

It seems unlikely, based on the statements about mistreatment made by the three chroniclers, that Matilda's actions were merely political, as if she separated from her husband because he was already conspiring against Roger. Despite the apparent dissonance of his younger brother, Richard, Ranulf himself does not seem to have expressed overt disapproval of Roger in the months before the spring of 1131, and he attended the coronation with Matilda the previous year.

Roger's defense of Matilda does not seem to have been motivated by politics. With a pope, two emperors and a pack of unruly vassals already acting against him, it was hardly expedient to lose the "Drengot contingent" of his army. In the end, Ranulf only became one more thorn in the king's side, and an unextractable one at that.

We must conclude that Matilda's grievances were real and painful. Their revelation contributed to the causes for the first war fought by a King of Sicily in his own kingdom.[318]

Grimoald and Lothair, Robert and Ranulf

While Matilda sought her brother's aid, Grimoald of Bari and Tancred of Conversano were again in open rebellion. Like the revolts that ended two years earlier, these were legitimized by papal sanction. Most of those opposing Roger were implicitly opposed to Anacletus, who saw his ecclesiastical influence diminishing in the contested regions, but in its essence this was not a war merely between papal factions, though a conflict fitting that description would soon emerge.[319]

During the late summer of 1131, Roger sailed with his sister to Sicily. Longstanding tradition has it that he was shipwrecked by a tempest and landed on the rocky coast of Cefalù, and that it was in thanksgiving that he erected a cathedral, the *duomo,* there and revived the town's diocese.[320]

A castle stood on the rocky mountain overlooking Cefalù near the site of a Sicanian temple to the goddess the Greeks worshipped as Artemis. In the town below, Roger erected a small palace, the Osterio Magno, along a narrow street, and a church dedicated to Saint George. Though Norman-Arab and Romanesque in style, the *duomo* of Cefalù is far more similar to what we usually associate with the cathedrals of Normandy. It has a long, narrow nave and a graceful transept. In the apse, overlooking the sanctuary, is an impressive mosaic icon of the Pantocrator rivaled only by that of Monreale. Critics debate which of the two is the more subtle or graceful. The mosaic of Mary with arms extended upward in prayer, flanked by four archangels, is typical of Byzantine art. This icon is called *Hagio Soritissa*. Initially, Roger probably intended for mosaics to cover the walls, but these were completed only in the main apse and in the ceiling above it. Some of the surviving rafter beams of the ceiling are original, bearing Koranic inscriptions in Kufic script. Cefalù's baptismal font is unique in Norman Sicily. It is carved of local stone with lions depicted in bold relief around it.

The king had little time to contemplate the construction of the magnificent church. The middle months of 1132 found him and his large army making its way from Campania into Lucania and Apulia, where his immediate objectives were Brindisi and Bari. That he ever formally recognized Grimoald as a prince is doubtful.[321] When Bari surrendered to royal authority in June of 1132, the "prince" was sent with his wife and children to Palermo's royal palace as "guests" of the gaolers who oversaw its dungeon. The family probably died there. Perhaps learning of their capture, Tancred of Conversano surrendered Brindisi, renounced his feudal lands in what was now the Kingdom of Sicily, and pledged to seek better fortunes in the Holy Land under the auspices of the family of his late patron, Bohemond II, though he never made this voyage.[322]

In late July, the king endured a debacle at Nocera, where he and his army were all but defeated by the forces of Ranulf and Robert. Roger had to retreat and hundreds of his knights were captured.[323] The fact that the rebels could inflict such humiliation upon the king showed the scope of their widespread support despite many losses during the previous year.

In the event, the king regrouped with his remaining knights and troops at Salerno, from which he ordered that his fortifications in the Benevento area be reinforced. With the death of Landolf of Garderisio, Benevento's archbishop, the citizens of the papal city would eventually accept Innocent as pope and therefore Gregory (or Gerard), the prelate he appointed to this see.

Leaving Benevento to the papacy where it belonged, Roger then launched yet another attack on Bari, where there were again riots. With this, the king had pacified Apulia, Lucania and Campania, at least for the moment.

By early 1133, Roger was back in Sicily, at Messina, but he would soon have to return to the mainland with his traveling court and, more importantly, his army. Though the king had, in fact, consolidated most of the realm, Ranulf of Alife and Robert of Capua were still at large, now joined by Sergio of Naples and an increasing number of barons.[324]

In June, Innocent II crowned Lothair Holy Roman Emperor in the Basilica of Saint John Lateran in one of the parts of Rome that was not controlled by Anacletus, who still held Saint Peter's.[325] The new emperor was constrained to return immediately to Germany to address the continuing Hohenstaufen threat, but the pontiff had granted him some of the lands in central Italy that once belonged to the late Matilda of Tuscany, who helped broker a resolution to end the Investiture Controversy. Meeting Innocent and Lothair in Rome, Ranulf and Robert were likely disappointed at the lack of military support.[326] Innocent made his way to Pisa.

Roger, meanwhile, was in Apulia and Lucania, accompanied by his chancellor, Guarino, and an army consisting largely of loyal Arab foot men and archers. Amongst his many acts, he renewed the privileges of monasteries at Gravina and Rapolla in September. Such magnanimity contrasted sharply with his treatment of the rebellious towns he punished.

The king stayed at Salerno in October before sailing for Sicily, where his devoted consort, Queen Elvira, had been acting as his effective regent, overseeing local affairs. Whilst in the capital, Roger undertook various tasks, such as the enfeoffment of some kinsmen of Anacletus.[327] His time with his family was to be brief.

Roger sailed back to the mainland in May 1134. Lack of military support from Lothair had left the rebels with limited resources to prosecute their war against the king. Even some of their own knights defected to the royal camp, and Robert's Pisans failed to appear. The summer saw both Ranulf and Sergio submitting to royal authority. Robert, who refused to return from Pisa to pay fealty to Roger, was divested of Capua *in absentia*. This ended the present hostilities but not the underlying hostility.[328]

Ranulf's wife, Matilda, returned to him, though Roger kept her dower as well as some lands his brother-in-law had misappropriated during the recent rebellion. Here was the perfect recipe for a rancid stew of hatred that only drove Ranulf and his allies more firmly into Pope Innocent's camp, where Robert of Capua was seeking assistance to entice Pisan support.

Back in Palermo, Roger, and then Elvira, fell ill late in 1134. The nature of the malady is not known, but it seems to have been a contagious virus resulting in a severe fever. Elvira died from this illness in February 1135, aged thirty-five. With this, Roger mourned in seclusion for several weeks, so long that many thought he was also dead. Elvira wasn't simply the first Queen of Sicily. She was Roger's confidante, and much beloved by the populace. That Roger loved her dearly is beyond doubt, and he did not soon remarry.

Rumors of his death seem to have spread far and wide, certainly to the ears of Ranulf, who exploited this opportunity to instigate another insurrection. For Robert, his accomplice, who had arrived with troops recruited in Pisa and Genoa, Capua was the immediate objective.

The king's chancellor, Guarino, was present in the region, along with the new *amiratus*, John, "son of Eugene," but their early efforts to maintain order ended in failure when both men were chased from Aversa. Guarino was more successful at Capua, which he defended from an assault by Robert.

In view of the rumors following Elvira's death, it is quite possible that neither Guarino or John, nor the other defenders of the kingdom who were presently in Campania and Basilicata, knew with certainty that the king was alive. His eldest son, Roger, his heir as Duke of Apulia, was now seventeen and old enough to fight in a war. The second-oldest, Tancred, who the king had made Prince of Bari, was about a year younger.

Roger sailed into Salerno's harbor during the spring of 1135 and immediately subdued Aversa. Ranulf took refuge with Sergio in Naples, which the royal army besieged, though the city would resist for nearly two years. The king's overzealous response was to attack and raze several towns around Naples, and to destroy what remained of Aversa. Robert's Pisans, unable to land at Naples, attacked and sacked Amalfi, a city that, besides being loyal to the king, was an occasional, if not terribly competitive, mercantile rival.[329] Among the booty was the oldest copy of the *Digest*, or "Pandects," of Justinian, a work compiled in the sixth century.

Though defeated, Robert was still defiant, refusing to pay fealty and homage to the king when given another chance to submit in June. For this he definitively lost Capua, which Roger gave to his own third-born son, Alfonso, who was about fifteen. The extended territory of the principality was quite large and, by tradition, it was a vassal state of the pope. For now, young Alfonso's counsellors administered the principality in that manner, almost as a semi-autonomous part of the *Regnum*, even though, according to the papal bull issued by Anacletus five years prior, it was to be a "province" of the kingdom.

Amidst this domestic chaos, Roger sent a fleet to the African coast to capture the island of Djerba, nominally a Zirid dominion in the Gulf of Gabés but ostensibly a "free" zone, that term being something of a euphemism for a pirates' lair. This conquest was successful, providing the Sicilians a foothold in Ifriqiya, where a new trade agreement was negotiated with Abul-Hasan al-Hasan ibn Ali.[330]

Meanwhile, Pope Innocent, who had been in Pisa for the last two years, convened a synod, or council, in that city to address ecclesiastical matters but also to confront the political predicament facing him. Here he received the acclamation, over his rival Anacletus, of bishops from many kingdoms. Truth be told, Innocent's election may have been of dubious canonicity, and no more valid than that of Anacletus, but his indefatigable effort to garner support across Europe had proven itself successful, effectively neutralizing his rival in almost every region except Rome, a few other cities of the Papal State, and the Kingdom of Sicily.

For good measure, he excommunicated Roger. This had little immediate effect on the king's actions in an age when Catholic monarchs viewed anathema almost as a normal part of dealing with the papacy. However, it bolstered the credibility of Innocent's war of words, which was soon to become a war of armies.[331]

While his papal patron was uniting the Catholic clergy, Lothair was unifying his empire. Here his most important accomplishment, amongst many challenges, was to defeat the rival Hohenstaufens, with Conrad III consequently renouncing his kingship. This finally left Lothair free to attack Roger in a campaign that would be prosecuted, in part, with financial support from John II Comnenus of Constantinople. These forces were joined by a small papal army and some opportunistic Pisans.

Invasion

By August 1136, the Holy Roman Emperor had begun his march southward through his Italian dominions with two imperial armies that would attack the *Regnum* from different directions. It would be a very long march.[332]

Not wishing to miss the spectacle of Roger's expected demise, Pope Innocent traveled from Pisa to the south of Italy, where he planned to meet Lothair once the *Regnum* was destroyed. To Bernard he entrusted the task of offering Roger a last chance to repent, renouncing his support of Anacletus and his family, before being destroyed.[333]

For the next few months, while Lothair's twin armies made their separate ways through Italy into the *Regnum,* Roger and his counsellors prepared for a major invasion. At Palermo on Christmas, the king knighted his sons Roger and Tancred, the former perhaps redundantly, along with forty other young men of the realm.

Guarino, the chancellor, attempted to negotiate with the monks of Mount Cassino to obtain permission from them to use the monastery, with its views of the surrounding country, as a strategic position in the forthcoming conflict. Henry "the Proud" of Bavaria, Lothair's son-in-law, would lead an army through this region on his way to Puglia. Despite being besieged, the monks refused to surrender and Guarino died in early January of 1137.[334]

How large were the armies? The numbers reported are often exaggerated and highly debatable, sometimes proffered to us with little distinction between knights, foot men and archers. So far as one can determine, each army was at least three thousand knights strong, perhaps much larger, with twice as many foot men.

This wasn't the only part of Europe readying itself for what was, in effect, a civil war. In England, where Henry I had died in 1135, his nephew, Stephen of Blois, seized the throne contrary to the late king's wish that his own intrepid daughter, Matilda, onetime Holy Roman Empress, succeed as queen regnant. Here, too, rebellion was in the air. Not for nothing would England's bloody conflict be remembered as The Anarchy. It will be recalled (from the last chapter) that Lothair owed his election as King of the Germans to the fact that Matilda and her first husband, Emperor Henry V, had no children.[335]

It was an Englishman, Robert of Selby, who Roger appointed as governor of Salerno and charged with preventing that city from falling to an invading army. The king was diligent in his efforts to prepare a defense. Would that he had more knights.[336]

Decisive Years

The invaders arrived in southern Italy at about the same time in the spring of 1137. Their attacks were coordinated reasonably well. Nevertheless, if they had a common objective in the short term, it was far from certain that they might share the same goals in the long term. Each had a reason or two for supporting an invasion of the Kingdom of Sicily at this moment.

Essentially, Lothair, who had been solicited directly by Innocent, wanted to obtain a few regions, such as Salerno, which at times during the Lombard era were imperial fiefs, while reinforcing his bond with the papacy, perhaps even reclaiming one or two of the prerogatives lost by the Holy Roman Empire with the recent resolution of the Investiture Controversy.

John, who retained the Asian parts of his Byzantine Empire only by endless battles, may have desired greater influence in Puglia and other Grecophone lands in southern Italy, and perhaps even a foothold in Bari, but first he wanted to suppress any hereditary claim Roger entertained to Antioch or other dominions of the late Bohemond II, territories that had once belonged to Constantinople. For now, the Byzantine Emperor himself was busy in Armenian Cilicia attacking Leo, who had recently plotted Bohemond's murder. John's emissaries to Lothair not only provided financial aid, but in chorus with their Venetian allies they complained about Roger's recent conquest of Djerba as a cause for concern, based on the presumption that the island should have belonged to the Byzantines.[337]

The Pisans and Genoans, as always, desired greater access to trade, yet they would have gladly accepted a territorial prize such as a convenient "satellite" port like Amalfi or Otranto, or even Malta or Pantelleria.[338]

Innocent's motives were the most transparent of all, though arguably the most "ideological." He wanted to remove from power the only remaining barrier to his absolute control of the papal lands, the city of Rome and Catholicism itself, since the defeat of Roger would bring about the demise of Anacletus. While Innocent might well expropriate a few of Roger's cities for the papacy, he was more immediately interested in acquiring souls than territory.

What occurred during 1137 was a rapid series of highly effective military actions beginning in the late spring.

In early May, Henry "the Proud" of Bavaria arrived at Mount Cassino, whose abbot, still nominally loyal to Anacletus, was initially reticent but soon capitulated. Capua was next; here Robert was restored to power but had to bribe the German troops to refrain from looting.

Innocent arrived in Benevento with his own small army, accompanied by the larger force led by Henry. It could be argued that taking this papal city was essentially symbolic, but because it was the pope's outpost, an enclave within the borders of the *Regnum,* its occupation reflected a victory over Anacletus that was both moral and material.[339]

At the same time, Lothair made his way rapidly down the Adriatic coast, pillaging Ancona, just north of the *Regnum,* and reaching Siponto. By the end of May he was besieging Bari, where he was joined by Henry and Innocent. It wasn't long before Bari, Taranto and other cities fell.[340]

Soon the imperial army was besieging Melfi, a traditional stronghold of the Hautevilles. Unlike some of the other cities, this one was still loyal to the king and a blood bath ensued, leaving a large number of defenders dead. By now, however, many of the imperial foot men, and even some of the knights, were tiring of the long campaign. Their exasperation led to a riot as they attacked the papal forces. Lothair himself had to intervene before Innocent was injured.

At Lagopesole, in Basilicata, in July, the irascible pontiff received the abbot of Mount Cassino, who had supported Anacletus, and reproved him severely and publicly.[341]

Now, in the hot summer, the imperial troops were growing increasingly irritated.

Meanwhile, a Pisan fleet arrived to attack Amalfi, which quickly capitulated. At Naples, which was still technically under siege by Roger's forces, they failed to penetrate the naval blockade. This prompted them to attack Salerno, where Robert of Selby was in charge. Here the fleet was joined by troops led by Robert of Capua, Ranulf of Alife and Henry the Proud. The Sicilian fleet blockading Naples abandoned that effort and sailed southward to relieve Salerno.

The city resisted until early August, when Lothair arrived with his formidable army. His generous terms of surrender annoyed the Pisans, who had planned on sacking a prosperous port whose merchants, like the Amalfitans, were their maritime competitors.

In early September, Lothair and Innocent, presuming total victory, invested Ranulf, Roger's brother-in-law, as Duke of Apulia. By then, the imperial knights and troops were sick and tired of the invasion, and the former had satisfied their feudal military obligation.

Where was Roger? Unfortunately, widespread disloyalty everywhere in the kingdom except Sicily and southern Calabria had left the king's military forces seriously depleted, certainly insufficient numerically to counter the invasion. Roger was raising an army in Sicily. His absence has been construed by some as reluctance to engage the enemy directly. That may be true, but no military leader wants to fight at a disadvantage.

Whether Roger ever attempted to negotiate with the invaders is fodder for debate.[342] At Palermo, he was still behaving as a king, issuing charters; clearly, not everybody in Campania and the other regions had lost faith in him.[343]

Lothair, whose health was failing, began the long trek back to Germany with his son-in-law, leaving about eight hundred knights to bolster the forces of Ranulf and Innocent. The Holy Roman Emperor died in Breitenwang, in Tyrol, in early December.

The invasion prosecuted by Lothair and Innocent was militarily successful for a glorious moment but its political effects were far from satisfactory. With the prominent exceptions of Naples and Capua, there was little to indicate that many localities in the conquered regions would be any more loyal to their new masters than they were to Roger. Indeed, fickle Naples was soon back in the royal camp.

In early October, Roger handily took back Salerno, but at the end of the month his army suffered a defeat by the imperial knights and Ranulf at Rignano, in the Gargano region in northern Puglia.[344] Sergio of Naples, now the king's ally, was killed at this battle. His death facilitated Roger's control of that city, whose patricians failed to agree upon a successor.

This left Ranulf in control of certain parts of Campania and the western reaches of Basilicata, and Robert at Capua, though the latter had to contend with a certain degree of dissent by the people of his own city. Innocent's plan to subjugate the King of Sicily, whose coronation he still refused to recognize, had failed abysmally, and it was obvious enough that the imperial troops couldn't remain in southern Italy forever.

By the end of November, Roger was in Salerno to ensure its protection. Bernard of Clairvaux, who had witnessed the recent battle, went to the city to meet with the king and propose an arbitration of the papal rivalry by a committee of six prelates, three partisans each for Innocent and Anacletus. That such negotiation was even attempted reflects the reality of the futility in trying to unseat Roger from his throne or his power.

With his adroit yet biased rhetoric, Bernard sought to persuade all and sundry of Innocent's case. Roger, however, remained unconvinced and returned to Sicily, leaving his sons and counsellors in charge of affairs at Salerno and elsewhere on the mainland.[345]

Any further campaign against the rebels could be prosecuted in the spring when the weather was better suited to it. Despite the debacle at Rignano and the loss of localities like Troia, some semblance of order had been restored in the more important cities of the mainland part of the *Regnum*. Ranulf's victory had been a hollow one.

With Lothair's death, and the rise of the rival Hohenstaufen party in Germany, many of the imperial knights began to make their way home, though some remained. This left the rebels, and hence the pope they supported, with a military strength that was greatly diminished from what it had been a few months earlier. Nevertheless, the death of Anacletus II in early January of 1138 relieved Innocent of a burden he had long been carrying. For the moment there was only one pontiff.

Yet there were other threats to the kingdom, such as occasional Almoravid raids on the coasts. Although trade with the Zirids had increased following the acquisition of Djerba, it was still rather modest and the terms were not always favorable to the Sicilians. Constant domestic strife on the mainland had diverted the attention of the king and his government from important affairs of state. There was much more to kingship than fighting wars against disloyal vassals and issuing charters to avaricious abbots, but little time available to address other concerns. Fortunately, an efficient administration permitted the function of government despite the constant military campaigns and other disturbances.

By no means was the Kingdom of Sicily the only realm in western Europe to find itself fighting enemies from within.

In March, Conrad III Hohenstaufen was crowned King of the Germans at Aachen. Henry the Proud, the son-in-law of the late Lothair, protested this and was consequently divested of his lands. This sparked a civil war that lasted for the next four years despite Henry's untimely death. The conflict led to the identification of the rival parties that came to be known, especially in Italian circles, as *Guelphs* and *Ghibellines*. The Guelphs derived their name from the House of Welf of Henry the Proud and almost always supported the papacy. The Ghibellines, whose name comes to us from that of the castle at Waiblingen inherited by the Hohenstaufens from the Salians (see Table 3), invariably supported the rights and sovereignty of the Holy Roman Emperor, usually against the papacy. An immediate effect of the troubles in Germany in 1138 was that Pope Innocent, who had endorsed Lothair against Conrad, could no longer count on imperial support against Roger; this was doubtless one of several factors that eventually led him to seek a better relationship with the King of Sicily.

In England, meanwhile, the year 1138 saw the first battles of The Anarchy, with Robert of Gloucester, the illegitimate half-brother of Matilda, challenging Stephen of Blois for power. Here, too, was subtle papal intervention, for Innocent supported Stephen.

A cardinal elected to the See of Peter in March as Victor IV, supported by the same faction of Romans that had sanctioned Anacletus II, renounced his "pontificate" in May.[346] In view of this development, the King of Sicily recognized Innocent II as pope.

By then, the sovereign was leading an army into Puglia, Basilicata and those parts of Campania that Ranulf and the other rebels had confiscated from royal control. This extended campaign saw a number of towns attacked but few that formally submitted to royal authority. Ranulf and his followers had convinced a great many barons to resist.[347]

Some of Roger's assaults on what were his own cities were overzealous and harsh, but the rebels could be even less disciplined. We find, for example, Raoul of Fragneto raiding the environs of Benevento and ordering his men to destroy vineyards, an act as vindictive as any perpetrated by the royal army.[348]

October 1138 found the king at Salerno before sailing to Sicily, where he could address matters besides papal and baronial dissent.

Innocent's next grand gesture was the Second Lateran Council begun in early April 1139. Here, among many other decisions, he made celibacy mandatory for priests, reiterating a canon established sixteen years earlier but not widely enforced. He excommunicated Roger for a second time and undertook to depose the bishops who had supported Anacletus.[349]

Ranulf of Alife died at Troia, a city he had occupied, in late April. This effectively ended the rebellion except for isolated pockets of resistance, notably at Bari.

On May twenty-ninth, Mount Vesuvius erupted, spewing ash over Naples, Salerno, Benevento, Capua and other localities for eight days.

In June, following the end of the council, Innocent led an army with Robert of Capua to the immediate north of the kingdom to meet with the king. At San Germano, the city at the base of Mount Cassino, days of negotiations stalled when the pope insisted upon the restoration of Capua to Robert, under papal authority, as a condition of recognizing Roger's dignity as king.[350]

With this, each army went its own way, but the pope and Robert decided to attack several towns *en route* to Capua, which they were intent on capturing. At Galluccio, knights led by Roger, Duke of Apulia, the king's eldest son, witnessed one of these gratuitous raids and decided to do something about it. They descended from high ground and attacked the papal army, the two forces being evenly matched numerically at perhaps a thousand knights each. The papal knights fled in disarray. Robert escaped but the pope and his entourage were captured. The Hautevilles and their knights accorded them every courtesy.

Three days later, on July twenty-fifth, at Mignano, Innocent recognized Roger as King of Sicily whilst recognizing his sons, Roger and Alfonso as (respectively) Duke of Apulia and Prince of Capua.[351]

King and pontiff rode to Benevento together. Here the former received emissaries from Naples pledging fealty on behalf of the council of jurats that had governed the city since Sergio's demise. The Duke of Apulia was received with honor at Naples, where his brother, Alfonso, became duke.

The king, meanwhile, tended to some unfinished business in Puglia. In early August he forced Troia, defended by some of Lothair's knights, to submit, and to desecrate the remains of Ranulf of Alife. Then Bari, long a haven for disloyal subjects, was besieged. When the city's "prince," Jaquinto, capitulated after two months, a knight who was released complained of having had an eye gouged out while imprisoned. This was a clear violation of the code of conduct regarding the treatment of knights. In reprisal, Jaquinto and a number of other citizens were executed.

With this, Roger made his way back to Salerno before sailing to Sicily in early November. Nearly a decade after his coronation, his sovereignty over the kingdom could finally be said to be absolute. If the kingdom's beginning had been less than auspicious, the monarch and his administration would now make up for lost time.

Cefalù Cathedral, founded by Roger II, viewed from the fortress overlooking the town. This was already the see of a bishop during the Byzantine era.

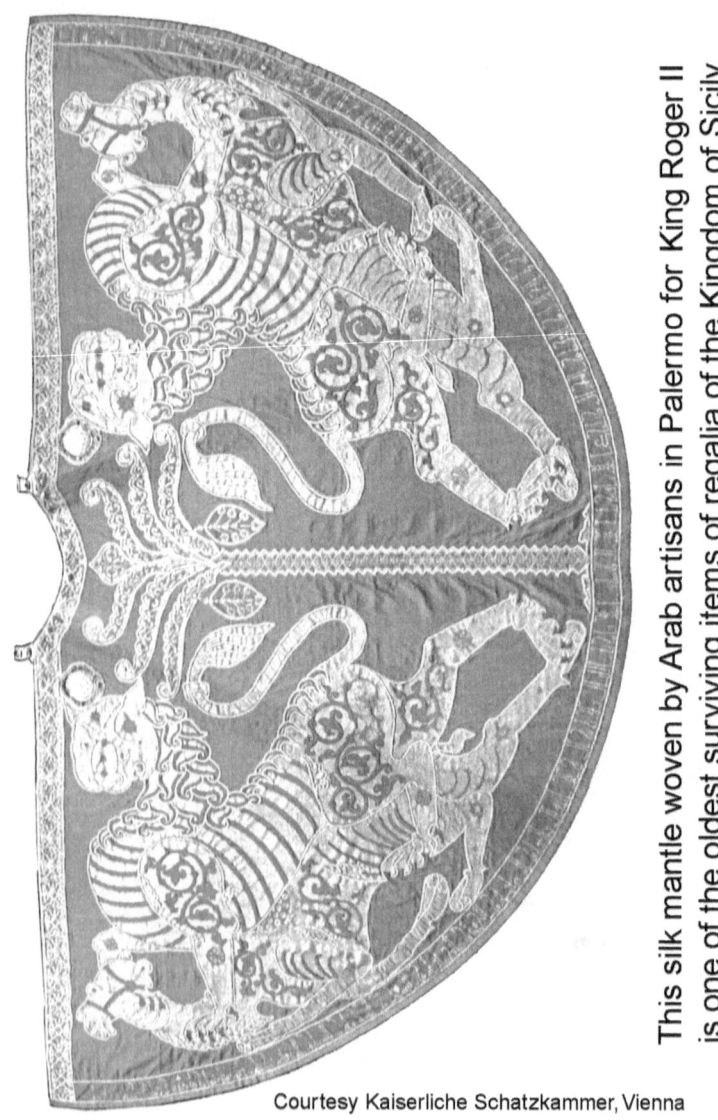

This silk mantle woven by Arab artisans in Palermo for King Roger II is one of the oldest surviving items of regalia of the Kingdom of Sicily

Courtesy Kaiserliche Schatzkammer, Vienna

Apse and cupola of the Palatine Chapel

Pisan Tower of the Norman Palace, Palermo

Cloister of Saint John of the Hermits, near the palace

Roger II crowned by Christ in a near-contemporary mosaic in the Martorana church in central Palermo

ΝΕΊΛΟΥ ΔΟΞΟΠΑΤΡΊΟΥ
ΤΆΞΙΣ ΤΩΝ ΠΑΤΡΙΑΡΧΙΚΩ͂Ν ΘΡΌΝΩΝ.
NILI DOXOPATRII
NOTITIA
PATRIARCHATUUM.

Σύγγραμμα γνώμενον παρὰ Νείλου Ἀρχιμανδρίτου τοῦ Δοξαπατρίου καθ᾽ ἃ κέλδυσιν τοῦ ἐυγενεστάτου μεγάλου Ῥηγὸς Ῥογερίου περὶ τῶν πέντε Πατριαρχικῶν θρόνων, κ̀ τ̃ ὑπ' αὐτοὺς Ἀρχιεπισκοπῶν, κ̀ Μητροπόλεων, κ̀ τ̃ ὑπὸ τὰς μητροπόλεις Ἐπισκοπῶν, κ̀ τῶν ἐνοριῶν ἑκάστου Πατριαρχικοῦ θρόνου, κ̀ πῶς κ̀ πότε συνέστη ἕκαστος πατριαρχικὸς θρόνος, κ̀ περὶ τ̃ τάξεως αὐτῶν, κ̀ τ̃ ἰδικῶν ἑκάστου ὀνομάτων, κ̀ πόσου λόγον ἐπέχουσι. συνεγράφη ἢ ἐτ̃: ϛχνα: Ἰνδικλιῶν Ϛ᾽:

Πανευγενέστατε Αὐθέντα μου, περὶ ἧς μοι ἔγραψας ὑποθέ-

Commentarius concinnatus à Nilo Doxapatrio Archimandrita, juſſu nobiliſſimi magni Regis Rogerii de quinque Patriarchalibus Thronis, & illis ſubjectis Archiepiſcopatibus, & Metropolitatibus, & qui Metropolitatibus ſubduntur, Epiſcopis,& Diœceſibus unius cujuſque ſedis Patriarchalis. Et quomodo & quando Patriarchici Throni inſtituti ſunt, & eorum ordine, & propriis nominibus, & cujus locum teneant, Concinnatus eſt anno 6651 Indictione ſexta.

Per quam illuſtriſſime Domine mi,de eo quod ad

Censorship in Catholic countries delayed publication of the treatise of Nilos Doxopatrios written for Roger II until 1685. It examines the roots of the patriarchal jurisdictions of the Orthodox and Catholic churches before the Great Schism.

Chapter 12

NORMANIZATION

In the second decade of Roger's reign, normalizing sometimes meant Normanizing. Yet life in the Kingdom of Sicily under the Hautevilles cannot be said to have been nearly as "Norman" as it was in Normandy or even England. Just as there were Celtic and Saxon cultural influences present in the Kingdom of England long after the Normans' conquest of 1066, we find the Greek and Arab cultures in the Kingdom of Sicily flourishing well into the thirteenth century, with a few vestiges surviving into our own times. Despite the slow Latinization of the church, neither Roger II nor his successors ever attempted to forcibly proscribe the use of Greek or Arabic by the subjects of the *Regnum Siciliae*.

The amalgamation was real. The Normans of southern Italy were mostly men, and always a small minority of the population that by the twelfth century usually married local women.

Compared to the essentially Latin, or "Italian," civilization of the eleventh-century Lombards, which was assimilated, even submerged, quite readily, the Byzantine and Fatimid cultures of southern Italy were distinct enough from that of the Normans to survive much longer than that of the Salernitans. Unlike the Lombards, whose only extant "mother culture" was the fading Longobardic society of part of northern Italy, those citizens having predominantly Byzantine or Arab roots could look to thriving Mediterranean empires where their languages, faiths and cultures were dominant. That connection was a cultural lifeline, for without it these peoples might well have been Latinized sooner than they were.

From Defiance to Compliance

By 1140, there was a very definite, indeed pragmatic, effort at political unification in view of the pacification of Puglia, Basilicata, Abruzzi and part of Campania. In that year, Roger confirmed royal privileges to the Palatine Chapel in the royal palace in Palermo, the edifice that was the kingdom's greatest architectural symbol of monarchical power, its "Tower of London."[352] That his ornate charter, with its colored ink, is one of only two known documents of this kind issued by his chancery during his reign says much about the importance he ascribed to this singular project.[353]

The king's eldest sons, Roger and Alfonso, were governing the mainland part of the *Regnum* with the help of competent advisors, encouraged by these men to impose their will as far north as the environs of Mount Cassino on the Tyrrhenian side of the peninsula and the Tronto River, in northern Abruzzi, on the Adriatic side, despite the fiefs in these areas belonging to the papacy. In effect, this expanded the kingdom northward.

Beginning in July of 1140, the elder Roger visited the peninsular part of the kingdom for what might be called an "inspection tour" to ensure that all was well. His itinerary took him to Benevento, Capua, Mount Cassino, Melfi and the abbey at Casauria (now Castiglione a Casauria) near Pescara. In October he reached Salerno and then sailed to Palermo.

To modern historians, the most salient part of this tour was Roger's visit to Ariano, now a royal city. Here he introduced a silver coin, the *ducat,* its name recalling the *duchy* of Apulia.[354] More significantly, he promulgated the kingdom's first general legal code.

The Law

The royal court of the Kingdom of Sicily, like that of other realms, was wherever the king was, and its system of law, which until now was riddled with inconsistencies, lacked a unifying code or the judges to enforce it. Feudal law, canon law, Maliki law and Hebrew law, a few of the general systems in place, were sometimes inadequate and potentially capricious. There might even emerge subtle complexities resulting from localized judicial traditions inherited from the Lombards of Salerno, the Ibadis of Enna, the Byzantine Greeks of Bari, and so forth. The Judaic traditions of Naples differed from those of Palermo. Certain Sunni practices might differ from those of the Shia.

The worst juridical practice in western Europe was the *judicium dei,* "the judgement of God," of which trial by ordeal is the most obvious example. Duels were little better.

In southern Italy, jurisprudence was what today's Italians call *un pasticcio,* an eclectic "pie" consisting of many confusing ingredients.

Modern colloquialisms aside, the difficulties were very real. If a Muslim and a Jew had a commercial dispute in a multiethnic, demesnial (non-feudal) town where there was no baron, it was not always clear what the proper legal venue for arbitration should be, much less the principles and norms to guide a decision in the case. Legal and geographic jurisdictions were not always very clearly defined. The royal court would be overwhelmed if the sovereign had to act as the last channel of recourse for the thousands of cases in the kingdom. What was needed was a legal framework that, among other things, set forth the rights of individual subjects as well as the king, church and nobility, with local judges empowered to render binding decisions.

Of course, the very idea of a "local" judge was itself complex. Clearly, it was impractical to place judges in any but the largest localities, perhaps coinciding with the seats of counties or bishoprics. To minimize bias, it would be best if these officers were "secular," not being priests, rabbis or imams, though it seemed likely that most would be Christians. The judges and advocates (attorneys) would have to be trained.

It was time for the warlord to become a lawgiver.

In, or shortly after, 1140 the king issued a legal code traditionally known as the "Assizes of Ariano," usually associated with that town.[355]

This was the cornerstone of the *corpus* of law of the Kingdom of Sicily in force until 1231, when it was supplanted by the Constitutions of Melfi. Taking a cue from the Code of Justinian, its underlying influence, it asserted royal authority in specific areas.

By no means was this a purely "secular" legal code, a concept that scarcely existed in twelfth-century Europe. Indeed, Catholic church law continued to be applied in many cases and places, particularly in view of the many bishoprics and monasteries being founded, usually with their own feudal estates and dependents, such as serfs.

The Assizes represented a concrete step in the Hautevilles' Latinization of their Kingdom of Sicily, both socially and ecclesiastically. In addition to Islamic and Judaic legal principles, certain Byzantine (Orthodox) Christian precepts were now subjugated to those of Rome. Evidence suggests that a few vestiges of "common law" remained in daily life, particularly among the Muslim population and especially in fields such as commerce.[356]

The Assizes were not, in the strictest sense, a "constitution," even as they clearly reflected the unifying jurisdiction established with the sovereignty of the Hautevilles under Roger. They cannot, however, be compared directly to the laws formulated during the same era by the rulers of England or France.

Unsurprisingly, Roger's code does not clearly address the role of the queen, either as consort or regent, matters left to traditional practice and law. There was no Queen of Sicily in 1140. As Roger was a widower when the Assizes were drafted, there was no reginal input.

There are two known, and slightly different, codices of the Assizes, one in the Vatican and the other at Mount Cassino. *Codex Vaticanus Latinus 8782* has forty-three statutes (clauses), or "assizes," and a preface. Copied late in the twelfth century, this is probably the more faithful to the original document. A later manuscript, *Codex Casinensis 468,* is abbreviated in form but includes seven additional statutes. Both codices were rediscovered during the nineteenth century.[357]

That the contemporary chronicler Falco of Benevento notes Roger's controversial introduction, at Ariano, of the ducat, without explicitly mentioning the new legal code suggests to some scholars that the Assizes were issued somewhat later and elsewhere. Moreover, the fact that the Assizes of Capua of Frederick II were deemed necessary in 1220 might lead a skeptic to question the application (or dissemination) of the earlier Assizes of Ariano. Thus far, a closely contemporary manuscript copy of the Assizes of Ariano dated accurately to *circa* 1140, if it survives, has yet to be discovered.

Yet modern historians seem to have known of the Assizes, sometimes mentioned generically as "Roger's laws," long before the nineteenth century, and Romuald of Salerno refers to "sundry legislation" at Ariano in 1140.

The Assizes asserted royal power in a formal way, affirming the monarch's fundamental role as lawgiver. All subjects had the same access to the law, even if their rights were not equal (as there was serfdom). Various crimes were addressed, particularly violent ones. Arming a mob, thereby inciting riots, was a grave act. Bishops, like nobles, were accorded certain privileges. Among Christians, apostates and heretics lost their rights of citizenship.

Rape was explicitly outlawed, though this statute was intended chiefly to protect nuns and virgins (maidens).[358] Treason was made a capital offense, Jews were forbidden the holding of Christian serfs, jesters were prohibited from blaspheming, simony was proscribed, fugitives were permitted asylum in churches. Sentences for crimes against public officials were to be taken seriously, taking into account that these acts were, in effect, offenses to the crown itself.

The forgery and theft of documents were unequivocally capital crimes. Counterfeiting or clipping coins was outlawed.

The code required that justiciars and notaries be descended from the nobility, royal assent being the only means of exempting this prerequisite.

Knights could be dubbed by senior knights, but only if these postulants were themselves the sons of knights. Only the king could elevate a man of low birth to knighthood, and he dubbed a number of knights at Naples in 1140.[359]

Infringement of demesnial lands (royal estates) was outlawed. Marriage was required as the basis for legitimacy of heirs. Adultery and prostitution were addressed, ditto kidnapping and robbery. Licensing of physicians is established (more at note 1159). Judges who accepted bribes could be executed.

We know not the extent to which the new legal code was copied and distributed; no manuscripts are known to be preserved from the time of Roger's reign. Were the Assizes a contemporary document, or were they a later "compendium" based on decisions Roger was known to have made, perhaps via several decrees over the course of a few years? We cannot know for certain.

Certain principles were affirmed or reiterated in successive years. In 1145, for example, the king decreed that capital crimes such as murder were to be punished only on royal authority, never by a bishop or abbot. To permit otherwise, apart from any question of the king's prerogatives being infringed, would have seen clerics advocating the shedding of blood. Nevertheless, it is clear that lesser officials occasionally enforced the law and meted out punishment, sometimes acting on the advice of justiciars, and so did barons.

Roger's justiciars were circuit judges responsible for specific regions or provinces, where they would travel from town to town to hear cases.

Whenever they were formulated, the Assizes, and decrees adhering to their principles, clearly reflected a Latin (Roman Catholic) theological orientation in the law. Nevertheless, Roger himself was amenable to hearing contrarian views, even those casting aspersions on papal primacy (see Chapter 4). What is more, Maliki law continued to govern certain aspects of commerce, such as contracts, especially in trade with Muslim states like Ifriqiya.

True, the Assizes were later eclipsed by the more complex Constitutions of Melfi, but as a cornerstone of the foundation of the kingdom they deserve more attention than they have received.[360]

At all events, while the Assizes took into account the existence of the three Abrahamic religious elements present in the kingdom, it is clear that the code itself had an underlying Christian orientation. The kingdom's Christians were beginning to differentiate themselves socially from the Muslims and Jews, and in an increasingly conspicuous manner. We find, for example, the word *christianus* used ever more frequently, as in the Italian *due cristiani,* "two Christians," and today it is sometimes synonymous in casual parlance with "person." When an Italian states that, *Non ho visto neanche un cristiano* ("I didn't see even one Christian"), the intent is not usually a distinction of faith but an observation that nobody, of any religion, was encountered. None of the chroniclers of the *Regnum* writing in Latin was especially sympathetic to non-Catholics.

The potentially severe penalties mentioned in connection with certain "capital" offenses reflect the "centralization" of government and law, an intolerance of the defiance of royal authority following a decade of rebellion.

Although there is clear evidence of common law existing in some form in the Kingdom of Sicily well into the Norman era, certainly in a few Maliki principles, it never seems to have made its way into general jurisprudence as it did in England.

The Function of Government

Apart from the exercise and application of the law, which can always be corrupted, feudalism and legal codes themselves are transparent enough. The daily function of government in the *Regnum* is more opaque in retrospect because contemporary references to it are sketchy and imprecise, woefully incomplete and even contradictory. Deciphering its mysteries would take more than the examination of a few charters, the evaluation of some passages in a chronicle, or comparisons to what was being done by the Normans in England and the Arabs in Africa.

While we should be wary of generalities, it is fair to state that the essential form of the kingdom's government was in place by the time the Assizes of Ariano were issued or shortly thereafter, albeit with a few modifications over the next few decades. While the Assizes may be said to reflect the culmination of the government's genesis, they seem to have achieved little in the way of addressing actual administration in practice.

Modern efforts to interpret the medieval government's structure are anything but satisfactory, partly because its organization varied somewhat with each reign and partly because some of the charters to which past historians made reference no longer exist to be consulted to confirm whether a certain court office was mentioned. Significantly, there were Arab, and even Byzantine, influences present that did not exist in many other European kingdoms, making direct comparisons difficult.

What we find in the *Regnum* was a blended system of government inspired by the cultures comprising the kingdom. It was essentially Norman, and probably influenced to some degree by the sophisticated system that existed in England, with some distinctively Arab elements.

That the kingdom's administration was formally "centralized" should not be construed to imply that there was not some local administration and, as ever, baronial dissent.

The church, whether through popes, bishops or abbots, would challenge royal jurisdiction into the nineteenth century, being the chief landholder after the crown itself. The civil judiciary and government generally did not interfere in matters concerning the church, which came to be viewed almost as "a state within a state." In Sicily proper the apostolic legateship governed this relationship to some limited degree, at least in the appointment of bishops, but this royal authority was rarely exercised. While certain prelates, such as the archbishops of Palermo, naturally enjoyed precedence at court, their position there didn't make them a formal part of government except, perhaps by participating in the "curia" in the same manner as major feudal lords. Only in the reign of Roger's grandson, William II, do we find an archbishop formally appointed as a *familiare* as part of the council sometimes called the *curia regis*.

Large demesnial cities like Salerno, Bari and Messina were known to elect jurats, sometimes *burgenses,* to form committees to decide local policy in a form of quasi-democracy not unlike what existed in some northern Italian communes. Even smaller demesnial cities, such as Enna (Kasr'Janni), Cefalù and Siracusa, occasionally engaged in this practice. However, it should be remembered that Roger had installed his sons at Salerno and Bari. While there might be factions, there were no formally-organized parties precisely comparable to the Guelphs and Ghibellines that emerged in Florence and Milan in response to conflicts between imperial and papal authority. However, Palermo is the quintessential example of a city having ethno-religious communities informally led by men respected by the people of these communities. These were not necessarily imams or rabbis, but prominent merchants or even men of letters.

Campanilismo is a modern term (from the word for the bell of the main "mother" church in a small town), but the roots of this idea are medieval. It refers to the tendency of towns to be self-contained, with little regard for central authority, though this should not be confused with simple provincialism. Granted that medieval life was generally "isolated" for the common folk, *campanilismo* describes a mentality which, at its extreme, can pit people against outsiders and even the monarch. Largely a result of the generally mountainous topography, the isolation of the kingdom's localities was exacerbated by the autocratic attitudes of many barons and some abbots. This is difficult to quantify based on the existing records, but under the Norman and Swabian kings we find most open conflicts within the kingdom to be motivated by issues other than disputes over royal succession (such as The Anarchy in England) or legitimate civic concerns (the independent-minded communes of northern Italy opposing imperial rule).

The first guilds, or *maestranze,* of tradesmen were localized organizations of those in the same profession or craft, such as metalsmiths, carpenters, weavers, tailors or shoemakers. Typically, these skilled artisans and craftsmen had workshops near others of their vocation. In Palermo the names of some streets in these medieval districts bear witness to this history. There are still metalsmiths' shops along Via Calderai ("Street of the Cauldron Makers"), bordering the city's erstwhile Jewish quarter. The greater number of craft guilds, like religious confraternities (discussed later in this chapter), emerged in the *Regnum* after the end of the Swabian era.

Most people lived outside the few major cities, and their usual contact with "government" was local by its very nature, via either a baron or an abbot. The demesnial (royal) cities were sometimes administered by bailiffs or constables. Hence in 1140 we find several of these cities governed by the king's sons as if they were his "delegates."

While domestic governmental functions and policies, such as taxation, trickled down to the general populace, specific operations were undertaken, in the first instance, between the crown and several *strata* of royal officers.

Roger's secondborn son, Tancred, Prince of Bari and Taranto, died in 1139 or 1140. Bari was eventually ceded to Tancred's younger brother, William, while Taranto ended up in the hands of a half-brother, Simon, Roger's illegitimate son (see note 404).

The Structure of Government

In its simplest outline, for which there are many hypotheses, this complex hierarchy had four major offices that answered directly to the crown: the chancellor (chancery), the treasurer (treasury), the highest-ranking justiciars (the judiciary), the "curia," officially the *magna curia regis*.[361] (The offices described here are indicated in the chart accompanying this chapter.)

In theory, the *justiciars,* or circuit judges, were outside "politics," and while there was no recourse to a "supreme judge" for appeals other than the king, there may well have been an administrator to whom the justiciars usually responded rather than the crown. For convenience, we may refer to this hypothetical officer as the "chief justiciar," though that term was not used, without suggesting that his office was a court of appeals.

Independent of the justiciars, yet peripherally part of the legal corps, were *notaries.* Learned in law, these were more than clerks or scribes, for they could issue and seal documents. There were several "royal" notaries who worked in or near the palace, and many "ordinary" notaries in major cities, where they worked as freelance professionals, charging fees for their services. In the normal course of affairs, the notaries, as a class, probably reported to the chancellor or the "chief justiciar," though there may have existed the intermediary position of *high notary,* sometimes known in later centuries as the *protonotaro.*

There is little doubt that certain notaries worked for specific justiciars, but most notaries were under the authority of the chancellor, who licensed them.

The *chancellor,* originally known simply as the *amiratus,* was the "prime minister." He answered directly to the sovereign and likely handled a great number of tasks, of which only a few are known to posterity. High military officers, such as *generals* and *admirals,* normally answered to the chancellor. By 1140, there was a clear distinction between the *chancellor,* who was essentially an administrator and the *amiratus,* who dealt chiefly with military matters, though both advised the sovereign.

The *treasurer* oversaw all aspects of financial administration, from taxation, excises and import duties to the minting of coinage and even certain aspects of feudalism. Under him were two secretaries, one responsible for the *royal diwan,* which handled the kingdom's finances, and another, the *baronial diwan,* whose tasks were concerned more with the baronage, lands and serfs. The secretary of the *royal diwan* might be a Muslim.

The *curia regis* was a corps of various court officers, and some high-ranking counts and barons, who had specific duties. Whereas most of the other officers were Christians, several in the *curia,* a kind of royal advisory council, were Muslims or Christianized Arabs. At times this may have even included the head of the royal bodyguard, usually an Arab, and perhaps a few palace eunuchs, also Arabs, from whose number were selected the palace chamberlain, several trusted messengers and other aides. Although the title of the counsellors known formally as *familiares,* or *archons,* was popularized after Roger's reign, officers who performed what were essentially similar functions doubtless existed in his time, when we sometimes, if rarely, encounter such terms.

The palace chamberlain, or seneschal (sometimes two different officers), might be considered part of the *curia regis.* In later times these members of the royal household would be regarded as a separate unit rather than part of the government.

There were also *bailiffs,* for whom Romuald of Salerno uses the term *camerarius* (though there were sometimes distinctions between the two). These were royal delegates whose duties varied, with some sent to preside over demesnial cities as if they were mayors. The authority of a bailiff in a demesnial town was comparable to that of a count or baron in a feudal town. A *constable* might serve the same role as a bailiff, perhaps as the protector of a royal castle, and this office sometimes implied the local function of law enforcement. There were occasional instances of justiciars serving as bailiffs, hence the confusion in the minds of some scholars.

In Palermo we find the position of *al-shaykh al-faqih al-qadi* long held by the Banu Raja family. This was a royal representative delegated to the city's Muslim Arab community. The same family may have overseen the *diwan al-mazalim,* or board of grievances, a kind of local law court based on Fatimid models to hear complaints.

The Hammudi clan was also important, and may have sponsored the political philosopher Ibn Zafar al Siqilli (mentioned in Appendix 6).

Historians generally agree that the judiciary was independent from the chancery and treasury. There may have been times when a specific *ad hoc* committee of the *curia* exercised power over one *diwan* or the other, but such evidence as exists suggests that the kings of Sicily oversaw the high offices directly, rather attentively and even adroitly.

Certain functions and duties were assigned to different officers over time. One of these was administration of the *baronial diwan* which, under Roger's successor (William I), was part of the treasury, though during most of Roger's reign it seems to have answered to the chancellor. Whereas the *royal diwan*, an institution inherited in its original form from the Kalbid emirs, was initially run by Muslims, the *baronial diwan* was operated by Christians.

While the *baronial diwan* could levy and collect various taxes from feudal vassals and demesnial towns, such as Capua, and even some monasteries, practices such as *scutage*, the payment of money by barons in lieu of military service, were not widely implemented in the *Regnum* during the Norman-Swabian period. Under Roger, the *baronial diwan* began to compile a registry of feudatories, the *Catalogus Baronum*, of which only part of the mainland portion survives, that was completed during the reign of William I. This is the "Domesday Book" of the Kingdom of Sicily. It is a list of vassals and their feudal obligations, usually expressed in the number of knights to be provided for military service to the king.[362]

Other taxes, such as those imposed upon merchants, such as excises and customs duties, were the province of the *royal diwan*. Indeed, the French *douane* and Italian *dogana*, for a customs duty, come to us from the Arabic *diwan*.

Whether the *counts* and *barons* could or should be considered part of a "government" may well be debated (few scholars include them in the formal schema). However, some of them controlled rather large districts and, at least in principle, they responded directly to the king. The nobles were certainly a key element in what might be termed "local government." In practice, they were not usually considered part of the *royal curia*, and in many circumstances they likely answered, in the first instance, to the *chancellor* or *justiciars* rather than the king himself.

Among those court officers who had little or nothing to do with government was the *royal falconer*, who during part of Roger's reign seems to have been a certain William.[363]

Coinage

In the government, one of the chief functions of the treasurer was the minting of coinage.

Under Roger II, coinage was standardized, with units generally comparable to what existed elsewhere, especially in Arab and Byzantine dominions. The design of a coin, particularly its reverse, might vary somewhat from one mint to another; the principal mints were at Palermo, Messina, Bari, Salerno, Capua and Amalfi, though other cities, such as Brindisi and Naples, sometimes produced coinage. Foreign coins circulated as well.

The *ducat*, as we have seen, was the standard silver coin. Though its format, influenced by Byzantine models, was not unique to the *Regnum,* it was the first coin exclusive to the kingdom, the others imitating those in use in other states.

The *follaris,* or *follis,* was copper (though a few were struck in bronze), eventually issued in larger or smaller sizes, hence the *trefollaris.* The *kharruba* was a silver coin generally smaller than the *follaris.*

The standard gold coin was the tiny *tarì,* from the Latin *tarenus,* sometimes *trappeso* (in the next section). The Fatimid and Norman versions of this coin were the same size, patterned after the Muslims' *ruba'i,* the popular quarter-dinar. The gold *dinar* sometimes seen in Sicily was usually slightly larger than the *tarì.*

The *schifati follari* (mentioned in the previous chapter) were even larger than the *dinar,* sometimes nearly the size of the *ducat.* The *schifatus* was later replaced by coins such as the *augustale* of Frederick II.

Despite similar names, not all these coins can be compared to those struck by the Angevins after 1266.

Apocryphal stories about William I and Frederick II issuing thick leather "coins" to pay their troops or retainers in lieu of metal coinage are not supported by surviving contemporaneous sources.

Among the common folk, many day-to-day transactions were concluded through barter, sometimes governed by written contracts where there were large quantities. Although there was no actual paper currency, the Arabs, and later the Templars, made use of what might be described as a "letter of credit," the *saqq* (mentioned in Chapter 9).

The standardization of coinage necessarily prompted a consideration of general measures, beginning with weight and mass.

Weights and Measures

While coinage was standardized, there was no system of weights and measures that was applied uniformly throughout the entire kingdom before 1266 despite an attempt by Frederick II to introduce one. Certain words were widely known, but a measurement identified with a term used in Basilicata might differ somewhat from what was employed for the same term in Sicily, the metrology itself varying slightly.

It was to be expected that each language spoken in the *Regnum* had its own words for common units of measurement, but the units themselves also varied. In practice, Palermitan merchants were disposed to use Arab measurements in trade with Africa, while Bariots used Greek terms in commerce with the Byzantine Empire. Trade with the states to the north of the kingdom generally used Latin terms.

Just as there were bilingual or trilingual charters and psalters, some bills of sale were issued in more than one language, and hence more than one system of measurement.

By the early years of the thirteenth century, several "native" units of measure were coming into common use, their names based on Latin, Greek and Arabic terms. These were some of the first words to make their way into the vernacular that became Sicilian. So far as we know (barring discovery of a prior charter fixing standard units in law), it was only about three decades later that these terms were recognized as "official" by Frederick II in his *Quaternus Excadeniciarum Capitinate,* useful legislation based on his more famous Constitutions of Melfi, which likewise regulate weights and measures.

Charters issued during the Norman-Swabian era that make reference to land only rarely utilize specific units of measure for distance and area, relying mostly, though not exclusively, on landmarks to define districts.

The term *salma,* sometimes *salmo,* plural *salmi,* from the Greek *sagma,* was used for both land area and the volume of dry products such as grain. An allied unit was the larger *canna,* which comes directly from the Greek.[364]

The *tomolo,* from the Arabic *thumn,* "one-eighth," was another term, a fraction of a *salma,* used to measure land area.

The *ruotolo,* from the Arabic *ratl,* was a unit of weight.

The *cafiso,* from the Arabic *kafiz,* was a unit of liquid measure, as was the *ciato,* from the Greek *kyathos.* A later introduction was the *quartuccio,* or "quart," which is slightly less than a liter. This "quart" is generally comparable to the volume of the *caraffa,* from the Arabic *garafa,* "to draw water," and the related *gurfa* or *gharraf,* a cup or dipper, probably derived in turn from the Persian *qarabah.*

The *cantaro,* from the Arabic *kintar,* was a unit of weight and volume mentioned by the mathematician Leonardo Fibonacci.

A few units inherited from the Roman era were still in use, particularly in ecclesiastical circles on the mainland. Notable among these was the *mille* (mile) for distance, from *mille passus,* a thousand steps.

For weight, the *libbra,* from the Latin *libra,* reformed under Charlemagne, was still used in Campania, Abruzzi and northern Calabria as part of the Lombard tradition.

The *oncia,* later the *onza,* finds its etymological origin in the Roman *uncia,* "one-twelfth." As a weight measure, however, it had many medieval iterations besides being a fraction of a *libbra.*

The *trappeso,* or *tarpeso,* was a unit of gold comparable to the weight of a *tarì* coin, theoretically a thousandth of a *ruotolo.* Indeed, the term *trappeso* was often used as a synonym for *tarì.*

Some of these terms were used formally into the twenty-first century, when a national law was promulgated to prohibit their use in official documents such as deeds. Indeed, a few, such as the *salma,* are still heard in rural areas today, especially in Basilicata, Calabria and Sicily, and wine is sometimes served in a *caraffa.*

Church and State

With the final submission of Bari, the largest Grecophone city of the *Regnum,* to royal control, social and ecclesiastical Latinization continued unabated, if slowly. There were still Orthodox monasteries, such as that of Stilo in Calabria, while Saint Philip, in the Nebrodian mountains, retained its Greek usages. For now, most Bariots, and the greater number of Messinians, were Greek speakers.

Conversion and assimilation were facts of life. The *Harley Trilingual Psalter* (shown in this book), with its text in Greek, Latin and Arabic, was composed in Palermo between 1130 and 1153. It is thought that this psalter was used at services in the royal presence in the Palatine Chapel. Most of the Greek text is drawn from the Septuagint, an early translation of the scriptures from Hebrew into Koine Greek. The Latin text is Saint Jerome's Gallican revision, completed around 384, itself formulated with an eye to the Greek texts. The Arabic is the eleventh-century translation *ex novo* by Abu'l-Fath Abdallah ibn al-Fadl ibn Abdallah al-Mutran al-Antaki.

Psalters were not the only useful liturgical devices. The Normans popularized the use of large, illuminated scrolls to record hymns. Especially popular for Paschal liturgies, these "Exultet rolls" were easy for the deacon and congregation to read during the mass (see the notes of Appendix 5).

The Benedictines were, without doubt, the most powerful and influential of the religious orders in the *Regnum,* though the Hautevilles introduced many others. Each order had its own rule and emphasis, but only with the establishment of the Franciscans during the reign of Frederick II do we see the inception of something significantly different.

While most Catholic monks lived a cloistered life, some being hermits in the Byzantine tradition, at least a few participated in local life. Most abbeys and monasteries, like the majority of the population, were outside the major cities, though there were clearly exceptions.

Certain abbots might bear the rank of bishop, but the archbishops of major centers constituted a power unto themselves, with that of Palermo governing the kingdom's primatial see and enjoying special esteem at court.

That most bishops and abbots exercised direct authority over a number of peasants and serfs was based not on ecclesiastical principles but on feudal norms, as if these prelates were counts or barons.

Late in 1140, Roger received some delegates of Bernard of Clairvaux who escorted Elizabeth of Champagne to the *Regnum* to wed his heir, Roger, Duke of Apulia. Consistent with his efforts as a builder of Latin Christianity, the king granted Bernard's Cistercians, a new order, the right to erect an abbey in Calabria.

Two years later, Roger approved the beginning of reconstruction of the Benedictine abbey of Saint John of the Hermits near the palace in Palermo. Its abbot would act as the king's confessor *ex officio.*

Although groups of devout Catholic men besides knights and pilgrims existed outside the religious orders, lay confraternities (considered in greater detail in Chapter 32) were not yet known. The focus of these devotional organizations might be the veneration of a local saint. Early use of the term *maestranza,* also descriptive of a craft guild (discussed earlier in this chapter), rather than the more accurate *confraternita,* sometimes creates confusion. Confraternities and guilds were both "brotherhoods," but neither type of organization thrived in the Kingdom of Sicily during the Norman-Swabian era to the extent that would be seen later.

An Orthodox prelate like Nilos Doxopatrios (whom we met in Chapter 4) might be welcomed by the king, and the presence of others at court who shared his faith is a possibility that cannot be excluded from consideration, but the greatest Christian influence was papal and Catholic. Some of the Christianized palace eunuchs eventually found places in the *curia,* particularly as chamberlains, but if they were considered particularly trustworthy or loyal it was probably more for being Arab than for their Catholicism. During the Norman era the royal bodyguard and archers seem to have remained mostly Muslim.

After 1140, it would develop that the greatest dissent to arise in the *Regnum* emanated not from the Muslims, though that was not unknown, but from Catholics, especially among the "Norman" baronage; Ranulf of Alife was not the last of his breed. While there is little doubt that some of the knights enfeoffed by the Norman kings bore Greek ancestry through one line or another, their identities are not generally known to us because, as vassals, their "surnames" were toponyms. That is what we usually find in the *Catalogus Baronum.*

To what degree was the *Regnum* a "papal" monarchy? Apart from reasons rooted in the kingdom's proximity to the Papal State, the popes certainly enjoyed a special prestige here. Not until the reign of Frederick II was the Kingdom of Sicily destined to confront much overt conflict emanating from Rome, and Frederick's problems were rooted mostly in the fact of his being Holy Roman Emperor and ruler of the northern Italian communes in conjunction with his rule of southern Italy, thus "isolating" papal territory between his dominions. Unlike many other European monarchies, the *Regnum Siciliae* was actually a recent papal foundation.

This should not be construed to suggest that the nature of Catholic religious devotion was much different in the Kingdom of Sicily from what one encountered elsewhere in western Europe. There were, however, a few favored saints, along with some colorful legends that have come down to us.

Legends

Two enduring legends that refer to the Norman period have proven to be more popular than courtly literature and certain other genuine artefacts. They have been transmitted orally. While neither is mentioned in records contemporaneous to the Norman era that are known to us, both have become emblematic of it.

Saint Rosalie may have lived in the twelfth century, yet precious little is known of her with certainty. The story that she was the daughter of a Norman baron during the reign of Roger II, or perhaps a lady-in-waiting to the king's second or third wife, is not supported by extant sources. She is said, by tradition, to have been born in 1130 and chosen the life of a hermit nun at a time when hermitages were being discouraged in favor of abbeys. Rosalie has been venerated since the thirteenth century in several towns of the hinterland, most notably Santo Stefano di Quisquina, the site of her grotto, and Bivona, where a medieval church dedicated to her still stands. She appears with Saint Elias, Saint Oliva and Saint Venera in a small icon of the thirteenth century preserved in Palermo, but it has been suggested that her name was added to the work long after its creation.

It was claimed, much later, that Rosalie had lived in a cavern atop Mount Pellegrino, overlooking Palermo, the city of which she is now the principal patroness. In modern iconography, she is depicted with red hair and a light complexion.

The origin of the legend of the "Saracen's head" is not known but it is not connected to religious belief. According to this tale, a beautiful maiden of Palermo's coastal Khalesa district met an Arab maritime trader during the Norman period (or the Kalbid era) and married him despite knowing that he often traveled between Sicily and Ifriqiya. Initially, she tolerated his absence during these voyages. The lady, who in some versions of the story was Christian, eventually learned that her husband had a wife and family in Ifriqiya, something he had initially denied, and one night she killed him, thereafter using his head as a pot for herbs she grew in her garden. The majolica vases sold in Sicily depicting the crowned head of a Moor recall this story of love, betrayal and revenge. Examples of such marriages were not unknown in the Muslim world.[365]

Both tales have a degree of historical relevance. The story of Rosalie seeks to identify a religiously devout Norman woman who becomes a nun and then a saint; this may be an indirect allusion to the Latinization of Sicily and the virtue of the unruly Norman baronage. The legend of the Muslim's head recalls the marital norms of Islam and the fact of trade between Sicily and Ifriqiya.

At least two legends associated with this era relate to Roger II directly. While these may have some basis in fact, their details appear to be apocryphal.

The Mikalis legend was mentioned in the Introduction. No sword is known with certainty to survive that belonged to the first King of Sicily. Extant contemporary records don't mention a named sword. The idea of the existence of a mystical royal sword, Mikalis, may have originated in the "Excalibur" given to King Manfred by Richard Lionheart, mentioned by the English chronicler Roger of Howden.[366]

Roger did not found an order of chivalry, though, like other kings, he seems to have supported the work of the Hospitallers and Templars (see note 336). The legend of his "Knights of the Golden Chain" was probably inspired by three developments. During his reign, there were those enfeoffed knights who had stayed loyal to him whilst many rebelled, and modern historians probably presumed that these men were recognized in a public way. Later in the twelfth century we meet the Teutonic Order, whose first royal patrons were the Hohenstaufens, including Henry VI, King of Sicily *jure uxoris* as the husband of Roger's daughter. In the fourteenth century, "collar orders" were founded to affiliate nobles with the sovereign (see the Conclusion).

Apropos patronage, while certain saints, such as Michael the Archangel, George of Lydda, Nicholas of Myra, Julian the Carthaginian and Mary Magdalene were indeed venerated by the Hautevilles, perhaps with a particularly adamant devotion, they cannot be said to have been "exclusive" patrons of the dynasty, nor did the kingdom have a specific heavenly patron during this era. The palace chapel, as we have seen, was dedicated not to one of these saints but to Saint Peter, and the names of specific saints were only rarely invoked in royal charters. The Norman veneration of Michael and George is rooted in these two saints being patrons of knights.

Like Michael and George, Julian the Carthaginian, whose relics were kept in the Palatine Chapel, is associated with knighthood. Jordan, the son of Roger I, invoked (and supposedly received) Julian's intercession at a battle against the Arabs at Erice, hence the renaming of the town during the Norman era.

The Christmas legend of Saint Nicholas (as Santa Claus) is based on the surreptitious gift-giving attributed to him. In fact, the tradition of the Christmas witch, or *Befana,* bringing children gifts on the eve of the Epiphany (from which she takes her name), antedates by centuries the popularization of the stories about Saint Nicholas in southern Italy. Although Saint Nicholas was venerated in the *Regnum* beyond Bari, his cult was not as widespread as a few historians claim.

Mary Magdalene, to whom a royal chapel was dedicated that was attached to Palermo's original cathedral, but replaced by another church that stands nearby, was long considered *de apostolorum apostola,* "the apostle to the apostles."

The veneration of these saints during the Norman era was consistent with Orthodox tradition and should not be confused with beliefs and practices that came later. Thomas Becket, whom we shall meet in a subsequent chapter, would be one of the first saints venerated in the kingdom whose cult was not both Orthodox and Catholic.

There were other forms of "soft" cultural power that helped to establish the prestige of the kingdom.

Mapping the Kingdom

It was probably around 1140 that Roger appointed a court geographer, Abdullah al Idrisi, who later mapped and described the *Regnum.* Although the most detailed part of this project to survive covers Sicily, it was clearly intended to assess the entire kingdom, with an eye to evaluating its resources, its strengths and weaknesses.

Abu Abd Allah Abdullah Muhammad ibn Muhammad ibn Ash Sharif al Idrisi (or Edrisi) was born in Sabtah, now Ceuta, Morocco, around 1100. It is possible that his family was traditionally associated, perhaps through commerce, with Sicily's northwestern emirate, and Idrisi certainly had kin on the island. Through one line, his direct ancestors were the Hammudids, a branch of Morocco's Idrisids, and it was at Cordoba and Marrakesh that Idrisi received his earliest education. He eventually visited the Holy Land and Asia Minor, as well as parts of France and possibly England.

According to the contemporary Arab traveller Ibn Jubayr, Idrisi was related to the Hammudi family that was influential among Sicily's Muslims. Notable among those thought to be his kinsmen was Abul Kasim ibn Hammud ibn al-Hajar, a caïd who was highly respected in the Muslim community of Palermo.

Idrisi's fame as a man of letters was known before his invitation to the royal court. He established his residence in Sicily around 1145, and may have first visited as early as 1139. Idrisi produced a number of works based on astute scholarly research, and it has been observed by modern Arabic scholars that he was an exceptional poet and writer of Arabic prose.

His famous planisphere, a large global map made of precious metal (mostly silver), did not survive the twelfth century, but it is known to have been a noteworthy work of geography, probably the most accurate map of Europe, northern Africa and western Asia to have been created during the Middle Ages. An atlas produced during this period survived. A multilingual "Book of Simple Drugs" is also known to us. A minor geographical treatise written during the reign of Roger's successor, William I, has been lost to time.

Idrisi's greatest surviving work is, without doubt, his "Pleasure Excursion of One Eager to Traverse the World's Regions," better known as the *Book of Roger*. Much of the information is secondhand. He describes England's dreary weather, for example, but does not seem to have set foot in that country.

Closer to home, the book provides much information about Sicily's economy. In a casual observation, Idrisi mentions the making of spaghetti in Trabia. It is to Idrisi that we owe much of our knowledge of the entire Mediterranean during this era. Some of the book's statements were unorthodox for their time, things like "the earth is round like a sphere." Today, the *Book of Roger* is considered one of the most important scientific works of the Middle Ages.

Like Marco Polo, Idrisi was a traveler who wrote about what he saw, but his work was much more scientific, and generally more objective, than Polo's. More importantly, it survives in several early manuscripts. The *Book of Roger* was completed in the first months of 1154. Part of this project was the *Tabula Rogeriana,* a map of the known world.

We know little of Idrisi's subsequent activities, but his life and career exemplify the extent of the intellectual and commercial relationship of the *Regnum* with the Islamic states to the west.[367]

By no means was Idrisi the only scholar at court conversant with science.

Medicine

Despite the political decline of Salerno as the Lombard capital, its distinguished medical school continued to turn out students. One of the better known among them is Romuald Guarna, the chronicler who was consecrated archbishop of that city and is thus known as "Romuald of Salerno." Romuald (who is described in Appendix 6) eventually became a professor of medicine at Salerno. As we have seen, Sichelgaita, the wife of Robert Guiscard, was also trained as a physician at this school. However, its most distinguished student may be a woman about whom virtually nothing is known. Trota, or Trocta, of Salerno lived in the second half of the eleventh century and probably into the twelfth.

Trota, sometimes "Trotula de Ruggiero," is not always identified very closely with a particular figure who lived during a very specific period.[368]

The focus of her treatise, the eponymous *Trotula,* is gynecology. Certain topics, such as abortion and contraception, are not considered directly (see Chapter 2). Trota is deservedly praised, but that is not to suggest that every idea in the work was very enlightened, even if it must be considered in the context of its time.

For example, one form of analysis suggested to ascertain a couple's fertility called for each spouse to urinate into a separate pot containing wheat bran, with infertility assumed if worms were thriving in it after nine or ten days.[369]

Unlike many of her contemporaries, Trota, whoever she was, believed that failure to conceive could be attributed to the husband as much as the wife.[370] This belief was not altogether unknown, but during the twelfth century most physicians and churchmen still preferred to place the blame for infertility on the woman. In many places, this mentality actually survived into modern times.

If a couple wanted a son, the husband was to consume the uterus and vagina of a hare, dried, powdered and mixed with wine. The woman should ingest a similar potion made from the testicles of a hare.[371] Other potions prescribed for the woman were made from the dried, powdered testicles and liver of a boar or pig.

In our times, the use of powders and potions of this kind are usually dismissed as "folk remedies" or even witchcraft (described in Chapter 32). However, a few seem to be rooted in medieval medicine.[372]

Certain treatments were purely cosmetic, intended to enhance beauty, and here the Christian women in Sicily learned much from their Muslim sisters, an observation that eventually appeared in *De Ornatu Mulierum,* sometimes called the *Trotula Minor* as it supplemented two principal texts, one on conditions and the other on treatments, that make up the main *corpus* of the *Trotula*.[373]

This treatise on cosmetics tells us something about the beauty standards of the time. Trota may have lived into the twelfth century, and treatments such as a potion, based on pomegranate rind, for darkening hair seem to defy the notion of blond hair and a light complexion as a "generalized" aspiration among women. There are descriptions of compounds and methods for such procedures as the removal of body hair.[374]

Not to be overlooked is the *Antidotarium Nicolai,* probably composed in Salerno around 1100, possibly by a certain Nicholas. This is essentially a collection of formulae for medicinal potions. Most derive from plants and minerals, and a few are made with sugar. Many are drawn from works written by experts around the Mediterranean. Notably, the slightly earlier *Antidotarium Magnum* of Constantine the African, a Tunisian monk at Mount Cassino, brought formulae known in Arabic and Greek into Latin translation. The compilation by Nicholas owes much to Constantine's larger collection. Other works were produced; a small compendium called the *Ars Medicinae,* or *Articella,* written at Salerno early in the twelfth century, influenced the practice of medicine around Europe.[375]

Among the teachers at Salerno's medical school, an institution praised across Europe, were Byzantines, Jews and Arabs as well as Lombards and other Latins. These professors brought their knowledge and traditions with them. Students came from far and wide.[376]

Rebecca Guarna, who was related to Romuald of Salerno, practiced medicine, including surgery, around 1200. She authored several treatises, including *De Urinis* and *De Embrione*. During this era, the most common surgical procedure known in the *Regnum* was circumcision. Though this was practiced chiefly among the Muslims and Jews, it was not unknown among Christians (see note 376).

Besides obvious illnesses from plagues and malaria, there were numerous allergies and other conditions which might be treated by the medicine of the time with varying degrees of success. Certain conditions that are commonplace today were less frequent in the Middle Ages. Celiac disease (gluten intolerance) was rare because medieval grain varieties, notably *tumminìa* and *russello* but also *bidì* and the distinctive *perciasacchi* (see Chapter 27), contained far less gluten than those introduced in modern times, while much rice was cultivated and consumed. Extreme obesity of the kind caused by overeating was unusual because most people ate less, at fewer meals.

Certain disorders were scarcely identified by the medical literature of the time except, perhaps, through vague descriptions of their most obvious physical manifestations. Here hereditary conditions that come to mind are thalassemia and multiple sclerosis; the former was long present in the populations of southern Italy and the latter was introduced principally with the Normans (see note 17).

In the twelfth century, the Kingdom of Sicily would become the first state in Europe to license physicians through the establishment of rigid regulations (see note 1159).

Trota, Sichelgaita, Rebecca and physicians like them, retroactively described as the "Women of Salerno," were exceptional for their era, but the Sicilian court became famous for other "exotic" things that were unknown in most of Europe.

Harems

The harem was one of the many traditions that Sicily's Christian kings inherited from the Kalbids. We find several references to it by people familiar with the palace and its court. Hugh Falcandus mentions it during the reign of William I in connection to the Bonello revolt (described in Chapter 16), when some of the concubines were raped and others abducted, but also in his "Letter to Peter."[377]

Later, the traveler ibn Jubayr mentions the harem in his diary during the reign of William II. He states, through hearsay, that Christian women converted to Islam and became concubines.[378]

In daily life, some of the women of the harem were silk weavers. Some may also have had other duties at court as artisans or even cooks. We do not know how many concubines there were, but in the reign of Frederick II, the last king known to have maintained the harem, they traveled with him; Frederick also seems to have had a harem at Lucera, a Muslim city in Apulia.[379]

The harem in the palace may have been guarded by eunuchs, as was the practice in Tunisia, yet we have no specific record of Sicily's court eunuchs performing this task. Although it is quite possible that a concubine could have given birth to a child of one of our kings, no such children are known to us by name or otherwise mentioned.

The precise location of the palace harem is unknown. It was probably somewhat isolated on a high floor of one of the towers, though not the tower that housed the Palatine Chapel and Roger's throne room.

Our knowledge of medieval harems like the one in Sicily comes to us from Fatimid history, though much that has been written about the institution itself concerns its modern incarnations.[380] It could be argued that little is known of the Sicilian harem because medieval harems, by their very nature, were discreet.

Some of the local leaders of Palermo's Muslim community, even during the Norman era, may have had small harems, which should not be confused with the habitation of four wives in the same large residence.

Ibn Jubayr observed Christian women in Sicily who dressed like the Muslim women, in veils or scarves.[381] This was also true of the Jewish women. Except for being exceptionally beautiful and well-dressed, a girl of the harem, if permitted to walk about Palermo, perhaps in the souk near the palace, would be indistinguishable from most other young women.

Whether the Sicilian concubines could be described as "slaves" is open to debate. Too little is known about the Sicilian royal harem to conclude much about it, but slavery was usually implied even by medieval standards, for these women were not free to leave. Although the women were secluded most of the time, it is quite possible that, perhaps accompanied by guards, they could occasionally venture beyond the palace walls.

Concubinage associated with harems of this kind was tantamount to slavery (considered below).

Eunuchs

Contrary to a popular belief implied by much literature, making boys into eunuchs was not a practice of Muslim Arab origin, nor even an official part of Islam. In fact, eunuchism was a practice known to the Byzantine Greeks, from whom the Muslims adopted it. There were eunuchs in antiquity.[382]

In the Middle Ages, part of the historical reasoning for appointing eunuchs to positions of trust was that they had no wives or children of their own, hence no conflicts of loyalty. This questionable logic endured in the Mediterranean region and some parts of Asia for many centuries.

Eunuchs were often charged with guarding harems but (as mentioned above) perhaps less so in Sicily than elsewhere. Most of the Sicilian eunuchs were slaves, at least initially, and most began their lives as Muslims. As the kingdom's Arab population gradually converted to Christianity, there were ever fewer eunuchs.

Questions of gender are unavoidable. To the modern mind, castration is usually viewed as a form of genital mutilation. In some societies, eunuchs constituted a "third gender." Castration affects sexual development, libido and even appetite.[383]

Several Sicilian eunuchs who converted to Christianity rose to become important, trusted court officers: Caïd Martin, Caïd Richard, Caïd Peter (Ahmed es-Sikeli), Philip of Mahdia.[384]

Besides men of such rank, there were a fair number of eunuchs at the court in the Norman era, for Hugh Falcandus mentions Norman rebels attempting to massacre many of them during a revolt in Palermo. Although it may not have been cited at the time, the tenuous Biblical pretext for such discrimination is found in Deuteronomy 23:1. The Koran does not mention eunuchs explicitly but Islamic law prohibits castration; the existence of eunuchism tells us that this proscription was not always put into practice.

Virtually nothing is known about Sicily's eunuchs as a group or community, and the only references made to them refer to those at court. We have no indication of the number that became Christian.

Too little is known to ascertain the precise motivations for the loyalty of most of Sicily's Muslims to the king, but it may be explained by the simple fact that the monarch was the guarantor of their safety in an environment increasingly hostile to them (see note 384).

Except for trusting certain eunuchs, we know little about what the kings and queens thought of the practice itself. The queens seem to have accepted eunuchism as part of life in Sicily, just as they accepted the reality of the royal harem.

Slavery and Incarceration

Some serfs were tied to the land, effectively "owned" by their feudal lords, who might be barons, abbots or the king himself. The concubines of the royal harem, as we have seen, lacked the freedom to leave in search of other living situations, and their everyday movements were generally controlled; they were, in effect, slaves.

Slavery, as an institution, had a long history in southern Italy, being known to the ancient Greeks and Romans, and the latter introduced the so-called "Roman villa system and economy," which in its workings vaguely resembled the manorialism, with its serfdom, that came later (considered in Chapter 2). As we have seen, late Roman usage may have influenced the practices of the Longobards who arrived in Italy during the sixth century.

Did actual chattel slavery exist in the Kingdom of Sicily?

Arab Palermo seems to have had a slave market, located in the Kala district near the seaside castle. Although its name persisted, the market itself appears to have been abolished by the time Roger II was crowned, with the Hautevilles discouraging the kind of slave trade known to exist in some measure among the Fatimids and Kalbids.

During the same century, we find the Norman kings forbidding the realm's Jews to hold Christians as slaves. A slave trade of sorts continued to exist, however, particularly at Messina, where it was accorded a single line by Roger's son, William I, in a decree incidentally reminding his subjects of the royal monopoly on it. If slavery persisted, even to a limited degree, during the Norman-Swabian era, it would at least be monitored and regulated by the crown.[385]

Yet the entire question of slavery is generally ignored in the sweeping legal codes promulgated by Roger II and Frederick II.

The term *servus* in legal codes, charters and chronicles often refers not to slaves but to serfs (see note 1028). In general practice, the nearest thing to slavery, as that term is connoted today, was the phenomenon of serfs being "sold" along with a manorial estate. It should be remembered that serfs were peasants but not all peasants were serfs, and not all land was strictly manorial (feudal).

Another case would be men taken prisoner in military campaigns. Since the church officially discouraged the enslavement of Christians, most prisoners of war forced into slavery were Muslims. Such cases were rare because, in practice, our kings were reluctant to enslave these men. Most often, prisoners would be exchanged or ransomed following a campaign or war, and there were infamous instances of kings ordering the killing of large numbers of captured men.

Most of the slaves were Muslims. By the middle of the thirteenth century, however, the alienation between the Catholic and Orthodox churches meant that Greeks might occasionally, albeit rarely, be enslaved.

Incarceration itself was exceptional because the *Regnum* lacked large prisons of the kind that could accommodate a great number of detainees for lengthy sentences. Other types of punishment, some quite harsh, were the norm; flogging and various forms of torture come to mind.

By no means did the Hautevilles and Hohenstaufens abolish slavery, but they made discreet efforts to curtail it.

Literacy

There is no question that the education of children was greater in the *Regnum* than what then existed in most parts of Europe. This was especially true in Sicily, particularly in the larger cities where there were traditionally Muslim schools. Until the emergence of a vernacular language around 1200, the spoken languages were Greek, Arabic, Norman French and an evolved form of Latin, a quasi-Italian, influenced by Longobardic.

It is worth considering the nature and extent of education during the reign of Roger's dynasty, bearing in mind the pedagogical distinction between reading and writing, as well as the varying types and levels of proficiency.

The clergy, of course, was highly literate, in Latin, Greek or both. Beyond the clergy, particularly amongst women, the literacy rate was generally lower except for noblemen, aristocratic ladies and nuns.

Many aristocrats in the laity were educated formally to attain reasonable proficiency in Latin, their official written language, usually by priests or nuns. Even among the nobility, however, the degree to which female literacy was achieved in traditionally "Latin" regions, such as Lombard Campania, is questionable.[386]

There is evidence that many inhabitants of the *Regnum* born into families that were Muslim, Byzantine or Jewish were afforded greater educational opportunities than what was historically made available to "Latins." Here there are several overlapping concepts.

The Aghlabids and Fatimids advocated the establishment of large libraries, comparable to those of major monasteries, but also the *dar al-hikma,* or "house of wisdom." One of the largest institutions of this kind was founded in Cairo in 1004 and eventually became what was essentially a "secular" university. In common parlance, *madrasa* is a generic term for any school.

Naturally, the use of paper facilitated writing, making study easier. Whereas "Latin" children might speak a language, such as Norman French, different from what was written, those raised speaking Arabic or Greek (or both) wrote in the same language that was spoken.

The Muslim schools were not very large, and for convenience were probably associated with mosques. Boys were educated separately from girls, perhaps on alternate days.[387]

The Jewish tradition was not unlike that of the Muslims except that it was more "private," probably relying upon families, rather than schools, to instruct younger children, except for actual Talmudical study (for boys) under a rabbi.[388]

In these populations there was a very practical reason for educating girls. One imagines, for example, the situation of an Arab or Jewish merchant who had daughters but no sons. Understandably, he would want his daughters to be literate. It should be remembered that the Jews of Sicily spoke and wrote Judeo-Arabic, with Hebrew as the formal and liturgical language.

The status of children's education among the Grecophone population is more difficult to gauge. Estimates of literacy at thirty or even forty percent would still place it far ahead of the populations of Campania, Tuscany and most of Europe. Even so, it was probably less dynamic than that of the Arabs and Jews of the Kingdom of Sicily.[389]

As regards the social view toward literacy, or the belief in its necessity, the most pronounced difference between the Muslims and Jews, on the one hand, and the Christians on the other, is that the Christians, and most notably the Catholics, were generally content to leave the reading and study of scripture to those in the religious vocations (priests, monks, nuns). In Islam and Judaism, contrarily, it was presumed that even "ordinary" worshippers would learn scripture; the words *imam* and *rabbi* originally meant "teacher."

The education of children in the Kingdom of Sicily cannot be said to be an amalgam of various systems. Rather, it was three or four distinct systems that co-existed comfortably.

With the exception of Trota of Salerno, about whom precious little is ever likely to be known, the first woman of the Kingdom of Sicily whose writing has been identified with reasonable certainty was born toward the end of the Swabian era. This was Nina of Messina, an aristocrat, the first poetess known to us to compose her work in a medieval Italian vernacular (see note 910).

Certain aristocrats, despite the benefit of education, are known to have been unable to read. Some of these cases may be explained by the presence of learning disabilities such as dyslexia. Only as an adult did Charlemagne learn to read, and despite his best efforts he never mastered writing very well.

Beyond basic education, the *Regnum* under the Hautevilles boasted its own multilingual literary tradition and became an important center for the translation and transcription of classical texts from Greek and Arabic into Latin. An oft-cited example is the Latin translation of Ptolemy's *Almagest* by Henry Aristippo (Henricus Aristippus), who also gave us Latin versions of works by Plato, Aristotle and the theologian Gregory of Nazianzus.[390]

Agriculture

There is little to suggest substantial changes in agriculture during the Hauteville and Hohenstaufen reigns.[391] Yet certain developments coincided with the Normans' arrival in Italy. There was, for example, the introduction of triennial, three-field crop rotation, accompanied by improved plowing methods.

Certain parts of southern Italy, especially where the landscape consisted mostly of valleys and coastal plains, had two annual harvests, in early autumn (or late summer) and early winter. In some regions there were indigenous crops, such as artichokes, cardoons, anise, broccoli and cauliflower, that were harvested from November into March.

It may be that certain methods, such as the Kalbid use of *kanats* for irrigation, made their way from Sicily to mainland regions of the kingdom. Statistics and land surveys are too few, and too unreliable, to offer us much in the way of empirical indications of, for example, deforestation.

Roger II encouraged the cultivation of wheat for export, and this led to the destruction of some forests. There were several types of wheat grown in southern Italy since Arab and Byzantine times, most originating in Asia, with the durum varieties being the most popular. Within this broad category are the three types already mentioned. *Tumminìa* (or *timilia*) is used to make the flour from which the "black bread" of Castelvetrano is prepared. *Russello* is named for its reddish color. *Perciasacchi* originated in Asia's vast central regions and is related to Khorasan wheat, while *margherito* and *bidì* were probably African. (The use of wheat in cookery is considered in Chapter 27.)

Rice was already being cultivated in Sicily and southern Puglia, and Asian livestock, such as the Girgentan goat, which we met in Chapter 1, was introduced in Arab times. The breed of water buffalo raised around Salerno was already present before the arrival of the Normans and is similar to those found in the Balkans.

Olive cultivars such as the Kalamata, of which several millennial trees planted in Norman times stand in southeastern Sicily, were introduced by the ancient Greeks.

Serfdom gradually increased as the greater number of smallholdings in Puglia, Calabria and Sicily were ceded to the control of barons and abbots.

Markets and Fairs

Connected with agriculture, but also the craft tradition, were markets and fairs. Some of the street markets in southern Italy, particularly in Palermo and Naples, have operated continuously since the Norman era.

What distinguished the markets in Sicily from most of those in peninsular Italy, and in Europe generally, was their origin in the souk (or bazaar) tradition of the Muslims, which is still seen in parts of Africa and Asia today. Chronicles and charters occasionally mention such places. In his "Letter to Peter," Hugh Falcandus notes an "Arab market" along the *Balat,* or "marble street," what is now Via Vittorio Emanuele, formerly Via Cassaro, in central Palermo (shown in one of this book's maps).[392]

Similar to a souk, a "standing" street market was a permanent site in a large European city where merchants sold all kinds of products, from fruits to jewels. Palermo's Ballarò, the oldest street market in Europe, was founded by the Aghlabids as the Balarah (or Balari) souk. The same city's Capo market in the Sari al Kadi district was founded later, during the eleventh century, as a boucherie (a site where meat was butchered).

Apart from the written record, the historical existence of street markets is evident because into the modern era these were continuously the chief marketplaces in cities and larger towns where, in some cases (such as that of Palermo) the positions of the streets and squares themselves have changed very little over time.[393]

In smaller localities, such markets might operate on just three days per week.[394]

A fair, in contrast to a market (or souk), was not permanent. It might be held just a few times in the course of a year and was much larger than the typical market. Normally, it would operate only with a royal license or the explicit permission of a local bailiff or governor.

Like the souks, the medieval concept of the fair survives in some sense in the former *Regnum.* Here we still encounter the "itinerant" street market, the weekly *mercatino.* Comprised of traveling merchants known (in English) in the Middle Ages as "chapmen," these smaller markets were operated in more recent times by vendors of agricultural produce, livestock, or farm-related items such as rakes and sheep bells. Yet this tradition is rooted in the medieval practice of the king granting the right of a small town to "hold a fair."[395]

Certain fairs were associated with festivals and other events, such as holidays and even tournaments. Established during the thirteenth century at the site of a jousting ground, the *Fiera Vecchia* ("Old Fair") of Palermo stood in what is now Piazza Rivoluzione near the Magione church of the Teutonic Knights in the Khalesa district.[396]

Tournaments and Heraldry

Tournaments, which included jousts, sword fighting and other forms of martial competition, had existed in some form for about a century before Roger's reign. In their most essential iteration, these were little more than public displays of knights practicing for warfare. By the middle of the twelfth century, however, they entailed much pageantry. Like the major fairs, tournaments usually took place in summer.[397]

At his Council of Clermont in 1130, Pope Innocent II condemned tournaments. Nine years later, the same pontiff's Second Lateran Council imposed certain strictures upon tournaments as well as actual combat. Use of the crossbow against Christians, while prohibited by the articles of this council, certainly continued. Jousts, in particular, were deprecated, yet these contests continued unabated, becoming public spectacles, a form of entertainment for the masses.

A true "code of chivalry" did not exist except in the abstract, as a warrior code governing the treatment of knights by other knights in matters such as ransoms for those taken prisoner. Despite this, we find Innocent's friend Bernard of Clairvaux, as well as John of Salisbury, writing about knightly ideals, as if a certain standard should exist. Taking the Templars as his inspiration, Bernard advocated a model based on crusading and the concept of fighting a just war. John's model was more encompassing, rooted partly in ancient Roman ideas. Neither principle gained much favor in the real world.

The warrior code, such as it existed at this early date, can be seen as little more than a classist, and generally sexist, guide for knights offering very little regulation over their often-harsh treatment of most women and children, or disdain for the majority of clergy on the lower rungs of the ecclesiastical ladder. This is not to suggest that most knights were miscreants, but they were not very concerned about the lives of ordinary people.

To the modern mind, a common image of the medieval knight is one of a mounted warrior facing an opponent. Indeed, several knights whose names are known to us became famous not for the battles they fought but for jousting and tournaments. William Marshal, who was born in England around 1146, is perhaps the most noteworthy of these men, and his biography affords us some of the most detailed observations about tournaments of this era.[398] No tourneyer of his prominence is known to have lived in the Kingdom of Sicily, though several sculpted capitals in Monreale's splendid cloister, completed before 1190, depict jousting knights.[399]

Lesser "tournaments" were displays such as the *bohort*, essentially an enactment, and the *tirocinio*, which might follow the dubbing of several young knights of royal families, such as Roger's sons.

A few legacies of the "Age of Chivalry" survive, courtly literature (considered later) being an obvious example. In our times, sportsmanship reflects modern perceptions of chivalrous conduct. Likewise, the idea that one should not "kick a man when he is down" is based on the way that knights were expected to treat fellow knights at tournaments, if not necessarily on the field of battle.

In the artistic sphere, heraldry, the use of coats of arms as personal, hereditary insignia, emerged in its fullness after the reign of Roger II. There is no contemporary evidence of his dynasty's use of the design attributed to the Hautevilles (see Table 18), which was later added to the mosaics depicting William II in Monreale's cathedral.

By definition, heraldry is the display of symbols on an escutcheon, or shield, and it developed its own rules and conventions.[400] It originated with the practice of knights emblazoning their shields and surcoats to distinguish themselves in combat, and especially in tournaments, when their faces were covered by helmets. One of the earliest heraldic designs known to us is attributed to Geoffrey "Plantagenet" of Anjou, the second husband of Matilda of England and father of Henry II. However, there is no conclusive evidence that Geoffrey, who died in 1151, used that design, consisting of six gold lions on a blue field, during his lifetime even though it may be the basis for the famous heraldic lions of England.

Although the lion was a symbol sometimes displayed by the Norman kings of Sicily, as on the wall behind the royal dais in the Palatine Chapel, it never found its way into formal heraldic use by them.[401]

Coats of arms eventually came to be used in coinage and seals. Among the first heraldic seals of this kind are those of Henry "the Lion" of Saxony and Bavaria, in 1144, and Ralph of Vermandois, in 1146.

The term "heraldry," in its widest usage, describes the duties of court officers responsible for maintaining an index of coats of arms and the families entitled to use specific designs, often recorded in a written form known as *blazon*. Heralds presided over tournaments and might also act as ambassadors at battles.

Very little is known about the heralds present in the *Regnum* during the Hauteville and Hohenstaufen eras. However, their true status in the Kingdom of Sicily during this early period does not seem to have been much more exalted than that of troubadours and minstrels. Elsewhere, as in England, they eventually attained a rank comparable to that accorded notaries.

Marriage

In the parts of the *Regnum* that were thoroughly Christianized, almost one-fifth of the adult population had religious vocations: priests, friars, monks, nuns. Among the rest, conjugal life was the norm.

Most Christian marriages were arranged, or at least approved, through the formal consent of the young spouses' parents. The majority of bridegrooms were at least eighteen, but brides might be as young as thirteen or even twelve. Although a widow or widower could remarry, divorce was highly exceptional among Christians even if it legally existed. A Catholic (or Orthodox) marriage could be annulled by the church; this was extremely rare in practice, more likely for aristocrats or royalty than the common folk.

Though a man might marry a young widow, the marriage of a menopausal woman, such as a widow aged around fifty, was rather unusual.[402]

A Muslim man might have as many as four wives, but even in Islam marriages were permitted only by parental consent, most often with the prospective groom negotiating with the father of the girl he wanted to wed. This was also the case among Jews.

Despite the flowery descriptions of courtship in romantic literature (see Appendix 4), rather few marriages resulted solely from the initiative of the spouses. Indeed, into the middle of the nineteenth century, parental permission was required for a young couple to marry (see Appendix 7).

The wedding normally took place in the parish church of the bride in the presence of witnesses. In Italy bridesmaids are still called *damigelle* (damsels). Here the "best man" and maid (or matron) of honor are simply *testimoni* (witnesses).

Among the Christians of the *Regnum,* certain usages of Germanic origin were gradually introduced. The idea of a "best man" (groomsman) probably began with the practice of a man who wed a maiden in another town being accompanied by a close male friend for extra protection from rural bandits *en route,* or from jealous suitors competing for the lady's hand in her own locality. Cases of a man kidnapping a young marriageable girl in another town, or anywhere, were quite rare, and the rape of maidens was formally criminalized in law as early as 1140, but there were elopements.

Elopement, preserved into modern times as the Sicilian practice known as the *fuitina,* from the word for "fleeing," seldom occurred in the Middle Ages, when a priest was unlikely to perform the nuptials of a couple in impromptu circumstances. Rare among aristocrats, the *fuitina* was sometimes tacitly sanctioned by a prospective bride's parents when they could not afford to furnish her with a dowry.

Most marriages involved dowries, dowers, or both. This was something of value, such as land, money or other assets. The dowry consisted of assets brought to the union by the bride, normally as a gift from her natal family. The dower, which was an additional element in the marriages of aristocratic spouses, was property, usually land, given to the bride by her husband. A few records of these, particularly for more prominent families, are conserved at archives in Palermo, Bari and Cava.[403]

In 1139, when Mount Sant'Angelo and several estates in its vicinity became part of the royal demesne, they were ceded to Simon, one of Roger's illegitimate sons. This territory would later become the dower of the queens of Sicily.[404]

The greatest freedom to choose one's spouse was enjoyed by peasants who owned very little, the least by royalty and high-ranking nobles. Among the common folk, most marriages were broadly endogamous.

The inhabitants of the *Regnum* who married outside the faith into which they were born were exceptional. Although there were doubtless instances of conversions, usually by the bride, prior to a wedding, there were not, in the literal sense, "mixed" marriages, nor were there "secular" (non-religious) unions.

Under feudalism, a baron could levy a nominal tax on weddings; this is what was later called the *droit du seigneur.*

For Christians, marriage, as an institution, was the province of the church, its strictures based on longstanding principles of canon law. Marriage and adultery are both addressed by Roger's Assizes, where it is made clear that, at least in theory, major vassals cannot grant betrothals of their daughters without royal assent. A few contemporary accounts refer to royal intervention, which we have already seen in the case of Roger removing his sister, Matilda, from an abusive husband.[405]

The Assizes make it clear that Catholic marriages must be performed physically in a church as a sacred place. The crown exercised very little control over non-Christian unions in the kingdom.

Cohesion

It had taken more than a century, but the Hautevilles had fashioned a polycultural region full of disparate power centers into a multiconfessional, multiethnic state. This was not very like the *Normanitas,* Norman society and its culture, that existed in Normandy and England, where one might speak of a *Gens Normannorum,* the Normans as a people. It was, however, the beginning of the *Gens Siculorum.*

While our focus is the kingdom rather than royal biography, the ethnicity of the royal family, as the "symbol" of the *Regnum,* merits mention. Granted that our Hauteville and Hohenstaufen kings and queens strongly identified with the state they ruled, there is much truth in the observation, popularized late in the nineteenth century during the reign of Britain's Victoria, the "Grandmother of Europe," that modern European royalty, if not literally a single family, was a unique clan or caste ancestrally outside the ethnic identity of one people or nation.

We find the seeds of this phenomenon germinating during our Norman era in practices that differed somewhat from those of the Lombard princes of Salerno, whose marriages were usually contracted with women from the Lombard regions of what is now Italy.

In the Kingdom of Sicily, the earliest attempt at an important inter-ethnic, and politically inter-dynastic, alliance was the marriage of Roger II to Elvira, a lady of the Jiménez dynasty of northern Spain (see Table 7), followed by the marriage of Roger's son, William I, to another Jiménez, Margaret, whose mother was Norman. Roger's daughter, Constance, was betrothed to a man whose ancestry was mostly "German" (originating in the German-speaking lands). The marriage of Constance's son, Frederick, to another "Spanish" lady, Constance of Aragon, followed this pattern of international unions.

These men and women were multilingual and, in light of the diverse origins that resulted in the existence of their natal and conjugal families, multiethnic. It is to be remembered that France, Spain and Germany did not yet exist as actual, unitary "states" so much as patchworks of occasionally-allied duchies and counties, even if they were evolving into the nations effectively established, through political and territorial unification, in (respectively) 1214, 1492 and 1871.

The evolution of states into nations makes for complex theses, with some arguing that true "nationhood" is a post-medieval development while others discern it at an early date (see note 15). Let us return to the Kingdom of Sicily in 1141.

Some Coins of the Norman-Swabian Era
Not shown to scale

Silver

Ducat of Roger II

Gold

Augustalis of Frederick II

Fatimid tarì   *Gold*   Norman tarì

KINGDOM OF SICILY

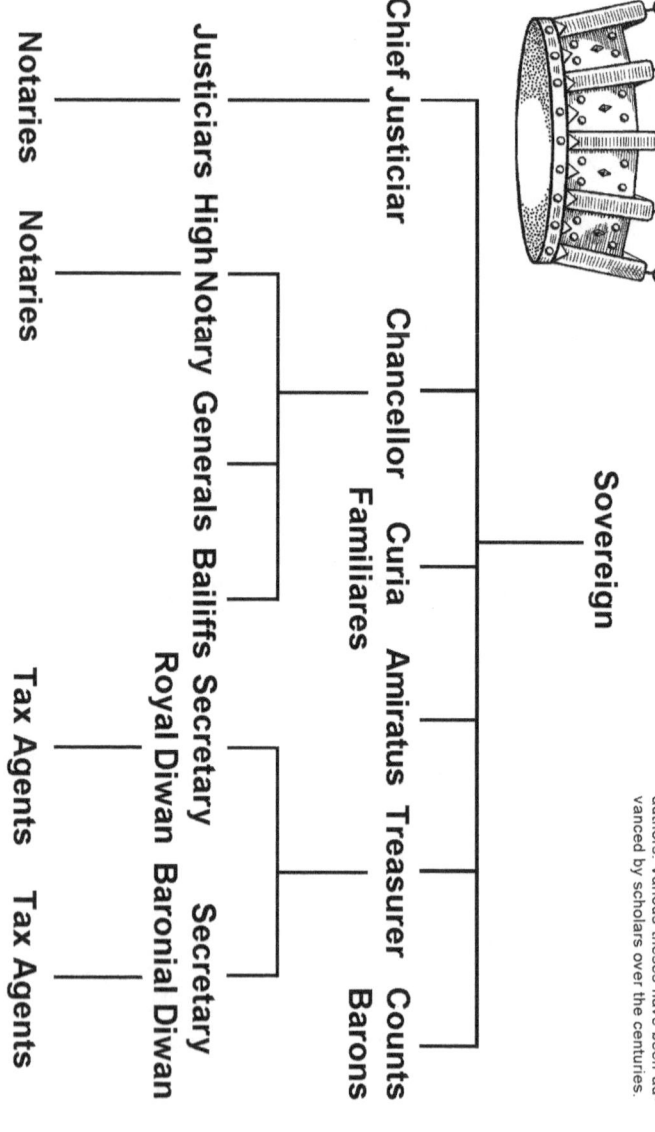

Early Government in the Kingdom of Sicily

Model of the hierarchy proposed by the authors. Various theses have been advanced by scholars over the centuries.

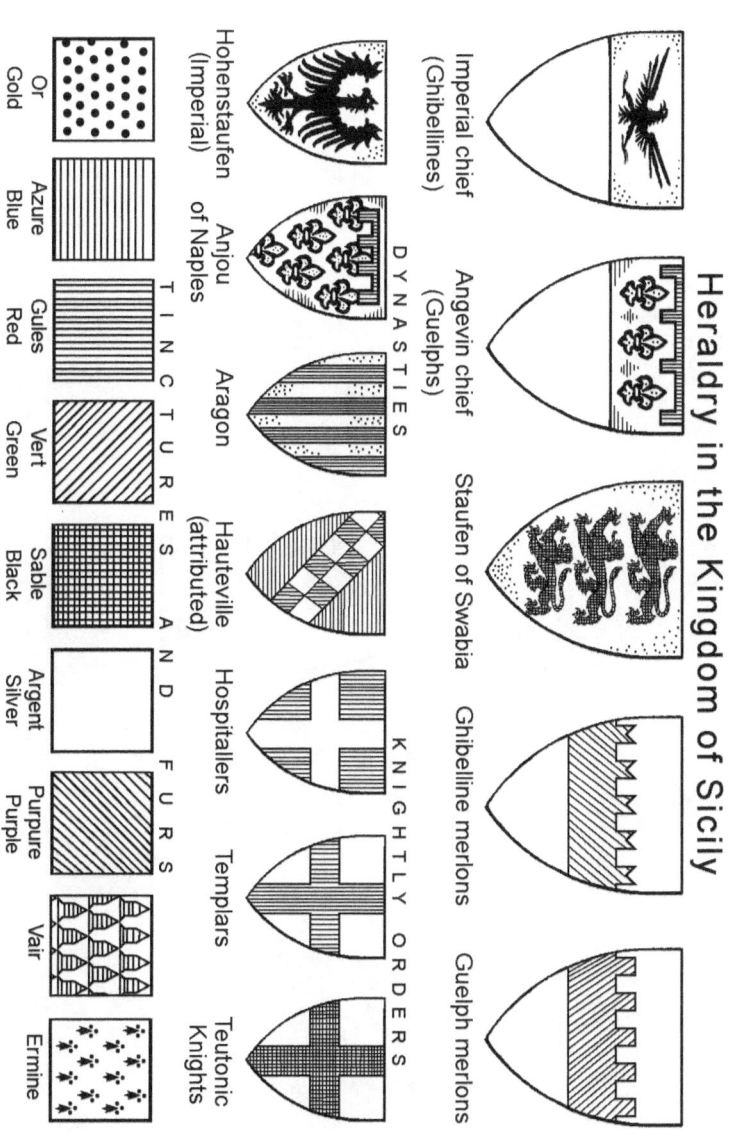

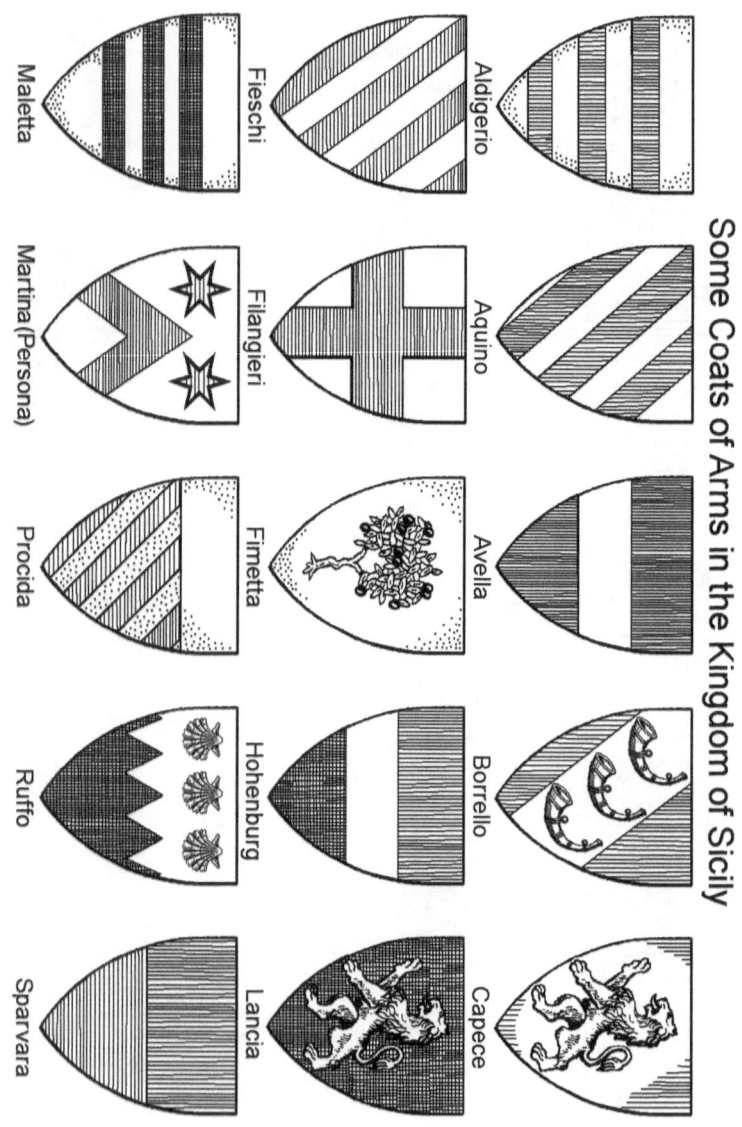

Harley Manuscript 5786, folio 106 verso, British Library, London

Composed in Greek, Latin and Arabic, the Harley Psalter reflects the Hautevillian efforts to unite the church while converting the Muslims.

KINGDOM OF SICILY

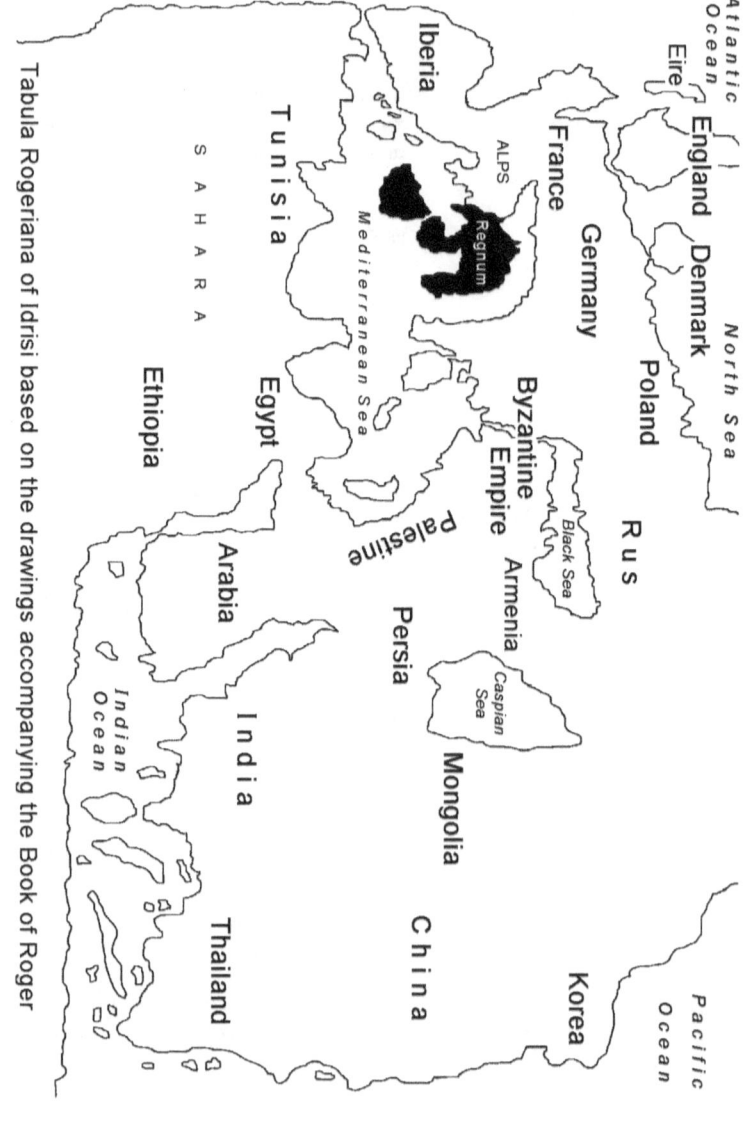

Tabula Rogeriana of Idrisi based on the drawings accompanying the Book of Roger

Chapter 13
POWER

By 1141, as we have seen, the kingdom's laws and government had been standardized following a decade of political chaos. The social milieu existed much as it would for another century. Prosperity was self-evident. This apogee would define Roger's reign and indeed the *Regnum* itself.

Ambitions

The territorial ambitions of the Kingdom of Sicily beyond its borders are difficult to gauge very precisely except from what actually transpired. It was generally believed that the king himself wanted Antioch as a dynastic hereditament. A few years earlier, in 1136, he had reportedly attempted to ambush Raymond of Poitiers while the Frenchman was traveling through Apulia on his way to the Holy Land to wed Constance, the young daughter of the late Bohemond II.[406]

However, in 1137 John II of Constantinople, never a friend of Roger, managed to bring Antioch, Edessa and Tripoli under Byzantine control, thus imposing a certain degree of power over the princes of the northern crusader states. This was achieved through what was essentially feudal homage, as if these rulers were vassals of the Byzantine Empire. Ever keen on an alliance with the Holy Roman Empire to counter Roger's power, in 1140 John negotiated a treaty with Conrad III. With this, Conrad betrothed his adoptive daughter, actually his sister-in-law Bertha of Sulzbach, to John's son, Manuel, though a few years were to pass before the nuptials were celebrated in Constantinople, where the bride was renamed *Irene* to accommodate Greek tastes. This made the prospective emperors of east and west brothers-in-law, Conrad being wed to Bertha's sister, Gertrude. However, Conrad, despite papal favor, was not destined to be crowned Holy Roman Emperor.

For his part, Conrad III had more pressing concerns than negotiating treaties with distant allies and arranging marriages. At Weinsberg in December 1140, he defeated the forces opposing him led by Welf VI of Bavaria, younger brother of headstrong Henry the Proud, who had died the previous year. Henry's son and heir, Henry "the Lion," was only ten years old, though he was supported by a faction of the German nobility opposed to Conrad's Hohenstaufens. Peace was in sight, to be negotiated in 1142. Conrad thus achieved an accommodation of sorts with Welf that lasted for the rest of the decade.

While John II may have had designs on Zirid Ifriqiya, that Muslim dominion was to remain beyond his grasp.[407] The recent Sicilian conquest of Djerba, off the coast of Tunisia, was beneficial for trade with Ifriqiya, but it was also a symbol of the influence of the *Regnum* that could be seen by the entire Mediterranean. Yet the Kingdom of Sicily could not be regarded as a true thalassocracy like the sea-empire of Venice or, eventually, that of Aragon despite the power emanating from Palermo.

The Pisans, Germans and Greeks had already experienced this power firsthand when they sought to defeat Roger in his own kingdom. In view of the papal recognition of Roger's kingship and sovereignty, Louis VII of France and other monarchs now recognized it as well.[408]

Like Roger, Louis had to face dissent, especially from the burgesses of Poitiers and Orléans, who wanted to establish communes similar to those of northern Italy. He also came into conflict with Pope Innocent II over the appointment of an important archbishop.[409] Yet he found time to patronize the arts. The Gothic movement in ecclesiastical architecture emerged in France, though it would never become very popular in the Kingdom of Sicily.

The Anarchy divided England ever more. "And men said openly that Christ and His angels slept," wrote the author of the *Peterborough Chronicle*. Matilda was now present in the country, which would suffer for years to come.

While these complexities were of little immediate concern to the Kingdom of Sicily, they very clearly reflected the present state of unrest across much of western Europe, where smoldering coals might burst into flame at any provocation.

Ifriqiya

Presently, the rapport of the Kingdom of Sicily with the Zirids of Ifriqiya, still ruled by Abul-Hasan al-Hasan ibn Ali, was pacific, governed by commercial interests administered on Djerba and supported by a fleet based at that island and Pantelleria. There was a workable relationship with the Fatimids of Egypt, who also ruled part of what is now Libya bordering Ifriqiya.

Now that Roger and his government no longer had to focus most of their attention on chaos in the *Regnum,* they looked to foreign conquests, with an eye to those that might bolster the kingdom's economy and political power. The most obvious objective was Ifriqiya itself, whose fragile economy made it a facile target.

The abundant imports of Sicilian grain and products such as dried meats had failed to resolve the dire consequences of occasional famines, and the influence of the Hammadids to the immediate west of Ifriqiya made it vulnerable to the control of that empire. Whether through mismanagement or misfortune, the Zirids were short of money to purchase grain, thus allowing their contracts with the Sicilians to lapse, and some citizens had even migrated to Sicily in search of better conditions. Most of the inland region of Ifriqiya consisted of desert terrain and rugged mountains, but the coastal plains were fertile, not unlike those of Sicily and Calabria (and greener in the twelfth century than they are today), fed by efficient irrigation systems. Now Mahdia, Tripoli, Gabés and other cities became overcrowded as the famines forced many Ifriqiyans to leave rural areas in favor of urban ones.

For the past five years, Abul-Hasan al-Hasan ibn Ali had relied upon the Norman military presence on Djerba as a defense against adversaries, most notably the Hammadids ruled from Bejaia (Bougie) by Yaha ibn Abd al-Aziz.[410]

Yaha himself was challenged by rivals — Bedouins, Berbers and Genoans. Now he would face open opposition from the Sicilians.

Roger's interests in Ifriqiya were based on expedience. He wanted uncontested control over shipping routes in the central Mediterranean, which was the reason for occupying Djerba and ousting its pirates, an action supported by the friendly Fatimids. Corollary to this, he desired improved commerce for his kingdom, something at risk now that the Zirids were in economic distress.

Not to be overlooked was the gold trade, which depended on mines in Africa. Begun under the Fatimids, this continued during Roger's reign. The principal trade routes for this precious metal crossed the Sahara northward through regions such as Sudan, ultimately reaching Ifriqiya and also what is now Morocco. Mercantile agents from cities such as Venice exploited their rapport with the Kingdom of Sicily to augment trade with northern Africa, and in many of these lucrative transactions gold coinage became the currency of choice even as silver was more commonplace in most of Europe. A parallel route brought gold through Iberia and into France. The phenomenon later known as medieval Europe's "commercial revolution" owed much to Italian coins minted from African gold, some of it likely mined by slaves.

A slave trade flourished along the same African routes as those used for gold, though slavery was far less prevalent in the *Regnum* than in some states, and not all slaves were African.

Other considerations were secondary at best. There was already a diocese at Mahdia and the King of Sicily was not interested in a "crusade" against the region's Muslims, though he would bring Ifriqiya's Orthodox Christians under the jurisdiction of the papacy.[411] Whether he wanted to establish an "empire" is a matter for debate, but the Hautevilles' traditional zeal for eastward expansionism into the Byzantine Empire supports the possibility that they might look southward as well.

Early in 1142, George of Antioch sailed to Mahdia at the head of a fleet to confiscate Zirid vessels and restore trade. Thus coerced, Abul-Hasan renewed Ifriqiya's trade conventions with the Kingdom of Sicily. George then initiated raids on Zirid territory to enforce Abul-Hasan's authority over contested localities, though this seems to have been a pretext for bringing Sicilian control to the region. Tripoli resisted, but Djidjelli, where Yaha had erected a pleasure palace, was taken, along with the island of Kerkennah and the town of Barasht.[412]

Precisely how long the Sicilian garrisons remained in these localities is not known, but George seems to have left some troops in Mahdia, where there were already commercial agents, while fortified Djerba, off the Gulf of Gabés, was not far away. The Zirid sultan, Abul-Hasan, accepted Sicilian support as a guarantee of territorial integrity and grain. The Arab chroniclers use terms such as "tyrant" to describe Roger II.[413] The Arab and Byzantine ethnicity and culture of Roger's representatives meant that little changed in terms of administrative style except for the presence of some Norman knights and officers.[414]

Governing the Kingdom

On the mainland, Roger ensured smooth administration by his older sons, especially his recently-married namesake, and was again at Ariano in July 1142.[415]

His travels also took him into papal territory, where he visited the abbey at Mount Cassino.[416] Yet his affinity for these monks wasn't sufficient to seduce him into granting them too much power in his capital. To avoid potential political entanglements, the Benedictine monks of the abbey of Saint John of the Hermits (mentioned in the previous chapter) were drawn from a more remote monastery of the *Regnum*.[417]

The Byzantine Emperor, John II Comnenus, died in Cilicia, near Antioch, in April 1143, from wounds suffered during a mundane hunting accident.[418] He was succeeded by his son, Manuel I, whose reign saw a continuation of the political resurgence fostered by his father. In August he was crowned by the new patriarch, Michael II. Manuel soon wed Bertha of Sulzbach, the sister-in-law (and adoptive daughter) of Conrad III Hohenstaufen, who sent some five hundred knights to Constantinople with the bride.[419]

Manuel's reign was nothing if not complex. His neglect of some of his father's allies, or vassals, left them to seek support elsewhere. Among them was Joscelin II, Count of Edessa, who saw his lands in constant peril. If any of Manuel's policies differed from those of his father, it was clear that his position regarding the Kingdom of Sicily was the same, and the recent Sicilian incursion into Ifriqiya confirmed that Roger was a formidable adversary.

Pope Innocent II died in September of 1143. His pontificate is generally recognized as a bridge linking an age of idealistic papal reformers to that of more pragmatic advocates of a "papal monarchy" which might assume a prominent place of power on the international stage. Yet, as recently as a year before his death, Innocent complained of Roger's use of authority in appointing bishops.[420]

Innocent's successor, Celestine II, born Guy of Castello, refused to accept the terms granted by his papal predecessor recognizing the sovereignty of the

Regnum.[421] On a more conciliatory note, in view of Louis VII, King of the French, finally sanctioning the papal appointment of Pierre, Archbishop of Bourges (see note 409), the new pontiff lifted the interdict that Innocent had placed on France. Though Celestine recognized the right of Matilda of England, and by *jure uxoris* her husband Geoffrey of Anjou, to rule, this decision did little to alter the abhorrent course of The Anarchy. Celestine's pontificate expired with him just five months after it had begun.

George of Antioch returned to Sicily from his African expedition, or raiding mission, soon enough to welcome Nilos Doxopatrios, whom we met earlier. The prelate's name figures among those of the parishioners of the appropriately-named church of Saint Mary of the Admiral, popularly the "Martorana," founded by George for the Byzantine Greek community of Palermo.[422] The very fact of a church being established explicitly for Orthodox Christians reflects the reality that by now most foundations in the *Regnum* were Roman Catholic.[423]

Even during this part of Roger's reign, when the kingdom had no queen, there were ecclesiastical patronages by royal women.[424] A noteworthy example is Adelisa, identified in charters as the king's niece. We find her ceding lands and serfs to the diocese of Cefalù.[425]

Robert of Selby, the chancellor, performed his duties efficiently, serving as the king's effective "regent" on the peninsula. This meant that some of his tasks were necessarily delegated to subordinates. We find Robert assisted by competent individuals such as Maio of Bari.[426] Robert was praised by his contemporary John of Salisbury, one of the greatest political theorists of the age, whom he met in the *Regnum*.[427]

The duties of George of Antioch, as *amiratus,* though much more than those of an admiral, were mostly military in nature and distinct from the tasks entrusted to Robert. As a member of the *curia regis,* he answered directly to the king, though in later times generals reported to the chancellor.[428]

The master of the *diwan* during Roger's reign was the Englishman Thomas le Brun, who had arrived as a child in Robert's entourage.

One of the many advantages afforded the kingdom by a government of loyal and expert officials was that this situation permitted stability in the capital even when the king himself was traveling, as was sometimes necessary. By the same token, Roger could send these officials around the kingdom in his stead.[429]

Economically, the Kingdom of Sicily at this point was the most powerful of the European states plying trade in the Mediterranean, able to protect its commerce with a persuasive navy.

Pope Celestine's successor was Lucius II, Gerard Caccianemici dal Orso, whose aristocratic surname is translated literally as "one who chases away the bear's enemies." Elected in March 1144, he would reign for eleven months in a pontificate marked by chaos as the citizens of Rome rebelled against him. Like his predecessor, he supported Matilda in England and opposed Roger in Italy.

Specifically, Lucius sought the return of Capua to papal authority while Roger claimed additional territory presently under the pontiff's control. A meeting in Ceprano in June left little doubt about the intransigence of both sovereigns. The king had his eldest son, Roger of Apulia, oversee the invasion of some papal lands in Campania. Under the supervision of Robert of Selby, Sicilian troops attacked towns as far north as Ferentino.[430]

In October 1144, Roger's thirdborn son, Alfonso, died while fighting papal forces shortly before Lucius recognized the king's rights and agreed to a seven-year truce based on the existing borders between the *Regnum* and the Papal State. With very few modifications, these boundaries, which guaranteed the integrity of papal Benevento, remained in place for the next seven centuries.

Alfonso's death was not only a personal tragedy. Politically, it was of concern because it left the king with only two living legitimate sons, namely Roger, Duke of Apulia, the firstborn, and William, presently the youngest.

As if by divine judgment, Lucius met with an equally dire end. Fighting the rebellious Romans in February 1145, his head was struck by a stone, leading to his death. His successor was Bernard Paganelli, a Cistercian from Pisa, elected immediately as Eugene III.

Although Roger sent Robert of Selby with troops to support the new pope, Eugene was not immediately able to reside in the city of Rome, which was in rebellion during most of his pontificate. Only later would Eugene negotiate anything like an accord with the irascible, factionalized Romans. A spiritual man, he held synods to address the reform of life among the clergy. His approval of the works of the Benedictine abbess Hildegard of Bingen reflects an effort to recognize the intellectual role of women in the Catholic ecclesiastical sphere. He was friendly to Orthodoxy, receiving a delegation of Armenian envoys early in his pontificate and encouraging the Latin translation of works of Greek patrology. Yet the effort for which he is most remembered would prove to be less than successful.[431]

Crusade and Conquest

On Christmas Eve of 1144, the County of Edessa, the first of the crusader states to be founded, fell to the forces of Imad al-Din Zengi, founder of the Zengid dynasty. This followed a month-long siege initiated in response to a military alliance of the county's Christian ruler, Joscelin II, with the Artuqids, who opposed the Zengids. Had Joscelin, a vassal of the recently-crowned Byzantine Emperor Manuel I, received imperial support, he might not have allied himself with Kara Aslan, the Artuqid leader, against the Zengids. In the event, help from Jerusalem and other quarters arrived too late to save Edessa (Urfa).[432]

Lying to the east of Antioch in what is now Turkey, near the Syrian border, Edessa was an ancient city founded by Greeks near the site of the world's oldest temples, at Göbekli Tepe. Although the Seljuk Turks had ruled it for a decade before its recent conquest by Europeans during the First Crusade, Edessa was a traditional center of Christian culture and learning. Its loss was sorely felt by Christians throughout the Holy Land. The incident became a catalyst, or pretext, for Bernard of Clairvaux to preach the Second Crusade called by Pope Eugene III with a papal bull in December 1145 mentioning support for the "Eastern Church."[433]

Convincing Catholics to "take the cross" was not very difficult, and indeed the King of the French was already contemplating an expedition to the Holy Land before the bull was issued, but the crusade itself was fated to end as little more than a debacle.[434]

While the kings of the French and the Germans, among others across Europe, were willing to participate in the expedition, the men running the Sicilian government seem to have had reservations about involving their king in such an enterprise. Roger himself could still remember the humiliation inflicted upon his mother by an earlier King of Jerusalem. There was also the irony of a crusade against Islam when many Sicilians were Muslim and there was amicable trade with Zirid Ifriqiya. Nevertheless, a belief was later propagated that Roger offered his support, which was ultimately rejected, or even rescinded, in order to claim, and perhaps occupy, the erstwhile Hauteville dominion of Antioch. Whatever the case, neither Conrad III or Manuel I trusted the King of Sicily, against whom they had formed an alliance, and Roger had no reason to trust either of them.

Even Pope Eugene entertained a doubt or two about Roger and the power at the king's disposal. In France, Louis VII, with the help of Bernard of Clairvaux to preach in favor of the venture, managed to raise a substantial army, but the prelate's efforts in Germany do not seem to have enjoyed pontifical approval since Eugene probably wanted to keep Conrad in Europe, either to suppress the rebellious Romans or to counter potential aggression by Roger.[435]

Despite the efforts of Louis to enlist Roger's help, and the transitory willingness of the latter to provide it, this never came to pass.[436] In the event, only a few knights of the *Regnum* are known to have participated in the Second Crusade as their service was required elsewhere by their king. Further afield, in the disunited Kingdom of England, recruitment met with less success owing to the obvious domestic challenges of The Anarchy. Yet an English-led multinational fleet stopped at Lisbon in July 1147 *en route* to the Holy Land to take the city and give it to Alfonso I, Portugal's first king.[437] A number of these crusaders chose to settle in Portugal rather than continue on to Palestine.

In Spain, the *Reconquista* continued, with navies from Genoa and Pisa assisting in the capture of Almería in October, the same month that Lisbon fell.

For the King of Sicily, there were other conquests to be had, and it was in these years that the *Regnum* began to pursue a policy of expansionism tantamount to imperialism. In the summer of 1146, the Sicilians, led by George of Antioch, finally occupied the coveted city of Tripoli, an action which led to control of most of Ifriqiya.[438]

Notwithstanding the importance of this acquisition, there is no evidence to suggest that the Sicilians or their kings ever considered Ifriqiya part of the kingdom. It was never more than a foreign province.[439]

To the east, meanwhile, the crusaders encountered one obstacle and defeat after another. In September 1147, some contingents of Conrad's German force clashed with those of Manuel at Constantinople on the way to the Holy Land. The following month, the Germans suffered a defeat at the hands of the Seljuk Turks at Dorylaeum in Anatolia. In November, an army led by Conrad's half-

KINGDOM OF SICILY

brother, Otto of Freising, was defeated by the Turks near Laodicea. Unbeknownst to the Germans, Manuel, fearing the Christians' possible designs on his empire more than those of the Muslims, had made a treaty with the Turks without telling Conrad or Louis.

The King of Sicily was not forgotten. When it was learned that a Sicilian force was attacking the Adriatic coast of the Byzantine Empire, some in the French camp advised Louis to ally himself with Roger against unreliable (or disloyal) Manuel.[440]

Instead, the remaining crusaders pressed on, eventually reached Jerusalem and then, in July, attacked the Zengids at Damascus.[441] Here the Christians met with the infamous defeat that brought the Second Crusade to a bitter end. Conrad returned to Germany via Constantinople, where he restored his alliance with Manuel. Louis remained in Jerusalem until 1149, increasingly estranged from his wife, headstrong Eleanor of Aquitaine, who was traveling with him.

George of Antioch led the Sicilian invasion of Byzantine territory in 1147, beginning by occupying the island of Corfu, and then proceeding to raid Corinth. At Thebes, he plundered the fabric workshops. The immediate strategy was probably pre-emptive in nature since Roger's counsellors expected an attack by Manuel and Conrad, but it reflected the longstanding Hauteville objective to control the Adriatic coasts of the Byzantine Empire, if not the entirety of Greece and perhaps even Constantinople itself.[442]

The people of Corfu welcomed Sicilian rule as a respite from Byzantine taxation, while a revolt by the Serbs, who were supported by the Hungarians, distracted Manuel's attention from the invaders. Whatever these Byzantine subjects wanted, the more general occupation was not to last. True, George made it to Constantinople, where his Arab archers loosed their arrows at the imperial palace, but that was little more than a nuisance. If anything, the incursion demonstrated to Michael that Roger's forces could penetrate Byzantine territory, as they had in the past.

George was back in Ifriqiya in 1148, where support from the governor of Gabés facilitated the occupation of most of the sultanate, including Mahdia, Sfax and Sousse, almost as if it were a fief of the Kingdom of Sicily. However, some cities to the west, such as coastal Annaba, remained outside Sicilian control.

In 1149, Manuel recovered Corfu following a months-long siege, aided by the Venetians who blockaded the island. The Sicilians had netted little more than some Theban silk weavers to augment that industry in Palermo. Even if the invasion had resulted in more insult than injury, the Byzantine Emperor would seek his revenge.[443]

Biding his time, he sought to appeal to Roger's detractors in the *Regnum* as pawns in his machinations. These vassals, among whom the disaffected holder of Conversano, near Bari, were now far fewer in number than they were a decade earlier. It was more effective to appeal to the Bariot citizenry, which for the most part was still very Byzantine in culture, temperament and faith. However, such an exercise would have to wait.

Chapter 14

CONTINUUM

At the beginning of the second half of the twelfth century, the foundations of the Kingdom of Sicily were solid and the economy was prosperous. Ifriqiya was an asset likely to elicit envy from the leaders of other European powers, certainly Manuel I of Constantinople. It irked the Venetians to see their maritime influence in the central Mediterranean curtailed by Sicilian primacy, indeed to the point that they were willing to support the Byzantine Empire against the *Regnum*. The Genoans, conversely, were more likely to plot a course of neutrality, if not cooperation.

Though this period was arguably the height of the reign of the first King of Sicily, it was a moment of transition. In May 1148, Roger, Duke of Apulia, heir to the throne as the king's eldest son, died, survived by his young wife, a niece of King Stephen of England. Roger of Apulia had fathered no legitimate sons known to posterity.[444]

Unions

Having lost three adult sons, Roger II was running out of heirs. That he now ceded the Principality of Taranto to an illegitimate son, Simon, did not alleviate these difficulties. To legitimize Simon would be extremely difficult.

A possible crisis was confronted in the simplest way. A wife was sought for his only surviving legitimate son, William, and also for Roger himself.

The bride chosen for William was Margaret Jiménez of Navarre, of the same dynasty as his mother, Elvira of Castile. This was a dynastic union but also a familial one; William and Margaret were third cousins, one generation removed (see Table 7). Raised in polycultural Pamplona by a Norman mother, the bride was thoroughly multilingual.

Roger wed Sibylla, daughter of the Duke of Burgundy (see Table 12), whose Capetian family was a branch of the French royal dynasty. It could be argued that this marriage was likewise a dynastic alliance, perhaps intended to foster friendship with a powerful lord whose dominions caressed the fringes of the Holy Roman Empire, but its main purpose was to provide Roger with another son or two.

The sea voyage of Louis VII and his consort, Eleanor, back to France on separate galleys was hindered by Byzantine assaults and bad weather. Storms blew the queen's ship off course, possibly as far as the coast of Ifriqiya. She made it to Palermo at the end of July in 1149, ill but safe. Her husband's ship, meanwhile, had landed in Puglia.

It is quite possible that three Francophone royal women met in Palermo that summer. Eleanor was lodged in the royal palace, where Sibylla gave birth to a son in August. During the time she spent in the city, Eleanor might have met Margaret of Navarre, whose precise date of arrival is not known. Eleanor was destined to return to Sicily, but this was the only time she may have met her future *consuocera*.[445]

Roger accompanied Eleanor to the mainland, where she was united with her husband. The two kings met at Potenza in late August. A quaint tale tells us that, in keeping with a certain tradition of a man being elevated to kinghood only by another king as his peer, Roger asked Louis to crown him, as if the coronation two decades earlier were insufficient. Roger then had the royal couple and their suite escorted to Tusculum to meet the pope.[446]

Eleanor and Louis prevailed upon the pontiff to grant an annulment of their marriage based on the pretext of close consanguinity through what was actually rather distant kinship. This was ridiculous considering the frequent marriages between royal cousins. It seems more likely that Louis was simply disappointed that Eleanor had produced two daughters but no sons, for it was stipulated upon their marriage that he could not rule Aquitaine *jure uxoris* and that the duchy would be inherited only by a male heir. Nonetheless, the annulment was granted two years later. One of its side-effects was to redraw the map of France.[447]

If not a marriage, the diplomatic relationship between the kingdoms of Sicily and France was at least useful while Conrad and Manuel were poised to strike Roger, but the King of Sicily had other potential allies.

Welf VI of Bavaria, Conrad's inveterate adversary, passed through the *Regnum* on his way home from the fiasco of the crusade and met with Roger. The two men seem to have commiserated. When he returned to Germany, Welf and his followers raided Conrad's Hohenstaufen dominions in Swabia, though that was not an exclusively pro-Sicilian gesture. Welf's more immediate objective was to revive the claim to Bavaria by his nephew, Henry the Lion, who was now twenty years old. In the event, Welf and his faction were soon suppressed.[448]

The Sicilian court also had cordial ties with that of Hungary, now supporting the Serbian rebellion against Manuel; Roger's cousin, Felicia (see Table 9), had wed King Coloman.[449]

In November 1149, Robert of Selby oversaw the restoration of Eugene in the city of Rome, but continued unrest would force the pontiff to withdraw from his capital seven months later. That Roger and his government supported the papacy was beyond doubt. Even so, at a meeting between king and pontiff at Ceprano in July 1150, Eugene expressed a lack of support for Roger's authority.[450] Unfortunately, the pope had allowed his rapport with Conrad, the "uncrowned Holy Roman Emperor," to compromise his relationship with the King of Sicily.

Eugene did not actively seek to deprive the German king, as emperor-elect, of the right to an imperial coronation. By tradition, however, this solemn rite was performed in one of Rome's great basilicas, something that presumed papal control of at least part of the city. Conrad, for his part, might descend into Italy with an army large enough to subdue the Roman rebels, attacking the *Regnum* as well. In view of the depletion of his forces during the recent crusade, and military campaigns at home against Welf and other detractors, this could not be accomplished.[451]

Meanwhile, the Almohads, who now ruled the northwest corner of Africa (Morocco), and part of Andalusia in southern Spain, having recently defeated the Almoravids, were advancing into the lands of the Hammadids to their east, in what is now Algeria. This left Yaha ibn Abd al-Aziz, the Hammadid emir, isolated, with the Almohads to his west and the Sicilians in Ifriqiya (Tunisia and the western part of Libya) to his immediate east. The days of Yaha's rule were numbered. Most of his emirate was being swallowed, one piece at a time, by the Almohads, and a coastal morsel of it would soon be annexed to Sicilian territory.[452]

Even if life for most in Ifriqiya changed very little under Hauteville rule, it cannot be denied that the conquest was one of the factors that ultimately brought about the political demise of the Zirid and Hammadid dynasties, facilitating the rise of the Almohads.

Transitions

Queen Sibylla of Sicily gave birth to a son, Henry, in August 1149. This child died early the following year. Sibylla herself died near Salerno in September 1150 from complications in giving birth to another son, who was stillborn. No sooner was the young queen entombed at the abbey of Cava when the royal courtiers began searching for another wife for their king.[453]

Concerned about the succession, Roger crowned his heir, William, who was already Duke of Apulia, *rex filius* on Easter in 1151. Margaret was probably crowned with him.[454]

Though strongly identified with the Normans, the practice of crowning a son during his father's lifetime was not unknown elsewhere in western Europe. Its purpose was to ensure that there would be no subsequent contestations, or at least none that were credible, regarding the right of the heir apparent to rule. An heir who became *rex filius* wore a crown but did not sit on a throne.

By the end of the year, Margaret was expecting her first child and Roger had wed Beatrice of Vitry of Rethel (see Table 13). Born around 1132 and barely older than Margaret, Beatrice was the eldest of at least six children of Guitier of Rethel and his wife Beatrice of Namur. The family was distinguished in the Ardennes region of what is now France, and an uncle of Beatrice's father was no less a personage than King Baldwin II of Jerusalem, who died in 1131, but the chief reason for this marriage was to provide Roger with a son.[455]

George of Antioch died in 1151, followed by Robert of Selby the next year.[456] With this, the king appointed Maio of Bari, whom we met earlier, as chancellor; Maio had already served as Robert's vice chancellor for the previous two years. To succeed George as *amiratus,* the king chose Philip of Mahdia, a eunuch from Ifriqiya who was said to be Greek.[457]

Conrad III of Germany died in February 1152, succeeded in his imperial claim by his nephew, Frederick I "Barbarossa," though some considered his lawful heir to be his own son, also Frederick, aged just six (see Table 3).[458]

Further afield, Stephen of England sought, but failed to obtain, papal approval for his son, Eustace of Boulogne, to become heir to the throne and end The Anarchy. Eustace was wed to Constance, the sister of Louis VII of France, and the two brothers-in-law raided Normandy as part of a longstanding feud between the French crown and Geoffrey of Anjou. Geoffrey's death in 1151 left Matilda of England a widow for the second time in her life. The following year the couple's eldest son, Henry, now claimant to the Duchy of Normandy, wed Eleanor, the former wife of Louis, thus obtaining Aquitaine.

Back in the Kingdom of Sicily, Roger received a request for aid from the governor of Annaba against the approaching Almohads. This coastal city, Saint Augustine's Hippo Regius, was to the immediate west of Ifriqiya. It would make a useful outpost against an encroaching power. That, however, would have to be carefully considered because it presupposed direct conflict with the Almohads, but such a result may have been presumed inevitable given their steady advance.

For now, Roger could content himself with the fine work of the geographer Idrisi, the theologian Nilos Doxopatrios and the other intellectuals at his court, amongst whom, perhaps, some personages unknown to posterity. He might listen to scholars like the classicist and translator Henry Aristippo engage in debate to defend their treatises. He could enjoy the poetry composed in Arabic by the royal secretary, Abu I-Daw, who was born into the prominent Banu Raja family of Palermo's Muslim community.

In March 1153, Frederick I signed the First Treaty of Constance with the papacy, promising to oppose any action by the Emperor of Constantinople to seize Italian territory and to subdue papal enemies in the city of Rome.[459] Mentioning Roger, this presumed the possibility of an incursion into the *Regnum* sooner or later.

Pope Eugene III died in July, accorded a funeral in Rome, the city to which he was forbidden entry during most of his pontificate. His successor, Anastasius IV, was a Roman, Corrado Demetri della Suburra, aged eighty when elected.

Bernard of Clairvaux, one of the great ecclesiastical thinkers of his time, died in August. His opinion of Roger II, and perhaps the *Regnum* itself, had changed over the years, from opprobrium to praise.

Meanwhile, Philip of Mahdia was leading a military expedition to occupy Annaba and fortify its defenses. This was successful, and the city was annexed to the Sicilian dominion of Ifriqiya. The citizens of Annaba were treated well.

Hailed upon his return to Palermo, Philip was not universally appreciated by his peers. It seems that some in the government were envious of his status and prestige. He was accused of apostasy based on allegations of his having converted to Islam while in Ifriqiya.

This provoked a disturbing incident. While the conversions of Muslims to Christianity were viewed as acceptable, even normal, for a Christian to embrace Islam was discouraged. Whether this was merely a pretext for attacking Philip is not known. Unfortunately, the accusation was taken seriously. Philip was imprisoned and eventually executed, supposedly on the king's orders. Yet the veracity of the account is questioned.[460]

Rex Mortuus Est

Roger seems to have fallen ill in Palermo during the late autumn of 1153, when he began to retreat from some of his public duties. Since being crowned as *rex filius,* William, the king's only surviving legitimate son, was ever more visible, though perhaps not sufficiently. It is clear that some found him to be a pale imitation of his father, or even his brothers.[461]

The king's poor health may have been brought on by exhaustion (according to Hugh Falcandus), but it ended in a terrible fever (Romuald of Salerno). A stroke or heart attack cannot be ruled out.

He was just fifty-eight years old when he died in Palermo on the twenty-sixth of February 1154.

William's succession was uncontested. Romuald states very simply that:

With the death of King Roger, his son, William, who had reigned alongside his father for two years and ten months, succeeded to the throne. Following the death of his father, and in the presence of the realm's great nobles, William was solemnly crowned on Easter, which was very near [4 April]. Among those in attendance was Robert of Bassonville, Count of Conversano and kinsman of the king.[462]

Roger's pregnant wife, Beatrice, was also present, consoled, perhaps, by the other queen, Margaret. A kingdom that, until a few years earlier, had no queen, now boasted two. It also had the royal and reginal culture and tradition that would be passed from one generation to the next.

Roger had wished to be buried at the cathedral in Cefalù, the splendid church that he founded. Despite repeated protestations by the canons of Cefalù, his porphyry sarcophagus was placed in Palermo's cathedral, where it remains.[463]

Rex mortuus est, vivat rex, goes a popular proclamation, from the French *Le roy est mort, vive le roi.* "The king is dead. Long live the king." The phrase refers to the continuity reflected in the new king immediately assuming the place of his predecessor, thus ensuring the survival of the dynasty and the monarchy.

It was a widely accepted principle that automatic succession occurred even before the son of a recently-deceased king was crowned. As we have seen, however, the Hautevilles and other sovereigns of their era ensured an unhindered succession through the practice of the regnant king crowning his son as *rex filius.*[464]

In the Kingdom of Sicily, the coronation was normally performed by the Archbishop of Palermo as primate of the realm, much as this prerogative was traditionally accorded to the Archbishop of Canterbury in England. It became a common European precept that the rite included both anointing and crowning, the former rooted in the practice described in the Tanakh of the Hebrews.[465] Another element of the ceremony, though not usually part of the rite itself, was the acclamation of the people, which is to say the baronage collectively. Coronations were meant to be public events.[466]

Writing early in the thirteenth century, the renowned jurist Tancred of Bologna, who was born in Germany and may have met Frederick II, affirmed that the King of Sicily was one of only six sovereigns of that era anointed at coronation, the others being the kings of England, France and Jerusalem, and the emperors of east and west. While his perception was not entirely accurate, what Tancred described did reflect a certain affinity, even uniformity, in the coronation practices of these monarchs as seen by contemporaries, and the placement of the Sicilian sovereigns in good company in terms of perceived importance.[467]

The *ordo,* the actual coronation rite, was based on royal (not imperial) models of the eleventh century (see Appendix 5).

Rogerian Retrospective

Very few of the chroniclers who wrote about Roger II ever met him or even saw the effects of his rule from a close vantage point. To the modern mind, the contemporaries whose impressions teach us the most are personages such as Louis VII of France, who met Roger, and observers like Romuald of Salerno, who lived in an important city of the kingdom and became an advisor to William, the king's immediate successor. Those in Ifriqiya and Greece, understandably, were less than flattering in their assessments, while Falco of Benevento, given his Lombard sympathies and anti-Norman leanings, was naturally critical, even cynical. Alexander of Telese was commissioned by the king's sister to pen a favorable narrative, but despite his partial disposition he brings us the essential facts.

The erection of the dominions of southern Italy into a kingdom was itself a supreme accomplishment replete with significance, the embodiment of spiritual as well as temporal authority. True, the King of the Germans, as the ruler of the imperial communes of northern Italy, might be crowned "King of Italy," but the Lombard kingdom was a thing of the past. During the time of the Hauteville and Hohenstaufen reigns the only kingdom in what is now Italy was the Kingdom of Sicily.

Not for nothing was coronation a religious rite, quasi-sacramental in nature. That kings and queens ruled by the grace of God was not an empty notion but a true reflection of perceived reality expressed through ancient beliefs dating from the time of King David. There was nothing hypothetical or imaginary about kingship and queenship, or the status of priesthood and knighthood.

It was natural that popular perceptions of a kingdom would be closely linked to its founding king. In no place was this truer than in the Kingdom of Sicily. Beyond this, Roger's century, and certainly his reign, witnessed the full emergence of the identity of the individual as a distinct reality.[468] It was thus no mere coincidence that Roger's sister commissioned a "chronicle" about her brother that reads like a biography.

Monarchy, by definition, is rule by one person. Autocratic a monarch may be, but much of the lustre attributed to monarchy is largely a myth. Roger's policy was never his alone. It was exercised based on the advice formulated by able counsellors and trusted friends. Many of his actions were almost instinctive, the fruit of the experience of his immediate ancestors and others who governed southern Italy before his birth, with papal input and Norman norms added to the mix.

By necessity, his rule was more Hautevillian than purely "Norman." Though he was raised in a polycultural society, the multiculturalism of his kingdom was incidental rather than purely intentional, something inherited from what already existed. A natural condition, the diversitude reflected no defined ideology or philosophy. If anything, it was generally, if sometimes subtly, contested by the very Latin papacy, which by the middle of the twelfth century, following a century of schism, could barely tolerate Orthodox Christians, much less Muslim Arabs, and offered little more than grudging acceptance of the presence of Jews.

Roger's public persona catered to papal sensibilities and aspirations. The king never claimed to be anything but Roman Catholic. Yet the Arab and Byzantine imagery of him as the ruler and protector of these peoples of the *Regnum* was very different from that of his contemporaries in France, England and Germany, while his accommodation of the Muslims and Greeks of his court reflected the old belief that actions often speak louder than words.

The "philosophy" of multiculturalism is a modern construct, and something of an ideal, but its medieval essence implied that each *ethnie* in a society was accorded the rights enjoyed by every other. This paradigm, or something reasonably close to it, was achieved under Roger II. Decade by decade, however, it would erode in successive reigns despite occasional attempts to maintain it, as Muslims became Christians and mosques were converted into churches. This was perhaps inevitable, yet the golden age of Roger's *Regnum* survived, after a fashion, into the reign of his grandson, Frederick.

What existed for some time in the kingdom, particularly in polycultural cities like Palermo, might be termed *co-culturalism,* defined here as a form of multiculturalism introduced not by design or even law but by happenstance and circumstance, yet naturally somewhat more tolerant and inclusive than such phenomena as the *convivencia* seen in Spain.

That Roger may have seemed like a man of contradictions says less about him as an individual and more about human nature and political circumstance. He was no more or less than a ruler typical of his times, if slightly more intelligent and enlightened than most. His actions were those of a pragmatist, an individualist, even a humanist. He was more than an opportunist. He does not seem to have been complacent. Here excessive analysis serves little purpose, for we can gauge the man best by his accomplishments.

Roger united southern Italy. Imperfect though this union may have been, with vocal dissent emanating from the baronage, the papacy, and cities such as Bari, the *Regnum* was a novel polity of diverse peoples that functioned reasonably well in an era when rebellion was the order of the day.

What is more, he managed to maintain the integrity of the kingdom despite attacks from within and without. He knew when to negotiate and when to fight. Whilst respecting the church and chartering its monasteries in his kingdom, he was not its slave; zealotry and crusading seem to have meant little to him. It was with reason that Roger's power was feared by popes and emperors alike. If certain barons resented him, it is clear that most Arabs and Byzantines in his kingdom respected him.

Roger instilled confidence and loyalty in most of those who did not cultivate a prior antipathy toward him based on politics or personal prejudice.

Whereas the earlier Hautevilles, even his own father, were chiefly warriors, Roger II bore the mantle of sovereign well, especially after 1140. In his era, of course, kings were at least part warrior by definition, but Roger was an able administrator. If his versatility were compared to that of the director of a modern company, it could be said that he was as adept in the field as in the boardroom.

His "boardroom" was packed with talent. He recognized competence when he saw it, and groomed young courtiers like Thomas le Brun and Maio of Bari to assume important responsibilities. That a fair number, perhaps even a few of lower rank and therefore unmentioned in chronicles and surviving charters, were "outsiders" from the Greek community or England suggests his trust in people, like his faithful Muslim bodyguard and archers, beyond fickle baronial circles.

His conquests outside Italy were carefully considered as part of a strategy to protect the kingdom's trade and shipping, hence its economy. Here again was a pragmatic, even opportunistic, response to an obvious need. The prosperity fostered by such politics likely mollified most detractors.

Given the challenges confronted by him, Roger can be forgiven if he failed to pursue a broader "grand" strategy for his nascent kingdom. By necessity, his most immediate objective was simple survival. So much the better if it led to a golden age.

That he was a Latinizer, both culturally and ecclesiastically, was intrinsic to his vision, yet very little in his reign can be considered excessively repressive of the "others," the ethnic and religious minorities. This period was, in a true sense, multicultural despite the growing dominance of the "Latin" element that united the kingdom's peoples. Under Roger's father and mother, the island of Sicily, more so than the other parts of what became the *Regnum,* was still essentially polycentric, with lingering Arabo-Berber and Byzantine Greek social forces predominant in certain localities and in entire districts of some larger cities. In view of continued revolts against the crown by the baronage, scholars have long argued about the true extent of the king's centralized control over the realm's feudal (Latin) faction, but it is clear that, guided by papal influence, Norman power would set the tone in the new state.

The euphonic concept of a multicultural society is fraught with unrevealed intricacies, leaving the degree to which, during the Hauteville era, the kingdom's peoples became a people open to debate. No single reign could span enough generations to make the idea a reality, and there were few efficacious models to emulate; the tenuous *convivencia* that existed in places like Iberia and the Holy Land was hardly ideal.

If the king himself was anything of an enigma, the kingdom he founded emerged as the least ambiguous kind of entity imaginable, destined to survive for seven eventful centuries.

Roger's reign marked the inception of the initial phase of the assumption of a "national" character which would slowly evolve into an ethnic identity. This may be seen as the inverse of the "natural" social evolution of a "typical" medieval state based on the overwhelming commonality of the language, culture, faith and ethos of the people living in it, the *ethnie* thereby becoming a state and nation. The Kingdom of Sicily was formed in a slightly less "organic" way. Its foundation differed from the practice of a generally homogeneous population choosing their first king from among themselves, and their *ethnie,* in a "tribal" manner. What is more, this "papal monarchy," as the term implies, owed much to support by the popes for its legitimacy.

That Catholic Roger was accepted as king by the great majority of people in a confessionally and ethnically diverse population is itself remarkable. Nothing quite like this existed in twelfth-century England, where the only religious minority in that kingdom ruled by a Norman dynasty was a small population of Jews.

Yet Roger was not a foreigner. Born and raised among the people he ruled, he was conversant with their faiths and spoke their languages. In many important ways he was one of them. The same would be true of the other kings of Sicily, his descendants, into the middle of the next century.

Despite the pivotal period during which he lived and ruled, Roger cannot be identified with a very specific, defining "founding myth" of the state he established. On the whole, the accounts of Hauteville rule in the *Regnum* are no more imaginative than those of the Normans in England. Milestones such as the Assizes of Ariano were soon overshadowed, to be obscured by the creeping mists of time. Yet a certain fondness for the dynasty characterized the histories published early in the print era. The Hauteville, or *Altavilla,* kings were never forgotten during the seven hundred and thirty years that the kingdom survived.

It has been seen that, despite frequent, and significant, contact with Normandy and England, the so-called "Plantagenet Empire," our Hautevilles fostered the growth of a composite culture, albeit with many typically western-European characteristics such as fundamental feudalism, an essentially Latin (Catholic) model of monarchy, and some Roman laws taken from those of Justinian. Except, perhaps, for certain Maliki influences in areas such as practices governing commercial contracts, Hautevillian rule cannot be said to have favored the establishment of common law principles like those that emerged in England, where they are still in force (see note 51).

The Lombards and Byzantines were certainly familiar with European kingship, even while Sicily's Arabo-Berbers looked to Muslim models, but our Normans brought the development of monarchy to its logical conclusion.

To the people of southern Italy, the saga of Roger II is remembered fondly as the stuff of romanticized legend, flawed in its details but glorious in its spirit. Here, grasping the hilt of magical Mikalis, was an Italian King Arthur, a cultural archetype for the ages. Not inappropriately, it was during Roger's era that his contemporary, Geoffrey of Monmouth, spun the yarn of the Arthurian mythos.

From artists we expect beauty. From justiciars we expect justice. From generals we expect protection. From royalty we expect divine greatness, for kings and queens are anointed by the hand of God and rule by His will. It was to kings and queens that nobles swore homage and fealty. It was to kings and queens that the clergy and the commonalty looked to ensure the persistence of social order in the face of whatever challenges the fates might muster.

Rooted in the concepts of the family and the tribe, the strength of monarchy transcended political power by reflecting the people of the kingdom. That is why monarchy, as an institution, has survived for so long. In our age, the mystique of royalty, the cornerstone of monarchy, has been marred by characteristics widely prevalent in society, when the dereliction of duty, the divulgence of secrets and the dissolution of marriages are all too commonplace.

But these blemishes so ubiquitous in society at large have not completely eroded the eternal substance of historical kinghood and queenhood, even if the perfect king and queen have yet to be born.

The king's mystical sword, along with his equally apocryphal order of chivalry, the "Knights of the Golden Chain," reflect a *Rogerian Legend* heretofore explored insufficiently even by the most astute scholars of the medieval culture of southern Italy.

Enlightened though he may have been, Roger was still a king of the kind who, through force of will and arms, erected kingdoms. His realm, like his sword, was forged from an elusive alloy of distinct elements, striving to be greater than the sum of its parts.

Often overlooked are the numerous men associated with the royal court. The names of many such men have vanished with the loss of a slew of charters over the parlous course of the Sicilian centuries. We shall shortly meet a few of the kingdom's women.

What Roger II bequeathed his successor and his people was a work in progress, laudable in its own right but boundless in its potential.

In the final, fruitful analysis, Roger II, like his father, was a man responding to the call of destiny.

Chapter 15

INHERITANCE

For better or worse, the *Regnum,* as a monarchy, was closely identified with its hereditary ruler, and William I was not destined to inspire the same kind of confidence as his father. Several courtiers left the kingdom soon after William I ascended the throne, and it was believed by some near the court that they did so because of a lack of confidence in his abilities.

By now, however, William and Margaret had two sons, and in November of 1154 Beatrice, Roger's widow, gave birth to a daughter named Constance.

By no means were Margaret and Beatrice the only two women linked to the Hauteville dynasty living in the *Regnum* during this period whose activities are known to us.

Women of the Kingdom

Lucy of Cammarata held a castle in Sicily's Sicanian Mountains guarding a town overlooking the Platani Valley. This locality, Kamrat, probably named for its oaks, is identified by the royal geographer Idrisi. Lucy seems to have been a niece of Roger I, possibly the daughter of one of his many brothers. By 1141, when she issued the first of half a dozen known charters ceding property and Berber villages to the diocese of Cefalù, Lucy was a widow caring for Adam, her son, invariably identified as her heir.

Cefalù, as we have seen, was erected into a diocese by the Byzantine Greeks in the seventh century but suppressed by the Aghlabids during the ninth, and refounded by Roger II. Lucy's donations of churches and lands were part of the endowment of this diocese even though Cammarata itself was some distance away, in the diocesan territory of Agrigento. Her patronage, which may be seen as part of the Norman effort to convert the local Muslims living in the villages under her control, had the king's approval. Besides a mosque, there was a synagogue at Cammarata.

In most of her charters, Lucy is styled simply "Lady of the Castle of Cammarata," as if she held the fortified town and the surrounding manors by her own feudal right rather than as "regent" for her son.[469] Indeed, the formula is rather similar to what we find in some of the charters later issued by Margaret as regent for William II.

It seems that Roger II gave Cammarata to Lucy following her husband's death but this cannot be stated with certainty; she may simply have succeeded her late spouse, of whom virtually nothing is known, with the king confirming her feudal tenure. Her estates were fairly extensive, including fertile lands in what are now the townships of Cammarata, Casteltermini and Mussomeli. After Adam died around 1154, the territory reverted to the crown during the reign of William I as part of the sovereign's normal right of escheat.

Lucy was not unique. The names of several ladies having Hauteville bloodlines or other connections to the royal family occur in charters of the twelfth century. An interesting case is Adelisa of Adernò, named in her charter of 1134 as "Adelisa niece of King Roger."[470]

Adelisa was the daughter of Emma Hauteville (see Table 8), a half-sister of Roger II, by Rudolf of Montescaglioso, whom we met in Chapter 10.

By 1134, Adelisa was the widow of Rainald of Avenella, a baron descended from the Drengot family. Over time, she donated some churches and estates in her dominions to the diocese of Catania and other episcopal jurisdictions in Sicily.[471]

By Rainald, she had at least two children, Adam and Matilda. Our scant information about Adelisa may be considered typical of what we find, or don't find, regarding the noblewomen of this era.[472]

Some women — notably Clementia of Catanzaro — were known to inherit substantial property from their fathers or uncles rather than their husbands, and in the next century this practice was formally permitted by statute in legislation that remained in force into the twentieth century, when the transmission of manors to heiresses was known as "Sicilian Succession" (see note 1027). This is not to suggest that this mode of inheritance by females had never occurred in the Lombard dominions, but the Normans seem to have viewed it more favorably.

Popes, Emperors and Rogues

In December 1154, Pope Anastasius IV died in Rome, succeeded by an Englishman, Nicholas Breakspear, who took the name Adrian IV. Unable to reach a very effective working rapport with Frederick Barbarossa, who wanted to be crowned Holy Roman Emperor but was reluctant to become a papal pawn, the new pontiff looked to the other emperor, Manuel I of Constantinople, as an ally against the King of Sicily.[473]

A few years earlier, Adrian had met William's kinsman, Raymond Berenguer

IV of Barcelona, in Catalonia, and was probably present at Lleida when that city was taken from Muslim hands in 1149 following a siege. As an avid supporter of the *Reconquista,* Adrian would not have looked kindly upon the Hautevilles' sympathy for their Muslim subjects in Sicily and Ifriqiya, but his more immediate interest was to seize control of the *Regnum.*

Most subjects, Muslim and otherwise, probably noted very few obvious changes in administration in the first few months following Roger's death, but some barons would exploit the opportunity of a new reign to achieve their old ambitions. While that may have been inevitable, some of William's actions were bound to elicit bad reactions.

It wasn't long before he deprived his half-brother, Simon, of the prosperous port city of Taranto because he thought it too grand a dominion for the illegitimate son of a king.[474] Even in the twelfth century, a bastard didn't usually enjoy attention being drawn to the fact of his rank being inferior to that of a legitimate son, especially when the affront entailed the loss of a tangible right.

Worse for William, the decision to divest Simon of this fief visibly contradicted the will of his late father. Here was not a question of entombing Roger in one cathedral rather than another, but of disinheriting one of his children in the eyes of the entire kingdom, for Simon's loss of Taranto could not possibly have gone unnoticed.

Thomas le Brun departed the *Regnum* to return to England, where Henry II had recently ascended the throne in view of the end of The Anarchy and the death of King Stephen. Whether his departure was precipitated by William's succession is debatable, but in England Thomas became the royal almoner. Idrisi, Roger's court geographer, withdrew from public life and seems to have retired to Sabtah (Ceuta), an Almohad territory in coastal Africa facing the Iberian Peninsula across the Strait of Gibraltar.

Maio of Bari, the chancellor, was appointed *amiratus* to replace the late Philip of Mahdia. To assume Maio's place as chancellor, William appointed Asclettin, a man of Norman extraction who had previously been a deacon in Catania. Although he would prove to be less than competent, early in 1155 he was entrusted with commanding an army and overseeing affairs in Puglia.

The king's recent appointments may have been resented by his treacherous kinsman, Robert of Bassonville, who had attended Roger's funeral. Honoring his father's dying wish, William gave Robert the prosperous County of Loritello (now Rotello in Molise), but the avaricious vassal seems to have thought this insufficient.

Hugh Falcandus states that Roger had declared in a will that Robert should take William's place if the king's son proved incompetent. However, there is no evidence to support this.[475]

William's hubris in his treatment of Simon seems to have been unprovoked and unjustified; his rationale may dwell in a personal feud whose details are lost to time. Conversely, the king's sour relationship with Robert was all too transparent, rooted in past conflicts between Roger II and the count's predecessors of the kind endemic to the realm's roguish nobility.

Papal, German and Byzantine politics were equally obvious in their origins and scope, and just as real. Kings for a mere quarter-century, the Hautevilles were still viewed as hegemons in undeserving control of territory and souls, and hence wealth, coveted by these other powers. If papal nuances varied slightly from one pontificate to the next, most differences were probably presumed to have been resolved before Adrian was elected. More generally, the popes, despite recent treaties, still presumed to control the Holy Roman Emperor as a vassal. Even a century of division, ostensible or real, between the Christians of east and west, failed to dissuade the papacy from regarding the Byzantine Emperor as an ally when that was convenient.

Before long, Robert was in rebellion, supported in his ambitions by Adrian, who refused to refer to William as anything more than the "lord" of Sicily.[476] Rebellious Robert awaited military support from Barbarossa that never materialized and conspired with Manuel I of Constantinople to invade Bari, an action the Greeks may have been planning while Roger was alive but cheerfully pursued now that he was dead. Papal support made it that much easier, but the very Byzantine Bariots needed little convincing.[477]

The first months of 1155 found William in Salerno and other localities fairly near some of the areas where revolts were beginning to occur.[478]

At the head of an army of some five hundred knights, disgruntled, disloyal Robert of Loritello exploited the prospect of Frederick Barbarossa's presumed invasion of the *Regnum* to lead a rebellious faction of the baronage against some localities loyal to William.[479] Very little of the exploits of disinherited, divested Simon of Taranto during this time is mentioned in the sources, but the high likelihood of his contact with the king's myriad detractors is beyond cavil.

Following some skirmishes and localized engagements, especially in Puglia, a major campaign was led by Asclettin while the king, inadvisedly, returned to Palermo in April 1155 to his family.[480] This now included a third son, William's namesake.

In June of 1155, Frederick Barbarossa made it to Rome to be crowned Holy Roman Emperor, though this did little to ameliorate his frosty rapport with Adrian, who resented the revived imperial pretension to the right to appoint bishops.[481] Despite the conditions of the Treaty of Constance, by which he was supposed to attack the Kingdom of Sicily, Frederick lacked an army sufficient to do battle against William or even to suppress the rebels in Rome who had protested his coronation; an exception was the ecclesiastical reformer Arnold of Brescia, who the emperor captured and hanged. Barbarossa's knights, some of whom were ill, were unmotivated to fight a war in the malaria-ridden south of the peninsula in the middle of summer after having spent much effort suppressing the imperial communes in the north, where a two-month siege of Tortona, near Milan, had proven particularly arduous.

Lacking military support, the English pope was soon constrained to leave Rome. Adrian might be forced to treat with William sooner or later, but first he would attempt to fight using what allies were available. After visiting several cities, he arrived at Benevento in November.

Unable to take Benevento but hoping to intimidate the pope, Asclettin attacked a number of towns on the southern fringe of the Papal State. This gave Adrian a pretext for excommunicating William.[482]

Barbarossa's failure to venture into Hauteville territory did not entirely discourage Robert of Loritello, who soon began receiving troops and gold from Manuel I, using Puglia as a base from which to launch occasional attacks northward and westward into other regions of the peninsular part of the *Regnum*.

It wasn't long before the Byzantines had captured Taranto, Trani, Andria, Giovinazzo, and their main objective, Bari. They then began an assault on Brindisi.

For his part, William wanted to respond to these attacks but he fell ill late in 1155. What struck him was probably a very debilitating, viral pneumonia. His absence from public life led many to think he had died, a supposition that encouraged a few isolated but effective revolts in Sicily.

With papal approval, exiled Robert II of Capua exploited this moment to return to the *Regnum* and retake the city he had lost nearly two decades earlier, aided by his equally embittered cousin, Andrew of Rupecanina (see Table 4).[483]

By spring of 1156, William was strong enough to ride to the Sicilian town of Butera to quash a revolt there. Then he made for Messina, where a large army and navy were awaiting him.[484]

Asclettin was chastised for his poor tactics against the rebels. William ordered him jailed.

With the imposing force assembled in Sicily, the king himself went to Puglia to excise the cancer infecting his kingdom. The royal army, with its Norman knights and Arab archers, made its way across Calabria to Taranto, along the way gaining strength through the support of loyal barons and eliminating token resistance. In May the navy reached the port city of Brindisi, whose coastal fortress had been resisting a long siege by the rebels and Manuel's Greeks.[485]

Victory was achieved soon enough. The traitors were punished, some put to death. Bari, which had fallen to Byzantine control, was largely razed, although its major churches were left unscathed.[486]

William then led his army westward into the Campania region around Naples and Salerno. He took back Capua and imprisoned Robert II, who died in captivity. Robert's son, Jordan, entered the service of Manuel I.[487]

Robert of Loritello was exiled, finding refuge at the court of Frederick Barbarossa.

Clearly, anybody who ever thought William incompetent or weak had underestimated him. Yet he was inclined to delegate authority whenever he could. This was shown by his appointment of Maio as a kind of "super minister" and his reliance on Asclettin to fight campaigns that he, as king, should have prosecuted himself. It was good to have competent ministers, but relying on them completely was a dubious strategy.

With his domestic enemies subdued, the king signed a treaty with Manuel I intended for a duration of thirty years.[488]

In view of evolving realities that could provoke open conflict at any moment, this treaty was expedient on both sides of the Adriatic. The two emperors may have been allies so far, but Barbarossa's strained rapport with the pope could not have escaped Manuel's ears. At the heart of the German-Byzantine alliance was little more than a mutual lust for territory in the *Regnum*. During the Second Crusade, a younger Barbarossa had shown himself just as willing as other westerners to ignore Byzantine prerogatives and sovereignty. His recent marriage to Beatrice of Burgundy augmented the territory under his rule, which extended into the imperial Duchy of Spoleto in central Italy. The thought that he might like to add a piece of Greece to his growing realm was hardly outside the realm of possibility, and Manuel had enough challenges to face elsewhere without having to worry about his western frontiers.

Treaty of Benevento

In June 1156, with Benevento on the verge of starvation, the English pope sued for peace. Here William was represented by Maio of Bari, and Adrian by Roland of Siena, a learned cardinal fated to become pope as Alexander III. Archbishop Hugh of Palermo was also present, accompanied by Romuald of Salerno. The young scribe who composed the text of the treaty normalizing relations between the papacy and the Kingdom of Sicily was Matthew of Aiello, a notary destined to play a greater role at court.

The Treaty of Benevento was signed in the papal city on the eighteenth of June.[489]

In this landmark accord, the Sicilian monarch remunerated to the papacy a tribute pledged by his late father and the pope finally, unequivocally recognized William as King of Sicily, the realm acknowledged to include those parts of Abruzzo annexed by William's older brothers. The apostolic legateship, the right of the sovereign to approve the appointment of bishops, was confirmed for the island of Sicily while papal prerogatives were maintained on the mainland.

The treaty explicates fifteen essential principles (the numbering is a modern addition). It is written from the point of view of the king, as a letter to the pope; an accompanying papal charter, or bull (see note 489), confirms it.

Past papal support of Hauteville sovereignty is acknowledged (1). The king refers to the recent Byzantine occupation of Bari in his kingdom as a disturbance of the peace at variance to what is normally desired in civil society (2). He names his delegates and states his intent to establish a perpetual peace with the papacy (3). He recognizes the pope as the ultimate venue of appeal to judge cases of disputes among clergy that occur on the mainland (4). Throughout the kingdom, the transfer of bishops from one diocese to another, an ever more frequent occurrence, is ultimately a papal prerogative (5). Episcopal consecrations, as well as visitations, are freely permitted as a papal right throughout the kingdom (6). Church councils may be convened in any city on the mainland without prior royal consent, which shall be required only if the king is resident in that locality at that time (7). Papal legates on the mainland shall not appropriate or usurp ecclesiastical assets in the kingdom (8). The crown's legatine authority is retained in Sicily, but prelates summoned from the island by the pope may travel to the mainland unhindered (9). Monasteries that are directly under papal jurisdiction retain that status (10). To avoid the possible conspiracy of subversive prelates against the crown, royal assent is required for the nomination of bishops and abbots, which shall be refused only in extreme cases (11). The territory and borders of the kingdom are definitively established to include Sicily, Apulia, Capua, Naples, Salerno, Amalfi and Marsia (northern Abruzzo), the last region having been occupied by William's elder brothers in the years after 1140 (12). The crown shall render an annual payment to the papacy of six hundred gold *schifati* for the kingdom excluding Marsia, for which four hundred *schifati* shall be paid, in gold or the equivalent value in silver (13). The terms of the treaty shall be honored not only by William but by his heirs (14). Adrian's successors shall likewise honor the treaty, its charter bearing a rare gold seal, in perpetuity, without the need for ratification during every pontificate (15).

In conjunction with the negotiations, William's excommunication was lifted. In Sicily, Palermo was formally recognized as a metropolitan see, with other bishops on the island suffragan to it. Hugh, consecrated Archbishop of Palermo six years earlier, was named Primate of Sicily. That is to say, he was the most senior prelate of the entire *Regnum,* outranking the bishops of Salerno, Bari, Capua, Syracuse and Messina. Adrian also confirmed Gentile as Archbishop of Agrigento.[490]

The Treaty of Benevento made the Kingdom of Sicily the closest ally of the papacy for the rest of the twelfth century. Frederick Barbarossa regarded the agreement as an affront because it effectively nullified his own, prior alliance with Adrian, but for now the Holy Roman Emperor was not in a position to invade the *Regnum* as he had hoped.

Barbarossa was soon facing his own rebellion by the vassals and cities of northern Italy.[491] William, on the other hand, found himself at peace with the papacy and most of the northern Italian communes. The king's ministers concluded a treaty with independent Genoa, one of the kingdom's most important trading partners, confirming special mercantile concessions in the realm. Before long, even Palermo had its Genoan quarter, located near the Kala port.

Neither William nor Adrian could have known that in later times the Treaty of Benevento would come to be viewed by historians as something of a turning point in papal diplomacy because it represented an approach as politically pragmatic as it was theological. Some jurists have posited that it was in 1156 that the papacy began to manage its affairs as a true European state rather than a theocracy, an idea reflected in the writings of John of Salisbury, who was present in Benevento for the signing.[492]

Like the apostolic legateship granted almost six decades earlier (see notes 225-227), the Treaty of Benevento guaranteed to the Sicilian monarchs a certain influence over the kingdom's ecclesiastical sphere that was generally lacking elsewhere. John of Salisbury was undoubtedly aware of these realities when they were confronted in his native England a few years later by his friend, Thomas Becket, who asserted the power of the church against that of the state.

In July, with the treaty concluded, William set sail for Sicily from Salerno.

Through force and diplomacy, and ultimately the force of diplomacy, he had survived a domestic crisis fomented by the same papal, imperial and baronial elements that had attempted to dislodge his father. Other nemeses would not be defeated as easily.

Ifriqiyan Destiny

While William was occupied with enemies in the *Regnum,* the Almohads had continued their advance eastward. They were again menacing Ifriqiya, making use of strategies both political and military. Some historians have taken to calling Ifriqiya part of a Hautevillian "empire," just as the English and French dominions of newly-crowned Henry II, if considered collectively, constituted a *de facto* "Plantagenet Empire" (or "Angevin Empire"). Neither supposition offers us a perfect model. Leaving Henry's legacy to his biographers, the Sicilian presence in Africa was never integral to the Hautevilles' dynastic identity, nor was it part of a "crusade" against Islam. From the beginning, its objectives, as we have seen, were chiefly, almost exclusively, economic.

This is not to suggest that differences in faith were insignificant; contemporary Islamic and Christian points of view about the Hautevilles' control of Ifriqiya were diametrically opposed to each other and reflected the religious bigotry of the era.[493] However, Almohad ideology was inspired by a Bedouin movement that challenged certain Muslim monarchies, such as those in southern Spain, as well as Catholic ones.

William and his government were now called upon to confront a geopolitical reality far greater than anything they were ever likely to face in Italy.

After Zirid power was lost in Ifriqiya, a man of that dynasty rose to a position of authority in Fatimid Egypt. Although other factors may have been involved, this would explain the reasoning behind a Sicilian raid on Tinnis in 1154. In the event, it meant that William would not be able to count on Fatimid support against the Almohads or anybody else.[494]

Besides the Almohad threat, though encouraged by it, there were revolts in several major cities beginning in earnest early in 1156. At least one, in Sfax, reflected discontent with the Sicilians' treatment of Ifriqiya's Muslims, who paid a tax from which Christians were exempted. Here again, certain details are unknown to us, but the resentment seems to have been longstanding. A chief insurrectionist was Umar ibn Abi al-Hasan al-Furryani, the governor of Sfax, whose father, before being taken to Sicily nearly a decade earlier to ensure the son's cooperation, had told him to rebel when circumstances permitted it. If true, the mere case of the man being made a hostage suggests more complexity, even repression, in Ifriqiya during its brief "Norman" period than some later historians have implied. When Umar refused to receive William's ambassadors, his father was hanged in Palermo.[495]

The Sfax uprising, which precipitated the massacre of most of that city's Christians, was merely the spark that ignited the fire. Before long, the conflagration of rebellion had spread to other cities and could not be stopped.

Little more than token assistance came from Sicily. Only twenty galleys arrived initially, and a Sicilian attack on Zawila led to much bloodshed. It was already obvious that most territories could not be held, and it wasn't long before devastated Zawila was taken by an Almohad force.

This kind of action became normal, the Almohads wasting no time securing such areas while expelling or killing the Sicilian occupiers. Though this was hardly a *jihad* in the traditional sense, most churches, even those that had stood for centuries, were either closed or immediately converted into mosques.

Despite continuous revolts beginning there in 1158, Tripoli fell only in the middle of the following year, leaving Mahdia as the last city of Ifriqiya under Sicilian control. Even the island of Djerba was lost.

Having seized control from the Sicilians, not all of the Ifriqiyans welcomed the Almohads with open arms. At Tunis in the summer of 1159, they at first offered resistance but were eventually forced to capitulate.

In September, a Sicilian fleet arrived to relieve the besieged city of Mahdia but could do little to help. In the end, the metropolis fell in January 1160 to the forces of the Almohad caliph, Abd al-Mumin.[496]

Cosmas, the bishop, was permitted to depart for Palermo, where he died later that year.[497] For the next two decades, Sicilian trade with Ifriqiya would be limited, and we find the Genoans, who had a treaty with the *Regnum,* filling the void (see note 732).

Commentators such as Hugh Falcandus were not entirely wrong to place the blame for the debacle with Maio of Bari, but the king himself was also at fault. The chronicler suggests that the monarch found Ifriqiya to be burdensome.[498] Materially, William was forced to expend resources to enforce his rights in his own kingdom that might have been used to address the situation in Ifriqiya.

The failure was not merely military. Though only sparse details are known about its causes, the Ifriqiyan crisis seems to have been aggravated by poor policies on the part of Sicilian administrators *in situ* who were unresponsive to local needs. This was easily exploited by the Almohads, whose African territory, following their conquest of Ifriqiya, now extended eastward to the Fatimid frontier.[499]

As can be imagined, the loss of Ifriqiya did little to enhance William's prestige at home, where it had an adverse effect on the economy now that a substantial part of the grain export market was gone.

Although some trade was eventually re-established, mostly by Muslim and Jewish merchants, very little in the subsequent political or social fabric of the *Regnum* during the Hauteville era is related directly to Ifriqiya. The lack of formal diplomatic relations did not dissuade Sicily's Muslims from traveling to Tunisia. Pantelleria and Malta remained military and commercial outposts for centuries.

The unflattering legend of the "Saracen's head" (described in Chapter 13) was inspired by the history of Sicily and Ifriqiya during the twelfth century.

Some commerce continued with the Fatimids, who ruled for another decade before being supplanted in Egypt by the Ayyubids. By then, the Almohads controlled the Maghreb and nearly all of Muslim Spain.

Closer to the palace, the king suffered a more personal loss when his secondborn son, Robert, aged about seven, died during one of those illnesses that claims the lives of young children.

Pope Adrian IV died at Anagni in September 1159. He was succeeded by Alexander III, born Roland of Sienna.[500] Almost immediately, Frederick Barbarossa supported Octavian di Monticella as the antipope Victor IV. Victor's successful occupation of most of Rome eventually forced Alexander to leave the city. The situation fostered an implicit conflict between the Holy Roman Emperor and the King of Sicily, with Barbarossa known to give hospitality to barons exiled from the *Regnum*. William continued to enjoy a good rapport with the papacy, which immediately confirmed the privileges of Archbishop Hugh of Palermo as Primate of Sicily.[501]

The remainder of William's reign saw virtually no invasive "disciplinary" actions directed at him by Alexander of the kind the pontiff addressed to the kings of France and England. For the next few years, most of the problems confronting the *Regnum* would be internal, some emanating from the king's family.

Chapter 16
PARENTI SERPENTI

"Kin are snakes" is a traditional expression among Italians. Among William's detractors were several of his kinsmen, legitimate and otherwise. By 1160, seeing that a frontal attack was futile, two of these men, abetted by a handful of chronically disgruntled barons, were conspiring to undermine the king through the use of covert tactics.

Simon of Taranto, as we have seen, harbored a longstanding, and arguably justified, grudge against his royal half-brother, with whom he does not seem to have been very familiar. Tancred of Lecce, the bastard son of William's elder brother Roger of Apulia, actually knew the king, and it is possible that there was an existing antipathy between the two men. Unlike demesnial Taranto, which was in the king's gift, Tancred's county was not a royal concession but a feudal estate inherited from his mother, Emma, herself a Hauteville descendant through her father, Achard II of Lecce. (For Simon and Tancred see Table 2.)

It is during the sixth year of William's reign that we encounter the first recorded court intrigues in the Kingdom of Sicily, with most of the details furnished by the poison pen of Hugh Falcandus, who knew many of the people about whom he writes.[502]

The daughter of Maio of Bari was betrothed to Matthew Bonello, who held lands around Caccamo and Prizzi, along with some estates in Calabria. Bonello's future father-in-law trusted him enough to send him to the mainland to assuage the doubts of some barons who were sufficiently annoyed with Maio to have sent missives to the king requesting his removal. While in Calabria, Bonello began to wander astray, first by courting a beautiful heiress and then by heeding the words of Roger of Martorano, one of Maio's most vocal detractors.[503] Among the malcontents was Gilbert of Gravina, a French cousin of Queen Margaret.[504]

The campaign against Maio was a dirty one, but the more imaginative allegations were ridiculous and readily dismissed. According to one rumor, the *amiratus* had tried to kill Archbishop Hugh of Palermo by poisoning, while Matthew of Aiello, Maio's protégé, had attempted to bribe the newly-elected pope, Alexander III, into deposing the king.

Even Margaret fell prey to the vicious rumors. According to Falcandus: "Voices flew around Sicily, one sometimes contradicting the other, saying that Maio had shown some of his confederates several crowns and other regalia, insinuating that the queen herself had sent him these objects from the palace. It was believed, in fact, that everything took place with her consent, linked as she was to Maio by bonds of undignified familiarity. However, many people thought these rumors false." Thus Falcandus himself tells us that the veracity of the gossip he savored was widely questioned.[505] Indeed, the allegation about the crowns being purloined from the royal treasury was later debunked.[506]

Maio was warned that a plot was afoot to kill him and that Bonello might be involved. However, he found himself reassured by the denial of his future son-in-law, who went so far as to request that the wedding be celebrated even sooner than had originally been planned. This led the *amiratus* to set aside any lingering doubts.

Meanwhile, the baronial conspirators planned the assassination fastidiously. As they saw it, the killer had to be somebody who could get close to Maio without arousing suspicion. Bonello was the ideal candidate.

Their plan was finalized shortly before Saint Martin's Day,[507] the feast on the eleventh of November that marked the end of autumn. The days were getting ever shorter, the nights ever cooler. It was as good a time as any to commit a murder. Bonello would not act alone.

Assassination

The day before Martinmas fell on a Thursday. Around dusk, not long after the sun had descended behind the conical summit of Mount Kuz, the highest of the mountains surrounding the city, Maio of Bari and a small entourage paid a visit to Archbishop Hugh at Palermo's archiepiscopal palace, which was located near the cathedral.[508] In the group was Matthew of Aiello.

After some time, the group left the archbishop's residence. By now it was completely dark and a bit chilly. For some, it would get colder still.

Maio and his cortege had made their way to Old Saint Agatha's Gate, where there was an imposing wall, beyond which the ground sloped toward the bed of the Papyrus River, whose waters had been diverted through a subterranean *kanat*.

Here the ambush took place. Bonello sprang upon Maio, slaying him with a sword. At the same time, his squad of knights attacked Maio's companions. Young Matthew of Aiello was wounded but managed to escape with the others.

Bonello and his company of rogues immediately fled the city, riding at full gallop to the castle at Caccamo in the dead of night. Back in Palermo, a crowd of exultant citizens dragged Maio's corpse along the streets.

So great was the tumult that it could be heard from the palace. The festivities seemed to be getting out of hand, and William demanded to know what was happening. It wasn't long before he was informed. The king immediately sent guards into the labyrinth of streets and squares to prevent a general insurrection. He had the presence of mind to dispatch some men to protect Maio's home to ensure that the dead man's family was not harmed.

If William was angry, Margaret was livid, expressing her rage in no uncertain terms. Her worst wrath was directed at Bonello and his accomplices, who by now were well on their way up the coast.[509]

If Margaret's reaction was crystal clear, William was indecisive, perhaps for the first time in his life. From the comfort of his window in a high tower of the palace, he could see the jubilant behavior of the Palermitans. The scene was disturbing. William's subjects seemed happy to be rid of Maio. The people who had lit bonfires for the vigil of Martinmas were now dancing around the flames to celebrate the death of a tyrant. This suggested to the king that the man he so long defended was indeed despised by the common folk as well as the barons.

Matthew Bonello, though a fugitive, had popular support. In the present climate, arresting the defiant baron would be an operation fraught with peril, and where there was one rebellious vassal there were usually others as well.

Corruption and Conspiracy

As inquiries were made, it became clear that some of the accusations made against Maio had been based on exaggerations while others seem to have been accurate. Falcandus tells us that incriminating revelations came from those in his family who worked as his assistants; his son and brother supposedly confessed to Maio's explicit acts of wrongdoing, such as the payment of bribes to ecclesiastics with money from the royal treasury. The chronicler states that a Calabrian bishop confirmed this by reimbursing money received from Maio.[510]

In practice, however, bribery was commonplace, while the popes still complained about widespread simony, the sale of ecclesiastical offices. No sources corroborate the allegation that Maio was truly corrupt, but his reputation as a bureaucrat may have lent an air of credibility to accusations of that kind.

Matthew Bonello was granted clemency for the murder on the pretext of Maio having deceived the king. With this, the baron returned to Palermo, where he was received at the palace and acclaimed by the people. If unpersuaded by Bonello's feigned sincerity, the king did not have to be convinced of his influence among both the baronage and the populace.

The queen entertained suspicions about Bonello. As if her own doubts were not enough, the palace eunuchs warned her of his amoral ambition.[511] Unbeknownst to the king, the late Maio had permitted his intended son-in-law to defer payment of a debt due the crown of sixty thousand gold tarì, an extremely large sum. Advised of this, the king now demanded remittance of these monies from Bonello and his guarantors.[512] As the months passed, Bonello found himself invited to court rather infrequently. He blamed this on Adenolf, the chamberlain, who had been a friend of Maio.[513]

With the recent death of his alleged ally Archbishop Hugh, Bonello's own friends in court circles were ever fewer.[514] The pompous baron correctly inferred that the king, supported by the queen, was trying to marginalize him. Not willing to accept his diminished status, he began to conspire with others of his ilk to obtain more. There were always a few malcontents about, but this time he didn't have to look beyond the putrid fruit of the stout Hauteville family tree, where covetous serpents concealed themselves among the leaves.

For good measure, Margaret's cousin, Gilbert, joined this elite company of bastards. Though he was born legitimately, his father was not (see Table 5).

Whatever one could say of Bonello, he was not lacking in ambition. Now his target was not an emir of emirs but the man on the throne. In early March, Bonello convened a secret meeting at his castle in Caccamo to finalize his plans.[515] What followed is an object lesson in how to execute the overthrow of a medieval monarch in his own capital.[516]

Palace Coup

Because the royal palace was heavily guarded, it was necessary to enlist the cooperation of two key figures if the plot were to have any hope of success. The palace castellan, the chief saboteur recruited, controlled the entrances. The guards' captain commanded some three hundred men and oversaw the jail. Enticed by coin, both were convinced to betray their king, leaving no more obstacles to the plan being set in motion.

Every step of the plan was worked out in detail, calling upon the knowledge and expertise of each player. For example, Simon, who had spent his childhood in the palace, was familiar with its corridors and chambers, as well as the maze of passages known only to those who lived there. This meant that he could help the others find the king. The possibility that the rebels' plan may have already been revealed to William forced Simon and Tancred to act prematurely, without waiting for Bonello to arrive in the capital.

Thursday, the ninth of March 1161, probably seemed like any other day in late winter. There was still a trace of snow on the rugged summits of the mountains visible from the towers of the palace, but wild asparagus was sprouting in the countryside, where the almonds were blossoming in shades of pink and white. Easter was around the corner, less than a month away, and William spent an early hour of daylight at liturgy in the chapel, where he was joined by Margaret and the children.[517]

The conspirators took advantage of this time to enter the palace and free all of its prisoners. By the time the royal family left the chapel, the rebels were already on their way to the Pisan Tower, the king's inner sanctum. Margaret and the children went to the royal apartments to begin the day's lessons, while William headed toward his throne chamber accompanied by Henry Aristippo, the archdeacon of Catania. An intellectual, Henry was one of the few advisors the king still trusted.[518]

Nearing the chamber he used as an office, William was walking down a narrow corridor with Henry when the pair saw half a dozen men striding toward them, brusquely and unannounced. It was unusual to see soldiers carrying swords and daggers in this part of the palace. The king did not yet know what had transpired whilst he was at holy mass, but he recognized Tancred of Lecce and Simon of Taranto. His first reaction was instinctive anger that these two undesirable kinsmen had been granted entry into the palace. It was obvious that this dastardly duo couldn't have overpowered the palace guards by themselves.

But William quickly realized that his immediate problem was far worse than the arrival of uninvited guests within the castle walls. With the two princes were irate nobles who, until a few minutes earlier, had been imprisoned in the palace dungeon. The mere fact of this confrontation meant that William's predicament was dire indeed.

Unarmed, and unaccompanied by a military escort, William glanced down the corridor behind him, thinking he might find a guard or two at the other end of the hall. If he acted quickly enough he might even slip into a secret passage to his tiny armory, where he kept swords and daggers. Outnumbered, he and Henry considered running but thought better of it.[519] They were seized by the intruders. After haranguing the king, the rebels ordered his abdication.

Now the group turned from regnal politics to unbridled thievery. Leaving the king under guard in one of the tower's rooms, the men, led by Simon, made their way into those chambers where money, regalia, rings, precious gemstones and silver vases were kept. Joined by the castellan and other traitors, they looted the premises. Some stole royal robes. Others hurled handfuls of glittering gold tarì coins out the windows to a boisterous crowd that was gathering below, seeking in this way to buy the Palermitans' loyalty.[520]

Some of the traitors preferred the pleasures of the concubines in the harem to material wealth. Each rebel plundered according to his own taste. Here was the epitome of rape and pillage. Henry Aristippo, though an ordained deacon, worshipped at the same altar of debauchery as the others. He abducted a few girls for himself and kept them at his house, where he set up his own small harem.[521]

Margaret and a few servants were in a room with her children. It wasn't long before some rebels arrived to ensure that they didn't leave.[522] Confined to a chamber on the fourth floor of the Pisan Tower, William was left alone to consider a course of action. The rebel cabal posted a guard outside the door but the room had a window from which the king could shout down onto the square for help. If anybody heard, nobody responded.[523]

Meanwhile, the knights of Bonello's beastly cohort gave chase to the few eunuchs remaining in the palace, most having fled at the first sign of danger.[524] As part of their plan, the revolt's ringleaders had already found sympathizers beyond the palace district to join the riot, and a number of knights, swords in hand, left the seaside castle overlooking the Kala harbor to murder some escaped eunuchs they found in the streets.[525]

The violence didn't end with the eunuchs and concubines. A great number of Muslim shopkeepers, along with those collecting taxes in the building that housed the *diwan,* or those walking along the streets, were killed by the same knights who had massacred the eunuchs.

When many of these Muslims, who Maio of Bari had disarmed the previous year, realized the extent of the knights' assault, they made for the part of the Sari al Kadi district outside the city wall, beyond the Papyrus River. Though they were pursued by the Christians, the fighting reached a stalemate because the aggressors had trouble attacking the defenders in the narrow alleys. In this way, the knights were repelled and the butchery minimized.[526]

Not content with the mayhem they had wrought, the leaders of the revolt incited the citizens to build a bonfire into which they tossed a great number of records. Not surprisingly, this included the tax rolls listing the barons' feudal obligations.[527]

The queen and her ladies-in-waiting could see the smoke and chaos from a palace window, even if they couldn't make out every skirmish taking place in the streets below. It was one thing to observe an isolated riot, but here was the better part of one of Europe's largest cities in utter turmoil.

Violent as the revolt was, regicide was not precisely what Simon and Tancred had in mind. What they wanted most was a friendly monarch they and Bonello could control, a puppet king.

Early in the afternoon, the two princes entered the chamber where the queen and her three sons were sequestered. The rebels demanded that her eldest son, Roger, Duke of Apulia, who was then nine years old, don some regal robes and then go with them to the stables. Seeing that she had no choice, Margaret complied with this request.

In late afternoon, the two renegade princes set young Roger upon a pony and led the boy around the streets of Palermo, presenting him as the new king to the cheering crowds.[528]

Walter, Roger's tutor, addressed the people, holding forth on how King William was a tyrant that now had to be replaced.[529] Young Roger was proclaimed king.[530]

That night, the rebels secured the palace, allowing nobody to enter. The next day, Friday, they repeated Thursday's spectacle, again parading Roger around the city. This failed to placate everybody, and there were isolated skirmishes between Muslims and Christians which led to a number of Arabs being killed, their shops looted.

By Saturday, Matthew Bonello still had not arrived at Palermo. There were those in the populace who began to question recent events, wondering why the legitimately crowned King of Sicily, whatever anybody thought of him, was still being held prisoner, and why the rebels' killing and pillaging should be justified. And anyway, who had appointed Simon and Tancred to act as kingmakers?

Increasingly worried about the atmosphere in Palermo, Tancred rode with several other rebels to Mistretta, in the Nebrodian Mountains, to confer with Bonello. Simon, meanwhile, was beginning to entertain serious thoughts of having himself crowned.

Goaded by several clerics, a large group of local men took up arms and stormed the palace, threatening to besiege it with ladders and towers unless the rebels freed King William.[531] Simon and the other conspirators held out initially but finally capitulated. They went to William, who promised to grant them safe conduct if he were freed. Once released, the king spoke to the populace from a tower window.

When the crowd demanded that the rebels be executed, William announced to his subjects that their loyalty to him was more than sufficient to satisfy any need for reprisal. With entente thus achieved, Simon and his henchmen rode off to Bonello's castle at Caccamo.

Margaret was relieved that the crisis was over. But in the commotion a stray arrow hit young Roger, who was standing near a window, mortally wounding him. He was dead within hours.[532]

Condolences were expressed by many who had once despised the king, but Margaret was inconsolable. She had lost her second child.[533]

Following a period of mourning, William met with local leaders, particularly the Muslims, to reassure them that henceforth they would be spared the bigotry and violence that characterized the recent upheavals. Bonello had not given up his ambition to unseat the king. Having assembled a rebel force, he marched toward Palermo from Caccamo, but he retreated as some of the king's galleys arrived from Messina with reinforcements to suppress an invasion.

Tancred, joined by the king's distant kinsman Roger Sclavo, attacked some Muslim communities in southeastern Sicily, such as that of Butera. These atrocities were supported by some of the Norman and Lombard barons in that region.

The defiant Bonello was eventually coaxed to the palace, where he was arrested. Some Palermitans protested this, but Bonello died in a dungeon within the palace walls late in 1161. A street is named for him near Palermo's cathedral not far from the site where he killed his almost father-in-law.

Cleaning House

William exiled Tancred and Simon, who went to the eastern Mediterranean, where they could go on pilgrimage in the Holy Land or render service as mercenaries in Constantinople. Gilbert of Gravina, the queen's cousin, was pardoned at Margaret's urging even though he had participated in the hellish folly that cost the life of her son. William ordered him back to the mainland to respond to some raids by Robert of Loritello.[534]

Beatrice, the "queen dowager" as the widow of Roger II, was with Constance, her young daughter, living undisturbed at San Marco d'Alunzio, the Hautevilles' familial castle set upon a rocky summit near a convent in the Nebrodian Mountains. Constance was now seven years old. Unlike Margaret's sons, Constance, being a girl, was not likely to be manipulated by plotters seeking to crown their own puppet monarch.

In the aftermath of recent events, William was left with very few people he could trust. He pardoned the notary Matthew of Aiello, who set about compiling a feudal tax roll to replace the one destroyed by the rebels.[535] The king was suspicious of the intellectual deacon Henry Aristippo, who had raided the harem, although he chose not to punish him.

Sporadic revolts in eastern Sicily were suppressed; the town of Butera was punished severely for having rebelled against the crown and persecuted the local Muslims.[536] Although the peasantry, encouraged by the baronage, participated in riots, these were not, strictly speaking, "popular" rebellions such as those that had recently been incited in Palermo. Outside the major cities, the revolts were usually baronial in nature, the result of vassals coercing peasants or serfs to join them in protesting royal authority. The relationship of most subjects to the monarch was indirect, exercised through a local baron or abbot as "intermediary." Even in demesnial cities, citizens' contact with the monarch and the highest *strata* of government was through local jurats.

If William could not tolerate open rebellion, he could make a sincere effort to mend his tattered ties with the barons by addressing their grievances. One of his measures in this direction was the restoration of the right of feudal inheritance to the sons of vassals killed in royal service.[537]

The early months of 1162 found the king on the mainland with a large army to quell some isolated disturbances that could not be left to the limited military resources of Gilbert of Gravina. William left Margaret in Palermo as his effective surrogate until he returned in the summer.

She was assisted by an Arab eunuch named Martin, a convert to Catholicism who undertook retaliation against people thought to be the king's adversaries. That Caïd Martin would be suspicious of Christians was not unreasonable in view of recent events, which had claimed the life of his brother.[538] Henry Aristippo, talented scholar and lecherous deacon, was apprehended, deprived of his mini-harem, and cast into a dark dungeon to die.

We do not know how influential Margaret was in these bloody reprisals. Confronted by adversity, she had become a she-wolf. Whilst the king was away, she did what her husband was unwilling, or at least less willing, to do.

Ruling the Kingdom

The status of Palermo's Muslim Arab population had suffered in the recent riots. For the first time since the Normans took the city almost a century earlier, its Muslims had been attacked in large numbers by Christian knights. This doubtless prompted many, in the interest of survival, to consider abandoning Islam.

Religious freedom, women's rights, prostitution, slavery and forced castration were important issues. Yet none of these things were viewed from the same perspectives as the sensibilities that color our times. Even if it were argued that the presence of eunuchs and harems reflected what were essentially Muslim practices inherited from the emirs who once ruled Sicily, William was unwilling to alter this aspect of the society over which he reigned.

When he returned to Palermo, William fell into some of his old habits. He still preferred passing his time hunting on the reserve to the immediate south of the Genoard park, delegating duties to his counsellors. A chapel dedicated to Saint Michael the Archangel was erected next to a royal hunting lodge at what is now the town of Altofonte so that the king could spend a few days at a time hunting in the woodlands without having to return to the city.

The serenity of this ennui was a mirage. A sobering moment in 1163 served as a reminder that danger lurked around every corner, even within the palace walls.

Following the recent revolts, the king had transferred important prisoners to a jail outside the palace. However, a few were still in the palace dungeon enclosed by thick Punic walls. It was only a matter of time before these men were moved to another jail, such as the round tower of Palermo's seaside castle.

Lacking any hope for being released, several prisoners convinced the guards to free them. With this accomplished, they made for a gate leading out of the palace. Their escape was foiled by the castellan, who quickly went through the gate, closing it from the outside and trapping the fugitives within the palace's curtain wall.

Next they entered the base of one of the towers, thinking they might find the king on one of the upper floors. Instead, they ended up in the room where young William and his brother, Henry, usually met for their lessons. Fortunately, the boys' tutor, Walter, had whisked the two to the safety of the bell tower as soon as he heard the commotion. Margaret was in a chamber upstairs and unaware of what was happening.

Martin managed to lock the escapees in a large room, where they were all killed. The knaves' lifeless bodies were literally thrown to the dogs, and what remained of the corpses was forbidden a burial.[539]

Perhaps at the queen's urging, the king ensured that henceforth no prisoners were ever to be jailed in the palace, even temporarily.

Overlooking the Kala harbor and protected by a moat, the sea castle was far more secure than the palace dungeon. Its master, sadistic Robert of Calatabiano, had made the fortress infamous for torturing the prisoners kept there.

His fief was on the other side of Sicily, near Catania, but Robert used his position to accrue wealth through corrupt means everyplace on the island. With the collusion of Caïd Martin, several avaricious justiciars would bring fraudulent charges against men whose estates they desired. The accused would be released only upon paying substantial bribes, or ceding a manor or two. This extortion seems to have touched many innocent Sicilians, but William was probably unaware of the problem (about which more later).

Apart from these chronic abuses, the *Regnum* was peaceful. Indeed, the king had told his three chief counsellors to avoid disturbing him unless it was absolutely necessary.[540] The most important royal counsellors came to be called *familiares* or *archons*. Martin was joined by Richard Palmer and Matthew of Aiello. William himself might issue an occasional charter in favor of a bishop or abbot.

The antipope Victor IV died in April 1164, having ultimately lost the support even of Frederick Barbarossa. However, the emperor immediately endorsed another antipope, Paschal III, born Guy of Crema.

Legacies

The Treaty of Benevento was not William's only lasting legacy. New monasteries and castles were constantly springing up around the *Regnum*.[541] One of the more interesting projects of this era was the Zisa palace, constructed beginning in 1165 on the edge of the Genoard park immediately outside Palermo's city walls. Its name comes to us from the Arabic *aziz,* for "splendid," preserved in the Sicilian verb *azizzare,* "to make beautiful." The Genoard itself takes its name from the Arabic *gennàt al-àrd,* "paradise on earth."

Hugh Falcandus tells us that it was William's wish that the Zisa, set amidst lakes and greenery, might surpass the splendor of the existing rural palaces around the capital, namely the Favara and the more austere Scibene.[542]

Wrote Romuald of Salerno: "At that time, King William ordered to be erected near Palermo a rather high palace, built with admirable technical competence, which he called the Zisa, surrounded by fruit trees and splendid gardens, rendering it pleasurable with numerous fountains and lakelets."[543]

The gardens and pools recently constructed in front of the palace do not conform to the original design, but are vaguely similar to those of the Alhambra in Granada.

The palace's shape recalls that of Fatimid palaces built in Tunisia and Egypt. The two lateral towers are part of a ventilation system engineered to cool the inner rooms during the hot summer months. The cornice along the top of the building was cut into a battlement over the centuries. Inside are preserved some of the ducts built into the floors of the three-story structure that supplied drinking water to the upper floors and also to flush the latrines. These were fed by large "tanks" in the spaces between the floors.

Part of an Arabic inscription survives at the entrance to the fountain room referring to the palace as "the most splendid residence in the realm, built in magnificence and delight," going on to mention "paradise on earth," namely the Genoard, and that its construction was ordered by "he who desires glory," William identified here by the Arabic *mustaziz.*

The Zisa has various Fatimid details, such as muqarnas, in its numerous chambers, and impressive mosaics in its entry hall, a kind of foyer, where water flowed to and from an impressive fountain immediately before the principal entrance, cascading into a pool in front of the building.[544]

Unfortunately, William I did not live to see its completion.

The year 1166 began well enough, but in March the king was struck by a terrible bout of dysentery. This illness seemed to have passed when a relapse made him suspect that his end was near. Seeking to settle his affairs to avoid contestations should he die, he formally decreed his elder son as his heir. He had taken the step of officially appointing Richard Palmer, bishop-elect of Syracuse, and Matthew of Aiello, now the high notary, as *familiares,* trusted counsellors, to assist in governing the *Regnum.*[545] The *familiares* would become a leitmotif in the government of the Sicilian kingdom.

Significantly, the moribund monarch named Margaret "keeper of the entire realm," regent.[546]

King William I of Sicily expired in May at the age of forty-six.[547] He was buried in the palace chapel.[548]

At the age of twelve, Margaret's son was now King William II of Sicily. He was crowned by Romuald of Salerno in Palermo's cathedral.[549]

Chapter 17

REGENCY

William's widow, Margaret of Navarre, Queen of Sicily, was now the most powerful woman in Europe and the Mediterranean.[550]

Though largely ignored by historians until recently, she is the queen of our Norman-Swabian era about whom the most is known, and the one whose regency lasted the longest.[551] This was a particularly important period, highly formative for the young king, William II, as well as a future queen, Constance, who was often at court. Margaret's regency thus directly influenced two monarchs. Later, even her young daughter-in-law, Joanna of England, who was not yet a teenager when she arrived in Palermo, doubtless looked to Margaret as something of a mentor despite being the daughter of another strong queen, Eleanor of Aquitaine.

During the regency, the Sicilian court saw women at its apex. Besides Margaret, as queen regent, Beatrice, the queen dowager, was sometimes present, perhaps acting as a discreet advisor and confidante. There were others, such as Adelisa, a daughter of Roger II who wed Margaret's half-brother.

Margaret herself is something of a nexus, a connection linking places and generations. She knew Roger II and may have met Louis VII of France and Eleanor of Aquitaine. It is likely that she met Tancred of Lecce. She was at court when Arab and Byzantine intellectuals were present. She had occasion to meet leading Muslims and barons of the kingdom. She was conversant with various cultures and instrumental in founding a great abbey that reflected them gloriously.

The details of the regency recorded by Romuald of Salerno and Hugh Falcandus, both present at court to witness most of the events about which they wrote, afford us rare insight into the kingdom's society, institutions and population. Indeed, we can learn more about the day-to-day workings of the *Regnum* from the events of these five years than from any other period of Hauteville rule. That is what makes the regency worth examining.

Raised in polycultural Pamplona as the multilingual daughter of a Norman lady, Margaret ruled a court she filled with kinsmen and allies. Though Norman French was spoken at court (see note 174), this was still a multicultural kingdom. Margaret was one of the few women of her era to rule a population that had a large number of Muslims.

During her regency, the queen and her government confronted a number of social ills that, unfortunately, taint our age as it did hers, including treason, larceny, corruption, racism, feuds, sexism, homicide and sex crimes, to mention just the most obvious ones.

Not that Margaret was the only one of our monarchs to contend with these perennial challenges, but we happen to know more about a few specific cases of this kind, in some detail, during her reign than those of most of the others.

Despite military action by the Holy Roman Emperor in regions to its immediate north, the *Regnum* fought no wars during the regency. It was at peace with the Byzantine Emperor.

A case could be made for Margaret being the greatest queen of the Kingdom of Sicily before 1266, on a par with earlier royal women such as Adelaide del Vasto and Sichelgaita of Salerno.

Considered collectively, the numerous characteristics and events that distinguished it made the regency unique for its time. Here, through a magnifying glass, it shall be viewed at some length.

A Queen's Rule

From the beginning, the queen's actions strongly suggest that she wished to avoid what some regarded as the errors of her late husband.[552] Her initial decisions were unusual enough to make people stand up and notice her. Margaret's intent, as regent, was that the subjects should ascribe these sage decisions to their sovereign, her son, William.

There was no model to follow except perhaps some of the policies of her father-in-law, the fondly-remembered Roger II. If there was a framework for Margaret's authority, it was established tradition and the kingdom's Assizes of Ariano, augmented by such developments as the Treaty of Benevento. She could not afford to be indifferent. Reasoning that bloody revolts were the progeny of dissent, Margaret sought to eliminate their root cause. She beguiled the restless baronage by redressing their unvoiced grievances. Her stratagems were simple.

The first decrees Margaret issued in the name of her son were intended to still troubled waters and to encourage loyalty toward the new monarch. These took several forms, all quite pragmatic.[553] According to Romuald of Salerno:

The queen, being a wise and prudent woman, and knowing well the spirit of the populace, which was very disturbed for the mistreatment the subjects had endured under the late William I, undertook through copious concessions to instill their love and fealty toward her son. Acting on sage counsel, she opened the jails and released many prisoners, restoring their lands and forgiving their debts. She allowed counts and barons who had left the realm to return, restoring to them the estates that had been confiscated. By royal grace, she very generously granted many lands to churches, counts, barons and knights. Through these and many other acts the fealty and spirit of affinity of the people for her son increased greatly, to the point that those who were already loyal became even more ardently loyal and those who were devoted became further devoted to him.

Many justiciars seem to have applied the law arbitrarily, meting out justice as they saw fit. This sometimes resulted in overzealous prosecution and excessively harsh sentences even for minor transgressions. A disturbing degree of corruption permeated officialdom.

Margaret abolished certain taxes that had been levied in recent years, particularly the "redemption fees" which had become a burden in Apulia and in the area around Salerno and Naples.[554] She made it clear that such taxes were not to be collected in the future.

Her sobriety of thought distinguished her. Presented in a velvet glove, her policy concealed an iron fist. It may have also hidden the fact that the *Regnum* was now being governed by a woman. If Margaret's authority as regent was unchallenged, her decisions did not always go unquestioned.

Reginal Authority

Margaret appointed the eunuch Caïd Peter, the head of the royal *diwan*, as her chief *familiare*, informing Richard Palmer and Matthew of Aiello that henceforth they had to answer to him. Neither Richard nor Matthew accepted this blissfully, but for now there was nothing they could do about it.

In appointing her own team, Margaret implicitly chose her own approach to government. But the ubiquitous court intrigues did not cease just because the queen was asserting her authority.

It didn't take long for some bishops to begin trying to convince Peter that Richard Palmer was planning to kill him. Yet Peter was reluctant to act against Richard despite the insistence of the bishops that he do something.

If Richard were removed, Gentile Tuscus of Agrigento or one of the other bishops could take his place. Gentile, in particular, was unabashedly ambitious; he had always behaved as a sycophant around William I but grew disillusioned when Richard, who was closer to the king, thwarted his proposals for various projects. According to Falcandus, one of the plotters was Romuald of Salerno. Matthew of Aiello, who also began to believe that Richard should perhaps be removed from power but still respected him as a colleague and peer, preferred to use his own methods to achieve the task.

According to Falcandus, a pretext for the antipathy towards Richard Palmer was his Anglo-Norman origin. Gentile and his unsavory ilk probably inferred that as an "outsider" Richard would never be easily manipulated. As the last influential Englishman at court, he was the only obvious obstacle to them taking control.

Caïd Peter, they thought, could be dominated more easily. An Arab convert to Catholicism, he had once served as a naval commander. Margaret herself did not cultivate a great liking for Richard Palmer, but she refused to dismiss him.

There was justification for her resentment. When her husband was alive, the queen had sought support from Richard for some of her proposals, only to receive from the pompous cleric cynical and condescending missives.[555] His arrogant comportment led Margaret to believe that he hated her, and she was probably right. Although Richard Palmer was bishop-elect of Syracuse, he spent little time in that city, preferring life in the capital. For now, the queen preferred marginalizing Richard to removing him altogether.

Meanwhile, Gilbert of Gravina, Margaret's cousin, having been advised of young William's accession to the throne, and Margaret's regency, made his way to Palermo. Couriers arrived at Palermo with this news when Gilbert was still at Messina, a few days away.

Gilbert was already the acting governor, or bailiff, of the mainland part of the *Regnum*. Now he sought to displace Caïd Peter, the chief *familiare*. He may have thought his cousin weak, yet her word alone had saved his hide from serious punishment for conspiring with Bonello a few years earlier. Arrogant Gilbert came to believe that he had been rewarded for his own merits; in reality, his "success" was little more than the product of nepotism. Quite simply, he was the queen's cousin. If King William I exiled his own kinsmen, Simon and Tancred, he certainly would have punished Gilbert.

The arrival of Gilbert imposed a temporary delay on the plans of the bishops to remove Richard Palmer from power. The company of knights traveling with Gilbert was not sufficient to attack Palermo, but it made an impression on Gentile of Agrigento and the other plotters. Richard Palmer also took note, and warned Gilbert about the conspirators. The queen's cousin assured Richard of his support.

Caïd Peter's faction, being loyal to Margaret, was not closely allied to any of the others. These men publicly commended Gilbert for having raced to Palermo to support his kinswoman. In private, however, they sought to convince the queen of her cousin's covert ambition to rule the kingdom. Their caveats were unnecessary, as Margaret already knew enough about Gilbert's character, or lack of it, to ascertain his objectives.

One day, Gilbert spoke to her in private audience, though in the presence of Caïd Peter. Here Gilbert defended Richard Palmer, spoke against the court eunuchs, and suggested that changes be made at court.

Margaret affirmed her faith in the people at court and her general approval with the organization her late husband had put in place. She offered her cousin a place as *familiare* under Peter. This enraged Gilbert, who found it offensive to be offered a position beneath that of a palace eunuch. He launched into a diatribe, ranting that Margaret's prestige in Apulia was abysmal, and before long his utterances degenerated into a series of vicious personal insults against his cousin.

Tears of disillusion gathered in the eyes of the woman who had done so much to help a wayward kinsman of middling birth. But the queen stood her ground throughout the tirade.[556]

Having thoroughly berated his cousin, Gilbert stormed out of the palace but he did not leave Palermo, where he began to contemplate ways of eliminating the chief *familiare*.

Peter surmised that Gilbert's knights could be divided into two groups. The enfeoffed knights were landed barons of the peninsular part of the *Regnum* who served Gilbert and the crown as part of their military obligation; looking toward their own interests, these barons preferred to see Gilbert appointed chief *familiare* in Peter's stead. The mercenary knights were generally indifferent about such matters; led by a salaried constable, Richard of Mandra, they need only be paid for their service, which was not a feudal obligation, and they would eventually return home, some beyond the Alps.

At Caïd Peter's suggestion, the queen enfeoffed Richard of Mandra with the County of Molise, which included wealthy baronies like Boiano and Venafro.[557]

Not only did Margaret know how to sew together a patchwork of supporters, she knew how to sow the seeds of dissent among her antagonists. The formal investiture of Richard with his prosperous county was an ostentatious event, and the first public occasion of its kind over which Margaret presided. Here the entire nobility could see the use of reginal power.

Gilbert and his followers were rankled by the elevation of Richard of Mandra, now Count Richard of Molise. There was nothing they could do to stop a feudal investiture, which was a royal prerogative, but they now conspired in earnest to kill Peter.

Thinking his position untenable and his life endangered, Caïd Peter departed Palermo under cover of night, taking a chest of gold tarì with him. He sailed to Africa, where he renounced Christianity, to which he had converted in youth, to embrace Islam anew under his original name, *Ahmed*.

It was rumored that Peter had taken some crowns and other regalia with him. The queen refuted this nonsense but to clear the air she summoned the barons, bishops and court officers present in northwestern Sicily to an audience at the palace.

It wasn't long before the convocation degenerated into a heated exchange, with Gilbert of Gravina insulting Peter and Richard of Molise defending him. In defense of Peter's honor, Richard challenged to trial by combat any baron present who persisted in defaming the absent *familiare*. The argument descended to the level of personal insults, with Richard calling Gilbert a coward unworthy to lead royal troops. These fighting words were precisely the kind of opening Gilbert was waiting for, and the two men squared off, swords drawn. Fortunately, some knights intervened to separate them before anybody was hurt. Margaret rose from her throne and ordered the two counts to desist, and they retracted the stream of invective they had unleashed upon each other. But their mutual acrimony remained, and Gilbert began a covert campaign to sully Richard's reputation.[558]

The *familiare* Matthew of Aiello was responsible for reading correspondence that arrived at court from around the *Regnum*. Seizing on rumors that

Frederick Barbarossa was again planning an invasion of southern Italy, Matthew had such a letter forged stating that the threat was imminent.[559] He read this message to an assembly of barons.

This gave Margaret a credible pretext for sending Gilbert back to Apulia. She flattered her cousin by telling him he was the best man to raise an army and defend that part of the kingdom. To reinforce his authority in the region, she made him governor of Apulia and Campania. Gilbert suspected there may be trickery behind his appointment to this mission, but open insubordination would make him an enemy of the court. Besides, he had already come to understand that, realistically, there was little more he could do to facilitate his ambitions in Palermo. Mollified, he departed for Apulia with his son, Bertrand.[560]

Although the actions of Gilbert and the bishops were not aimed solely at the Arabs, be they Muslim or Christian, the tenor of the insults directed against Peter reflected a subtle religious bigotry that was festering in the kingdom, particularly among the nobility.

In place of Caïd Peter, Margaret promoted Richard of Molise to *familiare*. Unlike his predecessor, Richard was a decisive man who commanded his own little army. This struck fear into his opponents.

The three *familiares* represented the feudal (Richard of Molise), bureaucratic (Matthew of Aiello) and ecclesiastical (Richard Palmer) spheres.

With Gilbert gone, the bishops resumed their efforts to subvert the position of Richard Palmer. This movement was led by Cardinal John of Naples, the pope's envoy.[561]

It was not with unbridled enthusiasm that Margaret countenanced the obnoxious, condescending Richard Palmer as a *familiare* at court. Apprised of this, John suggested to the queen a plan not unlike the strategy that was so effective in prompting Gilbert's recent *exeunt*.

Richard Palmer was still bishop-elect of Syracuse. During Margaret's regency this episcopal see was technically vacant and therefore depended directly from the Holy See.[562] It will be remembered that episcopal appointments in Sicily had to be confirmed by the monarch as the pope's apostolic legate, but here there was no hindrance as the queen wholeheartedly supported Richard's consecration. If he were summoned to Rome to be consecrated, Richard would consequently have to assume his duties in Syracuse, his designated diocese, on the other side of Sicily. Naturally, this meant he would spend less time at court in Palermo. The queen liked this idea as much as she disliked Richard.[563]

The plan was set in motion, and before long John was at the palace standing before Margaret, young King William, the *familiares,* several bishops and sundry barons reading the papal command to all of Sicily's bishops-elect to present themselves in Rome for consecration to regularize their positions. As a separate announcement, John added his own condition that the bishops-elect must comply with the papal directive within a certain date.

Richard Palmer craftily agreed to the papal order to be consecrated while refusing to accept any separate, additional conditions imposed by John of Naples. The aspiring prelate thus rejected the deadline. This abnegation was debated at length but resulted in an impasse.

Whilst Richard's obvious reason for the delay was to avoid abandoning the seat of power at court, he may have harbored an ulterior motive as well. Syracuse, where Saint Paul had preached, enjoyed great prestige as the oldest diocese of the *Regnum* and arguably the oldest in western Europe, but Richard aspired to more. If he could swap his Syracusan appointment for Palermo, he would emerge as one of the most powerful people in the kingdom after the regent herself.

The queen would have to devise another way to distance Richard Palmer from her inner circle. Word had reached the court that he was beginning to speak against her openly in public. That was something she could not tolerate, for a lack of respect of the regent's decisions might weaken the subjects' loyalty to their queen.

Cardinal John of Naples did not give up trying to get Richard to Rome, and the latter knew he could not forestall consecration forever. So Richard Palmer appealed to another Richard, namely his fellow *familiare* Richard of Molise, who enjoyed the queen's confidence, to aid his cause.

There was no way to force a change in policy, but the pope's envoy might be tricked into providing Molise a platform from which to defend Palmer. This tactic was to prove effective. At a subsequent audience at court, John of Naples responded negatively to requests that he delay the consecration deadline, prompting Richard of Molise to reproach him for threatening to enforce an order that would absent an important counsellor from royal service.

The cardinal responded that Richard Palmer would be free to return to Palermo following his consecration by Pope Alexander. Now, however, John's resolve offended the queen's sense of authority.

Annoyed that a papal prelate presumed to challenge her reginal prerogative by ordering a *familiare* away from Palermo, Margaret stood up and declared that, "The presence of the archbishop-elect is needed at court, so for now he cannot leave. He can depart in another moment when circumstances permit."[564]

It may be that the queen was made privy to the tactic of Richard of Molise before the gathering took place, and had reason to think she should make a point of her own by reminding those present that she was in charge. Her decision had the additional benefit of placing Richard Palmer in her debt, in the eyes of others if not his own. Henceforth his public criticism of her would ring hollow. Whatever motivated the queen, people would remember her willingness to take a decision long after they had forgotten its rationale or even what the decision concerned.

The extemporaneous pronouncement had the desired effect of imparting to her subjects the notion that Margaret was to be respected.

Manuel of Constantinople, having learned of the death of Margaret's husband, sent emissaries to propose the betrothal of his daughter and universal heiress, fourteen year-old Maria "Porphyrogenita" (see Table 6), to her son. This would presumably entail William's right to the Byzantine succession since the girl, born of Manuel's first wife, Bertha of Sulzbach, did not have any living brothers. The queen convoked a council to consider this proposal. She renewed the peace established with Manuel by William I, but the negotiation of the betrothal remained open, in effect inconclusive, for the numerous details that would have to be stipulated. Margaret's son wasn't the only monarch the Byzantine Emperor thought worthy of his daughter.[565]

Kinsmen

Before long, the queen's half-brother, Rodrigo (see Table 14), arrived in Palermo with a large contingent of Navarrese knights. Though named for Margaret's great-grandfather, the intrepid warrior El Cid, Rodrigo was not descended from him. Rather, he was fathered by a man with whom Margaret's mother had an extramarital affair and thus excluded from the Navarrese succession.

The queen probably summoned Rodrigo for additional protection at court, but his knights were little more than opportunistic rogues. Margaret encouraged Rodrigo to change his name to *Henry,* which the Sicilians found more acceptable and pronounceable.[566]

The queen enfeoffed her younger half-brother with the prosperous County of Montescaglioso, near Taranto, and several towns in Sicily, namely Noto, Sclafani and Caltanissetta. She also provided him with enough coin to support himself in a dignified manner during his initial travels.

First he spent some time in Palermo, entranced by its souks and atmosphere. Then, having squandered most of the money his sister gave him, Henry of Montescaglioso (as he shall now be called) made his way to his new county on the mainland, stopping first to inspect his Sicilian manors. Along the way to Montescaglioso, he had to pass through Messina. This port city, a springboard for European merchants, pilgrims, knights and pirates on their way to and from the eastern Mediterranean, was infamous for its vice and debauchery, attracting charlatans, beggars and prostitutes. To an inveterate gambler like Henry, the attractions of this place, a kind of medieval "Las Vegas on the Ionian," were irresistible.[567] If Palermo was a city of arrant luxury, Messina was an urban jungle of shameless sin.

News of Henry's impromptu sojourn reached the queen, who ordered him, as his sovereign and his older sister, to cross the Strait of Messina and make his way to Montescaglioso. It was summer and he had best reach his estates in time for the harvests. Almost as an afterthought, Margaret arranged for her brother to marry Adelisa, one of the daughters of King Roger (see Table 2).

The government was served well enough by the *familiares* Richard Palmer, Matthew of Aiello and Richard of Molise, with the treasury overseen by Caïd Martin and the palace by its chamberlain Caïd Richard. Of course, these were not the only important courtiers; archdeacon Walter, the tutor of Margaret's sons, was considered important enough to subscribe royal charters.[568]

But personal ambitions threatened to create fissures in this façade. Matthew wanted to become grand chancellor, while Richard Palmer envisaged himself as Archbishop of Palermo and Primate of the Realm. Richard of Molise was the most trusted of the *familiares,* and the one most likely to receive the political favors he requested.

No longer a neophyte, Margaret decided, as a matter of policy, to appoint councils of ecclesiastics to manage diocesan lands where there were no serving bishops, thus removing this power from the authority of bailiffs, who were easily corrupted. Requiring people who could be trusted, she sent a letter to her cousin, Rotrou (see Table 5), who had recently been consecrated Archbishop of Rouen, soliciting recommendations.[569]

There was a precedent in presuming to ask such a favor of him. Some years earlier, as Bishop of Evreux, Rotrou had sent Walter to Palermo to serve as the tutor of Margaret's sons. This was the same Walter who sheltered the children in the bell tower when some prisoners escaped the palace dungeon, the same Walter who served as a deacon of Cefalù. It was Walter who she sent to Rouen bearing her letter to Rotrou.

Margaret requested that her cousin might send to Palermo either Stephen of Perche or Robert of Neubourg, intellectuals known for their integrity and competence. It so happened that Stephen was already in Italy, where he was visiting Gilbert of Gravina, the son of his brother. Stephen and his company intended to go to the Holy Land, but made their way to Palermo when summoned.

In September, Stephen of Perche arrived in Palermo accompanied by the theologian Stephen of Blois and a company of thirty-six knights, esquires and friars. Margaret greeted him warmly, receiving him in audience in the crowded presence of her courtiers. Here she made a portentous pronouncement that she wanted heard by the entire court:

"Here I see myself finally achieving what I have ardently desired. To the sons of the Count of Perche I owe the same honor one accords a brother. The efforts of their father, in truth, gave my own father his kingdom. It was the Count of Perche who granted to my mother as his niece, and thereby to my father, a dowry of vast lands conquered in the face of great dangers and prolonged effort from the Muslims of Spain. You need not be surprised that I regard his son, Stephen, my mother's kinsman, as if he were my brother, welcoming him with joy the moment he arrives here from faraway lands. I desire and command that all who declare good wishes to me and my son will sincerely respect and honor Stephen. From your kind treatment of him, I will infer the depth of your fealty and affection toward us."[570]

Some of Stephen's knights and companions decided to stay with him in the *Regnum*. Among those persuaded to live in Sicily, at least for a few years, were Odo Quarrel, a canon of Chartres, and erudite Peter of Blois, a gifted writer, the latter appointed as the young king's tutor. By the spring of 1167, when Stephen had agreed to be the kingdom's chancellor, it was clear that Margaret had shown her mettle to all and sundry and was piloting a policy of her own.

Yet most of her routine duties were rather banal; a charter of March 1167 finds her acting in the transfer of ecclesiastical property in Palermo.[571]

Not all at court were enthralled by Stephen's appointment, but it was supported by an important cardinal who happened to be in Sicily on his way to France. This was William of Pavia, a papal diplomat whose presence was urgently required in England, where a dispute had broken out between King Henry II and Thomas Becket, Archbishop of Canterbury. Cardinal William would first stop in France, where Becket was living in self-imposed exile. The intrigues at the Sicilian court were tame compared to the storm raging beyond the English Channel.

Familial connections had long been intertwined across the Norman realms. One of Margaret's kinsmen, Richard of Aigle, held lands in Sussex, where in happier times he went hawking with Thomas Becket. At an audience with Margaret, Cardinal William expressed how worried he was about two of the exiled archbishop's nephews who had been expelled from England. Could they, he inquired, stay in Sicily until Henry permitted them to return to their homeland? Margaret gave them a home near the cathedral.[572] One of Becket's letters to the queen survives.[573]

As chancellor, Stephen set about governing the kingdom on his cousin's behalf. Margaret made it clear that all matters concerning administration should be submitted to him. Naturally, the other *familiares* were displeased by this, for it had the intended effect of restricting their access to the queen and their influence in the *Regnum*.

Outwardly, the prelates seemed to like Stephen. Before long, Romuald of Salerno, who had been Archbishop of Palermo for five years, ordained him a subdeacon. Soon the other bishops, acting on Romuald's suggestion, unanimously supported a decision to consecrate Stephen as Archbishop of Palermo and therefore Primate of Sicily, the first among equals in the kingdom's ecclesiastical hierarchy.

This permitted Romuald, who was also Archbishop of Salerno, to focus on his duties as a papal diplomat. However, as Romuald surely knew, Stephen's imminent consecration, which could be years away, created new complexities in the power structure.

At least two clerics at court were eyeing the appointment. Walter, as archdeacon of Cefalù and still a royal tutor, may have seemed the more likely candidate, but Richard Palmer, the bishop-elect of Syracuse, was equally ambitious. Romuald's maneuver thwarted their ambitions.

To Romuald — and perhaps even to Margaret — naming the same man to the highest civil and ecclesiastical offices of the realm may have seemed like a good idea. One of Stephen's first acts as chancellor was to appoint his friend Odo Quarrel as the master of his household. Just as it was necessary to go through Stephen to get to the queen, anybody seeking to reach Stephen needed Odo's consent and cooperation. The problem with this was that Odo's temperament was ill-suited to a secular environment beyond the walls of a monastery. Instead, Odo was given to greed, even extortion. He was easily bought, if for a high price. Stephen, on the other hand, was not tainted by such practices.

Until Stephen's appointment as chancellor, Richard Palmer drew a hefty salary for his services at court. As these duties diminished, so did his remuneration. In practice, this money was paid from the taxes levied upon a number of demesnial hamlets which belonged to the crown rather than a baron or abbot. Stephen permitted Richard to exchange these small settlements for two wealthier villages, not only compensating the financial loss but actually increasing his earnings. One town would be held by Richard *ex officio* only during his tenure as *familiare*, whilst the other was his to keep and someday hand down to his heirs.[574]

Margaret voiced no objection to this *quid pro quo*. Indeed, it reflected her policy of granting counties and baronies to loyal subjects. Although Romuald himself was instrumental in bringing about Stephen's planned consecration, if only to foil the ambitions of other likely candidates, he soon began to entertain grave misgivings about his decision, for the concentration of too much power in one man was risky.

Appointing Stephen chancellor was at least rational. Conversely, electing him archbishop was part of an attempt to attenuate the power of the omnipresent prelates. This annoying problem need not have existed. The cardinals and bishops should have been tending to matters elsewhere instead of conniving in the capital. Once appointed to a diocese, a bishop belonged in his bishopric serving the needs of his flock, not in Palermo stirring up trouble.[575]

Notorious Notaries

Avarice was ubiquitous, but many of the grievances against the chancellor were rooted in petty complaints rather than affairs of state. Some of the resulting incidents were nothing short of bizarre, and it is fortunate that the queen didn't have to deal with them herself.

Many nobles and prelates from other parts of the *Regnum*, even distant regions like Abruzzo, had to make their way to the court in Palermo to have important charters notarized, or witnessed. It was customary to pay for this service, although the payment was in the nature of an honorarium or gratuity rather than a fixed fee. There was no official schedule of fees, the clients paying what they thought was commensurate with the service rendered.[576]

Notaries did not simply subscribe (witness) documents; some were officers akin to what we now call a *barrister* or *attorney*, empowered to draft charters, contracts and treaties, and even to defend legal cases before a justiciar.[577]

A Palermitan notary named Peter, a kinsman of the *familiare* Matthew of Aiello, was rarely content with what was offered him and asked for much more. Far from aberrant, this kind of request was the norm. Refusing to pay the honorarium Peter demanded, several clients went together to Stephen, complaining not only about the high fee requested by Peter but the time the greedy notary required to seal a document. Stephen immediately referred the drafting and notarization of the documents in question to another notary present at court, who completed the work that same day.[578]

It didn't take long for Peter to realize that people who habitually requested his services in the past were no longer doing so. He correctly inferred that his regular clients were going to another notary. If he couldn't entice them to be his clients he would coerce them into it.

Of course, Peter wasn't the only greedy notary in the capital. Accompanied by some like-minded colleagues, he undertook surveillance of the streets his former clients had to traverse when leaving the offices of the competing notaries in the districts near the palace who charged lower fees. One day the angry notaries and a squad of thugs violently confronted the clients, beating and insulting them, and confiscated their notarized documents, tearing the charters to shreds and smashing the wax seals affixed to them.[579]

Apprised of the incident, Stephen summoned the perpetrators to court. Among those ordered to appear was Peter, the instigator, who was jailed following a perfunctory but fair hearing during which he readily admitted his guilt.

Richard Palmer took the occasion to denounce Peter's arrest as illegal and unreasonable. He scornfully affirmed, as if it were true, that in Stephen's native France the law might be enforced in this manner but not here in Sicily. According to Richard, the notaries, having great influence at court, did not deserve to be punished so harshly.

The chancellor was more than a little irritated by the belligerent tone of this criticism, especially coming from somebody for whom, just a few days earlier, he had guaranteed the income of two wealthy villages. He was especially annoyed that Richard voiced his vociferous criticism in public instead of speaking to him privately.

Rather than respond to this public insult, embittering as it was, the chancellor ordered that Peter be immured in a dungeon until a suitable sentence could be considered against a man capable of threatening the peace of the realm and thereby offending the dignity of the sovereign. But a few days later, acting on the request of the *familiares,* Stephen freed Peter, punishing him by rescinding his right to exercise the profession of notary.

To discourage future incidents of this kind, the chancellor fixed a limit on what notaries could charge for specific services.[580] Finding the profession a closed caste, he permitted the licensing of a number of new notaries, opening the ranks to many qualified men who, until now, had been unjustly excluded.

The notaries weren't the only officials adept at the unchecked abuse of power. The provincial and civic bailiffs were likewise out of control, inclined to impose illegal fines on the people under their authority.[581] Most of these monies found their way into the bailiffs' own coffers. This usually occurred in demesnial cities and other territories under royal jurisdiction, as opposed to the feudal lands held by barons.

Stephen's success in curtailing this profusion of abuses earned him the respect of the common folk. He instituted what today would be called an "open-door" policy. This meant that ordinary people could ask for justice. Men and women arrived at court in droves from every part of the *Regnum* seeking writs against their oppressors. So great was their number that there were scarcely enough notaries to draft their complaints or justiciars to hear their cases.

Some viewed Stephen as an angel sent by God, whilst others extolled the kingdom's new golden age.[582] Another element of the population, however, saw in the chancellor a perpetual nemesis.

Sadistic Gaoler

It was becoming apparent that, as grand chancellor, Stephen could not be corrupted. Besides this, he was now designated to become the premier ecclesiastic of the realm, something that only enhanced his moral authority. Indeed, it made him something of a "super enforcer" of the law, both religious and secular.

Aware of his power, some Palermitans prevailed upon the chancellor to rule on the position of Christians who had apostatized and embraced Islam, perhaps covertly. It was claimed that the deception perpetrated by these converts was encouraged by the eunuchs, many of whom were themselves Christianized Arabs of dubious religious conviction.

But the reality was rarely so simple. Some of the alleged "apostates" had begun their lives as Muslims, converted to Christianity as young adults, and then, after much contemplation and soul-searching, returned to the Islam of their parents.[583] This was not exactly the same thing as a person raised as a Christian abruptly becoming a Muslim.

This nuance seemed to escape Stephen, who began to prosecute the "apostates" zealously. Such a policy did not endear him to Sicily's Muslims.[584] Only judiciously should modern ideas be applied to medieval circumstances, but there was a perceptible conflict between Stephen's position as chancellor, from whence he represented all the subjects of the realm, and his status as a prelate who spoke only for its Catholics. If the queen was not yet *au courant* of Stephen's "apostate policy," she learned of it with the emergence of a specific case.

This involved Robert of Calatabiano. When we last encountered him, he was ensconced in Palermo's seaside castle, where he tortured prisoners and exacted bribes. His proclivity for violence and bribery had gone unpunished because the palace eunuchs concealed his misdeeds from royal eyes.

When it became obvious that Stephen's religious zeal was more than a mere gesture, a number of people took advantage of the situation to step forward to accuse Robert of Calatabiano of being a closet Muslim, a secret apostate. That, however, was only the tip of the iceberg.

Now Robert stood accused of everything from extortion to theft to murder. His accusers even claimed that he had forced Christian women and boys into prostitution at a private brothel frequented by Muslims. There was no telling where delusion ended and truth began, but the veracity of the allegations was presumed by many, including Stephen and the pope.[585] The people clamored for justice.

Unlike most of the other cases brought before Stephen and his justiciars, this one involved a high official, a great number of alleged victims and monstrous sums of money. Moreover, Robert was well-connected. In former times he was protected by Caïd Peter, who had fled the court and gone to Africa. He now enjoyed the friendship of the influential palace eunuchs. This helped Robert at the royal court but hurt him in the court of public opinion, for the alleged collusion of the eunuchs lent credibility to the hypothesis of the private brothel and sexual abuse by Muslims.

The case against Robert of Calatabiano ended up before the queen. Here the eunuchs begged Margaret to grant clemency to the accused, who they declared to be the victim of malicious slander. They further claimed that the fugitive Caïd Peter was the culpable party because it was he who had ordered, even coerced, Robert to steal and kill. Stephen saw how difficult the case was, effectively pitting the populace and the public interest against the eunuchs and even the *familiares*.

The queen likewise found herself in a trying predicament. She wanted to support the majority of her subjects without alienating her government, but attempting to appease both sides was like walking a tightrope strung across a chasm.

Without actually defending Robert, she asked her chancellor to reduce the number and severity of the charges being brought against the murderous sadist. When Stephen balked at this, she used her authority to overrule him, and ordered him to desist in prosecuting Robert for allegations lodged against him by individuals.[586] This did not exclude crimes against the crown and the Catholic hierarchy.

Margaret made it understood that she wanted an example made of Robert. She did not, and could not, condone his ungodly behavior. Yet her stance implied that, despite the gravity of his crimes, she did not wish to see him become a symbolic "martyr" for the *familiares,* eunuchs, bailiffs and barons, or a pretext for the populace of the entire kingdom to doubt the integrity of the institutions of the monarchy.

Without contradicting the regent directly, the chancellor responded that the best he could do was to suspend prosecution of Robert for civil charges. This would exclude offenses that might result in capital punishment. It seemed like a pragmatic compromise. Privately, Stephen told his royal cousin that he would resign from his positions if she ever again undermined him as she had during this trial.

He made it clear that for crimes in ecclesiastical jurisdiction Robert would be tried by a jury of bishops. This addressed perjury firstly, followed by incest and adultery, leaving aside larceny, robbery, murder, rape and corruption.[587] It could be argued that this legal remedy was flawed because, according to the Assizes of Ariano, perjury and adultery were civil crimes. One presumes that, in the first instance, they would be prosecuted by justiciars rather than bishops, even though they were also ecclesiastical offenses. Indeed, the queen was known to refer cases involving canon law to the ecclesiastical authorities (see note 405).

The verdict was announced at a later audience. To the extent that it did not mete out a death sentence, the *familiares* and eunuchs were placated. Robert of Calatabiano was flogged before a jeering crowd. His property was expropriated, and he was sentenced to a prison term in the same castle where he had tortured so many innocent men whilst prostituting women and children.

On the way to the seaside fortress, the condemned man was to be paraded along Palermo's main streets as his crimes were announced to the multitude, but the bishops thought better of this plan when they saw how many angry people were gathered in narrow passages from which to pelt the man with stones. Things were getting out of hand. The sword-bearing knights guarding the prisoner on all sides could barely restrain the relentless crowd, intent as it was on stoning Robert to death.

At that point a more circumspect approach was suggested. It was decided to hold Robert behind a wall of the cathedral until the crowd dispersed. A few days later he was taken to the jail in the seaside castle. By then, it had become clear that the rumors of the prisoner bribing his way out of confinement were greatly exaggerated. He died following some sporadic bouts of torture.

The common folk were happy to learn of the tyrant's fate, but others were less pleased by it. Robert's trial and punishment had the effect of cautioning the great of the realm that they too could be penalized for their crimes. This only exacerbated their dislike of Stephen of Perche.

Until now, the magnates were reluctant to speak ill of the queen except perhaps through whispers about her poor choice of a chancellor. Whilst Margaret, in the interest of keeping the peace, might reduce the charges against a corrupt castellan like Robert of Calatabiano, she was far less likely to tolerate overt treason against her son or herself.

Margaret's rule as regent was absolute. The occasional *curiae generales,* such as the meeting of barons summoned by King Roger on the eve of his coronation, was not a parliament (see note 306) and the baronage had no official say in royal decisions any more than priests and monks decided papal policies.

Apropos the church, Pope Alexander III was defending papal territory against a major incursion by Frederick Barbarossa. Margaret sent funds to assist the besieged pontiff, who was forced to leave Rome for Benevento in August of 1167. In the event, it was not papal military might but an epidemic among his imperial troops that drove Frederick out of Italy. This eliminated any foreign threat to Margaret during the regency. Most of her detractors were in the *Regnum* itself.

Slander

If it were difficult to find fault with Stephen of Perche, his detractors might invent flaws they could easily attribute to him and perhaps even the regent. Like most malicious rumors, these attacks were difficult to impute to specific persons; in effect, they were anonymous, emanating from the thin Mediterranean air. There was nothing novel in this form of defamation.

Certain conditions favored the wide and rapid diffusion of hearsay. Palermo was a very populous city, with a constant flow of people arriving and departing for other places in the *Regnum* and abroad. Of Europe's major capitals, Sicily's was the city nearest to papal power even if, for the moment, the pontiff was busy contending with the pretensions of Frederick Barbarossa in Italy, where he founded the Lombard League to resist imperial hegemony. Unlike most other royal capitals, Palermo, as we have seen, was the home of an uninvited cabal of cardinals and bishops who spent much of their time scheming and gossiping. The city was a rumor mill.

A revolt fomented by rumors had claimed the life of one of the queen's sons. However majestic its wonders, Palermo was no magical Camelot on the Tyrrhenian.

Although the kingdom's magnates did not savor the idea of taking orders from a woman, something to which they were unaccustomed, they knew that it was only a matter of a few years before William reached the age of majority. In the meantime, however, the chancellor could do much to delimit the scope of baronial power. He had already shown what he could achieve in the space of just one year.

It was easy enough to contrive rumors about "corruption" at court, and the agitators knew that vague allegations of wrongdoing, however outlandish, were difficult to refute very convincingly. Simple reasoning would dictate that the burden of proof lies with the person asserting a claim, for it is easier to show that something happened than to prove that it did not, but in the twelfth century the principles enshrined in the Socratic method were all but forgotten. Facts were whatever the hate mongers wanted them to be.

Yet besmirching the queen's name would not be a very simple matter. There was nothing in her conduct that was anything less than proper.

Somebody at court — so it was said — noticed the queen smile at the chancellor in a way that "somebody" deemed to reflect undue familiarity, even intimacy. "She devoured him with her eyes, and it was feared that an illicit love was hidden behind the guise of cousinhood," wrote Falcandus.[588] Lacking any legitimate grievance against the regent, some men resorted to the centuries-old practice of what in our era is sometimes called "slut shaming."[589]

This technique for attacking medieval queens was not terribly original, nor even very unusual. Indeed, accusing a queen of having a sexual affair with a highly-placed courtier was something of a cliché.[590] The path before many a woman was strewn with such innuendo.

The attacks directed at Stephen emanated from several quarters. The eunuchs despised him for imprisoning their ally Robert of Calatabiano. The barons resented him because most of the largesse and influence they monopolized in the past were now going to Stephen's friends. Sicily's most prominent Muslim, Abul Kasim, disliked the fact that his rival, Caïd Siddiq, Palermo's wealthiest Muslim, had become one of Stephen's advisors.

Little could be done to pacify those bemoaning the lust they thought revealed itself in Margaret's eyes, but Stephen sought to allay the laments that reached his ears.

Remedies

Although his efforts were earnest, Stephen's reputation was not helped by an incident that seemed to reflect an overzealous surveillance of his adversaries.

One of the men suspected of stirring up dissent was Matthew of Aiello, the *familiare*. When it was observed that he was sending more letters than usual across Sicily to his brother, John, an influential prelate in Catania, an attempt was made to intercept some of the couriers carrying these documents.[591] This mission was entrusted to Robert of Bellisina, whose men attempted to apprehend a messenger who was returning to Palermo.[592] While the courier bearing a letter from John got away, his colleague was caught. This man resisted arrest and was wounded. Matthew soon learned of the incident. Finding himself under suspicion, he decided to act.

Not long after the incident involving Matthew's courier, Robert of Bellisina fell ill with a grave fever. A physician named Salernus was recommended to administer a cure. Knowing Salernus to be a close acquaintance of Matthew, who had undertaken to get the physician appointed as a judge in the city of Salerno, Stephen sagely refused sending him to Robert. Instead, he ordered another doctor to treat him.[593]

Concealing his movements from the chancellor, Salernus nevertheless visited Robert several times. Despite treatment, the sick man failed to recover and soon died. Stephen was sad to learn of Robert's death.

The condition of the corpse was disturbing. Robert's hair fell out and patches of his skin separated from his muscle tissue. This suggested to some that poisoning had killed him, but to be certain the chancellor asked a team of physicians led by Romuald of Salerno to begin a medical investigation.[594] Those who had been close to Robert of Bellisina confirmed that Salernus had offered him a liquid, but what was in the potion?

It so happened there was living proof of its toxicity. A friend of Robert's showed the investigators a hand bearing a wound from a hemorrhage that erupted when, out of view of Robert and the servants, this man had poured the same liquid on his own palm, thinking to test it in this way before ingesting it.

Another witness, a notary named William, informed the investigators that a man in the employ of Matthew of Aiello often approached him to ask about Robert.

Thus informed, Stephen of Perche met with the *familiares,* Romuald and others, who agreed that the chancellor should summon Salernus for questioning.

Initially, the man denied ever administering a medicinal syrup to Robert of Bellisina but recanted this mendacious testimony when confronted by witnesses. Then he claimed to have given Robert innocuous rose water made by Justus, a local druggist. However, when interrogated, this apothecary swore that he had sold nothing to Salernus during the four weeks prior to Robert's death. It was clear that Salernus was not telling the truth.

The next day, the high justiciars of the court convened an audience. Under interrogation, Salernus responded to their queries in a desultory way, offering no exculpatory evidence.

He was found guilty of murder, the justiciars ordering his death and the confiscation of his property. Had Salernus decided to cooperate with the investigation by divulging the name of his fellow conspirator, the justiciars might have been inclined to grant him clemency, commuting his sentence to prison time and sparing his life. However, he could not be persuaded to disclose this information.

The queen was advised of the trial and sentence but played no part in it. If Matthew of Aiello were involved in some way, the incident was indeed disconcerting.

The fate of Salernus, unlike that of Robert of Calatabiano a few weeks earlier, was not important enough politically to warrant royal intervention. What is more, the evidence against Salernus was overwhelming.

As the weeks passed, there would be greater challenges to face.

Wayward Sibling

It will be recalled that for his steadfast loyalty Richard of Molise (Mandra) was granted a large county and made a *familiare*. This irritated his Apulian peers, who managed to turn Margaret's brother, Henry (Rodrigo) of Montescaglioso, against this man he barely knew. The pretext was that Richard was abusing his power, while Henry, as the regent's brother and the young monarch's uncle, deserved a lofty position at court.

Henry's arrogance was nourished by the support of the company of Spanish knights who came to Italy with him, their number augmented by others who had recently arrived from Navarre. With these knights and several influential barons allied with him, he crossed from the mainland to Sicily with the intention of intimidating Margaret, Stephen and the *familiares* into acceding to his demands.[595] If he knew that Gilbert of Gravina, who was his second cousin, had already failed in trying to achieve the same thing, it made no difference to him.

Advised of Henry's arrival at Messina *en route* to Palermo, the *familiare* Richard of Molise met with Stephen of Perche to warn the chancellor that these interlopers must not be granted any standing at court, even if it were necessary to subdue them through armed confrontation.

Stephen was no great admirer of Richard of Molise, but the last thing he wanted was to see blood spilled in the city. Acting prudently, he sent to Henry a letter written on the queen's authority ordering him to come to the capital but without his confederates, who were to remain at Termini, near ancient Himera, about midway between Palermo and Cefalù.

Meeting with Henry, Stephen was able to convince him to ignore the complaints of the Apulian barons. As the queen's brother, he had obtained much and might be further rewarded if he were loyal to her. Henry made peace with Richard of Molise, who he had been led to view as a rival.

Margaret was angry about her brother's insubordination on the mainland, where for months he had failed to follow her orders, but the chancellor managed to broker a reconciliation between the siblings. Henry promised obedience in the future. With this familial truce achieved, Stephen summoned the vassals who had come to Sicily with Henry and were waiting at Termini up the coast. At court, they reaffirmed their fealty once they realized that their plan had failed.

One amongst them, Bohemond of Manopello, who was distinguished for his exceptional intelligence, established a sincere friendship with the chancellor. Henry also became very friendly with Stephen.

This displeased those who were conspiring to obtain power. Having failed to achieve their ends through force of arms, these malcontents now sought to dissuade Henry's friendship with Stephen through words. They strove to convince his most trusted Spanish knights that befriending the chancellor was not in their noble lord's interest. Here they resorted to what they thought were effective methods, telling the knights that Stephen was having an incestuous relationship with the queen.[596] They went further, implying that Henry was naive, seeing as he was the only person at court unaware of this (alleged) liaison between Stephen and Margaret.

Henry was not wise. Indeed, he was credulous and rather easily duped. Nevertheless, at first he was disinclined to believe what he heard about the affable chancellor and the queen, people he knew and respected.

He changed his mind when the rumor's imagined veracity was reinforced by the very people who, unbeknownst to Henry, had hatched it in the first place.[597] This led him to forswear his loyalty to Stephen of Perche, believing the worst about his own sister. With this, the queen's brother joined the plotters.

Treachery

Henry of Montescaglioso was not alone. Within the palace walls, Caïd Richard, the chamberlain, who despised Stephen, was convincing ever more men-at-arms, from knights to archers, to join the plot against the chancellor.[598] Most of this he achieved through simple bribery.

Stephen was vaguely aware of this. He organized a fifty-man bodyguard that included many French knights, never going anywhere in Palermo without a company of at least twenty or thirty armed men.

One may argue the degree to which the hatred directed at the chancellor also reflected baronial resentment of the queen he served but, in the worst scenario, Stephen's death would certainly weaken Margaret's position. It would also spawn chaos at court. The *familiares* might remain loyal, but there was no way to tell where the unrest would end.

Stephen reasoned that confronting the conspirators at this point might be preferable to waiting for them to make the first move. For now, he lacked much evidence against any of them, yet he didn't want to give them more time to prepare a rebellion that could lead to a civil war. If, as he had been informed, there were plotters like Caïd Richard within the palace walls, that made the capital itself potentially dangerous.[599]

Disturbing as this was, expediency alone suggested that it may be best to address the problems growing outside the confines of Palermo. Whatever they were doing on the island, the more egregious offenders garnered their most effective support in Apulia, where royal authority was entrusted to a cadre of men whose loyalty sometimes seemed dubious, among them Margaret's kinsmen Gilbert of Gravina and Henry of Montescaglioso. The queen therefore contemplated an inspection tour of the mainland to begin during the spring of 1168. If nothing else, her appearance would remind any doubters of her authority throughout the realm, not only on the island of Sicily.

The strategic key to the kingdom was Messina, whose harbor was at least as important, both commercially and militarily, as the port of Palermo. From there, it was easy to follow Calabria's Ionian coast by land or sea to Taranto and then Bari.

With this in mind, Stephen proposed that the queen spend the approaching winter at Messina, from which a relay of couriers on fast steeds made it possible to get a letter to or from Palermo in three full days.

The queen's extended presence at Messina, where there was a fortified royal palace near the coast, might even discourage some of the city's infamous vices.[600]

Regardless of whether the queen ultimately decided to travel to Salerno or Bari, bringing the court to Messina from time to time was rooted in geographical reality. More than half the *Regnum* was in peninsular Italy, and for anybody coming from Calabria, Campania, or even more distant Abruzzo, a journey to Messina was far more convenient than riding another four or five days to reach Palermo after crossing into Sicily.

In September, Stephen summoned his kinsman Gilbert of Gravina to Messina, explaining that the court planned on passing the winter there.

The October of 1167 was rainier than usual, and the *familiares* used this as a pretext to try to dissuade the queen's departure during this season. Stephen was undeterred, ordering that the coastal roads to Messina be prepared for the arrival of young King William and the royal family.

In early November, word was received that the pope had ratified the nomination of Stephen as Archbishop of Palermo. The prelates of the kingdom swore their fealty to him as their primate, and Romuald intended to consecrate him in a solemn ceremony in the capital's cathedral. Yet he was never actually consecrated as planned.[601]

Stephen, like the queen, often tended to minutiae, such as confirming the privileges of the Benedictine monastery of Saint John of the Hermits near the palace.[602]

The weather improved by Martinmas, and on the morning of Wednesday, the fifteenth of November, the royal party set out for Messina. The chancellor left a small army of loyal knights behind to guard the capital. Caïd Richard, as the chamberlain, was left in charge of the palace, but couriers seeking to consign letters to the queen and chancellor knew where to find them.

Accompanied by the chancellor, high justiciars and some notaries, along with a large company of knights, the queen visited a number of towns *en route* to Messina. This included the fortress of San Marco d'Alunzio, where Beatrice, the widow of King Roger II, usually stayed with her young daughter, Constance.

The royal party finally arrived in Messina at the very end of November during the beginning of the Christmas season.

Law and Order

A number of nobles were waiting for the queen at Messina. One of them was Robert of Caserta.[603] This loyal count had heard that his cousin, William of San Severino, whose exile had recently been lifted, had convinced Margaret to restore his former lands to his possession.

Accompanied by several advocates, Robert petitioned the court requesting a revision of this decree on the basis that, in fact, certain lands now held by William legally belonged to the former. The reasoning for this was that in an earlier time William's father had come to possess the estates illegally through the use of force. In other words, these lands had never belonged to William by law. Although the queen understood Robert's complaint, the evidence suggests that she did not wish to alienate William by diminishing his property and wealth.

William had earned Stephen's trust; the chancellor considered him loyal. On the other hand, there were doubts in Stephen's mind about Robert's fealty. Nevertheless, there was no reason to offend this man to the point that he might be encouraged to join the kingdom's malcontents.

Acting on Stephen's advice, the queen gave Robert of Caserta, who seemed to have the stronger case, the lands he requested, compensating William of San Severino with other manors. She imposed the condition that this decision was final, and therefore the matter would never again be brought before the court.

The ecclesiastical sphere, as always, was full of complexities, even conflict. Margaret granted a charter to Nicholas, the Archbishop of Messina, confirming his episcopal rights following a local dispute in which the prelate's authority had been challenged.[604]

The next matter brought before the queen involved local taxes. King Roger had given the city certain privileges and tax exemptions, only to rescind these measures later. The rights eventually confirmed by his son seemed insufficient compensation for those that had been revoked.[605] Seeking to encourage Stephen to reinstitute these rights, the Messinians offered him bribes. The chancellor categorically rejected the gifts proffered him but convinced the queen to bestow anew the rights once granted by her father-in-law. This was a good way to garner some respect from the local people.

Stephen's strategy was effective. By December, there was always a crowd of subjects at court seeking justice. The people came from Calabria, eastern Sicily and elsewhere in the *Regnum*. The scene was not unlike what had occurred a few months earlier in Palermo, when the chancellor instituted his "open door" policy and began to assail corruption. The queen herself addressed very few cases, usually those involving important prelates and nobles, but every decision was rendered in the name of her son, King William II.

Richard of Aversa

Seeing that the queen and chancellor were just, a delegation of Messinians, came forth to denounce the abuses of Richard of Aversa, their city's governor.[606] Here the long litany of accusations was similar to that advanced against Robert of Calatabiano. Richard was said to have committed every kind of crime, often through accomplices acting as his proxies. The jeremiad included murder, robbery, thievery, even arson. It was said that the governor had illegally confiscated houses and vineyards. The people claimed that he excelled at bribing justiciars. Debauchery and adultery were not overlooked. If even a fraction of the allegations were true, Richard was the busiest man in the kingdom.

Stephen of Perche suspected that a few of the accusations might well be true, but he sought to control the governor rather than subject him to the rigors of a formal trial.

Having believed that the queen's presence augured well for them, the Messinians resented this procrastination, offended that everybody else in the kingdom obtained justice whilst the crimes perpetrated in their loyal city were neglected. Some leaders wrote out the grievances against the governor on signs they attached to long poles, displaying these during a raucous protest in front of the palace.

The Christmas season had already begun, but the clamoring crowd convinced Margaret that she had to resolve this matter here and now. Without hesitation, she commanded Stephen to accept the Messinians' petitions. He referred the case to the high justiciars, ordering them to begin an inquest and specifying that a hearing be held during the next few days.

The subsequent trial revealed that Richard of Aversa was unambiguously guilty of a great many offenses. He was imprisoned and his property was confiscated. Having left the trial to the justiciars, Margaret and Stephen now remonstrated with Richard, and there was no vocal opposition to the verdict except perhaps from the condemned man and his family.

To say that this decision bolstered local esteem for Stephen would be an understatement. The people loved him. Just as importantly, the subjects sang the incessant praises of their queen.

It was finally time to celebrate Christmas. These festivities, with their endless liturgies, extended into early January, culminating with the Epiphany.

The subtle contours of Margaret's policy were being shaped by pragmatism. She was not rewriting her late husband's script, merely editing it into a form resilient enough to survive into the first few years of her son's majority. She wanted to hand him a kingdom as free of disquietude as a medieval realm could be. In this she was selfless.

What emerges from a sober analysis of the first phase of the regency is an approach to governing that was meant to eliminate abuses whilst maintaining the essential organization of the monarchy. The high justiciars were a kind of "supreme court," whilst the other justiciars were, essentially, district judges.

There is nothing to suggest that Margaret was unduly harsh, but there can be no doubt that she was unafraid to wield the absolute royal authority she held in her son's name. At least a few criminals and traitors reluctant to live righteously under her rule died by it.[607] Anybody who presumed to break the law with impunity simply because there was a woman on the throne had best think again.

Falcandus tells us that there were subjects who resented the "Spanish woman," but there is no evidence to suggest that Margaret ever attracted much opprobrium from the common folk who, on the contrary, literally cheered when oppressive tyrants like Robert of Calatabiano and Richard of Aversa were tried and punished. The most obstreperous naysayers were to be found among the aristocracy.

The queen was resolute in her conviction that the kingdom should be ruled a certain way, but her approach was much more than an instinctive reaction to the way her husband had ruled.

By the middle of January in 1168, the majority of the Messinians seemed content. Unbeknownst to the queen, however, Henry of Montescaglioso, her troublesome half-brother, was up to his old tricks. In this he was abetted by Bartholomew of Parisio, whose sister was once married to Richard of Sai, a man granted a divorce on questionable grounds in order to wed a woman reputed to be a harlot (see note 405). Bartholomew's conniving may have had less to do with the perceived slight against his sister than with his own maneuvering to achieve greater power for himself through his close alliance with Henry. Not only did Bartholomew exercise a certain influence over some Messinians, a number of Calabrians present in the city to greet the young king were party to his covert machinations.

Traitors on Trial

No attempt at rioting was made during the Christmas season that had just ended, but it would transpire that Henry was contemplating a more specific operation, for which public disorder was merely a diversionary tactic.

Bartholomew was to some degree discouraged by the arrival of Gilbert of Gravina with a formidable company of a hundred well-armed knights. It was precisely to avoid potential dissension that Stephen of Perche had summoned Gilbert to Messina. Gilbert, of course, was Stephen's nephew.

Both were Norman to the core, and here was the root of yet another potential problem, for in recent weeks the French knights present in unruly Messina had taken to treating the local people with contempt, frequently insulting them.[608]

Bartholomew wanted more than an insurrection. He and his minions incited Henry to plan the assassination of Stephen, thinking that the chancellor's death might pave the way for the queen's half-brother to seize power. To that end, Henry solicited a certain Roger, a local justiciar, to join the plot. Roger feigned collaboration but secretly advised the chancellor of Henry's homicidal plan a day before it was to be set in motion.

Stephen instructed Roger the justiciar to behave with Henry and Bartholomew as if nothing had changed; in the meantime he informed the queen of the situation, advising her to act without delay.

The implications of the alleged murder conspiracy were myriad. Here was gross disrespect by a man toward the sister who had helped him in every conceivable way. Beyond that, he was a traitor to the kingdom she ruled in the name of her son. Henry had to be punished to dissuade others who might still attempt to carry out the assassination even after its chief plotter and beneficiary was unmasked.

The queen needed a strategy. First, she would convene a formal trial. Either Henry would be found guilty, or he would admit to his crimes of his own volition. Either way, he would then be expected to cooperate by identifying the other conspirators. If he were reluctant to name them, some time in a castle jail might loosen his tongue. Dungeons were cold this time of year.[609]

Margaret had Henry arrested, and ordered Stephen to summon the high justiciars, *familiares,* bishops and nobles who were to hear the case. The hearing took place ten days later under heavy guard.

Even though Henry himself was in custody, most of his co-conspirators were still at large; they posed a very real risk. In his opening statement, the accused man decried the value of his "paltry" income from the County of Montescaglioso. An aggrieved Henry wanted Taranto, even though that strategic port city was traditionally reserved to a member of the royal family. At the very least, he felt entitled to some wealthy lands in eastern Sicily. Ridiculous as this demand was, it did not lack for a pretext. If refused these prosperous lands, Henry hoped to more plausibly justify his hatred of Stephen of Perche for forcing the queen's half-brother into penury.

In response, Gilbert of Gravina thundered that Henry had tried to use the implicit threat of military force to coerce the queen into giving him lands which, had he behaved better in the first place, might have already been in his possession. He accused the queen's wayward half-brother of deception, stating that the man should not, by right, hold any lands in the kingdom. He then excoriated him for being a spendthrift whilst oppressing the peasants on his estates. Gilbert went on to cite Henry's foolish suggestion that Margaret fortify castles in his manors and hide money there against the future possibility that William II might not always be loyal to his own mother. He spoke of how Henry tried to manipulate young William into thinking that Margaret was somehow damaging the king and the kingdom, and how the boy responded (to Henry) that in distrusting his own mother he would also have to distrust her brother. Gilbert spoke of how Henry accused him, Gilbert, of disloyalty. He asked Henry what fault he found in Stephen so grave that it justified assassination. Gilbert concluded by saying that Henry, despite his maudlin appeal to clemency, deserved no lands in the Kingdom of Sicily. As a traitor, he deserved to be deprived of his property, along with his very life.

When Henry vehemently denied organizing any conspiracy to kill the chancellor, Roger the justiciar was brought in to testify, affirming the details of the plot. Henry's testimony became even more unseemly as he lost his temper and accused Roger of betraying a promise to collaborate in the conspiracy. Here the accused man contradicted himself, for just a few minutes earlier he had adamantly denied plotting to kill the chancellor. In this way Henry condemned himself with his own words. He was ordered detained in the palace, where the trial had taken place.

Before long, word reached Stephen that Henry's company of knights was assembling at the condemned man's residence in the city, and that many Messinians were taking up arms in expectation of a riot, or even a battle. The chancellor ordered his own knights, and those of Gilbert of Gravina, to guard the palace. Armed men were dispatched into the streets to restore order by assuring the populace that there was no need for alarm.

Whilst Henry languished in jail, his knights were ordered to surrender their weapons and immediately cross into Calabria, with the caveat that any men who failed to comply with this royal command would be imprisoned immediately.[610] Deprived of their swords, daggers and shields, the downtrodden knights made their way to the port and traversed the strait. Having heard about what had occurred over in Sicily, the local Greeks saw the opportunity for plunder and a touch of vengeance.[611] An angry mob assaulted the disarmed men, leaving them with little more than the clothes they were wearing. The beaten knights made their way northward but many died in the frozen forests of the Sila Mountains.

Back in Messina, an attempt was made to identify Henry's most pernicious partisans. One who approached the chancellor and voluntarily confessed was temporarily exiled whilst his lands were entrusted to an abbot friendly to the queen.[612] Another, Roger Sorello, who held estates near Naples, was imprisoned because he came forward only after the identities of the chief conspirators had already been divulged by Margaret's incarcerated half-brother. Under interrogation, and with no immediate hope of release, Henry had seen fit to disclose most of the plot's details.

Some at court propounded that Stephen of Perche pardon most of the offenders, even if many of the plotters clearly merited death or, at the very least, lengthy imprisonment. Gilbert of Gravina suggested otherwise. He had his own reason for this.

Richard of Molise, it may be remembered, had nearly come to blows with Gilbert of Gravina, the queen's cousin, during an argument about the flight of Caïd Peter to Africa. At Richard's urging, Matthew of Aiello successfully managed to have Gilbert sent away from the court on the pretext that he was needed on the peninsula to fend off an impending invasion by Frederick Barbarossa, who had to withdraw before invading the Kingdom of Sicily. Nevertheless, duplicitous Gilbert, who was envious of Richard's rank as *familiare*, had never forgotten this affront. He enmity was at least explicable.

At a royal audience, Bohemond of Manopello accused Richard of having covertly supported the recent conspiracy.[613] At first, Margaret found this absurd, but if her own brother could not be trusted, then who could she trust? On the other hand, Bohemond was a confederate of her brother.

For his part, Richard of Molise vigorously denied the ludicrous allegation that painted him as a miscreant, challenging to trial by single combat anybody who accused him of such a flagrant betrayal.

Further accusations followed, intended, more than anything, to erode Richard's credibility in the eyes of the queen. Their substance was that he continued, illegally, to hold the County of Mandra, as well as some royal towns around Troia. To this the *familiare* responded that Mandra had been entrusted to him temporarily by Caïd Peter and the Troian towns by Turgisio, that region's chamberlain. Turgisio, who was present, refuted this.

An impromptu jury led by the high justiciars, but excluding Matthew of Aiello, the other *familiare* present, then conferred to discuss the charges against Richard. This was not entirely proper but Margaret and Stephen did not object to it. In any case, the queen was the ultimate authority in the matter.

The sanctimonious "judges" decided that Richard held Mandra and the Troian towns legally so long as Caïd Peter guaranteed his possession, but effectively lost this tenure as soon as Peter fled the *Regnum*. Richard protested this casuistry, saying that justice was being corrupted, but Stephen did not wish to contradict a jury led by high justiciars. The travesty of justice that condemned Richard bore all the hallmarks of a vengeful show trial for which the verdict had already been determined.

The accused nobleman was not allowed to exonerate himself. Instead of his accusers being required to prove his guilt, Richard was expected to prove his innocence.[614] The *familiare* was arrested, and imprisoned in the castle on the rocky mountain overlooking Taormina to the south of Messina.

A number of others were condemned for being directly involved in the conspiracy. Most, like Bartholomew of Parisio, were imprisoned. Walter of Moac demanded trial by combat, and this duel was scheduled.[615]

Henry of Montescaglioso was imprisoned at Reggio in Calabria. Stephen ordered Odo Quarrel to hold him there until he could be taken to Spain. Margaret had decided to send him to the court of her brother, King Sancho, at Pamplona, with a thousand ounces of gold. The plan was for seven galleys under Odo's command to take Henry as far as Arles. From there, the fickle prince could make his way overland to Spain.

In exchange for Gravina, Gilbert requested the affluent County of Loritello. If this discouraged the return of Robert, its exiled holder, so much the better, at least from Gilbert's point of view. Stephen granted this request, which angered the residents of Loritello who had hoped that Robert might one day return to them.

Palermo

Margaret's presence in Messina had reminded the people of her power, but this was little more than a bittersweet victory. Like her kindred sovereigns, she was learning that royal authority was tenuous, and dangerous for whoever held it.

The queen found time in early March to grant the Agrò forest to the Most Holy Savior abbey.[616] These lands had belonged to a Greek Orthodox monastery, and the number of such communities was dwindling while those of the Roman Catholics increased. The queen also exempted a monastery from an import tax and ceded the manor of Rahal el Melum Rameth, near Milazzo, to the nunnery of Santa Maria delle Scale of Messina.[617] Following a visit to inspect Santa Maria, where a royal chapel was consecrated, Margaret and her sons left Messina on the twelfth of March.[618]

On the way to Palermo, they stopped at a number of coastal towns. The most important was Cefalù, where they were welcomed by the bishop, Boson of Gorron, who very much wanted the bodies of Roger II and William I to be entombed in his cathedral (see note 463). The royal party arrived at Palermo on the twentieth.

Richard of Molise was left imprisoned at Taormina on the other side of the island. Whatever he thought of his fellow *familiare,* Matthew of Aiello, who had spent the winter with the royal family at Messina, had made no effort to defend him. There was a certain logic to this, regardless of the working relationship that had existed between the two men. Quite simply, Matthew now had one less peer with whom to share his power.

As far as we know, the evidence against Richard of Molise was flimsy indeed, yet the queen never abjured her contention that he was guilty. She alienated a *familiare* who otherwise would have remained one of her staunchest allies. This left her somewhat isolated, with three more years to serve as regent before William reached the age of majority.

Disloyalty was rampant. The *familiare* Matthew of Aiello, the chamberlain Caïd Richard and Bishop Gentile of Agrigento probably perceived a changed situation now that Gilbert of Gravina and his large contingent of knights were no longer present to bolster the power of Stephen of Perche, the chancellor. The absence of Richard of Molise, who also commanded some knights, only reinforced their belief that Stephen was under-protected and could now be overthrown.

As usual, there were pretexts for the claim that the chancellor was acting inappropriately. One of the more credible among these was that the Frenchman John of Lavardin, to whom Stephen had given the Sicilian lands of the late Bonello, was mistreating the local people. This allegation bore a grain of truth because only those classified as serfs, be they Arab or Greek, were obligated to remit the kind of taxes the French baron was collecting.[619]

The meretricious complaint painted Matthew, Richard and Gentile as defenders of the populace despite their disdain for the common folk. Unfortunately, in rendering judgment in the matter Stephen relied on the advice of two French counsellors rather than Sicilians knowledgeable in local law.[620]

The traitorous triumvirate wasted no time contemplating an attack on Stephen, conspiring to kill him on Palm Sunday, the Sunday before Easter, which fell at the end of March. Their scheme called for him to be struck down whilst leaving Palermo's cathedral with the royal cortege.[621]

Obviously, the assassination plot required the participation of a certain number of accomplices if it were to be successful. The chief conspirators were adept at stabbing somebody in the back verbally, but the task of doing so literally, with a real sword, was assigned to a professional. In the event, the plan was aborted after several knights involved in it were arrested and divulged some of its details.[622]

For now, Stephen's detractors sought wider support for their cause. One of their tactics presented itself in the reaction of Stephen's counsellors to the French baron's taxation on peasants. Exploiting this, the trio disseminated the rumor that the populace of the entire *Regnum* would soon be subjected to these taxes, which until now were unheard of.

It didn't take long for Stephen to determine the source of these detrimental rumors. He suspected that Matthew of Aiello might be the mastermind of the most recent defamation scheme. Matthew was summoned to court, where he was formally accused of treason. Unable to defend himself against such an accusation, the *familiare,* who was also high notary of the realm, was summarily incarcerated. The chroniclers differ slightly in their assessments of Matthew's character.[623]

The chancellor didn't stop with Matthew of Aiello. Stephen wanted to arrest Caïd Richard, who he felt certain was involved with Aiello in the disinformation campaign that was eroding his prestige.

But here the queen drew the line, forbidding the arrest of the palace chamberlain.[624] The most that Stephen achieved was having Richard confined to the palace and prohibited from communicating with his company of knights.

By 1168, Margaret found herself in the midst of ruling and, for the most part, governing a kingdom of more than two million people.[625]

Agrigento

It wasn't long before Gentile, the Bishop of Agrigento, realized that the plan to discredit Stephen, and perhaps even kill him, had been foiled. What was worse, the other two conspirators in his malevolent trio had been removed from circulation.[626] Gentile, despite his name, was anything but gentle. Indeed, his perfidy was well known.

Gentile was one of the prelates who spent more time in the capital than in his own bishopric. Now he found a reason to justify his presence in Agrigento. Accompanied by a few knights, he headed there covertly, traveling along obscure roads.

There was a reason for such secrecy. Bedeviling as certain prelates were, the queen had come to prefer having the more troublesome bishops in Palermo, where she could keep an eye on them.

The Agrigentans themselves rarely lamented Gentile's prolonged absences. Its timeless Greek temples attested to the city's survival over many long centuries. If the most heinous tyrants of antiquity had failed to break Agrigentan will, the local bishop hardly stood a chance of doing so.

Suppression was not always in Gentile's interest. Early in April of 1168, his strategy consisted chiefly of manipulation. Many of the people in the towns around Agrigento were recent converts from Islam.[627] The ardor of these new Catholics led a good number of them to embrace Christianity just as zealously as they had professed the Muslim faith of their ancestors, and they held bishops in high esteem.

Resorting to the usual tropes, Gentile sought to exploit his flock's confidence in him. He impudently announced that Matthew of Aiello had been imprisoned illegally, and that Stephen of Perche planned to usurp royal authority by marrying Margaret.

In his crazed rantings, the bishop underestimated the Arabs' loyalty to the queen, whilst straining their credulity. In Agrigento and the surrounding manors he convinced nobody. Open rebellion was the last thing anybody wanted.

Within days, those at court noted Gentile's absence; perhaps they missed his habitual tirades and chronic gossip. Margaret sent to the bailiff of Agrigento a justiciar named Burgundio bearing an order for the bishop to report to the royal court at once, accompanied by the same justiciar.

Back in Palermo, Gentile faced a hearing. There was no dearth of witnesses to offer evidence against him, and their testimony was unassailable. His treachery exposed, he was held in custody, but the punishment of a prelate was more appropriately handled by the Holy See. To that end, the queen sent a letter to Pope Alexander soliciting a response to the situation. Meanwhile, Gentile was escorted to the royal fortress at San Marco d'Alunzio, where he was detained pending a papal reply.

Any hope of a successful conspiracy or rebellion might have ended with Gentile's arrest. It so happened that troubles in northeastern Sicily began to take on a life of their own, threatening the peace of the entire *Regnum*. Most of this can be attributed to one man, Odo Quarrel.[628]

Messina

Just days after sending Bishop Gentile to San Marco, Stephen had to contend with problems created by Odo. It may be recalled that Odo Quarrel was supposed to accompany Henry of Montescaglioso, Margaret's bothersome brother, to France.

The chancellor was annoyed to learn that his assistant was still in Messina long after he was scheduled to depart. Knowing something of Odo's avarice, Stephen hastily dispatched a letter tactlessly ordering him to set sail within three days, telling him to forget exploiting Messina for his own gain.

Odo had embarked on a scheme to exact his own tax from ships leaving Messina, or simply passing through its straits, on the way to the Holy Land. This was tantamount to extortion, and it enraged the Messinians, as well as the merchants and pilgrims. But the abuses didn't end with Odo himself.

Some of his French companions, who were given to getting drunk as they wandered aimlessly through the city's streets, entered a gaming house and began to insult the men gambling there. At first the gamblers, fearing reprisal from Stephen if they responded to the aggressors, tolerated the unprovoked abuse. Finally, unable to further endure the pejorative words of the foreigners, they beat the men.

When news of this incident reached Odo's ears, he summoned Andrew, the city's governor, and demanded that the gamblers be apprehended immediately and brought to him. Andrew demurred, suggesting that any punishment be delayed until the local populace was more tranquil; he explained that in recent weeks the Messinians had been growing restless as the result of rumors, so it might be imprudent to arrest the gamblers at this moment. Seeking a conciliatory tone, the governor stopped short of excoriating Odo. Vilifying the chancellor's assistant directly would hardly be politic; indeed, it could have dire consequences. For now, comity and appeasement might be more effective than bitter words. Having witnessed, just months earlier, the demise of his predecessor, Richard of Aversa, Andrew thought it possible to catch more flies with honey than with vinegar.

Odo's approach, on the other hand, was to swat any fly that crossed his path. Known for his intolerance and short temper, the haughty mandarin bristled that the supposed influence of peasants did not concern him. The prosecution of these men would serve as a deterrent for others.

Given no choice, Andrew went to the house where the altercation had transpired. The crowd of men gathered there had no intention of being scolded. They began to assault the governor, who quickly mounted his horse and fled amidst a flurry of stones being hurled at him.

The Messinian gamblers and their friends were speakers of Greek. The "Latins" of the city, along with foreign merchants who were there on business, had other grievances, such as Odo's tax on shipping. These men incited the Greeks, saying, among other things, that Queen Margaret had married Stephen of Perche, and that young King William was in danger, if indeed he was not already dead. The governor and his judges were reluctant to enforce order for fear of provoking a general riot.

Within days, news of the unrest engulfing Messina and its purlieus reached Margaret back in Palermo.

Before pandemonium ensued, the queen took the uncommon step of composing a letter to be read publicly at Messina. Issued jointly in her name and that of her son, the king, it sought to assuage the Messinians' fears, exhorting the people to remain loyal to the sovereign and his officers. It explained the reasoning behind the recent decisions against Bishop Gentile, Caïd Richard and Matthew of Aiello, and how Stephen, as chancellor, ensured that the three conspirators were not punished too harshly despite the gravity of their treason. Margaret's missive was not intended to prompt panegyrics for the queen or her chancellor; it was only meant to placate the vast swath of society that was getting ready to rebel against royal authority. The final passage of the text reassured the people that Queen Margaret and King William were well and unharmed.

Unfortunately, nobody but the governor and his judges (and Hugh Falcandus) ever learned the contents of the royal letter.

Andrew called the people together at the new cathedral. Here, as the governor procrastinated reading the letter aloud, rumors circulated among the crowd. Existing falsehoods were embellished and new ones were hatched. By the time Andrew finally began to read the letter, his voice was drowned out, lost in a sea of shouts and screams. The unruly horde had been carried away by a wave of imaginative lies: Stephen of Perche had been crowned king. William was dead, his younger brother besieged at Palermo's seaside castle. Geoffrey, the brother of Stephen of Perche, was coming to Sicily to marry Constance, the young daughter of King Roger II, and rule in her name.

Finally, a self-appointed leader enjoined the people to assassinate Odo Quarrel, suggesting that they then liberate the queen's half-brother, Henry of Montescaglioso, who, the man said, had always been benevolent to the Messinians. Andrew, whose purview it was to maintain order, implored the mad mob to abandon these ideas, but his words went unheeded.

Wasting not a moment, the people assaulted Odo's house, which was adjacent to the royal palace. This initial attack failed, and Odo managed to escape to the palace, which an angry crowd surrounded once it became known that he was inside.

At the harbor, some of the people armed themselves, commandeered seven galleys, boarded the ships and crossed the strait to Calabria, where John of Calomeno, the bailiff of Reggio, permitted the Messinians to enter the gates of that demesnial city. There a local crowd escorted them to the fortress where Henry was imprisoned.

The knights guarding this castle attempted to defend it by tossing stones upon the intruders, who nonetheless persisted in demanding that Henry be freed. The knights refused, declaring that they would hand the prisoner over to the Messinians only if ordered to do so by a competent authority. The rebels accepted this proposal, crossed back to Messina, and returned with James the Innkeeper, the man who the chancellor had sent to outfit the galleys that were to take Henry to France. The knights were expecting a justiciar, if not the governor himself; at the same time, there was only enough food in the castle to last three days. They reluctantly acceded to the Messinians' demand.

As soon as Henry of Montescaglioso was freed, he crossed over to Sicily, where he was acclaimed by the Messinians. The revolution had begun.

A few days were to pass before detailed reports of the most recent events at Messina arrived at the court in Palermo during the middle of April 1168.[629] For now, Henry of Montescaglioso had seized control of one of Europe's most important cities, a key to shipping and a gateway to the eastern Mediterranean. Ironically, the Messinians were not supporting Henry out of affinity for him so much as the belief that he was their best hope of supporting the monarchy which they believed had been threatened. The unsubstantiated rumors of the young king's death led the people to embrace his uncle.[630]

Odo Quarrel

The people wanted odious Odo Quarrel, dead or alive. For the moment, he was still in the royal palace near the shore. The castellan responsible for protecting the palace was reluctant to turn him over to an angry horde, but he cooperated with Henry, who sent a squad of men with a notary to take an inventory of Odo's possessions, and especially the money he had accumulated from his illegal tax.

At this point Odo was taken into custody. During the night he was removed from the palace, placed on a boat, and transported to the old seaside castle near the harbor, where he was imprisoned.[631] The more astute Messinians suspected that Henry was protecting Odo to ensure that the corrupt cleric, being the assistant and close friend of the chancellor, might intervene on the rebels' behalf with the royal court, whoever was running it. At the very least, as a hostage Odo would make an effective bargaining chip in the negotiations Henry envisaged with Margaret.

The best way to avoid this, the leaders of the avenging mob reasoned, was simply to eliminate Odo, but nobody seems to have said anything about killing him.

Instead, the throng demanded that Henry consign Odo to them for corporal punishment. Here they made mention of the grave offenses the treacherous man had perpetrated against the monarch he served, and against the people of Messina. Reluctant as he was to comply with this request, Henry thought it impolitic to defy the popular sentiment of people whose support he may yet need.

Odo had already been divested of his money and precious gems, so no harm was seen in placating public desires.

Therefore, the queen's half-brother permitted the mob to attach the tyrant's feet to a sturdy donkey that then dragged him naked down the streets. Some scraped skin, along with a few superficial bruises inflicted by a mild cudgeling, would ensure that Odo emerged from the experience chastened but essentially unscathed. This scenario, terrible as it is to the modern mind, was not altogether unorthodox in the twelfth century. Henry intended to throw the man into prison following the macabre spectacle. The premise in this reprisal was that a generous dose of humiliation might serve Odo well.

Henry was expecting little more than a token gesture that would satiate the public appetite for justice.

That is not what was delivered. The queen's half-brother had neglected to recognize the fact that he was witnessing the excessive response of an unruly mob, not a sentence, however harsh, meted out by a justiciar and supervised by guards. Before long, Odo was stabbed to death. Then his body was chopped into pieces. His head was placed at the end of a lance and paraded along the city streets. It was this savage spectacle that set the stage for what was to come.

Seized by an uncommon furor, the Messinians began running amok, killing any men they could find in the city who hailed from beyond the Alps. In this they were motivated in large measure by a loathing for French knights like those who had arrived with Odo Quarrel and harassed the gamblers a few days earlier. Even here, the splenetic mob's frenzy was misdirected, for there were many German, French and English merchants and pilgrims in Messina who had nothing to do with Odo Quarrel or the chancellor he had served.

Henry put an abrupt end to this wanton violence by announcing that anybody who committed murder would be tried and summarily punished. Clearly, there was a method to Henry's madness. Indeed, he was not mad at all.

Escalation

Undaunted, the queen considered a response to the burgeoning rebellion led by her half-brother. She was told that a number of knights could be mustered hastily from Palermo and some towns to the east. They could be sent along the Tyrrhenian coast toward Messina. Even though the April rains might hamper the knights' advance somewhat, it was fortunate that these coastal roads had been widened and repaired on the chancellor's orders the previous autumn, and in the worst case galleys could be used to transport the men by sea.

The immediate problem was a question of numbers. At the very least, the size of such a force would have to be sufficient to dissuade the Messinians from rebelling further. For this a full-fledged army was required, and raising one would take time.

Henry's advisors surmised the royal court's reaction, even if they suspected that King William himself might be dead. They had to defend the areas to the west of Messina, and for that they needed Rometta.[632] This fortified city straddling the Peloritan Mountains overlooked the Tyrrhenian coast near Milazzo, where there was a seaside castle. Controlling it was a paramount strategic necessity because any troops arriving by land from Palermo had to pass through this area.

Rometta had no baron; it was a royal town where the castellan guarded a small fortress. Most of the inhabitants were speakers of Greek. A few promises were sufficient to dislodge the castellan, and the Messinians left a small garrison at Rometta's castle.[633] The next operation would be far more onerous.

Its objective was Taormina, where Richard of Molise was imprisoned in a castle atop a rocky mountain overlooking the Ionian Sea far below. The town (now a popular resort) was famously impregnable, being one of the last strongholds in Sicily to fall to the Normans during the previous century.[634] Bearing this reality in mind, Henry led an army of Messinian knights and archers to Taormina as furtively as he could, along obscure mountain passes.

The element of surprise worked to the attackers' advantage, and the town was subdued with minimal effort. The problem was the fortress; here their efforts were repulsed.

Like Rometta, this was a royal town. Matthew, the castellan, defiantly refused to relinquish his prisoner. He could not be enticed, bribed or intimidated. But perhaps he could be persuaded.

Exasperated, Henry sent the brother of Matthew's wife with entreaties. This man begged the castellan, his brother-in-law, to release the prisoner, saying that he should think of the lives of his sister, nieces and nephews, who were being held hostage in Messina pending Richard's release. Matthew was unmoved, responding that, as a question of honor, he would not capitulate, even if the cost of refusal was his own life or that of his sister.

Matthew's brother-in-law finally took another approach. He persuaded the jailer, with whom he was acquainted, to free Richard while Matthew was asleep. This led to a skirmish and the death of the castellan. With this, Henry's forces took the castle.

Henry of Montescaglioso and Richard of Molise now controlled a strategic chunk of Sicily. Significantly, the northeastern region was the gateway to the peninsular part of the *Regnum*.

The two men had never been very fond of each other, but now politics united them. Margaret's half-brother had always been troublesome, even disloyal. Richard, on the other hand, had been imprisoned following a trial motivated by little more than envy; his loyalty to the queen had never wavered, and he probably did not deserve the fate that befell him.[635]

Henry and Richard might share doubts about Margaret's wisdom in acquiescing to their imprisonment, but this was overshadowed by their visceral hatred of Gilbert of Gravina and Stephen of Perche.

Back in Palermo, Stephen was alarmed at the fall of Taormina and the release of Richard of Molise, a competent warrior. An immediate response was necessary, but this was not forthcoming with any urgency, for there was an unforeseen impediment at court.

One of the figures at larger European courts, such as Sicily's, was the astrologer, something of a cross between a sorcerer and an astronomer. The most sophisticated among them came from the Muslim lands, and in Palermo astrologers were probably part of the Arabs' *dar al-hikma,* or "house of wisdom," a secular place of learning. The study of astrology found its way into other fields, such as meteorology and agriculture.

One of the era's better known astrologers was Adelard of Bath, who visited Sicily and then introduced the Muslims' knowledge of astronomy and geometry to England, where he served as the tutor of a young Henry II. Adelard is considered the most important English scientist of his time.[636]

Not surprisingly, there were astrologers among William's teachers.[637] Peter of Blois, the chief tutor, did not object to the young king learning about the zodiac, the stars, comets, eclipses and the phases of the moon, and neither did Margaret. The boy was developing a serious interest in astrology, and it was indeed considered a science in the twelfth century, when it was distinguished from astronomy little more than alchemy was differentiated from chemistry. Seen in its best light, astrology was usually thought to complement religion rather than contradict it.

Margaret herself does not seem to have been very interested in astrology, but her son, who was present at ever more meetings, was growing obsessed with it. Therefore, it was not surprising that the young monarch turned to astrologers to determine a good time to attack the rebels in Messina.[638]

Here the queen was left with little choice. Even if she thought the horoscope useless, by mitigating the influence of the court astrologers she would be casting doubts upon their legitimacy. Worse, she would be seen to be contradicting, even chastising, her son before the eyes of his subjects. This may explain why she did not act, but her indolence delayed action when every passing day was crucial. The result was grave inefficiency at a moment when nothing short of a timely response would suffice.

If Stephen of Perche could not immediately attack Henry and Richard, he would attempt to cripple them logistically. Because the rocky hills around Messina yielded little grain, the city's ravenous demand was usually satisfied with wheat from Calabria; that source was not viable this year because the region had suffered a preternaturally meager harvest the previous autumn. Knowing this, the chancellor cut off the supplies from Catania, whose plains produced plenty of grain.

Requiring a large army, the chancellor sought allies on the island to participate in the postponed military attack. The Lombard towns expressed their unequivocal support for the queen.[639] Between knights, footmen and archers, these communities alone could raise an army twenty thousand strong.[640] These loyal subjects encouraged Stephen to act soon, and he assured them that a day had been chosen to march on Messina. He did not mention that the day had been selected by astrologers.

Henry and Richard were more than capable of leading an army. Killing was their stock in trade. By now, they may have known that William and Margaret were alive and well. If so, the fact did not dissuade them. What they really wanted was to topple Stephen of Perche from his lofty perch. Then they would deal with Gilbert of Gravina.

With the widening dissent, Roger of Gerace, one of the barons who had conspired with Bishop Gentile of Agrigento but escaped notice, saw an opportunity to further his interests. To that end, he rode to Cefalù to solicit the support of Boson, its bishop, who controlled the royal city on the Tyrrhenian coast and was known to be one of Stephen's critics. Although Boson was, in principle, amenable to supporting the Messinians, there was little he could offer them materially, for the chancellor had already stationed a garrison of knights in the mountaintop citadel that overlooked the cathedral and town. From this vantage point, it was possible for sentinels to guard the coast for many miles; on a clear day one could see the volcanic Aeolian Islands to the northeast.

This made it obvious to the insurgents that the mobilization of troops to be used against them was proceeding, however sluggishly. Rapid as the rebels' advance had been thus far, its success was by no means assured. Fortunately for Henry and Richard, some allies of like mind were working toward the same objective on another front.

Fortitude

Like Richard of Molise, the *familiare* Matthew of Aiello had been imprisoned following a trial on the basis of sketchy evidence. Were both arrests no more than a ploy by Stephen of Perche to eliminate the two men most likely to challenge his authority? This we shall never know.[641]

What emerges from the scant facts known to us is the distinct possibility that, as chancellor, Stephen of Perche was occasionally overzealous, even unwise, inclined to paint several men with the same scornful brush. Whilst Margaret's capricious half-brother merited discipline for his treason, the *familiares* had never shown themselves to be overtly disloyal, nor had they ever confessed to their purported guilt. Had Stephen succumbed to hubris? Some thought so.

The rebels' hatred was never targeted directly at the queen except through surreptitious rumors. Perhaps they viewed her as a victim of Stephen's thirst for power. Of course, Henry, Richard and Matthew wanted to slake some ambitions of their own; they sought control. Apart from that, however, there was no common thread running through the motivations of Stephen's detractors. The men shared no ideology or political view significant enough for the chroniclers to record. They were, quite simply, European Christian men of their time. That they resented the presence of somebody they viewed as a usurper of their perceived birthrights reflected little more than nastiness nurtured in the depths of the mind.

"The queen can do no wrong." Crown immunity is a modern legal concept rooted in medieval practice. It was one of the fundamental principles underpinning the lengthy reign of England's Queen Victoria, and the even longer reign of Britain's next queen regnant, Elizabeth II. Another legal doctrine that survives in England is appointment, dismissal or even incarceration "at the queen's pleasure." In the Kingdom of Sicily this principle was enshrined in the Assizes of Ariano, which confirmed royal authority as the ultimate law of the realm. This idea had existed long before the twelfth century; no medieval monarch of Europe ruled without it, and there is nothing to suggest that Margaret ever abused her reginal rights, which she exercised in favor of her son.

The queen and the young king were unimpugnable, indeed untouchable. They were not simply "above the law." They themselves were the final arbiters of the law. Anybody brazen enough to openly defame the monarch or regent risked permanent incarceration, even death.

The rebels knew this. It was a sacrosanct fact of life, and it meant that any maneuvering against the chancellor would have to result in a "surgical strike" against him, and against him only, were it to bear fruit. This was not just a question of law. A handful of knights and barons could not hope to control a city the size of Palermo if things turned violent. The loyalty of the people was, first and foremost, to the sovereign; Bonello's revolt had shown the bedlam that ensue when the populace rebelled against the rebels.

As a purely military operation could be haphazard, the rebels resorted to trickery within the palace walls, where Matthew of Aiello was being held prisoner.

Matthew's incarceration was something more akin to "house arrest" than conventional captivity. His imprisonment in the royal palace did not confine him to a jail; indeed, the palace dungeon no longer served that purpose. Since the deposed *familiare* was not isolated, he communicated with people in the palace. In this way, he learnt of the revolts in northeastern Sicily and the recent transfer of some men in Stephen's elite corps of bodyguards to Cefalù and other strategic towns.

It so happened that the royal castellan, Ansaldo, a close ally of Stephen of Perche, was absent from his post, confined by illness to a high floor in another tower of the palace. This gave Matthew an opportunity to convince the man's colleague, Constantine, to enlist the majority of the palace personnel to assassinate the chancellor on an appointed day.[642] The plan was for them to attack Stephen and the two close associates, Roger of Avellino and John of Lavardin, who arrived with him most mornings at a certain gate.[643]

The threshold of the palace, at least in theory, was a kind of Rubicon; within its walls no visitors, not even knights, were allowed to carry swords and daggers.[644]

As there were, in total, some four hundred men between servants and guards, this diabolical strategy stood a good chance of success.[645]

Opportunism was rife in Palermo, where it took very little for some greedy ruffians in the Kasr district near the palace and cathedral to agree among themselves to attack whichever faction seemed more likely to be overpowered once the expected fighting began. Ideally, from their warped point of view, this would be Stephen, whose death might permit the criminals to pillage the wealth of gold they thought was kept in his house.

Insurrection

Stephen suspected that something was afoot; there usually was. Ansaldo confirmed that there was a plot against the chancellor, and that a large number seemed to be involved thus far. Stephen's life was in danger. The castellan went on to counsel his friend to go to a fortified town of the hinterland that he could use as a base. From such a place, he could summon the troops he needed from the towns where the fealty of the populace had not yet been compromised.

Ansaldo suggested that Stephen depart the capital immediately, paying no heed to the date established by the astrologers to march on the enemy. In this way, he could assemble a force without delay. Then the young king and, presumably, the regent could join him.

Ansaldo's plan was essentially sound, but Stephen of Perche did not follow through on it. Instead, he took the advice of some of his French knights, and particularly that of Robert of Meulan.[646] These men advised him against leaving the king in Palermo, believing the capital to be safe. The fundamental flaw in this counsel was that these men-at-arms, being foreigners, had no idea of the degree to which the Palermitans were capable of conspiring.

The day finally dawned for the attack planned on Stephen. That morning found a few of the murderous servants waiting just inside the gate the chancellor usually entered. Upon arriving, Stephen was expected to step through with two or three trusted associates, leaving his company of armed knights outside the wall.

But this morning he did not arrive. Somehow, Odo, the master equerry, the man responsible for the horses stabled within the palace's curtain wall, had learned of the plan. Early in the morning he went to Stephen's house to alert him. Having been warned of the plot, the chancellor dismissed the knights waiting outside his house to escort him to the palace. Several of his friends remained with him.

As soon as he learnt of this, Constantine, the traitorous assistant of the palace castellan, ignited a rebellion by sending a large number of servants into the city with orders to incite the populace against the chancellor. Claiming that Stephen was about to abscond from Palermo by sea with chests of gold belonging to the king, the servants goaded the citizens into taking up arms and encircling Stephen's house.

Nearby, Hervé "the Florid," who was resented not for his loyalty to Stephen but because he was a braggart, and Roger of Avellino were trotting their horses outside the palace. A large mob attacked the two. Hervé was struck off his horse and stabbed to death with swords. Roger rode into the flat area south of the city gate at the edge of the Genoard.[647] Here the crowd was about to assault him with lances when King William, who had heard the noise, suddenly appeared at a window and ordered the people to desist, threatening them with punishment if Roger was harmed.

The events unfolded with an uncommon fury as a frail decorum devolved into chaos. Partaking in the rebellion were the chancellor's most vociferous critics, whose steady stream of gossipy propaganda spurred hundreds of ordinary Palermitans to join them just as the rabid Messinians had acted against Odo Quarrel. The stark difference was that Odo's sins were real, whilst most of those attributed to Stephen had been crafted by fabulists animated by vested interests to remove him from power, by force if necessary. The chancellor's denouement, the rebels hoped, would be fast and fierce.

From a tower window, Margaret could see the violence enveloping the Kasr district. Fearing the worst should the insurrection sweeping the city go unchecked, she ordered Roger of Avellino to be taken to the seaside castle in the Kala, where he could be protected and assist in its defense.

Meanwhile, the crowd at Stephen's house was growing larger by the minute. Among these people were the royal longbow archers who, Falcandus tells us, were never the last to arrive at riots when there was any chance for lucre to be had.[648]

Stephen had left the protection of his residence to Simon of Poitiers. This man-at-arms placed knights and foot men around the perimeter of the house's wall, but the crowd's sudden onslaught threatened to overwhelm them.

Seeing that the situation was critical, the chancellor moved quickly to escape with a few trusted friends into the bell tower of the church adjacent to his house, along with several other French knights.[649] Amongst them was Robert of Meulan, who just a few days earlier had advised Stephen to remain in Palermo because a revolt in the city seemed unlikely. Overconfident Robert might live to eat his presumptuous words, but first he had to survive the present peril. It was turning into a long day.

To better see what was happening, the queen ascended the steps along a narrow passage to the roof of the Pisan Tower. Much of her view of the streets below was blocked by the low buildings, but she could see the bell tower where Stephen and his companions had taken refuge, and the scene didn't look good.[650]

William was with his mother. The young king was learning firsthand the form a rebellion could assume in a large city. Here was a sober lesson in the reality of ruling a kingdom.

Accompanied by a company of knights, Roger of Tiron, a high constable, made his way to the bell tower and assailed the most aggressive attackers.[651] Unfortunately, he and his men were overwhelmed by the onslaught of the armed mob and forced to retreat.

Meanwhile, the mob attacked Stephen's house even more truculently than before. The knights besieged within its walls fought back just as ferociously.

With the collapse of public order, Matthew of Aiello and Caïd Richard were able to leave the palace unopposed. The pair ordered the servant musicians to go sound horns and drums outside the chancellor's house. Summoning the people to battle in this way was a royal prerogative, so another segment of the populace, consisting of Muslims as well as Christians, assuming that the signal had been given on the queen's orders, arrived to reinforce the assault.

Margaret and William could see that the violence was concentrated in the area around Stephen's house and the church next to it. The palace, though by now largely abandoned by the guards, was not under attack. What the queen and her son were witnessing was unchecked street fighting on an unprecedented scale. Numbering fewer than a hundred, the loyal knights did their best to defend the chancellor and themselves against thousands.

The fighting at the house was intense, but in the end the edifice was overrun by rioters who gained entry to it through a passage from the church next door. This led to the knights at the house being taken prisoner by rebels led by Constantine, the disloyal castellan who had instigated the disorder in the first place.

With the chancellor's house finally taken, the crowd could focus its efforts on the bell tower, where Stephen and his company continued to defend themselves. Having reached an impasse, the rioters began to consider ways to overcome the resistance, perhaps by building a siege engine to attack the tower, or simply by piling wood and igniting a fire whose heat would force the structure's porous bricks to crumble.

The queen was now desperate. She wanted the people to desist. Something had to be done, and right now.

Not without grave misgivings, the queen proposed that she and William leave the palace to go speak to the people. Matthew of Aiello forestalled this, explaining that all the arrows and stones flying about made an unannounced public appearance too risky.[652] His words were not devoid of reason, for safety was indeed a factor to consider; Margaret probably remembered how an earlier revolt had claimed the life of one of her sons. Nonetheless, Matthew's words conveniently camouflaged the fact that the young king's presence would almost certainly convince the Palermitans to cease the hostilities, which were initiated earlier in the day on the pretext of a royal order.

By the end of the afternoon, the conspirators were beginning to succumb to some fears of their own. A problem appeared just as the sun began to disappear behind majestic Mount Kuz to the south of the city. The crowd was likely to disperse at dusk, with no guarantee that even a few of the fickle Palermitans would remain to prevent the chancellor and his knights escaping in the darkness. Short of imprisoning Margaret and her sons, it would be impossible to prevent the young king from emerging to address his subjects the next day; indeed, the people might even demand it, just as they did during Bonello's revolt years earlier.

All along, the rebels' objective had been to eliminate Stephen of Perche, yet they had failed to overpower him. In seeking to checkmate their nemesis, they had achieved nothing more than a sour stalemate. It was time to negotiate. This was done in the king's name, if not with his willing consent.

In the haggard twilight, the voice of reason emerged from the smoldering embers.

If he agreed to leave, Stephen would be guaranteed safe conduct out of the realm. He and the men who had come with him from France would be supplied armed galleys to take them to whatever land they wished, and the Sicilian barons with him in the tower could retain their estates in the *Regnum*. Stephen's mercenary knights were given the choice of continuing their service to the king or accepting passage to a place of their choosing. These terms were accepted. The deposed chancellor and a small company would sail to Jerusalem via Constantinople.

Caïd Richard, Matthew of Aiello, Richard Palmer, John of Malta and Romuald of Salerno jointly gave their word that the conditions of the agreement would be respected. The next morning, after bidding his cousin a sad farewell, Stephen renounced his status as Palermo's archbishop-elect and boarded his galley, setting sail on a westward course around Sicily. The only encumbrance proved to be a problem with his galley that forced him to purchase another vessel at Licata. Before long he was in the Holy Land.[653]

Queenship

The queen needed solid advice. Unfortunately, it was not forthcoming from any quarter except, perhaps, the feckless astrologers or a handful of sycophants. Having placed so much faith in one man, Margaret had alienated some who otherwise might have been more willing to take up her cause. Peter of Blois, the royal tutor, was a worthy confidant, but he had left shortly after his friend Stephen.

A few days after Stephen of Perche departed, Henry of Montescaglioso arrived in Palermo's harbor with a score of armed galleys. Accompanying him were Bishop Gentile of Agrigento, who he had freed from San Marco d'Alunzio, and his ally Richard of Molise.

The queen was coerced into appointing a number of *familiares*. The list included the notary Matthew of Aiello, the archdeacon (and royal tutor) Walter, Caïd Richard, Bishop Gentile of Agrigento, Richard Palmer, Bishop John of Malta, Archbishop Romuald of Salerno, Roger of Gerace, Richard of Molise and, worst of all, Henry of Montescaglioso. The only consolation in having ten headaches instead of two or three was that they might fight enough among themselves to permit Margaret to serve as an effective referee. The doctrine of *divide et impera* would serve her well.

Collectively, these *familiares* represented the most important elements of the ruling class, namely the baronage, the bureaucrats and the clergy. In principle, this might provide political stability.

A certain coterie of historians has taken to referring to this expanded group of *familiares* as a "council of regency," a characterization predicated on the belief that the queen's authority suddenly evaporated under the torrid Sicilian sun. There is a morsel of truth in this. However, it was rare for more than four or five of these men to be present at court at the same time.[654] Margaret was still the nexus of power in the Kingdom of Sicily.

A complementary theory, little explored until now, is that the effect of the "council," whatever its initial intent, was to give a voice to the baronage. Here, arguably, we see the first seeds of representative government, which eventually took root at the end of the next century with Sicily's first parliament. Although it cannot be compared to England's *Magna Carta,* which was a formal charter of baronial rights, the "council" certainly gave the nobles a greater influence at court than they otherwise could have expected.[655]

In the other great Norman realm, King Henry's Assize of Clarendon introduced certain rights that, in a perfect world, could redress perceived injustice of the kind claimed by Sicily's rebellious baronial element. Trial by jury, novel disseisin and other elements of what came to form the foundation of common law might well have been introduced in the *Regnum*. This may have obviated the very premise of some complaints because it is possible, based on what little we know, that Matthew of Aiello and Richard of Molise would not have been found guilty had their cases been heard by a competent jury.[656]

Continuously forced to respond to immediate challenges to her authority, Margaret had little time to address fundamental legal questions. Even if she did, some subjects might well have questioned her prerogative, as regent, to do so.

Apart from the crisis that saw the expulsion of Stephen of Perche, grave as it was, there was very little to stimulate the queen to effect sweeping additions to existing law. Unlike the English king, whose actions were motivated in part by a burgeoning jurisdictional "turf war" with the Catholic Church, Margaret's relationship with the papacy was consolidated by such things as the apostolic legateship. For now, the Assizes of Ariano would have to suffice, and Margaret would have to endure an expanded cadre of *familiares*.

The first act of the newly-appointed *familiares* was to expel Gilbert of Gravina (and Loritello) from the *Regnum*. Sensing that she had no choice, the queen agreed to this, however reluctantly.[657] She drew the line at their request to attaint or exile Hugh of Catanzaro, a kinsman of Stephen of Perche.[658]

Falcandus tells us that the *familiares* relented for two reasons. On the one hand, Hugh was violent and unpredictable, and therefore capable of waging an insurgency against them; on the other, the *familiares* wished to mitigate the queen's anger.[659]

Apart from Margaret's feelings and Hugh's belligerent temperament, the *familiares* had good reason to fear the Count of Catanzaro. Unlike Stephen's other companions, who had few ties to the Kingdom of Sicily, Hugh had a link to it that was worth fighting for. The large chunk of Calabria he controlled was held by right of his wife, the heiress Clementia, who, as a maiden, once flirted with Matthew Bonello. Hugh had enough resources, and enough support from the Calabrian baronage loyal to his wife's family, to raise a formidable army of his own.

After the first few chaotic months, the power of the *familiares* was more like a placid pond than a raging river, but even a docile lake can be dangerous for those unable to swim. Fortunately, Margaret knew how to survive in perilous waters, and she refused to let herself drown in her own tears.

As individuals, some of the *familiares* wielded considerable influence at court. Matthew of Aiello ensured that John, his brother, was consecrated Bishop of Catania as planned. This took place in July. John was not altogether unenlightened; he permitted the Jews in his diocesan jurisdiction to be judged by their own laws.[660]

The queen restored to Richard of Molise the prosperous lands he had held until his imprisonment.

Henry of Montescaglioso was finally granted his wish for more territory when he was invested with the Principate, a large county that included territories around such cities as Salerno and Avellino. The queen reasoned that this concession, ludicrously generous as it was, would keep her half-brother far away from the royal court. Margaret's only modicum of satisfaction in this gesture came the moment Henry made submission by kneeling before her and William to swear fealty to the monarch.

The *familiare* Walter, archdeacon of Cefalù, had no hope of being consecrated bishop of that diocese so long as Bishop Boson was alive, and he was hardly content to serve exclusively as rector of the palace chapel.[661] Almost as soon as Stephen had left the *Regnum,* overbearing Walter began seeking supporters who might endorse his appointment as Archbishop of Palermo. He reassumed the role of royal tutor held until recently by Peter of Blois, soon emerging as the most important *familiare*.

By the autumn, exiled Robert of Loritello learnt of recent events. For months, he had been sending Margaret letters requesting that she lift his exile. Reasoning that he might reclaim his old manor now that Gilbert of Gravina was no longer in the *Regnum,* he began sending insistent letters to the regent asking for it back. Margaret had to think about this.

She was busy dispatching correspondence of her own, to such people as Thomas Becket, who had sent letters to the queen and to her chancellor thanking them for providing hospitality to his nephews.

Not surprisingly, Richard Palmer corresponded with his countryman. Ostensibly acting on behalf of the King of France but perhaps at Margaret's urging, the Archbishop of Canterbury asked Richard to intervene to recall Stephen of Perche to Sicily.[662] Richard, of course, wished to keep Stephen as far away as he could.

By the end of 1168, a certain calm had been restored to the kingdom. The queen regent's authority had diminished slightly, but hers was still the most powerful voice in the *Regnum*.

Views of the Zisa's facade, muqarnas and mosaics

Santa Maria della Valle, or Santa Maria della Scala, refounded near Messina by Roger I and Adelaide
19th century print

Chapter 18
LEADERSHIP

Despite the presence of several *familiares,* the queen regent continued to make her own decisions. She decided to permit Robert of Loritello, her son's distant cousin, to return from exile; this might bring him into her camp. Other problems she faced in 1169 were more complex.

In the wake of the resignation and departure of Stephen of Perche, the chancellorship was not filled and the archbishopric of Palermo was vacant. The queen's failure to make these appointments might elicit subtle dissent in certain quarters. Not being eager to see the concentration of power in one courtier, the *familiares* voiced no objection to this lacuna.

As the Archbishop of Palermo was, *ex officio,* the Primate of Sicily, a position that brought with it its own privileged place in the kingdom's power structure, the queen, at least for the moment, saw no urgency in advancing any names for it. For now, reticence was expedient. The taciturn regent would have her way eventually. It would be best for her political detractors not to view her silence to imply consent.

Primate

As the royal tutor, Walter, who was also the rector, or dean, of the palace chapel, spent more time at court than any other *familiare*. He even had a tiny "office" in the palace. Although he never became chancellor, Walter was, effectively if unofficially, the chief *familiare,* and we find his signature as the first witness subscribing many royal decrees.

Like Stephen of Perche, Walter had been sent to Sicily by Margaret's kinsman Rotrou of Rouen. However, having arrived earlier than, and separately from, Stephen and the hated French knights, Walter never came to be closely associated with this faction in the public mind. Spared the bitter animus directed at them, he was not expelled with the others.

If Walter was related to Margaret or Stephen, it was only through a very distant, tenuous kinship.[663] He may not have been a close friend of Stephen, but neither was he an outright enemy. In any case, he never defended him with much vigor, and in the end he added his voice to the opposition. With Stephen of Perche and Peter of Blois gone, Walter was the best advisor the queen could expect to find, even if he would never be anything like a trusted confidant.[664]

He was tireless in his efforts to garner enough support to justify being elected the capital's archbishop. Before long, he renounced his position in the diocese of Cefalù to be appointed archdeacon of Agrigento, a more important see. This suggests a certain amity with Gentile Tuscus, Agrigento's bishop.[665]

Falcandus claims that Walter attempted to gain the appointment as Archbishop of Palermo by paying a violent mob to frighten the local clergy into supporting him. The palace may have hoped Rome would refuse to ratify this election on the grounds that Stephen, having renounced his archiepiscopal status under duress, was still archbishop-elect. The chronicler contends that Margaret sent Peter of Gaeta, subdeacon of the papal curia, seven hundred gold ounces to give the pope to encourage Rome's support.[666] This account, if truthful, implies that the regent's actions were tantamount to bribery. In this she was not alone, for the baronage, which endorsed Walter, made its own entreaties to the Pontiff, along with a bribe even more substantial than Margaret's.

After contemplating the situation, the pope decided to confirm the election of Walter who, by February, had already begun to behave as if he were archbishop, subscribing charters with that title and celebrating liturgy in the cathedral.[667] Alexander kept the gold the queen had sent him but, seeking to spare her feelings, he delayed sending Walter's charter of appointment to Palermo.

Earthquake

Early in the morning of the fourth of February a violent earthquake shook eastern Sicily and southern Calabria. Its epicenter was near the city of Catania, which it all but leveled.[668] Some fifteen thousand Catanians perished. Most of the people in Lentini were killed. There was damage from Messina down to Syracuse. Castles crumbled at Modica and other towns, and from Taormina the snow-capped summit of Mount Etna was observed to sink somewhat.[669]

Lending the catastrophe an apocalyptic air was its occurrence during the vigil of the feast of Saint Agatha, Catania's heavenly patroness. The city's cathedral was dedicated to her, and its collapse crushed Bishop John of Aiello, the brother of Matthew the *familiare,* along with forty-five monks inside for matins.[670]

Margaret and her sons made their way to Catania to comfort the people as best they could. Here William spoke publicly in his first official address to his subjects: "Let each of you pray to the God he worships. He who has faith in his God will feel peace in his heart." Such words reflected William's kind disposition to all the Abrahamic faithful he ruled.[671]

Nothing could portend such a catastrophe, let alone explain it. To the medieval mind, a disaster of this magnitude could be nothing less than an act of a wrathful God. Some thought it foretold even worse cataclysms to come. In a letter to Richard Palmer, Peter of Blois expressed the opinion that the earthquake was God's vengeance.[672] According to Falcandus, there were people who believed that Stephen of Perche, said to be at the court of Constantinople, might return, flanked by Robert of Loritello and a faction of the baronage, to take control of the court.

This speculation ended when news arrived that Stephen had died in Jerusalem, where he was buried with honor in the Templars' chapter house.[673]

Decisions

Three years earlier, when Emperor Manuel of Constantinople proposed betrothing his daughter to Margaret's son, the queen's reaction was tepid. The young king was now fifteen; he would reach the age of majority in two years. Recent events had shown that he was becoming a decisive young man, intelligent and confident. It was time to begin the search for an appropriate bride for him.

The Byzantine proposal, interesting as it was, did not appeal to the queen. Her affinity for Norman society prompted her to look toward the northeast. She was not the only one in her family to entertain such a notion.

Alfonso VIII of Castile, the son of Margaret's late sister, Blanca, was making overtures to Henry II of England to marry one of the English king's daughters. Alfonso was the same age as William. Matilda, one of the daughters of Henry and Eleanor, had recently married the Duke of Saxony. There were two unwed princesses left, and Eleanor (Leonor), the elder, was not yet eight years old. Despite the girls' tender years, however, it could not hurt to make a discreet inquiry.

For the moment, Margaret had to rule the *Regnum*. This entailed establishing policy when necessary, but more often confirming feudal grants, founding monasteries and, of course, protecting the rights of all the subjects. She had little time to think about those who had left. The eunuch and onetime *familiare* Caïd Peter, for example, was now an admiral in the service of Abu Yaqub Yusuf, the Almohad emir. It will be remembered that once he left the kingdom Peter reassumed his original name, Ahmed; to this he had since added the surname *es-Sikeli*, "the Sicilian." Although Sicilian merchants traded with Almohad Ifriqiya, the *Regnum* presently lacked a formal treaty with it.

In February, the queen permitted Matthew of Aiello to establish a tax-exempt monastery on his property in Palermo. The salutation of this charter, which is typical of those issued during the regency, refers to "William, benevolent King of Sicily, Duke of Apulia and Prince of Capua, with Lady Margaret his Queen Mother, resplendent in their great and glorious royal generosity."[674] Another charter, dated May 1169, confirms the rights to an abbey in northeastern Sicily formerly granted by John of Aiello, Matthew's late brother. This monastery, which seems to have been uninhabited by this time, once housed Byzantine monks.[675]

These charters reveal something of the form the court had assumed. Caïd Richard was the master chamberlain, assisted by Caïd Martin, the royal chamberlain. The *familiare* Matthew of Aiello was high notary. Richard of Molise was also present.

Stephen's death removed the last theoretical impediment to Walter's formal appointment as Archbishop of Palermo, and Pope Alexander formalized it by decree in June.[676] The queen then had to endure attending the petulant prelate's consecration in Palermo's cathedral in late September.[677]

Walter convinced her to appoint his brother, Bartholomew, as a *familiare*, but the archbishop's avarice did not end there. He also prevailed upon the queen to concede to him the feudal rights of the mills of the manor of *Bur-Ruqqad,* or Brucato, as well as other lands.[678]

The queen had her own tactic for reminding pompous Walter that the Kingdom of Sicily wasn't his personal theocracy. This involved adding a layer of power to the court hierarchy. She appointed Matthew of Aiello, the *familiare* and high notary, her vice chancellor. This was a slightly ironic title as there was no high chancellor for him to serve under. Nevertheless, it sent the clear signal that the *Regnum* was a monarchy, not a dictatorship, and that Margaret was still in charge.[679]

In October 1169, a force sent by the Byzantine Empire and the Kingdom of Jerusalem besieged Damietta, in Egypt, but the city failed to capitulate. This debacle, which did not involve the Kingdom of Sicily directly, foreshadowed the rapid rise of the Ayyubid dynasty under Saladin, supplanting the Fatimids.

By Christmas, Henry II had expressed his consent to the marriage of his youngest daughter, Joanna, to King William. This was not a formal, binding decision, and Joanna was just four years old, so the wedding was still some years away, but the English monarch's agreement was a hopeful sign. Without delay, the queen sent ambassadors to discuss the matter with the pope.

The beginning of 1170 was a good time to think about the year just ended. There was peace and stability in the kingdom, whilst the treasury, the *diwan,* was as rich as ever. If the queen found Walter and his ilk overbearing, perhaps downright obnoxious, she managed to achieve a tolerable coexistence with them. More important than her needs was the necessity of rebuilding Catania and the other localities destroyed during the previous year.

To the north of the kingdom's border, Pope Alexander III spent a good part of his pontificate exiled from the city of Rome, which was a hotbed of unrest rooted in the ambitions of Frederick Barbarossa and the occasional antipope. The pontiff resided instead at Benevento, Gaeta and Anagni. Gifts like the gold he received from Margaret and the Sicilian barons the previous year made this exile bearable.

In January, the pontiff received as Margaret's ambassadors Robert of Loritello and Richard Palmer, whose brief it was to seek approval for the idea of the marriage of William to Joanna, the youngest daughter of the King of England. These emissaries were more reliable than others the queen might have sent; Robert was distant kin to her son and Richard was English by birth.

At England's royal court, like Sicily's, life proceeded unhindered despite political complexities. King Henry's dispute with Thomas Becket, who Pope Alexander supported, had yet to be resolved.

The Sicilians were anything but oblivious to what was transpiring in England, and the matter was doubtless discussed, if perhaps perfunctorily, by the two Sicilian ambassadors and the pope. It did not impede the negotiations, but Becket himself was displeased, personally offended by what he viewed as disloyalty on the part of the two emissaries, with whom he was familiar, and perhaps even Margaret. In a letter to the Bishop of Ostia he wrote that, "Even the King of Sicily, in whose dominions you live, has been promised the daughter of the King of England if he will join in effecting our ruin."[680]

That criticism was misplaced and simply erroneous. Margaret was merely seeking to secure a marriage for her son. Like many, she hoped for a resolution to a conflict that had already dragged on for years. Thomas Becket further asserted that Richard Palmer was offered the bishopric of Lincoln, as if this were comparable to the importance (and climate) of Syracuse, if he supported King Henry politically and financially.[681] There seems to be no basis for Becket to have believed such a thing; most of the money he mentions would certainly have to come from the treasury of the *Regnum,* and that would require Margaret's approval.

Margaret supported Becket whilst Matthew of Aiello, who was now her vice chancellor, was inclined to endorse King Henry's views.[682] Yet the Kingdom of Sicily took no official position in the dispute, and during the summer of 1170 the Archbishop of Canterbury and the King of England seemed to reach a compromise.

As the months passed, the queen continued the business of running a kingdom. As always, the greater number of decrees she issued in her son's name dealt with feudal and ecclesiastical rights. Typical of these is a charter of October, in which she granted a hermit monk of the Byzantine tradition a small manor and the rights to a mill.[683]

Margaret's improvised strategy of "divide and conquer" was beginning to achieve its desired result. Archbishop Walter viewed Matthew of Aiello as a rival, and their rapport was sometimes difficult. Over time, however, the two men developed a reasonably efficient working relationship.[684]

By the Christmas season of 1170, it seemed as if the marriage agreements of William II to Joanna of England and that of his cousin Alfonso VIII of Castile to her elder sister, Eleanor (Leonor), would soon be confirmed.

The English monarch hoped to benefit from these unions. Princess Leonor's marriage to Alfonso would provide Henry more security along the southern border of Aquitaine and other regions he ruled by right of his wife. Joanna's marriage to William would more closely link England, Normandy and Henry's various French lands to the affluent Kingdom of Sicily.

No account was taken of love. Henry's daughters would be expected to embrace the husbands chosen for them, just like Margaret herself had done many years earlier.

For his part, Alfonso wanted support from Henry, whose lands extended to the Pyrenees, to offset the territorial ambitions of his avaricious uncle, Sancho VI of Navarre. By surrounding Navarre in this way, the young King of Castile hoped to restrict Sancho's expansion into Castilian territories beyond La Rioja.

Margaret's motives were more nuanced. She had no lofty political or economic objectives in arranging her son's marriage to Henry's daughter, but closer ties with Henry and his dominions on the continent would not be unwelcome.

These incipient wedding plans were torn asunder by an event that occurred in the last days of December, when Thomas Becket was murdered in Canterbury by four of Henry's knights. In the aftermath of this tragedy, the English sovereign risked becoming a pariah.

Thomas Becket

He was one of the most influential prelates of his century. In death, if not in life, Thomas Becket came to be admired, and then venerated, across Catholic Europe. His letter to Queen Margaret is the only snippet of her correspondence that survives, but his eloquent epistles fill many volumes, painting a punctilious portrait of his personal character and his theological views. No discourse on the concepts of national sovereignty, ecclesiastical authority or the separation of church and state during the High Middle Ages is truly complete without a consideration of the unholy feud between Henry II, King of England, and his onetime friend, Thomas Becket, Archbishop of Canterbury, and the topic has a special relevance to the *Regnum Siciliae*.[685]

Thomas Becket was born in London around 1119, son of Gilbert, a prosperous merchant who eventually became a property holder and sometime sheriff. Of Norman ancestry, he had at least three sisters but no surviving brothers. A wealthy friend of Gilbert Becket was Richard of Aigle, a cousin of Margaret of Navarre through her mother. Young Thomas went hunting and hawking with this baron, who he came to regard almost as an uncle.

The boy's education began at Merton Priory and continued in London, perhaps at the school of Saint Paul's Cathedral.[686] Being residents of Cheapside, his parents had a connection with this church.

Around the age of twenty, Thomas studied for a year in Paris. By the time he returned, his mother had died and his father's business was suffering. To avoid penury, Thomas made use of his writing skills by earning a living as a clerk (scrivener), first for a kinsman who was a justiciar, and then for Theobald of Bec, Archbishop of Canterbury. Thomas did not declare a calling to the priesthood, but before long Theobald was sending him on missions to the papal court. The archbishop then sponsored the young man's education in canon law in Bologna and Auxerre.

Such an education was not unlike that of Stephen of Perche and Peter of Blois. In this social class we find the promising sons of wealthy families destined for scholarly pursuits rather than service as knights, notaries or merchants. These intellectuals were the kind of young men likely to become the advisors to kings and cardinals.

Not only did his sojourn across the channel provide Thomas an exceptional education, it had the benefit of removing him from the strife of The Anarchy. Yet the scholar had to return to his homeland sooner or later, and Theobald, his sponsor, found him a succession of posts in ecclesiastical service. In 1154, Theobald made Thomas the Archdeacon of Canterbury.

However devout he may have been, Thomas still was in no hurry to be ordained a priest, but through his exemplary service to Theobald he became known as a learned and pragmatic man, more thinker than scrivener. In 1155, Theobald recommended him to become the chancellor of King Henry II.

This post involved collecting monies owed the crown, whether from barons or bishops. Thomas performed his duties efficiently, bringing order to the royal accounts. He and the king become good friends, passing much time together hunting and conversing. Thomas was Henry's closest confidant. Being thirteen years the king's senior, he may even have been something of a mentor to him. Close as they were, the two men had very obviously different mentalities. Henry's lifestyle was austere; he enjoyed simple pleasures. Even his attire was simple, virtually indistinguishable from what any rustic baron wore whilst hunting. A pragmatist, he deplored ceremony for its own sake. Thomas cultivated a slightly more elegant image that reflected his taste for luxury.

The story is told of how Henry sent Thomas ahead of him to Paris in 1158 to negotiate the marriage of the young heir apparent to the daughter of King Louis VII of France. Henry suggested that the chancellor make an effort to impress the French. Taking this recommendation to heart, yet relishing the task, Thomas brought with him every kind of fur and silk garment, along with lush carpets and exquisite furnishings, in eight large carts and on the backs of a dozen mules. Over two hundred foot men led the endless train of courtiers, esquires, heralds, archers, falconers and servants who preceded Thomas and his elite company of knights and prelates. The king himself arrived later, dressed unpretentiously, with just a few knights in tow.[687]

Henry's ideals transcended his ascetic approach to life. The monarch believed that justice should be available to all his subjects, and that some semblance of equality could prevail under the law. True, there were barons and there were serfs, and a feudal order that kept every man in his place, with little thought given to women, but the long civil war he witnessed as a boy convinced the king that just laws could bring about a fundamentally just society.

Thomas Becket agreed with these principles. Amongst their prominent proponents were Richard of Luci, England's highest judge as the chief justiciar, and Ranulf of Glanville, the erudite scholar who succeeded him.[688]

With Henry's introduction of civil (secular) tribunals, a law emerged that was "common" throughout England. Decisions might establish precedent, ensuring consistency in the prosecution of the same crime in different parts of the realm.

Henry's common law did not completely supplant existing principles.[689] His grandfather, Henry I, had proclaimed a very rudimentary legal code, the Charter of Liberties.[690] Yet the new laws added much to England's juridical landscape.

The legal system instituted by Henry II, with its itinerant judges, was effective so long as the bishops did not encroach on its jurisdiction by claiming immunity for the clergy, which was about one-sixth of the population. The king wanted his legal system to function on its own, independently of papal influence, but he reasoned that ecclesiastical support was necessary if his reforms were ever to be accepted without resistance.

In 1161, an opportunity presented itself with the death of Archbishop Theobald of Bec. Henry's simple solution was to ensure that somebody who shared his own views assumed this important post as Archbishop of Canterbury, and thus Primate of England.[691]

To Henry, the obvious choice, or at least the most expedient one, was Thomas Becket, whose perspectives about royal authority and the law were not unlike his own. The next year, Thomas was ordained to the priesthood and elected archbishop. Following his consecration, he seems to have realized that it would be difficult to serve two masters, so he resigned from the office of chancellor.

In accepting the pallium, Thomas Becket seems to have reconsidered some of his ideas about ecclesiastical rights. Only rarely did he seek to ingratiate himself with antagonists, and now his dogmatism revealed itself. Whereas, as chancellor, his knowledge of canon law never impeded his support of the new system of justice, as archbishop he became its critic.

Although Becket's greatest criticisms seemed to focus on just a few laws, much more was at stake. The archbishop thought that conceding one or two points would lead to the collapse of the authority of the Holy See altogether. Greater accommodation may well have been reached if both the archbishop and the monarch were less adamant in the totality of their views, and differences in character certainly aggravated matters. Henry was known for his violent temper, Thomas for his stubbornness. It was an explosive combination.

In January 1164, the Constitutions of Clarendon were enacted. Their preamble mentions the earlier laws of Henry's grandfather, "which should be observed and enforced in the realm."[692] Yet these new statutes were very clearly intended to curtail the power of the ecclesiastical courts and papal authority. Becket was saddened to see among the names of the signatories supporting the Constitutions that of his old friend, Richard of Aigle.

Disputes between laymen and clerics were to be decided by the civil courts, in some cases by a jury of "twelve lawful men." The Constitutions forbade the excommunication of English subjects, and even prohibited clergy from leaving the kingdom without prior royal consent.

A few church powers were retained in some form. For example, clerics accused of crimes could be tried in ecclesiastical courts, but with an officer of the civil (secular) court present; if convicted, the cleric would be remanded to the civil court for punishment. Because the judges of the ecclesiastical court could not order a punishment that would spill blood, a priest found guilty of murder might be defrocked but penalized no further, whereas a civil court would more likely order mutilation or even death.

The Constitutions found consent with the other prelates but enraged Thomas Becket, who viewed the laws as an affront to the apostolic authority of the church, and therefore an offense to God Himself. In this he was "more Catholic than the pope" who, oddly enough, advocated less obstinate positions in some of these matters. This did not reflect Pope Alexander's sympathy for Henry's views, but rather his fear that strong opposition might drive the King of England to support the antipope, a threat being used by Frederick Barbarossa in an effort to manipulate the papacy.

Thomas eventually voiced assent to the Constitutions but never confirmed his approval with a seal or signature. If Henry had even the faintest shadow of a doubt about Becket's opposition to the reforms, it vanished as the months passed.

The defiant Archbishop of Canterbury knew that repercussions would follow, but in this the king was creative. Taking what he thought to be the path of least resistance, Henry accused Thomas of malfeasance committed during his tenure as chancellor. He summoned him to appear at a great council at Northampton to answer these charges. When convicted, Thomas stormed out of the trial and fled to France, where he received sanctuary from King Louis VII.

In 1166, with Thomas in exile, Henry enacted the Assize of Clarendon.[693] Very little of this dealt with ecclesiastical authority. Instead, it transferred much power from the barons to the royal judges. Trial by jury was instituted based on an evidentiary model, replacing such methods as compurgation, an accused person being released if a certain number of his friends swore that they believed him, and trial by single combat, a knight dueling an opponent to decide his case.[694]

Henry took reprisal against the prelate's family, which he exiled, and (as we have seen) eventually two of Becket's nephews were granted hospitality by Queen Margaret in Sicily.

By 1167, Pope Alexander III was actively intervening in the dispute through the diplomacy of one emissary after another. Whilst he agreed with Thomas in theory, the pontiff saw no point in allowing the controversy to drag on for years. A meeting between the king and the archbishop east of Paris early in 1169 resolved nothing, ending with both parting in exasperation.[695]

Henry was just as obdurate as Becket. He arranged for his young son, Prince Henry, to be crowned *rex filius* by the Archbishop of York, whose see contested Canterbury for primacy in England. This was meant to humiliate the exiled Becket, as everybody knew that the privilege of coronation belonged to Canterbury alone. The coronation took place in June 1170.

Becket's reaction was to excommunicate the Archbishop of York, along with the bishops of London and Salisbury who assisted him in crowning Henry the Young King.[696]

Convinced that the senior Henry had gone too far, Pope Alexander confirmed Becket's excommunications of the bishops and others, though young William II of Sicily, through his mother, intervened with the pontiff on behalf of at least one of them, Jocelin de Bohun (see Appendix 2). Fearing that an interdict on England might be the next misfortune to befall his reign, the king met with Thomas in France in late July. The exile formally ended and the two tacitly agreed to ignore, for now, the myriad jurisdictional complications arising from the Constitutions of Clarendon.

Thomas Becket returned to England in early December. In Normandy, Henry was distressed to learn that his erstwhile friend refused to lift the excommunication of the Archbishop of York. Worse yet, the archbishop excommunicated other subjects in what seemed like an attempt to test Henry's resolve, if not his laws.

Seeing Henry's displeasure, four of his knights went to Canterbury to confront the archbishop. There, in the cathedral, they struck down Thomas Becket with their swords at the hour of vespers on the evening of Tuesday, December twenty-ninth, 1170.

Henry repudiated this heinous act, disavowing any responsibility for it. The assassins, though publicly condemned, went unpunished except for banishment from the court and excommunication. Saint Thomas of Canterbury was canonized in February 1173. Remorseful King Henry II did public penance at the martyr's tomb in Canterbury Cathedral in July of the following year. This involved being flogged by monks, but it permitted the king's reputation to be rehabilitated in the eyes of the pope and other sovereigns. Although some of the laws contested by Thomas Becket were suspended for a time, the greater number survived. In England, trial by jury supplanted trial by ordeal and principles of common law endured. Henry faced squabbles not with churchmen but with his own wife and sons.

Thomas Becket's story was widely recounted; in Sicily it was described by Romuald of Salerno. The next decade saw a great number of churches founded in the saint's name across western Europe. The Sicilians dedicated the mother church of Marsala to Thomas Becket, and the earliest public holy image of him is a mosaic icon in Monreale Abbey. A small church was erected in his honor in Palermo near the place where his nephews lived. In England, meanwhile, pilgrims like those famously described by Chaucer flocked to Canterbury.

Religions

In Palermo, nothing in the first days of 1171 represented overwhelming problems.[698] There were no serious conflicts within the *Regnum*, and no foreign threats.

Yet the news of the murder of Thomas Becket was startling not only for the death itself, but for the brutality with which the archbishop was said to have been killed. Ultimately, a king was held responsible for the actions of his knights, especially when a few of them acted together and claimed to be exercising his will. There was no telling how long it would take for the King of England to emerge from this quagmire, but the fingers being pointed at him as the presumed culprit did not bode well for his reputation abroad.

Henry's problem with the church would have to be resolved with alacrity, for he now risked excommunication for himself and interdict for his kingdom. The betrothals of his daughters to the sons of the two Jiménez sisters were probably the last things on his mind. Yet, like many other matters, they were predicated on a solid rapport with the papacy.

There was still time to find William a suitable bride. Indeed, another offer soon arrived from the Emperor of Constantinople. This reiterated his proposal of several years earlier. Manuel's daughter was still available, although no longer his universal heiress as a son had been born since he last tendered Margaret a proposal that William wed Maria. This time, Margaret decided to accept the offer.[699]

As the most influential *familiares*, Matthew of Aiello and Walter the Archbishop of Palermo worked together well enough for a later chronicler to describe them as "two firm pillars" supporting the Kingdom of Sicily.[700] That portrayal may well have reflected popular sentiment. For now, most of the queen's tasks were almost routine

In March, for example, she restored to Gentile, Bishop of Agrigento, a mill of which, according to a surviving charter, the prelate had somehow been defrauded.[701] Other decrees defended the rights of Muslims and Jews.

Cities like Jerusalem and Palermo might accommodate all of their religious factions in something approaching harmony, but that was not true everywhere. In May, the Christians of Blois, a city on the Loire, massacred some forty Jews on the contrived pretext of the murder of a Christian child.

By 1171, the composition of the population of the realm Margaret ruled in her son's name could be identified by religion in a general way. The Jews were the only religious minority of note in the peninsular part of the Kingdom of Sicily. On the island of Sicily, perhaps one in four subjects were Muslim, and no more than one in ten were Jewish.

In Egypt, a Sunni family succeeded a Shia dynasty. The death of the last Fatimid caliph brought changes to the African lands running along the Mediterranean all the way to the Red Sea. Cairo, the family's capital, had been founded not long after the Fatimids made their way to Egypt from Tunisia. In September 1171, Saladin, a Kurd, formally established what was to become a new ruling house. His Ayyubids, who had a natural religious affinity for the Sunni Abbasids of Baghdad, were intent on asserting their power around Jerusalem. Islam spanned three continents, influencing regions from Spain to what is now Pakistan.

The Christianity of some regions on the fringe of Europe was being brought into line with Rome's customs and rites. After a band of English knights had occupied part of Ireland, King Henry, not wishing to see them establish a rival kingdom on the island, reminded them that he was their lord. He and a large invasion force would land in Ireland in October. Pope Alexander approved the conquest of Eire so long as Henry encouraged its people to embrace the same liturgy and traditions as the Catholics in England, setting aside certain distinctively Celtic practices. The same pontiff made an effort to more firmly integrate the people of Finland into Rome's fold.

In Sicily, as we have seen, the Christians were becoming ever more Latin. Margaret was eyeing some abandoned Greek monasteries on the eastern side of the island with a view to establishing Catholic houses for the religious orders, especially for nuns.

Building churches was becoming something of a competition, a kind of medieval one-upmanship, in Norman Sicily. Maio of Bari built San Cataldo to challenge the Martorana of George of Antioch next door; Matthew of Aiello built Saint Mary of the Latins in the Saqaliba district and later endowed the Magione in the Khalesa quarter, while Walter wanted to leave his mark on Palermo with a new cathedral. Each power player had his own "pet project."

A unique occasion occurred in the middle of 1171 when one of Margaret's most famous countrymen visited Sicily. It was to be the last noteworthy event of her regency.

Benjamin of Tudela

Benjamin of Tudela had been traveling around the eastern Mediterranean for years before reaching Sicily along his return route to Spain.[702]

Benjamin ben Jonah was born in the prosperous, multicultural town of Tudela around 1130. It will be remembered that this town came into the possession of Margaret's mother as a gift from Rotrou of Perche. Tudela was the most important center of learning in Navarre. During the twelfth century, Jews and Muslims made up at least half its population.

Benjamin was chiefly a rabbi and merchant, but his travel diary is the best record of its era for its descriptions of the Jewish populations of southern Europe and western Asia. It is also something of an ethnography, and a census of Jews. His expedition may have begun as a pilgrimage; it ended up being an adventure. Whilst there is some ambiguity about the precise dates that he passed through each place he describes, some in great detail, we know that he set out upon his journey from Zaragoza, in Aragon, in 1165. He followed the Ebro River to Tarragona before heading toward Barcelona and Girona. He then traveled along the French coast to Marseilles, where he boarded a galley that took him to Italy.

Here he stopped at Genoa, Lucca, Pisa and Rome before crossing the peninsula to Apulia, from whence he set sail for Greece. He visited Salonika and then Constantinople. From there, he followed the coast of Asia Minor southward. A highlight of his trip was the Kingdom of Jerusalem. Benjamin eventually made his way to Mosul and then opulent Baghdad, the largest city known. Next he ventured into Persia, and thenceforth into the desert of Arabia. It is thought that, embarking at Basra, he sailed around the peninsula and up the Red Sea to Egypt.

Whether by land or by sea, Benjamin and his companions arrived at Damietta and Cairo, taking time for an excursion to visit Alexandria. They then sailed from Damietta to Messina. This nautical voyage took almost three weeks.

Writing in Hebrew, Benjamin describes Messina and the orchards around it, mentioning that there were around two hundred Jews in the city. From there, it took him two days to arrive at Palermo, where some fifteen hundred Jews lived. He notes that there was still a large Muslim population in the capital.

Like Ibn Jubayr some years later, Benjamin of Tudela paints the picture of a splendid city full of gardens fed by rivers and springs. The royal palace and the mosaics of its chapel are mentioned.

Benjamin stayed at the royal court and among the city's Jews for a week or two. The queen doubtless enjoyed a chance to reminisce about Navarre with a native. His diary suggests that Benjamin visited Trapani, as he mentions the coral harvested there, but this is uncertain.

He saw Palermo's magnificent synagogue, described by a fifteenth-century visitor, Obadiah ben Abraham of Bertinoro, as a squarish structure boasting a splendid courtyard enclosed by a colonnade.[703]

Brief though his visit to Sicily was, Benjamin's account offers us information of the kind not readily found in other sources. It is invaluable for its insight by an outsider who saw good reason to note things unlikely to be pondered by a native who viewed them as commonplace. That, of course, is the great advantage of travelogues.

Benjamin of Tudela visited over three hundred localities, including such places as Saint Catherine's Monastery in the Sinai and various ancient archeological sites. Although he did not visit the African coast beyond Egypt, he covered the European and Asian parts of the Mediterranean world. In many of these areas, all three Abrahamic faiths flourished. By 1173 he was back in Spain. He seems to have died there in that year.

Majority

Late in 1171, William II reached the age of majority, ruling without a regent.[704]

There may have been a public celebration to mark the rite of passage. If so, the details of this birthday feast are unknown to us. As William was already a crowned monarch, there was no need for another coronation. Majority meant that he no longer had any need for tutors. Henceforth, Walter the archbishop would be an advisor but little more. The queen regent became the queen mother.

One of William's first acts as king ruling in his own right was to confirm to the Archbishop of Palermo the right to try adulterers (see note 704).

In the early days of May in 1172, the king and his young brother, Henry, who was then twelve, left with a large entourage for Taranto, where they were to meet Maria of Constantinople, to whom William was betrothed the previous year.[705] This was the first time that Margaret's sons left their mother's presence for more than a day or two.

Lost Princess

It had been agreed with Manuel I of Constantinople that his daughter would arrive with several galleys and a number of emissaries, knights, ladies-in-waiting and servants. A legation of Sicilian ambassadors had visited the Byzantine court to ensure that Maria, who was nearly two years older than William, was sufficiently healthy, intelligent and attractive to become Sicily's queen consort.

With the birth of her half-brother, Alexios, Maria was no longer Manuel's universal heir to the Byzantine throne, but she was just as eligible as any other princess to become William's bride, for her father's empire was an important ally. Unstated was another aspect of the union that was not to be overlooked.

In the event of the childhood death of her brother, who was not yet three, Maria would again become Manuel's heiress, an eventuality that might well open the door for William to claim the Byzantine Empire by marital right. This possibility did not escape Manuel or, for that matter, any other monarch whose interests touched Mediterranean shores, especially Frederick Barbarossa.

William waited at Taranto for about ten days. Presuming a timely departure from Constantinople, there was no immediate explanation for a delay in Maria's arrival. The seas were calm this time of year. The route of her flotilla would take Maria through the Aegean, following the Greek coasts into the Ionian to Corfu and then to Apulia.

Not wishing to spend too much time idly waiting, William left a company of prelates and nobles at Taranto to receive Maria while he and his brother went to pray at the sanctuary of Saint Michael on Mount Gargano, a site very important to the Hauteville dynasty. They then went to Barletta for a few days.

As the days passed, it became obvious that Maria was not going to arrive. An armed flotilla sailing through friendly coastal waters did not risk an attack by pirates, and there were no storms, so the royal court could only conclude that Manuel had reneged on his word. If that matter were not grave enough, the event itself left William greatly dismayed. The young man had expected to meet the woman who would be his wife. Instead, he departed Apulia without so much as an explanation for her failure to appear.

Not only was this annoying, it was highly offensive to royal dignity. The lack of an explanation, or indeed any communication, from the Byzantine court only added insult to injury.

Manuel I, admittedly, had other matters on his mind which may be construed to explain the situation, if only partially, as these involved maritime transport. The previous year had seen the beginning of a sea war pitting the Byzantines against the Venetians, who resented the emperor granting equal trade privileges to their perpetual rivals, the Genoans and Pisans. Most of these hostilities ended in 1172, not through battle but because of an epidemic of plague among the Venetians, but there were still isolated incidents. Only five years later was a formal truce negotiated.

Lost Prince

From Apulia, William and his company headed to the western side of the peninsula. Before long, he was passing through Benevento. At this point, young Henry began to complain of illness. The king thought it best to send his brother to Salerno. Not only did that city have a good medical school and exceptional physicians, it was a convenient port from which to embark for Sicily.

Matthew of Aiello and Archbishop Walter remained with William. Despite their concern for Henry, both *familiares* wanted to be as near to the king as possible.

From Salerno, young Henry returned by sea to Palermo accompanied by a small retinue. During the sea voyage, his physical condition did not improve. In Sicily, the illness only worsened. Henry died in the middle of June.

Having visited Capua, William soon headed to Salerno, where the royal galleys were waiting to take him to Sicily. He embarked without further delay and set sail for his capital. Upon reaching Palermo, William learned of his brother's death. He did not take it well.

But the political repercussions of young Henry's premature passing transcended even a family's anguish. His death brought with it dynastic ramifications that could change the course of history. The young prince had been first in line to the throne after William. Now there were no legitimate male heirs in sight.

Constance, the posthumous daughter of Roger II, would become heiress presumptive to the throne. It will be remembered that she was around William's age, even though she was his aunt. The idea that she might become queen in her own right was antithetical to the principle of Salic Law that excluded females from the line of succession; male primogeniture was the norm.

If Constance were to marry, her husband might rule in her name *jure uxoris,* by marital right. Until now, Constance's mother, Beatrice of Rethel, the widow of Roger II, had made no effort to find the girl a husband, and neither had Margaret. Married life did not seem to interest the young woman.

Finding William a wife to produce heirs was more important than ever. A proposal came from the Holy Roman Empire when ambassadors representing Frederick Barbarossa offered the hand of his daughter, Beatrix Hohenstaufen. This German offer was not accepted, but neither was it immediately refused. The issue was complex.

Margaret and William both knew that Pope Alexander and Frederick Barbarossa had yet to negotiate a peace with each other. Jeopardizing Sicily's rapport with the Papacy was not a good idea, especially now that papal support was being sought for the ambitious project at Monreale.

After careful contemplation, William refused to wed Frederick Barbarossa's daughter. The rebuke, accompanied as it was by William's refusal to negotiate a new treaty with the Holy Roman Emperor until the dispute was resolved, enraged Barbarossa.

Other monarchs were more willing to cultivate good relationships with the papacy, if only out of necessity. In England, Henry II reached what seemed like an accommodation with Alexander III in the wake of the Thomas Becket assassination.[706]

Faced with uprisings in France supported by his own sons, Henry could be forgiven for ignoring the subject of the betrothal of his daughter to the King of Sicily. Letters from the English king advised fellow monarchs of developments in his realm. One such letter arrived at Palermo. William responded amicably early in 1173.[707]

William II

The same year, Margaret visited the Nebrodian Mountains to inspect the monastery being built at Maniace. Several charters relating to the monasteries she founded in the region cite her authority exclusively.[708] We find, for example, the phrase *dominae Margaritae gloriosae reginae matri,* without William being mentioned explicitly.[709] Within a few years, Maniace became a vast network of holdings outside the ecclesiastical jurisdiction of the Archbishop of Messina, ceded to the authority of the abbot of Monreale.[710] Using the royal castle at San Marco d'Alunzio as her base, the queen mother exercised her authority with a certain degree of autonomy.

One of the people Margaret, as regent, had permitted to return from exile was Tancred of Lecce, the illegitimate grandson of Roger II who had participated in the Bonello revolt. During the middle of 1173, William decided to entrust the wayward prince with commanding a fleet to support a Fatimid uprising against Saladin's ambitious Ayyubid government, which had designs on the Holy Land.[711]

The plan, a response to a request by Amalric, the King of Jerusalem, was for the Sicilian fleet to land at Alexandria. Tancred's forces were to be supported by the Fatimid insurgents and, more importantly, an army sent by Amalric from Palestine. The attack was to take place in July of the following year. This meant that William had to invest in the construction of at least two hundred galleys at the shipyards of Messina and Brindisi.

If all went according to plan, William would assert his authority in the eastern Mediterranean. In July of 1174, the Sicilian fleet commanded by Tancred arrived at Alexandria to support the friendly Fatimids in their struggle against the adversarial Ayyubids. Here two unexpected problems presented themselves, and Tancred might have elected to abort the principal assault had he known about either one. In Egypt, Saladin had recently captured and killed the leaders of the Fatimid insurgency; in Palestine, Amalric had unexpectedly died, so no army arrived from Jerusalem. This left the Sicilians alone. Formidable as the landing force was, it was beaten back, suffering heavy losses. In the end, Tancred had to content himself with some raids along the African coast, while Saladin's acquisition of territory and power continued unabated.[712]

In England, the public act of penance by Henry II was the defining step in his spiritual rehabilitation. It paved the way for the Sicilian king to again solicit the English king for his daughter's hand in marriage. News reached the Sicilian court that William's cousin, Alfonso VIII of Castile, intended to resume his own plan to marry Eleanor, the daughter of Henry II, in view of the English monarch's formal reconciliation with the papacy.

LEADERSHIP

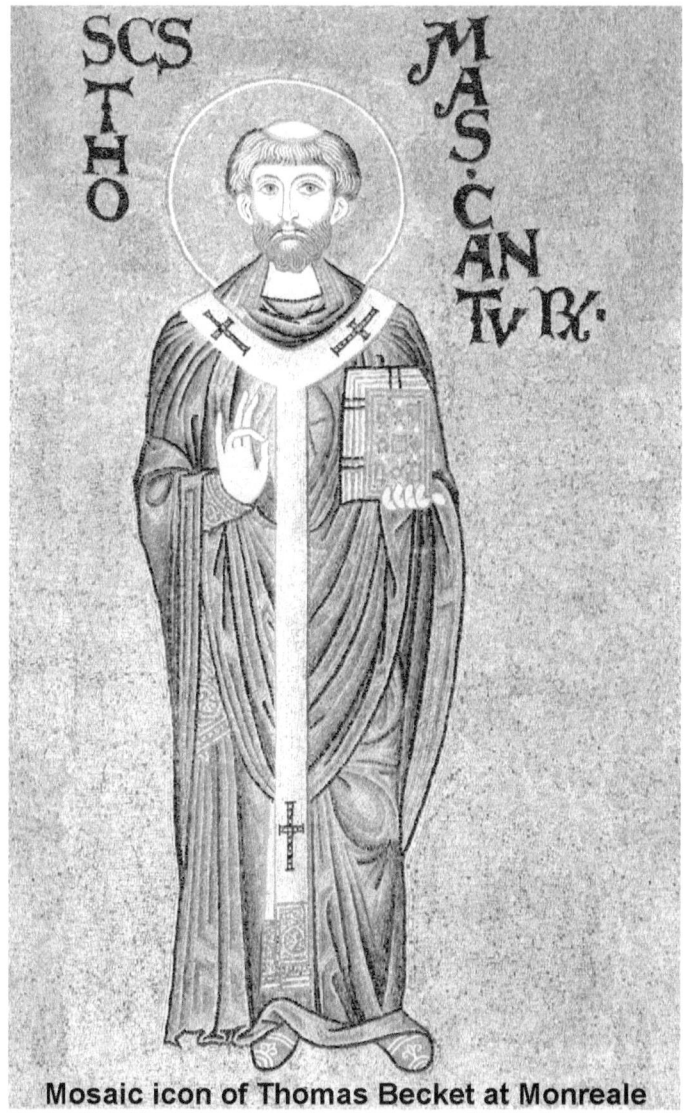

Mosaic icon of Thomas Becket at Monreale

Margaret's charter of November 1171 in Latin and Greek confirming privileges granted by Roger II to abbeys in the Nebrodian Mountains

Chapter 19

MULTICULTURAL MONASTERY

Places of worship embody the power of God and the identity of His people. In the *Regnum* during the Norman period, the very concept of royal patronage was concerned principally with Latin foundations, even if our monarchs occasionally lent their support to Greek churches, whilst protecting Jewish and Muslim communities. Though royal patronage might help to pave a monarch's path to Heaven, in the earthly realm it was, more immediately, a sign of power. Battlefield victories may be forgotten, but cathedrals were meant to last forever. Life was ephemeral; souls were eternal.

We find ladies mentioned in connection with churches from the very beginning of the Norman era, sometimes as patrons.[713] This was consistent with what occurred elsewhere in Europe. Reginal patronage, or matronage, reflected their use of "soft" power.

If we seek a singular, imposing benefice that epitomizes the favor of a medieval Sicilian queen, it is Monreale Abbey. Indeed, one might go so far as to suggest that familiarity with this place is a necessary key to understanding the intricate social, juridical and cultural rapport amongst the Sicilian monarchs, their subjects, and the papacy. Nothing in chronicles, letters and charters can prepare visitors for what awaits us in this unique monastic complex, where Komnenian, Norman, Fatimid and Provençal art come together in a syncretic symphony that transcends any single work or movement. It is here that one encounters the quintessential spirit of one of Sicily's greatest medieval queens and her son.

Invisible Hand

The planning and construction of Monreale's church and cloister began shortly after the end of Margaret's tumultuous regency of William II. As we have seen, this period found her efforts directed toward the abbey at Maniace and a nunnery outside San Marco d'Alunzio. Her most personal model, albeit a woman she scarcely knew, was her own mother, whose name appears in a charter of 1135 confirming certain privileges to the Diocese of Pamplona.[714]

As an exercise in power, Monreale reflected, amongst nobler motives, William's rebellion against the yoke of Archbishop Walter of Palermo, his onetime tutor. Wiley Walter wanted a new cathedral in Palermo. The zealous prelate was destined to get what he desired, but only following Margaret's death.

In its essence, Monreale's abbatial complex was similar to those elsewhere in western Europe, where the cloister was a normal component of most monasteries.[715]

Work on the abbey seems to have begun before papal confirmation arrived in 1174.[716] Margaret's name is not given as the issuer of any known decree involving its construction, or establishment of its Benedictine community. This is reasonable, both socially and juridically, for while Maniace, though an abbey (rather than a simple monastery), was small and geographically isolated, Monreale, from the outset, was to be large and very visible, literally standing guard over Palermo. There was a garrisoned castle dedicated to Saint Benedict, now called *Castellaccio,* on the mountain overlooking Monreale itself (the fortress can be seen from the Porta Felice gate near the Palermitan coast), to remind the Muslims on the other side that the erstwhile emirate was now a Catholic kingdom. The abbey itself, visible from the valley below, was surrounded by walls with embattled towers, and the church had two stout, crenelated towers of its own. Here was the ultimate symbol of royal authority and patronage, but, apart from its obvious purpose as a religious community, it was not meant to show the personal power of the queen mother. Rather, this was intended as a sign of the independence of Sicily's third king, the son whom Margaret had raised, and whose birthright she had adamantly defended for five years.

The architecture and art of Monreale were actually very different from Maniace, and altogether more complex. The church is, however, rather similar to Cefalù's cathedral and cloister, which were erected four decades earlier. Indeed, his grandfather's foundation of Cefalù's cathedral may well have inspired William II to make his own mark.

If Monreale was an exercise in defiance against Archbishop Walter, that was hardly its only statement. While the burgeoning Gothic movement was redefining ecclesial architecture across western Europe, Monreale's cathedral was conceived as an expression of the cultures of the Kingdom of Sicily consecrated to the glory of the Divine Maker in one place. Here, in one of Europe's most important realms, was proof that the eminently traditionalist Romanesque was not dead. For now, at least, gargoyles and grotesques would have to content themselves in other dominions.

Foundations

One of the peaks overlooking the Genoard park and hunting grounds to the immediate south of Palermo has come to be called *Mount Caputo.* Except perhaps for a tiny Arab village, the mountain was largely uninhabited until 1172.[717] Favored for its hunting, it afforded the visitor a commanding view of the city and the entire valley formed by the rugged mountains surrounding it. The site was known for its springs. With royal involvement, the place was renamed, appropriately enough, *Mons Regalis,* "Royal Mountain." It soon came to be called *Monreale.*

Writing long afterward, the chronicler Richard of San Germano believed that the construction of the abbey church at Monreale was suggested to the king by Matthew of Aiello. He further reports that Monreale reflected a certain diminution of Walter's effective power.[718]

Peter of Blois, like Walter a former tutor of the young king, seems to have surmised William's intention to distance himself from the archbishop upon reaching the age of majority, if not earlier. This the monarch did by interrupting his formal studies as soon as he could. Peter later exploited this fact to compare William II of Sicily unfavorably to a much older Henry II of England: "Although your king has studied well, ours is far more learned. In fact, I have had the chance to assess the practical education of both monarchs. As you know, the King of Sicily was my pupil for a year, having already studied with you to acquire a knowledge of general studies and literature. He was able to benefit from my special efforts to motivate him, but as soon as I departed from the kingdom he fell into the habit of reading frivolous books and enjoying royal pleasures."[719] There may be some truth in this, since few sovereigns were as erudite as Henry. However, Peter may have overlooked, or chosen not to see, William's quest for autonomy.

Although the King of Sicily and his guests could stay at the castle above Monreale, there would also be a comfortable palace on the north side of the church's apse (what remains of this edifice is now part of the city hall). From the highest floor of the palace, the royal family could see Palermo, just a short ride away, yet enjoy the privilege of being, quite literally, above the fray whose petty intrigues infested the court in the city far below.

From the outset, Monreale Abbey, officially "New Saint Mary's," was intended to be part of a vast monastic complex of the Benedictines, far larger than Saint John of the Hermits. The monks of Cava, near Salerno, were happy to oblige the king by sending some of their number to Monreale.

By longstanding tradition, major Benedictine abbeys like Cassino and Cava were autonomous, answering, through their order's hierarchy, to the pope himself. Local diocesan bishops had little say in monastic administration. Pope Alexander III granted Monreale's Benedictines a similar privilege.[720] This meant that they were outside Walter's jurisdiction. All he could do was watch as the new church took shape.

King William endowed the monastery with extensive lands and towns populated largely by Arabs: Corleone, Jato, Partinico, Battallario, Calatrasi.[721] The Arabs' villages bore names like *Rahal Algalid* and *Menzil Zarsun.* This was a vast, fertile territory bordering the Archdiocese of Palermo.

With papal and royal approval, the abbot of Monreale gradually obtained authority over numerous monastic estates in Sicily, such as those Margaret founded around Maniace, and some in regions as far afield as Apulia.

The greater part of the church's sturdy superstructure was completed by 1180. Although a Gothic cathedral of comparable size might take decades to build, a church like Monreale's could be completed in less time so long as the work went uninterrupted and there were enough men assigned to the project. Yet it would be another decade before most of the mosaics in the church, and the columns in the cloister, were completed, with some work continuing after 1190 and even into the next century.

Building such a monument required a monumental effort. What follows is a very concise overview.

The Church

Whether one refers to it as a basilica, *duomo* or cathedral, the church around which Monreale was built is impressive. The layout is a classic cross plan with a transept. The two massive towers were meant to serve as fortifications. The floor area measures slightly over four thousand square meters (more than forty thousand square feet), the nave being just over a hundred meters (at three hundred thirty feet) in length.

The nave is positioned generally, though not precisely, on an east-west axis *ad orientem,* with the apse toward the east. This tradition dates from the early centuries of the church in Greece and elsewhere in Europe. In former times, the celebrant faced the altar and apse during liturgy; this is still true in Orthodoxy, and it was the case in Catholicism until the twentieth century, when altars were repositioned so that the priest faced the congregants.

There was initially a Byzantine *templon,* essentially a low iconostasis (icon screen), separating the sanctuary from the nave.

Inside the church is a wide central aisle between two narrower ones, for a total nave width of forty meters. Eighteen columns support the arches. These pillars were not built for the church; they were taken from a temple in Rome, and many of their capitals bear the likeness of Roma, one of that city's deities.[722] Most of the columns are made of syenite, an igneous rock very similar to granite but bereft of more than rare traces of quartz. It takes its name from Syene (Aswan) on the Nile, where the Romans quarried it.

The church's wooden roof replaces the one destroyed by fire in 1811. The original ceiling had muqarnas "stalactites" similar to those of the chapel in the palace in Palermo.

An interesting detail is the occasional use of *strata* of timber between some of the large stones of which the thick walls are constructed; this serves as a soft buffer to absorb seismic shock that creates fissures during earthquakes.

Among the distinctively Arab features are the geometric motifs of the exterior of the three apses, typical of Fatimid designs.

The Mosaics

What most strikes the visitor are the walls covered with mosaics set upon an endless field of gold tesserae. At six thousand three hundred and forty square meters (nearly seventy thousand square feet), thus eclipsing the wall area of the mosaics of Saint Mark's in Venice by around thirty percent, this is the largest medieval display of its kind in Italy. It was inspired by the mosaics of the Palatine Chapel in Palermo.

Many figures are icons, while others are Biblical scenes. The Old Testament is depicted on the walls of the central aisle. The mosaics of the lateral aisles and those above the sanctuary depict the New Testament. Some are accompanied by inscriptions in Latin or Greek. The Biblical cycle was readily understood and appreciated by most worshippers, accustomed as they were to hearing these stories and parables. For others, the mosaics themselves were instructive, perhaps prompting the occasional explanation of a Biblical detail by monks to visitors.

All the saints but one are venerated in the Orthodox church. The lone exception is Thomas Becket, depicted in the central apse. It is unsurprising to see Queen Margaret's saintly patron, elusive Margaret of Antioch, guarding her tomb.

Overlooking the royal thrones in the presbytery, one mosaic shows King William II offering the church to the Virgin Mary, while another shows the same king being crowned by Christ, recalling the mosaic in Palermo's Martorana depicting Roger II receiving the crown from Jesus; here the symbols on his robe are clearly crosses. The two lions *passant guardant* facing each other in the triangular mosaic immediately above the royal throne on the north wall resemble the heraldic beasts in the royal coat of arms of England (displayed by English kings beginning with Richard Lionheart) and the lions flanking the royal throne dais in the Palatine Chapel in Palermo's Norman Palace.

Dominating everything is the imposing icon of Christ Pantocrator, "Ruler of All," looking down from high in the central apse above the main altar. At thirteen meters wide and seven meters high, this is thought to be the largest medieval image of the Pantocrator to survive. Indeed, the extent of Monreale's mosaics dwarfs that of any similar display that survives from the Middle Ages in what was once the Byzantine world. Beneath the Pantocrator is the *Theotokos,* the Mother of God; below this is a window of fine Fatimid design. (See this volume's map section for a diagram describing some images.)

The dating of the mosaics is usually based on the comparison of certain styles and compositions seen in particular images to those of artists whose work is present in other churches. It is through this (imperfect) method that specific figures or renderings are identified with one artist or another. It is believed that some of the mosaicists were monks from the Grottaferrata monastery near Rome, others from Greece (see note 310).

The Cloister

If Monreale's mosaics leave an impression, so does its large cloister. The colonnade is formed of two hundred twenty-eight pillars, most in pairs.

The Fatimid fountain in one corner is very similar to the one in Palazzo Falson in Mdina, Malta. The water spouts from the faces of men and lions carved in relief into a sphere set upon a column of zigzag motifs. When the water spurts out, the fountain's ensemble gives the appearance of a palm tree, representing life. The fountain was probably intended to be placed in the center of the cloister in representation of the spring of eternal life in the garden of paradise of all three Abrahamic faiths.

Most of the cloister and its decoration are essentially Provençal in style. Some of the same artisans carved similar capitals at Maniace and elsewhere. The columns and capitals in Cefalù's cloister are quite similar.

The columns were carved by a number of sculptors working under a few masters who seem to have been Provençal, Greek, Norman and Lombard (northern Italian). This explains the widely varying styles, themes and symbolism, from Biblical and mythological scenes and figures to representations of kings, Norman knights and Arab warriors.

There are archers, lions, mermen, boars, and Norman knights bearing long shields devoid of heraldic devices. The Arab warriors are depicted holding round shields. Also present are owls with monks' heads symbolizing vigilance. There are grapes representing autumn and even the depiction of blowing leaves. One scene shows lions devouring men and stags.

The double-tailed mermaid sitting among the evangelists and their symbols is Melusina. Her presence here may not be entirely coincidental, for a legend says that Eleanor of Aquitaine, and therefore her daughter Joanna, Queen of Sicily, were descended from Melusina, presumably through the Merovingians and Angevins. The family of Joanna's father, Henry II of England, boasted some of the same lineage.[723]

Along the eastern colonnade is a capital showing William II offering the cathedral to the Blessed Virgin Mary and Baby Jesus.

A few capitals are particularly informative about aristocratic life. Though we have no written record detailing tournaments involving participation of a "Sicilian William Marshal," the jousting knights suggest that such things existed here in the Kingdom of Sicily, as in England and France.

Most of the carved images are reasonably clear expressions of myth, scripture or the social currents of their age. They seem intended to be understood by informed observers. There are no cryptic messages or symbols that could be viewed as "esoteric."

The columns themselves vary in design superficially. Some bear sculpted motifs while others are decorated in patterns with mosaic tiles. The alternating pairing of smooth and decorated columns was meant to create a subliminal sense of endless movement linked to the infinity of God or Allah. (A few designs are indicated in a diagram in the map section.)

Bordering the cloister are a refectory and dormitory. Beyond these is a large courtyard, the *belvedere,* from which the entire Gulf of Palermo is visible, as well as the mountains to the south where the smallholdings of the Arabs were located. In Altofonte, across the valley, is the royal chapel of Saint Michael and a segment of a wall of a small castle (now part of the mother church) that served as a hunting lodge.

The Royal Tombs

Queen Margaret and two of her sons, Roger and Henry, whose remains were transferred from Mary Magdalene in Palermo, rest in the north semitransept. In the opposite (south) semitransept are the two Williams.[724]

Margaret's original sarcophagus was porphyry, which preserved her body remarkably well until 1811, when lightning struck the cathedral's wooden roof, setting off a fire. Fed by the resinous Nebrodian fir (a timber harvested in northern Sicily) of which the ceiling was constructed, the flames severely damaged her tomb and those of her sons Roger and Henry. The queen's remains were subsequently placed into a sarcophagus constructed in 1846 modelled on the original one but made of marble. An epitaph in mosaic appears in the wall above the tomb.

Nearby is an altar dedicated to Saint Louis of France, who died whilst crusading in Tunisia. Here his heart is preserved (see note 31).

The Bronze Doors

Two impressive sets of bronze double doors bearing panels depicting biblical scenes grace the church. Forged in 1186, the doors beneath the main portico at the end of the nave are by Bonanno "Pisano" of Pisa, architect of his city's leaning tower. The pair of Byzantine design under the north portico is the work of Barisano of Trani. Similar bronze doors designed by both sculptors are conserved in churches elsewhere in Italy.

Palermitan Benefices

By early 1178, a number of Margaret's projects were nearing completion. An impressive church, dedicated to the Holy Spirit, was being erected outside Palermo's city walls near the Oreto River.[725] It was given to the Cistercians but assigned to the episcopal jurisdiction of Archbishop Walter, perhaps as something of a consolation to him for the lack of a new cathedral in Palermo.[726] Indeed, Walter was showing himself to be uncharacteristically cooperative in order that he might obtain royal support for the grand church he envisaged; he even conceded some additional rights to Monreale's abbot.[727]

In addition to recent foundations, the crown supported a number of existing monasteries. Amongst the Benedictine abbeys outside local episcopal jurisdiction was one in Calabria where the poet William of Blois had once been the abbot.[728]

A King's Reign

Even though he probably looked to his counsellors and his mother for advice, William, at twenty, was no longer a mere boy.[729] Much as we may ascribe many of the efforts at Monreale to Margaret, we must not overlook the king's role. Nevertheless, monarchical rule was "collective" in significant ways.

Romuald of Salerno and his fellow Salernitan, Matthew of Aiello, who seem to have shared the king's suspicion of Archbishop Walter, may well have encouraged the foundation of Monreale. Both were benefactors of their own projects. Matthew famously constructed the church of the Magione for the Cistercians, who interred Tancred of Lecce and his son there, though both tombs were later cast out by Henry VI and Constance Hauteville (see note 25).

Monreale's abbot was permitted to wear a mitre and exercise authority similar to that of a bishop. This was a rare ecclesiastical rank. A mitred abbot was, indeed, accorded a status almost equal to that of a bishop. The first monks took up residence in Monreale in 1176. An indication of the abbot's power is the fact that by 1177 charters identified him as a bishop even though he was not yet consecrated as such. Monreale became a metropolitan archdiocese in February 1183.[730]

A Popular Aesthetic

The large monastic complex of Monreale is one of the most imposing physical exemplifications of the thriving culture of the *Regnum*.

It is fair to say that the various elements of the kingdom's artistic, cultural and social syncretism were greater than the sum of their parts, together forming something unique, or at least highly distinctive. Each component contributed to the aesthetic, even ideological, character of Hautevillian society and its ideals, to coalesce into a comprehensive whole. Certainly, a great degree of planning is evident at sites like the Palatine Chapel and the abbeys of Monreale and Cefalù.

In part, the cosmopolitanism probably reflected a desire to transcend a slavish *Normanitas*. More than a rigidly conceived "grand design," however, it was the result of a natural development in view of the presence of varied cultural influences. The monarchs and their people were intrinsic to an evolution rooted in what, by the end of the twelfth century, defined the kingdom itself.

Though this visual aesthetic was inherited by the Hohenstaufens, their thirteenth century is identified more closely with essential fortifications and, in the ecclesiastical sphere, certain subtle Gothic influences over the Romanesque; the Swabians brought us Castel del Monte in Puglia and the basilica of Saint Francis of Assisi in Palermo.[731]

Beyond architecture, the Norman era found art, dress, jewelry, iconography and the written word complementing each other seamlessly, with nary an element ever seeming out of place. Visually arresting as they are, the crowns, garb and other imagery never deviate from what the viewer expects to see. This harmony results from a fusion of sundry precursors, as if mythos were meeting ethos.

Despite its sophistication, the manifestation of this material culture was intended to be understood and appreciated by all. While it might be explained to those encountering it, or to modern observers, by a teacher or guide, it was never meant exclusively for an educated elite consisting of "experts" but for the general populace. Naturally, prior knowledge varied from one visitor to another, but nothing in the mosaics or capitals of Monreale, or the painted muqarnas ceiling of the Palatine Chapel a few miles away, was designed to be cryptic or esoteric.

In an era that sometimes finds the very study of the Middle Ages characterized by some critics as "ornamental," as if the medieval era were extraneous or irrelevant to the essential needs of modern society, polyculture brings us a timeless message.

Monreale's cathedral and monastery epitomize the visual, even spiritual, union of faiths and faith. Here humility is caressed by the shadow of greatness.

Apse of Monreale Cathedral viewed from the roof

Fatimid fountain in Monreale's cloister

Apse of Monreale Cathedral viewed from the nave

Corner of Monreale's cloister near the Fatimid fountain

Chapter 20
REIGN

By 1175, King William II of Sicily had launched a military campaign and secured jurisdictional independence for a major abbey he had founded. If actions spoke louder than words, there could be little doubt about his authority, and no question of his maturity.

In September of that year, he signed a twenty-year peace with the Venetians to protect shipping and trade. Following a rather similar agreement with the Genoans, who had extensive interests in the *Regnum,* it excluded galleys in the service of the Byzantine Empire from the protection of the King of Sicily.[732] For the moment, the diplomatic rapport of the Venetians with Frederick Barbarossa was not quite so cordial. Considering their lingering difficulties with Manuel of Constantinople, this left the Venetians with William as one of their most important allies, another being the pope. By now, Barbarossa had another antipope in his camp, John of Struma, known to supporters as Callixtus III.

The real pope, Alexander III, knew that William had refused a political alliance that would have been facilitated by marrying Barbarossa's daughter who, as fate would have it, died in 1174.

As we have seen, William had even postponed planning a marriage to a young daughter of Henry II of England until that king might return to papal graces. Late in 1175, Alexander decided to remind Henry about the agreement made with Queen Margaret before Thomas Becket's murder. Henry, for his part, needed solid alliances as much as Alexander needed safe borders.

Joanna of England

Joanna had been raised, for the most part, in France with her mother,

Eleanor of Aquitaine, the estranged wife of Henry II. Queen Eleanor had taken her sons' side in their war against her husband, a conflict that ended in September 1174. Although this was not the royal couple's only marital squabble, it led to Henry imprisoning his own wife in England; in 1176 Eleanor was living under "house arrest" in Winchester.

We know far more about the details of the betrothal of Joanna of England to William of Sicily than we do about the great majority of royal unions negotiated in Europe during the twelfth century. So complete are the surviving records of it that the event is the very archetype of royal weddings in this era of the history of the *Regnum*.[733]

To ensure that all went well, William's mother turned to a trusted prelate, Rotrou of Rouen, the kinsman who had sent Stephen of Perche to her court years earlier. Rotrou offered to go to England to meet with Henry. Accompanying him were two bishops, Elias of Troia and Arnolf of Capaccio, along with a faithful nobleman and justiciar, Florio of Camerota. With a company of knights and servants, these four ambassadors reached England early in April 1176.

There was never really any doubt that Henry would consent to this marriage; he had already agreed to its conditions a few years earlier. In the meantime, as we have seen, he had also approved the betrothal of another daughter to William's cousin, the King of Castile.

Nevertheless, the King of England followed the formality of meeting in council with the prelates and high nobles of his court to grant his royal assent before sending William's ambassadors to meet Joanna at Winchester.

Considering Joanna's tender years, this was a precocious betrothal even by the standards of the twelfth century; the girl was six months shy of her eleventh birthday.

At Winchester, the ambassadors were presented to Eleanor, who permitted them to meet the young princess. Her beauty and poise were obvious enough. The men were curious about the girl's health and intelligence.

Communication was no obstacle, as Joanna spoke French. The men asked her a few questions. Having heard something about the fiery temperaments of her mother and father, they were at least a little interested in Joanna's personality.

Eleanor and her daughter probably had a few questions about William, especially if, perchance, the Queen of England, who had visited Palermo many years earlier during the reign of Roger II, had heard the rumor that the King of Sicily kept a harem. The ambassadors overwhelmingly approved of Joanna.

Brooking no delay, they made their way back to London to discuss the betrothal details with the king. There they explained that, as Queen of Sicily, Joanna would receive a large dower that included, among other lucrative manors, the wealthy county of Mount Sant'Angelo.

Rotrou of Rouen was present, along with Cardinal Hugh Pierleoni, the pope's permanent ambassador to the English court. Henry's next step was to send his own ambassadors to Palermo to convey his personal greetings to William, his future son-in-law.

Meanwhile, the Sicilian ambassadors, Elias, Arnolf and Florio, remained in England as Henry's guests whilst Joanna and her ladies-in-waiting prepared for the voyage, as the three would accompany her to Sicily. The party would be ready to depart in four months.

Henry visited his daughter during the middle of August to wish her well, and to remind her of the importance of the role she was about to assume.

The Journey to Sicily

In October, Henry received a letter from William thanking him and setting forth some details of Joanna's journey.[734] The day of the departure eventually arrived. Joanna embraced her mother, Eleanor, knowing she might never see her again. Her retinue then set out for Sicily with a large company of prelates and nobles. With them Henry sent his future son-in-law gifts of fine horses, clothes, gold and silver, and precious vases.

The English royal party included Archbishop Richard of Canterbury and Bishop Geoffrey of Ely, along with Bishop Giles of Evreux and Hugh of Beauchamp. Among the travelers was Hamelin of Warenne, King Henry's half-brother. Not all of these clerics, courtiers and kinsmen would accompany Joanna all the way to Sicily. Some would go only as far as Saint-Gilles, on the French coast, where a flotilla of Sicilian galleys would meet Joanna. Elias of Troia, Arnolf of Capaccio and Florio of Camerota, being William's ambassadors, were to travel with the company to Palermo.

Joanna, of course, was the youngest of the travelers, and one of the few women. On the leg of the journey over land, the large royal party, with its many wagons, traveled much more slowly than a pair of couriers or a company of knights would have ridden over the same distance.

Having crossed the English Channel, the company was met in Normandy by Joanna's eldest brother, Henry the Young King, who accompanied them to Poitiers. From there, her brother Richard escorted the company southward through Aquitaine. In late November, Joanna and her suite arrived at Saint-Gilles, where twenty-odd Sicilian galleys were waiting for them. She had just celebrated her eleventh birthday.

Unfortunately, the two galleys bearing precious gifts that William had sent his father-in-law were lost at sea. This was reported by Bishop John of Norwich, one of Henry's returning ambassadors, who described a terrible voyage from Messina to Saint-Gilles.

Leading the Sicilian flotilla were Alfano, Archbishop of Capua, Richard Palmer, Bishop of Syracuse, and Robert, Count of Caserta. Most of the royal retinue embarked, but Richard of Canterbury and Geoffrey of Ely returned to England to report to Henry that the first part of the journey was successful.

The galleys set out along the Italian coast, occasionally stopping along the way. The waters of the Tyrrhenian, the same sea that had claimed the galleys carrying gifts for King Henry, were choppy this time of year. Joanna was unaccustomed to sea travel. She suffered a bout of sea sickness that necessitated stops along the coast more frequent that what had been planned.

Joanna and her suite finally reached the waters of the Kingdom of Sicily. They disembarked at Naples to celebrate Christmas and give Joanna a few days' rest. At this point it was decided to travel over land, stopping at Salerno and Calabria. This took longer than an itinerary by sea, but it was less injurious to Joanna's physical condition. It also offered the advantage of affording her a glimpse of the peninsular part of the *Regnum*. Naples was gradually increasing in population and importance, while Salerno, with its splendid cathedral and palace, was one of the kingdom's most important cities.

Royal Wedding

When Joanna reached Palermo in early February 1177, William was waiting for her at one of the city's eastern gates. It was nearly nightfall when Bishop Giles of Evreux presented her to the King of Sicily. Joanna mounted a palfrey and rode with William through a city lit by lamps and torches. Exultant crowds hailed the couple and their endless entourage.

Accompanied by her ladies-in-waiting and servants, the bride-to-be was lodged at the Zisa palace on the other side of the Genoard.[735]

On Sunday, the thirteenth, Joanna was wed to William in the chapel of the royal palace beneath the benevolent gaze of the Pantocrator. Here she was crowned and anointed Queen of Sicily.

On this occasion, according to Romuald of Salerno, William was crowned for the second time, *in cappella sua desponsavit, et se et eam gloriose coronari fecit, et solemnes de illa nuptias celebravit*.[736] The nuptials and twin coronations were performed by Archbishop Walter, who could finally enjoy the satisfaction and prestige of having crowned a king.

Back in England, Henry and Eleanor received a report of the magnificent event. The only disappointment was the loss of the two galleys transporting gifts for Henry and, perhaps, for Eleanor.

One of the gifts Joanna brought for her mother-in-law was sent from Bishop Reginald of Bath. This was a gold reliquary, formed into a pendant, bearing relics of martyred Thomas Becket (see Appendix 2). Significantly, it reflects the widespread extent of the veneration of Saint Thomas of Canterbury that existed in 1177. Joanna could be counted among those who accorded the saint a special devotion; in Spain, her sister, Leonor, erected a shrine to him in Toledo's cathedral.

Joanna may be credited with introducing a troubadour tradition at court not unlike that of southern France. Her mother tongue, which she learned in childhood, was actually Occitan, the *langue d'oc*.

Peace

In July, Romuald of Salerno, along with Roger of Andria, represented William at the negotiations that culminated in the Treaty of Venice.[737] Apart from the treaty specific to the Kingdom of Sicily bearing the golden imperial seal, the emperor swore pacts with the papacy and the Italian communes. Abandoning his support of an antipope, Frederick Barbarossa recognized Alexander III as pontiff. Peace with the *Regnum* was to last at least fifteen years, that with the imperial communes six.[738]

South of the Alps, the chief effect of this heretofore elusive treaty, delivered by the emperor's emissaries during a visit at William's court in May the next year, was a rare era of peace over the next few years. For the Kingdom of Sicily, it meant domestic security throughout William's reign. It generally established a more amicable rapport with Barbarossa, whose son, young Henry, is mentioned in the treaty as his heir, having already been crowned King of the Germans.

The *Regnum,* like other European kingdoms, had its shortcomings. Romuald of Salerno recounts a peculiar incident that occurred following the meeting in Palermo. According to established practice, Barbarossa's ambassadors were escorted from Sicily northward through the *Regnum* on their return by a company of knights led by a military commander.[739] This journey proceeded through the mountains without incident until the party reached the wooded environs of Lagonegro at the northern boundary of Calabria. There they were attacked by a large crowd of peasants. The ambassadors sought refuge in a house which the peasants assaulted by hurling stones. The crowd of thieves managed to seize the trunk borne by one of the ambassadors, stealing a silver cup and the royal charter William was sending to Frederick; their interest in the charter was its gold seal.

As soon as the company reached Salerno, they reported the incident. Romuald, who had recently established his residency in the city, thus heard about it, and notified the king. Enraged at the news, William immediately sent justiciars to the scene of the crime with an armed force bearing explicit orders to find, try and hang the perpetrators. The robbers were found at Barletta, Troia, Salerno, Capua and San Germano, and duly hung publicly to send a message that law and order would prevail in the kingdom. William then issued another charter bearing a gold seal and sent it to Frederick.

Another violent incident occurred around the same time at Faiano, near Salerno, when Matthew, a Benedictine abbot, was hacked to pieces with swords and lances; some claimed this murder was instigated by monks who hated the unpopular cleric. Led by Florio of Camerota, William's justiciars investigated the crime, learning that, indeed, the peasants who did the killing were acting on the orders of some local monks. Speedy justice in this case made it clear that clerics were not exempt from royal authority.[740]

Some subjects were disgruntled for legitimate reasons. Nearer the capital, Monreale's abbot, being the feudal lord of a chunk of the Sicilian hinterland comparable to a vast barony, was beginning to act the part of a zealous baron. When several Muslims, not wishing to accept their status as his serfs, left the territory only to be repatriated, the perfervid prelate made the men swear on the Koran never to leave again, for they were tied to the land.

William occasionally had to travel around the *Regnum,* accompanied at times by Matthew of Aiello. By now, the king probably had other trusted advisors, nearer his own age, whose names are unknown to posterity. Then there were the older advisors he consulted often: Tancred of Lecce, the abbot Theobald of Monreale, the justiciar Florio of Camerota.

Romuald of Salerno had retired from the court and his chronicle ends in 1178. In the following year he attended the reformative Third Lateran Council, which, perhaps at his urging, infamously condemned the Albigensians as heretics.[741]

Amongst the many architectural projects being undertaken was construction of a palace similar in style to the Zisa, though slightly smaller. Situated on the opposite side of the Genoard, near the Kemonia River not far from the road leading to Monreale, the Cuba, being surrounded by a lake, was equally impressive. Like the Zisa, the Cuba, which takes its name from the Arabic *qubba,* "cupola," is still standing.[742] Giovanni Boccaccio later mentioned it in his *Decameron,* where it is a setting in the sixth story of the fifth day, involving John of Procida.

Manuel I Comnenus of Constantinople died in 1180, leaving his heirs to fight over the Byzantine succession. The best way to ensure against such a catastrophe in the Kingdom of Sicily was for William to have a few sons. It may be presumed that Joanna was living with her husband by then, when she was fifteen.

It was long believed that during 1181 Joanna gave birth to a child, rumored to have been named Bohemond and to have died in infancy. However, only one chronicler, Robert of Torigni, reports the event, and he was not in Sicily. Significant as his chronicles are, Robert's statement about Bohemond is probably inaccurate.[743]

Robert of Torigni also tells us that the same year, 1181, saw the arrival in Palermo of an embassy from Tunisia that confirmed a decade-long treaty with the Kingdom of Sicily. The Arabs state that a Sicilian embassy went to Mahdia to meet the Almohad caliph, Abu Yaqub Yusuf (Yusuf I). The impromptu impetus for this trade accord was an event that occurred two years earlier, when a Sicilian flotilla encountered a floundering ship taking the caliph's daughter to her wedding to a Muslim emir and returned the girl to her grateful father.[744] The agreement found the *Regnum* supplying much-needed grain to Tunisia.

His exact date of birth is unknown to us, but when Romuald Guarna of Salerno died in 1181 he may have been seventy. This distinguished prelate, politician, diplomat and chronicler was succeeded as Archbishop of Salerno by Nicholas of Aiello.

Tasks

Pope Alexander III, who had long been an ally, died in August 1181. His most lasting achievement was the Third Lateran Council, largely a dilatory attempt to curtail corruption and make the papacy more efficient. Many occupants of the See of Peter were wicked misanthropes. Alexander, a true man of God, was the exception. His successor was Ubaldo Allucingoli, an octogenarian cardinal who took the name Lucius III. Perhaps not surprisingly in view of his age, Lucius was a bit of a reactionary; his pontificate was destined to last just four years.

It would take longer than that for William to realize his next project.

Monreale's splendid church was clearly visible from Palermo. It was an impressive sight that envious Archbishop Walter could not ignore. The king began to contemplate the avaricious prelate's request for a new cathedral in Palermo. It was normal to draft the details of such a project a year or two before construction was scheduled to begin. In this case, the availability of a work force was a determining factor; these hundreds, even thousands, of men would not be free until the structural work on Monreale was complete.

The dimensions of the new cathedral would compensate for whatever it lacked in beauty. As the church of the Primate of Sicily, it would be larger than any other cathedral in the *Regnum*. Its nave was intentionally longer than that of Monreale's *duomo*.

The squarish nave of Palermo's earlier basilica, which had been altered by such details as muqarnas when it was converted to a mosque, was perpendicular to that of the new cathedral being planned; a few parts of this original structure would be preserved.

The cathedral Walter inherited was already somewhat larger than what William and Margaret were building at Monreale. Writing in the tenth century, the visitor Muhammad ibn Hawqal, who knew magnificent mosques in his native Baghdad, described what was then the Great Friday Mosque of Palermo as being large enough to accommodate seven thousand worshippers. It had at least seven large mihrabs; what is thought to be the vestige of one of these can still be seen near the stairs leading down to the crypt.

Except for the later addition of a Catalan Gothic portico and an unsightly cupola, the exterior has been altered rather little over the centuries. Unfortunately, most of the interior, which is now covered in stucco, reveals very little of the original Romanesque design, which featured Norman, Fatimid and Byzantine details.

William and his mother had a personal concern about the construction of Walter's cathedral. Attached to Palermo's original basilica was the chapel dedicated to Mary Magdalene that housed the royal tombs. Plans called for these to be transferred to another church of the same name to be hastily built at a site nearby.[745]

In January of 1182, a series of storms swept across southern peninsular Italy that seem to have had hurricane force. A contemporary chronicler claims, perhaps accurately, that agriculture was affected.[746]

Politically, the *Regnum* was more serene. Except for sending a flotilla to the island of Majorca as part of a half-hearted Christian effort to oust the Muslims, William's military exploits during this period were few.[747] Most of his time was occupied with domestic affairs. Elsewhere, however, events transpired that had a subtle ripple effect on the Kingdom of Sicily.

In April 1182, the Greeks of Constantinople, incited perhaps by Andronikos Comnenus (see Table 6), erupted against the many Italian merchants in the city. Few of the victims in this "Massacre of the Latins" were Sicilian and even fewer were Venetian; most were Genoan or Pisan.[748] Yet many Roman Catholics were attacked and killed indiscriminately. Not even the papal ambassador was spared. This prompted William and other European monarchs west of the Adriatic to contemplate an invasion of the Byzantine territories. However, the Kingdom of Sicily still had a treaty with the Byzantine Empire. Andronikos seems to have had his cousin, the young emperor Alexios II, son of Manuel I, killed so that he could have himself enthroned. For good measure, he also eliminated Maria "Porphyrogenita," who was once betrothed to William II.

By January 1183, William was making one of his periodic tours of the peninsular part of the *Regnum*, visiting Capua, Salerno and the Benedictine abbey at Cassino, among other localities.[749] With the vice chancellor and the *familiare* Archbishop Walter attending the king during his travels, the two queens, Margaret and Joanna, were left in charge at Palermo as the *de facto* "governors" of Sicily in William's absence.[750]

Meanwhile, the new pope, Lucius III, erected Monreale into a metropolitan archdiocese.[751]

William was back in the capital by April, when he issued a charter relegating to serfdom a great number of Sicily's rural Muslims.[752] By now, this was a general policy.

These Muslims were hardly the only subjects to organize themselves to act against the law. On the peninsula, the constables and justiciars sought to capture the leader of a large band of outlaws perpetrating robberies and other crimes. The head of this group, the so-called *Vendicosi* (Avengers), was identified as a certain Adenolfo, from Pontecorvo, who may have been an aristocrat, and it is possible that he was abetted by the clergy.[753] The *Vendicosi* do not seem to have been connected to the peasants who robbed the German ambassadors a few years earlier. Although this "Robin Hood" phenomenon may not have been very widespread, robbery in the countryside was not at all unusual.

Queen Margaret, who was now forty-eight, died at the end of July. A few days later, her funeral at Monreale, where she was interred, was attended by thousands who hiked up the mountain to commemorate their queen. The chief celebrant was a certain William, recently consecrated as Archbishop of Monreale.

The queen's epitaph is eloquent in its simplicity: "Here in regal dignity lies Queen Margaret, distinguished by her noble spirit, the consort of a king, the mother of princes, the regent for King William II the son she bore. Commended to Heaven on the Feast of Saint Peter in Chains, in the year one thousand one hundred and eighty-three. Amen."[754]

In a sense, her death presaged the end of an era.

Margaretine Retrospective

The outlines of Margaretine policy may be inferred from the queen's actions in the name of her son. Even as her official duties ended with the arrival of William's majority and the inception of his personal (active) rule as king, the abbeys of Monreale, Maniace and several smaller foundations would reflect the last tangible effects of a series of reginal efforts.

Rarely have historians debated the merits of Margaret's decisions as regent.

Most often, in histories of the *Regnum* written by men, there is no debate whatsoever, with Margaret ignored altogether. By tradition, and into recent times (and arguably even our own), the overwhelming majority of men in southern Italy were inclined to take very little true account of female merit beyond women's roles as wives, mothers and wenches. That a woman might exercise authority in the social or political spheres was a prerogative of a few ladies in the aristocracy.

Yet even the works authored by women fail to mention this singular woman, who held the reins of power longer than Constance Hauteville, the Sicilian queen of this era who receives the most attention from historians (see note 23).

But whereas Constance is generally, if inaccurately, seen as a royal woman "born to be queen," Margaret's destiny never envisaged her as more than a regent. In the event, the "girl from Pamplona" rose to the occasion dutifully, unequivocally, gloriously. Following in the footsteps of predecessors such as Adelaide del Vasto, and perhaps even her own Norman mother, Margaret was a feminist before feminism.

We have seen the complexity in the historiography that relates to her. Except for a few charters and fewer letters, most of what we know of Margaret of Navarre comes to us from a single source, the curmudgeonly chronicler Hugh Falcandus.

For a few years after William reached the age of majority, Margaret continued to advise him, though little is known with exactness about her role during this period except for her support of the abbeys mentioned above. This period, which might be defined as a *post-regency,* existed in other kingdoms as well, especially when royal kin were few, leaving mother and son to govern the realm with little help from an extended family.

At about the age of thirty-six in 1171, Margaret, like Adelaide before her, could have remarried. Even in the Middle Ages, there were women of forty or fifty who were considered attractive, perhaps ravishing. Instead, the life of the queen regent segued to that of queen mother.

In an age that often sees womanhood itself reduced to prurience and even exploitation, with royal women, now called *princesses* and often regarded as little more than celebrities, it is important to view Margaret and her contemporary queens for what they really were. Here was the fullness of womanhood in its timeless magnificence.

Jubayr

In May of 1184, a major earthquake struck Calabria with enough force to collapse Cosenza's cathedral.[755] Accompanied by Joanna, the king went to direct efforts to assist the population.

In December of that year, the traveler Abu Hussain Muhammad bin Ahmad ibn Jubayr was shipwrecked at Messina, where he was given hospitality by an Arabic-speaking King of Sicily. His Sicilian travels took him westward by ship, with stops at Cefalù, Termini, Solunto and finally Palermo.

Following a week in the capital, he departed by land for Trapani, passing Alcamo along the way.

Among many other details, he describes several castles which no longer exist. He refers to a military fleet under construction, probably galleys for William's planned invasion of Greece. In Palermo he found a city of gardens and streets in a metropolis that combined "the benefits of wealth and splendor," comparing it to Cordoba. He mentioned its limestone buildings, its springs and its rivers.

Ibn Jubayr remarked that the Christian women dressed with much the same modesty as their Muslim sisters, and wore scarves or veils (see note 381). His description leads us to infer that many of the Christian women spoke Arabic.

He also described Palermo's Martorana church, and specifically its bell tower (perhaps higher then than now). He observed that the city of Messina was predominantly Greek, with a dwindling Muslim community. Some of his comments are cryptic. He mentions a tax on Muslims, without making clear whether this tax was also levied upon Christians and Jews.

It is obvious from his writings that Jubayr was devout in his Sunni faith, perhaps even something of a dogmatist. However, the winds of religious intolerance and change were gathering force, and perhaps that is what he concluded from what he saw in Sicily, where he might have hoped to see more Muslims.

A number of mosques had already been converted to churches to accommodate the growing number of Muslims becoming Catholic. For example, five years earlier the Archbishop of Catania had granted permission to John of Messina, a pastor, to transform Catania's great mosque into a church dedicated to Saint Thomas Becket.[756]

Jubayr's record is useful in establishing the continuity of the Sicilian cultural atmosphere over the centuries. It is, in effect, a link in a chain. Muhammad ibn Hawqal, a merchant from Baghdad with a penchant for geography, described an Arab-Byzantine Sicily in the time long before Idrisi and Jubayr, and a capital just as prosperous. In Palermo alone he counted three hundred mosques when this city was ruled by Muslims.

Jubayr also visited Jerusalem and other places, and wrote about these.[757]

Decisions

In 1184, William arranged the marriage of his aunt, Constance, to Henry, King of the Germans, the son and heir of Frederick Barbarossa. This may have reinforced Sicily's bonds with the Holy Roman Empire, but any child of Constance would be a Hohenstaufen, not a Hauteville.

Even so, Constance herself was now officially recognized as heiress presumptive. That is to say, she was first in the line of succession barring the birth of a child to Joanna.

The Sicilian royal family found itself in one of those occasional genealogical bottlenecks formed by a dearth of male heirs. William and his counsellors must have known this. The queen dowager, Beatrice of Rethel, Constance's mother, would have been aware of such a reality. She died a few months after the betrothal.

Constance, who was nearly thirty, seems not to have considered marriage before this point. It certainly had not been thrust upon her. While it is possible, if unproven, that she was living in a convent, there is nothing to suggest she had taken vows. Subsequent events imply that she did not suffer fools gladly, especially, it seems, when the fools were men, and she may have generally preferred the company of women.[758]

The year 1185 found Constance making her way northward to Germany with her endless train of knights, ladies, servants and belongings, along with a dowry consisting of plenty of coin. The lavish nuptials were celebrated at imperial Milan in January 1186. On this occasion, Constance was crowned Queen of the Germans as Henry's consort.

In 1185, William launched an invasion of the Byzantine lands to the east of the *Regnum,* something he had been contemplating ever since the Byzantine massacre of the Latins at Constantinople a few years earlier. In reality, this may have been little more than a pretext for supplanting the shipping, mercantile and political influence of the Genoans, Pisans and Venetians in this region. In the event, the Sicilians sought to exploit the unrest that existed in Constantinople since the crowning of Andronikos, who had grown to be despised by the majority of the population. Yet William's advisors may have been unaware of a more recent power shift developing in the Byzantine Empire even as they began the invasion.

Leading the incursion was Tancred of Lecce, along with Margaritus of Brindisi, an able admiral. The fleet landed at Durrës in June.

Following the Sicilians' infamous sack of Thessaloniki in August, Isaac II Angelus Comnenus (see Table 6) seized power from his kinsman. For his recent military defeat, amongst other offenses, Andronikos was tortured to death by an angry mob.

The Sicilian advance toward Constantinople was arrested in November with a defeat at Demetritzes by the highly competent Alexios Branas.[759] Here Richard of Acerra, brother-in-law of Tancred of Lecce and one of the leaders of the invasion, was captured, though eventually released.

A kinsman of the emperor, another Isaac Comnenus, had occupied the island of Cyprus. In June 1186, the Sicilians managed to defend it against imperial forces. Meanwhile, Pope Lucius III had died, succeeded by Urban III, born Uberto Crivelli.

Only three years later did William make peace with Emperor Isaac. Ambitious Margaritus, who probably began his career as a pirate, was able to retain the islands of Cephalonia and Zante as a county which remained part of the Kingdom of Sicily for a decade.

Presently, the Byzantines, confronted by renewed Muslim threats to their south and east, gave little further thought to the Sicilians and Cephalonia to the west.

Jerusalem

As we have seen, the Hautevilles had established a presence at Antioch and elsewhere in the Holy Land as early as the First Crusade, but Roger II refrained from participating in the Second Crusade, which followed the disastrous marriage of his mother, Adelaide del Vasto, to the King of Jerusalem. Except for some trade, and the obvious familial connections, the relationships between the crusader states and the Kingdom of Sicily had never been quite so close as circumstances, and even proximity, might suggest. Apart from the contingent at Antioch, where Bohemond I had established a principality, and perhaps a few Hospitallers and Templars, rather few knights from the *Regnum* are known to have ended up at that end of the Mediterranean during the Hauteville reigns. The unsuccessful military expedition to Egypt by Tancred of Lecce in the summer of 1174 was noteworthy for being the exception to this tendency, and it certainly did not lead to anything like a permanent presence.

By the early months of 1187, Saladin, having exploited a moment characterized by a certain lack of unity among the Christians of the region, had occupied some of the lands around Jerusalem.[760] Even the knightly orders were underprepared for this series of assaults. The Battle of Hattan, in July, was a dismal turning point for the Christians and the Jews allied with them. Tyre resisted, but Acre, Nablus, Jaffa, Toron, Sidon, Beirut and Ascalon capitulated by September, when Saladin advanced on the Holy City itself.

The defense of Jerusalem was left to Balian of Ibelin, a feudal lord wed to Maria Comnena, who was the widow of King Amalric of Jerusalem and a grand-niece of Manuel I of Constantinople. Following failed negotiations, the siege began on September twentieth. Despite their best efforts, the Hierosolymitans were forced to surrender on the second of October.[761]

With the capture of Jerusalem, the only military assistance of note to arrive from Europe was a Sicilian fleet of some sixty galleys led by the admiral Margaritus. The next year, he relieved the Knights Hospitaller, who were being besieged by Saladin at their large fortress, Krak des Chevaliers. There was very little more than this that Margaritus could do.

The recent campaigns left the Christians holding very little of what had been the crusader states. With other kings, William began contemplating a crusade to take back the Kingdom of Jerusalem.

In late October 1187, during his very brief pontificate as the successor of Urban III, Pope Gregory VIII, born Albert of Morra, issued a bull, *Audita tremendi,* calling for the Third Crusade.[762] He blamed the sinful Christians for leaving the Holy Land vulnerable not only to attack by men but to the wrath of God. Indeed, the wording was rather similar to that of the bull calling for the Second Crusade (see note 433). It seemed to chide the Christians for a lack of devotion.

A King's Legacy

Amongst the Catholics who needed no prodding for their devotion was Matthew of Aiello, arguably the most important person in the Kingdom of Sicily after the king himself. It was probably around 1187, if not earlier, that construction began on the church of the Holy Trinity, or Magione, under his patronage, attached to a small Cistercian monastery near the site where a mosque had stood on the edge of Palermo's Khalesa district.[763] Its popular name comes to us from the Norman French word for a large house, which in this case referred to a conventual house of monks. While this project could hardly compare to Archbishop Walter's grandiose cathedral being erected near the palace, it was more rapidly completed. Generally considered the last church in the Norman-Arab style constructed in Sicily, the Magione boasts an interior of graceful, quasi-Gothic arches, while its lack of cupolas distinguishes it from churches such as the Martorana erected just a few decades earlier. Although traces of frescos survive, there do not seem to have been mosaics on its walls. The significance of this church, now a minor basilica, is to be found in its subsequent association with the royal family. Architecturally, it represents the very beginning of a direction that the Norman-Arab style might have taken had it been permitted to evolve into the next century.

By early 1189, architecture may have been the last thing that William was contemplating. The possibility of a crusade was probably one of his chief reasons for negotiating a treaty with the Byzantine Emperor. It would hardly do to be at war with Isaac if Christians were expected to unite against a common foe in a "religious war."

For his part, Isaac was a bit suspicious of Catholic kings, whose knights were given to raiding Byzantine territories they passed through on the way to the Holy Land. That is what had happened in Anatolia during the Second Crusade, and the Byzantines wished to avoid the same problem this time.

Isaac's sister, Theodora, was married to Conrad of Montferrat, a crusader descended from the same dynasty as Adelaide del Vasto. Conrad was understandably rankled by the murder of his brother, Renier, husband of Maria "Porphyrogenita," by Andronikos. Out of loyalty to Isaac, however, he fought a Byzantine campaign against his own cousin, Frederick Barbarossa, in Italy. Conrad also defended Isaac against a revolt led by Alexios Branas, whom his troops killed. In 1189 Conrad, who was now a widower, was holding the city of Tyre against Saladin's forces.[764] With his brother-in-law awaiting relief, Isaac, against his better judgment, permitted Frederick Barbarossa to march through Byzantine lands. Unfortunately, his suspicions about the Germans proved to be correct.[765]

Back in the Kingdom of Sicily, treaties with both Isaac and Barbarossa permitted William to remain aloof of such intrigues. The precise extent to which he planned to contribute anything to the crusade is not known. It seems that his chief duty was to protect ships transporting crusader armies.[766] In the event, despite encouragement from all quarters, Sicilian participation would again be minimal.

The summer of 1188 witnessed the new pontiff, Clement III, born Paolo Scolari, confirming the existing papal relationship with the *Regnum*.[767] He also took the time to confirm the privileges of Monreale's bishop, which reflected growing influence.[768]

Sadly, King William II of Sicily died on the eighteenth of November 1189, perhaps following a brief illness, at the age of thirty-six.

Later accorded the epitaph "the Good," compared to his father, William I "the Bad," he is fondly remembered by history for his good rapport with the baronage. Nearer his own time, the praise from his subjects may not have been quite so generous, but he ultimately made peace with the kingdom's foes.

His patronage of churches and monasteries was significant even by the standards of his august Hautevillian predecessors. His reign saw very little rebellion or overt dissent in his dominions. To the extent that medieval prosperity can be measured, the kingdom seems to have been reasonably prosperous. The arts flourished. William's most impressive cathedrals stand as a lasting testament to his legacy.

The most obvious personal shortcoming of William's reign was his lack of children. This would have political consequences. Barons and bishops who had been faithful to the late king would reveal themselves to be slightly less loyal to his widow, Joanna, and his aunt, Constance. There was a certain logic in their rationale, and it transcended mere misogyny.

Chapter 21

DYNASTICISM

This was a moment of potential transition. While other western realms were readying themselves for the Third Crusade, the Kingdom of Sicily found itself threatened by a dynastic crisis prompted by one of the guiding precepts of European monarchy.

As we have seen, it was Constance Hauteville, now wed to Henry VI and living in Germany, who had been designated heir presumptive to the throne by her nephew, William II. This status was not contested during William's lifetime.[769]

However, while the Assizes of Ariano did not address the Hauteville line of succession directly, in practice it was governed by the principle in Salic Law that recognized legitimate male primogeniture, or agnatic succession, as the primary basis for the inheritance of royal rights.[770] In general, the transmission of these dynastic rights through a female was permitted only if the deceased monarch had no sons or brothers, or patrilineal nephews or male cousins, to succeed him. Since familial identity was inherited from fathers rather than mothers, this meant that Constance's children would be Hohenstaufens.

The problem was not specifically a change of dynasty, but the particular house that would inherit the Sicilian throne if Constance ever had a son.

Neither the baronage nor the papacy was amenable to a Hohenstaufen, or any Holy Roman Emperor, being King of Sicily. The barons saw the likelihood of a foreign ruler upsetting the *status quo,* while the pope feared his territory, and hence his power, being "surrounded" by one monarch, with imperial lands to Rome's north and the Kingdom of Sicily to its south. These were valid concerns in view of the politics of some of these emperors, most recently Frederick Barbarossa.

Dynastic Continuity

Though there was no perfect candidate, there was an obvious one.

Despite the misadventures of his younger days, when he abetted the rebels seeking to depose William I, illegitimate Tancred of Lecce, nephew of William II, had earned the esteem of the recently-deceased king and much of the baronage. Tancred's military campaigns may not have been very successful, but they reflected decisiveness and courage that were quintessentially Hautevillian. By now, at the age of fifty, Tancred had matured into a solid leader, the father of several children, and the patron of monasteries around Lecce.[771]

Encouraged by Matthew of Aiello, the barons had little difficulty encouraging Archbishop Walter of Palermo to crown him King of Sicily.[772] The coronation took place in January 1190.[773]

Whether Tancred's *de facto* reign was a *de jure* right has been debated, but its form was correct and neither Constance nor her husband could do anything about it in the immediate future. They had very few sympathizers in the *Regnum*, and the pope himself approved of the coronation.[774]

Tancred's case was not without precedent. A famous example of a bastard king from a Norman dynasty was William I "the Conqueror" of England (see Table 15). By comparison, Tancred is much maligned, perhaps unjustly.[775]

Amongst Constance's few vocal supporters in the *Regnum* was his descendant, the widowed Joanna, now queen dowager, who Tancred placed under house arrest, probably in the Zisa palace, while confiscating assets such as her dower lands in Apulia.

Tancred's rationale for his unpleasant treatment of Joanna was rooted in two fundamental presumptions. Firstly, if granted too much freedom of movement around the kingdom, especially in the capital, she might instigate an insurrection against him, an insurgency that could threaten social stability for years. Secondly, his own wife, Sibylla of Acerra (see Table 16), was now Queen of Sicily, and thus entitled to the dower.

Given the domestic affairs in the kingdom, it was clear that there would be even less Sicilian participation in the crusade than what had been planned. This was a relief to some, a disappointment for others. Yet there is nothing to suggest anything like a major upheaval in the *Regnum*. On the contrary, Tancred's kingship was generally accepted as normal, even desirable, by the majority of barons and prelates. We find him reigning and governing much as his predecessor did.[776] The highest level of administration did not change, and Matthew of Aiello was promoted from vice chancellor to chancellor.

Tancred attempted a rapprochement with some rebel barons and even enticed a few Muslim bandits of the Palermitan hinterland to conform to the law.[777] The greatest thorn in his side was Roger of Andria, an envious cousin who, having been a high justiciar and high constable, felt himself more suitable than Tancred to kingship.[778] If Roger could not have himself crowned, he would spearhead an effort by a faction of barons to depose Tancred and enthrone Constance.[779]

The only way Constance could challenge Tancred was through the use of military force, but presently there were pressing problems in the Holy Roman Empire. For the moment, with his father on crusade, Henry VI was constrained to confront the renewed ambitions of Henry the Lion, Duke of Saxony and Bavaria, exponent of the Welf dynasty that had often contested the Hohenstaufens. The Lion, it will be remembered, was married to Matilda, a sister of Joanna.

It so happened that Joanna's brother, Richard "Lionheart," who had recently succeeded to the English throne, planned on passing through the Kingdom of Sicily on his way to the Holy Land. Destiny would prompt Constance and her husband southward around the same time.

The first few months of 1190 transpired without incident. Tancred named his son, Roger, heir apparent as Duke of Apulia, and the Messina mint began coining *follari* bearing their names. The storm was to arrive the following year.

Henry and Constance

Fortunately the imperial couple could readily muster an army by diverting some of the forces already engaged to fight Henry the Lion in Germany. A treaty being negotiated with him obviated the need to use it there.

In May 1190, Henry VI sent a large advance force led by the *ministerialis* Henry "Testa" of Kalden southward while he stayed in Germany to settle succession questions arising from the recent death, on crusade, of his imperial vassal Louis III of Thuringia and to conclude the treaty with Henry the Lion. The departure of the army led by Henry Testa without a definitive victory left Roger of Andria to fend for himself. Late in 1190, he was captured by Richard of Acerra following a siege and put to death.[780]

Before Constance and her husband departed for Italy, news arrived at the imperial court that Frederick Barbarossa had died in Asia Minor in June 1190. Since the imperial crown was now Henry's as Frederick's heir, it was opportune for him to go to Rome to claim it from the pope. That this was on the way to Naples and Salerno meant that two birds, coronation and conquest, could be hit with one stone. One objective would prove easier to achieve than the other.

Along the way, Constance and Henry met Eleanor of Aquitaine and her future daughter-in-law, Berengaria, at Lodi, near Milan, in January 1191. The two ladies were going to Sicily to meet Richard "Lionheart," who would stop at Messina *en route* to the Third Crusade.[781] Told of Constance's plight, Eleanor lent a sympathetic ear, and even subscribed a charter issued by Henry, but she could not know that her son was soon to recognize Tancred's right to the Sicilian throne. Eleanor's true opinion about the Sicilian dispute is not known. Of course, her daughter, Joanna, supported Constance and opposed Tancred.

Joanna and Lionheart

While Tancred's Hautevillian kinswoman was attempting to enforce her dynastic rights on the peninsula, King Richard I "Lionheart" of England and King Philip II "Augustus" of France stopped at Messina late in 1190 *en route* to the Holy Land.[782] The English fleet had sailed around the Iberian peninsula to arrive in the Mediterranean.

Consisting of more than a hundred vessels, Richard's fleet arrived at the Sicilian city in the middle of September ahead of its lord, who undertook the last leg of the journey over land, working his way down the Italian peninsula.[783] Philip and his French force arrived at Messina a day or two after the English.

Richard was delayed for another week in Calabria, where some local peasants took him to task for claiming a falcon that was theirs.[784] This bizarre incident near Mileto would be all but insignificant except that it may have informed the king's condescending opinion about the local folk and his subsequent actions toward them. Across the strait, his people were not welcomed very cordially by the Messinians.

At Messina the French were received by the populace no more kindly than the English, but it was the latter under Richard who decided to take the city following a series of skirmishes in which Philip initially sided with the Messinians.

This was achieved in a single assault, with plenty of rape and pillage in its wake, although Richard sagely put an end to the violence before it led to mass carnage. Philip and the French disapproved of the occupation, if only because they felt deprived of their share of the plunder, and protested. Fortunately, the two kings brought matters under control before their armies began a major battle against each other.[785]

Walter of Coutances, Archbishop of Rouen, who was traveling with Richard, threatened to anathematize whomever did not restore to the Messinians the silver taken from them.

With Messina occupied, Richard sent a party of trusted emissaries, led by Hugh III of Burgundy and Robert of Sablé, to Tancred's court to demand compensation for losses to the crusaders resulting from the Messinians' aggression.

More importantly, they also conveyed Richard's explicit demand that his sister, Queen Joanna, be freed immediately and her dower lands restored, along with the portion of her late husband's money due her. On his sister's behalf, Richard further demanded a golden throne to which she was entitled by Norman tradition, along with two dozen silver goblets and plates. For himself he wanted a golden table, a silk pavilion large enough to cover two hundred knights seated at dinner, and some ships and provisions.[786]

The fact that the English sovereign had just conquered one of the kingdom's largest cities "in less time than a priest could chant matins" lent an implicit gravity to this request.[787] Seeing that Messina was impossible to repossess, Margaritus of Brindisi abandoned it as soon as he could.

Joanna's support of Constance did not waver. Whether Richard seriously considered a conquest of Sicily on Constance's behalf, which was well within his army's capability, Tancred probably understood the scope of the English king's military might.

At all events, while the King of Sicily immediately took steps to free Joanna, he stalled for time regarding the dower and money on the pretext that he first had to consult with his advisers. In this he may have been secretly encouraged by Philip, whose trust in Richard was beginning to wane.

Tancred's delay in paying Richard emboldened some Messinians, who began to obstruct English supply ships whilst cooperating with the French, who had curried favor with the local leaders. However, Tancred and his subjects relented when Richard began the construction of a castle called *Mategriffon* on a hill overlooking Messina, a gesture that suggested he might be willing to stay in Sicily for a while.

In late September, Joanna was freed, released to her brother's protection. She traveled by galley from Palermo to Messina. Philip, a widower, was entranced by her beauty.

To shield his sister from wayward arrows and lusting eyes, Richard arranged for her to be lodged at the monastery in Bagnara, across the strait in Calabria, where he left a small garrison to guard her. With this in mind, he had already ordered his engineers to fortify the abbey founded there a century earlier by Roger I.[788]

Richard's friendship with Philip, who had supported him in a series of battles against his own father, the late Henry II, was growing strained, especially after Richard called off his planned marriage to Philip's half-sister, Alys.

Tancred eventually paid Richard twenty thousand gold ounces for Joanna's dower. Another twenty thousand was paid to accommodate Richard's other requests, though according to one chronicler this was ostensibly a dowry for Tancred's daughter, Elvira, to wed Richard's young nephew, Arthur of Brittany, whom Richard had declared heir presumptive to the English throne. This betrothal was never finalized; the contract for Elvira's dowry may have been little more than a ploy by Richard to justify his theft of Joanna's money.

Joanna's dower lands in Apulia were not restored to her, and Richard never gave her much of the remuneration remitted to him by Tancred.[789]

Richard accepted an invitation to meet Tancred at Catania, where the two monarchs made peace, sending a copy of their treaty to the pope. It was here that Tancred received the sword "Excalibur" mentioned by Roger of Howden (see note 366). Then Richard returned to Messina and Tancred to Palermo. Much to the chagrin of the Messinians, the English and French armies wintered in Sicily.

On Christmas, Joanna attended Richard's lavish feast at Mategriffon.[790] Philip of France, who was present, was already admiring the widow's beauty with an eye to marrying her.[791]

In March 1191, Philip set sail for Palestine while Richard crossed the strait to Calabria to meet his mother, Eleanor, who arrived with his fiancée, Berengaria of Navarre.[792] Eleanor, who had lived through much since her previous visit to Sicily four decades earlier, had not seen her youngest daughter in fourteen years. In the event, she stayed into the first days of April before returning to England, stopping *en route* to visit the pope, leaving her daughter and future daughter-in-law at Messina to proceed to the Holy Land.

Third Crusade

The Lionheart's peace with Tancred hardly suggested him being very kindly disposed to his Mediterranean allies.

In early April of 1191, Richard sent Joanna and Berengaria ahead of him to Palestine with a small flotilla while he tended to some final preparations before setting sail with his main fleet a few days later.[793] Among many other tasks, he destroyed most of Mategriffon, the castle he had built of timber and stone to keep an eye over the Messinians.[794]

Along the way to the Holy Land, the large galley transporting Joanna and Berengaria was blown off course by a violent storm. The ladies and their retinue found themselves off the coast of Cyprus.[795] Richard landed at Rhodes, where he spent a few days recuperating from an illness while Philip was already besieging Acre. Before long, Richard's fleet was sailing again.

Anchored in deep waters near the port of Limassol, the galley carrying Joanna and Berengaria waited for several days in late April while some pilgrims from other ships went ashore. Unfortunately, these pilgrims were attacked, robbed and imprisoned.

About a week later, the ruler of Cyprus, Isaac Comnenus, with whom Tancred was allied, began to coax the ladies and their entourage into coming ashore. They were on the verge of accepting when Richard's fleet arrived and routed the Byzantine force, constraining Isaac to come to terms.[796]

On the twelfth of May, with Cyprus under his control, Richard wed Berengaria at Limassol, where she was crowned Queen of England.[797] Now Isaac, safely ensconced in a castle, demanded that Richard leave Cyprus and began waging a campaign against him. This consisted of little more than a series of skirmishes, but it took the king a fortnight to conquer the entire island. He then deposed and imprisoned Isaac whilst leaving his own men in charge of Cyprus.

Joanna and Berengaria arrived at Acre on the first of June, joined by Richard two days later following his engagement and defeat of a Saracen vessel.[798]

The besieged city capitulated in July. With this, the crusading kings established contact with Saladin through emissaries. On July twenty-first, Richard brought his wife and sister into the city, lodging them in its palace.[799] Ten days later, Philip returned to France to confront domestic problems, leaving Hugh of Burgundy in charge of the French troops. The Arab chronicler Baha ad-Din tells us that two Catholic attendants in Joanna's service who were converts from Islam escaped to the Ayyubid camp, where they embraced their former faith and were received by Saladin.[800]

Having waited a month for a reply from Saladin, on August twentieth Richard ordered the execution of over two thousand Muslim prisoners. Saladin retaliated by killing his Christian prisoners.

In early September, the Christians won an important battle at Arsuf. The crusaders' victory forced Saladin to the negotiating table. He sent his brother, Al-Adil ("Saphadin"), to meet with Richard.

Incredibly, one of Richard's proposals was that as part of a peace agreement his sister, Joanna, should marry Al-Adil and the couple could then rule Jerusalem together.[801] This unorthodox idea was discarded after perfunctory discussion about the incompatibility of the hypothetical spouses, although

Richard reportedly put forward the name of his niece, Eleanor of Brittany, after Joanna refused to be bartered. The Muslim chronicler from whom the account comes suggests that neither Saladin nor his counsellors sincerely believed that Richard was serious in advancing the idea.[802]

After the negotiations failed, Richard pressed on to Ascalon, which he fortified. A series of battles fought in 1192 culminated in September of that year with a compromise, the Treaty of Jaffa, that gave Christian pilgrims and clergy access to Jerusalem. Under the circumstances, which had been reached only through much bloodshed, little more could be expected of either the Christian "Franks" or the Muslim Ayyubids.[803]

Intersections

In Italy, meanwhile, Christians were fighting Christians. By the time Henry and Constance were to be crowned in 1191, a new pope, Giacinto Bobone, had just been elected as Celestine III. This pontiff's only initial request was to be ceded the city of Tusculum, a wish Henry granted.[804]

The imperial coronation of Henry and Constance took place on Easter Monday.[805] They still did not have any children.

Despite the couple's entreaties, Celestine, even after crowning the new Holy Roman Emperor, was reluctant to issue a declaration nullifying Tancred's coronation as King of Sicily.[806] Other churchmen were more accommodating. At Cassino Henry demanded, and received, a pledge of loyalty from the monks, but this served little purpose beyond the confines of the abbey's quasi-sovereign territory.[807]

Other gestures would be enforced under the threat of arms. Capua and Aversa submitted to Constance's authority readily enough. With the help of Pisan and Genoan navies, Henry besieged Naples into the summer, but Margaritus of Brindisi successfully defended the city.[808]

Now an old, familiar beast reared its ugly head as an epidemic swept through the imperial ranks, prompting its withdrawal. Henry himself was infected but recuperated. He accepted the invitation of the Salernitans to leave Constance, who had fallen ill from the torrid summer temperatures, in their city with a small garrison as a sign of her sovereign authority and his solemn promise to return. Salerno's medical school had competent physicians present to treat her.

The queen's presence was significant as Salerno was still the largest city of the peninsular part of the kingdom, and Constance was lodged in its royal fortress, Terracena. Henry's presence was required back in Germany so he could address the kind of domestic problems that only the emperor could resolve.

Having survived the imperial siege and forced Henry to withdraw, the Neapolitans exploited this moment to score a facile victory. Some nobles led by Nicholas of Aiello, the son of Tancred's chancellor Matthew, contacted the Salernitans, claiming that Henry was dead and encouraging the citizens to attack Constance at her stronghold in order to prove their loyalty to Tancred. Fearing a bloody reprisal by Tancred for having negotiated with Henry, the Salernitans complied with this demand.

The empress herself suspected that her husband might be dead. She attempted to negotiate with the besiegers but the best she could obtain from their leader, her distant kinsman, Elias of Gesualdo, was safe conduct for the knights of her garrison. This surrender left her a prisoner of Tancred.

Making his way out of the kingdom, Henry, who was still ailing, was resting at Cassino when he received news of his wife's capture. Enraged, he took hostages at San Germano, the town beneath the abbey, but did not draw blood. After he departed the *Regnum,* several of his vassals remained behind to wage a piecemeal war in isolated areas. If nothing else, this served to remind Tancred that his power on the mainland was neither absolute nor uncontested.

Constance would not forget the treachery of Nicholas of Aiello and the others, but for now she was to be taken by galley to Sicily. What was most important, for the moment, was that she live to fight another day. It was becoming crystal clear that claiming her crown, no less sitting on her father's throne, was going to be an exercise in perseverance.

She donned regal attire and let herself be escorted to the port of Salerno. By the time Constance arrived at Messina late in 1191, the kings of England and France, who had spent several months in the city before departing for the Holy Land in the spring, had recognized Tancred as King of Sicily. Like so many other irksome annoyances of recent months, that affront to her dignity would not be forgotten, but she would have to endure others.

At Messina, Constance was brought before Tancred. She was thirty-seven, her captor fifty-three. If Peter of Eboli is to be believed, Constance was slender and stately, Tancred short and ugly. Though they may have met in the past, it is unlikely that they ever exchanged many words with each other. Their terse conversation as it is recounted in Peter's verse chronicle lends us an impression of the queen's reasoning.

"Was the entire world not enough to satisfy you?" Tancred asked. "Why do you desire my lands? Know that God will judge us fairly for what we do, and take his wrath upon those who take the law unto themselves. Fate has delivered you into my hands because you inflicted injury upon my kingdom. As we have seen, your husband, who was ill, has retreated."

"Do not forget what I am saying to you now, Tancred," Constance replied. "Before long, your rising star shall turn against you, just as my star has fallen upon me. Destiny cannot be changed. I do not seek your kingdom but that of my father, which is mine by right. Are you Roger's son? Not by any means. I am the king's heiress because I am his legitimate child by my mother. The legal rights of both my parents bequeath me the realm you presently hold as a usurper. You have not yet confronted the man who shall obtain these lands for me by the sword. What laws and oaths gave you the realm that appertains to me? It was only the benevolent grace of King William that permitted you to keep even Lecce."[809]

Having uttered these defiant words, Constance engaged in no further conversation with Tancred. She was sent to Palermo, where she resided with Tancred's wife, Sibylla, who did not relish the task of being a gaoler.

Back on the mainland, meanwhile, the towns that had recently submitted to Constance's authority were being taken back, one by one, by Tancred's vassals.

At Henry's urging, Pope Celestine used the threat of excommunication to persuade Tancred to release his imperial prisoner to papal custody. Nevertheless, in June 1192 pontiff and king concluded agreements confirming the relationship between the papacy and the kingdom, leaving no doubt that Rome continued to recognize that Tancred ruled lawfully in the eyes of the church.[810]

During the same month, Constance was accompanied to Messina, and then onto the mainland, by Giles of Anagni, a cardinal, who was the papal chancellor.

The entourage escorting Constance was intercepted at Ceprano, just inside papal territory, by some imperial knights led by Roffred of Liri, a cardinal who was formerly the abbot of Cassino. The loyalty of this Benedictine, who had been imprisoned briefly for supporting Tancred, was for the moment reasonably secure because his brother, Gregory, was being held hostage by Henry in Germany. Constance was soon reunited with her husband at Trifels Castle.

Her next attempt to conquer the *Regnum* was to be funded with money from an unexpected source.

King's Ransom

The phrase "a king's ransom" comes to us from the medieval practice of paying a high price to free an important personage taken prisoner in combat, with kings being the most valuable of all. Only rarely did this go beyond the battlefield; Tancred freed Constance not for money but at the pope's request.

By the autumn of 1192, it was clear to Henry VI that determination alone would not be enough for a proper conquest of the kingdom claimed by his wife. A serious campaign would require a massive investment, perhaps more money than he could generate through taxes and other sources of revenue. An opportunity was to present itself from unexpected quarters.

After the deaths of Henry's father and brother on the Third Crusade, Leopold, Duke of Austria, hastened to Palestine to assume command of the imperial contingent while Henry was being crowned emperor and prosecuting the unsuccessful campaign against Tancred in Italy. Following the capture of Acre, Leopold expected the same courtesy accorded the other sovereigns present. Instead, Richard ordered the duke's banner removed from its staff alongside the others flying atop the city's ramparts. Enraged at this affront, Leopold and his knights decamped and immediately returned home.

By the time the aggrieved duke complained to the emperor about the banner incident, Henry was already nurturing his own grievance against Richard based on the English king's support for Tancred's claim to the *Regnum*.

A third matter may have contributed to the emperor's animosity. Conrad of Montferrat, the recently murdered King of Jerusalem (see note 764), was a cousin to both Henry and Leopold. Richard, a vocal opponent of Conrad, with whom he had quarreled, was suspected of complicity in the assassination of this fellow monarch.[811] Naturally, this matter was far more grievous than Richard's refusal to fly a comrade's flag.

In December 1192, the Lionheart, whilst returning from the crusade, was captured by Leopold, who confined him at Dürnstein Castle. Henry probably approved of this.

At Speyer in March of the following year, Richard was transferred to Henry's custody and taken to Trifels Castle, where he was formally accused of murdering Conrad of Montferrat. The Holy Roman Emperor demanded a ransom of a hundred fifty thousand silver marks to release the King of England.

Following much effort to raise this sum to defray the cost of a "king's ransom," Richard's mother, Eleanor, came to remit the monies. It was the second time she and Constance met, and the younger woman had yet to sit upon her father's throne. Richard was finally released in February 1194.[812]

Tancred died during the same month, having been predeceased by his eldest son, Roger, in December.[813] Both were entombed in the Magione church. The prospects for continued Hauteville rule were buried with them.

Palermo Cathedral as it appeared before the addition of the unsightly cupola and other Baroque details

Following their coronations in Palermo Cathedral, kings and queens were acclaimed at this dais nearby.

Roger I on a copper follaris minted at Messina

Chapter 22

REGNANCY

The spring of 1194 found the Kingdom of Sicily being ruled by Tancred's widow, Sibylla, as regent for her younger son, William.[814]

Back in Germany, with the imperial treasury replenished by enough English silver to defray the expense of a major military campaign, Henry raised a large army and launched a serious effort to place Constance on the Sicilian throne.

Sibylla's regency for her young son would prove ephemeral. Only a few of her charters survive, but their appellation was not unlike the formula sometimes employed by Margaret. We find, for example, the phrase *domina Sibilla gloriosa regina matre*.[815]

Matthew of Aiello had died the previous year, leaving few capable leaders to assist the queen and her young son. The task of defending the kingdom fell, first and foremost, to intrepid Margaritus of Brindisi, who was married to a daughter of Roger II.

Regina Siciliae

By August 1194, Henry VI had conquered Naples. He was in Palermo by November, when Margaritus surrendered the city's sea castle to the invaders. Constance, who was now pregnant, traveled separately through imperial lands with her retinue.[816]

Sibylla sent her son and daughters to Caltabellotta Castle for safety, but she seems to have remained in Palermo to defend the city.[817]

Henry had promised Sibylla a comfortable "domestic exile" at Lecce, even offering her son the County of Taranto. Alas, this offer was too good to be true. Before long, he would accuse Sibylla and several prominent nobles, including Margaritus, of plotting a conspiracy to overthrow him. Similar allegations were also made against Eugene, the *amiratus,* an intellectual known for his translations from Arabic to Latin, whose family had long served the Hauteville dynasty. This was likely nothing more than a pretext to eliminate potential opponents, who were summarily arrested and sent to Germany.[818] Young William was blinded and castrated, then made to disappear following a year or two of imprisonment at Hohenems Castle.[819]

Tancred's remains, along with those of his eldest son, were cast out of the Magione. The royal tombs were destroyed as part of an effort to cancel every trace of both father and son from the annals of history, though this gesture did not escape the notice of a distant chronicler.[820] Wasting no time, Henry betrothed Irene Angelina, the young widow of Tancred's son Roger, to his brother, Philip of Swabia.

It wasn't only Tancred's physical remains that were cast into the ether of time. Most of the laws he had promulgated were abrogated. This included the so-called "Concordat of Gravina" negotiated with the papacy two years earlier permitting the unhindered, uncensored entry of the pope's legates into Sicily.

On Christmas in 1194, Henry had himself crowned King of Sicily *jure uxoris* in Palermo Cathedral by right of his wife. He now ruled more territory and more people than any other monarch in Europe.[821]

The next day, Constance went into labor in the March of Ancona. At the town of Jesi, in imperial territory not far from the border of the Kingdom of Sicily. Longstanding tradition says that the queen ordered her attendants to erect a pavilion where she could give birth in view of witnesses such as clerics and courtiers.[822] Her worry was that the maternity of a quadragenarian who had not yet given birth during nine years of marriage might later be placed in doubt by naysayers. Constance's red-haired son was christened Frederick.[823]

On that day the torch that lit the flame of the Sicilian monarchy was passed from the Norman Hautevilles to the Swabian Hohenstaufens. The survival of the *Regnum Siciliae* founded by Constance's father was assured.

In March of 1195, Constance was crowned Queen of Sicily at Bari following her husband's first major convocation of the baronage, at which he announced his intention of leading a crusade to occupy Jerusalem, where the truce with the Ayyubids had expired. Henry then returned to Germany to address imperial matters, *en route* suppressing pockets of dissent in the mainland part of the *Regnum* and rewarding loyal allies such as Conrad Lutzelinhart, also known as Corrado Moscencervello, to whom he gave the County of Molise.[824] Constance, meanwhile, went to Palermo, where she established her own court and began her effective reign.

After leading a brief insurgency on the mainland, Sibylla's brother, Richard of Acerra, was captured, and then summarily executed as a traitor for having supported Tancred against Constance and killing Roger of Andria.[825]

In outward appearance, Constance's queenship was not too different from that of any other heiress of royal rank whose husband ruled *jure uxoris* on her behalf. However, if not precisely a queen regnant according to the most rigid definition, Constance was the nearest thing to it in Sicily's Norman-Swabian era.[826]

The daily operation of the kingdom did not change any more than it had when Tancred assumed power following the death of Constance's nephew, the fondly-remembered William II. Its fundamental laws and institutions remained in place. There was no ideological transformation, and no serious attempt by Henry to integrate the Kingdom of Sicily into the Holy Roman Empire as if it were a German duchy. Young Frederick's grand inheritance would be a personal union, not a political one. This was significant because, despite frequent baronial unrest and localized laws, the *Regnum* was by now an essentially "centralized" monarchy with a unitary legal code rather than a conglomeration of quasi-sovereign duchies and counties such as those that comprised the Holy Roman Empire.[827]

The only truly hereditary territory the Hohenstaufens had in the Holy Roman Empire was Swabia. The Kingdom of Sicily, conversely, was a great patrimony inextricably linked, through Constance, to an undeniable familial inheritance.

This inheritance consisted of more than land. As soon as he had reached Palermo, and without immediately notifying his wife, Henry withdrew much money from the treasury and sent it to Germany.[828] Just as significantly, he enfeoffed some German barons in Sicily and installed the faithful Teutonic Knights in Messina and Palermo. In the capital, he gave this chivalric order the Magione. Commanderies were also established in Apulia.

The Teutonic Order was founded in Palestine a few years earlier under the patronage of Henry's late brother, Frederick of Swabia. Unlike the knightly orders of the Hospital and the Temple, which were multiethnic and independent, the Teutonic Knights, though ostensibly autonomous, were closely linked to a specific culture and dynasty, the German Hohenstaufens.

Experience had taught Henry and Constance that the very thought of trusting the baronage and populace of the *Regnum* was fraught with risk. Here, on "foreign" soil, the German knights and barons were unlikely to rebel against one of their own.

This policy of Germanification led to Sicily's Muslims, whose numbers were already diminishing, being excluded from government.

Greek appointments all but disappeared. To replace Margaritus, Henry named as admiral William Grasso, a Genoan, giving him Malta as a fief.

Henry's attempt — in his own way — to calm a sea of potential Sicilian troubles was successful at first, and it seems to have met with Constance's approval. The most turbulent waters were those bubbling up from the murky flow of the Tiber. Thanks to Constance's delivery of a healthy boy, the papacy's worst fears had come to pass. In an undercurrent destined to shape papal policy for the next seven decades, there was now a legitimate male heir to the powerful realms that engulfed the lands ruled by the pope. From London to Kiev, temporal sovereigns took notice of the power that bisected Europe in a line extending from the North Sea to the central Mediterranean.

In April 1195, the pope approved Henry's crusade. The papal bull addresses him as emperor but not, as he desired, King of Sicily.[829]

By June, Constance was in Palermo issuing decrees in her own name and under her own seal as Queen of Sicily.[830] Her surviving charters reflect the typical duties undertaken by a monarch as the court of final appeal in matters involving barons, abbots and serfs.

As if one empire were not enough, Henry began eyeing the Byzantine Empire to the east.[831] For now, however, he had more than enough on his plate. It was nearly as challenging for Henry to rule the combined territories of the Holy Roman Empire, the northern Italian communes and the Kingdom of Sicily as it was for his contemporary, Genghis Khan, to control the vast, growing Mongol Empire to the east. Henry's family was much smaller than that of his Asian counterpart; appropriately, he delegated some duties in northern Italy to his only surviving brother, Philip of Swabia.[832]

Knowing that the pretensions of the rival Welf dynasty could rekindle themselves at any time, Henry sought to consolidate his young son's position in Germany. At Frankfurt in 1196, young Frederick was elected King of the Germans, or "King of the Romans," a status that qualified him, under imperial law, to be crowned king and then emperor.[833] Unfortunately, some important electors in other regions dissented, leaving the election in limbo.

The empire was not the only realm where rebellion could erupt, and early the next year, 1197, Henry was back in the *Regnum,* where he convoked a baronial meeting at Capua. Accustomed to the comparative laxity of administration under William II and Tancred, some barons resented Henry's rigidity and tax increases. Constance may have shared their view, though not their decision to start a violent rebellion.[834]

Henry's untimely death at Messina on the twenty-eighth of September 1197 made Constance the regent for young Frederick.[835] Henry was interred in Palermo's cathedral in a tomb of porphyry befitting his imperial rank.

In retrospect, little can be discerned about Henry's brief rule of the Kingdom of Sicily. He and Constance seem to have had rather different ideas regarding taxation and finances, and slightly contrasting temperaments about the use of power. In some ways, Constance may have had a greater affinity for the common folk.

Regent

Ruling from Palermo, Constance could control the Kingdom of Sicily, but grasping the reins restraining the headstrong German princes was another matter altogether.

Even as arrangements were being made for his brother's funeral, Philip raced to Germany in an attempt to defend Frederick's rights there.[836] This was a daunting task, made more so by the opposition of the recently-elected pope, Innocent III, an aristocrat born Lothar of Segni.[837]

Now, as regent, Constance was exercising the sovereign rights of her son.[838] She had an efficient chancellor in Walter of Palear.

Frederick's education was a paramount concern, naturally, but there were competent tutors to tend to this. The boy was to be taught several languages, including Arabic and some Greek, and an appreciation of the diversity of cultures that made his kingdom unique. Constance had to think about more than her son's education, and on Saturday, the seventeenth of May 1198, the three year-old was crowned King of Sicily in Palermo Cathedral. The coronation, and Frederick's rights, received unequivocal pontifical recognition.[839] We find papal correspondence bearing the wording "Empress Constance, glorious Queen of Sicily and her dear son, Frederick, illustrious King of Sicily, her Heir in perpetuity," with the pontiff recognizing traditional prerogatives such as the apostolic legateship of Sicily.[840]

By then, Philip, Frederick's uncle, hoping to placate imperial elector princes reluctant to embrace administration by the mother and courtiers of a boy king in another country, had already had himself elected King of the Germans. In September, he was crowned at Mainz. At this juncture there was little choice, for some German princes were already throwing their support behind the rival Welfs.[841] Constance's reaction to her brother-in-law's decision is not known, but she certainly would have understood the complexities facing the Hohenstaufens in Germany.

With this in mind, she tacitly, though not explicitly, renounced her son's imperial claims by omitting any mention of these at his coronation or in her subsequent charters. By no means was this a formal abdication of Frederick's inherent dynastic rights as a Hohenstaufen. Rather, it was a pragmatic effort to permit his uncle, Philip, to defend that inheritance in any way possible while avoiding the ire of a pope who felt threatened by the dynasty's power in Italy.

This permitted Constance, as queen, to focus on local problems. Relying upon the expertise of local advisors, she sent most of her late husband's counsellors back to Germany. Those enfeoffed in the *Regnum* remained. In at least one case this was problematic.

Markward of Anweiler, the imperial seneschal who held lands in the northern marches of the *Regnum,* came forth claiming to possess the "genuine" will of the late emperor making him, and not Constance, the regent of the kingdom.[842] This, the vassal affirmed ridiculously, was because Frederick was not actually born of Constance. The queen responded to this nonsense by banishing Markward from the kingdom.[843] Unfortunately, he would eventually return to foment still more chaos.

With Henry dead and the Holy Roman Empire in disarray, Pope Innocent III protested Sibylla's imprisonment just as his predecessor had once objected to the detainment of Constance by Tancred. He threatened excommunication and interdict. In the event, Sibylla and her daughters escaped the nunnery where they were imprisoned, making their way to France, where they were received with honor at the royal court.[844] There Elvira, King Tancred's eldest daughter, was betrothed to Walter III of Brienne, an enterprising lord.

Now the dearth of Hohenstaufen males was proving just as problematical as the shortage of Hauteville heirs had been during Constance's youth. Showing uncommon foresight, the queen made certain provisions for her son's future. Most importantly, she named Pope Innocent III the young king's guardian in the event of her death.[845] This would have made the pontiff the *de facto* regent of the Kingdom of Sicily until Frederick reached the age of majority. As Frederick's guardian, the pope was to receive thirty thousand gold tarì per year.

Constance also renounced certain provisions of the apostolic legateship enjoyed by her Norman forebears, though some of her successors asserted this privilege. By the autumn of 1198, the queen was already thinking about a bride for her son, perhaps a sister of Peter II, the young, recently-crowned King of Aragon.[846]

These years represent the continuation of a liminal period stretching from late Hautevillian to early Hohenstaufen rule evident in court culture and usages, a trend reflected in subtle changes in government and, eventually, a certain degree of papal intervention.

It is quite possible that Constance's immediacy in addressing some of these matters was motivated by a persistent illness which led her physicians to make a pessimistic prognosis of her chances for survival. On the other hand, she was the last of her house, and personal experience had taught her the importance of establishing matters involving dynastic succession in a clear, unequivocal fashion that would leave such details beyond subsequent contestation.

Constance died in Palermo on the twenty-seventh of November in 1198. Her legacy is one of certitude, rectitude and fortitude. Long viewed as a termagant, she has come to be regarded as the very avatar of Sicilian queenhood.

Thanks to her efforts, the continued life of her father's kingdom was assured. Yet her death marked the end of its Norman era.

Constancian Retrospective

Although she was queen regnant, ruling in her own name as her father's lawful heiress, Constance's reign in the kingdom was, in practice, similar to that of a consort or regent. While she was giving birth on the peninsula, her husband was being enthroned in Palermo, where he was ruling in her name from her natal city.

Constance has the distinction to have succeeded, upon her nephew's death, as the first Queen of Sicily born in the *Regnum,* even if her coronation was much delayed. Guelph writers, and particularly Tuscans, disparaged her for bearing the son they despised. Apart from their intrinsic hatred, it is to be noted that they wrote their nasty missives long after her death; they did not know her.

Despite that unflattering literary treatment, and the negative stereotype of the tempestuous redhead, very little in what is known of Constance's life indicates hubris.[847] The most we can infer about her is that she was assertive. She asserted her right to rule and the rights of the people she ruled.

Like Margaret, who may have been her queenly model, she had to take unpopular decisions. Unlike Margaret, whose essential reginal information comes to us from a single chronicler, Constance enjoys reports from several sources. However, it is the chronicle of Peter of Eboli, which she commissioned, that brings us the greatest number of facts.

It is not surprising that Peter omits the detail of the queen ordering the remains of her kinsman, the bastard she viewed as a usurper, cast out of Palermo's Magione, a fact reported by another chronicler (see note 25).

Now a minor basilica, it is one of several "unknown" royal churches of the kingdom.

Even if her elite sisterhood included bold regents like Adelaide and Margaret, Constance remains the royal woman of our Norman-Swabian era about whom the most has been written in successive centuries. Most of this is owed to her being the living link between our two greatest kings, her father and son, and a bridge between dynasties.

Like Margaret, and probably our other queens and countesses, Constance was generally untrusting of men. That female characteristic has made its way into our times, perhaps not without reason in an Italianate patriarchy historically reluctant to recognize the fundamental rights of women (see note 20).

Constance's travels and trials were hardly indifferent. Her road to reginality was paved with neither sympathy or simplicity. Her experiences are vaguely indicative of the challenges confronted by many women at a "later" stage in life. Forty years of age in her time might well be perceived as fifty in ours, and vice versa.

In Constance Hauteville we see the supreme dedication to duty by a woman who never asked to be queen, and may not have had to rise to that occasion had her kingly nephew fathered a child or two. Here is circumstance as the arbiter of destiny.

Had her reign been longer, her achievements would have been even greater. The oeuvre of her life thrived in a place beyond all contention.

Courtesy Archdiocese of Palermo

On 15 April 1196 Constance issued this charter under her own name and seal, ceding authority over some serfs (named in the decree) to a certain jurisdiction. Here she is referred to as Roman Empress and Queen of Sicily.

The Magione, where Tancred and his son were entombed

Teutonic knight depicted on a tomb in the Magione, Palermo

Chapter 23
REGNUM VIVUM

The Kingdom of Sicily was alive, destined to remain distinct in almost every way from the Holy Roman Empire. If it now found itself linked to still another culture, that was just one more layer to enhance the patina of its polycultural patrimony.

Initially, there were a few vestigial influences from the reign of the late Henry VI, and some residual chaos. Pope Innocent III, as Frederick's guardian, appointed Cencio Savelli, the future Honorius III, as the young king's principal tutor. In 1199, Philip of Swabia, the boy's uncle, permitted arrogant Markward of Anweiler to invade the kingdom to oust Walter of Palear, the chancellor and acting regent, from power, something achieved completely more than a year later. Markward accomplished this by overpowering the token force left in Palermo by Walter's brother, Maniero of Manopello, who was on the other side of the island at Messina, and exploiting the disloyalty of the castellan who was supposed to defend the palace.[848]

The local baronage didn't like this, and neither, it seems, did anybody else except, perhaps, the German knights, who caused much destruction on their way through the kingdom to Palermo. The pope was not amused, and took an instant dislike to the transalpine men who were now running the *Regnum*. In stark contrast to erudite Walter, who was Archbishop of Troia in Puglia, most of this cabal were soldiers by training, willing to use any means necessary to stay in power. It is thus unsurprising that we find Markward instigating Muslims to act against his Christian detractors.[849]

The Staufen Century

Papal concerns were largely political. The German barons and administrators in the *Regnum* were comparatively few in number, and the lives of most people do not seem to have been greatly affected by the dynastic transition.

KINGDOM OF SICILY

There were no great societal changes except, perhaps, the further depletion of the treasury. Trade continued abroad, while Genoan and Pisan merchants were permanent fixtures in Palermo and other large cities of the kingdom, to the point of building their own churches in the districts where they lived.

There was no direct involvement in foreign wars. Even Henry's recent "German Crusade" was joined by very few knights from southern Italy.[850]

There was, however, a subtle socio-cultural evolution. Speakers of Greek and Arabic were ever fewer. The Normans' French was rarely heard. Even the architecture was becoming slightly more typically "European," with construction of a Gothic church in Messina for the Teutonic Knights.[851] Most significantly, new languages were growing from the cacophony of tongues still spoken. Like the dominant church, these vernacular languages were essentially Latin.

Inevitable though this social momentum may have been, it does not seem to have been overbearing. It was a natural consequence of recent history. Nevertheless, there were now Catholics who could remember their grandparents speaking Arabic or Greek. Older people might remember Roger II and lament the passing of his daughter. Indeed, some would remember Queen Joanna, now married to Raymond VI of Toulouse, by whom she bore children. Sadly, she would not live into the next century.[852]

Sicilian society itself may have been fundamentally sound, yet the *Regnum* was haphazardly administered, with the zealous courtiers given to squabbling amongst themselves. This kind of unrest left the kingdom vulnerable to attacks from outsiders.

Tancred's exiled consort and her son-in-law solicited Innocent for his approval of an ambitious plan to take back the *Regnum*.[853] However, while the pontiff approved the claim of Walter of Brienne to Lecce and Taranto as Elvira's birthright, he did not condone an outright conquest of the entire kingdom. In 1201, Walter, accompanied by his wife, made an incursion into the kingdom at the head of an army that was intended to fight in what became the Fourth Crusade. Presumably, Walter would leave Elvira with a strong garrison at Lecce or Taranto while he departed for Palestine. His success ultimately proved elusive and he was killed by Dietpold of Schweinspünt, who had assumed a place of power following Markward's death in September 1202.[854] Walter's brother, John of Brienne, was destined to occupy a slightly more auspicious niche in history.[855]

After Markward's death, William of Capparone, another German, served as the effective regent, approved for this role by Philip of Swabia but not by the pope. As "great captain" of Palermo, William was essentially a military man who seems to have had some experience in the service of the Pisans.[856] He was infamously intolerant of dissenting opinions. Urso, the Archbishop of Agrigento, was expelled from his own archdiocese for refusing to swear fealty to him. Needless to say, William was not universally loved, even if his administration was reasonably efficient. He was hardly an inspiring leader.[857]

What followed were several dark years for the kingdom, beginning with a widespread famine owing to poor harvests in 1202, perhaps due to a drought. On the mainland, a hurricane in late December was severe enough to uproot trees.[858]

These "acts of God" may have seemed consistent with Pope Innocent's negative opinion about William and his administration, but papal actions were even more indicative of the poor rapport. In 1200, when William recommended that Walter of Palear become Archbishop of Palermo, the nomination was blocked by Rome because the pope believed the prelate to have been corrupted by Markward.[859] A certain Peter was consecrated the next year, but following his death in 1204 no successor was named for another six years since the pope did not wish to relinquish what little real authority he exercised over those governing the kingdom in Frederick's name.

In concrete terms, there was not much to be done by the papacy to discourage abuses outside ecclesiastical circles. Innocent was given to using excommunication as a tool to discipline *pro tempore* administrators of whom he did not approve. This tactic does not seem to have been very effective.[860]

Fourth Crusade

For the moment, the Sicilians had no direct interest in crusading, but there was a Hohenstaufen connection to an expedition being planned.

Philip of Swabia, being married to Irene Angelina of Constantinople, a daughter of Emperor Isaac II Angelus Comnenus, had contact with the Byzantine court.[861] In 1201, Prince Alexios, Irene's brother, made his way, via Sicily, to Germany to solicit Philip's help in restoring his father, the recently deposed Isaac, to the throne. Isaac had been unseated by his belligerent brother, Alexios III, six years earlier. It was only with the help of crafty Pisan merchants that Irene's brother, who was also held captive, managed to escape his wicked uncle.[862]

Irene was doubtless influential in helping her brother to garner western European support for a campaign to oust her uncle and restore her father. Philip wished to assist his brother-in-law, who promised to heal the schism between the Christians of east and west if placed on the Byzantine throne.

With this objective in mind, in 1203 the Fourth Crusade was diverted to Constantinople with the help of Venetian galleys. This was facilitated by the fact of the Venetians being owed a large debt from the Byzantines that Alexios was willing to pay if installed in power. Tragically, it resulted in a horrific bloodbath the next year perpetrated by a fanatical faction of the Latin Franks against the Byzantine Greeks.[863]

This led to the establishment in Constantinople of a "Latin Empire" that flourished for the next few decades at the expense of Byzantine sovereignty and culture. Yet the Latin conquest of Byzantine territory was hardly complete. In April 1205, the Bulgarians scored a victory against these "Franks" at Edirne, while a branch of the Comnenus dynasty established itself at Epirus in western Greece (see Table 21).

Philip was not directly involved in this, even if his desire to assist his brother-in-law had been a key factor in the crusaders' decision to go to Constantinople.[864]

Instead, he was forced to remain in the German lands to discourage the pretensions of his ambitious Welf rival, Otto of Brunswick, whose claims were supported by the pope in an attempt to break the Hohenstaufen hold on Germany. This left Philip little time to address the challenges facing the reign of his young nephew in Palermo.

The Fourth Crusade is usually regarded as a signal event in the separation of the church into Catholic and Orthodox spheres (see Chapter 4).

Irene Angelina was living proof that the actions of a deposed Queen of Sicily could alter the course of history.

Liberation

In October 1204, Pope Innocent nearly concluded a sort of "truce" with William of Capparone through a papal ambassador and cardinal, Gerard of Sant'Adriano. This probably involved lifting the regent's excommunication. Unfortunately, with little accommodation of substance offered by William, who, among other things, refused to compensate the church for some lands he had confiscated, the negotiations ended with Gerard leaving Palermo for Messina.[865]

Gerard was at least able to see the king long enough to ensure the boy's health and safety. At the same time, Innocent was already thinking about a possible marriage of Frederick with a sister of King Peter II of Aragon.[866] Freeing the young King of Sicily from William's control was becoming something of a papal priority.

Royal charters issued in Frederick's name during these years are few; many seem to have been lost to time. While Sicily was tranquil enough, Dietpold of Schweinspünt was busy on the mainland, where he was engaged in a series of battles against Walter of Brienne and his knights, some in rather remote areas. The end of these campaigns in June 1205 (see note 854) finally permitted Dietpold to respond to concerns that Walter of Palear and others had about William of Capparone. The next year the pope invited Dietpold to Rome, where he lifted his excommunication and ordered him to install Walter of Palear as Frederick's personal guardian.

Although William of Capparone acceded to this request, he refused to leave Palermo's royal palace. His expulsion was achieved through military force early in 1207.

Witnessing this upheaval must have made several impressions upon the young king, none of them very good. In reality, however, the kingdom he had inherited wasn't too different from others in this regard. The stories told about Frederick, as a boy, wandering around the streets and souks of Palermo may not be very accurate, but he was certainly conversant with the cultures of the people he was destined to rule.

Walter, who now found himself as regent and chancellor, viewed Dietpold with suspicion and ordered his arrest. The highly resourceful Dietpold escaped to Salerno. In May he defeated Walter's allies at Naples.[867]

Into the next year, there followed some military engagements between "Latin" and "German" baronial factions, both ostensibly loyal to the young king, in whose name they fought. For the most part, these were skirmishes in the northern part of the kingdom.⁸⁶⁸ Peering through the fog of rhetoric that emanates from the chronicles, one distinguishes the faint outlines of age-old conflicts over territory. True, some of the "native" barons had seen their lands and prerogatives infringed upon by the newcomers, but others had no such axe to grind. One chronicler tells us that:

In July of the year 1208, Pope Innocent III held a meeting of the curia at San Germano near Cassino. Here he made Count Peter of Celano, Count Richard of Aquila [Fondi] and many other counts and barons, and also rectors of cities, swear to respect in a scrupulous manner his mandate to keep peace in the Kingdom of Sicily and to help the cause of King Frederick, their lord, who was still in his minority. He appointed the aforesaid counts Peter and Richard as justiciars of the kingdom for Apulia and Terra di Lavoro.⁸⁶⁹

Here the pontiff was seizing his last opportunity to establish the administrative hierarchy in two important mainland districts of the *Regnum* before Frederick reached the age of majority later in the year, when the sovereign himself would be able to make changes. At all events, Innocent was planning Frederick's wedding, if not his very future.⁸⁷⁰

Around the same time, the murder of Philip of Swabia by a deranged nobleman left the King of Sicily without a close senior kinsman.⁸⁷¹

Keys to the Kingdom

By most accounts, Frederick reached the age of majority on his birthday in December of 1208 when he was fourteen, the minimum age for a king to be considered an adult. The pope was already planning the young man's marriage to Constance of Aragon, a widow at least ten years his senior.⁸⁷² A daughter of King Alfonso II of Aragon and Sancha of Castile, she had been married to King Emeric of Hungary, by whom she bore a son, now deceased. She was already a queen and her ability to bear children was not in doubt.⁸⁷³

In principle, a woman like Constance was a good choice not only for Frederick but, more importantly, for the kingdom. She had experienced hardship in Hungary, from which she was forced to flee following the death of her husband. She had a personal familiarity with central Europe as well as the Iberian lands, the kings of Aragon having a close relationship with the kings of Sicily. Indeed, she had Hauteville blood, her great-grandfather, Raymond Berenguer III, being the son of a daughter of Robert Guiscard (see Table 26). Constance was known to be able to confront adversity pragmatically. More than Frederick's wife, she would be his chief confidante and advisor.⁸⁷⁴

The marriage agreement stipulated that Constance would receive a dower consisting of Mount Sant'Angelo and the nearby towns, the same lands once conceded to Queen Joanna. Additionally, she would have Taormina and a number of smaller fiefs in Sicily.⁸⁷⁵

Departing Aragon in early June 1209, Constance was accompanied to Sicily by her brother, Alfonso, and a company of five hundred knights. She was wed at Messina in August.[876]

The Queen Dowager of Hungary was now crowned Queen of Sicily. There wasn't much time for celebrating.

The murder of Frederick's uncle, Philip of Swabia, in 1208, opened the way to the Welf claimant, Otto of Brunswick, to be crowned Holy Roman Emperor in October 1209.[877] Riots forced him out of Rome but did not dissuade him from further adventures in papal Italy.

No stranger to conflict, Otto was the son of Henry the Lion, Duke of Bavaria and Saxony, and Matilda of England, sister of Richard Lionheart and the fondly-remembered Joanna. Indeed, Otto had spent part of his childhood at the English court of his mother's father, Henry II, and was therefore conversant with affairs in France and England, a fact which made him that much more dangerous in papal eyes.

Otto's loyalty to the papacy was far from absolute, and he could not resist reclaiming papal lands that had once been imperial fiefs. He was encouraged by victories at Ancona and Spoleto, where he defeated loyal Hohenstaufen vassals. Farther south, on the northern fringe of the *Regnum,* in Abruzzo, he was abetted by a few disloyal ones. He soon launched a successful military incursion into Puglia and Basilicata, eventually making it as far as Calabria. However, control of even part of the Kingdom of Sicily would place Otto in the same strategic and political position toward the papacy as the hated Hohenstaufens, most notably the late Henry VI.[878]

Constance of Aragon had brought with her a large contingent of five hundred knights accompanied by their supporting esquires and troops. The prowess and fealty of these men was beyond cavil; their very presence encouraged the submission of barons on the island of Sicily who otherwise might have proven reluctant to restore crown lands usurped during Frederick's minority. Unfortunately, many of the Aragonese and Catalonian knights fell prey to a fatal epidemic. The illness also claimed the life of their leader, Constance's beloved brother, Alfonso. In view of this tragedy, the remaining Spanish knights returned to their homeland.[879]

Thinking his position ironclad, Otto, who by the end of 1210 held most of the peninsular part of the *Regnum,* arrogantly demanded that Frederick recognize him as an overlord in this region.[880] When Frederick ignored this demand to pay homage, the usurper claimed these areas outright. Otto's march on Rome to attempt to constrain papal concessions to a proposed imperial prerogative to appoint bishops prompted Innocent to excommunicate him late in 1210.[881]

Before confronting Otto, Frederick had to get his own house in order. Acting on his wife's advice, he dismissed Walter of Palear, who was now Bishop of Catania, from the chancellorship, although the prelate was later reinstated at the pope's urging.[882]

Back in Germany, the high nobility soon grew tired of Otto's behavior, and at the Diet of Nuremberg in 1211 a vocal faction elected Frederick their king with Innocent's assent.[883] This resulted in the emperor's withdrawal from

Italy with his tail between his legs, leaving most of the occupied territories under Frederick's control. Otto may have presumed that his short-lived marriage to a Hohenstaufen lady would bolster his position.[884] If so, he was sorely mistaken.

Amidst this unrest, Constance gave birth to a son, christened Henry, in 1211.

If Frederick were to reclaim the peninsula and accept the German crown, the first order of business was to raise an army. There were also political considerations. Yet it may have seemed ironic that the pope, normally opposed to rule of the lands surrounding papal territory by a sole monarch, would now acquiesce to such a situation. The arrangement was accepted on the condition that Frederick's newborn son become King of Sicily whilst Frederick himself was crowned Holy Roman Emperor. With young Henry thus crowned, Frederick tended to further diplomatic details that might put the pontiff's mind at ease. For example, he reiterated his late mother's renunciation of the apostolic legateship in Sicily.[885]

In March 1212, Frederick sailed with a flotilla and a modest force to Gaeta, north of Naples, from whence he would trek northward, meeting with the pope on the way to the imperial communes and then Germany.

Hohenstaufen Rule

The king left the queen in Sicily as his regent, effectively his surrogate or governor. Whilst Frederick and his company of knights were wending their way toward the Alps and into Germany, avoiding cities allied with Otto, Constance addressed daily affairs and cared for her infant son. She had to contend with the effects of a famine and adjudicate legal cases that could be decided only by the crown.

As a strategic base, Constance generally preferred Messina to Palermo because it facilitated closer contact with the mainland. Yet in 1212, while Frederick was attending Christmas mass at Speyer's magnificent cathedral, Constance and Henry attended the liturgy at Palermo's equally impressive basilica.[886]

Constance issued a number of charters jointly in her name and that of her young son, with the formula "Constance, Queen of the Romans, Queen of Sicily, together with Henry, King of Sicily, her son." Most of these decrees involved ecclesiastical matters.[887] The queen lent her personal patronage to the abbey at Fiore in Calabria's mountainous Sila region.

Apart from his wife, Frederick had several trusted advisors during this time. One of them was Berardo of Castagna, who eventually became Archbishop of Palermo. Another was the chancellor Walter of Palear, presently Archbishop of Catania. Herman of Salza, Grand Master of the Teutonic Order, sometimes offered advice. Frederick's chief admiral was Henry of Malta, the Genoan who had succeeded William Grasso, whose daughter he married. One of his law experts was Thaddeus of Suessa. William of Montferrat, once a supporter of Otto as emperor, came to be a faithful counsellor of Frederick.

Frederick was crowned King of the Germans at Mainz in December of

1212. It would take a few more years for him to consolidate his power in Germany, where he did not yet enjoy the support of all the elector princes and bishops. The enmity between the rival factions that came to be known as Ghibellines and Guelphs (whom we met in Chapter 11) continued in earnest, complicated by occasional wars emanating from other quarters.

One of these conflicts, the Anglo-French War, led to the crushing defeat of Otto of Brunswick at Bouvines in July 1214 by a French army led by King Philip II, effectively ending Welf military power and quashing Otto's aspirations to imperial greatness.[888] Meanwhile, in April 1213, Pope Innocent had called for a Fifth Crusade, but several years were to pass before it would materialize.[889]

His coronation at Aachen in July 1215 left little doubt of Frederick's status as King of the Germans, and the death of the Hohenstaufens' perennial rival, Otto of Brunswick, isolated and abandoned, three years later, left the younger man unopposed to claim the imperial crown.

The effect of German affairs on the Kingdom of Sicily was, if anything, the result of Frederick's complex relationship with the papacy. Other kingdoms were no more fortunate in their dealings with Innocent.

In England, the loss of the war against France precipitated problems that led King John, the younger brother of Richard Lionheart, to issue the *Magna Carta* in June 1215.[890] This was meant to protect baronial liberties. Among its many lofty principles, it was intended to restrain the capricious use of *vis et voluntas*, "force of will," by the crown. Innocent, of course, disapproved of the charter, a decision that precipitated the First Barons' War against the English king by his own vassals. John's death the next year left the matter to be settled by his son, who revived the charter.

In November 1215, Pope Innocent's Fourth Lateran Council saw some bishops protest the proposed coronation of Frederick as Holy Roman Emperor. Frederick's envoy, William of Montferrat, had to defend him against supporters of Otto. In this debate, William was supported by Berardo, Archbishop of Palermo.[891] Ecclesiastically, very few of the precepts iterated at the council were truly novel. Their focus was crusading, church reform, and the suppression of heresy. Two canons were particularly relevant to the *Regnum*. One called for the reunification of the Orthodox and Catholic churches. Interestingly, a canon forbade secular law from interfering with ecclesiastical law, and vice versa. Another canon, which does not seem to have been enforced very widely, if at all, dictated that Muslims and Jews be distinguished by their dress. The council was attended by more than four hundred bishops and at least eight hundred abbots. Some Orthodox prelates were present, along with ambassadors sent by many monarchs. This major synod is generally considered the most important Latin council up to that time, perhaps the most significant of the Middle Ages.

Frederick was not yet called upon to revise the fundamental laws of the *Regnum* where, it might be argued, *vis et voluntas* was the norm. Compared to John of England, who had lost Normandy and now Anjou, Frederick's territorial position was solid, even expanding his dominions somewhat. His allies the Teutonic Knights were beginning to conquer German and Slavic lands in central and eastern Europe which would eventually accrue to imperial control.

Before he could leave his German lands, Frederick had to address a number of fiscal matters. In some cases, this meant devolving more rights to the imperial ("free") cities and to the bishops controlling ecclesiastical towns. Of equal importance was the delegation of local authority to loyal vassals; there was no telling when, or even if, Frederick would return to Germany to enforce the law himself.

He ensured peace with other sovereigns, such as Valdemar II of Denmark.[892] The chief scope of these treaties was to protect the territory and interests of the Holy Roman Empire. However, a few of these agreements were construed to apply to the Kingdom of Sicily as well.[893]

In July 1216, Frederick promised Pope Innocent that the Kingdom of Sicily would not be annexed to the Holy Roman Empire.[894] Indeed, such a union appears never to have been very seriously contemplated. It seemed more than sufficient that both crowns might henceforth be balanced on the same head, though even that arrangement was unacceptable to the popes. The loose confederation that was the Holy Roman Empire, famously said by Voltaire to be neither holy, nor Roman, nor an empire, was not very much like Sicily, with its comparatively centralized government, and there was nothing to compel anybody trying to make one fit the mold of the other.

Innocent III was soon gone, succeeded by Cencio Savelli, Frederick's onetime tutor, who took the name Honorius III.

With his position consolidated, Frederick summoned his family to Germany. The queen and young Henry set out from Messina with six galleys in July. First they sailed to Gaeta. At Capua, the queen berated Bartholomew, the Bishop of Chieti, for his dispute with the pope.

Nicholas of Aiello, Archbishop of Salerno, and his brother, Richard, visited Constance to show their allegiance to her son as King of Sicily and to ask forgiveness for supporting Otto as emperor a few years earlier.[895] The royal party then traveled through Bologna and Cremona.[896] Constance and Henry were at Nuremberg in December 1216.

There was economic and social stability. The harvests of 1216 were exceptionally good and the *Regnum* was still exporting some of its wheat and other foodstuffs.[897] Its dried olives were a delicacy in England.

Through Frederick, the Kingdom of Sicily was linked to the Holy Roman Empire and the Italian communes through trade. Yet the *Regnum,* as a political entity, remained sovereign and distinct from these imperial realms. Here many ideas, old and new, some concerning ethics and morality, transcended mere law.

Animal Rights, Environmentalism, Pacifism, Vegetarianism

As we shall see, Frederick's ideas about ecology, through the care of birds and protection of the environment, were ahead of their time, but several other "modern" concepts that originated early in his reign, to become known to the common folk, are generally overlooked.

Francis of Bernardone was born around 1181 to a prosperous silk merchant in Assisi, a Ghibelline commune in Umbria to the north of the *Regnum* that often found itself under imperial influence, having formerly been in the Duchy of Spoleto. As a young man, Francis "of Assisi" abandoned a life of leisure to dedicate himself to the alleviation of the suffering of the poor. With papal approval, he founded the Order of Friars Minor (the Franciscans) and preached a message devoid of the triumphalist tone of some other religious orders.

His work inspired the establishment of the Order of Poor Ladies, or "Poor Clares," an order of nuns, by a devout woman of Assisi; their largest church, Santa Chiara, was later erected at Naples in the Angevin Gothic style under royal patronage that continued into the nineteenth century.

Organized along the lines of the Franciscans, the order established by Clare of Assisi, born Chiara Offreduccio, lacked the hierarchy of most religious orders even though its foundress was an aristocrat. This was a departure from tradition because orders such as the Benedictines typically reserved the highest positions to those born into the nobility. Unlike the Franciscans, who traveled often, Clare's sisters were not itinerant. She did not reach the Kingdom of Sicily but, in a sense, it arrived at her doorstep. Clare faced the troops of Frederick II during his incursions into papal territory, notably when her prayers, and the Eucharist, drove a Muslim contingent from her convent at San Damiano, outside Assisi, in 1240. This was just one miracle attributed to Clare, who came to be identified as something of a feminist symbol among Catholic women.[898]

An unequivocal pacifist, Francis famously traveled to Egypt seeking to end the Fifth Crusade. Although he spent some time in Puglia and other parts of the *Regnum,* he is not known to have met Frederick despite a legend that he did.

Like Frederick, he favored an early "Italo-Romance" vernacular over Latin. Francis used a form of Medieval Umbrian akin to Tuscan. His most famous work, written shortly before his death, is the *Canticle of the Sun.* A good part of the *corpus* of his work survives.

Francis identified elements of the environment, such as water, being so closely linked to human well-being that they were "brethren."

He defended the rights of domestic animals in an age when, rather than pets, dogs were often pressed into service to herd sheep or guard homes while cats were kept to control pests such as mice. It is believed that Francis protested when he witnessed such behaviors as a peasant beating a dog into submission.

His rationale for this position was that animals were God's creatures and therefore kindred to humans. On a more "pragmatic" note, he posited that somebody who mistreated animals was just as likely to mistreat people. In the thirteenth century, such views were considered unorthodox, perhaps even radical. The Bible does not generally speak well of dogs. Indeed, the Haditha state that angels will not enter a home where there are dogs, hence the traditional Muslim antipathy toward canines.

In the western world, the modern concept of vegetarianism, for philosophical reasons, is sometimes attributed to the initiative of Francis, who was almost certainly a pollotarian or pescatarian. This was linked to his advocacy of the humane treatment of animals, but it was not without precedent in Christianity. Monks sometimes abstained from animal flesh. (Jesus ate fish and probably meat.)

Francis of Assisi died in 1226 and was canonized two years later, when his follower Thomas of Celano began writing the saint's first biography, but centuries were to pass before the ideas espoused by him became part of everyday life. The greatest church of his order erected in the *Regnum* was built in the Italianate Romanesque Gothic style immediately following Frederick's reign; now a minor basilica, it stands guard over a medieval square in Palermo.

Except for being baptized in the same cathedral, Frederick and Francis would seem to have had little in common. Yet both were learned men who viewed peace as a way forward. Both had a certain tolerance for people of other faiths, such as the Muslims and Jews.

It was only under papal coercion that Frederick ostensibly supported the long "crusade" against the Albigensians, the Cathars of Languedoc, while his brother-in-law actually fought against papal forces (see note 879). Frederick may have benefitted from the conquests of the Teutonic Knights on the eastern fringes of the empire, but these were not his initiatives.

It would develop that, like Francis, he desired peace with the Muslims of the eastern Mediterranean, and for this he received the barbs of papal censure.

The early efforts of the Franciscans, who sought to help the poor, were supported by Frederick. Only later, following the death of Francis himself, was it necessary for the king to take certain modest measures against the order, and then only in response to the papal politics that led to the monarch's excommunication. Unfortunately, the papacy eventually used the Franciscans as a weapon against Frederick.

Naturally, Frederick's character changed with age, colored by experience. However, most of the negative traits attributed to him were hatched after his death by chroniclers and poets from the imperial communes who harbored strong Guelphic biases against him. Dante Alighieri is the most obvious example, but another is Salimbene di Adam, a Franciscan born in Parma in 1221.

Conversely, we find very little criticism of Frederick in the Kingdom of Sicily, where his policies, formulated at least in part by Constance, seem to have been viewed as more acceptable. Even in the communes north of Rome, the first two decades of his reign are generally free of the harshest condemnations.

Detractors of Francis were few in number. He is generally credited with bringing a refreshingly simple spirit to Catholic thought. Despite this simplicity, he is considered, with Frederick, one of the greatest thinkers in Italy, and perhaps all of western Europe, to live during the first half of the thirteenth century.

In different ways, both men may be viewed as "secularists" in the abstract sense that they advocated for less involvement of the church, as a political entity, in everyday life and affairs of state.[899]

More than overt dogmatism, their efforts were tantamount to a dignified, if muffled, *cri de coeur,* a pragmatic reaction to authoritarian mentalities prevalent in the church that were virtually unchanged during the preceding centuries.

In practice, Frederick patronized the arts and sciences, often with very little direct reference to the divine. Francis viewed nature as an extension of God, but without the comparatively complex philosophy of Bernard of Clairvaux, a thinker of the previous generation, or Thomas Aquinas, a theologian of the next.

Whereas Bernard preached crusades, Francis preached against them. Even Frederick, though scarcely a pacifist, was reluctant to prosecute a war when a truce might suffice.

Toward the end of his life, Francis withdrew from active involvement in the order he founded, which he considered to have strayed somewhat from its original mission by becoming something too complex or worldly for his taste. Here his actions were more personal, attributed to nobody but himself, while Frederick's policies were largely those of his advisors.

Frederick was a monarch whose ideas about monarchy, if not exactly radical, would prove to be at least discreetly evolutive, inspiring his support of novel developments in law, learning and language. Francis was a monk who entertained a new monasticism, one that brought its friars into a more active participation in society than those of the older religious orders. For a time, these subtle heterodoxies may have served to inspire the common folk to view kings and clerics as part of their extended community, and this very concept might make the social hierarchy, later known as the "three estates" (nobility, clergy, commonalty), more cohesive as a whole. This is rather difficult to gauge from the surviving record because the voices of the common folk were only rarely preserved in the written word.

Frederick and Francis stood out in their time. While it would be inappropriate to ascribe to either man a personality based on our modern norms, each represented a small step forward in thirteenth-century thought.[900]

Imperial Kingdom

With his wife and son at his side, Frederick continued to address imperial affairs in Germany, from whence a number of princes and knights were preparing to depart for the Fifth Crusade. Yet the knights of the Kingdom of Sicily were, for the most part, conspicuously absent in this endeavor, even as they saw foreign crusaders march through the *Regnum* to embark at ports like Gaeta and Brindisi.[901] Pope Honorius was hardly pleased by this lack of participation by the man he was planning to crown Holy Roman Emperor. In consolation, he at least had an opportunity to oversee another imperial coronation.

In April 1217, the pontiff crowned Peter II of Courtenay, a patrilineal descendant of the kings of France, as the "Latin" emperor of Constantinople. Peter was one of many monarchs supporting the crusade, but in Epirus *en route* to Constantinople by land, he was captured by the forces of his rival Theodore Comnenus (see Table 21), Lord of Epirus and pretender to the Byzantine throne, and imprisoned. His wife, Yolanda of Flanders, escaped this fate and reached Constantinople, where she reigned briefly as regent for her son.[902]

It wasn't only the political developments that distinguished this era. There were also important social trends, such as the evolution of language.

Chapter 24

LINGUA DELLU REGNU

By the second decade of the thirteenth century, we find several "native" languages in the *Regnum*. The earliest of these tongues to achieve vernacularity in daily use, and the one about which the most is known, is Sicilian.[903] The emergence of Sicilian was one of the most obvious results of the gradual Latinization of the kingdom. A common spoken language such as Sicilian provides insight into society at large because, like cuisine, it touched everybody, not only the nobility and the clergy.

Although we can never know if our kings and queens listened to troubadours or minstrels recite specific verses, a body of the poetry of the Sicilian School survives. It is collectively the first known literature of any of the Italian languages although, as we have seen, Francis of Assisi composed prayers in an early form of Umbrian.

The geographical focus of Sicilian was Palermo, where the sonnet was born as part of this movement, but it was also spoken in much of Calabria, as well as parts of Puglia, especially around Taranto and Lecce. In Campania we find the early development of Neapolitan, which is somewhat more similar to the languages of central Italy. Though Dante and his contemporaries knew of Sicilian, it did not directly influence Tuscan or Umbrian, which developed on their own from Latin.

Until around 1200, most of the poetry heard in Sicily was written, and recited, in Siculo-Arabic, Hebrew or Norman French. We know something of the Arabic works, such as the *qasidas* of Abd al Gabbar ibn Hamdis, but virtually nothing of those composed in French save for one significant example.[904]

Set mostly in Calabria, the *Chanson d'Aspremont,* part of the Charlemagne Cycle, is an epic of over eleven thousand lines composed in Calabria or Sicily, perhaps shortly before 1190, possibly to encourage participation in the Third Crusade.[905] The author himself seems not to have been from the Kingdom of Sicily. The poem became popular in England and Italy, with later copies of the work reflecting English or Tuscan linguistic influences. Unusually long for a *chanson de geste,* it was favored by Richard Lionheart and his dynasty. Prominent amongst its themes is the story, or backstory, of Durendal, a mystical sword obtained from a Muslim owner in the context of a tale that is an allegory for the forthcoming Third Crusade.

Not all poetry known in Sicily before the thirteenth century was, strictly speaking, *court* poetry, which is part of the courtly tradition that began to flourish in the Norman era during the reign of William II. As we have seen, William's time on the throne coincided with the introduction of Provençal culture and art (exemplified in the carved capitals of Monreale's cloister), tournaments, heraldry and the politesse that, in common parlance, has come to be called "chivalry." It also coincided with the arrival, in 1177, of Joanna of England, whose mother was a great patroness of the troubadour tradition.

Although Sicilian began its evolution as a vernacular language during the last decades of the twelfth century, probably taking shape by 1200, the surviving examples of actual poems can be dated accurately only to the majority of Frederick II.

Classified as Italo-Dalmatian (and also "Italo-Romance"), the earliest Sicilian was a Romance language having French, Arabic, Greek and even German influences. It was influenced by Catalan after 1282, when Sicily, but not the peninsular part of the kingdom, was ruled by the royal house of Aragon. A distinction may be drawn between the medieval (or "Middle") Sicilian spoken and written into the fourteenth century and the modern form of the language sometimes heard today.

The Sicilian Tongue

Interesting as the language is, it is no longer spoken as it was in Frederick's time. A few observations are in order.

Succinctly, we may note that it is a slightly guttural tongue, sounding vaguely like Catalan, lacking a true future tense or (historically) a standard orthography. The long "u" is often used in words similar to Italian ones which use the long "o." We find *picciottu* instead of *giovanotto* (young man), *chiddu* for *esso* (it), *chistu* for *questo* (this), *iddu* for *egli* (he) and *idda* for *ella* (she), and so forth. Its verb forms make Sicilian as distinct from Italian as it is from Spanish. Certain nouns and adjectives are rather peculiar: *parrinu* instead of *prete* (priest), *beddu* for *bello* (beautiful).

The Sicilian word *tascio,* which means "tacky," falsely sophisticated or lacking in good taste, is understandably offensive in fashion-conscious Italy, though to refer to somebody as *vastaso,* "uncouth," is far more insulting. Certain Sicilian phrases seem appropriate sometimes. *Ammunì* sounds much more persuasive than the mellifluous Italian *Andiamo* ("Let's go").

Some words come directly from Arabic: *babbaluci* (also the Greek *boubalàkion*) for *lumache* (snails), *dammusu* for ceiling, *saia* (from *saqiya*) for "canal," *gébbia* for "reservoir," and *azzizare* ("to make beautiful") from *aziz*. Other words rooted in Arabic: *favara* (a well), *mischinu* (an unfortunate person), *zagara* (orange blossom), *zammù* (anise), *balata* (stone), *cafìsu* (a liquid measure, from *qafìz*), *tarì* (a gold coin).

A number of Sicilian words derive from Norman French: *buatta* (jar, from *boîte*), *custureri* (tailor, from *coustrier*), *largasia* (largesse), *racìna* (grape), *vuccèri* (butcher, from *boucher*), *accattari* (to buy, from *acater*, modern *acheter*), *cavallu* and *cavaddu* (horse, from *cheval*).

From Medieval Greek we find: *carusu* (boy, from *kouros*), *cona* (icon, from *eikona*), *crastu* (ram, from *krastos*), *pistiari* (to eat, from *apestiein*), *naca* (cradle, from *nake*), *bucali* (pitcher, from *baukalion*), *grasta* (a terracotta vase, from the classical *gastra*).

Among words from Middle High German are: *arbitrari* (to work, from *arbeit*), *vardari* (to wait or watch, from *warten*), *sparagnari* (to save money, from *sparen*), *guastari* and *vastari* (to waste, from *wastjan*).

Provençal has made a few contributions, notably: *lascu* (thin or sparse, from *lasc*), *addumari* (to light, from *allumar*), *aggrifari* (to kidnap, from *grifar*).

There are, of course, many words from Latin and Catalan.

On a more hypothetical note, the Indo-European etymologies of a few Sicilian words may be connected to the language of the Sikels who already populated the island's eastern region when the Greeks arrived in antiquity. Two oft-cited examples are *dudda* (various red berries, akin to the Welsh *rhudd* meaning "pink" and the Romanian *dudà*), and *scrozzu* ("short" or "undeveloped," similar to Germanic *scurz* and Lithuanian *su-skurdes*).

Contrary to a notion popularized during the nineteenth century, Sicilian and Neapolitan are not "dialects" of Italian.[906] Recent years have seen a renewed interest in Italy's regional languages.[907]

Neapolitan

While Sicilian was predominant in Sicily, southern Calabria and parts of Puglia, Neapolitan was spoken in other peninsular regions of the kingdom during Frederick's reign, even though use of this tongue became more generalized in southern Italy after 1266. The growth of Naples, and its newfound status as a capital, displaced the cultural influence of Salerno.

Issued between 960 and 963, the so-called "Campanian Placets" are considered the oldest legal (judicial) documents in Italy to include text written in an "Italo-Romance" vernacular, offering us a glimpse of the language spoken by the Lombards of Salerno and its environs when the Normans arrived. The oldest one, the *Placet of Capua* of March 960, records the oft-cited decision in a case between Rodelgrimo of Aquino and the abbot of Mount Cassino. The testimony of a witness was written in an early form of Neapolitan (or "Salernitan") so that it reflected his actual spoken words. This text suggests much about just how Latin or "Italian" the Lombard society of southern Italy (and its language) had become by the tenth century.

Recorded by a judge, Arechisi of Capua, the oldest of the placets (like the others) explicates an important legal principle, namely protection of the long-standing right to land held by a gastald or other landholder in the event that the property was contested by the church, or vice versa. Such land could not be assigned to the challenging claimant (petitioner) if the holder could prove continuous possession during the immediately-preceding thirty years. The church often prevailed.

In the charter of 960 we read phrases such as: *Sao ko kelle terre, per kelle fini quei ki contene trenta anni le possette parte Sancti Benedictj.*[908]

This "Italo-Romance," quasi-Neapolitan language spoken by the Lombards of *southern* Italy is distinguished from the more "Longobardic" tongue spoken in parts of *northern* Italy by, for example, Adelaide del Vasto and her knights who established several towns in the Nebrodian region of Sicily (see notes 42 and 639).

In the fourteenth century we find Giovanni Boccaccio writing a famous letter in Neapolitan, which by that time had been influenced somewhat by the Angevins' French. Shortly before 1350, the *Cronaca di Partenope,* a major history of Naples, was written in a Neapolitan which, by then, could be understood by those accustomed to reading Tuscan or even Castilian, hence: *Onde el dicto Re Gulielmo con soi navilij laccompagno per mare in fino a la cità de Venecia alla quale el dicto papa volea andare per più securita di lui, a ziò che Federico imperatore non lo podesse offendere.*[909]

Other vernaculars developed in southern peninsular Italy. Prominent among these are Calabrian and Puglian, which have more Greek influences than Neapolitan.

In the literary sphere, Neapolitan, like Sicilian, was eclipsed in most of what is now Italy during the fifteenth century by Tuscan movements. Interestingly, however, certain fairy tales of medieval origin were introduced in Europe through Neapolitan. Of particular note is the work of Giovan Battista Basile, whose *Pentamerone,* originally published in 1634 as *Lo Cunto de li Cunti* ("The Tale of Tales"), included such stories as *Cinderella,* set in the Kingdom of Naples and later published in other versions by Charles Perrault and the Grimm brothers. Basile's version of *Sleeping Beauty* was also adapted by foreign authors, while his *Petrosinella* became *Persinette* in French and *Rapunzel* in German.

The Sicilian School

The best known poets of the Sicilian School are Giacomo of Lentini, by profession a notary, and Cielo of Alcamo. Although Cielo's *Contrasto* (in Appendix 4) is the longest surviving poem, and the most popular among Sicilians, Giacomo's known body of work surpasses that of his peers in quantity.

Amongst the other poets are the Abbot of Tivoli (whatever his name), Roger d'Amici, Otto delle Colonne, Guy delle Colonne, Rinaldo of Aquino, Stephen the Pronotary, Mazzeo of Ricco, Jacopo Mostacci, Percival Doria, Giacomino the Apulian, Tommaso of Sasso and Arrigo Testa of Lentini.

Those boasting important court connections include Peter della Vigna, John of Brienne, and Frederick's sons Enzio (Enzo) and Manfred.

The only female poet usually mentioned in connection with the Sicilian School is "Nina of Messina," who wrote later and whose exact name is unknown. She is the first poetess known to have composed poems in an "Italian" language. Her poem, *Sad Me Who Loved a Sparrowhawk*, in the original orthography:

Tapina jnme camaua vno fparuero, amaualu tanto chio menemoria, alorichiamo bene mera manero, edumque troppo pafciere noi douia. ore montato efalito fialtero, afai più alto chefare nomfolia, edè afifo dentro auno uerzero, vnaltra dona lotene jm balia. Jsparuero mio chio tauea nodrito, fonalglio doro tifaciea portare, p'ché delluciellare foffe piu ardito. Orfe falito ficome lomare, edarotti ligieti efe fugito, quando eri fermo neltuo vciellare.

Sad me who loved a sparrow-hawk, So much that I was dying over him; When I called him he would heed me, And I never had to feed him very much. / Now he has flown off and he has soared, So high that he cannot rise any further; And he is perched in a garden, Where another woman has him under her power. / My sparrow-hawk, whom I had nurtured myself; I had you wear a golden bell, So that you were more daring in your hunt. / Now you have risen just like the sea tide, You have torn your jesses and you have fled, While you were resting from your hunting.[910]

Frederick himself composed a number of poems, and five surviving works are usually attributed to him. The French and Provençal influences on the Sicilian School are obvious; Cielo's *Contrasto* is a Sicilian adaptation of *Le Roman de la Rose*. (A *romance* such as the *Contrasto* tends to focus on the individual, while a *chanson de geste* is more general in tone.)

When did Sicilian become the principal court language? This is difficult to estimate precisely, but during the regency of Constance, the mother of Frederick II, both German and French were the predominant spoken languages at court, while there were ever fewer speakers of Arabic and Greek at the palace.

Sicilian developed, in the first instance, as the spoken language of the ordinary people as they became "Sicilian" rather than remaining identifiably Arab, Norman or Greek. It is a product of the gradual amalgamation of cultures and the eventual dominance of Latin in liturgy, along with the conversion of Muslims to Christianity and, however insidiously, the Byzantine Greeks to Catholicism.

Most of the poems translated from Sicilian into English as recently as the middle of the twentieth century were rendered in a slightly "Victorian" style that attempted to maintain their rhyme and prosody. The translations in this chapter are almost literal, with no attempt at rhyme or poetic style, as the original words should, in a sense, speak for themselves.

The work selected for this chapter is the poetry generally attributed to Frederick II. Some of this has already been translated for publication elsewhere. However, what follow are original translations, effected without reference to any others. As the poems of Frederick presented here were slightly "Tuscanized" by copyists, they are not available in "pure" Sicilian. Apart from that, the orthography of the poems as they were copied in the earliest known codices differs slightly from the texts presented here.[911] Some of the orthography varies slightly between manuscripts, and in some instances it is more typically "Sicilian," with frequent use of the "k" and the "u" as well as "j" in place of "i."

This phenomenon should be viewed in the context of the emergence of a "Siculo-Tuscan" school after Frederick's death, which explains how this poetry and vernacular became known in northern Italy by 1260. Although the Sicilian language itself influenced Tuscan only minimally, poets such as Chiaro Davanzati and Guittone of Arezzo adopted styles that inspired a generation of poets.

Frederick himself presents us with some complexities. His falconry treatise reflects an unusual proclivity for scholarship by a monarch of his era. This was likely dictated to scribes, who wrote it in Latin. His poems, on the other hand, were probably his own words, even if they were dictated.

Though Frederick's patronage of the Sicilian School and its language was not purely political, it was consistent with his efforts to assert himself and his Kingdom of Sicily in the face of continued papal opposition. It is quite possible that he was seeking to establish an independent culture.

Significantly, many poems of the Sicilian School were intended to be recited rather than sung to an instrumental accompaniment. Frederick's *Dolze Meo Drudo* may be an exception, but its only known musical accompaniment was written long after the poem itself was composed.[912] The song-like, lyrical *canzone* (from the Provençal *canso*) was suitable to be sung; this form gave rise to the sonnet. The poems of the Sicilian School are broadly divided into those two categories.

Some traditional folk music, particularly that having lyrics in Sicilian or Neapolitan, seems to have medieval origins. Its provenance is difficult to trace precisely, but by the sixteenth century we find a number of songs being recorded (transcribed), though not necessarily published, for posterity. In the eighteenth century, Alfonso Liguori, a prelate who was eventually canonized, transcribed several old Neapolitan songs. More recently, certain melodies have been "reconstructed" as part of a revival, and performed with medieval instruments.

The thirteenth century saw a number of musical instruments in use. Besides various string instruments such as the harp, psaltery, and early forms of the violin and guitar, we find the bagpipes, or *zampogna,* in the Kingdom of Sicily. The shawm, or *ciaramella,* was a woodwind instrument often regarded as a precursor to the oboe. An early form of the flute was also known, and of course there were drums. Various wind and string instruments were used that today are associated chiefly with folk music; the *colascione* was similar to a mandolin or lute but had only three strings and a very long neck. The rebec, or *ribeca,* resembled a violin but usually had three strings; a musician depicted in the ceiling of Palermo's Palatine Chapel is shown playing a ribeca or lute. The organistrum, or *ghironda,* was closely associated with poetry readings.

The ephemeral Sicilian School dissipated and disappeared upon the death of its last royal patron, King Manfred. It has been suggested that, had the Hohenstaufen dynasty survived and prospered, ruling the Kingdom of Sicily and the northern Italian comunes for a few more generations, perhaps even into the fifteenth century, Sicilian, rather than Tuscan, might have emerged as the principal Italian vernacular.

The lengthiest original work composed in Middle Sicilian before the widespread emergence of Tuscan as Italy's literary language is a prose chronicle, the *Rebellamentu di Sichilia contra Re Carlu*. Thought to be the memoir of John of Procida, this narrative recounts the history of the War of the Sicilian Vespers of 1282 from the Ghibelline point of view. It was probably written a few years before John's death in 1298. The work is significant because, unlike most of the existing texts of the poems of the Sicilian School, its language has not been Tuscanized. It is, in fact, the earliest known narrative of substantial length written in one of the Italian languages. Later, in the fourteenth century, we find *La Conquesta di Sichilia Fatta per li Normandi* of Simon of Lentini, essentially a Sicilian translation of certain parts of the Latin chronicle of Godfrey Malaterra, complemented by additional details about later history. Here the language is strikingly similar to that of the *Rebellamentu*.

In reality, the surviving texts of most of the poems are problematical because, being transcribed from around 1280 onward, apparently by speakers of Tuscan, they do not accurately reflect Sicilian as it was actually spoken.

Apart from its orthography, it is obvious that the language of the following excerpt from the sixty-fourth chapter of the *Rebellamentu*, based on the *Spinelli Codex*, the oldest known manuscript (kept in Palermo), is quite different from the poetry we find in *Codex Vaticanus Latinus 3793* and *Codex Urbinas Latinus 697*, with their words altered by Tuscan influences. This is a Sicilian nearer to what the poets actually spoke and wrote:

Quandu lu re di aragona audiu quisti palorj, sì appj grandi dubitanza, audendu chi lu re carlu avia tantu putirj. Et incontinenti mandau currerj per l'isula di sichilia, chi si re carlu vinissi inver palermu. Et in quilla nocti vinni unu notaru inbaxaturi di parti di lu comunj di missina, e quillu missaiu dissi a lu re di aragona comu in missina non avia vidanda exceptu per octu iorni et non per chuj e kj "vuj nj dijati dari ayutu e ssiccursu di gentj e di victuagli, chi per nixunu modu nuj non putimu pluj resistirj dananti di lu re carlu, sì kj nuj nj rindirimu ad ipsu, kj nuj non putimu altru farj." [913]

In their original form, the poems of Frederick II and the other poets of the Sicilian School probably sounded more like this than what appears in the following section and in Appendix 4. Fortunately, a number of texts were transcribed from manuscripts that have since been lost.[914]

Analogies are rarely precise, but we may view the older ("Medieval" or "Middle") Sicilian spoken before 1300 the way that native speakers of English regard the language of Chaucer, and the more modern Sicilian, influenced by Catalan, as the language of Shakespeare.[915]

Although Sicilian continued to be spoken, evolving with time, it was no longer the important literary language it had once been. By 1500, official documents such as the *riveli* (a tax roll) were recorded in what was essentially Tuscan with a few Sicilian phrases and usages. Yet most Sicilians still spoke Sicilian into the early years of the twentieth century.

The five works presented here constitute the entire "Frederican Canon" of the emperor's poems, about which much has been written.[916] Wherever possible, words were preferred in the manuscript texts which reflect the Sicilian language of Frederick's era over the more Tuscanized versions.[917] The first work is a sonnet.

Misura, Providenzia e Meritanza

Misura, providenzia e meritanza fanno l'uomo eser sagio e conoscente e'n ogni nobeltà l'uom se n'avanza e ciascuna riccheza fa prudente.

Judgment, consideration and merit make a man wise and knowledgeable propagating every sign of nobility, and every wealth earned makes him prudent.

Nè di riccheze aver grande audanza faria l'omo ch'è ville esser valente, ma della ordinata costumanza discende gentileza fra le gente.

A man lacking wealth in great measure, even if lowborn, will be seen as worthy, by consistently behaving honorably, and he'll be esteemed by the folk as a gentleman.

Omo ch'è posto in alto signoragio e in riccheze abunda, tosto scende, credendo fermo stare in signoria.

Instead, a man who enjoys aristocratic rank and abundant wealth quickly loses status by thinking himself better than others.

Unde non salti troppo omo ch'è sagio, per grande alteza che ventura prende, ma tutt'ora mantegna cortesia.

Contrarily, a wise man who is discreet in manners, confronting his every destiny with dignity, will always remain courteous to all.

Poi Ch'a Voi Piace Amore

Poi ch'a voi piace, amore, che eo degia trovare, faronde mia possanza ch'io vegna a compimento. Dat'agio lo meo core in voi, madonna, amare, e tutta mia speranza in vostro piagimento; ed eo non mi partiragio da voi, donna valente, ch'eo v'amo dolzemente, e piace a voi ch'eo agia intendimento. Valimento: Mi date, donna fina, chè lo meo core adesso a voi s'inchina.

Since it pleases you, my love That I should write poems I will do everything I can To succeed in bringing you joy. My heart is devoted To loving you, milady, And all I hope for Is for your appreciation; I will not leave you, worthy lady. Because I love you sweetly And my aspiration pleases you. Give me strength, perfect woman, Because my heart now bows to you.

LINGUA DELLU REGNU

S'eo inchino, rason agio di sì amoroso bene, ch'eu spero, in voi sperando ch' ancora creio avire allegro meo coragio; e tutta la mia spene, ch'ò data in voi amando ed in vostro piacire ca veio li sembianti di voi, chiarita spera, ca spero gioia intera ed ò fidanza ne lo meo servire a piacire, di voi che siete fiore sor l'altre donn'e avete più valore.

If I bow down to you, it is with reason, Before such a loving woman That I await and hope for, And that I still have to achieve, But joyful is my courage. And all my hope Was devoted to loving you And pleasing you And I see your face, oh bright star, For I desire complete happiness And I trust in my ability to serve you in love, And to please you, who are much more beautiful Above all other women and you are more worthy than them.

Valor sor l'altre avete e tutta caunoscenza, ca null'omo porria vostro pregio contare, che tanto bella sete! Secondo mia credenza non è donna che sia alta, sì bella, pare, nè c'agia insegnamento 'nver voi, donna sovrana. La vostra ciera umana mi dà conforto e facemi alegrare: s'eo pregiare — vi posso, donna mia, più conto mi ne tegno tuttavia.

You have more virtue than any other woman And you are full of wisdom, So much so that no man can Grasp the depth of it, Because you are so beautiful! I believe there is no other woman who equals you in beauty, nor any one as intelligent compared to you, regal woman. Your kind human face Comforts me and makes me happy; If I were to praise you, oh perfect woman, I could always boast and be proud of it.

A tutt'or vegio e sento, ed ònne gran ragione, ch' amore mi consenti voi, gentil criatura. Già mai non n'ò abento, vostra bella fazone cotant' à valimenti. Per vo'son fresco ognura; a lo sole riguardo lo vostro bello viso, che m'à d'amore priso, e tegnolomi in gran bonaventura. Spreio à tuttura — chi al buon segnore crede però son dato a la vostra merzede.

I always see and feel, And with good reason, That Love makes me feel in touch With you, oh gentle woman. I am never at peace, Because of the strong virtue Emanating from your beautiful face. I am always calm for you: In the sunlight I see your beautiful face, Which has made me fall in love, And I keep it as a sign of good luck. He who trusts in a good lord is always hopeful: This is the reason why I trust in your mercy.

Merzé pietosa agiate di meve, gentil cosa, chè tutto il mio disio e certo ben sacciate, alente più che rosa, che ciò ch'io più golio è voi veder sovente, la vostra dolze vista, a cui sono ublicato, core e corp' ò donato. Allora ch'io vi vidi primamente, mantenente — fui in vostro podere, che altra donna mai non voglio avere.

Have mercy on me, oh gentle lady, Because of all my desire. And you know very well, More fragrant than a rose, That what I most desire Is to see you often: It is for the sweet vision of you Before which I fade, That I have given up my heart and body. From the very first moment I saw you I suddenly fell under your power, for I don't ever wish to have another woman but you.

De le Mia Disïanza

De la mia disïanza ch'ò penato ad avere, mi fa sbaldire, poi ch'ï n'ò ragione, chè m'à data fermanza com'io possa compire lu meu placire, senza ogne cagione, a la stagione, ch'io l'averò 'n possanza. Senza fallanza, voglion le persone, per cui cagione, facciamò membranza.

The object of my desire, For which I suffered to conquer, Makes me joyful now that I have reason to be so Because it assures me that I can carry out my pleasure Without any deceptive obstacle During the time I will have her in my power. Without any delay I want the person Of whom for now I dream about.

A tuttt'or membrando de lo dolze diletto ched'io aspetto, sonne alegro e gaudente. Vaio tanto tardando, chè'n paura mi metto ed ò sospetto, de la mala gente, che per neiente, vanno disturbando e rampognando, chi ama lealemente; und'io sovente, vado sospirando.

I am constantly contemplating The sweet delight That awaits me. I am happy and content. If I continue to delay It is only because I am fearful And suspicious of those evil people, Who without any reason disturb And criticize those who truly love; And this often makes me suffer.

Sospiro e sto 'n rancura; ch'io son sì disioso e pauroso, mi fate penare. M'a tanto m'asicura lo suo viso amoroso, e lo gioioso, riso e lo sguardare e lo parlare, di quella criatura, che per paura, mi face penare e dimorare, tant'è fine e pura.

I suffer and feel afflicted For having this strong desire And with fear they make me suffer. But that is when I find reassurance Thanks to her loving face, And the joyous laughter and the way she looks at me And the manner of speech of that good woman, Thus I am afraid to suffer and to be doubtful And to delay; she is so perfect and pure.

Tanto è sagia e cortise, no credo che pensasse, nè distornasse, di ciò che m'à impromiso. Da la ria gente aprise da lor non si stornasse, che mi tornasse, a danno chi gli ò ofiso, e ben mi à miso in foco, ciò m'è aviso, che lo bel viso, lo cor m'adivise.

She is so wise and courteous, That I cannot even contemplate her changing her mind Nor pulling back from what she promised me. Evil people's behavior has made her understand Not to be lured by their ideas, As to avoid being hurt by those who I offended, And this has made me happy, On fire, it seems to me, That her lovely face has divided my heart.

Diviso m'à lo core e lo corpo à 'n balia, e tienmi e mi lia, forte incatenato. La fiore d'ogne fiore prego per cortesia, che più non sia, lo suo detto fallato, nè disturbato, per inizadore, nè suo valore, non sia menovato, nè rabassato, per altro amadore.

My heart is divided And my body has power over it, It holds me and bonds me tightly in chains. The most beautiful flower above all others I pray, in all kindness, That her words will never again be lies, Nor that they will ever again be disturbed By those who sow discord, Nor that her worthiness will ever be lost, Or diminished by another lover.

Dolze Meo Drudo, e Vatène

Dolze meo drudo, e vatène! Meo sire, a Dio t'acomano, ché ti diparti da mene ed eo tapina rimanno.

My sweet lover, begone! Milord, I entrust you to God from the moment you leave me and I, in misery, remain here.

Lassa, la vita m'è noia, dolze la morte a vedere, ch'io non penso mai guerire membrandome fuor di gioia. Membrandome che te'n vai,

Oh, life for me is misery, death seems a liberation, for I believe there is no cure for me as I think of myself deprived of joy,

Lo cor mi mena gran guerra; di ciò che più disïai mi tolle lontana terra. Or se ne va lo mio amore ch'io sovra gli altri l'amava.

Just thinking of you leaving me makes my heart fight against me. A faraway land deprives me of what I most desire. The love I cherished above all others has abandoned me.

Biasmomi de la Toscana, ch'è mi diparte lo core. Dolce mia donna, lo gire non è per mia volontate, ché mi convene ubidire quelli che m'ha'n potestate.

I curse Tuscany, who has stolen my heart. My sweet lady, my departure is not by my own choice, but I must obey who has power over me.

Or ti conforta s'io vado, e già non ti dismagare, ca per null'altra d'amare, amor, te non falseraggio.

Now be brave even as we part, and don't lose faith, for I shall never betray you, my love, for another.

Lo vostro amore mi tene ed hami in sua segnoria, ca lealmente m'avene d'amar voi sanza falsìa. Di me vi sia rimembranza,

Your love holds me under your dominance, and keeps me faithful to love you without deceit. Remember me.

E non mi aggiate 'n obria, c'avete in vostra balia tutta la mia disïanza. Dolze mia donna, 'l commiato domando sanza tenore,

And don't forget me, for you have in your power all of my desires. My sweet lady, I pray that you bid me farewell without further delay,

Che vi sia racomandato, ché con voi riman mio core. Cotal è la 'namoranza degli amorosi piaceri, che non mi posso partire da voi, mia donna, in lleanza.

As I commend to you my heart so that it remains with you. So pleasing is the memory of our time together that in perfect faith, I cannot truly leave you, my lady.

Per la Fera Membranza

Per la fera membranza, de lo mio gran disio malamente fallio che mi fece partire e dipartire la gran gioia ch'avea; ma senza dubitanza lo meo signor sentio, alorché mi partio del mio pregio gradire che fallire, non vol né non porea; e non comportaria la mia pena sapesse, che tanto mi stringesse quanto temesse, de la vita mia. Per che si converria che tal gioia si desse, che, s'altri l'aprendesse, dir no 'l potesse, ch'eli sofferia.

For the tormented memory Of my intense desire A grave error was made That made me leave And separate from the intense joy that I felt; But without a doubt, when I left I felt that my lord Appreciated my worthiness As he would never and could never be mistaken; And he would not allow Me to suffer if he knew That this saddens me so much As to fear for my life. So it may be better For someone to give me such joy, So that if someone were to learn of it They would not mention it due to envy.

Farò come l'ausello quand'altre lo distene, che vive ne la spene la quale à ne lo core, e no more, sperando di campare; e aspettando quello viveraggio con pene, ch'io non credo aver bene tant'è lo fino amore e lo grande ardore, ch'aggio di tornare a voi, donn' ad amare di tutte giò compita, ch'avete la mia vita di giò partita, e da ralegranza; e mille anni mi pare che fu la dipartita, e parmi la redita quasi fallita, per la disïanza.

I will be like a bird Held as a prisoner, Living for the sole hope That it keeps in its heart. It does not die hoping to survive; And anticipating That way of living whilst suffering, But I don't believe I have a like virtue. For my love is so precious And my desire to return to you is so strong, Oh loving woman, endowed with joy, You have taken away from my life Joy and happiness; And it seems to me that a thousand years Have passed since I left, And it seems to me that my return Has failed because of my desire.

Jvausi misser palmeri abbati & diss.
signuri Re laudatu sia deu & ben
chi esti vinutu effactu nru intendimentu
p uostra bontati equilla di misser iohanni
di prochita sipo v plaza di quista cosa i
asa bon mezu ebonu fini si comu d/auutu
bonu incomezamentu ma ben vuria ki
om Russium vinutu cum phi genti ch
silu Re carlu dixonisi p tucta la ysola di
sichilia luquali ani ben gndichi milia
homini accauallu siki nuj auiximu t ppu
affari accumbactiri cum ipu et sipero m
pari ki penzamu di kauiri phi agenti di
quali partikauiri sindi p uassi sipo eu
ceiyu ki mi sima sia p dicta tantu ora
ristricta et in succaren di vidanda

Vandu lu Re di aragona audiu qsti
paroli si appi grandi dubitanza
audendu ch lu Re carlu auia tantu pu
tiri et incontineti madau diieri per
li sula di sichilia ch si Ro carlu vinissi

Dopo che fo stato il dicto papa alexandro lon gamente in franza, & in quello de ingel terra, tornata La corte sua in italia p mare et capitando in sicilia, che allora cera signore Re gulielmo diuotamente ui fo receiuuto honorato et fauorito, riconoscendosé fidele di sancta ecclesia & che la isola de sicilia tenea da lui: per La qual cosa el dicto papa si lo confirmo re de sicilia, & rendereli puglia. Oue el dicto Re gulielmo con soi nauilij L accompagno per mare infino alla ci ta de uenecia, alla quale el dicto papa uolea an dare per piu securita di lui, a zio che federico r imperatore non lo podesse offendere, et fe sua stantia nella dicta cita per fauorire i fidelli de sancta ecclesia, da lombardi & uenetiani fo re ceuuto et honorato reuerentemente: per Lo cui fauore i milanesi si ferono la lor citade de mila no, nel anno de christo. M clxviiij Dopuo poco tempo li milanesi collo aiuto de piacentini & cremonesi, & de alcune altre cita de lombar dia le quale obediano ad sancta ecclesia si fe ceno una terra in Lombardia, quasi per una bastia & bactifolle in contra alla cita de pauia che sempre fo contra ad milano tenendose con lo imperadore. Et quella cita facta per honore de lo dicto papa alexandro & perche la fosse piu famosa la chiamorno allexandria, et dopo fo sopranominata da la paglia, in dispregio de qi de lombardia, el papa gli concesse el uescouo

Page from the Modena codex of the *Cronaca di Partenope*, the first general narrative of the history of Naples written in Neapolitan

Chapter 25

HEGEMONY

That stability prevailed in the *Regnum* under the chancellor, Walter of Palear, during the absence of the king and queen belied an undercurrent of isolated discord. A few vassals in the northern regions would have to be placated and the complaints of some Muslims in western Sicily addressed, but these matters, which had persisted for a decade as a chronic condition were not, for the moment, very pressing.

For the moment, the rapport between Frederick and his onetime tutor, Pope Honorius III, was reasonably solid. The pontiff was directing the Fifth Crusade from afar. The failure to raise an army in the Kingdom of Sicily, and the absence of Frederick himself to lead it, would have consequences.

Fifth Crusade

If nothing else, the debacle known as the "Children's Crusade" of 1212 reflected the crusading fervor present in much of central Europe, even among the common folk, and it encouraged the more serious effort that followed five years later.[918]

Despite a combined Christian force exceeding thirty thousand, the Fifth Crusade preached by Honorius and his predecessor never achieved the level of participation that was expected. It wasn't only the knights of the Kingdom of Sicily who were mostly absent. Many French knights were too busy prosecuting the Albigensian Crusade to join an expedition to the eastern Mediterranean, and some were reluctant to fight alongside the Germans. There were very few English knights.[919]

Among the crusaders were knights and troops from Germany, France,

Hungary, Constantinople and elsewhere. Contingents were also sent from the knightly orders, with the Teutonic Order led by Frederick's advisor, Herman of Salza. John of Brienne, now titular King of Jerusalem, a city he ruled only tenuously by right of his late wife and an expiring truce with the Ayyubids, was also present, though he did not lead the entire crusade as some claimed. Compared to prior crusades, this one was more directly controlled by the pope, who hoped to avoid repeating the disaster of 1204. Its effective leader was Pelagio Galvani, the papal legate, a dogmatic cardinal openly hostile to Orthodox Christians.

The Ayyubids were led by Al-Adil, or Saphadin, whom we met earlier, and his son Al-Kamil, or Meledin.[920]

As sultan, Al-Adil had granted a degree of autonomy to the Christians of Palestine, but the papacy sought complete control of the former territory of the Kingdom of Jerusalem. The first phase of the campaign began with battles initiated by Andrew II of Hungary and John of Brienne around Acre in October 1217, resulting in a stalemate and the failure to take Damascus. Complaining of illness, Andrew then withdrew from the crusade.

It was next decided to attack the Ayyubids' capital in Egypt. Here, beginning in June 1218, the focus was a long siege of Damietta. This is where Francis of Assisi, whose temperament was very different from that of Pelagio, met Al-Kamil.

The crusaders managed to occupy the city and its port, which the defenders abandoned. It wasn't long before Al-Kamil, whose father was now dead, began to negotiate terms. The sultan was willing to cede control of the city of Jerusalem to John of Brienne, but Pelagio intervened to prevent such an accord. The zealous prelate wanted the entire region, not just a tiny piece of it, and had good reason to view this objective as attainable.[921]

In December 1220, Honorius notified Pelagio that Frederick would be sending an army by March of the following year.[922] In May 1221, Ludwig "Kelheimer" of Bavaria (see Table 24) finally arrived with imperial troops and the order to delay major campaigning until Frederick arrived, but this force was not the large army Pelagio had been expecting. Equally underwhelming was the small fleet that arrived led by Henry of Malta, accompanied by the chancellor, Walter of Palear, its cost defrayed by donations collected from bishops and peasants in the *Regnum*.[923]

This seemingly half-hearted effort by Frederick was insufficient to further Pelagio's military objectives, and in August he agreed to an eight-year peace with Al-Kamil.

This outcome was disappointing. For his part, Frederick removed and exiled his chancellor, Walter of Palear, and divested Henry of Malta of his rank.[924] Yet Frederick himself was blamed by many for the failure of the crusade's final phase, and Honorius expected him to make amends.

The Return

The imperial coronation of Frederick and Constance took place in Rome on November twenty-second, 1220. A great number of nobles of the *Regnum* attended.[925] The emperor used the occasion to issue a summary of his policies regarding ecclesiastical prerogatives of the church, the treatment of heretics and even such details as the rights of farmers in his imperial dominions.[926] Although Frederick had been issuing decrees in Germany for several years, this may be viewed as something of a prelude to his first institution of a formal legal code in the Kingdom of Sicily.

It is noteworthy that some of the men in the service of Frederick's court were involved with matters in both the Holy Roman Empire and the Kingdom of Sicily. This was the case of the notary and advisor Peter della Vigna, who arrived around this time.

Frederick visited Mount Cassino in December *en route* to Capua. Then, returning to the *Regnum* following an absence of eight years, he ordered the suppression of several rebellious vassals in the realm's northern regions, particularly their leader, Thomas Berardi of Celano, a kinsman of deposed Walter of Palear and perhaps the most powerful count in the kingdom. Thomas Aquino of Acerra, who was present at the recent coronation, was appointed grand justiciar for Apulia and Terra di Lavoro, effectively the "governor" of these regions, and sent to Abruzzo and Molise to subdue the rebel, whose complaints dated back more than a decade to the era of unrest following Frederick's minority.[927]

Frederick also addressed economic details. A new gold *tarì* was struck at Amalfi. Only later would the *augustale* be instituted, minted at Messina and Brindisi.

At Capua in, a city that still cultivated traces of its spirit of independence, Frederick held a meeting of barons and issued a legal code, the Assizes of Capua. With this, he decided to tighten his grip on the barons, who had run amok during his minority and in some cases even supported an intruder. He would pursue an effort to update the Assizes of Ariano instituted by his grandfather, but for now these Capua laws were intended to amend the code of Roger II rather than to replace it altogether. This represented a definite attempt to accrue more power to the crown. The laws issued at Capua in 1220 were nothing like a "major" legal code and the convocation of barons bore little resemblance to a parliament (see note 306).

In January 1221, Frederick and his family continued on to Apulia.[928] In May they reached Messina, where a meeting of barons and bishops was held in conjunction with the issuance of the Assizes of Messina. These added several statutes to the Assizes of Capua, such as laws to control the gambling for which Messina was famous. Bowing to papal pressure, Frederick infamously imposed a dress code on Jews. Whether this statute was ever put into practice is debated.[929] Jews would not be the only religious minority in the kingdom to be the subject of public policy.

The royal family stayed in eastern Sicily until July.[930] From Catania, they then set out for Palermo at the end of that month, stopping for a few days in Caltagirone. They were in Palermo by the middle of August.[931]

In November 1221, they traveled to Agrigento, and from there to Catania, where they celebrated Christmas. In early 1222 Constance remained in Catania while Frederick went with Henry to Apulia and then Naples and Capua.[932] At Anagni the emperor met the pope.

Malcontent Muslims

A localized but violent revolt by the Muslims of Jato, near Palermo, brought Frederick back to the island in May 1222, when he was met by his wife at Messina.[933]

Muhammad ibn Abbad, sometimes "Morabit" or even "Benaveth" in Latin chronicles, was one of the last important Muslim Arab leaders of note in Sicily, controlling estates beyond Monreale as if he were a feudal lord. It seems that the Aghlabid-Fatimid system of smallholding, inherited in turn from the Byzantines, had been preserved in these areas.

The immediate rebellion was rooted in a complaint by the neighboring Abbot of Monreale, who now controlled a large chunk of Sicily as his archdiocese, that his lands, along with the attendant feudal rights, were being infringed upon.[934] Little is known about this archbishop, named Caro, but he had been a *familiare* at the court of Frederick's mother and seems to have had little tolerance for the Muslims; he was present when Markward of Anweiler received papal censure for an alliance with them.[935]

Amongst the localities the Muslims controlled were Entella, Calatrasi, Corleone and coastal Cinisi. This constituted a strategic swathe of the island. Abbad was even minting his own coins and being called an *emir al-muminin,* a title identifying a Muslim leader as a "prince of believers." That some of Palermo's remaining Muslims supported him posed a potential threat in the capital. That his ambitions might be bolstered by the Tunisians under the Almohad caliph Abu Yakub Yusuf "al Mustansir" was of even greater concern, since Abbad maintained diplomacy with them and others.

In practice, Frederick's government had been willing to accommodate the needs of Sicily's dwindling Muslim population, which seems to have numbered about sixty thousand by this time, but quasi-sovereignty of the kind preferred by Muhammad ibn Abbad was out of the question.

The provocations of the revolts that occurred in 1222 were many, and the sources offer differing accounts about their causes.[936] Whatever the catalyst for the recent uprisings, it would be incorrect to view the unrest as an isolated phenomenon; a few years earlier there was violence against Christians at Agrigento. The fact that direct royal intervention was now required says much about the gravity of the situation.[937]

Rather than an action directed chiefly against the baronage or the lay peasantry, or even the crown, the rebellion seems to have been a reaction to ecclesiastical zeal. Here again, it had festered for a few years, aggravated perhaps by recent papal pronouncements and the Fifth Crusade, factors which were an incentive to prelates of Caro's ilk to preach against Islam. In Sicily, anti-Muslim sentiment was not merely ideological; it might lead to material oppression and even the confiscation of land.

Following a two-month siege at Jato during the summer, Muhammad ibn

Abbad capitulated and was publicly executed, along with two of his sons and two merchants, or pirates, present in Sicily who may have been providing shipping.[938]

Abbad's daughter is known, though not by name. One account says that the enigmatic "Bint Muhammad ibn Abbad" was taken hostage, another that she led a resistance in the hinterland following her father's death; the latter is more likely accurate, though the insurgency was short-lived.[939]

The fall of Jato to royal power in 1222 marks a turning point in the history of the kingdom's Muslims, who henceforth were relegated to a lesser status than that to which they were long accustomed. Beginning the following year, they were gradually resettled in several mainland localities, most notably Lucera in Puglia, which they could govern without being disturbed by the church. That progress of migration would take a generation to complete.

This was an opportune moment for many Muslims to embrace the predominantly Catholic, and Latin, culture that was enveloping the *Regnum,* a trend some would defy for the remainder of the thirteenth century.

The Frederican attitude toward the kingdom's Muslims and Jews does not lend itself to facile descriptions. It clearly reflected papal influences, though it also exemplified an effort to keep peace in the realm.[940] While the policies toward the Muslims were evolving, most of those regarding the kingdom's Jews had changed little despite the recent legislation. In the kingdom's major cities, the Jews found themselves under the judicial authority of the local bishop.[941]

Frederick's wife died at Catania on the twenty-third of June 1222.[942] A funeral was held there, with a second one following in Palermo, where Constance, Queen of Sicily, Queen of the Germans, Holy Roman Empress and Queen of Hungary was entombed. In death, she wore rings befitting a queen, and a splendid jeweled crown of Byzantine design.

The king had little time to grieve. Many Muslim rebels were still at large in the mountains and he was encouraging them to move into the valleys, away from the fortified towns.[943]

There were, as ever, lethal disasters. In August the town of Fondi, north of Naples, caught fire and burned to the ground. The causes are not known.[944]

In 1223, Frederick started a fire of his own by ordering a raid on Djerba, whose pirates were aiding Sicily's Muslim dissidents. Jews of the occupied island were invited to migrate to Sicily.[945]

Meanwhile, troublesome Thomas Berardi of Celano was exiled from the kingdom, sent to live in Rome, though his family was permitted to keep some of his manors in Abruzzo, measures decreed by Frederick while on the mainland. Royal justice could be harsh. The town of Celano was condemned to destruction by fire, most of its citizens sent to live in exile on Malta and Gozo.

By now, Henry of Morra, a *familiare,* was the master justiciar of the royal *curia* of the Kingdom of Sicily. This meant that he was, in effect, its "chief justice," and he sometimes acted as Frederick's governor or "regent" in the mainland territories. We find him enforcing the law as it was expressed in the Assizes of Capua, often in favor of the church in cases involving the baronage. The crown stopped minting gold tarì at Amalfi in favor of similar coins, commonly called *imperiali,* struck at Brindisi, a decision bolstered by legislation confirming recent laws such as those issued at Capua and Messina.[946]

Only a fraction of the kingdom's foreign trade was undertaken by Frederick's subjects. The Genoans, with their privileged mercantile and shipping status, were responsible for much of it, and in cities like Palermo and Messina they had their own little communities and churches near the ports. Muslim merchants were still important, of course, and it was through them that people as far away as China heard about the kingdom. Based on their reports, a Chinese geographer of this period compared Sicily to the Rhum Sultanate in Asia Minor.[947]

Although there were many Sicilians of Arab ancestry whose ancestors had converted from Islam quite recently, no practicing Muslims are known to have been introduced into Frederick's government.[948] Nevertheless, the monarch retained Muslim bodyguards and archers whose loyalty to the crown was less fickle than that of the kingdom's Christians.[949]

Despite this very imperfect treatment, there is nothing to suggest that Frederick or his Hohenstaufen successors sought, in a blatant or even deliberate manner, to coerce the kingdom's Muslims into converting to Christianity. While the transfer of the population to Lucera was a means of controlling Muslim activity, it also ensured the preservation of the community and its faith, albeit in a restrictive form compared to what had existed until this time.

In this Frederick swam against the current, for both church and baronage were predominantly anti-Muslim. It wasn't long before the zealous, recently-founded Dominicans, whose Italian name, *Domenicani,* was interpreted as "God's hounds," attempted to convert the kingdom's "infidel" Muslims and Jews, albeit not very successfully.[950]

The same rabid mentality cannot be said to have tainted the crown. It is even possible that Frederick's initial procrastination to embark on a crusade was motivated, if only in part, by his reluctance to engage directly in an unnecessary war against Palestine's Muslim population.

Ultimately, Frederick's crusade would be his alone, prompted mostly by personal ambition and involving many knights of the *Regnum* but comparatively few from his other dominions. It was integral to his claim to the crown of Jerusalem.

Jerusalem

John of Brienne was not King of Jerusalem through ancestry but by *jure uxoris* as the widower of Maria of Montferrat, herself the daughter of an heiress, Isabella, whose father was King Amalric (see Table 20 and note 764). There were, of course, several familial connections to the Kingdom of Sicily. Most notably, the Aleramid dynasty of Montferrat was that of Adelaide del Vasto, while John of Brienne was the brother of Walter, who had wed a daughter of King Tancred of Sicily and invaded the *Regnum* during the minority of Frederick II.

The death of Maria of Montferrat shortly after childbirth left John's daughter, Yolanda, as Queen of Jerusalem by hereditary right.[951] In the strictest terms,

John reigned not by right of his late wife but as regent for his daughter.[952] A cunning if sometimes incompetent ruler whose actions had helped turn the recent Fifth Crusade into a disaster, John held Jerusalem only tenuously, more as a guest than a king. The truce with the Ayyubids would expire eventually. In reality, John controlled very little territory except the city of Acre.

Seeking allies, he betrothed Yolanda to Frederick, who had promised to undertake a crusade to Palestine as soon as conditions permitted it. The girl's fate was decided during a meeting at Ferentino in March 1223 that Frederick held with John and Honorius, at which the forthcoming crusade was the main focus of the negotiations.[953] The papal view, or understanding, was that the marriage agreement was predicated on Frederick's promise to go on crusade. With less justification, John seems to have inferred from the meeting that a successful crusade would make him the lawful governor of the city of Jerusalem whilst his daughter resided in Europe with her new husband. Frederick clearly expressed the position that he would undertake such a crusade only as King of Jerusalem by right of Yolanda, regardless of John's pretensions. Thus each man entertained a slightly different, personalized perception based on his own objectives. In the spirit of the times, any views that might be held by Yolanda, the young woman whose destiny was the subject of the negotiations, were considered inexistent, if they were considered at all. Around the time Frederick was negotiating for Yolanda's hand, he fathered a child, Frederick "of Antioch," born to a woman whose identity is debated.

Following further negotiations, the wedding was arranged. To avoid the kind of controversy that might arise afterward, the pope granted a dispensation from the canonical impediment of the spouses' distant kinship, Yolanda and Frederick being third cousins.[954] The ceremony would be celebrated, in the first instance, by proxy two years later.[955]

At all events, this bolstered Frederick's claim to be King of Jerusalem, albeit, for the moment, uncrowned.[956]

Back in Sicily early in 1224, he confirmed privileges to the Teutonic Knights. This was, without doubt, the knightly order most loyal to him and his dynasty. For the next decade, they were to be favored over the Hospitallers and Templars, to become the most important crusading order in the kingdom.[957]

Domestic affairs were not Frederick's only concern. The "Treaty of Catania" of November, 1224, affirmed his promise to Louis VIII of France that he would not take the side of young Henry III of England in the event of an open conflict.[958]

Intellectual Life

The same year saw what was arguably Frederick's greatest accomplishment as King of Sicily until this time, the foundation of the school that became the University of Naples. An effort was made to afford poor boys an education here through what might be called "scholarship grants."[959] Operating continuously since then, it is generally considered the first secular university to be founded in Europe by charter.

Although many of its teachers were drawn from the clergy, the school itself was not operated by a religious order, answering directly to the crown. One of the objectives behind establishing the institution was the education of the kingdom's leadership class. This included future judges, lawyers and notaries. An early student was Thomas Aquinas. Early teachers were Peter of Ireland and Arnold the Catalan.

The existence of this school eventually found the geographic focus of learning in the *Regnum* redirected from Palermo to Naples and nearby cities such as Salerno and Capua. The *Studium* at Naples did not initially offer much instruction in the sciences, yet Frederick's personal interests generally ran more toward the scientific. He ordered the medical school of Salerno to perform the *anatomica publica* (public autopsies) for the benefit of its students.

Frederick welcomed the presence of scholars like Michael Scot, a gifted mathematician, reprising the intellectual splendor the court enjoyed during the reign of Roger II.[960] Michael Scot, who was an astronomer and mathematician in his own right, translated, among other works, *On the Sphere* by the Arab astronomer Al-Bitruji, or "Alpetragius." His own *Liber Physiognomiae* is dedicated to Frederick, though physiognomy itself would now be considered pseudoscience.

Scot befriended Leonardo Pisano Bigollo, later known as "Fibonacci," the mathematician whose *Liber Abaci* is credited with popularizing the use of Hindu-Arabic numerals in northern Italy and certain other parts of Christian Europe.[961] Completed in 1225, his *Liber Quadratorum,* on the Diophantine equations of algebra, is dedicated to Frederick.[962]

One of Fibonacci's friends was John of Palermo, the court philosopher, about whom little is known. Nearly as elusive is Theodore of Antioch, a Syrian known as a translator; by some accounts he was an astrologer and philosopher but also a physician.

In the event, neither Scot or Fibonacci, who each may have inspired Frederick to write about scientific subjects, remained at the royal court as long as John, whose name appears in several charters. Frederick's most noteworthy scientific effort was his treatise on falconry and the care of birds, *De Arte Venandi cum Avibus,* "The Art of Hunting with Birds."[963]

Another mathematician sometimes present at court was Guido Bonatti, who lived most of his life in northern Italy.

The Sicilian language and the poetry composed in it were becoming ever more popular, encouraged by Frederick and his notaries, but it is also quite possible that scientific work was written that has been lost to time (a reality considered in Appendix 6).

Some of these works were likely written by Jews, who seem to have filled an academic void left by the isolation, or suppression, of the Muslims. Each major city of the *Regnum* had its Jewish quarter, and in the next century many practitioners of the medical profession were Jews. Precise numbers are not known, but by the end of Frederick's long reign the Jews, not the Muslims, had become the kingdom's largest religious minority.

Two Jewish intellectuals invited to Frederick's traveling court come to mind.

Jacob ben Abba Mari ben Simson Anatoli, who knew Michael Scot, translated some texts of Averroes. Judah ben Solomon ha-Kohen was a mathematician and astronomer.

Frederick's correspondence with the Sufi philosopher Abd al-Haqq ibn Ibrahim ibn Sabin al Mursi (Ibn Sabin) led to the *Al-Kalam ala al-Masail al Siqilliyah,* or *Sicilian Questions,* composed in Andalusia.[964]

Marginalized as they may have been, Muslims and Jews boasted a place at the Hohenstaufen court that they would never enjoy under subsequent dynasties.[965]

By no means was intellectual life at Frederick's court unique for its time, but it shone more vividly than what was typically encountered in other parts of Europe, where the king himself might not be very interested in science, philosophy or literature. Indeed, some monarchs of the thirteenth century were unabashed philistines. In some cases, the church itself hindered education, especially where Muslims and Jews were its proponents, or where a discipline's "secular" orientation might challenge those scientific or philosophical views traditionally espoused in ecclesiastical circles.

Politics as Usual

In July of 1225, Frederick met with some prelates and barons at San Germano, near Mount Cassino. He restored to ecclesiastical authority certain lands in the Kingdom of Sicily that belonged to the church, not as sovereign papal territory but by feudal right, to be held by the church as if by a count or baron of the *Regnum.* He committed to the much-delayed crusade in two years' time, with at least a thousand knights. This promise was made to the papacy on the pain of excommunication.[966]

In August, the admiral Henry of Malta, who had been "rehabilitated" after being punished for his role in the debacle that was the Fifth Crusade, sailed to Acre to transport Yolanda to the Kingdom of Sicily. In early November the fourteen year-old bride was met at Brindisi by her father and her husband. Frederick soon began styling himself King of Jerusalem.[967] If John found this offensive, there was nothing he could do about it.[968]

Later in November, Frederick's son, Henry, married Margaret, the daughter of Leopold VI of Austria, at Nuremberg. This too was a forced dynastic union; Henry was fourteen and Margaret was twenty-one.

The transfer of Sicily's Muslims to Puglia had begun slowly, but now it was involving an ever greater number of families, from Jato as well as other localities. This "resettlement" was not achieved without great distress to those being removed from the only homes they had ever known.[969] Most of the lands confiscated from the Muslims were ceded to the royal demesne or given to the church rather than to barons. Even Corleone, which was initially given to Oddo of Camerana as a fief to populate with some people from northern Italy, was soon expropriated from him and assigned to the crown, remaining under direct royal jurisdiction for centuries.[970]

In addition to Lucera, the Muslims were transferred to Stornara nearby and, initially, to Girifalco in Calabria and Acerenza in Basilicata. Lucera, an imposing city protected by a hilltop fortress, eventually came to resemble an emirate, as if a Muslim monarchy had been transplanted to Puglia.

Meanwhile, an actual Muslim monarch sent an emissary to the Sicilian court. This was the Ayyubid ambassador Fakhr al-Din ibn Shaykh al-Shuyukh, who sought peace on behalf of Al-Kamil.[971] It was no secret that the European Christians would undertake a crusade at some point, and Al-Kamil presently found himself in an internecine conflict within his own family. This raised the specter of one brother siding with Frederick against the other. Besides negotiations, Fakhr's visit permitted him to see for himself if material preparations for a crusade had commenced; construction of a large fleet of galleys had not yet begun.

Apropos crusading knights, in January of 1226, while traveling with Frederick in Apulia, Yolanda issued a decree confirming privileges to the Teutonic Order.[972] Amongst military-religious orders, these were the knights upon whose loyalty the king-emperor could count. By comparison, the Hospitallers, and certainly the Templars, could be fickle about lending their support.

It was unusually cold. Richard of San Germano tells us that Lake Fucino, in the Abruzzo region, froze enough to permit horses to cross it.

By February, the royal couple was at their palace in Salerno.[973] This sojourn was rather exceptional, as Yolanda did not travel very extensively with her husband. In March, Frederick left her at Salerno. While he trekked northward to the imperial cities of Italy, holding an imperial diet at Cremona in the spring of 1226, Yolanda sailed to Sicily, with Henry of Morra as acting regent for the mainland part of the *Regnum*.

At the diet, and in its immediate aftermath, the Milanese and others of the imperial communes reconstituted the Guelph-oriented Lombard League to oppose Frederick's attempted reorganization of the administration of northern Italy by giving himself more authority.[974] The ensuing chaos prevented Frederick's son, Henry, and some German princes from reaching imperial Italy in time for the diet. This disaster had little immediate impact on the Kingdom of Sicily except to attenuate material support, such as knights and money, from the communes for the forthcoming crusade.

The summer of 1226 saw Louis VIII of France, as part of the Albigensian Crusade, besieging and taking the imperial town of Avignon, irritating both Frederick and Henry. The death of the French king in November obviated any action against him. His son and successor, pious Louis IX, was just twelve years old.[975]

The same month found Frederick back in Puglia, and he crossed over to Sicily in January of 1227.[976]

It was early in 1227 that Pope Honorius requested grain from Sicily to relieve a potential famine in and around Rome. This was provided. The cause of the shortage seems to have been a poor harvest, but it is also possible that some greedy Roman merchants were withholding supplies in an attempt to drive up prices.

The forced migration of the Muslims to Lucera was proceeding without any major interruptions. That Lucera was fortified by a large ring wall protecting the city reflected current policy. While the crown banned the construction of feudal castles by overly ambitious barons, it undertook the erection of its own fortresses in royal territories. Obvious demesnial examples are Ursino Castle in Catania and Castel del Monte near Andria in Puglia.

Much to the pope's chagrin, the crusade to Jerusalem was endlessly delayed.[977] Honorius was somewhat indulgent of his former student, but his death in March left a more obstinate man, Ugolino of Segni, as pope, with the name Gregory IX. An avowed authoritarian, this kinsman of Innocent III was an adamant advocate of the use of papal power against heresy.

We find the roots of the "Inquisition," as this institution came to be known, used against "heretics" such as the Cathars as early as the twelfth century.[978] In the imperial lands, the Waldensians were a tempting target. As a juridical process of the church, though involving the state, the Inquisition was initially intended for Catholics, not Muslims or Jews, and the Greek Orthodox hierarchy never instituted anything similar. Amongst its few commendable objectives, it discouraged the homicides perpetrated by common folk given to burning witches and other eccentrics. At first, the Inquisition was administered by bishops rather than the papacy. Gregory formalized it under papal control, entrusting the Dominicans, and even the Franciscans, with identifying heretical activity as "inquisitors."[979] This led to occasional abuses as localized tribunals took church law into their own hands, though nothing like the widespread torture that characterized the revived Inquisition of the modern era.

That Frederick disagreed with some of the Inquisition's fundamental tenets is well known, and it was one of his reasons for the crown opposing the power of these two religious orders during Gregory's pontificate. An underlying cause for Frederick's defiance was the potential erosion of royal authority inherent in an ecclesiastical effort of this kind, but royal concerns transcended papal policy regarding Catholic heretics.

Gregory's overt antipathy toward Muslims, and his more nuanced resentment of Jews, represented a severe contrast with the policies of Frederick, who defended *all* the subjects in what was still a polycultural kingdom. As king, he might suppress Muslim insurrections, but that represented no personal animus toward Islam as a faith, and the church itself was charged with the protection of the realm's Jews.[980]

By the late spring, Frederick was with his wife in Puglia, where he was overseeing the finishing touches of the construction of a large fleet to sail to Palestine. In the middle of August he bid her farewell at Otranto, going to Brindisi where his crusader army was gathering.[981] Unlike the forces mustered for past crusades, the army assembled for this one consisted mostly of knights and archers from the Kingdom of Sicily, though there was a contingent from the German lands. Before embarking, Frederick met with some French emissaries to renew with Louis IX the terms of the treaty made with his father.[982]

That Thomas Aquino of Acerra, recently-appointed bailiff (governor) of the Kingdom of Jerusalem, and Herman of Salza, head of the Teutonic Order, were sent ahead of the main force to ensure a cordial reception by Al-Kamil says much about the form the expedition was to take. Odo of Montbéliard, the bailiff under John of Brienne, was removed, while the role of the Hospitallers and Templars would be less than that of Herman's German knights. Both decisions set the stage for a more unified effort by Christian forces under Frederick once he arrived in Palestine, where Al-Kamil, based in Egypt, was at odds with his nephew, An-Nasir Dawud, who held Syria. With a bit of good fortune, the strategy of "Divide and Conquer" might be just as effective for this Roman Emperor as it was for the Caesars of antiquity.

Significantly, most of the landed nobles, and even some prelates, of the Kingdom of Jerusalem already recognized Frederick, not John, as their sovereign, and were waiting for their new lord to arrive.

Following years of delay, the crusading effort was finally nearing its realization, but no sooner had the first part of the fleet of fifty ships set sail when Frederick fell ill and was forced to turn back while twenty galleys continued on to Acre. Thus Al-Kamil received Thomas, along with Berardo of Castagna.

Doubting the monarch's sincerity despite clear evidence of a fatal epidemic among the crusaders, Gregory excommunicated him late in September 1227.[983] Compared to Frederick's malady, whatever it was, the excommunication was little more than an annoyance. For his part, Gregory, who was born in papal Anagni, where he publicly proclaimed the excommunication, had never been an imperial apologist. In early December, he received a lengthy response from the excommunicant mentioning some events of recent years and explaining the causes for the various delays of the long-awaited crusade. This failed to change the pontiff's mind, and the excommunication remained in force.[984]

On the thirtieth of April 1228, Yolanda died at Andria after having given birth to a boy christened Conrad.[985] She was entombed in that city's cathedral. Her funeral was attended by many magnates of the kingdom present for a meeting with Frederick at Barletta.

Meanwhile, in July, Gregory oversaw the canonization of Francis of Assisi, whose order he had long supported and even helped to establish. Now, however, he sought to bring the Franciscans under more direct papal control. In tandem with the Dominicans, this order began to exercise ever greater influence amongst the people of the *Regnum,* especially on the peninsula, a trend that did not go unnoticed by Fredrick and his advisors, who would have to respond to what was tantamount to an encroachment upon royal authority.

While Gregory was wary of Frederick's control of Germany and most of Italy, this was not the moment to challenge him directly. For now, excommunication was sufficient, if not highly effective in concrete terms, and though the prospect, indeed the threat, of this anathema had been considered by Honorius two years earlier, Gregory imposed it without so much as a second thought.[986] Yet the pontiff knew that Thomas Aquino of Acerra and Herman of Salza had already sailed in August 1227, their force augmented by those of Richard Filangieri, whose family held Nocera as a fief, transported with another fleet sent in April of the following year. He also knew that Frederick was constrained to defray the expense of this crusade on his own, chiefly by a tax on his subjects in the Kingdom of Sicily, without the financial assistance normally provided by the papacy for such projects. Further, it was generally known that

Frederick's archers were the Muslims so resented by Gregory, willing to serve their king even against their co-religionists if called upon to do so.

That the majority of feudal knights were from the *Regnum* reflected Frederick's greater power and direct authority here compared to the Holy Roman Empire and the rebellious Italian communes. Moreover, a certain apathy about crusading had infected Germany, as well as England and France. The result was an army far smaller than what was presumed to be necessary. It is believed that there were around eight hundred knights of the *Regnum* led by Thomas Aquino of Acerra, followed by some five hundred from northern Italy under the command of Richard Filangieri of Nocera.

Sixth Crusade

Not for nothing is the Sixth Crusade sometimes called "Frederick's Crusade" or even the "Emperor's Crusade." Frederick's personal fleet, some seventy galleys led by the rehabilitated admiral, Henry of Malta, departed from Puglia during the last days of June 1228.

The first major "conquest" was not Muslim territory but the island of Cyprus, which was governed by the Ibelin family, ostensibly as regents of the King of Jerusalem. As king, Frederick now had a legitimate claim to the island, where he deposed John of Ibelin, half-brother of Isabella I of Jerusalem, the late Yolanda's grandmother (see Table 20). Nevertheless, the Sicilian occupation of Cyprus was to end soon after Frederick departed. His rule of the Kingdom of Jerusalem itself would later be contested by fellow Christians during the so-called "War of the Lombards." For the moment, however, Cyprus was a convenient springboard to Palestine, and it might prove useful in the event that a naval retreat was required.[987] What is more, the mere fact that Frederick had taken possession of this strategic island, where he remained for five weeks, served to convince friends and foes alike that his campaign was part of a diligent effort.

With its groundwork thoroughly laid, the next phase of the expedition was reasonably predictable. In September, Frederick's force joined the rest of his army at Acre, one of the few cities in Palestine occupied outright by Christians. He was well received by this multinational army, which had already begun repairing some castles in the region, such as those at Caesarea and Jaffa.[988]

None of this impressed Pope Gregory sufficiently to lift the excommunication, despite entreaties by Rainald of Spoleto, Frederick's regent back in the *Regnum*. In Palestine, some local prelates and the Templars complied to the papal position, refusing to support the *de jure* King of Jerusalem beyond the minimal effort necessary. The local barons, by comparison, were more disturbed by Frederick's authoritarian treatment of John of Ibelin, which they suspected might eventually be applied to them as well.

For his part, Al-Kamil, having consolidated his position against his troublesome nephew in recent months, made it known that he no longer needed Frederick's alliance or support.[989] In view of the crusaders' confiscation of a few coastal towns *en route* to Jerusalem, he may not have realized that the invading army was smaller than what was expected. It was necessity, more than anything else, that had motivated Al-Kamil's alliance with Frederick in the first place. With the threat from his rival kin much diminished, the presence of a large army of "Franks" was potentially problematic.

With this in mind, he sent emissaries, including Fakhr al-Din, to negotiate with Frederick. In February 1229, the "Treaty of Jaffa and Tell Ajul" was sealed. Besides certain terms among the Ayyubids themselves, this established a ten-year peace with the Christians, entailing Frederick's control of Jerusalem and his pledge to support Al-Kamil against all enemies.[990]

This may be construed to apply to Christians as well as Muslims, thereby leaving the feudal monarchies of Antioch and Tripoli undefended by the King of Jerusalem in the event of an attack by the Ayyubids. The present holdings of the Hospitallers and Templars were to be left undisturbed, but these orders would not be permitted to increase their material influence by obtaining lands or building castles. It is clear enough that Frederick, who would be an absentee king, wished to avoid further conflict in the region once he returned to Italy, but such provisions may also reflect more immediate realities.

None of these polities had shown much support for Frederick since he arrived, and they seemed unlikely to do so in the future. As sovereignties, they might well act without consulting him beforehand, perhaps even inviting John of Brienne to return as king. The peace was already fragile enough without these threats to its stability.

It was hardly surprising to find opposition to the treaty in these quarters. The most vociferous opponent seems to have been Gerold of Lausanne. Though he had arrived in the Holy Land only two years earlier with the first contingent of the crusader army, he was the leader of the kingdom's Catholics as Jerusalem's archbishop and patriarch. There were, in fact, very few Christians left in Jerusalem itself, and Gerold had not yet been installed there.

Frederick's excommunication had prevented the patriarch from supporting him wholeheartedly. However, what angered Gerold most was that under the treaty the Ayyubids would retain the Temple Mount and other holy sites, along with ecclesiastical property around Jerusalem, such as churches converted into mosques. He made his pronouncements from Acre.

On March eighteenth, Frederick was crowned in Jerusalem's Church of the Holy Sepulchre.[991] The following day, Peter, Archbishop of Caesarea, arrived in Jerusalem with a letter, dated the seventeenth, placing the city under interdict, an act initiated by Gerold. Peter did not try to enforce this, but Gerold sent a letter critical of Frederick's treaty to the pope, who in turn dispatched a nasty missive to several European monarchs.[992]

In concluding this treaty for such a short term, Frederick was hardly myopic. Muslim law forbade anything more than a ten-year truce with infidels. The emperor departed from Acre on the first of May, returning via Cyprus, arriving at Brindisi on June tenth.

During the same month, Al-Kamil and his brother, al-Ashraf, defeated their nephew, An-Nasir Dawud, at Damascus, thus ending the overt rivalry within the Ayyubid dynasty.

Frederick's expedition set precedents as the first crusade led by just one monarch, with little direct involvement by the papacy and without combat. It was the only crusade led by a King of Sicily, exceptional for being comprised largely of knights from the *Regnum,* accompanied by Muslim archers.[993] Frederick's presence in the Kingdom of Jerusalem is a memory of which few physical traces survive.[994]

The newly-crowned King of Jerusalem had been advised of pressing problems in the Kingdom of Sicily.

War of the Keys

Frederick returned to find the mainland part of the *Regnum* under attack by his father-in-law, John of Brienne, as part of an invasion encouraged by Pope Gregory IX.[995] Nobody expected better of John, but fellow monarchs, such as Louis IX of France, found it reprehensible that a pontiff would launch a "crusade" against a Christian king, especially one away from his own domain while crusading. Whatever their differences, Europe's Catholic sovereigns constituted an elite caste. That a pope could instigate a war against one king implied that he could do so against others in the royal brotherhood.[996]

Declaring Frederick's truce with Al-Kamil "anti-Christian" gave Gregory one more pretext to claim part of his kingdom. His complaints formed a lengthy list.

Presently, Frederick had to determine who his allies were. Fortunately, most of the baronage of the *Regnum* supported him, along with the knights of the Teutonic Order. On the mainland, he had already confiscated some Templar and Hospitaller estates before departing for Acre; he now appropriated those of the former located in Sicily.[997] Most of these lands and castles would eventually be restored to the crusading orders, though in Sicily a few of the estates of the disloyal Templars were ceded to the Hospitallers and the Teutonic Knights.[998]

The war owes its popular name to the term used by Richard of San Germano for the pope's soldiers, *clavesignati,* or "key bearers," a reference to the keys of Saint Peter as a traditional papal symbol.[999]

The greatest nobles of the *Regnum* were unwavering in their fealty: Henry of Morra, Thomas Aquino of Acerra, Roger of Galluccio, Reynold of Balbano, Nicholas of Cicala.[1000] Early in 1229, Nicholas, who was responsible for imposing the tax to cover the costs of the Sixth Crusade, was one of the first knights to organize a resistance to the invasion in the northern part of the kingdom. In this he was joined by Reginald of Spoleto, who ruled what was still an imperial duchy.[1001]

Reginald engaged John directly in a series of skirmishes. Involvement by ordinary citizens was generally limited but some towns actively rebelled against the invaders. Gaeta initially chose interdict over papal rule.

Most of the invaders were Italian, but Gregory and John had solicited knights from France, Spain, England, and eventually Portugal and Sweden, albeit generally with limited success. Most were recruited not by kings but by prelates such as Milo of Beauvais and Hugh of Clermont in France. Indeed, the chief commanders flanking John were cardinals, namely John Colonna and Pelagio of Albano. With him was his nephew, Walter IV of Brienne, who made an ancestral claim to Taranto and Lecce as a grandson of King Tancred.[1002]

Incredibly enough, Gregory managed to levy a tax across Europe to pay for this invasion, sometimes as a tithe, as if it were for a crusade. This is generally considered the first instance of the papacy raising money in this way to finance a campaign against a Catholic king. Though resisted in England, it was successful in France despite the reluctance of King Louis to condone it. In Germany, where Frederick's son, Henry, had recently taken direct control of government, the response was abysmal.

Gaeta and other coastal towns eventually capitulated, and the papal forces made an incursion into Puglia in May 1229. The Muslims still living in Sicily refused to collaborate with the papacy.

In view of the king's return to the kingdom, the papal armies converged at Capua. Meanwhile, Frederick remained in Puglia into the autumn gathering troops. He then made his way northward. John retreated into papal territory but Frederick decided to restrict his own actions to the *Regnum* itself. His action against the Templars and Hospitallers left them without sufficient resources in the Kingdom of Sicily to do much more than observe the counteroffensive that was transpiring.

Confronted by the prospect of a real war against a major army led by a warrior king, Gregory decided to negotiate a truce. With German help, this was brokered at San Germano in July 1230.[1003] Frederick's excommunication was lifted at Ceprano the following month, and he returned most of the confiscated estates of the troublesome Templars and Hospitallers. He wisely granted an amnesty to subjects who had supported the pope, and he ceded to the papacy certain rights over Gaeta, almost as if it were a papal city like Benevento.

Much contemporary commentary about the war followed across central and western Europe, generally reflecting either ecclesiastical or royal sympathies depending upon the chronicler or troubadour. Within the *Regnum*, the war served as a gauge of loyalties. It effectively ended John's political pretensions, if not those of Gregory.

That the rapport between Frederick and Gregory would be cordial from 1230 until 1238 meant that the Kingdom of Sicily could at least pretend to an undisturbed period of calm.

In April of 1231, Frederick signed a ten-year trade treaty with the Hafsid leader Abu Zakariya Yahya, who had recently seized power to become the Sultan of Ifriqiya.[1004] This firmly re-established commerce and permitted an official Ifriqiyan presence on Pantelleria, where the sultan could appoint a delegate to oversee the needs of that island's Muslims. Here we see Frederick facilitating a pragmatic arrangement that increased the kingdom's tax revenue and guaranteed a market for its wheat rather than insisting on the outright occupation of Djerba or other territories. The agreement incidentally ensured that the Muslims of the *Regnum* had access to links to Islamic northern Africa.

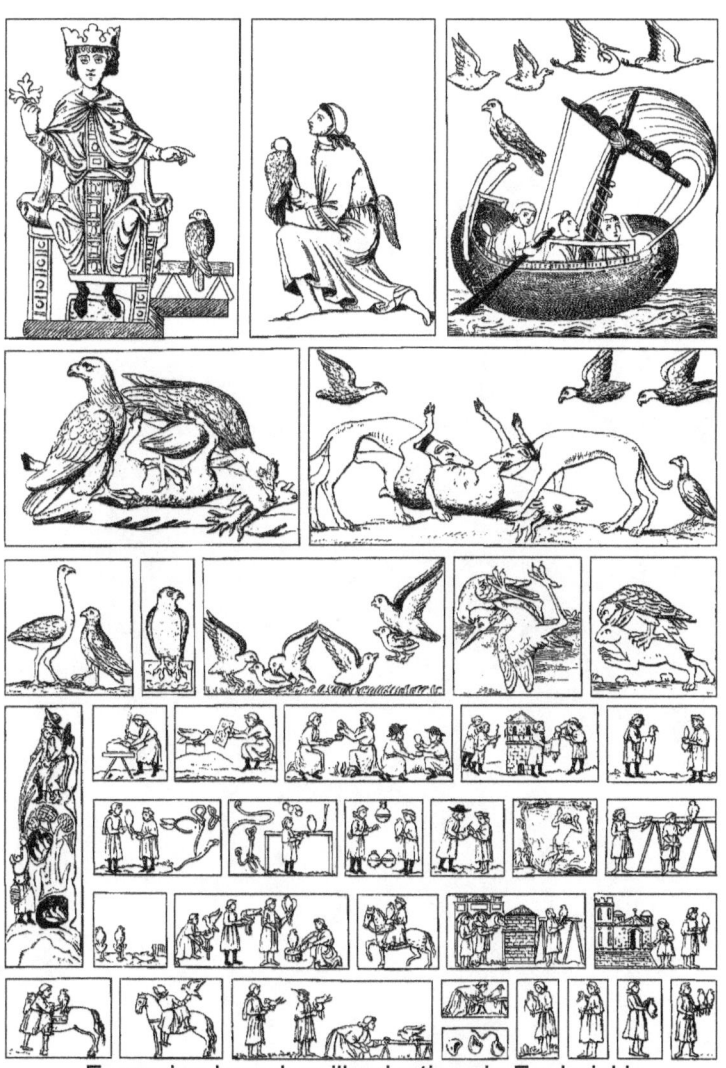

Engraving based on illuminations in Frederick's treatise on falconry. Frederick is the first figure.

KINGDOM OF SICILY

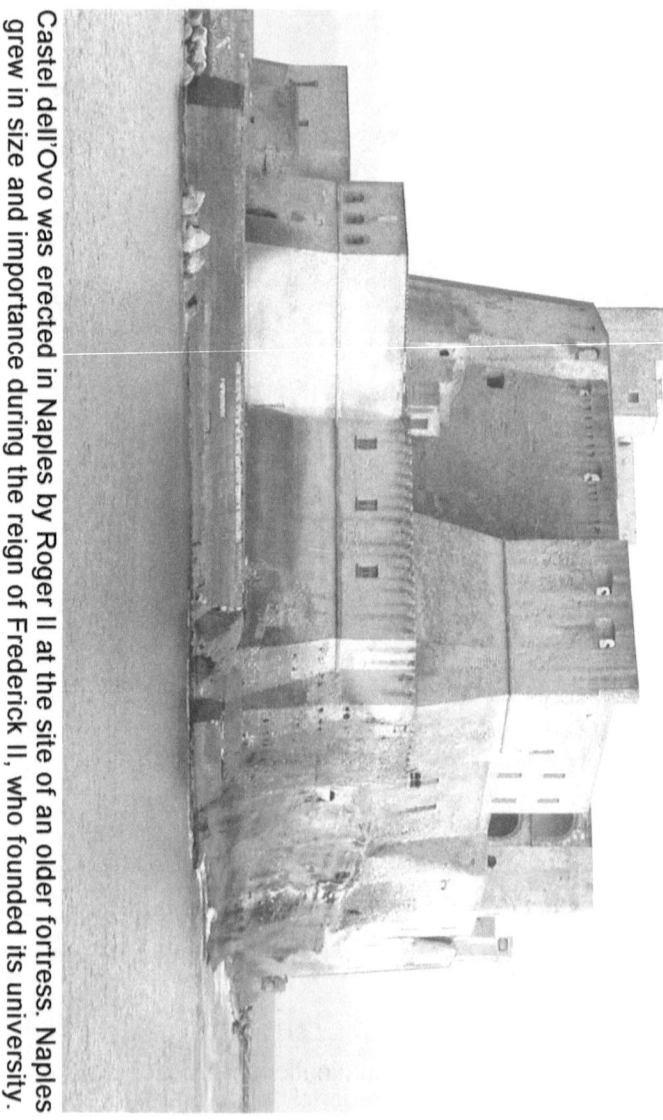

Castel dell'Ovo was erected in Naples by Roger II at the site of an older fortress. Naples grew in size and importance during the reign of Frederick II, who founded its university.

Chapter 26
SOCIETY AND LAW

Whatever somebody living in the thirteenth century may have perceived, the society of the *Regnum* had undergone some identifiable changes since the Norman era. This reflected more general changes in Europe over the course of nearly two centuries.

The policies, even "reforms," of Pope Gregory IX were part of a gradual evolution in the papacy and its influence that began around the time of the rise of Norman power in southern Italy in the middle of the eleventh century, continuing through the reign of Frederick II. The concept of the "papal monarchy" spread far beyond Italy, northward to the German lands and eastward to the Byzantine and Slavic territories, even if it was especially evident in the Kingdom of Sicily.[1005]

Much that came to be identified with Catholicism, and with central and western European culture generally, emerged during this period of papal "innovation." Broadly speaking, these developments included the foundation of universities and hospitals in a form that would be recognizable to modern people, increased commerce and sophisticated banking in cities, and a more sophisticated papal government prepared to intervene in the affairs of sovereign states. Catholic canon law grew more complex, along with western theological thought. The crusades and inquisitions were outgrowths of these trends. Even the Gothic architectural movement was the result of a slightly novel way of thinking. Society witnessed an increasing "internationalization" as monarchs across central and western Europe cooperated in enterprises such as the crusades while supporting the religious and knightly orders founded during this period; the Cistercians, Dominicans, Hospitallers and Templars were present in many kingdoms. Trade between states was greater than ever. European ver-

461

nacular languages became acceptable in literature. A certain "European" identity emerged, something obvious in the Kingdom of Sicily.

The amalgam of various developments would lead a few modern historians to characterize intellectual Frederick II, the most powerful European king of the moment, as a "man of the Renaissance." Others viewed the entire era as a "renaissance" of its own.[1006] While such descriptions can be debated, there is no doubt about the presence of significant social changes.

The Siculo-Neapolitan ethnogenesis spawned in this environment embraced both the cultural and political spheres. A sign of the latter was a noteworthy legal code.

The Constitutions of Melfi

The Assizes of Ariano had sufficed for ninety years, but changing times necessitated evolving laws. Frederick had already undertaken this, if only in a small way, with his assizes of Capua and Messina, which augmented the existing code without nullifying it. The new code would reform the Assizes of Ariano.

Much could be said about the inspiration behind the *Liber Augustalis*, or *Constitutiones Regni Siciliae*, popularly the "Constitutions of Melfi" for the city where the new code was issued in August 1231. In its essence, it reflected an effort at greater uniformity in the application of justice in the kingdom, integrating traditional Roman law, such as the ideas in the Code of Justinian, with some broad but well-defined precepts of canon law as these now existed. At the same time, it took into account those fundamental feudal principles common to most European monarchies. Even a few Lombardic legal notions found their way into the code, along with some statutes added to the Assizes of Ariano by William I and William II. The result is a symbiotic array of statutes that generally complement each other. Considered *in toto*, the code is far greater than the sum of its parts.[1007]

Despite the eclectic influences underpinning the Constitutions, the statutes were a step forward, forming the framework for subsequent legislation in what, beginning a half-century later, became the "twin kingdoms" of Naples and Sicily under (respectively) the Angevins and Aragonese.[1008] In stark contrast to the Assizes, the Constitutions, which were later published with commentary in several notable editions, enjoyed a certain prestige throughout Europe and were generally known.[1009]

The Constitutions addressed such matters as administration and the legal system, with an eye to efficiency. An underlying principle was the effective support for a strong "centralized" monarchy, something construed by Gregory as a threat to the papacy and to the church generally. The pontiff's reaction was at least rational insofar as the code was largely a response to recent papal challenges to the authority of the Sicilian crown. Despite later criticisms of Frederick as a "freethinker," which is probably accurate, or even an "atheist," which is not, the Constitutions are not exclusively "secular," though they discouraged slavish hierocracy in favor of temporal law.[1010]

More generally, the Constitutions reflected an effort to make procedural law less "subjective," a noble idea in the thirteenth century. This meant that authority could be exercised based on principles of law, but not merely at the whim of a bishop or baron. According to this model, power emanated from law, not vice versa. More than the Assizes of Ariano, the Constitutions of Melfi addressed "non-public" life, the everyday activities of ordinary people outside the clergy and aristocracy, protecting some "personal" rights that were not previously recognized to this degree. Despite what some optimistic scholars have construed from it, the code did not literally "make all equal in the eyes of the law," but it offered the realistic *possibility* of a peasant obtaining justice in a system that generally favored the church and the nobility over the common folk. Here was an attempt at "peace and justice," a standard that the great majority of subjects could see and perhaps appreciate.

The code did not introduce common law such as that present in Plantagenet England or the Maliki principles known among the Muslims (see note 51). Yet the latter were known in the *Regnum* and may have been applied in areas such as commercial contracts with the Hafsids, to whom the Sicilians sold wheat according to the recent trade treaty (mentioned at the end of the previous chapter).

While a nuanced term such as "absolutism" may be imperfect, and perhaps slightly anachronistic, there should be no misperception of the reality that, first and foremost, the Constitutions advanced the power and interests of the crown. Nothing in the statutes attenuates the authority of the monarchy, and there is no hint of the kind of baronial rights that scholars have inferred from England's *Magna Carta*.

Nevertheless, the Constitutions reflect the scholasticism of their age, exemplified by thinking at the great universities of Europe. In Italy, and certainly at Frederick's court, this was represented by those who studied law in Bologna.

The formulation of the statutes, which took at least six months, was the work of a committee led by Peter della Vigna, who was then the emperor's closest advisor, and James Amalfitano, the Archbishop of Capua.[1011] Thaddeus of Suessa was probably consulted. Herman of Salza seems to have made suggestions, likewise Berardo of Castagna. The work of the distinguished jurist Roffred Beneventano may have been an influence. Frederick himself seems to have contributed much to the code. At the very least, he studied it carefully before approving it.[1012]

Over two hundred statutes, or clauses, in the original manuscripts are divided into three sections (or "books") dedicated to public law, judicial procedure, and private (and criminal) law.[1013] The "categories" of a few of these statutes overlap slightly from one book to another.

In practice, the Constitutions are a general code that deals with government, including the judicial system, as well as feudalism, the church, individual rights and even certain aspects of sexual behavior. It addresses "civil" (sometimes "case") law involving matters such as contracts, and "criminal" (sometimes "penal") law concerning crimes committed against individuals or society. The principle of *mens rea,* or the conscious intent to commit an act, is generally recognized, with a clear distinction drawn between, for example, murder and manslaughter.

Because there was no common law (on the English model), decisions rendered by justiciars, or even the crown itself, did not establish precedent for similar cases. The code made it possible for law to function efficiently, with less need for decisions to be made by the monarch personally. The Constitutions dictated that justiciars themselves could not adjudicate cases in jurisdictions where they had personal ties, such as feudal estates. This limited instances where there might be clear conflicts of interest.

Although it failed to bring about certain important rights, like trial by jury, established by the *Magna Carta,* Frederick's code reiterated some fundamental principles encapsulated in his grandfather's Assizes, such as the criminalization of rape.[1014]

That questions of public health and the environment were considered was highly exceptional for a legal code of this era. It is impossible not to see in the Constitutions an interest by the crown, the kingdom's ultimate authority, in cultivating the welfare of society and its people, regardless of their place in the social hierarchy: nobility, clergy, commonalty.

Greater royal control was enforced over things like the sale of fiefs, subinfeudation, and property inheritance. Even the construction of castles and the marriages of a nobleman's children were regulated. Demesnial cities could not elect councils of jurats in the manner of the northern communes or erect protective walls without royal consent although (as we shall see) such councils were often formed unofficially.

It may not be very accurate to ascribe to Frederick, as some have, a quasimystical sense of himself beyond that of most other European monarchs of his era. To identify him as the very founder of the concept of the prototypical secular state is equally overzealous. Yet the Constitutions clearly reflect a recognition of the importance of the duties of a king. The code is boldly indicative of a certain view of the *Regnum* as a sovereign state by Frederick and his trusted advisors. This differs markedly from the identity of the Holy Roman Empire as a polity, and any notions about distant Jerusalem.

The advent of the Constitutions should be considered in the context of the "papal monarchy," and particularly Frederick's rapport with Gregory IX. Yet the code, however "universal" some of its themes may appear, was intended for only one kingdom.

The Constitutions cannot be viewed apart from the society of the Kingdom of Sicily during the preceding decade, and in some respects the *Regnum* as it existed under Frederick's Hauteville predecessors. The Constitutions were part of a continuum.

Compared to the Assizes of Ariano, the Constitutions of Melfi tend to reflect a defined, sophisticated perception of the monarch and the state, a luxury not afforded Roger II, who had to actually found a state for his successors to inherit.

Some supplementary statutes, the so-called *Novellae,* were promulgated in the years immediately after 1231.[1015] What follows is a concise summary and commentary, with reference to some specific statutes (or "titles").[1016]

SOCIETY AND LAW

The Constitutions Summarized

The very first text in the code is a *prooemium* (preamble).[1017] The three *libri* (books) follow, each with its own series of *tituli*.

Book 1 begins with two statutes condemning the behavior of heretics and Patarines.[1018] Statute 3, taken from the Assizes of Ariano, establishes punishment for apostates from Christianity.[1019] Statutes 4 and 5, also from Roger II, protect royal authority. Statute 6 governs the activity of usurers, while Statute 7 regulates tithing. Statutes 8 and 9 punish those inciting war. Statute 10 proscribes all except knights from bearing arms (swords). Statutes 11, 12 and 13 prohibit foreign knights to bear swords or wear armor in the kingdom, outlaw the menacing with a weapon by anybody, and forbid the unlawful striking with a weapon. Statute 14 outlaws murder but permits homicide in self-defense. Statute 15 obligates castellans, who in some cases are barons, to send knights to serve at the royal court or perform military service. Statutes 16 to 19 govern judicial procedures regarding the legal representation and defense of citizens, including Muslims and Jews.[1020] Statutes 20 to 24 outlaw the rape of maidens, nuns and prostitutes while proscribing false accusations (made against men) of violence against women.[1021] Statutes 25 and 26 establish punishment for theft of land. Statute 27 lists penalties for arson and vandalism committed covertly. Statute 28 outlines penalties for those who hide criminals. Statute 29 prohibits theft from shipwrecks or the scenes of fires. Statute 30 metes out penalties to those who attack the families or property of officials absent from their homes whilst performing service for the crown. Statutes 31 and 32 mandate respect for justiciars during trials. Statute 36 addresses embezzlement by officials and justiciars. The next few statutes establish the roles of various officers, such as the master justiciars, the master chamberlain, the bailiffs (governors), and the masters of the *diwan* (treasury). Statute 45, a law dating from the reign of William I, requires that clergy accused of crimes be judged by ecclesiastical (not secular) authority. Statute 46 requires that subjects (other than clerics) accused of theft be remanded to the custody of justiciars. Several following statutes consider how chamberlains and bailiffs are appointed, with clergy and justiciars prohibited from being bailiffs in order to ensure that conflicts of interest are avoided. Then castellans (of demesnial towns) and sergeants are considered. The duties of justiciars are explicated at length. Statute 47 defines the rights of counts, barons and knights and their property. Then the appointment and number of judges and notaries are set forth, and the format of documents is established. A number of judicial procedures are codified. Statute 101 ascribes more weight to the word of a baron than a commoner during a trial. Statutes 104, 105 and 106 apply broadly to what might be described as the right to a speedy trial, addressed more explicitly in Book 2, penalizing litigants (in non-criminal cases) who fail to appear before a justiciar when summoned. The contumacy of communes (demesnial cities), the refusal of urban administrators or governors to comply with a summons to appear before a justiciar, is addressed in Statute 107, which establishes that, if necessary, such a city must levy an extraordinary tax to defray the cost of a judgment it is ordered to pay.[1022]

Book 2 begins with a law, its Statute 1, which governs the payment of a penalty ordered by a judge in a criminal case. Statute 2 permits married women and communes to appoint lawyers for their own defense at trials. Statute 3 imposes exile for individuals who perpetrate "contempt of court" by not appearing at trial when summoned. Statute 4 governs the humane treatment of captives. Statute 5 determines that the identities of criminals should be made known publicly. Statute 6 permits the treasury to sell property confiscated for contumacy. Statute 7 provides for the crown to care for the children of nobles who have been exiled and Statute 8 considers their wives and parents, while Statue 9 specifies that fathers are not to be held accountable for the actions of their sons. Statute 10 allows for "parole," a pledge by the accused, depending on social rank, circumstances and the nature of the alleged crime, to appear for trial as prescribed instead of being jailed in the interim; it also states that an accused suspect who has been jailed awaiting trial must be tried as soon as possible and not be presented before the justiciar in chains.[1023] Statute 11, a clause from the reign of Roger II, establishes that a husband who reunites with an adulterous wife thereby renounces the right to lodge a complaint against her for the crime she has allegedly committed. Statutes 12 and 13 state that an accuser who fails to appear at trial must pay a fine. Statute 14 establishes a penalty for calumny, defined as a false accusation of criminal activity.[1024] Statutes 15 and 16 consider accusers and defendants appearing (or not) at trial and reaching settlements among themselves. Statute 17 abolishes distinctions between certain Norman, Roman and Longobardic practices involving trials, and establishes uniform procedures. Chapter 20 governs exemptions from military service.[1025] Statute 22 accords greater authority and precedence to the requests of higher justiciars when a person is being tried in different jurisdictions for different offenses at the same time. Several statutes govern legal procedures, evidentiary standards and perjury. Statute 31 abolishes trial by ordeal. Statutes 32 and 33 generally proscribe trial by combat except in very specific cases, without outlawing duels between knights. The next few statutes concern feudal homage (a knight's obligation to his lord), combatants and champions. Statute 41, established by Roger II, offers equal legal protection for women at hearings and trials; Statute 44 also addresses this. Statute 42 extends juridical protection to minors. Statute 48 governs appeals. Statute 49 guarantees the right to a speedy trial.[1026] Statute 50, inherited from the reign of Roger II, establishes a penalty for justiciars who rule poorly or accept bribes to rule a certain way. Statute 52 clarifies how evidence must be gathered and presented in appeals.

Book 3 begins with a statute protecting demesnial (crown) property. Statute 2 prohibits the ordination of vassals and serfs without the prior consent of their feudal lords, but the following clause, dating from the reign of William I, permits the ordination of peasants who are not encumbered by serfdom. Statute 4 enforces royal rights over all demesnial cities, towns, castles and villages, even in cases where this has not been actively asserted by the crown during previous Hauteville and Hohenstaufen reigns; it imposes a harsh penalty upon counts and barons who, perhaps in usurping demesnial lands, claim control over serfs to whom they are not entitled. Statute 5 reiterates a law of Roger II that fiefs (baronies and other manors) cannot be alienated without royal consent; nor can such property be transferred (sold) if it is entailed by fees payable to the crown. The next statute, number 6, permits subjects of demesnial lands who have recently been enserfed by being transferred, perhaps unlawfully, to feudal estates (see preceding Statute 4) to reclaim their freedom as peasants under direct royal authority. Statutes 7, 8, 9 and 10 concern related principles. Statute 13, first promulgated by William I, governs the assignment and administration of dowries; Statutes 15, 16 and 17 also concern dowries. Statutes 18, 19, 20 and 21 govern vassalage, the relationship between greater lords, such as counts, and the minor lords, such as barons and enfeoffed knights, who pledge fealty and homage to them. Statutes 22 and 23 govern marriages among the nobility, which must have royal sanction. Statutes 24 to 27 govern feudal succession. Statute 26 permits succession by females in the absence of males.[1027] Statute 31 ensures proper administration of church property following the death of a bishop. The next two statutes prohibit the unauthorized construction of castles or urban fortifications (walls). Statute 34 addresses the status of serfs who flee from the estates to which they are tied.[1028] Statute 37 details exceptional conditions under which unclaimed feudal property may be claimed; this is addressed by several following clauses. Statutes 42 and 43 cover personal offenses against commoners as well as nobles, setting forth the recourse available. Statutes 44 and 45 establish the licensing of physicians (see note 1159). Statute 47 regulates the activity of apothecaries in the formulation of potions and pills. Statute 48 declares the importance of air and water quality, proscribing the deposit of hemp and flax in rivers near towns; entombment of cadavers is also regulated.[1029] Later, Statute 72 prohibits fisherman disposing of yew leaves in water. Statute 49 constrains merchants to ensure the quality and safety of merchandise; jewelers, metal-smiths, armorers and saddle makers are mentioned.[1030] Statute 51 governs the accuracy of weights and measures. Several statutes address cattle rustling but also the destruction of forests and other lands by cattle left to wander too widely. Statute 59 reiterates the law from the Assizes of Ariano that only men of noble rank may be knighted except by royal authority. The following statute restates this for knights while holding judges and notaries to the same standard. Each of the next few statutes are concise but clear, outlawing forgery (61), the counterfeiting of coinage (62), coin shaving (63), suborning perjury (65), the concealment or destruction of wills (66, 67), and poisoning (69). A number of statutes deal with adultery or other sexual activities, such as prostitution.[1031] Statute 81 permits a husband to immediately kill his adulterous wife and her lover ("co-respondent") if he catches the two in the sexual act; the very next statute facilitates the charge of pimping against the cuckolded husband if he willingly permits the co-respondent to escape.[1032] Reiterating a law of the Hauteville era, Statute 83 establishes that adultery cases should be tried by the church rather than the secular authorities.[1033] Statute 78 permits simple divorce.[1034]

A New Order

We thus find the crown governing certain aspects of conjugal life. Frederick himself was not married in 1231, but his relationship with a Piedmontese noblewoman named Bianca Lancia brought him a son and two daughters. Manfred, born of this union around 1232, may have been his favorite son.

The institution of the gold *augustalis* coin coincided with the promulgation of the Constitutions. Issued in full and half versions, this was based on the Roman *aureus,* featuring a representation of Frederick as a classical Roman emperor on the obverse and the image of a Roman imperial eagle on the reverse. This new gold coin, with a purity greater than that of the traditional *tarì* of the Normans and Fatimids but roughly comparable to that of the Hafsid *dinar,* came to be preferred, even required, in major transactions with the republics of Genoa and Venice at a time when silver coinage was becoming the norm in northern Italy and across Europe. This reflects the prosperity of the *Regnum* at this time. That silver coinage was preferred, sometimes even mandated, for most "domestic" trade within the kingdom permitted the crown to augment its own gold reserves. What is more, the circulation of foreign gold coins in the kingdom was discouraged, their use banned even in certain transactions with the Genoans and Venetians, who might be constrained to trade in bullion. Ifriqiyan commerce was a good source of gold that was mined south of the Sahara.

Here was a subtle but real economic policy.

Like the coinage, the increased facilitation of commerce correlates to the arrival of the Constitutions. Of course, trade would have continued with Africa and the northern communes even in the absence of a new legal code, but Frederick's reorganization, such as it was, made business somewhat simpler, or at least accountable. The code addressed potential corruption and its consequences, such as tax evasion.[1035]

A curious section (to the modern mind) is the proscription on the use of paper for important legal documents, with requirement of the use of parchment or vellum for this purpose. Parchment was, of course, more durable, less susceptible than paper to damage from moisture, folding or even ink. Sicily was ahead of most of Europe in the use of paper, introduced by the Arabs during the ninth century.

Naturally, certain existing practices in the secular sphere antedated the Constitutions and even the Assizes, and most of these remained unchanged, being rooted in past decrees, canon law or feudal custom. As we have seen, trial by ordeal was all but abolished while trial by combat continued as a traditional right of the knightly class, but there were other social conventions. That the power of the nobility diminished somewhat hardly meant that the historical rights of this class disappeared. The rights of ladies (aristocratic women) still exceeded those of ordinary ("common") maids and maidens. For an obvious example we may look to an incident that occurred in the royal palace during the regency of Queen Margaret when, in her presence, Gilbert of Gravina, squared off against Richard of Molise, both men drawing their swords. Margaret herself ordered the two to desist, and both complied (Chapter 17). Yet the mere act of a knight drawing his sword in this manner in the presence of a lady, much less a queen, was a serious affront to acceptable behavior. It would have been well within the queen's rights to cast both men into the palace dungeon for a few days as punishment.

SOCIETY AND LAW

There are clear attempts in the Constitutions to regulate local government and, as we have seen, the construction of towers and castles, to the point of the crown ordering the destruction of certain fortifications built by barons without royal consent. This policy curtailed baronial power as well as the hypothetical development of communes similar to the northern Italian cities that continuously challenged Frederick. At the same time, we see the construction of large royal (demesnial) castles, such as that of Catania.

Not all of the statutes were enlightened beyond their era. Though a husband might not be punished if he killed his adulterous wife and her lover immediately upon catching them in the sexual act *in flagrante delicto,* there is no similar recourse for a wife against an adulterous husband. A peasant who struck a knight or noble might have the offending hand chopped off unless he could prove that he acted in self defense.

There were, of course, a few subsequent "refinements" that addressed specific matters, such as trade and taxation. Whilst at San Germano in 1232, the king reduced the taxes on wine and fruit, likewise the duties on leather, cotton and fish, as well as livestock. In most cases, these duties were reduced to a level that had existed years earlier. A few master justiciars rebelled against the increased discipline. At Messina, disgruntled Richard of Montenegro, the high justiciar for Sicily, plotted a conspiracy against the crown and was disciplined.[1036]

Besides disloyal Richard, the king had recently appointed as high justiciars: Sansone of Bari for Basilicata (Lucania), Philip of Zuncolo for Abruzzo and Molise, Godfrey Busardo for the Otranto region, Robert of Aquino and Hector of Montefusculo for Terra di Lavoro (Campania), William of Spinosa for Calabria, Philip of Aquino for the Principate near Benevento. These districts were further divided over the next few years.

The justiciar Thomas Aquino of Acerra was appointed bailiff (governor) of the kingdom, effectively a "prime minister," as he had been in Jerusalem. He wed Frederick's daughter, Constance.

At the same time, Frederick made a continued effort to meet with the barons of the *Regnum,* whether at Capua, Foggia, Messina or elsewhere. This access to the sovereign helped to ensure a certain serenity in the kingdom.

There can be little doubt that the new laws reflected changes to certain aspects of the monarchy itself. If nothing else, Frederick's Constitutions were more complex than Roger's Assizes, concentrating more power in the crown while forming a larger, fairer, and perhaps more authoritative, judiciary to enforce it. More, perhaps, than the others who ruled the *Regnum* during the Norman-Swabian era, both of these sovereigns exercised the right of the king as "fount of justice," a principle recognized in some form by, amongst others, John of Salisbury, who was familiar with the Kingdom of Sicily.[1037] Yet most historians have refrained from ascribing to Frederick and his jurists the credit for bringing about fundamental changes to the nature of kingship or society.[1038] It would be more accurate to say that both Roger and Frederick implemented a slightly evolved approach in the application of royal power, with the king as the "vehicle" of justice, which was ultimately God's alone. This was linked to an evolving medieval concept of "natural law" developed more fully shortly after Frederick's reign by Thomas Aquinas.[1039]

Whereas Roger's Assizes adhered rather slavishly to Justinian's laws, Frederick's legislation, like that of some of his contemporaries, clearly transcended these. Yet both monarchs probably would have agreed that kingship had to be based on law, or at the very least clearly expressed through it. While this was hardly a novel notion, few European rulers of their era truly embraced it.[1040] In reality, contemporary references to Frederick with terms such as *lex animata,* "the living law," make it clear that the true power of the crown was undiminished by the Constitutions. What changed somewhat were the *channels* through which justice arrived.

The merits of Frederick's code, which was intended solely for the Kingdom of Sicily, may have been recognized by a few jurists in other realms, but we cannot point to laws beyond the *Regnum* that were influenced directly by the Constitutions.

Even if some of his closest counsellors served him *ad personam,* irrespective of his Italian or German jurisdictions, Frederick legislated very differently for each of his dominions. As we shall see, his son, Henry, was busy making laws for the Holy Roman Empire.

In one of the *Novellae* enacted at a meeting of his court and baronage at Syracuse late in 1233, Frederick decreed that no subject born in the Kingdom of Sicily could marry a foreigner except with prior royal consent, either from the sovereign himself or through his representatives.[1041] Whether this law was applied, save for a few cases, is not known.

Confidence

Little can be inferred with great certainty about the general reaction to the Constitutions in the decades immediately following their implementation except from what is known about a few individual cases brought before the justiciars. The *Novellae* suggest the perceived need for certain refinements. However, there may have been a wider, more substantive, impact than what has usually been noted by historians.

Six centuries after Frederick's death, Alexis de Tocqueville identified a phenomenon he called the "shadow of the law." Here he referred to the social environment nurtured by widespread perceptions such as the general presumption that statutory law would usually be enforced with a certain degree of rigor, fairness and alacrity. This gave rise to conditions motivating the greater part of the populace, even people lacking direct experience with the judiciary, to respect the government and the law courts.

In other words, so great was the "moral force" of the law that society as a whole was reassured by the mere presence of the sophisticated legal code and the judiciary charged with enforcing it. The very existence of efficient justice enhanced the ethos and function of the state by instilling confidence in the minds of most people. It could be argued that a sense of "freedom from tyranny" thus prevailed.

This is hardly tantamount to a reflection of the principle of *vox populi,* for there were nothing like elections except, in a very rudimentary form, within the councils of jurats that governed the day-to-day administration of demesnial (royal) cities on behalf of the crown. In an age lacking true democracy, the long shadow cast by the law was one aspect of life that afforded every social class (nobility, clergy, commonalty) enough trust in the monarchy to identify itself as part of a cohesive state.

To be sure, Tocqueville's theory was the fruit of a modern constitution, based on certain principles of the Enlightenment, that guaranteed an array of individual rights in a fundamentally democratic nation, a reality quite distant from what existed in medieval states such as the Kingdom of Sicily. Nonetheless, it is quite possible that something vaguely like this collective trust was felt in the *Regnum* for the remainder of Frederick's reign, and during the reigns of his dynastic heirs. A contemporary European example of this phenomenon, albeit different in significant ways, was the effect of the *Magna Carta,* mentioned earlier, on the rights of the English baronage; like the Constitutions, it marked a significant milestone along the path to true nationhood.

Despite the name later given to the *Liber Augustalis,* it was not a constitution in the true sense. It was, however, a step toward constitutional law and away from the limitations of early feudalism. Although Italy saw little progress in that direction in the centuries immediately following the Hohenstaufen reigns, Frederick's Constitutions were indeed part of a western European trend toward centralized government based on the codification of efficient laws. An ambitious objective of such legislation was to make conceptual law practical, an effort begun in the *Regnum* almost a century earlier by Roger II. During Frederick's reign, this represented a departure from some of the essentially Frankish, Longobardic and Maliki norms of the Hauteville period, though some principles of Roman law, embodied in the Code of Justinian, were retained.

Inherent in this "proto-constitutional" process was an evolution in the idea of what the monarchy, as a state, should be. This was considered by legal scholars such as Andrew of Isernia (see note 1009). Alas, by the time Andrew died, early in the fourteenth century, the progress represented by Frederick's laws was little more than a memory, with the kingdom itself divided into two states. There were, however, true parliaments (see note 306).

However they are viewed by the modern eye, the Constitutions were a legal cornerstone of the Swabian era, proof that a few royal counsellors were addressing questions of law even as others were composing poetry in a new vernacular. Nothing in the *Regnum* was static. Even the cuisine was evolving.

KINGDOM OF SICILY

CONSTITUTIONUM
REGNI SICILIARUM
LIBRI III.

Cum Commentariis Veterum Jurifconfultorum

ACCEDIT NUNC PRIMUM

DOMINICI ALFENI VARII J. C.

COMMENTARIUS

AD

FRIDERICI II.

IMPERATORIS ET REGIS CONSTITUTIONEM

De Rebus non alienandis Ecclefiis.

EDITIO ABSOLUTISSIMA.

NEAPOLI MDCCLXXIII.
SUMPTIBUS ANTONII CERVONII.

Constitutions of Melfi published in Naples in 1773

Chapter 27

CULINARY CULTURE

What did the people of the *Regnum* eat? Like language and literature, cuisine was an important part of the social milieu of the times, and a very significant aspect of identity. A number of culinary delights of the thirteenth century are known through recipes present in the historical record. Most of what was written pertains to courtly "aristocratic" cuisine, but a few dishes popular among the common folk are also known. There was not always much distinction between the two culinary spheres.

Beyond its more obvious purposes, food could be symbolic, representing everything from power and privilege to piety and humility. The recipes associated with certain events, such as religious festivals, evolved over time.[1042]

Apart from what was served, hospitality toward guests was the hallmark of royal courts, baronial households and monasteries, and, in Sicily, the homes of the emirs who came before them. Peasants were as hospitable to guests as their means allowed them to be. Certain attitudes are difficult to trace across centuries, but the sense of hospitality still evident in southern Italy today seems to be a legacy of the Greeks, Arabs and Jews more than the Normans and Lombards. As in many other aspects of social culture, a certain cohesion was becoming evident in cookery toward the middle years of the thirteenth century.

A few courts — certainly Frederick's — were wealthier than most others. The role of the queen as hostess likely came to the fore during the regencies of Margaret of Navarre and Constance Hauteville, though virtually nothing is known in the particulars with regard to feasts and the precise foods served at these events, or even such occasions as tournaments and festivals.[1043]

It is impossible to ignore the most ancient fundaments of medieval culinary culture, which brings us traditions such as the myth of the Sicilian maiden

Persephone associated with the pomegranate and, more importantly, the wheat harvest. The "wild" flora and vegetation of southern Italy is remarkably varied. Oleasters are still found, along with tender asparagus, cardoons, capers, truffles and even the manna ash. Lentils were known to the Phoenicians and Greeks, and perhaps the indigenous Sicanians. The region's recorded culinary history dates from Greek and Roman times. Ovid, for example, wrote about the "sweet mullet and tender eel" to be fished in Ionian waters. Pliny the Elder mentioned the lamprey as well as wine from the Etna region, local bread, delicious capers, and Sicilian cheese made from the milk of goats; wheat, of course, was an important staple. Plato mentions the lavish cuisine of Syracuse but also the gluttony of the Syracusans. Archestratus, a Siceliot of Gela, wrote "Life of Luxury," or "Gastronomy," a poem dedicated to food and one of the earliest descriptions of ancient European cookery. The recipe collection of the Roman writer Apicius, whose identity is debated, is conserved in a manuscript of his *De Re Culinaria* copied around 900, published in the sixteenth century.

Geography was influential. Somebody who lived in Potenza or any city of the kingdom's mountainous interior might rarely visit the sea or taste its fruits, but plenty of goat, lamb, pork, chicken and rabbit was available. A person born and raised in Enna might never see a roasted squid, cuttlefish or prawn.

While almonds were an imported luxury in England, they were ubiquitous in Puglia, Calabria and Sicily. We read of Jacqueline of Settesoli, who was later canonized, bringing almond cookies to Francis of Assisi.

Beyond culinary history, the sociological aspects of medieval food and diets have been the subject of insightful study in recent times. Apart from such phenomena as halal and kosher observance, there were "prestige" foods and those considered more "common." There were also medicinal uses for certain foods, particularly herbs, thought to cure everything from headaches to infertility (Chapter 12). Preservation existed in a rudimentary but efficacious form. Drying and pickling were both commonplace; olives were conserved using either method. Fish was dried and salted, such as the *baccalà* still made from cod fillets. In a certain cultural sense as well as a nutritional one, we are what we eat.

It should be remembered that the ordinary person might consume two meals per day, in the late morning (or early afternoon) and in the evening after the sun had set. A third meal, or even a very large one, was a luxury; an actual breakfast was unusual. For the common folk, many meals were as simple as a piece of cheese with bread and perhaps a seasonal vegetable or a few nuts, and ordinary people consumed less meat than the aristocracy. The Italian word *pranzo* (lunch) comes to us directly from the Latin *prandium,* and *cena* is the same in both languages.

Such foods as roasted meat were typical of more formal meals. To graze and feed livestock was more costly than fishing, or raising chickens. Most fish and seafood has become far less abundant (and comparatively more expensive) in the Mediterranean than it was in centuries past, but in medieval times fish was normally more available or affordable than mutton or beef in cities and towns fairly near the coast. Whilst fasting, monks at monasteries near coastal areas might consume crustaceans, but crabs and shrimp, though widely consumed, were not prized as particularly "estimable" or desirable foods. At the court, an important guest was more likely to be served roasted meat than fried fish.

In the culinary hierarchy, hunted game such as deer, hare and boar were seen to be more "noble" than the meat of domesticated sheep, goats, pigs and rabbits. Doves, pheasant, partridge, storks, starlings and peacocks outranked chickens and geese. Tuna and swordfish were prized, but smaller fish, along with such creatures as urchins, prawns, squid and cuttlefish, were considered "common."

Enough contemporaneous reporting exists for a good picture of the agriculture of southern Italy in Arab and Norman times. Mohammed ibn Hawqal, Abdullah al Idrisi, Mohammed bin Ahmad ibn Jubayr al Kenani and Hugh Falcandus all left us ample descriptions. The *Jamsilla Chronicle* of the thirteenth century brings us this description of the environs of Stilo, in Calabria:

The castle's position and fortifications made it virtually impossible either to assault or to starve into surrender by siege. Set upon rocky cliffs overlooking steep chasms, it was surrounded by vast valleys whose woodlands and grassy fields, even left uncultivated, could feed sixty people. Edible, wild cabbages grew there, and the pastures sustained much wild game.

Here the generic Latin term *caules,* from which the Italian *cavolo,* refers to various edible plants, such as cauliflower, or *cavolfiore,* and broccoli, or *cavolo broccolo,* and even *rapini* (brassica rapa), harvested in Calabria in late winter and early spring, and again in autumn.

Much of the agriculture (surveyed in Chapter 12) was greatly augmented during the Aghlabid and Fatimid eras, when sugar cane, mulberries, lemons, citrons and oranges were cultivated on a large scale. Wheat, almonds, olives, figs, artichokes, cardoons and other foods had been present since antiquity. We know of the Arabs' irrigation systems, the *kanats.*

The present is not always a clear window to the past. Some fruits and vegetables were more widely cultivated in southern Italy during the Middle Ages than in later times. Here mulberries come to mind, as these trees were used in silk production, which greatly diminished by 1300. With the European colonization of the Americas, sugar cane production decreased in Italy. Over time, rice production also diminished.

Lacking in most of the colorful accounts left to us in Latin and Arabic are recipes or detailed descriptions of specific prepared dishes. There is no eyewitness account of a meal at court sufficient to conceive of a menu. Fortunately, enough is known of Arab cuisine elsewhere in the Islamic world to form a picture of what was served.

Though some of our foreign-born queens may well have brought cooks or recipes to Sicily from their countries of birth, it is reasonable to believe that they partook of the local cuisine, which was diverse enough to accommodate most tastes.

Context suggests that, as early as the eleventh century, the Normans adapted to the flavors and tastes present in the Italian lands they conquered. If anything, there was a greater variety of fruits and vegetables in southern Italy than what was available in Normandy. (Italy has a greater diversity of native flora than any other European country except Russia.) Early Latin chroniclers, notably Amato of Montecassino, William of Apulia and Godfrey Malaterra, did not refer to cookery in explicit terms; at best, they alluded to terrain, agriculture and wine.

The delicious cuisine of the Sicilian court may be divided into several direct ethnic influences and two dynastic eras: Hauteville and Hohenstaufen.

The court's greatest kitchens were in the Norman Palace in Palermo, possibly in one of the towers that is no longer standing. In addition to the large kitchens, there was probably a small kitchen in the Pisan Tower near Roger's Chamber, a suite the king used as a kind of "office" and throne room. In reality, the court traveled; it was wherever the king was, and some cooks traveled with their monarch. Some of our queens spent more time in the capital while their husbands were off besieging the kingdom's rebellious cities or disciplining barons.

There were, of course, regional cuisines throughout the kingdom, with that of the mainland influenced more by the Lombards and Greeks than the Arabs.

As we have seen, the widowed Adelaide del Vasto raised her children mostly in Messina and San Marco d'Alunzio, bringing them to Palermo when her sons neared the age of majority. Western Sicily was then more Arabo-Berber than Byzantine, and the inception of a court cuisine was essentially an Arab development. Even the comital court of Roger II was impressive, but in 1130 it became a royal court to rival those elsewhere in Europe. The food had to be good.

The next nearest court, just north of the kingdom's border, was papal Rome, where the greatest similarity to Sicilian cuisine was to be found during the Hohenstaufen era, when we find the early evolution of what is now regarded as the quintessential "Italian" cookery, which itself varies from region to region. That a few Sicilian cooks or recipes ended up at the English court would be expected considering the ties between the two capitals.[1044]

The first consort to reside in Palermo's palace most of the time was Elvira of Castile. The contact of her Jiménez dynasty with the Almoravids to the south of Castile probably fostered culinary influences that would have given her a foretaste of Sicilian cuisine. Elvira herself was something of an "outsider" as the first Sicilian consort born beyond the more "familiar" territories of Italy and Normandy.

Although the cooking was, for the most part, left to the palace cooks, it was part of a noblewoman's training to recognize good meat, vegetables and fruit, and to be able to prepare some dishes herself. Even if our queens spent little time in the kitchen except for supervising, they certainly knew their way around it.

There were two major markets near the palace. The Balarah souk, now the Ballarò street market, was Palermo's largest marketplace. The market now called *Capo* was chiefly a boucherie just beyond Old Saint Agatha's Gate near the church dedicated to this saint; this was right outside the city walls along what had once been the course of the Papyrus River, in the Sari al Kadi district.

While the commerce of the Balarah souk was based on a great diversity of foods, spices and various products, the boucherie was chiefly a meat market. Each was just a short stroll from the palace. There were other markets, but the Vucciria, whose name recalls the Boqueria of Barcelona, was established later, after 1300, during Sicily's Aragonese period.

With the obvious exceptions of modern transatlantic introductions like tomatoes and peppers, most of the fruits and vegetables cultivated in southern Italy by 1900 were already present in the eleventh century, many introduced by the Byzantines or Arabs. Only a comparatively small number, such as the artichoke and certain broccoli varieties, were truly indigenous to what became the Kingdom of Sicily.

As we shall see, at least a few recipes that are popular today survive from the Norman-Swabian era.

Arab Cookery

When he arrived in Sicily during the reign of William II, probably late in 1184, the traveler Ibn Jubayr noted that the palace chef was a Muslim.[1045] Arab cuisine was still dominant in most of Sicily at that point, even if the culinary traditions of the eastern third of the island probably ran more to the Greek. Some of the recipes were doubtless similar to many in the *Kitab al-Tabikh* (the Baghdad Cookery Book) and other compilations known to us, such as the earlier collection of ibn Sayyar al Warraq.[1046] In Sicily, there were probably some subtle African influences, thanks to the Aghlabids' historical contact with the Berbers they ruled.

Many dishes were quite simple. Chicken or beef would be roasted and served with a sauce of walnuts, pistachios or hazelnuts. Lamb or goat might be stewed, served with rice or couscous. The Aghlabids of the ninth century introduced spices formerly unknown in Sicily, some from Asia.

They may also have introduced certain ovine and caprine varieties. The Girgentan goat, *capra girgentana,* with its spiralled horns, resembles the Asian markhor, *capra falconeri.* It was brought to southern Sicily by the Arabs or Berbers. Today, this breed is prized for its milk.

A typical recipe, *tardin,* calls for finely chopped, pounded lamb or goat meat to be mixed with onions and egg whites, with a bit of olive oil, flavored with powdered coriander, anise seed, cumin, cinnamon, grated galangal, murri (fermented barley paste) and mustard paste. This is then fried.

A popular Palermitan specialty, *pane con milza,* a sandwich made of slices of fried beef spleen, may be medieval in origin.

Mustard seed paste was similar to the yellowish condiment served today. There were also mustard greens. *Mostardo* was wine must boiled into a dense paste and seasoned with spices.

There were also simple broths. Olives and cucumbers were pickled in brine.

Idrisi, the court geographer of Roger II, mentions *itriya* (spaghetti) being made in Trabia, outside Palermo, probably from a variety of durum wheat introduced by the Aghlabids, but we know virtually nothing about the sauces (if any) with which it was served before the thirteenth century. Among the more common varieties of hard wheat were *tumminìa* (timilia) and *russello*. The *perciasacchi* type is a variant of the Khorasan known in Asia, and *margherito*, along with the kindred *bidì*, probably originated in Africa. These have been reintroduced in recent times, having been largely substituted by other varieties since the Middle Ages. It is believed that dozens of varieties or sub-varieties of wheat were cultivated in Sicily alone into the end of the medieval era. Despite its name, what Italians call *grano saraceno* is not "Saracen grain" but buckwheat.

Couscous is still popular in western Sicily, though the recipes have been altered a bit over time since ingredients such as potatoes and tomatoes came from the Americas during the sixteenth century.

Tuna might be roasted over an open flame. The *mattanza*, the practice of capturing tuna in huge nets, originated in Arab times and existed until recently off the coast around Trapani, where the head fisherman was still called the *rais*. Dried fish was also popular, as was *bottarga*, tuna roe. *Agrodolce*, sometimes *stemperata*, fried fish cooked with onions in white vinegar and sugar, is an Arab recipe.

Sugared fruits were made, and sorbet. Almond paste biscuits, and baked cookies consisting of almonds and sugar ("brittle") are still made. Despite Italian stories claiming a later origin, *confetti*, sugar-coated almonds presented to guests at weddings, probably began as the *mlabbas* of Palestine or the *noghl* of Persia, brought to Sicily when it was ruled by Arabs.

Dairy products included ricotta (cottage cheese from curded sheep's milk), yogurt and *kamakh rijal*. The typical aged cheese, as opposed to uncultured curds like ricotta, was similar to what is now called *caciocavallo*, still popular in southern Italy.[1047]

It is quite likely that the sugary cheese cream used in *cassata* and *cannoli* was influenced by a recipe known to the Fatimids. *Cassata* is an example of a recipe having vague Arab influences rather than a proven Arab pedigree. It is a tort of sweet ricotta cheese filling inside a thickly frosted crust topped by candied fruits. Every indication, including the candied fruits, points to it being a Fatimid creation, at least in some form, yet we have no precise evidence of it in the Arabic record.[1048] Its name comes either from the Arabic *kas'at*, for a bowl, or *caseus*, the Latin for cheese. *Cassata*, as it has come down to us, seems to bear the mark not only of Arab cookery but, as well, the cuisine of northern Spain. This may be a culinary influence that arrived with Elvira's Jiménez dynasty. *Cassata* probably evolved over time; the sponge cake base used today may have begun as a simple crust similar to the crispy *cannolo* shell.

Although *gelo di melone*, watermelon gelatin, seems to be Arab in origin, there is no evidence of it in Sicilian medieval records.

The *sfincia*, from the Arabic *isfang* (fried pastry), was made of a light dough of flour, eggs and butter, formed into a ball and quickly deep fried to a light, spongy, porous consistency. After it was removed from the oil, strained, and allowed to cool to room temperature, it was served with honey poured over it. The traditional folk recipes for the dough are far superior to what is used in Sicilian pastry shops nowadays, when *sfince* are stuffed with ricotta cream (with no honey in sight) as if they were Neapolitan *zeppole*.

Sfogliatella, a word derived directly from the Latin *torta defoliata,* loosely translated "leafy tort," was a small "puff pastry" made of light, powdery flour formed into a paste that is fried in lard to a flaked, thinly-layered consistency. This may be filled with cream or served with honey poured over it. In the *Liber de Coquina* (described below) its preparation is explained very simply: *Ad faciendum tortam defoliatam, recipe farinam distemperatam cum aqua calida et misce lardum minutim incisum, sale apposito, et pone in tiolla calefacta, aliam tiellam desuper apponendo.*

Almond nougat, called *turrón* in Spain and *torrone* in Italy, seems to be Arab in origin, though *cupedia,* a Roman confection, was similar. It is mentioned in a medical treatise, the *Book on the Simple Medicines,* written by Ibn Wafid Abul Mutarrif, a physician of Cordoba, and translated by Gerard of Cremona.

The *Kitab al Tabikh fil Maghrib wa'l Andalus,* a cookbook compiled in Andalusia during the thirteenth century, identifies a certain mutton recipe as Sicilian. This calls for varied pieces of mutton or lamb steamed with three times as much chopped onion. Once this meat is nearly cooked, one adds oil, pepper, cinnamon, spikenard, saffron and Chinese cinnamon, boiling down the liquid mixture into a gravy.

In his chronicle, Godfrey Malaterra mentions the Arabs of Troina getting drunk on wine in winter: "The Normans' adversaries, being accustomed to the warm waters of summer, began to feel the coldness of the air and tried to warm themselves by drinking wine. This, however, made them drowsy. Thus they began to neglect their vigilance of the town during the nights" (see note 148).

Few of the native grape varieties of Sicily survived the phylloxera epidemic of the nineteenth century, but Nero d'Avola, which seems to be indigenous to Sicily or Calabria, is still used to make a hearty red wine. Nerello Mascalese, another red, survived due to its cultivation in the volcanic soil on the lower slopes of Mount Etna. Zibibbo, a grape of the muscat family, takes its name from the Arabic *zabib* (raisin), and it was the Arabs who introduced this grape on Pantelleria.

Though some of Sicily's Arabs consumed wine, it is unlikely that they were so lax regarding certain meats. The dearth of pork recipes in modern Sicilian cuisine is usually attributed to its proscription by Muslims and Jews. However, the boarish Nebrodian black swine may have been raised by the Greeks of northeastern Sicily, being isolated to that region.

There are recipes containing chickpeas and *tahini* that are similar to *hummus,* and aubergine (eggplant) salad recipes not unlike Sicilian *caponata.*

Caponata is a cold salad of Arab origin which, in its simplest form, consists of chunks of fried aubergine along with celery, olives, onions and capers (and in modern times some tomato). It has a sweet/sour flavor from traces of sugar and vinegar. It is vaguely similar to French *ratatouille.* An old theory posits its name coming from that of the *capone* (dolphinfish), still an ingredient in some recipes, perhaps with the aubergines substituting the fish.

A medieval Arab recipe for *capone* survives in *stemperata,* a method of preparing fish in a sauce containing ingredients similar to those of *caponata,* in addition to raisins and mint. *Agrodolce* (mentioned earlier) is a simplified variation of this.

It is obvious enough that some recipes of Arab origin are, in one iteration or another, still present in Italian cuisine. It would not be unreasonable to ask what happened to the others. Some probably waned in popularity over time as others evolved. A good example is the *arancina*.

Rice Balls

The *arancina*, or *arancino*, is the stuffed rice ball, its Sicilian name (literally "small orange") coming to us from the Norman French *poume d'orange*, and the name of the fruit deriving from the Arabic *narang*, from the Sanskrit *naranga*. It has an orangish color. There was a trend in using saffron, a spice known in southern Italy in antiquity, in medieval recipes.

The rice ball, which in eastern Sicily is conical rather than round, is coated with a light batter that forms an exterior crust when deep fried. The traditional recipe calls for a filling of cooked, seasoned beef in a spicy gravy.

The *arancina* is rather like a ball of *paella*, even if the latter, as it is prepared today, is based on a modern recipe. Rice was introduced in Sicily by the Arabs, just as it was brought by them to Spain, though the chief variety cultivated was slightly different. Today, the rice most often used to make *arancini* is Italian *originario*, sometimes called *tondo*, while that typically used in Valencian *paella* is *senia* or *bomba*.

The *poume d'orange* introduced in England during the Norman period was a meatball that sometimes contained saffron but no rice. The theory that an Arab cook from Sicily brought it to the English court is at least plausible. The recipe is documented in an extant manuscript, written in Norman French, dating from the thirteenth century.[1049]

An eccentric notion that rice was imported into Sicily during the Fatimid period but not cultivated on the island is unsupported by fact. Just as Ifriqiya raised wheat while also importing it, the Emirate of Sicily probably imported some rice to augment its native production to meet the great needs of a growing population. Rice was introduced into northern Italy during the fifteenth century.

We find rice widely cultivated in Sicily into the nineteenth century, long after the Fatimid irrigation systems had faded from memory. A flood plain outside Ribera, in southern Sicily, provided the ideal environment. This was where the Verdura River neared the coast. The towns in this region were dominated by the Norman castle of Poggiodiana. The name Ribera, akin to *riviera*, may be translated from a Sicilian phrase meaning "river basin." Deforestation and climate change have sealed the stream's sad fate, and a golf resort named for it stands nearby.

In 1841, Ribera was the largest rice producer south of Rome, with five thousand quintals. When did it cease producing rice?

The town was the birthplace of the unificationist Francesco Crispi. In reprisal for a slight he suffered at Ribera during a visit following Italian unification, he convinced the crown to prohibit the cultivation of rice in that part of Sicily, thereby giving Piedmont, the home region of the ruling House of Savoy, a national monopoly henceforth, although a small amount of rice was still produced around Siracusa into the beginning of the twentieth century. Rice has been reintroduced in Sicily in recent years, and Italy is Europe's largest producer of this grain.

What evidence is available suggests that the rice ball is one of the few "native" Sicilian recipes to survive from the Norman-Arab era.

There is debate about whether *panelle* (chickpea fritters), *caponata* and *cannoli* were conceived during this period or invented later. Nevertheless, a few surviving recipes seem to have been inspired by Arab cuisine, which has left us certain Sicilian words, such as *fastùka*, from the Arabic *fatùk*, for pistachio.

It is difficult to trace the exact origins of most modern Sicilian recipes, but historians postulate that many more are, in fact, of Arab creation than the few mentioned here.[1050]

Another rice recipe, *tummàla*, was popularized after 1200 yet is thought to owe its name to an emir of Catania, Muhammad ibn al-Thumna, who we met in Chapter 6. This is a complex casserole, or *timbale*, of chopped chicken, livers, eggs, rice and cheese.

Turks' Heads

An interesting example that seems to survive from the Norman era is called the *Testa di Turco*. It is difficult to know with certainty whether any of the recipes bearing this name actually derive from medieval ones, but it has been suggested that, at the very least, they are all similar in being filled pastries.[1051]

There are distinct sweet pastry recipes called *Testa di Turco* at Scicli and Castelbuono; the former takes its name from the dough being swirled to resemble a turban, the latter is a layered cake filled with cream and berries.

Another recipe is a pastry filled with meat and cheese. This seems to be similar to recipes brought to Plantagenet England, perhaps through its contact with Sicily.[1052] A kindred example of this "Turk's head" was a kind of pasta pie filled with rice, chicken (or even eel), flavored with spices and sugar, then roasted until browned, hence the name.

One might expect *Testa di Saraceno* to be more descriptive if the name referred to the Arabs of Sicily, who the Sicilian chroniclers called *Saracens*. The *Testa di Moro*, conversely, is not a food but a majolica pot shaped and painted to resemble the head of a Moor wearing a crown (Chapter 12).

The name of the food may well be a modern misnomer. By way of analogy, *Piazza Meschita*, in Palermo, was not the site of a mosque (here the majestic *Mezquita* of Cordoba comes to mind) but a synagogue. By the time the living memory of the conversions of 1493 had faded, so had the Palermitans' distinction between Muslims and Jews. Distinctions between Moors and Turks may have been equally ambiguous.

Sagra

The term *sagra*, still used today, refers to various feasts and festivals but especially those related in some way to agriculture or certain local foods. Many *sagre* are directly connected to harvests. There are *sagre* for almost every kind of produce, from chestnuts to cherries to artichokes, and even simple prepared foods such as cheeses.

By their nature, most *sagre* are rural, though they are known in certain districts of larger cities. While some modern *sagre* focus on meat, most of the celebrations having medieval origins are "vegetarian" because of their emphasis on local produce for which a township was known.

Because *sagre* were traditionally medieval, those for foods, such as tomatoes, introduced in southern Italy in modern times are rare.

Patronal celebrations are not, strictly speaking, *sagre*, but certain saints, or their feast days, are associated with particular foods. That the word *sagra* derives from the term for "sacred" is not mere coincidence. Thanksgiving for a good harvest was the religious basis for many *sagre*, and this necessarily related to local saints (see Chapter 32).

The precise origins of certain feasts are difficult to identify. The dinner traditionally associated with Saint Stephen's Day (December twenty-sixth) is usually linked to the translation of some relics of this early martyr, brought to Italy by the Hospitallers following the fall of crusader rule in the Holy Land, to Putignano, near Bari, in 1394. Yet Frederick II proclaimed the observance of this feast, coinciding with his birthday, in 1233, with meals to be offered to the poor at royal expense (see note 1078). This, however, was not a *cuccagna*.

Cuccagna

Certain medieval terms fell into disuse with the extinction of the events they described. The Sicilian word *cuccagna* derives from the Medieval Latin *cocania*, "a country of abundance," from which the German *kuchen* (which now refers to a cake) may also come to us. In the Middle Ages, it connoted the game of climbing a greased or soaped pole, the *albero di cuccagna*, to snatch sweets or other tasty food attached at the high end as a prize; this survives as the Spanish *cucaña*. Details of this form of *cuccagna* in the Kingdom of Sicily are sparse before 1266, but it was an event popular across Europe.

Better known is a festival that came more than two centuries later, when Sicily's prosperity was on the wane. At this "cuccagna" a vast table of food was placed in a large square or field protected by guards and a cordon. At a signal, the crowd surrounding it was allowed to throng the table and eat the food that had been prepared. The sadistic aristocrats watching this spectacle found it entertaining to see the poor trample each other to reach the food. A medieval king would not likely countenance such a humiliation of his own people, but by 1415 the island was administered by viceroys representing kings who lived in Spain.

European Cookery

As we have seen, there is no conclusive evidence to suggest that the Normans introduced any of their recipes in the Italian lands they conquered during the eleventh century. The cuisine of the urban centers, large and small, that they occupied in Puglia and Calabria was based on longstanding Greek culinary traditions. This was also true of oeniculture.

Though known to the Arabs, the hunting culture was popularized in Sicily by the Normans. On the mainland, it was already commonplace among the Lombards who ruled cities like Salerno. Deer, boar, partridge and hare thus made their way into Sicilian cookery, whereas the Arabs had consumed more goat, mutton, rabbit and chicken. The Christians used lard, pork fat and butter.

Despite such additions, the cuisine seems to have remained predominantly Arab in orientation into the reigns of William II and Tancred. The next step in its evolution occurred during the Swabian period. At least, this is when the greater number of "European" recipes known to us were recorded. These have come to be identified with Frederick II and his successors, particularly Manfred.

Although the Sicilian language that flourished during the Swabian era did not have a continued, long-lasting impact on Italian culture beyond a few regions after Manfred's death in 1266, the cuisine of southern Italy during this period survived and evolved to form the foundation for what exists in Italy today.

Spaghetti, as we have seen, was already being made in Sicily during the twelfth century. In the next century we find recipes for such things as ravioli. Risotto recipes have their origins in Piedmont during the fifteenth century, but the cultivation of rice in Sicily and other southern regions may account for its introduction in the north.

This is not to suggest that every recipe known at the court of Frederick II originated south of Rome. Many were known in the northern Italian comunes that he ruled, and a few may have come from his German lands.

Because Frederick's court traveled often, almost constantly, not only throughout his dominions in northern Italy but into his Holy Roman Empire, some of these recipes were known in these regions. Therefore, by 1250, not every recipe was exclusively "Sicilian."

The chief sources for court recipes during the Swabian era come to us from several manuscripts copied early in the fourteenth century. The *Liber de Coquina* is conserved as two codices (Lat 7131 and Lat 9328) in the Bibliothèque Nationale in Paris. Its first section is usually called the *Tractatus,* which may be the work of a French copyist, and the second part, the *Liber de Coquina,* which was probably composed by an Italian. A reference to Frederick II suggests that the recipes probably date from his reign; in other places his son, Manfred, is mentioned. Specifically, we find such phrases as *secundum usum imperatoris* ("according to the emperor's preference") in the second recipe of the *Liber,* on the preparation of *caulles,* which may refer to either cabbage or to plants such as cauliflower (and broccoli), the latter being more likely, especially when stems are mentioned. Yes, certain words present in these medieval texts are open to interpretation based on etymology and context.

Another codex containing recipes from this era is called the *Meridionale* because it was written in Neapolitan.[1053] Many of these recipes first appeared in the *Liber.* Significantly, both the *Liber* and the *Meridionale* laid the groundwork for what became Italian cuisine.[1054]

In general, the *Tractatus* has recipes for meat, poultry, fish, legumes and sauces, while the *Liber* concentrates on pastry as well as fish, poultry and vegetables. The *Meridionale* is rather general and highly informative. *The Forme of Cury* written in England was influenced by these works, which should not be confused with compilations of Neapolitan recipes that came later.[1055] It is interesting to speculate that certain medieval recipes and cooking methods which came to be known in England and elsewhere in northern Europe originated in Italy and Spain.

There also exist other compilations including Sicilian recipes which, in some cases, may date from the end of the Middle Ages, some recorded in monastic records during the early modern era.[1056]

Very few "canonical" recipes include exact measurements in the original, leaving the preparation open to a certain degree of interpretation.[1057]

Let us consider some of the actual recipes.

A typical recipe is chicken with fennel sauce. Here chicken is cut into pieces, then cooked and browned in lard. The cooked meat is then removed from the lard and broth, to which is added finely chopped fennel leaves, a bit of chopped parsley and crushed almonds, along with water, olive oil, salt and spice (a mixture of ground cinnamon, pepper, saffron and cloves). This green sauce is either served over the chicken or the individual pieces of meat are coated with it (a similar recipe follows below). Some of these recipes are similar to what one encountered in Ifriqiya and Iberia.

A simple recipe called *laudo* in the *Meridionale* calls for broiling chicken, to which is added onions, wine, saffron and other ingredients.

Saffron was ubiquitous, present in many recipes of the Swabian era. Except for desserts, about one out of four recorded recipes called for it. We also find the liberal use of lard and butter.

The *Meridionale* brings us a number of curious recipes of Arab origin. *Eucabam,* its name a corruption of the Arabic *ukaybiya,* was chicken served in a sauce of milk, egg yolks, almonds and saffron, with bread. *Aaneth* was broiled mutton browned, then cooked in vinegar, flavored with spices, almonds, egg yolks, parsley and saffron. *Schinchinelli* was a kind of large raviolo filled with almond paste, dried fruit, perhaps preserved pears, and honey, then baked; its name derives from the Arabic *kuskenole.*

There are recipes for small birds such as doves and pigeons, and offal, such as stuffed pig's stomach.

There are several recipes for fava beans. The simplest is to boil and flavor the fresh beans. This is similar to *fritedda,* or *fritella,* a dish popular in spring which consists of whole, fresh fava beans, peas and pieces of fresh artichokes cooked together and flavored with salt and black pepper. Another recipe, *maccu,* is a thick soup which is usually made in the winter with dried beans. This contains beans without the skin, crushed, boiled, and flavored with some chopped onion, olive oil and finely chopped parsley, salt and pepper. The medieval recipe had a bit of honey in it.

There are a few very simple recipes for boiled, fresh, green fava beans. Indeed, many of the recipes in these collections are so strikingly elementary that they are really little more than very concise notes of instructions.

Among the seafood recipes was one for prawns in pastry (heavy batter) served with almonds or pine nuts, flavored with saffron. The prawns, of which there are several varieties, are cleaned and peeled except for the tails.

There are similar recipes for many fish and seafoods, including lamprey and trout. A simple recipe for stuffed sardines is present in the *Liber,* and though it is not very similar to the modern *beccafico* it may have been an early inspiration.

We find numerous recipes for *frittate,* or omelets, made from eggs and various vegetables, such as chards and mushrooms, though not usually with more than one kind of vegetable. This was almost a genre unto itself. Some of these omelets, made with the addition of flour, were rather similar to quiche (which is baked). Not all these recipes called for cheese.

Cheeses, though not described extensively, have changed little over time based on the milk source, the culture used and the process of ageing. Many were made from the milk of sheep or goats, as were milk products such as *ricotta* (cottage cheese), curds without a culture. *Ricotta salata,* as its name implies, was salted, aged ricotta but without a culture.

One recipe that called for cheese was *lassanis* (the recipe appears in English below), the precursor of modern lasagna. It was a baked pie of flat pasta noodles layered with spices, eggs, cheese and bacon.[1058]

In one form or another, lasagna remained popular at court into the nineteenth century; it was the favorite food of Francesco II of the Two Sicilies (see Appendix 7), who reigned until 1861, nicknamed "The Lasagna King" or simply *Lasa.*

In the Neapolitan of the *Meridionale* we find this description of a simple sauce for flavoring fried fish: *Affare sapore per pescie fricto tolli salsa verdi che è scricta desopra et suco de citranguli o agresta et gecta sopre.*

Another dish, the *torta de montano,* was similar to a roasted "meat pie," while *torta defoliata* was more like a meat loaf.

In the *Libro di Cucina* of the "Anonimo Veneziano" compiled in northern Italy late in the fourteenth century we find two pie recipes, one for chicken livers with bacon (number 111) and the other for fava beans with bacon (number 109), favored by King Manfred and bearing his name.

Some recipes are virtually unchanged in centuries. In antiquity, the Syracusan dramatist Epicharmus of Kos wrote a play called "The Sausage." The Roman culinary writer Apicius mentions foods of this kind, and indeed many still prepared today. Today, pork sausage with fennel seeds is based on the same simple preparation as that described in the *Meridionale.*[1059] Another form of sausage was stuffed with fish.

There is a recipe for a sauce made from black cuttlefish ink. A very similar sauce is still used for spaghetti.

Frederick II favored *scapece,* which could be conserved in a jar. known as *askipecia* or *scapetia* in Latin, the word *scapece* ultimately derives from the Arabic *sikbaj,* aubergines marinated in vinegar. Frederick's version was made of fried eggplant (alternatively zucchini), anchovies preserved (or cooked) in vinegar, some mint, a bit of garlic and pepper, and perhaps a touch of saffron.[1060] This was prepared during Frederick's travels by his chef, Bernard. It brings to mind the *caponata* and *stemperata* mentioned earlier; like these, it was influenced by Arab cuisine. Interestingly a variation on the original *scapece* recipe has survived in Puglia into our time.

We find a number of Sicilian names for prepared foods of the Norman era. *Itria* (vermicelli), *cubaita* (sesame brittle) and *cuscusu* (couscous) come to mind; all derive from Arabic for foods known in Arab-speaking lands. Although Angelo Senisio's *Declarus*, a Sicilian dictionary written around 1350, refers to some foods that may have been known a century earlier, it is not intended as a description of recipes.

Crespelle, which are still made in our times, are extremely thin, crispy, fried "cookies" made with white flour and eggs, flavored with sugar or honey. Known as *chiacchiere* in Sicily, these are described below.

Ricettariu di lu Regnu di Sichilia

It seemed appropriate to present a sampling of recipes from the two earliest written collections known in the kingdom.

Though the surviving copies of both works were written in the fourteenth century, many recipes in the *Liber* are also present in the *Meridionale,* where we encounter a few linguistic subtleties. In the Latin of the *Liber* the word *lardum* is usually bacon, whereas in the Neapolitan of the *Meridionale* the term *lardo* may sometimes be simple fat (lard) from pork. Because certain ingredients, such as pomegranate wine, could be difficult to find, substitutions were sometimes indicated. The *vernaccia* mentioned was probably a slightly fortified wine from Liguria rather than the white table wine made today; *Greco* was a Neapolitan white wine that may have aged to a light amber. The Latin *cavli* may refer to either cauliflower (or broccoli) or, less often in southern Italy, cabbage. "Fennel" is not always true fennel, *foeniculum vulgare,* but anise (Florence fennel), *pimpinella anisum,* which has a large white bulb. Even the modern diction often varies; around Palermo *sparacelli* refers to broccoli while in central Sicily the same word refers to asparagus.

It is possible that certain recipes calling for "bread crumbs" actually require a small amount of whole-grain durum flour as a thickening agent.

Some recipes were seasonal. Broccoli had a long season, from October through March, while fava beans were harvested in the spring but could be dried. Nuts, grains, olive oil, honey, sugar and spices were easily conserved. Although fish could be dried and salted, most recipes call for using it fresh. The comparatively cooler climate of the Middle Ages facilitated the natural preservation of many ingredients. Bread was usually made from whole-grain wheat; it had a thick crust and, if placed in a cool, dry place, might last for several days. Grain and other products were stored within thick walls, in places similar to the crypts of churches.

Certain ingredients were a bit different in times past. Almond milk, for example, was somewhat viscous and unsweetened; it is made by soaking almonds in water for ten or twelve hours, then removing the skin and crushing the soft nuts into a juicy puree to which more water might be added. The term "bitter herbs" may refer to such things as arugula.

If there were a cryptic element in a recipe, it was most likely ingredients such as the specific spices used. This makes some of the recipes recorded in the *Liber de Coquina* rather difficult to replicate precisely today. Generic references to "spices" are sometimes enigmatic and these will vary by recipe. In the absence of more detailed information, an imperfect general solution is a mix of these powdered spices: cloves, saffron, cinnamon, pepper, ginger. For desserts: cinnamon, cloves, ginger. For a stronger flavor: cloves, black pepper, nutmeg.

A potential problem is posed by the fact that quantities are not indicated, though experienced modern cooks have sometimes resolved this through experimentation. In fact, the descriptions recorded for many recipes were imprecise even by medieval standards.

Visitors to Sicily sometimes wonder why so few restaurants serve chicken except for the small establishments that sell it skewered (rotisserie). In modern times, the Sicilians have come to regard chicken as something "informal" to be prepared and consumed in a family setting, much like turkey on American Thanksgiving. Roasted chicken is sometimes made in homes, and the most common Sicilian recipe for stuffing (bread crumbs, eggs, grated cheese, minced onions and chopped parsley) may well be medieval in origin.

Actual restaurants, as opposed to simple trattorias frequented by travelers, were quite rare in southern Italy until the nineteenth century except for a few establishments in a few cities.

The repertoire of recipes from this era is impressive. What follow are a few simple examples present in both codices; sometimes there are variations in ingredients and cooking method between the same recipe in the *Liber* and the *Meridionale*. As the recipes presented here are intended to be suitable to modern tables, such delicacies as peacock, stork and dove, though included in both books, were not considered. Likewise, lamprey is usually difficult to find.

Poultry Sauce: Add powdered marjoram and cardamom to a puree of chicken livers cooked in olive oil with pomegranate wine. If you have no such wine, use Greek wine with a touch of vinegar. (This gravy is suitable for chicken that is simply grilled or fried and not otherwise seasoned.)

Fennel Chicken: Fry chicken pieces in olive oil until they are almost completely cooked. Then add some water, finely chopped chicken liver, finely chopped wild fennel leaves (not anise) and parsley. Add spices to taste and cook the mixture. (This varies slightly from the similar recipe noted earlier.)

Lemon Chicken: Cook chicken pieces in lard and onions. Add (unskinned) almonds and some water to the mixture, which should be thickened by the addition of a beaten egg yolk. When fully cooked, sprinkle liberally with lemon juice and serve.

Fruity Chicken: Fry chicken pieces in lard until mostly cooked. Then add water and saffron to cook completely. After a few minutes, add to this mixture sugared (pitted) dates, (pitted) plums or prunes, raisins and almonds. Allow to simmer another few minutes before serving.

Stuffed Chicken: Into the cavity of a clean, dressed chicken, place a mixture of ground pork (or bacon), chopped chicken liver, chopped leeks, chopped parsley, spices, saffron, eggs and grated cheese. Roast the stuffed chicken (on a spit) until brown and fully cooked.

Partridge: Cut the dressed birds into pieces and cook these in lard with chopped onions. When they are cooked and browned, let simmer in pomegranate wine with sugar and add vernaccia wine. (This recipe is equally suitable for pheasant, quail or other birds.)

German Chicken Soup: Boil chicken pieces until cooked. Set aside broth. Remove bones and chop the chicken meat finely. Add meat to the broth with chopped parsley, mint, marjoram and rosemary, sage and a bit of saffron. Bring this to a boil. Salt to taste.

Saracen Chicken Soup: Broil small pieces of chicken and chopped liver in lard until partially cooked. Add wine and spices and continue cooking. Add water as necessary. Finally, add pitted dates, raisins, and sugar. Serve with crumbled, dried bread. (This a typical Arab sweet-and-sour recipe. The recommendation for the use of pork lard in the text probably reflects later usage.)

Imperial Soup: Boil chopped green broccoli (the florets but not the stems or leaves) with a small quantity of very finely-chopped whole fennel (anise), including the bulb as well as the leaves. Add beef or chicken broth, a bit of olive oil, and salt to taste. (This vegetable soup was a favorite of Frederick II.)

Ceci Soup: Boil ceci (chickpeas) until soft. Remove ceci from water and mash, adding a touch of olive oil, with spices and powdered white pepper. Place the mashed ceci mixture back in the remaining water adding some chopped parsley and a few chopped, roasted chestnuts. Bring to a boil. Serve hot.

White Meat Broth: To the broth of lamb or kid add finely-chopped, skinned almonds and grated white ginger. Boil. Add salt and white pepper to taste. (For modern cooks chicken broth is a good substitute for the broth of lamb or kid.)

Creamy Chicken Rice: Cook white rice and allow it to cool. In another pan, cook some boned chicken chopped into small pieces. Then combine the two, adding sheep's milk, and bring the mixture to a boil. Add sugar and spices before serving. (The more recent recipe calls for the further addition of pieces of fried bacon.)

Poultry Innards: Clean and chop livers and gizzards. Mix together with eggs and cheese and form into flat cakes. Fry or deep fry in oil and lard.

Meat Balls: Beef, pork or mutton are very finely chopped and ground. Add saffron and other spices as preferred, chopped onions and egg. Mix thoroughly, form into balls and fry.

Mamonia: Prepare boned, chopped mutton or goat meat. Boil this with wholegrain white rice in bitter almond milk and spices. When cooked, add honey. (This was a variation of the Arab *mamunya,* of which there were other, very distinct, forms in Syria and England.)

Ravioli Pork Filling: Chop and boil pork meat until most of the liquid has evaporated. Remove from heat and let it cool. Then chop it very finely. Add grated cheese, eggs, spices and salt. (For a modern approach, grind the pork before cooking.)

Herring in Broth: Boil Greek wine in a pan. Add fresh, cleaned, boned sardines without overcooking. There should be just enough wine to cover the fish. Add pepper, saffron and sugar. Then add oil and let the mixture thicken. (This is similar to stemperata.)

Tench: Steam very briefly so the fish is just tender enough to cut and clean easily without breaking the backbone. Sprinkle the inside with almond milk and stuff with marjoram, parsley and mint. Then fry the fish in olive oil to cook it. Serve with green sauce. (Tench is a freshwater fish but this recipe is equally suitable for saltwater fish of this size having white flesh.)

Fish Sausage: Clean the fish, then steam it just enough to easily remove the scales and bones. Next, chop it finely, adding chopped grassy herbs with the desired spices. Stuff it into goat or sheep intestines and fry it. Alternatively, form it into a cylinder wrapped in a sheet of thin, clean linen, remove it and then boil it in oil until cooked.

Roasted Squid: Clean the squid, leaving the tentacles attached to the body, which should be slit along its length to form an open butterfly shape when cooked. Roast over an open flame until cooked. Flavor with lemon or citron juice, or rose water.

Simple Shrimp: Place live shrimp in boiling water. Do not overcook. Remove, strain, and sprinkle with verjuice or red vinegar. Salt to taste. (Verjuice is preferable to vinegar.)

Cuttlefish and Octopus Broth: Clean both, setting aside the ink gland of the cuttlefish. Cut these into pieces and sauté in chopped onion and olive oil until cooked. Gradually add just enough water to cover this mixture, adding marjoram and chopped parsley. As soon as this comes to a boil, add some crumbled bread crust. Then add more water with spices, saffron, chopped almonds and the cuttlefish ink. If a sweet-and-sour flavor is desired, add citron juice and sugar.

Cuttlefish: Thoroughly clean the cuttlefish, removing the ink and bone. Fry it in olive oil. Add salt and pepper. Serve it with a green sauce (see below).

Green Sauce: Finely chop parsley leaves, adding (in a lesser quantity) chopped mint leaves. Flavor with powdered nutmeg, cloves, cardamom and ginger. Add bread crumbs and oil, mixing the ingredients thoroughly. Then add salt and a small amount of vinegar to taste.

Wild Mushrooms: Boil mushrooms until cooked. Drain. Cut into pieces if necessary. Sauté with finely chopped onion in olive oil or pork lard. Flavor with spices or chopped, grassy herbs such as chives.

Mushroom Tart: Add steamed chopped mushrooms to eggs and Comino pecorino cheese (made from sheep's milk in Abruzzi) with spices. Bake in a greased pan. (This may be cooked as an omelet or poured into a pie crust like a quiche.)

Lentils: Boil the lentils with aromatic herbs (such as chives), olive oil, salt and saffron. When cooked and soft, almost a paste, mix into the lentils a beaten egg and grated cheese before serving.

Lentils and Pork: Boil lentils with fresh, boned pork, without adding eggs or cheese.

Fried Spinach: Clean spinach thoroughly, then boil for a few minutes until partly cooked. Remove from water with a fork and press to strain well. Next, sauté chopped onion in olive oil, then adding bitter spices and saffron. Salt to taste, sprinkling with lemon juice if desired. (This is a variation of the *isfanak muttajan* known in Arab cookery.)

Green Soup: To meat broth add chopped swiss chard (the main ingredient) and a lesser quantity of chopped escarole (or spinach). Let this boil until cooked, then add a bit of chopped mint and chopped parsley just before serving. Salt and pepper to taste.

Gnocchi: Mix white flour with eggs, water and a small quantity of white bread crumbs. Form into small balls. To cook, place these into water that is already boiling. Remove after a few minutes. Serve with butter and grated cheese.

Lasagna: Roll pasta (see the gnocchi recipe) into thin sheets cut into rectangles. In a shallow, flat, greased pan, form these into three or four layers between a mixture of chopped hard-boiled eggs, chopped bacon, spices (which may include finely-chopped chives and parsley), grated or chopped cheese and small pieces of boiled pork sausage. The sheets of pasta should be soft (freshly-made). Bake.

Pancakes: Add egg whites to white flour with water and some chopped, fresh flower blossoms such as lavender. Add salt or sugar to taste. Mix, but do not whip, to a smooth, pasty consistency. Fry in butter or lard. Serve with honey or a sauce.

Fried Cheese: Coat chunks of soft, slightly-aged sheep's cheese with a mixture of beaten eggs and green herbs dredged in bread crumbs. Fry in oil or lard until a crust is formed.

Stuffed Figs: Fill large, fresh figs with small pieces of skinned apples and pears, adding pieces of walnut and ground cinnamon.

Crespelle: Mix white flour with water, egg and saffron, and very little yeast. When it has risen, roll the paste into a very thin layer and cut into long, narrow strips. Deep fry in oil with lard until cooked and crispy but not browned. Set the cookies on a cloth to drain the oil. When cool, coat with sugar or honey and serve. These are the *frittelle ubaldini* mentioned in the *Meridionale,* so-called because they were preferred by Ubaldino della Pila, brother of the cardinal Ottaviano degli Ubaldini, a contemporary of Frederick II. (The recipe mentioned earlier is identical but without the eggs or saffron, and the strips are cooked in oil without lard.)

Candied Violets: Gently rinse edible blue violets, holding the delicate flowers by their stems, and allow to dry. Heat cane sugar in a pan with a little water as needed until the mixture is melted and liquid. Remove from heat. Carefully dip the flowers into the liquid and set to dry on a lightly oiled cutting board or other surface. (These were said to be a favorite of Frederick II.)

Biancomangiare: Slowly heat milk and cream in a pot with cane sugar and a bit of chopped, crushed vanilla bean. Permit the sugar to dissolve but do not boil the mixture. Then stir in a bit of liquefied *amidon* (wheat starch) and let the whole mixture thicken before removing it from the heat and pouring it into small bowls to let it cool in the coldest part of the cellar. Sprinkle ground cinnamon or crushed almonds over the top. This is just one variation on this confection popular in France and Spain, and nowadays cornstarch can be substituted for wheat starch. The medieval recipe is derived from the Arab *isfidabaj.*

Wren Pie: Bake a large, bowl-shaped pastry shell and let it cool to room temperature. Then use a knife to make an opening at the bottom of it. At the top or along the side, fashion a series of rectangular holes to resemble the bars of a cage. Shortly before serving place a few live birds into the pastry via the hole in the bottom and set the pie upon a heavy plate. Present it to a diner with a knife to carve into the top and free the birds. (It is not suggested that any reader attempt to prepare this, but it is a fine example of what was sometimes made for royalty.)

Courtly Dining

For the common folk, dining was simple enough, but what was a formal meal like at the Sicilian court? It should be remembered that, unlike the courts of many parts of Europe, Sicily's was influenced initially to a great degree by Byzantine and Arab culinary traditions, which in certain ways were more refined and sophisticated than those known in England, France, Germany and some parts of northern Italy.

Fragments of medieval plates of the Norman-Swabian era survive that were discovered in the royal palace in Palermo; some of this pottery is decorated with Fatimid or Byzantine motifs. These items were somewhat similar to majolica but without the white glaze undercoating that characterized that medium.

The use of knives and wooden spoons was normal at court. Indeed, it is even possible that simple forks (with two tines) were used at court meals in Sicily before this was common practice in most of Europe. At her wedding feast in 1004, Maria Argyropoulina, the niece of Basil II of Constantinople, scandalized many of the Venetian guests present when she ate her meat with a fork, and a golden one at that, but over time the utensil came to be viewed as slightly less eccentric.[1061] The story about the Byzantine princess is rather significant because it informs us of one of the first public uses of what became the modern fork, and the church's view of the dining utensil as a sinful luxury. Yet it is difficult to imagine any of the Hautevilles or their spouses worrying about offending the clergy by using a fork to eat food.

Another detail worth remembering is that spaghetti was known in Sicily as early as the reign of Roger II, and this food is sometimes mentioned as a reason for Italians' early use of the fork, albeit some time later. Even so, this suggests that forks may have been used in Sicily before the rest of Italy.[1062]

Nevertheless, guests would eat some foods with their hands, and finger bowls and linen napkins were provided.

Though a guest might bring his own knife and cup to dinner at a comparatively humble baronial castle, this was less necessary at a royal palace, where it was usually presumed that these things would be provided.

We do not know exactly which service tradition prevailed at which time, and it is quite possible that particular practices continued from one reign into another. The Arabs might place several different dishes on the table simultaneously, whereas the Greeks and Normans might prefer sequential courses. Naturally, the king and queen could dictate their preferences not only for the food served but for the mode of service. Elvira may have preferred one approach, Margaret another. Whatever the case, by the Hohenstaufen era, service probably began to conform more to the prevailing European norm.

Where were the meals served? So extensively have the major medieval palaces been restructured or destroyed that it is impossible to determine where a "great hall" was located in most of them. Little remains of the Favara (in Palermo's Brancaccio district) or the royal palace at Monreale. The palace at Messina is long gone. Some royal residences, like Arechi Castle in Salerno, have been extensively modified since 1266, though Castel del Monte, Frederick's Apulian refuge, survives unscathed. There were, in fact, many other castles where the traveling court stayed occasionally, particularly during the Swabian era, such as the imposing fortresses still standing in Bari and Catania.

The Barons' Hall in Palazzo Steri, overlooking Piazza Marina in Palermo, though built later (it was completed in the fourteenth century), offers a glimpse of what a Sicilian royal dining hall looked like. It is spacious, its wooden ceiling painted with typical medieval figures, scenes and coats of arms. This was larger than the great hall of the typical baronial castle, and the edifice was eventually used as the royal palace of Palermo.

The great hall at San Marco d'Alunzio, the first castle erected by the Hautevilles in Sicily, was certainly smaller than this. Like the castle at Mileto, in Calabria, it has fallen victim to earthquakes. The castle at Melfi is in better condition, though much altered over time, while that at Ariano has been largely reconstructed.

A few of our queens sometimes had what were, in effect, their own castles and households. We thus find Adelaide at San Marco d'Alunzio and later (following her marriage to the King of Jerusalem) at Patti, and Joanna at the Zisa in Palermo. Would that we knew more about the dinners served in these residences. Each cook doubtless had his own specialties, each woman her own food preferences.

Entertainment at formal court dinners and royal feasts would be provided by minstrels and troubadours, who were ever more present beginning with the reign of William II and the influence of his wife, Joanna of England. Even before then, there were fine musicians in Sicily, and the painted Fatimid muqarnas ceiling of Palermo's Palatine Chapel depicts them playing lutes and harps.

The meal served at midday or in the early afternoon was the chief meal of the day (until recent times this was still true in Italy). Formal royal meals were more likely to be served at this time than in the evening, even if a major banquet lasted until dusk. There was a general sense of order, with meat dishes following lighter foods such as soups. Menus, and even the scheduling of a banquet, were planned around Christian feasts, which might entail fasting, and days on which it was customary to refrain from consuming either meat or fish; into modern times fish was popular on Fridays during Lent. Some clergy eschewed meat generally.

Halal and kosher requirements were easily accommodated given the nature of most recipes and the possibility of substituting olive oil for pork lard. Historians disagree about the reasons for the increasing use of lard, and even butter, by the thirteenth century; the thesis that olive oil was somehow scarce or particularly costly in regions such as Sicily, Calabria or Puglia is questionable. Much of the salt used was extracted from sea water; there are still salt evaporation ponds near Trapani.

Almost everybody of note who visited the court in Palermo probably dined with the king or queen at some point, even if some of these dinners were less formal than others. This included Eleanor of Aquitaine during the reign of Roger II and the nephews of Thomas Becket during the reign of William II. More so than most European medieval kings, Sicily's monarchs were likely to invite intellectuals to court.

Often, formal dinners were distinguished not only by the Sicilian court's polycultural cuisine but by the company itself. At times, there may have been a diversity of guests present. Travelers arrived from the Arab and Byzantine lands of the Mediterranean, naturally, and the Plantagenet dominions in France and England. Beginning with the marriage of Roger II to Elvira of Castile, there was increasing contact with northern Spain. The Hohenstaufen reign brought with it greater contact with Germany. This was also an opportunity for the sharing of recipes.

During the Norman era, there were initially certain differences between the food served at the royal court, with its Arab cooks, and the cuisine at the castle of a typical Norman or Lombard baron in the hinterland in Campania or Basilicata. Yet a heretofore unfamiliar cuisine could be introduced more rapidly than a language or faith because it was intrinsically easier to learn a new recipe than a new tongue or ideology. When the barons and their companies attended meals at court, either in Sicily or during the king's travels around the peninsular part of the kingdom, they would have a chance to sample this cuisine. Little effort was required for a baron to introduce the recipe to his wife and cook once he returned to his own lands. This is likely how *scapece* became known in Puglia and other regions that Frederick II visited often. Other recipes of Arab or Byzantine origin were likely introduced as a consequence of contact with the eastern Mediterranean during the crusades and the Normans' incursions into regions such as Greece.

Obviously enough, a great celebration like the banquet at a wedding or coronation was much more complex and impressive than a "routine" dinner for a visiting diplomat. Some wedding celebrations lasted for days.

Though certain banquets and feasts in the Kingdom of Sicily, such as the wedding of William II and Joanna of England in 1177, stand out for their grandeur, virtually nothing is known about the menu or the quantity of food served.[1063] We know that the wedding celebrations of Frederick II and Isabella of England in Germany in 1235 lasted at least four days but we have only sparse details about the food. For a general idea of this we may look to the magnificent feasts known elsewhere in western Europe during that era.[1064]

For the wedding on the day after Christmas in 1251 of Margaret, the daughter of Henry III of England, to Alexander III, the young King of Scotland, the festivities lasted a week, and Matthew Paris tells us that sixty bulls constituted the first and main course.[1065] Whether, as the chronicler claims, more than a thousand knights attended with their spouses and esquires, is debatable. Even so, it is reported that the guests consumed seventy pigs, almost two thousand hens, sixteen hundred partridges, three hundred rabbits, and a large number of peacocks, pheasants and of course swans, along with plenty of fish. Nearly seventy thousand loaves of bread were baked. In fact, the planning and preparation began months before the wedding in York. The detail with which the feast was described was rather exceptional for its time because it reflected a personal account; Matthew seems to have been present.

Bovine livestock was rarer in the kingdom of Sicily, but it is reasonable to presume that the amounts of other kinds of protein served at some celebrations held in the *Regnum Siciliae* rivalled those known in England and France.

It was during this era that Bartholomew the Englishmen, while living in Magdeburg, wrote his encyclopedic *De Proprietatibus Rerum,* which describes, among many other things, the character of society. Here he considers aristocratic dining etiquette, stating that bread is served first, followed by wine and meat, and then fruit:

Meat and drink is ordained and convenient to dinners and to feasts, for at feasts first meat is prepared and made in a readiness, guests be called together, forms and stools be set in the hall, and tables, cloths and towels be ordained, disposed, and made ready. Guests be set with the lord in the chief place of the board, and they sit not down at the board before the guests wash their hands. Children be set in their place, and servants at a table by themselves. First knives, spoons and salts be set on the board, and then bread and drink, and many diverse messes, household servants busily help each other to do everything diligently and talk merrily together. The guests be gladded with lutes and harps. Now wine and now messes of meat be brought forth and divided. At the last cometh fruit and spices, and when they have eaten, board, cloths, and relief be borne away, and guests wash and wipe their hands again. Then grace is said, and guests thank the lord. Then for gladness and comfort drink is brought yet again. When all this is done at meat, men take their leave, and some go to bed and sleep, and some go home to their own lodgings.[1066]

Here, incidentally, we find the origin of the phrase "set the table" rooted in the practice of laying a board across a trestle, then covering it with a linen cloth.

While Bartholomew was writing his "encyclopedia," another Englishman, John of Garland, was working on his *Morale Scolarium,* which considered, among many other things, table manners.

Medieval eating could be a messy affair, especially without the use of forks, and one imagines noble ladies taking care not to splatter gravy on their elegant silken gowns.

The significance of the medieval precursor of what nowadays would be termed a "state dinner" cannot be understated. This was a chance for a sovereign to impress upon his guests that he and his kingdom were truly important. Everything, from the food to the entertainment to the palace itself, enhanced this impression.

As we have seen, the court was wherever the monarch was. Frederick II, as emperor, had to travel constantly; indeed, he spent very little of his reign in Palermo. In truth, his imperial status spoke for itself. Even a meal under a tent could not diminish the prestige of a man so powerful. For the Hautevilles, Palermo itself was impressive enough.

Palermo's souks were more alluring than most European fairs; only Spain offered anything comparable. London, Paris and Milan were destined for greatness, but this was Palermo's moment.

One thing about Palermo's royal residences was especially helpful in the preparation of food. Unlike many European castles and palaces of its era, Palermo's royal palace had rudimentary plumbing, with water supplied by the *kanats* running to the city from the rivers and springs near Monreale and Baida. (Such a *kanat* connected to the Kemonia River fed the mikveh of the great synagogue near the Balarah souk.) This meant that water for cooking did not have to be carried from a river or well. Some of the springs, such as the Sorgente del Gabriele, which feeds a *kanat* near Via Nave and the Scibene palace, still supply Palermo with water.

Guests might be entertained at one of the smaller royal palaces around the city, especially during warmer months. The Zisa, the Cuba, the Favara and the Scibene, all surrounded by gardens, were also provided water through *kanats*. These palaces had ponds or pools similar to those of the Alhambra in Andalusia.

Conclusions

Both the courtly and common cuisines of southern Italy evolved noticeably from the foundation of the kingdom in 1130 until the fall of our second royal dynasty in 1266, something confirmed by recent scientific research.[1067]

The gradual culinary changes shadowed trends in other areas of society, particularly its Latinization and the diminishing influence of Islam and Arab culture generally. Furthermore, many of the foundations of the cookery that survived over the centuries paralleled trends in other areas, such as language.

And hospitality.

Chapter 28
PERMANENCY

Along with the Constitutions of Melfi, the mercantile and military institutions of the *Regnum* were reinforced. The Muslims of Lucera, a city whose population grew larger every year, manufactured bows and armor for the entire kingdom. Melfi and Canossa also produced fine equipment of this kind. Excellent crossbows were imported from Acre. There were great shipyards at the major ports. Once again, the kingdom's merchant fleet rivalled those of the Genoans and Venetians. It was a Genoan, Nicholas Spinola, who Frederick eventually appointed as admiral of the fleet.[1068]

Day by Day

While the Kingdom of Sicily was enjoying a prosperous period of general calm, Frederick's other dominions experienced sporadic bouts of unrest. This meant that the attention of the king and his counsellors was sometimes diverted away from the *Regnum* to these other areas. The imperial communes in northern Italy were hotbeds of chronic rebellion, but even Frederick's Kingdom of Jerusalem was showing overt signs of dissent rooted in endemic local factionalism and a general antipathy to his rule.

On June fifteenth, 1232, a battle was fought at Agridi (on Cyprus) between the forces of Frederick II and those loyal to Henry I of Cyprus as a campaign in the "War of the Lombards."[1069] Naturally, the loss of Cyprus meant the loss of special trade privileges on that island by merchants of the Kingdom of Sicily.

In the same year, the Venetians were granted trade concessions at ports in Puglia just as the price of the kingdom's grain was becoming more affordable.

KINGDOM OF SICILY

Sicilians who traded with Venice were granted advantages, such as tax exemptions in the kingdom. This lasted for the better part of a decade, until Venice sided with the papacy against Frederick.

Farther north, imperial power in the German lands was being reshaped by some of Henry's policies. In response to the reaction of the nobility against the privileges he had granted to free (non-feudal) cities, he issued a law favoring the princes, planting the seeds of what in later times came to be called "federalism."[1070]

This differed from Frederick's comparatively "authoritarian" view of the ideal exercise of the crown's power over major vassals, a concept upon which the Kingdom of Sicily was founded by his Norman ancestors. Frederick doubtless understood the distinctions that made the Holy Roman Empire unique, but he disapproved of his son's initiative to grant the imperial magnates even more power than they already had. That he would have to acquiesce to these changes to keep the peace drove a wedge between himself and Henry.

Frederick renewed his peace with Louis IX of France.[1071] Other operations were more delicate, and certainly more difficult. We find Pope Gregory IX brokering a fragile, ephemeral peace between Frederick and the imperial communes following the inconclusive diet held at Ravenna late in 1231.[1072] This brought benefits to the *Regnum* because it facilitated trade between northern and southern Italy, though in truth such commerce had always been conducted remarkably well despite the endless quibbles and conflicts that plagued the peninsula.

Whilst at Ravenna, Frederick paraded his zoo through the city to public amazement. This menagerie included camels, elephants, panthers and what was probably the first giraffe ever brought to Europe, all gifts of the Sultan of Egypt, with whom he had negotiated a ten-year truce during the Sixth Crusade. There may even have been a cockatoo or two among the prized birds.[1073]

Our focus, of course, is the Kingdom of Sicily, not the Holy Roman Empire or its Italian communes, but it was no random coincidence that Frederick's *augustale*, a coin minted for circulation in the *Regnum,* bore the legend *AVGVSTVS IMPERATOR,* or that the chronicler Richard of San Germano invariably referred to the sovereign not as *Rex Siciliae* but simply as *Caesar.* The imperial appellation was the first in Frederick's decrees, even those relative to the Kingdom of Sicily.

It may be that Frederick wished to impose the same kind of centralized authority north of the Papal State that he enforced to its south. Yet it was clear that the communes, led by Milan, would have none of it. Milan, more than any other city, defied the recent peace, supporting the principles of independence represented by the Lombard League, which was revived despite imperial condemnation.

Just as he attempted to bring stability to imperial northern Italy, Gregory IX now encouraged the warring factions in the Kingdom of Jerusalem to compromise, even to the point of recognizing Frederick as their distant but lawful sovereign. In the event, Frederick sent a contingent of troops to Acre, where John of Ibelin had encouraged some citizens to rebellion, to reinforce those already stationed in the region.

The papacy would maintain a tacit acceptance of Frederick's rule of Germany and northern Italy for the better part of the decade, generally approving of his policies in the Kingdom of Sicily.[1074]

By the early months of 1233, Frederick was in Puglia, where he assembled a large and intimidating army. He further fortified Muslim Lucera while razing the walls of Christian Troia. He ordered the fortification of Bari, Naples, Brindisi and Trani, and the construction of octagonal Castel del Monte on the edge of a demesnial forest near Andria.[1075] We are told that on April twenty-fifth a fierce tempest of rain and hail flooded the valleys around Mount Cassino, carrying away entire houses.[1076]

Assuming, or reclaiming, the control of territory without the use of force, be it human or divine, required more effort. Richard, Duke of Spoleto, an imperial vassal, was brought before the emperor by Henry of Morra for usurping the town of Antrodoco, near Rieti; he submitted, ceding the town to the Kingdom of Sicily.

It was generally accepted, if rarely stated explicitly in law, that even the high justiciars had to petition the crown in the kind of criminal case that involved numerous persons rather than just a few suspects. Returning to Messina, Frederick meted out justice to a rebel instigator named Martin Mallone, who may have conspired with the seditious justiciar Richard of Montenegro (Chapter 26). Martin and his accomplices were variously hanged or immolated, a fate of which Richard, as an aristocrat, was spared.

There were other pockets of rebellion in Sicily, where Frederick destroyed the town of Centuripe, forcing its inhabitants to settle elsewhere. He ordered Gaeta, a city north of Naples that had rebelled during the War of the Keys a few years earlier, when its citizens preferred papal rule, to submit to royal authority, which it did. He then commanded the high justiciars to convoke meetings with prelates of the kingdom who, it was reported, felt themselves offended, so that they might air their grievances; such a convocation took place in August at Teano under Hector of Montefusculo, but none of the churchmen voiced any complaints against royal officials.[1077]

To commemorate his birthday in 1233, Frederick ordered large public feasts in a number of cities for the poor to be held on Saint Stephen's Day, the twenty-sixth of the month.[1078]

At a baronial meeting in Messina in January 1234, he instituted seven major fairs around the kingdom. These were strictly regulated by a discreet protectionism. Merchants or tradesmen who were not licensed to operate at the fairs were banned from participating, and nobody in the immediate region could sell their wares anyplace except at the fair. The fairs were to be held at Sulmona, Capua, Lucera, Bari, Taranto, Cosenza, and Reggio (in Calabria), but not in Palermo or Messina, which had large, permanent souks.

Frederick also decreed a greater frequency of public convocations by bailiffs and justiciars around the kingdom, in cities such as Piazza Armerina, Gravina, Sulmona and Salerno, to be attended by barons and other subjects.[1079] By February he was in Puglia, where an unusually cold winter, with an exceptionally great snowfall, had killed much livestock beginning the previous month.

Even deer, boar and wild birds were not spared the consequences of this weather, which also had effects on agriculture.[1080]

Making his way westward, the monarch ordered the expansion of the castles and fortifications of Capua, Naples and Gaeta, and among his other appellations Frederick became known to posterity as a great builder of fortresses. He visited Mount Cassino and San Germano before meeting Pope Gregory at Rieti. There he presented his five year-old son, Conrad, to the pontiff, to whom he pledged support against the rebellious factions in Rome, and reasserted royal claims to the border territories around Rieti. At Viterbo, Frederick assembled an army, besieging Rospampano, which some Romans had occupied. Due, perhaps, to a lack of motivation by the papal and royal forces, this effort was still unsuccessful after two months, and in September Frederick returned to the kingdom.[1081]

He undertook to reopen the *Studium* (university) of Naples, which had been closed due to the recent conflict between the kingdom and the papacy.

Meanwhile, some rebel Roman troops from Rospampano launched a failed attack against papal Viterbo. Some German knights based in that city killed some of the rebels, chasing the others to the castle, which eventually capitulated.

Imperial Diversions

Back in Puglia, Frederick received news that his son, Henry, was acting against his policies by depriving the German princes of some of the privileges that had recently been granted to them. The true extent of these purported abuses is not easily quantified, while the veracity of the information contained in reports and chronicles is difficult to ascertain, but it is clear that there were problems. Indeed, the emperor had criticized some of his son's actions publicly at the Diet of Aquileia in 1232, reluctantly but firmly confirming the delegation of power to the German princes during a meeting at Cividale shortly thereafter (see note 1070).

It seems that Henry was not enforcing imperial authority adequately. As well as the major German vassals, the northern Italian communes, notably Milan, were ever malcontent when it came to central rule, accustomed as they were to governing themselves semi-independently even before the Lombard League was established to challenge the attempts of Frederick's grandfather, Barbarossa. Beyond this, two oft-cited examples of a cause for the conflict between father and son were the fruit of a particularly thorny predicament in Germany, both involving papal authority.

Conrad of Marburg was a bishop who had prosecuted the Cathars, something Frederick officially condoned. In 1227, Pope Gregory empowered this sadistic cleric to eradicate heresy in Germany. Henry saw the bishop's activity as overzealous, considering that most of the "heresies" identified seemed to exist only in Conrad's fertile imagination. Acting against Conrad was moral but not very politic, as it cast a pall over Frederick's simultaneous efforts to garner papal support against the Lombard League, with which a tenuous peace had been negotiated. Bishop Conrad's murder by several knights in July 1233 only made matters worse.

Henry also intervened when Gerhard, Archbishop of Bremen, applied harsh measures in a quasi-crusade against some peasants at Stedingen, branding them "heretics" when their only obvious offense was to demand a few essential rights over the soil they tilled. Unsurprisingly, Conrad of Marburg had preached a crusade against the hapless Stedinger. The problem was that Pope Gregory supported Gerhard.[1082]

Now, in 1234, Frederick impetuously outlawed his son as King of the Germans while the pope excommunicated him for opposing Gerhard. Before long, Henry was in league with the League and a few rebellious German vassals against his father's politics.[1083]

These were problems of a kind unlikely to occur in the Kingdom of Sicily, where royal power was essentially centralized, all but absolute, and reinforced by the recent Constitutions. The situation in Germany and the communes was dire, and it would necessitate Frederick's departure from the *Regnum*.

Henry's insolence, if such it was, highlighted a problem facing the emperor-king and his small dynasty, namely a paucity of heirs. Presently, he had only two legitimate sons, Henry and Conrad. With this in mind, a delegation led by Peter della Vigna undertook a search for a woman to wed their sovereign. It was presumed that she would be somewhat younger than Frederick, and the daughter of a king. A marriage to Bianca Lancia, the mother of Frederick's son Manfred, was not seriously considered.[1084]

By November, the pope was preaching another crusade, intended to take place before Frederick's truce in Jerusalem expired.

In early January 1235, Frederick imposed a general *collecta* tax throughout the *Regnum* to defray, amongst other expenses, the cost of an expedition through the Italian communes and into Germany.[1085]

Meanwhile, Peter della Vigna was traveling to England to arrange the marriage of Isabella, the sister of King Henry III, to Frederick.[1086] This marriage uniting dynasties on both sides of his kingdom so disturbed Louis IX that Pope Gregory had to write him as if in reassurance that it posed no menace. Nevertheless, the King of France had good reason to fear this formidable alliance capable of attacking, and defeating, him on opposite fronts.[1087]

Like Frederick, Henry levied an extraordinary tax. In this case, however, it was to defray most of the cost of his sister's dowry of thirty thousand marks. This money would be spent on the efforts of Henry's new brother-in-law to rein in the imperial communes of northern Italy.

Shortly after Easter, Henry of Mulnarken, Archbishop of Cologne, and Henry of Louvain, Duke of Brabant, accompanied by a large imperial suite, met Isabella and escorted her into Germany. As Queen of Sicily, her dower would include Mount Sant'Angelo, in Puglia, and the estates near it.[1088]

The Puglia region was near and dear to Frederick's heart, and he seems to have preferred the Kingdom of Sicily to his other dominions.[1089] Had he wished, he could have lived and reigned in the Holy Roman Empire, but being nearer the seat of papal power offered definite advantages when dealing with contentious pontiffs. In favor of this choice, it could also be argued that the route to the imperial communes from Campania or Puglia was less arduous than a trek through the Alps from the German lands.

While his bride was traveling toward Germany via Antwerp, Frederick was making his way with a tiny force across his Empire, where he was suppressing revolts stirred up by his son, to Worms. Here the rebellious heir submitted himself to paternal judgment.

Once Isabella reached Cologne, where the crowds were ecstatic to see her, she and her large entourage waited for Frederick's son to be tried at Worms.

In early July, Frederick had his eldest son and heir dragged off to jail in chains for opposing policies that some viewed as repressive, even draconian. It is a punishment that seems too great for the crime. Hinting at little more than a lingering bitterness, the written record tells us of no plangent entreaties between father and son, but there must have been conversations.

The wedding was celebrated at Worms on July twentieth, followed by four days of celebrations.

Whatever Frederick's opponents thought of him, they grudgingly respected him, especially now that he was at the apogee of his power. His army had increased in size with the growing support of the German princes.

Conrad was named Frederick's heir in Henry's stead.[1090] Henry's young sons by Margaret of Austria, named Henry and Frederick, were disinherited; in the event, neither boy lived quite long enough to succeed to the throne.[1091]

It was around this time that the newest round of laws promulgated by zealous Pope Gregory began to become known in Frederick's dominions as copies were distributed. Completed in 1234, these *Decretals* decreed, among other things, that Jews were destined for "perpetual servitude" according to the doctrine of *perpetua servitus judaeorum*. To apply this idea, Frederick himself instituted the principle of *servitus camerae imperialis,* subjecting Jews in the Holy Roman Empire to direct imperial authority. This was enforced slightly less rigorously in the Kingdom of Sicily, where archbishops had long been "protectors" of local Jewish communities, than in the imperial lands, where policies regarding treatment of the Jews varied somewhat from one state to another. Frederick himself does not seem to have embraced the new doctrine beyond what was strictly necessary to placate the popes. Nor did he condone Gregory's revived "Inquisition," which now used the Franciscans, and especially the Dominicans, as its pawns. Unfortunately, however, his overt agreement with these papal pronouncements seemed to proclaim otherwise.

At Mainz in August 1235, Frederick implemented a public peace, or *landfriedensgesetz,* as a fundamental right. He maintained a continuous correspondence with his English brother-in-law. The subject of these letters ranged from the emperor's rapport with the papacy to Henry's chronic conflicts with the French king.[1092]

Pope Gregory reached a peace with the rebellious faction of Rome, which now ceded to the pontiff the towns and castles around the city that had been appropriated. As long as it lasted, this made the pope somewhat less dependent on Frederick for military security.

Frederick left Isabella in Germany while he crossed the Alps to subdue some Lombard towns, a task that would occupy him over the next few years. He probably sent her to stay for some months at Trifels, the imperial fortress in the Palatine Forest, where she gave birth to a daughter, Margaret, late in

1236.[1093] The empress does not seem to have had a very happy life, either before or during her marriage.[1094]

To the south, the *Regnum* was governed competently in Frederick's absence by Henry of Morra and Thomas Aquino of Acerra, supported by the network of bailiffs and justiciars appointed over the last few years. Henry and Thomas spent a fair amount of time in Capua, Naples and other northern cities of the kingdom.[1095] Not only were some of these localities likely to seek more independence along the lines of communes such as Milan, they were fairly near the border with the Papal State. Like Frederick, these high officers of the kingdom trusted the demesnial cities and the pope only to a finite degree.

Summoned to report personally on the state of the kingdom, in December 1236, Henry and Thomas went to meet their sovereign lord in Lombardy only to learn that by then he was on the other side of the Alps subduing the long defiant Frederick "the Quarrelsome," Duke of Austria. This was the brother of the emperor's daughter-in-law, Margaret.[1096]

In February 1237, with the Duke of Austria suppressed, or at least placated, young Conrad was crowned King of the Germans at Vienna.

Meanwhile, in Rome, Peter Frangipane, whose family held the Colosseum and much of the city, broke the tenuous peace that had recently been negotiated with Pope Gregory. Although the Frangipani had not always sided with the Hohenstaufens, Peter himself did.[1097] In papal circles, Frederick, considered guilty by association, was blamed for the riots that ensued. This combined with the suppression of the northern communes to rekindle the rapacious papal antipathy that had characterized the infamous War of the Keys.

In April of 1237, Peter della Vigna and Herman of Salza met with Gregory to defend Frederick's actions in northern Italy. At the same time, peace was restored in Rome.[1098]

There were, as ever, occasional outbreaks of dissent in the kingdom, motivated by one catalyst or another. James of Molino, a builder of fortifications, was arrested for inciting a riot. He was imprisoned at Naples while his co-conspirators were incarcerated in other castles.

Traveling to the communes from Germany, Frederick crossed the Alps in November. A few more years were to pass before he returned to his Kingdom of Sicily, from which he drew resources, including thousands of Arab archers from Lucera.

On the twenty-seventh of November, the emperor's multinational force drawn from Germany, the Kingdom of Sicily and some Ghibelline communities in northern Italy scored a decisive victory at Cortenuova, near Bergamo, a battle counting at least ten thousand men on each side. Thus far, it was the largest single engagement fought by Frederick during his reign, and the one to see the greatest involvement by knights, foot men and archers from the *Regnum*. This was followed by the fall of Cremona and other cities, but Milan failed to capitulate despite a siege.[1099]

Following his victories, Frederick delegated the short-term care of the vanquished and their cities to counsellors from the *Regnum* such as Thomas Aquino of Acerra and Henry of Morra, along with several important barons.

Frederick's troops confiscated the *carroccio* from the Milanese when they abandoned it in a muddy road. In a triumphalist gesture, he had a single elephant from his zoo pull this large wagon, usually drawn by several oxen, into Cremona, as if to represent the imperial power of one intrepid monarch outweighing that of many communes. Bearing heraldic signs and banners, the *carroccio* was the very symbol of municipal autonomy, serving as a rallying point in battle. Significantly, its cross, relics and small altar made the *carroccio* a religious symbol as well as a secular one. Frederick's gesture was not mere hubris, as the *carroccio* also represented the defeat of his grandfather, Barbarossa, at Legnano in 1176. Following the display at Cremona, he sent it to Rome. Pope Gregory was not amused at this fateful reminder of the scope of Hohenstaufen power.

Most of the protracted military campaign against defiant imperial communes was subsidized by money from the *Regnum,* some of it generated from the sale of grain, and even salt, to Africa and Europe. One of the least pleasant duties falling to Henry of Morra was the collection of taxes. The kingdom's total reserves are not known, but in 1238 the revenue accumulated from the *collecta* amounted to over a hundred thousand gold onze. As an indication of the collection according to region, the rural, sparsely-populated valleys around Mount Cassino that fell within the *Regnum* usually generated about a hundred fifty *onze* for the crown. There were also certain taxes paid by Muslims and Jews that were not usually remitted by Christians. Among these were the head tax (poll tax), a tax on wine, and taxes on the slaughter of certain animals in conjunction with halal and kosher observance.[1100]

At Ravenna in February 1238, Isabella gave birth to a boy christened Henry (sometimes called "Henry the Younger" by historians). Nobody seemed bothered by the fact that Frederick's elder son of the same name was rotting away in prison, his political rehabilitation all but impossible because he was suffering from leprosy.[1101] The same year, illegitimate Enzio was wed in Sardinia to Adelasia of Torres, a union that gave Frederick influence over another large Mediterranean island.[1102] Another illegitimate son, Frederick "of Antioch," born of a certain Matilda (or Maria), was wed about this time to Margaret of Poli.

Frederick's consort, meanwhile, stayed at Andria, in Puglia, possibly in the Castel del Monte, from September 1238 until December of that year, when she traveled to Palermo. She does not seem to have been given any official duties as her husband's regent in the *Regnum* during his long absence. For the present, with exceptions such as his son-in-law Thomas Aquino of Acerra, Frederick relied for assistance on everybody except close members of his family, though this was to change.

As we have seen, Pope Gregory's *Decretals* were destined to make life more difficult for Jews. Though Frederick was remiss in accepting such a doctrine, his sagacity shone at other moments. When, in December 1238, thirty-four Jews were killed in Fulda, in Hesse, allegedly for having murdered several Christian boys, the emperor instituted an investigative commission composed of Jews and former Jews. The people who had been lynched were exonerated and measures were taken to protect the Jewish communities in the future.

By the end of 1238, Thomas Aquino of Acerra, the justiciar Roger Porcastrella of Urbe and the Archbishop of Palermo Berardo of Castagna had made serious efforts to reassure Pope Gregory that, despite the recent defeats of most of the communes, Hohenstaufen rule posed no threat to papal authority in Italy.[1103] Gregory's ambassador to Frederick was Elias of Cortona, minister general of the Franciscans.[1104] Whether Elias ever shared Gregory's view of Frederick as a "baptized sultan," or even "the antichrist," is not known, but he became a friend of the emperor.

Ever riddled by perplexing complexities, the relationship between the emperor and the communes, mirrored in the chronic conflicts between Ghibellines and Guelphs, was rarely an easy one. It was now clear that whatever hopes for coexistence had emerged from the peace negotiated a few years earlier by Pope Gregory were now little more than indistinct, shifting *strata* of the muddy Lombard soil.

The powdery soil of Palestine could be just as capricious, and another truce, the one established a decade earlier with the Muslims in the Holy Land, was due to expire. The pontiff wanted the emperor to participate in a crusade being planned. Here Frederick, as King of Jerusalem, had a vested interest, but this proposal had been advanced before Cortenuova.

Still another *collecta* was levied throughout the kingdom in January 1239, and at Brindisi new *augustales* were soon being struck.[1105]

Paying a tax to cover the cost of what was essentially a foreign war could not have been a very pleasant proposition, but no major protests against the *collecta* are known to us. Most subjects in the *Regnum* were probably unaware of the battles being fought by their king in northern Italy.

In March, Stephen, the newly-elected abbot of Mount Cassino, went to northern Italy to meet Frederick, to whom he pledged friendship.[1106]

Gregory does not seem to have disapproved of this link being established. Nevertheless, on the pretext that Frederick, being more powerful than ever, might unseat him, the pontiff excommunicated the emperor-king on Palm Sunday, March twentieth, provoking a conflict that would last for years.[1107]

If Frederick was excessively disturbed at being excommunicated, it seems to have had little adverse effect on his actions as monarch. Not that he could have been indifferent to such a thing, but he was already conditioned by the previous excommunication. It was about this time that he wrote his treatise on falconry and composed most of his poetry. At all events, he would be forced to respond to a series of papal provocations across his dominions, with some notable aggression in the Kingdom of Sicily. Indeed, Gregory's tactics were to prove similar to those employed a decade earlier, when he sought, unsuccessfully, to enlist other sovereigns in a war against the King of Sicily.

If the general reaction among the clergy and populace in Fredrick's dominions was not more loudly expressed, that was because the counterpoise of imperial and papal authority had long been a fact of life, and even the defining power dynamic, of Catholic Europe.

Eloquent Peter della Vigna, among others, defended Frederick. Apart from public pronouncements, this meant sending letters to European kings to rebut papal accusations connected to the excommunication. Pious Louis IX of France rose to Frederick's defense, refusing Gregory's request that he fight a "crusade," against another Christian king. This too was a reprise of the events of a decade earlier.[1108]

Frederick's supporters were also to be excommunicated, even if this directive was applied rather haphazardly; among the monarch's early defenders, and one of the first to be anathematized, was Elias of Cortona.[1109]

These challenges left little opportunity to address the question of the proposed crusade to the Holy Land.[1110]

Another detail involving Muslims was the fate of Abd al-Aziz, who was present in the *Regnum* as a political exile when Frederick was excommunicated. Pope Gregory accused Frederick of detaining the Tunisian prince, a nephew of the Hafsid sultan Abu Zakariya Yahya, on the pretext that he wanted to go to Rome to be baptized. Frederick sent Abd al-Aziz to Lucera.[1111]

At the pope's instigation, some religious orders preached against Frederick. Gregory particularly favored the newly-founded Franciscans, who Frederick promptly suppressed in Sicily, effectively banishing them and prohibiting the foundation of new monasteries. For security, he ordered Franciscans and Dominicans having ancestry in Lombardy to depart from the kingdom. He also commanded any prelates of the Kingdom of Sicily present in the papal curia to leave Rome. Property in the kingdom belonging to "foreign" clergy who were not subjects was confiscated. At the same time, the lands of major churches and abbeys in the *Regnum* were taxed, though Mount Cassino, which had estates in the kingdom, was exempted from this.

Enzio, now styled "King of Sardinia," was made imperial vicar for the communes of northern Italy, with special authority in Lombardy. Naturally, Gregory excommunicated him. Enzio was assisted by several administrators from the Kingdom of Sicily, notably Pandulf of Fassanella in Tuscany and Walter of Manopello in Romagna. James of Morra was left in charge of the Duchy of Spoleto, which at times had been an imperial fief but most recently had fallen under papal control.

Frederick soon began planning a march southward through papal territory. This was not initially the "invasion" sometimes described, though Enzio occupied the Marches and Romagna which, unlike the Duchy of Spoleto, had long been held by the popes.

Traversing these lands separating the Hohenstaufen dominions in Italy was a normal practice. However, it was inevitable that a few papal localities, such as strategic Viterbo, would be occupied in the course of a war in which the pope attempted an invasion of the *Regnum* and the destruction of its king, and more towns would follow. One way or another, Frederick now had to return to the Kingdom of Sicily, where he would remain until the summer of 1240.

He delegated some subsequent attacks on papal cities, notably Assisi, to generals such as Vitale of Aversa, a Muslim. Although religious houses were to be left undisturbed, this policy was occasionally violated, hence the defense of San Damiano, near Assisi, against Vitale's overzealous troops by the intervention of Saint Clare, who resided there.

506

Regnum Aeternum

While at Foggia in April 1240, Frederick issued legislation clarifying the duties of justiciars, but the prosperous realm had managed remarkably well in the absence of its king.

Trade with other countries was good. The Hafsids had recently begun to render an annual tribute in gold when the Sicilians assumed complete control of the Tunisian ports importing wheat, and the *collecta* was efficient enough to repay money Frederick had recently borrowed from Pisan merchants to cover some of the initial costs of his suppression of the communes. Jews from Djerba arrived in Sicily to cultivate indigo and henna.[1112]

The *Regnum* was the most loyal of Hohenstaufen dominions. It was much changed from the polity that existed a decade earlier during the War of the Keys.

The pope obtained very little assistance from the states he solicited to fight Frederick. An exception was the Venetians. Having suffered at Frederick's hands during the recent campaign, they attacked Sicilian shipping along the Adriatic coasts, sacking Brindisi late in 1240.[1113]

The next year found forces of the *Regnum* attacking major papal strongholds such as Benevento. Some of these sieges were highly destructive.

Meanwhile, the "Barons' Crusade" led by, amongst others, Frederick's brother-in-law Richard of Cornwall, reclaimed Jerusalem, along with additional territory, leading to control of the Holy Land by Christians for the next few years.[1114] Returning from the crusade during the summer of 1241, Richard stopped in Sicily, where he landed at Trapani, hoping to find Frederick and Isabella at Palermo. Instead, he met Frederick, in whose name he had taken the Kingdom of Jerusalem, at Faenza, which he was besieging. It seems that the emperor initially brushed aside Richard's wish to visit Isabella, who was in the first trimester of pregnancy and perhaps unwell. Finally, after a few days of waiting, he made a formal request, to which the emperor acceded. The esteemed Earl of Cornwall was then accompanied to meet his sister.[1115]

In correspondence with Frederick, Isabella's other brother, Henry III of England, expressed dismay at reports that she did not participate in public ceremonies and was not often seen wearing a crown.[1116] A concise but curious entry by Matthew Paris mentions "the rising hopes of Isabella."[1117]

There were some reassignments of bailiffs and justiciars around the kingdom. This resulted from Frederick's belief that change of this kind was a good thing.[1118] Among diplomats, Roger de Amicis was sent to Egypt and Oberto Fallamonaca to Morocco.[1119]

Knights around the kingdom were told to prepare for war, and more taxes followed to pay for it. At Capua, a city sometimes given to papal sympathies, the justiciar Richard of Montenegro instituted patrols at night.[1120]

Not every cardinal in Rome supported the pope's action against Frederick; John Colonna famously opposed it. Stephen, the abbot of Mount Cassino, whose lands bordered the *Regnum,* was reluctant to endorse the pontiff very overtly, but neither did he wish to be seen supporting Frederick. To avoid a possible pillaging of the abbey by overzealous knights seeking an additional source of revenue to fight the war, he moved many treasures in gold and silver to the church of Saint Mary in the town of San Germano nearby. Among clergy, he was not alone in his concerns about the course this "civil war" was taking, with Gregory's forces attacking a few papal towns where there was rebellion.[1121]

Frederick continued a general mobilization of knights and naval forces in the kingdom. In view of the recent raids by the Venetians, the Adriatic coasts were a high priority.[1122]

These royal efforts were highly efficacious. The Kingdom of Sicily had become machine-like in its efficiency. Baronial disloyalty was now rare despite frequent taxation. Whether guarding the border near Aquino and San Germano or serving in Frederick's army, the enfeoffed knights of the realm were ready to perform their duties. Assisi and Spoleto, both sometimes imperial cities, were both forced to submit to Frederick's authority. The March of Ancona, the part of the Duchy of Spoleto bordering the *Regnum*, was for a time governed by a Genoan cardinal appointed by Gregory named Sinibaldo de' Fieschi, who was on amicable terms with Frederick.

Gregory's effort to convene his cardinals in Rome to act against Frederick failed when some of the key prelates being transported by the Genoans were intercepted and detained *en route* to the Papal State by a Sicilian fleet led by Enzio, in tandem with the allied Pisans, at the Battle of Giglio on May third, 1241.

In June, news arrived at Frederick's traveling court from the King of Hungary that Batu Khan's formidable Mongol-Tatar army was making its way westward after having sacked Kiev. A contemplated invasion of imperial dominions by this emergent "Golden Horde" (Ulug Ulus) was eventually called off despite its early victories in the eastern reaches of the German lands. Richard of San Germano tells us that the invaders were "at Germany's gates."[1123] Their withdrawal was fortuitous, for it spared Frederick the cost and effort of a major campaign to defend his Empire, something which would have forced him to abandon Italy yet again.

Hierocracy

The death of Pope Gregory IX in August brought with it an equally auspicious respite. The pontificate of Gregory's successor, Celestine IV, born Godfrey of Castiglione, lasted only a few days until November tenth. Following Celestine's untimely death, more than a year would pass before the next pope was elected by the divided papal curia.

Until then, Rome would find itself in a certain factional disarray in a papal interregnum, effectively a lengthy *sede vacante*. Presently, there was rather little pro-papal civil dissent in the Kingdom of Sicily, even while some of the Guelphic cities of northern Italy were still in open rebellion against Frederick. Since the excommunication, Frederick's agents had sown enough discord in the Eternal City to discourage anything like a military onslaught on the *Regnum*, and even much of the clergy now supported king against pontiff.

That papal policy often spilled into social policy in Catholic countries was hardly novel. It was rooted in the longstanding belief that the pope, as the Vicar of Christ, in answering only to God, must enjoy an authority greater than that of other monarchs. This reasoning led to conflicts such as the one that ended with the murder of Thomas Becket.

Now, however, Catholic monarchs, and even quasi-elective local leaders like those who governed the small imperial states of northern Italy, began to question the value of blind obedience to the pope in what were essentially secular matters.

In ecclesiastical circles, there would be theological holdouts, such as Thomas Aquinas, who defended the role of the church in most aspects of life. In the secular sphere, commentators such as Dante Alighieri might defend the papacy, whilst criticizing the Hohenstaufens, when it suited their political needs. None of these ideologies are perfectly quantified by the paradigms offered by modern political philosophy, and they transcended the differences between Guelphs and Ghibellines. More generally, there were few true "atheists" and "anticlericals" in thirteenth-century Europe.

Intrinsic to the reinstituted Inquisition, reflected in such actions as the renewed attempt by the papacy to subjugate Europe's Jews, was a certain degree of injustice, even malice. Thus was forged a mentality about a minority population that would prevail in Europe into the modern era.

An obvious example of this kind of intolerance was the confiscation of most of the copies of the *Talmud* that could be found in France. This occurred in 1242. Louis IX of France was not the only Catholic king ordered to find and confiscate thousands of books and scrolls, but he was far more compliant to papal whims than the others, almost to the point of zealotry. The French king eventually burned the Hebrew scriptures.[1124]

On its surface, Frederick's gentle suppression of the Dominicans and Franciscans of the *Regnum* was prompted by the simple need to defend the kingdom against subversion. Whether it was motivated by something more than that, such as a desire to uphold the rights of the realm's Muslims and Jews to worship freely, could be debated. Yet Frederick maintained the Muslim city of Lucera while inviting Jews from Tunisia to settle in Sicily, gestures that could not have pleased the popes of the day.

The very concept of the "papal monarchy" was moving toward a conclusion, in the Kingdom of Sicily as elsewhere. The passing of visionary, even idealistic, figures such as Joachim of Fiore (in 1202) and then Francis of Assisi (in 1226) foreshadowed the inception of a "pragmatic" Catholicism, not only in monasticism but in secular life. Not without nuance, the social influence of the papacy diminished slightly even as faith itself remained an important part of life for most people.

This, perhaps, made it easier for Frederick to defy papal political authority more openly now than when he was excommunicated over a decade earlier (in 1227).

Even the people of Rome had grown tired of the whims of the pontiffs living in their midst. Gregory spent much of his pontificate outside the city and so would the pope who was elected after Celestine IV. Interdict and excommunication continued to be powerful tools, but their overuse, often to negligible effect, left popes vulnerable to ridicule.

Society itself changed little. Kings still ruled by the grace of God. Corollary to that belief, nobles maintained the self-serving belief that their right to special status emanated from God. Yet the idea that a pope could dissolve the Kingdom of Sicily, or any kingdom, was disappearing into the Tiber's mists.[1125]

We see Italian polities other than the *Regnum* increasingly willing to contest papal hegemony, especially when doing so was consistent with their political or commercial objectives. It is thus unsurprising that the Pisans, who were already in competition against the Genoans, supported the Sicilian navy at the Battle of Giglio. The resulting interdict that Gregory placed upon the commune of Pisa was viewed by the Pisans themselves as little more than a distasteful nuisance.

The true extent to which hierocracy might have been challenged more overtly, and effectively, during the thirteenth century is open to question.[1126] At all events, the greater development of legal codes, such as the Constitutions of Melfi that Gregory IX found so offensive, tended to emphasize a sense of social order and ethics which, if not purely "secular," existed in the temporal environment outside the general purview of the church.

Excommunication and interdict were legitimate, if distasteful, papal prerogatives rooted in ecclesiastical authority. Beyond this, popes could still stir up trouble for kings and queens in the temporal realm. As we shall see, a pontiff was to issue a declaration deposing Frederick II.[1127]

Certain papal pronouncements, such as the proscriptions on knightly tournaments (jousts) and the use of the crossbow, were routinely ignored. Even some practices legitimately governed by canon law, such as those concerning the requirements for Catholic marriage, were disregarded if deemed inconvenient; here the marital impediment of close consanguinity between spouses comes to mind.

That the natural sciences were cultivated at Frederick's court did not diminish a general belief in the divine, with its apparitions and miracles. A waning confidence in the papacy as an institution cannot be said to reflect a diminution in theism *per se*.

Few doubted the sacrality of kingship, but some were beginning to question the right of a pope to abrogate something that emanated from God. This is what had happened to Frederick's ancestor, Henry IV, who was deposed by Pope Gregory VII.[1128]

For its part, the papacy was reluctant to renounce its traditional powers where these overlapped those of the crown. The attempt by Henry II of England to limit the use of ecclesiastical courts for the trials of clergy was one of the causes for his rift with Thomas Becket.

Eternal kingmakers, the popes continued to arrogate to themselves an authority over temporal affairs for centuries to come, long after that pretension was divorced from reality.[1129] What we see during the mature phase of Frederick's long reign are the first embryonic signs of the changing attitudes of

Catholic kings in the face of the generally immutable world view held by the supreme pontiffs. Even Louis IX, despite his exceptional piety and devotion, and his adamant support of the popes, was reluctant to endorse the papal prerogative of *plenitudo protestatis* (fullness of power) being used to depose a fellow European sovereign.

It wasn't long before detailed treatises were being formulated on the use of pontifical and royal power.[1130] That so many theologians took up this cause as a papal apologia suggests the church's need to respond to the ever more frequent doubts being expressed about the practice of hierocracy.

The formal separation of church and state, as that principle is enshrined in law today, is a modern one. Yet history shows us that the demarcation of spiritual and temporal authority was pondered by at least a few medieval thinkers in Catholic Europe, inspired in no small measure by events such as those that transpired during the age of "papal monarchy."

Further afield, the continued efforts of Gregory IX to negotiate ecclesiastical harmony with the Orthodox Christians ended inconclusively. This curtailed the papacy's ecclesiastical influence in certain Grecophone regions on the other side of the Adriatic, notably the state of Epirus ruled by the exiled Comnenus dynasty (Table 6).

In an age that saw the emergence of scholasticism, humanism and other significant movements, the nature of the relationship between crown and mitre was evolving decade by decade. While the state became less dependent on the church, a broad idea of Christendom survived.

Church of Saint Francis of Assisi, built in Palermo after 1250

Chapter 29
EUROPEAN KINGDOM

Whatever machinations emanated from outside the realm, even from the papacy, by the middle years of the thirteenth century the Kingdom of Sicily had achieved a certain maturity, along with its longest-reigning king.

Frederick's third wife was not destined to live very long. Isabella died at Foggia on the first of December in 1241 giving birth to a child who did not survive. She was entombed at Andria in the same church as Yolanda of Jerusalem. Her dying wish was that her husband and her brother should remain friends, which they did.[1131] The *Regnum* was again without a queen.

Few traces of Isabella survive. Even her tomb was eventually destroyed. The most substantial thing that remains is her illuminated psalter of Byzantine design, a gift from her husband.

Isabella's death left Frederick more time with his mistress. Bianca Lancia of Agliano was now around thirty years old. She was born into a family thought to have shared the Aleramic lineage of Adelaide del Vasto. Her paternity is much debated, but her father was probably Boniface of Agliano.

The State

The two French cardinals Frederick had detained at the Battle of Giglio, preventing their participation in the last synod called by Gregory IX and the conclave that elected Celestine IV, were still in his custody in 1242, when Louis IX requested the release of his countrymen. Ever a faithful son of the church, the French king disapproved of Frederick's efforts to shape papal policy, and urged the cardinals to elect another pope as soon as possible.[1132]

Frederick's attempt to intercede in the papal election had been successful only so long as Celestine had lived.[1133] This changed with the pontiff's death and the consequent papal interregnum. While the cardinals might squabble among themselves, they now understood the necessity of electing another pope. To escape the violent factionalism and Ghibelline influence in Rome, they transferred the curia to Anagni.

Frederick's interference was anything but subtle, nor was it lacking in an effective strategy. Quite simply, the papacy was intimidated by most of Italy being controlled by one monarch, presently the most powerful man in Europe. Recent battles and sieges in the Papal State itself, along with continuing unrest in Rome, were more than sufficient to convince any doubters that Frederick was able to suppress, or redirect, papal power at its source. He had the means to march on Rome and might just do it. Besides his own knights and troops, he enjoyed the support of the Teutonic Order, which had commanderies in Puglia and elsewhere in the *Regnum* and was presently making incursions into the Baltic region.

Frederick had good reasons for wishing to curtail papal militancy. Much of his reign had been tainted by papal politics which, as we have seen, transcended strictly ecclesiastical matters to encroach upon royal jurisdiction, an old habit that was not easily broken. At no point, however, did Frederick threaten the pope himself, nor did he seek to usurp the papal role in the purely spiritual sphere. He seemed to know where to draw the line.

What was needed, from the point of view of Frederick's traveling court, was a pope at least reasonably accommodating of the emperor-king. Much like Henry II of England, who ensured that his friend, Thomas Becket, was installed as Archbishop of Canterbury, Frederick sought a sympathetic candidate for the Holy See, and in some ways history would repeat itself. Sinibaldo de' Fieschi, a Ligurian aristocrat of a Ghibelline family and sometime governor of the March of Ancona, the land of Frederick's birth, was friendly to the emperor.[1134] This distinguished canonist was about the same age as Frederick and had served in the papal curia, to which he had recently returned, yet he did not seem to be an apologist for all of the policies of Gregory IX.[1135]

In the *Regnum*, the *collecta* was now being levied every year, and in 1242 this occurred in January. Early in the same year, whilst present in Puglia, Frederick ordered a general judicial inspection to identify criminals who might be at large. This included bandits, operators of illegal gambling rings, and any commoner carrying a weapon, such as a sword, dagger or crossbow, illegally.[1136]

In compliance with royal directives regarding urban and feudal fortifications, several unauthorized towers were ordered destroyed at the city of Bari. This may have seemed counterproductive in view of recent coastal attacks by the Venetians, but Bari had a large seaside castle in addition to its city walls. At the same time, the construction of galleys and other large ships was ordered for possible action against the Pisans and especially the Venetians. Despite the problems at Bari, it was during this period that Frederick began a serious, and very effective, program of castle building and repair, restructuring Norman fortresses and constructing some of his own.[1137]

Meanwhile, Frederick sent emissaries to the papal court to encourage peace between the papacy and his Italian dominions, particularly the Kingdom of Sicily. The men chosen for this mission were Gerhard of Malberg, recently elected as grand master of the Teutonic Order, Marino Filangieri, the Archbishop of Bari, and Roger of Porcastrello, a court chaplain and almoner.[1138] This was more than a token gesture, for it was hoped by all parties that Frederick's relations with the next pope, whoever it was, might be an improvement over those with the late Gregory IX. Unfortunately, however, Frederick was still attacking papal towns, a fact that must have made some cardinals doubt his sincerity.

In February, Henry, Frederick's eldest son, died when he fell from a horse while riding with his gaolers near Martirano in Calabria. It is possible that he was riding ahead of them at a fast gallop in an attempt to escape. He was interred in Cosenza's cathedral nearby, survived by his wife and two sons. Frederick publicly lamented his eldest child's death, and it may be that he had summoned him to court with the intention of rehabilitating him in some way now that Pope Gregory was gone, though Henry's leprosy would have made this difficult. Frederick's eulogy, as reported by Richard of San Germano, reflects much bitterness, implying that the acrimony of the father toward the son was even greater than what might be inferred from the facts reported several years earlier in other sources.[1139]

Frederick had long trusted some of his advisors more than he trusted his eldest son. By now, the chief among them was Peter della Vigna, a native of Capua a few years Frederick's senior. Peter had been in royal service for two decades, having begun his career as a notary and scribe recommended by the Archbishop of Palermo. His talents ran the gamut from jurist to diplomat to poet. Although he was not always identified by a title other than *master*, he became Frederick's *de facto* chancellor, part of an elite team present at court that ensured the smooth operation of the kingdom. The clear, eloquent Latin of many of Frederick's decrees and laws reflects Peter's style.[1140]

Like some of the other counsellors, he served Frederick *ad personam*, not only for the Kingdom of Sicily but for other dominions as well. Peter could usually be found with the traveling court, wherever it was. Beginning around 1230, he was probably the most important person in the day-to-day operation of the kingdom after the king himself.

Even when Frederick was in the kingdom, it was easy to forget that the capital was Palermo. In recent times, with his attention required elsewhere, he spent very little time in this city. It simply wasn't expedient for the monarch to be in Sicily, or even southern Calabria, when his presence might be needed to confront problems in northern Italy, if not the German lands. Thanks to the delegation of tasks to reliable counsellors such as Peter della Vigna, Thaddeus of Suessa and Berardo of Castagna, as well as the various bailiffs (governors) and justiciars, Frederick's administration of the Kingdom of Sicily was highly efficient even without his constant presence, a fact reflected in his few surviving registers of day-to-day minutiae.[1141]

Nevertheless, the king's lack of immediate access to the royal archive kept in Palermo was certainly a disadvantage. Here Frederick might have been assisted by officers such as Oberto Fallamonaca, who became *secretus* of Palermo, but there is little to suggest that he called upon them, for many decisions had to be taken long before a response could arrive at the traveling court from Sicily, which could take weeks if not months. This explains why certain decrees regarding localized affairs might not always be consistent with policies established by earlier kings of Sicily.[1142]

By May 1242, Frederick was in Abruzzo, having stopped at Naples and Capua after leaving Foggia. Several of his generals were ordered to attack cities in the borderlands between the Papal State and the Kingdom of Sicily. Andrew of Cicala sacked Rieti. Conrad Guiscard of Urslingen, the Duke of Spoleto, though technically a papal vassal, led an army to attack Narni and its environs. The imperial army attacked, but did not annex, Ascoli, in the Marches to the immediate north of Abruzzo.[1143]

In July, Frederick led an army to attack the outskirts of Rome. By some accounts, this became a siege of the under-defended city, where a Ghibelline faction controlled certain districts. In August, the siege was lifted, but for good measure, and perhaps as a sign of his contempt for papal attempts to convert the Muslims, Frederick had his troops remove a large bronze statue of a man and a calf from the formerly-Byzantine abbey at Grottaferrata and transport it as a gift to the Islamic city of Lucera.

Henry of Morra died in 1242, when there were efforts to address problems in Frederick's other dominions. Thomas Aquino of Acerra was sent to the Kingdom of Jerusalem, where royal power was always tenuous, to assert Frederick's authority as best he could. Bernard of Manopello was sent to Sardinia, where factionalism was quite normal.[1144]

In this way we still find trusted experts from the *Regnum* being "exported" to places where they were needed, a practice that had begun over a decade earlier. One who remained at the king's side was John of Procida, an alumnus of Salerno's medical school and now the royal physician. The scion of a noble family of the kingdom, John became a confidant of Frederick and a tutor of his son, Manfred.

Early 1243 saw the *collecta* again being levied to defray the expenses of recent military campaigns and those to come.[1145] By February, Frederick himself was at Foggia to raise a large army, and perhaps to ensure that the tax was collected. Though the army was recruited along traditional feudal lines, with barons providing knights, the kingdom's larger demesnial cities, such as Bari and Capua, had to supply a certain number of foot men. Lucera, of course, provided Europe's finest archers.[1146]

While most of the Lucerans seemed to be reasonably content, there was lingering bitterness among some of the comparatively few Muslims who were still in Sicily, particularly at Jato and Licata, where there were localized revolts.[1147] Presently, as Frederick was obviously occupied with other matters, he delegated to Richard of Caserta the task of transferring these subjects to the mainland. This would take at least two years.[1148]

In the Kingdom of Jerusalem, meanwhile, Frederick's greatest challenges, at least for the moment, were posed not by Muslims but by Christians. He hoped that Thomas Aquino of Acerra might succeed where Richard Filangieri had not. Alas, this was not to be, and to compound the complexities the realm was again being ruled not from Jerusalem, which Muslim forces were planning to seize, but from Acre. Yet a solution of sorts was devised despite the endless conflicts among the Christian families of the kingdom and the ambitious knightly orders. A regency was established *in situ* on behalf of Frederick's son, Conrad, who was presently in Germany, under his great-aunt, Alice of Champagne.[1149]

The Cities

By the time Frederick's reign as King of Sicily had reached a stage of stability, a number of trends could be discerned in the administration of the demesnial (royal) cities and towns of the *Regnum* compared to its feudal (baronial) localities. Here the government was markedly different from what existed in the imperial communes of northern Italy and in the Holy Roman Empire. Yet there were still certain signs of local autonomy in organs such as quasi-representative city councils of jurats, or *giurati*. The most noteworthy examples were Messina, Capua, Bari, Brindisi, Salerno and Naples, while Palermo, as the capital, saw less administrative independence. It was not by happenstance that these cities had been ruled by Lombards, Greeks or Arabs well into the Norman era, when they occasionally formed urban councils even during the reign of Roger II, but it was probably inevitable that large localities of this kind, whose prosperity was rapidly increasing, would adopt such practices sooner or later.[1150]

Only a comparatively small fraction of subjects resided in cities of this size compared to those who lived in the many smaller (typically feudal) localities sprinkled across the kingdom. Even so, we find thriving demesnial towns such as Calascibetta and Piazza Armerina, and small cities like Agrigento and Troia, under royal control being administered by bailiffs (governors) rather than counts or barons. Described in charters and chronicles by various names, such as *secretus,* these bailiffs, whose role was somewhat similar to that of a modern mayor, were often assisted by informally-appointed councils, or committees, of nobles, notaries and jurists drawn principally from outside the clergy.

Even though most of their duties were superficially similar, the bailiff or *secretus* of a locality in the kingdom could not be compared directly to the *podestà* of an imperial commune. An obvious difference is that the bailiff was a royal appointee while the *podestà* was elected, or approved, by the communal council. In theory, of course, the *podestà,* like the bailiff, answered to the emperor.

Until the Norman era Amalfi, as a maritime republic, had an *arengo,* or committee of local clans and families.[1151] A similar system was found in San Marino, a papal town that became a republic.

By now, the overwhelmingly Latinized, Catholic social composition of the Kingdom of Sicily meant that the local bailiffs and the men on the councils had essentially similar backgrounds wherever in the realm they were found, reflecting the gradual development of a monocultural *ethnie.*

The obvious exception was Lucera, where there was a local emir, and even in that city there was a council of caïds as this was Muslim tradition.[1152] The kingdom's Jews had standing committees of elders within their own communities but were generally excluded from the major local councils. Large abbeys like those of Cava and Monreale had what were essentially administrative councils, and the latter, with its vast estates, exercised a feudal influence far beyond the monastic community.

The urban councils of the demesnial cities had historical roots, having existed in some form in the Lombard, Byzantine and Arab cities when the Normans arrived in southern Italy. Even in Frederick's time their character varied somewhat from city to city, not to be compared directly to what existed in Milan, Venice, Pisa or Genoa. Collectively, some of their members came to constitute what was sometimes called a *patriciate,* an untitled urban aristocracy whose status and wealth was based more on commerce, and even banking, than on strictly feudal and agricultural activity. In the *Regnum,* a civic council in a major city, despite the rather restrictive limits placed on its power, might even be referred to colloquially as a "senate."

In the kingdom, naturally, the crown, church and baronage were reluctant to facilitate the rise of this emergent class, which is rarely identified very clearly in charters and other records. In cities such as Bari, not all men who erected their own towers were of the feudal nobility; some belonged to the patriciate. However, the imperial communes, not the kingdom's cities, are known for this practice, and here San Gimignano (near Siena) comes to mind.

In the Kingdom of Sicily, the jurats, or *burgenses,* were not, strictly speaking, a hereditary class, but a place on a civic council might well be passed from a man to his son or nephew. Because this system, in contrast to that of Milan, was not very formalized, such usages as term limits were not the norm.

Because of their internal power structure, the communes sometimes saw violent feuds between local factions, families and clans. Stories like the legend of Romeo and Juliet were based on at least a few morsels of fact. That kind of rivalry was probably less commonplace in the cities of the kingdom than the imperial communes.

Beyond these generalities, the realities in each demesnial locality of the *Regnum* were unique.[1153] The local history of Lombard Salerno differed somewhat from that of traditionally Byzantine Bari, while historically polycultural Palermo was in a class of its own. Even without rabid familial rivalries or the conflicts between Guelphs and Ghibellines seen in imperial and papal Italy, demesnial cities experienced the emergence of factions based on quarters or districts.

In Salerno, for example, there were the *seggi,* where influential families eventually came to be regarded as aristocratic. In Messina, the city council met only occasionally.[1154]

Whereas Roger II, who ruled just one kingdom, was able to place his sons in Campania and Puglia as his surrogates while he was in Sicily, Frederick lacked this luxury. As we have seen, he left Conrad in Germany (as king) and Enzio in northern Italy (as imperial vicar). This meant that local administration was necessarily delegated to the governors.

Naturally, most of the knights and squires of the royal army came from feudal towns controlled by counts and barons, but, as we have seen, many of the foot men were drawn from the demesnial cities.

Significantly, the larger demesnial localities of the kingdom were undergoing increasing economic growth through the steady development of a true mercantile class not unlike that of Venice or Genoa. Despite this, most of the cities of the *Regnum* lacked the plenary fiscal authority to levy taxes of their own. For the most part, such local taxes as there were could be collected only with the approval of the crown, acting through the local governor. It was important that local taxes, which at all events were minimal, did not infringe on revenue intended for the *collecta*.

Although a *curiae generales* convened by the king was usually a meeting of barons and clergy, in a large demesnial city it would necessarily include at least a few of the local *notabili*, and *magnati*.[1155] These were not "parliaments," which were instituted later.[1156]

Lives and Deaths

By 1240, the *Regnum* probably had between three and four million souls living within its borders, but the precise population of the kingdom's major cities toward the middle years of the thirteenth century can only be estimated. There is little doubt that Palermo and its environs still had at least a hundred fifty thousand inhabitants during this period, making it one of the most populous cities in Europe. Salerno and Bari each may have had some sixty thousand citizens, which was probably comparable to the number thought to have lived in Milan, the most notable imperial commune, and in Genoa.[1157]

It was during the next century, in the prelude to the Renaissance, that the cities of Italy, from north to south, truly began to attract people from rural areas. For now, most people were content to live outside the cities.[1158]

The greater risk of living in the larger cities concerned health. Plagues and other contagions spread rapidly in densely-populated environments, with urban sanitation leaving much to be desired compared to what one encountered in towns and rural areas. Many lives were claimed by illnesses such as dysentery and malaria.

Estimates of medieval life expectancy vary widely. By the middle of the thirteenth century, most people who survived to the age of about twenty could reasonably expect to live another thirty-five or forty years. Except for the knightage, with its obvious risks, aristocrats generally lived longer than commoners. Rare as they were, there were nonagenarians, but poor healthcare meant that the general quality of life was not to be envied (see note 1158).

Around 1241, Frederick undertook to regulate the practice of medicine in the *Regnum* with his "Edict of Salerno." This simple code, which complemented principles set forth earlier in the Assizes of Ariano and the Constitutions of Melfi, gave Salerno's medical school a virtual monopoly on the licensing of physicians, with some authority accorded the *Studium* at Naples, permitting the issuance of an actual diploma, for which the text was composed by Peter della

Vigna. A medical education entailed five years of study and a year of internship, emphasizing practice as well as theory. To become a surgeon required additional training. Physicians could prescribe drugs but they could not make or sell these; that was the exclusive domain of pharmacists. For clarity, however, rules are established for the preservation and expiry of potions. Although the Muslims of Sicily licensed physicians, Frederick's effort, which may have been undertaken on the advice of John of Procida, is generally considered a milestone as the first *formal* medical licensing of its kind. It fundamentally altered the treatment and care that his subjects in the Kingdom of Sicily could expect from their physicians.[1159]

There is much truth to the cliché that in medieval Europe the idea of childhood did not truly exist.[1160] By the time a child was a teenager, hard work was a fact of life, with marriage just a few years away.

Infant mortality was high. Giving birth was as dangerous to the mother as it was for her child, even among the aristocracy where health was thought to be good and midwives were presumed to be highly competent. It may be remembered that one wife of Roger II (Sibylla), and two wives of Frederick II (Yolanda and Isabella) died from complications of childbirth.

More generally, the increases in Europe's population that began early in the eleventh century, coinciding with the arrival of the Normans in southern Italy, resulted largely from improvements in agriculture (considered in Chapter 3), such as triennial, three-field crop rotation and better plowing methods. This led to an agricultural policy far more sophisticated than what had existed previously. The conversion of many woodlands to pasturage and wheat fields greatly increased the amount of food produced, facilitating the growth of larger families. The Fatimids and Kalbids had already begun this process in Sicily, but by the early decades of the twelfth century we find the Normans encouraging barons and abbots to make land more productive than it had ever been, even in Basilicata, Campania and Puglia. The fact that Sicily exported wheat to Africa and other regions reflected the success of this approach, much as we may lament the loss of many forests.

The written record offers us only general ideas about how novel agricultural ideas were exchanged, but it is clear that the Kingdom of Sicily, boasting social contact with most of Europe and the Mediterranean, was the beneficiary of such exchange.

Politics

By the middle of 1243, the armies of the Kingdom of Sicily had occupied a good part of the Papal State, even if outright annexation of the borderlands was not part of Frederick's strategy. Control of the city of Rome was still divided between Ghibelline and Guelph factions.

Before a conclave to choose a new pope was convened formally, the cardinals meeting at Anagni and elsewhere had long deliberated over how they might elect a pontiff who could defend the papacy and its territory against Frederick's forces. To counter this, the emperor and his delegates sought to convince, even coerce, the cardinals to elect as pope a man who supported Frederick, or, at the very least, did not contest most of his politics in Italy. This condition presupposed papal acceptance of Hohenstaufen rule to the north and south of Rome's temporal dominions.

In conclave in late June, nine cardinals, mostly Italians, elected Frederick's friend, Sinibaldo de' Fieschi, as Pope Innocent IV.[1161] In July, Frederick sent his first embassy to the newly-elected pontiff. This consisted of his most trusted counsellors, namely the Archbishop of Palermo Berardo of Castagna, the grand justiciar Thaddeus of Suessa, and the kingdom's master (chancellor) Peter della Vigna, who were kindly received.[1162]

On the evening of July twenty-fifth, the feast of Saint James, an unusually large number of meteors of the Delta Aquariids filled the sky over the part of the kingdom bordering papal territory, as if hurled upon the *Regnum* from God. Those seeing in this a sign, either good or bad, would not be disappointed.[1163]

The new pope was to reconsider the relationship of the papacy with Frederick and perhaps with the kingdom itself, if he was not already thinking about this complex matter. Like Thomas Becket, who as Archbishop of Canterbury took positions contrary to those of his friend Henry II in England, Sinibaldo, as pope, now opposed most of Frederick's ideas about imperial power in Italy. A major point of contention was Milan and the entire Lombardy region, which the pope wanted to see ceded to papal rule, a request Frederick categorically refused.

In August, instigated by Cardinal Ranieri Capocci, the people of the occupied papal city of Viterbo rebelled against Frederick. In response, the emperor besieged it, not wishing to lose control of a key locality near Rome. Pope Innocent urged the Viterbans to capitulate in November, but then, after Frederick's army departed the city, Capocci killed many of the citizens for making peace. This incident did little to encourage confidence in the pontiff's actions regarding government in the papal dominions.[1164]

In September, Innocent's papal bull *Qui justis causis* formally authorized the Baltic Crusades, prosecuted by the Teutonic Order and other Catholics.

It was during the early autumn that Raymond VII of Toulouse visited Frederick. Raymond (see Table 15) was the son of Joanna of England, Queen of Sicily as the consort of William II. Having suffered defeat in the recent Saintonge War waged alongside Henry III of England and Hugh X of Lusignan against Louis IX of France and his younger brother Alphonse of Poitiers, Raymond may have been seeking a special alliance with Frederick. While Frederick was generally supportive of Henry, his brother-in-law, he had no interest in acting against Louis, with whom he was on amicable terms, in the sundry wars over French territory.

Presently, following some time hunting, Raymond sought to negotiate a peace between Frederick and Innocent.[1165] Raymond visited Innocent in Rome, to which the pontiff had returned despite continuing local unrest.

While at Grosseto in January 1244, Frederick issued several *Novellae* to his Constitutions of Melfi regarding justiciars, notaries and lawyers. These amendments addressed the organization and function of the judiciary to provide greater efficiency and prevent potential abuses, whilst making it clear that "by no means do they infringe upon the authority of the earlier laws." This followed similar legislation issued at Foggia four years earlier.[1166]

Richard Filangieri had made his way back to the Kingdom of Sicily in 1243. Upon arriving in Puglia, he was captured by Frederick's agents and imprisoned on royal orders for having ineptly governed the Kingdom of Jerusalem, where he had recently been replaced by Thomas Aquino of Acerra. Raymond of Toulouse gained Richard's release early in 1244, but he was forced into exile and became an avowed enemy of the Hohenstaufens.[1167]

Aided by Raymond of Toulouse, Frederick's efforts to achieve a true peace with the papacy continued unabated into the spring of 1244, but there was little progress.[1168]

In the *Regnum,* and indeed throughout most of Italy, even in the Papal State, the events of the past few years, nurtured by a steady stream of propaganda from Frederick's camp, had resulted in much antipathy toward the pope. The Ghibellines in the city of Rome still detested their ruler.[1169]

On June seventh, 1244, Innocent fled the Papal State instead of meeting Frederick to discuss their differences. The pontiff was soon in his native Genoa, planning an itinerary to France. The self-exiled pope still found support in the rebellious communes, where there was strong Guelph activity and papal sympathy was the norm. Elsewhere, Innocent left several prelates behind to make his case among doubters; they encountered resistance from most of the towns in papal regions where Frederick had made inroads, and Rome itself remained divided.

Further afield, the city of Jerusalem was completely and definitively lost to the Khwarazmian Turks in August, and the Battle of Hiribya (La Forbie) against the Ayyubids in October failed to salvage much Frankish power in the Holy Land. With this, Frederick's Kingdom of Jerusalem was effectively dissolved, a fact that clearly annoyed him.[1170] Meanwhile, Batu Khan's Golden Horde was again menacing Slavic Europe and the northern Balkans, thus threatening the eastern fringe of the Holy Roman Empire.

Clearly, Frederick, Conrad and their counsellors had much to think about besides their relationship with the pope. In the event, Innocent's departure removed the immediate threat of military action in the Kingdom of Sicily by papal forces, if that was ever seriously contemplated. As we shall see, Innocent's war of words against Frederick was to prove uncommonly aggressive even by papal standards, but it would be a nuisance rather than an existential threat.

It brought certain benefits. Frederick's continued marginalization of the Dominicans and Franciscans, a policy facilitated by the pope's absence, granted a respite to the kingdom's Muslims and Jews, even if Innocent remained zealous in his conviction that people of these faiths should be converted. In contrast to Innocent's "conservative," or "papalist," element of the church, the Benedictines and other orders, along with secular (diocesan) clergy, were generally indifferent about the conversion of non-Christians in the *Regnum.* In the event, the Muslims were ever fewer, and even the Jewish population was diminishing.[1171]

Consistent with his Constitutions of Melfi, Frederick had recently reiterated his promise to suppress Christian heretics, such as Cathars, Patarines and Waldensians, in his northern Italian dominions, a practice that differed from his more protective policy toward Muslims and Jews in the *Regnum*.[1172]

These weren't the only "infidels." The military movements of the Golden Horde were far from predictable compared to those of the Ayyubids and Turks who now occupied most of Palestine, the lost Kingdom of Jerusalem. Louis IX of France, perhaps more than any other king, was already considering the possibility of a crusade to the Holy Land.

There was no guarantee that Frederick would participate in a crusade advocated by a pope who despised him. Such reluctance had wide implications, for it meant that knights from the *Regnum* and Germany would not likely join such an expedition.

When Baldwin II, Latin Emperor of Constantinople and a papal ally, expressly requested help against resistance led by John III Doukas Vatatzes, Emperor of Nicaea and a claimant to the Byzantine throne, Frederick supported the latter. To seal the alliance, he even betrothed Constance, one of his daughters by Bianca Lancia, to John, who thus became his son-in-law (see Table 23).[1173] This sent yet another signal of Frederick's intentions to the papal court, namely the fact that his loyalty to the pope could no longer be taken for granted in matters involving Mediterranean affairs.

The loss of most temporal papal influence in Italy had a material cost, and the pope was soon soliciting England for extraordinary funds.[1174]

Meanwhile, Ranieri Capocci, who Innocent had left in Italy to wage psychological warfare on the Ghibellines, was dispatching texts that sought to defame Frederick as the "antichrist" and a "heretic," terms usually reserved for the kind of enemy against whom crusades were directed. The papacy would have to decide which target to attack first, the Muslim menace or a Catholic king.

That decision was not long in coming.

Lyon and Deposition

There can be little doubt that Innocent and his closest advisors were considering action against Frederick long before they arrived in France. Most of the principal work of the "First Council of Lyon" was directed at Frederick and his interests in some way, either as Holy Roman Emperor, King of Sicily or, where a crusade was concerned, King of Jerusalem.

Innocent reached Lyon in December of 1244. The council was convened in June of the following year, attended by well over a hundred prelates from around Europe, along with sovereigns such as Baldwin II of Constantinople, Raymond VII of Toulouse and Raymond Berenguer IV of Provence. The kings of England and France were represented. Frederick's delegation was led by Thaddeus of Suessa and Walter of Ocra.[1175]

Very little that was considered at this uncommon council was purely doctrinal. The council was primarily an exercise in whatever political power remained in the pope's hands. In contemplating a crusade to reconquer

Jerusalem, Innocent wished to cede rule of that kingdom to somebody other than Frederick. By condemning Frederick's tolerance of Muslims as behavior unbefitting a Christian, the pope was seeking a pretext for other monarchs to act against him as a traitor in a "crusade."

Since those gestures were insufficient to remove Frederick from power, Innocent excommunicated him and, for good measure, deposed him as king and emperor. The papal bull explicating this, dated the seventeenth of July 1245, is *Ab apostolicae dignitatis apicem*. The other terms of the bull may be summarized succinctly. It accuses Frederick of perjury for promising a peace with the papacy that he did not keep. Frederick is accused of disregarding pontifical authority and invading the pope's sovereign territory, the latter assertion being accurate in view of the sieges of cities in the Papal State. It is stated that Frederick persecuted the church in the Kingdom of Sicily and kidnapped prelates *en route* to Rome. He is accused of conspiring with Muslims against the church, specifically with "the sultan" and "the Saracens."[1176] Frederick is further accused of failing to remit monies due the papacy from the Kingdom of Sicily, and condemned for betrothing his daughter to a "schismatic."[1177] Finally, the bull absolves Frederick's subjects of loyalty to him, not only in the *Regnum* but in his other dominions, including the Holy Roman Empire and, by way of implication, the imperial communes in northern Italy.

This was more than sufficient to discourage, or infuriate, Frederick's delegates, who defended him in debate but now had to return to their lord with news of Innocent's offensive proclamation.[1178]

The pope chastised Frederick for the Muslim archers he used in the campaigns against the Christians in the imperial communes, and the Muslim women in the harem.

Another detail, though seemingly little more than a "footnote," was the papal accusation that Frederick had ordered the murder of Ludwig "Kelheimer" of Bavaria, who fought in the Fifth Crusade, at Kelheim in 1231, supposedly in reprisal for his having sided with the papacy against the emperor in the War of the Keys. Here too was a suspected Muslim connection, for the murderer, who was immediately captured and lynched, was believed by some to have been a member of the secretive *Assassin* sect. Presently, Frederick's son, Conrad, was betrothed to Ludwig's granddaughter, Elisabeth (see Table 24), and Innocent may have been seeking to prevent this wedding from being celebrated.

There was, of course, no way for the pope to remove Frederick from the throne short of military intervention. For the moment, Innocent refrained from commanding the other Christian sovereigns of Europe to undertake a "crusade" against deposed, excommunicated Frederick similar to the War of the Keys preached by his onetime mentor, Gregory IX. This idea, however, does not seem to have been far from his mind, and Louis IX of France made a serious, if futile, effort to negotiate a peace between pontiff and emperor.

A number of other issues were considered at the council. Chief among these was a crusade to reclaim the Kingdom of Jerusalem. In connection with this planned Seventh Crusade, the pope reiterated the longstanding proscription on knightly tournaments, not only for the traditional reasons but now because they might detract from preparations for the greater military effort.[1179]

Excommunication procedures were reviewed, and a response to the real but diminishing threat posed by the Golden Horde was set forth. Procedures were revised for cases brought before ecclesiastical tribunals.

For his part, Frederick was forced to respond to the pope excommunicating and "deposing" him. He sent letters to other monarchs, such as his brother-in-law, Henry III of England, decrying the pontiff's pretexts and the abuse of papal power. The actual effects of the "deposition" were minimal, but the excommunication thwarted Frederick's proposed betrothal to Gertrude, the daughter of Frederick II of Austria.[1180]

On June twenty-fourth, Innocent issued the bull *Grandi non immerito* to "depose" Sancho II of Portugal. In that case there was a disloyal brother, Alfonso of Boulogne, willing to march on the deposed monarch, thus prompting a civil war. Frederick, fortunately, had no siblings or other *parenti serpenti* to challenge his sovereignty.

Louis IX was an outspoken apologist for the pope, Henry III far less so. Yet no regnant European sovereign openly endorsed the authority claimed by Innocent to depose a king in this way. For now, most were silent on the issue, maintaining diplomatic relations with the "deposed" Frederick, who had been anathematized both spiritually and temporally.

Here actions spoke more loudly than words. In the months to follow, Louis found very few brother monarchs willing to contribute more than token forces to the forthcoming crusade, which was destined to become a predominantly French effort. Whereas Frederick, Henry and Sancho might have marshalled substantial armies to the cause, Innocent's politics alienated them and others to the point of greatly restricting, even eliminating, participation. What is more, rather few of the French king's vassals shared his enthusiasm, having fought enough over the last few years to slake their thirst for blood. Though Innocent was a reasonably skilled rhetorician, he was an uninspiring leader. The words of this implacable foe of the King of Sicily and Holy Roman emperor failed to deprive Frederick of his thrones.

A young Thomas Aquinas, son of one of Frederick's knights, was studying at Paris but soon followed his theological mentor, Albert Magnus, who was Bavarian by birth, to Cologne in the Holy Roman Empire. The scholasticism associated with Thomas Aquinas eventually became quite popular, greatly influencing Catholicism in a "philosophical" way by advancing thoroughly-reasoned ideas about many doctrines, even those, such as the transubstantiation of the Eucharist, that had existed in some form for centuries. Although Aquinas himself rarely took positions expressly opposing the politics of the Hohenstaufens, his work was critical of the tenets of Islam, Judaism and even Greek Orthodoxy.[1181]

Along with the increasing intolerance that characterized the papacy of this era, such developments furthered the evolution, or devolution, of the Kingdom of Sicily into a monocultural society.

Frederick sought to protect the Muslims and Jews of his kingdom from this onslaught, and he obviously had no reservations about his daughter marrying a man of the Orthodox Christian tradition. In this he differed from Catholic contemporaries such as Louis IX.

Historians have sometimes viewed this situation as the Catholic churchmen and most European monarchs being men of their time while Frederick was in some way ahead of his. Such a perception ignores the fact that the Kingdom of Sicily, from the time of its foundation, was a beacon of cultural and religious tolerance in an age of generalized bigotry. Though enlightened, even inspired, Frederick was merely attempting to salvage something of the society of the century into which he was born.

Another consideration concerns writing about the Middle Ages long after that era ended. It would be erroneous to think of social, philosophical or even theological criticism of Gregory IX, Innocent IV, Louis IX, Thomas Aquinas and others of their time as little more than an intellectual exercise by modern writers to judge medieval men and their ideas by today's standards. Even in the thirteenth century there were those who disagreed with some, if not many, of the opinions expressed by these thinkers.

One of those dissenters was Frederick II.

Chapter 30
CATHOLIC KINGDOM

By 1246, while Louis IX of France was looking to Jerusalem, Frederick was being forced to focus his gaze on his European dominions, and especially his subjects in Italy. For the Hohenstaufen dynasty, the Kingdom of Jerusalem was lost, and there could no longer be serious thought of conquests in Africa or on the other side of the Adriatic.

Corollary to the deposition of Frederick as emperor was that of Conrad as King of the Germans, and in May Germany's ecclesiastical princes elected Henry Raspe IV of Thuringia to replace the young man. Nicknamed the "Papist King" for his lack of support by the secular elector princes, Henry, who had once been Conrad's guardian, managed to defeat some imperial forces near Frankfurt in August, not out of military prowess but because of betrayal in Conrad's ranks. The usurper unsuccessfully besieged Ulm in January of 1247, and died the next month. In one of his texts, Matthew of Paris famously depicted Henry's heraldic escutcheon upside down to symbolize dishonor and defeat.[1182]

Innocent's efforts in Italy weren't much more successful than those in the German lands, though there was increasingly active rebellion in the communes. Nevertheless, Frederick reached a truce with the Milanese.[1183]

Business as Usual

A letter circulated criticizing the clergy was thought by papal advisors to have been written by Frederick or his counsellors, to whom a plan to assassinate the pontiff was likewise attributed.[1184] For his part, the pope sent emissaries around Europe to convince entire states to oppose Frederick and Conrad. This effort met with very little success. Not only did these various monarchs lack the military means to subdue Frederick and his son, there was little genuine incentive to provoke an open conflict, or "crusade," against the Hohenstaufens, especially after the fate of Henry Raspe became known, nor were boycotts and other economic measures a real possibility.[1185]

At the same time, Louis IX was trying to persuade these European kings to support a *genuine* crusade to the Holy Land to revive the lost Kingdom of Jerusalem. Even the Kingdom of Sicily contributed something to this effort, in the form of horses, arms and food supplies. Louis exploited this assistance as an opportunity to encourage the pope to reconsider his actions against Frederick, but his efforts were for nought.[1186]

At Vohburg in September 1246, Conrad wed his third cousin, Elisabeth Wittelsbach of Bavaria (see Table 24).[1187]

Following the death of Henry Raspe, Innocent appointed William II, Count of Holland, as King of the Germans, but this pretender, or "anti-king," would have little success in Germany so long as Conrad was alive. Despite strife between Guelphs and Ghibellines in the papal lands, life and government to the south, in the *Regnum,* continued almost as if the pope had never acted against Frederick at all. Bishops still recognized him as their king, while abbots and abbesses accepted royal favor. This belied the fact that the pope began to direct his most serious aggression toward Frederick as King of Sicily.

Yet the subtle dissent among the kingdom's Christians during this period does not seem to have been a result of the papal attacks on Frederick. In the event, the discontent was addressed by the reassignment of governors and justiciars. The Muslim revolts in western Sicily, though still a reality in 1246, finally diminished as this population continued to be transferred to the mainland.[1188]

Loyalty was ever important, and while self-exiled Innocent's political influence in Italy was presently minimal it was not absent. A plot to assassinate Frederick had been foiled at Grosseto when he was *en route* to the *Regnum*. Disturbingly, one of the conspirators was James of Morra, who for a time had been the imperial governor for the Duchy of Spoleto after that dominion was seized from papal control. Whether the pope himself planned the assassination cannot be known with certainty, but he may have condoned it. Frederick was convinced that it was part of a papal plan.[1189]

While Frederick and his counsellors may still have been somewhat suspicious of the Hospitallers, and even more so the Templars, the loyal Teutonic Knights still enjoyed a privileged place in the *Regnum,* with its existing possessions confirmed or new ones granted. In the years to come, their commanderies in Puglia were to assume an important role in support of the kings of Sicily.[1190]

Frederick's prestige in the Holy Land was still great amongst the Muslims. The Ayyubid sultan, Al-Malik as Salih Najm al-Din, when solicited for peace by Innocent, responded that he would treat with the pontiff only if granted Frederick's prior consent.[1191]

In his own kingdom, clerics such as Berardo of Castagna, Archbishop of Palermo and Primate of Sicily, showed no overt signs of disloyalty. Frederick, as king, continued to issue charters granting or confirming the rights of bishops and abbots, his kingship uncontested.[1192]

Despite his being primate, Berardo did not have literal, direct hierarchical authority over all the bishops of the kingdom. At best, he might exercise such power over the bishops of the island of Sicily, several of whom were his suffragans. However, as a trusted royal confidant throughout Frederick's reign, he was a point of reference for the prelates of the *Regnum,* especially during the pope's absence from Rome.[1193]

Perhaps wishing to avoid what might have escalated into an open, factional rift among the prelates of the kingdom during Frederick's reign, something similar to the violent rivalry between Guelphs and Ghibellines in the papal lands and imperial communes, Innocent refrained from criticizing Berardo very explicitly. Such a tactic might have revealed most of the realm's clergy to be in opposition to the papal mistreatment of their king. The highly ineffectual "deposition" of Frederick by Innocent represents what may well be considered the first major case of papal action of this kind being all but useless. There can be little doubt that other monarchs and their advisors saw this as an object lesson in how a powerful king could defy the papacy's worst, exemplified in deposition, and survive.

The War of the Keys of two decades earlier was a "crusade" only in the minds of a few zealots. Innocent was now preaching an actual crusade against Frederick. The problem was that he lacked a competent general to lead the attack. The nearest thing was a pompous prelate in his papal court.

In the spring of 1247 Manfred, Frederick's son by his mistress Bianca Lancia, was betrothed to Beatrice of Savoy (see Table 25), whose family ruled an imperial territory straddling what are now France and Italy, along with some important Alpine passes and Piedmontese flatlands.[1194] When, during the summer, Innocent's "general," Cardinal Ottaviano degli Ubaldini (about whom more in later chapters), sought to invade Italy via this route, he found no support among the vassals loyal to Beatrice's kinsmen.

It was probably late in the same year that Frederick wed Bianca Lancia of Agliano, who thus became the uncrowned Queen of Sicily shortly before her death following an illness.[1195] She received the traditional reginal dower of Mount Sant'Angelo in Puglia while her son, Manfred, was henceforth publicly recognized as a Hohenstaufen, a fact destined to influence the history of the *Regnum.*[1196]

By February 1248, Frederick was outside Parma hoping to bring that city back into the imperial fold following successful rebellions by its Guelphic elements. While he was unsuccessfully besieging the city, his camp, which he optimistically named *Victoria,* was raided and much treasure stolen, including coins, regalia and even a copy of his treatise on falconry. Worse was the capture, torture and murder of Thaddeus of Suessa. The loss of Parma precipitated the sporadic but inevitable loss of most of imperial northern Italy, yet the pope still could not unseat Frederick in the Kingdom of Sicily or the German lands of the Holy Roman Empire.[1197] During the summer the *collecta* was levied in the Kingdom of Sicily to replenish the treasury and cover the costs of the campaign. This continued taxation must have irked some barons, abbots and civic aldermen, but the overt protests were minimal. By this time, the *collecta,* which defrayed military expenses, may have been seen as a fact of life in a kingdom that played an important role in Italian, imperial and even European politics. Even so, there survives very little in the historical record to suggest that the prominent people of the kingdom regarded their country as a "superpower" that influenced the fate of other states.

In August, Louis IX and his army embarked at Marseilles for the Seventh Crusade, landing at Cyprus after three weeks. It was here that the horses, arms and victuals furnished by Frederick arrived.[1198] The Ayyubids, for their part, knew that Frederick's son, Conrad, King of the Germans, was the *de jure* King of Jerusalem and that the Hohenstaufens were not involved in this war. Only in May of the next year did the French, joined by Christian allies from Acre and elsewhere, sail from Cyprus to Egypt, where the crusaders captured Damietta. Their early victories were to prove misleading. Later, when the greater part of the crusader force was taken prisoner, Jean de Joinville, a knight and chronicler, received superior treatment by identifying himself as a kinsman of Frederick II.[1199]

Frederick himself was more immediately concerned with those kinsmen who were closer to him genealogically and geographically. He ensured that the baronage of the Kingdom of Sicily swore homage and fealty to Henry "the Younger," his son by Isabella of England, as a potential heir to the throne.[1200]

Frederick still had to defend the religious minorities of his kingdom, especially the Muslims, against papal condemnation, whilst defending his own position as monarch.[1201]

While the kingdom itself was secure, a few territories to the immediate north of the border that had recently come under royal control were reclaimed by papal forces. This included Jesi, Frederick's birthplace, along with some other lands in the March of Ancona in the Duchy of Spoleto. Nevertheless, in October 1249, a papal army attempting to cross the border into the *Regnum* was handily repulsed by a Sicilian army. Early in 1250, some papal territories, such as Cingoli, were actually reclaimed by Frederick's forces.[1202] In the kingdom, as elsewhere, the Teutonic Order remained loyal to the Hohenstaufens.[1203]

While there could be no doubt that some of the papal cities and northern communes were slipping from Frederick's grasp, the feudal and demesnial cities of the *Regnum* remained loyal. The same could not be said of everybody at court, where in 1248 there was evidence of embezzlement and, early the next year, a second plot to kill Frederick, this time by simple poisoning.

The hypothesis that Peter della Vigna, the *de facto* chancellor, sometimes identified as imperial protonotary and (for the Kingdom of Sicily) logothete, colluded in either episode is debatable.[1204] Yet the record shows Frederick's suspicion that his chancellor was disloyal as the stated reason, in the spring of 1249, for imprisonment of the man who for decades was one of the most trusted counsellors of both kingdom and empire. For many years, Peter had been the face of public affairs of Frederick's royal and imperial court. That he may have been tainted by a touch of avarice, having amassed a fortune in feudal wealth through his office, was not terribly unusual for the times during which he lived. Much about his fall from grace will always be an enigma. At all events, Peter's removal left a void in the administration of the kingdom, where there were some new appointments.[1205]

The spring of 1249 found Frederick back in the *Regnum,* first at Naples, with a stop in papal Benevento in June, and Melfi in August. By October, he was in Foggia in Puglia, his favorite region, where he remained until June of 1250. During this time, in addition to indulging his passion for hawking, he addressed the needs of the kingdom, making a few appointments.[1206]

In these years, many of Frederick's decrees dealt with the administration of the Italian communes by his sons, Henry and Enzio, and his faithful delegates. There was also correspondence with his ally, Louis IX, who was facing monumental challenges in his crusade. Whatever challenges the ruler faced in his other Italian dominions, and in the papal territories he occupied in the central part of the peninsula, the Kingdom of Sicily was as serene as it had ever been.

Perhaps the years of ceaseless conflict, frenetic activity and constant travels had taken their toll. Frederick was struck down by fever on the thirteenth of December 1250, at Castel Fiorentino, a fortified town near Torremaggiore, north of Lucera in Puglia, following an illness that had resulted in dysentery and abdominal pain. He died just before his fifty-sixth birthday and was interred in the cathedral of his royal capital, Palermo, where he rests next to his first wife, Constance.

It was with simple eloquence that Matthew Paris recorded: "Frederick, peerless wonder of the world, died in Apulia on Saint Lucy's Day." *Obiit insuper stupor mundi Frethericus, die Sanctae Luciae, in Apulia.* It is here, immediately after his death, that Frederick was attributed the enduring appellation *Stupor Mundi,* not by one of his own subjects but by a foreign admirer.[1207]

We know that Manfred, Frederick's son by Bianca Lancia, was present at his death. Frederick's testament was subscribed a few days earlier by a number of counsellors, including John of Procida. Amongst the others were Berardo of Castagna, Berthold of Hohenberg, Richard of Caserta, Peter Ruffo of Calabria, Fulco Ruffo, John of Ocrea, Robert of Palermo, and Richard of Montenegro. The charter was drafted by Nicholas of Brindisi. It was clear that Manfred would be bailiff, or regent, of the Kingdom of Sicily for his elder half-brother, Conrad, King of the Germans.[1208]

The testament accurately reflects what we know about Frederick's policies, convictions and appointments. It is reasonable that he would order it if there were a grave fear of his death during an acute, worsening illness. The testament cedes funds to the church for the reconquest of the Holy Land and to Frederick's sons. It establishes succession to the Kingdom of Sicily, the Holy Roman Empire and the Kingdom of Jerusalem.[1209]

At his death, Frederick was a slightly balding man of average height, still distinguished by his green eyes and reddish hair. His counsellors saw to it that his lifeless body was dressed in silk robes of Arab design to be entombed in Palermo.

If describing his physical appearance is simple enough, composing a profile of Frederick's personal character has proven rather elusive. He rarely displayed hubris. His personal religious beliefs were slightly ambiguous; he was not especially devout, yet he respected traditional Catholic law, if not the excessive political zeal of certain pontiffs.

The fiercest modern criticisms of Frederick's personality reflect a view of him as taciturn, obstinate, perhaps slightly sardonic. He was an absolute monarch.

Frederick's death signalled the end of a great multicultural experiment, a decline that culminated in the rise of a Siculo-Neapolitan monoculture, a natural ethnogenesis fostered in some measure since the beginning of his reign, and indeed initiated during the reign of his Norman grandfather.

Frederican Retrospective

Whereas Roger II is identified, first and foremost, as the King of Sicily, his famous grandson is most often linked, in the mainstream flow of consciousness, to his status as Holy Roman Emperor. Though it was not an exclusively modern phenomenon, that emphasis saw a revival when Frederick was "rediscovered" in Germany in the twentieth century during a rabidly nationalistic phase of the nation's history at a time when he was largely ignored in his native Italy.

In their attempts to shed light on Frederick's character, or personality, while inferring the reasons for his actions, too many biographers have wandered into the realm of psychoanalysis, and there are several distinct schools of thought about the man and his reign.

Another complexity arises from the very real distinctions to be found in Frederick's rule of his various dominions, where there was rarely anything like a "grand plan." Not only were these different states, they were different *kinds* of states, readily distinguished by means of a simple taxonomy. The Holy Roman Empire was a proto-federalist union ruled by a hereditary monarch whose rights had to be confirmed through election by his peers and coronation by the pope. The communes of northern Italy were a loose conglomeration (not a true confederation) of city-states of varied origin and government, some rooted in Longobardic feudalism and others in the medieval mercantile tradition, closely connected to the Holy Roman Empire but not always a formal part of it. The duchies of Tuscany and Spoleto sometimes found themselves under imperial suzerainty, likewise Burgundy and Savoy. The Duchy of Swabia was the hereditary domain of the Hohenstaufen family. The Kingdom of Jerusalem was a western European state founded under papal auspices in western Asia as a Catholic outpost bordering Muslim monarchies. The Kingdom of Sicily was a multicultural Euro-Mediterranean monarchy established by a Norman dynasty sanctioned by the papacy.

The knights of the Teutonic Order, of which the Hohenstaufens were *de facto* patrons, were given free rein by Frederick on the fringe of the Holy Roman Empire in eastern Europe, a fact which led to wars against Prussians, Lithuanians and others in what became the Baltic Crusades. In the German lands, this knightly order was almost a state within a state.

Each of Frederick's dominions had something that made it unique. Were his actions exclusively his own, and not largely the result of work delegated to his advisors, governors, jurists and generals, one would be forgiven for thinking there were four or five Fredericks. Here is a detail overlooked by many historians, for most of any king's policies, decrees and decisions, though issued in his name and with his approval, are not his efforts alone. Despite what some scholars would have us believe, single rule, whether in medieval monarchies or modern dictatorships, is largely a myth. Frederick relied heavily upon his counsellors, especially Peter della Vigna, who died in prison.

It is true that Frederick and his counsellors entertained definite ideas about what the state should be, and we see nothing less in the Constitutions of Melfi. However, the most likely explanation for Frederick's policies and "ideology," particularly in the Kingdom of Sicily, is simple survival in the face of aggression. The geographic extent and ethnic diversity of his dominions made it difficult to focus exclusively on one or the other group or region for very long.

The *Regnum,* where he lived most of his life, and which he usually ruled directly, entailed certain challenges unlike those of his other realms. Yet here, as elsewhere, the greatest obstacles emanated from papal Rome. Opposition to hierocracy was no small part of his reign. The first stirrings of belief in the desired separation between church and state, the spiritual versus the temporal, can be said to have emerged, as something tangible and lasting, during his long reign, when we see the beginning of the end of "papal monarchy." Integralism, the influence of the church over the government in predominantly Catholic countries, eventually faded from view thanks largely to the efforts of leaders like Frederick.

Characterized by certain tendencies and trends, Frederick's reign as King of Sicily enjoyed more dynastic and political stability than that of his other dominions. Yet even here Frederick had to defend his rights, first in the infamous War of the Keys instigated by a pope and an obnoxious father-in-law, and then in a conflict initiated by another, equally zealous, pontiff.

In some respects, his rule of the *Regnum* could be seen as that of a reformer, his "anti-papal" policy bearing certain parallels to that of Henry II of England, with Pope Innocent IV as his "Thomas Becket." Like Henry, Frederick found himself acting harshly against his own adult son.

Though exceptionally enlightened in some significant respects, Frederick was a man of his time. His actions were generally pragmatic if pertinacious. If he was sometimes excessively suspicious, this was an understandable reaction to the challenges to his authority, either from the church or from the more rebellious elements of the nobility.

He astutely distinguished friends from foes. The Dominicans were adversaries, the Teutonic Knights allies.

Reading the words — flattering or not — of his contemporaries, one is inclined to think of a youngish, vigorous Frederick more than the avuncular figure that he was becoming. Frederick seemed to delight in frustrating his detractors. Papal impositions only made him more defiant of irrational strictures, so it's no surprise that overtures from the Latin Emperor of Constantinople for support against the Byzantine claimant convinced Frederick to affiance his daughter to the latter, probably to spite the pope.

Frederick's rule cannot be said to have been either unduly lax or excessively rigid. His Sicilian laws far transcended those of his grandfather, Roger II, in impact, relevance and scope, but it was fortunate that the Rogerian code offered a solid foundation upon which to build.

There was a general consistency in Frederick's administration. The degree to which he may be considered "duplicitous" is difficult to gauge very accurately. Here again, circumstances determined his actions, with the man responding to the conditions and realities confronting him. It must be remembered that this was an age that found a pope encouraging the invasion of a kingdom while its king was away on crusade. Only the fact that the behavior of certain pontiffs was so frequently bizarre could make such a thing seem "normal."

Like Roger II, Frederick stood out as a promoter of science, literature and the arts. This was significant in an era that found kingdoms closely identified with their kings. There is something to be said for Europe's most powerful monarch finding time to compose poetry and a scientific treatise.

His duties far and wide allowed for very little time in Palermo, and the establishment of the *Studium* at Naples gradually displaced the kingdom's center of learning to that city, along with Salerno and even Capua. By the end of his reign, the great scholarship in Arabic and Greek that once distinguished the *Regnum* had all but vanished.

If a trend toward a Latin monoculture was inevitable, attempts were made to preserve Muslim Arab society within the wider context of the Christian kingdom. Ecclesiastical and social Latinization spelled the end of the kingdom's Grecophone communities, but Frederick's encouragement of the written use of a unifying vernacular cannot be underestimated.

The Jews, who by 1250 probably comprised only about three or four percent of the society of the *Regnum,* were now the largest religious minority. The Hohenstaufens' dynastic successors, the Angevins and Aragonese, would not treat them very kindly.

Were we to compare Frederick to the European thinkers of the next few centuries, he was not, as some have posited, comparable so much to a man of the Renaissance as to an activist of the Enlightenment. Though Catholic, he actuated vaguely "secularist" policies that might well stand on their own without a strictly theological foundation, even in our modern times. His tolerance for those of other faiths and his consideration for nature place his views nearer those of Francis of Assisi than Thomas Aquinas.

Time has favored the ideals not of pontiffs like Gregory IX or Innocent IV but those of rulers such as Frederick II, who triggered these popes to react violently to his rule and even his opinions. Little can be known about Frederick's thoughts; his observable reasoning, reflected in his actions, was shaped at least as much by empiricism as by spirituality. Among his contemporaries, only Frederick's acrimonious detractors in the papacy ever characterized him as anything like an atheist.[1210]

CATHOLIC KINGDOM

A freethinker forms opinions based on reason, independent of authority or imposed tradition, particularly where religion and politics are concerned; although they are sometimes associated with atheism, freethinkers may hold certain religious beliefs without advocating rigid dogma, perhaps as simple deists.[1211] A secularist believes that religion should not be involved with the normal function of government.[1212] Based on these broad definitions, Frederick was what today would be considered a freethinking secularist. He was also a multiculturalist (or polyculturalist).[1213] It may be argued that he was even something of a visionary.

But he was far from perfect. Frederick's life, like those of all leaders, is a story of both tragedy and triumph. It is, of course, closely linked to the people and places he ruled.

Anybody seeking an overarching "philosophy" in Frederick's government of the Kingdom of Sicily, in contrast to his administration of the imperial German lands (which was based on a model that had existed since the reign of Charlemagne), may be left wishing for more. In the event, his rule left the *Regnum* in a sophisticated phase of development sufficient to continue after his death, unburdened by pedantic questions about the precise duties of a bailiff (governor), justiciar or treasurer, or the "perfect" application of law. The rights of nobility, clergy and commonalty were defined fairly well along lines which, for better or worse, would exist for centuries.

The Kingdom of Sicily attained its last true greatness under Frederick. Following his premature death, barely more than three decades would pass before it was dismembered, to pass into Angevin and Aragonese, or Neapolitan and Palermitan, states that were, quite literally, a fraction of the realm's former self.

Although the Kingdom of Jerusalem survived Frederick's death in piecemeal form, the Holy City itself was already lost by the time he died.

It is cliché to affirm that Frederick was the greatest European monarch of the first half of the thirteenth century. Politically, such kudos are at least partly justified by the fact that he ruled more of Europe than any of his contemporaries, and never lost any pitched battles. Socially, some plaudits are substantiated by his intellectual accomplishments. If his merits were long overlooked, that had much to do with Guelph propaganda and other developments in Italy after his death (see Appendix 6).

Staggering as his achievements were, Frederick's temperament probably left something to be desired. Yet strength of will permitted him to grasp the reins of the dominions inherited from his ancestors, marshaling their peoples into a time of prosperity despite chronic papal meddling. The challenges Frederick faced, and usually overcame, were far more daunting than those thrust upon contemporaries like Henry III of England and Louis IX of France.

As one point of reference — among many — for an ethnic identity, Frederick is something of a "mythomoteur" in southern Italy; Germany, it can be argued, never truly needed him as a symbol because it had Charlemagne. In contrast to Roger II, we know more about Frederick and his reign.

There is no doubt that Frederick's rule of the Kingdom of Sicily differed from that of his other dominions. The greatest distinction is that here he was a nation-builder.

Much has been misattributed to Frederick, such as words he never uttered (see note 24). This has led to a great deal of misunderstanding about his personality.

Historians have rarely agreed about the intentions, ideologies or character of Frederick as king, emperor, intellectual, Christian, husband or father. Many biographers are plainly ambivalent, as perhaps they should be. Views in the wider scholarly community are eclectic.

Authors' perspectives are colored to some degree by their personal backgrounds and the ideas instilled in them by their professors and fellow scholars. There are traditionally Catholic, Protestant, Jewish and Muslim views about Frederick, imbued with southern Italian, northern Italian, German or other orientations, and in literary circles even a lingering, residual Guelph-over-Ghibelline bias thanks to Dante and his confederates.

Even the least biased commentators are endlessly inclined to question whether an absolute monarch was ahead of his time, behind the times, or in step with the times during which he lived. While those questions need not concern us at length, it is to be remembered that, unlike his mother's father, Roger, who founded a kingdom, Frederick was the heir to several. He did not construct what he ruled in southern Italy. True, he had to assert and enforce his claims to the German and imperial lands of his Hohenstaufen forebears, and that of a wife as heiress to Jerusalem, but his inheritance of the Kingdom of Sicily, despite an occasional papal contestation, was never truly in doubt. His sons were destined to face even greater, more tenacious, resistance from Rome.

A perspective little explored by historiographers until recently is related directly to the people of the former *Regnum,* and thus it is usually minimized or ignored by historians from other parts of Italy and Europe. This "Siculo-Neapolitan," pseudo-nativist view of Frederick is not "Italian" (Guelphic or, post-1861, "unificationist"), nor is it "regionalist" (a term descriptive of the constituent parts of Italy *after* 1861, before which there were no Italian "regions" but pre-unitary states). Rather, it reflects the positions supported by many historians in the Kingdom of the Two Sicilies (see Appendix 7), effectively the continuation, or "revival," of the *Regnum,* from the seventeenth century until 1861. Although a few advocates of the *Risorgimento* saw in Frederick a quasi-unificationist figure for the fact of his ruling most of what is now Italy, including Sicily and Sardinia, to most unificationists he was anathema. As an early symbol of *il Regno,* he was an inconvenient reminder that the *Mezzogiorno,* as the former *Regnum* came to be called, had long been a sovereign nation. To the extent that Frederick was overlooked in mainstream publications and school texts, that was consistent with the official Italian policy toward the despised, deposed, exiled *Borboni* (Bourbons) of Naples, who, like Frederick, advocated the arts and even spoke a local vernacular, Neapolitan.[1214]

More than any other ruler of Sicily during the Norman-Swabian period, Frederick and his reign lend themselves to counterfactual theorizing. What if he had responded differently to the circumstances that confronted him? What if he had formulated different laws? What if he had lived longer? What if he had more actively supported the Gothic architectural movement in the Kingdom of Sicily? It is perfectly legitimate to question how a change to some past event might have affected subsequent history. Often, however, such speculation is an attempt to escape the determinism of history, and in historical studies it lends itself to excessive theorizing.

At all events, there is little doubt that Frederick and his era significantly influenced the development of the society and culture of southern Italy, at least for a time. Here the exceptionalism of the Kingdom of Sicily was exalted and preserved.

Finally, precisely how much of our modern concept of the desired separation of church and state is justifiably attributed to Frederick may well be debated, for society's general knowledge of his advocacy of such ideas was subsumed following his death, to be claimed, in a later time, by movements like the Enlightenment. In our times the most rabid apologists for Gregory IX, Innocent IV, and even Thomas Aquinas, are few in number, found more in Catholicism's dogmatically traditionalist circles than in the wider world, where secular power, polyculturalism and multiconfessionalism are generally accepted. Despite a few violent hiccups into the twentieth century, today even Frederick's native Italy and ancestral Germany can claim a good measure of tolerance and diversity compared to just a few decades ago.

No longer are Frederick's appreciation of wildlife and the environment considered mere eccentricities. Would that this virtue were more generally imitated in an era of climate change, rampant pollution, and the extinction of species.

Those seeking to view a medieval personage through a modern lens are confronted by an intrinsic relativism. Even so, it isn't too difficult to imagine Frederick, in contrast to his contemporary sovereigns, as a competent, perhaps distinguished, head of state or government in our century, particularly in one of those (few) nations where freedom and democracy are the norm.

Frederick has become a social, political and cultural synecdoche for the first half of Europe's thirteenth century, a status that is largely merited. In our secular age, his conflict with the papacy engenders less controversy than it once did. As a figure, Frederick, seen in the light of a new day, stands taller than any of the contemporaries who contested him.

PETRI DE VINEIS
JUDICIS AULICI ET CANCELLARII
FRIDERICI II. IMP.
EPISTOLARUM

Quibus
Res gestæ ejusdem Imperatoris aliaque multa ad Historiam ac Jurisprudentiam spectantia continentur

LIBRI VI.

Novam hanc Editionem adjectis
variis Lectionibus
curavit

JOH. RUDOLPHUS ISELIUS JC.

Accedit
Simonis Schardii Hypomnema de fide, amicitia & observantia Pontificum Romanorum erga Imperatores Germanicos.

Tom. I.

BASILEÆ,
Sumptibus JOH. CHRIST, MDCCXL.

Early printing of the letters of Peter della Vigna, one of the closest advisors of Frederick II. Peter drafted decrees and important legislation.

Chapter 31
HEREDITAMENT

There were few obvious changes in the kingdom at Frederick's death in 1250. Institutions and government of the *Regnum* were unaltered. The copious *corpus* of law was generally undisturbed. The arts and literature continued to flourish. Leadership was initially based on Frederick's wishes. The greatest threat to the *Regnum* was Pope Innocent IV, whose efforts to subdue Frederick had failed but who now began making plans to return to Italy. By late January 1251, the pontiff was dispatching letters encouraging prelates and abbots to rebel against the Hohenstaufens, and overtly criticizing Berardo of Castagna for his longtime loyalty to Frederick.[1215]

Frederic was entombed in Palermo on the twenty-fifth of February, when snow still capped the Madonian Mountains visible from the city and the very first almonds were blossoming in the valleys. Celebrated by Berardo of Castagna as Primate of Sicily, this somber, solemn liturgy belied the ferocity of the coming storm.

Heirs

Who would rule the Kingdom of Sicily? Officially, it would be Conrad, who was presently in Germany but planning a journey to the *Regnum*. Of course, Frederick had several other sons.

Henry "the Younger," Frederick's son by Isabella of England, was named King of Jerusalem, a right that appertained to Conrad, but neither claimant would actually rule the distant kingdom.

In imperial northern Italy, Enzio, King of Sardinia, was taken prisoner, destined to spend the rest of his life in captivity in Bologna. Frederick of Antioch, another of the late emperor's natural sons, would play a small role in affairs.

Manfred, the royal regent or vicar (or bailiff) for Conrad, was eighteen years of age and already a husband.[1216] Manfred's chief counsellor, who would become his chancellor, was his former tutor John of Procida, the royal physician and one of the late Frederick's most trusted confidants. Among his advisors were several relatives in his mother's Lancia family.

Born at Venosa, where some of the Hautevilles were entombed, and raised chiefly in the *Regnum,* Manfred had a greater knowledge and familiarity of southern Italy than his half-brothers. Compared to them, he seems to have spent more time with his father. Formally schooled in Bologna and Paris, he bore a *forma mentis* similar enough to that of Frederick to be regarded as an intellectual.

Frederick's testament named Manfred Prince of Taranto, and he inherited his mother's dower lands in Puglia. He also held Gravina and other territories.

He would soon have to defend the kingdom against two principal adversaries, namely the papacy and a faction consisting of those barons and cities that supported the pope. In the Kingdom of Sicily this was not always a "formal" war between the Guelph and Ghibelline parties, which were typical of northern and central Italy, but it was often tantamount to such a conflict.

Manfred ensured a sense of continuity in the kingdom by retaining his father's counsellors, bailiffs and justiciars. He appointed his younger half-brother, Henry "the Younger," vicar for Sicily and Calabria.[1217]

Among Manfred's staunchest allies were some loyal vassals and the councils of certain demesnial cities, along with a number of German barons and enfeoffed knights present in southern Italy. He also had the support of the knights of the Teutonic Order, which had commanderies and preceptories in Puglia and Sicily.[1218]

Acting on behalf of his brother, Conrad, Manfred attempted negotiations with the papacy to bring an end to the hostilities of the last few years. Initiated formally in the summer of 1251, this effort was undertaken on the sage advice of prelates such as the octogenarian Berardo of Castagna, Archbishop of Palermo. Innocent IV was implacable, especially now that his most formidable nemesis was gone. The pontiff desired nothing less than direct control over the *Regnum.*

Despite the military campaigns he prosecuted in the years immediately before his death, Frederick was generally inclined to make use of negotiation when it might prove effective. With the support of his ally Louis IX, the emperor had hoped to go to France to seek a peace with Innocent. That, alas, was not to be. Now a serious military effort by the pope left Conrad and Manfred with fewer choices.

Yet Innocent was not destined to return to Rome; for now, he was busy stirring up rebellion in the imperial communes of northern Italy, an effort in which he was generally successful despite the resistance of a few stubborn Ghibellines. He efficiently harassed Conrad and Manfred from a distance. His exile had not tempered Innocent's zeal, and he soon made torture an official practice of the Inquisition.[1219]

On a wider stage, Catholic Europe was paying a high price for the absence of Hohenstaufen forces on the Seventh Crusade. While Conrad and Manfred were confronting realities in Italy, Louis IX was working tirelessly to obtain freedom for the larger part of his army, which had been taken prisoner. Popular support to assist the pious French king was not lacking, but the Shepherds' Crusade, an effort similar to the debacle that was the Children's Crusade four decades earlier, ended with riots in Paris and attacks on clergy. For the moment, Louis was at Acre, serving as *de facto* King of Jerusalem. In France, his mother, Blanche of Castile, threatened to confiscate the lands of any vassal who prosecuted Innocent's "crusade" against Frederick's heirs. This meant that, for the moment, the conflict between the Hohenstaufens and the papacy was "contained," having few immediate consequences beyond Italy and Germany.

With papal support, a certain resistance to royal authority began to grow in Puglia and Campania. Its first effects were seen at Andria, Foggia and Barletta, and among the Capuans and Neapolitans. At Capua and Naples the rebels were united into a quasi-Guelphic "confederation" by the local aristocrats, who sided against Manfred partly out of sympathy for the pope but largely out of their hatred for Berthold, Margrave of Hohenberg.

Berthold had been the valet of Frederick II, from whom he received lands, and he had served as ambassador to Nicaea. The emperor made him Manfred's guardian, although John of Procida, as the boy's tutor, also seems to have had this role for a time. Berthold's rapport with Manfred was to go through many vicissitudes.

Certain that the civic councils of Naples and Capua would not support him, and lacking an army sufficient to subdue them, Manfred initially remained in Puglia, where, during the spring of 1251, he raised a force large enough to put down the rebellious magnates of those two cities. This was to be the pattern over the next few years, indeed throughout the next decade, particularly in Campania, Basilicata and Puglia.

By the summer, Manfred was leading an army through Campania, mostly as a show of force, though he took some small localities such as Nola. For the most part, there were skirmishes but no major battles, even at Pozzuoli, near Naples, which he briefly besieged. In the autumn he made his way across the peninsula to Trani in Puglia. In December, Pope Innocent instigated further unrest by "liberating" Naples from royal authority.[1220]

Conrad

While Manfred and Berthold were bringing the dissenting elements of the kingdom under control, the pope was "giving" their lands to nobles sympathetic to the papal cause and Conrad was making his way southward. In his absence from Germany, Conrad left his brother-in-law, Otto of Bavaria, as his vicar. After suppressing a few rebel cities in northern Italy, the King of Sicily arrived in Istria, where he embarked on an Adriatic voyage southward to the *Regnum*.

Early in 1252, Conrad arrived at Siponto by sea to meet with Manfred and to address matters transpiring in the kingdom. A public coronation does not seem to have been seriously contemplated, but the king met with a number of counsellors and other officials of the *Regnum* during a large *curiae generales*.

Meanwhile, Berthold of Hohenberg, Walter of Ocra and Archbishop James of Trani solicited the pope to recognize Conrad. This effort failed. Innocent was destined to travel near Rome but not within the city, whose citizens still resented him. He lacked the military strength to enter the metropolis.

Though born in Puglia, Conrad, the son of Frederick's wife Yolanda Brienne of Jerusalem, had spent most of his adult life in Germany. His personal knowledge of the Kingdom of Sicily was rather limited. However, with the help of the counsellors of his late father, he quickly grasped the gravity of the present predicament, which saw two major cities in open rebellion and papal spies infiltrating the realm, especially on the mainland.

He really did not know Manfred very well. Perceiving his young, charismatic half-brother as something of a rival, Conrad was dissatisfied with the situation he found in Italy. He divested Manfred of Mount Sant'Angelo, Brindisi and every territory except Taranto itself.

Moreover, he exiled several of Manfred's loyal Lancia kinsmen from the kingdom. There were rational reasons for this. Manfred's uncle, Manfred Lancia, had once been the imperial vicar for territories around Milan; after Frederick's death he usurped Lodi and other lands while apparently sympathizing with the pope. The Lancias found refuge with Manfred's sister, Constance (Anna), in Greece. Learning of this, Conrad sent Berthold to protest, but she refused to expel her kin. The Lancias would soon return to the *Regnum*.

By the summer, the two Hohenstaufen brothers were in Campania, where they subdued Aquino, Sessa and several other fortified towns that had rebelled. They besieged Naples and Capua.

Sicily, where the Lancias had managed to retain order, was now administered by Henry "the Younger," who was just fourteen years old. Thanks to the efforts of competent court officers and justiciars, dissent on the island was kept to a minimum. Henry's chief counsellor, appointed by Conrad, was Peter Ruffo, formerly one of Frederick's advisors. Being a major feudatory in Calabria, Peter had a vested interest in the political stability of the kingdom, yet he eventually rebelled against the dynasty to which he had sworn fealty.[1221]

In March 1252, Conrad's wife, Elisabeth of Bavaria, gave birth to a son at Wolfstein in Swabia. Christened Conrad, he became known as Conradin. Significantly, he was the heir apparent to the throne of the Kingdom of Sicily.

In September, Berardo of Castagna, Archbishop of Palermo and longtime counsellor of Frederick II, died in the kingdom's capital. This left something of a power vacuum in the large city and in northeastern Sicily, where Berardo was serving as the king's unofficial representative, maintaining order and loyalty.

Henry "the Younger," the governor of Sicily, half-brother of Conrad and Manfred, died in May 1253.[1222]

Only in October of that year did Naples, besieged by land and blockaded by sea, its citizens on the verge of starvation, finally capitulate to Conrad's forces.[1223] In what seems an act of vindictiveness, Conrad transferred the city's *Studium* to Salerno, a decision that would later be reversed.[1224] Equally vindictively, the pope excommunicated Conrad in February 1254.

The king was preparing to return to Germany when he died at Lavello on the twenty-first of May 1254, aged twenty-six, probably of malaria. He was interred at Messina.[1225] He had appointed Berthold of Hohenberg as the guardian for his newborn son, effectively making him the boy's regent.[1226]

The author of the *Jamsilla Chronicle,* who was probably a counsellor of Manfred, noted that, by law, the role of regent should have been assigned to Manfred based on kinship (as the boy's uncle), as well as the testament of Conrad, who knew that, in view of the death of Frederick, the young heir's duties in the *Regnum* would be assumed *pro tempore* by Manfred. Nevertheless, Manfred feigned unequivocal satisfaction when Berthold assumed the regency. He wished, on the one hand, to slake Berthold's ambition while, on the other, to minimize the potential threat of an attack by the German knights.[1227]

With Berthold having assumed the regency, the entire royal treasury, consisting of gold, silver, precious gems and valuable objects, ended up in his possession. As Conrad's last will and testament regarding his son and the Kingdom of Sicily left young Conradin to the guardianship of the pope, Innocent exploited the opportunity to claim the realm for the papacy. When Berthold, as regent, sent ambassadors to the pope to request the papal spiritual protection for the young king, as established by Conrad's will, Innocent interpreted the gesture as a sign of weakness rather than a sign of devotion. The pontiff replied explicitly that the papacy wished to maintain possession and domination of the realm, promising to grant the young monarch, upon reaching the age of majority, the recognition of his royal rights, if indeed they appertained to him. The pope began to treat with some high nobles of the kingdom to determine how the papacy might come to possess the realm materially.

A number of great nobles of the realm already seemed inclined to support the Guelph cause. Berthold lacked the power sufficient to oppose such a grave and urgent challenge, and envisaged himself confronting great difficulties now that the pope had begun to raise an amy to invade the kingdom. Many important nobles already seemed to be siding with the papacy, while others were openly asking the pope for help.

In view of this, Berthold began to regret having accepted the regency. Not without discomfiture, he understood that he should free himself from the weight he had so imprudently assumed.[1228]

For the moment, though Manfred was effectively in charge of the kingdom, he was expected to answer to Berthold.

Manfred

In July 1254, a royal delegation led by Manfred and Berthold, accompanied by Frederick of Antioch, went to Anagni to meet the pope and negotiate a peace. Predictably, this failed, despite Berthold recognizing Innocent as young Conradin's guardian.[1229]

Berthold soon renounced the regency in favor of Manfred but soon began to kowtow to the papacy for his own benefit. At all events, Manfred was now free to defend the kingdom without the strictures imposed by the late Conrad's conditions.

The pope had excommunicated Manfred. However, a détente of sorts was reached in September, when Innocent made him "papal vicar" of the Kingdom of Sicily.

Early in October, Manfred met the pontiff at Ceprano.[1230] By the end of the month, Innocent was in Naples, where, despite his overt statements of conciliation, he attempted to consolidate his support against the Hohenstaufens. This was to be his last malicious gesture, for here he died on December seventh.[1231]

A few days later, the cardinals gathered at Naples elected Rinaldo di Jenne, a nephew of Gregory IX, as Pope Alexander IV. Whereas his predecessor may have been moving toward a compromise of sorts, Alexander had no intention of doing so. Indeed, he appointed Cardinal Ottaviano degli Ubaldini as his legate, or "ambassador," to Manfred, despite the prelate very undiplomatically leading an army into the kingdom.

It was in 1254 that Frederick Lancia of Squillace and the others of his family returned from Greece. These were Manfred's greatest human assets, but there were others; he recruited the archers of Lucera to augment his army for the coming conflict.

Manfred's forces included not only enfeoffed vassals of the *Regnum* but a number of mercenaries, along with some knights of the Teutonic Order. The mercenaries would have to be paid from the kingdom's assets, which were kept at loyal Lucera.[1232]

On December second, a papal army was defeated by Manfred's forces at a major battle outside Foggia.[1233]

In May 1255, Manfred appointed his uncle, Frederick Lancia of Squillace, to govern Sicily and Calabria, where Peter Ruffo had stirred up a caldron of dissent and disorder, being forcibly expelled from Messina three months earlier. In truth, the island was to present the least severe of Manfred's problems, which were simmering on the mainland.

The Battle of Foggia was hardly the end of armed conflict. Military force was used to convince cities such as Barletta to remain loyal to the crown. In the political sphere, the crown and the papacy competed for localized power. Although this principally involved the baronage, and the councils of demesnial cities, it also concerned bishops and abbots. In general, Puglia and Sicily were royalist while Campania and parts of Calabria had an increasingly papalist influence.

The monastic environment was far from monolithic, but the Dominicans and Franciscans were permitted to return to the *Regnum*. Here we find the latter erecting a major church in Palermo.[1234]

In August of 1255, Manfred's chief military adversaries, Ottaviano degli Ubaldini and now Berthold of Hohenberg, sought a truce in view of the arrival of delegates of Louis of Bavaria on behalf of the king, young Conradin. This agreement, by which Manfred renounced control of part of Campania, did not last.[1235]

Brindisi and Messina were predominantly supportive of the Hohenstaufens, while Naples, Bari and Capua were mostly papalist, or anti-Hohenstaufen.[1236]

Many barons and prelates, and even entire cities, were ambivalent. Some were outwardly opportunistic, changing alliance depending on whether they were most recently encouraged, or coerced, by the "influencers" of the pope or the king.

Although there were exceptions, Manfred's supporters were generally reluctant to resort to actual bribery. Papal agents were more likely to appeal to a subject's avarice; this became a familiar pattern.

A typical case was that of William Borrello of Agnone, to whom the pope offered Manfred's fiefs of Mount Sant'Angelo, historically demesnial as the dower of the queens of Sicily, and Lesina. Earlier, Conrad had knighted William, restoring to him some estates that Frederick had confiscated from the Borrello family. Now, when Manfred offered him lands in place of those illicitly given him by the pope, William insolently refused, going so far as to insult Manfred personally.

When traveling near Teano to resolve the matter with the pope, Manfred and a small company of loyal knights unexpectedly encountered William Borrello and several of his confederates. William was killed in the fight that ensued.[1237]

A greater menace was Peter Ruffo, Count of Catanzaro, who held a large chunk of Calabria. The region, but not Peter himself, submitted to royal authority following a series of skirmishes.[1238] Peter fled the kingdom and was murdered in exile, possibly by Hohenstaufen agents.

Manfred's policy toward penitent traitors was generally forgiving, but he eventually captured and imprisoned traitorous Berthold of Hohenberg and his three equally seditious brothers. He entrusted high offices only to those he found most loyal. At a *curiae generales* in Barletta in February 1256, he invested one of his uncles, Galvano Lancia, as Count of the Principality of Salerno. He also declared Berthold of Hohenberg and Peter Ruffo of Calabria to be felons.

His other uncle, Frederick Lancia of Squillace, remained vicar general for Calabria and Sicily.[1239] Frederick was presently on the mainland but sent representatives to encourage barons and towns on the island to remain loyal to the crown. For the most part, these efforts were successful, but the passing of Berardo of Castagna four years earlier resulted in a dearth of royal influence in Palermo, still the kingdom's largest, wealthiest city. In the capital, to which the Franciscans had been allowed to return, a friar named Rufino, a legate of the pope, was pursuing a campaign to bring important clerics and other citizens to the papal camp. This man was readily apprehended and incarcerated, and there were doubtless other incidents of this kind around the kingdom.[1240]

In April 1256, a royal army marched on Messina, where a Roman elected as podestà sought to make the city a commune similar to Milan, something that had been attempted by the rebels of Rome. Elsewhere in Sicily, Roger of Fimetta, a rebel baron, was likewise subdued.

In May, Frederick Lancia of Squillace rapidly brought most of Calabria under control, forcing the Ruffo family to submit to royal authority.

Meanwhile, Manfred led an expedition into Campania. At Naples, whose council welcomed him, some Capuan emissaries declared their city's loyalty. Richard of Avella, an influential baron, pledged fealty to Manfred.

Boniface Lancia, another of Manfred's uncles, placated Molise.

Fickle Brindisi, which was under siege, capitulated early in 1257 along with several other cities in Puglia, notably Oria and Otranto. In March, Ariano was taken, and largely destroyed. Aquila soon surrendered. Several rebelling towns in eastern Sicily capitulated.

This found the kingdom in a rare, tenuous peace. With this, Manfred went to Sicily early in 1258. He had heard, or perhaps invented, a rumor that his young nephew, Conradin, was dead. In fact, the boy, officially Conrad II of Sicily, was alive.

Nevertheless, Manfred was crowned in Palermo on the tenth of August 1258.[1241]

Chapter 32
KINGSHIP

While Manfred was being crowned, Pope Alexander IV was seeking other candidates for the coveted Sicilian throne. Indeed, he had been working on that project for quite some time, having inherited the task from his predecessor.

In a development that might be considered unexpected, Manfred's agents in the Italian communes managed to restore a number of cities and towns to imperial power.[1242] The Florentines even declared Manfred to be "Protector of Tuscany."

This kind of acceptance resulted from many complexities. An obvious reality reflected the popular Ghibelline view that loyalty to the emperor was more expedient than fealty to the pope. People who under normal circumstances might be inclined to embrace Guelphic sympathies now realized that, since Frederick's death, there was no emperor. The time it might take the pontiff to crown one could be put to good use in the exercise of self-government under lax absentee rule. The Florentines thus found nominal imperial rule acceptable for the moment. This arrangement was viable as long as the Hohenstaufens had other fish to fry. Most of those fish were to be caught south of Rome.

In immediate material terms, Manfred and his supporters had proven themselves adroit in the military strategies and tactics required to suppress a city. Those who were inclined, a decade earlier, to dismiss Manfred as a young man unable to command a formidable army were now confronted by the presence of an experienced leader in his late twenties who reminded many of Frederick.

The Eternal Chessboard

During Conrad's brief reign, Pope Innocent IV had offered the *Regnum*, which he viewed as a fief in his gift, to young Edmund "Crouchback," second son of King Henry III of England (see Table 22). Henry's taxation of his barons to defray the cost of ousting Manfred rekindled English memories of the fiscal policies of his father, King John, whose unbridled military spending only aggravated the baronial indignation that led to the *Magna Carta*. This "Sicilian business" became a contributing factor, if only a peripheral one, to the conditions culminating in the Second Barons' War.[1243]

During his brief stay in Palermo following his coronation, Manfred took up residence in the opulent Norman Palace. As King of Sicily, he could now appoint his own officers unencumbered, and his former tutor John of Procida was soon named chancellor. Before long, the king was back on the mainland defending his dynasty's sovereign rights.

The fact that young Conradin was not, in fact, dead, did not cause Manfred to renounce the crown he now wore. Rather, he justified his position on the basis that the *Regnum* needed a steady hand as a bulwark against papal ambitions, and that to achieve this a crowned monarch might be more effective than a regent or vicar representing a child king living in a far country. Events since Conrad's death had shown this to be the case.

At Trani's cathedral in early June 1259, not long after the death of his first wife, Beatrice of Savoy, Manfred wed Helena Angelina (see Table 21), the daughter of the Despot of Epirus.[1244] This afforded him an ally in western Greece immediately across the Adriatic and a coastal foothold in his wife's dower lands, which included Vlore.

Helena's father, Michael II Comnenus Doukas, exploited the advantage of having an ally like the King of Sicily in an attempt to seize Nicaea from Michael VIII, his Greek "frenemy" to the east in Asia Minor. The brief war that erupted ended in a stalemate, but Manfred retained a few coastal territories.

Arduous as the previous few years had been, the real challenges confronting Manfred were just beginning. By no means was his control over territory any more absolute or secure than that of the pope. There were isolated pockets of resistance, such as Mount Saint Julian (Erice), near Trapani, where some citizens rebelled against royal authority by murdering Frederick Maletta, Manfred's uncle by marriage (see Table 23), in May 1260. Although this Frederick was a brother-in-law of the late Berthold of Hohenberg, his own loyalty to the Hohenstaufens was beyond cavil. Frederick Lancia of Squillace punished the rebels by destroying much of the town.[1245]

When Pope Alexander IV died in May 1261, he was succeeded three months later by a Frenchman, Jacques Pantaléon, who took the name Urban IV. This coincided with the loss of Constantinople by the "Latin" emperors who had ruled it since the shameful Fourth Crusade fifty-seven years earlier. What remained of the Byzantine Empire was thus restored to Greek control under Michael VIII. One of Urban's first acts as pontiff was an unsuccessful attempt to initiate a "crusade" against Orthodox Christians to reclaim Constantinople. This effort generated little enthusiasm in Catholic Europe.

The pope was still the common thread running through the complex fabric of European life and politics. Faith, expressed through the church, was a *sine qua non* of everyday existence. The papacy was ubiquitous in Europe, its tendrils reaching into the Baltics, the Balkans and the Byzantine lands. It was a state within every state, and in central Italy it was a state unto itself, a theocracy dividing the Hohenstaufen dominions.

Pity the king who found himself targeted by the Vicar of Christ. Pity still more the Waldensians and Cathars, and the Jews, not to mention the Muslims. Even the Orthodox Christians of the east were not safe from the clutches of Rome. The worthy work of good Francis of Assisi was condoned by the papacy; that is because it posed no obvious risk to the church as an institution. *Res Publica Christiana,* a phrase erroneously attributed to Frederick II, attempted to express the concept, vaguely similar to "Christendom," of one Europe under one church.[1246]

The pope viewed himself as *dominus mundi,* "lord of the world." In that scenario, any King of Sicily would be entitled to little more than a few crumbs from the papal table. Nevertheless, Manfred still attempted to negotiate with the new pope, only to be excommunicated.[1247]

Whatever one thought of Manfred, he enjoyed a certain amount of support, even esteem, among the baronage. Never lacking in self-confidence, he wed his daughter, Constance, to Peter III of Aragon in June 1262. Predictably, the pope protested this.[1248]

Meanwhile, as English support for the "Sicilian business" evaporated, other candidates were sought. Surely, if *Pontifex Maximus* could decide who was to be crowned king, he might just as easily cast aside one designee in favor of another. Urban formally annulled the offer of the Kingdom of Sicily that had been tendered to Edmund of England. His new candidate was a fellow Frenchman, Charles of Anjou, younger brother of the ever-crusading Louis IX.[1249]

Louis himself was initially unconvinced. Having supported Conrad as Frederick's legitimate heir, he subsequently endorsed the papal choice of Edmund. Now, despite his antipathy for Manfred, he saw no immediate justification for an Angevin to be crowned King of Sicily. Yet he eventually consented to it in spite of these reservations.

While Manfred was asserting his family's dynastic rights in Italy, Hohenstaufen power in Germany was clearly in decline. In 1262, the agents of young Conradin, led by his spiritual guardian Eberhard II, Bishop of Constance, affirmed the boy's rights over a diminishing Duchy of Swabia. At the same time, Conradin's uncle, his temporal guardian Louis of Bavaria, even tried to position him as an alternative to Manfred in communes such as Florence, an idea that appealed to some Guelphs and even to a faction in the papacy, but was never pursued much beyond the initial proposal.

Government and Culture

The economy of the Kingdom of Sicily was solid. The essential system of feudalism and taxation had not changed since Norman times, and there were no discernible changes under Manfred, who required money for his army. Whether through excises or the infamously unpopular *collecta* preferred by his father, Manfred, as king, sought to generate useful income. This did not exempt ecclesiastical estates and other church lands, or even those of the highly-respected Teutonic Order.[1250]

The kingdom's foreign policy remained constant. The Hafsids of Ifriqiya continued to remit the "tribute" they had paid during Frederick's reign. Muhammad al-Mustansir, who became caliph in 1256, followed the practices of his father, the sultan Abu Zakariya Yahya. Like Frederick and Manfred, al-Mustansir was an intellectual; he authored a book on hunting with dogs and falcons.[1251]

In nearly every respect, the social and intellectual culture of the *Regnum* under Manfred was a continuation of that of his father. A sign of this policy was the restoration to its original status of the *Studium* of Naples, that institution having been suppressed by Conrad during his short reign.

Manfred himself epitomized Frederick's appreciation of the intellectual life and its cultivation in the kingdom. He translated a Hebrew text, the *Liber de Pomo,* originally an Arabic work based on Plato's *Phaedo.* He debated Peter of Ibernia on the philosophical aspects of nature, or rudimentary physics. Manfred encouraged the work of court translators such as Bartholomew of Messina and Stephen of Messina.[1252]

As king, Manfred even founded a city, Manfredonia, on the Adriatic coast near Siponto.

A certain prosperity encouraged widespread support for the sovereign. It didn't take much imagination for the subjects of the *Regnum,* like many citizens in the imperial communes, to ascertain their immediate future under the Hohenstaufens compared to their likely fate under the pope and his minions. The Muslims and Jews, in particular, were likely to view matters in this light.

Even the chronicler Saba Malaspina, who despised Manfred, had to concede the fact that his reign was generally a good one, or that most of his subjects supported him.[1253]

Magic and Mysticism

A number of "mystical" traditions and practices encountered in the society of southern Italy in later centuries were known during the Swabian era. Some of these were connected to religious devotion (considered at the end of this chapter).

Various traditions associated with Catholicism beyond formal liturgical practice involve what might be called "esotericism" based on specific folk customs.

In the formal sphere, there are also recurring sacred events. In Naples, the liquefaction of the blood of Saint Januarius (San Gennaro) was first recorded in the fourteenth century but seems to have occurred before then.[1254]

Beyond Christianity, mystical traditions still existed among the kingdom's Jews as the *Kabbalah* and among some of its Muslims as *Sufism.*[1255]

Mysticism outside religion, or that which existed only on the periphery of religious faith, was usually regarded as witchcraft. The horn of a goat, or a representation of one, to ward off curses or evil spirits, was not a votive symbol but a talisman.

Witchcraft, or *stregoneria,* was practiced by individuals, usually women, outside the church, and southern Italy had its own distinct form of these arcane arts.

The use of powders and potions in witchcraft occasionally overlapped what was found in the more legitimate field of medicine.[1256] Witchcraft sometimes involved *veneficium,* the use of potions for poisoning.

There were also incantations (spells) and other practices. Although the Inquisition and the Constitutions of Melfi forbade Catharism and other movements thought to involve rituals of this kind, the typical town of the *Regnum* had one or two resident "witches" to offer simple "supernatural" assistance to those in need in an age of widespread superstition. The activities of these local witches were generally harmless and usually escaped the notice of the ecclesiastical hierarchy beyond the local clergy. In the thirteenth century, the church in southern Italy only rarely expressed public disapproval for witchcraft performed privately, in a witch's home.

Witchcraft was more likely to be condemned when it openly challenged the tenets of Catholicism. Certain women commonly identified as "witches" were simply proponents of unorthodox forms of devotion. Wilhelmina of Bohemia, who lived in Milan after 1260, advocated a greater role for women in ecclesiastical life, perhaps as clergy (priestesses), becoming known as a *pinzochera,* a religious woman who lived outside the convent. In this sphere we find Maifreda of Pirovano, a noblewoman who, as one of Wilhelmina's followers, was regarded as a mystic and executed as a heretic.

Very little about medieval *stregoneria* was recorded, and tarot was popularized only after 1400. The grimoire attributed to Pope Honorius III, who died in 1227, is, in fact, a modern work. Transmission by oral tradition has led to many of witchcraft's practices in southern Italy being lost to time.

Astrology and alchemy, by comparison, were the subjects of treatises by the precursors of astronomers and chemists. Compared to a witch, a court astrologer was an eminently respectable personage.

When witchcraft wandered into the realm of the occult, or supernatural sorcery involving such phenomena as the intervention of evil spirits, it attracted greater attention from the ecclesiastical authorities. Because suspicion was a normal part of life in an age when little was understood about nature, certain forms of witchcraft and sorcery thrived for centuries.[1257]

Beyond this, there were legends about named witches, notably Janara in Campania. Some of these fictive personages were inspired by mythological figures, such as Artemis, the Romans' Diana.

Magical objects were not unknown, particularly in the public sphere. Prominent examples were presumably "mystical" swords such as apocryphal, perhaps legendary, Mikalis (mentioned in Chapter 12). As a matter of fundamental feudal law, swords were generally revered as symbols of aristocratic power that ordinary folk could not possess, common people being restricted to the use of knives and other arms.

Swords endowed with magical powers characterized legends consisting of dragons, unicorns, and personages such as King Arthur. In Italy during Manfred's reign we find the *Golden Legend,* initially the *Legenda Sanctorum,* compiled by the chronicler Jacob de Voragine, embellishing the lives of the saints with details typical of medieval fantasy. Later, as Archbishop of Genoa, Jacob was famously authorized by the papacy to absolve the Genoans for supporting the Sicilians against the Angevins during the War of the Vespers.

Saint George, a patron of knights, is usually depicted slaying a dragon, but those winged beasts weren't the only fantastic creatures popular in medieval times. The legend of Colapesce (Nicholas the Fish) tells us about a young man of the *Regnum* who, according to some accounts, became a merman (half-fish). Noted by the chroniclers Richard of San Germano, Gervase of Tilbury and Salimbene di Adam, the tale mentions Colapesce meeting Frederick II.

Melusina, a mermaid having two tails, is depicted in a capital of Monreale's cloister (Chapter 19). There are numerous medieval stories about her (see note 723).

Certain stories rooted in reality are equally enduring but rather imprecise. Near Sant'Alfio, on the lower slopes of Mount Etna, in what was once the Carpineto Woods, we find the Hundred Horse Chestnut, one of Europe's oldest trees, dating from at least 200 BC, which some writers regard as "mystical" (see note 1280). It owes its name to the longstanding belief that a medieval Queen of Sicily, possibly Frederick's third wife Isabella of England (though this fact is debated), found shelter under its branches during a rainstorm, accompanied by a large number of knights and retainers. By tradition, chestnut trees were Christian symbols of chastity, honesty and fertility. While the Hundred Horse Chestnut is not known to be associated with complex legends (or myths) such as those linked to Yggdrasil, the sacred tree of Norse mythology, its lore reflects the importance ascribed to the relationship between humans and nature.

Magic and mysticism flourished at an intersection of reality and imagination, a locus in the endlessly complex world of the mind.

Power Games

In 1263, the ambitious Charles Anjou of France accepted a papal offer of kingship weighed down by cumbersome conditions. Papal control of his Italian realm would be burdensome indeed. Legatine powers in Sicily were to be abolished, and armies were to be provided the papacy whenever requested. A substantial annual tribute was to be remitted to Rome. Naturally, there were to be no claims made by Charles on the Holy Roman Empire or any of its territories in northern Italy. Charles was expected to materially support the obvious papal objective of a new conquest of Constantinople from Michael VIII; presumably, this would be planned in conjunction with Baldwin II, the recently-ousted "Latin" Emperor.

The pope imposed a total of twenty-six conditions. No wonder some critics came to regard Charles as a papal puppet.[1258]

The throne itself was a more than sufficient incentive, but Charles may have accepted these outrageous terms partly due to his wife's endless prodding.

Behind every ambitious man there was a woman, and here it was Beatrice of Provence. Her sisters were already the queen consorts of England, France and Germany, and it irked her to be accorded lesser precedence than them.[1259]

While the cities of the kingdom were generally pacific, conflicts between Guelph and Ghibelline factions continued in the papal lands, where even smaller localities such as Sutri fell prey to violent contestation.[1260] Rome itself still had a vocal, powerful anti-papal faction.

As Manfred's army was marching up the peninsula, Urban IV, in flight from his Hohenstaufen foes, died in Perugia in early October 1264. Elected in February the next year, his successor, Clement IV, was also a Frenchman, Guy de Foulques. Guy had once been an advisor to the Angevins and strongly supported Charles.

As Charles made his way across Savoy and Piedmont into northern Italy, he negotiated cooperation, or at least indifference, from most of the cities and sovereigns in the region, Ghibelline as well as Guelph. The family that ruled Savoy, having ties through marriage to both Charles and Manfred, chose neutrality.[1261]

In January 1265, Charles made a pact with the Torriani clan, which had taken effective control of Milan and Bergamo. In October, he gathered his forces in Lyon.

Part of his voyage to Rome followed the Tyrrhenian coast southward by sea. A tempest saved his forces from a squadron sent northward by Manfred.[1262]

Charles reached Rome in May and the next month he was proclaimed King of Sicily by the pope, who was still in Perugia. With this, several of Manfred's allies betrayed him. Notable among them were Peter of Vico in Campania and Peter Romani, a leader of the Ghibellines in Rome. Meanwhile, Charles managed to obtain much-needed monetary support from the papacy and some bankers of the northern communes.

Charles was crowned on the Epiphany, the sixth of January 1266.[1263] Beatrice, his ambitious wife, was finally a queen. Naturally, Manfred protested the coronation, with Charles as well as the pope.[1264]

Now a direct confrontation between Manfred and Charles was inevitable. The wait would not be a long one.

Benevento

In late January there were some skirmishes around Capua, where Charles occupied several castles. San Germano, near Cassino, was captured by the Angevins in early February. The adversaries knew where to find each other.[1265]

Charles, who had participated in the Seventh Crusade with his elder brother and been taken prisoner, had the advantage of a monolingual "Angevin" force drawn principally from various parts of what is now France, led by Philip of Montfort and other vassals, though there was also a Guelph force from northern Italy. Manfred's army, by contrast, was drawn from the kingdom and from Germany, and most of the Muslims from Lucera spoke only Arabic. Manfred's force was led chiefly my his Lancia kinsmen.

The Angevin force numbered around twelve thousand, the Sicilian army one or two thousand more. Charles had some six hundred knights, Manfred perhaps three times that number. There were also "light" horsemen, especially on the Sicilian side. The Angevins had some eight thousand footmen. Charles had more crossbowmen than longbow archers; Manfred had thousands of longbow archers.[1266]

On the morning of February twenty-sixth, Manfred's army attacked Charles' forces outside the papal city of Benevento. What followed was one of the major battles of the thirteenth century and a pivotal moment in Italian history. Here, along rapid streams and rugged hills, two large armies of several thousand knights each met head-on.

The battle was noteworthy for its technology. Some of the German knights were outfitted with the newest military innovation, an early form of plate armor. Their faces concealed, it was the knights' shields and surcoats that distinguished them. Here heraldry was a useful science.[1267]

On the Sicilian side, the Germans and Muslims were positioned to the fore. Manfred personally stayed behind them with a reserve consisting of his own feudal knights, whose loyalty might be suspect. Manfred's cousin, Frederick of Castile, a brother of King Alfonso X of Castile, was present to fight alongside the King of Sicily.

The battle began in the morning on the Calore River. The new German armor seemed impenetrable until some of the Angevin knights realized that in raising their arms to strike, Manfred's knights exposed their armpits, a vulnerable area to stab.[1268]

The fighting was intense.

Most battles have their tactical "turning points." In this one it seems to have been a bottleneck formed by Manfred's cavalry while trying to cross a bridge over the Calore in a charge against the Angevins. To his credit, Manfred was leading the attack that led to his demise. He died audaciously, just as he had lived.[1269]

Between knights and other horsemen, Manfred lost some three thousand mounted warriors, with only around six hundred surviving. Thousands of Muslim archers and foot men were slaughtered during the battle or immediately afterward.

Though Charles forbade Manfred, as an excommunicated Catholic, a Christian burial, he was interred in a grave at the end of a bridge in Benevento, where each Angevin who passed deposited a stone, thus erecting a crude cairn. An inscription marks this spot, but it was rumored that in 1267 Bartholomew Pignatelli, Archbishop of Cosenza (and later Messina), removed the corpse from Benevento and interred it along the banks of the Liri River, in papal territory near Ceprano.[1270]

To the pope's consternation, the Angevin army sacked Benevento, still one of the largest papal cities.

Manfred's defeat, which saw the imprisonment of his widow and sons, was not just part of a political power struggle. In many respects, it determined the fate of southern Italy for the next five centuries, shaping the form that the region's society and culture ultimately assumed.

Conradin and Tagliacozzo

The Hohenstaufens still had their supporters. In September 1267, a fleet led by Frederick of Castile landed at Sciacca to support a rebellion that had been fomented in Sicily against the Angevins. Frederick's brother, Henry, supported Charles of Anjou but had grown disillusioned with him for not being repaid a loan. While they initially found themselves on opposite sides in the dispute between Charles and Manfred, Frederick and Henry shared a mutual hatred of their older brother, King Alfonso, who had deprived them of their estates in Spain, thereby forcing them to seek their fortunes abroad. In the tangled web of dynastic genealogies, the brothers were related to both Charles and Manfred.

Frederick of Castile was based at Tunis, where he held a position in the service of Muhammad al-Mustansir. Although Palermo and Messina refused to join him, the rebellion spread to Calabria and Puglia. Undeterred by excommunication, Frederick won a naval victory over a flotilla launched by Charles.

Whilst Charles attempted to consolidate his power in the *Regnum*, the enmities between Guelphs and Ghibellines simmered to the surface, as they were wont to do every so often. So long as a Hohenstaufen heir lived, the Ghibellines would have a rallying point. Young Conradin responded to their pleas, leaving his Duchy of Swabia to reach Verona, a Ghibelline stronghold, in October of 1267.

This, of course, earned Conradin an ample dose of papal approbation.[1271] Yet in July 1268, he was received by the crowds of Rome with unbridled enthusiasm.

Meanwhile Charles was besieging Lucera, trying to convince its Muslims to surrender to his royal authority and convert to his Catholic faith. Learning of Conradin's approach, he lifted the siege and made his way up the peninsula.

On August twenty-third, the two armies did battle near Tagliacozzo in western Abruzzi. This time, Henry of Castile fought against Charles. Like Manfred, Conradin had the support of Muslim troops from Lucera, foot men as well as archers. Here too the battle was decided by factors fortuitous to Charles, who was all but defeated until one of his companies, having hidden itself, ambushed Conradin, who in the confusion managed to escape.[1272]

Conradin and his faithful supporter Frederick of Baden tried to make their way to Genoa, perhaps with the intention of sailing to Sicily. Had they achieved this objective they might well have changed the course of history. Unfortunately, they were betrayed by their onetime supporter John Frangipane, captured and tried. The trial itself was ridiculous, branding the two men as "traitors" and "murderers," but it suited the purposes of Charles and his allies. Along with several military companions, the two were beheaded in October 1268, in Naples, which by then Charles had made into his official capital. Conradin was sixteen.[1273]

The would-be king was entombed in the Carmelites' church of Santa Maria del Carmine not far from the place where he was killed.

John of Procida, his estates confiscated by the Angevins, fled the *Regnum*.

The Duchy of Swabia was absorbed into adjacent regions of what are now Germany, Switzerland, Austria and Italy.

The Hohenstaufen kings were gone. They would not be forgotten.

Sorellanza Siciliana

Medieval war was the violent domain of men-at-arms whose brotherhood relied upon the enforcement of will through brutal force guided by a common loyalty to other men, namely popes, kings, bishops and barons. But in significant ways men, the hallowed heroes of our medieval chronicles, represented only half the population, and even less if the inherent rights of children, boys as well as girls, were taken into account.

Whether their familial loyalties were Ghibelline or Guelph, the wives and daughters of the barons and knights who opposed each other at the battles of Benevento and Tagliacozzo were "sisters" who, under other circumstances, might well have been friends or at least confederates. Indeed, many were probably friends or kinswomen who found themselves divided by politics beyond their control in what was essentially a civil war, if indeed any war is ever truly "civil" or civilized.

Little is mitigated by the purported rules of conduct on the battlefield, for death is death, and the loss of a son, be he an infant or a knight, is the emotional antipode of motherhood. No war that ever touched the trimillennial history of southern Italy, from the fabled days of Helen of Troy to the destructive global conflict that ended in 1945, was instigated by a woman. Not without reason, it has long been postulated that a world governed by a sisterhood of mothers might be prone to fewer wars.

The Italian *sorellanza* is a seldom-heard term for sisterhood, and even if the medieval connotation bears little similarity to its modern incarnation, it stands as a reflection of history. In its widest usage, sisterhood describes women having common interests, or, nearer our times, women generally.

The roles of women (considered in Chapter 2) underwent a certain evolution in the centuries before the foundation of the *Regnum,* leaving us, early in the Middle Ages, with such phenomena as hagiography and queenhood. There were many implicit sisterhoods. There was the sisterhood of abbesses and nuns, the sisterhood of noblewomen, a sisterhood of mothers, a sisterhood of midwives, perhaps even a sisterhood of shepherdesses. Some "vocational" sisterhoods, such as those of queens or physicians, were truly elite.

The sisterhood of queens was tenuous because there were not always many occasions for royal women to meet each other. In the *Regnum,* we find a remarkable concurrence of sisterhood consisting of Margaret of Navarre, Beatrice of Rethel, and young Constance Hauteville, later joined by an even younger Joanna of England. Little is known of the bonds of friendship between these once and future queens, but they certainly existed in some measure. It was noted earlier (though the fact is ignored by most historians) that Margaret and Beatrice represent a rare moment of female rule of the Kingdom of Sicily. There were also the nieces and various female cousins of King Roger II, an extended Hauteville family full of kinswomen whose names make only fleeting appearances in the historical record. Lucy of Cammarata, whom we have met, was such a woman.

The sisterhood of physicians, particularly those in Salerno, included women such as Sichelgaita, Trota and, later, Rebecca Guarna. These women may not have been contemporaries or "classmates," but they shared education and experiences.

Where did the generic concept of sisterhood, a term that rarely shows itself in studies about medieval women, come from?

Unlike many parts of Europe, where the fullness of recorded history begins with the ancient Romans, southern Italy, like Greece, boasts a long tradition of sisterhood based on religious practice.

In the sisterhood of antiquity we find priestesses overseeing shrines to goddesses. Among the deities venerated in *Megale Hellas* were Artemis (the Romans' Diana) at Cefalù, Athena (Minerva) at Syracuse and Paestum, and Aphrodite (Venus) at Eryx. Associated with Enna and its environs, Demeter (Ceres) and her daughter, Persephone, are truly, unequivocally, ours.

By the fourth century, the monotheism of Christianity was supplanting goddesses and other mythological women with early saints such as Agatha (at Catania) and Lucy (at Syracuse). Bolstered by the power of the universal church, their saintly cults soon eclipsed anything known in the ancient world.

How much of the classical patrimony of Greco-Roman mythology was known to very many people living in the kingdom during our twelfth and thirteenth centuries is fodder for debate. Many of the temples, such as that to Athena in Syracuse, had long been converted into churches. Was ancient sisterhood forgotten, to be rediscovered only during the Renaissance?

The sisterhood of our Norman-Swabian era is indistinct, obscured by the opaque shadows cast by the men who wrote history at a time when most societies were intrinsically androcentric, even misogynistic. Except in charters issued by abbesses and queens, we find very few women writing about other women, and in the kingdom before 1266 no known chronicler was female. In the neighboring Byzantine Empire, Anna Comnena, who died in 1153, is a rare exception, writing about Sichelgaita of Salerno (see note 145).

While the law took some account of the inherent rights of some women, the great majority of females, young and old, were defined by the identities of their fathers and husbands. Even Lucy of Cammarata, despite being a royal woman ("princess") of the reigning dynasty, ultimately found herself identified via her husband.

There were distinctions between sisterhood and brotherhood, the latter reflecting the social position of the dominant sex. Rarely was the symbiosis between women and men a comfortable one.

Some of the orders of chivalry had serving sisters. Before marrying Frederick II, the widowed Constance of Aragon lived in such a community, Santa María of Sigena, founded by her mother for the Knights Hospitaller (see note 713). For most women, religious sisterhood meant life in a cloistered convent, even if Clare of Assisi broke with this tradition by establishing an order that cared for the sick.

Few women besides nuns were closely, formally associated with other women in a defined community. More commonplace were localized friendship networks, where bonds of sisterhood existed between cousins or sisters-in-law.

Like a queen, the mistress (baroness) of an aristocratic household might have a coterie of ladies with whom she associated closely. While few of the women in her castle were her peers, some might become her friends.

Sisterhood, in one form or another, was never countercultural. It was an essential part of social culture, for it represented the manifestation of what originated as an instinct among all women, regardless of ethnicity, faith or rank.

The imprecise term *patriarchy,* referring to the general dominance of men over women in society, does little to explain the specific strictures against which women might seek to rebel in such a hierarchy. By the twelfth century, an entrenched mentality in Catholic circles associated young women with sin, identifying their personalities with the temptress Eve in the Garden of Eden. This served to discourage dissent. The papacy disavowed this characterization of Eve only in the twenty-first century.

The modern, multivalent concept of sisterhood is usually linked to our ideas about feminism, for which there are several principal paradigms. Yet the notion that medieval women, as women, might have a natural affinity for each other, if only in view of their common struggles against the obstacles imposed upon them in an androcentric society, presumes no complexity of reasoning. It is natural, almost instinctive.

In that context, it is to be remembered that a medieval girl's initiation to life as a woman might begin socially at the age of thirteen or fourteen or shortly thereafter, usually as a wife and soon as a mother of at least two or three children.

In its most essential form, sisterhood, or *The Sisterhood,* was expressed through companionship. It was part of a femininity that flourished from a woman's earliest years until her death in an era when friendships, like most marriages, were presumed to last a lifetime. Loyalty and respect were integral to this. There were certain implicit standards of behavior; for example, a woman did not normally defame another woman in the presence of men. Maidens were expected to be courteous to matrons. Mothers, and older women generally, were accorded a certain deference by younger women. Sisterhood implied women's shared experience in education and in life generally.

Sisterhood was not a medieval development, nor was it extinguished after the Middle Ages. It can transcend time. Sichelgaita, Margaret, Constance and their contemporaries were the elder sisters of today's women, and especially those of southern Italy. Like Demeter and Persephone, they are ours.

Saints, Devotion, Pilgrimage, Confraternities

In death, one distinction proved notably elusive to the Hautevilles and Hohenstaufens. A few of their contemporaries came to be venerated as saints through formal canonization. That was the case, quite conspicuously, of Louis

KINGSHIP

IX, who became the heavenly patron of France. However, none of the medieval Sicilian monarchs who appear in the preceding chapters seem to have been considered seriously for sainthood, at least not by the hierarchy of the church. Indeed, between the efforts of successive pontiffs, the conquering Angevins of Naples, and Tuscan poets of Guelphic orientation, there was a determined effort to vilify these sovereigns (see Appendix 6).

If, based on the standards of the era, we were to view any of our queens in a saintly light, it might be Margaret of Navarre, the mother of William II.

A superficial reading of the history of the Norman-Swabian era would seem to imply little respect for our kings, given the many rebellions. In reality, the greatest dissent emanated from the higher echelons of the church and the nobility. Most clergy, and most of the commonalty, were little more than pawns in these conflicts. In liturgy, the *laudes regiae* (Appendix 5) proclaimed the status of the king while invoking his protection by saints for which there was then special veneration in the Kingdom of Sicily and in Catholicism generally. In the time of Frederick II those mentioned were: Saint Michael, Saint Gabriel, Saint John the Baptist, Saint Peter, Saint Paul, Saint Stephen, Saint Laurence, Saint Sylvester, Saint Mary Magdalen, Saint Christina, Saint Agatha.

By the end of the Hohenstaufen era in 1266, and definitively, irrevocably, two years later, the *Regnum* was overwhelmingly Latinized in every way. The Christians were Roman Catholic despite some vestigial Byzantine usages and traditions. The Muslims and Jews together comprised perhaps six percent of the population, and the faith of the former would soon vanish entirely. The plenitude of polyculturalism was gone.

Christening (baptism) necessitated a given name based on that of a saint. Since each saint was commemorated on a certain day of the year, a child, in addition to a birthday, had a "name day," which in Italy is still observed as an *onomastico*. Into the twentieth century in many places south of Rome, the *onomastico* was celebrated instead of the birthday. In some cases, of course, a child was simply named for the saint of the day.

Devotion implied patronage, even protection, in this world and the next. It is thus unsurprising to see Saint Margaret in a mosaic icon overlooking the tomb of Margaret of Navarre in Monreale.

Certain saints of an earlier era had already become more widely venerated in the kingdom through Norman efforts. Yet Saint George and Saint Michael were recognized as the patrons of knights long before the arrival of the Drengots and Hautevilles in southern Italy.

Many local saints lived in the Byzantine era. Venerated in several towns of Sicily, where he died in 561, Saint Calogero was a Greek born in Calcedonia.

Latinization brought with it new saints, such as Francis of Assisi and Thomas Becket, whom we have met. Many would follow, including Saint Rosalie, whose alleged origins are somewhat conjectural.

Some saints are associated with certain groups or causes; today Saint Lucy, martyred in 304, is the patron of the blind, while Saint Agatha, martyred in 251, is the protector of women afflicted by breast cancer.

Every city and town ended up with its chief patron. Palermo had four:

Agatha, Cristina, Ninfa, Oliva. The cults of Saint Rosalie (see Chapter 12) and Benedict the Moor became popular in later centuries. Saint Nicholas of Myra, who died in 343, was venerated as the patron of Bari beginning in 1087 when his relics were translated to Puglia. Even the smallest chartered locality had at least one annual patronal feast.

Typical of this localized veneration was Saint Gerland of Besançon, Bishop of Agrigento, who died in 1100. Canonized in 1159, this kinsman of Roger I was known for converting many of that Sicilian city's Berbers to Christianity. Like Gerland, Catald of Taranto, whom we met in Chapter 4, was canonized long before there was a congregation for that purpose.

Like the church itself, religious devotion was parallel to the concept of monarchy, linked to it but in certain ways distinct from it. True, Catholic monarchs were expected to be religiously devout and to support the church, yet they had little say about who was venerated and canonized, a procedure placed under papal control in 1170.

While Roger II supported a pontiff regarded as an antipope, and though Frederick II opposed the hegemony of certain men who occupied the See of Peter, neither monarch contested the inherent right of the papacy to determine who was to be canonized.

Typically, the medieval veneration of a recently-deceased person began as a "grass roots" trend, a local cult among the common folk or minor clergy. Prominent figures such as Thomas Becket, Francis of Assisi and Louis IX, canonized in (respectively) 1173, 1228 and 1297, were the exceptions.

It was mentioned earlier (in Chapter 12) that the Hautevilles, as a ruling dynasty, did not venerate one saint exclusively as their familial patron. Unlike France, where Louis IX became the national patron, and Hungary, where King Stephen I, who died in 1038, became that country's saint, the Kingdom of Sicily under the Hautevilles and Hohenstaufens lacked such a figure. Both of these saints were part of a medieval trend to make a member of the ruling dynasty the people's official patron. Sicily itself was sometimes associated with the patronage of Saint George.

For the most part, the patrons of the major cities were those venerated since the fall of the Roman Empire in what is now Italy. In these important Christian centers, the Ostrogoths, Vandals and Longobards made comparatively few efforts to introduce saints of their own. We find Saint Januarius in Naples, Saint Matthew in Salerno, Saint Agatha in Catania and Saint Lucy in Siracusa.

It is erroneous to regard as "Greek" all those Grecophone saints of southern Italy canonized before 1054, not because none were ethnically Greek but because the term is often imprecise. Saint Venera, who was martyred in Sicily in 143, may not have been "Italian" or Byzantine by birth or upbringing.

Over the centuries, beliefs and legends accrued to the stories of these saints. Miracles were attributed to them. The most famous of these is a recurring event, the liquefaction of the blood of Saint Januarius in Naples (see note 1254). There were, however, other phenomena, unexplainable in the medieval mind, in smaller localities around the kingdom. Many are long forgotten. The so-called "myrrh" exuded from the bodily relics of Saint Nicholas in Bari was principally water resulting from condensation in a humid environment.

Pilgrimages to saints' shrines, sanctuaries or tombs were not uncommon. Here the most famous example associated with our Normans is Mount Sant'Angelo, the shrine of Saint Michael, in Puglia, mentioned in Chapter 2. The route to this shrine came to be called the *Via Micaelica.*

In southern Italy, the best-known pilgrimage route was traveled by those trekking southward from Rome on foot to reach ships for the Holy Land. This route also took them to Mount Sant'Angelo. As early as 725, the *Iter Francorum,* later known as the *Via Francigena,* extended along the peninsula to Brindisi, where pilgrims embarked for Palestine (see note 252). It is attested in detailed descriptions written in the first half of the eleventh century describing a route along ancient Roman roads still in use at that time, with an extension running between Palermo and Messina. Indeed, a segment from southern England through France to Rome was described by Sigeric of Canterbury in 990. The fame of the *Via Francigena* (which has seen a revival of interest) coincided with the crusades and the increasing popularity of the *Camino de Santiago,* or "Way of Saint James," a pilgrimage route to the shrine of Saint James of Campostela in Galicia, now part of Spain.

In western fashion, we find statues supplanting icons by the end of the Hohenstaufen era, not only in churches and chapels, where they were sculpted in marble, but in religious processions, for which many were carved of wood. This coincided with movements such as the Italianate "Romanesque Gothic," with its heavy pillars, stout walls and rose windows, in turn influenced by the architecture of France and Spain.

Among clergy outside the secular (diocesan) sphere, monastic communal life was now the norm. Gone were the hermit monks of Orthodoxy, which lacked religious orders. In Italy the Greek language was little more than a memory, evoked by a few words in Sicilian and Neapolitan.

In theological thought, the scholasticism of Thomas Aquinas, Bonaventure (John of Fidanza) and their contemporaries came to dominate Catholicism. This theology, however, was not foremost in the daily lives of most people.

Many devotional practices among ordinary people, those outside the clergy and the aristocracy, were established that have continued in some way into our times.

An obvious example, the use of votive tokens similar to Spanish *milagros* or Byzantine *tama,* originated in older Christian practices derived from ancient Greek usages involving terracotta figurines. Certain traditions, such as arranging low chairs in a semi-circle at a Catholic wake, something known in Calabria, were clearly Judaic in origin. Particular rituals were associated with prayer or the devotion to specific saints.

Certain foods have long been associated with religious feasts, some for many centuries. At least a few of these connections existed before 1300. Hard biscuits marked the feast of Saint Martin, *sfince* (see Chapter 27) that of Saint Joseph, and fava beans that of Saint Nicholas. We find bread formed into particular shapes, some resembling the sculpted figures of saints. The consumption of roasted lamb or goat on Easter was traditional long before the arrival of the Normans.

Localization was the norm. The patron saints of large cities were known to comparatively few people in an age that found the greater part of the population living outside urban areas such as Naples and Palermo.

True lay confraternities were not very commonplace before the fourteenth century. However, we find groups of laymen sharing a devotion to a local saint organizing processions, feasts and other events. These informal brotherhoods gave rise to the earliest confraternity tradition in southern Italy, a development which seems to have been influenced by older institutions such as the knightly and religious orders.

In particular, the "tertiary order" of the Franciscans had existed since 1221 for men ineligible to take full vows and live the communal life in a friary (or monastery). Six years later, Pope Gregory IX granted canonical protection to groups of laity that came to be called "brothers and sisters of penance."

One of the earliest confraternities in the Kingdom of Sicily was said to be the *Gonfalone,* believed to have been established in Palermo in 1264 as a branch of the archconfraternity of the same name in Rome approved by Saint Bonaventure with formal statutes. These were penitents distinguished by their white habits.

In Naples we find the Company of the Holy Cross being founded in 1290. Like some other important confraternities established in major cities around that time, this one had its own church, which is still standing.

Besides their participation in ecclesiastical functions, confraternities became active in their local communities. Complementing the religious orders, they were, in effect, early charitable organizations. Confraternities brought about the greater participation of the laity, ordinary people, in the life of the church.

Another type of organization, the "noble company," was a form of confraternity that drew its membership from amongst the aristocracy throughout the kingdom. While the noble companies were no more "secretive" than confraternities, their intrinsic exclusivity made them seem so to outsiders.

These legitimate institutions should not be confused with covert organizations such as the *Vendicosi,* or "Avengers" (see note 753), and much later, in the eighteenth century, the shadowy brotherhood in Palermo apocryphally called the *Beati Paoli.*

Certain orders of chivalry founded for aristocrats by the Angevins of Naples very much resembled noble companies superficially; here an early example was the Order of the Knot (described in the Conclusion). Unlike confraternities and noble companies, which could be established in an autonomous fashion and later confirmed by bishops or the crown, orders of chivalry, which conferred the rank of knight, could be founded only by the monarch, acting as the kingdom's fount of honor.

EPILOGUE

The years immediately following the last Hohenstaufen reign saw a reorganization of the kingdom's government, even if the existing system of law and justiciars was not immediately disturbed. Transferring certain offices from Palermo to Naples was part of this, but the process was not so unsettling as might be imagined. The essential chancery had always traveled with the king, and during Manfred's reign much of the intellectual life of the kingdom had gravitated toward Naples and Salerno, and to some degree even Messina.

In 1267, Charles of Anjou signed the Treaty of Viterbo with Baldwin II of Constantinople, the ousted Latin claimant to the recently-restored Byzantine Empire. Ever since 1261, forces in the papacy had hoped to reseat Baldwin on his throne, and Manfred had considered a "crusade" to accomplish that objective, partly to earn papal favor. Now, as part of the treaty, Charles even betrothed one of his daughters to Baldwin's son.

In Tunisia, Muhammad al-Mustansir no longer considered himself bound by the treaties the Hafsids had made with the Hohenstaufens. This obviously affected trade and eliminated the taxes long remitted to the King of Sicily. At the same time, the Angevin policy toward the kingdom's Muslims was now becoming altogether more aggressive than what had existed until 1266, a policy actively encouraged by the pope, acting through the dogmatic Dominicans.

While Charles attempted to suppress the remaining Muslims of the *Regnum*, his brother, Louis, contemplated a crusade to northern Africa.

The Dominicans, who so fervently wanted to integrate the Muslims and Jews into the Catholic population, were themselves reintegrated into the kingdom, where they eventually became its most influential religious order. A Latin monoculture dominated life.

In 1270, Louis led the Eighth Crusade to Ifriqiya. Frederick of Castile took this opportunity to fight against the French king. This campaign, the so-called "Tunisian Crusade," ultimately failed with the death of Louis on August twenty-fifth just as a relief force led by Charles arrived at Tunis.[1274]

The heart of King Louis was deposited at Monreale in conciliation to the Palermitans, who much lamented the loss of their city's status as a royal capital (see note 31). Charles himself reclaimed diplomatic and commercial rights for the kingdom through the Treaty of Tunis signed with Muhammad al-Mustansir in November; this also included agreements with France and Navarre.

By 1271, Charles was making inroads into the Balkans, and particularly Albania. This occupation was to prove ephemeral. His true objective, Constantinople, was elusive. At the Second Council of Lyon, in 1272, the papacy made serious efforts to heal the rift of the Great Schism, an effort that failed.

The next decade saw more pacific government on the peninsula than in Sicily, where there was baronial unrest if little open rebellion.

A good number of French were brought to the kingdom, where they were appointed as governors and justiciars. A famous case was that of John of Saint Rémy, the high justiciar for Val di Mazara. Exceptionally, he had a reputation among the Palermitans for being kind and fair, but most appointees behaved like "commissars" in a conquered country. This lent certain parts of the kingdom the aura of an occupied nation.

Charles proceeded to lay plans for an invasion of what remained of the Byzantine Empire. At home, he attempted, with some success, to forge the kingdom into an "Angevin" state.[1275] Both efforts were torn asunder in 1282 by the War of the Vespers. The expedition to Constantinople was scrapped, while the island of Sicily seceded from the peninsular part of the kingdom.[1276]

In its traditional telling, the Vespers revolt was initiated on Easter Monday, March thirtieth, near the Holy Spirit church outside Palermo's city walls when an Angevin soldier molested a local woman. Her husband and some other men present attacked the soldier and his companions, who may have been drunk, and chaos quickly enveloped the city, soon spreading across the island. Other accounts suggest a conspiracy organized by John of Procida.

Whatever spark ignited it, the uprising was immediately exploited by an embittered, vindictive baronage full of Ghibelline sympathizers.

United by a singular fury, the frenzied populace killed French men and women wherever they could be found. Even monasteries were not immune to this communal rage, and French monks and nuns were murdered in cold blood. It was necessary to unmask the foreigners, so the revolutionaries quickly devised a simple linguistic test. Those suspected of being French were ordered to pronounce the Sicilian word *ciciri,* for chickpea. Any Frenchman unable to pronounce it with an acceptably Sicilian accent instantly sealed his fate, and perhaps that of his wife and children.

Charles was incredulous. Pope Martin IV, a Frenchman of Angevin sympathies, was equally stupefied. The reports arriving from Sicily were shocking, inexplicable.

In September of 1282, King Peter III of Aragon was proclaimed King of

Sicily based on the fact of his wife, Constance, being the daughter of Manfred. In a series of battles at sea and skirmishes on land, the Angevin forces were defeated by Aragonese-Sicilian ones. Some of the fighting took place on the peninsula.

In April of the following year, Queen Constance arrived at Messina with her children and John of Procida, who Peter named chancellor.[1277]

Frederick's descendants had returned.

In one of the war's memorable "non-events," Charles and Peter were to meet for a duel to decide the fate of Sicily, each accompanied by a hundred fighting knights. This was to take place in June 1283, at Bordeaux, capital of the neutral French territories of Edward, King of England.[1278] Each warring king agreed to appear with his suite but it was tacitly understood that each would arrive at a different time. Then each sovereign claimed that the other was a coward. Most of the military engagements were more serious than this charade, but not much more decisive.

In a significant incident, King Charles' son and heir, Charles "the Lame," was taken prisoner by Roger of Lauria during a naval battle near Naples in June 1284 and held in the citadel of Cefalù.

By the time King Charles died early the next year, Angevin power in Sicily had all but vanished. His son, now Charles II, was still a prisoner, and the papacy was at first reluctant even to recognize him as the late monarch's heir. In the event, Pope Martin himself died a few months after the elder Charles.

In a gesture of alliance with his Angevin cousins, Philip III of France attacked Aragon, but his army was quickly defeated, as much by malaria as by force of arms, thus ending the "Aragonese Crusade."

All the key players were dead by the end of 1285: Charles I of Anjou, Philip III of France, Peter III of Aragon, Pope Martin IV.

Attempts to end the war resulted in several ineffective treaties, notably those of Tarascon in 1291 and Anagni in 1295.

Charles II definitively suppressed the subaltern Lucerans in 1300. Many Muslims were converted, a few deported and a good number killed. This was the effective end of organized Islam in southern Italy.[1279]

Finally, in 1302, the year of Constance's death, the Peace of Caltabellotta officially ended two decades of conflict, even if disputes continued. As there were now two rival claimants to the throne of the Kingdom of Sicily, there were two "Sicilies," the island ruled from Palermo by the Aragonese and the mainland ruled from Naples by the Angevins. These states eventually became known as the kingdoms of (respectively) Sicily and Naples, in view of a treaty definitively ending the hostilities in 1372.

Though some kings, especially those from Spain, would coincidentally rule both realms at the same time in a "personal union," sometimes employing the name "Two Sicilies" in royal decrees (see Appendix 7), political reunification was achieved formally only in 1816.

Serfdom, one of the things that distinguished manorialism, disappeared in southern Italy, and in most of western Europe, in the middle of the fourteenth century as the result of two catastrophic events that left fewer people alive to farm the land, thus affording serfs more freedom to leave the estates to which they were attached. An exceptionally terrible famine swept the continent beginning in 1315. Next, the bubonic plague pandemic known as the "Black Death," which arrived in Sicily in 1347, claimed many millions of lives. Even if the plague tended to spread more rapidly in populated centers such as cities, its aftermath saw an increase in the number of people seeking to live in urban areas.

Certain religious orders continued their ascent to power. The Dominicans, in particular, came to predominate monastic life into the nineteenth century. That has all but disappeared; the large monastery the order founded at Taormina is now a luxurious grand hotel.

While the Benedictines were regarded as a pillar of western monasticism, the Dominicans, who eventually founded many schools, came to be associated with the zealous defense of the Catholic faith and even the Inquisition. Later, the Jesuits, who also founded schools, were known for supporting Catholicism against the Reformation. The humble Franciscans and Poor Clares preached among the people.

The kingdom's mystique was scarcely forgotten. In the literary sphere, we find a metrical romance, *King Robert of Sicily,* making its way into several European vernaculars, including English, in the decades before 1400.

The Norman-Swabian era, a time so important for Europe and the Mediterranean, is part of the people of the former kingdom.

Conclusion
THE LIVING KINGDOM

It is instinctive to wonder what we should learn from history. Beyond education, even enlightenment, history is worth contemplating for the simple purpose of knowing something about our past. That is our right.

The legacy of the Norman-Swabian Kingdom of Sicily brings us a few lessons but transcends any simple, universal "meaning." Here there are many truths. Though, as we have seen, Arab, Lombard and Byzantine families ruled monarchies in southern Italy, it was the Normans who erected a sovereign kingdom that eventually spawned a complex ethnogenesis, and with it a true sense of statehood, even nationhood.

In the former *Regnum,* as elsewhere in Europe and in the world, there exists a certain "philosophy" of ethnic identity based on collective cultural memory. Naturally, there are various interpretations of what such a philosophy is, or what it should be. Yet the belief that there is a *right* to express ethnic identity, and the prerogative to a view of the history that informs it, is generally accepted in free societies today.

Carl Jung identified what he called the "collective unconscious," broadly defined as an inherited commonality of all people beyond the conscious level. In our times such a theory might well be seen as abstract, but it is at least reasonable, descriptive of essential values and even ethics. *Napoletanità* and *Sicilianità* are more social than psychological, linked to a collective sense of self-perception and self-identity over many centuries.

Although its true socio-cultural exceptionalism, or "uniqueness," ended with the extinction of the Hohenstaufen dynasty, the *Regnum* and its sundry social developments contributed a great deal to the collective *personality* of the people of southern Italy during the successive centuries unto our times. Were this element absent from our history, those of us having roots in this fascinating region would not be who we are. The *Regnum* was the cornerstone for much of what has existed into the modern era. It may be thought of as one *stratum* among many *strata* of history, similar to a layer in a multi-layered cake.

Since ethnic and national identity are not static, and because the medieval record is far from complete, it is sometimes difficult to discern the existing elements inherited from the Middle Ages, much less those that have spanned millennia to survive from antiquity. At Siracusa, the cathedral dedicated to the *Theotokos,* the virgin mother of God, was built upon the standing structure of the temple of Athena, a virgin goddess venerated by the Greeks. Whether the greater number of the city's first Christians distinguished very clearly between the two is a matter of debate.

An everyday example of a modern practice that survives from medieval times can be seen during the celebration of mass in certain Catholic churches in small towns in Sicily, Calabria and Basilicata. This is the congregants' raising of both arms, palms facing forward, during prayer, rather than simply folding the hands together; this variation of the *orans* posture is a very old Greek custom popularized at the dawn of Christianity. If Saint Paul prayed when he visited southern Italy, this is how he did it, for the outstretched arms and open hands "reaching up to God" originated with Hebrew prayer. The folded-hands position popular in parts of western Europe by the Middle Ages probably began as a sign of servility associated with Roman slaves or shackled prisoners.

If generally overlooked by historians, the magical sword of Roger II and Sicily's mystical chestnut tree are medieval elements of the literary culture of the *Regnum* of the kind found in kingdoms elsewhere in Europe.[1280] Another is Adenolfo of Pontecorvo, the "Robin Hood" figure mentioned in these pages (see note 753). Overlapping poetry such as the *Chanson d'Aspremont* and Cielo's *Contrasto,* this is part of what makes the medieval culture of southern Italy distinctive and unique.

Like magical Mikalis, the apocryphal legend of King Roger's "Knights of the Golden Chain," an order of chivalry that probably never existed, may have been part of an attempt to imitate the essential elements of the tales of King Arthur (here the Knights of the Round Table). Yet the very creation of such legends reflects a quest to assert a defining monarchical identity for the people, something that might survive over the centuries. This is significant when we consider that these legends were likely formulated *after* the Norman-Swabian era, as if to commemorate our early kings by embellishing their legacy in the popular mind. The notion of the Rogerian "Golden Chain" parallels the inception of knightly court orders such as England's Order of the Garter, founded in 1348, inspired by Arthurian legend (see note 366) and the romanticized ideals of chivalry then in vogue.

In the "twin kingdoms," an early example of such an institution was the Order of the Knot founded by King Louis I of Naples in 1352. In 1381, another Angevin monarch, Charles "the Short" of Durazzo, who was briefly king of both Naples and Hungary, founded the Order of the Ship; its insignia was the image of a galley suspended within an anchor, and for a short time its

CONCLUSION

"chapel" was the Basilica of Saint Nicholas in Bari, its knights being expected to follow the Rule of Saint Basil. The Order of the Ermine was founded by King Ferrante I Trastámara of Naples in 1464; this was dedicated to Saint Michael the Archangel. Its insignia was the figure of an ermine, or stoat, representing fealty, suspended from a chain. The motto of this ephemeral order, inspired by an order of the same name bestowed by the Duke of Brittany, was *Malo mori quam foedari* (Better death than dishonor). The same Neapolitan sovereign bestowed the Order of the Urn, *l'Ordine della Giara*.

Southern Italy boasts at least thirty centuries of clearly delineated history, and monarchy is the political system that has most shaped our society. That is true in most of Europe. With a few notable exceptions, such as Venice and San Marino, the greater number of Europe's republics emerged quite recently, since the eighteenth century, France being the quintessential example.

The mystique of kingship and queenship was part of the Norman-Swabian ascendancy. Certain traditions, institutions, and even rituals, distinguish major royal monarchies, such as that of the *Regnum,* from lesser monarchies and other forms of nationhood and government. Beyond the written word and some lasting traditions, history has bequeathed us contemporaneous royal images in the form of everything from coins to mosaics to illuminations.

Coronation (see Appendix 5) reflected a quasi-mystical transformation affecting not only the monarch or consort being crowned but the state itself, which thenceforth became associated with a new ruler. Feudal and knightly investiture came to be integral elements of medieval monarchy. That these rites were long regarded as something akin to sacraments says much of their significance.[1281]

More generally, our Norman-Swabian centuries coincided with an evolution in Catholicism substantial enough to define western Christianity into our time, even in the formation of the first Protestant churches.

A parallel development was a sense that individual, or personal, identity was something real and significant (see note 468). In viewing the lives of medieval persons and events, some commentators wander into the realm of "presentism," judging people or situations of the past by today's values and mores. While we may well make occasional comparisons regarding certain monarchs, humanists and scientists as people ahead of their time, it is best to view their lives through the prism of the era in which they lived.

Only the people in the kingdom can determine the manner in which they define and appreciate their own monarchical history. The sixteenth century and the popularity of printing witnessed the arrival of major general histories by Thomas Fazello (1498-1570) in Palermo and, in Naples, Angelo Di Costanzo (1507-1591) and Giovanni Antonio Summonte (1538-1602). Each of these historians entertained definite ideas about the connection of the identity of the people to that of the state.[1282]

This, of course, was intertwined with the institution of absolute monarchy. It was in the nineteenth century that constitutions were seriously contemplated in the "twin kingdoms" of Naples and Sicily, reunited as the Kingdom of the Two Sicilies (see Appendix 7).

Today, Italy's socio-cultural-political "regionalism" is as tangible as ever, but the value Italians place on history can be contemplated only in the context of the nation's complex social fabric. One of the reasons it was so difficult to unify "Italy" during the nineteenth century, and into the twentieth, is because most parts of it, such as Tuscany, Veneto and the Two Sicilies, were characterized by very distinctive cultures that had existed for countless centuries, seemingly since time immemorial. Europe is full of "regions" endowed with their own social cultures: Catalonia, Navarre, Bavaria, Scotland.

No extended consideration of the current ethnic identity of southern Italians can ignore the recent political developments that have colored the discussion. Despite nineteenth-century attempts to conglomerate what is now Italy, whose very name Klemens von Metternich famously described as little more than a "geographical expression," into a nation, true nationalists are a rarity. Public, state-sponsored festivities, such as those celebrating unification, attract very few citizens. Many parades are attended only by the participants and a handful of curious bystanders. The veterans of Italy's last war were never accorded much esteem. Liberation Day, observed on April twenty-fifth, is little more than a pretext for picnics and cynical observations about "the only country that celebrates its own defeat." By comparison, traditional religious festivals, such as those commemorating the heavenly patrons of Naples and Palermo, are true celebrations that attract thousands. This transcends *campanilismo,* attachment to one's locality. It represents a link to the medieval past.

These identities are not found only among "native" Italians. There exists a "diasporic" population of those descended from ancestors who emigrated from southern Italy, perhaps generations ago. Many of these descendants, such as those present in the Americas, preserve ethnic traditions known in the land of their forebears. An obvious example is the observation of the feast of San Gennaro in New York, where it is marked by a festival (see note 1254).

In the sphere of living history, as we have seen, much has come to us from our Norman-Swabian era in art, architecture, language and cuisine, along with some legal and theological precepts and even a few words, such as *admiral.*

A number of folk customs linked to religious traditions originated in the Middle Ages. For example, bonfires of dried branches marked the Assumption, or Dormition, of Mary so that the rising smoke would make it easier for her to ascend into Heaven.

Some traditions that seem medieval are modern revivals. The *palio* tournament at Piazza Armerina was instituted in the twentieth century, and even the one held at Siena dates only from the seventeenth. The marionettes seen in plays depicting the story of Roland and his knights were popularized after 1700.

In southern Italy, the most recent effort to overtly resist the authority of the centralized state ruled from Rome occurred during the twentieth century in time of war.[1283] More recently, there has been resistance to cultural appropriation when foreigners attempt to introduce their "interpretations" of the history and culture of southern Italy.[1284]

Various social and political phenomena are associated with ethnic identity.

CONCLUSION

"Identity politics," as that term is usually defined, relates to the status of a minority *ethnie* in a larger, perhaps multiethnic, society.[1285] This was descriptive of the Christians in Palermo in 1072, the Muslims of the *Regnum* in 1250, and the Jews of the "twin kingdoms" into the fifteenth century. Thus the dawn of the modern era found southern Italy essentially homogeneous.

Beyond its political connotation as "the authority and control over a state or territory," the term *sovereignty* can describe the proprietary right of a nation, people or *ethnie* over its identity and heritage. This may be termed "cultural sovereignty."[1286] It is a suitable paradigm for considering the status of a people as the heirs of a medieval legacy in a modern era that finds personal, ethnic (and even national) identity under threat.

Here in southern Italy, there exist certain "Siculo-Neapolitan" perspectives of our Norman-Swabian era. Internationally, there are highly eclectic views about it.

Whether or not it reflects sound reasoning in every instance, revisionism is a normal part of the writing of history. It's understandable that views have changed since the days of Fazello, Di Costanzo and Summonte, and today we find historians attempting to distinguish themselves for "originality" by challenging even the most essential facts.[1287]

A general awareness of history relies upon the diffusion of information about it. Twenty-first century technology has made this easier than ever. Even so, except for academic papers (journal articles) and slender monographs, rather little work by history scholars from southern Italy finds its way into English. In English-language publications, that reality has left many topics, indeed entire fields, vulnerable to the misperceptions (or misrepresentations) of Anglophone scholars, even where modern history is concerned.[1288]

The best generalist works to consider the medieval identity of the people of southern Italy as it is perceived and understood today emanate from the former *Regnum,* being the fruit of the efforts of authors who, as natives, are intimately familiar with what our society has inherited from the past. Here there has been occasional revisionism.[1289]

Theories of ethnic identity paradigms abound.[1290] An ethnic or national identity is much more than a label or "brand." Yet, as was stated in the Introduction, each *ethnie* has its own "aesthetic," while history is an integral, if incorporeal, part of ethnic and national heritage. However, even if we extol its virtues, characterizing an entire society is an exercise fraught with pitfalls; to advance generalizations risks sowing the seeds for stereotypes.

There's an old saying that when two Italians enter a room and engage in debate, they leave with three opinions. Academia isn't much different. Asking five historians to formulate the "correct" or "appropriate" view of the merits, character and legacy of the Kingdom of Sicily will yield at least five different responses. While there can not be one "canonical" or "correct" view about the reign of a particular dynasty, the positions presented in the preceding chapters generally reflect those that you are likely to encounter most frequently here in the former *Regnum*.

Whether there exists a true model or "philosophy" of southern Italian identity might well be debated. Yet certain political trends of the twenty-first century suggest that, at the very least, a few identifiable tendencies emerge from time to time.[1291]

What is sometimes called *expressionism* is the personal or "psychological" impact of events or trends on people beyond what is usually reflected in a written account. This aspect of social (as opposed to purely political) history touches emotions and perceptions, and hence ethnic self-identity. It is typical of narratives that seek to explore meaningful insights into history, such as the forces motivating the actions of kings and queens and the behavior of ordinary citizens. This complements, or even completes, our knowledge of people and events. It fosters empathy, adding to the pattern and form of history's indelible story while affording us a means to avoid presuppositions. Expressionism reflects a story, but not necessarily the only story, of a people and its ethnic (or national) culture.[1292] It has been argued that the memoir of John of Procida, who was present at the Battle of Benevento, is an early precursor of this.[1293]

In Italy, reference works and school texts often define the country's constituent parts (regions) by the social culture, or *perceived* social culture, of the state founded in 1861 and reconstituted in 1946. Neither the identity of the former *Regnum,* nor that of its modern successor, the Kingdom of the Two Sicilies (see Appendix 7), relies on the cultures of other parts of what is now Italy. Although the "Italianist" approach is legitimate for comparison and context, the testimony of the *Regnum* must be viewed apart from, even in contrast to, later developments such as Tuscan poetry and the Renaissance.

A people has an inalienable right to its own history, not something imposed upon it by coercion or sufferance.[1294]

Knowledge of history can be edifying. While the dignity of a people is rooted largely in its collective historical identity, the dignity of an individual can be edified by consciously belonging to an *ethnie*. In our times, the increasing interest in family history (genealogy) among the descendants of southern Italians reflects an obvious curiosity about ancestry. This is nothing like the Shinto veneration of ancestors, but here there exists a link between past and present that seems to be expressed more explicitly, and perhaps more willingly, than what we encounter elsewhere in Italy. Indeed, it is not unusual for an ordinary family in southern Italy, and especially Sicily, to trace a precise, generation by generation lineage to 1500, something which in most countries is possible only among the aristocracy.[1295]

The degree to which an individual's ancestral (natal) *ethnie* is, or should be, part of a personal identity evokes discussion in certain circles.[1296]

The affinity for familial history over national history is common to the people of most societies. In southern Italy, where this phenomenon is particularly evident, it partly explains why modern nationalist movements, such as Fascism, were never embraced very adamantly by most of the citizenry. It also suggests reasons why there is very little overt "patriotism," in contradistinction to ethnic pride, in Italy today.[1297]

More obvious to the general public are the festivals mentioned elsewhere. Given the importance of the medieval Kingdom of Sicily as a place visited by those from around Europe and the Mediterranean, it is unsurprising that foreign saints are the focus of some of these observances.[1298]

Ethnic identity cannot be viewed as something extrinsic to social history. It was the church that ensured the continuation of many traditions, including a fair number based on the lives or martyrdom of saints who lived in antiquity.[1299] The populace wholeheartedly embraced such things, for there were few other public festivals of note except for such events as celebrations marking good harvests and changes of the seasons. The "secular" (diocesan) clergy was highly respected.[1300]

Today, only a fraction of those having roots in the *Regnum* live in southern Italy. By 1880, the hardships imposed by Italian unification prompted mass emigration (see Appendix 7), seeding a "diaspora" of descendants from medieval ancestors that now spans generations. Naturally, the profundity of identification with this heritage varies by individual, but it is a birthright.[1301]

This remains relevant because, apart from shaping one's opinions about the past, ethnic identities go a long way in determining an individual's beliefs, values, behavior and aspirations. This begins in childhood, when an individual begins to identify as part of a group based on ancestral identity.[1302]

Very distant influences upon the kingdom are difficult to ascertain. It was Muslim traders who introduced paper making from China and Hindu-Arabic numerals from India, and facilitated references to Sicily in Chinese literature (see note 947). It was this extensive trading network that brought a knowledge of creatures such as the Komodo dragon and the cockatoo to the *Regnum*.[1303]

A few cynical commentators view our current knowledge of the Middle Ages as something of a "revival," as if it were somehow long forgotten, and indeed a renewed interest in that era was fostered in the eighteenth century (see Appendix 7). However, while most ordinary people in southern Italy knew little, if anything, about such things as the chronicle of Hugh Falcandus or the Constitutions of Melfi until the twentieth century, a general knowledge of our medieval history was always present, if only because of visual testaments like Monreale's abbey and various churches and castles in the former *Regnum,* and the existence of a Siculo-Neapolitan kingdom until 1860. The presence of ancient temples at Paestum, Agrigento and Segesta, and the society represented by them, was scarcely a secret, even to people who had never heard of the books written by Fazello, Di Costanzo and Summonte.[1304] In other words, many people of the former Kingdom of Sicily require little, if any, prodding to see the relevance of our Middle Ages.

To neglect the medieval era is to neglect a part of ourselves.

Identity formation — or ethnogenesis — is nothing if not complex. One need not accept the reductive view advocated by Hegel, among others, that a people exists chiefly for the purpose of establishing a state, but statehood is certainly an important, if sometimes unplanned, result of ethnogenesis.[1305]

The preceding chapters deal with monarchy as part of ethnic identity and the guarantor of statehood (and eventually nationhood), a paradigm thought by some scholars to have originated many millennia ago in tribal societies. Yet the conservation of ethnic identity is not intrinsically linked to a particular form of leadership or government. What is important is that the people and their rights are genuinely represented in a tangible way. When Frederick II transferred Sicily's Muslims to Lucera, he guaranteed them the practice of their religion, the use of their language, and local rule by their own emirs.

Ethnicity and ethnicities can thrive in a republic, where the potential for fanatical nationalism is just as real as it is in a monarchy, obvious parallel examples being monarchical Italy and republican Germany, with their infamous fascist movements, before and during the Second World War. The ignoble actions of the Italians and Germans epitomized the potential danger that the majority *ethnie* of a polycultural society might suppress, or even extinguish, an ethnic minority.[1306]

Whatever form of government is present, authenticity is key, with the people writing their own history while maintaining their own culture and traditions. It should not be written for them, not by the state in authoritarian fashion and certainly not by "transethnic" foreigners.[1307]

It is significant that, whatever their precise sympathies, some of our most important "local" chroniclers, people such as Godfrey Malaterra and Falco of Benevento, were not men in the employ of the Hautevilles about whom they wrote. They were anything but sycophants. This served to counterbalance the writings of men such as Alexander of Telese and Peter of Eboli, who were, in effect, commissioned to record views favorable to certain rulers whilst disparaging others.

We have seen that an ethnic identity can emerge from several distinct cultures. The present century has witnessed an influx of Asians and Africans into Italy, where they are generally received with greater acceptance in Naples and Palermo than in Milan and Turin. Too many centuries have passed since the times of our medieval forebears to discern a causal effect in today's attitudes, but certain obvious differences between Italy's south and north are rooted in the past.

No society or *ethnie* is truly formed *ex nihilo*. It is born of earlier influences and elements. History is a collective memory.[1308] It is a continuum, almost a form of time travel, for while heroes are mortal, their stories are forever.

A true appreciation of medieval history as part of a collective identity will rely on more than "traditional" study. The fact that we share experiences makes our common past relevant to society now and in the future.[1309]

Individual identity within a group will always present us with challenges in both thought and practice.[1310]

While the preceding chapters do not purport to be a "manifesto" for the identity of the people of the *Regnum* or their modern descendants, this narrative is more mindful than most of that heritage. It recognizes something that can be unseen but never truly lost.

Multidisciplinary as many fields are, it is usually the domain of philosophers, more so than historians, to glean the "truth" from history. Like the chroniclers, couriers and heralds of the Middle Ages, historians convey information that they did not create. Commentary may complement the facts but should not seek to alter their substance.

CONCLUSION

History is an antidote to indifference. It can teach us how to view the past, and how to live the present. The study of history was never meant to be an arcane gnosticism reserved to a privileged few.

The Norman-Swabian age has given us a great deal to consider. It is ours, a precious gift from the people of southern Italy of centuries past to the entirety of humanity living today.

There can be no single, canonical *corpus* of "lessons" from the reigns of Roger II and Frederick II, for views are ever interpretive, contemplative, and often subjective, changing with minds and times; today's zeitgeist is tomorrow's fossilized relic. Naturally, perspectives have changed since Thomas Fazello published his history.[1311]

As long as the Kingdom of Sicily was a multiethnic, multiconfessional society, it was discernibly different from what came later. That aspect of its existence cannot be overlooked, but neither can the emergence of a distinctive Siculo-Neapolitan *ethnie* be ignored, for it too was something different, and retrospective efforts to paint it as generically "Italian" have been less than successful.[1312]

The kingdom's capital city remains interesting, with more medieval sights and sites preserved than one might expect. Not only does Palermo have more standing churches and chapels of the twelfth century than any other city in Europe, the old city itself is an unpolished gem, a diamond in the rough full of visible history.[1313]

The people of the *Regnum* were participants in an unplanned journey. The multicultural kingdom's history is a long moment in time that serves to remind us that, in reality, we are part of something far greater than ourselves.

We are all Normans, Lombards, Greeks, Swabians, Arabs and Berbers. And Christians, Muslims and Jews. Even those of us who have yet to discover it. Knowing something about the past helps us to confront the future.

De peregrino in die lune pasche

Ec est dies est quod hec facta sunt

Qui sunt hii sermones quos confertis ad inuicem ambulantes & estis tristes alleluia alleluia. Et solus peregrinus es in iherusalem & non cognouisti que facta sunt in illa in his diebus, alleluia. Que? De ihesu nazareno qui fuit uir ppheta potens in opere & sermone corum deo & omni populo alleluia alleluia.

O stulti & tardi corde ad credendum in omnibus, his que locuti sunt pphete alleluia. Nonne sic oportuit pati xpistum & ita intrare in gloriam suam alleluia. Cum autem appropinquaret castello quo ibant ipse se finxit longius ire & coegerunt illum ut remaneret cum eis. Mane nobiscum quoniam aduesperascit & inclinata est iam

Chant from a troparium that may have been used as early as 1100 in Palermo, possibly in the first Palatine Chapel

AFTERWORD

Beginning in 2016, the British government made a formal effort to define and popularize the phrase "Global Britain." Amongst its other connotations, this implied Britain's continuing role in the world, particularly in the cultural, commercial and intellectual spheres, despite its withdrawal from certain European treaties and even the increasing challenges confronted by the United Kingdom to uphold its international political position in an ever-changing environment.

The term *Global Siculo-Neapolitan* describes the cultural and social legacy born of the culture and society of the Kingdom of Sicily as this state existed until 1266. Although the concept itself was easier for historians to identify before the demise of Italy's pre-unitary states, such as the Kingdom of the Two Sicilies, in the nineteenth century (see Appendix 7), it has re-emerged in recent times. Today it refers to the influence of the social culture of southern Italy around the world, largely through the diasporas resulting from migration after 1860. While much of this culture is plainly modern, many of its foundational elements, such as those involving language, cuisine and various traditions, are patently medieval.

In the popular mind, this often transcends the generic "Italianism" that some in Italy, including those in officialdom, attempt to promote abroad, because even many non-Italians who may not be too familiar with, for example, the work of Dante, are certainly familiar with lasagna, spaghetti, mozzarella and a few Sicilian and Neapolitan words. Certain medieval arts, such as mosaicry, are part of this dissemination of culture.

Globally, the focus of most of the social culture identified with "Italians" actually pertains to those having roots in the parts of Italy to the south of Tuscany and the Marches. This development may be intrinsically "populist," but it is highly effective. It is far more than an aperçu.

In significant respects, the phenomenon is not unlike the diffusion of the diasporic culture of Judaism that has prospered in the Americas and elsewhere beyond Europe and the Mediterranean. Not every family that originated in southern Italy is Catholic, yet a collective "Catholic culture" predominates even among those who are not. This is a product of our Norman-Swabian era, and especially the thirteenth century. The resurgence of interest in our medieval multicultural, multiconfessional heritage is meaningful and real, but what is experienced daily in Naples and Palermo is the result of a complex ethnogenesis that has left us with a distinct identity that, in a sense, is greater than its Norman, Lombardic, Byzantine and Arab parts.

Integral as it is to the propagation of culture, the written word is just one element among many that facilitates its transmission from generation to generation and place to place. History, such as that presented in the preceding pages, must be recorded for posterity if a memory of it is to survive, but the greatest dissemination of the culture bequeathed us by the past does not come to us from one social or intellectual class. It comes to us from the people generally as part of their collective identity.

If the quintessence of that identity will always be found in southern Italy, it is occasionally expressed, in some measure, in New York, Toronto and Buenos Aires. This is not very different from what has occurred in the global diffusion of many Old World cultures.

History tells us who we were and who we are. At its best, it tells us who we will be. "We know what we are," proclaims Ophelia in *Hamlet*, "but know not what we may be."

To adduce facts and ascertain their effects is merely the most tangible part of the telling of the story. Sometimes we must infer realities and truths from a place just beyond the threshold of our senses, as if from an undiscovered dimension. It is in grasping those elusive elements that our distant past becomes meaningful to our complicated present, and perhaps to the lives of generations yet to be born.

Is significance a constant over time? Clearly, certain values, concepts and institutions considered important in the Middle Ages have changed. In our times, faith, law, spirituality, marriage, and perhaps even love, are very different from what our medieval ancestors knew. Love of our Maker, love of our country, love of our spouse, love of our earthly environment, love of our society and its culture, and love of the eternal precept that whatever unites us is greater than what divides us.

An interest in history reflects love for ourselves. History's indifference to our feelings makes her a difficult companion. But failure to see her means relinquishing any hope of understanding her. History is an Italian woman, at once maiden, goddess, saint, sinner, queen, wife and mother. She is Arethusa, Athena, Agatha and Adelaide. She is kind and wise yet demanding and stern, and rarely transparent. Sometimes, if gently coaxed, she deigns to share a secret or two.

To live without passion is to never have lived at all, for the strength of character is the essence of survival. Those seeking less are contented with the repetition of a few tired clichés and the consumption of yesterday's stale cannolo.

AFTERWORD

The Kingdom of Sicily will always be more than a piece of peninsula and a few wayward islands washed by a sea of complexity.

Whether a few left-over morsels of knowledge from the table of medieval sovereigns is deemed significant many centuries from now cannot be known. Whatever history's lessons may be, curiosity about our antecedents is more than sufficient to justify our best efforts to preserve a few memories of their lives and times, and hence our own.

History is personal, presuming realizations beyond what can be expressed on the page, for here is the timeless continuum of humanity.

The Cubola, a pavilion in Norman-Arab style, survives in Villa Napoli, Palermo, in what was once the Genoard park.

GENEALOGICAL TABLES

KINGDOM OF SICILY

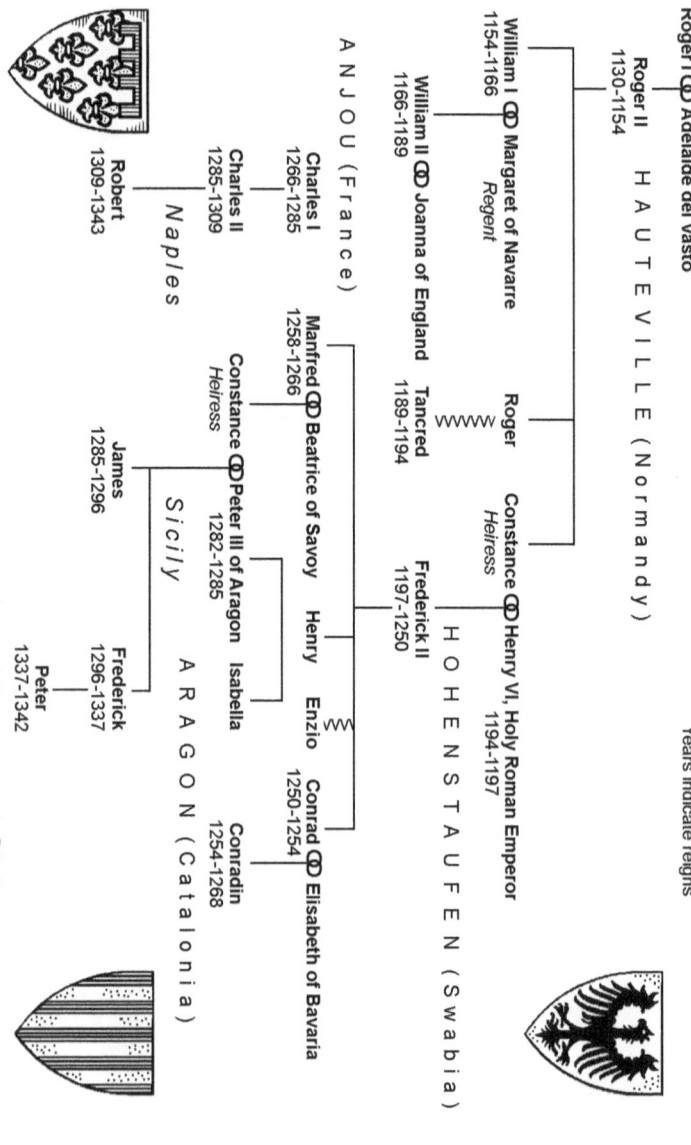

Table 1: Medieval dynasties of the Kingdom of Sicily

GENEALOGICAL TABLES

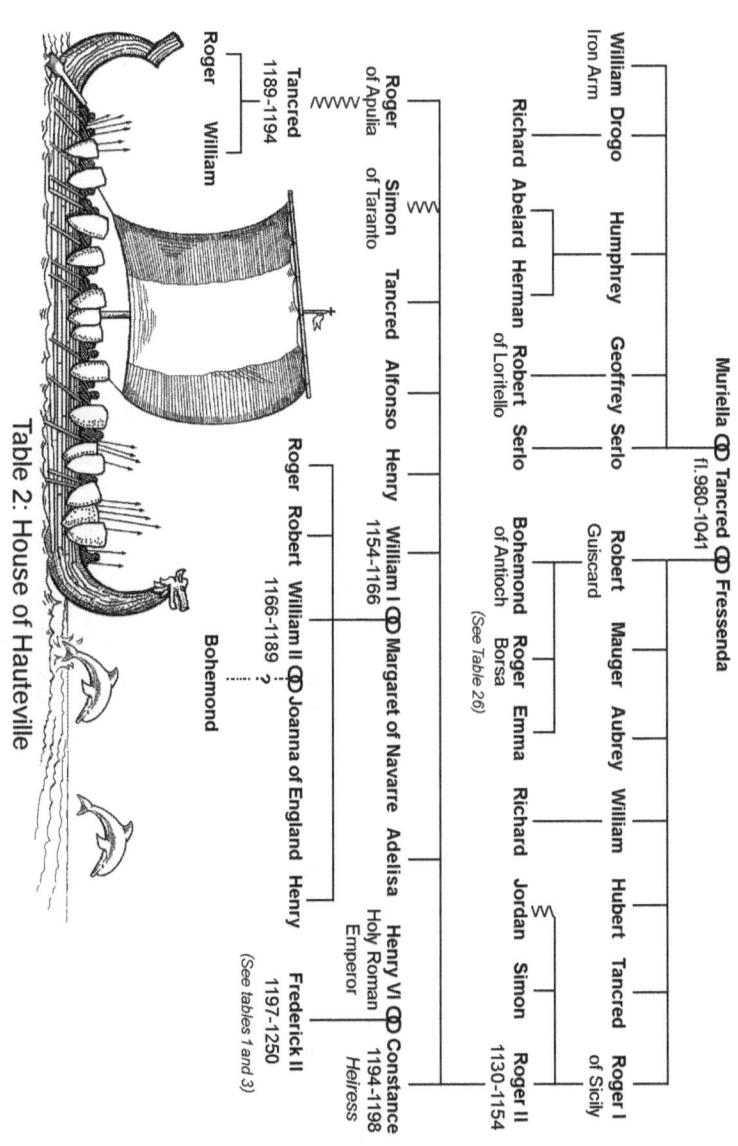

Table 2: House of Hauteville

KINGDOM OF SICILY

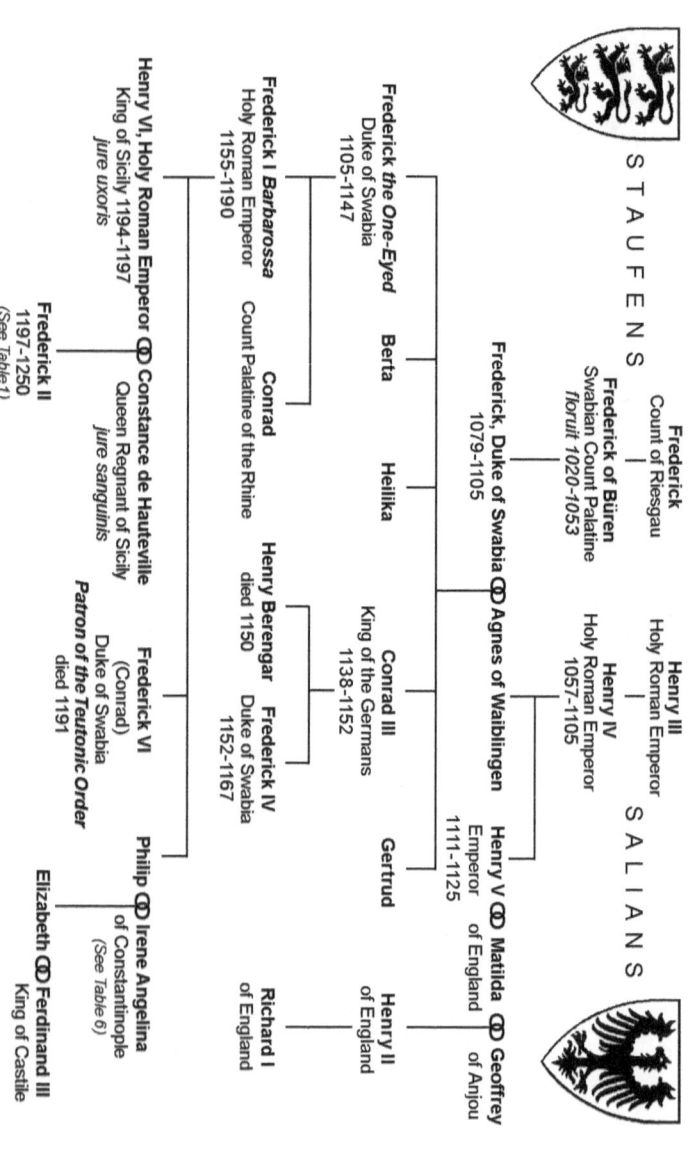

Table 3: Ancestry of Frederick II

GENEALOGICAL TABLES

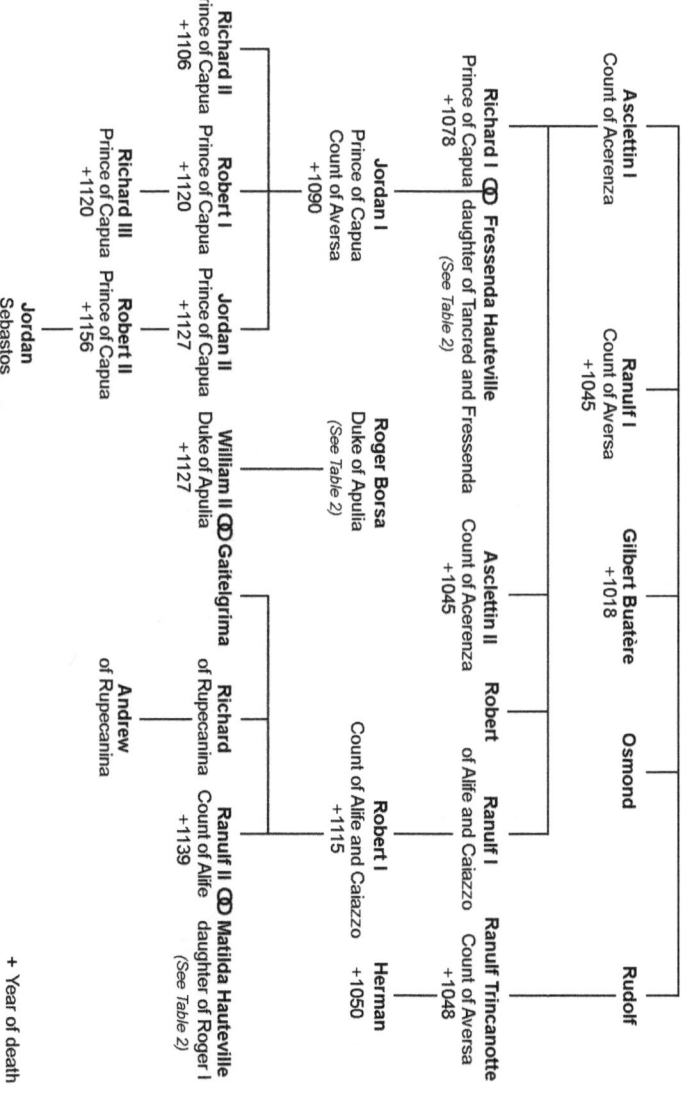

Table 4: Drengot Dynasty of Capua and Aversa

+ Year of death

KINGDOM OF SICILY

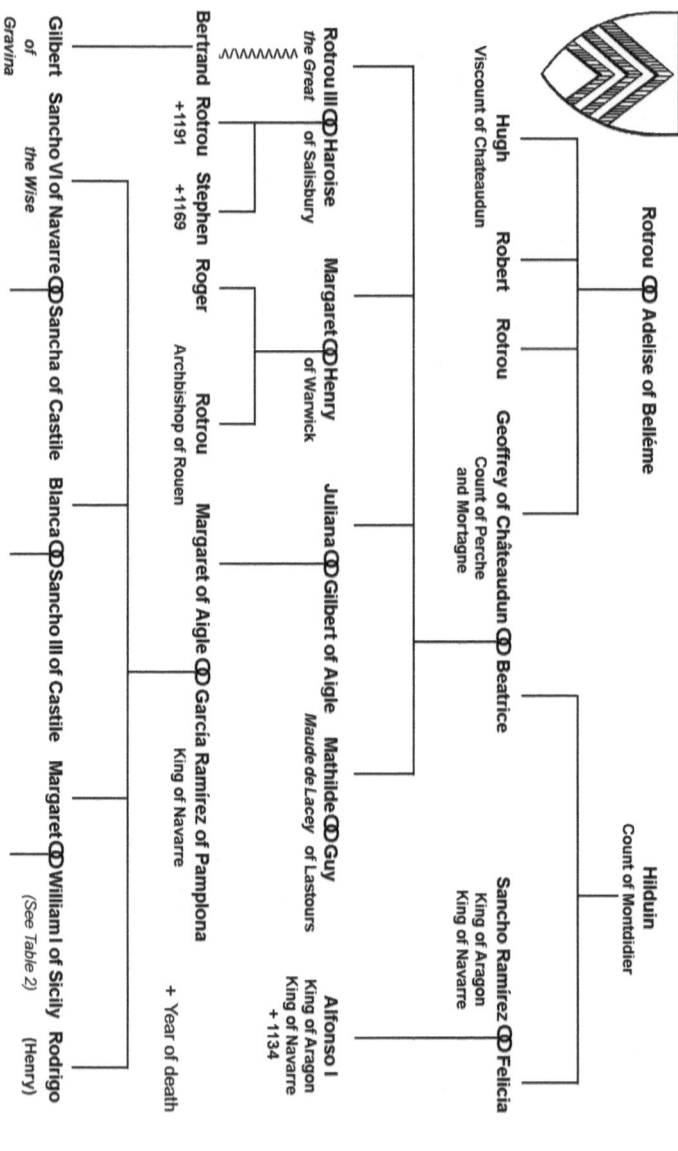

Table 5: Perche Family of Normandy and France

GENEALOGICAL TABLES

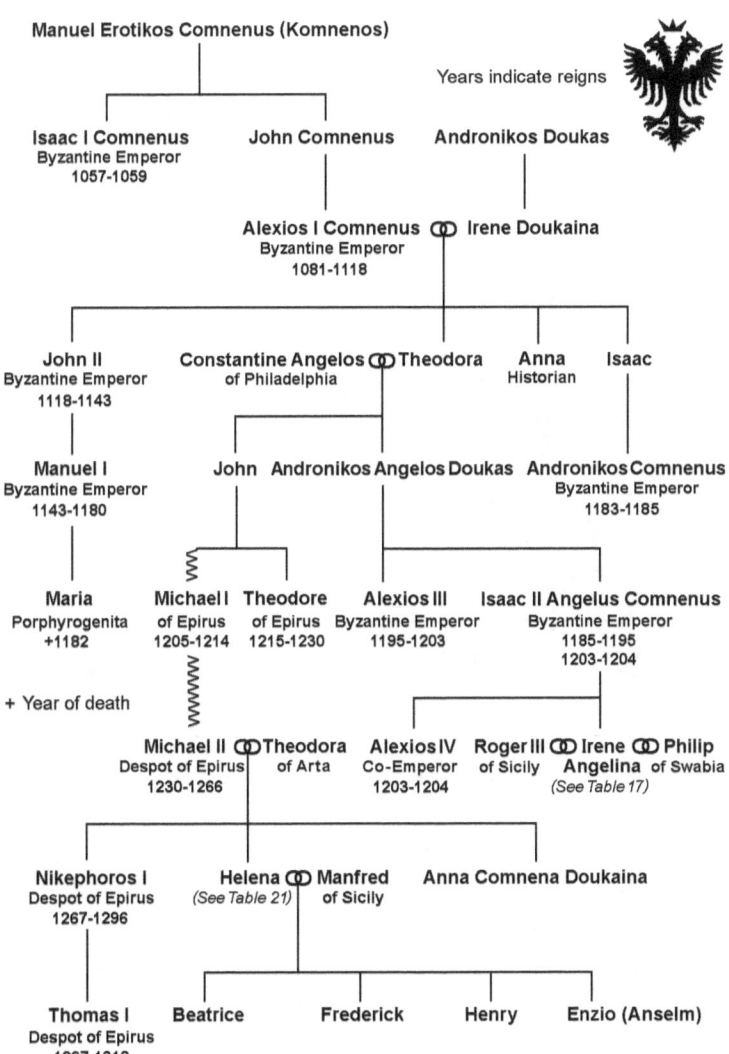

Table 6: House of Angelus Comnenus of Constantinople

KINGDOM OF SICILY

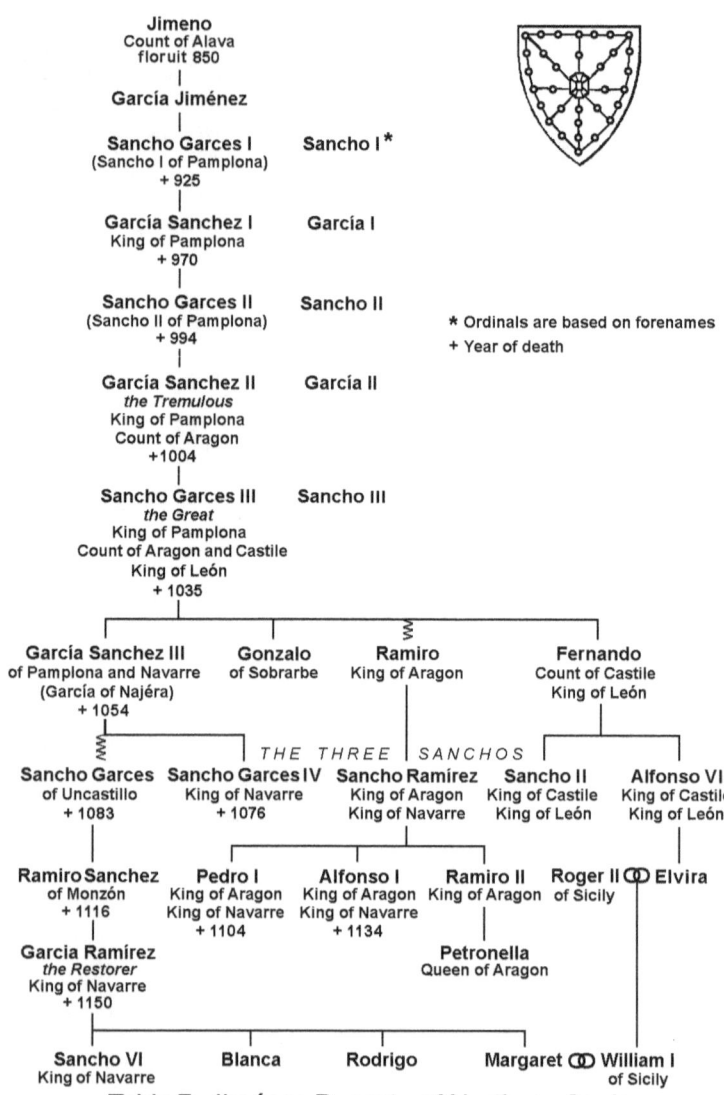

Table 7: Jiménez Dynasty of Northern Spain

GENEALOGICAL TABLES

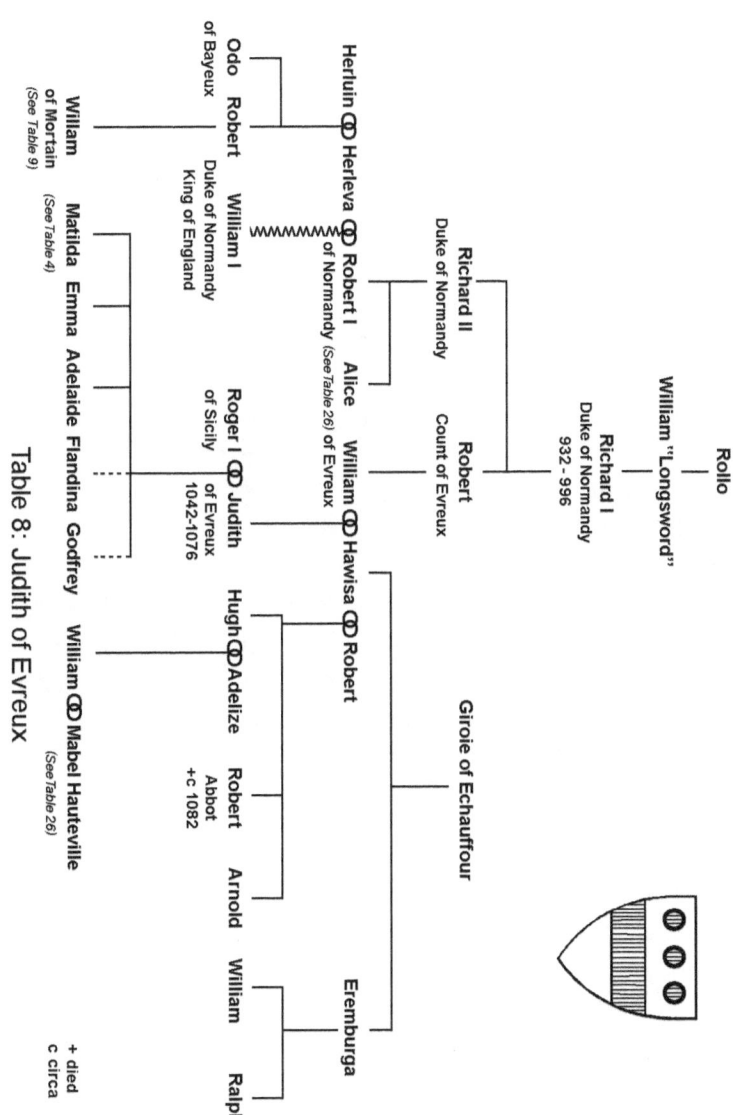

Table 8: Judith of Evreux

+ died
c circa

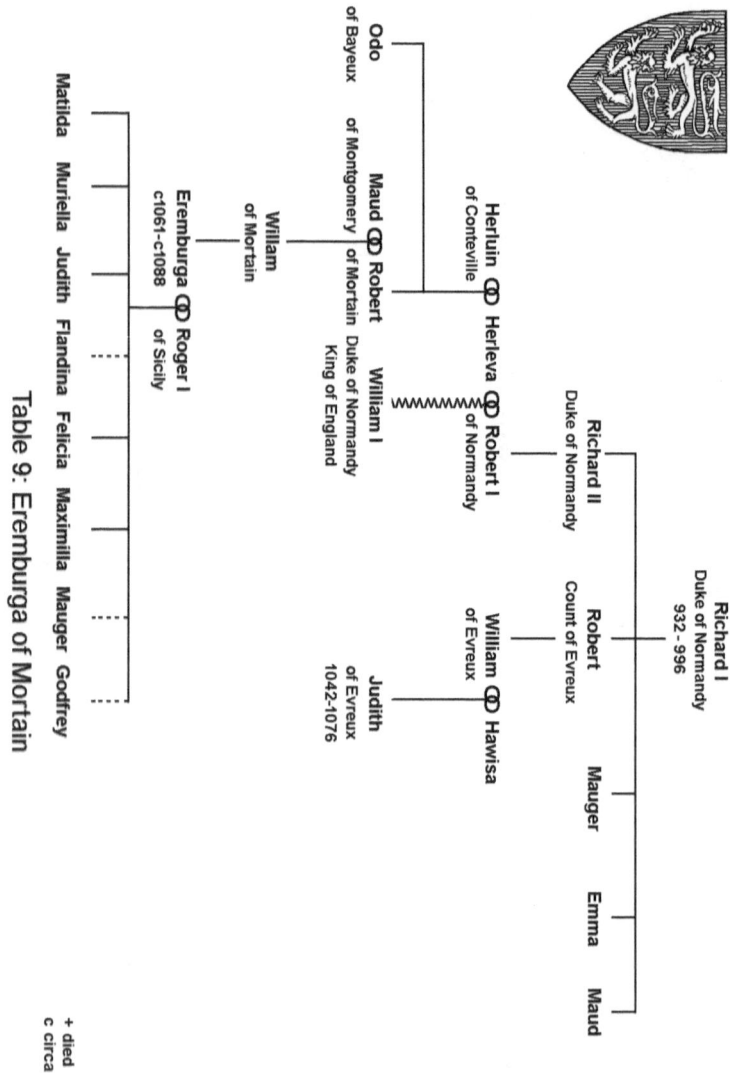

Table 9: Eremburga of Mortain

GENEALOGICAL TABLES

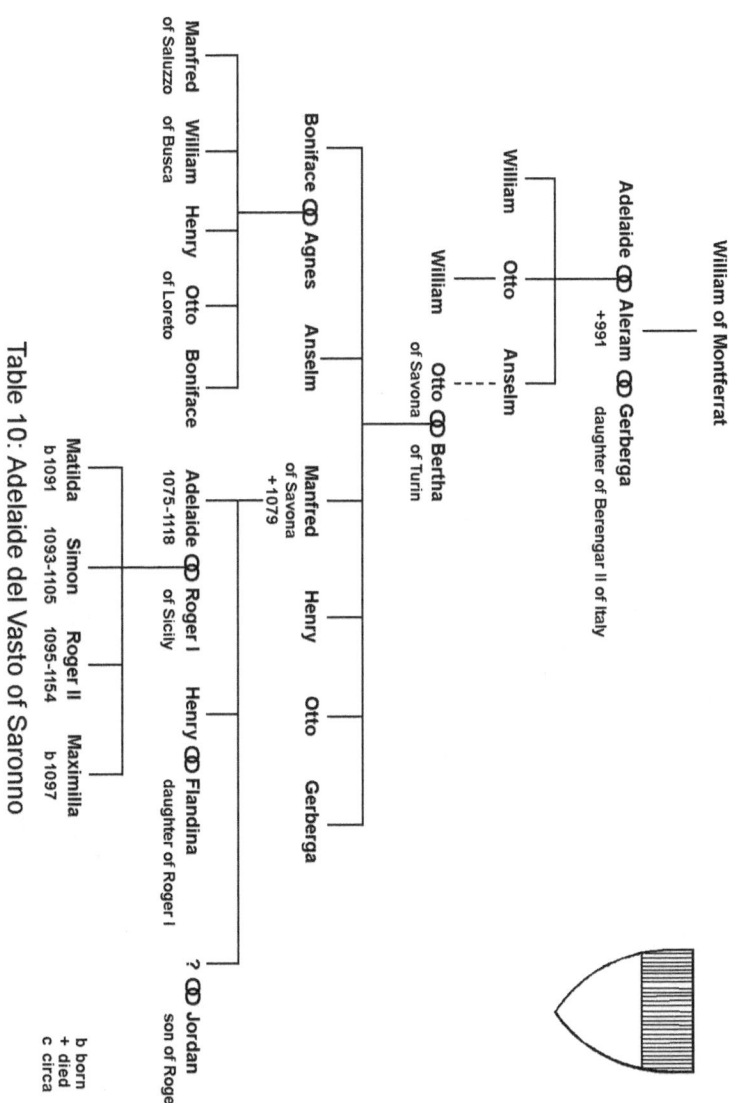

Table 10: Adelaide del Vasto of Saronno

b born
+ died
c circa

KINGDOM OF SICILY

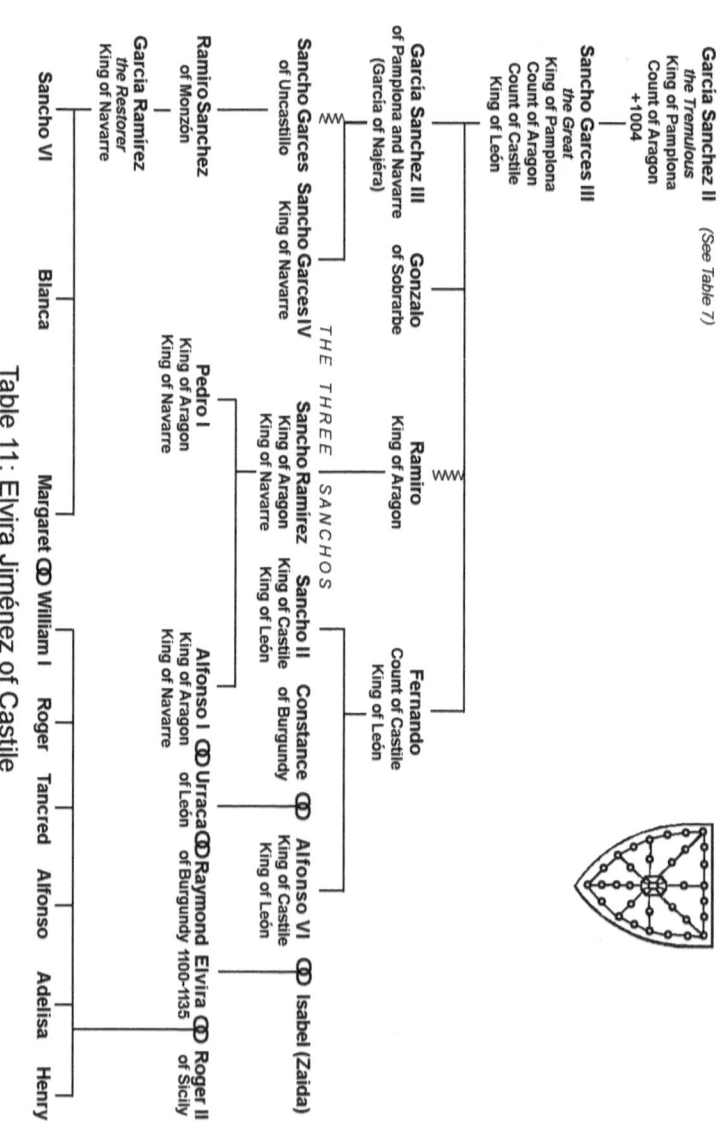

Table 11: Elvira Jiménez of Castile

GENEALOGICAL TABLES

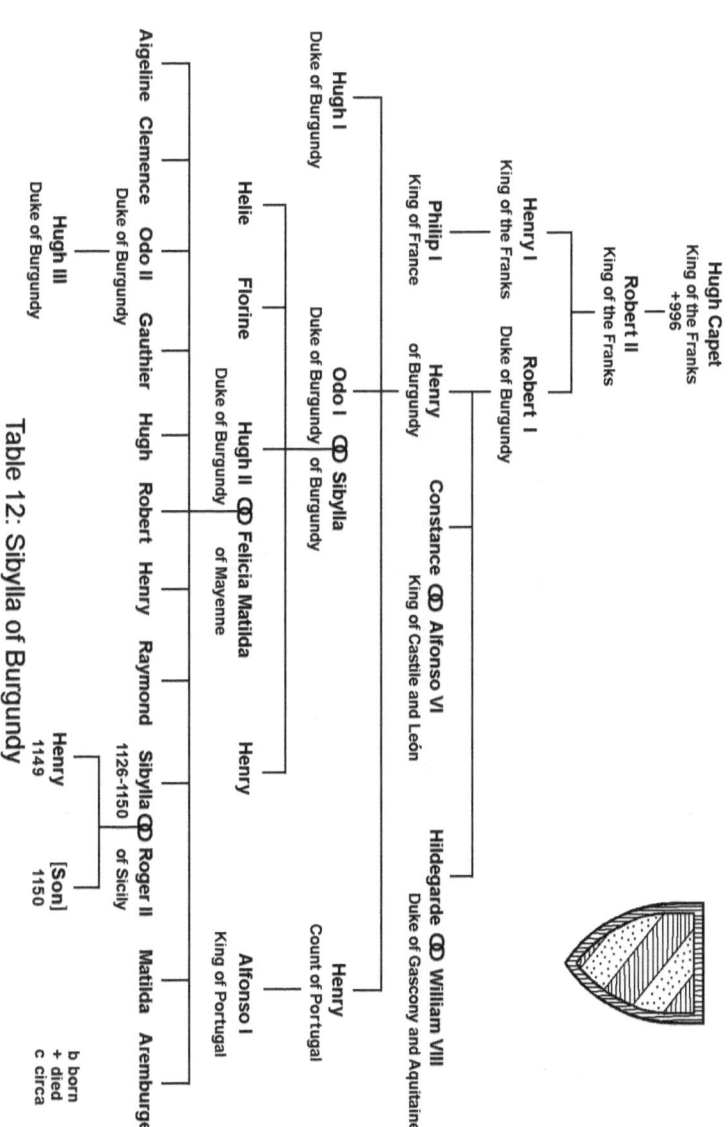

Table 12: Sibylla of Burgundy

KINGDOM OF SICILY

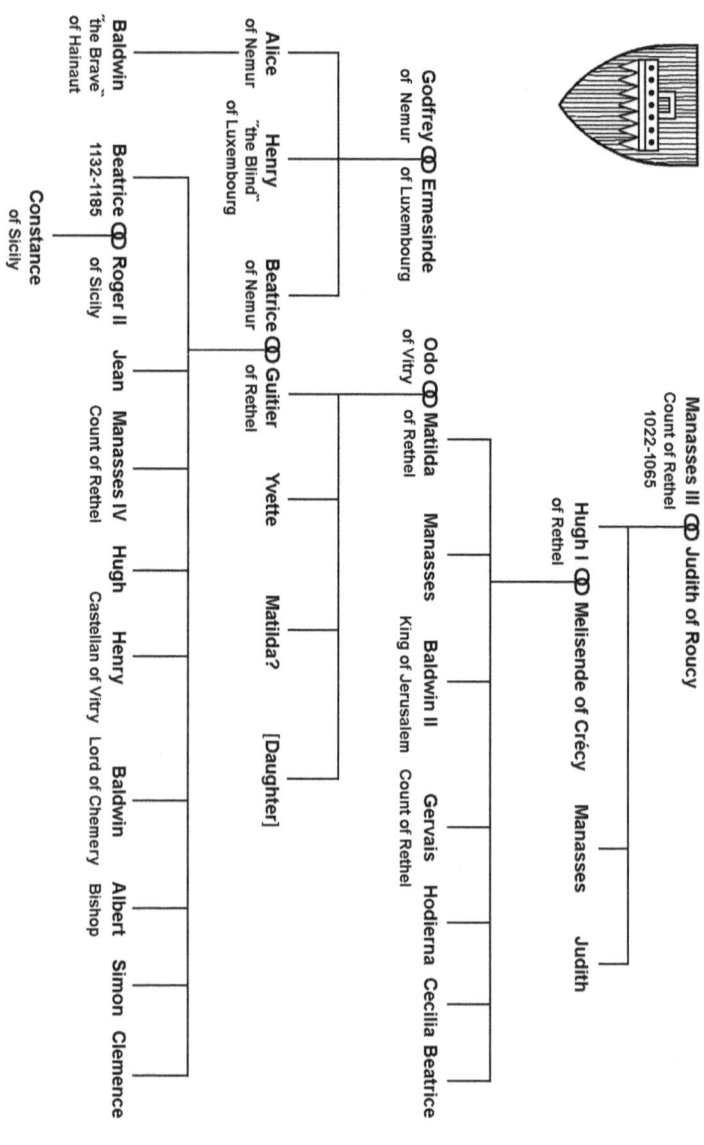

Table 13: Beatrice of Rethel

GENEALOGICAL TABLES

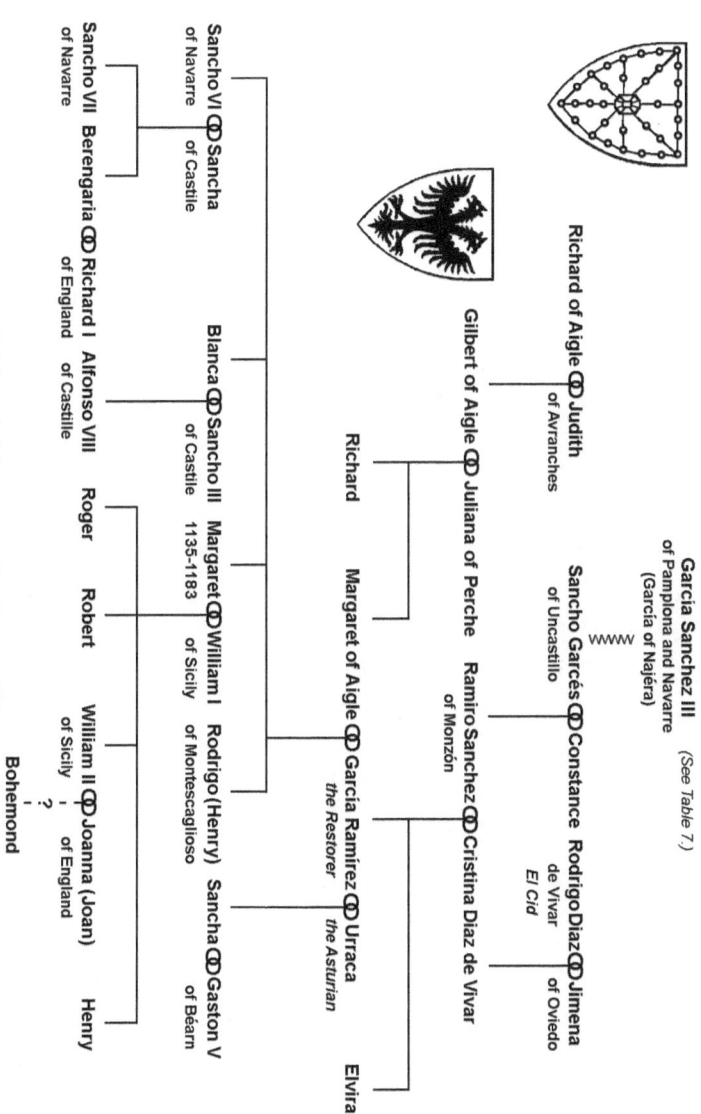

Table 14: Margaret Jiménez of Navarre

KINGDOM OF SICILY

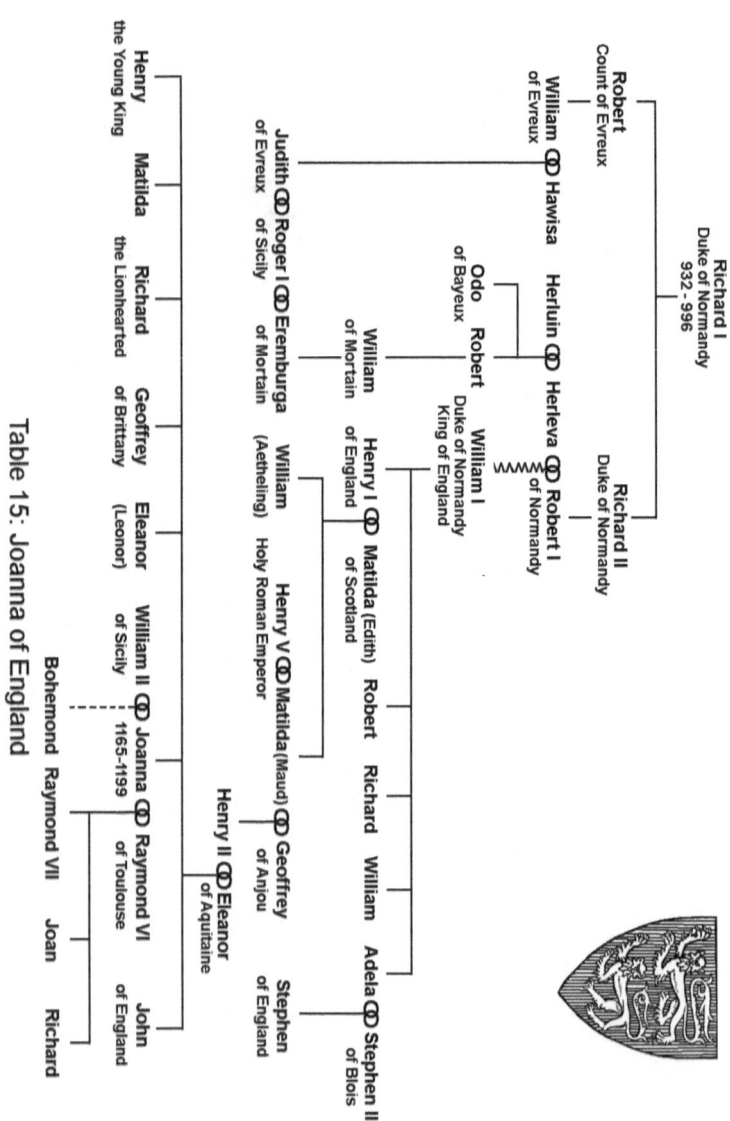

Table 15: Joanna of England

GENEALOGICAL TABLES

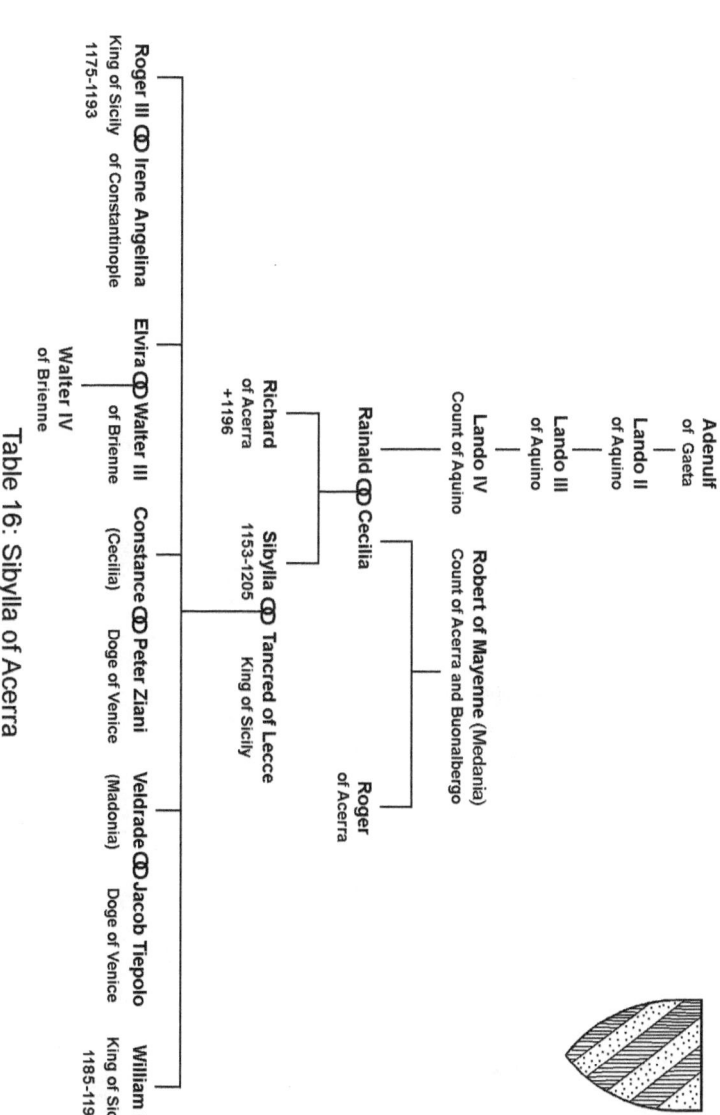

Table 16: Sibylla of Acerra

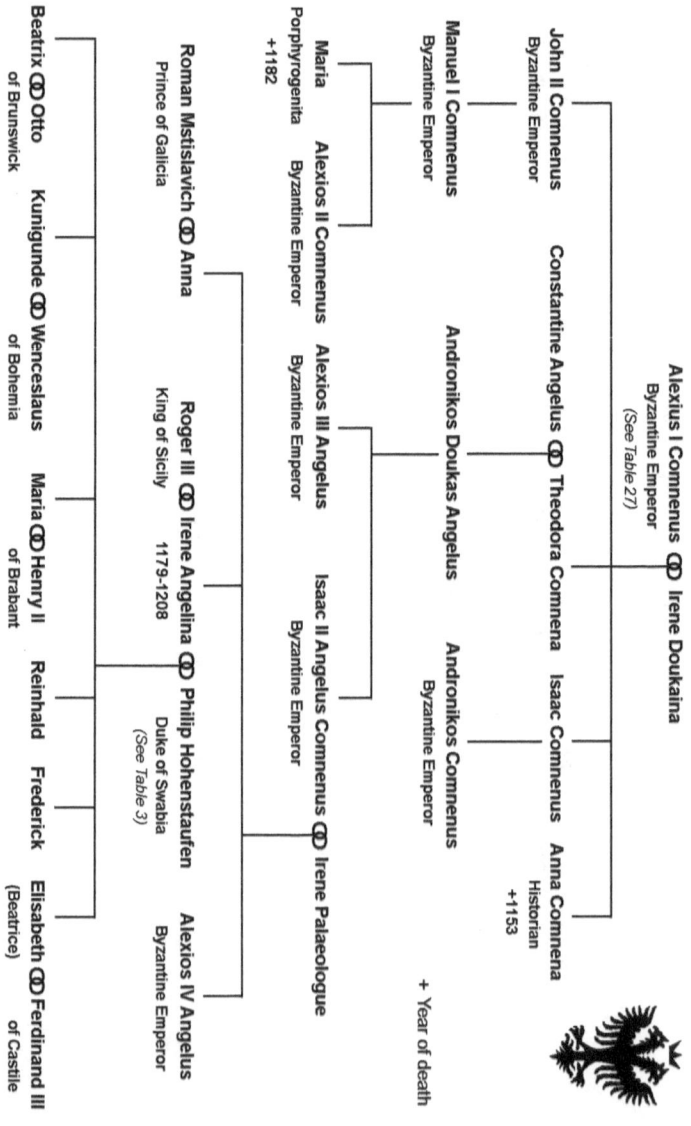

Table 17: Irene Angelina of Constantinople

GENEALOGICAL TABLES

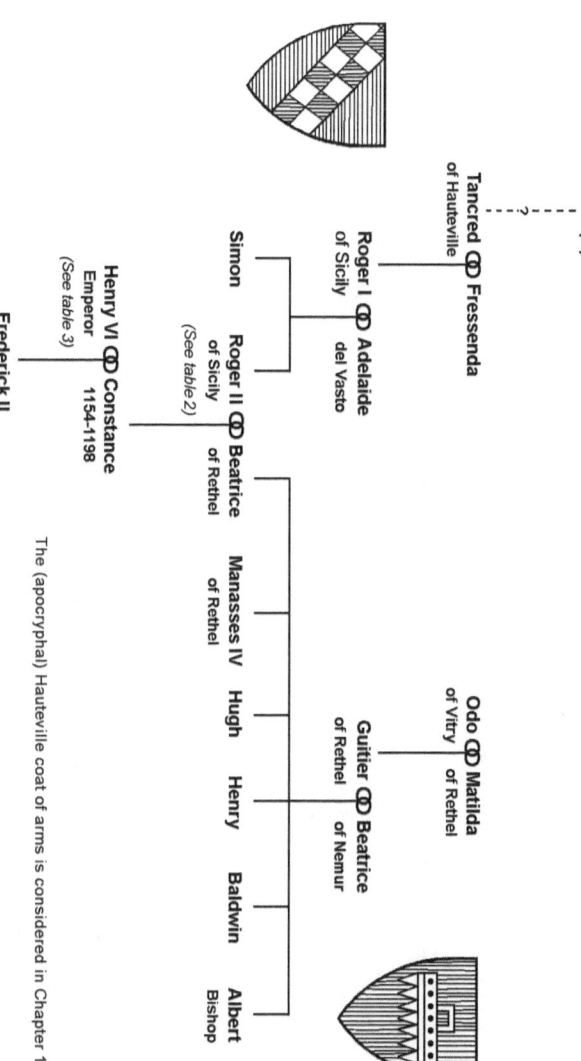

Table 18: Constance of Sicily

The (apocryphal) Hauteville coat of arms is considered in Chapter 12.

KINGDOM OF SICILY

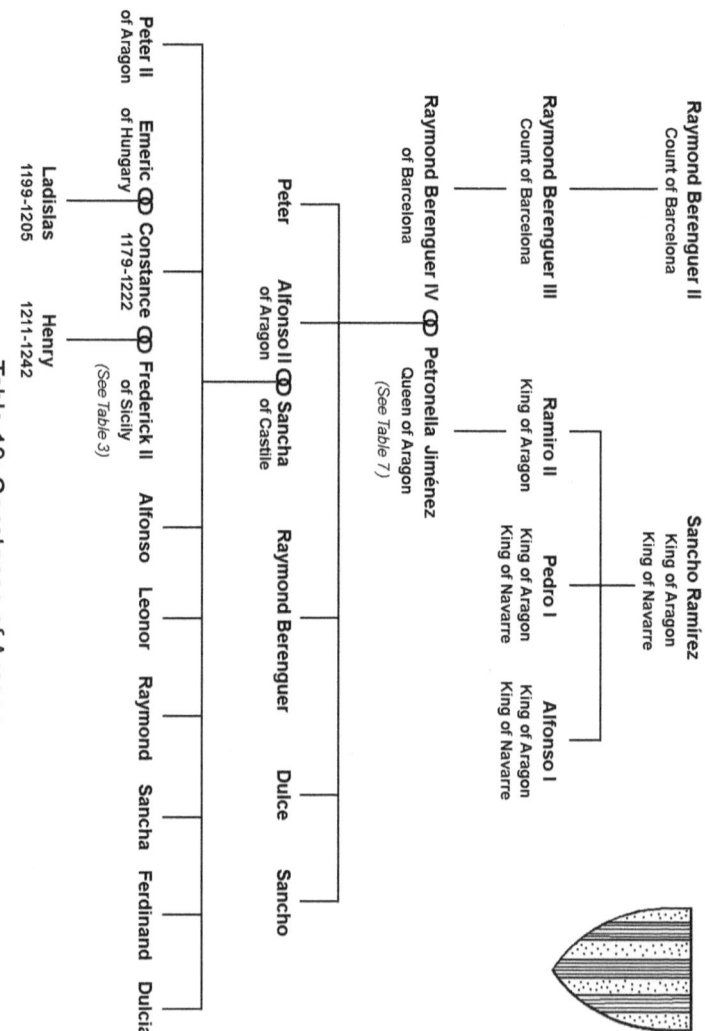

Table 19: Constance of Aragon

GENEALOGICAL TABLES

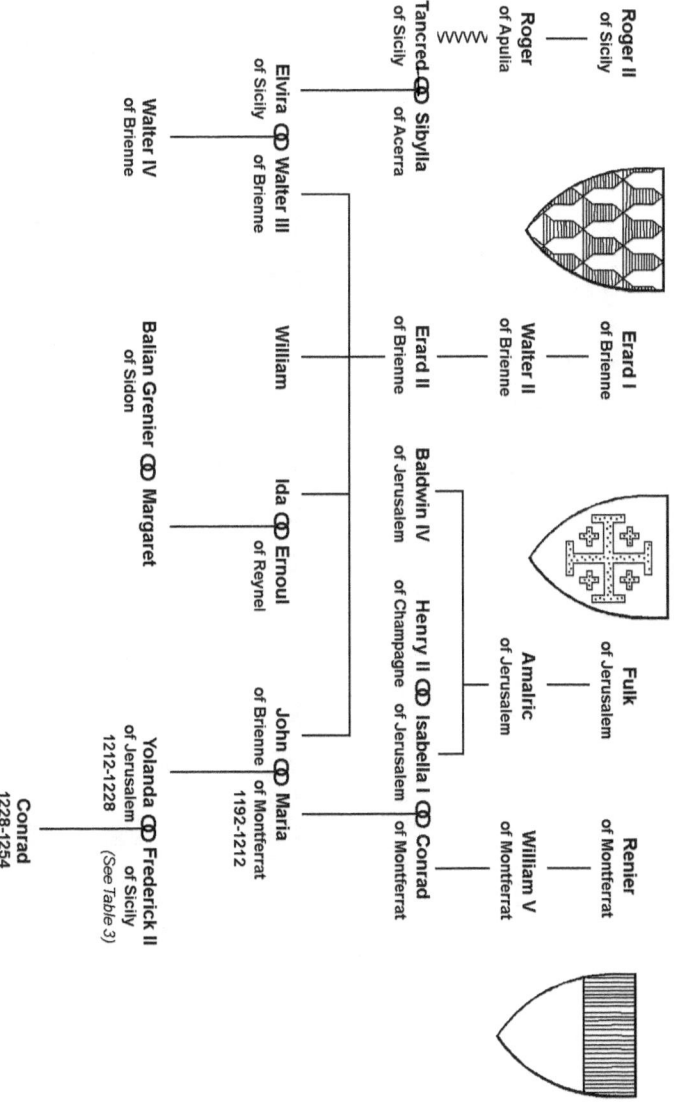

Table 20: Yolanda (Isabella) of Jerusalem

KINGDOM OF SICILY

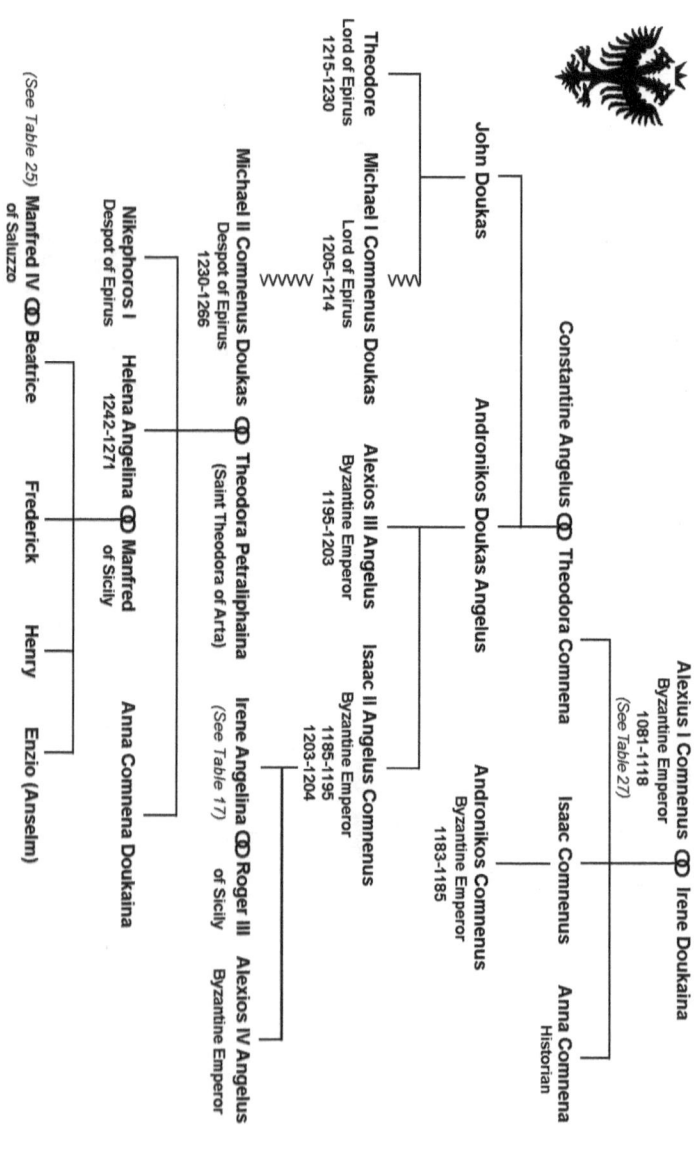

Table 21: Helena Angelina of Epirus

GENEALOGICAL TABLES

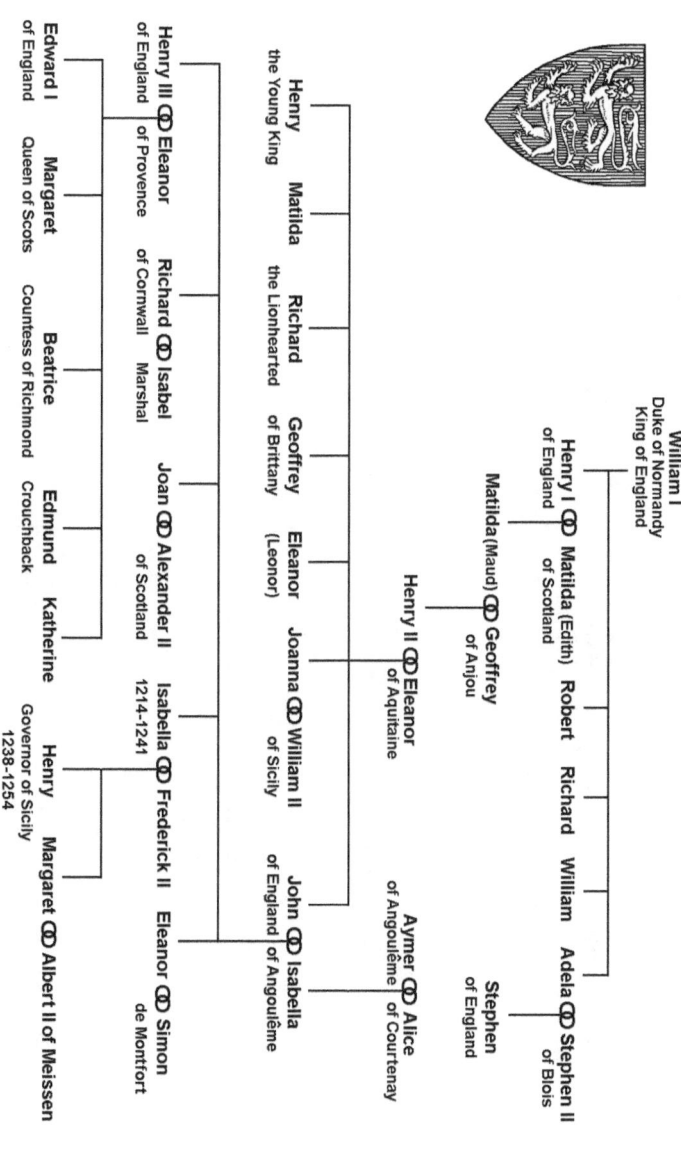

Table 22: Isabella of England

KINGDOM OF SICILY

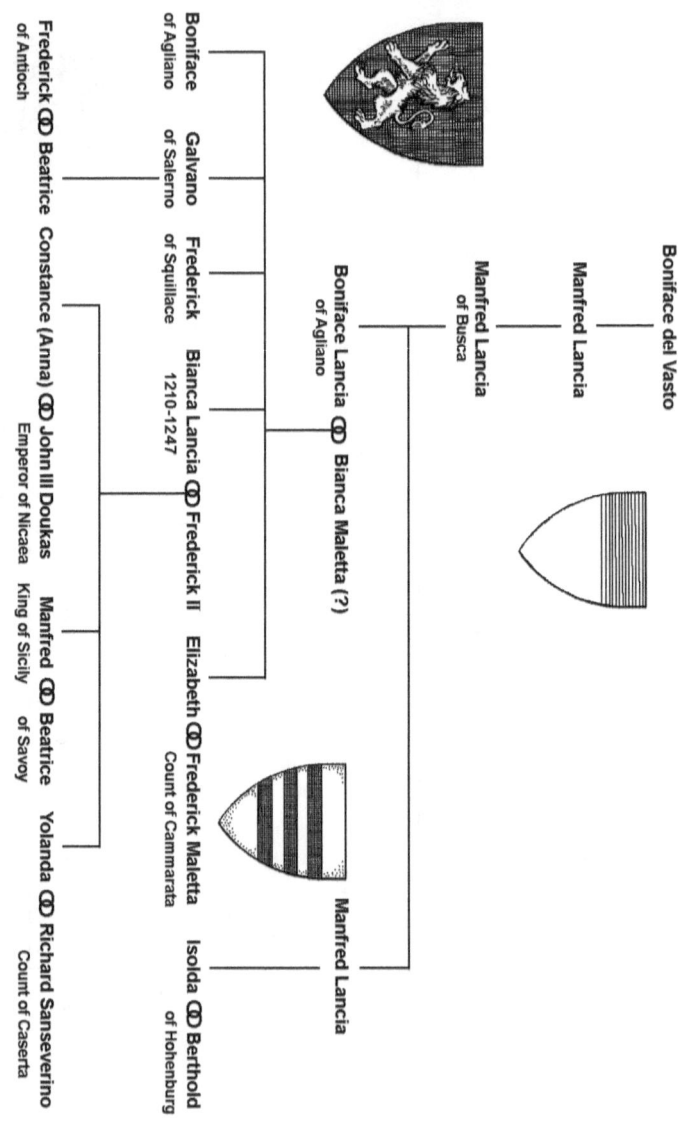

Table 23: Bianca Lancia of Agliano

GENEALOGICAL TABLES

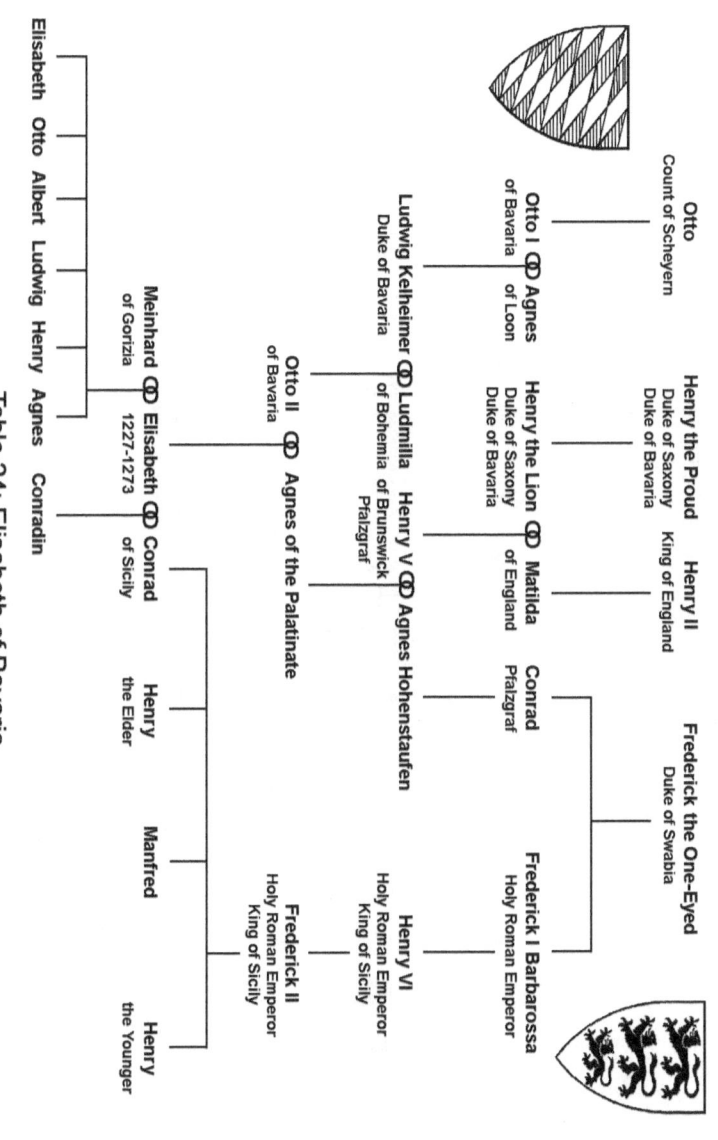

Table 24: Elisabeth of Bavaria

KINGDOM OF SICILY

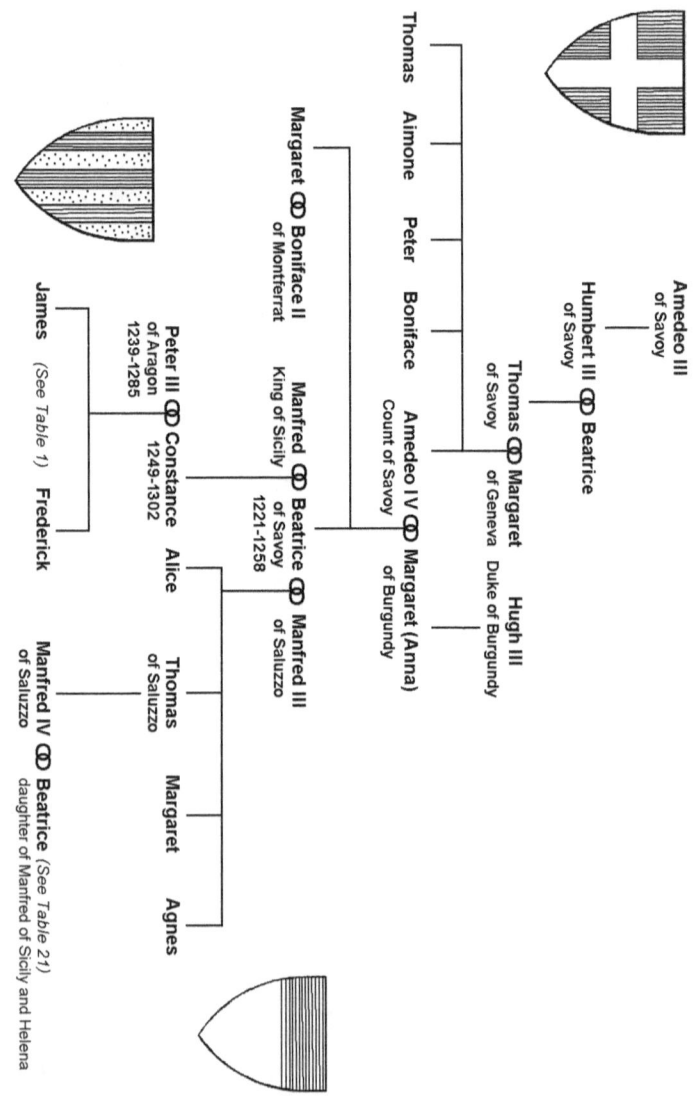

Table 25: Beatrice of Savoy

GENEALOGICAL TABLES

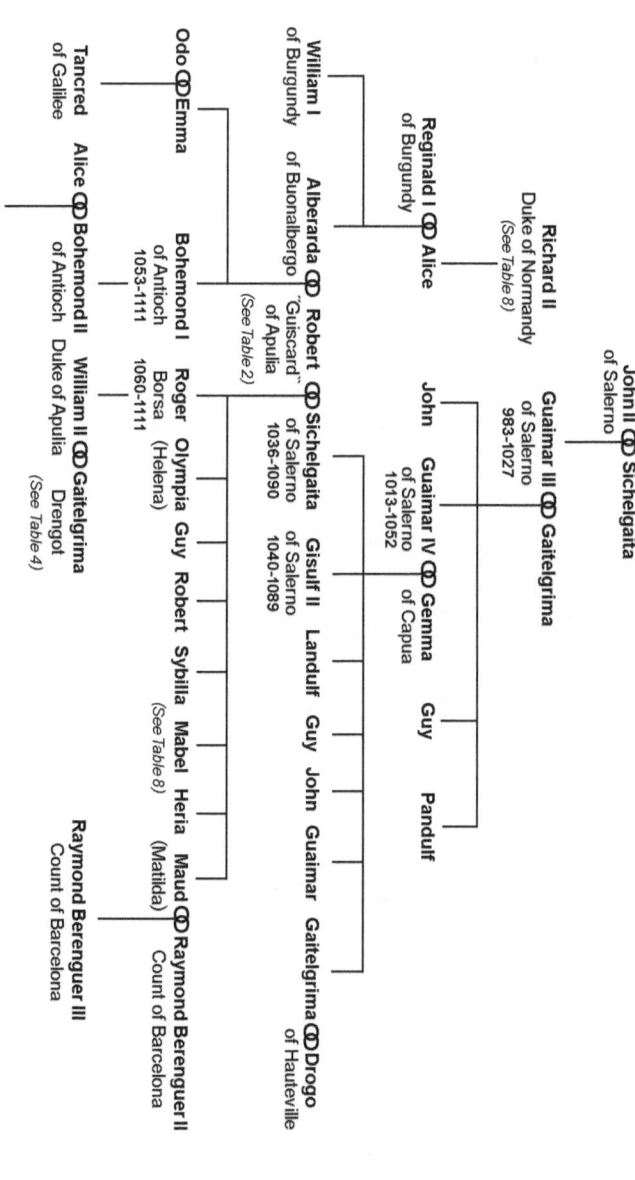

Table 26: Sichelgaita of Salerno

KINGDOM OF SICILY

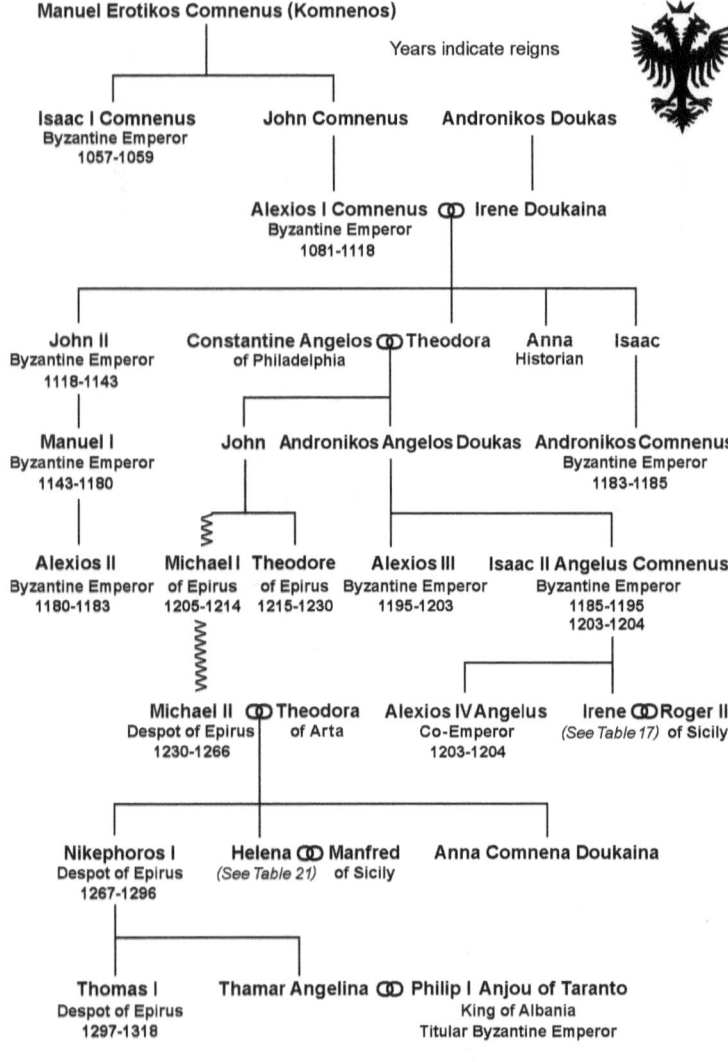

Table 27: House of Angelus Comnenus Survey

TIMELINE

This succinct chronology is intended merely as a general framework to lend context to the history and events recounted in the preceding pages. It is not meant to present in detail those events that occurred during this period, or to substitute the narrative text. Those seeking an accurate timeline for Sicily's Fatimid era are commended to Leonard Chiarelli's book, *A History of Muslim Sicily* (2018 edition), pages 353-358.

Fatimid-Lombard Period

992 - Death of Jawhar al-Siqilli, founder of Cairo.

994-1027 - Guaimar III, son of John II, rules Lombard principality of Salerno.

998/999 - Possible arrival of Normans at Salerno.

998-1019 - Rule of Jafar al-Kalbi (Taj al Dawlah) in Sicily under Fatimids, construction of Favara palace in Palermo. Norse civilization in northwestern France (Normandy) assimilates with local culture. Normans arrive in southern Italy.

1002 - Defeat of al-Mansur ibn Abi Aamir (Almanzor) leaves most of Navarre and Catalonia in Christian hands.

1004 - Fatimids establish large library and *dar al-hikma* (house of wisdom) in Egypt.

1008 - Fatimids re-establish diplomatic relations with China.

1016 - Norman knights first participate in battles in Italy. First Turkish raids in Armenia.

1017 - Norman victory at Arenula.

1018 - Bulgarian lands conquered by Byzantines, who also defeat Italians (Lombards) at Battle of Cannae, in Apulia, where many Norman knights are felled.

1019-1037 - Rule of Ahmed al-Akhal in Sicily.

1021 - Approximate foundation date of Norse settlements in Newfoundland.

1027-1052 - Guaimar IV, son of Guaimar III, rules Lombard principality of Salerno.

1037-1040 - Rule of Sicily by Abdallah Abu Hafs, usurper.

1038 - Hautevilles attack Capua.

1038-1042 - Byzantine forces of George Maniakes briefly occupy parts of eastern Sicily; army includes Greeks, Normans, Lombards, and Norse Varangian Guard under Harald Sigurdsson Hardrada, later King of Norway (killed in battle in England in 1066).

1040 - Hasan as-Samsam begins his rule in Sicily; deposed in 1044.

1041 - Normans defeat Byzantine Greeks in battles in Puglia.

1042 - Normans establish Melfi as their Italian capital; Guaimar IV of Salerno recognizes their authority in Puglia.

KINGDOM OF SICILY

1044 - Sicily divided into four qadits; rivalry among its emirs worsens.

1045 - Zirids of Tunisia rebel against Fatimids to unite with Abbasids of Baghdad. Cathedral of Gerace (Calabria) consecrated.

1046 - Byzantine catepan Eustathios Palatinos defeated near Taranto.

1052-1078 - Gisulf II, son of Guaimar IV, rules Lombard principality of Salerno.

1053 - Normans defeat Lombards at Battle of Civitate. Following death of Hasan as-Samsam and extinction of Kalbid dynasty, three important emirs divide control of Sicily: ibn al Hawas at Kasr' Janni (Enna), ibn al-Thumna (Timnah) at Syracuse and Catania, Abdullah ibn Hawqal at Trapani and Mazara.

1054 - Great Schism between eastern and western Christianity. Supernova observed by astronomers in Asia; becomes Crab Nebula.

1055 - Seljuk Turks occupy Baghdad.

1057 - Tunisia invaded by Banu Hilal of Arabia, with Zirid lands reduced in size.

1059 - Treaty of Melfi grants papal recognition of Norman claims in southern Italy.

1060 - Unsuccessful Norman attack in coastal northeastern Sicily.

Norman Period

1061 - Battle of Messina, with parts of Nebrodian and Peloritan region occupied; permanent Norman presence in Sicily.

1062 - Roger I weds Judith of Evreux.

1063 - Battle of Cerami results in Norman victory.

1065 - Kingdom of Castile founded. Seljuk Turks invade Georgia.

1065-1067 - War of the Three Sanchos among three Jiménez cousins ruling Castile, Navarre and Aragon.

1066 - Battle of Hastings leads to complete Norman conquest of Saxon England. Battle of Messina forms partial pattern of this invasion of an island from a continent (some Norman knights fight at both campaigns).

1068 - Battle of Agrigento leaves Ibn al-Hawas dead.

1071 - Normans attack Palermo; Norman invaders are led by Robert of Hauteville, Arab defenders by Ayub ibn Temim. Byzantines lose Battle of Manzikert to Seljuk Turks.

1072 - Battle of Palermo ends in January with Norman occupation under Roger and Robert of Hauteville. Bishop Nicodemus removed from authority over Christian community.

1074 - Hautevilles sign treaty with Byzantine Empire. Seljuk Turks seize Jerusalem from Byzantine control.

1075 - Normans sign treaty with Zirids of Tunisia. Investiture Controversy begins as conflict between Papacy and Holy Roman Emperors.

TIMELINE

1077 - Robert Guiscard takes Salerno, deposing his brother-in-law Gisulf II and ending Lombard power in southern Italy. Excommunicated Henry IV, Holy Roman Emperor, does penance at Canossa.

1078 - Arab poet ibn Hamdis leaves Sicily.

1079 - Frankish settlement begins along Way of Saint James in northeastern Spain.

1081 - Suppression of revolt led by self-appointed "emir" Bin al Wardi (Bernavert) at Catania; another of his revolts is quashed at Syracuse in 1085.

1083 - Roger I appoints Latin (rather than Orthodox) Bishop of Palermo and Gallican Rite is introduced in new churches.

1084 - Bruno founds Carthusian Order in Germany.

1085 - Alfonso VI of Castile seizes Toledo from Moors.

1087 - Ibn Hammud, Emir of Kasr'Janni (Enna), last major Arab stronghold in Sicily, surrenders to Normans.

1089 - Roger I weds Adelaide del Vasto.

1091 - Fall of Noto to Normans. Byzantine Greeks defeat Pechenegs at Battle of Levounion.

1094 - El Cid conquers Valencia.

1095 - Roger II, future King of Sicily, is born. Pope Urban II preaches First Crusade.

1096 - First Crusade begins; some Norman knights participate under Bohemond of Hauteville (later Prince of Antioch).

1097 - Odo of Bayeux, younger brother of William the Conqueror, dies in Palermo *en route* to the Crusade while visiting Roger I.

1098 - Roger I, as Great Count of Sicily, becomes apostolic legate, with right of approval over bishops. Cistercian Order founded in France.

1099 - Crusaders conquer Jerusalem. Death of El Cid in Spain.

1100 - Crusaders control Palestine in the wake of First Crusade and crown Baldwin first King of Jerusalem.

1101 - Roger I, Great Count of Sicily, dies, succeeded by Simon, his eldest living, legitimate son, who is still a minor. Roger's consort, Adelaide del Vasto, is regent.

1104 - Alfonso I "the Battler" becomes King of Aragon and Navarre.

1105 - Roger II succeeds his elder brother Simon (1093-1105) as ruler of Sicily under Adelaide's regency.

1108 - Bohemond of Antioch becomes vassal of Byzantine Emperor.

1109 - Bertrand of Toulouse occupies Tripoli (Lebanon).

1112 - Roger II is knighted by his mother.

KINGDOM OF SICILY

1113 - Adelaide weds Baldwin I of Jerusalem. Order of Saint John (Knights Hospitaller) based in Palestine chartered by Pope Paschal II; establishes commanderies in Sicily.

1117 - Roger II weds Elvira of Castile.

1118 - Death of Adelaide del Vasto, widow of Roger I.

1119 - In Spain, Alfonso the Battler takes control of Tudela from Moors. Knights Templar founded in Palestine.

1120 - Council of Nablus establishes legal code for Kingdom of Jerusalem.

1121 - Presumed year of birth of William I of Sicily.

1122 - Concordat of Worms between Papacy and Holy Roman Empire.

1123 - First Lateran Council forbids Roman Catholic clerics wives or concubines; until now Catholic priests were permitted to marry before ordination.

1125 - Christian army defeats Seljuk Turks at Battle of Azaz.

1127 - William II of Apulia dies at Salerno.

1128 - Portugal declares independence from León, which recognizes its monarch, Alfonso Henriques, in 1143.

1130 - Roger II crowned first King of Sicily. Palatine Chapel rebuilt to present form during this period.

1131 - Cathedral of Cefalù erected.

1135 - Death of Elvira of Castile in Palermo; birth of Margaret of Navarre. Beginning of "Anarchy," a civil war over royal succession, in England.

1136 - Construction of Saint-Denis near Paris; Gothic movement begins.

1138 - Death of Anacletus II ends papal schism (which began in 1130); Innocent II universally recognized as pope. Major earthquake around Aleppo.

1139 - Second Lateran Council, convened by Pope Innocent II, makes celibacy mandatory for Roman Catholic priests, reiterating a canon established in 1123 but not widely enforced. Innocent recognizes Roger II as King of Sicily.

1140 - Roger II promulgates Assizes of Ariano, introduces ducat.

1143 - Martorana Church (Palermo) built in Norman-Arab style for Greek Orthodox community by George of Antioch. Nilos Doxopatrios, Orthodox cleric, authors a theological treatise supporting Orthodoxy. Legal principles expressed in Assizes of Ariano are in force by this time.

1145-1148 - Second Crusade; participation by Sicilian knights is limited.

1147 - Almohads displace Almoravids in northwestern Africa and southern Spain.

1148 - Roger II weds Sibylla of Burgundy.

1149 - Eleanor of Aquitaine calls at Palermo. William I weds Margaret of Navarre.

TIMELINE

1150 - Death of Sibylla of Burgundy. Death of King García Ramírez, father of Margaret of Navarre; accession of Sancho VI of Navarre.

1151 - Roger II weds Beatrice of Rethel. William I crowned *rex filius*.

1152 - Birth of Roger, first son of William I.

1153 - Birth of Robert, second son of William I. End of "Anarchy" in England. First Treaty of Konstanz between Papacy and Holy Roman Empire to prevent Byzantine conquests in Italy.

1154 - Death of Roger II; birth of his daughter, Constance of Sicily. Reign of King William I begins. *Book of Roger* completed by court geographer Abdullah al Idrisi. Accession of Henry II in England.

1155 - Birth of William II, third son of William I and Margaret. Birth of Alfonso VIII of Castile, son of Blanca (Margaret's sister). Frederick I "Barbarossa" Hohenstaufen crowned Holy Roman Emperor.

1156 - Treaty of Benevento normalizes relations with papacy.

1158 - Birth of Henry, fourth son of William I and Margaret. Thomas le Brun (Thomas Brown), treasurer at William's court, returns to England to reform exchequer of Henry II, thus influencing European accounting principles.

1159 - Death of Robert, secondborn son of William and Margaret. Arrival in Sicily of Gilbert of Gravina, Margaret's cousin.

1160 - Mahdia, last Norman stronghold in North Africa, is lost.

1161 - Matthew Bonello leads revolt of Norman barons, resulting in death of Roger, firstborn son of William and Margaret. Rhum Sultanate makes peace with Byzantine Empire.

1165 - Birth of Joanna "Plantagenet" of England to Eleanor of Aquitaine and Henry II. Construction of Zisa palace begins in Palermo.

1166 - Death of William I; reign of young King William II begins under Margaret's regency. Arrival in Sicily of Rodrigo (Henry), Margaret's half-brother.

1167 - Margaret appoints her cousin, Stephen of Perche, chancellor.

1168 - At Messina, Margaret oversees trials of Rodrigo (Henry) and others. Stephen of Perche deposed and expelled.

1169 - Major earthquake in Catania and southeastern Sicily. Walter becomes Archbishop of Palermo.

1170 - Tancred of Lecce weds Sibylla of Acerra (approx. year). Thomas Becket murdered in Canterbury.

1171 - Margaret's regency ends when William II reaches age of majority. Benjamin of Tudela visits Sicily. Saladin deposes Fatimids, establishes Ayyubid rule.

1172 - Death of Henry, Margaret's fourthborn son. Planning and construction begin on Monreale Abbey.

1173 - Thomas Becket canonized.

1174 - Sicilian fleet led by Tancred of Lecce attacks Alexandria.

KINGDOM OF SICILY

1175 - William II signs treaty with Venetians. Henry II of England signs treaty with Irish.

1176 - Betrothal of William II to Joanna of England. Byzantines lose much of Anatolia to Seljuk Turks.

1177 - Joanna of England marries William II. Treaty of Venice between pope and Holy Roman Emperor.

1178 - Sicilian treaty with Holy Roman Empire. Romuald Guarna of Salerno leaves Sicily.

1179 - Birth of Constance of Aragon. Birth of Irene Angelina of Constantinople (approx. year). Third Lateran Council convened by Pope Alexander III.

1181 - Sicilian treaty with Tunisia. Pope Alexander III dies.

1182 - Massacre of the Latins in Constantinople.

1183 - Death of Margaret of Navarre. Monreale becomes archdiocese.

1184 - Major earthquake in Calabria. Ibn Jubayr visits Sicily. Construction of Palermo's new cathedral begins.

1185 - Death of Beatrice of Rethel, widow of Roger II. William II invades Byzantine lands.

1186 - Constance, daughter of Roger II, weds Henry VI, future Holy Roman Emperor.

1187 - Saladin captures Jerusalem. William II sends fleet to Palestine.

1189 - Death of William II. Richard I "Lionheart" crowned King of England.

1190 - Tancred of Lecce crowned King of Sicily. Richard Lionheart, brother of Queen Joanna of Sicily, occupies Messina with Philip II of France for several months *en route* to Third Crusade. Death of Frederick I "Barbarossa," Holy Roman Emperor; succeeded by Henry VI.

1191 - Joanna of England, widow of William II, goes on Third Crusade. Henry VI and Constance defeated in attempted invasion of *Regnum,* with Constance captured.

1192 - Constance is rescued. Roger III (son of Tancred) weds Irene Angelina. Isabella I crowned Queen of Jerusalem.

1193 - Death of Saladin.

1194 - Death of Tancred of Lecce; Constance becomes queen, gives birth to son, Frederick II. Holy Roman Emperor Henry VI arrives in Palermo and rules by right of his wife, Constance.

Swabian Period

1195 - Constance crowned Queen of Sicily.

1196 - Joanna, widow of William II, weds Raymond VI of Toulouse.

1197 - Henry VI dies; Constance becomes regent for Frederick II. Widowed Irene Angelina weds Philip of Swabia. Basilica of Saint Nicholas (begun in 1089) consecrated in Bari.

1198 - Death of Constance; she is survived by her son, Frederick II. Constance of Aragon weds Emeric of Hungary. Teutonic Order founded under Hohenstaufen patronage.

TIMELINE

1199 - Death of Joanna of England at Rouen.

1204 - Constance of Aragon widowed in Hungary. Latins ("Franks") sack Constantinople during Fourth Crusade, establishing "Latin Empire."

1205 - Death of Sibylla of Acerra.

1206 - Mongols unite under Genghis Khan (Temujin), who conquers large parts of Eurasia.

1208 - Death of Irene Angelina of Constantinople.

1209 - Frederick II weds Constance of Aragon.

1210 - Pope Innocent III recognizes Order of Friars Minor (Franciscans). Albigensian Crusades begin. Otto IV invades Italy.

1211 - Constance of Aragon gives birth to Henry, eldest child of Frederick II.

1215 - Fourth Lateran Council. *Magna Carta* in England. Dominic of Osma (of Caleruega, Spain) founds Order of Preachers (Dominicans or "Blackfriars"), confirmed by Papacy in 1216.

1217 - Cleric and scientist Michael Scot translates *On the Sphere* by the Arab astronomer Al-Bitruji (or Alpetragius). Fifth Crusade begins.

1220 - Frederick II issues Assizes of Capua.

1221 - Frederick II issues Assizes of Messina.

1222 - Death of Constance of Aragon.

1223 - Following execution of Arab rebel leader Morabit in Sicily (in 1222), thousands of Muslims from Jato (Iato) area, who had revolted with their leader Ibn Abbad (or Bernavert), are deported to Lucera and other towns in Apulia. Many Muslims have already converted to Catholicism. Jews from occupied Djerba (in Tunisia) invited to Sicily. Transfers of Muslims to mainland Italy continue until around 1246.

1224 - University of Naples founded by Frederick II.

1225 - Frederick II weds Yolanda of Jerusalem. Zhao Rukuo completes *Zhu Fan Zhi*.

1226 - Frederick II summons Imperial Diet of Cremona.

1228 - Yolanda dies giving birth to Conrad.

1229 - Frederick II, accompanied by Saracen guards and Italian and German knights, goes on Sixth Crusade as King of Jerusalem. Signs peace with Ayyubids without war.

1230 - Upon his return from Jerusalem Frederick suppresses Templar preceptories in Sicily and defeats John of Brienne, his father-in-law, on the mainland.

1231 - Constitutions of Melfi become legal code for Kingdom of Sicily under Frederick II.

1233 - Cathars of France persecuted as heretics by first Inquisition.

1235 - Frederick II weds Isabella of England.

KINGDOM OF SICILY

1240 - Cielo of Alcamo composes poetry in Sicilian. First of a series of major revolts by Sicilian Arabs, including some Christian converts, but Frederick retains trusted Saracen guards and court officers.

1241 - Queen Isabella dies giving birth. Mongol-Tatar army of Batu Khan arrives in central Europe after having sacked Kiev; leads to foundation of "Golden Horde."

1244 - Fall of Jerusalem to Khwarazmian forces.

1245 - First General Council of Lyon convoked by Pope Innocent IV.

1246 - Conrad, son of Frederick II and Yolanda, weds Elisabeth of Bavaria.

1248 - Frederick II weds Bianca Lancia shortly before her death. Manfred, son of Frederick II and Bianca, weds Beatrice of Savoy. Crusade to Egypt by Louis IX of France.

1250 - Death of Frederick II. Elisabeth of Bavaria becomes queen as consort of Conrad.

1252 - Elisabeth of Bavaria gives birth to son, Conrad (Conradin). Papal bull *Ad Extirpanda* institutes use of torture on heretics in Inquisition.

1254 - Death of Conrad; Manfred, natural but legitimized son of Frederick, becomes regent for his young son (Conradin). Death of Pope Innocent IV.

1255 - Manfred is excommunicated by Pope Alexander IV but reclaims much of southern Italy from papal control.

1258 - Manfred crowned King of Sicily. Beatrice of Savoy crowned, dies. Baghdad falls to Mongols.

1259 - Manfred weds Helena Angelina of Epirus. Widowed Elisabeth of Bavaria marries Meinhard of Gorizia.

1261 - Byzantine Empire restored when Constantinople falls to Greek (Nicaean) control.

1262 - Constance, daughter of Beatrice of Savoy and Manfred, weds Peter III of Aragon.

Angevin Period

1266 - Charles of Anjou (brother of Louis IX of France) becomes King of Sicily following defeat and death of Manfred at Battle of Benevento; establishes capital at Naples.

1268 - Young Conradin, a (legitimate) grandson of Frederick II and last male Swabian claimant, is executed following defeat at Battle of Tagliacozzo.

1270 - Following Eighth (Tunisian) Crusade, funeral of Louis IX of France at Monreale, where his heart is preserved; canonized in 1297.

1271 - Helena Angelina dies in captivity; Charles of Anjou captures some of her dowry lands in Albania and Epirus.

1273 - Rudolf of Hapsburg becomes king in Germany; his dynasty will succeed Hohenstaufens as Holy Roman Emperors.

1281 - Angevin forces defeated by Byzantine troops in Albania and Greece.

TIMELINE

Aragonese Period

1282 - Constance, daughter of Beatrice of Savoy and Manfred, crowned Queen of Sicily following Vespers revolt that expels Angevin French from Sicily and makes Peter III of Aragon its sovereign. Neapolitan invasion of Constantinople (to restore "Latin Empire") is aborted as military resources must be diverted to Sicily.

1285 - Deaths of Charles I of Anjou and Peter III of Aragon, succeeded by their sons.

1290 - Approximate year the *Rebellamentu,* memoir of John of Procida, was written.

1298 - Death of John of Procida, chancellor of Frederick II and Manfred.

1300 - Destruction of Lucera by Charles II and conversion of its Muslims marks end of organized Islam in medieval Italy.

1302 - Death of Constance, daughter of Manfred of Sicily and Beatrice of Savoy. Peace of Caltabellotta treaty signed between Aragonese and Angevins.

Endotaph of Constance of Aragon (see page 635)

Dignum et necessarium est opere et／
siq[ui]d[em] de nobis et uniu[er]si regni n[ost]ri
statu meritis n[ost]ro p[re]sumim[us]. a largitate
divina q[uod] cõsecuta. recepim[us]. divinis beneficiis qu[i]b[us] ualem[us] obsequiis respõdea[mus].
ne tante gr[ati]e penit[us] ingr[a]ti sim[us]. Si g[ratia]
sua m[isericordi]a nob[is] d[eu]s p[ri]us p[ro]stratis hostib[us] pace[m]
reddidit. integritate[m] regni. tranq[ui]llitate[m]
gratissima[m]. tã incarnalib[us] q[uam] insp[irit]ualib[us]
reformau[it]. reformare cogimur’ iust[i]tie
simul et pietatis tr[a]mite[m]. ut uidem[us] eam
et mirabilit[er] ee distortam. h[oc].n[amque].ip[su]m q[uo]d
air. inspirari[m]. de munere ip[s]i[us] largitoris
accepim[us]. dicente ip[s]o. p[er] me reges regna[n]t.
et c[on]ditores legum decern[un]t iustitiam.
H[o]c.n[amque].gr[ati]ar[um] b[on]o ee putam[us]. q[uod] s[ui]d s[im]pl[icite]r
offerim[us]. q[uod] eum ee cognouim[us]. m[iser]iam s[uam]

Text of the facing page in the Vatican manuscript

Appendix 1
ASSIZES OF ARIANO

The Assizes are described in Chapter 12. The following texts incorporate minor stylistic editing, such as full words in place of abbreviations. Numeration of the statutes in the second codex was added by Jacqueline Alio in 2016 when these were published in the first biography of Margaret of Navarre.

Codex Vaticanus 8782

Dignum et necessarium est o proceres si quod de nobis et universi regni nostri statu meritis non presumimus; a largitate divina gratia consecuta recepimus; divinis beneficiis quibus valemus obsequis respondeamus, ne tante gratie penitus ingrati simus. Si ergo sua misericordia nobis deus pius prostratis hostibus pacem reddidit, integritatem regni, tranquillitate gratissima, tam in carnalibus quam in spiritualibus, reformavit, reformare cogimur iustitie simul et pietatis itinera, ubi videmus eam et mirabiliter esse distortam. Hoc enim ipsum quod ait, inspiramentum, de munere ipsius largitoris, accepimus, dicente ipso: per me reges regnant et conditores legum decernunt iustitiam. Nichil enim gratius deo esse putamus, quam si id simpliciter offerimus, quod eum esse cognovimus, misericordiam scilicet atque iustitiam. In qua oblatione regni officium quoddam sibi sacerdotii vendicat privilegium.

Unde quidam sapiens legisque peritus iuris interpres, iuris sacerdotes appellat. Iure itaque qui iuris et legum auctoritatem per ipsius gratiam optinemus, eas in meliorem statum partim erigere, partim reformare, debemus et qui misericordiam consecuti sumus in omnibus eas tractare misericordius, interpretari benignius, presertim ubi severitas earum quandam inhumanitatem inducit. Neque hoc ex supercilio quasi iustiores aut moderatores nostris predecessoribus in condendis legibus interpretandisve nostris vigiliis arrogamus, set quia in multis delinquimus et ad delinquendum et ad delinquendum procliviores sumus, parcendum delinquentibus cum moderatia nostris temporibus apta conveniens esse censemus.

Nam et ipsa pietas ita nos instruit dicens: Estote misericordes sicut et pater vester misericors est.

Et rex et propheta: Universe vie domini misericordia et veritas. Et proculdubio tenebimus, quia iudicium sine misericordia erit ei qui iudicium fecerit sine misericordia.

Volumus igitur et iubemus ut sanctiones quas in presenti corpore sive promulgatas a nobis, sive compositas nobis facimus exhiberi, fideliter et alacriter recipiatis.

I. De legum interpretatione

Leges a nostra maiestate noviter promulgatas pietatis intuitu asperitatem nimiam mitigantes mollia quodam moderamine exaucuentes; obscura dilucidantes, generaliter ab omnibus precipimus observari, moribus, consuetudinibus, legibus non cassatis pro varietate populorum nostro regno subiectorum, sicut usque nunc apud eos optinuit, nisi forte nostris his sanctionibus adversari quid in eis manifestissime videatur.

II. De privilegio sanctarum ecclesiarum

Noverint ergo omnes nostre potestati subiecti, quoniam in voto nobis semper fuit, et erit, ecclesias dei pro quibus dominus Ihesus sanguinem suum fudit, protegere, defensare, augere modis omnibus, sicut et proienitores nostri consueta liberalitate, id ipsum facere studuerunt, ideoque multa et innumera beneficia a deo consecuti sunt semper in melius. Itque sacrarum ecclesiarum res omnes et possesiones in nostra post deum et sanctos ejus custodia collacatas atque commissas ab omnibus incursibus malignantium, gladio materiali nobis a deo concessas defendimus et inviolatas custodimus; principibus, comitibus, baronibus et omnibus nostris fidelibus commendamus, scituri, quod nostrum decretum quisquis violare voluerit, nostram se sentiat ledere majestatem.

III. Monitio generalis

Monemus principes, comites, barones, maiores atque minores, archiepiscopos, episcopos, abbates, cunctos denique qui subditos habent cives, burgenses, rusticos, sive cuiuscumque professionis homines, eos humane tractare, misericordiam adhibere, maxime cum debitum adiutorium conveniens et moderatum valent ab ipsis quos habent subditos, postulare. Gratum enim deo faciunt, et nobis maximum gaudium, cuius potestati atque regimini divina dispositio, tam prelatos subdidit quam subiectos. Quod si fuerit neglectum, nostram spectabit sollicitudinem male factum in melius reformare.

IV. De rebus regalibus

Scire volumus principes nostros, comites, barones universos archiepiscopos, episcopos, abbates, quicumque de regalibus nostris magnum vel modicum quid tenet, nullo modo, nullo ingenio, possit ad nostra regalia pertinens alienare, vel vendere, vel in totum vel in partem minuere, unde iura rerum regalium minuantur, aut subvertantur sive aliquod etiam dampnum patiantur.

V. De sanctarum reliquiarum venditione

Sanccimus nemini licere martirum, vel quorucumque sanctorum reliquias vendere, vel comparare. Quod si presumptum fuerit, nondum pretio numerato nichil ets consecuturus si venditor emptorem voluerit convenire. Si autem numeratio facta est, emptori repetitionem non esse, fiscum vero vendicare. Nostram spectabit providentiam temeritatem contrahentium cohercere, et ubi decuerit, reliquias cum consilio antistitum collocare.

VI. De confugio ad ecclesiam

Presente lege sanccimus per loca regni nostri omnia deo propitio in perpetuum valitura nullos penitus, cuiuscumque condicionis de sacrosantis expelli ecclesiis, aut protrahi confugas, nec pro his venerabiles episcopos, aut yconomos exigi, que debentur ab eis qui hoc moliri aut facere presumpserit, capitis periculo, aut bonorum omnium ammissione plectendis. Interim confugis victualia non negentur. Sane si servus, aut colonus, aut servus glebe se ipsum subtraxerit domino, vel furatus res ad loca sancta confugerit, cum rebus quas detulit, domino presentetur, ut pro qualitae commissi subeat ultionem, aut intercessione procedente restituatur et gratie. Nemini quippe ius suum est detrahendum.

VII. De privilegiis ecclesiarum non violandis

Si venerabilis ecclesie privilegia cuiscumque fuerint temeritate violata dolove suppressa commissum iuxta dampnositatem ecclesie compensetur. Quod si non sufficiat ad condempnationis mulctam, regis iudicio vel officialium arbitrio committetur. Nichilominus pro qualitate commissi regis providentie, vel officialium arbitrio subiacebit.

VIII. De episcoporum privilegio

Episcopus ad testimonium non flagitetur, nisi forte in causis ecclesiasticis, vel publicis, cum necessitas, aut regis auctoritas postulaverit. Presbiteri non cogantur corporale sacramentum in negotiis exibere; diacones, subdiacones et infra positos altari sacri ministros, ab obsequiis sordidis alienos esse precipimus; presbiteros tantum non etiam ceteros omnibus angariis personalibus prohibemus.

IX. De illicitis conventiculis

Conventiculam illicitam extra ecclesiam in privatis edibus celebrari vetamus, proscriptionis domus periculo imminente, si dominus eius in eam clericos novam vel tumultuosam conventiculam celebrantes, susceperit non ignarus.

X. De ascripticiis volentibus clericari

Ascripticios sine voluntate et assensu eorum quorum iuri subditi sunt, et potestati, nullus episcoporum ordinare presumat, neque de aliensa parrochia, per litteras commendatorias secundum canonum instituta, vel ab episcopo, vel a proprio capitulo. Hii quorum ascripticii sunt, si quod premium pro data licencia consecrandi suscepisse convicti fuerint, huiusce ascriptii perdant qui dedit pecuniam ab ordine cadat, fisco vero cum omnibus rebus suis vendicetur. Solent sancto voto atque proposito sanctis occasionibus pravitas se ingerere, et dei servitium atque ecclesie ministerium perturbare. Ne ergo sinistrum aliquod aliquando possit nostris institutionibus obviare, si forte in rure vel in vico ecclesia assignatos habuerit sacerdotes quibus decedentibus sint alii (subrograndi et) domini ruris vel vici super ascripticiis, episcopo fieri subgorationem negaverint, presertim cum ex ipsis ascripticiis persona ydonea ab episcopo expectatur, dignum nostre clementie videtur, atque iustissium ad iustam petitionem ecclesie ascripticiorum dominum iure cogendum; filii vero decedentis presbiteri ad asripticiorum condicionem reddatur omni occasione remota.

XI. De raptum virginum

Si quis rapere sacratas deo virgines aut nondum velatas causa iungendi matrimonium presumpserit, capitali pena feriatur, vel alia pena quam regia censura decreverit.

XII. (sic)

Iudeus paganus servum christianum nec vendere, nec comparare audeat, nec ex aliquo titulo possidere seu pignori detinere. Quod si presumpserit, omnes res eius inficentur, et curie servus fiat. Quem si forte ausu vel nefario vel suasu circumcidi vel fidem abnegare fecerit, capitali supplicio puniatur.

XIII. De apostatantibus

Apostantes a fide catholica penitus execramus, ultionibus insequimur, bonis omnibus spoliamus, a professione vel voto naufragantes legibus coartamus, succesiones tollimus, omne ius legitimum abdicamus.

XIV. De ioculatoribus

Mimi et qui ludibrio corporis sui questum faciunt, publico habitu earum virginum, que deo dicate sunt, vel veste monachica non utantur, nec clericali; si fecerint verberibus publice afficiantur.

XV. De pupillis et orphanis

Pupillis et orphanis pietatis intuitu, multa privilegia priscis legibus confirmata pro qualitate temporum quibus absolverint in ultimo delegamus nostri iudicibus ubi iactura tollerabilis non est, favorabiliter commendamus. Mulieribus nichilominus ubi non modice lese sunt, propter fragiliorem sexum, legum equitatem sectantes tam per nos, quam per officiales nostros ex pietatis visceribus subveniendum decrevimus, sicut decet et oportet.

XVI. De indigne anelantibus ad sacerdotum

Nemo sacerdotum dignitatem pretio petere audeat, contumeliam pro premio reportaturus et penam, mox ut fuerit propria petitione detectus. Ille enim honore se privat, qui inpudenti fronte, velud importunus expostulat.

XVII. De sacrilegiis

Disputari de regis iudicio, consiliis, institutionibus, factis non oportet. Est enim par sacrilegio disputare de eius iudiciis, institutionibus, factis atque consiliis et an is dignus sit quem rex elegerit, aut decernit. Multe leges sacrilegos severissime punierunt, set pena moderanda est arbitrio iudicantis, nisi forte manufacta templa dei fracta sunt violenter, aut dona et vasa sacra, noctu sublata sunt, hoc enim casu capitale est.

XVIII. De crimine maiestatis

Quisquis cum milite uno vel cum pluribus, seu privato scelestem inierit factionem aut factionis dederit, vel susceperit sacramentum, de nece etiam virorum illustrium, qui consiliis et consistorio nostro intersunt, cogitaverint et tractaverint, eadem severitate voluntatem sceleris qua effectum puniri iura voluerunt, ipse quidem ut pote reus majestatis gladio feriatur, bonis eius omnibus fisco addictis; filii vero eius nullum unquam beneficium sive a nostro beneficio seu iure consensum optineant. Sit ei mors solacium et vita supplicium. Quod si qiusquam de factiosis mox sine mora factum detexerit, veniam et gratiam mox sequatur. Crimen majestatis post mortem rei etiam incipit et tractatur; rei ù memoria condempnatur, adeo ut quicquid contraxerit, fecerit, statuerit, a die criminis nullam habeat firmitatem; set omne quod habuit, fisci iuribus vendicetur. Hoc crimine qui parentem purgaverit, eius successionem meretur. Hoc crimine tenentur omnes, quorum consilio fugiunt obsides, armantur cives, seditiones moventur, concitantur tumultus, magistratus necantur, exercitus deseritur, ad hostem fugitur, socius proditur, dolo malo cuneus discinditur, bellis ceditur, ars desolatam relinquitur, sociis auxilium denegatur, cetaraque hujusmodi sicut regii consilii explorator, summissor et publicator, et qui susceperit hospitio hostes regni, et ductum prbeuerit non ignarus.

XIX. De nova militia

Divine iustitie consentientes probanda probamus contrarium refutamus. Sicut, enim, nullatenus exasperandi sunt boni, ita beneficiis non sunt fovendi mali. Sanccimus, itaque tale proponentes edictum, ut si quicumque novam militiam arripuerit, contra regni nostri beatitudinem, atque pacem, sive integritatem, militie nomine et professione, penitus decidat, nisi forte a militari genere per successionem duxerit prosapiam. Idemque statuimus de sortientibus qualiscumque professinis ordinem, ut puta si vel auctoritatem iudicii optinuit, sive notariorum officium, ceterisque similibus.

XX. De falso

Qui litteras regias aut mutat aut quas ipse scripsit notho sigillo subsignat, capitaliter puniatur.

XXI. De cutendibus monetam

Adulterinam monetam cudentibus, vel scienter eam accipientibus, penam capitis irrogamus, et eorum substantiam publicamus; consentientes etiam hac pena ferimus. Qui nummos aureos vel argenteos raserint tinxerint, vel quocumque modo imminuerint, tam personas eorum, quam bona omnia publicamus.

Ubi questio falso inciderit, diligens inquisitio mox sequatur, argumentis, testibus, collatione scripturarum, et aliis vestigiis veritatis. Non solum accusator probationibus honeretur, set inter utramque personam iudex sit medius, ut omnibus que competunt exquisitis, demum sententiam ferat. Capitali post probationem supplicio secuturo si id exigat magnitudo supplicii, vel alia pena pro qualitate delicti.

XXII. De falso instrumento

Qui falso instrumento nesius utitur, falsi crimine non punitur. Qui falsitatem testibus astruxerit, falsi pena cohercetur.

XXIII. De abolitione testamenti

Amator testamentorum, publicorum instrumentorum, celator, delator, perversor, eadem pena tenetur. Si quis patris testamentum deleverit, ut quasi ab intestato succedat, patris hereditate privatur.

XXIV. De officialibus publicis

Qualitas persone gravat et relevat penam falsi. Officiales reipublice, vel iudicis qui tempore amministrationis pecunias publicas subtraxerint, obnoxii crimini peculatus, capite puniantur, nisi regia pietas indulserit.

XXV. De bonis publicis

Qui sua negligentia bona publica deperire, vel minui permiserit, in persona propria et rebus suis, constituetur obnoxius, et hoc prospectu pietatis rege. Qui sciens furantibus assensum prebuerit, eadem lege tenetur.

XXVI. De coniugiis legitime celebrandis

Quoniam ad curam et sollecitudinem regni pertinet leges condere, populum gubernare, mores instruere, pravas consuetudines extirpare, dignum et equum visum est nostre clementie, quandam pravam consuetudinem, que quasi clades et lues huc usque per diuturna tempora, partem nostri populi perrependo pervasit edicti nostri mucrone decidere, ne liceat vitiosas pullulas de cetero propagare. Absurdum quippe moribus repugnans sacrorum canonum institutis, christianis auribus inauditum est, matrimonium velle contrahere, legitimam sobolem procreare, indivisibile vite consortium alligare, nec dei favorem et gratiam nuptis nuptiarum in stabulis querere, et tantum in Christo et ecclesia ut dicit apostulus sacramentum confirmandum per sacerdotum ministerium creare. Sancimus itaque lege presenti deo propitio perpetuo valitura, volentibus omnibus legitimum contrahere matrimonium necessitatem imponi, quatinus post sponsalia nuptias celebraturi sollempniter quisque pro suo modulo seu commodo, limen petant ecclesie sacerdotum benedictionem post scrutinium consecutum anulum ponat, pretii postulationique sacerdotali subdantur, si volunt futuris heredibus successionem relinquere.

Alioquin noverint ammodo molientes contra nostrum regale preceptum, neque ex testamento, neque ab intestato se habituros heredes legitimos, ex illecito per nostram sanctionem matrimonio procreatos. Mulieres etiam dotes, et aliis nubentibus legitime debitas non habere. Rigorem cuius sanctionis, omnibus illis remittimus, qui promulgationis eius tempore, iam matrimonium contraxerunt.

Viduas vero volentibus ducere, huius necessitatis vinculum relaxamus.

XXVII. De adulteris

Generali lege presente sancimus pietatis intuitu, cui viscera tota debemus, quotiens a nostra provisione et ordinatione iura regentibus accusatio adulterii aut stupri fuerit presentata, oculo non caligante personam despicere, condiciones notare, etates et consilium animi investigare, si deliberatione vel consultatione, vel lubrico etatis proruperint, ad facimus, vel prolapse sint. Utrum earum fortuna tenuis sit an torosa, petulantia stimulate fuerint, an dolore maxime materiali. Ut, his omnibus perquisitis, probatis vel manifestis, non de rigore iuris, set de lance equitatis, super commissis excessibus, lenior vel asperior sententia feratur. Sic, enim, perfecta iustitia divine iustitie respondebit. Nam nec nos poterit illa divina sententia: in qua mensura mensi fueritis remetietur vobis.

Legum igitur asperitate lenita, non ut olim gladio agendum, set rerum ad eam pertinentium confiscatio inducetur, si filios legitimos ex eo matrimonio violato, vel alio non habuerit. Periniquum est successione quippe fraudari, qui nati sint eo tempore quo thori lex legaliter servabatur. Aut viro traenda est, nullatenus ad vite periculum servituro, set ultionem thori violati, nasi truncatione, quod sevius et atrocius inducitur persecuturo. Ultra enim, neque viro, neque parentibus sevire licebit. Quod si vie eius noluerit in eam dare vindictam, nos huiusmodi maleficium non sinemus inultum, precipimus publice flagellandum.

Qui coram se spectante, vel arbitrio, permittit cum ganeis suam coniugem lascivire, non facile poterit vero iudicio accusare. Viam quippe mechandi aperit, qui cum possit prohibere consentit.

Quamvis uxorem suspectam quis habeat, eum lenocinii non dapnamus. Quis enim alieni thori iure inquitet quietem. Quod si patenter deprehendimus quempiam habere uxorem questuosam, dignam nostris temporibus mox sequimur pene vindictam, eum quoque pena infamie condempnamus. Femine penitus, et adulterii et stupri severitate iudiciaria prestentur immunes, quas vilitas vite dignas legum observatione non credit.

XXVIII. De eodem

Que passim venalem formam exhibuit, et vulgo prostitutam se prebuit, huius criminis accusationem ammovit. Violentiam tamen ei ingeri prohibemus, et inter boni testimonii feminas, ei habitationem vetamus. Adulter, adultera simul accusari non possunt, alter singulariter est accusandus, et rei exitus expectandus. Nam si adulter defendi poterit, mulier est secura, nulli ulterius responsura. Si vero fuerit condempnatus, tunc demum mulier accusatur.

Lex delectum non facit, quis primum conveniri debeat. Set si uterque presens est, vir conveniendus est primum.

Repudium in accusatione est semper permittendum; neque violentia seu detentio est adhibenda.

XXIX. De lenocinio

Lenas sollicitantes alienam scilicet castitatem genus criminis pessimum, tamquam ipsas adulteras puniendas presente lege sancimus. Matres virgines filias venalicias proponentes, et maritalia federa fugientes, ut lenas ipsas persequimur, scilicet ut nasus ejus abscidatur. Castitatem enim suorum viscerum vendere inhumanum est et crudele. Quod si filia se ipsam tamen prostituerit, mater vero solummodo consentit, iudicum arbitrio relinquatur.

XXX. De violatione thori

Si providentia rege celsitudinis nullo modo patitur inter regni nostri militem baronum nostrorum quemlibet alterius castrum invadere, predas committere, cum armis insurgere, vel inique fraudari, quin pro commisso bonorum omnium iactura ipsum afficiat, quanto amplius dampnandum censemus si compatris et vicini thorum violare presumpserit. Intolerabile prorsus de iure videtur. Sanccimus itaque si de tali facto nobis aliquando fuerit proclamatum, manifestum fuerit, vel probatum, bonorum omnium mulctatione plectendum. Si maritus uxorem in ipso actu adulterii deprehenderit, tam uxorem, quam adulterum occidere licebit, nulla tamen mora protracta.

XXXI. De adulterio

Lex maritum lenocinii pena cohercet, qui uxorem in adulterio deprehensam, retinuerit, adulterumque dimiserit, nisi forte sine sua culpa ille diffugit.

XXXII. De desistendibus ab accusatione

Qui post crimen adulterii intentatum uxorem receperit, destitisse videtur ab accusatione ideoque suscitare qustionem ultra non poterit.

XXXIII. De iniuriis privatis personis illatis

Quod iuri et rationi est consentaneum satis iure cunctis est gratum, et quod a ratione equitatis dicrepat, universis ingratitudinem representat. Nulli igitur mirum si quod in homine deus carius et dignius posuerit, cum negligitur atque despicitur, et inprobo iudicio vilipenditur, sapiens et honestatis amicus rationabiliter indignatur. Quid enim absurdius quam equa lance pensari ubi iumenti cauda decerpitur, et ubi honestissimi viri barba depilatur.

Pro suggestione ergo populi nostro regno subiecti atque supplicantie legum suarum ineptitudinem cognoscentis hanc legem et edictum proponimus. Ut cuicumque de popularibus excusato, tamen et deliberatione barba fuerit depilata, reus talis commissi pena huiusmodi feriatur solidis aureis scilicet regiis sex; si vero in rixa factum fuerit, sine deliberatione et studio, de eisdem solidis III.

XXXIV. De iniuriis personis illatis curialibus

Observent diligentissime iudices, ut in actione iuriariarum, curialium dignitatem personarum considerent, et iuxta personarum qualitatem sententiam ferant, eorum scilicet quibus fiunt, et eorum qui faciunt, et quando ubi temeritas presumitur, et iuxta qualitatem personarum sententiam ferant; ipsis autem facta iniuria, non ad ipsos dumtaxat, set etiam ad regie dignitatis spectat offensam.

XXXV. De mederi volentibus

Quisquis ammodo mederi voluerit, officialibus et vicibus nostri se presentet, eorum discutiendus iudicio. Quod si sua temeritate presumpserit, carcere constringatur, bonis ejus omnibus publicatis. Hoc autem prospectum est, ne quilibet nostro regno subiecti periclitentur imperitia medicantum.

XXXVI. De plagiariis

Qui sciens liberum hominem vendiderit hac pena legitima teneatur, ut ex bonis suis venditus redimatur; ipse vero maleficus curie nostre servus sit, bonorum suorum residuo publicato. Quod si non poterit redimi, pro servo tradatur parentibus venditi, bonis eius curie addictis. Quocumque autem venditus redeat, maleficus curie servus fiat, fillis etiam post hunc casum nascentibus subiectis curie perpetue servituti.

XXXVII. De siccariis

Qui aggressorem vel latronem in dubio vite discrimine constitutis occiderit, nullam ob id factam calumpniam metuere debet.

XXXVIII. De infantibus et furiosis

Infans sine malignitate animi et furiosus si hominem occiderit, non tenetur. Quia alterum innocentia consilii, alterum fati infelicitas excusat.

XXXIX. De fure

Nocturnum furem qui occiderit, impune ferat si aliter comprehendi non potuerit, dum modo clamore id fiat.

XL. De incendiariis

Qui dolose domum incenderit capitis pena plectatur, velud incendiarius. In maleficiis voluntas spectatur non exitus; nichil enim interest occidat quis an mortis causam prebeat.

XLI. De precipitatoribus

Qui de alto se ipsum precipitat, et hominem occiderit, et ramum incautus prohiciens, non proclamaverit, seu lapidem ad aliud iecit, hominemque occidit, huic pene non succumbit.

XLII. De poculo

Mala et noxia medicamenta, ad alienandos animos, seu venena quis dederit, vendiderit, habuerit, capitali sententia feriatur. Poculum amatorium, vel aliquem cibum noxium, quisquis instruxerit, etiam si neminem leserit, impunis non erit.

XLIII. Si iudex litem suam fecerit.

Iudex si accepta pecunia reum quem criminis et mortis fecerit, capitis periculo subiacebit. Si iudex fraudulenter atque dolose sententiam contra leges protulerit, auctoritate iudiciaria inrecuperabiliter cadat, notetur infamia, rebus eius omnibus publicatis. Quod si ignorantia a iuris sententia oberraverit, ferens iudicium pro simplicitate animi manifesta, regie misericordie et providentie subiacebit.

Codex Casinensis 468

Leges a nostra maiestate noviter promulgatas, generaliter ab omnibus precipimus observari, moribus, consuetudine, et legibus non cassatis, nisi forte nostris his sanctionibus adversari quid in eis manifeste videatur.

1. De privilegiis ecclesiarum

Primo itaque iura sanctarum ecclesiarum, res omnes et possesiones earum in nostra post deum et sanctos ejus custodia collacatas ab omnibus incursibus malignantium, gladio materiali a deo nobis concesso defendimus et inviolatas custodimus; quisquis hoc nostrum decretum violare voluerit, nostram senserit ledere maiestatem.

2. Ut domini subiectos humane tractent

Monemus, princeps, comites, et barones, omnesque dominos, subiectos humane tractare, misericordiam adhibere, maxime cum debitum adiutorium et moderatum et conveniens volent ab ipsis, quos habent subiectos, postulare.

3. Ut regalia non minuantur

Quicumque de regalibus nostris magnum vel modicum quid tenet, nullo modo, nullo ingenio possit ad nostra regalia pertinens donare, vendere, vel alienare, vel in totum vel in partem minuere.

4. De sacrosanctis ecclesiis, et episcopis, et clericis

Sancimus nemini licere sanctorum reliquias vendere vel comparare. Sancimus sub capitis periculo nullos penitus cuiuscumque condicionis de sacrosanctis ecclesiis expelli aut protrahi confugas; nec pro his venerabiles episcopos vel iconomos exigi que debentur ab eis; nec ipsis confugis interim victualia negentur. Servus vero, colonus, seu gleba servus, subtrahens se domino, vel furatus res ad loca sacra confugiens, cum rebus quas detulit domino presentetur.

Privilegia ecclesiarum inconcussa serventur. Episcopus ad testimonium non flagitetur, nisi forte in causis ecclesiasticis vel publicis, et cum summa necessitas, aut regis auctoritas postulaverit. Diaconos et subdiaconos et infra positos altari sacri ministros, ab obsequiis sordidis, alienos esse precipimus. Presbiteros vero tantum non etiam ceteros ab angariis personalibus prohibemus.

5. De illicitis conventiculis

Conventiculam illicita extra ecclesiam in privatis edibus celebrari vetamus.

6. Ne servi vel ascripticii clericentur

Ascripticios sine voluntate eorum quorum iuri subditi sunt, nullus episcoporum ordinare presumat. Iudeus, paganus, servum christianum, nec compare audeat nec ex aliquo titulo possidere.

7. De ioculatoribus

Mimi et mime, et qui ludibrio corporis sui questum faciunt, publico habitu veste monachica, vel clericali non utantur; quod si fecerit, verberibus publice afficiantur.

8. De raptu

Si quis rapere sacratas virgines, aut nondum velatas causa iungendi matrimonium presumpserit, capitali pena feriatur.

9. De apostatis

Apostatas insequimur ultionibus, bonis omnibus spoliamus. A professione vero naufragantes seu voto legibus coartamus, succesiones tollimus, omne ius legitimum abdicamus.

10. De pupillis et orphanis

Leges que pro pupillis et orphanis faciunt relevamus. Mulieribus lesis ex pietatis visceribus propter fragiliorem sexum subveniendum decrevimus sicut decet, et quatenus oportet.

ASSIZES OF ARIANO

11. De sacrilegis consiliis

Disputari de regis iudiciis, consiliis, institutionibus et factis non oportet; talis disputatio par sacrilegio computatur. Multe leges sacrilegos severissime punierunt, set pena moderata est arbitrio iudicantis, nisi forte manu facta templum dei fractum est violenter, aut dona et vasa sacra noctu sublata sunt, hoc enim casu capitale est.

12. De crimine maiestatis

Quisquis cum milite uno aut pluribus seu privato villano scelestam inhierit factionem aut factionis dederit vel susceperit sacramentum, de nece etiam virorum illustrium, qui consiliis et consistorio nostro intersunt, cogitaverint et tractaverint, eadem enim severitate voluntatem sceleris qua effectum puniri iura voluerint, ipse quidem ut pote reus majestatis gladio feriatur, bonis eius fisco addictis. Filii vero eius nullum unquam beneficium sive a nostro beneficio seu iure confertum optineant;sit ei mors solacium et vita supplicium. Quod si quisquam de factiosis mox sine mora factam detexerit, et premio a nobis et honore donabitur.

Is vero qui usus fuerit factione, si vero tamen incognita adhuc patefecerit et conciliorum archana absolutione tantum ac venia dignus habebitur; sic tamen, si suis assertionibus veri fides fuerit opitulata, laudem maximam et premium a nostra clementia consequetur; alioquin capitali pena plectetur.

Crimen maiestatis post mortem rei etiam incipit et tractatur, et rei memoria condempnatur adeo ut quicquid contraxerit, fecerit, statuerit, a die criminis nullam habeat firmitatem; hoc crimine qui parentem purgaverit, eius successionem meretur.

Hoc crimine tenentur omnes quorum consilio fugiunt obsides, armantur cives, seditiones moventur, concitantur tumultus, magistratus necantur, exercitus deseritur, ad hostem fugitur, dolo modo cuneus scinditur,socius proditur, bellis ceditur, arx desolatur vel relinquitur, sociis auxilium denegatur, cetaraque huiusmodi, ut regii consilii explorator, sive missorum publicator et qui susceperit hostes regni hospitio, vel ductum prebuerit non ignarus.

13. De jnjuriis curialium

Observent iudices diligentissime, ut in actionem injuriarium curialium personarum dignitatem et qualitem eorum quibus illate sunt, et eorum qui faciunt, et quando, et ubi, huiusmodi temeritates presumuntur, et sic ferant sententiam; quia non ad ipsos dumtaxat, sed ad regie dignitatis spectat offensam.

14. De crimine falsi

Qui litteras regias aut mutat, aut quas ipse scripsit notho sigillo subsignat capitaliter puniatur. Qui falso instrumento utitur nescius, falsi crimine non punitur.

Adulterinam monetam cudendibus vel scienter eam succipientibus, et utentibus, penam capitis irrogamus, et eorum substantiam publicamus; consentientes etiam, hac pena ferimus.

Qui nummos aureos vel argenteos raserit, tinxerit, vel aliquo modo minuerit, tam personas eorum, quam bona omnia publicamus.

Qui falsitatem testibus astruxerit falsi pena coherceantur.

Motor testamentorum publicorum, instrumentorum celator, deletor, perversor, eadem pena tenetur.

Si quis patris testamentum aboleverit, ut quasi ab intestato succedat, patris hereditate privetur.

Qualitas persone gravat et relevat penam falsi.

15. De coniugiis

Sancimus lege presenti, volentibus omnibus legitimum contrahere matrimonium necessitatem imponi, quatenus post sponsalia celebraturi nuptias sollempniter quisque pro modulo suo seu quomodolibet limen petat ecclesie, sacerdotum benedictionem post scrutinium consecuturum anulum ponat, preci postulationique sacerdotali subdantur, si voluerint futuris heredibus successiones relinquere. Alioquin amodo molientes contra regale nostrum edictum, neque ex testamento neque ab intestato, habituros se legitimos filios heredes ex illicito matrimonio per nostram sanctionem noverint procreatos; mulieres etiam aliis nubentes legitimas dotes debitas non habere. Viduas vero volentibus ducere hoc necessitatis vinculum relaxamus.

16. De crimine adulterii

Generali lege sancimus quotiens nostra provisione et ordinatione iura regentibus accusatio adulterii vel strupi fuerit presentata, oculo non caligante personas despicere, condiciones notare, etates et consilium animi investigare, si deliberatione, consultatione, vel lubrico etatis proruperint ad facinus vel prolapse sint, an dolore maxime maritali; ut, his omnibus perquisitis, probatis vel manifestis, non de rigore iuris set de lance equitatis super commissis excessibus levior vel asperior sententia proferatur. Sic enim profecto iustitia nostra divine iustitie respondet.

Legum igitur asperitate lenita, non ut olim gladio agendum, set rerum ad eam pertinentium confiscatio inducetur, si filios legitimos ex eo matrimonio violato vel alio non habuerit. Iniquum enim est eos successione privari, qui nati sunt eo tempore quo thori lex legaliter servabatur. Aut viro tradenda est nullatenus ad vite periculum servituro, set ultionem thori violati nasi truncatione quod sevius et atrocius inducitur persecutor; ultro enim nec viro nec parentibus sevire licebit. Quod si vir eius noluerit in eam dare vindictam, nos maleficium huiusmodi non sinemus inultum; precipimus igitur publice flagellandum.

Qui coram se spectante, vel arbitrio permittit cum ganeis coniugem suam lascivire non facile nostro iudicio poterit accusare. Viam quippe peccandi mechandi aperit, qui cum possit pohibere consentit.

Quamvis uxorem suspectam quis habeat, quamvis famosam, si tamen fidem habet, eum lenocinii non dampnamus; quis enim iure thori alieni inquietet quietem. Quod si patenter deprehendimus quempiam habere incestuosam uxorem, dignam mox sequemur pene vindictam; eum quoque pena infamie condempnamus.

Femine penitus et adulterii et stupri prestentur immunes iudiciaria severitate, quas vilitas vite dignas legum observatione non credidi, sicut ministre caupone.

17. De meretricibus

Que passim formam venalem exhibuit, et vulgo prostitutam se prebuit, huius criminis accusationem amovit; violentiam tamen ei ingeri prohibemus, et inter boni testimonii feminas habitare vetamus.

18. De accusatione adulterii

Adulter et adultera simul accusari non possunt, alter singulariter est accusandus, et rei exitus expectandus; nam si adulter defendi poterit, mulier est secura, nulli ulterius responsura. Si vero fuerit condempnatus, tunc demum mulier accusatur.

De crimine adulterii pacisci non licet, et par delictum accusatoris prevaricatoris et refugientis veritatis inquisitionem. Qui autem pretium pro comperto stupro accepit, pena legis Julie de adulteriis tenetur. Crimen adulterii maritum retenta in matrimonio uxore, inferre non posse nemini dubium est.

Lex delectum non facit, quis primum debeat conveniri, set, si uterque est presens, vir convenendus est primum. Repudium in hac accusatione pretermittendum, neque violentia seu detentio adhibenda.

19. De officialibus rei publice

Officiales rei publice vel iudices qui in tempore amministrationis pecunias publicas subtraxerint, obnoxii crimine peculatus, capite puniuntur, nisi regia pietas indulserit.

Qui sua negligentia bona publica deperire vel minui permiserit, et in persona propria et in rebus suis constituetur obnoxius; et hoc prospectu regie pietatis.

ASSIZES OF ARIANO

20. De furtis

Qui sciens, furanti sinum prebuit, eadem pena tenetur.

21. De crimine lenocinii

Lenas sollicitantes alienam castitatem genus criminis pessimum tamquam ipsas adulteras puniendas, presenti lege sancimus.

Matres virgines filias venalicias proponentes et maritalia federa fugientes, ut lenas ipsas persequimur, scilicet ut nasus earum abscidantur; castitatem enim et virginitatem suorum viscerum vendere inhumanum est et crudele; quod si filia se ipsam tamen prostituit, mater vero tantum consentit, iudicis arbitrio relinquetur.

Crimen lenocinii contrahunt, qui deprehensam in adulterio uxorem in matrimonio tenuerit, non qui suspectam adulteram habuerunt.

22. De eodem

Si providentia rege celsitudinis nullo modo patitur inter regni nostri limitem baronum nostrorum quemlibet alterius castrum invadere, predas committere, cum armis insurgere, vel inique fraudari, quin pro commisso bonorum omnium ipsum iactura afficiat; quanto amplius dampnandum censemus, si compatris vel vicini thorum violare presumpserit quis intolerabile prorsus de iure videtur. Sancimus itaque si de tali facto nobis aliquando fuerit proclamatum, et manifestum fuerit vel probatum, bonorum omnium mulctatione plectendum.

23. De vindicta adulterantium

Si maritus uxorem in ipso actu adulterii deprehenderit, tam adulterum quam uxorem occidere licebit, nulla tamen mora protracta. Lex maritum lenocinii pena cohercet, qui uxorem in adulterio deprehensam retinuit, adulterumque dimisit; nisi forte sine sua culpa ille diffugerit.

24. De desistentibus ab accusatione

Qui post crimen adulterii intemptatum uxorem receperit, destitisse videtur, ideoque suscitare questionem ultra non poterit.

25. De plagiariis

Qui sciens liberum hominem vendiderit, hac pena legitima teneatur, ut ex bonis suis venditus redimatur; ipse vero maleficus curie servus sit, bonorum suorum residuo publicato; quod si ex rebus ipsius redimi non poterit, pro servo tradatur parentibus venditi, bonis eius curie addictis; quocumque autem casu venditus redeat, maleficus curie servus fiat, filiis etiam post hunc casum nascentibus subiecti sint curie perpetua servitute.

26. De sicariis secundum legem corneliam

Qui aggressorem vel latronem, in dubio vite discrimine constitutis occiderit, nullam, ob id factum, calumpniam metuere debet. Qui aggressorem ad se venientem ferro repulerit, non homicida set defensor salutis est.

Nocturnum furem qui occiderit, impune feret, si aliter comprehendi nequiverit, si modo cum clamore id fiat.

Infans sine malignitate animi et furiosus si hominem occiderit, non tenetur; quia alterum innocentia consili alterum facti infelicitas excusat

Nichil interest occidat quis, an mortis causam prebeat.

In maleficiis voluntas spectatur non exitus.

Qui de alto se ipsum precipitat et hominem occidit, qui ramum incautus deiciens non proclamavit, seu lapidem aut aliud deiecit hominemque occidit, huic pene succumbit.

27. De incendiis

Qui dolose domum incenderit, capitis pena plectetur velut incendiarius.

KINGDOM OF SICILY

28. De noxiis medicaminibus

Poculum amatorium vel aliquem cibum noxium quisquis instruxerit, etiam si neminem leserit, impunis non erit.

29. De eisdem

Mala et noxia medicamenta ad alienandos animos, seu venena qui dederit, vendiderit, habuerit, capitali sententia feriatur.

30. De iudice depravato

Si iudex accepta pecunia reum quemlibet criminis et mortis fecerit, capitis periculo subiacebit.

Si iudex fraudulenter atque dolose sententiam contra leges protulerit, auctoritate iudiciaria irrecuperabiliter cadat, notetur infamia, rebus eius omnibus publicatis. Quod si iuris ignorantia a iuris sententia aberraverit, ferens iudicium pro simplicitate manifestum regie misericordie subiacebit.

In maleficiis voluntas spectatur non exitus.

31. De arripientibus novam militiam

Quicumque novam militiam arripuit contra regni nostri beatitudinem et pacem sine integritate militie nomine et professione penitus cadat, nisi forte a militari genere per successionem duxerit prosapiam.

32. De tironibus

Nullus tiro ga aut veteranus aut censibus obnoxius ad militia accedat.

33. De iniuriis privatorum

Cuicumque de popularibus ex consulto tamen et deliberatione barba fuerit depilata, reus soldorum aureorum VI regalium pena condempnetur; si vero in rixa factum fuerit, sine deliberatione, solidorum III.

Vel iumenti cauda decerpitur.

34. De fugacibus

Si quis temerario ausu presumpserit bona in quiete et tranquillitate regni habita, cum pro ipso laborare expedit, labores fugiendo obmittere, omnia bona sua dominus eius habeat, et illius persona curie assignetur.

35. De seditionariis

Si quis in exercitu seditiones, iurgia seu aliud fecerit, uti exercitus noster turbetur, persona eius cum omnibus suis bonis mercedi curie subiacebit.

Si quis ficte vel fraudulenter ad magnum exercitum non venerit, seu, postquam venerit, ab exercitu sine licentia curie recesserit, capitalem subibit sententiam, vel in manibus curie tradetur, ut ipse et eius heredes culusti fiant.

36. De mordisonibus

Comperit nostra serenitas infra regni nobis a deo concessi fines quorundam immanitate clandestina incendia, tam in urbanis quam rusticis prediis, perpetrari, arbores quoque et vites furtim cedere. Proinde hac edictali pragmatica sanctione in perpetuum valitura deo propitio sancimus, ut si quis amodo de hujusmodi reatu fuerit appellatus, si suspectione careat et eius conversatio per bonorum testimonia illibata consistat, pro tenore veterum legum, aut cuiuscumque loci consuetudine se expurget. Si vero tanti reatus non levis suspitio de eo fuerit, vel preterite vite sue probrosus cursus extiterit, opinionemque eius apud bonos et graves dehonestaverit, de calumpnia prius actore iurante, non ut actenus set ceteris super hoc legibus sopitis et moribus, igniti ferri subeat iudicium. Predicti denique criminis confessus aut convictus, dampno prius lese partis de eius facultatibus resarcito, vite sue periculum, vel membrorum suorum privatione pro bene placito maiestatis nostre incurret.

37. Que sit potestas justitiarii

Sancimus ut latrocinia, fracture domorum, insultus viarum, vis mulieribus illata, duella, homicidia, leges parabiles, calumpnie criminum, incendia, forisfacte omnes, de quibus quilibet de corpore et rebus suis mercedi curie debeat subiacere, a iustitiariis iudicentur, clamoribus supradictorum baiulis depositis, cetera vero a baiulis poterunt definiri.

38. De intestatis

Nuper ad nostri culminis pervenit audientiam quod cum aliquis burgensium vel aliorum hominum civitatum intestatus decedit, sive filii ex eo existant sive non, res eius ad opus curie nostre capiebantur, quod admodum maiestati displicuit et grave tulimus.

Nos itaque, ex solita nostre benignitatis gratia, hanc pravam consuetudinem penitus resecare volentes, precipimus, ut, si quis burgensium vel aliorum, qui in ipsa civitate devenerit, intestatus decesserit, si ex eo filii vel filia exiterit, ipse sui patris heres existat, et tertia pars omnium rerum eius pro ipsius anima erogetur.

Si vero nulli filii ex eo existant, tunc proximiores eius tam ex linea ascendentium et descendentium quam ex latere venientium, qui de iure ei succedere debent, heredes existant, si de feudo vel de servitio non fuerit, tertia tamen parte rerum suarum pro defuncti anima distributa.

Si autem filius vel filia ex eo nullus exiterit, vel alius tam ex linea ascendentium quam et descendentium, vel ex latere venientium, qui de iure ei succedere debeat, tunc etiam tertia parte omnium rerum suarum ut dictum est integre pro defuncti anima prestita, residuum ad opus curie nostre capiatur.

Si vero cum herede seu sine herede testatus decesserit, ultima eius voluntas in integrum observetur.

39. De excessu prelatorum et dominorum

De prelatis autem ecclesiarum sic a regia munificentia statutum est, ut in his tantum ab hominibus suis adiutorum exigant, vidilicet, pro consecratione sua, cum ad concilium a domino papa vocantur, pro servitio exercitus nostri, si quando in exercitu servierint, vel si vocati fuerint a rege vel missi, pro corredo nostro si quando in terris eorum nos hospitari vel corredum ab eis recipere contigerit. Et in his tantum casibus a prelatis omnibus, comitibus, baronibus et militibus moderate secundum facultates hominum suorum audiutoria exigant et accipiant.

40. Rescriptum pro cleris

De eo autem quod male interpretatum est videlicet quod de nostre maiestatis constitutione villani non audeant ad ordinem clericatus accedere, sine voluntate et assensu dominorum suorum, ita statutum est, quod si aliquis villanus est et servire debet personaliter intuitu persone, ut sunt ascripticii et servi glebe, et alii huiusmodi, qui non respectu tenimentorum vel alius beneficii servire debent, set intuitu personarum, que persone eorum sunt obligate servitis isti quidem, sine assensu et voluntate dominorum suorum ad ordinem clericatus accedere nequerunt. Illi vero, qui non intuitu personarum set respectu testimentorum vel aliquorum beneficiorum que tenent servire debent dominis suis, si voluerint ad ordinem clericatus accedere, liceat eis etiam sine voluntate dominorum suorum, prius tamen renuntiatis his que tenent a dominis suis.

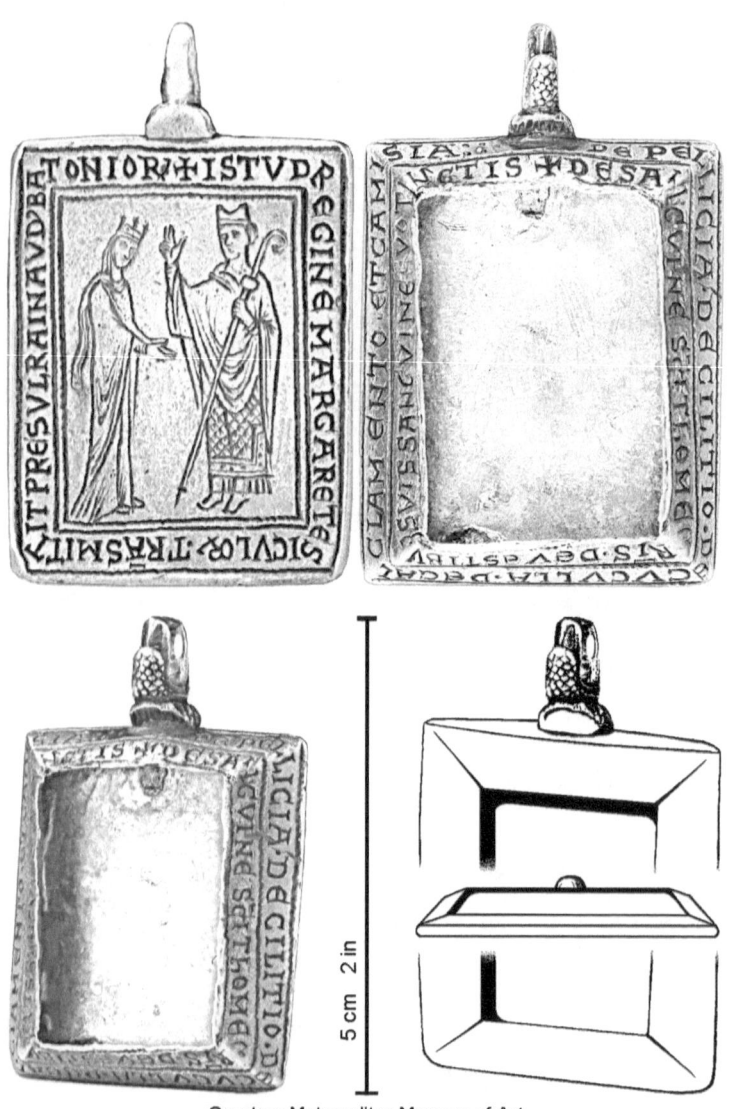

Courtesy Metropolitan Museum of Art

Appendix 2
MARGARET'S PENDANT

Except for a few small fragments of what is thought to be the crown of Roger II, the oldest surviving royal jewelry of the Kingdom of Sicily is the pendant of Margaret of Navarre, consort of William I and mother of William II. This is not, strictly speaking, regalia, because it was not associated with her coronation or queenship.[a]

The only contemporary image of Margaret known to us, which may indeed be a merely symbolic representation, is this gold reliquary pendant (a color photograph appears on this volume's back cover) made by skilled goldsmiths in Canterbury, a center of this craft. This was given to her by Bishop Reginald of Bath, whose name appears on it: "Bishop Reginald of Bath consigns this to Queen Margaret of Sicily." Clockwise, beginning from the cross at the middle-top of the border, this Latin inscription on the obverse reads: ISTUD REGINE MARGARETE SICULORUM TRANSMITTIT PRESUL RAINAUDUS BATONIORUM.

Seven tiny relics of Saint Thomas Becket were once preserved under a rock crystal. These are described in the inscription on the reverse side: DE SANGUINE SANCTI THOME MARTYRIS DE VESTIBUS SUIS SANGUINE SUO TINCTUS DE PELLICIA. DE CILITIO. DE CUCULLA. DE CALCIAMENTO. ET CAMISIA. "Of the blood of Saint Thomas Martyr. Of his vestments stained with his blood: of the cloak, the belt, the hood, the shoe, the shirt."

The majuscule characters are typical of the ecclesiastical engraving and inscriptions of the twelfth century; the lettering rendered in mosaic in the epitaph above Margaret's tomb in Monreale is very similar.

Bishop Reginald "Fitzjocelin" (de Bohun) of Bath, whose ambivalent relationship with Thomas was described by Herbert of Bosham, probably ordered the design of this pendant for Margaret on the occasion of her son's marriage, in 1177, to Joanna, the daughter of King Henry II of England. Margaret had intervened with Pope Alexander III, with whom she had a good rapport, when Reginald's father, Jocelin, was excommunicated by Thomas Becket.[b]

The pendant was likely sent to Palermo as a gift from Eleanor of Aquitaine to her *consuocera* (see note 445), whom she may have met at Palermo in 1149, but it is not noted explicitly in the chronicles of the time or in the surviving Pipe Rolls of Henry II. The nearest description comes to us from the chronicle of "Benedict of Peterborough" (Roger of Howden), which mentions "horses, clothes, gold and silver, and precious vases."[c]

Becket was murdered in late 1170 and canonized in 1173. Fashioned between 1174 and 1176, the gift was probably an acknowledgment of Margaret's support for Becket, specifically for giving refuge to his kinsmen in Sicily, and for her support of the papacy generally. There is debate as to whether the image depicts Margaret being blessed by Reginald, or by Becket himself, though the latter is the majority view among scholars.

Measuring 5 x 3.1 x .7 centimeters (nearly two inches in height), the pendant is exceptional for the mere fact of its preservation. The great majority of English goldsmiths' work of this period was melted down over the centuries. Hallmarks were not used in the twelfth century; the gold purity of the pendant is approximately twenty-two karats, which is slightly less than that of gold coins minted during the same period.

The essential form of the pendant was cast using what is now known as the "lost wax" process, with the reverse pounded into position and detailing, such as the lettering and the obverse image, engraved.

The engraving is quite similar in style to various drawings and illuminations of its era. For comparison, particular reference is sometimes made to those of the unfinished *Winchester Bible,* and specifically its Ecclesiastes (folio 268 recto). Forming the pattern of what were to be painted illuminations, the manuscript's drawings resemble the lines of the pendant's figures.

Margaret is shown bowing slightly for the bishop's blessing. Her gaze seems to be fixed on something she is holding in her hands, perhaps the reliquary itself. Not much can be inferred from this simple representation except that Margaret is depicted as rather slender and statuesque, nearly as tall as the prelate invoking the benediction (Thomas Becket was taller than average).

Long and tortuous has been the reliquary's journey from Canterbury to Palermo to Munich and then Florence, finally crossing the Atlantic during the middle years of the twentieth century. Removed from Margaret's tomb following the fire at Monreale in 1811, it was presented to Queen Maria Carolina of Naples with the relics already destroyed.

In 1861, Maria Sophia von Wittelsbach of Bavaria (1841-1925), the last Queen of the Two Sicilies, took the pendant with her into exile, eventually selling it to an agent of the Florentine firm of Stefano Bardini and donating the proceeds to poor veterans of the war that ended with the unification of Italy.[d]

It is now part of the collection of the Metropolitan Museum of Art in New York, where it is usually displayed in the Treasury gallery at the Cloisters Museum in Fort Tryon Park in Upper Manhattan, catalogued under accession number 63.160. The pendant was part of a significant bequest made in 1963 to the museum by Joseph Pulitzer (1913-1993), who acquired it from the Italian collector and art dealer Piero Tozzi, Stefano Bardini's son-in-law.

The fire of 1811 necessitated the replacement of Margaret's sarcophagus, which was mostly porphyry, with the marble one seen today.[e] Another consequence of the fire is that her remains, and her gown of reddish silk, were largely destroyed. Little is known of her crown, which resembled that of Constance of Aragon (see Appendix 3), but it is believed that its gold and gems were stolen shortly after the fire. In death, Margaret wore at least one ring bearing a large gemstone; this also disappeared.

Medievalists working in southern Italy from 1860 until the end of the Kingdom of Italy in 1946 seem to have been unaware of its very existence. The pendant has occasionally been mentioned by historians writing after 1965, when it was first described at length.[f] However, it has received very little attention in the former kingdom, where it is virtually unknown and where (as of this writing) it has never been publicly exhibited.

Many art treasures fashioned of gold kept in what is now Italy "disappeared" between the bloody unification war of 1860 and the tumultuous global conflict that ended in 1945. While fine collections are to be found in the museums of southern Italy, their administration and security leave much to be desired and they are generally poorly promoted and under-visited. It seems appropriate that the personal jewelry of the queen of a multicultural kingdom is displayed in one of the world's great "universal museums" in one of its most polycultural cities. The only superior circumstance would be to see the pendant worn by Margaret herself.

Notes

a. The mantle is the oldest "complete" item of royal regalia. For this and other items see Dolezalek, Isabelle, *Arabic Script on Christian Kings: Textile Inscriptions on Royal Garments from Norman Sicily* (2017).

b. The pope's letter to Jocelin in March 1172 states "King William of Sicily and his mother." Transcription in *Materials for the History of Thomas Becket, Archbishop of Canterbury* (in Sources), volume 7, pages 509-510 (document number 768).

c. *Gesta Regis Henrici Secundi Benedicti Abbatis* (in Sources), volume 1, page 120: *Tunc dominus rex tradidit filiam suam nunciis regis Willelmi simulque nunciis suis, et praeparavit eis necessaria sua, et dedit eis equos et vestes, et aurum et argentum, et vasa pretiosa.* See also *The Great Roll of the Pipe for the Twenty-Second Year of the Reign of King Henry II, AD 1175-1176,* in *The Publications of the Pipe Roll Society* (1904), volume 25, pages 198-199.

d. This detail was discovered in private records of the royal family now kept in Rome in the custody of Prince Carlo di Borbone of the Two Sicilies, Duke of Castro.

e. Margaret's tomb and other details before 1811 are described in Lello, Giovanni Luigi, *Descrizione del Real Tempio, e Monasterio di Santa Maria Nuova di Morreale* (1702 edition), especially page 82. See also note 754.

f. See Hoving, Thomas. "A Newly Discovered Reliquary of St Thomas Becket," *Gesta,* volume 4, spring 1965 (New York 1965), pages 28-30.

Appendix 3
CONSTANCE'S CROWN

This is the only royal crown of the Norman-Swabian *Regnum* to survive in its totality. The crown of Constance of Aragon, the first consort of Frederick II, was worn by her in death. Three of Constance's rings (out of a total of five known) are also preserved.

Fashioned of gold, leather and gemstones in the Byzantine style, the crown (shown on this book's cover) is typical of the head-dresses of the emperors and empresses of Constantinople, being a "skull cap" type of *kamelaukion* rather similar in design to a *kippah* or *taqiyah*.

It was manufactured in the workshops of Palermo, the *tiraz,* for a queen, though perhaps for an earlier consort.

The silk-lined crown is decorated with numerous pearls, ten garnets, nine rubies, fourteen sapphires, three topazes and one amethyst, including one stone bearing an Arabic inscription (in reverse for sealing) and another engraved with a heraldic beast (possibly a dragon).

A pair of fillet pendants is suspended from the crown. These frame the face of the person wearing it. Its roughly hemispherical shape makes the kamelaukion appear vaguely similar in form to the Crown of Saint Stephen of Hungary, which is also of Byzantine design and has pendilia.

Constance died in Catania on June twenty-third, 1222. A silver endotaph placed on her corpse reads: *Hoc est Corpus Domine Constancie Illustris Romanorum Imperatricis Semper Auguste et Regine Sicilie Uxoris Domini Imperatoris Frederici et Filie Regis Aragonum Obiit Autem Anno Dominice Incarnacionis Millesimo CCXXII, Die XXIII Iunii X Indicione in Civitate Catanie.*[a]

The crown was partially restored in 1491, the year it was first removed from Constance's tomb, which was also opened in 1781. It underwent a somewhat more extensive restoration in 1848 and is now displayed in the "treasury" museum of Palermo Cathedral.

It lacks the cross typical of royal crowns and obviously differs from the multifaceted diadems of Sicily's Norman kings (shown in mosaics in the Martorana church in Palermo and the cathedral of Monreale). This has led to much speculation.

It is possible that this kamelaukion crown was intended for less formal occasions. Perhaps it was worn when the queen walked among the common folk (not that she would have always worn a crown in such circumstances). This "informal" crown may have been designed without a cross because a Christian symbol would have been seen to alienate the Muslims and Jews of the kingdom, even though these subjects knew that their monarch was a Christian.[b]

The crown's history has been much debated, with some twentieth-century authors speculating that it was made for a king.[c] More recently, still others have made their views known.[d]

It is likely that Constance had other crowns besides this one, and those may have been more similar to the royal crown worn by Frederick II.

Regardless of its history, the crown adorned Constance of Aragon in death and in memory.

Notes

a. Body of Our Lady Constance, August Empress of the Romans, Queen of Sicily, Consort of Emperor Frederick, Daughter of the King of Aragon, Deceased at the City of Catania 23 June 1222 of the Tenth Indiction.

b. See Lipinsky, Angelo, "Sicaniae Regni Corona" and "Le Insegne Regali" in Sources.

c. See Lipinsky (the preceding note); also Maria Accascina's commentary in *Oreficeria di Sicilia,* pages 78-79, and Josef Deér's passing remarks in *The Dynastic Porphyry Tombs,* page 171. In his short monograph *La Corona di Costanza,* Gregorio La Grua, by stated intent (on page 7) does not respond directly to all of the affirmations of Lipinsky, Accascina or Deér.

d. In "From Her Head to Her Toes," Christopher Mielke examines Deér's tenuous thesis while citing several papers published after 1990.

Constance's crown

Appendix 4
THE CONTRASTO

Little is known of Cielo (Ciullo) of Alcamo, whose given name may be a form of *Michele* (Michael); in medieval Sicily *Celi* was often the shortened form of *Miceli*. Perhaps instead *Cielo* was short for *Marcello,* but what little evidence exists suggests that the poet was Sicilian and that he probably came from the town of Alcamo on the western side of the island.

The oldest surviving manuscript of his poem, the lengthiest of the Sicilian School, was copied in a "Tuscanized" tongue and script late in the thirteenth century, *Codex Vaticanus Latinus 3793*.

Intended to be literal and clear, this translation was effected without reference to any other. Previous English translations, such as those of Dante Gabriel Rossetti (1861) and Lorna Lancaster de'Lucchi (1922), rendered flowery, rhyming poetry which, though eloquent and appealing to the Victorian mind, was not very true to the original. That of Frede Jensen (1986) was a significant improvement.

As mentioned in this volume's Introduction, Dante Alighieri and others knew of Cielo's work, which was part of an early nexus that inspired the literary, and not merely spoken, use of an Italian vernacular even though it did not influence Tuscan directly.

The *Contrasto* with which the Tuscans were familiar may have been a version more faithful to the Middle Sicilian text. It was Angelo Colocci (1474-1549), an expert in Provençal poetry and secretary to Pope Leo X, who undertook the first serious effort to identify its author, perhaps based in part on supporting documentation now lost. The first modern analysis of note was that of Bruno Panvini published in 1962, and others have since followed.

The poem was most likely composed between 1234 and 1242.[a] It might reflect an attempt to parody the Provençal themes popular in that era (see note 74 for another possible example), but too little is known about Cielo or his intentions to draw a sound conclusion about this. Like his fellow court poet Giacomo of Lentini, Cielo may have been a royal notary or scribe. As mentioned above, his toponym suggests an association with the Sicilian town of Alcamo. Unlike Giacomo, he lacks a very substantial body of work. Indeed, the *Contrasto* is the only poem we know to be his.

As the story of a knight's successful effort to court a beguiling damsel, the *Contrasto,* or "Dialogue," is a fine example of the troubadour tradition. Was it read in the presence of Isabella of England or even Bianca Lancia? This we shall never know, but the possibility that one (or both) of these ladies heard it cannot be excluded from consideration.

The *Contrasto* was part of a trend, indeed a movement, during the age of chivalry. Cielo seems to have been familiar with *Le Roman de la Rose,* which was written a few years earlier and was widely disseminated. Here he plays on *Rosa* as the flower and the name of the damsel.

At times the author has the suitor calling the woman *madonna*, *mia donna* and *donna*, all terms used at court. Then in another stanza he switches to *vitama*, *càrama* and *amika*, typical usage amongst commoners, as if the dialogue were actually taking place between a troubadour and a peasant girl. However, the two protagonists switch to more intimate forms of speech as the poet's intent of bedding the lady is made clear. This is evident in the use of words such as *villana*, for *peasant*, towards the lady, indicating a lower social class, and *canzoniere* (troubadour) or *zitello* (young boy) by the lady towards the suitor so as to diminish his status within the court and socially.

Whilst Cielo's *Contrasto* imitated the vernacular poetry already being composed in France and Spain, it stood at the vanguard of its form in Italy. Here in Sicily, the most obvious vestiges of the age of chivalry must be dated to the next century, when the wooden ceiling of the barons' hall in the Steri castle in Palermo was painted with colorful images depicting the persons and heraldic designs typical of courtly culture.

For all the mystery about its author, the *Contrasto,* first published in Naples in 1661, is the earliest court poetry of its length written in any of the Italian languages. It stands at the apex of the Sicilian School.

The Poem

1. Knight: *Rosa fresca aulentissima, ki apparj inver la state, le donne ti disirano, pulzelle et maritate, Trajimi de 'ste focora, si de'ste a boluntate, per te non aviu abbento notte e dia, penzando pur di vuy, madonna mia.*

Oh, fresh and fragrant rose that blooms during the summer, envied by dames and damsels alike, I ask you to deliver me from this raging flame, for I can rest neither night nor day thinking of you, my lady.

2. Damsel: *Si di meve trabagliti, follia lo ti fa fare: lu mari potj arromperj avanti a semenare, l'abere de 'sto seculo tutto quanto assembrare. Avereme no' poteri a 'sto monnu, avanti li cavelli m'aritonno.*

If you are suffering because you keep thinking of me, you are terribly foolish. You would have more luck plowing the sea and then attempting to sow it.[b] You can try to collect all the goods of the earth but you still will never have me in this world. I would sooner cut off all my hair first and become a nun.

3. Knight: *Si li cavelli attònniti, avanti fossi morto, kà eu sì mi pèrdera lu sullazzo e diporto. Quanno ci passo e veioti, rosa fresca dell'orto, bono confortu donimi tutt'ore, poniamo ki s'aiunga nostro amore.*

If you were to cut off your hair, I would rather be dead, for I would lose all my solace and delight. When I walk by and see you, oh, fresh rose of the garden, you always give me a sense of pleasure. Let us allow our love to unite us!

4. Damsel: *Ki nostro amori aiungasjf?! No'boglio maltalenti! Si ci ti trova patremo co' l'altri miei parenti, guardanò t'aricolgono questi forti currenti. Como ti seppi bona la venuta, consigliu ki ti guardi la partuta.*

That our love were to unite us is something I do not even wish to desire. If my father and my other kinsmen were to find you here, beware, for if they return they'll catch you even if they have to chase you. As it was easy for you to get here, I advise you to be careful as you leave.

5. Knight: *Si toy parenti trovammi, ki mi pozzono farri? Una difensa mettoci di dumilia gostari, non mi toccara patreto per quanto ave a Bari. Viva l'imperaduri 'n grazi'a Deu! Intendi, bella, ki ti dico eu?*

If your father and relatives were to find me here, what could they do to me? They would have to pay a fine of two-thousand augustales.[c] Not even your father would try to harm me for all the riches in Bari. Long live the emperor, thanks be to God! Do you understand, my beautiful one, what I am saying to you?

6. Damsel: *Tu mi no' lasci vivere né sera né mattino! Donna mi so' di perperi, d'àuro massamotino, si tant'avé donassemi quant'ave Saladino, et per aiunta quanto lu Soldanu, toccaremi no' poteri a lu manu.*

You will not let me live in peace neither by day nor by night. I am a wealthy woman with Byzantine bezants and Berber gold. If you were to give me as much as Saladin's gold, and moreover all that the sultan owns, you would not even be able to touch my hand.

7. Knight: *Multi sono le fimmini c'hanno dura la testa, et l'omo, co' parabole, l'adimina et ammonesta, tanto intorno percazzala, fin ki l'ave in podesta. Femmina d'omo non si po' tenere, guàrdati, bella, pur di ripentere!*

There are many stubborn women but a man is able to conquer them and persuade them; he hunts them down until he has them under his power. A woman cannot keep a man away. Watch out, my beautiful one, for one day you may regret it!

8. Damsel: *K'eu mi repentéssendi? Avanti fossi accesa, ca nulla bona femmina per mi fosse ripresa. Aersera passastici, correnno a la discesa, acquistiti riposo, canzoneri! Le to' paraole no' me piaczo gueri.*

I will regret it one day? I would rather die than learn that an honest woman could be blamed because of me! I saw you walking by my home last night, running quickly from one side to another. Calm down, chansonnier, I do not like your words at all.

9. Knight: *Quanti sono le schiantora ki m'hai mise a lu cori! E solo purpenzànnonde, la dia quanno vo fori!*

THE CONTRASTO

Fimmina de 'sto secolo tanto no'amai ancori, quant'amo teve, rosa invidïata, bene creo kj mi fosti distinata.

How much pain you have caused me to feel in my heart, and all alone I think about it as I go out each morning! I have never loved a woman in this world as much as I love you, oh much envied rose. I truly believe that you are the woman destined to be with me.

10. Damsel: *Si distinata fosseti, cadèra de l'altezze, kè male messe forano in teve mie bellezze, Si tutto addivenissemi, tagliàrami le trezze! Eu consori m'arenno a una magione, avanti ki m'attoccano persune.*

If you were destined to be with me, I would be lowering my expectations too much, for my beauty would be lost on you. If all this were to happen, I would prefer to cut off my braids and become a nun in a convent, before you can touch my body.

11. Knight: *Si tu consore arenneti, donna col viso kleri, a lu mosteru venoci et arennomi confreri, per tanta prova vencierti, faràllo volonteri! Con te co'stao la sera et lu mattino, besogna ki ti tenga al meo dimino.*

If you were to become a nun, oh radiant-faced woman, I would come to the abbey and become a monk. I would do this immediately to win you in this trial. I would be with you both night and day. I must have you!

12. Damsel: *Oy me tapina misera, com'ào reo distinato! Gesù Cristo l'altissimo, de 'ntutto se' airato? Concepistimi a 'mbàttere in omo blestiemato? Cerca la terra, ch'este granne assai, kiù bella donna di me troverai.*

Alas, poor me, what a cruel destiny is mine! The most holy Jesus Christ must truly be angry with me for He has allowed me to encounter a sacrilegious man. Search the world that is very vast, for you will find a woman more beautiful than I.

13. Knight: *Cercat'aio Calabria, Toscana et Lumbardia, Pugla, Costantinopoli, Genoa, Pisa, Soria, Lamagna et Babilonia, tucta Barbaria. Donna non ci trovai tanto cortese: per donna sovrana di mi te prese.*

I searched in Calabria, in Tuscany, in Lombardy, in Apulia, in Constantinople, in Genoa, in Pisa, in Syria, in Germany, in Babylonia, and in all of North Africa.[d] In none of these lands have I found such a noble woman as you. Therefore, I have chosen you as my sovereign lady.

14. Damsel: *Poy tanto trabagliastiti, faccioti meo prigheri, ki tu vai et domannimi a mia mare et a mon peri. Si dare mi ti degnano, menami a lu mosteri et sposami davanti da la iente: eu poi farò le to' comannamente!*

As you have already gone through so much distress, I beseech you to go see my mother and my father tomorrow and ask them for my hand. If they deign to offer me to you in marriage, take me to the monastery[e] and marry me before everyone. And then I will obey your every command.

15. Knight: *Di ciò ki dici, vitama, neiente non ti bale, ca de le to' parabole fatto n'ao ponti e scale, penne penzasti mettere, sonti cadute l'ale. Eu dato t'aio la bolta sottana, dunque, si poy, manteniti villana.*

What you tell me, love of my life, will not bring you anywhere, for I won't even mention what you just told me. You thought you were growing feathers and instead your wings fell off and I gave you the final blow. Therefore, if you can, defend yourself, peasant girl.

16. Damsel: *En paura no' mettimi di nullo manganiello! Eu staomine 'n 'sta groria de 'sto forte castiello, prezzo le to' parabole meno de 'no zitiello. Si tu no' levi e vàitine di quace, si tu ci fosse morto ben mi kiace.*

Don't even think that you are frightening me with a mangonel.[f] I am well-protected in my strong castle and I consider your words less than those of a child. If you do not leave and go away from here, I'd be glad if you were dead.

17. Knight: *Dunque vorresti, vitama, ka per te fosse 'strutto! Si morto essere debboci od intagliato tutto, di kuaci no' mi mossera, si non ayo lu frutto lo quale staci ne lo to' jardino disìrolo la sera et lu mattinu.*

Therefore, love of my life, you wish that I be dead? Even if I were to die or if somebody were to cut me up into pieces, I would not leave this spot until I eat the fruit that's in your garden. I desire it morning and night.

18. Damsel: *Quello frutto non àvvero conti né cavaleri, molto lo disirarono conti et iustizieri, avere no' nde pottero, gìronde molto fieri. Intendi bene ki bole dicére me n'este di mill'unzi lo to' abere.*

Neither counts nor knights have ever partaken of that fruit. Marquesses and judges have long desired it, but they couldn't have it. Thus they were very angry when they left. Understand what I am trying to tell you; your property is worth less than a thousand ounces.[g]

19. Knight: *Molti so' li garofani, ma non ki salma nd'hai bella, no' dispregiaremi s'avanti no'massai. Si vento è 'n proda, et girasi, agiunge da li prai, arimembrare t'ao 'ste parole, ka de 'st'ira, animella, assai mi dole.*

You have many cloves[h] but not enough to make up an entire plot of land.[i] My beautiful, do not despise me before first granting me a chance. If the wind is in the sails and it changes direction instead so that I meet up with you on the shore, remember what I told you, for in my soul I feel a terrible pain.[j]

20. Damsel: *Macara, si dolesseti, ki cadesse angosciato la iente ci corressoro da traverso e da lato, tutt'a meve dicessoro 'accorri 'sto malnato! Non mi degnara porgere la mano, per quant'ave lu Papa et lu Soldano.*

Even if you were to feel so much pain that you fell down in agony, and people would come to you from left and right telling me, "Help this poor man!" I wouldn't even hold out a hand to help you for all the wealth of the Pope and the Sultan.

21. Knight: *Deu lo volesse, vitama, ka fossi morto in casa l'arma n'andèra cònsola ka di notte fantasa, la iente ti chiamarano 'oi periura, malvasa c'ha' morto l'omo in càsata traìta, sanz'ogni colpo levimi la vita!*

If only God would allow that I were to die in your home, oh love of my life! My soul that is in a delirium both day and night will leave comforted. People would call you: Oh evil liar! You killed a man in your own home, traitor! Alas, you kill me without even stabbing me.

22. Damsel: *Si tu no' levi e vàitine co' la maladizione, li frati miei ti trovano dentro kissà magione, bell'omi so s'eu soffero, perdici le persone, ka meve se' venuto a sormonare. Parente oy amico non t'ave a itare.*

If you don't get up and leave, then you shall be cursed; my brothers will find you in this house, and I would gladly accept that they kill you because you came here to bother me. Neither a kinsman nor a friend can come and save you.

23. Knight: *A meve non aì tano amiki né parenti stranio mi sono, carama, enfra 'sta bona ienti. Ora fa 'n'anno, vitama, ce'entrata mi se'n menti, dicènnoti: 'Vististi lu'ntaiuto?' Bella, da quello jorno so' feruto.*

My friends and relatives cannot help me. I am a foreigner, my dear, amongst these good people. It's been a year, oh my life's love, since you've entered my thoughts. Ever since you wore that dark dress of mourning.[k] Since that day, my beauty, have I been wounded.[l]

24. Damsel: *A tanto 'namorastiti, Iuda, hàilo traìto, como si fosse porpora, iscarlatto o sciamito! S'a le Vangelie iurimi ki mi sia marito, avereme no' poteri a 'sto monno, avanti in mari ièttomi a perfonno.*

Oh! So it was on that occasion that you fell in love, oh Judas the Traitor, as if I were wearing a scarlet dress or one made of another precious cloth![m] Even if you were to swear on the gospels that you'll become my husband, you cannot have me for any price in the world. I would rather throw myself out into the deepest sea!

25. Knight: *Si ne lu mari ièttiti, donna cortesi et fina, deretro mi ti misera per tucta la marina. Da poi ca annegàsseti, trobàrati a la rina solo per questa cosa adimpretare, con teco m'ayo a junjiri et peccare.*

If you were to throw yourself out into the sea, oh noble and fine woman, I would follow you all along the harbor, and after you've drowned I would find you on the shore to do this one thing: I must commit a sin by having you for my pleasure.

26. Damsel: *Segnomi in Patri et 'n Filio ed in Santo Matteo, si ka non se' tu retico, figlio de lu giudeo, e cotale parabole n'odio redire anch'eu! Mortasi la fimmina, a lo 'ntutto perdeci lu saboru et lu desduttu.*

I make the sign of the cross in the name of the Father, and of the Son and of Saint Matthew.[n] I know that you are neither a heretic nor a Jew, and I've never heard such words before. If a woman is completely dead, you lose all the fun and pleasure.

27. Knight: *Bene lo faccio, carama; altro no' pozzo fare, si quisso non accomplimi, lassone lo cantare. Fallo, mia donna, plàzati, kj bene lo poi fare. Ancora tu no' m'ami, molto t'amo, sì m'hai preso come lu pesci a l'amo.*

I know that well, my dear. There is nothing else I can do. If you do not fulfill my desire now, I will stop singing. Fulfill it, my woman, please me, for I know you can. Even if you don't love me, I love you dearly. You have caught me like a fish on a hook.

28. Damsel: *Sazzu ki m'ami; amoti di core paladino, lèvati susu e vattene, tornaci a lu mattino. Si ciò ki dico facimi, di bon cor t'amo e fino. Quisso eu ti 'mprometto sanza faglia, te' la mia fede, ki m'hai in toa baglia.*

I know you love me, and I love you with a noble heart. Now get up and leave. Come back tomorrow morning. If you do as I tell you, I will love you with all my heart and faithfully. I promise this to you truthfully. You have my word; I put myself under your command.

29. Knight: *Per zò ki dici, carama, neiente non mi movo. Innanti prenni e scannami, to 'sto cortello novo, 'sto fatto fare potesi innanti scalfi 'n'ovo. Accompli mio talento, amika bella, kè l'arma co' lu cori mi si 'nfella.*

Because of what you're telling me, my dear, I won't move from here at all. I would prefer that you slaughter me. Here take this new knife to do it. We can do this before you cook an egg.[o] Fulfill my desire, my beautiful friend, because my soul and my heart are overcome with sadness.

30. Damsel: *Ben sazzu: l'arma doleti, cumo mo k'ave arsura. 'Sto fatto no' potèrasi per null'altra misura, si non hai le Vangelie, ki mo ti dico: 'Jura!' Avereme no' poi 'n toa podesta. Innanti prenni et tagliami la testa.*

I know this well. Your soul hurts like a man who is suffering from thirst.[p] This cannot be done in any other way. You need to have the gospels with you so that I can ask you to swear by them. Otherwise I will not surrender to you, unless you take me and cut off my head.

31. Knight: *Le Vangelie, carama? K'eu le porto 'n sino, a lu mostero presile, non c'era lu patrino. Sovra 'sto libro juroti: mai non ti vegno mino. Accompli mio talento in caritate, kè l'arma me ne sta 'n suttilitate.*

The gospels, my dear? I am carrying them in my coat pocket; I stole them in church while the priest wasn't there. Upon this book I swear never to betray you. Fulfill my desire, I beg you, for my soul is destroying me!

32. Damsel: *Meu sire, poy jurastimi, eu tucta quanta incenno. Sono a la toa presenzia, da voy non mi difenno. S'eu minespreso àioti, merzè, a voy m'arenno. A lo letto ne gimo, a la bon'ora, ki kissà cosa n'è data in ventur.*

KINGDOM OF SICILY

My lord, thanks to your oath my entire body is now burning with passion. I stand here before you and I give in to your requests. I ask you to forgive me if I've mistreated you as I now surrender. Let us finally go to bed together, for this is our destiny!

Notes

a. This dating reflects two important facts. Firstly, the gold *augustale* coin mentioned in the fifth stanza was instituted in 1231. Secondly, the *Contrasto* was clearly influenced by a French poem composed around 1230, namely *Le Roman de la Rose* (by Guillaume de Lorris with later additions by Jean de Meun), which may have taken a few years to make its way to Italy. (For further commentary see the works by Panvini, Mangieri and Spampinato Beretta in Sources.)

b. This is a proverb still in use in Calabria and Sicily, *zappari a l'acqua e siminari a lu ventu*, that refers to something impossible or inconclusive.

c. The *augustale* was a gold coin issued under Frederick II beginning in 1231 and minted in Messina and in Brindisi. It was patterned after the Roman *aureus*. The obverse showed the bust of the emperor according to the classical Roman style while the reverse bore Frederick's imperial eagle. The fine refers to a statute in Frederick's Constitutions of Melfi, where article 16, *De defensis imponendis, et quis eas imponere possit,* states that somebody who was attacked could have defended himself by invoking the law, and if this was not sufficient, the victim could have decided on a sum as compensation for having been attacked.

d. *Babylonia* probably refers to Cairo or Baghdad.

e. By *monastery* the poet simply means a church.

f. The mangonel was a medieval siege weapon. With the use of military terms such as mangonel, castle and the final blow, the poet is comparing the sexual conquest of a woman to a military battle. This was common use both in classical and medieval times.

g. The *ounce* was a Sicilian gold coin. One *oncia* was worth thirty *tarì*, another type of gold coin used in Sicily since Arab rule. The damsel is telling the knight that he is too poor for her.

h. Cloves refers to the spice. Many spices arrived from the east so they were quite expensive. The poet wants to say that even if the girl has much to offer, it is not enough to make her precious.

i. Here the term used is *salma,* a Sicilian form of measurement for both land and weight, q.v. Chapter 12.

j. The knight is reminding the damsel that, although she is despising him at the moment with the excuse of being wealthier than he, her fortune can change just like the wind.

k. For "dark dress of mourning," the poem states, *ti vististi di maiuto,* "you wore maiuto." Much has been debated regarding what kind of dress the author refers to, but the term is rooted in a Sicilian word of Arabic origin: *tabùt* meaning *tomb* in Arabic is still used in Sicily as *tabùto* with the same meaning. *Maiuto* is probably a corruption of this term, referring to a dress worn for mourning. The original text probably read, *ti vististi lo'ntavuto*.

l. That is to say, "wounded by your love," as Cupid wounds one's heart with his arrows.

m. Here the lady ridicules the suitor for having fallen in love with her while she was dressed in mourning as if what she was wearing were made of precious scarlet cloth or something similar.

n. Perhaps Saint Matthew was the woman's patron saint; for example she may have been from a town where he was venerated as the local patron (such as Salerno or Scicli).

o. "Before you can cook an egg." In the poem we find *inanti che scalfi un uovo,* which is a typical Sicilian expression, still in use, referring to something that happens quickly.

p. The term used here is *arma,* which means *soul* in Sicilian but *weapon* in Italian. There might be the use of a double meaning referring to the man's sexual organs. This is supported by the fact that in the same stanza the damsel is comparing the poet's sufferance to that of a man dying of thirst.

Appendix 5

CORONATION RITE

Christian coronation was a religious rite of a quasi-sacramental nature, rooted in "mystical" practices and traditions, some dating from antiquity. The first distinctly Christian coronation may have been that of Theodosius II of Constantinople, performed by the city's patriarch in 408, but little is known of the ceremony. When he was enthroned in 672, Wamba, a Visigothic king who ruled much of Spain and part of France, was anointed with holy oil, yet we do not know that a crown was placed on his head.[a] The "Iron Crown of Lombardy" was originally a votive symbol, not regalia.

It was a scholar in Charlemagne's Frankish empire who undertook to further develop the coronation ceremony. Hincmar of Rheims, who died in 882, formulated a rite that would serve as a model for those that followed, beginning with its use by the Carolingians. His *ordo* (order) owed much to episcopal consecration, and for centuries coronation was regarded as a sacrament.[b]

The rite came to consist chiefly of the *anointing* (blessing with holy oil or chrism) and the *crowning* (placing the crown upon the monarch's head), which were considered the two essential elements. Other features were the *vesting* (placing a mantle upon the monarch's shoulders), a simple *oath* sworn by the king, his *girding with a sword*, the *delivery of the sceptre and orb* as symbols of office, and the *delivery of the ring*.[c] The final step was royal *enthronement*.[d]

This was followed by the *acclamation of the people* (homage of the baronage in attendance), not to be confused with the "liturgical acclamation," or *laudes regiae*, which might be sung at the first mass the king attended after his coronation.[e]

The coronations of the kings of Sicily included *all* of these elements at a time when, it seems, those of some European kings did not (see note 467).

Beginning with the first Sicilian coronation in 1130, the Hautevilles, and then the Hohenstaufens, followed established Latin and Catholic usage. The form and wording of the coronation *ordo* observed in the Kingdom of Sicily was thus traditional, conforming quite closely to what was known elsewhere in the dozen or so "Latin" kingdoms then extant in central and western Europe. The *ordo* used in Norman England was quite similar to that of Norman Sicily, which it may have influenced.[f]

In theology and law, the king ruled by the grace of God, not by the will of the clergy or nobility. The idea of royal power emanating from the divine was reflected in imagery such as the mosaic in Palermo's Martorana church depicting Roger II crowned directly by Christ.[g] Yet the king's oath was nothing less than a covenant with the church and with all the people he ruled.

The *ordo* represented an intersection of the ecclesiastical (anointing) and the political (crowning), or even the spiritual and the temporal. It made the king a living symbol of heavenly authority in a secular environment. Coronation distinguished kings from uncrowned monarchs such as the princes of Salerno and the dukes of Spoleto.

Coronations were public rituals performed in cathedrals or royal chapels with witnesses present. Though there are records of some of our kings and queens being crowned more than once in the course of a lifetime, chroniclers mentioned very few details about the actual ceremonies. As we have seen (in Chapter 9), the knighting of a young king, or a youth destined to become one, was a ceremony distinct from coronation. A coronation might occasion a tax on the nobility, but this does not seem to have become the norm in the Kingdom of Sicily until the thirteenth century.

The *ordo* itself is thoroughly Latin, and played a part in the gradual Latinization of the kingdom. Yet Byzantine influences in the ambience are obvious enough from royal and ecclesial iconography. In illuminated liturgical scrolls of this period we see clergy depicted wearing Byzantine vestments. The chanting or singing of hymns in certain liturgies, such as those celebrated immediately before and during Easter, is reflected in some distinctive parchment scrolls that survive. Indeed, such a scroll may have been used in the mass following an actual coronation when it occurred around Easter.[h]

The *ordo* used for Sicilian queens differed from that for kings, and only one recension (version) of it survives.[i] Most queens of Sicily were crowned at marriage or when their husbands were crowned. The only Sicilian queen of the Norman-Swabian period crowned in her own right (as queen regnant) was Constance Hauteville, the daughter of Roger II. The

KINGDOM OF SICILY

others were crowned upon marriage to the king (Sibylla of Burgundy, Beatrice of Rethel, Joanna of England), or when the king himself was crowned (Elvira of Castile).

Not every queen was crowned in the capital (Constance Hauteville was crowned in Bari) but the kings were crowned in Palermo. The rite for crowning a *rex filius* (William I in 1151) or a child (Frederick II in 1198) was presumably somewhat simpler that what appears here.

Copied around 1200 in Beneventan script, the best-known manuscript of the coronation rites, and what seems to be the oldest text, probably taken from a charter written decades earlier, is conserved in the Biblioteca Casanatense (Casanata Library) in Rome as *Codex 614*. In earlier times it was housed in the archive of Benevento's cathedral, where it may have been the papal copy of the *ordo* during the pontificate of Innocent III.

Besides the coronation rite for queens, *Incipit Ordo ad Reginem Noviter Benedicendam,* the Casanata manuscript contains two for kings, namely *Incipit Ordo ad Regem Benedicendum Quando Novus et Clero et Populo Sublimatur in Regnum,* possibly the *ordo* used for Roger II, and the shorter *Ista est ordinacio de sollempnitate coronacionis regis,* probably used for his successors. In addition to these three texts, four "redundant" copies (for kings) from the Kingdom of Sicily are known.[j]

The celebrant was usually the Archbishop of Palermo as Primate of Sicily. (The coronation rites of Frederick II as King of the Germans, Holy Roman Emperor, and King of Jerusalem were different from the *ordo* presented here.) Based on the well-established norms set forth in codices contained in the "Roman-German Pontifical," the so-called *Pontificale Romano-Germanicum* (popularly the "PRG"), the three rites in the Casanata manuscript are generally similar to the orders used for other western European kings, not only those of England, during this period.[k]

Much in the rites is not only liturgical but Biblical. The coronation rite was followed by the celebration of the mass, significant because it is the first liturgy attended by the king as a crowned sovereign.

Though slightly condensed, the following text incorporates the most essential elements, retaining the idiosyncrasies of the Sicilian orders.[l] Spoken (or chanted) sections are in *Italics*. The rubrics are presented with clarity in mind.

Ordo Coronationis

The celebrant (the metropolitan archbishop) and other bishops process into the church ahead of the king and queen. The lesser prelates carry the regalia, namely the sceptre, orb, mantle and crown and ring, with the holy oil (or chrism) and holy water, the Gospel book and relics. A cross, two candles, an icon and the royal sword are also borne into the church. The regalia is blessed with holy water. The celebrant recites the prefatory prayer:

Celebrant: *Omnipotens sempiterne Deus, qui familum tuum regem nostrum* [name] *regni fastigio dignatus es sublimare, tribue ei, quesumus, ut ita in huius seculi cursu cunctorum in commune salutem disponat, quatinus e tue veritatis tramite non recedat.*

A responsorial prayer follows, ending with *Ecce mitto angelum meum,* to which the verse is recited: *Audi, Israel, mandata vitae.*[m]

Some psalms are recited.[n] Then the Kyrie and the Lord's Prayer are chanted: *Kyrie eleison, Christe eleison, Kyrie eleison. Pater noster, qui es in caelis, sanctificetur nomen tuum. Adveniat regnum tuum. Fiat voluntas tua, sicut in caelo et in terra. Panem nostrum quotidianum da nobis hodie, et dimitte nobis debita nostra sicut et nos dimittimus debitoribus nostris. Et ne nos inducas in tentationem, sed libera nos a malo. Amen.*

Celebrant: *Domine exaudi orationem meam.*

Congregants: *Et clamor meus ad te veniat.*

Celebrant: *Dominus vobiscum.*

Congregants: *Et cum spiritu tuo.*

CORONATION RITE

Celebrant: *Deus qui scis genus humanum nulla virtute posse subsistere, concede propicius, ut familus tuus rex noster* [name] *quem populo tuo voluisti preferri, ita tuo fulciatur adjutorio, quatinus potuit preese valeat et prodesse. Per dominum nostrum.*[o]

Congregants: Amen.

Celebrant: *Omnipotens sempiterne Deus, celestium terrestriumque moderator, qui famulum tuum* [name] *ad regni fastigium dignitatus es provehere, concede, quesumus, et cunctus adversitatibus liberatus et ecclesiastice pacis dono muniatur ad ad eterne pacis gaudia te donante pervenire mereatur. Per dominum nostrum.*

The king prostrates himself for the following prayer by the celebrant and then rises: *Ut hunc famulum tuum* [name] *in regem eligere digneris. Te rogamus, audi nos. Ut eum benedicere et sublimare digneris. Te rogamus. Audi. Et cum ad imperii fastigium perducere digneris. Te rogamus.*

Celebrant (to king): *Vis sanctam fidem a catholicis viris tibi traditam tenere et operibus observare?*

King: *Volo.*[p]

Celebrant (to king): *Vis sanctis ecclesiis ecclesiarumque ministris tutor ac defensor esse?*

King: *Volo.*

Celebrant (to king): *Vis regnum tibi a Deo concessum justicia regere et defendere?*

King: *Volo. Et in quantum divino fultus adjutorio ac solacio omnium suorum valuero, ita me per omnia fideliter acturum promitto.*

Celebrant (to the entire congregation): *Tali principi ac rectori vos subicere ipsiusque regnum firmare, firma fide stabilire atque jussionibus illius obtemperare debetis juxta apostolum. Omnis anima potestatibus subdita sit regi quasi precellenti.*

The entire congregation says: *Fiat. Fiat. Amen.*

The celebrant prays over the king: *Benedic, domine, hunc regem nostrum, qui regna omnium moderaris a seculo, et tali eum benedictione glorifica, ut davitice teneat sublimitatis sceptrum et glorificatus in eius protinus reperiatur merito. Da ei, te inspirante, cum mansuetudine ita regere populum, sicut Salomonem fecisti regnum obtinere pacificum. Tibi semper cum timore sit subditus, tibique militet cum quiete. Sit tuo clipeo protectus cum proceribus, et ubique tua gratia victor existat. Honorifica eum pre cunctis regibus gentium. Felux populis dominetur, et feliciter eum naciones adornent. Vivat inter encium catervas magnanimus. Sit individue equitatis singularis protector. Locupletet eum tua previdens dextera. Frugiferam obtineat patriam, et eius liberis tribuas profuturam. Presta ei prolixitatem vite per tempora, et in diebus eius oriatur justicia et eterno glorietur in regno. Per dominum nostrum.*

The prayer continues: *Omnipotens eterne Deus, creator omnium, imperator angelorum, rex regnancium dominusque dominancium, qui Abraham fidelum famulum tuum de hostibus triumphare fecisti, Moysi et Iosue populo prelatis multiplicem victoriam tribuisti humilemque David puerum tuum regni fastigio sublimasti, et Salomonem sapiencie pacisque ineffabili munere ditasti, respice, quesumus, ad preces humilitatis nostre, et super hunc famulum tuum* [name] *quem supplici devotione in regem eligimus benedictionum tuarum dona multiplica, eumque dextere tue potentie semper ubique circumda, quatenus predicte Abrahe fidelitate firmatus, Moysi mansuetudine fretus, Iosue fortitudine munitus, Salomonis sapiencia decoratus, tibi in omnibus placeat, et per tramitem justicie in offenso gressu semper incedat, ecclesiamque tuam deinceps cum plebibus sibi annexis ita enutriat ac doceat, muniat et instruat, contraque hostes visibiles et invisibiles eiusdem potenter regaliterque tue virtutis regimen administret, et ad vere fidei pacisque concordiam eorum animos, te opitulante reformet, ut horum populorum debita subjectione fultus, cum digno amore glorificatus, ad paternum decenter solium tua miseracione conscendere mereatur. Tue quoque proteccionis galea munitus, et scuto insuperabili jugiter protectus, armisque celestibus circumdatus, optabilis victoriae triumphum feliciter capiat, terroremque sue potencie infi-*

delibus inferat, et pacem tibi militantibus letanter reportet. Per dominum nostrumqui virtute sancte crucis tartara destruxit, regnoque diaboli superato ad celos victor ascendit, in quo potestas omnisque regni consistit victoria, qui est gloria humilium et vita salusque populorum. Qui tecum.

Another bishop in attendance recites the following: *Deus inenarrabilis auctor mundi, conditor generis humani, gubernator imperii, qui ex utero fidelis amici tui patriarche nostri Abrahe preelegisti reges seculi profuturos, tu presentem regem hunc cum exercitu suo per intercessionem omnium sanctorum uberi benedictione locupleta et in solium regni firma stabilitate conecte. Visita eum sicut Moysen in rubo, Iesu Nave in prelio, Gedeon in agro, Samuelem in templo, et illa eum benedictione sydera ac sapiencie tue rore perfunde, quam beatus David in psalterio Salomonem filium eius te remunerante percepisse decantat e celo. Sis ei contra acies inimicorum lorica, in adversis galea, in prosperis paciencia, in proteccione clipeus sempiternus, et presta, ut gentes illi teneant fidem, proceres sui habeant pacem, diligant caritatem, abstineant se a cupiditate, loquantur justitiam, custodiant veritatem. Et ita populus iste sub eius imperio pullulet coalitus benedictione eternitatis, ut semper maneant tripudiantes in pace atque victores. Quod ipse.*

The celebrant then anoints the king with holy oil or chrism and says: *Ungo te in regem de oleo sanctificato, in nomine Patris et Filii et Spiritus Sancti. Amen.*[q]

The celebrant, assisted by bishops, girds the king with the royal sword, reciting: *Accipe gladium per manus episcoporum licet indignas vice tamen et auctoritate sanctorum apostolorum consecratus tibi regalitir impositum nostreque benediccionis officio in defensionem sancte dei ecclesie divinitus ordinatum. Et esto memor de quo psalmista dicit: Accingere gladio tuo super femur tuum, potentissime, ut in hoc per eundem vim equitatis eiusque exerceas, molem iniquitatis potenter destruas et sanctam dei ecclesiam eiusque fideles propugnes atque protegas, nec minus sub fide falsos quam christiani nominis hostes execres ac destruas, viduas et pupillos clementer adiuves ac defendas, desolata restaures, restaurata conserves, ulciscaris injusta, confirmes bene disposita, quatenus hec in agendo virtutum triumpho gloriosus justicieque cultor egregius cum mundi salvatore, cuius typum geris in nomine, sine fine merearis regnare. Qui cum Deo.*

Assisted by bishops, the celebrant vests the king with the mantle and (on each arm) armils, and places a ring on his finger, reciting: *Accipe regie dignitatis anulum et per hunc in te catholice fidei cognosce signaculum, quia ut hodie ordinaris caput et princeps regni ac populi, ita perseverabis auctor ac stabilitor christianitatis et christiane fidei, ut felix in opere, locuples in fide cum rege regum glorieris. Per eundem qui est honor. Amen.*

The celebrant places the sceptre in the king's right hand and says: *Accipe virgam virtutis et equitatis, per quam intelligas mulcere pios, terrere reprobos. In nomine Patris et Filii et Spiritus Sancti. Amen.*

The celebrant places the orb in the king's left hand and says: *Accipe regnum, intende, prospere procede et regna. In nomine Patris et filii et Spiritus Sancti. Amen.*[r]

Lastly, the celebrant blesses the crown and places it upon the king's head, saying: *Accipe coronam regni, que licet ab indignis, episcoporum tamen manibus capiti tuo imponitur quamque sanctitatis gloriam et honorem et opus fortitudinis expresse signare intelligas, et per hanc te particopem ministerii nostri non ignores, ita ut, sicut nos in interioribus pastores rectoresque animarum intelligimur, tu quoque in exterioribus verus dei cultor strenuusque tuo regimini commissi utilis executor regnatorque proficuus semper appareas, ut inter gloriosos athletas virtutum gemmis ornatus et premio sempiterne felicitatis coronatus cum redemptore ac salvatore Iesu Christo cuius nomen vicemque gestare crederis sine fine glorieris. Qui vivit et imperat deus cum Deo Patre in unitate. In nomine Patris et Filii et Spiritus Sancti. Amen.*

There follows the archiepiscopal benediction, and the proclamation confirming the coronation:

Benedicat tibi Deus custodiatque te et, sicut te voluit super populum suum esse regem, ita in presenti seculo felicem et eterne felicitatis tribuat esse consortem. Amen. Clerum ac populum, quem sua voluit opitulatione in tua sanccione congregari, sua dispensacione et tua amministracione per diuturna tempora faciat feliciter gubarni. Amen. Quaternus divinis monitis parentes, adversitatibus carentes, bonis omnibus exuberantes, tuo imperio fideli amore obsequentes, et in presenti saeculo tranquillitate fruantur, et tecum eternorum civium consorcio potiri mereantur. Amen.

CORONATION RITE

Celebrant: *Domine salvum fac regem.*[s]

Congregants: *Et exaudi.*

The king is thus acclaimed and then enthroned in or near the sanctuary. The celebrant recites: *In hoc regni solio confirmet et in regno eterno secum regnare faciat Iesus Christus dominus noster rex regum et dominus dominancium. Qui cum deo Patre.*

A mass follows that includes prayers for the king.[t] Among these are the following:

Deus qui miro ordine universa disponis et ineffabiliter gubernas, presta, quaesumus, ut famulus tuus rex noster [name] *hec in huius seculi cursu implenda decernat, unde tibi in perpetuum placere prevaleat. Per dominum nostrum.*

Concede, quesumus, omnipotens Deus, his salutaribus sacrificiis placatus, ut famulus tuus [name] *ad peragendum regalis dignitatis officium inveniatur semper idoneus et celesti patrie reddatur acceptus. Per dominum nostrum.*

Following the pontifical benediction:

Hec, domine, salutaris sacrificii percepio famuli tui [name] *peccatorum maculas diluat et ad regendum secundum tuam voluntatem populum idoneum illum reddat, ut hoc salutari misterio contra visibiles atque invisibiles hostes reddatur invictus, per quod mundus est divina dispensacione redemptus. Per dominum nostrum.*

Deus cuius regnum est omnium seculorum, supplicationes nostras clementer exaudi et christianissimi regis nostri protege principatum, ut in tua virtute confidens et tibi placeat et super omnia regna precellat. Per dominum nostrum.

At the dismissal:

Deus qui diligentibus te facis cuncta prodesse, da cordi regis nostri inviolabilem caritatis affectum, ut desideria de tua inspiracione concepta nulla possint temptacione mutari. Per dominum nostrum. Amen.

The episcopal and royal corteges process out of the church. Outside, barons and knights draw their swords, extending their arms to point upwards in a sign of respect for the sovereign.[u]

Notes

a. For the account of Julian of Toledo in the *Historia Wambae,* see *PCC, Patrologiae Latinae,* volume 96 (1852), column 765-766.

b. Combining anointing and crowning, Hincmar's *ordo* is the earliest of its kind to survive; he actually formulated several orders. For the background and original texts see Prou, Maurice (translator), *De Ordine Palatii* (1885); Jackson, Richard, *Ordines Coronationes Franciae* (1995), volume 2, pages 73-123.

c. The placement of the mantle, along with presentation of the sceptre and orb, is sometimes called "investiture."

d. For useful introductions see Woolley, Reginald, *Coronation Rites* (1915); Stubbs, William, *The Constitutional History of England in Its Origins and Developments* (fifth edition, 1891), pages 161-166; Maskell, William, *Monumenta Ritualia Ecclesiae Anglicanae* (1847), volume 3.

e. The *laudes regiae* was a royal acclamation, usually in the form of a hymn, beginning with the phrase "Christ conquers, Christ reigns, Christ commands." See Kantorowicz, Ernst, *Laudes Regiae: A Study in Liturgical Acclamations and Mediaeval Ruler Worship* (1958), which considers the Kingdom of Sicily under the Normans on pages 157-166. The liturgical acclamation for Frederick II: *Christus vincit, Christus regnat, Christus imperat. Exaudi Christe. Domino nostro regi Friderico magnifico et triumphatori ac invictissimo vita perpetua. Exaudi Christe, Salvator mundi, tu illum adjuva. Adjuva Redemptor mundi, tu illum. Sancta Trinitas, tu illum adjuva. Sancta Maria, tu illum adjuva. Sancte Michael, tu illum adjuva. Sancte Gabriel, tu illum adjuva. Sancte Johannes Baptista, tu illum adjuva. Regi nostro Friderico glorioso et triumphatori pax sempiterna. Exaudi sancte Petre, tu illum adjuva. Sancte Paule, tu illum adjuva. Sancte Stephane, tu illum adjuva. Sancte Laurenti, tu illum adjuva. Pacifico rectori et piissimo gubernatori regi nostro Friderico lux indeficiens et pax eterna. Exaudi Christe. Sancte Sylvester, tu illum adjuva. Sancta Maria Magdalena, tu illum adjuva. Sancta Christina, tu illum adjuva. Sancta Agatha, tu illum adjuva. Christus vincit, Christus regnat, Christus imperat. Exaudi Christe. Ipsi soli honor et gloria, virtus et victoria per infinita secula seculorum. Amen.* Transcribed by Di Giovanni, Giovanni, in *Sanctae Panormitanae Ecclesiae Canonici de Divinis Siculorum Oficiis Tractatis* (1736), pages 117-118, from a contemporary manuscript. The most important surviving manuscripts conserving music from the Kingdom of Sicily during the Hauteville period are kept in the Biblioteca Nacional in Madrid as *E-Mn 288* (probably from Palermo around 1100), *E-Mn 289* (Palermo around 1150), *E-Mn Vitr 20/4* (Palermo around 1150), and *E-Mn 19421* (Catania around 1160); for commentary see Hiley, David, and Manfredi, Agnes, "Quanto c'è di Normanno nei Tropari Siculo-Normanni?" *Rivista Italiana di Musicologia,* volume 18, number 1 (1983), pages 3-28.

f. For comparison to the similar rite used in England during the twelfth century, possibly for Henry I in 1100, see Legg, Leopold, *English Coronation Records* (1901), pages 30-42. The *ordo* used at Henry's coronation was itself influenced to some degree by that of King Ethelred in 978. Whether Henry's *ordo* was a direct influence on the form of the rite used in Sicily is not known, but it is quite possible that English clergy present in Sicily were familiar with it. In fact, there was a general similarity in the coronation rites used in western Europe in this era.

g. See Chapter 11; the image is hardly unique in Byzantine iconography, viz. the Coronation of Constantine VII in the tenth century, a sculpted icon conserved at the Pushkin Museum of Fine Arts, Moscow. Some observations about visual imagery connected to Sicilian royalty are presented in Barber, Richard, *Magnificence: Princely Splendour in the Middle Ages* (2020); also Vagnoni, Mirko, *Dei Gratia Rex Siciliae: Scene di Incoronazione Divina nell'Iconografia Regia Normanna* (2017).

h. The long, illuminated *rotulus* (scroll) of the type used in the Kingdom of Sicily, particularly for the *Exultet* of the *Praeconium Paschale,* was virtually unknown elsewhere; as the scroll was read, the deacon would unroll it over the ambon so that congregants nearest the sanctuary could see the illuminations and follow the chanting (in some scrolls the illustrations are inverted to facilitate this motion). See Avery, Myrtilla, *The Exultet Rolls of South Italy* (1936); Delisle, Leopold, "Un Livre de Choeur Normano-Sicilien Conservé en Espagne," *Journal des Savants,* year 6 (January 1908), pages 42-49; Kantorowicz, Ernst, "A Norman Finale of the Exultet and the Rite of Sarum," *Harvard Theological Review,* volume 34, number 2 (April 1941), pages 129-143; Lander, Gerard, "The 'Portraits' of Emperors in Southern Italian Exultet Rolls and the Liturgical Commemoration of the Emperors," *Speculum,* volume 17, number 2 (April 1942), pages 181-200. See also Kelly, Thomas, *The Exultet in Southern Italy* (1996); Zchomelidse, Nino, *Art, Ritual and Civic Identity in Medieval Southern Italy* (2014).

i. *Queens of Sicily,* pages 567-574.

j. *Codex Vaticanus Latinus 6748* (folios 103-111) is from Monreale and *Codex Vaticanus Latinus 4746* (folios 17-22) is from Siracusa, both manuscripts retained in the Vatican Apostolic Library; *Codex 678* (folios 130-141) and *Codex 742* (folios 75-85) are both from Messina and conserved in the National Library of Madrid.

k. The first publication of *Codex 614* was accompanied by notes published by Jacob Theodor Schwalm (1865-1931) in his "Reise nach Italien im Herbst 1894," in *Neues Archiv der Gesellschaft für ältere Deutsche Geschichtskunde,* number 23 (1898), pages 21-22. For the definitive transcription and notes see Elze, Reinhard, "Tre Ordines per l'Incoronazione di un Re e di una Regina del Regno Normanno in Sicilia" in *Atti del Congresso Internazionale di Studi sulla Sicilia Normanna* (Palermo 1974), pages 438-459. It is worth noting that although Professor Elze did not wish to publish a "composite" text of a coronation rite, he effected some corrective edits to both of those for kings from *Codex 614,* based on established usage and the reading of abbreviations. For comparison, a later rite is published in *Pontificale Romanum Clementis VIII* (1595), pages 224-242, standardizing the *ordo* for use in Catholic monarchies. See also Andrieu, Michel, *Les Ordines Romani du Haute Moyen-Age* (1931) and *Le Pontifical Romain au Moyen-Age* (1938).

l. Whether an *ordo* recorded for posterity was, in fact, used at a specific coronation cannot be known with certainty. These texts reflect what was *intended* to be used, not necessarily what actually was.

m. "Hear Israel, the commandments that give life." Baruch 3:9. All Biblical references are to the Latin Vulgate.

n. Usually, according to the *Ista est ordinacio*, these are: Psalm 83 *Quam amabilia sunt tabernacula tua Domine virtutum,* Psalm 84 *Benedixisti Domine terram tuam,* Psalm 85 *Inclina Domine aurem tuam,* Psalm 115 *Credidi propter quod locutus sum,* Psalm 122 *Ad te levavi oculos meos,* Psalm 129 *De profundis clamavi ad te,* Psalm 131 *Memento Domine.*

o. Sometimes: *Per Dominum nostrum, Iesum Christum, Filiam tuum, regem aeternum.*

p. This is the oath.

q. First the king's hands are anointed, then the forearms (or shoulders), upper breast, the upper back between the shoulders, and head.

r. The shorter (perhaps more recent) *Ista est ordinacio* specifies the hand into which the scepter and orb are placed.

s. "Lord, save the king," from Psalm 19:10. This constitutes an acclamation by the nobility.

t. For the Gallican liturgical rite used in the Kingdom of Sicily, see Di Giovanni, op. cit. supra.

u. Another sign of acclamation by the nobility. It is likely that, following the mass, the king stood on the dais next to the cathedral, where he could be seen by his people. This may explain the association of the nearby chapel with the coronation.

Silver gilt anointing spoon used in Norman England similar to that used in the Kingdom of Sicily

Appendix 6
HISTORIOGRAPHY

The way history is written is almost as important as the subject itself. What researchers usually refer to as *historiography* may be defined very loosely as "the history of history," and the term's use here is very general. Historiography includes, among other things, the body of research by scholars who have studied sources such as documents contemporary to the events they describe, as well as the work of peers. Historiography is more than a generic bibliography listing every work ever published in a field; it is a reflection of a scholar's informed choice about which works are worth considering as indicative of legitimate additions to the *corpus* of our collective knowledge about a subject. *Historicism,* which has several meanings (including a few formulated during the twentieth century), generally considers the ways that sources are interpreted in view of their era and context. The *historical method* is based on the scientific method, a reading of *all* the available data, not a selective interpretation of *some* of it. Accurate historical writing relies upon solid epistemology, ontology and evidentiary standards. It should be rooted in contemporary (primary) evidence rather than subsequent analysis, rhetoric, semiotics or hypothesis.

Many of the original sources for this work, such as charters, were consulted in the libraries and archives listed in the Acknowledgments, most being published (the compendia are listed in Sources), and a few of the following topics were mentioned in passing in the Introduction.

It is important to note that there are various perspectives about the interpretation of sources and the conclusions to be drawn from research, some provoking heated debates.

Multidisciplinary Methodology

The use of the diplomatic and epistolary record is straightforward enough, and it constitutes the greater part of research. Most of the more important charters have been published or at least catalogued. The more significant chronicles and poems of our Norman-Swabian era have been transcribed and published; indeed, most have been translated into English from Latin, Arabic, Greek, Middle Sicilian or Norman French.

As the authors stated in the Introduction, history is not religion; history has experts but no authorities. The only dogma of the historian is a factual, accurate chronology with a precise attribution of people and events. This should be arrived at through research based on sound epistemology and solid investigative methods. Fortunately, these methods are increasingly multidisciplinary (or interdisciplinary), taking into account the wider context of historical events. They may involve such fields as genetic (DNA) research, most notably phylogeography, and climatology.

Rather few historians writing about Italy's Norman-Swabian history have even mentioned these "new" scientific fields, much less utilized them. This omission may be attributed, at least in part, to the fact that so few historians who write in English about southern Italy have spent much time here, not in just several important localities and archives, but traveling around this region. The *Regnum Siciliae* wasn't just Palermo, Bari and Salerno but Enna, Potenza and Brindisi.

Even without referring to actual genetic studies, one observes the numerous blue-eyed and red-haired Italians in Campania, Puglia, Calabria and Sicily; in Palermo children with red hair are actually called *Normanni* and women with black hair are called *More,* not as derogatory terms but as simple descriptions based on ethnology. The presence of multiple sclerosis in southern Italy's population is a legacy of the northern peoples: Goths, Vandals, Norse, Lombards, Normans.

Climate change (caused mostly by global warming) is no secret, but those who live here in Sicily actually experience it acutely. The winters are ever shorter and milder while the summers are increasingly longer and hotter, with bananas and mangoes now grown in Sicily. On August tenth, 2021, the Sicilian city of Siracusa set a European heat record when the temperature hit 120 degrees Fahrenheit (48.8 degrees Celsius). In the decades to come, rising water levels are likely to alter the coastlines of the former *Regnum,* with the effects of desertification evident in some regions.

KINGDOM OF SICILY

How are science and modern technology relevant to the study of history?

A consideration of climate change, specifically global warming, is necessary if we wish to accurately gauge the accounts of certain events, such as the Normans' experience at the Nebrodian town of Troina in the early months of 1062, for which Godfrey Malaterra cannot provide a precise indication of the temperatures beyond mentioning that it was colder than most recent winters and there was much snow. Here in Sicily, today's concept of "much snow" certainly differs from that of the eleventh century. (Your authors tend to gauge it informally by the amount of snow visible each winter on Mount Cuccio overlooking Palermo, and the Madonian Mountains visible to the east of the city.) Attribution science provides models to gauge global temperatures over time.

The genetic record identifying haplogroups, which are linked to specific populations, serves to enlighten historians who might otherwise consider the "disappearance" of Sicily's Muslims an "enigma." Though Islam disappeared, the Arabs themselves did not "vanish" but, for the most part, simply converted. We Sicilians are the descendants of our island's historical Arabs, Greeks, Phoenicians, Romans, Normans, Swabians, Angevins, Catalans and Jews.

Genetic factors can explain certain personality traits. The same gene that gave Constance Hauteville red hair may have colored her character and that of her son (see note 847).

Genetic testing also serves a forensic purpose. It can identify remains, such as those of the two queens in a tomb in the crypt of Andria's cathedral. Paleopathology can inform us about physiological details such as the possibility that Henry (1211-1242), the eldest son of Frederick II, probably suffered from the effects of leprosy (see note 1101). This is an example of the influence of context on biography, and on historiography in general.

Chemical analysis of medieval cooking pottery confirms the presence of substances present in certain foods (see note 1067).

As we have said, travel and physical observation are important because, even if a biographer need not consult archival records in a certain locality, it is beneficial to explore the places themselves.

In writing about the Bonello revolt that claimed the life of a son of William I, it was necessary to trace every step of the uprising based on the episode as it was recounted by Hugh Falcandus. Parts of the medieval city of Palermo mentioned in that chronicle and other sources are barely recognizable today. As one example among many, a city gate, the Arabs' *Sant'agat,* that once stood near the paleo-Christian church of Saint Agatha, is long gone, and should not be confused for another "Saint Agatha's Gate" still standing in the Norman wall that shadows Corso Tukory at the eastern end of the Ballarò street market. It was at the former, near the cathedral, that Matthew Bonello and his accomplices killed Maio of Bari in November 1160. The church remains, and a street follows the path that once led to the gate, but the gate itself, along with the medieval wall, is gone, though a segment of the city's ancient Punic wall survives nearby. The site is not much to see (a photo of it appears in *Sicilian Queenship* on page 362), and this exemplifies the condition of certain castles and other edifices.

In connection with the later revolt that led to the expulsion of Stephen of Perche, Falcandus mentions the riots ending as the sun set beyond the high mountain, Mount Cuccio (from the Arabic *Kuz* for its conical summit), to the south of Palermo. For this, one need only observe that the sun disappears beyond that mountain about a half-hour before dusk, depending on the season. In the Middle Ages, before there were lights lining the road (now Corso Calatafimi) to Monreale, this meant that darkness enveloped the city's older districts rather early.

Arguably, these may not be determining details in a general history. However, even if the results of such research are not reported explicitly in the narrative or notes, they facilitate an author's understanding of the subject. We can know more about medieval people if we know more about their environment. That includes things like poetry and cuisine, considered in this volume.

Political systems involving feudalism, the church and the law are well known. For the Kingdom of Sicily, the legal framework of society was rooted in the two major law codes, namely the Assizes of Ariano and then the Constitutions of Melfi, augmented by Catholic canon law and certain feudal practices. Based on the Code of Justinian, the two codes were not tantamount to a constitution, whether written or unwritten, nor were they comparable to such milestones as England's *Magna Carta,* but they were the nearest thing to it in the Kingdom of Sicily.

HISTORIOGRAPHY

Charters are extremely important, and many have been destroyed, some quite recently (see notes 28, 1009, 1141).

The general term "digital humanities" usually refers to the use of current information technology to facilitate our consultation and analysis of sources.[a]

When a medieval narrative such as a chronicle is published for the first time, the editor of the *editio princeps* (first print edition) is sometimes forced to divide a single, continuous text into sections such as chapters for the convenience of readers. Thenceforth, subsequent editions and translations should follow that format, as we see with the chronicles cited in this work. Much like the division of the Bible and Koran into sections, this facilitates ready, universal citation regardless of the edition being consulted. Some early editors did not do this, and the authors of this work were constrained to do so in the first English translations of the *Ferraris Chronicle* and the *Jamsilla Chronicle*. Even a codex of the Assizes of Ariano published here (Appendix 1) required the numeration of statutes (sections) as these were not standardized, not having been published in their entirety in the original Latin in an English monograph until the publication of *Margaret, Queen of Sicily* in 2016.

Historians must sometimes formulate or introduce concepts that may seem novel, hence *co-culturalism* and *post-regency* in this volume. *Rogerian Legend* is another such phrase used in these pages. *Global Siculo-Neapolitan* describes a phenomenon that is well known in modern contexts but rarely considered in medieval studies. Certain foreign terms are *ex novo* translations, such as *Sicilianistics* from *sicilianistica*.

Sicilian and Allied Writers

Historians distinguish between *annals,* which are essentially "diaries" that record a sequence or chronology of events as they occur, and *chronicles,* "narratives" which typically lend more detail and insight to the events they recount. In many cases, however, the difference between the annal and the chronicle is rather subtle. By definition, both are contemporaneous to the events they describe, and one imagines their writers recording notes before composing "finished" entries in an annal or narratives in a chronicle.

Writing in 1867, William Stubbs drew the distinction in these terms:

The difference between chronicles and annals was not, as it has been sometimes stated, that the former belong to universal, the latter to national or particular history, but that the former have a continuity of subject and style, whilst the latter contain the mere jottings down of unconnected events. The annals are the ore, the chronicles are the purified metal out of which the historian elaborates his perfect jewel.[b]

Not every chronicle cited in this work was written in southern Italy. For our purposes, however, what might be described as the most "relevant" contemporary chronicles are those written in southern Italy around the time of the events they describe. In considering the *Regnum* specifically, we are not overlooking contemporaneous writings by authors in, for example, the Muslim and Byzantine lands, or even the work of Orderic Vitalis. We are merely recognizing the accuracy and detail of firsthand accounts of day-to-day events. Apart from occurrences in the *Regnum Siciliae* itself, the travels of, in particular, Frederick II to northern Italy, the Holy Roman Empire and the Kingdom of Jerusalem are relevant, though our emphasis in this volume is the Kingdom of Sicily rather than events such as the Sixth Crusade. Herewith, the more important chroniclers and historians in order of their chronological relevance to this work. To this list could be added a number of Spanish, French, German and English chroniclers who made passing references to the Hautevilles and Hohenstaufens, perhaps in connection with their own dynasties, such as England's Plantagenets. Here the chronicles of Roger of Howden, Gervase of Tilbury, William of Puylaurens and Robert of Torigni come to mind. In the eastern Mediterranean we find Nicetas Akominatos Choniates and William of Tyre.

Paul the Deacon. Baptized *Winfrid,* Paul, an aristocratic Lombard monk at Mount Cassino who died around 798, wrote his *History of the Langobards* after 787. Paul met Charlemagne, who appreciated his talents as a writer. His work is significant for being the first substantial

653

history of the Lombards, including those who ruled part of southern Italy from Salerno. Derived from earlier sources, which in some cases were subsequently lost, it presents a useful overview of the relationship between Lombard society and Charlemagne's Franks to 744.

Muhammad ibn Hawqal. In his *Kitab al-masalik wa l-mamalik,* this merchant from Baghdad with a penchant for geography described an Arab-Byzantine Sicily in the year 972 (361 AH), long before Idrisi and Jubayr, when Palermo was already a prosperous capital. He spent much time in Asia and Africa. He died shortly after 978.

Ali ibn al-Athir al-Jazari. Abu al-Hassan Ali ibn Muhammad ibn Muhammad ash-Shaybani, who was either Kurdish or Arab, was born into an aristocratic family of the Banu Bakr tribe in 1160 in what is now Cizre in Turkey and died in 1232 or 1233 in Mosul, now part of Iraq. The early parts of his invaluable "Complete History," the *al-Kamil fi at-Tarikh,* were drawn from prior Arabic sources, some now lost, but the sections beginning around 1190 were contemporaneous. Ali ibn al-Athir knew Saladin and writes authoritatively about such events as the crusades of his own era, which involved Frederick II. His information about the Kalbids and Zirids before the arrival of the Normans in Sicily in 1061 is considered reliable, being based on the work of Shaddad (see below).

Amato of Montecassino. Amato, whose ancestry may have been Lombard, began writing his chronicle around 1080, possibly from notes he had compiled for decades. *L'Ystoire de li Normant,* survives in its entirety only in a French copy written in the fourteenth century, but many of its details are attested in the *Cassino Chronicle* of Leo Marsicano, which incorporates excerpts from Amato's original (Latin) text.

Godfrey Malaterra. Godfrey (or Geoffrey) Malaterra, a Benedictine monk and possibly Norman, wrote his chronicle toward the end of the eleventh century but mentions facts garnered from earlier sources. He was likely present at the wedding of Roger and Judith. For a time he lived at the abbey in Calabria founded by Judith's brother. His chronicle, the *De Rebus Gestis Rogerii Calabriae et Siciliae Comitis et Roberti Guiscardi Ducis Fratris Eius,* which ends in 1099, mentions details about the conquest of Sicily unattested by others. Malaterra died before 1130.

William of Apulia. Written in hexameters before 1099, the focus of William's chronicle is Robert Guiscard, for whom he could be said to be an apologist. Unlike his contemporaries Godfrey and Amato, William appears to have been a layman. His chronicle, the *Gesta Roberti Wiscardi,* is highly detailed for certain events, such as the Battle of Palermo in 1071-1072. He probably died before 1120.

Abd al Gabbar ibn Muhammad ibn Hamdis al-Azdi al-Siqilli (Ibn Hamdis). Born in Syracuse around 1056, Ibn Hamdis was chiefly a poet. However, his poetry relates certain historical attitudes among Sicily's Muslim population in Norman times. He left Sicily in 1078 and subsequently lived in Africa and Spain. He died in 1132 or 1133.

Abd al Gharib Izz al-Din al Sanhaji (Abd al-Aziz ibn Shaddad). This Zirid chronicler wrote a history, now lost, about Ifriqiya early in the twelfth century. As a nephew of Yahya ibn Tamim, he was closely connected to both the sultan and his son, Ali, and therefore privy to certain matters involving the court at Mahdia. He lived in Palermo in 1156, and then went to Syria. His "Kairouan Chronicle" is the source for much in the writings of Athir, Tijani, Khaldun, Abulfeda and others whose work was composed much later.

Leo Marsicano. Born around 1046, Leo "of Ostia" was a monk at Mount Cassino, where he wrote his chronicle based partly on the work of Amato (q.v.) before becoming a bishop. Leo's work on the chronicle ends in 1075. It was continued during the next century by Peter the Deacon, whose work was generally less accurate.

HISTORIOGRAPHY

Anna Comnena. Anna was the daughter of the Byzantine Emperor Alexios I (see Table 6). Her history, the *Alexiad,* generally considered the first work of its kind written by a European woman, is useful for its description of the incursion of Robert Guiscard into the Byzantine lands and details such as Sichelgaita's courage at the Battle of Dyrracheion (Durrës) in 1081. Like Ali ibn al-Athir, she brings us a point of view that contrasts with those of the Latin chroniclers based in Italy.

John Kinnamos (Cinnamus). This Greek chronicler is sometimes considered a continuator of Anna Comnenus. His known work takes the reader to the end of the twelfth century, complemented by that of Nicetas Choniatas (see below), whose style is very different.

Alexander of Telese. Completed around 1136, the *Ystoria Rogerii Regis,* sometimes *De Rebus Gestis Rogerii Siciliae Regis,* was reportedly commissioned by a sister of King Roger II. Alexander was a monk in the Calabrian town of Telese, where he is thought to have lived until around 1143. His work is, arguably, the first "biography" in the Kingdom of Sicily.

Ibn Zafar al Siqilli. Hujjat al-Din Abu Abdallah Muhammad ibn Abi Muhammad ibn Muhammad ibn Zafar al Siqilli lived in Sicily, where he may have been born, but was educated in Cairo. He was in Sicily by 1154 but soon left. One of many intellectuals at court, he wrote a political treatise, the *Sulwan,* or "Waters of Comfort," reflecting these times, translated by Michele Amari and first published in Italian in 1851. Noted for his insights into the use of power, ibn Zafar is sometimes regarded as a precursor to Niccolò Machiavelli. Part of his work was intended as advice for the monarch, and may well have been considered in that light by the first kings of Sicily. At least one of the allegorical fables in his treatise, a story adopted from older Asian sources, is represented in the painted ceiling of the Palatine Chapel, namely that of the "two foxes."

Hugh Falcandus. His identity is not known, but whoever Hugh Falcandus was, it is clear that he had close, if not privileged, access to the royal court in Palermo. The tone of his writing is often cynical, even sardonic, and historians have long questioned his objectivity, as well we should. Yet his chronicle has been seriously studied for centuries. Evelyn Jamison cogently argued that Falcandus was quite possibly Eugenius of Palermo, who died in 1202. Gwenyth Hood advanced another widely-supported theory, specifically that Falcandus was Hugh Foucault (who died in 1197), Prior of Saint-Denis and Argenteuil, whose surname, sometimes *Foucaud,* is readily latinized to something very similar to *Falcandus,* there being no "universal" orthography for Latin surnames derived from Norman French or most other languages.[c] It is generally accepted that the essential details cited by Falcandus are reasonably accurate, and indeed some are readily corroborated by contemporaneous sources. The challenge for the modern scholar lies in discerning what is most likely factual from what probably is not. For the most part, Falcandus is blatant enough in his character assassinations for us to distinguish fact from subjectivity. Indeed, a few of his descriptions of personalities may be quite precise. Falcandus disliked Romuald Guarna of Salerno, whom he almost certainly knew personally.

Romuald of Salerno. Archbishop of the prosperous diocese of Salerno from 1154 until his death in 1181, Romuald Guarna of Salerno was born into the nobility that held estates in parts of southern Italy. His *Chronicon sive Annales* covers part of the middle of the twelfth century, complementing other works such as those of Hugh Falcandus. Accompanied by Bishop Hugh of Palermo, in 1156 he negotiated the Treaty of Benevento with Pope Adrian IV. Two decades later, he concluded the Treaty of Venice. He was Archbishop of Palermo from 1161 to 1166 (though apparently not consecrated). Romuald's self-serving chronicle, but not his ambitious career, ended by 1179, the same year that saw him attending the Third Lateran Council that condemned the Albigensians (Cathars) as heretics. He was one of the *familiares* appointed to assist Queen Margaret in governing the *Regnum,* and he performed the coronation of William II. His chronicle is less opinionated than that of his contemporary Hugh Falcandus, or at least less overtly critical of its subject.

KINGDOM OF SICILY

Abu Abd Allah Abdullah Muhammad ibn Muhammad ibn Ash Sharif al Idrisi (or **Edrisi**). Living in Sicily by 1145, Idrisi (whom we met in Chapter 12) became the court geographer. Descended through a long line of distinguished and aristocratic personages from the Prophet Muhammad, Idrisi seems to have spent his youth in Sabtah, now Ceuta (in Morocco), where he is thought to have been born, but his family had commercial interests in Sicily. His *Book of Roger* is a key record of Sicilian geography in the twelfth century. Idrisi left the *Regnum* during the reign of William I.

Benjamin of Tudela. Benjamin ben Jonah was born around 1130 in the same region as Queen Margaret. Rabbi Benjamin's travels offer us much information about the Mediterranean world, and not just that of the Jews, during the twelfth century. He arrived in Sicily during the summer of 1171. Benjamin was chiefly a rabbi and merchant, but his travel diary is the best record of its era for its descriptions of the Jewish populations of southern Europe and western Asia. He stayed at Sicily's royal court and among Palermo's Jews for a week or two. By 1173 he was back in Spain. He seems to have died there in that year.

Ibn Jubayr. Abu Hussain Muhammad bin Ahmad ibn Jubayr (or Jubair) al-Kenani was born around 1145 in Valencia, then a thriving region of "Moorish" Spain, and by 1182 he was high secretary for the Emir of Granada. The following year Jubayr left for a Hajj (pilgrimage) to Mecca. His travels took him across the Mediterranean, reaching Alexandria in the spring of 1183. On his way back to Spain, in early December 1184, he reached Sicily, where he was shipwrecked at Messina but given hospitality by an Arabic-speaking monarch, William II. His Sicilian travels took him westward by ship, with stops at Cefalù, Termini, Solunto and finally Palermo. Following a week in the capital, he departed by land for Trapani, passing Alcamo along the way. He died in Alexandria in 1217.

John Skylitzes. John composed his chronicle, the *Synopsis of Histories,* in Greek during the eleventh century (see *Historia Bizantina* in Sources). The best-known surviving codex is not an autograph but a copy made in Palermo in the next century. As the only Byzantine chronicle of length that is illuminated, it is an invaluable source for costume and other visual imagery.

Nicetas Choniates. The focus of the chronicle of Nicetas Akominatos (his actual name) of Chonae is the second half of the twelfth century and the early years of the thirteenth. He witnessed the sack of Constantinople in 1204. His work is useful for its Byzantine Greek perspective of the Kingdom of Sicily.

Falco of Benevento. Born around 1070, this chronicler wrote the *Chronicon Beneventanum* and other works. Of Lombard ancestry, he was antipathetic toward the Normans. Despite his obvious bias, Falco, who died during the reign of Roger II, is a good source for essential information and major events.

Peter of Blois. This Breton cleric educated in Bologna arrived in Sicily in September 1166 with his brother, William. He became tutor of the young king and one of Margaret's advisors. He left shortly after Stephen of Perche departed, ending up at Canterbury and then Bath, although he was back in Sicily with Richard Lionheart in 1189. A number of Peter's letters survive. He lived until around 1211. Peter's brother, William, was the abbot of a monastery in Calabria.

Peter of Eboli. This chronicler served at the court of Constance, daughter of Roger II. His *Liber ad Honorem Augusti* is a good source for the early years of the Hohenstaufen reign, but also such figures as Archbishop Walter of Palermo and Matthew of Aiello. Peter's view of Tancred of Lecce is infamously biased. He died after 1220.

Richard of San Germano. Born around 1165, this cleric was a notary at the Benedictine abbey at Cassino, San Germano being a medieval name for it. His *Chronica Regni Siciliae* covers the history of the *Regnum* from the death of William II in 1189 until 1243. Richard, who served at the court of Frederick II, died in 1244. His chronicle is generally regarded as the most important narrative source for the early decades of Frederick's reign.

HISTORIOGRAPHY

Peter della Vigna. The letters of the diplomat Peter della Vigna, sometime chancellor of Frederick II and probably the chief author of the Constitutions of Melfi, have much to offer about the emperor and his times. Peter negotiated the betrothal of Isabella of England to Frederick, who later imprisoned him based on the (likely mistaken) belief that he had committed treason. He was a poet of the Sicilian School.

The Monk of Santa Maria di Ferraria. Little is known about the author of the *Ferraris Chronicle*, but he was a monk at a monastery near Naples and met Frederick II. Discovered in the nineteenth century and translated in the twenty-first, this work ends in 1228 and for the Norman period owes much to the chronicle of Falco of Benevento. A case could be made that this is the first "history" of the Kingdom of Sicily, covered from its inception. It is especially useful to complement the chronicle of Richard of San Germano and other sources.

Nicholas of Jamsilla. Ascribed to a personage bearing an anachronistically attributed name, this chronicle about Manfred Hohenstaufen was completed in 1258. It is the best source for the reigns of Conrad, and then Manfred, following the death of Frederick II. A number of candidates have been advanced for its authorship, such as Nicholas of Brindisi, the court notary Nicholas of Rocca, Manfred's confidant Godfrey of Cosenza, and the archbishop (and onetime notary) Belprand of Cosenza. The names of James and Rudolph of Poggibonsi, both notaries, have also been propounded. Among scholars the favorite seems to be Godfrey of Cosenza, who figures in the pages of the chronicle and may have been Manfred's kinsman.

John of Procida. Born into the family that ruled the island of Procida and educated at Salerno's medical school, John became the physician, confidant and counsellor of Frederick II and later his son, Manfred, to whom he was a tutor. He subscribed some of Manfred's charters and was an instigator of the unrest, and possibly a conspiracy, that led to the War of the Vespers in 1282, the catalyst for the division of the *Regnum Siciliae* into two separate states until 1816. Although he doesn't seem to have written much history before 1266 except a few letters, he was present at the Battle of Benevento and his chronicle, or third-person "memoir," of the Vespers uprising is the earliest known narrative written in an Italian language.

Matthew Paris. Matthew's *Chronica Majora*, though written in England and France, is useful for the years of the reign of Frederick II after the death of Richard of San Germano in 1244. Unlike the writings of Saba Malaspina, Bartholomew of Neocastro and Salimbene di Adam, it is contemporary to the reign of Frederick. Though Matthew was sympathetic of Frederick in the Chronica Majora, he was more critical in his *Historia Anglorum*. For the reigns of Frederick's sons, Conrad and Manfred, the contemporary source nearest the court, and most sympathetic to the Hohenstaufens, is that of "Jamsilla."

Saba Malaspina. The chronicle of Saba of Malaspina, *Rerum Sicularum Historia*, was completed in 1285. It is noteworthy for covering such events as the Battle of Benevento from a papal, almost theocratic, point of view. A Guelph, possibly from Calabria or Rome, Saba was Bishop of Mileto from 1286 and died in 1298.

Andrew of Hungary. *Andreas Ungarus* wrote a detailed account of the Battle of Benevento. He was a chaplain to two Hungarian kings of the Arpád dynasty, Béla IV and Stephen V. He arrived in Italy in the suite of Mary, daughter of Stephen V, who was betrothed to Charles "the Lame," later crowned as Charles II. The only surviving codex of Andrew's account, the *Descriptio Victorie Beneventi*, completed at the French court, most likely around 1271 shortly after the death of King Louis IX, is a manuscript in Paris, of which the *editio princeps* was published in 1649 in *Historiae Francorum Scriptorum* (volume 5, pages 826-851); another edition appeared in the *Monumenta Germaniae Historica Scriptores* series in 1882 (volume 26, pages 560-580).

Bartholomew of Neocastro (Nicastro). Bartholomew, a jurist who died in 1294 or shortly thereafter, is best known as a supporter of the Sicilian rebellion against the Angevins. His *Historia Sicula* begins with the death of Frederick II in 1250 and is highly favorable to the

Aragonese dynasty that ruled Sicily after 1282. To Bartholomew is owed our knowledge of details such as the exploits of Macalda of Scaletta (see note 75).

Salimbene di Adam. The *Chronica* of Salimbene di Adam is an important source for northern Italy for the reign of Frederick II, whom he probably met. It seems to have been written beginning around 1282. As a Franciscan of Guelphic sympathies, Salimbene entertained a somewhat biased view of the monarch who suppressed his order and his city, Parma (see note 964).

Anonymous Works. Several less famous, if significant, chronicles were composed by authors whose names are not known to us, with very few biographical or contextual details about them revealed in the work. One of the more important works of this kind is the *Anonymous Historia Sicula*, which largely echoes the information provided by chroniclers such as Godfrey Malaterra while adding a few details. Transcribed from two manuscripts in the Vatican, this was first published by Giovanni Battista Caruso in 1723. It is possible that it was drawn not only from Malaterra's work but from chronicles contemporary to his that have not survived into modern times. Certain records, such as the so-called "Cambridge Chronicle," which covers the ninth and tenth centuries, are of incertain provenance.

Early Secondary Literature

As stated in the Introduction, the first printed general history of note to consider the *Regnum* was Thomas Fazello's *De Rebus Siculis*, published in Latin 1558 and in Italian in 1573. (Fazello lived from 1498 until 1570.) His work isn't studied very widely outside Italy, but he is credited with having popularized the epithets for William I "the Bad" and William II "the Good," though these nicknames may already have been in use. The impact of his work cannot be overstated. Fazello, who was the prior of the Dominicans in Palermo, came to be known by an epithet of his own as "the Father of Sicilian History." By comparison, the work of his contemporary and rival, Francesco Maurolico, of Messina, was not nearly as well known.

In its Italian translation, *Le Due Deche dell'Historia di Sicilia,* Fazello's history runs to more than a thousand pages. It became the blueprint for perceptions of the *Regnum* by subsequent scholars, including those in Naples. It was consulted at some length by Denis Mack Smith and Moses Finley for their history of Sicily published in 1968.

As a humanist of the Renaissance era, Fazello sought to make his tome more than a history. Significantly, he brings us a morsel or two of *Sicilianità* (see note 14).

However one views his work, it stands as something that formed perceptions of the *Regnum* that have been with us for centuries. No study of the published (print) historiography of the first two centuries of the Kingdom of Sicily and its influence in shaping attitudes about identity is complete without a glance into its pages.

A number of histories that followed Fazello's are too often overlooked, or even derided, by today's historians, yet these are useful for general historiography and reference. Examples are Angelo Di Costanzo's *Le Istorie del Regno di Napoli dal 1250 fino al 1498* (1572), Giovanni Antonio Summonte's *Historia della Città e Regno di Napoli* (1601), Rocco Pirro's *Sicilia Sacra* (1647) and *Chronologia Regum Siciliae* (1643), Giovanni Battista Caruso's *Bibliotheca Historica Regni Siciliae* (1723), Giacinto Dragonetti's *Origine dei Feudi nei Regni di Napoli e Sicilia* (1788), Alessandro Di Meo's *Annali Critico-Diplomatici del Regno di Napoli* (1805), Michele Amari's *Storia dei Musulmani in Sicilia* (1854), and Giuseppe De Blasi's *La Insurrezione Pugliese e la Conquista Normanna nel Secolo XI* (1864), amongst many others.

In fact, despite what some scholars occasionally imply (perhaps to bolster the prestige of their own efforts), work of this kind, most of it written before the unification of Italy, affords the reader a great deal of accurate information, just as Ferdinand Chalandon's major history of the Normans of Italy has much to offer us. The clarity of Michele Amari's translations of Arabic texts is unsurpassed.

The work of a few of these writers was translated into other languages, making it known internationally at an early date. Amari's history of the War of the Sicilian Vespers was promoted as a metaphor for the Italian unification movement, in which he participated, and a legal treatise penned by Giacinto Dragonetti influenced the politics of Thomas Paine.

HISTORIOGRAPHY

These native scholars' views of the *Regnum* and its people have sometimes been overshadowed by influences from farther afield. Two phenomena have exercised particular influence in Italy upon the telling of the history of the Norman-Swabian era.

Ghibellines and Guelphs

The first blow was delivered during the Middle Ages. The defeat of the last Hohenstaufens, at the battles of Benevento in 1266 and Tagliacozzo in 1268, signalled the end of the multicultural golden age of the Kingdom of Sicily. By 1300, the victorious dynasty, the House of Anjou, which had lost Sicily during the War of the Vespers in 1282, was suppressing Islam at Lucera, the last major Muslim community in Italy.

With the defeat of the Ghibellines who had supported the Hohenstaufens as Holy Roman Emperors, the rival Guelphs of northern Italy redoubled their efforts to denigrate that dynasty, something seen in the work of Dante and Boccaccio. Such tropes became ingrained in Italian literary culture, where they generally went unchallenged. Whereas Sicilian had once been the most important literary language in Italy, Tuscan took its place, eventually making inroads even in Sicily. As the Renaissance enveloped the regions north of Naples, the south generally embraced this significant movement somewhat belatedly.

Not until the twentieth century were the biographies of our Swabian kings, particularly Frederick II and his son Manfred, "corrected" in most major historical works. In English, noteworthy examples were the translation of Ernst Kantorowicz's *Kaiser Friedrich der Zweite,* first published in the original in 1927, and Steven Runciman's book on the War of the Sicilian Vespers; Kantorowicz and Runciman both enjoyed a certain celebrity and are the subjects of biographies (see note 10).

Unification

The nineteenth century saw the arrival of the Italocentric movement called the *Risorgimento,* or "rebirth" (though your authors prefer the more literal "resurgence"). The philosophical facet of these efforts existed long before 1800, but the chief political objective of the *Risorgimento* was the unification of Italy, a movement with which the word has become synonymous. Its greatest impetus came following the Congress of Vienna, which ended in 1815, mostly outside the Kingdom of the Two Sicilies (see Appendix 7) and the Papal State, in regions such as Tuscany, Lombardy and Piedmont.

An underlying — often unstated — pretext of the *Risorgimento,* if not the subsequent political unification movement, was that "Italians" were already "united" culturally. This presupposition was, at best, only partially correct considering the differences between the populations of various regions, particularly those, such as Veneto and Calabria, that were not very near each other. Owing to history, the Sicilians, for example, had more in common with the Catalonians than with the Ligurians.

During the middle of the nineteenth century, parts of northern Italy were painted as "progressive" or "liberal" while the Papal State and the Two Sicilies were represented as repressive or reactionary. Following the unification in 1861, it was deemed necessary to dispel any belief that might challenge this notion.

The most obvious strategy was simple censorship. While a professor in Italy might publish an article on Frederick II in an academic journal such as the *Archivio Storico Siciliano,* a lengthy biography with wide distribution was out of the question because it would probably remind southerners of a glorious medieval past. It is therefore unsurprising that the first major "modern" biographies of Frederick II, one of the greatest monarchs of his era, were published not in Italy but in Britain and Germany.[d]

Arab culture was maligned. The Italian historian (and sometime Fascist) Benedetto Croce infamously, and ridiculously, declared that Arab Sicily was "an invention of Michele Amari."

Italian schools taught (and to an extent still teach) a revised version of history, both medieval and modern. Amongst various deceptions that one could mention, the curriculum generally ignores the medieval Kingdom of Sicily, the modern Kingdom of the Two Sicilies, and Fascism, whilst proclaiming that an Italian invented the telephone.

The use of "regional" languages like Neapolitan, Sicilian and Friulian was officially discouraged. In a propagandistic claim divorced from reality, such languages were disparaged as "dialects" of Italian, which is essentially a modern form of Tuscan. There are uncanny parallels with Spain, where Catalan and other tongues were discouraged in public life in favor of the dominant Castilian.

Later, the arrival of Fascism saw the teaching of English banned in Italy's public schools, a policy whose dire effects stretched into the last decade of the twentieth century, when the nation still suffered a dearth of English teachers, the education ministry advocating French instead.

In this milieu women were generally ignored (see note 551).

In recent decades, Italy's warped historiography has been described by historians, especially foreigners such as the late Denis Mack Smith.[e] Due to the government's control of relevant information, reforms were not possible until the fall of the Kingdom of Italy following the Second World War. Even today, access to certain records regarding, for example, the Italian occupation and genocide in Ethiopia (1936-1941), kept at the *Archivio Centrale dello Stato* in Rome, is restricted.[f] Much documentation has simply "disappeared" and Italy has nothing like a freedom of information act.

Today, when the internet makes it possible for Italians to obtain information about Italy formerly available only in other nations, it is more difficult to "conceal" or distort Italian history.

Yet some original sources have been destroyed or merely misplaced; even certain poems of the Sicilian School survive only as single copies. Obvious examples relevant to the medieval Kingdom of Sicily include the codices of the Assizes of Ariano, the only known manuscript of the *Ferraris Chronicle,* and texts of certain coronation rites, rediscovered since the middle of the nineteenth century.[g]

Where the original manuscripts no longer exist, scholars sometimes debate whether later copies are, in fact, outright forgeries; some almost certainly are.[h]

Caveat Lector

In the preceding chapters, your authors have resisted the temptation to respond to novel socio-political theories, preferring instead to present factual information on the subject at hand. Though some of it is quite good, the more "analytical" work published during the present century regarding medieval and modern Italy should be viewed with a critical eye, considering its objectives and also factors such as its conformity to controversial (or at least novel) models that include, among others, deconstructionism and "new historicism," as opposed to "old historicism" and allied movements.

In advocating the careful use of original sources while discouraging slavish empiricism (positivism), Edward Carr famously defined history as "an unending dialogue between the present and the past," challenging some of the ideas advanced by Leopold von Ranke and others of an earlier generation. Carr, in turn, was contested by Geoffrey Elton. Hugh Trevor-Roper, among others, entered the fray, leaving us a diversity of opinions. More recent times have brought us paradigms such as autohistory (see note 12) and ethnohistory.

An increasingly popular trend in foreign (non-Italian) academic circles, and one about which few scholars are willing to comment openly for fear of sparking public feuds, is a cynical, condescending revisionism that seeks to challenge whether, for example, the society of the kingdom ruled by the Hautevilles was "truly" multicultural, as if we (the numerous scholars in southern Italy) somehow fail to understand our own history. This sometimes leads to surreal conclusions that ignore obvious artistic, social or physical (e.g. genetic) evidence in favor of the arcane hyper-analysis of a few charters, perhaps interpreted outside their natural or intended context; among the motives for this kind of approach is the desire to present something "original" or "revelatory." In stark contrast to scholars who live and work in the former *Regnum,* and therefore have a strong basis for comparing our medieval society to what has existed here in southern Italy in later centuries, most foreigners lack a "native" point of reference, a reality mentioned in the Introduction (see also notes 12, 13, 34). Some Anglophone historians who write about Italy lack a fundamental knowledge of

HISTORIOGRAPHY

Italian (note 30), much less Sicilian and Neapolitan, languages as important in these studies as Latin, Greek and Arabic.

Where the kingdoms of Sicily, Naples and the Two Sicilies (see Appendix 7) are concerned, anybody outside this region, even a Tuscan, writes as a "foreigner." Their commentaries and "critiques" on social practices in southern Italy should be viewed in that context. Being an Italophile scholar does not bestow the prerogative of non-Italians lecturing Italians about our society and politics, any more than cultivating an interest in Spain makes one Spanish.

Each country has its own character. Those societies known in the Middle Ages which lack a state in modern times have sometimes attempted to establish one based on old traditions, witness Kurdistan and Israel. The people of southern Italy are fortunate for their kingdom having survived so long. People are linked to the places where their ethnogenic history occurred. This is not an eccentric idea, and it is unsurprising that foreign scholars come to Sicily to learn about Sicilian history (would that more of them spent at least a few years living here).

Into the middle of the nineteenth century, and indeed into the twentieth, the Neapolitans and Sicilians writing our history were, almost without exception, raised in southern Italy and educated in schools operated by the Dominicans and other religious orders. While we should praise the changes in perspectives that have been propagated in social studies since that era, certain factors are still important. Today, the true substance of the social orientation of the medieval kingdom as an institution, even as a "papal monarchy," founded in the sphere of Catholicism, is too often treated inadequately by those writing history. Granted that the presentation of history must be neutral, perhaps even "secular," a close knowledge of Catholicity and its implications is vital to our studies. Naturally, scholars raised in a southern Italian environment, and educated in Catholic schools, bring highly-developed insight when evaluating the social and political realities that colored every aspect of life in the kingdom founded by Roger II, even for those of other faiths.

It should be noted that publications such as monographs adapted from doctoral dissertations were not always the hyper-theoretical, bluntly-revisionist essays seen so frequently today. In former times, they reflected genuinely beneficial additions to the conversation, not something that was different merely for the sake of standing out in a crowded field. Two fine examples of works that are still useful for reference despite a few new discoveries since they were written are *Irene von Byzanz*, about Irene Angelina of Constantinople (see Table 17), defended at the University of Innsbruck in 1936 by Maria Luise Mumelter (1912-2005), and *Bohemond I, Prince of Antioch,* defended at Princeton University in 1917 by Ralph Yewdale (1892-1921) and published shortly after his death.

Deconstructionism (post-structuralism) and postmodernism may have their place, particularly in literary studies, but in medieval historical studies they sometimes lead to misinterpretations, for while it is necessary to examine social context closely and comparatively from a multidisciplinary perspective, the principles advocated by Michel Foucault, Jacques Derrida and scholars of like mind, when applied to the canvas of history with too broad a brush, can facilitate dubious conclusions about facts and the "truth." Ditto the overzealous application of semiotics, which can lead to the perception that texts have meanings at variance to what was intended, and intertextual analysis, which is more applicable to pure literature than to chronicles and charters.

Some authors, even in the banal academic settings of courses and conferences, cultivate a certain *protagonismo*. It is to be remembered that, epistemologically, history and historiography are not religion and historians do not speak from authority. A history or thesis presented by a younger or lesser-known scholar can be just as valid as that of an older or famous one.[i]

The accurate presentation of medieval topics to young students and the general public sometimes requires the correction of erroneous tropes that have made their way into popular culture and even politics.[j]

These arcane complexities need not concern the reader at length, but they should be borne in mind by historians, even junior scholars, when evaluating the quality of work in this field, and when writing history. Here the reader is commended to the works by McCullagh, Munslow, Kimball and Paglia listed in the following section.

KINGDOM OF SICILY

Suggested Reading

Writing history can be a challenge even for a seasoned historian. A wide diversity of views is expressed in the following monographs: Carr, Edward, *What is History* (1961); Elton, Geoffrey, *The Practice of History* (1967); Marwick, Arthur, *The Nature of History* (1970); Tuchman, Barbara, *Practicing History: Selected Essays* (1981); Tosh, John, *The Pursuit of History* (1984); Kimball, Roger, *Tenured Radicals: How Politics Has Corrupted Our Higher Education* (1990); Jenkins, Keith, *Rethinking History* (1991); Munslow, Alun, *Deconstructing History* (1997); McCullagh, C. Behan, *The Truth of History* (1997); Evans, Richard, *In Defence of History* (1997); Cannadine, David, *What is History Now?* (2002); Burke, Peter, *What is Cultural History?* (second edition, 2008); Mortimer, Ian, *What Isn't History?* (2017); Skinner, Patricia, *Studying Gender in Medieval Europe: Historical Approaches* (2018).

For additional commentary see: Paglia, Camille, "Ninnies, Pedants, Tyrants and Other Academics," in *The New York Times*, 5 May 1991 (section 7, page 1), adapted from "Junk Bonds and Corporate Raiders: Academe in the Hour of the Wolf," in *Arion: A Journal of Humanities and the Classics*, volume 1, number 2 (spring 1991), pages 139-212; Samuel, Raphael, "What is History?" in *History Today*, volume 35, number 3 (1985); Stearns, Peter, "Social and Political History," in *Journal of Social History*, volume 16, number 3 (1983); Eley, Geoffrey, "What is Cultural History?" in *Cultural History and Cultural Studies* (spring-summer 1995); Gurevich, Aaron, *Historical Anthropology of the Middle Ages* (1992).

For the writing of history anonymously in open-source publications see Rosenweig, Roy, "Can History be Open Source? Wikipedia and the Future of the Past," *The Journal of American History*, volume 93, number 1 (June 2006), pages 117-146.

Notes

a. See Morreale, Laura, and Gilsdorf, Sean, *Digital Medieval Studies: Practice and Preservation* (2022). This is distinguished from "artificial intelligence."

b. See Stubbs, William, *Gesta Regis Henrici*, Preface, page xii.

c. For a letter to Hugh Foucault from Peter of Blois see *PCC, Series Secunda*, volume 207 (1855), letter 116, columns 345-346 (and footnote 48); for commentary see Gwenyth Hood's paper, op. cit. in Sources.

d. By Thomas Kington (1862) and Ernst Kantorowicz (1927). For the impact of historical narratives on politics, see Gottschall, Jonathan, *The Story Paradox: How Our Love of Storytelling Builds Societies and Tears Them Down* (2021).

e. For commentary on distorted historiography in Italy, see the late Mack Smith, Denis, "Documentary Falsification and Italian Biography" in *History and Biography: Essays in Honour of Derek Beales* (Cambridge 1996), pages 173-187, and the introduction of his *Italy and Its Monarchy* (1989). Also *The Pursuit of Italy: A History of a Land, Its Regions, and Their Peoples* (2011) by David Gilmour; *Under the Volcano: Revolution in a Sicilian Town* (2013) by Lucy Riall. *Memorie del Sud* (1999), edited by Andrea Orlandi, presents a number of revelatory details regarding the peninsular half of the Two Sicilies and the war of 1860-1861. Another insightful work is *Darkest Italy: The Nation and Stereotypes of the Mezzogiorno 1860-1900* (1999) by John Dickie.

f. For Italian crimes against humanity (in addition to generic war crimes), see Campbell, Ian, *The Addis Ababa Massacre: Italy's National Shame* (2017).

g. See Kestemont, Mike, et al., "Forgotten Books: The application of unseen species models to the survival of culture," *Science*, volume 375, number 6582 (February 2022), pages 765-769; Wilson, Richard, *The Lost Literature of Medieval England* (1970 edition).

h. One of the most infamous examples in the Kingdom of Sicily during the Norman era is a charter of privileges supposedly conceded by Roger II to the city of Messina in 1129 but generally regarded as spurious or (at the very least) highly embellished. See La Mantia, Vito, *I Privilegi di Messina con Documenti Inediti* (1897), pages 1-22.

i. A candid exposition is Friedman, Hershey, and Weiser, Linda, "A Treatise on the Jackass in Academe: How Arrogance and Self Centeredness Destroy the Credibility of Higher Education," *Journal of Intercultural Management and Ethics,* number 2 (2019), pages 9-27. See also note 11 supra.

j. In studies of southern Italy by foreigners, this involves, for example, the fallacy that the Mafia originated in the Middle Ages (see note 34). More generally, and for new approaches, see Gabriele, Matthew, and Perry, David, *The Bright Ages: A New History of Medieval Europe* (2021); Albin, Andrew, and Erler, Mary (editors), *Whose Middle Ages? Teachable Moments for an Ill-Used Past* (2019).

KINGDOM OF SICILY

St Januarius Francis I

St Ferdinand

St George of the Reunion Constantinian St George

Last knightly orders bestowed by the kings of the Two Sicilies. During the Norman-Swabian era we find the Hospitallers, Templars, Knights of Saint Lazarus and Teutonic Knights present in the Kingdom of Sicily. The Order of the Golden Chain, like the sword Mikalis, is probably legendary.

Engravings by Raffaele Ruo, 1832

Appendix 7
TWIN KINGDOMS

Mentioned in the Introduction and elsewhere in the preceding pages, the "twin kingdoms" of Naples and Sicily grew out of the War of the Vespers of 1282, which resulted in the separation of the Kingdom of Sicily into the peninsular (Angevin) and Sicilian (Aragonese) states that existed for the next six centuries. Occasionally ruled by the same monarch in a "personal union," especially after 1500, these two states were formally reunited in 1816 as the Kingdom of the Two Sicilies which, in a sense, restored the *Regnum Siciliae* founded by Roger II.

Historical Legacy

The modern history of the "twin kingdoms" is much more than a mere *coda* to our Middle Ages. As direct, if slightly punctuated, outgrowths of the medieval era, these two monarchies were complex and scarcely idyllic but by no means irrelevant.

After 1372, when its kings finally renounced their effective claims on Sicily, the peninsular state ruled by the Angevins descended from Charles I was ever more frequently known as the Kingdom of *Naples,* to be distinguished from the Kingdom of *Sicily* ruled from Palermo by the Aragonese and their descendants. The phrase *Two Sicilies* came to be used during the modern era when both realms were ruled by the same king. The most noteworthy of these monarchs was Charles de Bourbon, who was crowned king of both Naples and Sicily in Palermo in 1735. Like some of his predecessors in the immediately preceding centuries, he was born outside Italy into a dynasty that usually ruled from a distance through viceroys and other administrators. Unlike them, Charles actually resided in the two Italian kingdoms he ruled.[a]

The reign of Spanish-born Charles de Bourbon, *Carlo di Borbone,* a great-grandson of Louis XIV of France, ushered into the "twin kingdoms" an era of prosperity, with occasional comparisons of his enlightened rule to that of Frederick II. He reformed the government and treasury, undertook major construction projects, facilitated efficient banking and trade, and addressed the needs of the poor. Charles made successful efforts to limit the power of the papacy, the Inquisition and the Jesuits in his realms. At the University of Naples he instituted Europe's first chair in economics. He erected Europe's largest royal palace at Caserta. The wealth, population and magnificence of Naples rivaled those of Paris and London. "See Naples and die," went a popular adage.

The concept of the "Neapolitan Nation" popularized during the fifteenth and sixteenth centuries was revived, as if Calabria, Abruzzi and Puglia were merely suburbs of the capital and its culture.

With a generous dose of hyperbole, the historian Santi Correnti (1924-2009) famously declared that it was Charles who truly brought southern Italy out of the Middle Ages. Yet it was under this king that the Two Sicilies witnessed a revival of interest in its medieval past. This was evident in the publication of works about the Hautevilles and Hohenstaufens, and in the foundation of an order of knighthood in honor of Saint Januarius, the heavenly patron of Naples.[b]

In 1759, Charles abdicated the Neapolitan and Sicilian thrones to succeed an elder half-brother as King of Spain, becoming the ruler of the Spanish Empire and an early ally of the United States of America (he sponsored construction of the first Catholic church in New York). In Italy, he was succeeded by his thirdborn son, Ferdinando, who was raised in Naples and spoke Neapolitan as his mother tongue.

Wed to a sister of Marie Antoinette, Ferdinando I of the Two Sicilies instinctively opposed revolution in all its forms. The British occupation of Malta during the Napoleonic Wars deprived him of that island long held as a fief by the Knights Hospitaller, but the Congress of Vienna confirmed his authority over the Two Sicilies, the state he founded.

Though the constitution Ferdinando established in Sicily in 1812 was rescinded in view of the reunification of the "twin kingdoms" a few years later, some of its principles, such as the abolition of feudalism, were retained, while the legal codes he enacted guaranteed personal rights, such as divorce, unknown in other parts of Italy. Reactionary Ferdinando's reign is justly criticized, but his realm boasted men of the Enlightenment such as Gaetano Filangieri, whose work inspired the American statesman Benjamin Franklin, with whom the Neapolitan aristocrat corresponded.

665

KINGDOM OF SICILY

Ferdinando's son and heir, Francesco I, ruled from 1825 until his death in 1830. Francesco's son, Ferdinando II, began his reign as a progressive but became conservative in view of revolts such as that of 1848, which shook Italy and much of Europe. He proved reluctant to guarantee the British a monopoly on Sicily's sulphur. The stalwart sovereign fended off the material efforts of proponents of the *Risorgimento,* a movement to unite the various states in Italy, including the papal dominions, into a single nation. The Two Sicilies was the wealthiest of these polities, boasting the most territory and the largest standing army. The king's willingness to use this formidable force discouraged attacks.[c]

Besides a few statutes inherited from the Constitutions of Melfi of Frederick II, a number of social practices survived from medieval times. This concerned, for example, marriages. Into the middle of the nineteenth century, betrothals required parental consent unless the groom was at least twenty-five and the bride twenty-one years of age (Code of the Kingdom of the Two Sicilies of 1848, title 5, chapter 1, article 163). At all events, the spouses had to be, respectively, at least fourteen and twelve (ibid, article 152).

Ferdinando's death in 1859 left his son, Francesco II, as king. The young man proved too religiously devout to confront worldly realities. He resisted the proposal of his Piedmontese cousin, Vittorio Emanuele II of Savoy, to unite Italy. In 1860, British naval support, bolstered by the disloyalty of some of Francesco's generals, facilitated an invasion by "independent" troops secretly abetted by the Piedmontese. Francesco surrendered at Gaeta, north of Naples, in February of 1861. Rigged referenda reporting an improbable ninety-eight percent of eligible voters to favor the neocratic regime "confirmed" Vittorio Emanuele as king of an Italy that was now unified but hardly united.[d]

Repression and punitive taxation followed. Catholic schools were forcibly closed without enough public schools to replace them. With this, general literacy decreased. At the same time, increased poverty in the former Two Sicilies prompted emigration. Whether a true sense of unified "Italian" nationhood exists among the great majority of Italians is much debated.[e]

Censorship became the norm and worsened during the twentieth century with the advent of Fascism. The Second World War was a military debacle for the Italians and highly destructive in Palermo. The republic that, under Allied auspices, supplanted the hapless kingdom in 1946, introduced democracy, and with it a balanced reconsideration of the history of the Norman-Swabian era of the *Regnum* (see Appendix 6).

The strong sense of "historical" identity in southern Italy persists in some circles and under certain circumstances is occasionally noted in the Anglosphere.[f]

Living Legacy

The Introduction and other sections in the preceding pages make mention of many traditions and institutions rooted in the Norman-Swabian period, or preserved from an era antecedent to it, known during modern times. Some survived into the nineteenth century in the Kingdom of the Two Sicilies and a few are still known in southern Italy and its diaspora. This is sometimes called "cultural transmission," though that term only partially describes such phenomena. In summary, and to encapsulate a few of the more salient and "tangible" among these hereditaments:

- The Sicilian and Neapolitan languages, lexicon and literature (Chapter 24).
- Foods and recipes known in the thirteenth century (Chapter 27).
- Celebrations of religious feasts and *sagre* known in the medieval kingdom.
- Byzantine usages in Catholicism (triple immersion at baptism, orans posture).
- Judaic usages at Catholic funerals and wakes (Chapter 32).
- Arab irrigational technology and words such as *gebbia,* from *jabh* (reservoir).
- The *Befana* and other Christmas and holiday traditions.
- Female inheritance rights inspired by "Sicilian Succession" (note 1027).
- A woman's use of her natal "maiden" surname after marriage.
- Kinship identities such as *consuocera* and *commare* (note 445).
- Late use of some medieval measures, units and coinage.
- Certain laws governing taxation and the administration of land.
- Systems of district and circuit judges.

TWIN KINGDOMS

- Principles of Maliki Law in commerce (reinstituted).
- Laws permitting divorce (reinstituted in the twentieth century).
- Laws against rape (reinstituted in the twentieth century).
- Control (licensing) of the practice of medicine by trained physicians.
- Universities (Naples) and medical schools (Salerno).
- Local councils based on the jurat system of demesnial cities (reinstituted).
- Certain titles of courtesy, viz. *signore* from Norman French *seigneur.*
- Chivalric institutions (knightly orders).
- Monasticism (Franciscans, Dominicans).
- Some architectural forms (castles, churches, cloisters, *palmenti,* dry stone walls).
- Certain traditional artforms, such as iconography and mosaic.
- Architectural and artistic movements, such as the Gothic.
- Certain marriage practices, such as dowries.
- Developments leading to establishment of guilds and confraternities.

Notes

a. A good outline of the dynastic lineage is to be found in Louda, Jirí, and Maclagan, Michael, *Heraldry of the Royal Families of Europe* (first edition, 1981), chapter 33, pages 245-252.

b. By the eighteenth century, the Neapolitan knightly orders mentioned in the Conclusion were abeyant. The Hospitallers, who maintained commanderies in the Two Sicilies, held Malta as a fief of the Kingdom of Sicily from 1530 until 1798 (the "Order of Malta" has been based in Rome since 1834). In 1734, the Bourbons of the Two Sicilies inherited the Constantinian Order of Saint George (founded in Venice during the sixteenth century) through Elisabeth Farnese, wife of Philip V of Spain and mother of Charles III, from the dukes of Parma; see Mendola, Louis, "The Sacred Military Constantinian Order of Saint George of the Two Sicilies," *The Journal of the Orders and Medals Research Society,* volume 32, number 4 (London 1993), pages 310-314. Charles founded the Order of Saint Januarius in 1738 as the premier order of chivalry of the Kingdom of Naples; see Mendola, Louis, "The Distinguished Royal Order of Saint Januarius," *The Journal of the Orders and Medals Research Society,* volume 29, number 3 (London 1990), pages 194-199. For neo-medievalism into the nineteenth century see Maggio, Nicolò, "Medievalismi Siciliani: Il Mito del Medioevo nel Risorgimento Siciliano," *Materialismo Storico,* volume 8, number 1 (2020), pages 221-266.

c. For biographies see Acton, Harold, *The Bourbons of Naples* (1956), *The Last Bourbons of Naples* (1961); also Petrie, Charles, *Charles III of Spain: An Enlightened Despot* (1971).

d. See Mendola, Louis, *The Kingdom of the Two Sicilies 1734-1861* (2020), pages 187-189 (referendum of 1860), 277 (referendum of 1946), that monograph being a general introduction to the history of the kingdom.

e. In English, see: Mack Smith, Denis, *Italy and Its Monarchy* (1989); Katz, Robert, *The Fall of the House of Savoy* (1971); Graziano, Manlio, *The Failure of Italian Nationhood: The Geopolitics of a Troubled Identity* (2010); Gilmour, David, *The Pursuit of Italy: A History of a Land, Its Regions and Their Peoples* (2011). Also Gentile, Emilio, *La Grande Italia: Il mito della nazione nel XX secolo* (2011). During the Second World War, the Allied invasion of southern Italy saw many citizens overtly supporting the Americans against the Italians, with General George Patton warmly received by large crowds in Palermo after the women of Licata had hurled rubbish from their balconies onto the heads of Italian soldiers taken prisoner by the Americans marched down the town's narrow streets; see Atkinson, Rick, *The Day of Battle: The War in Sicily and Italy 1943-1944* (2007).

f. See, for example, Minahan, James, *Encyclopedia of Stateless Nations: Ethnic and National Groups Around the World* (2016 edition), pages 298, 383; Bucher, Michael, "Re-Discovering the Italian Kingdom of the Two Sicilies," *Time* ("Lightbox" section), 25 August 2016; Shugaar, Antony, "Italy's Own Lost Cause," *The New York Times* ("Disunion" section), 2 May 2012.

KINGDOM OF SICILY

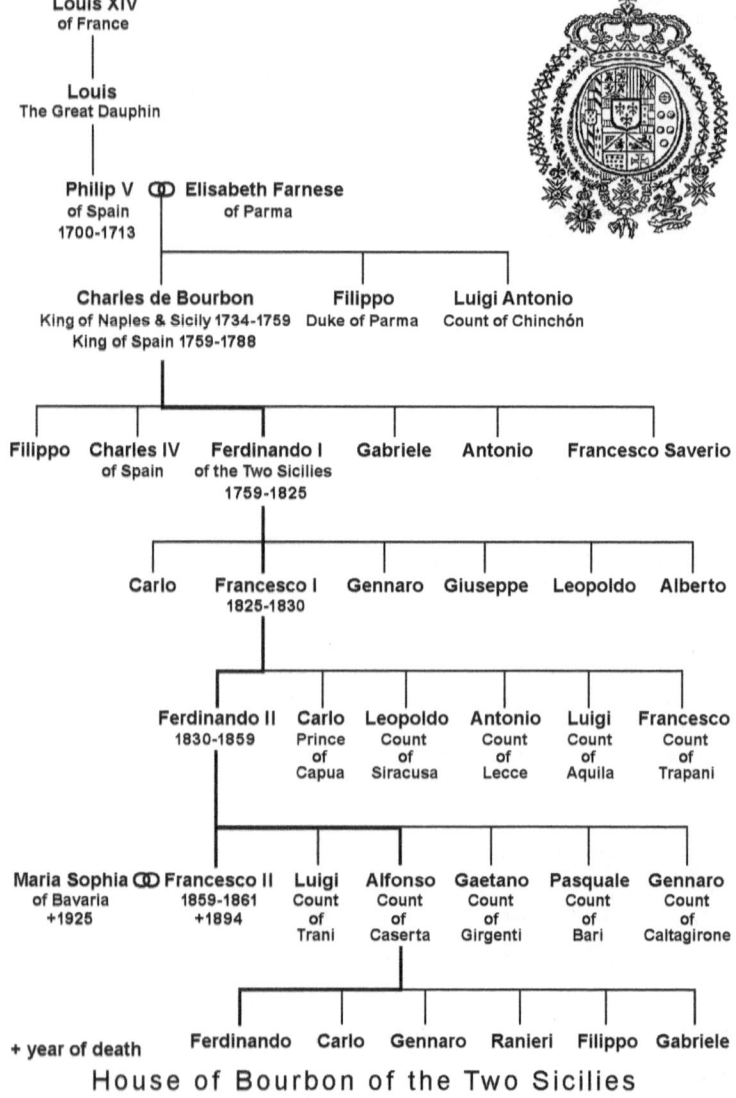

House of Bourbon of the Two Sicilies

GLOSSARY

These terms are defined in a way consistent with their usage in this book, with some explained further in the main text, Introduction or notes. For Arabic terms generally, the reader is referred to Leonard Chiarelli's book, *A History of Muslim Sicily* (2018 edition), pages 419-423.

Abbasids - dynasty that ruled most of the Muslim world from 750, when it displaced the Umayyads, until 861, thenceforth controlling Baghdad and certain regions until 1258.

abbey - monastery, typically large in size, overseen by an abbot or abbess.

Aghlabids - Arab dynasty of the Nadji of Banu Tamim that ruled Ifriqiya from 800, under *Abbasids* (q.v.), supplanting Muhallabids and conquering Sicily.

Almohads - Rulers of Berber caliphate founded in northern Africa in 1121, embracing Morocco, southern Iberia, and eventually Tunisia, dissolved in 1248.

Almoravids - Berber dynasty in Morocco, overthrown in 1147 by *Almohads,* q.v.

Amazigh - endonym for *Berbers* (q.v.), plural *Imazighen*.

amir - See *emir*.

amiratus - highest-ranking officer in royal service to Norman rulers of Sicily.

Apulia - Latin for southeastern peninsular Italy; Puglia.

Arab - generally speakers of Arabic and its dialects, other than *Judeo-Arabic* (q.v.), in Arabia and other lands.

arancina - fried, meat-filled rice ball, probably Arab in origin, also *arancino.*

archimandrite - superior abbot in *Orthodox* (q.v.) churches.

archon - in Sicily the Greek term for a *familiare,* q.v.

apse - semi-circular termination of the end of a church behind the *sanctuary,* q.v.

Assassins - secret society founded by Muslims in western Asia in 1090.

augustale - gold coin instituted by Frederick II.

babbaluci - small, edible snails (Sicilian).

baccalà - dried, salted codfish fillets.

baglio - bailey; walls built around a fortified courtyard, sometimes with low towers.

bailiff - royal representative administering a city; governor.

baron - holder of two or more *manors* (q.v.) forming a single large estate; any holder of a large feudal estate smaller than a duchy or *county,* q.v.

baronage - barons collectively; feudal lords collectively regardless of rank.

barony - the land and dignity of a *baron,* q.v.

basilica - large church given a canonical distinction for its importance.

Bedouins - nomadic tribes in desert regions of Arab lands in Africa and Arabia.

Befana - Christmas witch, from *Epifania* (Epiphany), antedating Saint Nicholas (Santa Claus) tradition in Italy.

Benedictines - monks of the oldest religious order, founded by St Benedict in 529.

Berber - the *Amazigh* (q.v.) society of coastal northern Africa.

KINGDOM OF SICILY

bint - Arabic for *daughter* or *maiden*, used as a *nasab*, q.v.

bull - the most formal type of official papal decree; *bulla*.

Byzantines - Grecophone population of the eastern part of the Roman Empire; descendants of these Byzantine Greeks.

cafiso - a small unit of liquid measure, from the Arabic.

caïd - among Muslims, a high official, governor, judge or chief; an Arabic title of respect.

caliph - Muslim leader claiming spiritual and temporal rule as a successor of Prophet Muhammed.

canna - a unit of volume measurement for dry products such as grain.

cantaro - unit of weight and volume, from Arabic *kintar*.

canonization - formal process of elevation to sainthood.

caponata - eggplant (aubergine) and olive salad thought to be Arab in origin.

caraffa - a unit of volume measurement for liquids such as wine.

cardinal - title of Catholic ecclesiastical officials immediately below the pope in rank, who formerly need not have been bishops.

cardoon - a plant, *cynara cardunculus*, Sicilian *carduna*, of which the stalk is eaten, indigenous to the central and western Mediterranean and related to the artichoke.

Carthusians - religious order founded by Bruno of Cologne in 1084.

castrum - fortified town; castle.

catepan - military leader or governor appointed in Byzantine imperial lands.

cathedral - principal church of a diocese as ecclesiastical see of a bishop or archbishop, sometimes *duomo*, q.v.

Catholic - the church in the west (under Rome), esp after 1054, cf. *Orthodox*.

cerveru - Sicilian variety of the Norman deerhound.

Christendom - Christian states collectively, esp those ruled by Catholic monarchs.

chrysobull - important decree issued by emperors bearing a gold seal.

Cistercians - religious order founded in France in 1098 as offshoot of *Benedictines*, q.v.

cloister - monastic residence, esp the quadrangle and garden of a monastery or abbey.

co-culturalism - multiculturalism resulting from natural circumstances, more inclusive than *convivencia*, q.v.

collecta - occasional general tax on property levied at royal discretion.

commandery - smallest administrative division of certain knightly orders.

commare - godmother of one's child, from Latin *cum mater*.

commonalty - people, such as peasants and serfs, outside the clergy and *nobility*, q.v.

common law - body of law based on legal precedents established by the courts rather than legal codes.

commune - city-state of northern Italy under imperial rule, e.g. Milan.

constable - officer having defined authority, sometimes a *bailiff*, q.v.

Constancian - relating to Constance Hauteville, queen regnant 1194-1198.

consuocera - co-mother-in-law; relationship between women whose children are married to each other.

GLOSSARY

convivencia - coexistence of populations of various faiths, esp in Spain, cfr *co-culturalism*.

count - holder of a feudal territory usually larger than a *barony* (q.v.) but smaller than a *duchy*, q.v.

county - feudal territory held by a *count*, q.v.

crusade - military expedition by Christians, usually against non-Christians, motivated by religious belief.

curiae generales - a large royal convocation of barons and prelates.

curia regis - royal council of *familiares* (q.v.) and other high officers answering directly to the king.

Dar al-Islam - society where Muslim majority is ruled by Muslims.

Dar al-Kufr - society where Muslim minority is ruled by non-Muslims.

demesnial - said of cities/lands appertaining directly to the royal demesne rather than vassals (barons); royal or crown territories, cfr. *manorial*.

destrier - any sturdy "war horse" favored by knights, such as (in the Kingdom of Sicily) the Arabian and Sanfratellan.

dinar - a gold coin slightly larger than a *tarì*, q.v.

diptych - in Orthodox churches, list of the names of prelates for whom prayers are offered.

diwan - the royal treasury, esp under Muslim administration.

donativo - modern word for *collecta*, q.v.

dower - property given to an aristocratic bride by her future husband.

dowry - assets of a bride, given to her by her father, that she contributes to her marriage.

dubbing - elevating a young man or *squire* (q.v.) to knighthood in a public ceremony.

ducat - silver coin instituted by Roger II.

duchy - a duke's lands, usually being larger than a *county* (q.v.) and sometimes sovereign.

duomo - Italian term for a very large church, usually one built as a *cathedral*, q.v.

editio princeps - first printed edition of a medieval work that previously existed only in manuscript form.

emir - title of various Muslim rulers, esp those who are *Arab*, q.v.

emperor - ruler of an empire, specifically the Byzantine Empire or Holy Roman Empire.

enfeoffment - in the feudal system, the granting of land to a knight or other noble in exchange for military service; infeudation.

excommunication - the formal exclusion of a Catholic from participation in church life.

familiare - familiaris; member of the *curia regis* (q.v.) appointed by the sovereign.

Fatimid - relating to the Shia caliphs of a dynasty founded in 909, ruling from Egypt after 969 but deposed in 1171; the culture associated with this dynasty.

fealty - loyalty pledged by a baron or knight to his lord under the feudal system, usually in conjunction with *homage*, q.v.

feudal - related to the system governing the rapport between nobles, such as *counts* (q.v.) and *barons* (q.v.), and the crown. Cfr. *manorialism*, which describes the internal administration of fiefs (manors).

feudo - Italian for a fief, *manor*, q.v.

fief - a *manor*, q.v.

follaris - a coin made of copper or bronze.

Frankish - the medieval society and culture of most of what are now France and Germany; exonym for Catholic Europeans in the eastern Mediterranean during the crusading era.

Franks - People from lands under *Frankish* (q.v.) rule; Catholic crusaders and pilgrims from central and western Europe in the Holy Land.

friar - name given to men in certain religious orders, esp Dominicans and Franciscans.

fritola - fried, sugared doughnuts popular in Venice.

fritella - a Sicilian dish made with fresh fava beans, artichoke hearts and peas; also *fritedda* and *frittella*.

frittola - in Sicily, fried remnants from the butchering of beef; also *frittula*.

frittoli - in Calabria, fried remnants from the butchering of pork; also *frittuli*.

furusiyya - in Arab countries, equestrian martial exercise and traditions, comparable to those of knighthood.

gastald - in southern Italy, a Lombard noble rank comparable to that of *baron,* q.v.

Germans - speakers of German, esp in central Europe.

Global Siculo-Neapolitan - describes the diffusion of the culture of southern Italy outside Italy.

hadith - in Islam, a tradition or statement outside of Koranic scripture governing daily life and religious practice.

hagiography - the study of saints and sainthood.

hammam - Arabic term for a public bath fed by a spring or aqueduct, used by either men or women (but not both sexes together).

harem - part of a household reserved for concubines.

heraldry - system of representing a knight through symbols and designs painted on his shield; the activities of heralds as court officers and diplomats.

hermitage - in Orthodoxy, residence of a hermit monk, living outside a monastery; *kellion*.

hierocracy - belief that papal authority was temporal as well as spiritual; papalism.

homage - in feudalism, pledge of a baron or knight acknowledging his tenure and duty to his lord, usually in conjunction with *fealty,* q.v.

Hospitallers - knights of the Order of St John, founded in 1099 to operate hospitals and aid pilgrims in the Holy Land, now the Sovereign Military Order of Malta based in Rome.

Ibadi Islam - sect or school of Islam founded in the Khawarij movement at Basra, later present in Sicily, cfr *Sunni Islam* and *Shia Islam*.

icon - in Christianity, a devotional rendering of a holy figure in flat, stylized manner, as a painting, fresco or mosaic, adhering to a traditional format.

iconography - the art, tradition and interpretation of icons, particularly according to *Orthodox* (q.v.) principles.

iconostasis - in churches of Orthodox or Byzantine design, a wall of icons separating the nave from the *sanctuary,* q.v.

Ifriqiya - coastal regions of northern Africa, particularly Tunisia and parts of Libya.

incipit - the first three words in a papal bull or other decree, serving to identify it.

incunable - said of a book printed in Europe before 1501.

interdict - in the *Catholic* (q.v.) church, the act of an authority banning worship and sacraments by people in a locality or large community.

GLOSSARY

investiture - the act of *dubbing* (q.v.) a knight, esp in an order of chivalry; the act of *enfeoffment* (q.v.) of a baron or landholding knight; the ceremony elevating a non-royal sovereign (e.g. a prince of Salerno) to his office.

loros - in Byzantine culture, a long, narrow ceremonial stole, usually embroidered and sometimes jeweled, worn by rulers and bishops.

jihad - in Islam, a war undertaken for religious purposes.

Judeo-Arabic - vernacular language of the medieval Jews of Sicily and *Ifriqiya,* q.v.

judicium dei - in law, justice by divine judgment, esp in trials by combat (duel) or ordeal.

jurat - member of the civic council of a *demesnial* (q.v.) city.

jure uxoris - the right of a man to an office, esp *kingship* (q.v.), through that of his wife.

justiciar - a judge appointed by, and acting through, royal authority.

Kalbids - Muslim dynasty of Sicily from 948, originally under Fatimids.

kanat - canal or subterranean aqueduct for transporting water from an aquifer to the surface for irrigation or other purposes.

kingship - the office, status, reign or position of a king.

knight - man who performs mounted military service in exchange for feudal tenure, or as part of a knightly order such as the *Hospitallers* (q.v.) or *Templars* (q.v.).

lady - woman of aristocratic rank.

latifondo - a large agricultural estate, whether manorial or not, typically for grain cultivation.

Latin - said of the culture of much of Italy or western Europe compared to that of the Byzantine Greek lands; the language and liturgy of the western (Catholic) church compared to those, such as Greek and Slavonic, of the eastern (Orthodox) churches.

Lombards - the residual civilization of the *Longobards* (q.v.) in parts of Italy during the Middle Ages.

Longobardia - Greek term for southern peninsular Italy, esp regions ruled by *Lombards* (q.v.) of Salerno; Lombardy, region of northern Italy ruled from Pavia or Milan by Lombard dynasties.

Longobards - people of a Germanic civilization that settled in the Apennine Peninsula during the sixth century.

maestranza - in Italian, a guild; sometimes a confraternity.

Mafia - secretive criminal organization established in rural Sicily around 1790.

Maghrebi Jews - Jews of northern Africa and Sicily during the Middle Ages.

malik - in Arabic, a king.

malikah - in Arabic, a queen or other high-ranking female ruler; wife of a king.

Maliki - a major school of jurisprudence in *Sunni Islam* (q.v.), founded by Malik ibn Anas, popularized in *Ifriqiya,* q.v.

manor - the smallest unit of hereditary property of a nobleman, the essential estate in the *feudal* (q.v.) or *manorial system,* q.v.

manorial - said of a manor (q.v.) that is *feudal* (belonging to a vassal) rather than royal or *demesnial,* q.v.

manorial system - administration of *manors* (q.v.) and *serfs* (q.v.) by those, such as *barons* (q.v.), holding these estates. Cfr. *feudal,* which refers to the relationship, based on *fealty* (q.v.) and *homage* (q.v.), of barons under the king.

Margaretine - relating to Margaret of Navarre, queen regent 1166-1171.

mattanza - Iberian method of capturing tuna in nets, introduced in Sicily.

Mezzogiorno - term popularized after 1861 for the former Kingdom of the Two Sicilies (Appendix 7), often in disparagement.

mikveh - in Judaism, a ritual bath fed by a spring or aqueduct.

Mizrahim - Jews of the eastern Mediterranean.

monastery - residence of *monks* (q.v.) living communally.

monk - celibate male who has taken vows, usually in a religious order in a *monastery*, q.v.

multiple sclerosis - hereditary chronic disease that can affect function of the brain, spinal cord and optic nerves, thought to have been introduced chiefly through the Norman gene pool (see note 17).

muqarnas - in Islamic architecture, intricate ornamented vaulting of ceilings and walls.

Muslim - follower of Islam, in Italy usually *Sunni* (q.v.), *Shia* (q.v.) or *Ibadi,* q.v.

Napoletanità - distinctive character of being Neapolitan in identity, origin and culture, cfr. *Sicilianità*.

nasab - patronymic construction in Arabic, *bint* for women, and either *ibn* or *bin* for men.

nave - long central part of a church where congregants worship facing the altar.

Neapolitans - people of Naples and its environs; esp after 1282, people of the peninsular kingdom ruled from Naples.

nobility - hereditary aristocracy, consisting of counts, barons, knights, prelates and court officers.

Normanitas - said of the distinctly Norman character of society, culture, literature or architecture.

Norse - any of several Nordic civilizations of medieval Scandinavia.

oncia - small unit of measurement for weight and coinage, sometimes *onza*.

ordeal, trial by - determination of guilt/innocence by subjecting a suspect to a dangerous physical test, cfr. *judicium dei*.

Orthodox - the Byzantine churches of the east, esp after 1054, cfr. *Catholic*.

Outremer - *Frankish* (q.v.) states in the Holy Land founded by crusaders, lit "beyond the sea."

Palestine - territory including what are now Israel, southern Lebanon and parts of western Syria and Jordan, constituting the Kingdom of Jerusalem; the Holy Land.

palmento - house for pressing grapes, making and storing wine.

parlamentu - in Sicilian, a meeting or conversation.

parliament - meeting of barons empowered to enact legislation or impose policy.

patriarch - the highest-ranking bishops in Orthodoxy.

peasantry - chiefly agricultural social class, including *serfs* (q.v.), below the *nobility,* q.v.

post-regency - period following a regency when a former queen regent continues to advise her son (the young king) unofficially.

preceptory - in some knightly orders, such as the *Templars* (q.v.), a community of knights and serving brothers.

primogeniture - reference to inheritance by the firstborn child.

prince - ruler of a principality, such as Salerno; later, the legitimate son of a king.

GLOSSARY

princess - female ruler of a principality; wife of a prince; later, the legitimate daughter of a king.

Principate - region around Salerno after 851, *Principato*.

priory - monastery of men or women under a prior, esp in orders such as Dominicans and Franciscans, which in turn may answer to the jurisdiction of *abbeys*, q.v.

qadit - a large administrative district, comparable to a *taifa* (q.v.), under Arab administration.

qanat - See *kanat*.

qasida - form of Arabic poetry similar to the ode.

queen consort - the wife of a king during his reign.

queenhood - the state of being a queen.

queen regent - a queen who exercises royal authority on behalf of her young son, as heir, before the age of his majority.

queen regnant - a queen who rules in her own right.

queenship - the exercise of authority and power by a queen.

Reconquista - the military effort by Christians to reclaim Iberia from Muslim control, until 1492.

regent - man or woman who rules in place of a king or queen, typically one who has not reached the age of majority.

reginalità - Italian for *queenship*, q.v.

regnu - *kingdom* in Sicilian and Neapolitan, from *regnum*, modern Italian *regno*.

Regnum Siciliae - Kingdom of Sicily.

rex filius - a young royal heir crowned before the age of majority while his father still reigns as king.

rivelo - tax roll based on the *donativo*, q.v.

Rogerian Legend - characteristics attributed to Roger II similar to those of King Arthur.

ruotolo - unit of weight equal to a thousand *trappesi* (q.v.) or *tarì*, q.v.

sacrament - Christian rituals that impart divine grace, e.g. baptism, penance, matrimony, etc.

sagra - annual festival to mark a harvest or a specific food.

salma - unit of measurement for land area and the volume of dry substances such as grain, sometimes *salmo*, plural *salmi*.

sanctuary - the part of the church near the *apse* (q.v.), where the altar is located.

Saracen - medieval exonym for *Muslims* (q.v.), esp Arabs.

scholasticism - medieval Catholic theological movement based largely on the philosophy of Aristotle and early Christian teachings, emphasizing the reasoned study of tradition and dogma.

secretus - later term for a court officer, such as a governor or *bailiff*, q.v.

secular - said of clergy in a diocese rather than an order such as the *Benedictines*, q.v.

seigneur - manorial lord (usually an enfeoffed knight) under Frankish/Norman feudalism and *manorialism*, q.v. Sometimes a *baron*, q.v.

Sephardic Jews - Jews of the Iberian Peninsula.

serf - member of the peasantry tied to the land in the *manorial system*, q.v.

Shia Islam - sect or school of Islam based on succession through Ali ibn Abi Talib as heir of Prophet Muhammad, cfr. *Sunni Islam*.

Sicilianist - scholar specialized in *Sicilianistics,* q.v.

Sicilianistics - study of the language, culture and society of Sicily and the Kingdom of Sicily, from *sicilianistica.*

Sicilianità - distinctive character of being Sicilian in identity, origin and culture, cfr. *Napoletanità.*

Sicilians - people of the island of Sicily; people of the Kingdom of Sicily from 1140 until 1282.

Sicilian Succession - the right of women to inherit feudal property (see note 1027).

Siculo-Arabic - Arabic spoken by the Arabs of medieval Sicily, conserved as Maltese.

Siculo-Neapolitan - of or relating to southern Italy and its kingdoms.

souk - in Arabic, a permanent market or fair, also *suk.*

squire - attendant of a *knight* (q.v.) while being trained for knighthood, sometimes *esquire.*

stratigotus - alternate term for a governor or *bailiff,* q.v.

subscribe - to witness a decree or other official charter by signing it or affixing a seal.

sultan - title used by certain Muslim sovereigns, usually below a *caliph* (q.v.) but above an *emir,* q.v.

Sunni Islam - sect or school of Islam based on succession through Abu Bakr following the death of Prophet Muhammad, cfr. *Shia Islam.*

taifa - chiefly in Iberia, a small Muslim state after the fall of the *Umayyads* (q.v.) of Cordoba in 1031; the *qadits* (q.v.) of Sicily ruled by independent emirs after 1044.

tarenus - Latin for *tarì* (q.v.).

tarì - small gold coin introduced in Sicily by the Arabs and also minted by the Normans.

Templars - knightly order founded in Jerusalem in 1118 to protect pilgrims, later known for its financial power, abolished in 1312.

thalassemia - hereditary blood disorder that causes a decrease in hemoglobin production, fairly common in the Mediterranean and parts of Asia and Africa.

thema - in the Byzantine Empire, a province under a governor or *catepan,* q.v.

tomolo - a fraction of a *salma* (q.v.) as a unit of area measurement, also *tumolo.*

trappeso - unit of gold measurement equal to weight of a *tarì* (q.v.).

Umayyads - dynasty that ruled most of the Muslim world until 750, thenceforth controlling certain regions, notably Al-Andalus (Spain) until 1031.

Vikings - *Norse* (q.v.) raiders; Scandinavians generally.

Zibibbo - a grape variety, from Arabic *zabib.*

Zirids - *Berber* (q.v.) dynasty that ruled part of coastal Mediterranean Africa from 972 until 1148, sometimes under *Fatimids* (q.v.).

NOTES

1. Generally, the period from 1000 to 1300 in Europe, marked by discernible socio-political change, an increase in population, and a certain degree of prosperity and artistic development.

2. For example, Walter "of the Mill," who as Archbishop of Palermo and Primate of Sicily was the highest-ranking prelate of the kingdom, owes his peculiar Anglice nickname to the gadfly notion that he was English (he was actually Norman) and that *offamilias,* which denoted his status as a *familiaris,* or royal counsellor, referred to a mill someplace in England. The idea that, while in her twenties, Constance, the daughter of Roger II, had lived in a convent in Palermo, perhaps even taking vows, was formulated in Tuscany long after her death (a notable reference appears in John Villani's *Nuova Cronica,* book 5, chapter 16). More recently, other dubious theories have been advanced (see note 34).

3. See Tuchman, Barbara, *Practicing History: Selected Essays* (1981), page 9.

4. One of the better expositions of this approach is Abulafia, David, "Mediterranean History as Global History," *History and Theory,* volume 50, number 2 (May 2011), pages 220-228.

5. The exhibit ran from 18 November to 15 December 1994 at the Norman Palace, Palermo. Amongst the speakers at the conference was Professor David Abulafia, of Cambridge University, whose biography of Frederick II was published in the original in 1988 and in Italian translation in 1990. In Italy, one of the staunchest advocates for considering the Norman and Swabian periods together was Antonio Marongiù, for which see "A Model State in the Middle Ages: The Norman and Swabian Kingdom of Sicily," *Comparative Studies in Society and History,* number 6 (1964), pages 307-320. See also Tramontana, Salvatore, *La Monarchia Normanna e Sveva* (1986).

6. Jamison, Evelyn, "The Norman Administration of Apulia and Capua, More especially under Roger II and William I, 1127-1166," *Papers of the British School at Rome,* volume 6, number 6 (January 1913), pages 211-481 (specifically page 219).

7. Haskins, Charles Homer, *The Normans in European History* (1915), page 192. So highly respected were the views of Haskins that he was appointed a delegate for the United States at the Paris Peace Conference of 1919.

8. Ibid, pages 2 and 128, where the Muslims of Sicily are referred to as (respectively) *paynim* and *infidels,* although this reflected the terms used by medieval Christians themselves. Haskins also used now-outmoded words such as *Saracen* for Arab and *Basilian* for Greek Orthodox.

9. Women were admitted to public universities in the Kingdom of the Two Sicilies until its annexation to the Kingdom of Italy in 1860; successively, however, in the Kingdom of Italy they were admitted beginning only in 1875. See Mendola, Louis, *The Kingdom of the Two Sicilies 1734-1861* (2020), page 92; Polenghi, Simonetta, "Striving for Recognition: The first five female professors in Italy 1887-1904," *Paedagogica Historica,* volume 56, issue 6 (2020), pages 748-768. For the current situation see Filandri, Marianna, and Pasqua, Silvia, "Being good isn't enough: Gender Discrimination in Italian Academia," *Studies in Higher Education,* volume 46, issue 8 (2021), pages 1533-1551.

10. In the third (1877) edition of his *magnum opus* detailing the Norman conquest of England, Edward Freeman, who later wrote a history of Sicily, undertook to respond to subjective criticisms voiced by an envious colleague (see *The History of the Norman Conquest of England,* volume 1, pages vi-ix). For another example, see *Outlandish Knight: The Byzantine Life of Steven Runciman* (2016), where Runciman's biographer, Minoo Dinshaw, refers to the possible motive for vitriolic comments by Helene Wieruszowski in *Speculum,* volume 34, number 2 (1959), pages 323-326, despite her work being cited on page 338 of the first edition of *The Sicilian Vespers* (1958). See also James Powell's review of Salvatore Tramontana's monograph, *Gli Anni del Vespro: L'Immaginario, la Cronaca, la Storia,* in *Speculum,* volume 66, number 3 (July 1991), pages 700-701. Ernst Kantorowicz, who died in 1963, was often subjected to overt scorn that clearly transcended academic commentary on his work; see Lerner, Robert, *Ernst*

Kantorowicz: A Life (2017). As regards motivations: Hauptman, Robert, *Authorial Ethics: How Writers Abuse Their Calling* (2011), pages 14-122; Cohen, Nicholas, *You Can't Read This Book: Censorship in an Age of Freedom* (2012); Martin, Brian, "Jealousy, Happiness and the Quest for Status and Salaries," *Campus Review* (Australia), 23-29 October 1996, page 9; Damrosch, David, *We Scholars: Changing the Culture of the University* (1995); Leahy, Robert, *Emotional Schema Therapy* (2015), pages 246-248; Menon, Tanya, and Thompson, Leigh, "Envy at Work," *Harvard Business Review*, April 2010, pages 3-7; Smith, Richard, et al., *Envy at Work and in Organizations* (2016); Friedman, Bonita, "Envy: The Writer's Disease," *The New York Times* (26 November 1989); Billan, Rumeet, and Humber, Todd, *The Tallest Poppy: Successful Women Pay a High Price for Success* (2019); Garland, Douglas, *The Tall Poppy Syndrome: The Joy of Cutting Others Down* (2022). For the diminishing opportunities in humanistic fields, see *State of the Humanities 2022*, published by the American Academy of Arts and Sciences. See also the following note.

11. One of the finest (and most sobering) case studies of defective peer review in the field of medieval studies is presented by the late Plinio Prioreschi in *A History of Medicine*, volume 5 (2003), pages xix-liii. In *Peer Review: A Critical Inquiry* (2004) David Shatz identifies three major forms of bias that frequently taint peer review: ad hominem, affiliational, ideological. See also: Skinner, Patricia, *Studying Gender in Medieval Europe: Historical Approaches* (2018), page 18; Gould, Thomas, *Do We Still Need Peer Review? An Argument for Change* (2013); Hechinger, Fred, "Peer Review in Social Fields is Faulted," *The New York Times* (30 September 1986); Weale, Albert (editor), "Peer Review: The challenges for humanities and social sciences," *British Academy Report* (2007). Professor Davina Cooper observed: "A European friend recently told me she had been warned to keep her best ideas off her grant applications in case they were taken and used without attribution. Others worry about submitting articles to academic journals in case anonymous peer review leads their ideas astray. What is lost in this fear that ideas will be taken and used without acknowledgment by academically ravenous others? Are we developing a culture with the injunction to keep our best thoughts private until their provenance has been secured by publication?" See "Whose ideas are they anyway? Academic work as a form of public action, rather than possession," *LSE Impact of Social Sciences Blog*, 26 September 2014 (blogs.lse.ac.uk/impactofsocialsciences/2014/09/26/whose-ideas-are-they-anyway/, retrieved in September 2021). Similarly Grossberg, Michael, "History and the Disciplining of Plagiarism," in *Originality, Imitation, and Plagiarism* (2008), pages 159-172. In a lighter vein, a professor of German literature wrote: "Think of your meanest high school mean girl at her most gleefully, underminingly vicious. Now give her a doctorate in your discipline, and a modicum of power over your future. That's peer review." She notes that criticisms are often "hidden amidst the venting of petty vendettas and pettier agendas." See Schuman, Rebecca, "Revise and Resubmit!" *Slate*, 15 July 2014 (slate.com/human-interest/2014/07/the-easy-way-to-fix-peer-review-require-submitters-to-review-first.html, retrieved in September 2021). Robert Hauptman (op. cit. at note 10) considers ethics in book reviews. Amongst many problems that could be mentioned regarding the study of Norman Italy, a pervasive issue is that most Catholics and Protestants writing about Eastern Orthodoxy bring a millennium of "Latin" bias to their field, making them inappropriate choices to referee (peer review) work dealing with, for example, the differences between Catholicism and Orthodoxy in the Kingdom of Sicily. Double-blind peer review is reasonably efficient where the author's name can be kept anonymous, as in the case of a little-published junior scholar, but established authors encounter difficulties when they are known as the only historians working in a specialized sub-discipline. According to Hauptman (ibid, page 17), if "the paper is in a highly specialized and delimited disciplinary area, referees, who are intimately familiar with their peers and their perspectives, can often deduce who the author is."

12. Two early expositions of this model are set forth in Paulo Freire's *Pedagogia do Oprimido*, first published in 1968, a foundational work on the topic of critical pedagogy, and Edward Said's *Orientalism*, published a decade later; for a more recent interpretation see *For an Amerindian Autohistory: An Essay on the Foundations of a Social Ethic* (1992), by Georges Sioui. These works and others were reactions to the fact that, in the twentieth century, the outsider's view was normal in works published in English. That sometimes yielded bizarre results, especially when the typical British or American (and white) male wrote, perhaps condescend-

ingly, about societies that were not his own. Such "colonialism," sometimes a result of prior imperialism, tainted much of the reporting of "foreign" history by propagating misperceptions, biases, stereotypes, clichés and even racism, especially where Asia and Africa were the objects of study. It was sometimes deceptive, sacrificing veracity and depriving the reader of accurate information. In our time, the criticism of that kind of work reflects a reaction against longstanding bias; scholars even use the term "decolonization" to describe this. See: Ashcroft, Griffiths, Tiffin, *The Empire Writes Back: Theory and Practice in Post-Colonial Literatures* (1989); Shuttleworth, Kyle, *The History and Ethics of Authenticity: Meaning, Freedom and Modernity* (2020); Keita, Maghan, *Race and the Writing of History: Riddling the Sphinx* (2000); Carson, James, "Teaching Amerindian Autohistory," *American Indian Quarterly,* volume 27, number 1/2 (2003), pages 155-159; Goldberg, Susan, "For Decades, Our Coverage Was Racist. To Rise Above Our Past, We Must Acknowledge It," *National Geographic: The Race Issue* (April 2018); Fuglestad, Finn, "The Trevor-Roper Trap or the Imperialism of History," *History in Africa,* volume 19 (1992), pages 309-326. An underlying problem is the underrepresentation of certain ethnic minorities and people of color in the academy, obviously in Italy but even in Britain and the United States. See Bhopal, Kalwant, "Academics of Colour in Elite Universities in the UK and the USA: The 'unspoken system of exclusion,'" *Studies in Higher Education,* volume 47, number 11 (2022), pages 2127-2137; Adams, Richard, "Fewer than 1% of UK university professors are black, figures show," *The Guardian* (27 February 2020); Bitar, Jinann, *Faculty Diversity and Student Success Go Hand in Hand, So Why Are University Faculties So White?* (2022); Curtis, John, *Faculty Diversity and Minoritized Student Outcomes: An Analysis of Institutional Factors* (2021). For autoethnography see *Handbook of Autoethnography* (2021 edition), edited by Tony Adams, Stacy Holman Jones and Carolyn Ellis, and *Essentials of Autoethnography* (2021), by Christopher Poulos; and see also the following note. Among Anglophone Italians writing (accurate) monographs in English about some aspect, direct or peripheral, of the many topics covered in this volume we find: Leonard Chiarelli, William Tronzo, Ronald Musto, Dawn Marie Hayes, William Granara, Anne Maltempi, Laura Morreale, Gay Talese, Lisa Marie Basile, Marianna Gatto, Conchita Vecchio, Allison Scola, Diana Giovinazzo, Lisa Scottoline, Adriana Trigiani, Leigh Ann Esposito, the late John Marino.

13. This situation was acknowledged in comments by the English author of a book on the Kingdom of Sicily under the Normans: "If we became aware of foreign authors regularly selecting a chunk of English history, such as the Civil War, and not bothering with what came before or after, I think we would likely feel entitled to point out the importance of studying problems in their proper context. We might also, as Englishmen, I think, rather wonder at, even resent, perhaps, foreigners meddling with our history and wonder about their motives for doing so." See Matthew, Donald, "Modern Study of the Norman Kingdom of Sicily," *Reading Medieval Studies,* volume 18 (1992), pages 34-56 (specifically page 37). For bias in British views of Italy, see Comiati, Giacomo, and Piperno, Martina, "Italy Made in Britain: British Perspectives on Italian Culture," *Modern Languages Open,* volume 1 (2018), page 3; also Willman, Kate, "Contemporary British Travel Writing on Italy and British Broadsheets," *Modern Languages Open,* volume 1 (2018), page 8. A foreign scholar's xenocentric interest in southern Italy is typically based on little more than the recommendation of a dissertation advisor, viz. the comment by Professor David Abulafia: "I think when one starts as a historian, obviously one is guided to some extent by interests derived from one's teachers and so on," in Li, Hansong, "Humanity and the Great Seas," *Chicago Journal of History,* number 7 (autumn 2016), pages 20-29 (specifically page 20). An example of xenocentrism by Italians is reflected in publication of the journal *Studi Irlandesi* by the University of Florence since 2011. For commentary on xenocentrism as a wider trend see Schulman, Sarah, "White Writer," *The New Yorker* (21 October 2016); de Waal, Kit, "Don't dip your pen in someone else's blood: Writers and 'the other,'" *The Irish Times* (30 June 2018); Magner, Denise, "When Whites Teach Black Studies," *The Chronicle of Higher Education* (1 December 1993); Young, James (editor), *The Ethics of Cultural Appropriation* (2012); Keeshig-Tobias, Lenore, "Stop Stealing Native Stories," *Borrowed Power: Essays on Cultural Appropriation* (1997), pages 71-73; Mishan, Ligaya, "What Does Cultural Appropriation Really Mean," *The New York Times* (30 September 2022); Greenwalt, Kyle, and Leahy, Patrick, "Situating the Nation: History Pedagogy for the 21st Century," *Contempo-*

rary Social Studies: An Essential Reader (2011), chapter 18, pages 335-356; Moore, Laurence, "Insiders and Outsiders in American Historical Narrative and American History," *The American Historical Review,* volume 87, number 2 (April 1982), pages 390-412; Merton, Robert, "Insiders and Outsiders: A Chapter in the Sociology of Knowledge," *American Journal of Sociology,* volume 78, number 1 (July 1972), pages 9-47; Isai, Vjosa, "Doubts Over Indigenous Identity in Academia Spark 'Pretendian' Claims," *Canada Letter,* in *The New York Times* (15 October 2022); Cyca, Michelle, "The Curious Case of Gina Adams: A 'Pretendian' Investigation," *Maclean's,* 1 October 2022; Viren, Sarah, "The Native Scholar Who Wasn't," *The New York Times* (25 May 2021); Teillet, Jean, "There is nothing innocent about the false presumption of Indigenous identity," *The Globe and Mail,* 11 November 2022. For published examples of foreign historians' misperceptions about medieval Sicilian history see note 34 below.

14. For a view of the impact of Thomas Fazello see Maltempi, Anne, "Writing History in Renaissance Sicily: The Formation of Sicilian National Identity in the Work of Tommaso Fazello," *Mediterranean Studies,* volume 29, number 1 (2021), pages 4-31. For some observations about the influence of chroniclers and other writers in the fourteenth century see Musto, Ronald, *Writing Southern Italy Before the Renaissance: Trecento Historians of the Mezzogiorno* (2018). The major "modern" historical works to which reference is made are Chalandon, Ferdinand, *Histoire de la Domination Normande en Italie et en Sicile* (Paris 1907), and Kantorowicz, Ernst, *Kaiser Friedrich der Zweite* (Berlin 1927), for which there is a supplement of references, *Kaiser Friedrich der Zweite: Ergänzungsband* (1930); see also note 32. Some reasons for the lack of major Italian publications on these subjects until recently are noted in Appendix 6.

15. See Davies, Rees, "Nations and National Identities in the Medieval World: An Apologia," *Belgisch Tijdschrift voor Nieuwste Geschiedenis: Revue belge d'historie contemporaine,* volume 34, number 4 (2004), pages 567-577. Also Smith, Anthony, *The Ethnic Origins of Nations* (1991); Eller, Jack David, "Ethnicity, Culture and 'The Past,'" Michigan Quarterly review, volume 36, number 4 (Fall 1997); Hastings, Adrian, *The Construction of Nationhood: Ethnicity, Religion and Nationalism* (1997); and the Introduction and essays in Jensen, Lotte (editor), *The Roots of Nationalism: Identity Formation in Early Modern Europe 1600-1815* (2016). A perennially interesting entry is Kantorowicz, Ernst, *The King's Two Bodies: A Study in Mediaeval Political Theology* (1957, 1997). See also: Llobera, Josep, *Foundations of National Identity: From Catalonia to Europe* (2004); Balcells, Albert, *El Nacionalismo Catalán* (1991); Lledó-Guillem, Vicente, *The Making of Catalan Linguistic Identity in Medieval and Early Modern Times* (2018); Armstrong, John, *Nations Before Nationalism* (1982); also Davies, Norman, *Vanished Kingdoms* (2012). For overviews of the European trends, see Elliott, John, "A Europe of Composite Monarchies," *Past and Present,* volume 137, number 1 (November 1992), pages 48-71; Leyser, Karl, "Concepts of Europe in the Early and High Middle Ages," ibid, pages 25-47; Dunbabin, Jean, *France in the Making 843-1180* (1985, 2009), Ruddick, Andrea, *English Identity and Political Culture in the Fourteenth Century* (2013); Geary, Patrick, *The Myth of Nations: The Medieval Origins of Europe* (2002). For some foundational concepts still considered valid today, see Barth, Fredrik, *Ethnic Groups and Boundaries: The Social Organization of Culture Difference* (1969); Anderson, Benedict, *Imagined Communities* (1983). For the importance of ethnicity despite some academic attempts to minimize its relevance, see Winant, Howard, "Race, Ethnicity and Social Science," *Ethnic and Racial Studies,* volume 38, number 13 (2015), pages 2176-2185. Also Appendix 6 and notes 1308 and 1310.

16. Some commentators subjectively correlate these perceived differences to such phenomena as northern localities generally being somewhat tidier, and perhaps better-administered, than their southern counterparts. The "kingdom versus commune" thesis was cited in explanation of differences between north and south in Putnam, Robert, *Making Democracy Work: Civic Traditions in Modern Italy* (1993). See also Galasso, Giuseppe, "Due Italie nel Medioevo?" *Mediterranea: Ricerche Storiche,* number 22 (August 2011), pages 217-236; Abulafia, David, *The Two Italies: Economic Relations Between the Norman Kingdom of Sicily and the Northern Communes* (1977). However, at the unification of Italy in 1861 Naples was the wealthiest city in the country, and the Kingdom of the Two Sicilies was its most prosperous constituent state; see Mendola, Louis, *The Kingdom of the Two Sicilies 1734-1861* (2020).

NOTES

17. Genetic haplogroups do not always correlate precisely to the presence of specific peoples (and can be affected over time by such phenomena as "genetic drift"), but they offer us a broad "footprint" left by the past. Research undertaken during the last two decades reveals the following Y-chromosome haplogroups (and others) in southern Italy in approximately the following percentages: J (35), R (25), I (15), K (10), H (10), Others (5). These are very broadly identified with the following populations (and others) patrilineally: J1 (Arabs, Berbers, Carthaginians, Jews), J2 (Greeks, Romans, Jews), R1b (Germans, Normans, Lombards), I1 and I2b (Vikings and Normans), I and I2a (Elymians), G (Arabs and Elymians), N (Norsemen and Normans), E1b1b (Arabs and Berbers), K (Arabs, Greeks, Berbers, Carthaginians), H (Arabs), T (Phoenicians, Carthaginians). In matrilineal (mtDNA) lineage we find, among others, the "Seven Daughters of Eve," namely the haplogroups H (Helena), J (Jasmine), K (Katrine), T (Tara), U5 (Ursula), V (Velda) and X (Xenia). The reader seeking an introduction to this area of phylogeography is referred to *The Journey of Man: A Genetic Odyssey* (2004) by Spencer Wells, Explorer-in-Residence of the National Geographic Society and former student of the late Luigi Luca Cavalli-Sforza, the author of *Genes, Peoples and Languages* (2000), and *The Seven Daughters of Eve* (2001) by Bryan Sykes. While published surveys by geneticists are highly informative, the statistical samples available through firms such as Family Tree DNA are infinitely larger and potentially more useful if evaluated critically. For the geographic distribution of multiple sclerosis see, amongst other studies, Savettieri, Ragonese, Aridon, Salemi, "Epidemiology of Multiple Sclerosis in Sicily," *Neurological Sciences,* volume 22 (April 2001), pages 175-177. For origins see the sixth map in this book.

18. A good example of this is Sara McDougall's book, *Royal Bastards: The Birth of Illegitimacy 800-1230,* published in 2016, though it could be argued that medievalists were already reasonably familiar with most of the concepts presented in that work. See also Armstrong-Partida, Michelle, "Concubinage, Illegitimacy and Fatherhood: Urban Masculinity in Late-Medieval Barcelona," *Gender and History,* volume 31, number 1 (March 2019), pages 195-219; Matthews, Helen, *The Legitimacy of Bastards: The Place of Illegitimate Children in Later Medieval England* (2019). Two of Sicily's monarchs of the Norman-Swabian era were born outside marriage, namely Tancred and Manfred, each the last regnant king of his dynasty.

19. See: Bennett, Judith, "Medievalism and Feminism," *Speculum,* volume 68, number 2 (Spring 1993), pages 309-331; Pierson, Ruth, and Prentice, Alison, "Feminism and the Writing and Teaching of History," *Atlantis,* volume 7, number 2 (1982), pages 37-46; Skinner, Patricia, op. cit. at note 11; Lerner, Gerda, *The Creation of Feminist Consciousness: From the Middle Ages to 1870* (1994).

20. In 2020, the *Global Gender Gap Report* published by the World Economic Forum found Italy in 76th place compared to Ireland in 7th, Spain in 8th, France in 15th and Britain in 21st. During the same year, Italy (with a population of some 59 million), had 112 femicides. ISTAT, the Italian national statistics agency, reports that 43.6 percent of Italian women (nearly 9 million) between the ages of 15 and 65 have been sexually harassed in the workplace, 15.4 percent in the three years immediately prior to the report; see *Statistiche Report: Le molestie e i ricatti sessuali sul lavoro 2015-2016* (13 February 2018), published in English in condensed form under the same date as *Sexual Harassment and Sexual Blackmail at Work.* See also Van Cleave, Rachel, "Rape and Querela Law in Italy: False Protection of Victim Agency," *Michigan Journal of Gender and Law,* volume 13, January 2007 (Ann Arbor 2007), pages 273-310; Galli, Natalie, *The Girl Who Said No: A Search in Sicily* (2019); Bubola, Emma, "Locker-room talks: Italian politics and normalized sexism," *AlJazeera* (11 March 2018); Donadio, Rachel, "The Missing Piece in Italian Politics: Women," *The Atlantic* (10 March 2018); Pianigiani, Gaia, "Women Could Decide Italy's Election, but They Feel Invisible," *The New York Times* (3 March 2018); Soncini, Guia, "The Failure of Italian Feminism," *The New York Times* (26 October 2017); Giuffrida, Angela, "Italy's highest court accused of victim blaming over rape case," *The Guardian* (17 July 2018); Horowitz, Jason, "In Italy, #MeToo is More Like 'Meh'" in *The New York Times* (16 December 2017); Vigo, Julian, "Tight Jeans, Rape and Technology," *Forbes* (22 July 2018); Winfield, Nicole, "Italian Court Ruling That a Woman Was Too Ugly to Be Raped Sparks Outrage," *Time* (14 March 2019). The Italian version of #MeToo is #QuellaVoltaChe. For history see notes 1021 and 1032.

21. For example, the Society for Medieval Feminist Scholarship is dedicated to studies in this field, publishing the *Medieval Feminist Forum,* formerly the *Medieval Feminist Newsletter.*

22. An overview of strategy in the study of medieval women is set forth by Patricia Skinner (op. cit. at note 11), who has researched in Italy. Of note are Stafford, Pauline, "Writing the Biography of Eleventh-Century Queens," *Writing Medieval Biography 750-1250: Essays in Honour of Frank Barlow* (2006), pages 99-110; Chibnall, Marjorie, "The Empress Matilda as a Subject for Biography," ibid, pages 185-194; Parsons, John (editor), *Medieval Queenship* (1993); Erler, Mary, and Kowaleski, Maryanne (editors), *Gendering the Master Narrative: Women and Gender in the Middle Ages* (2003); Stafford, Pauline (editor), *Gendering the Middle Ages* (2001).

23. Constance Hauteville is mentioned only perfunctorily in recent reference works, where Margaret is ignored. See Fösser, Amalie, "The Political Traditions of Female Rulership in Medieval Europe," *The Oxford Handbook of Women and Gender in Medieval Europe,* pages 75-76, 79; also the concise entry on pages 165-166 of *Women and Gender in Medieval Europe: An Encyclopedia.* Constance is mentioned in passing in Skinner, Patricia, *Women in Medieval Italian Society 500-1200* (2001), page 161. Theresa Earenfight mentions Constance Hauteville and her daughter-in-law, Constance of Aragon, in her fine study, *Queenship in Medieval Europe* (2013). The first monographic biography of Constance Hauteville in English is Mary Taylor Simeti's *Travels With a Medieval Queen: The Journey of a Sicilian Princess to Reclaim Her Father's Crown* (2001), though the book is partly a memoir of its author's experiences. An exhibit held in New York in March 2022 was dedicated to Constance and her daughter-in-law (Constance of Aragon), without the catalogue essays even mentioning Margaret; q.v. *Constancia: Women and Power in the Mediterranean Empire of Frederick II* (2022). Our English queens, Joanna and Isabella, are included in Mary Anne Everett Green's *Lives of the Princesses of England from the Norman Conquest* (1850). See also note 551.

24. Various apocryphal phrases are incorrectly attributed to Frederick II, such as *Si regnum meum Siciliae vidisset Deus Palestinam non elegisset* ("If God had seen my Kingdom of Sicily, He would not have chosen Palestine"). For defamatory allegations see note 964; those made during Frederick's lifetime are mentioned at note 1210.

25. *The Annals of Roger de Hoveden* (in Sources), volume 2, page 341.

26. In the chronicler's own words: *Audivimus a quibusdam quod Johanna uxor Guillelmi regis Siciliae, filia Henrici regis Anglorum, peperit ei filium primogenitum, quem vocaverunt Boamundum. Qui cum a baptismate reverteretur, pater investivit eum ducati Apuliae per aureum sceptrum, quod in manu gerebat.* See *The Chronicle of Robert of Torigni,* page 303; also *The History of William of Newburgh and the Chronicles of Robert de Monte* in *The Church Historians of England: Pre-Reformation Period,* volume 4, part 2, page 806. Several factors argue against the accuracy of this account. Firstly, it is not corroborated elsewhere, not even by an inscription on a tomb (no tomb of a child of William and Joanna exists). Secondly, Robert was far away in Normandy, not in Sicily, so he was not a witness to events in the *Regnum.* Thirdly, a firstborn son would most likely have been named William, Roger, or even Henry (for Joanna's father or William's beloved brother), not Bohemond. Lastly, Joanna bore no other children by William, although she later gave birth to the children of her second husband, a fact that raises questions about William's ability to father children. In his *Decameron* (day 4, story 44), Giovanni Boccaccio states incorrectly that William had two children. See also note 743.

27. Whilst searching through some uncatalogued, unindexed (and then unedited) parchment manuscripts in the Vatican Secret Archive (in 1992) which had been acquired from another collection, one of the authors of this book found an apparent reference to the Assizes that may be dated tentatively to around 1146 referring to issuance of certain "laws" in a year inferred as 1141 or 1142 (sic), suggesting that the traditional presumption of the code's dating is accurate. Unfortunately, photography of the charter was not possible. See also note 355.

28. See Matthews, Herbert, "Germans Burned Library in Naples: 200,000 Volumes Destroyed Systematically in Action That Recalled Louvain," *The New York Times,* 12 October 1943, page 3; Filangieri, Riccardo, "Report on the Destruction by the Germans, September 30, 1943, of

the Depository of Priceless Historical Records of the Naples State Archives," *The American Archivist,* volume 7, number 4 (October 1944), pages 252-255. This incident coincided with the "Four Days of Naples" (see note 1283). See note 1009 for Carcani's fortuitous transcription of the registry of Frederick II for 1239-1240 long before it was destroyed.

29. Tuchman, Barbara, op. cit., page 19. She also states, on page 42: "If I were a teacher, I would disqualify anyone who was content to cite a secondary source as a reference for a fact."

30. For examples of the infiltration of (literal) fantasy into medieval studies: *Queenship and the Women of Westeros: Female Agency and Advice in Game of Thrones and A Song of Ice and Fire,* published by Palgrave Macmillan (Springer Nature) in 2019 as part of its "Queenship and Power" series (page liii of the introduction by the editors gives us *La Correra de la Serra* for the *Corriere della Sera,* one of Italy's major newspapers); Carroll, Shiloh, *Medievalism in A Song of Ice and Fire and Game of Thrones,* published by Boydell and Brewer in 2018 as part of its "Medievalism" series. See also note 34.

31. King Louis IX was canonized in 1297. Following the destruction (by revolutionaries) of most of his remains at Saint-Denis, more of his bodily relics may have been conserved at Monreale than anyplace else. The small chest of Catalonian manufacture that formerly contained the king's heart and viscera is kept in Monreale's diocesan museum. Geoffroy of Beaulieu, long the king's confessor, was present in September 1270 when the relics were translated to Monreale, for which see *Recueil des Historiens des Gaules et de la France* (1840), volume 20, page 24 (sections XLVI and XLVII). Geoffroy's "Life of Louis IX" is considered at some length in De Wailly, Natalis, "Examen Critique de la *Vie de Saint Louis* par Geoffroi de Beaulieu," in *Bibliothèque de l'École des Chartes* (1844), volume 5, pages 205-231. French scholars have long questioned whether anything more than the saint's viscera and (perhaps) two fingers was ever present at Monreale. For a review of the analysis of the remains of the relics in 1843, see Letronne, Antoine, *Examen Critique de la Découverte du Prétendu Coeur de Saint Louis* (1844); more recently, Charlier, Philippe, et al., "Schistosomiasis in the Mummified Viscera of Saint Louis (1270 AD)," *Forensic Science, Medicine and Pathology,* volume 12, number 1 (March 2016), pages 113-114. Further observations appear in Bourassé, Jean Jacques, *Dictionnaire d'Épigraphie Chrétienne* (1852), volume 1, columns 908-912; the Monreale entry ends with column 939 following extensive historiography regarding the heart of France's heavenly patron. See also notes 971, 975, 1274.

32. See Abulafia, David, "Kantorowicz and Frederick II," *History,* volume 62, number 205 (June 1977), pages 192-210; also notes 10 and 14 supra.

33. From the 2002 (Pimlico) edition of David Abulafia's *Frederick II: A Medieval Emperor,* page 457: "There have been several popular biographies in German and Italian which are mostly competent enough, but which are spelled out in a glow of admiration for the *Stupor Mundi,* often without much willingness to address the doubts and reservations in this book." An interesting comment by Charles Homer Haskins appears in his book on the Normans (op. cit. at note 7), page 248, where he states that the book by Isidoro La Lumia needs revision.

34. Responses to various theories, whether tenable or not, serve no constructive purpose in this kind of work, where there is no reason to cite a fallacious idea simply to express disagreement with it. Moreover, it is not the intent of the authors to denigrate the efforts of fellow scholars by describing their errors in a way that might identify those making the mistakes. To cite an inventive notion about medieval Sicily: A British academic teaching at a university in England construed a remark made by the chronicler Hugh Falcandus to imply that a "mentality" (pattern of behavior) known amongst the Arabs of Palermo in the twelfth century fostered attitudes that still existed in Sicily in the twentieth, leading to organized crime. For accurate information on that topic see Lupo, Salvatore, *History of the Mafia* (2009); Mendola, Louis, *The Kingdom of the Two Sicilies 1734-1861,* pages 99-101; more generally, O'Connor, Cailin, and Owen, James, *The Misinformation Age: How False Beliefs Spread* (2019). Other misperceptions are mentioned at notes 2 and 1288; see note 31 for the attempt by French historians to discredit the fact of the heart of their patron saint being at Monreale.

35. See Chapter 6 of Kulikowski, Michael (op. cit. at note 37), pages 123-143; also Eisenberg, Robert, "The Battle of Adrianople: A Reappraisal," *Hirundo,* volume 8 (2009-2010), pages 108-120.

36. For a good introduction to this period see Ward-Perkins, Bryan *The Fall of Rome and the End of Civilization* (2006); a lengthier study is Heather, Peter, *The Fall of the Roman Empire: A New History of Rome and the Barbarians* (2006). See also the following note.

37. The oldest surviving manuscript of the *Getica,* or *De Origine Actibusque Getarum,* is the *Codice Basile* at the Palermo Archive of State, while the definitive English translation is *The Origin and Deeds of the Goths* (1908), by Charles Mierow. A fine general history of the Gothic War based on recent historiography is *Rome's Gothic Wars* (2007) by Michael Kulikowski. For the earliest medieval European civilizations of southern Italy see *People and Identity in Ostrogothic Italy, 489-554* (1997) by Patrick Amory, and *The Vandals* (2010) by Andrew Merrills and Richard Miles, also *On Barbarian Identity: Critical Approaches to Ethnicity in the Early Middle Ages* (2002), a collection edited by Andrew Gillett. An early Italian entry that sought to present a balanced view was Gabriele Pepe's *Il Medio Evo Barbarico d'Italia* (1941). See also the preceding note.

38. An excellent introduction in English is to be had in Christie, Neil, *The Lombards: The Ancient Longobards* (1999). However, the defining studies are those of the late Nicoletta Francovich Onesti, notably her collections of articles in *Le Regine dei Longobardi e Altri Saggi* (2013) and *Goti e Vandali: Dieci saggi di lingua e cultura medievali* (2013); see also note 41.

39. See *Edicta Regum Langobardorum.* For fine English translations see Drew, Katherine, *The Lombard Laws* (1973). A facsimile edition of the *Codex Legum Longobardorum,* copied at Benevento around 1005 and conserved at the Cava abbey (Codice 4, Badia di Cava dei Tirreni), was published in Italy in 2017 by CAPSA Ars Scriptoria, accompanied by a transcription with an Italian translation by Stefano Gasparri, Claudio Azzara and Flavia de Rubeis. A fine general history of the Lombards' Principality of Salerno is Taviani-Carozzi, Huguette, *La Principauté Lombarde de Salerne* (1991). For the Papal State a good introduction is Noble, Thomas, *The Republic of Saint Peter: The Birth of the Papal State 680-825* (1986).

40. See *Scriptores Rerum Langobardicarum et Italicarum,* which also has a number of allied texts. For a translation see William Dudley Foulke's *History of the Langobards by Paul the Deacon* (1907). A facsimile edition of the ninth-century *Cividale Codex* (Codice XXVIII, Museo Archeologico Nazionale di Cividale di Friuli) was published in Italy in 2015 as *Historia Longobardorum* by CAPSA Ars Scriptoria, accompanied by a transcription and lengthy commentary by Laura Pani, Stefano Gasparri and Elisa Vittor.

41. See Francovich Onesti, Nicoletta, *Le Regine dei Longobardi* (at note 38), also the concise but useful synopsis published digitally shortly before her death, *La Lingua dei Longobardi: Caratteristiche e Problemi* (2014). A fine local study is Falluomini, Carla (editor), *Goti e Longobardi a Chiusi* (2009).

42. Influenced by the northern dialect of Lombardic rather than the Neapolitan form of it then widely spoken in the south (at Salerno and Capua), this "Gallo-Italic of Sicily" was introduced by Adelaide del Vasto and her retainers late in the eleventh century (for Neapolitan see Chapter 24). The knights were from Saronno, in what is now the province of Varese in Lombardy, but also certain parts of Piedmont and Liguria ruled by Adelaide's family. This philology was researched extensively by Giovanni Tropea between 1960 and 1970 and published in a number of articles, e.g. "Effetti della simbiosi linguistica nella parlata gallo-italica di Aidone, Nicosia e Novara di Sicilia," *Bollettino dell'Atlante Linguistico Italiano,* New Series number 13-14 (1966), pages 3-50. (For influences on Tuscan see the preceding note.) For insight into the Nebrodian communities see La Via, Mariano, "Le Così Dette 'Colonie Lombarde' in Sicilia," *Archivio Storico Siciliano* (Palermo 1899), pages 1-35. For the language (Neapolitan) spoken in Salerno and Capua by 1000 see notes 132 and 908.

43. See Christys, Ann, *Vikings in the South* (2015), pages 59-60. Also Kunz, Keneva, and Sigurdsson, Gisli (translators), *The Vinland Sagas* (2008); Wallace, Birgitta, "The Norse in Newfoundland: L'Anse aux Meadows and Vinland," *Newfoundland Studies,* number 19, number 1

NOTES

(2013), pages 5-43; Anderson, Rasmus, *America Not Discovered by Columbus* (1891); Kuitems, Margot, et al., "Evidence for European Presence in the Americas in AD 1021," *Nature*, number 601 (2022), pages 388-391. As we shall see, Norsemen made up the elite Varangian Guard of the Byzantine Empire.

44. For the uninitiated, three informative general histories of the Byzantine Empire are Steven Runciman's *Byzantine Civilisation* (1969 edition), John Julius Norwich's three-volume opus, *Byzantium* (1988), and George Ostrogorsky's *History of the Byzantine State* (1956). For a focus on Italy's Norman-Swabian period a fine entry is Angold, Michael, *The Byzantine Empire 1025-1204: A Political History* (1997 edition). A useful work for the era leading up to that period is Holmes, Catherine, *Basil II and the Governance of Empire 976-1025* (2005).

45. See Antonopoulos, Panagiotis, "Emperor Constans II's Intervention in Italy and its Ideological Significance," *Byzantine War Ideology between Roman Imperial Concept and Christian Religion* (Vienna 2013), pages 27-32.

46. Essentially, a vocal faction in Constantinople accused those having or venerating icons of idolatry. Although this controversy erupted not in the Latin west but in the Byzantine Empire in the eighth century, the Carolingians of the Holy Roman Empire embraced it, fostering disdain for the Christians of the east. See Noble, Thomas, *Images, Iconoclasm and the Carolingians* (2013); for a general exposition see Martin, Edward, *A History of the Iconoclastic Controversy* (1930).

47. There are various books about the Lombards and Byzantines in Italy, but for an emphasis on their presence in the south see Barbara Kreutz's *Before the Normans: Southern Italy in the Ninth and Tenth Centuries* (1991), and Luigi Berto's *Ethnic Identity, Memory and the Use of the Past in Italy's 'Dark Ages'* (2022). For the Byzantines, see: Cosentino, Salvatore, and Zanini, Enrico (editors), *A Companion to Byzantine Italy* (2021); von Falkenhausen, Vera, *La Dominazione Bizantina nell'Italia Meridionale dal IX al XI Secolo* (1978); Lavermicocca, Nino, *Puglia Bizantina: Storia e cultura di una regione Mediterranea 876-1071* (2012 edition); Savvides, Alexios, *Byzanto-Normmanica: The Norman Capture of Italy and the First Two Invasions in Byzantium* (2007). For a general view, see Wickham, Chris, *The Inheritance of Rome: A History of Europe from 400 to 1000* (2009).

48. Bucaria, Nicolò, and Cassuto, David, "La Sinagoga e il Miqweh di Palermo alla Luce dei Documenti e delle Scoperte Archeologiche," *Archivio Storico Siciliano*, Series 4, Volume 31 (Palermo 2005), pages 171-209; Scandaliato, Angela, and Mulè, Nuccio, *La Sinagoga e il Bagno Rituale degli Ebrei di Siracusa* (2002).

49. This was stated by the Jewish author of the *Chronicle of Ahimaaz*, who probably lived in Amalfi; his text covers the period from 850 to 1054. For a general introduction see Simonsohn, Shlomo, *Between Scylla and Charybdis: The Jews in Sicily* (2011). See also Moshe, Gil, "The Jews in Sicily under Muslim Rule in the Light of Geniza Documents," *Italia Judaica 1* (1983), pages 87-134, and the more recent (1995) article is the bibliography. The best published collection of charters relative to the Jews of Sicily is the *Codice Diplomatico dei Giudei di Sicilia* (1884), compiled by Bartolomeo and Giuseppe Lagumina. An early history, which reflects the biases of its time, is Di Giovanni, Giovanni, *L'Ebraismo della Sicilia* (1748). See also Abulafia, David, "The Jews of Sicily under the Norman and Hohenstaufen Rulers," in *Ebrei in Sicilia* (2002), pages 69-92.

50. In English, and perhaps any language, the definitive history of the Muslim Arabs in Sicily is Chiarelli, Leonard, *A History of Muslim Sicily* (second edition, 2018), which, in addition to its fine narrative, has a good timeline, list of rulers and bibliography. Another fine entry is Granara, William, *Narrating Muslim Sicily* (2019). A concise overview is Ahmad, Aziz, *A History of Islamic Sicily* (1975). For a wider context, see Brett, Michael, *The Rise of the Fatimids* (2001); a reliable summary is Jiwa, Shainool, *The Fatimids: The Rise of a Muslim Empire* (2018). Other works in the bibliography are informative, and much in the books by Salvadore Morso and Michele Amari has withstood the test of time quite well despite what some recent critics claim.

51. Makdisi, John, "The Islamic Origins of the Common Law," *North Carolina Law Review*, volume 77, number 5 (June 1999), pages 1635-1737. See also note 656.

52. Johns, Jeremy, *Arabic Administration in Norman Sicily: The Royal Diwan* (2002).

53. See Broadhurst, Ronald, *The Travels of Ibn Jubayr* (1952, 2008); Granara, William, "Ibn Hawqal in Sicily," *Alif: Journal of Comparative Poetics,* number 3, (Cairo 1983), pages 94-99; Gabrieli, Francesco, "Ibn Hawqal e gli Arabi in Sicilia," *L'Islam nella Storia: Saggi di storia e storiografia musulmana* (1966), pages 57-67. For language see Agius, Dionisius, *Siculo Arabic* (1996). Cordoba, with its magnificent mosque-cum-cathedral, is still an impressive city. The Nasrid palaces in the Alhambra of Granada, and the splendid salons in Seville's Alcazar, are equally majestic. The surviving testaments to the Mudéjar style in Andalusia and Navarre differ somewhat from what one finds in Sicily, but before it fell to ruin the *hammam* at Cefala Diana may have been similar to the Bañuelo in Granada; see Nef, Annliese, and Bagnera, Alessandra (editors), *Les Bains de Cefalà: Pratiques thermales d'origine islamique dans le Sicile médiévale* (2018). A medieval passive cooling system (most of those that survive are modern constructions) remains in the medieval tower of Palazzo Conte Federico, Palermo, where it was once fed from the same Kemonia spring that supplied the mikveh nearby.

54. Chiarelli, Leonard, "The Ibadi Communities in Muslim Sicily," *Ibadi Jurisprudence: Origins, Development and Cases*, in the series *Studies on Ibadism and Oman,* volume 6 (2015), pages 159-166.

55. For some translations from the Arabic see Mallette, Karla, *The Kingdom of Sicily 1100-1250: A Literary History* (2005). See also Schippers, Arie, "Arabic and Hebrew Love Poetry in Sicily in the Middle Ages and Their Contacts with Early Romance and German Poets in Sicily," *Quaderni di Studi Arabi,* volume 10 (2015), pages 87-102; Miller, Nathaniel, "Muslim Poets under a Christian King: An Intertextual Reevaluation of Sicilian Arabic Literature under Roger II," *Mediterranean Studies,* volume 28, number 1 (2020), pages 51-87; Carpentieri, Nicola, "Adab as Social Currency: The Survival of the Qasida in Medieval Sicily," *Mediterranea,* volume 3 (Córdoba 2018), pages 1-18. See also note 367 and the works of Umberto Rizzitano (in the bibliography).

56. This phrase, more often "western culture," sometimes used (incorrectly) as a metaphor for "Eurocentric," has fallen out of favor among scholars in recent decades; its use here is merely descriptive.

57. Mediterraneanist studies abound, spawning eclectic views. See, for example, Herzfeld, Michael, "The Horns of the Mediterraneanist Dilemma," *American Ethnologist,* volume 11, number 3 (August 1984), pages 439-454; Haller, Dieter, "The Cosmopolitan Mediterranean: Myth and Reality," *Zeitschrift für Ethnologie,* volume 29, number 1 (2004), pages 29-47. The trans-Mediterranean focus has become topical (timely) regarding the Norman period in almost every area; for textiles see Goskar, Tehmina "Material Worlds: The Shared Cultures of Southern Italy and Its Mediterranean Neighbours in the Tenth to Twelfth Centuries," *Al-Masaq: Journal of the Medieval Mediterranean,* volume 23, issue 3 (London 2011), pages 189-204.

58. Sometimes the *Mozarabic Chronicle* or the *Continuatio Hispana,* where we encounter the word *europenses* in reference to the victors. Written by a Christian, the chronicle offers us one of the few reliable accounts of the famous battle.

59. Biographies of Charlemagne abound. Three recent entries: McKitterick, Rosamond, *Charlemagne: The Formation of a European Identity* (2008); Nelson, Janet, *King and Emperor: A New Life of Charlemagne* (2019); Fried, Johannes, *Charlemagne* (2016).

60. For a good contextual biography see Fouracre, Paul, *The Age of Charles Martel* (2000).

61. For the Franks during the Merovingian period see James, Edward, *The Franks* (1991). For essays on the Franks generally, see Fouracre, Paul (editor), *Frankland: The Franks and the World of the Early Middle Ages* (2008). For biographies of Charlemagne see note 59; for his dynasty, see Costambeys, Marios, et al., *The Carolingian World* (2011).

62. A few notably clear works about this popular, complex topic: Oliver, Neil, *The Vikings* (2013); Winroth, Anders, *The Age of the Vikings* (2016); Haywood, John, *Northmen: The Viking Saga, AD 793-1241* (2016); Price, Neil, *Children of Ash and Elm: A History of the Vikings* (2020); Wallace-Hadrill, John, *The Vikings in Francia* (1975).

NOTES

63. Much has been published about the Normans. Good recent works are: Rowley, Trevor, *The Normans: A History of Conquest* (2021); Green, Judith, *The Normans: Power, Conquest and Culture in 11th-Century Europe* (2022); Crouch, David, *The Normans: The History of a Dynasty* (2006); Webber, Nick, *The Evolution of Norman Identity 911-1154* (2005); Bates, David, *Normandy Before 1066* (1982). See also Johnson, Ewan, "Origin Myths and the Construction of Medieval Identities: Norman Chronicles 1000-1100," in *Texts and Identities in the Early Middle Ages* (2006), pages 154-164.

64. For one early examination, among many, of the differences between Longobard and Frankish feudal law, see Dragonetti, Giacinto, *Origine dei Feudi nei Regni di Napoli e Sicilia* (1788), pages 229-232.

65. Amato of Montecassino, *L'Ystoire de li Normant,* book 1, chapter 17: *Avan mille puis que Christ lo nostre Signor...* The surviving manuscript of this work is a copy translated into French during the fourteenth century and apparently altered somewhat in the process. The citations used here refer to the system of books and chapters (rather than pages) in the edition of Robert Viscart published in Paris in 1835 followed in that of Alberto Tamburrini published in 1999. These are essentially the same as those in the system employed by Vincenzo De Bartholomaeis in his *Storia de' Normanni di Amato di Montecassino* published in Rome in 1935 and Prescott Dunbar's English translation published in 2004 (which is based on that text). Interestingly, Orderic Vitalis repeated this story; see *The Ecclesiastical History of England and Normandy by Orderic Vitalis,*volume 1, pages 411-412. For Amato see Appendix 6.

66. The statement that the Normans assisting Melus against the Bariots in 1016 were joined by their companions from Salerno implies that some were already living in that city by then; Amato, book 1, chapter 23: *Mès, quant fu seu à Salerne que ensi avoient combatu li Normant por aidier à Melo et estoient mort, vindrent cil Normant de Salerne.* Interestingly, Rodulfus Glaber, a Burgundian monk whose chronicle was completed by 1035, long before that of Amato, mentions Norman mercenaries in the service of abbots in southern Italy by around 1010.

67. See the *Cassino Chronicle,* the *Chronica Monasterii Casinensis* of Leo Marsicano, book 2, chapter 37, pages 236-237: *Ante hos circiter sedecim annos quadraginta numero normanni in habitu peregrino a Ierusolimis revertentes Salernum applicuerunt...* See also the *Cassino Annal,* the *Annales Casinenses,* page 305, referring to two codices and the year 1000. Orderic Vitalis, who lived much later, likewise repeated the story, writing around 1115. For additional commentary see Dunbar, Prescott, *The History of the Normans by Amatus of Montecassino* (2004), page 50, note 12.

68. For context, it is worth noting that the Muslims of Sicily sometimes acted as mercenaries; such may have been the case when they fought against Emperor Otto II near Stilo, in Calabria, in July 982 (mentioned in Chapter 1), having made a pact with Italy's Byzantines in 967. Amato's dating of the Normans' arrival at Salerno to 999 is consistent with the presumed succession of Guaimar III to the princedom in 998 (it may have been earlier), while the *Bari Chronicle* (see note 93) and other contemporary sources mention numerous Arab raids along the Italian coasts during this era. The church of the Holy Sepulchre was later rebuilt, beginning around 1042, and became a focal point for crusaders as well as pilgrims. For the quote from the *Ferraris Chronicle* see Alio, Jacqueline, *The Ferraris Chronicle: Popes, Emperors and Deeds in Apulia 1096-1228* (2017), page 85.

69. This story begins with the first book of William's chronicle, where line 4 refers to the *Gens Normannorum* as an ethnic group being "distinguished for its ferocious knights." The *editio princeps* of the chronicle of William of Apulia, *Gesta Roberti Wiscardi* (The Deeds of Robert Guiscard), was published in 1582 based on the only complete manuscript known to survive, a twelfth-century copy from the abbey of Mont Saint-Michel now conserved in the city library of Avranches. The lines in that first edition are not clearly numbered. Like many other chronicles, this was republished in the excellent *Monumenta Germaniae Historica* series, in *Scriptores,* volume 9 (1851), pages 239-298. The line numeration used here is based on what is published in that edition, followed by, amongst others, Francesco De Rosa in 2003. For information on William see Appendix 6.

70. Notably, in the *Chronica Monasterii Casinensis,* book 2, chapter 37, pages 236-239. See also the *Cassino Annal* as cited at note 67.

71. An early study on the "Gargano" and "Salerno" traditions is Joranson, Einar, "The Inception of the Career of the Normans in Italy: Legend and History," *Speculum,* number 23, number 3 (July 1948), pages 353-396. A number of others have followed, some contesting the credibility of the "Salerno" tradition. See, for example, France, John, "The occasion of the coming of the Normans to southern Italy," *Journal of Medieval History,* volume 17, issue 3 (September 1991), pages 185-205. Writing around 1028, the chronicler Adémar de Chabannes mentions the arrival of the Normans, if only in passing, in his *Ademari Chronicon,* book 3; see Chavanon, Jules, *Adémar de Chabannes, Chronique* (1897); also *PCC,* Series Secunda, volume 141 (1853), columns 29-80; commentary at Bauduin, Pierre, "Ademar of Chabannes and the Normans," *Lives, Identities and Histories in the Central Middle Ages* (2021), pages 161-179.

72. Certain information about the Drengot clan is too sketchy and contradictory to facilitate reliable conclusions. Their fief, Quarrel, was near Alençon. They would prove to be one of the few families to seriously challenge the power of the Hautevilles in Italy. It is known that Osmond (or possibly Gilbert) Drengot was exiled from his homeland for murdering William Repostel, a kinsman of Richard II of Normandy, in 1016. It is reported that Repostel had seduced (or raped) a daughter of Gilbert or Osmond. Amato (op. cit. supra, book 1, chapter 20) states that Repostel was killed by Gilbert; Orderic Vitalis identifies the perpetrator as Osmond. More generally, see Johnson, Ewan, "The Process of Norman Exile into Southern Italy," *Exile in the Middle Ages: Selected Proceedings* (2004), pages 29-38.

73. Amato of Montecassino, *L'Ystoire de li Normant,* book 1, chapters 22-23; also *Chronica Monasterii Casinensis,* book 2, chapter 37, pages 238-241. The annals/chronicles of Cava and Bari also mention these events. From William of Apulia, book 1, lines 71-92: *Maii mensis erant aptissima tempora Marti: Hoc ad bella solent procedere tempore reges. Fortunaque pari primo pugnatur utrimque. Auctis militibus comites fuit inde secutus Turnicius, sed terga dedit victusque recessit. Conflictu belli Pacianus corruit huius. Normannis auget validas victoria vires, Expertis Graecos nullius roboris esse, Quos non audaces sed cognovere fugaces. Imperii fama insinuat rectoribus arva Appula Normannos Melo duce depopulari. Hunc, his auditis, sibi curia iudicat hostem. Si capitur, capitis fieri caesura iubetur. Multa Graecorum cum gente Basilius ire Iussus, in hunc audax anno movet arma sequenti, Cui catapan facto cognomen erat Bagianus. Quod catapan Graeci, nos iuxta dicimus omne. Quisquis apud Danaos vice fungitur huius honoris, Dispositor populi parat omne quod expedit illi, Et iuxta quod cuique dari decet omne ministrat. Vicinus Cannis qua defluit Aufidus amnis, Circiter Octobris pugnatur utrimque Kalendas.* Cannae was the site of a Roman defeat by Hannibal in 216 BC (BCE) during the Second Punic War.

74. Morris Bishop's book, *The Middle Ages* (1970), places knighthood into a wider medieval context. Fine introductions are *The Knight and Chivalry* (revised edition, 2000), by Richard Barber, and *Chivalry* (1984) by Maurice Keen. Another reliable entry is Richard Kaeuper's *Medieval Chivalry* (2016). A useful examination of the literary sources and mythos is presented by David Crouch in *The Chivalric Turn: Conduct and Hegemony in Europe before 1300* (2019). For "courtliness," the respectful ("chivalrous") treatment of women by men, a seminal study is Kelly-Gadol, Joan, "Did Women Have a Renaissance?" in *Becoming Visible: Women in European History* (1977 edition), pages 137-164. Perhaps intending satire (though some scholars question that thesis), André the Chaplain, whose work was known in Sicily, mentions a knight raping a peasant woman, for which see: Parry, John Jay, *The Art of Courtly Love by Andreas Capellanus* (1969), pages 148-150; Heneveld, Amy, "The Falcon and the Glove or How the Courtly Exemplum Teaches Love in Andreas Capellanus' Tractatus de Amore," *Cahiers de Recherches Médiévales et Humanistes,* number 23 (2012), pages 49-60; Croce, Orazio, *Influssi del 'De Amore' di Andrea Cappellano nella Scuola Poetica Siciliana: Una Revisione Critica* (2010).

75. Rather little was recorded in much detail about the education of children in southern Italy between 1130 and 1266, but in England we find Walter of Bibbesworth writing about it near the end of this era, offering advice to a noblewoman on how to teach her children French. Chess was popular among aristocrats; one of the most distinguished chess players of the Norman-Swabian era was Macalda of Scaletta, who was afforded a military education, as if

NOTES

destined to be a knight, and could wield a sword. The War of the Vespers of 1282 found her governing Catania while her second husband (the first was William Amico), Alaimo of Lentini, was away in Messina doing battle against the Angevins. She became a lady-in-waiting to Constance, the daughter of King Manfred of Sicily, and she knew John of Procida, who had been a counsellor of Frederick II. Macalda is known to posterity for her pompous personality and court intrigues; she infamously tried to seduce Constance's husband, Peter III of Aragon. In 1285, she was placed under arrest and imprisoned in Mategriffon, the castle erected by Richard Lionheart at Messina. Macalda, who died around 1309 aged about seventy-two, famously played chess against the emir Margam bin Sebir, who was held captive at Mategriffon following an Aragonese raid on his Tunisian dominions. The chief contemporary source for Macalda is the *Historia Sicula* of Bartholomew of Nicastro, particularly chapters 50-51, 87-89, 91; she is mentioned (though not named) as Alaimo's wife by the Catalan chronicler Bernat Desclot in his *Crónica del Rey en Pere*, chapter 96. A few years earlier, Alfonso X of Castile, a kinsman of Frederick II, had commissioned the translation of an Arabic manual, as the *Libro de Acedrex, Dados e Tablas* (or "Book of Games"), in which women are depicted playing chess (e.g. on folio 58 recto); this is conserved in *Libro de los Juegos* in the Biblioteca del Real Monasterio de El Escorial, Madrid, Manuscript T-1-6. In the ceiling of Palermo's Palatine Chapel is a depiction of men playing chess (see Chapter 11).

76. The precise circumstances of the Drengots being enfeoffed with Ariano are the subject of debate. However, see Cuozzo, Errico, "Intorno alla prima contea normanna nell'Italia meridionale," *Cavalieri alla Conquista del Sud: Studi sull'Italia Normanna in Memoria di Lèon-Robert Ménager* (1998), pages 171-193.

77. Amongst other sources, see *Chronica Monasterii Casinensis,* book 2, chapter 37, pages 245-251. Here the term *citizen* is used loosely to refer to urban inhabitants; true modern *citizenship* emerged in Italy during the fourteenth century, beginning in the *communes.*

78. Amato of Montecassino, op. cit. supra, book 1, chapter 33, offers a description, though in that entry the number of adversaries confronting the Normans is certainly overstated.

79. Ibid, book 1, chapter 34.

80. Ibid, book 2, chapter 6; *Chronica Monasterii Casinensis,* book 2, chapter 56, pages 275-276. From William of Apulia, op. cit. supra, book 1, lines 169-172: *Post annos aliquot Gallorum exercitus urbem, Condidit Aversam Rannulfo consule tutus. Hic opibus plenus locus utilis est et amoenus. Non sata, non fructus, non prata arbustaque desunt.* Sergio IV also gave his sister to Ranulf in marriage. It would seem that Ariano, which may have been held by Ranulf a few years earlier (see note 76), was no longer in his possession. The rulers in the "Sergian" dynasty of Naples founded by Sergio I, who was elected by the local populace in 840, may have had Byzantine Greek ancestry patrilineally, but they were not always aligned formally with the Byzantine emperors; indeed, Sergio I sided with the Aghlabids against the Byzantines of Bari and Messina.

81. This was in 1038, as noted in *Chronica Monasterii Casinensis,* book 2, chapter 63, pages 292: *Rainulfum quoque ipsius Guaimarii suggestione de comitatu Aversano investivit.* See also the biography of Conrad II by Wipo of Burgundy, *Wiponis Gesta Chuonradi II, Scriptores Rerum Germanicarum in Usum Scholarum,* volume 7 (Hanover 1878), chapter 17 (page 28) and chapter 37 (page 43).

82. William of Apulia, op. cit. supra, book 1, lines 167-168: *Moribus et lingua, quoscumque venire videbant, Informant propria, gens efficiatur ut una.*

83. Pandulf went to Sant'Agata de' Goti, which was his fief, before departing for Constantinople. His withdrawl represents a change in fortune for the Byzantines in Campania, though they still controlled some localities in the region.

84. From Godfrey (Geoffrey) Malaterra's *De Rebus Gestis Rogerii Calabriae et Siciliae Comitis et Roberti Guiscardi,* book 1, chapters 4 and 5, where we read: *Erat miles quidem praeclari admodum generis, qui, ab antecessoribus suis haereditario iure sibi hanc villam relictam possidens, Tancredus nomine, duxit uxorem, moribus et genere splendidam mulierem, nomine Moriellam, ex qua legali successione annorum quinque filios, postea futuros comites, suscepit: Willelmum videlicet cognomine Ferrea Brachia, Drogonem,*

Humfredum, Gaufredum et Serlonem. Horum matre defuncta, cum ipsa aetas adhuc viridis patri continentiam denegaret, vir honestus inhonestos coitus abhorrens, secundas nuptias celebravit, malens una et legitima esse contentus, quam se foedo concubinarum amplexu maculari, memor illius apostolici dicti: Unusquisque accipiat uxorem propter fornicationem devitandam, et quod sequitur: Fornicatores et adulteros iudicabit Deus. Ducta vero Frensendis vocabatur, generositate et moribus priore non inferior, quae legitimis terminis marito septem peperit filios, non minoris pretii vel dignitatis a praedictis fratribus, quorum nomina subtitulamus hic: primus Robertus, dictus a nativitate Guiscardus, postea totius Apuliae princeps et Calabriae dux, vir magni consilii, ingenii, largitatis et audaciae; secundus Malgerius, tertius Willelmus, quartus Alveredus, quintus Hubertus, sextus Tancredus, septimus Rogerius minor, postea Siciliae debellator et comes. Mater vero accuratissime et materno affectu filios suos nutriens, tanto amore ipsos, qui non sui sed mariti sui ex praecedenti uxore erant, amplectabatur, ut vix discernere posses, nisi ex aliqua causa didicisses, quis filius vel quis non filius eius esset: unde et a marito plus amabatur et a circummanentibus plurimum appretiabatur. Infantes vero, ut aetas illis administrabat, pueriles annos transcendentes, cum iam adolescentiam, unus post alium, attigissent, coeperunt militaribus disciplinis adhaerere, equorum et armorum studia frequentare, discentes seipsos tueri et hostem impugnare. There are several surviving manuscripts in various states of conservation, with the first text published in the sixteenth century. The numeration of books and chapters used here corresponds to those in *RIS,* volume 5, part 1, *Raccolta degli Storici Italiani,* edited by Ernesto Pontieri, published in Bologna in 1925; these were used in Vito Lo Curto's *Ruggero I e Roberto il Guiscardo* (2002). Some redundancy of Godfrey's chronology, and a few additional or slightly differing details, appear in the *Anonymous Historia Sicula,* published in 1723 (see Appendix 6).

85. By his first wife, Muriella, Tancred (980-1041) fathered William "Iron Arm," Drogo, Geoffrey, Serlo, Humphrey and Beatrice; by his second wife, Fressenda, he sired Robert "Guiscard," Mauger, William, Alberic, Hubert, Tancred, Roger and Fressenda. Serlo, Alberic and Tancred remained in Normandy. There were probably other daughters besides Beatrice and Fressenda. According to *Domesday Book,* a certain Alverardus of Hauteville once held manors across the Channel in Somerset; this was probably Alberic. The origin of the name of the French locality called *Hauteville* is disputed, but it may simply mean "High Town," the story attributing it to an eponymous ancestor named *Hiallt* perhaps being legendary.

86. Gaitelgrima (who died after 1027), the mother of Guaimar IV (died 1052) and wife of Guaimar III (died 1027), was the sister of Pandulf IV of Capua (died 1050), both being children of Pandulf II of Benevento (Pandulf III of Capua), who died in 1014.

87. Malaterra, book 1, chapters 6 and 7. Malaterra, a Norman apologist, reports that Guaimar was negatively influenced by Lombards at his court who were envious of the Normans' military prowess and worried that they might try to seize power in view of recent victories such as that over Pandulf IV at Capua. It should be remembered that the Norman and Lombard knights likely had squires or other retainers (see "Knighthood" in Chapter 2), which added to their number.

88. Amato, book 2, chapter 8. Sometimes Arduin "of Melfi" for the city he took, where his control was recognized by the catepan (he died in 1041).

89. William of Apulia, book 1, line 198.

90. Malaterra, book 1, chapter 7.

91. Amato, book 2, chapter 9. The relics were taken to Constantinople, from whence they were translated to Venice in 1204 following the Fourth Crusade.

92. John Skylitzes (see *Historia Bizantina* in Sources), Godfrey Malaterra, William of Apulia and Amato of Montecassino each give somewhat differing accounts, even regarding the identity of the offender (either Maniakes or his successor Michael Dokeianos). See William of Apulia, book 1, lines 206-231; Malaterra, book 1, chapter 7; Amato, book 2, chapter 14.

93. *Chronicon Ignoti Civis Barensis,* pages 149-151; this is the *Bari Chronicle,* or *Anonymi Barensis Chronicon.* John Skylitzes and the other chroniclers also mention these events. Two additional records emanate from the same source as the *Bari Chronicle,* these being the annals of Bari and those of Lupus Protospatharius, for which see *Annales Barenses*

NOTES

and the commentary by William Churchill.

94. William of Apulia suggests that Atenulf bribed the Normans into nominating him. As Atenulf was not himself the Prince of Benevento, he may have seen an alliance with the Normans as a means to encroaching upon the power held by Guaimar and others.

95. Amato, book 2, chapter 19; William of Apulia, book 1, lines 245-247; Malaterra, book 1, chapter 9. The Sicilian chroniclers differ slightly in their accounts of these events.

96. Amato, book 2, chapters 21-28; William of Apulia, book 1, lines 297-401; Malaterra, book 1, chapters 9-10.

97. See note 86.

98. See note 96 and, for concordance, *Chronicon Ignoti Civis Barensis,* loc. cit.; *Annales Barenses,* anonymous and Lupus Protospatharius entries for 1040, 1041, 1042.

99. Guy of Sorrento, who was gastald of Conza, was a brother of Guaimar IV, both being sons of Guaimar III.

100. Amato, book 2, chapter 35; William of Apulia, book 2, lines 23-24; Malaterra, book 1, chapter 12.

101. For an examination of texts see, Ghignoli, Antonella, and Bougard, François, "Elementi Romani nei Documenti Longobardi?" *L'Héritage Byzantin en Italie VIIIe-XIIe Siècle: La fabrique documentaire* (Rome 2011), pages 241-301.

102. Amato, book 3, chapter 16. The Norman Benedictine abbot John of Fécamp wrote to Pope Leo IX criticizing the Normans of southern Italy; see *PCC, Patrologiae Latinae,* volume 143, columns 797-800.

103. This occurred at Monte Ilaro, where Drogo was lodging, whilst on his way to hear mass on the feast of Saint Laurence, 10 August. It is reported by Amato, book 3, chapter 22; Malaterra, book 1, chapter 13. For the location of the abandoned locality (near Bovino) and clarification of the lacuna of its nomenclature in the chronicles, see Di Meo, Alessandro, *Annali Critici-Diplomatici del Regno di Napoli della Mezzana Età* (1802), volume 7, page 317. According to Malaterra, the perpetrators were probably encouraged by Lombards, aided by a certain traitor named Riso: *Longobardi igitur Apulienses, genus semper perfidissimum, traditionem per universam Apuliam silenter ordinant, ut omnes Normanni una die occiderentur. Determinato die, cum comes Drogo apud castrum Montis Olei, quod corrupte ab incolis Montolium dicitur, moraretur, summo diluculo ad ecclesiam, ut sibi mos erat, properans, cum iam ecclesiam intraret, quidam, Risus nomine, eiusdem comitis compater et sacramento confoederatus, post ianuam latens, foedere rupto, ferro eum suscepit: sicque cum pluribus suorum, paucis aufugientibus, occisus est. Sed per diversa Apuliae loca plures hac traditione occubuerunt.*

104. Malaterra (loc. cit.) states that: *Porro Umfredus Abagelardus, nece fratris turbatus, honorem sibi vindicans, castra, quae frater possederat, insiluit. Normannosque, qui periculum traditionis evaserant, sibi alligans, in vindictam fraternae necis insurgit, multoque tempore castrum, in quo frater suus occisus fuerat, oppugnans, tandem devicit; fratrisque interemptorem, cum sibi assentientibus, diversis cruciatibus afficiens, eorum sanguine iram et dolorem cordis sui aliquantulum extinxit.* See also William of Apulia, book 2, lines 286-294.

105. Amato, book 3, chapters 38-42; William of Apulia, book 2, lines 180-266; *Chronica Monasterii Casinensis,* book 2, chapter 84, pages 332-333. The account by William is the lengthiest and most detailed. From Malaterra, book 1, chapters 14-15: *Apulienses vero, necdum traditionibus exhausti, per occultos legatos nonum Leonem apostolicum, ut in Apuliam cum exercitu veniat, invitant, dicentes Apuliam sibi iure competere et, praedecessorum suorum temporibus, iuris Ecclesiae Romanae fuisse, se illi auxilium laturos. Normannos imbelles, viribus enerves, numero paucos. Ille, ut assolet, quamvis prudentissimus esset, ambitione captus, Alamannorum exercitu ab Imperatore sibi in adiutorio accepto, confidens in auxilio Longobardorum, Apuliam intrat. Comes vero Humfredus, sibi honestius ducens potius cum honore vitam finire quam cum dedecore privari, commoto exercitu, audacter hostibus occurrit, ordinataque acie suorum, certamen iniens, cum primo congressu fortiter, ut solitus erat, agere coepisset, Longobardi, territi, fuga seipsos tueri nituntur, Alamannis in proelio relictis. Qui, cum fortiter dimicarent, nullum refugium nisi in armis*

691

habentes, Normannis vincentibus, pene omnes occubuerunt. Apostolicus, fuga vitae asylum expetens, intra urbem provinciae Capitanatae, quae Civitata dicitur, sese profugus recepit. Quem hostes insequentes, armato milite obsident. Aggeres portant, machinamenta ad urbem capiendam parant, incolas minis terrent, ut apostolicum reddant. Illi vero, ut semper perfidissimi, nulla pactione ad utilitatem apostolici, nisi ut se ipsos tuerentur, exquisita, eum per portas eiciunt. Quem hostes suscipientes, ob reverentiam Sanctae Romanae Sedis, cum magna devotione eius provolvuntur pedibus, veniam et benedictionem eius postulantes. Sed et usque ad loca, quibus exercitus castra et tentoria fixerat, cum omni humilitate illi servire executi sunt... For a competent esposition see Loud, Graham, *The Latin Church in Norman Italy* (2007), pages 68-70; for a fine narrative see Norwich, John Julius, *The Normans in the South* (1967), pages 80-96.

106. The thesis that some medieval knights may have suffered from post-traumatic stress disorder (PTSD) has emerged from analyses of descriptions by Geoffroi de Charny (who died in 1356) and others. It may have been mitigated somewhat by firm religious conviction and a knight's training from youth, resulting in exceptional mental conditioning that, to some degree, prepared men-at-arms for the atrocities encountered in war. Very little in the chronicles most relevant to our study (see Appendix 6) makes clear reference to this phenomenon. See Kaeuper, Richard (commentary), and Kennedy, Elspeth (translation), *The Book of Chivalry of Geoffroi de Charny: Text, Context and Translation* (1996); also Taylor, Craig, "Military Courage and Fear in the Late Medieval French Chivalric Imagination," *Cahiers de Recherches Médiévales et Humanistes*, number 24 (2012), pages 129-147; Ben-Ezra, Menachem, "Traumatic Reactions from Antiquity to the 16th Century: Was There a Common Denominator?" *Stress and Health*, volume 27, number 3 (August 2011), pages 223-240; Kerth, Sonja, "13 Narratives of Trauma in Medieval German Literature," *Trauma in Medieval Society* (2018), pages 274-297; Shay, Jonathan, *Achilles in Vietnam: Combat Trauma and the Undoing of Character* (1994).

107. See, for example, Cilento, Adele, and Routt, David, "Foundation of a Monastery in Byzantine Calabria 1053/54" *Medieval Italy: Texts in Translation* (2009), pages 506-507. Examples of new towns were Andria and Corato, founded by Peter of Trani; see William of Apulia, book 2, lines 30-31.

108. Only nine centuries later, in 1965, did the patriarchs of Rome and Constantinople, in the spirit of ecumenism, lift the mutual excommunications of the eleventh century. This chapter considers the distinct traditions of the Catholic and Orthodox churches more than the Great Schism as an event, an approach reflecting the authors' contention that most accounts, particularly those written by the non-Orthodox, overlook much of the nuance involved. Even terms such as "Basilian," sometimes used by non-Orthodox historians in reference to the Greek church as it existed in southern Italy before (and after) 1054, are misleading.

109. See *PCC, Patrologiae Latinae*, volume 143, columns 744-769, for the lengthy letter sent by Pope Leo IX to Patriarch Michael I Cerularius asserting papal primacy, and hence power over the entire church, based on the infamous "Donation of Constantine," a forged charter by which Constantine the Great supposedly ceded universal authority over both halves of the Roman Empire to the early bishops of Rome. Later, in 1059, Bishop John II of Trani was deposed by Pope Nicholas II for supporting the Patriarch of Constantinople.

110. Ibid, columns 1000-1004, Latin text of the letter of excommunication written by Humbert of Silva Candida.

111. Ibid, columns 929-999, correspondence of Humbert of Silva Candida with clergy, including Niketas Stethatos, his counterpart in Constantinople, regarding the theology behind the Schism. Humbert would later work to ensure papal recognition of the Hautevilles' position in Italy. The events prompting the Great Schism were widely recorded, as in *Chronica Monasterii Casinensis*, book 2, chapter 85, pages 333-334.

112. Most of what one reads about the Great Schism of 1054 is slanted toward either the Catholic or Orthodox point of view. *The Eastern Schism: A Study of the Papacy and the Eastern Churches during the XIth and XIIth Centuries* (1955), by Steven Runciman, approaches its subject with a fair degree of balance. Also recommended are John Meyendorff's *Orthodoxy and Catholic-*

NOTES

ity (1966), Aidan Nichols' *Rome and the Eastern Churches: A Study in Schism* (second edition, 2010), and Edward Siecienski's study, *The Papacy and the Orthodox: Sources and History of a Debate* (2017). See also the following note.

113. Doxopatrios was a distinguished theologian, onetime deacon of Saint Sophia in Constantinople and, in Sicily, a parishioner of the Martorana church founded by George of Antioch. Composed in Greek at King Roger's court by 1143, his treatise is titled *Orders and Ranks of the Patriarchal Thrones*. For the text in Greek and Latin see *PCC, Series Graeca Posterior,* volume 132, columns 1083-1114; for commentary Angeli Murzaku, Ines, and Crostini, Barbara, *Greek Monasticism in Southern Italy: The Life of Neilos in Context* (2017); Caruso, Stefano, "Echi della Polemica Bizantina Antilatina dell' XI-XII Secoli nel De Oeconomia Dei di Nilo Doxapatres," *Atti del Congresso Internazionale di Studi sulla Sicilia Normanna* (Palermo 1974), pages 403-432; Morton, James, "A Byzantine Canon Law Scholar in Norman Sicily: Revisting Neilos Doxapatre's 'Order of the Patriarchal Thrones,'" *Speculum,* volume 92, number 3 (July 2017), pages 724-754. More generally, Neocleous, Savvas, *Heretics, Schismatics or Catholics? Latin Attitudes to the Greeks in the Long Twelfth Century* (2019). For the church in Sicily during the Arab period see Lancia, Domenico, *Storia della Chiesa in Sicilia* (1884).

114. By 1200, there were very few active Orthodox monasteries in southern Italy. Beginning around 1478, a great number of Albanian refugees from Ottoman expansionism reintroduced Orthodoxy here. Today these Arbëreshë are Catholics with their own Byzantine rite; the Martorana is one of their churches. In this rite married men may be ordained to the priesthood but not consecrated as bishops. Italians often refer to these Catholics with the misnomer *Ortodossi* rather than *Bizantini.*

115. Amato, book 4, chapters 7-9.

116. William of Apulia, book 2, lines 286-297.

117. Ibid, book 2, lines 364-369.

118. Theophanes Kerameus (1129-1152), Bishop of Rossano, in Calabria, was writing his homilies in Greek as recently as 1140, a fact indicative of the widespread use of that language in liturgy well into the reign of Roger II. See *PCC, Series Graeca Posterior,* volume 132, columns 135-1078.

119. For general discussions and some examples, see Fonseca, Cosimo Damiano (editor), *L'Esperienza Monastica Benedettina e la Puglia* (1983); Loud, Graham, *The Latin Church in Norman Italy* (2007).

120. *Chronica Monasterii Casinensis,* book 3, chapter 12, page 373.

121. The papal bull *In Nomine Domine* was a key development in the evolution of the College of Cardinals. The more general conflict was at the root of what became known as the "Investiture Controversy." This clash between ecclesiastical and civil authority led to much strife between the Holy See and the Holy Roman Empire, finally culminating in the Concordat of Worms in 1122.

122. Hildebrand was eventually elected pope as Gregory VII. The expedition against Mincio was organized later in 1059.

123. Robert Guiscard had very recently wed Sichelgaita of Salerno as his second wife, though the precise date of their nuptials, late in 1058 or early in 1059, is not known. See Malaterra, book 1, chapter 31; William of Apulia, book 2, lines 424-439; Amato, book 4, chapters 18-21. There were obvious political reasons for the union, but the marriage seems to have been a happy one, with Sichelgaita accompanying her husband in many of his travels. See note 145. Robert's marriage to his first wife, Alberarda, had been annulled on the basis of alleged consanguinity; see Amato, book 3, chapter 11; *Chronica Monasterii Casinensis,* book 3, chapter 15, page 378.

124. For a good exposition see Kamp, Norbert, *Vescovi e Diocesi nell'Italia Meridionale nel Passaggio dalla Denominazione Bizantina allo Stato Normanno* (1977).

125. Like Hildebrand of Sovana, Desiderio was a future pope, as Victor III.

126. See Malaterra, book 1, chapter 35; also *Chronica Monasterii Casinensis,* book 3, chapter 15, pages 377-378,

127. Malaterra, loc. cit.; William of Apulia, book 2, lines 384-404. Also *ITP,* volume 10, pages 186-187; volume 8, pages 11-13. Robert Guiscard had been excommunicated, and this was lifted.

128. See *ITP,* volume 10, entry 73 on page 186.

129. For Gaitelgrima's marriage to Jordan Hauteville, bastard son of Roger I, see William of Apulia, book 2, lines 430-439; for Sichelgaita see note 123 supra. Another Gaitelgrima (sometimes Altrude), a daughter of Guaimar III, wed Drogo.

130. For example, William of Apulia states that "the entire population of Italy feared Humphrey and his brother Drogo" (book, 2, lines 27-29) and later, describing the Battle of Civitate, refers to the *Italiae populo,* "the people of Italy" (book 2, line 164). He occasionally uses the term "Latins" (book 1, line 47), particularly when distinguishing the Lombards from the Byzantine Greeks. Elsewhere, of course, he also refers to the Lombards, sometimes as *gens Longobarda,* "the Lombard people" (book 2, line 441). For Lombard family identity see Skinner, Patricia, *Family Power in Southern Italy: The Duchy of Gaeta and Its Neighbors 850-1139* (1995); Drell, Joanna, *Kinship and Conquest: Family Strategies in the Principality of Salerno during the Norman Period 1077-1194* (2002). For the Byzantines see notes 118 and 132.

131. For some observations see Loud, Graham, "How 'Norman' was the Norman conquest of southern Italy?" *Nottingham Medieval Studies,* volume 25 (1981), pages 13-34.

132. See Francovich Onesti, Nicoletta, *I Longobardi nel Sud: Culture Scritte e Tracce Linguistiche* (2016); Bozzarello, Luca, "Napoli e Bisanzio," *Bizantinistica: Rivista di Studi Bizantini e Slavi,* volume 21 (2020), pages 37-76. For various papers see Cosentino, Salvatore (editor), *A Companion to Byzantine Italy* (2021), particularly Marazzi, Federico, "Byzantines and Lombards," chapter 5, pages 169-199. The *Placet of Capua* is described in Chapter 24; see also note 908.

133. Leaving aside the particular case of Kasr'Janni (Enna was traditionally considered the geographic center of Sicily), the eastern third of the island was probably about sixty-five percent Byzantine Greek, though this cannot be measured precisely and in cities such as Syracuse and Catania the Byzantines usually made common cause with the Arabs against the Normans. For an examination of the Muslim Arab presence in Calabria during this period see Burgarella, Filippo, "Greci e Arabi nella Calabria Medievale," *La Calabria nel Mediterraneo: Flussi di persone, idee e risorse* (2013), pages 179-187.

134. Usage of these titles varied considerably. In common parlance, the term *emir,* sometimes *amir,* could refer to various civilian or military rulers of substantial territory regardless of their official status. Most often, however, the territory called an *emirate* had a defined status in law, sometimes as part of a *caliphate* (Catania was never formally an emirate). A *caïd* was a local official who might oversee a *qadit,* or the highly-placed counsellor to an emir, but the title was sometimes used for men of high importance regardless of their official position. The occasional characterization of these Sicilian emirs or caïds, typically by non-Arab historians, as "warlords" is inaccurate; they were respected leaders of their communities.

135. For the problematic discord amongst the Arabs of Sicily, see Ali ibn al-Athir al-Jazari, *al-Kamil fi at-Tarikh,* in Amari, Michele, *BAS,* volume 1, pages 443-449. For the *qasidas* ("odes") of the Kalbid era, see note 55 supra.

136. Amato, book 5, chapter 11. See also note 133.

137. Amato, book 5, chapters 8-9; Malaterra, book 2, chapter 1.

138. Amato, book 5, chapters 10-12; Malaterra, loc. cit.; *Chronica Monasterii Casinensis,* book 3, chapter 15, page 378. As noted elsewhere, a Byzantine army had tried to retake Rometta in 954. It is quite possible that the Normans under Maniakes occupied the town in 1038.

NOTES

139. The next few paragraphs in the text are based chiefly on the account by Malaterra, considered the most reliable writer for these facts. See also *The Ecclesiastical History of England and Normandy* by Orderic Vitalis, volume 1, pages 437-438. There exists no detailed Arab account of the Battle of Messina, though there are a few references to it in the Arabic sources. See Malaterra, book 2, chapters 4-14; Amato, book 5, chapters 10-19.

140. See Agius, Dionisius, *Siculo Arabic* (1996). This language has been preserved as Maltese.

141. See *The Ecclesiastical History of England and Normandy by Orderic Vitalis,* volume 1, pages 149, 400-401.

142. Amato, book 5, chapter 25. This locality is highly significant for the Hautevilles' chief familial castle in Sicily into the reign of William II. The Greek city was Alontion, from which the Latin Aluntium, which minted its own coins. The vestiges of a Greek temple remain. When the Normans arrived, the inhabitants of the village were chiefly Greek Orthodox, perceived as less menacing than Muslims, and there was a Byzantine monastery dedicated to Saint Theodore. The date of the castle's construction (1061) comes to us from Malaterra (book 2, chapter 17), who mentions it almost as an afterthought to his report of the Normans' zealous raids around Kasr'Janni (Enna): *Cum redit, spoliis et praeda totum exercitum abundanter replevit. Per mensem itaque ibi perdurantes, totam provinciam, diversis incursionibus lacerantes, afflixerunt, sed Castro-Iohannis minime praevaluerunt. In ipso anno dux castrum Marci fecit.*

143. Malaterra refers to *Graeci* and *Sarraceni* based on the languages they spoke (see note 147), though there was an obvious religious correlation as most Byzantine Greeks were Orthodox Christian while most "Saracens" were Sunni Muslim. There were Jews in Messina and various towns; they spoke Judeo-Arabic, for which see Wansbrough, John, "A Judaeo-Arabic Document from Sicily," *Bulletin of the School of Oriental and African Studies, University of London,* volume 30, number 2 (1967), pages 305-313.

144. Malaterra, book 2, chapter 27.

145. In the *Alexiad* (book 4, chapter 6), Anna Comnena refers to Sichelgaita's courage at the Battle of Dyrracheion in October 1081. For commentary see Skinner, Patricia, "Halt, Be Men! Sikelgaita of Salerno, Gender and the Norman Conquest of Southern Italy," *Gender and History*, volume 12, issue 3 (2000), pages 622-641; Eads, Valerie, "Sichelgaita of Salerno: Amazon or Trophy Wife?" *Journal of Medieval Military History,* volume 3 (2005), pages 72-87; Memoli Apicella, Dorotea, *Sichelgaita tra Longobardi e Normanni* (1996).

146. This castle stood in something like its original condition until the summer of 1943, when protracted fighting between Germans (who had occupied it as a defensive position) and Americans resulted in its destruction.

147. Malaterra, book 2, chapter 29: *Graeci vero et Sarraceni, quibus omnis patria favens pro libito patebat, plurima replebantur abundantia.* "Instead, the Greeks and Saracens received provisions from the entire region and were supplied abundantly."

148. Ibid, book 2, chapter 30: *Quamobrem hostes balnearum aestuationibus aestuari assueti, frigidori aura flante, dum vini potationibus naturalem calorem intra se excitare nituntur, somno propter vinum, ut assolet, subsequente, tardiores ad excubias vigilarum urbis esse coeperunt.* The Koran (Sura 5, 90) and hadiths proscribe the consumption of alcohol as an intoxicant. The Muslims probably obtained the wine from the Greeks.

149. Ibid, book 2, chapter 31: *Quae, quamvis juvencula, tanta strenuitate coepit esse sollicita circa castrum tuendum, ut, diatim circuens, ubi meliorandum videbat, studeret ut fierent vigiles. Reliquos omnes, quos sibi dominus suus abiens dimiserat, blande alloquens, ut sollicite, quae servanda erant, providerent, hortabatur, multa in reditu domini sui repromittens. Sed et transactum periculum, ne, segniter agendo, quid simile incurrerent, ad memoriam reducebat.* The military "siege" of the Normans at Troina lasted from December into late February or early March.

150. This was in 1061; the assault on Kasr'Janni took place in 1062. See Malaterra, book 2, chapter 17.

151 Amato, book 5, chapter 23; Malaterra, book 2, chapter 32. Kasr'Janni, formerly Castrogiovanni and now Enna, at 931 meters (3054 feet) above sea level, is the highest of Italy's provincial capitals. In antiquity, it was associated with the cult of Demeter and Persephone.

152. Malaterra, book 2, chapter 33. For the Arab perspective expressed in the history of Ali ibn al-Athir al-Jazari, *al-Kamil fi at-Tarikh*, see Amari, Michele, *BAS,* volume 1, pages 447-449.

153. A chain of this kind also protected Palermo's main harbor, the Kala, to the west of the Oreto, which was guarded by a castle. Unlike the smaller harbor attacked by the Pisans, the Kala was heavily fortified. The course of the Oreto has since been diverted; it once flowed near the church of Saint John of the Hermits.

154. Malaterra, book 2, chapter 34; Amato, book 5, chapter 28; *Annales Pisani* in *RIS,* volume 6, part 2 (1936), page 5.

155. Malaterra, book 2, chapter 35-39; Amato, book 5, chapter 24. For Palermo see Malaterra, book 2, chapter 36; Amato, book 5, chapter 26 (where the entry is out of order).

156. *Anglo Saxon Chronicle,* folio 337, published in *The Anglo Saxon Chronicle According to the Several Original Authorities,* translated by Benjamin Thorpe (1861), volume 2, pages 169-170; Orderic Vitalis, book 3, chapter 14, in *The Ecclesiastical History of England and Normandy by Orderic Vitalis,* volume 1, pages 480-491. A fine biography is Hollway, Don, *The Last Viking: The True Story of King Harald Hardrada* (2021).

157. Malaterra, book 2, chapter 41. A *Geniza* letter mentioning a Norman attack on Palermo around this time may, in fact, refer to the fighting at Misilmeri; see Moshe, Gil, "Sicily 827-1072 in Light of the Geniza Documents and Parallel Sources," *Italia Judaica 5* (1995), pages 96-171.

158. That the challenges facing the Byzantine Empire were known to those in Italy besides the Bariots is suggested by the lengthy description by William of Apulia, book 3, lines 1-110.

159. Chief contemporary sources for the long siege of Bari are Malaterra, book 2, chapters 40 and 43; Amato, book 5, chapter 27; William of Apulia, book 3, lines 1-179; and the *Chronicon Ignoti Civis Barensis.*

160. *Chronicon Ignoti Civis Barensis,* Lupus Protospatharius, entry for 1070 (page 44), which states that their heads were sent to the emperor.

161. Joscelin had rebelled against Robert Guiscard; see Amato, book 5, chapter 4.

162. There is no unequivocally accurate estimate of the city's population, which some historians have sought to ascertain by examining such statistics as the number of mosques and butchers, as well as contemporary comparisons to other Muslim cities, notably Baghdad and Cordoba, which were both larger than Balharm.

163. This reflected a wider Fatimid policy; see Rustow, Marina, "Jews and the Fatimid Caliphate," *Al-Masaq: Journal of the Medieval Mediterranean,* volume 33, issue 2 (London 2021), pages 169-187.

164. Malaterra, book 2, chapter 45. The church, of which little remains besides the main portal and a segment of the austere façade, was referred to as "Saint Cyriacus." Now deconsecrated and called *Santa Ciriaca* or even *Santa Domenica,* it is located at Via Case Santa Domenica number 24 (off Via Saitta Longhi) in a semi-rural area between Monreale and Molara, near Strada Statale 186. For the charter mentioning it, Tabulario di Santa Maria Nova, Monreale (in the Biblioteca Centrale della Regione Siciliana), manuscript number Balsamo 31, of 30 December 1174 (in which Pope Alexander III grants status and privileges of "major abbey" to Monreale's Benedictine monastery); also Garufi, Carlo Alberto, *Catalogo Illustrato del Tabulario di Santa Maria Nuova in Monreale* (1902), pages 8-9; *ITP,* volume 10, page 275. For the consecration of Alcherio as the city's first Roman archbishop (following the Schism) on 16 April 1083 see *ITP,* volume 10, page 229, which mentions the suppression of the Muslims but nothing of Nicodemus, though the previous entry states he was recognized as archbishop

in 1072, usually presumed as the year of his death; for the full text of Gregory VII confirming privileges to Palermo Cathedral see Mongitore, Antonino, *Bullae, Privilegia et Instrumenta Panormitane Metropolitanae Ecclesiae Regni Siciliae Primariae* (1734), pages 1-3. See also notes 175 and 181 below. For a study of Nicodemus and the Kyriaca church in Palermo, with an examination of the original records, see Alio, Jacqueline, *Notes on Norman-Swabian Sicily: New Research in Old Sources* (2021), pages 221-228.

165. The full name of Ibn al-Ba'ba was Abu Abd Allah Muhammad ibn Abd al-Rahman al Saigh.

166. This fortified palace takes its name from the Arabic *fawwara,* for a fountain or spring. It is located in what is now the Brancaccio district, being erected by Jafar al-Kalbi II, Emir of Sicily from 998 to 1019. In the time of Roger II it was still known as *Kasr Jafar.*

167. See Malaterra, book 2, chapter 45, who states that the Catania action was a diversion to deceive the Arabs into thinking that he was planning to attack Malta; also Amato, book 6, chapter 14.

168. For Palermo about a century earlier, see the part of the description by Abu al-Kasim Muhammad ibn Hawqal dedicated to this city, translated by Michele Amari in *BAS,* volume 1, pages 10-27. Though this is a work in translation Amari's familiarity with Palermo ensured the accurate identification of the places mentioned.

169. Amato, book 2, chapters 15-16. The main engagement before the Normans reached Palermo took place near what is now the church of Saint John of the Lepers (see note 177) in a flat area east of the city near the Oreto River. See also note 153.

170. The Battle of Palermo is described in Amato, book 2, chapters 17-20; William of Apulia, book 3, lines 204-339; Malaterra, book 2, chapter 45. It is noted in *Chronica Monasterii Casinensis,* book 3, chapter 15, page 378. For some general observations about this campaign and others during this period, see Theotokis, Georgios, "The Norman Invasion of Sicily, 1061-1072: Numbers and Military Tactics," *War in History,* volume 17, number 4 (November 2010), pages 381-402. For other views see Norwich, John Julius, *The Normans in the South* (1967); King, Matthew, *Dynasties Intertwined: The Zirids of Ifriqiya and the Normans of Sicily* (2022); Loud, Graham, *The Age of Robert Guiscard: Southern Italy and the Norman Conquest* (2000).

171. A fast ship could make it between Sicily and Tunisia in six days in the good conditions that generally prevailed in the summer. Allowing a week for the Zirids to supply their fleet, perhaps using the island of Bint al-Riyah (Pantelleria) as a stepping stone to Sicily, this suggests that they may have arrived in Palermo as soon as three weeks after Ibn al-Ba'ba sent for help. It is most likely that the Zirid fleet arrived in late September or early October.

172. Now Via Alloro. Virtually nothing of this wall remains, but the preserved timber gate, the *Bab al Fotik* ("Gate of Victory"), is preserved in the Oratory of the Bianchi at the corner of Vicolo della Salvezza and Via Spasimo. There are numerous studies of these fortifications; one of the better ones is Pezzini, Elena, "Un tratto della cinta muraria della città di Palermo," *Mélanges de l'école française de Rome,* volume 110, number 2 (1998), pages 719-771.

173. Michele Amari considered him at length; see also Granara, William, *Ibn Hamdis the Sicilian: Eulogist for a Falling Homeland* (2021).

174. In chapter 50 of his chronicle, Hugh Falcandus, referring to the half-brother of Margaret of Navarre, states that, *Quibus ille Francorum se linguam ignorare, que maxime necessaria esset in curia, nec eius esse, respondebat, industrie ut oneri tanto sufficeret.*

175. The year of death of Nicodemus is debated, but there is no surviving, contemporary, documentary reference to him acting after 1072. The date of his burial, long accepted by the Archdiocese of Palermo, is usually placed in late 1072. His sarcophagus (presently number 8 in the crypt of Palermo Cathedral) is of Paleo-Christian design and bears no inscription. The presumed date of his death (in 1072) seems to be based on an inscription, now lost, in the Santa Ciriaca church. See also notes 164 and 181.

176. The church, near the sea castle and Kala, was demolished in 1834 and what little remained was bombed in 1943. The Greek inscription commemorating its dedication in 1081 is preserved in the regional museum housed in Palazzo Abatellis in Palermo. Saint Peter's church was affiliated with the Bagnara monastery (in Calabria) from 1117. See Alio, Jacqueline, *Sicilian Queenship: Power and Identity in the Kingdom of Sicily 1061-1266* (2019), page 101.

177. The precise years of foundation of these churches are disputed. Saint John of the Lepers, for example, supposedly built soon after the invasion of 1071, is referred to in a decree of William I in 1155 which suggests that it had already been in existence for some time, possibly for decades; see Archive of State of Palermo, Tabulario della Magione, Manuscript number 6, 1154-1155 (lands ceded to a hospital by Roger II confirmed by William II).

178. This church was erected in the Roman city, probably in the fifth century. The present superstructure of Saint Agatha "alla Guilla" dates from the sixteenth century. See the map of Palermo around 1180.

179. For the texts of these charters see Mongitore, Antonino, *Bullae, Privilegia et Instrumenta Panormitane Metropolitanae Ecclesiae Regni Siciliae Primariae* (1734), pages 4-5 (Roger Borsa in 1086) and pages 12-14 (Roger I in 1095)

180. Ibid, pages 6-8. This charter was issued by Sichelgaita in 1089. For the original (examined by the authors), Archivio Storico Diocesano di Palermo, Tabulario della Cattedrale di Palermo, Manuscript number 3.

181. Ibid, pages 8-11, for a charter mentioning Nicodemus that may be a forgery (or a poor copy); see a discussion at Vargas Macciucca, Francesco, *Esame delle Vantate Carte e Diplomi di Santo Stefano del Bosco in Calabria* (1765), pages 250-256.

182. As recently as 1144, we find Roger II granting an unnamed, formerly-Byzantine church confiscated by the Arabs in the Sari al Kadi district to the local Venetian community to be rebuilt and dedicated to Saint Mark; see *DNS,* number 18 (pages 44-45). This structure, which no longer exists, replicated the older Venetian church of the same name in Bari, mentioned in Chapter 7, which is still standing. For the Kyriaca church see note 164 supra.

183. For references to myriad original sources, see *ITP,* volume 10 (entries for Calabria and Sicily by year). Much analysis has been published about this phenomenon, particularly in Italian. See Enzensberger, Horst, "Fondazione o 'rifondazione'? Alcune osservazioni sulla politica ecclesiastica del Conte Ruggero," *Chiesa e Società in Sicilia: L'Età Normanna* (1995), pages 22-49; Di Giovanni, Giovanni, *Storia Ecclesiastica di Sicilia,* volume 2 (1847). For good overviews in English, see White, Lynn Townsend, *Latin Monasticism in Norman Sicily* (1938); Loud, Graham, *The Latin Church in Norman Italy* (2007).

184. A number of these charters survive. For two issued by Roger I to monasteries in 1092 see *DNS,* number 1 (pages 3-7), number 2 (pages 7-9). For general discussions see Nef, Annliese, and Prigent, Vivien, "Contrôle et exploitation des campagnes en Sicile," *Authority and Control in the Countryside: From Antiquity to Islam in the Mediterranean and Near East* (2018), pages 313-366; Bresc, Henri, "Féodalité Coloniale en Terre de Islam: La Sicile," *Structures Foédales et Foédisme dans l'Occident Meditérranéen* (1978), pages 631-647; Dalli, Charles, "Contriving Coexistence: Muslims and Christians in the Unmaking of Norman Sicily," *Routines of Existence* (2009), pages 31-43.

185. As recently as the reign of Frederick II, revolts in the mountains to the south of Palermo were rooted in complaints from Muslims about such issues as the unpopular feudal administration of manorial towns by the abbot of Monreale (see Chapter 25). A few major abbeys were granted a status tantamount to quasi-sovereignty.

186. For example, a charter relative to the city of Tudela issued in 1138 assigns to the Bishop of Pamplona the Church of Saint Mary at Tudela (and its estates), "with all the assets therein appertaining to Moors and Christians." That this was issued by Margaret of l'Aigle, the niece and heiress of Rotrou of Perche, a Norman who held the city of Tudela as a fief, indicates that, at least in this regard, the policy of the Hautevilles was similar to that of their country-

men who appropriated Muslim lands elsewhere. This record is conserved in the Gran Cartulario de la Catedral de Pamplona, *El Libro Redondo,* folios 72-73; for a transcription see *Colección Diplomática de la Catedral de Pamplona,* pages 191-192.

187. See the preceding note; also Nelson, Lynn, "Rotrou of Perche and the Aragonese Reconquest," *Traditio,* volume 26 (1970), pages 113-122. For Bohemond of Antioch the original source of most information is the *Gesta Francorum et Aliorum Hierosolymytanorum* (The Deeds of the Franks), for which there is an English translation, with the Latin text, by Rosalind Hill in an edition of that title published in 1962; confirmed Latinists may prefer the critical edition by Heinrich Hagenmeyer, *Anonymi Gesta Francorum et Aliorum Hierosolymytanorum,* published in 1890. A "parallel" account, the *Historia de Hierosolymitano Itinere,* was written by Peter Tudebode; published in *RHC, Historiens Occidentaux,* volume 3 (Paris 1866). Good biographies are: Theotokis, Georgios, *Bohemond of Taranto: Crusader and Conqueror* (2020); Russo, Luigi, *Boemondo: Figlio del Guiscardo e Principe di Antiochia* (2009); Flori, Jean, *Bohémond d'Antioche: Chevalier d'Adventure* (2007); Yewdale, Ralph, *Bohemond I, Prince of Antioch* (1924). For Tancred of Galilee see note 223 below. For various studies, see Morreale, Laura, and Paul, Nicholas (editors), *The French of Outremer: Communities and Communications in the Medieval Mediterranean* (2018).

188. See *DNS,* number 7 (pages 16-18), for the concession by Roger II to Ansaldo of Arri of some land near Messina having thirty-two serfs in 1127.

189. A recorded example in our Norman era occurred early in 1168 during the reign of young William II when his mother, Margaret of Navarre, was regent. Walter of Moac (Modica) demanded trial by combat after being accused of treason. Hugh Falcandus (chapter 52) reports that, *Gualterius autem Modicensis super eadem coniuratione sollempniter accusatus, pacta cum accusatore suo monomachia datisque fideiussoribus, diem constitutam iussus est expectare.* Walter obviously survived (if indeed this duel ever took place), since he subscribed charters long after this date.

190. These campaigns are mentioned by various chroniclers. For accounts by those close to the Normans: Amato, book 6, chapters 24-29, and book 7, chapters 4-25; William of Apulia, book 3, lines 360-664 Malaterra, book 3, chapters 2-4.

191. Early in 1074, Gregory solicited the help of William of Burgundy to subdue the Hautevilles in Italy and then attack the Turks who were menacing Constantinople's authority in the east; see *PCC, Series Secunda,* volume 148 (1853), 325-326 (book 1, letter 41). Despite these vicissitudes, Pope Gregory VII, as we shall see, would eventually need Robert's aid to counter a military assault of the Holy Roman Emperor on Rome.

192. Amato, book 7, chapter 26; Malaterra, book 3, chapter 13; William of Apulia, book 3, lines 498-502, and book 4, lines 1-15. See Anna Comnena, *Alexiad,* book 1, in Sewter, Edgar, *The Alexiad of Anna Comnena* (1969), pages 57-59; John Skylitzes, in PCC, *Series Graeca,* volume 122 (1889), 453-456; John Curopalates (who mentions the union in passing), in *Corpus Scriptorum Historiae Byzantinae,* volume 35 (1839), page 720. The departure of young Olympia is noted in *Chronicon Ignoti Civis Barensis,* Lupus Protospatharius, entry for 1076 (page 45). For the letter of Pope Gregory VII to Michael VII in 1073 in response to an imperial request for aid against the Turks, *PCC, Series Secunda,* volume 148 (1853), 300-301 (book 1, letter 18); for an appeal to the Apulians and Calabrians in 1080, ibid 578-581 (book 8, letters 5 and 6). For the text of the treaty, or letter, of 1074 in French translation (the original source is *Codice Medicea Laurenziana Pluteo 57,* part 40, folios 218-222, in Florence), see Bibicou, Hélène, "Une Page d'Histoire Diplomatique de Byzance au XI Siècle: Michel VII Doukas, Robert Guiscard et la Pension des Dignitaires," *Byzantion,* number 29/30 (1960), pages 45-73; the surviving manuscript, signed by Michael VII, his younger brother (and co-emperor) Andronikos, his son Constantine, and Patriarch John VIII of Constantinople, states that Olympia, as empress, "will be accorded every imperial honor." See also Chalandon, Ferdinand, *Essai sur le Règne d'Alexis I Comnène* (1900).

193. Malaterra, book 2, chapter 8.

194. Ibid, chapter 9.

195. Amongst the many labors of Pope Gregory VII was an attempt to suppress the so-called Mozarabic, or Visigothic, liturgical rite in Spain. The "Missal of Silos" was written for this rite at Santa María la Real of Nájera, in what was then Navarre, some time before 1080 and it is one of the earliest paper documents in Europe, antedating anything known in Italy (even the letter of Adelaide shown in these pages). It is presently conserved as Codex 6 in the archive of the Abadía del Monasterio de Santo Domingo de Silos. See Vivanco, Miguel, "Liber Misticus," *Hispania Vetus: Musical-Liturgical Manuscripts from Visigothic Origins to the Franco-Roman Transition* (2007), pages 290-291. For more about liturgy in Spain, see Vones, Ludwig, "The Substitution of the Hispanic Liturgy by the Roman Rite in the Kingdoms of the Iberian Peninsula," ibid, pages 43-59.

196. The most detailed contemporary source for this incident is that of Lambert of Hersfeld, who also offers information regarding the Investiture Controversy; see *Lamperti Annales* in Holder-Egger, Osvald (editor), *Scriptores Rerum Germanicarum in Uso Scholarum ex Monumentis Germaniae Historicis,* volume 38 (1894), pages 289-299. For excommunication as a practice, see Vodola, Elizabeth, *Excommunication in the Middle Ages* (1986).

197. Except for a few generalities, the chroniclers provide us very little in the way of detailed descriptions of the personnel in Roger's army after 1072, though Anna Comnena offers us a few clues about Robert's troops. However, the sieges of the Sicilian cities are described. Because of their loyalty, Muslims eventually comprised the royal bodyguard. On the carved capital of a column in Monreale's cloister they are depicted holding swords along with round shields bearing a lion, a royal symbol. Visiting Roger I at a siege of Capua in 1098, Anselm of Canterbury famously observed that "the brownish tents of the Arabs were innumerable," and Arab archers from Lucera fought at the Battle of Benevento in 1266.

198. For Judith, see Alio, Jacqueline, *Queens of Sicily,* pages 83-100. She seems to have had no surviving sons (see Table 8); it has been suggested that Godfrey, reportedly a leper who became a monk, may have been her child, but it is possible that he was born to Roger's second wife (Table 9) or fathered by Roger outside marriage (see note 232).

199. For Eremburga of Mortain, ibid, pages 101-106. Sichelgaita led a siege of Trani in 1080; see Willian of Apulia, book 3, lines 668-672.

200. For the battle against Ibn al Wardi near Caltagirone, see Malaterra, book 3, chapter 10; for Trapani, ibid, chapter 11; for Taormina, ibid, chapters 15-18.

201. Robert Guiscard's oath and investiture of 1080 was published in *Sancti Gregorii VII Epistolae et Diplomata Pontificia,* volume 1 (Paris 1877), book 8, pages 438-439. For Gregory's letter (addressed to his archbishops in Apulia and Calabria) soliciting Robert's aid to restore Michael VII to the Byzantine throne, ibid, book 8, page 445. The pontiff's relevant letters and charters also appear in Migne's *PCC, Series Secunda,* volume 148. These documents were drawn from the epistolary of Pope Gregory VII, sometimes the *Dictatus Papae Gregorii VII,* conserved in the Vatican collection, which have also been published in the *Monumenta Germaniae Historica* series and elsewhere. Robert's oath of fealty set the stage for what became the kingdom: *Ego Robertus, Dei gratia et sancti Petri, Apuliae, et Calabriae et Siciliae dux; ab hac hora et deinceps ero fidelis sanctae Romanae Ecclesiae, et apostolicae Sedi et tibi, domino meo Gregorio, universali papae. In consilio vel facto, unde vitam aut membrum perdas, vel captus sis mala captione non ero. Consilium, quod mihi credideris et contradixeris ne illud manifestem, non manifestabo ad tuum damnum, me sciente. Sanctae Romanae Ecclesiae tibique adjutor ero ad tenendum, acquirendum, et defendendum regalia sancti Petri, ejusque possessiones pro meo posse contra omnes homines, excepta parte Firmanae marchiae, et Salerno atque Amalphi, unde adhuc facta non est definitio, et adjuvabo te ut secure et honorifice teneas papatum Romanum. Terram Sancti Petri, quam nunc tenes vel habiturus es, postquam scivero tuae esse potestatis, nec invadere nec acquirere quaeram, nec etiam depraedari praesumam absque tua tuorumque successorum, qui ad honorem sancti Petri ordinati fuerint, certa licentia, praeter illam quam tu mihi concedes, vel tul concessuri sunt successores. Pensionem de terra Sancti Petri, quam ego teneo aut tenebo, sicut statutum est, recta fide studebo ut illam annualiter sancta Romana habeat Ecclesia. Omnes quoque ecclesias, quae in mea persistunt dominatione cum illarum possessionibus dimittam in tua potestate, et defensor ero illarum ad fidelitatem sanctae Romanae Ecclesiae. Et si tu vel tui successores ante me ex hac vita migraveritis, secundum quod monitus fuero a melioribus car-*

dinalibus, clericis Romanis et laicis, adjuvabo ut papa eligatur et ordinetur ad honorem sancti Petri. Haec omnia suprascripta observabo sanctae Romanae Ecclesiae, et tibi cum recta fide, et hanc fidelitatem observabo tuis successoribus ad honorem sancti Petri ordinatis, qui mihi, si mea culpa non remanserit, firmaverint investituram a te mihi concessam. This was followed by Pope Gregory's confirmation as a response: *Ego Gregorius papa investio te, Roberte dux, de terra quam tibi concesaerunt antecessores mei sanctae memoriae Nicolaus et Alexander. De illa autem terra quam injuste tenes, sicut est Salernus, et Amalphia et pars marchiae Firmanae, nunc te patienter sustineo, in confidentia Dei omnipotentis et tuae bonitatis, ut tu postea exinde ad honorem Dei et sancti Petri ita te habeas sicut et te agere et me suscipere decet sine periculo animae tuae et meae.*

202. Ibid, 300-301, 325-326, 329-330, 385-387, 390. Whether this was a catalyst for the First Crusade is a matter of debate; see, for example, Charanis, Peter, "The Origin of the First Crusade," *Byzantion,* number 19 (1949), pages 17-36.

203. See note 192. Robert Guiscard's eldest daughter, Maud (Matilda), wed Raymond Berenguer II, Count of Barcelona (assassinated in 1082), while a younger one, Emma, married Odo, a Norman nobleman in southern Italy; see William of Apulia, book 4, lines 1-15. The fate of Olympia/Helena is not known, but she seems to have resided with her uncle and his wife, Eremburga, in Sicily.

204. For the Diocese of Troina, Malaterra, book 3, chapter 19; *Sancti Gregorii VII Epistolae et Diplomata Pontificia,* volume 1 (Paris 1877), register 9, pages 496-497; for various other sources see *ITP,* volume 10, entry 1 on pages 137-138. For the marriage of Matilda, see Malaterra, book 3, chapter 22.

205. William of Apulia, book 4, lines 160-174; *Alexiad,* book 1, chapter 12, where Anna Comnena identifies the impostor as a certain Raiktor but considers that Guiscard may have concocted the entire story.

206. Robert's decision to invade the Byzantine Empire was conditioned by the known reasons mentioned, and perhaps one or two for which a written record is lacking. This question is much analyzed and debated by historians. See Charanis, Peter, op. cit. at note 202; also Upsher Smith, Richard, "'Nobilissimus' and Warleader: The Opportunity and the Necessity Behind Robert Guiscard's Balkan Expeditions," *Byzantion,* volume 17, number 2 (2000), pages 507-526. See also Savvides, Alexios, *Byzanto-Normmanica: The Norman Capture of Italy and the First Two Invasions in Byzantium* (2007), pages 45-70; Loud, Graham, *The Age of Robert Guiscard: Southern Italy and the Norman Conquest* (2000), pages 209-222. The analytical narrative by Ferdinand Chalandon is not to be overlooked, but neither is that by Edward Gibbon, in *Decline and Fall of the Roman Empire* (1826 edition edited by Thomas Bowdler), volume 5, pages 50-65.

207. This is a conservative estimate; the figures are much debated. The chief contemporary sources for the invasion are Anna Comnena, the daughter of Alexios I (see Table 6), and William of Apulia, book 4. For Anna Comnena, *Alexiad,* book 1, chapter 16, where she states 150 ships bearing 30,000 men.

208. For the succession in favor of Roger Borsa declared publicly by Robert Guiscard in 1081 before departing for Greece, see *William of Apulia,* book 4, lines 185-192. Already in 1086, we find Roger Borsa issuing decrees as "Duke of Apulia," q.v. note 179. Coins were also struck in his name.

209. Malaterra, book 4, chapters 4 and 10.

210. Malaterra, book 4, chapter 2.

211. For the workings of the *diwan* see Johns, Jeremy, op. cit. at note 52.

212. Roger I was already issuing charters as "Count of Calabria and Sicily" at least as early as 1080, and chroniclers sometimes referred to him by this titulature. For Robert Guiscard ceding Sicilian territories to Roger, see Amato, book 6, chapter 21; Malaterra, book 2, chapter 45. Roger Borsa ceded some of his claims in Calabria to his uncle in 1085, and his part of Palermo in 1092.

213. Malaterra, book 4, chapter 6; Ali ibn al-Athir al-Jazari, *al-Kamil fi at-Tarikh*, in Amari, Michele, *BAS*, volume 1, chapter 35, pages 442, 449-450.

214. The chief source is *Chronicon Ignoti Civis Barensis*, Lupus Protospatharius, entry for 1087 (page 45), but it is also described in considerable detail by Orderic Vitalis (book 7, chapter 12) and other chroniclers. Later, during the First Crusade, some Venetian sailors removed what bones of the saint remained at Myra. Despite what has sometimes been claimed, Nicholas was never the chief patron of the Normans of Italy, who venerated Saint Michael as well. A clear study in English is Hayes, Dawn Marie, "The Cult of St Nicholas of Myra in Norman Bari, c1071-c1111," *The Journal of Ecclesiastical History*, volume 67, number 3 (2016), pages 492-512.

215. Malaterra, book 4, chapter 3; also Ali ibn al-Athir al-Jazari, *al-Kamil fi at-Tarikh*, loc. cit. at note 213 (above), pages 451-452. For the Pisan account of the attack with an English translation and notes, see King, Matthew, *Perceptions of Islam in the Carmen in Victoriam Pisanorum* (2015).

216. For Adelaide, see Alio, Jacqueline, *Queens of Sicily*, pages 107-126; *Sicilian Queenship*, pages 76-78, 276-282. Also: Houben, Hubert, "Adelaide 'del Vasto' nella Storia del Regno di Sicilia," *Itinerari di Ricerca Storica*, number 4 (Lecce 1990), pages 9-40; von Falkenhausen, Vera. "Zur Regentschaft der Gräfin Adelasia del Vasto in Kalabrien und Sizilien 1101-1112," *AETOS: Studies in Honor of Cyril Mango Presented to Him on April 14, 1998* (Stuttgart 1998), pages 87-115; Pontieri, Ernesto, "La madre di re Ruggero: Adelasia del Vasto, contessa di Sicilia, regina di Gerusalemme," *Atti del Covegno Internazionale di Studi Ruggeriani*, volume 1 (Palermo 1955), pages 327-432.

217. See note 24. There are local dialects of Sicilian, Calabrian and other vernacular languages that developed in southern Italy during the thirteenth century. By that time, as stated in the Introduction, chroniclers such as Hugh Falcandus, who was probably from France, drew a distinction between the Lombards of northern Italy and those (who may have seemed more Italianized) from the south.

218. Malaterra, book 4, chapter 16. The islands would remain part of the kingdom for the next seven centuries. Their continuous rule by Arabs led to the preservation of the Siculo-Arabic language, which became Maltese.

219. There are many fine general histories of the First Crusade. Three of the best are: Riley-Smith, Jonathan, *The First Crusade and the Idea of Crusading* (1986); Frankopan, Peter, *The First Crusade: The Call from the East* (2012); Runciman, Steven, *A History of the Crusades: Volume 1, The First Crusade and the Foundation of the Kingdom of Jerusalem* (1951). See also: Prawer, Joshua, *The Crusaders' Kingdom: European Colonialism in the Middle Ages* (1972), Tyerman, Christopher, *The Debate on the Crusades* (2011), and the collection *The Social Structure of the First Crusade* (2008), edited by Conor Kostick.

220. No detailed extract of the actual deliberations of the Council of Bari survives, though Anselm of Canterbury mentions the event in his *De Processione Spiritus Sancti*, while his biographer, Eadmer, describes it (see note 224 below). For a good English translation of Anselm's text see Hopkins, Jasper, and Richardson, Herbert, *Complete Philosophical and Theological Treatises of Anselm of Canterbury* (2000), pages 466-514. For a recent discussion (from the Catholic point of view) see McKenna, Thomas, "Greek and Latin Gods: Anselm's Defense of the Filioque," *Saint Anselm Journal*, volume 14, number 1 (2018), pages 111-131. Anselm, who is sometimes described as "Italian Norman" but was Lombardic through his father, is credited with developing the ontological argument for the existence of God. For William II of England see Barlow, Frank, *William Rufus* (1983); Mason, Emma, *King Rufus: The Life and Murder of William II of England* (2008).

221. For a good overview see Hailstone, Paula, *Recalcitrant Crusaders? The Relationship Between Southern Italy and Sicily, Crusading and the Crusader States, c. 1060-1198* (2020).

222. Orderic Vitalis, *Historia Ecclesiastica*, book 10, chapter 4, in *The Ecclesiastical History of England and Normandy*, volume 3 (translation by Forester, Thomas), page 206. For a long glance

NOTES

at Odo's eventful life see Bates, David, "The Character and Career of Odo, Bishop of Bayeux," *Speculum*, volume 50, number 1 (January 1975), pages 1-20.

223. For the *Gesta Francorum* recounting the story of Bohemond of Antioch see sources at note 187. A comparable biography of Tancred of Galilee is the *Gesta Tancredi* of Raoul of Caen. See *Gesta Tancredi in Expeditione Hierosolymitana*, in *RHC, Historiens Occidentaux*, volume 3 (Paris 1866), pages 603-716; also the fine English translation by Bernard and David Bachrach, *The Gesta Tancredi by Ralph of Caen: A History of the Normans on the First Crusade* (2005). A competent modern biography is Nicholson, Robert, *Tancred: A Study of His Career and Work* (1978).

224. Anselm, Archbishop of Canterbury, was present at Capua to witness this. His biographer, Eadmer, writes at some length about the thousands of Arabs, their devotion to Roger and courtesy toward Pope Urban II, and the Council of Bari, in *Vita Sancti Anselmi*, book 2, chapters 32-34; for the Latin text with a parallel English translation see Southern, Richard William, *The Life of Saint Anselm, Archbishop of Canterbury, by Eadmer* (1962), pages 109-113. See also Malaterra, book 4, chapter 28.

225. Text of conferral of apostolic legateship from Pope Urban II in July 1098 reported in Malaterra, book 4, chapter 29: *Urbanus Episcopus, servus servorum Dei, carissimo filio Rogerio, comiti Calabriae et Siciliae, salutem et apostolicam benedictionem. Quia propter prudentiam tuam supernae maiestatis dignatio te multis triumphis et honoribus exaltavit, et probitas tua in Saracenorum finibus Ecclesiam Dei plurimum dilatavit, sanctaeque sedi apostolicae devotam se multis modis semper exhibuit, nos in specialem atque carissimum filium eiusdem universalis matris ecclesiae assumpsimus, idcirco de tuae probitatis sinceritate plurimum confidentes, sicut verbis promisimus, litterarum ita auctoritate firmamus: quod omni vitae tuae tempore, vel filii tui Simonis, aut alterius qui legitimus tui haeres extiterit, nullum in terra potestatis vestrae, praeter voluntatem aut consilium vestrum, legatum Romanae Ecclesiae statuemus; quinimmo, quae per legatum acturi sumus, per vestram industriam legati vice cohiberi volumus, quando ad vos ex latere nostro misserimus, ad salutem videlicet ecclesiarum, quae sub vestra potestate existant, ad honorem beati Petri; sanctaeque eius Sedis Apostolicae, cui devote hactenus obedisti; quamque in opportunitatibus suis strenue ac fideliter adiuvisti. Si vero celebrabitur concilium, tibi mandavero quatenus episcopos et abbates tuae terrae mihi mittans, quot et quos volueris, alios ad servitium ecclesiarum et tutelam retineas. Omnipotens Dominus actus tuos in beneplacitu suo dirigat, et te, a peccatis absolutum, ad vitam aeternam perducat. Datum Salerni per manum Iohannis, sanctae Romanae Ecclesiae Diaconi Cardinalis, tertio nonas Iulii; indictione septima, anno Pontificatus nostri undecimo.* See also *PCC, Series Secunda*, volume 151, columns 506-507.

226. Text of confirmation of apostolic legateship from Pope Paschal II in October 1117 reported in *Codex Ottobonianus Vaticanus*, number 3057, folio 151: *Rogerio comiti Siciliae. Ante Sarracenorum invasionem Siciliae insula Romane ecciesie adeo familiaris fuit, ut semper in ea Romani pontifices et patrimoniorum suorum curatores et sue vicis representatores habuerint. Patri autem tuo divina gratia prerogativam contulit, ut suo et suorum labore et sanguine Sarraceni ab eadem insula pellerentur, et in ea dei ecclesie restituerentur. Unde, sicut in tuis litteris suggessisti, antecessor meus patri tuo legati vicem gratuita benigni, tate concessit. Nos quoqne tibi post ipsnm eius successori concessimus, ea videlicet ratione, ut si quando illuc ex latere nostro legatus dirigitur, quem profecto vicarium inteiligimus, que ab eo gerenda sunt, per tuam industriam effectui mancipentur. Sic enim in ecclesia seculares potestates dispositas legimus; ut qnod ecclesiastica humilitas minus valet, secularis potestas sue formidinis rigore perficiat. Nam personarum ecclesiasticarum seu dignitatum indicia nusquam legimus laicis vel religiosis fuisse commissa. Porro episcoporum vocationes ad synodnm, quas unquam sibi legatus aut vicarius usurpavit quod aliquando singularibus, aliquando pluralibus litteris per quoslibet solet nuncios fieri. Cognosce fili carissime modum tuum et datam tibi a domino potestatem, noli contra dominicam erigere potestatem. Sic enim a domino Romane ecclesie potestas concessa est, ut ab hominibus auferri non possit. Disce in comitatu tuo bonorum imperatorum exempla, ut ecclesias non inpugnare studeas sed iuvare, non indicare aut opprimere episcopos, sed tamquam dei vicarios venerari. Que a patre tuo nobilis memorie Rogerio comite ecclesie data sunt, per te nullatenus minuantur, sed potius augeantur. Noli deum precedere sed sequaris, quia eo duce non offendes, sed vite lumen habebis. Hec tibi tamquam filio carissimo precipio, hec moneo; si, ut spondes, obedieris et obtemperaveris, tuam profecto salutem obtemperabis. Omnipotens dominus suo te beneplacito dirigat, conservet atque custodiat. Datum Anagniae, Kalends Octobris 1117.* See also *RPR* (1851), charter 4846, pages 516-517; *PCC, Patrologiae Latinae* (1893), volume 163, columns 425-426.

227. As regent for her young son, Frederick II, Queen Constance is believed to have renounced the apostolic legateship in return for the pope's protection of her only heir. In the event, she died in 1198 and no pontiff ever defended the boy's interests with much conviction. After the Hohenstaufen era, the next monarch known to assert such rights, or at least the next one to do so openly and formally (with a legal declaration), was Ferdinand the Catholic late in the fifteenth century. King Philip II of Spain instituted the juridical office of *Judex Monarchiae Siciliae* in 1597. In 1715, Pope Clement XI revoked the privileges of the so-called *Monarchia Sicula,* but this did not end the academic (or juridical) debate. An early treatise is Nicola Maria Tedeschi's *Istoria della Pretesa Monarchia di Sicilia,* published in Rome in 1715, followed by Pietro Giuseppe Zappata's *Difesa Storica della Monarchia Siciliana,* published in Turin in 1716. For other competent studies see Sentis, Franz, *Die Monarchia Sicula* (1869); Caspar, Erich, "Die Legatengewalt der Normannisch-Sicilischen Herrscher," *Quellen und Forschungen aus Italienischen Archiven und Bibliotheken,* volume 7 (Rome 1904), pages 189-219. For a more recent analysis see Salvatore Fodale's *Comes et Legatus Siciliae: Sul privilegio di Urbano II e la Pretesa Apostolica Legazia dei Normanni in Sicilia* (1970).

228. For the text of the papal bull of 20 July 1098, still conserved in the Vatican, see *BRP,* volume 2, pages 190-192. The archbishops of Conza and Acerenza (noted in the bull) were already suffragans, but the text recognizes the erection of the recent cathedral and the keeping of the tomb of Saint Matthew in its crypt as factors arguing for the elevation of its archbishop to the status of primate, without stating or implying primatial authority over any other part of the Duchy of Apulia. In another Norman dominion, in 1071 Pope Alexander II decided that Canterbury was to be the primatial see of England, though in 1118 Pope Callixtus II released the archbishops of York from that authority; in 1352 Pope Innocent VI established that the Archbishop of Canterbury would be Primate of All England while the Archbishop of York would be Primate of England. In 1353, a similar arrangement was made for the Archbishop of Armagh as Primate of All Ireland and the Archbishop of Dublin as the Primate of Ireland.

229. In a Greek charter of September 1094, Roger refers to Bruno as his "spiritual father," i.e. perhaps his confessor; see Becker, Julia, *Documenti Latini e Greci del Conte Ruggero I di Calabria e Sicilia* (2013), document 44, page 182.

230. Manuscript GG in Sources.

231. Apart from the chronicles, a perusal of the places and dates mentioned in some of his charters (not all of these indicate the place) confirms his movements. Most recently we find him in: Mazara in 1093, Palermo in December 1094 and early February 1095, Messina in late February 1095, Squillace and Mileto in 1096, Mazara in 1097, Maida (Calabria) in May 1098, Squillace in August 1099. Of course, he was at Capua in 1098. Although little can be known about Roger's health, this suggests a fair amount of activity in his final years and there is no evidence to suggest that a courtier, or his wife, was undertaking duties in his name.

232. For Simon's birth see Malaterra, book 4, chapter 19. Among Roger's legitimate sons, Mauger (Malgerio), Count of Troina, was probably deceased by this time, and the Godfrey whom we met earlier (see note 198), if living, was a leper (or suffered from some other ailment) considered unsuitable to rule. Roger seems to have fathered another son named Godfrey, possibly outside marriage (though he may have been Judith's son), and it was probably this "second" Godfrey who subscribed some of Roger's charters and became Count of Ragusa, and died around 1120. See Sortino Trono, Eugenio, "Il Conte Goffredo di Ragusa 1093-1120," *Archivio Storico per la Sicilia Orientale,* volume 12 (1915), pages 181-185.

233. See *ITS,* volume 9, columns 426-427, relative to the church in Squillace (Calabria) in 1096; see also note 244. In cases where Adelaide's charters are lost, her activities are implied by mention of her in several of those later issued by her son, ibid pages 32-33 (in 1133).

234. Falco of Benevento wrote his chronicle beginning around the time Roger reached the age of majority. Alexander of Telese began his chronicle still later. Both make reference to earlier events but very little pertaining directly to Adelaide's regency of approximately thirteen years.

NOTES

235. Comparatively little is known with certainty about the administration of Apulia, Sicily and Calabria during this period; see Takayama, Hiroshi, *The Administration of the Norman Kingdom of Sicily* (1993), pages 25-46.

236. The text: "Issued by me, Adelaide, Countess of Calabria and Sicily, to the monastery of our holy father Saint Philip of Demenna, also called Melitiro, and with he who holds the same, the monk Gregory the successor to the abbot, and with him in turn his successors in monastic life, in the month of October of the tenth indiction, myself residing in the Demenna district at San Marco d'Alunzio with my son Simon, having seen cured my son, Roger, from an ear ailment at Saint Philip, having seen with my own eyes, and also heard, of the multitude of miracles that our holy father Saint Philip performs, and knowing of the constant prayers of the serene holy men lifted up to the Lord God in our favor and that of the late Count Roger and our ancestors and all Christians our brethren. Having seen the monastery in poverty with the pangs of hunger, and touched by your needs, I have donated to you four serfs named Stephen Philamacos, Peter de Theodore, Constantine Porcelli and Theodore Daneste, that they and their children, and their children's children, along with their land and belongings, may serve your monastery. By these presents I command all those appertaining to my authority and lands, whether bailiffs, viscounts, or my successors or heirs, to refrain from harassing, disturbing, impeding, imprisoning, taxing or judging the monk and his clerical and lay dependents. Further, I grant to the monastic estate the vineyards of the Oria manor numbering six hundred vines, the Vajitza manor numbering two hundred vines, and the Erepi manor numbering two hundred vines, lands which have sometimes been disputed. I grant you the right to erect a mill along the Panagia River. I further grant lands on this side of the river, beneath Pauliano, fields of four modii, in the manors of Pauliano, Galati and Patera, to be administered by the monastery for your use. That these rights be irrevocable. Whomever shall violate our seal shall be subject to no small punishment by me or my heirs and successors. In the most avowed faith and trust has our leaden seal been affixed to this our diploma consigned to the said monastery, in the abovementioned month and indiction, in the year of the world 6610. Countess Adelaide with her sons Roger, and Simon Count of Sicily and Calabria." Translation by the authors. For the manuscript see entries A, B and C in Sources. The donations in memory of Roger being cured are described in manuscripts number 7 (October 1101) and number 12 (November 1112); transcriptions in Spata, Giuseppe, *Le Pergamene Greche Esistenti nel Grande Archivio di Palermo* (1862), document 5 (October 1101), pages 191-196; document 11 (November 1112), pages 233-236. Michele Amari mentions some of Adelaide's charters in his *Storia dei Musulmani in Sicilia* (1868), volume 3, page 346, notes 1 and 2.

237. Here our source is Orderic Vitalis in his *Ecclesiastical History*, volume 4, book 13, chapter 15 (pages 134-135 in the English edition of 1856); Thomas Forester, the translator, believes the girl was Adelaide's niece. Her name (Yolanda or Violante) is likely apocryphal, and we don't know if she was the daughter of Judith or of Eremburga, or perhaps born outside marriage. Robert was the son of Robert I of Burgundy (died 1076), himself the brother of King Henry I of France. In contrast to what was likely the *unofficial* status of Robert, Christodoulos was the official *amiratus* of the County of Sicily; see, for example, *ITP*, volume 10, pages 104-105.

238. A fine overview of Adelaide's monastic foundations and endowments is presented by Vera von Falkenhausen in "Zur Regentschaft der Gräfin Adelasia del Vasto in Kalabrien und Sizilien 1101-1112." See also White, Lynn Townsend, op. cit., pages 87, 95, 98, 145, 153, 155, 209, 210, 241. For the Greek monasteries specifically, see White, pages 40-46.

239. In the original, *mulier prudentissima*. See book 1, chapter 3 of the *De Rebus Gestis Rogerii Siciliae Regis* of Alexander of Telese.

240. Alexander of Telese, op. cit., book 1, chapter 2, *Rogerii indotes*. This oft-quoted passage was based on hearsay, as Alexander of Telese wrote his account, essentially a biography of Roger I, around 1136. It seems unlikely that young Matilda, the witness, was even present with her brothers and their friends (all males) playing the game. Nonetheless, Alexander states that the fight between brothers also involved opposing bands of boys fighting on behalf of each, which may explain little Roger's "victory."

241. Ibid, book 1, chapter 3.

242. Her charter of 1109, Manuscript B in Sources, is shown in these pages, recorded in *DGA,* volume 1, part 1, document 10, pages 402-403. For commentary see La Mantia, Giuseppe, *Il Primo Documento in Carta (Contessa Adelaide, 1109) Esistente in Sicilia e Rimasto Sinora Sconosciuto* (Palermo 1908); Johns, Jeremy, "Parchment versus Paper: Countess Adelaide's Bilingual Mandate of 1109," *Documenting Multiculturalism* (Oxford, November 2018). Conferatur Spanish specimens at note 195 supra.

243. A few churches are indicated in the map in this book, but many more that were erected before 1200, and later destroyed, are mentioned in charters and even in chronicles. For this reason, the identification of "Norman sites in Palermo" published in some recent works is woefully incomplete.

244. For the text of Adelaide's charter, with a few barons listed, see *ITS,* volume 9, columns 429-430. For the papal bull of 1110, see also *BRP,* volume 2, pages 258-259.

245. For Samuel Lang's English translation of the account of Sigurd's visit in Snorri Sturluson's *Heimskringla* see *The Heimskringla or the Sagas of the Norse Kings* (second edition, 1889), volume 4, page 124. The *Fagrskinna,* another of the kings' sagas, written around 1220, also mentions this visit, and that Sigurd I referred to Roger II as a *jarl* (count) worthy of becoming a *konongr* (king); see the original text in Jónsson, Finnur (editor), *Fagrskinna Nóregs Kononga Tal* (1903), chapter 73, page 331. A good study is Jakobsson, Armann, "Image is Everything: The Morkinskinna Account of King Sigurd of Norway's Journey to the Holy Land," *Parergon,* volume 30, number 1 (2013), pages 121-140. For a later example of a king performing an impromptu coronation see note 446.

246. Essentially, Eleazar (whose name is not conclusive from the surviving texts), the lord of the fortified manor of San Filippo of Argirò, now Agira, claimed that the Bishop of Troina (by this time a "suffragan" of the Archbishop of Messina), who held the neighboring manor of Regalbuto, had usurped some of his lands along their common border. Adelaide delegated this case to Robert Avenel and other nobles, who met at the disputed border, where Eleazar wanted to resolve the dispute with the sword. The dispute was ultimately settled without the use of violence. See Spata, op. cit. at note 236, document 13, pages 241-244. This is discussed by Michele Amari, loc. cit. at note 236, pages 348-349, who cites it as an example of the pacific efficacy of Adelaide's administration.

247. Riley, Henry (translator), *The Annals of Roger de Hoveden* (1853), volume 2, page 50. For analysis of this see Boulton, D'Arcy Jonathan, "Classic Knighthood as Nobiliary Dignity: The Knighting of Counts and Kings' Sons in England 1066-1272," *Medieval Knighthood V: Papers from the Sixth Strawberry Hill Conference 1994* (1995), pages 41-100.

248. The event of Adelaide knighting Roger here may be the basis for a later (mistaken) belief that coronations were performed in this chapel or on its dais. Writing only about twenty-four years after the knighting ceremony, and most likely informed by Roger's sister, Matilda, who was probably present, Alexander of Telese (book 1, chapter 4) refers to Roger "reaching adulthood and being knighted." *Cum autem adolevisset, factusque miles...* Not long afterward, we find Constance of France (1078-1125), widow of Bohemond I of Antioch (see Table 26), who died in 1111, knighting her young son, Bohemond II (1107-1130).

249. Roger was probably knighted late in 1111 or early in 1112. Historians usually determine the date by references to Roger as *miles* (knight), rather than simply *comes* (count), in certain Latin charters. Unlike the hereditary status of count, based on automatic succession upon the death of his brother, knighthood had to be conferred *ad personam.* For a charter of June 1112 see *Rogerii II Regis Diplomata Latina,* number 3, pages 7-9; see also the manuscripts under entries A and B (in Sources), transcribed in Cusa's *I Diplomi Greci ed Arabi.* Another indicator may be Adelaide's release of some serfs in San Marco d'Alunzio to a nearby abbey in 1112, ostensibly in gratitude for her son's recovery from an illness more than a decade earlier but coincidental to him reaching majority.

250. William of Tyre, writing long after the facts mentioned, describes Adelaide's betrothal and marriage to Baldwin, and her subsequent separation from him, in book 11, chapters 21 and 29, of his chronicle, *A History of Deeds Done Beyond the Sea*. His chief source seems to have been an account by Albert of Aix (or Aachen). This will be found in the *Chronicon Hierosolymitanae Expeditionis*, book 12, chapter 13, *Quomodo conjux ducis Siciliae ad thalamum regis Baldevini cum magno apparatu properavit*, and although he seems never to have visited Palestine himself, Albert may well have had access to works such as the *Chanson d'Antioche* and he probably interviewed crusaders returning from Jerusalem. He describes Adelaide's arrival and reception thus: *Rege dehinc cum omni manu sua ab insecutione hostium Ptolemaidem reverso, mense augusto inchoante, pervenit ad aures regis quomodo nobilissima conjux Roggeri ducis Siciliae, fratris Boemundi magnifici principis, post obitum et exsequias praefati mariti ad thalamum regis magnopere properaret in apparatu copioso magnarum divitiarum et plurimo militum comitatu. Fuerunt ei duae triremes, singulae cum quingentis viris bello doctissimis, cum navibus septem, auro, argento, ostro, gemmarum vestiumque pretiosarum multitudine onustis; praeter arma, loricas, gladios, galeas et clypeos auro fulgidissimos, et praeter omnem armaturam, quam ad defensionem navium solent viri potentissimi comparare. In ipsa denique nave, in qua praedicta matrona manere decreverat, malus auro purissimo tectus, procul radios ad solis claritatem exerebat, et utraque navis cornua auro et argento fabrili opere vestita, spectaculo admirationis omnibus erant ea intuentibus. In una de septem navibus viri Sarraceni et sagittarii, viri fortissimi et claritate pretiosarum vestium fulgentes inerant, dono regi adducti, et qui nullis in regione Jerusalem sagittandi arte inferiores haberentur. Hujus itaque matronae adventu et gloria audita, rex tres naves, quas vocant galeidas fetas viris egregiis et marino certamine peritissimis, misit illi in occursum; sed ventorum turbine mari intumescente, nequaquam illi occurrere aut sociari potuerunt. Ventorum enim potentia naves longe jactatae, tandem portu sinuque Ascalonis vespere sunt receptae circa horam nonam, nequaquam nautis valentibus aut frustra conantibus iter per aquas tenere, propter ventum qui eis nimium contrarius repugnabat.*

251. In Orderic Vitalis we find blunt defamation of a kind divorced from reality. From Forester's translation of the *Ecclesiastical History*, volume 4, book 13, chapter 15 (page 137 in the 1856 edition), one reads that Adelaide, "having collected money from all sources after her husband's death, amassed a great treasure. Baldwin the younger, King of Jerusalem, hearing this, coveted her wealth and sent noble proxies to demand her hand in marriage. Adelais (sic), insatiably greedy of pride, of rank, and honour, accepted the proposals of the illustrious suitors, and went to Jerusalem with a large retinue and a vast treasure. King Baldwin was pleased enough to receive her money, which he lavished on the stipendiaries who fought in the name of Christ against the pagans; but he repudiated the woman who was wrinkled with age, and had rendered herself infamous by many crimes. In consequence, the old woman returned to Sicily in confusion at her failure, and spent her declining years in general contempt." Adelaide was in her early forties.

252. The papal bull *Pie Postulatio Voluntatis* (preserved in the National Library of Malta in Valletta) was issued to the Knights Hospitaller at Benevento in February 1113; it mentions by name the order's hospices in southern Italy. A good introduction to the history of the order is Nicholson, Helen, *The Knights Hospitaller* (2001) but see also the late Desmond Seward's book at note 254. (The Order of the Hospital is now the Sovereign Military Order of Malta based in Rome.) The *Via Francigena*, the pilgrimage route in central and southern Italy, is described in Chapter 32; it was mentioned by Constance Hauteville in a charter of April 1198 referring to a donation of land near Milazzo by Godfrey Borrello to the Archdiocese of Messina in 1089, transcribed in Piaggia, Giuseppe, *Illustrazione di Milazzo* (1853), pages 86-87. More generally, see Stopani, Renato, *La Via Francigena: Una Strada Europea nell'Italia del Medioevo* (2003 edition); Arlotta, Giuseppe, "Vie Francigene, Hospitalia e Toponimi Carolingi nella Sicilia Medievale," in *Tra Roma e Gerusalemme nel Medioevo* (2005), volume 3, pages 815-886.

253. These observations are necessarily somewhat speculative because very little early documentation survives regarding this church and the foundation of its community (see note 177) or even the Order of Saint Lazarus. However, Adelaide was undoubtedly familiar with the work of this order in Jerusalem. During the thirteenth century the Order of Saint Lazarus founded a leprosarium at Capua.

254. The best general history is Seward, Desmond, *The Monks of War: The Military Religious Orders* (1996 edition).

255. This title, sometimes *amiratus amiratorum,* from the Arabic *amir al umara* (emir of emirs), may be the origin of the modern *admiral,* but in Norman Sicily it was the highest official of the realm, outranking the chancellor. See Carbonaro, Francesco, *The Norman Admiralty: History of an Office Between Two Worlds* (2021).

256. See note 123. Jordan's father, Gerard, who died in 1086, was Alberarda's brother. Gerard was a faithful knight of Robert Guiscard who fought at the Battle of Civitate.

257. Falco of Benevento, year 1113, states that Jordan and his cohorts were envious of the wealth of Landulf of Graeca (whose surname is a toponym for a manor near Benevento), the papal constable of Benevento, who had razed a castle erected in Beneventan territory by Robert of Alife at Mount Sableta (now Saglieta).

258. See *ITP,* volume 10, entry 6 on pages 112-113; also *Chronica Monasterii Casinensis,* book 4, chapter 49, page 516. In 1117 Paschal II gently reminded Roger II not to stray beyond his prerogatives; see note 226.

259. For the beginning of this revolt, *Chronicon Ignoti Civis Barensis,* pages 155-156. Grimoald's given name suggests Lombard ancestry through one line or another.

260. There are several known references to this, most notably a few decades later by Hugh Falcandus, early in chapter 21 of his chronicle, where he mentions that the scholar and deacon Henry Aristippo kidnapped several concubines during the revolt against William I (see also his "Letter to Peter" at note 377 below). The phrase "baptized sultan" (attributed to Gregory IX and other popes) was used to describe our early Sicilian kings, particularly Frederick II.

261. The wedding between Roger and Elvira was celebrated late in 1117 but its precise date is not known with certainty.

262. Information about Zaida/Isabel, possibly the widow of Abu al Fatah al-Mamun of Córdoba, remains sketchy and much debated, but most scholars agree about her identity. She seems to have converted to Christianity before her marriage to Alfonso. The given name *Zaida* comes to us from the Arabic masculine name *Zaid,* "to prosper," which is Koranic. A traditionalist view about this queen is expressed in Florez, Enrique, *Memorias de las Reynas Catholicas de Castilla e de Leon* (1761), volume 1, pages 203-211; more recently Montaner Frutos, Alberto, "La Mora Zaida, entre Historia y Leyenda," *Historicist Essays on Hispano-Medieval Narrative* (2005), pages 272-352. Zaida's purported descent from the Prophet Muhammad is based on later Christian claims, contradicted by earlier Muslim sources, that she was the daughter, rather than the daughter-in-law, of Abbad III of Seville (Al Mutamid Muhammad ibn Abbad al-Lakhmi), who died in 1095.

263. Urraca's nickname is sometimes translated "the Brave." For Elvira see *Queens of Sicily,* pages 127-146, from which some of this information is excerpted. The chief source for Elvira's natal family and what little we know of her betrothal is the *Chronicon Regum Legionensium,* or *Liber Chronicorum,* of Pelayo of Oviedo, which ends with the death of her father in 1109. For a good summary see Reilly, Bernard, *The Kingdom of León-Castilla under King Alfonso VI 1065-1109* (1988); see also *The Kingdom of León-Castilla under Queen Urraca 1109-1126* (1982) by the same author. For Urraca see also note 284.

264. The revisionist thesis that the marital union between Roger and Elvira was contracted between two "unimportant" dynasties is not supported by the entirety of the evidence. In fact, both the Hauteville and the (extended) Jiménez families had contracted marriages with important European dynasties at a time when the western part of the continent was a patchwork of rather small states in, for example, what are now France and Germany.

265. Earthquakes claimed much of the church erected by order of Roger I in 1094, of which little survives except a facade and an arched portal. The "Castle of Adelaide" was likewise largely destroyed. Adelaide's tomb is not the original sarcophagus but one designed in the Renaissance style in 1557. The inscription reads: HIC JACET CORPUS NOBILIS DNE ANDILASIE REGINAE MULIERIS SERENISSIMI DNI ROGERII PRIMI REGIS SI-

NOTES

CILIE CVIVS ANIMA PER MISERICORDIAM DEI REQUIESCAT IN PACE. AMEN MCXVIII. This seems to be essentially consistent with an earlier inscription, but see also various recorded notations, such as *Necrologia Panormitana,* page 472.

266. Arab chroniclers noted the Muslim institutions (chamberlains, bodyguards eunuchs, etc.) at the Sicilian court. See Ali ibn al-Athir al-Jazari, *al-Kamil fi at-Tarikh*, in Amari, Michele, *BAS,* volume 1, chapter 35, pages 449-450.

267. Ibid, pages 452-453.

268. Ibid, pages 454-455.

269. Ibid, volume 1, pages 455-457 (al-Athir); volume 2, pages 52-55 (Tijani), and 208-209 (Khaldun).

270. There was a large chancery in Palermo. However, no central registry (similar to those for papal bulls and letters) survives. Published compendia are drawn from charters in various archives and libraries. Charters issued during this period usually gave a date and indiction but not always a location.

271. Raymond of Burgundy, who died in 1107, had fathered a son who became Alfonso VII of Castile and León, and a daughter, Sancha, who was about the same age as Elvira, her aunt.

272. First proposed by the papacy in the tenth century, the "Truce of God" was generally ignored. A parallel idea, the "Peace of God," proscribed knights' attacks on women, children and unarmed clergy. It also forbade robbery and the destruction of homes and property. See also the following note.

273. Falco of Benevento, year 1115, near the end of that chapter; also *Chronica Monasterii Casinensis,* book 5, chapter 55, pages 519-520. This was actually the "Truce of God," *Treugam Dei,* and not the "Peace of God" (see the preceding note). However, the promise to which the barons and knights swore in 1115 seems to have conformed more closely to the "Peace of God."

274. Falco of Benevento, year 1117; *Chronicon Ignoti Civis Barensis,* page 156. In June 1123, Grimoald infamously issued to the church of Saint Nicholas an ornate charter (in purple ink) of the type considered the prerogative of emperors and kings; see von Pflugk-Harttung, Julius, *Iter Italicum,* volume 1 (1883), document 49, pages 458-460.

275. Falco of Benevento, year 1121; Romuald of Salerno, year 1122. For the text of the papal mediation see *PCC, Series Secunda,* volume 163 (1854), document 163, columns 1227-1229; also Ughelli, Ferdinando, *ITS,* volume 9, columns 367-368. This is subscribed by numerous bishops, including those of Messina, Reggio and Potenza.

276. The example cited in note 246 reflects such a dispute. Rivers and streams made convenient boundaries (in modern Italy the Po famously divides Piedmont from Lombardy) but the phraseology in the charters issued by our Norman and Swabian monarchs was generally quite vague, and in Sicily they sometimes referred to places named in Arabic for which precise maps were lacking even in Idrisi's time.

277. A good study of this phenomenon in a wider context is Sunderland, Luke, *Rebel Barons Resisting Power in Medieval Culture* (2017).

278. A fine introduction is Spencer, Charles, *The White Ship: Conquest, Anarchy and the Wrecking of Henry I's Dream* (2021).

279. Falco of Benevento, year 1122; Romuald of Salerno, year 1123. This is what may have led to Roger sometimes being identified in subsequent charters as "Count of Sicily and Italy," *Italia* being an ancient term for Calabria, which had a mythical king named *Italo,* though in some instances we find both *Calabria* and *Italia* mentioned in the titulature, viz: *Privilegium factum a me Rogerio Magno Comite Sicilie, Calabrie et Italie,* in *DNS,* number 7 (pages 16-18), the original charter of 1127 conserved in the Archive of State of Palermo.

280. Ali ibn al-Athir al-Jazari, *al-Kamil fi at-Tarikh*, in Amari, Michele, *BAS,* volume 1, chapter 35, page 458.

281. Ibid, pages 454-458. The incident was noted further afield, if not always very accurately; see William of Tyre, book 13, chapter 22. Although historians have sometimes blamed Christodoulos for the failure of the attack on Ifriqiya, there is no evidence to suggest that he was at fault, and Roger did not remove him. Indeed, Christodoulos was a leader of the next campaign, to Montescaglioso in mainland Italy.

282. Ibid, volume 2, pages 208-209 (Khaldun).

283. See Makdisi, John, op. cit. Also Mansouri, Tahar, "Produits Agricoles et Commerce Maritime en Ifriqiya aux XII-XV Siècles," *Médiévales,* volume 33 (autumn 1997), pages 125-139; Davis-Secord, Sarah, "Muslims in Norman Sicily: The Evidence of Imam al-Mazari's Fatwas," *Mediterranean Studies,* volume 16 (2007), pages 46-66.

284. The source for this is the contemporaneous *Historia Compostelana,* containing the texts of numerous charters as well as information about Urraca's difficult reign and unhappy marriage. This appears in the original in *PCC, Patrologiae Latinae,* volume 170 (1894), columns 879-1236; also *España Sagrada* (1765), volume 20, edited by Henrique Florez. For a modern Spanish translation, see Suárez, Manuel, *Historia Compostelana o sea Hechos de Diego Gelmirez, Primer Arzobispo de Santiago* (1950). For an insightful discussion, see Fletcher, Richard, "Reconquest and Crusade in Spain c. 1050-1150," *Transactions of the Royal Historical Society,* volume 37 (1987), pages 31-47. A reconsideration of the term *Reconquista* and its context is presented in Rios Saloma, Martin, "La Reconquista: Génesis de un Mito Historiográfico," *Historia y Grafía,* number 30 (2008), pages 191-216. See also note 263.

285. The chief evidence that Constance ceded part of the city of Bari, which was not in her gift, to Tancred of Conversano in 1117 is based on a charter which may be a contemporary forgery; see Nitti, Francesco (editor), *Codice Diplomatico Barese, Volume 5: Le Pergamene di San Nicola di Bari 1075-1194* (1902), page 111. However, several authentic charters track the activities of Tancred of Conversano and his mother, such as their endowment of a monastery in Brindisi in 1107; see Monti, Gennaro (editor), *Codice Diplomatico Brindisino, Volume 1: 492-1200* (1940), pages 20-23. For an exposition regarding the presence of Constance and Emma in Taranto based on suspect charters see Di Meo, Alessandro, *Annali Critici-Diplomatici del Regno di Napoli della Mezzana Età* (1804), volume 9, pages 304-305.

286. The Montescaglioso incident may be viewed as still another example of baronial unrest during the reign of William II as Duke of Apulia. Over the centuries, most Italian historians have acknowledged the great difficulties Roger II confronted in uniting southern Italy, with its rebellious baronage, into a cohesive state, a fact noted during the print era by authors such as Fazello, Di Costanzo, Pirro, Summonte, Amari, Ughelli and others. As we shall see, a tenuous unity was achieved by 1140 despite sporadic revolts after that time.

287. There is no surviving contemporary copy of this bull but it is mentioned subsequently by Pope Alexander III and other pontiffs. Historically, we find similar papal pronouncements by Pope Gregory I addressed to the Neapolitans and Palermitans, through their bishops, late in the sixth century. *Sicut Judaeis* became the term to describe a body of several decrees addressing the rights of Jews; notably, in 1272 Pope Gregory X issued a bull protecting the Jews.

288. Sometimes Lothair II. The best biography is Wilhelm Bernhardi's *Lothar von Supplinburg* (1879), presented as a lengthy timeline of sources.

289. See *Annales Ceccanense,* the "Fossa Nova Chronicle," years 1125-1128.

290. See Falco of Benevento, year 1125.

291. See *Chronica Monasterii Casinensis,* book 4, chapter 88, pages 548-550; for commentary, Di Meo, Alessandro, op. cit. at note 285, pages 309-312, 317-319.

NOTES

292. The status of these lands is much debated. Romuald of Salerno (year 1127) states that Alexander of Conversano was entrusted as a bailiff of Taranto. Alexander of Telese (book 1, chapter 12) states, less probably, that Bohemond II ceded these lands to the pope. William of Tyre (book 12, chapter 21) states that the young prince made a pact with his kinsman, William II of Apulia, that whoever died first would leave his lands to the other. Falco of Benevento (year 1128) states that Taranto belonged, by right, to the pope. For Bohemond's arrival and marriage in Jerusalem, William of Tyre, book 13, chapter 21.

293. For a discussion regarding Alfano, Bishop of Capaccio, see Volpi, Giuseppe, *Cronologia de' Vescovi Pestani ora detti Capaccio* (1752), pages 5-6.

294. Romuald of Salerno, year 1127; Falco of Benevento, year 1127; Alexander of Telese, book 1, chapter 10; *Chronica Monasterii Casinensis,* book 4, chapter 96, pages 556-557.

295. For the texts see Amari, Michele, *Storia dei Musulmani in Sicilia* (1868), volume 3, pages 388-390, mentioned in Caspar, Erich, *Roger II und die Gründung der Normannische-sicilischen Monarchie* (1904), act number 53, pages 498-499. For Raymond's kinship to the Hautevilles see Table 26.

296. Romuald of Salerno, loc. cit. supra ; Falco of Benevento, year 1128; Alexander of Telese, book 1, chapter 10.

297. Romuald of Salerno, year 1127; Falco of Benevento, ibid; Alexander of Telese, book 1, chapters 12-13.

298. Romuald of Salerno, years 1128-1129; Falco of Benevento, year 1128; Alexander of Telese, book 1, chapter 15.

299. Alexander of Telese, book 1, chapters 14 and 24. Falco of Benevento (under year 1129) states that Naples did not submit to Roger's authority.

300. Alexander of Telese, book 1, chapters 15-16; also Falco of Benevento, year 1129.

301. In book 12, chapter 7 of *A History of Deeds Done Beyond the Sea,* William of Tyre states there were only nine knights at this time, but that with Bernard's support the order grew.

302. See *PCC, Series Latina* (1859), volume 182; columns 921-940.

303. For Bernard's letter to Roger II some years later, ibid, column 374.

304. As Honorius lay dying, a hastily-assembled commission of six voting cardinals elected Innocent with the support of the Pierleoni family's longtime antagonists, the Frangipani. At least fourteen cardinals viewed this election as uncanonical and immediately elected Anacletus. Despite the politics involved, there is much to suggest that Anacletus was, in fact, the legitimate pope. For a general study see Palumbo, Pier Fausto, *I Precedenti, la Vicenda Romana e le Ripercussioni Europee dello Scismo di Anacleto II* (1995).

305. Amongst the sources for this is William of Tyre, book 13, chapter 27.

306. Falco of Benevento, year 1129 (sic); Romuald of Salerno, year 1131 (sic); Alexander of Telese, book 2, chapter 2. Sicilian historians have taken to calling this a "parliament." It was not, nor can the baronial convocations at Ariano (around 1140), Capua (in 1220), Messina (1221), Melfi (1231), or even Palermo (1282), be considered parliaments as that term is usually understood. The first Sicilian parliament, leading to the barons' election of Frederick of Aragon as [Frederick III] King of Sicily, took place in 1295 and 1296. Aside from prefatorial developments such as the *Magna Carta* (in 1215), the inception of an "effective" parliament in England is usually dated to 1258 (following one held three years earlier); interestingly, it was prompted by baronial opposition to the support of a proposed Papal-sponsored invasion of Sicily by King Henry III. More generally, see Pakenham, Frank, *A History of the House of Lords* (1988); Calisse, Carlo, *Storia del Parlamento in Sicilia dalla Fondazione alla Caduta della Monarchia* (1887).

307. Dated 27 September 1130 at Benevento, this confirmed Roger's prerogative to become "King of Sicily, Calabria and Apulia," defining the dominions constituting the realm whilst

authorizing the Archbishop of Palermo to crown him with other bishops attending, naming those of Syracuse, Agrigento, Mazara and Catania. For the text see *PCC, Series Secunda,* volume 179 (1855), columns 715-717; also Baronio, Cesare, *Annales Ecclesiastici,* volume 18 (1746 edition), pages 453-455; Pirro, Rocco, *SIS,* volume 1 (1733 edition), pages xv-xvi.

308. There is very little of substance in the surviving record to shed much light on the socio-political paradigm intended for the Kingdom of Sicily in 1130 or during its first few years of existence. Conjecture is usually based on assessments of the *Regnum* as it existed by around 1140 when Roger issued a unifying legal code and appointed justiciars.

309. Romuald of Salerno, year 1131 (sic); Falco of Benevento, year 1130. The precise rite used for Elvira's coronation is not known, but see *Queens of Sicily,* pages 567-574. Little is known of Peter, the archbishop, who had formerly been a bishop in Calabria; he was sent to Palermo by Pope Callixtus II in 1122.

310. The essential construction, begun in 1129, was "dedicated" by Archbishop Peter in 1132; for the text of this charter see, amongst other compendia, Garofalo, Luigi, *Tabularium Regiae ac Imperialis Capellae Collegiatae Divi Petri in Regio Panormitano Palatio* (1835), number 2, page 7. The chapel was consecrated on 28 April 1140, an act confirmed by an ornate royal charter (issued later) conserved in Palermo; ibid, number 2, pages 11-13. For this charter see also notes 274 and 327, and Garufi, Carlo Alberto, "I Diplomi Purpurei della Cancelleria Normanna ed Elvira Prima Moglie di Re Ruggero," *Atti della Reale Accademia di Scienze, Lettere e Belle Arti di Palermo,* series 3, volume 7 (1904), 31 pages. The work on the chapel's sanctuary mosaics and ceiling was probably completed for the inauguration in June 1143, though the wall mosaics in the nave were added after Roger's reign. That the wooden muqarnas ceiling, probably commissioned the same year, was constructed separately as a unit and then lowered into position as one piece using specially-constructed apparatus is indicated by the directionality of paint drops (this book's authors examined the ceiling closely, from the scaffolding, during the restorations of 2008). Because some analyses written about the art of the Palatine Chapel are seriously flawed, publications should be read critically; we find, for example, the misidentification of certain figures in the painted ceiling, with many scholars ignoring, or minimizing, influences such as that of Ibn Zafar (see the study by Costantino and Appendix 6), and presuming that a stylized Komodo dragon, which could have been known via Muslim visitors to eastern Asia (see notes 947, 1073, 1303), was merely an imaginary beast. For reference: Kitzinger, Ernst, "The Mosaics of the Cappella Palatina in Palermo," *Art Bulletin,* number 31 (New York 1949), pages 290-319; Brenk, Beat, *La Cappella Palatina a Palermo* (2010) and "The Mosaics of Cefalù Revisited," *Codex Aquilarensis,* number 34 (2018), pages 13-34; Kapitaikin, Lev, *The Twelfth-century Painted Ceilings of the Cappella Palatina, Palermo* (2011); Costantino, Antonino, *La Cappella Palatina di Palermo: Essenza di un Regno* (2021); Johns, Jeremy, "Muslim Artists and Christian Models in the Painted Ceilings of the Cappella Palatina," in *Romanesque and the Mediterranean* (2015); Britt, Karen, "Roger II of Sicily: Rex, Basileus, and Khalif? Identity, Politics, and Propaganda in the Cappella Palatina," *Mediterranean Studies,* volume 16 (2007), pages 21-45; Kitzinger, Ernst, *I Mosaici di Monreale* (1960); Demus, Otto, *The Mosaics of Norman Sicily* (1950, 1988); Borsook, Eve, *Messages in Mosaic: The Royal Programmes of Norman Sicily 1130-1187* (1990); Naro, Massimo, and Abulafia, David, *Il Duomo di Monreale: Lo Splendore dei Mosaici* (2009). Useful for comparison to the works in Cefalù is Gelfer-Jorgensen, Mirjam, *Medieval Islamic Symbolism and the Paintings in the Cefalù Cathedral* (1986).

311. Romuald of Salerno, year 1153, authors' translation.

312. See, amongst others, *DNS,* number 10 (pages 21-24), of May 1131, where Roger signs as *Rogerius in Christo Deo pius potens rex et christianorum adiutor.*

313. Not to be confused with her elder half-sister (daughter of Judith of Evreux), who wed Raymond IV of Toulouse in 1080, as noted in chapter 22 of Malaterra's chronicle, this Matilda, born around 1091, was probably a daughter of Adelaide del Vasto, the third wife of Roger I. There exists a hypothesis that she was born around 1087 as the daughter of Eremburga of Mortain, Roger's second wife. This seems somewhat less likely given the presumed year of birth of Ranulf of Alife around 1093 and Matilda bearing a child around 1125, but it is far from impossible.

NOTES

314. See Alexander of Telese, book 2, chapters 14, 15, 17.

315. Reilly, Bernard, *The Kingdom of León-Castilla Under Queen Urraca* (1982). Alfonso's death in 1134 paved the way for García Ramírez, father of Margaret of Navarre (destined to wed Roger's son, William I of Sicily), to become King of Pamplona (and Navarre).

316. See Falco of Benevento, year 1132.

317. Translation from *The Ferraris Chronicle,* pages 102-103.

318. Matilda's story is adapted from *Sicilian Queenship,* pages 117-123.

319. Certain dates of specific events, such as the assaults on feudal towns, are reported differently by different chroniclers.

320. There may be some truth to this. However, although it is a later copy dated to the fourteenth century, the oldest surviving record to mention the incident is a charter, manuscript number 317 in *Pergaminos del Tiempo de Ramón Berenguer III,* conserved in the Archivo de la Corona de Aragón (Barcelona). Raymond III, Count of Barcelona, was the son of Matilda, the daughter of Robert Guiscard (see Table 26 and note 203). The original document was supposedly issued by Cefalù's first Catholic bishop, Boson of Gorram; for its text see Carini, Isidoro, "Una Pergamena sulla Fondazione del Duomo di Cefalù," *Archivio Storico Siciliano,* new series, year 7, numbers 1-4 (1883), pages 136-138; also *Els pergamins de l'Arxiu Comital de Barcelona from Ramon Berenguer II to Ramon Berenguer IV* (2010), document 878, pages 1417-1419. The story was popular by the sixteenth century, when it is mentioned by Fazello in the first printed history of Sicily. For the refoundation of the diocese by Pope Anacletus II at Priverno on 4 September 1131, see *ITP,* volume 10, entry 1, page 364; for its establishment as suffragan to Hugh, Bishop of Messina, on 14 September 1131, see *SIS,* volume 1 (1733 edition), pages 388-389. That foundation of Cefalù as a diocese was not recognized by Pope Innocent II, prompting a further refoundation by Pope Alexander III in 1171.

321. Alexander of Telese, book 2, chapters 12, 19-21.

322. Ibid.

323. Falco of Benevento, year 1132; Romuald of Salerno, year 1132; Alexander of Telese, book 2, chapters 29-34. For another contemporary description see the letter of Henry, Bishop of Sant'Agata de' Goti, suffragan to the Archbishop of Benevento and adamant supporter of Innocent II, in Jaffé, Phillip, *Monumenta Bambergensia, Bibliotheca Rerum Germanicarum,* volume 5 (1869), number 259, pages 442-444.

324. Falco of Benevento, year 1133; Romuald of Salerno, year 1133; Alexander of Telese, book 2, chapters 36-37.

325. See *PCC, Series Secunda,* volume 179 (1855), columns 47-50.

326. Ibid, columns 188-189. There is much scholarly work on Matilda and her reign; a good biography is Spike, Michèle, *Tuscan Countess: The Life and Extraordinary Times of Matilda of Canossa* (2004). For Ranulf and Robert see Alexander of Telese at note 324.

327. For a charter given at Rapolla, near Potenza, in 1133, see *ITS,* volume 9, columns 32-33. For the ornate charter (bearing a rare gold seal) ceding manors to the Pierleoni in 1134, see Kehr, Paul, "Diploma Purpureo di Re Roggero II per la Casa Pierleone," *Archivio della Reale Società Romana di Storia Patria,* number 24 (1901), pages 253-259, 511; conferatur at note 274 above.

328. Alexander of Telese, book 2, chapters 62-63, 67; Falco of Benevento, year 1134; Romuald of Salerno, year 1134.

329. Alexander of Telese, book 3, chapters 11-13; Falco of Benevento, year 1135.

330. Ali ibn al-Athir al-Jazari, *al-Kamil fi at-Tarikh,* in Amari, Michele, *BAS,* volume 1, chapter 35, page 459-461. According to al-Athir, the Zirid sultan had requested Roger's assistance against the Hammadids to the immediate west of Ifriqiya. For the account by Abu Abd Allah

al Tijani, op. cit., volume 2, chapter 45, page 55; for that by Wali al Din ibn Khaldun, ibid, chapter 50, page 222.

331. *RPR* (1851), pages 577-580; also *RIS,* volume 6, part 2 (1936), page 9; for other sources see von Hefele, Karl, *Conciliengeschichte,* volume 5 (1886), pages 425-435.

332. Besides the Italian chronicles (Alexander, Falco, Romuald), see Scheffer-Boichorst, Paul, *Annales Patherbrunnenses* (1870), year 1136, page 163.

333. *Chronica Monasterii Casinensis,* book 2, chapters 103-105, pages 564-568. For an example of Bernard's communication with Roger at a later date, see note 303.

334. Ibid.

335. Matilda of England is a fascinating figure but she is not ours. A fine modern biography is Hanley, Catherine, *Matilda: Empress, Queen, Warrior* (2019); also Chibnall, Marjorie, *The Empress Matilda: Queen Consort, Queen Mother and Lady of the English* (1991).

336. The copy of a royal charter allegedly subscribed by Guarino in October 1136 ceding a church in Messina to the Knights Hospitaller is probably a forgery. For the text see *SIS,* volume 2 (1733 edition), page 931; also Delaville Le Roulx, Joseph, *Cartulaire Général de l'Ordre des Hospitaliers de S. Jean de Jérusalem* (1894), volume 1, number 119, pages 99-100. For a discussion see Caspar, Erich, *Roger II und die Gründung der Normannische-sicilischen Monarchie* (1904), pages 529-530. However, it is likely that Roger did indeed support this order.

337. For the succession to the Principality of Antioch see William of Tyre, book 14, chapter 9. For Lothair's invasion of the Kingdom of Sicily and the Byzantine donation see the *Annales Erphesfurdenses Lothariani* in Holder-Egger, Osvald (editor), *Monumenta Erphesfurtensia Saec XII, XIII, XIV: Scriptores Rerum Germanicarum in Usum Scholarum,* volume 9 (1899), pages 41-44; also *Annalista Saxo,* in *MGH, Scriptorum,* volume 6 (1844), pages 770-777. See also the following note.

338. For a concise commentary on the Pisans and Lothair see *Annales Pisani,* page 11, note 2; for the Byzantines and Roger see Chalandon, Ferdinand, *Les Comnène* (1960 edition), volume 2, pages 164-167.

339. Romuald of Salerno, year 1137; Falco of Benevento, year 1137.

340. Ibid; also German sources at note 337.

341. *Chronica Monasterii Casinensis,* book 4, chapter 108, pages 571-572.

342. That Roger might consider reaching an accommodation with Lothair by offering him Apulia (see *Annalista Saxo* at note 337) seems uncharacteristic of the king.

343. On 25 August 1137, Roger confirmed rights to William, the abbot of Montevergine near Naples; Garufi, op. cit. at note 310, pages 29-31.

344. Falco of Benevento, year 1137.

345. Ibid; also note 303.

346. Gregory of Ceccano; see Falco of Benevento, year 1138, where it is suggested that Roger II confirmed this choice.

347. Falco of Benevento, year 1138.

348. Ibid.

349. Ibid, year 1139; for the council see von Hefele, Karl, op. cit. at note 331, pages 438-442. The council constrained the removal from their ecclesiastical offices of those priests or deacons who have taken wives or concubines. Monks are prohibited from working as lawyers for pay in the civil (secular) sphere. Nuns are forbidden the foundation of convents outside the established religious orders. Use of the crossbow against Christians is prohibited, although it certainly continued. Jousts in tournaments are condemned, yet these continued unabated. Churches are considered a sanctuary for fugitives. Arsonists are denied Christian burial. Chil-

dren born of incest are banned from inheriting property, while the children and other kin of priests are forbidden the inheritance of church property. The sons of priests may serve as clergy only in monasteries, not in diocesan churches. The laity has no power over ecclesiastical estates; neither a baron nor the son of a priest can claim church land. Bishoprics are not to be left vacant for more than three months; this provides for the speedy election of bishops without inordinate delay.

350. Falco of Benevento, year 1139.

351. For the confirmation dated 27 July 1139, see *BRP,* volume 2, number 61, pages 442-443; also *PCC, Series Secunda,* volume 179 (1855), columns 478-479; *SIS,* pages xvi-xvii. Also *ITP,* volume 8, entries 156-162, pages 42-43. For Pope Celestine II, see note 421.

352. The comparison is only a general one, recalling similarities that are more political than architectural. The Palermo palace stands on high ground and never had a moat; here there was an entire walled district rather than a protective wall encircling a castle. Like the Tower of London, the palace in Palermo was erected upon the site of an ancient edifice (though Phoenician rather than Roman) and had a generally squarish structure. Similarly, both edifices were arguably palaces as much as castles; each had a Romanesque royal chapel and luxurious quarters. Each palace was situated near the edge of its city, affording the king a view of his subjects. Both were conceived by Norman architects and constructed during the same era, though the Palermo palace reflects definite Fatimid influences. The palace in Palermo had four square "towers," namely the Pisan (the only one to survive largely unscathed), Greek, Ioaria (part of this survives) and Kirimbi, connected by passages and courtyards. Peter of Eboli also describes a great hall, possibly connected to the central courtyard, supported by forty pillars. Unlike their cousins in England, the kings of Sicily had several secondary palaces in their capital, such as the Scibene and Favara (and later the Zisa and Cuba), and another castle (on the coast). Into the nineteenth century, the roof of the Pisan tower of Palermo's palace was the highest point in the city; it was in its astronomical observatory that Giuseppe Piazzi identified Ceres, the first known dwarf planet, in 1801. (Unfortunately, some medieval sections of the Norman Palace fell prey to disastrous "restorations" after 1880.) The "reconstructions" proposed in recent decades are highly speculative and should be viewed critically.

353. See notes 274, 310 and 327; also Buchtal, Hugo, "The Beginnings of Manuscript Illumination in Norman Sicily," *Papers of the British School at Rome,* volume 24 (1956), pages 78-85.

354. Falco of Benevento (year 1140) claims that this was not a very popular coin.

355. It is quite possible that the new legal code, or collection of statutes, was promulgated a year or two after 1140, but not likely long afterward, as there were soon justiciars applying its principles. A charter issued in 1142 is sometimes identified in connection with the "Assize of Silva Marca" for a locality near Ariano. See also note 27.

356. Some of Sicily's Muslims were Shiites, but they were a minority viewed as a ruling elite. The Maliki School of jurisprudence was rooted in Sunni legal principles brought to the island in the ninth century by the conquering Aghlabids, most of whom were Sunnis. Some principles believed to emanate from the Maliki School are the right not to testify to incriminate oneself, proscription of the use of hearsay as evidence in trials, the accused's right to trial by jury, the weight of a contract as right to possession or transfer of property (rather than actual physical possession as sole proof of title), and the importance of judges' decisions in establishing legal precedent. Among the English institutions thought to have been influenced by Islamic law are the Inns of Court and perpetual endowment. As early as 1955, Henry Cattan noted the striking similarity between the perpetual endowment of a trust and the Muslim principle of *waqf.* In contract law we find such similarities as *force majeure* and rescission. Another example is that a contract (as for the sale of goods) becomes effective immediately upon acceptance of an offer. This is expressed in Ranulf of Glanville's definition of a valid contract based on agreement and consideration. Some of the earliest efforts in this direction can be seen in the Assize of Clarendon decreed by Henry II in 1166. For more about this, see Makdisi, John, op. cit.

357. There exist fine published translations of the text into Italian, French and English. In Appendix 1, for the benefit of jurists and scholars, and to avoid ambiguity in interpretation, are the original texts of both extant manuscripts; these were copied decades after Roger's reign.

358. This statute was reiterated by Frederick II, King Roger's grandson, with the Constitutions of Melfi in 1231. By the end of the Middle Ages, it had fallen into disuse, and only rarely was anybody in Sicily charged with rape after 1500. In dilatory legislation formulated in 1930, the united Italy defined rape as a crime, but only as "an offense against public decency" akin to pornography, which rarely resulted in prison sentences. Finally, in 1996 (sic), Italy made rape a felony crime as a form of violent assault. It remains a very underreported crime, and the statute itself is not very effective; see Van Cleave, Rachel, op. cit.

359. Falco of Benevento, year 1140.

360. For further commentary see Zecchino, Ortensio, *Le Assise di Ariano: Testo Critico, Traduzione e Note* (1984); Paratore, Ettore, "Esame delle Varianti dei Codici Vaticano e Cassinense delle Leggi," *Atti del Congresso Internazionale di Studi sulla Sicilia Normanna* (Palermo 1974), pages 477-479; Brandileone, Francesco, *Il Diritto Romano nelle Leggi Normanne e Sveve del Regno di Sicilia* (1884); Perla, Raffaele, *Le Assise de' Re di Sicilia: Osservazioni Storico-Giuridiche* (1881); Pennington, Kenneth, "The Birth of the Ius Commune: King Roger II's Legislation," *Rivista Internazionale del Diritto Comune,* number 17 (2006); Loud, Graham, *Roger II and the Creation of the Kingdom of Sicily* (2012), which includes a translation of one of the codices. The text of the Constitutions of Melfi, discussed in a later chapter, appears in Latin and Greek in *Constitutiones Regum Regni Utriusque Siciliae Mandante Friderico II Imperatore,* published by the Royal Press in Naples in 1786.

361. There exists no definitive model of the structure of government under the Hautevilles. For an eclectic range of conjecture see: Garufi, Carlo Alberto, "Sull'Ordinamento Amministrativo Normanno in Sicilia: Exhiquier o Diwan?" *Archivio Storico Italiano,* series 5, volume 27 (1901), pages 225-263; Haskins, Charles, "England and Sicily in the Twelfth Century," *The English Historical Review,* number 26 (1911), pages 432-447, 641-665; Mazzarese Fardella, Enrico, *Aspetti dell'Organizzazione Amministrativa nello Stato Normanno e Svevo* (1966); Amari, Michele, *Storia dei Musulmani di Sicilia* (1868), volume 3; Takayama, Hiroshi, "The Administrative Organization of the Norman Kingdom of Sicily," in *Studi in Onore di Salvatore Tramontana* (2003), pages 415-429, and *The Administration of the Norman Kingdom of Sicily* (1993); Johns, Jeremy, *Arabic Administration in Norman Sicily: The Royal Diwan* (2002); Nef, Annliese, *Conquérir et Gouverner: La Sicile Islamique aux XIe et XIIe Siècles* (2011), pages 243-301; Davis-Secord, Sarah, *Where Three Worlds Met: Sicily in the Early Medieval Mediterranean* (2017).

362. The name *Catalogus Baronum* was attributed to the registry in later times. See Del Re, Giuseppe, *Cronisti e Scrittori Sincroni Napoletani,* volume 1 (1845), pages 571-616; Jamison, Evelyn, *Catalogus Baronum* (1972); Cuozzo, Errico, *Catalogus Baronum: Commentario* (1984).

363. William the Falconer, *Guilielmus Falconarius,* is mentioned in the *Liber Guilielmi Falconarii,* or *De Falconibus,* sometimes recorded as a *coda* to the *Liber de Natura Falconum* associated with the legendary Armenian king "Dancus" and regarded as one of the earliest falconry treatises in Europe. Manuscript copies (from around 1300) of William's work are conserved in the Vatican (e.g. Reg. Lat. 1446, pages 74r-76r) and elsewhere, the texts varying slightly in phraseology. William informs us: *Iste magister non fuit mendax sed verax, iste medicine sunt bone et perfecte et multum probate. Guilielmus falconarius, qui fuit nutritus in curia Regis Rogerij, qui postea multum moratus fuit cum filio suo, habuit quendam magistrum, qui vocatus fuit Martinus, qui fuit sapiens ed doctus in arte falconum. Et iste discipulus suus Guilielmus scrivit omnia que ipse scrivit, et tanto plus quod ipse composuit libellum unum de arte ista, cuius principium tale est. Nolite dubitare sed firmiter sciatis quod nullus talis magister vivit modo in mundo. Incipit quedam alia capitula de infirmitatibus falconum et postaea de remediis earundem doctrinam magistri Guilielmi.* The entire text was published in Tilander, Gunnar, *Dancus Rex, Guillelmus Falconarius, Gerardus Falconarius* (1963), pages 134-175. In his *De Animalibus,* completed before 1280, Albert of Cologne identifies *Guilelmi regis Rogerii falconarii* several times, for which see Stadler, Hermann, *Albertus Magnus De Animalibus Libri XXVI* (1920), volume 2, book 23: chapter 10 (page 1465), chapter 14 (page 1468). Commentary at Haskins, Charles

Homer, "Some Early Treatises on Falconry," *The Romanic Review*, volume 13 (1922), pages 18-27 (esp. pages 20-22). See also Mortara, Alessandro, *Scritture Antiche Toscane* (1851); Ceruti, Antonio, "Trattato di Falconeria, Testo di Lingua Inedito del Secolo XIV," *Il Pugnatore*, volume 2, part 2 (1869), pages 221-230 (esp. pages 228-229). More generally, Epstein, Hans, "The Origin and Earliest History of Falconry," *Isis*, volume 34, number 6 (autumn 1943), pages 497-509; Oggins, Robin, *The Kings and Their Hawks: Falconry in Medieval England* (2004). England still has a Grand Falconer, a title vested in the dukedom of Saint Albans by hereditary right.

364. These units and etymologies were found in various sources spanning centuries. For the text of the *Quaternus Excadeniciarum Capitinate*, which was issued around 1249, see Amelli, Ambrogio, *Quarternus de Excadenciis et Revocatis Capitinatae de Mandato Imperialis Maiestatis Federici Secondi* (1903). We find Frederick II enforcing the system established in 1231 (with the Constitutions of Melfi) as early as July 1238, when his register shows a charter issued for this purpose at Cremona to Thomas of Acco, the master chamberlain (governor) of Abruzzi; see Winkelmann, Eduard, *Acti Imperii Inedita seculi XIII, Urkunden un Brief* (1880), number 818, pages 634-636. For legislation regarding the *salma* during the reign of King James I of Sicily after 1285, see *Regni Siciliae Capitula* (1573), volume 1, chapter LXII, page 20.

365. Cfr. Roxelana (Aleksandra Lisovska), born around 1505, who became a concubine of Suleyman the Magnificent, whom she eventually married. She died in 1558, probably in Istanbul.

366. For Excalibur as a gift to King Tancred see *The Annals of Roger de Hoveden* (in Sources), volume 2, page 194. A certain sword mentioned by chroniclers and attributed to King Roger II is unnamed (it may have been Mikalis) and likely no longer exists; this is considered by David Abulafia in "The Norman Kingdom of Africa," *Anglo-Norman Studies VII: Proceedings of the Battle Conference 1984* (1985), pages 41, 48-49. It is likely that the Arthurian legend promoted so famously by Geoffrey of Monmouth arrived in southern Italy independently of the Plantagenets, though details are sketchy. We find, for example, King Arthur depicted in a mosaic in Otranto's cathedral, and even, according to Gervase of Tilbury and others, banished to the fires of Mount Etna; see Crofts, Thomas, "Geoffrey of Monmouth's Byzantine Reception," in *A Companion to Geoffrey of Monmouth* (2020), pages 427-431; De Falco, Fabrizio, "The Reception of the Work of Geoffrey of Monmouth in Italy," ibid, pages 477-481. For the origin of the Durendal legend see note 905.

367. See Appendix 6, also the *Book of King Roger*, viz. Rizzitano, Umberto, *Il Libro di Ruggero* (2008); Santagati, Luigi, *La Sicilia di al-Idrisi ne Il Libro di Ruggero* (2010); also Amari, Michele, *Carte Comparèe de la Sicile* (1859); general commentary at Kapitaikin, Lev, "The Daughter of al-Andalus: Interrelations between Norman Sicily and the Muslim West," *Al-Masaq: Islam and the Medieval Mediterranean*, volume 25, number 1 (2013), pages 113-134.

368. This has given rise to questions of Trota's existence, or even whether she may have been a "composite" of two or more unnamed women. However, page 65 of Manuscript 544 in the Wellcome Library (London), copied in France early in the fourteenth century, depicts her standing while holding a gold orb, implying that she was traditionally identified as one woman. Although Francesca Cenci is thought to have been licensed to practice medicine in 1321 by royal decree (see note 28 for absence of the original charter), the first woman in the kingdom known with certainty to be formally licensed was a Jewish lady, Virdimura of Catania, wife of a physician named Pasquale, on 7 November 1376, viz. Real Cancelleria (Archive of State of Palermo), volume 16, number 57 recto, transcribed in *Codice Diplomatico dei Giudei di Sicilia*, volume 1, part 1, document 69, page 99.

369. See Green, Monica (translation and notes), *The Trotula: A Medieval Compendium of Women's Medicine* (2001), pages 94-95. This is a recommended edition as it is faithful to the manuscript record, while many earlier published texts were compendia of various sources.

370. Ibid, pages 112-115.

371. Ibid, pages 94-97.

372. Ibid. See Pitrè, Giuseppe, *Medicina Popolare Siciliana* (1896); and note 1256. The possible utility of certain medieval therapies is considered by Harrison, Freya, and Connelly, Erin, in "Could Medieval Medicine Help the Fight Against Antimicrobial Resistance?" *Making the Medieval Relevant* (2020), pages 113-134.

373. Generally considered the first treatise on women's cosmetics, *De Ornatu Mulierum* was written in the male voice, either because the author was a man or for wider acceptability. See Cavallo, Proto, Patruno, Del Sorbo, Bifulco, "The First Cosmetic Treatise of History: A Female Point of View," *International Journal of Cosmetic Science,* number 30 (2008), pages 79-86; also Green, Monica, op. cit. supra, pages 45-48.

374. Green, Monica, op. cit. supra, pages 168-175. Certain practices, such as the shaving of pubic and underarm hair by women, were known in the *fitra* of Islam but practiced by some Christian ladies; like circumcision (see note 376), this diminished after the Swabian era. See Muallaaziz, Didem, et al., "Pubic Hair Removal Practices in Muslim Women," *Journal of Basic and Clinical Sciences* (Izmir), 2014, number 3 pages 39-44. Yet the practice was not unknown in southern Italy before the arrival of Islam; statues and other art indicate that depilation of pubic hair had existed among Mediterranean women, and particularly the Greeks and Romans, in antiquity, reflecting part of a feminine aesthetic ideal that seems to have diminished in the early Middle Ages among our Lombards and Byzantines.

375. There exist numerous manuscripts of the *Antidotarium Nicolai* but no confirmed autograph copy. The earliest publication is *Nicolai Alexandrini Medici Graeci* (Venice 1543); in French see Dorveaux, Paul, *L'Antidotaire Nicolas* (1896). More generally, Prioreschi, Plinio, *A History of Medicine,* volume 5 (2003), pages 229-243; also Lawn, Brian, *The Prose Salernitan Questions, Edited from a Bodleian Manuscript* (1979).

376. A good, if now oft-challenged, general history is De Renzi, Salvatore, *Storia Documentata della Scuola Medica di Salerno* (second edition, 1857); more generally, see García-Ballester, Luis (editor), *Practical Medicine from Salerno to the Black Death* (1994). A fine overview is Kristeller, Paul, "The School of Salerno," *Bulletin of the History of Medicine,* volume 17, number 2 (1945), pages 138-194. By the end of the thirteenth century the number of circumcisions was much reduced compared to earlier times owing to the diminution of the Muslim population and, albeit to a lesser degree, that of the kingdom's Jews, though it was not yet proscribed for Catholics. See Jiwa, Shainool, *The Fatimids: The Rise of a Muslim Empire* (2018), volume 1, pages 109-112; Alahmad, Ghiath, and Dekkers, Wim, "Bodily Integrity and Male Circumcision: An Islamic Perspective," *Journal of the Islamic Medical Association of North America,* number 44, volume 1 (2012), 7903; Kacker, Seema, and Tobian, Aaron, "Male Circumcision: Integrating Tradition and Medical Evidence," *The Israel Medical Association Journal,* volume 15, number 1 (January 2013), pages 37-38; Thomas Aquinas, *Summa Theologiae,* part 3, question 70, articles 1-4; Jones, David, "Infant Male Circumcision: A Catholic Theological and Bioethical Analysis," *The Linacre Quarterly,* volume 85 (2018), number 1, pages 49-62. There exists insufficient data to ascertain the prevalence of sexually transmitted infections, or even urinary tract infections, in medieval women, but see Morris, Brian, and Hankins, Catherine, et al., "Does Male Circumcision Reduce Women's Risk of Sexually Transmitted Infections, Cervical Cancer, and Associated Conditions?" *Frontiers in Public Health,* volume 17 (January 2019), article 4. We find Catholic policy declared at the eleventh session of the Ecumenical Council of Florence, in the bull *Cantate Domino* (4 February 1442) of Pope Eugene IV addressing union with the Copts, condemning the practice.

377. From Hugh Falcandus: *Nec deerant qui puellarum pulchritudinem crederent lucris omnibus praeferendam. Sic homines aetate, moribus genereque diversi, variis nichilominus dissonisque rerum studiis agebantur.* For the "Letter to Peter," see Siragusa, Giovanni Battista, *La Historia o Liber de Regno Sicilie e la Epistola ad Petrum Panormitane Ecclesie Thesaurarium di Ugo Falcando* (1897 edition), pages 169-186. See also note 260 above, and *Queens of Sicily,* page 192.

378. Broadhurst, Ronald, *The Travels of Ibn Jubayr* (2008 edition); page 341. This supposition seems unlikely to be accurate.

379. See Abulafia, David, *Frederick II: A Medieval Emperor* (2002), pages 81, 147, 397.

NOTES

380. For a good general introduction, though its emphasis is Ottoman Turkey, see Croutier, Alev, *Harem: The World Behind the Veil* (1989). For European kingdoms influenced by Islamic practices, see Murrell, Stacey, "Concubinage in New Contexts: Interfaith Borrowings and the Rulers of Castile-León in the High Middle Ages," *Authorship, Worldview, and Identity in Medieval Europe* (2022), chapter 4.

381. Broadhurst, op. cit., page 350. Apart from observers like Ibn Jubayr, certain illuminations, such as those in the chronicle of Peter of Eboli, depict women's hairstyles. The paintings in the ceiling of the Palatine Chapel (Palermo) are rather few, but one notes those rendered later in the painted ceiling of the Barons' Hall of Palazzo Steri in the same city.

382. El-Azhari, Taef, *Queens, Eunuchs and Concubines in Islamic History 661-1257* (2019); Scholz, Piotr, *Eunuchs and Castrati: A Cultural History* (1999).

383. For the physical and psychological effects of castration, chiefly on adults, see Brett, Roberts, Johnson, Wasserug, "Eunuchs in Contemporary Society," *Journal of Sexual Medicine*, volume 4 (2007), pages 930-955.

384. For recent work see Catlos, Brian, "Who Was Philip of Mahdia and Why Did He Have to Die?" *Mediterranean Chronicle*, volume 1 (2011), pages 73-103; Birk, Joshua, *Norman Kings of Sicily and the Rise of the Anti-Islamic Critique: Baptized Sultans* (2017), pages 173-205; also Dalli, Charles, "Contriving Coexistence: Muslims and Christians in the Unmaking of Norman Sicily," *Routines of Existence: Time, Life and After Life in Society and Religion* (2009), pages 30-43.

385. *Servos autem et ancillas, pannos, vel alias res curiae de coetero nullus vestrum invitus emere compellatur.* The royal charter dated 12 May 1160, copied as manuscript Qq.H.17 in the Biblioteca Comunale di Casa Professa (Palermo), deals principally with questions of taxes at a port of entry, its terms noted in a subsequent charter of 20 August. See La Mantia, Vito, *I Privilegi di Messina con Documenti Inediti* (1897), pages 23-24 (documents 2-3). Evidence suggests that slavery actually increased after the Swabian era; see Gaudioso, Matteo, *La Schiavitù Domestica in Sicilia Dopo i Normanni* (1926); Campagna, Giuseppe, "Note sulla Schiavitù in Sicilia tra Tardo Medioevo e Prima Età Moderna," *Rivista dell'Istituto di Storia dell'Europa Mediterranea,* volume 4, number 2 (June 2019), pages 99-123. For slavery by Jews see *Codice Diplomatico dei Giudei di Sicilia* (1884), volume 1, part 1, documents 13-14, page 11. See also Smith, Romney, "The Business of Human Trafficking: Slaves and Money between Western Italy and the House of Islam before the Crusades," *Journal of Medieval History*, volume 45, number 5 (2019), pages 523-552.

386. For the Lombards see Skinner, Patricia, "Women, Literacy and Invisibility in Southern Italy 900-1200," *Women, the Book and the Godly: Selected Proceedings of the St Hilda's Conference 1993* (1995), pages 1-11. More generally, Peters, Sarah, "Reading Regina: Revisiting the Education of Upper-Class Women in the Middle Ages," *Lucerna*, volume 1, number 1 (2006), pages 48-56; Bäuml, Franz, "Varieties and Consequences of Medieval Literacy and Illiteracy," *Speculum*, volume 55, number 2 (April 1980), pages 237-265; Briggs, Charles, "Literacy, Reading and Writing in the Medieval West," *Journal of Medieval History*, volume 26 (2000), number 4, pages 397-420; Orme, Nicolas, "Lay Literacy in England 1100-1300," *England and Germany in the High Middle Ages* (1996), pages 35-56. For some concise observations about the aristocratic laity of Norman Sicily, see Thompson, James, *The Literacy of the Laity in the Middle Ages* (1960 edition), pages 72-73.

387. That there were great thinkers in the *Regnum* is not debated, but the presence of schools for children, both boys and girls, is suggested more by context, and via comparisons to kindred societies, than by specific surviving records. See Halm, Heinz (editor), *The Fatimids and Their Traditions of Learning* (1997); Cortese, Delia, *Women and the Fatimids in the World of Islam* (2006); Kharanbe, Saleh, and Asaqli, Eisam, "Intellectual Life During the Reign of the Two Fatimid Caliphs: al-Amir bi-Ahkam Allah and al-Hafiz li-Din Allah," *International Journal of Humanities and Social Science*, volume 6, number 3 (March 2016), pages 222-233; Daftary, Farhad, *The Isma'ilis: Their History and Doctrines* (second edition, 2007).

388. See Baskin, Judith, "Some Parallels in the Education of Medieval Jewish and Christian Women," *Jewish History*, volume 5, number 1 (1991), pages 41-51; Simonsohn, Shlomo, *Between Scylla and Charybdis: The Jews in Sicily* (2011), pages 369-370.

389. See Mullett, Margaret, *Letters, Literacy and Literature in Byzantium* (2007); Holmes, Catherine, "Political Literacy," *The Byzantine World* (2010), pages 137-148.

390. See Haskins, Charles Homer, "The Sicilian Translators of the Twelfth Century and the First Latin Version of Ptolemy's Almagest," *Harvard Studies in Classical Philology*, volume 21 (1910), pages 75-102. For a recent overview citing earlier studies, see Angold, Michael, "The Norman Sicilian Court as a Centre for the Translation of Classical Texts," *Mediterranean Historical Review*, volume 35, number 2 (July 2020), pages 147-167.

391. The topic of agriculture during this era of the *Regnum* is generally overlooked by foreign historians. A fine bibliographic guide for recent works is Cortonesi, Alfio, and Passigli, Susanna, *Agricoltura e Allevamento nell'Italia Medievale: Contributo Bibliografico 1950-2010* (2016).

392. For the text, Siragusa, loc. cit in note 377.

393. Indeed, Via Vittorio Emanuele (the Cassaro), which follows Palermo's "Marble Iter," was paved during the Punic era, possibly as early as 700 BC (BCE). It was the city's main "upmarket" shopping street for centuries and is still lined by shops. This is one of the oldest, longest straight streets in Europe.

394. For its clarity, one of the better primers remains Verlinden, Charles, "Markets and Fairs," in *Cambridge Economic History of Europe* (1963), volume 3, pages 119-154.

395. In larger cities, a *mercatino* is usually held weekly in districts distant from the street markets, which in Naples and Palermo are found in the historical urban centers. For general commentary on markets and fairs see Corrao, Pietro, "Fiere e Mercati," *Strumenti, Tempi e Luoghi di Comunicazione nel Mezzogiorno Normanno-Svevo* (1995), pages 345-361.

396. The place name appears in a charter of the Magione from 1291, while a decree by Peter II of Sicily (son of Frederick III) in 1340 confirms the privilege. Other references at Fazello, Thomas, *Le Due Deche dell'Historia di Sicilia* (1573), page 260; Palermo, Gaspare, *Guida Istruttiva per Potersi Conoscere Tutte le Magnificenze della Città di Palermo* (1816), volume 2, pages 291-292; *Commenda della Magione* (in the Palermo Archive of State), *Inventario*, number 9 (March 1464).

397. A good introduction is Barber, Richard, and Barker, Juliet, *Tournaments: Jousts, Chivalry and Pageants in the Middle Ages* (2000 edition).

398. Meyer, Paul (editor), *L'Histoire de Guillaume le Maréchal* (1891).

399. That early Siculo-Norman escutcheons, which resemble those of the Bayeux Tapestry commemorating the Battle of Hastings (1066), and the shields depicted in Monreale's cloister, are not embellished with heraldic insignia suggests that armorial heraldry was introduced in the Kingdom of Sicily after 1180. See Mendola, Louis, "English and Italian Legacy of the Norman Knight Figures of Monreale" in Sources.

400. See Mendola, Louis, *Sicilian Genealogy and Heraldry* (2014); more generally, Boutell, Charles, and Brooke-Little, John, *Boutell's Heraldry* (1970 edition).

401. See Mendola, Louis, "Pre-Armorial Use of the Lion Passant Guardant and the Fleur-de-lis as Heraldic Badges in Norman Sicily" in Sources.

402. See Amundsen, Darrel, and Diers, Carol Jean, "The Age of Menopause in Medieval Europe," *Human Biology*, volume 45, number 4 (December 1973), pages 605-612; also note 743.

403. For the Campania region see Drell, Joanna, *Kinship and Conquest: Family Strategies in the Principality of Salerno during the Norman Period 1077-1194* (2002).

404. Simon, with whom we shall become acquainted in a later chapter, received Taranto in 1148 but as king his elder (and legitimate) half-brother, William I, divested him of it. The first queen to receive Mount Sant'Angelo as her dower was Joanna of England, consort of William II. A similar arrangement, from 1302 until 1537, was the *Camera Reginale*, a reginal dower comprising several towns in southeastern Sicily.

NOTES

405. Hugh Falcandus (chapter 29) recounts a noteworthy case that came before Margaret as regent for William II: Richard of Sai, master constable (governor) of Apulia, arrived at court accompanied by his wife, whom he wished to divorce in order to marry Theodora, a girl who happened to be the niece of Alfano, archbishop of the important diocese of Capua. Richard's estranged wife was a noblewoman. Because the couple seeking legal separation was Catholic, their case had to be referred to the ecclesiastical authorities. The queen instructed her counsellors to ask the prelates to convene a hearing so that both husband and wife could present their cases. Despite her uncle being a cardinal, Theodora was reputed to be a sexual libertine. The mere fact of a woman taking up with a married man was sufficient "justification" for "slut shaming." The queen did not hold an opinion of this case strong enough to dissuade her from giving a prosperous feudal town to a loyal subject like Richard of Sai; in a stance redolent of modern sentiments, she was more concerned about Richard's professional life than his adultery. Richard's chief witnesses were two knights who claimed to have seen him, some time before his marriage, conducting a romantic affair with a pretty cousin of the woman he eventually married. This would seem to violate the law regarding affinity, a legal form of kinship acquired through marriage "in law," which defined such relationships as a brother-in-law or sister-in-law. Witnesses for Richard's wife accused the two knights of perjury, claiming they could demonstrate that the two men had lied. Some of these witnesses, being cousins of Richard's estranged wife, felt their kinswoman had been maliciously slandered by her husband's very allegations. However, their chief legal argument was that the canon regarding affinity simply did not apply to this case because Richard of Sai had never actually been married to his wife's cousin, with whom he claimed to have had sexual relations. Cardinal John of Naples granted the divorce (or annulment) and, as was normal in such settlements, he made the ex-spouses vow not to engage in sexual relations with each other henceforth. Not every prelate was happy with the decision rendered by the cardinal, for it did not conform to canon law. Ubaldo of Ostia felt that his fellow cardinal had been compromised ethically through bribery. Others also criticized John. When they asked him if they could apply a similar sentence in like cases, he arrogantly responded that his decision did not establish a legal precedent, and that anyway it was his personal prerogative to do what they could not. In any case, Richard of Sai was now free to wed Theodora.

406. William of Tyre, book 14, chapter 9.

407. See the German chronicles cited in note 337. In fact, the rulers of the Byzantine Empire had long hoped to conquer, or re-conquer, Tunisia. Roger's conquest of Djerba was merely one more affront to other European powers active in the Mediterranean.

408. Louis VII was formally "King of the Franks," crowned in 1137, the same year he wed Eleanor of Aquitaine. As long as this marriage lasted, it greatly extended his territory.

409. Pierre de Chatre, Archbishop of Bourges. This conflict led to an interdict; after that was resolved, in 1145 Louis, supported by Bernard of Clairvaux, sought papal favor by promising to lead what became the Second Crusade. Meanwhile, with The Anarchy raging in England, Geoffrey of Anjou, in the name of his wife, Matilda, completely conquered Normandy but ceded part of the key territory of Vexin to Louis.

410. The chief source for this is Ali ibn al-Athir al-Jazari; see note 330. For one of the recent famines see note 412.

411. The "crusading thesis" advanced by a few scholars based on tenuous evidence and much supposition is unconvincing. Several churches were long present in Ifriqiya and there was periodically a diocese at Mahdia, whose bishop, Cosmas, probably a Greek, died in September 1160 in Palermo, to be entombed in the cathedral (in the sarcophagus now numbered 24 supporting an altar in the crypt), where some items from his own church were kept. For the inventory see Garofalo, Luigi, *Tabularium Regiae ac Imperialis Capellae Collegiatae Divi Petri in Regio Panormitano Palatio* (1835), number 15, pages 34-36; for the tomb of Cosmas see Casano, Alessandro, *Del Sotterraneo della Chiesa Cattedrale di Palermo* (1849), page 56. Hugh Falcandus refers to Cosmas only generically but mentions the loss of Ifriqiya by William I; see commentary at La Mantia, Giuseppe, "La Sicilia ed il suo Dominio nell'Africa Settentrionale," in *Archivio*

Storico Siciliano, new series, year 44 (1922), page 168, note 1. No major effort was made to convert the Muslim population of Ifriqiya; even in Sicily this was not a high priority during Roger's reign, and it would develop that his ephemeral support for the Second Crusade was lukewarm at best. Only a few chroniclers, notably Robert of Torigni, imply any religious motivation whatsoever for the Sicilian conquest of Ifriqiya, which received no formal endorsement as a "crusade" from the papacy; Hugh Falcandus and Romuald of Salerno noted the invasion but with less emphasis on anything conforming closely to the concept of a "crusade." For views see Wieruszowski, Helene, "The Norman Kingdom of Sicily and the Crusades," *Politics and Culture in Medieval Spain and Sicily* (1971), pages 1-50; also other works cited at note 414.

412. Ali ibn al-Athir al-Jazari, *al-Kamil fi at-Tarikh,* in Amari, Michele, *BAS,* volume 1, chapter 35, pages 461-463 (the invasion generally), 469 (the famine of 1141-1142. For the account by Wali al Din ibn Khaldun, op. cit., volume 2, chapter 50, page 223.

413. For Tijani, perhaps after Shaddad, see Amari, Michele, *BAS,* volume 2, chapter 45, page 54. Also Romuald of Salerno, year 1142.

414. A detailed analysis is Abulafia, David, "The Norman Kingdom of Africa," *Anglo-Norman Studies VII: Proceedings of the Battle Conference 1984* (1985), pages 26-49. See also Amari, Michele, *Storia dei Musulmani di Sicilia* (1868), volume 3, pages 403-407; Wieruszowski, Helene, op. cit. at note 411; more generally King, Matthew, op. cit. at note 170.

415. See note 355, also Caspar, Erich, *Roger II und die Gründung der Normannische-sicilischen Monarchie* (1904), acts 146-147, pages 546-547.

416. *Annales Casinenses,* page 309, gives the date as 4 November 1142.

417. *ITP,* volume 10, entries 1-3, pages 242-244. For other references see Caspar, op. cit. at note 415, pages 570-571.

418. William of Tyre, book 15, chapters 22-23.

419. This wedding was finally celebrated in January 1146. The chief source for Constantinople during this period is Nicetas Choniates; see *Nicetae Choniatae Historia,* also William of Tyre, book 16, chapters 19- 23.

420. See the *Ferraris Chronicle,* pages 129-130. Recent studies are published in Doran, John, and Smith, Damian (editors), *Pope Innocent II (1130-43): The World vs the City* (2016).

421. *ITP,* volume 8, entries 165-166, pages 43-44; this is reported by Falco of Benevento and in the *Ferraris Chronicle.* Also Romuald of Salerno, year 1143. For the acts of Pope Innocent II see note 351.

422. *ITP,* volume 10, entry 1, pages 245-246; Morso, Salvadore, *Descrizione di Palermo Antico* (1827), pages 73-106; Caspar, Erich, op cit. at note 415, act 153, page 548; Cusa, Salvatore, *DGA,* volume 1, pages 68-70; *DNS,* number 30 (pages 73-75). Based on the charter of 1146, the church's foundation is usually dated to that year.

423. This contradicts some ideas expressed by historians insufficiently conversant with Orthodoxy. Although, as stated earlier, Greek was widely spoken during the Norman era, with vestiges of Byzantine liturgical and sacramental practice evident in Puglia, Calabria and Sicily for centuries thereafter (e.g. infant baptism by triple immersion in Bari), very few of the ecclesiastical foundations of the twelfth century, whether "secular" (diocesan) or monastic, were established under Orthodox clergy or jurisdiction; the Martorana was a rare exception.

424. The term "royal woman" is used in fields such as queenship studies to identify women in ruling (imperial, royal, ducal) families who are not actually queens or empresses. The word *princess* was not yet used.

425. The charter of June 1140, which mentions six serfs, was subscribed by knights, burgesses and clergy. See *DNS,* number 15 (pages 38-41).

426. Ibid, number 19 (pages 45-49). This royal charter of October 1144 granting privileges

NOTES

to a monastery in Calabria states it being witnessed in Messina in the absence of Robert (who was probably on the mainland), by Maio, who was responsible for the royal chancery and its archive as the *scriniarius*. In 1149, Maio became vice chancellor.

427. See *Policraticus, sive De Nugis Curialium et Vestigiis Philosophorum* (Leiden, 1639), book 7, chapter 19, pages 479-483. John of Salisbury, who knew Bernard of Clairvaux and (later) Thomas Becket, was in the *Regnum* from 1149 to 1153, when he wrote his *Historia Pontificalis*. It was probably here that he met Robert of Selby, who died in 1152. Commentary at Dickinson, John, "The Mediaeval Conception of Kingship and Some of Its Limitations, as Developed in the Policraticus of John of Salisbury," *Speculum*, volume 1, number 3 (July 1926), pages 308-337.

428. As noted in Chapter 12, the precise hierarchy of the government changed over time and is much debated.

429. From the autumn of 1144 until late in 1147, the king seems to have remained in Sicily, mostly in Palermo and Messina, perhaps with a few forays into Calabria. This is indicated by the chroniclers but corroborated by royal charters; for an outline see Caspar, Erich, op. cit. at note 415, acts 168-209, pages 553-567.

430. There are several contemporary references to the frosty rapport of Lucius II with the King of Sicily. See *ITP*, volume 8, entries 167-168, page 44; *RPR* (1851), charters 6085 and 6096, pages 612-613; also Romuald of Salerno and Falco of Benevento, year 1144.

431. For some fine essays see Fonnesberg-Schmidt, Iben, and Jotischky, Andrew (editors), *Pope Eugenius III (1145-1153): The First Cistercian Pope* (2018).

432. Joscelin II returned to occupy Edessa in 1146, only to be defeated again by the Zengids.

433. This bull, *Quantum Praedecessores*, addressed to Louis VII, is widely published; see, amongst other sources, *PCC, Patrologiae Latinae*, volume 180, columns 1064-1066.

434. For a fine survey of original sources and historiography see Constable, Giles, "The Second Crusade as Seen by Contemporaries," *Traditio*, volume 9 (1953), pages 213-279; also Berry, Virginia, "The Second Crusade," *A History of the Crusades* (1958), volume 1, pages 463-512. Reliable general works are Phillips, Jonathan, *The Second Crusade: Extending the Frontiers of Christianity* (2010); and Steven Runciman, op. cit. at note 219, volume 2.

435. This is implied in a reference to a papal letter (no longer extant) mentioned in subsequent correspondence from Conrad to Eugene in March 1147; see *Die Urkunden Konrads III und seines Sohnes Heinrich*, in *MGH, Diplomata Regum et Imperatorum Germaniae*, volume 9 (1969), pages 332-333. Moreover, the bull of December 1145 (see note 433 above) was indeed addressed to Louis VII.

436. See Odo of Deuil, *Protectione in Orientem de Ludovici VII Regis* (1660), chapter 4, pages 46-47; also published in *PCC, Patrologiae Latinae*, volume 185, columns 1227-1228.

437. Odo of Deuil, op. cit. supra, states that the siege resulted in the massacre of the city's Muslim inhabitants despite a promise to spare them, a description corroborated by contemporary accounts, such as that of Helmold of Bosau, and the *De Expugnatione Lyxbonensi*.

438. See Ali ibn al-Athir al-Jazari, *al-Kamil fi at-Tarikh*, in Amari, Michele, *BAS*, volume 1, chapter 35, pages 463-477. For later descriptions, op. cit., volume 2: Wali al Din ibn Khaldun, pages 224-229; Tijani, pages 49-50; Abulfeda, pages 100-102.

439. Although Roger II might be referred to as *malik* (often translated "king") in Arabic coins and charters, and a few inscriptions, there is no known evidence of the formal use of the term *rex* in Latin titulature in royal charters in reference to his rule of Ifriqiya. However, the title seems to have been used informally during his reign. At the beginning of his chronicle, Falcandus states that, *Tripolim namque Barbarie, Affricam, Faxum, Capsiam aliasque plurimas barbarorum civitates multis sibi laboribus ac periculis subiugavit*.

440. Odo of Deuil, at the end of chapter 3 in his *Protectione*, op. cit. at note 436.

441. One of the more detailed accounts of this battle, and of the crusade generally, is William of Tyre, book 16, chapters 18-29; book 17, chapters 1-8.

442. Although this is mentioned by other chroniclers, the nearest source to the events is Nicetas Choniates, Manuel I section, book 2. For the Greek text and a Latin translation see Bekker, Immanuel (editor), *Corpus Scriptorum Historiae Byzantinae, Nicetas Choniata* (Bonn, 1835), pages 96-131. Another edition is *PCC, Series Graeca Posterior,* volume 140 (1865), where some writings of his brother, Michael, also appear. In English translation see Magoulias, Harry, *O City of Byzantium: Annals of Niketas Choniates* (1984). A contemporary source, useful as a counterweight to Nicetas, is the *Epitome* of John Cinnamus (Kinnamos), first published by Cornelius Tollius as *De Rebus Gestis Ioannis et Manuelis* (1652), with later editions, most notably Meineke, Augustus, *Corpus Scriptorum Historia Byzantinae, Ioannis Cinnami* (Bonn, 1836); these include the original Greek with a Latin translation. (The *Corpus Scriptorum* series, or "Bonn Corpus," has sometimes been criticized for somewhat inattentive editing.) For some comments on Kinnamos see Lopez-Santos Kornberger, Francisco, "Byzantine Perceptions of the West in John Kinnamos' Account of the Reign of Manuel Komnenos," *Bisanzio e l'Occidente,* number 3 (2021), pages 1-10.

443. A good general study is Magdalino, Paul, *The Empire of Michael I Komnenos 1143-1180* (1993).

444. Most necrologies give May 1148. Romuald of Salerno, who was probably present at court, states 1149, probably in error. Elizabeth of Blois, the widow of Roger of Apulia, wed William of Perche-Gouët. Roger had fathered a natural son, Tancred of Lecce (born around 1138), with Emma, a noblewoman in Puglia. Little is known of his other son, William, likewise born outside marriage. The king may have already been planning to remarry even before his son's death.

445. The Italian term *consuocera* refers to the affinity of two women who are "co-mothers-in-law," being the mothers of children married to each other. In 1177, Margaret's son, William, wed Eleanor's daughter, Joanna (see Chapter 20). The term *commare,* from the Latin *cum mater,* refers to the godmother of a woman's child, from the point of view of the mother; the masculine (for a godfather) is *compare.*

446. The chief account is found in the letter of Louis VII to his trusted counsellor, Suger of Saint Denis, for which see *Recueil des Historiens des Gaul el de la France,* volume 15, pages 513-514, where the French monarch writes that: *In Calabriae* (sic) *partibus secundum depositionem divinam primus reditui nostro desideratae securitatis portus occurrit, applicuimusque IV kalendas augusti. Ibi siquidem ab hominibus dilectissimi nostri Rogerii, Regis Siciliae, devote reverenterque suscepti, et ab ipso quidem directis ad nos frequenter tam literis quam ninciis magnificentius honorati, fere jam per tres hebdomadas Reginae hominumque nostrorum praestolabamur adventum; quae seorsum a nobis delata navigio, post multos tandem circuitus terrae et maris, per Dei gratiam Panormum Siciliae felici cursu pervenerat, atqe inde ad nos cum omni incolumitate et gaudio properabat. sed et Lingonensis episcopi gravis quidem et incerta inter mortem et vitam infirmitas non minima causa dilationum exstiterat; et habendum cim praefato Rege colloquium redituus nostri accelerationem pariter retardabat. Eo itaque viso, caeterisque paratis quae nostro videbantur expedire itineri, viam nostram accelerare curabimus; quatinus et vos in nostris amplexibus, et nos in vestris, praestante Domino, pariter guadeamus.* (Earlier correspondence to Suger and to King Roger of Sicily appears on pages 495-496, and in the same volume see page 425 for a description from *The Deeds of Pope Eugene III* of the two kings meeting at Potenza and then going to see the pope, also the *Annales Casinenses* entry for 1149 mentioning their visit to that abbey in October.) Writing much later, William of Nangis mentions the episode with an emphasis on Louis rather than Eleanor; see *Chronique Latine de Guillaume de Nangis,* volume 1, page 46. Louis himself wrote that he landed "in Calabria," but his trek to Potenza argues for Taranto, Bari or some other port in Apulia. The *Historia Pontificalis* of John of Salisbury also records the incident, though slightly differently, stating that the galleys of Eleanor and her husband were intercepted by Byzantines but rescued by the ships of Roger II, which took the couple to Palermo; see *John of Salisbury's Memoirs of the Papal Court,* pages 60-61 (but in her footnote on page 61 Marjorie Chibnall, the editor, postulates that the copyist may have simply written

NOTES

Palermo instead of *Potenza*). For the account of Louis VII crowning Roger see Mas Latrie, Louis, *Chronique d'Ernoul et de Bernard le Trésorier* (1871), chapter 3, pages 13-14 ("Sire, se vous plaisirs estoit que vous me mesissiés ceste couronne d'or en ma tieste, pour savoir comment elle me serroit?"); for the story of Sigurd I Magnusson of Norway crowning a young Roger years earlier see note 245.

447. In 1152, Eleanor wed Henry II of England, by whom she bore sons. The most significant result of this union, apart from the births of Henry's successors Richard and John, was that Aquitaine henceforth fell under Plantagenet rule. A great deal has been written about Eleanor, much of it flattering. Two biographies that stand out for their thoroughness are those of Jean Flori and Ralph Turner.

448. Welf VI and Conrad III may have tolerated each other during the crusade, but the former was defeated at the Battle of Flochberg in February 1150 by troops (nominally) led by Conrad's son, Henry Berengar, who predeceased his father in 1150 at the age of thirteen; q.v. *Annales Aquenses* in *MGH*, volume 24 (1879), page 38.

449. A fine study is Makk, Ferenc, *The Arpáds and the Comneni: Political Relations Between Hungary and Byzantium in the 12th Century* (1989).

450. In ecclesiastical matters, such as the appointment of bishops, this reflected complaints unresolved since the pontificate of Innocent II, q.v. note 420 supra; more generally, Romuald of Salerno, year 1150. John of Salisbury may have been present at the meeting in Ceprano, mentioned in passing in his *Historia Pontificalis*. See Chibnall, Marjorie (translator), *John of Salisbury's Memoirs of the Papal Court: Historia Pontificalis* (1956), page 66.

451. For some papal letters to Conrad following the Second Crusade see *RPR* (1851), charters 6488 and 6501, pages 638-639. See also *PCC, Patrologiae Latinae,* volume 180: June 1149, columns 1393-1394; October 1149, column 1397; November 1149, columns 1402-1403; June 1150, columns 1422-1423. For Conrad's letter to Eugene relative to the Battle of Flochberg, ibid, column 1628; for Conrad's planned expedition into Italy, ibid, January 1152, column 1501. The definitive modern biography of the uncrowned emperor is Ziegler, Wolfram, *König Konrad III* (2008). For commentary see Roche, Jason, *The Crusade of King Conrad III of Germany* (2021).

452. Ali ibn al-Athir al-Jazari, *al-Kamil fi at-Tarikh*, in Amari, Michele, *BAS,* volume 1, chapter 35, pages 477-479.

453. Sibylla's year of death being 1150 was determined largely from context (Roger's movements in peninsular Italy based on the dates of his charters). Conversely, in the *Annales Casinenses* the entry for 1151, page 310, reports it as occurring in that year (1151), stating simply, *Obiit Sibilla regina,* with the additional note that during the same year *Rex Roggerius constituit Wilielmum filium suum ducem Apuliae regem,* "Roger crowned his son, William Duke of Apulia, king." Sibylla's original funerary epitaph no longer exists, but see *Necrologio del Liber Confratrum di San Matteo di Salerno,* pages 136 and 336, which supports the year 1150 as being correct, and *Necrologium Salernitanum,* page 475, which concurs with this. More about Sibylla at Alio, Jacqueline, *Queens of Sicily,* pages 147-154.

454. For Margaret of Navarre from childhood until this time see Alio, Jacqueline, *Margaret, Queen of Sicily,* pages 59-117.

455. More about Beatrice at Alio, Jacqueline, *Queens of Sicily,* pages 155-162.

456. The chronicler al-Athir refers to George of Antioch suffering from digestive tract disorders, op. cit. at Amari, note 452 supra, volume 1, page 475.

457. Chief sources for Philip of Mahdia are al-Athir, ibid, volume 1, pages 479-480; Khaldun, ibid, volume 2, page 229; and Romuald of Salerno, year 1153.

458. It was alleged that Conrad III, on his deathbed, designated Barbarossa, who had accompanied him on the Second Crusade, as his successor. He was crowned King of the Germans at Frankfurt and Aachen in March 1152, King of Italy at Pavia in April 1155, and Holy Roman Emperor in June of that year.

459. For the text, *PCC, Patrologiae Latinae,* volume 180, columns 1638-1640.

460. See note 457. For an analysis see Catlos, Brian, "Who Was Philip of Mahdia and Why Did He Have to Die? Confessional Identity and Political Power in the Twelfth-Century Mediterranean," *Mediterranean Chronicle,* volume 1 (2011), pages 73-103.

461. Falcandus wrote harshly of William that, compared to the esteem in which Roger held his other sons, "only reluctantly did the father consider him worthy of being a prince," *quem vix pater eodem dignum principatu censuerat.*

462. Robert's mother, Judith, was King Roger's sister.

463. See, most notably, *DNS,* document 46, pages 106-109, addressed to Margaret, as regent for William II, in 1169.

464. In England, the principle of *Le mort saisit le vif* dates from 1272, when the death of Henry III occurred while his eldest son, Edward I, was absent from the country, participating in the Ninth Crusade, to be crowned two years later. However, earlier kings of England, notably Henry II, sometimes arranged the coronations of their own sons as *rex filius.* A recent example of automatic succession in England was Charles III in 2022.

465. See 1 Samuel, chapter 16, verses 12-13. Though referring to prior events, this was probably written around 550 BC (BCE).

466. To dispel two bizarre misconceptions (among many) that have made their way into the academic literature in recent times, the installations (investitures) of the princes of Salerno were not coronations and the coronation of Roger II was not a "self-coronation." (Certain scholars entertain ahistorical ideas about the nature of kingship.)

467. See Selden, John, *Titles of Honor* (1614 edition), chapter 7, pages 128-131, especially 130; Beckmann, Johann, *Noticia Dignitatum Illustrium Civilium, Sacrarium Equestrium* (1677 edition), pages 92-93. However, the fact that certain texts of coronation rites for other kingdoms mention anointing suggests that Tancred may have been misinformed.

468. A concise but defining study of this paradigm is Morris, Colin, *The Discovery of the Individual 1050-1200* (1974), in which the Hautevilles are mentioned.

469. For the texts of the Latin diplomas (two are in Greek) see *DNS,* document 27, pages 64-65; Pasca, Cesare, "Cenno Storico e Statistico del Comune di San Giovanni e Camerata," *Giornale di Scienze Lettere e Arti per la Sicilia,* volume 60, number 178 (October 1837), pages 41-46. For an additional charter and commentary, see White, Lynn Townsend, *Latin Monasticism in Norman Sicily,* pages 192-193, 257-259. Having examined both charters of 1141 in manuscript QqD3, folios 66-68 and 76-79 at Palermo's Biblioteca Comunale di Casa Professa (manuscript HH in Sources), one of which being thought by Professor White to be a near-contemporary forgery, Jacqueline Alio believes the diploma in question more likely to be a slightly inaccurate transcription rather than a malicious deception; in either case, the reason for mentioning Lucy here is to recognize her role as a benefactress, not to scrutinize every minute detail of one charter among several.

470. For these charters see Garufi, Carlo Alberto, "Per la Storia dei Secoli XI e XII," *Archivio Storico per la Sicilia Orientale,* volume 9 (1912), number 2, pages 342-343, 353-365.

471. Ibid. For a donation to the diocese of Cefalù see also *DNS,* document 15, pages 38-41 (the original charter from June 1140 is in the Tabulario di Cefalù, number TVC008, formerly 8, at the Catena division of the Archive of State of Palermo); for another donation, document 31, pages 76-77 (number TVC011, formerly 11, in the Tabulario di Cefalù).

472. The content of this section is adapted from *Sicilian Queenship,* pages 81-82.

473. This was consistent with Adrian's cordial rapport with the Patriarch of Constantinople; see William of Tyre, book 8, chapter 6, amongst other sources. The Plantagenet invasion of Ireland (in 1169) was later rationalized by Adrian's infamous "Laudabiliter" bull, not conserved as an original charter but cited by his successors and alluded to by his friend John of Salisbury

NOTES

in the *Metalogicon*. Minutiae about Adrian's eventful pontificate dwell beyond the scope of this work. See Bolton, Brenda, and Duggan, Anne (editors), *Adrian IV The English Pope: Studies and Texts* (2003).

474. Hugh Falcandus, chapter 33. The precise date of Simon's divestiture of Taranto is uncertain. The best secondary literature for William's reign, and a fine guide to historiography, remains Siragusa, Giovanni Battista, *Il Regno di Guglielmo I di Sicilia Illustrato con Nuovi Documenti* (1885).

475. Hugh Falcandus, chapter 2.

476. Romuald of Salerno, year 1154.

477. Ibid. See also the history of John Kinnamos, op. cit.

478. Hugh Falcandus, chapter 1.

479. Ibid, chapter 2. The estimate is not unrealistic.

480. Ibid, chapters 1-2.

481. *Annales Casinenses*, entry for 1155, page 311. The essential source for Frederick Barbarossa is the *Gesta Friderici Imperatoris* of Otto of Freising.

482. Ibid loc. cit., amongst other sources. For the excommunication, *ITP*, volume 8, entry 178, page 46; William of Tyre, book 18, chapter 2.

483. Hugh Falcandus, chapter 3.

484. Ibid, chapters 6-7.

485. *Annales Casinenses*, entry for 1156, page 311. For a detailed account of the Italian intrigues and campaigns from a Byzantine point of view according to John Cinnamus, see *Corpus Scriptorum Historiae Byzantinae, Ioannis Cinnami* (Bonn, 1836), book 4, pages 134-176.

486. Hugh Falcandus, chapters 8-9; William of Tyre, book 18, chapter 8.

487. See note 485. Jordan Drengot of Capua (see Table 4) became a *sebastos*, or diplomat, for Manuel I. In 1166 he traveled to Rome attempting to broker a unification of the Catholic and Orthodox churches; see Ellis, George (translator), *Boso's Life of Alexander III* (1973), pages 69-70.

488. Romuald of Salerno, year 1154 (sic).

489. The oldest surviving manuscript of the Treaty of Benevento is in the Vatican Secret Archive, catalogued as Archivium Arcis, Armadio I-XVIII, number 4421. Following this text (numeration was added to printings in the nineteenth century) is the papal bull confirming the treaty. *In nomine Dei eterni et salvatoris nostri Iesu Christi amen. Domino Adriano Dei gratia sancte Romane ecclesie summo pontifici, karissimo domino et patri suo reverendo eiusque successoribus Willelmo eadem gratia rex Siciliae, ducatus Apulie et principatus Capue:* (1) *Nostre semper consuetudinis extitit animum nostrum in triumphis et maximis humiliare successibus et tunc nos attentius ad omnipotentis Dei obsequium et cultum mansuetudinis exponere, cum ad maiorem prosperitatem et gloriam nos vidimus pervenisse, tales in tranquillis et prosperis rebus erga nostri redemptoris obsequium inveniri volentes, qui et perceptorum a rege omnium regum beneficiorum non appareamus ingrati et maiores successus atque victorias de brachio virtutis Dei iugiter sperare possimus.* (2) *Huiusmodi quidem nostre consuetudinis consideratione inducti, cesis et comprehensis in manu bellica ad laudem et gloriam nominis Dei Grecis et barbaris nationibus que regnum nostrum nulhi eorum vi set proditorum nostrorum dolositate intraverant, devictis et fugatis de finibus regni nostri turbatoribus pacis et proditoribus nostris, humiliandos nos sub omnipotenti manu Dei decrevimus et ad cultum humilitatis propensius intendendum.* (3) *Discordie igitur illi, que inter Romanam ecclesiam et nos fuerat agitata, finem congruum imponere cupientes, cum appropinquavissemus civitati Beneventi et inimici nostri ante faciem indignationis nostre fugissent, venerabiles patres vestros Hunbaldum scilicet tituli Sancte Praxedis et Iulium tituli Sancti Marcelli presbiteros cardinales et cum eis Rollandum tituli Sancti Marci presbiterum cardinalem et cancellarium vestrum, quos ad nostram presentiam direxistis, eo quo decuit honore suscepimus et desiderium ac monita vestra de bono pacis ex ore ipsorum libenti animo audientes, ipsis et*

KINGDOM OF SICILY

Maione magno ammirato ammiratorum dilecto fideli et familiarissimo nostro et Hvgone Panormitano et Romoaldo Salernitano venerabilibus archiepiscopis et Willelmo Troiano episcopo et Marino Cavensi abbate fidelibus nostris mediantibus, in hunc vobiscum per eos pacis devenimus concordieque tenorem, videlicet de capitulis illis, de quibus inter maiestatem vestram et nos controversia vertebatur, quod subscriptum est observetur. (4) De appellationibus quidem ita: Si aliquis clericus in Apulia et Calabria et aliis terris, que Apulie sunt affines, adversus alium clericum de causis ecclesiasticis querelam habuerit et a capitulo aut episcopo vel archiepiscopo suo seu alia ecclesiastica persona sue provincie non potuerit emendari, libere tunc si voluerit ecclesiam Romanam appellet. (5) Translationes in ecclesiis fient, si necessitas et utilitas ecclesie aliquem de una ecclesia ad aliam vocaverit et vos aut vestri successores concedere volueritis. (6) Consecrationes et visitationes libere Romana ecclesia in omni regno nostro habebit. (7) Sane celebrationes conciliorum Romana ecclesia faciet, in quacumque Apulie vel Calabrie civitate voluerit aut illarum parcium, que Apulie sunt affines, civitatibus illis exceptis, in quibus persona nostra vel nostrorum heredum in illo tempore fuerint, remoto malo ingenio, nisi cum voluntate nostra nostrorum ve heredum. (8) In Apulia et Calabria et partibus illis, que Apulie sunt affines, Romana ecclesia libere legationes habebit. Illi tamen, qui ad hoc a Romana ecclesia fuerint delegati, possessiones ecclesie non devastent. (9) In Sicilia quoque Romana ecclesia consecrationes et visitationes habeat. Et si de Sicilia personas aliquas ecclesiastici ordinis vocaverit, eant. Magnificentia nostra auteni nostrorumque heredum pro christianitate facienda vel pro suscipienda corona remoto malo ingenio retinebit, quas providerit retinendas. Cetera quoque ibidem habebit Romana ecclesia, que habet in aliis partibus regni nostri, excepta appellatione ac legatione, que nisi ad peticionem nostram et heredum nostrorum ibi non fient. (10) De ecclesiis et monasteriis terre nostre, de quibus a Romana ecclesia questio mota fuit, sic fiet: Vos quidem et vestri successores in eis habebitis, quod habetis in ceteris ecclesiis, que sub nostra potestate consistunt, que solite sunt aceipere consecrationes seu benedictiones a Romana ecclesia et debitos insuper et statutos ei census exsolvent. (11) De electionibus quidein ita fiet; Clerici convenient in personam idoneam et illud inter se secretum habebunt, donec personam illam excellentie nostre pronuntient. Et postquam persona celsitudini nostre fuerit designata, si persona illa de proditoribus aut inimicis nostris vel heredum nostrorum non fuerit aut magnificentie nostre non extiterit hodiosus, vel alia in ea causa non fuerit, pro qua non debeamus assentire, assensum prebebimus. (12) Profecto vos nobis et Rogerio duci filio nostro et heredibus nostris, qui in regnum pro voluntaria ordinatione nostra successerint, conceditis regnum Siciliae, ducatum Apuliae et principatum Capue cum omnibus pertinentiis suis, Neapolim, Salernum et Amalfiam cum pertinentiis suis, Marsiam et alia que ultra Marsiam debemus habere et reliqua tenimenta, que tenemus a predecessoribus nostris, hominibus sacrosancte Romane ecclesie, iure detenta, et contra omnes homines adiuvabitis honorifice manutenere. (13) Pro quibus omnibus vobis vestrisque successoribus et sancte Romane ecclesie fidelitatem iuravimus et vobis ligium hominium fecimus, sicut continetur in duobus similibus capitularibus quorum alterum penes vestram maiestatem sigillo nostro aureo, alterum vero sigillo vestro signatum penes nos habetur. Et censum sexcentorum skifatorum de Apulia et Calabria, quadringentorum vero de Marsia vel equivalens in auro vel argento nos ac nostros heredes Romane ecclesie statuimus annis singulis soluturos, nisi forte impedimentum aliquod intervenerit, quo eessante censum ex integro persolvetur. (14) Omnia vero predicta, que nobis concessistis, sicut nobis ita etiam et heredibus nostris conceditis quos pro voluntaria ordinatione nostra statuerimus, qui sicut nos vobis vestrisque successoribus et ecclesie Romane fidelitatem facere et que prescripta sunt voluerint observare. (15) Ut autem que supradicta sunt tam vestro quam vestrorum successorum tempore perpetuam optineant finnitatem et nec nostris nec nostrorum heredum temporibus alicuius valeant presumptione turbari. Presens scriptum per manum Mathei nostri notarii scribi et bulla aurea nostro tipario impressa insigniri ac nostro signaculo decorari iussimus. (seal) *Dat. ante Beneventum per manus Maionis magni ammirati ammiratorum, anno domini incarnationis millesimo centesimo quinquagesimo sexto, mense Iun. quarte indictionis, anno vero regni domini Willelmo Dei gratia magnifici et gloriosissimi regis Siciliae, ducatus Apuliae et principatus Capue sexta. Feliciter amen.*
The preceding text and the following bull (usually *Licet ex Injuncto* for its incipit), appear in *MGH, Legum Sectio IV, Constitutiones et Acta Publica Imperatorum et Regum*, volume 1 (1893), pages 588-591. The bull, from *Codex Vaticanus Latinus 8486* (the "Liber Censuum"), is also published in *ITP*, volume 8, entries 182-189, pages 47-49; *PCC, Patrologiae Latinae*, volume 188 (1855), columns 1470-1471, number 102; Mansi, Giovanni Domenico, *Sacrorum Conciliorum*, volume 21 (1776), columns 801-803: *Adrianus episcopus, servus servorum Dei, karissimo in Christo filio Willelmo illustri et giorioso Siciliae regi, ejusque haeredibus, quos pro voluntaria ordinatione sua statuerit in regnum, in perpetuum: Licet ex injuncto nobis a Deo apostolatus officio universos Christi fideles paternae charitatis brachiis debeamus amplecti, atque ad pacen eos et concordiam invitare; reges tamen et sublimiores quasque personas tanto amplius diligere et honorare debemus, atque de bono pacis eos tanto studiosius commonere, quanto Ecclesiae Dei et fidelibus Christianis major inde fructus spiritualiter ac temporaliter dignoscitur*

NOTES

provenire. Constat, charissime in Christo fili Willelme, gloriose Siciliae rex, te inter reges et celsiores personas saeculi, eximiis operibus, potentia opibusque clarere: ita ut ex vigore justitiae, quam in terra sub tua ditione constituta conservas, ex securitate pacis, qua omnes per eamdem constituti laetantur, et ex terrore quem inimicis Christiani nominis per opera magnifica incussisti, usque ad extremos angulos fama tui nominis et gloria protendatur. Quod siquidem nos, dilectissime in Christo fili Willelme eximie, diligentius attendentes et inspicientes pariter quantae utilitates Romanae Ecclesiae valeant provenire, si celsitudo tua per firmam pacem ei et concordia conjungatur, dum in civitate Beneventana securi et liberi cum fratibus nostris essemus, ad pacem tecum habendam diligenti studio decrevimus intendere. Misimus ergo ad excellentiam tuam quosdam fratrum nostrorum, scilicet: ut supra; et proposuimus per eos nostrum de bono pacis et concordiae desiderium: et invitavimus attentius, et monuimus excellentiam tuam ad pacem. Et illius inspirante virtute qui ad coelum iturus discipulis suis ait: Pacem do vobis, pacem meam relinquo vobis (Joan. xiv); talem animum tuum invenimus, qualem filii pacis et catholici principis decuit inveniri. Et mediantibus praefatis filiis nostris, et cetera, ut supra, in hanc formam pacis libera et spontanea voluntate nostra devenimus, ut videlicet de capitulis illis, de quibus inter nos et excelleniiana tuam controversia est, per omnia, et cetera. Ut autem quae supra diximus tam nostro, quam successorum nostrorum tempore perpetuam obtineant firmitatem, et nec tuis, nec tuorum haeredum temporibus, ali cujus valeant praesumptione turbari; nos ea de communi consilio et voluntate fratrum nostrorum, auctoritate apostolica confirmamus, et valitura in perpetuum praesentis scripti pagina communimus; et tam a nobis, quam a nostris successoribus perpetuis temporibus statuimus observanda. Nulli ergo omnino liceat hanc paginam nostrae concessionis et conflrmationis infringere, vel ei ausu temerario contraire. Si quis autem hoc attentare voluerit, omnipolentis Dei, et beatorum Petri et Pauli apostolorum ejus indignationem incurrat. Amen, amen, amen. Datum anno Dominicae Incarnationis 1156, mense Junii IV indictionis. A fine translation of the treaty appears in Loud, Graham, and Wiedemann, Thomas, *The History of the Tyrants of Sicily by 'Hugo Falcandus' 1154-1169* (1998), pages 248-252.

490. For the royal and papal decrees see *SIS*, volume 1 (1733 edition), columns 88-99; *ITP*, volume 10, entries 26-27, page 231. Today the title *Primate of Sicily* is largely symbolic. However, it should be noted that the only other primate in Italy is the pope. Other traditional titles of this kind held by Italian archbishops are the *Patriarch of Venice* and *Archimandrite of Messina*, both of Byzantine origin. For comparison, the Archbishop of Canterbury is the *Primate of All England.*

491. Romuald of Salerno mentions this as it diverted the emperor away from southern Italy.

492. John of Salisbury was at Benevento with Adrian from November 1155 until July 1156. See *Policraticus,* book 6, chapter 24, op. cit. at note 427 supra, page 386. The effective duration of the Treaty of Benevento may be debated in view of the division of the *Regnum* in 1282, after which the kings of Naples and Sicily (see Table 1) continued to recognize it. The apostolic legateship in Sicily was asserted for centuries (see note 227) and the papacy formally recognized its borders with the Kingdom of the Two Sicilies until the Lateran Treaties of 1929.

493. The Muslim chroniclers, almost without exception, decry the Sicilian Christians, and especially the kings, as tyrants; while this sentiment was a trend, some of these writers were probably imitating Shaddad's earlier, lost chronicle. Hugh Falcandus referred to the Muslims of Ifriqiya in equally unflattering terms.

494. The nearest sources for the Tinnis raid are Ali ibn al-Athir al-Jazari, *al-Kamil fi at-Tarikh*, in Amari, Michele, *BAS,* volume 1, chapter 35, page 480; Abulfeda, op. cit, volume 2, page 102.

495. The chief contemporary source for the Sfax uprising is Khaldun, ibid, volume 2, pages 209-211; see also al-Athir in volume 1, pages 481-482.

496. For the events in Ifriqiya according to the Arab chroniclers, op. cit at note 494 supra: volume 1, pages 482-491 (al-Athir); volume 2, pages 209-211 (Khaldun); pages 102-103 (Abulfeda); pages 78-84 (Tijani). For the Sicilian chroniclers nearest the court: Hugh Falcandus, chapter 17; Romuald of Salerno, year 1154 (sic).

497. See note 411. A number of prelates and nobles were granted safe passage to Sicily.

498. Falcandus (chapter 17) states that the king and others believed defending Ifriqiya, and

specifically Mahdia, was not worth the effort and expense. Although this idea may have been expressed at court in 1160, it belies the value of an asset like Ifriqiya to the Kingdom of Sicily: *Nam admiratus falso regi suggesserat frumentum Africae, quod per totum annum sufficeret, se iubente, fuisse repositum; foris autem publice predicabat in ea regem esse sententia, ut diceret si caperetur Africa, nihil se dampni passurum, eamque civitatem plus oneri sibi esse quam honori; cum in stipendiis militum aliisque ad urbis tuitionem necessariis maximos quidem sumptus faceret, unde nihil unquam emolumenti speraret. Hoc autem ab admirato, sicut dictum est, eo fiebat animo ut insani capitis esse regem ostenderet, qui nobilissime civitatis amissione regnum suum mutilari iacturam non duceret, cum eidem posset facillime subveniri; nec animadverteret rei turpitudinem aut quod inde Siciliae periculum immineret. Igitur ubi Africae cognitum est legatos elusos esse, cum iam nichil sperarent auxilii, sed neque fames ultra poterat sustineri, prehabite transactioni stari placuit; ac tunc demum Masmudis urbe tradita, acceptisque navibus, que ad transfretandum sufficerent, in Siciliam transierunt.*

499. For commentary, see the works cited at note 414; also Johns, Jeremy, "Malik Ifriqiya: The Norman Kingdom of Africa and the Fatimids," *Libyan Studies,* number 18 (1997), pages 89-101; Dalli, Charles, "Bridging Europe and Africa: Norman Sicily's Other Kingdom," in *Bridging the Gaps: Sources, Methodology and Approaches to Religion in History* (2008), pages 77-93.

500. The chief contemporary source for Alexander is the *Life of Alexander III* by Boso of Santa Pudenziana. For a fine translation see note 487. Commentary in Clarke, Peter, and Duggan, Anne (editors), *Pope Alexander III (1159-81): The Art of Survival* (2012).

501. *ITP,* volume 10, entry 28, pages 231-232

502. Much of this chapter was adapted from *Margaret, Queen of Sicily.*

503. Clementia of Catanzaro, holder of a prosperous town, spent much time in Palermo. Falcandus (chapter 13) quotes a speech which is partly a diatribe against Maio of Bari and partly a plea for Matthew Bonello to marry Clementia and join some rebels in overthrowing Maio.

504. Romuald of Salerno mentions Bohemond of Monopoli, Roger of Acerenza, Philip of Sangro and Roger of Tricarico. Falcandus (chapter 13) mentions other malcontents, including several who had participated in the baronial revolts in Apulia and Campania suppressed by William a few years earlier.

505. In the original (chapter 11): *Iamque totam fere Siciliam varii super hoc dissonique rumores impleverant, passimque vulgatum erat, admiratum diademata quedam aliaque regis insignia, quae sibi praeparaverat, multis familiaribus suis ostendisse, nec deerant qui reginam haec ei de palatio dicerent transmisisse. Nam et eius consensu totum hoc fieri eamque Maioni putabant inhonesti contractu foederis obligatam. Plerisque falso videbatur id dici.* Defamatory innuendo about Margaret is absent from the chronicle of Romuald of Salerno.

506. Crowns were indeed discovered among Maio's possessions following his death, and Falcandus (chapter 14) believed this convinced the king of his guilt, but it was later revealed that, in fact, the crowns were gifts being readied for presentation to William the following year. Maio had commissioned their design and manufacture.

507. Saint Martin's Day was an important feast in the Middle Ages. It meant that the olives had been harvested and the winter wheat planted. It no longer marks a transition of seasons.

508. Falcandus believed (or at least stated) that Hugh was complicit in the plot to kill Maio. This seems unlikely, though the archbishop did not greatly lament Maio's untimely passing.

509. According to Falcandus (chapter 13): *At regina mortem Maionis multo molestius nec adeo patienter audivit, et in Mattheum Bonellum eiusque socios majori quidem impetu indignationis exarsit.*

510. Falcandus (chapter 14) makes specific reference to Bishop Erveo of Tropea repaying more gold to the king than he had received from Maio.

511. According to Falcandus (loc. cit.): *Itaque reginae ipsius freti consilio, sollicitudinis suae regi causas aperiunt asseruntque non negligendum eius capiti, nisi mature praecautum fuerit, periculum impendere.*

512. Falcandus (loc. cit.) does not elaborate on the details, but this may have been a loan

NOTES

against some of Bonello's landed estates: *Interim tamen, LX milia tarenorum, tam ab eo quam ab illis qui pro ipso fideiusserant, repeti iubet, quos idem olim, ut patrimonium suum reciperet, curiae spoponderat se daturum. Eorum autem solutionem admiratus, genero parcens, ignorante rege, distulerat.* The debt was grudgingly paid.

513. Adenolf, who was from northern Italy, had served at the palace since 1155.

514. Romuald Guarna of Salerno (the chronicler) became Archbishop of Palermo in 1166 and remained so into the reign of William II. Falcandus, perhaps out of envy, seems to have disliked him.

515. It is presumed that such a meeting took place in Caccamo Castle, and that is the long-standing historical tradition. Documentation supporting this is lacking.

516. The telling of the events in the following section relies almost entirely on a single account, that of Hugh Falcandus, which seems to be accurate in its essential details.

517. Falcandus and Romuald give very slightly differing (but essentially complementary) accounts of the events in this section. Falcandus' description is the more detailed but the less flattering of the king.

518. Sometimes *Henricus Aristippus,* a scholar of Greek who undertook the first known Latin translation of the *Phaedo* of Plato and the *Meteorologica* of Aristotle. As an ambassador to Constantinople for two years until 1160, he brought back a copy of Ptolemy's *Almagest* for translation into Latin. William initially trusted him but changed his mind in 1162.

519. Falcandus states that William and Henry were chased down a corridor and caught. In Romuald's account William was confronted by the intruders in a room (which had a window) in the Pisan Tower.

520. From Falcandus (chapter 14): *Nonnulli quoque, per fenestras palatii in plebem quae foris stabat, tarenos habundantissime dispergebant.* The tarì coins were tossed out of a high window of the Pisan Tower, which overlooked a wall (much altered over successive centuries) that faced the city's Halkah district. Compared to the copper follis and silver ducat, the gold tarì was small enough that an adult pelted with a few of these coins would not likely be injured as a result.

521. Although his intent is clear, Falcandus (loc. cit.) does not refer literally to "concubines" but to "pretty girls." He wrote: *Nec deerant qui puellarum pulchritudinem crederent lucris omnibus praeferendam. Sic homines aetate, moribus genereque diversi, variis nichilominus dissonisque rerum studiis agebantur.*

522. According to Romuald of Salerno: *Sed rex ipse captus est et in carcere positus, regina quoque cum filiis suis in quadam camera honeste est custodita.*

523: From Romuald: *Rex autem huius rei nescius et ignarus et de tam repentino casu attonitus, ad fenestram turris pisane venit, et quosque transevntes cepit ad suum auxilium convocare. Sed cum nullus esset qui succurreret, captum est palatium nemine repugnante, et ex magna parte expoliatum.*

524. The massacre was not entirely arbitrary. The eunuchs, most of whom lived in the palace, had long been viewed as partisan, given to gossip and conniving, and some among their number were known supporters of the late Maio of Bari.

525. From Falcandus (chapter 14): *Eunuchorum vero quotquot inveniri potuerunt nullus evasit. Plures autem eorum in initio rei ad amicorum domos confugerant, quorum plerosque repertos in via, milites occiderunt qui de castello maris exierant, aliique qui iam coeperant per civitatem discurrere.*

526. From Falcandus (loc. cit.): *Multi quoque Sarracenorum, qui vel in apothecis suis mercibus vendendis praeerant, vel in duaniis fiscales redditus colligebant, vel extra domos suas improvidi vagabantur, ab eisdem sunt militibus interfecti. Postea vero Sarraceni, perturbatione cognita, viribus se quidem ad resistendum impares arbitrati, cum eos praecedenti anno admiratus omnia arma sua curie reddere coegisset, relictis domibus quas plerique eorum in civitate media possidebant, in eam partem quae trans Papiretum est secesserunt, ubi Christianis in eos impetum facientibus, aliquam diu frustra conflictum est. Nam illi ad introitus et angustias viarum nostris tutius resistebant.*

527. The *Catalogus Baronum*. See note 362.

528. Falcandus and Romuald are in agreement that the rebels paraded young Roger through the streets of the city.

529. Walter was destined to be consecrated Archbishop of Palermo. For now, he was archdeacon of Cefalù, serving under Boson of Gorron, its bishop, but he spent most of his time at court, eventually becoming dean, or rector, of the Palatine Chapel as well as the royal tutor.

530. However, this was not formalized and the boy was not crowned.

531. According to Romuald, this included (besides himself) Robert of Messina, Richard Palmer of Syracuse and Tustin of Mazara. It will be remembered that Romuald was Archbishop of Palermo, thus especially influential in the capital.

532. Romuald states that the arrow hit young Roger in an eye. That is probably what happened. It is difficult to ascribe much credibility to the theory, advanced by Falcandus (who claims merely to be reporting rumors), that the arrow did not kill Roger but that an angry William brutally kicked the boy out of resentment for his having been proclaimed king by Walter and the people.

533. Roger was entombed with his brother in the chapel dedicated to Mary Magdalene (see note 745).

534. According to Falcandus (chapter 23): *Illi se coniunxerant, praeter Gillebertum Gravinae comitem, qui regis gratiam consanguineae suae reginae precibus impetraverat, et relicta societate comitum, exercitui praeerat in Apulia, Roberti comitis impetum quantum poterat moraturus.*

535. See note 362.

536. Falcandus, chapter 24.

537. See manuscript V in Sources.

538. Falcandus, loc. cit.

539. From Falcandus (loc. cit.): *Illi vero spe frustrati, ad inferiorem ingressum palatii se transtulerunt, sive ut ad regem indeflexo gressu contenderent, sive ut ibidem in scholis regis filios invenirent, quos eorum preceptor Gualterius, Cephaludensis archidiaconus, in campanarium, primis rei motibus praecognitis, asportarat. Acciderat autem gayto Martino post primum januam in introitu sedenti viros quosdam assistere, quorum unus, irruentibus illis, obvium se dedit, et primos ictus excipiens, eorum impetum retardavit spemque sustulit. Interim enim gaytus Martinus, foribus obseratis, intra palatium se recepit. Ita, cum nihil eorum quae speraverant effecissent, subita virorum multitudine circumventi, quae cum Odone magistro stabuli repente confluxerant, ad unum omnes interfecti sunt. Cadavera eorum, proiecta canibus, prohibuit curia sepeliri.*

540. Here the chief source is Falcandus (chapter 25): *Cum ergo regnum ab extrinsecis tumultibus aliquando quievisset, rex autem interim otio quietique vacaret, timens ne quaevis occasio voluptuosum otium impediret, familiares suos premonverat ut nihil ei quod mestitiam aut sollicitudinem posset ingerere nunciarent.*

541. A decade earlier, Idrisi counted only 130 towns, villages and other places of note in Sicily. In fact, there were hundreds of named manors on the island, many held by barons or abbots, and the surviving portion of the *Catalogus Baronum,* for which the Sicilian section is missing, lists a multitude on the mainland. For observations regarding castles in the kingdom during this era see Maurici, Ferdinando, *Castelli Medievali in Sicilia: Dai Bizantini ai Normanni* (1992); Severini Giordano, Franco, *I Castelli Normanno-Svevi di Calabria nelle Fonti Scritte* (2014).

542. Hugh Falcandus, chapter 25, where *Minenius* may refer to the Scibene palace in what is now Mezzomonreale: *...cogitans ut quia pater eius Favariam, Minenium aliaque delectabilia loca fecerat, ipse quoque palatium construeret, quod commodius ac diligentius compositum, videretur universis patris operibus premillere. Cuius parte maxima, mira celeritate, non sine magnis sumptibus expedita, antequam supremam operi manum imponeret, dissenteriam incurrens cepit diuturno morbo dissolvi.*

543. Romuald of Salerno, year 1165: *Eo tempore Rex Guilielmus palatium quoddam altum satis et miro artificio laboratum prope Panormum aedificari fecit, quod Zisam appellavit, et ipsum pulchris pomiferis et amoenis viridariis circumdedit, et diversis aquarum conductibuset piscariis satis delectabile reddidit.*

NOTES

544. Unfortunately, the Zisa's restoration, featuring brick of a color not used in the original structure, is mediocre. Nevertheless, most of the original supporting walls remain. A useful reference to the muqarnas is Garofalo, Vincenza, "A Methodology for Studying Muqarnas: The Extant Examples in Palermo," *Muqarnas,* number 27 (2011), pages 357-406.

545. This is based directly on the account of Romuald of Salerno, year 1166.

546. Romuald and Falcandus both use the same phrase, *totius regni* (the entire kingdom), in defining the scope of her authority. Romuald: *Margaritam reginam uxorem suam totius regni et filiorum suorum tutricem et gubernatricem,* "entrusting Queen Margaret his wife with the governing of the entire realm and the care of his sons." Falcandus: *Reginam autem praecepit totius regni curam et administrationem, quae vulgo balium appellatur,* "to the queen was entrusted the care and administration of the whole kingdom as what is commonly known as a governor," thus explaining that this is what in common parlance was then called a *balius* (a "governor"). In the Latin of Margaret's time and place a precise cognate for *regent* was not used, and in Italy the term *viceré* (viceroy) came into use much later.

547. Falcandus gives the date of death as 15 May. Romuald states 7 May. Historians generally favor the date provided by Falcandus, which is what one reads in most books published during the last two centuries.

548. Falcandus states that the king's death was kept secret for a few days until arrangements could be made for his son's coronation, and that the late monarch's entombment in the palace was meant to be temporary. This differs slightly from Romuald's account.

549. Romuald states that young William was proclaimed king and crowned on 9 May, two days following his father's death. This seems credible as Romuald himself performed the coronation in Palermo's cathedral; it does not seem that the boy was already crowned *rex filius.* There is an additional discrepancy between Falcandus and Romuald regarding the young king's age (Falcandus states he was at least thirteen), but Romuald, as his tutor, might be presumed to be better informed on this detail.

550. Here reference is made specifically to the years of Margaret's regency (1166-1171). By contrast, Eleanor of Aquitaine, the heiress of a wealthy duchy, was Queen Consort of England (and Duchess of Normandy) as the wife of Henry II from 1154 to 1189, but she never wielded economic or military power comparable to that of the Kingdom of Sicily. Margaret's stepmother, Urraca of Castile, was Regent of Asturias (part of the Kingdom of León) until 1165, but no single Spanish kingdom of the twelfth century could compare to the Kingdom of Sicily in terms of sheer wealth and political influence. The contemporary European queen whose effective power most nearly approximated Margaret's was the Empress Maude, or Matilda, daughter of Henry I of England and consort of the (Salian) Holy Roman Emperor Henry V; by the time she died in 1167, Maude had been Imperial regent in northern Italy (for her first husband), led troops into England (for her second husband Geoffrey of Anjou), and served as regent in Normandy (for her son Henry II of England). In this regard, and though the authors do not wish to engage in pedantry, it may be noted that none of the three regions (Normandy, England, northern Italy) Maude governed at one time or another was as wealthy or important as the Kingdom of Sicily during this period. Another queen worthy of inclusion in this elite sorority is Melisende of Jerusalem, who died in 1161.

551. Until recently, Margaret was completely overlooked by most major references on European queens and medieval women; see note 23. Constance was regent for Frederick II from September 1197 until her death in November 1198, before which her reign as queen regnant, from December 1194, was through her husband, Emperor Henry VI, who ruled in her name *jure uxoris,* a total of four years compared to Margaret's five. As a widow, Margaret arguably exercised more direct authority, at least for the first few years of the regency.

552. Following the death of his son, William I was accorded the unflattering nickname "the Bad," an epitaph rooted largely in the criticisms recorded by Romuald and especially Falcandus, but popularized in the sixteenth century by Thomas Fazello.

553. Hugh Falcandus (chapter 25): *Itaque regina, ut plebem ac proceres sibi filioque gratos efficeret, statuit eorum gratiam copia meritorum elicere, et fidem, si fieri posset, immensis saltem beneficiis extorquere ac primum universa recludi iussit ergastula plurimamque multitudinem virorum, tam in Sicilia quam in adiacentibus insulis, liberavit. Inde redemptionis onus importabile, quod totam Apuliam Terramque Laboris ultima iam desperatione concusserat, omnino censuit amovendum, scripsitque magistris camerariis ut a nemine deinceps quicquam nomine redemptionis exigerent.*

554. In his last days, William I had abolished the redemption tax in Apulia. Margaret's policy was distinctive because it abrogated such taxes altogether, throughout the kingdom; in addition to Apulia, which included part of Lucania (Basilicata), Falcandus mentions *Terra di Lavoro*, the region of Naples.

555. According to Falcandus (chapter 26): *Regina vero nihilominus eisdem consentiebat consiliis, nec illius ipsi persecutio displicebat, eo quod adhuc vivente marito suo, cum pro quibusdam negotiis suis aliquotiens electo preces porrigeret, ille ut in prosperis semper elatus, contemptorem induebat animum, superbe nunciis mordaciterque respondens, nunquam eius petitiones efficaciter admictebat.*

556. Ibid.

557. Molise had reverted to the crown when the man who previously held it died without heirs some years earlier. The territories given to Richard of Mandra made his personal feudal power far greater than Gilbert's.

558. Hugh Falcandus, chapter 26.

559. Frederick Barbarossa was indeed planning an invasion, but his chief objective was Rome, which he reached the next year, where he wished to install an antipope, and Ancona, to the immediate north of the *Regnum*, which had declared allegiance to the Byzantine Emperor. For now, a few disgruntled barons acting as his surrogates were making raids along the border the Kingdom of Sicily shared with the Papal State.

560. Falcandus (chapter 26) does not state explicitly that Margaret was privy to Matthew's maneuver (although she probably was), but explains that she exploited the occasion, *Hinc oportune regina, quaesitam occasionem eliciens.*

561. Cardinal John of Naples (see note 405) was a Papal diplomat and not, as his name seems to imply, the Archbishop of Naples. He was the ambassador of Pope Alexander III to the Sicilian court and later played a role in the conflict between Thomas Becket and Henry II of England.

562. Richard Palmer was nominated (but not immediately consecrated) shortly after the death of Syracuse's last bishop and by 1166 the post had been vacant for more than a decade.

563. According to Falcandus (chapter 26): *Assentiente regina idque sibi gratum fore modis omnibus attestante.*

564. From Falcandus (chapter 28): *Regina mutato consilio respondit: Electi praesentiam curie necessariam esse, nec eum ad praesens posse quopiam proficisci, alias iturum, cum temporis oportunitas pateretur.*

565. Romuald of Salerno, year 1166. This probably coincided with negotiations for a betrothal of Maria to Béla III of Hungary, to whom Manuel accorded the name *Alexios* in anticipation of a marriage; see *Corpus Scriptorum Historiae Byzantinae, Ioannis Cinnami* (1836), book 5, chapters 5-6, pages 214-215. As we shall see, the negotiations for Maria's marriage to William were eventually revived in 1170, but by that time she was no longer sole heiress as she had a younger half-brother, Alexios II, born in September 1169, who succeeded to the Byzantine throne (though he died in 1183). In 1180 the oft-betrothed Maria wed Ranier of Montferrat.

566. Falcandus (chapter 31) states that, *Hunc ergo regina cum antea Rodericus dicereturm idque siculi nomen abhorrentes velut ignotum et barbarum irriderent, Henricum, appellari praecepit.* For Margaret's natal family and the circumstances of Rodrigo's birth see *Margaret, Queen of Sicily.*

567. Not that there were large casinos in Messina, but there were small gaming houses. Most of Henry's money was lost rolling dice or playing "tiles," a game somewhat similar to domi-

NOTES

noes. The city's gambling was later addressed by Frederick II in his Assizes of Messina of 1221, q.v. Chapter 25.

568. See manuscript D in the Sources.

569. Rotrou of Rouen was Queen Margaret's first cousin, one generation removed, being the son of Henry of Beaumont, first Earl of Warwick, and Margaret, daughter of Geoffrey of Perche. See Table 5.

570. From Falcandus (chapter 34), who was almost certainly present, the Latin of words spoken in Norman French: *"Ecce, completum video quod plenis semper votis expetii. Nec enim aliter quam fratres proprios diligere quidem et honorare debeo filios comitis Perticensis per quem, ut verum fatear, pater meus regnum obtinuit. Nam idem comes patri meo terram amplissimam cum nepte sua, matre mea, dotem dedit, quam in Hispania multis periculis ac diuturnis laboribus expugnatam, Sarracenis abstulerat. Nec ergo mirari potestis si filium eius, matris meae consobrinum, loco mihi fratris habendum censeam, et de remotissimis partibus ad me venientem gratanter excipiam, quem quidem volo jubeoque, ut qui me filiumque meum diligere se fatentur, propensius diligant et honorent, ut eorum gratia erga nos ex hoc ipso fidei dilectionisque quantitatem emetiar."*

571. See manuscript D in Sources. The charter was subscribed by a *familiare* (Matthew), the treasurer (Martin) and the royal tutor (Walter), but not by Stephen; Walter's presence is explained by his being rector of the palace chapel which is dealt with in the charter. Relying on the date indicated in a forged charter, Chalandon and others report Stephen being appointed chancellor in late 1166, yet the earliest surviving (authentic) charters referring to him as chancellor were issued the following year. Falcandus does not suggest his appointment before spring 1167.

572. A small church dedicated to Saint Thomas Becket was consecrated along what is now narrow Vicolo del Lombardo in Palermo around 1180 and much altered during subsequent centuries. It was extensively damaged during the bombings of 1943. This was probably the site of the local home of Becket's nephews. It is mentioned in the so-called *Ruolo dè Tonni* compiled in 1439, for which one may consult, amongst other references, Gioacchino Di Marzo's *Opere Storiche Inedite sulla Città di Palermo* (1873), volume 3, page 489, footnote 1.

573. See *Epistolae Sancti Thomae Cantuariensis,* volume 1, document number 192, pages 392-394. Becket makes reference to the queen's request to assist in prompting the return of her cousin, Stephen of Perche, when exiled. The letter is borne by Thibauld, Prior of Saint-Arnoult de Crepy, who shall elucidate (verbally) more information than Thomas does in the correspondence itself. *Serenissime domine, et in Christo carissimae Margarete, illustri reginae Siculorum, Thomas divina dispensatione Cantuariensis ecclesiae minister humilis, salutem, et sic temporaliter regnare in Sicilia, ut cum angelis aeternaliter exultet in gloria. Licet faciem vestram non noverimus, gloriam tamen non possumus ignorare, quam et generosi sanguinis illustrat claritas, et multarum magnarumque virtutum decorat titulus, et famae celebritas numerosis praeconiis reddit insignem. Sed inter caeteras virtutes, quas cum aliis auditoribus gratanter amplectimur, liberalitati vestrae debemus, et qua nunc possumus devotione, gratias referimus ampliores, quae coexules nostros, proscriptos Christi, et consanguineos nostras, fugientes ad partes vestras a facie persecutoris, consolata est in tribulatione sua, quae profecto magna pars verae et Deo gratissimae religionis est, si pro justicia patientibus clementia ferat solatium, si pauperibus opulentia suffragetur, si sanctorum necessitatibus absoluta potestatis communicet amplitudo. Talibus enim hostiis promeretur Deus, exhilarescit et dilatatur gloria temporalis, et omnium bonorum gratiosus conciliatur affectus. His meritis inter alios specialiter tamen promeruistis et nos, qui totum id quod sumus et possumus ad vestrum devovimus obsequium. Cujus devotionis primitias, quas pro tempore potuimus excellentiae vestrae nuper optulimus, preces vestras apud regem Christianissimum promoventes, sicut perpendere potestis ex precibus ejus dilecto nostra illustri regi Siciliae porrectis, et ex verbis venerabilis prioris Crispiniacensis, quem et eruditio litterarum, et vitae sinceritas et integritas famae bonis omnibus amabilem et commendabilem reddunt. Est enim vir probatissime conversationis sanae doctrinae, et quantum ad humanum spectat examen, perfectae pro tempore sanctitatis, quem tanta reverentia a sublimitate vestra desideramus et petimus exaudiri, quanta totam occidentalem ecclesiam, si vestris pedibus assisteret, audiretis. Et hoc quidem tum pro suae personae reverentia, tum pro merito et auctoritate Cluniacensis ecclesiae, cujus procurat necessitates, quae in orbe Latino dinoscitur, a diebus patrum nostrorum in monastica religione perfectionis gloriam quasi propriam possedisse. In caeteris, quae*

vobis ex parte nostra dixerit, ei, si placet, credatis ut nobis. Valete. The translation from the book by John Allen Giles published in 1846: To the most serene lady and dearest daughter in Christ, Margaret, the illustrious Queen of Sicily, Thomas, by divine appointment humble minister of the church of Canterbury, sends health, and thus to reign temporally in Sicily, that she may rejoice forever with the angels in glory! Although I have never seen your face, I am not ignorant of your renown, its fame supported by nobility of birth and by greatly numerous virtues. But amongst other perfections which we and others praise, we owe a debt of gratitude to your kindness, which we are now endeavoring to acknowledge, for the generosity with which you gave refuge to our fellow exiles, Christ's poor ones, our own kin who fled to your realm from him who persecutes them. You have consoled them in their distress, which is a great duty of religion. Your wealth has relieved their indigence, and the amplitude of your power protected them in their needs. By such sacrifices God is well pleased, your earthly reputation is enhanced and made known, and every blessing is poured upon you. By these means you have bound ourself also to you in gratitude, and we devote all that we possess and all we are to your service. As the first fruits of our devotion, we have used our good services to present your request to the most Christian king, as you may know by the requests which he had made to our dear friend, the King of Sicily, and by the words of the venerable prior of Crepy, whose literary attainments, single-mindedness and sense of justice make him dear to all good men. He is a man of correct life, sound doctrine, and perfect sanctity in human judgment. We beg of you to hear him with as much reverence as you would listen to the entire Western Church were it assembled at your feet. And I beseech you, not only out of respect for his person, but in high regard for the Church of Cluny, whose necessities he is charged with and which is reputed throughout all the Latin world to have possessed, within its walls, all the glory of virtue and perfection from the time of our first ancestors. In other respects also, I ask you, if it so please you, to place as much confidence in all that he shall tell you as coming from me, as if I myself had said it. Farewell. (See also note 662.)

574. Falcandus (chapter 38) uses the phrase *eius successores,* literally "his successors" (heirs generically), who might have been nephews; it was not unusual for a bishop to leave a substantial bequest to his kinsmen. Stephen's generosity thus enfeoffed Richard Palmer, making him a lesser manorial lord. It will be remembered that Richard had come to Italy from England, and therefore held no estates of his own in Sicily. However, the village Richard received, albeit wealthy, was not a walled town (for which the Latin word *castrum* was used) or a locality protected by a castle but what in Italy is still called a *casale,* from the Latin *casalia.* During this period many smallholdings of Sicily's Arabs and Greeks were being consolidated and absorbed into baronies (and their inhabitants forced into serfdom) while others were acquired by Catholic bishops or abbots; the *casale* granted to Richard Palmer may have been a village amidst such farms.

575. A decade later, Pope Alexander III ordered the prelates who had been living in Palermo for more than six years to report to their bishoprics. By then, the power-hungry clerics had already done much to harm the monarchy.

576. Falcandus implies, but does not state, that the clients were parsimonious.

577. It is interesting to note that in Italy today one must be an attorney to become a notary; this is a holdover from the Middle Ages.

578. The authors cannot help commenting that in Italy notary fees are still infamously exorbitant, even subjective, and the bureaucracy is sluggish. Not without reason, Italians sometimes describe our nation's officialdom as "medieval."

579. Many charters issued in Sicily were paper rather than parchment or vellum and thus fragile; in 1231 Frederick II outlawed paper for the most important documents. Not all seals were wax or metal (gold or lead); some were drawn on the charter in crimson ink.

580. This is essentially a translation of the account of the incident by Hugh Falcandus (chapter 39). It is interesting that in Italy today there is no fixed limit on what notaries can charge their clients for witnessing documents (see note 578).

NOTES

581. Here Falcandus prefers the term *stratigotus,* but in some charters the word *balius* (bailiff) is used, q.v. Chapter 12.

582. According to Falcandus (chapter 40): *Cuius rei fama totum regnum brevi pervadens, plebisque gratiam et favorem ei concilians, tanta nomen eius celebritate diffudit, ut omnes assererent velut consolatorem angelum a Deo missum, qui curiae statu in melius immutato, aurea saecula revexisset.*

583. For some notes on the conversions of Muslims to Catholicism in Sicily during this era, see Metcalfe, Alexander, *Muslims and Christians in Norman Sicily: Arabic Speakers and the End of Islam* (2011).

584. Very little evidence survives to suggest that Stephen of Perche conducted anything like a mass pogrom against the "heresy" of these relapsed converts. It appears that the allegations against them were addressed on a case-by-case basis, which is essentially the kind of approach Pope Alexander suggested for worse crimes allegedly committed by Muslims (see note 585).

585. A letter from Pope Alexander III to Stephen of Perche in late 1167 refers to the matter of punishing Muslims who (allegedly) have raped Christian women and boys, *agendum sit de Sarracenis qui mulieres christianas et pueros rapuerint.* See *ITP,* volume 10, page 232, entry number 31.

586. From Falcandus (chapter 41): *Harum regina precum assiduitate permota, cancellarium primo rogat, deinde renitenti praecipit ut neminis adversus Robertum Calataboianensem accusationes admictat.*

587. To quote Falcandus (loc. cit.): *Convocatis ergo curiae familiaribus et episcopis aliisque personis ecclesiasticis, Robertus sub multa frequentia plebis introducitur, omissisque furtis, rapinis, iniuriis civium homicidiis et illata constupratae virgini violentia, periurii, incestus, adulterii quaestio ventilatur.*

588. In the original (chapter 43): *Reginam, cum hispana sit, francum hunc consanguineum appellare, nimis ei familiariter colloqui et velut rapacibus eum oculis intueri, verendum ne sub nomine propinquitatis amor illicitus occultetur.*

589. By the most widely-accepted definition, *slut shaming* is the defamation or stigmatizing of a woman whose behavior is judged (especially by men) to be promiscuous or sexually provocative; the Middle English *slutte* dates from around 1400. An infamous victim of such defamation was Theodora, the consort of Emperor Justinian I, in the "Secret History" of Procopius of Caesarea; for the original Greek with an English translation see Dewing, Henry, *Procopius: Volume 7, The Anecdota or Secret History* (1935); a fine biography is Cesaretti, Paolo, *Theodora, Empress of Byzantium* (2004); commentary in Betancourt, Roland, *Byzantine Intersectionality: Sexuality, Gender and Race in the Middle Ages* (2020).

590. See McCracken, Peggy, *The Romance of Adultery: Queenship and Sexual Transgression in Old French Literature* (1998); Stafford, Pauline, *Queens, Concubines and Dowagers: The King's Wife in the Early Middle Ages* (1983).

591. John of Aiello was consecrated Bishop of Catania on 26 July 1168, having been elected in February. See *ITP,* volume 10, page 291, entry 24; also page 292, entry 25.

592. Bellisina may be *Beauce* or *Bellême,* both in France.

593. Falcandus, chapters 47-48. Aside from feudal toponyms, men were sometimes given nicknames for their towns of origin. Salerno was known for its medical school and, as Falcandus informs us, Salernus the physician was a judge in that city.

594. It will be remembered that Romuald was the best-known physician at court.

595. Among whom were Bohemond of Manopello (who Falcandus tells us was intelligent and eloquent), William of Gesualdo and Richard of Balbano.

596. In the words of Falcandus (chapter 50): *Nunc reliquum quidem esse, ut aut inhonestis reginae votis deservire credatur ipsiusque cancellarii libidini seu potius incestui consentire, aut illicitam eorum familiaritatem se nescire fateatur.* At one point Henry of Montescaglioso, who was no great judge of character, suspected (or was led to believe) that Richard of Molise, rather than Stephen of Perche, was having an affair with Margaret.

597. This passage implies that Falcandus (ibid) himself did not believe the rumor, which (unfortunately) has made its way into what little has ever been written about Margaret's character: *Qui, cum primum mente dubia vacillaret, dehinc ab ipsis rei principibus qui confinxerant ea cumulatius eadem audiens, plenam hiis quae sibi dicta fuerant fidem adhibuit, relictoque cancellario, consiliis eorum adhesit, quod inde suaderent se facturum pollicitus.*

598. The knights were Christians; most of the archers were Muslims.

599. Falcandus presents the conspiracy of Caïd Richard as a fact.

600. What little was left of this edifice in modern times was completely destroyed by the earthquake of 1908.

601. Neither Falcandus nor Romuald give a specific date for the supposed consecration. For papal approval, see the letters from Pope Alexander III in *ITP,* volume 10, page 232, entries 29 and 30. A charter Stephen subscribed at Messina in March 1168 refers to him simply as "bishop-elect" of Palermo, *datum Messane per manus Stephani Panormitane ecclesie electi et Regii Cancellarii,* for which see *DNS,* pages 101-102, document 44.

602. For a transcription see White, Lynn Townsend, *Latin Monasticism in Norman Sicily* (1938), pages 266-267, document 26. The date (and the year of young William's reign) is very clear from the text: *Anno dominice incarnationis millesimo centesimo sexagesimo septimo, mense novembris, indictionis prime, regni vero domini Guillelmi dei gratia gloriosissimi et magnificentissimi Regis Siciliae, Ducatus Apuliae, et Principatus Capuae, anno secundo feliciter.*

603. Hugh Falcandus, chapter 52. This man was Robert of Lauro, sometime high justiciar of northern Apulia. He came to Messina with his son, Roger of Tricarico.

604. See manuscript S in the Sources.

605. See manuscript V in the Sources. However, it is unclear whether the Messinians petitioning Margaret were referring to these same taxes.

606. Hugh Falcandus, chapter 53. For the title see note 581. This was the "mayor" of Messina.

607. Here it should be remembered that in the twelfth century the death penalty was the norm in Europe.

608. Falcandus (chapter 53) uses the phrase *Graecos et Longobardos,* literally "Greeks and Lombards" but actually the native Messinians, many of whom spoke Greek, and the (non-Norman) barons from the Italian mainland who had settled in eastern Sicily.

609. From Falcandus (loc. cit.): *Quod ubi regina cognovit, anxia cepit distrahi sollicitudine multaeque fluctuationis aestibus agitari. Durius enim in fratrem decernere quippiam tantamque praesumptionem animadversione digna punire crudele quidem tyrampnidique proximum videbatur, sed et si fratri parceret, intelligebat cancellario non dubium capitis periculum imminere, neque posse proditores ab eo quod coeperant absterreri; simulque considerabat indignum eum esse, cui fraternus exhiberetur affectus, qui sororis posthabita reverentia, qui tot eius beneficiorum immemor id solum agere decrevisset quod ad eius dedecus et infamiam non ambigeret retorquendum, multisque rebellandi praebens materiam, regni pacem et quietem niteretur modis omnibus impedire. Huic ergo deliberationi justa succedens indignatio, fraternam ab eius animo clementiam exturbavit, placuitque, congregata curia, comitem sollemni judicio conveniri, convictumque vel confessum interim in aliqua munitionum servari, donec eius indicio ceteri possent proditores agnosci.*

610. Most of these knights were from Navarre and the other kingdoms of northeastern Spain.

611. Falcandus refers to these subjects as "Greeks," because (like the Messinians) the majority of Calabrians spoke this language and frequented Greek Orthodox churches.

612. This was Bartholomew of Lusci, whose lands near Lecce were placed in the care of Giles, the abbot of Venosa (who probably came from Navarre).

613. Bohemond of Manopello (and Tarsia), who had accompanied Henry to Palermo and befriended Stephen of Perche, was the son of another Bohemond (who died after 1156) briefly imprisoned by King William I for allegedly usurping royal lands. See also note 595.

614. The account by Falcandus is, in itself, insufficient as an analysis of the case against Richard of Molise, which probably involved more than what is known to us. Superficially, the accusations seem to reflect little more than the longstanding grievances against him.

615. Little is known of the duel, or if it even took place, but Walter of Moac (Modica) was a master constable by 1171 and he subscribed the dower charter of Joanna of England in 1177.

616. See manuscript T in the Sources.

617. See manuscript J in the Sources.

618. See *DNS,* pages 101-102, document 44, where Stephen of Perche is identified as "bishop-elect of Palermo," not as a consecrated bishop. This abbey, the so-called *Badiazza* located in the San Rizzo region of the Peloritan Mountains overlooking Messina, was formerly known as *Santa Maria della Valle* (Saint Mary of the Valley), being a Greek Orthodox monastery that became Roman Catholic. In Margaret's time it was a center for the covert forgery of charters. Resembling a fortress, the structure suffered damage in the earthquake of 1908 but was restored and is still impressive.

619. Specifically, these were periodic tithes (which might be paid in kind) and an annual monetary tribute. The point was that in Sicily these taxes were regulated, whereas in the baron's native France they were left more to the discretion of the local feudatory. It is implied, and indeed suggested by the available evidence, that the serfs of Norman Sicily were treated better than those in France and other regions during the same period.

620. Robert of San Giovanni and Roger of Tiron.

621. This comes to us from Falcandus. Romuald does not mention the plot explicitly but does tell us that Matthew of Aiello and Caïd Richard were accused of treason.

622. These knights were already in jail by the time Matthew of Aiello was accused, shortly thereafter. According to Falcandus (chapter 55): *Inde capti sunt plerique milites, quos de morte ipsius jusiurandum praestitisse constabat.* The imprisoned knights probably knew the identities of the plot's three organizers; this may have been the basis for Stephen of Perche implicating Matthew of Aiello and Caïd Richard.

623. Falcandus states that Matthew of Aiello "exceeded the others in cleverness," *qui ceteris astutia praeminebat* (implying that Matthew was crafty and conniving). Romuald uses the phrase "sage and prudent," *sapiens et discretus* (thereby implying that the *familiare* was intelligent and probably loyal). This is a good example of the chroniclers describing the same person in somewhat contrasting terms; indeed, Romuald adds that Matthew was arrested "for no reason," *sine causa capi fecit.*

624. Falcandus (chapter 55): *Cumque regina nullatenus consentiret ut Richardus gaytus caperetur.* The chronicler then reiterates that Caïd Richard was a chief instigator.

625. Estimates of the population of the Kingdom of Sicily before 1200 are based to a great extent on such factors as taxation, agriculture, military capacity and the number of churches and mosques, as the Normans undertook nothing like a general census and there were many peasants but (compared to most European kingdoms) few serfs to be counted. Palermo, Messina, Bari and Salerno were quite large by contemporary standards. Although there is a dearth of demographic information for this period, it seems unlikely that there were more than three million people living in the *Regnum* in Margaret's lifetime. For comparison, this may have been roughly equal to the combined population of England and Wales during the twelfth century. Italy, with its wealthy northern communes, was rather highly (and densely) populated compared to most parts of Europe.

626. There were, of course, other sympathizers, such as Roger of Gerace, an important baron, and William of Leluce.

627. This part of Sicily had once boasted a large Berber population.

628. This is the thesis advanced by Falcandus. Romuald, conversely, does not speculate in this

regard. Not only is Falcandus the principal source for most of the events that transpired at Messina in 1168, for most of these he is the *only* source.

629. Romuald states mid-April (a week after Easter) for the release of Henry of Montescaglioso, but a necrology at Chartres gives 6 April for the death of Odo which, according to Falcandus, occurred a day after Henry arrived in Messina; see *Recueil des Historiens de la France, Obituaires de la Province de Sens* (Diocese of Chartres), volume 2 (1906), page 55. Andrew, the governor of Messina, probably sent a messenger to Stephen of Perche explaining the situation.

630. This important point overlooked by many historians is crucial to the analysis of subsequent events. Henry was not acting against the king or regent, but against the chancellor.

631. Like the palace, this edifice was destroyed long ago. What little of it survived into recent centuries was leveled by the earthquake of 1908.

632. For Rometta see Chapter 1.

633. Romuald does not mention the incident explicitly, and Falcandus refers to "promises," using the Latin cognate *promissis*, rather than monetary bribes.

634. Using the zodiac as a reference, Godfrey Malaterra (book 3, chapter 18) states that in the summer of 1079 Roger I took control of the town following a six-month siege: *Sextus erat mensis quo fervidus eminet ensis. Piscibus obsedit servente leone recedit.*

635. See note 614.

636. See Haskins, Charles Homer, "Adelard of Bath," *The English Historical Review*, volume 26, number 103 (July 1911), pages 491-498; Kraye, Jill (editor), *Adelard of Bath* (1987); Cochrane, Louise, *Adelard of Bath: The First English Scientist* (1994); Burnett, Charles, *Adelard of Bath: Conversations with His Nephew* (1998); Wallis, Peter (editor), *Adelard of Bath: The First English Scientist* (2013); Webb, Simon, *The Life and Times of Adelard of Bath* (2019). More generally, Carey, Hilary, *Courting Disaster: Astrology at the English Court and University in the Later Middle Ages* (1992), pages 10, 27-31.

637. William's affinity for astrology was later observed by Ibn Jubayr.

638. We cannot know precisely what it was that influenced the astrologers in casting and interpreting William's horoscope. The most noteworthy astronomical event of this period was the annual Lyrids meteor shower; the more spectacular solar eclipse of 9 April 1168 was not visible over Sicily.

639. Here the term *Lombard* refers in some cases to the southern peninsular Italians (such as Salernitans) who settled in Sicily with the Normans and spoke an early form of Neapolitan (see Chapter 24 and note 908). The towns mentioned by Falcandus are Capizzi, Maniace, Nicosia, Randazzo and Vicari, but there were others having large Lombard (northern Italian) populations that arrived with Adelaide del Vasto, namely San Filadelfo (San Fratello), Sperlinga, Aidone and Butera (see notes 42 and 132).

640. This estimate comes to us from Falcandus, and it may be based on a larger number of towns than the five he mentioned (q.v. the preceding note).

641. Falcandus and Romuald differed in their perceptions of Matthew of Aiello.

642. The master castellan was Ansaldo; Constantine was his assistant. Little is known of either one.

643. Roger of Avellino was a distant kinsman of the king; the ancestors of John of Lavardin held a manor on the Loire.

644. According to Falcandus (chapter 55), *ubi nemini liceat armis se vel militibus praemunire*, although there would have been exceptions to the rule. The analogy to the Rubicon, of course, refers to Julius Caesar crossing that Italian river with an armed legion in 49 BC (BCE) on his way to Rome, making him and his troops outlaws.

NOTES

645. Falcandus (loc. cit.) refers to "four hundred" servants, *qui fere quadringenti erant,* a number that probably included the guards present during the day shift.

646. Scion of a Norman family, crusading Robert of Meulan was the nephew of Robert of Leicester, sometime justiciar of Henry II of England; like Stephen of Perche, he was related to Rotrou of Rouen.

647. Outside what is now Porta Nuova, into the present Piazza Indipendenza.

648. *Tunc vero sagittarii curiae, qui nunquam in seditionibus ubi lucri spes appareat ultimi consueverunt occurrere.*

649. Falcandus mentions Carbonello and Bohemond of Manopello, William of San Severino, Alduin Cantuese, Hugh Lupino (now wed to Clementia of Catanzaro, with whom Matthew Bonello had flirted), and Robert of Meulan (who lived until 1203).

650. There was a church and some buildings in what is now Piazza delle Vittorie between the palace and cathedral.

651. Robert of Tiron, who held several manors in Sicily, was a competent knight and trusted advisor of Stephen of Perche.

652. According to Falcandus (chapter 55): *Interea cum rex ad matris petitionem e palatio vellet exire ut ab obsidione populum amoveret, Mattheus notarius ceterique conspiratores qui aderant prohibuerunt egredi, dicentes non esse tutum illuc accedere, nam sagittarum ac lapidum circumquaque turbinem agitari.*

653. Stephen of Perche died in Jerusalem the following year; see William of Tyre, book 20, chapter 3.

654. Over the next few years, the *familiares* rarely acted in unison, although we find one or another (or several at a time) witnessing royal decrees throughout the remainder of the regency. They did not all serve at the same time, and some were more influential than others. However, we find several of them witnessing the dower charter of Joanna of England in 1177.

655. As the "council of regency" consisting of numerous *familiares* did not survive in that form into William's majority, it did not become an enduring element in royal rule.

656. For English common law under Henry II, Hudson, Richard, "The Judicial Reforms of the Reign of Henry II," *Michigan Law Review,* volume 9, number 5 (Ann Arbor 1911), pages 385-395. For common law in Sicily see Makdisi, John, op. cit. at note 51. For comparison, in 1168 England did not have a "statutory" legal code quite so complex or complete as the Assizes of Ariano; however, the Charter of Liberties (issued by Henry I in 1100) is regarded by some scholars as an early precursor of the *Magna Carta.*

657. Like Stephen of Perche, Gilbert of Gravina ended up in the Holy Land. This is stated by Falcandus; for concordance see *Annales Casinenses,* entry for 1168, page 312.

658. Hugh of Catanzaro (Hugh Lupino) was one of the signatories of the dower charter of Joanna of England.

659. Falcandus (chapter 55): *Sed quia nullius consilii audaciae homo erat ut vel occulte paraturus insidias, vel ex praecipiti magnum ausurus aliquid timeretur, maluerunt ei parcere, sperantes eo ipso posse reginae indignationem aliquatenus mitigari.*

660. For the consecration see note 591. For John's policy regarding the Jews see *Codice Diplomatico dei Giudei di Sicilia* (1884), volume 1, part 1, document 15, page 12; this charter was issued in December 1168.

661. Boson was Bishop of Cefalù until his death in 1172.

662. For these letters: *Epistolae Sancti Thomae Cantuariensis,* volume 1, document number 192, pages 392-394 (translated supra at note 573); document number 193, pages 394-395; document number 150, pages 319-320. See also Giles, John, *The Life and Letters of Thomas à Becket,* letters 24-25, pages 303-305.

663. For the name sometimes attributed to Walter see note 2.

664. The queen bore the indelible memory of how years earlier, during the revolt that claimed the life of her son, Walter was one of the opportunists who exploited the public sentiment of the moment to advocate the abdication of her husband.

665. Walter may also have had another motive in asserting his influence in southern Sicily, as his brother, Bartholomew, became Archbishop of Agrigento in 1171.

666. Hugh Falcandus (chapter 55): *His accedebat quod Petrus Caietanus romanae curiae subdiaconus certissime promiserat electionem hanc nihil roboris habituram, septingentasque auri uncias opera studioque reginae acceperat romano pontifici deferendas.*

667. The dating is obvious from several charters referring to Walter as "archbishop-elect." See, for example, the charter issued in February 1169 permitting the construction of a small convent by Matthew Aiello, in *DNS,* number 47 (pages 109-111); more at note 674.

668. The description suggests the earthquake's magnitude at approximately 8.0 on the Richter scale.

669. The greater part of this description comes to us from Falcandus, although a few details were reported by Romuald. See also the letters of Peter of Blois in *Petri Blesensis Opera Omnia,* number 46 on pages 138-140 and number 93 on pages 290-291.

670. Much of the apse survived, and it is the only part of the original structure standing today.

671. This is the view of Ibn Jubayr, who visited Sicily late in 1184. Though recorded years after the event, the quote seems to have been widely known and is probably not merely apocryphal.

672. See letter 46 in *Petri Blesensis Opera Omnia,* pages 138-140, written following the murder of Thomas Becket.

673. See note 653 supra. Stephen's death is the last event mentioned by Hugh Falcandus (chapter 50): *Dum igitur adversus ea que accidere poterant multis se consiliis et artibus premunirent, repente de morte cancellarii certissimus ad curiam rumor perlatus, et regine prorsus animum deiecit, et partem contrariam in id roboris ac securitatis evexit ut nichil sibi deinceps estimarent difficultatis ac periculi formidandum.*

674. See note 667. This grants Matthew of Aiello the right to establish a convent for nuns on his property on high ground in Palermo's Saqaliba district (corrupted into *Carrabule* in the Latin text). Completed two years later, this was the Benedictine convent that came to be known as "Saint Mary of the Latins," and later "Saint Mary of the Chancellor," erected along what is now Via del Celso between Vicolo Ragusi and the aptly-named Vicolo del Gran Cancelliere (a school now stands on the site). This charter was sealed with the prestigious gold seal reserved for use with the most important royal documents, typically those addressing questions of policy, diplomacy or the general populace.

675. *DNS,* number 48 (pages 111-112). This confirms a privilege granted to the Monastery of the Holy Savior of Mount Calanna, located near Alcara li Fusi (although Mount Calanna itself lies along the slopes of Mount Etna); a Sicilian saint, Nicholas Politi, was interred there in 1167. The charter of May 1169 is one of many that reflects the Latinization of Sicily's Greek Orthodox monasteries; the principal abbey at Calanna, where some icon frescos were discovered and restored in 2014, came to be known as Saint Mary "del Rogato."

676. This was issued at Benevento on 22 June 1169. See *ITP,* volume 10, pages 232-233, entry 32.

677. Ibid, page 233, entry 33.

678. Manuscript E in the Sources.

679. See, for example the charter of October 1170, in *DNS,* number 54 (pages 124-126).

680. *The Life and Letters of Thomas à Becket,* volume 2, page 201.

681. Ibid.

NOTES

682. This is the consensus of scholars based on the available evidence; no explicit statement (such as a letter) in support of Thomas Becket by Margaret survives.

683. Ref. note 679.

684. This is the opinion of chroniclers such as Peter of Eboli; Peter was sometimes critical of Matthew of Aiello. Yet both *familiares* became fixtures at court throughout William's reign; Walter lived until 1190, Matthew until 1193.

685. This narrative is not intended as a detailed biography. See the Sources for contemporary records, and the books by Duggan and Barber on the lives of (respectively) Thomas Becket and Henry II. Among those who wrote about Becket shortly after his death are John of Salisbury, Herbert of Bosham and Alan of Tewkesbury. Accounts of his death appear in the chronicles of Roger of Howden, Ralph Diceto and others.

686. This church, whose construction was begun by William the Conqueror in 1087, was completed in the Gothic style in 1314 (sic). It was destroyed by the Great Fire in 1666, after which the present cathedral was erected.

687. The source of this account is William Fitzstephen's biography of Thomas Becket.

688. Ranulf of Glanville later wrote a detailed summary of these laws, the *Tractatus de Legibus et Consuetudinibus Regni Angliae*.

689. There may have been Maliki influences that arrived via Sicily. See note 356 supra.

690. Except for a single statute protecting church property, the emphasis of this simple proclamation of Henry I was the guarantee of baronial rights (see also note 656). Other pre-existing laws were known, if rarely applied during the reign of Henry II. Written around 1115, the *Leges Henrici Primi* (Laws of Henry I) was a legal treatise that sought to compile the entire body of law that existed in England. This was later superseded by Glanville's treatise (see note 688). Theobald of Bec, as Archbishop of Canterbury, advocated the study of canon law and Roman law, and to that end he brought Vacarius of Mantua, a leading scholar, from Bologna to teach it in England. Vacarius founded the law school at Oxford. See Re, Edward, "The Roman Contribution to the Common Law," *Fordham Law Review*, number 447 (New York 1961), pages 447-494.

691. The primacy of the Archbishop of Canterbury was challenged by the Archbishop of York in 1118, and in Henry's reign both archiepiscopal sees claimed it. (See also note 228.)

692. See *Select Charters*, pages 135-140.

693. Ibid, pages 140-146.

694. This was the kind of trial requested by Walter of Moac in Sicily when accused of treason in 1168.

695. Accounts of this encounter come to us from Herbert of Bosham and Alan of Tewkesbury.

696. Henry the Young King lived from 1155 to 1183, predeceasing his father.

697. For methods used to determine the beginning of the year during this period see Poole, op.cit., pages 41-47.

698. For methods used to determine the beginning of the year during this period see Poole, Reginald, *Medieval Reckonings of Time* (1918), pages 41-47.

699. Romuald of Salerno, year 1171.

700. Richard of San Germano, whose chronicle begins in 1189, uses this phrase verbatim, adding that the great men of the realm referred, in the first instance, to these two courtiers: *His duobus, quasi duabus columnis firmissimis, omnes regni magnates obsequendo adhaeserant, cum per eos quicquid a curia regia peterent, facilius impetrarent*. This may be an accurate description for the last years of the reign of William II, but it is only a retroactive (and anachronistic) characterization;

being born in peninsular Italy around 1165, Richard did not have a firsthand knowledge of Margaret's regency.

701. *DNS,* number 56 (pages 127-128).

702. For most of the information presented about Benjamin of Tudela in this chapter, see the translation by Marcus Nathan Adler, which is based on three manuscripts, and the book by Adolf Asher (both in Sources).

703. Today the synagogue site is marked by a church, San Nicolò da Tolentino, whilst the mikveh is preserved under the Jesuit cloister of Casa Professa.

704. The text of a charter issued at Palermo on 27 November 1171 in Greek and Latin begins (in both versions) with Margaret's name and in the latter language refers to the queen as *Margarita dei gratia regina mater domini regis,* a formula that differs, if only very slightly, from that used in most royal charters issued until this time. (See manuscript K in the Sources.) The subtle variation in wording may reflect Margaret's new status in view of her son reaching the age of majority, or it may be nothing more than a stylistic choice by the scrivener writing the text. In either case, we know that by the spring of 1172 William was acting on his own, as when (in April) he confirmed to the Archbishop Walter of Palermo the prerogative of trying adulterers; see manuscript F in sources, also Mongitore, Antonino, *Bullae, Privilegia et Instrumenta Panormitane Metropolitanae Ecclesiae Regni Siciliae Primariae* (1734), pages 46-48.

705. Most of the details about Maria's planned arrival at Taranto come to us from Romuald of Salerno, year 1172.

706. With the Compromise of Avranches (May 1172), Henry II of England promised to go on crusade. He also swore to guarantee papal legal jurisdiction in his kingdom in certain cases, effectively renouncing some of the rights he had obtained through the legislation that led to the conflict with Thomas Becket. The king was absolved of any guilt for Becket's death.

707. From Henry Riley's *Annals of Roger de Hoveden,* volume 1 (1853), pages 368-369: To Henry, by the grace of God the illustrious King of the English, Duke of Normandy and Aquitaine, and Count of Anjou, William, by the same grace King of Sicily, Duke of Apulia and Prince of Capua, wishes the enjoyment of health, and the desired triumph in victory over his foes. On the receipt of your letter, we learned a thing of which indeed we cannot without the greatest astonishment make mention, how that, forgetting the ordinary usages of humanity and violating the law of nature, the son has risen in rebellion against the father, the begotten against the begetter. The bowels have been moved to intestine war, the entrails have had recourse to arms, and, a new miracle taking place, quite unheard of in our times, the flesh has waged war against the blood, and the blood has sought means how to shed itself. And, although for the purpose of checking the violence of such extreme madness, the inconvenience of the distance does not allow of our power affording any assistance, still, with all the loving kindness we possibly can, the expression of which, distance of place does not prevent, sincerely embracing your person and honour, we sympathize with your sorrow, and are indignant at your persecution, which we regard as though it were our own. However, we do hope and trust in the Lord, by whose judgment the judgments of kings are directed, that He will no longer allow your sons to be tempted beyond what they are able or ought to endure; and that He who became obedient to the Father even unto death, will inspire them with the light of filial obedience, whereby they shall be brought to recollect that they are your flesh and blood, and, leaving the errors of their hostility, shall acknowledge themselves to be your sons, and return to their father, and thereby heal the disruption of nature, and that the former union, being restored, will seal the bonds of natural affection.

708. The foundation date of Maniace (1172) is given in the *Annales Siculi,* in *RIS,* volume 5 (edited by Muratori, Lodovico, 1774, reprint Bologna 1928), page 116. See also the charters of Nicholas, Archbishop of Messina, in March 1174 (in *Catalogo Illustrato,* page 7); Theobald, Archbishop of Monreale, in April 1177 (ibid, page 14); Nicholas, Archbishop of Messina, in May 1178 (ibid, pages 15-16). For a detailed summary of sources, see White, Lynn Townsend, *Latin Monasticism in Norman Sicily,* pages 146-148. See also Radici, Benedetto, "Il Casale e l'Abbazia di Santa Maria di Maniace," *Archivio Storico Siciliano* (Palermo 1909), pages 1-104.

NOTES

709. See the charter of March 1174 cited in note 708; also manuscripts G and U in Sources.

710. See *Catalogo Illustrato,* pages 15-16;

711. Saladin advanced on several fronts over the next decade; he conquered Jerusalem in 1187.

712. William of Tyre, book 21, chapter 3; al Athir, *BAS,* volume 1, chapter 35, pages 495-499.

713. To cite just a few specific examples, Judith of Evreux endowed her brother's abbey at Saint Euphemia in Calabria and Constance Hauteville founded Saint John's Abbey at Fiore in the Sila Mountains, later endowed by her daughter-in-law, Constance of Aragon. Sibylla of Acerra and her consort, Tancred, were patrons of Saints Nicholas and Catald at Lecce. Elisabeth of Bavaria endowed Saint Mary (a Carmelite basilica) in Naples in memory of her fallen son, Conradin, and, with her second husband, the Cistercian monastery at Stams in Tyrol. Further afield, Sancha of Castile founded Santa María de Sigena in Aragon in 1183, and her daughter, Constance, resided there before marrying Frederick II. Although she did not herself found Fontevrault, Eleanor of Aquitaine was a notable benefactress and, in death, so was her daughter, Joanna, widow of William II of Sicily and then wife of Raymond VI of Toulouse. Joanna's sister, Leonor (Eleanor) of England, founded Santa María la Real de las Huelgas with her husband, Alfonso VIII of Castile, in 1187. To the east, Melisende of Jerusalem, who was descended from the same dynasty as Beatrice of Rethel, the third wife of Roger II, founded and endowed the Benedictine convent of Saints Mary and Martha at Bethany (now Al-Eizariya) near the tomb of Saint Lazarus; she died there in 1161. Urraca of León and Castile was a patron of the Basilica of San Isidore in León.

714. Margaret of l'Aigle (see Table 14). The charter is conserved in the Gran Cartulario de la Catedral de Pamplona; *El Libro Redondo,* folio 61 recto. For a transcription see *Colección Diplomática de la Catedral de Pamplona* (edited by José Goñi Gaztambide, 1997), volume 1, page 173.

715. See Horn, Walter, "On the Origins of the Medieval Cloister," *Gesta,* volume 12, number 1 (1973), pages 13-52.

716. See manuscript M in Sources, also the papal charter of 1174 at note 164 supra. Numerous records attest to the details of the foundation of this monastery and diocese and its subsequent status. See, for example, *ITP,* volume 10, pages 272-281; also *Catalogo Illustrato,* pages 6-32. For a list of additional original sources, see White, Lynn Townsend, *Latin Monasticism in Norman Sicily,* pages 132-145.

717. That an Arab village near the site of Monreale Abbey was called *Ba'lat* or *Ba'lara* is open to question. The claim that a Greek Orthodox chapel was already located on the site of Monreale's *duomo* is based on an erroneous reading of the phrase *super sanctam Kuriacam,* properly "the place overlooking" an existing church (not literally "on top of" it) in William's charter of August 1176. See Garufi, Carlo Alberto (editor), *Catalogo Illustrato,* page 11, footnote number 1.

718. From the chronicle of Richard of San Germano: *Quod idem archiepiscopus ad instinctum ipsius cancellarii factum intelligens (nam odio se habebant ad invicem, quamquam se in publico diligere viderentur, et per invidiam detrahentes libenter unus alteri in occulto) hanc suam injuriam et capitis diminutionem patienter portavit ad tempus. Qui tandem processu temporis cum non posset quod factum fuerat per ecclesiam revocare, hoc fieri subdole procuravit.*

719. The letter was written to Archbishop Walter of Palermo in 1177: *Nam quum rex vester bene litteras noverit, rex noster longe litteratior est. Ego enim in litterali scientia facultatus utriusque cognovi. Scitis, quod dominus rex siciliae per annum discipulus meus fuit, et qui a vobis versificatoriae artis primitias habuerat, per industriam et sollicitudinem meam beneficium scientiae plenioris obtinuit.* For the entire letter, see number 66 in *Petri Blesensis Opera Omnia* (edited by Giles, John, 1847), volume 1, pages 192-197.

720. This privilege was granted in late 1174 and repeatedly confirmed over the next few years; see *Catalogo Illustrato,* pages 7-13. Monreale was eventually erected into an archdiocese. Reference is made to it in several subsequent papal bulls and royal decrees (see note 716). In 1174, Alexander III also chartered the monastery of Saint Mary of the Latins erected by Matthew of Aiello in Palermo; see *DNS,* number 64 (pages 155-161).

721. This area is still part of the Archdiocese of Monreale. For an example of some Arab smallholdings in each fortified locality (Jato, Corleone, Calatrasi, Battallario) see *Catalogo Illustrato,* pages 18-20.

722. Located in the forum near the Colosseum, the site of temples dedicated to Roma and Venus is easily identified by the remains of capitals nearly identical to those installed at Monreale.

723. Richard Lionheart, Joanna's brother, mentioned his descent from Melusina in words known to the chronicler Gerald of Wales. See Brewer, John (editor), *Giraldus Cambrensis, De Instructione Principum Libri III* (London 1846), page 154; this is translated in Stevenson, Joseph, *The Church Historians of England* (1858), volume 5, part 1, page 224. A romance written about Richard, *Richard Coeur de Lion,* retold this story, but with Eleanor of Aquitaine (as "Cassodoren, Princess of Antioch'') in the role of Melusina. Though the legends of Melusina are quite old, being known around Europe long before 1100, they are hardly the province of just one dynasty, and a poetic variation of the story was widely propagated only later. For the popular literary version written by Jean d'Arras during the fourteenth century see *Melusine* (1895), translated by Alexander Donald; a competent introduction is Knight, Gareth, *The Book of Melusine of Lusignan in History, Legend and Romance* (2013).

724. Carved from a porphyry column, the sarcophagus of King William I was transferred to Monreale in 1182 and still survives. That of Frederick II in Palermo's cathedral is very similar.

725. This church, restored to its original state, stands amidst what is now a large cemetery. It is known as the site of the Vespers uprising in 1282. For some observations regarding its foundation and Margaret's known role, see White, op. cit. supra, pages 169-170.

726. Founded in France in 1098 as a splinter from the Benedictines, the Cistercians were growing in importance. To some degree, the establishment of a major Cistercian church in Palermo, in the shadow of the rival Benedictines, probably reflected Walter's attempt to assert his own influence in the monastic environment. At all events, as Primate of Sicily Walter was still the senior prelate of the *Regnum.* His brother, Bartholomew, was now Archbishop of Agrigento (see the following note).

727. For the charter of March 1177 exchanging the tithes of the churches of Corleone for episcopal jurisdiction over Baida, a village on the southern edge of the Genoard, see *Catalogo Illustrato,* page 13. Since 1171, Walter's brother, Bartholomew, had been Archbishop of Agrigento, for which see, *exempli gratia,* the charter in *Catalogo Illustrato* (op. cit.), pages 20-21.

728. Not to be confused with the Bishop of Lincoln who died in 1209, the talented William of Blois was the abbot of the monastery of Santa Maria della Matina at San Marco Argentano in Calabria. See Conti, Emanuele, "L'Abbazia della Matina," *Archivio Storico per la Calabria,* volume 35 (Rome 1967), pages 11-30. He was once considered for the bishopric of Catania, an appointment which went to John of Aiello. This rejection probably saved William's life, for John perished in the earthquake of 1169. Despite what some modern historians have written, there is no contemporary evidence that William of Blois was ever the abbot of Maniace; charters issued in 1177 and 1178 refer to the abbot of that monastery as "Timothy" (see *Catalogo Illustrato,* pages 14-16). The confusion probably results from poor interpretation of a phrase in letters from William's brother, Peter, *abbas matinensis,* "abbot of Matina," as if it were *abbas maniacensis,* "abbot of Maniace."

729. William II was probably born in December 1153. For insights into accurate historiography regarding the role of queens, see Earenfight, Theresa, "Without the Persona of the Prince: Kings, Queens and the Idea of Monarchy in Late Medieval Europe," *Gender and History,* volume 19, number 1 (April 2007), pages 1-21.

730. See note 751. A "formal" consecration of the church in 1267 is sometimes cited as "proof" that it was not completed until that date. It is more likely that the event was part of a strategy by Charles I Anjou of Naples, who had recently defeated Manfred of Hohenstaufen at Benevento, to link this personal symbol of the kings of Sicily to him and his dynasty. For the crown's relations with the Sicilian church in 1267, see *SIS,* volume 1 (1733 edition), page

NOTES

406. Similarly, the translation of the heart of King Louis IX to Monreale three years later reflected an effort to gain favor with the Palermitans, who were less than enthusiastic about Charles having made Naples his capital and, by some accounts, mistreating the Sicilian baronage; see the memoir of John of Procida in Mendola, Louis, *Sicily's Rebellion against King Charles* (2015).

731. For Norman movements generally, see Reilly, Lisa, *The Invention of Norman Visual Culture: Art, Politics and Dynastic Ambition* (2020). For the Hohenstaufen movements see Licinio, Raffaele, *Castelli Medievali: Puglia e Basilicata dai Normanni a Federico II e Carlo d'Angio* (1994); Nancarrow, Jane-Heloise, "Normanitas and Memorial Traditions in the Apulian Architecture of Emperor Frederick II," *Mediterranean Studies,* volume 27, number 1 (2019), pages 36-62.

732. For the Venetian treaty, see the *Chronicon Venetum* of Andrea Dandolo in Muratori, Lodovico (editor), *RIS,* volume 12 (1728), page 301: *Rex Vilielmus ducis nuncios alacriter videns, fedus cum eis usque ad XX annos et plus, si de parcium consensu proceserit, composuit, et Venetis in regno negociantibus immunitates contulit, et hec nuncii redeuntes duci referunt, et tunc, omnium conlaudacione, nuncii Emanuelis, iuxta solitum dilaciones exquirentes, licenciati sunt.* Romuald of Salerno alludes to this, and a succinct summary is published in Abulafia, David, *The Two Italies* (1977), page 143. Manuel I of Constantinople seems to have attempted to encourage the Venetians to break this treaty, q.v. Nicetas Choniates, Manuel I section, book 5. The Genoan treaty appears in *Liber Iurium Reipubblicae Genuensis,* book 1, in *Historiae Patriae Monumenta,* volume 7 (Turin, 1854), page 300; ibid page 190 for the treaty of 1156 and page 202 for privileges granted by William I in 1157.

733. See *Margaret, Queen of Sicily,* pages 399-408, for texts drawn from the following sources. Henry Riley's eloquent, Victorian translation of the account of the wedding and the text of the marriage charter (and dower inventory) was published in the *Annals of Roger de Hoveden,* volume 1 (1853), pages 413-417. The *Ymagines Historiarum* of Ralph of Diceto also offers details, such as a letter from William to Henry; see Stubbs, William, *The Historical Works of Master Ralph de Diceto* (1876), volume 1, pages 413-414, q.v. the following note.

734. To Henry, by the grace of God most noble King of England, your friend William, by the grace of God King of Sicily, Duke of Apulia and Prince of Capua, sends greetings. We have received your ambassadors in honor, and we thank you for so kindly receiving the three nobles sent to your court asking for your consent in granting us the hand of your daughter in matrimony. Likewise, your ambassadors have expressed to me your gracious consent. As my ambassadors are authorized to act on my behalf, I did not swear a prior oath to this undertaking, but by this letter I hereby confirm their promises to you. As the ambassadors have explained, we shall send a fleet of galleys to Saint-Gilles to meet your embassy, from there securely transporting your daughter to our court, and I hope that the nuptials can be celebrated as soon as possible. Given at Palermo on the twenty-third of August, 1176.

735. Roger of Howden mentions "a certain palace," an observation similar to that of Romuald of Salerno.

736. Romuald of Salerno, year 1177.

737. Ibid. Romuald's chronicle provides one of the most important accounts of this diplomatic event, and the text of the treaty between the Holy Roman Empire and the Kingdom of Sicily, but there are several others of importance, notably the detailed description by Boso, q.v. Ellis, George (translator), *Boso's Life of Alexander III* (1973), pages 100-111. The text of the treaty: *In nomine Patris et Filii et Spiritus sancti. Amen. Nos Fridericus Dei gratia Romanorum imperator et semper augustus, et Heinricus rex filius noster, interventu venerabilis patris nostri Alexandri Dei gratia summi pontificis et fratrum suorum cardinalium, pro parte nostra et heredum nostrorum paciscimur vobiscum, domine Willelme, eadem gratia illustris rex Siciliae, quod amodo usque ad quindecim annos observabimus vobis et heredibus vestris et universo regno vestro et toti terre dominationis vestrae eram et firmam pacem. Et quod per nos vel per quoslibet alios, mari vel terra, vos predictum illustrem regem et heredes vestros aut regnum vestrum et terram dominationis vestre, sicut prescriptum et determinatum est, usque ad quindecim annos non invademus nec invadere faciemus, nec vobis aut regno vestro et iam dicte terre dominationis vestre*

guerram aliquo modo faciemus. Et ut hec omnia suprascripta firmiter et illibata a nobis supradicto Friderico Dei gratia Romanorum imperatore et semper augusto et Heinrico filio nostro rege et heredibus nostris tam vobis supradicto illustri regi Willelmo, quam heredibus vestris et regno vestro et toti terre dominationis vestre attendantur et obseruentur, nos predictus imperator bona fide, sine fraude et malo ingenio, in presentia beatissimi patris nostri papae Alexandri et cardinalium et legatorum vestrorum, Romoaldi venerabilis Salernitani archiepiscopi et Roggerii egregii comitis Andriae, et principum ac fidelium nostrorum a comite Henrico de Diessa in anima nostra supra sancta Dei evangelia et sanctorum reliquias iurari fecimus, et Henricum filium nostrum per interpositam dignam personam in anima sua id ipsum iurare faciemus usque ad medium futurum Septembrem indictionis undecime. Et principes nostros idem iurare fecimus, videlicet Christianum Maguntinum archiepiscopum, Arnoldum Treverensem archiepiscopum, Corradum Guormaciensem electum, Godefridum imperialis aule cancellarium, Guorwinum protonotarium, markyonem Theodericum de Lusiz, Florentium comitem Holandiae, comitem Dedonem de Groyx, comitem Henricum de Diessa, comitem Robertum de Durna. Ad huius autem pacti, promissionis et iuramenti nostri et Heinrici regis filii nostri et principum nostrorum memoriam et inviolabile firmamentum presens privilegium nostrum per manus Guortwini protonotarii nostri scribi fecimus, et imperiali sigillo nostro aureo sigillatum et predictorum principum iuramento communitum vobis suprascripto illustri regi Willelmo fecimus assignari. Anno dominicae incarnationis millesimo centesimo septuagesimo septimo, mense Augusti, decima indictione.

738. Romuald of Salerno, loc. cit. supra. Italy's northern communes, being under imperial authority, were vitally important to Frederick Barbarossa. Beyond their strategic significance, they were far wealthier than most of the cities he ruled in what are now Germany and Austria, thus providing a greater tax base. Frederick's alliance with the Kingdom of Sicily eliminated a potential threat from the south.

739. Romuald's original text uses the generic term *armigero* for an armed man of noble rank: *Qui accepta a rege licentia, reversi sunt, quodam regis armigero eos, ut moris est, usque ad fines regni deducente.*

740. This case was somewhat similar, though not identical, to the kinds of circumstances that led to the jurisdictional dispute between Henry II and Thomas Becket, but Romuald of Salerno supported William's decision to punish the murderous monks.

741. For historians, Romuald's departure leaves a dearth of detailed information from chroniclers present at court after 1178. As an example of the kind of sources consulted for subsequent periods, a charter of March 1180 given by William II and witnessed by Archbishop Walter, Matthew of Aiello and Richard Palmer indicates Palermo as its place of issuance. See *DNS,* pages 171-172, number 71. For a good summary of the Third Lateran Council see Summerlin, Danica, *The Canons of the Third Lateran Council of 1179: Their Origins and Reception* (2019).

742. This palace is located along what is now Corso Calatafimi.

743. See note 26. We do not have it on reliable authority that William fathered children even outside wedlock. The average age of menarche in Europe in Joanna's time was around thirteen; see Amundsen, Darrel, and Diers, Carol Jean, "The Age of Menarche in Medieval Europe," *Human Biology,* number 45, volume 3 (Detroit 1973), pages 363-369.

744. See *The Chronicle of Robert of Torigni,* page 285 (folio 229 in the manuscript); also Ali ibn al-Athir al-Jazari, *al-Kamil fi at-Tarikh,* in Amari, Michele, *BAS,* volume 1, chapter 35, page 499.

745. The church of Mary Magdalene standing today is found within what is now a military complex inside the city walls near Porta Nuova. Not all of its royal tombs survive. See Garofalo, Luigi, *Tabularium Regiae ac Imperialis Capellae Collegiatae Divi Petri in Regio Panormitano Palatio* (1835), number 17, pages 39-40.

746. *Anonymous Cassino Chronicle* (in *Cronisti e Scrittori Sincroni Napoletani,* volume 1), year 1182.

747. For more about Majorca and the complexities of western Mediterranean politics during this period, see David Abulafia's study, *A Mediterranean Emporium: The Catalan Kingdom of Majorca* (1994).

NOTES

748. This was described by several chroniclers. For the most complete account see William of Tyre, book 22, chapters 10-13; also Nicetas Choniates, Andronikos section, book 1. A fine general study is Nicol, Donald, *Byzantium and Venice: A Study in Diplomatic and Cultural Relations* (1988).

749. William's presence at Capua in January is attested by a charter issued there; see *DNS*, pages 188-190, number 76. For his visit to Cassino in February, see *Annales Casinenses*, entry for 1183, page 313.

750. Archbishop Walter, Matthew of Aiello, and Richard Palmer (by now Archbishop of Messina) all subscribed the charter issued at Capua. This was logical, as the royal court was, in effect, wherever the king was.

751. This is attested by several surviving charters dated February 1183. See, in particular, *ITP*, volume 10, pages 276-278, entries number 6-11; *Catalogo Illustrato*, pages 22-24.

752. *Catalogo Illustrato*, pages 25-26.

753. Adenolfo was executed in 1184 or 1185. See *Anonymous Cassino Chronicle*, year 1185; *Fossanova Chronicle/Annales Ceccanenses*, year 1186. (It is worth noting that the bandit Ghino di Tacco, the "Italian Robin Hood," was born during the next century.)

754. *Hic regina iaces regalibus edita cunis Margarita tibi nomen, quod moribus unis, regia progenies per reges ducta propago, uxor regis eras et nobilitatis imago, si taceam quibus ipsa reples preconia mundum, regem Wilelmum satis est peperisse secundum, undecies centum decies octo tribus annis. Post hominem Christum migras necis eruta dampnis. Lux ea qua populis dant petri festa catene. His te de nebulis tulit ad loca lucis. Amene.* In the necrology of Saint Matthew, published in 1922, Carlo Alberto Garufi makes an unconvincing argument for another date of Margaret's death based on the citation of inaccurate information; here his opinion differed from, among others, that of Rocco Pirro, who, writing in the seventeenth century, considered the epitaph above Margaret's tomb accurate despite a seemingly contradictory charter. Even if a few years passed before the epitaph was produced, it should be remembered that masses were celebrated annually to mark the date of Margaret's death, and there were people living, including her son and daughter-in-law, who remembered it.

755. *Anonymous Cassino Chronicle*, year 1184.

756. For the charter of January 1179, subscribed by thirteen monks, see Grossi, Giovanni Battista, *Catana Sacra* (1654), pages 98-99.

757. See Broadhurst, Ronald, *The Travels of Ibn Jubayr*.

758. For more about Constance's story see *Queens of Sicily*, pages 381-408; also *Sicilian Queenship*, pages 79-80, 125-128.

759. For the detailed Byzantine account see Nicetas Choniates: Andronikos section, books 1-2; Isaac section, book 1.

760. The nearest contemporary account of the events leading up to the siege seems to be William of Tyre, book 22, chapters 16-30, but see also the following note.

761. See Mas Latrie, Louis, *Chronique d'Ernoul et de Bernard le Trésorier* (1871), pages 178-188; *De Expugnatione Terrae Sanctae per Saladinum, Libellus* in Stevenson, Joseph, *Radulphi de Coggeshall Chronicon Anglicanum* (1875), pages 209-262; Ali ibn al-Athir al-Jazari, *al-Kamil fi at-Tarikh*, in Amari, Michele, *BAS*, volume 1, chapter 35, page 499-501. Another source is the account of al-Imad al-Din al-Katib al-Isfahani, a secretary of Saladin.

762. *PCC, Patrologiae Latinae*, volume 202 (1855), columns 1539-1542.

763. Historians have sometimes dated the beginning of construction to 1191. However, after much investigation, the authors favor a slightly earlier date.

764. In 1190, Conrad of Montferrat wed Isabella, daughter of King Amalric of Jerusalem and Maria Comnena, and thus claimed the crown, but he was assassinated in 1192. Maria, Conrad's daughter with Isabella, became Queen of Jerusalem in 1205. See Table 20.

KINGDOM OF SICILY

765. Isaac's suspicions were well-founded. Frederick Barbarossa was making alliances with the Bulgarians and Hungarians who were seeking to annex Byzantine territory. The Germans fought and won a battle against the Byzantines at Philippolis (Plovdiv in present-day Bulgaria) in November 1189, q.v. Niketas Choniates, Isaac section, book 2.

766. *RPR* (1851), charter 10131, dated December 1188, page 876; *PCC, Patrologiae Latinae,* volume 204 (1855), columns 1415-1416; Reusner, Nicolaus, *Epistolarum Turcicarum Variorum et Diversorum Authorum* (1598), pages 16-17. This sets forth the duties of each monarch on the crusade, stating that, *Guilielmus, Rex Siciliae, pacato a piratis mari, annonam ex Sicilia et Apulia provecturis ministravit.*

767. *PCC, Patrologiae Latinae,* volume 204 (1855), column 1486; *ITP,* volume 8, page 56; Mansi, Giovanni Domenico, *Sacrorum Conciliorum,* volume 22 (1776), columns 556-557: *Caritatis amica simplicitas nulis verborum fallaciis, nullis appetit ambiguitatum involucris offuscari. Frequentur igitur est necese ut quae minis plenae dicta videntur et ambiguitatis scrupulos possent sane dicta generare, explanatione veridica clarins elucescant, ea propter benigne in Domino fili, audito quod in magnitudinis tuae praesentia quaestio meta fuerit, utrum ex nostri tenere rescripti colligeretur quod singuli haeredum singulis successoribus fidelitatis praestare debeant hujusmodi iuramentum. Intellecta etiam expositione dilectorum filiorum Arduini in titulo Sanctae Crucis in Jerusalem, et Petri in titulo Sancti Laurentii in Damaso Presbyterorum Cardinalium, Sedis Apostolicae Legatorum, quae ad nos fuit sub sigillorum suorum testificatione transmissa, a sano eorumdem intellectu nolentes aliqatenus dissentire, Serenitati Regiae duximus intimandum, quod cum intentio nostra sit nil intolerabile tibi, nel haerdibus tuis imponere, talitur in hoc titulo tibi duximus respondendum, ut haeredes tui, qui nobis vel alicui successorum nostrorum iuraverint, aliis iurare minime compellantur, catholicis tamen successoribus nostris et hominii et fidelitatis puritatem nihilominus, ac si iurassent, omni tempore teneantur absque tergiversatione aliqua fideliter observare, nisi forte alicui eorum, sicut personae tuae, fuerit hominium de benignitate sedis apostolicae relaxatum, qui tamen non se propterea credit a fidelitatis observatione immunem. Datum Laterani.*

768. The list of rights, prerogatives and territories was lengthy. See *PCC, Patrologiae Latinae,* volume 204 (1855), columns 1385-1390.

769. The fact that Constance was William's designated successor (heiress) is confirmed by the chroniclers Richard of San Germano, Peter of Eboli and Roger of Howden, as well as the author of the *Annales Casinenses.* This was known even to the author of the *Itinerarium Peregrinorum et Gesta Regis Ricardi.* For commentary see Fröhlich, Walter, "The Marriage of Henry VI and Constance of Sicily: Prelude and Consequences," *Anglo Norman Studies 15* (1993), pages 99-125.

770. Specific reference is made to *succession* according to Salic Law, which was actually an entire legal code developed during the reign of the Frankish king, Clovis I, around 500. Agnatic seniority and agnatic primogeniture were principles applied by Charlemagne, not only for royalty but for feudal succession to manors and baronies. As we shall see, female line succession was instituted in the Kingdom of Sicily by Frederick II for feudal property.

771. Tancred and his wife invested in the town of Lecce, erecting such structures as the Benedictine monastery of Saints Nicholas and Catald. Tancred's grandfather (his mother's father), Achard, who had founded the nunnery of Saint John the Evangelist, where Emma, Tancred's mother, later became the abbess.

772. Peter of Eboli, book 1, chapter 6, lines 142-165, *Epistola ad Tancredum.* The sections and verses cited refer to those used in the editions of Giovanni Battista Siragusa (1906) and Francesco De Rosa (2000). In her fine critical edition and translation, *Book in Honor of Augustus* (2012), Gwenyth Hood does not use this system.

773. Peter of Eboli, book 1, chapter 7, lines 166-199, *Spuriosa unctio regni.* Here the infamous physical description of Tancred as a "monster, crime of nature, dwarf, ape and half-man" in lines 185 -187: *Ecce vetus monstrum, nature crimen, aborsum; Ecce coronatur simia, turpis homo. Huc ades Alecto, tristis proclamet Herinis; Exclament Satiri, 'semivir ecce venit.'*

774. Explicit papal references are sparse, but there were no protests from those circles and

NOTES

diplomacy continued into Tancred's reign. Walter was not reprimanded by Celestine III for crowning Tancred, and the pontiff, despite eventually crowning Henry VI emperor and Constance empress, expressed no support for their Sicilian claims. According to Richard of San Germano, year 1189: *Romana in hoc curia dante assensum.*

775. See note 18 for good studies of bastardy. The most important local chronicles of Tancred's reign come to us from two contemporary writers. The work of Richard of San Germano is reasonably objective. That of Peter of Eboli, commissioned by Constance, is highly biased against Tancred.

776. Several interesting papers presented about Tancred at a conference held in Lecce in 1998 were published in *Tancredi Conte di Lecce Re di Sicilia,* edited by Hubert Houben and Benedetto Vetere.

777. For a few exceptions, Peter of Eboli, book 1, chapter 11, lines 292-305.

778. Richard of San Germano, year 1190. The diplomatic record (charters) suggest that most of Roger's official authority was in Apulia, where he sometimes acted as if he were bailiff (governor). See also the following note.

779. Descended from the Ollia family of the knight Warren (from Ouilly-le-Teson in Normandy), mentioned in Chapter 10, Roger obtained Andria in 1168 after Gilbert of Gravina, its former holder, left the kingdom (q.v. Hugh Falcandus, chapters 26 and 55), and he accompanied Romuald of Salerno to Venice to negotiate the Treaty of Venice in 1177. For his royal pretensions, see Cuozzo, Errico, "Ruggiero, Conte d'Andria: Ricerche sulla nozione di regalità al tramonto della monarchia normanna," *Archivio Storico per le Province Napoletane,* number 20 (1981), pages 129-168.

780. Richard of San Germano, year 1190; *Annales Casinenses,* entries for 1190, page 314. Henry "Testa" of Kalden of Pappenheim was imperial marshal for Frederick Barbarossa. Confusion sometimes results from the possibility of a father and son having the same name; if that was the case, it was probably the elder Henry of Kalden who was sent to southern Italy.

781. See *The Historical Works of Ralph de Diceto,* volume 2, page 81.

782. Since our knowledge of the activities of King Richard I in Sicily comes to us from several overlapping sources which often contradict each other in their details (and especially their chronologies), every chronicler offers us a different interpretation of the events. The eyewitness account of Geoffrey of Vinsauf, published in English in *Chronicles of the Crusades* (pages 162-176), is available in the original Latin in the *Itinerarium Peregrinorum* (pages 153-177) edited by William Stubbs. The chronicle of "Benedict of Peterborough" (actually Roger of Howden) in *The Chronicle of the Reigns of Henry II and Richard I,* volume 2 (pages 124-161 passim), edited by William Stubbs based on the Cotton Manuscript, is a fine narrative. A good English translation is found in *The Annals of Roger de Hoveden,* volume 2, by Henry Riley. Other chroniclers, such as William of Newburgh and Ralph of Diceto, address these events to some degree.

783. See *Itinerarium Peregrinorum,* pages 153-157.

784. See *The Chronicle of the Reigns of Henry II and Richard I,* volume 2, page 125. Though taller than average, Richard was dressed casually, like any squire on pilgrimage, and thus not recognized by the local people as royalty. Peasants possessing a falcon is explained by the fact that in this region hawking was not the exclusive prerogative of the aristocracy.

785. *Itinerarium Peregrinorum,* pages 158-163.

786. Ibid, pages 165-166.

787. Ibid, page 163.

788. For details about Bagnara see *The Chronicle of the Reigns of Henry II and Richard I,* volume 2, page 127; *The Annals of Roger de Hoveden,* volume 2, page 158 mentions this and also Philip's interest in the pretty widow (see also note 791).

789. One chronicle reports that later, at Acre, Richard borrowed Joanna's dower funds with the intention of repaying her; see *La Continuation de Guillaume de Tyr,* page 104. A fine analysis is Colette Bowie's paper "To Have and Have Not" (in Sources).

790. *Itinerarium Peregrinorum,* pages 172-173.

791. Philip's wife, Isabella of Hainault, had died earlier in the year. William of Newburgh tells us of a marriage proposal made by Philip to Joanna in 1195; see *Chronicles of the Reigns of Stephen, Henry II and Richard I,* volume 2, page 459.

792. *Itinerarium Peregrinorum,* pages 174-176.

793. Ibid, page 176-177.

794. Part of a tower of this castle is located in Viale Principe Umberto at the Sacrario di Cristo Re, a domed church overlooking the old city.

795. *Itinerarium Peregrinorum,* page 182. An alternate account states that the ladies were shipwrecked.

796. Ibid, pages 183-194; *Chronicle of the Reigns of Henry II and Richard I,* volume 2, pages 162-167.

797. *Itinerarium Peregrinorum,* pages 195-196.

798. *Chronicle of the Reigns of Henry II and Richard I,* volume 2, pages 168-169.

799. *Itinerarium Peregrinorum,* page 182, where we read that: *Eodemque die introduxit ad se in palatium, uxorem suam reginam Angliae, et Siciliae reginam sororem suam.* A good biography of Berengaria is Storey, Gabrielle, *Berengaria of Navarre: Queen of England, Lord of Le Mans* (2022).

800. This incident is reported by the chronicler Baha ad-Din in *The Life of Saladin* (1897), pages 253-254; for a more recent translation see *The Rare and Excellent History of Saladin,* page 154.

801. This is reported by Baha ad-Din in *The Life of Saladin,* pages 310-312, 326; also *The Rare and Excellent History of Saladin,* pages 187-188, 195-196. See also *Suite de la Troisieme Croisade,* pages 334-336.

802. Indeed, the marriage proposal may not even have been tendered. No European chronicler mentions it.

803. The Third Crusade and its vastness of complexities are far too great to consider at length in this volume. The reader is referred to books dedicated to the subject, such as James Reston's *Warriors of God.*

804. There are several contemporary references to this detail. See, for example, *The Annals of Roger de Hoveden,* volume 2, page 197.

805. The coronation is mentioned in numerous sources, such as the *Annales Casinenses,* entries for 1191, pages 314-315; others noted in *RPR* (1851), page 887.

806. *Annales Casinenses,* loc. cit. supra.

807. Ibid.

808. Ibid; also Richard of San Germano, year 1191; Peter of Eboli, chapters 13-14, lines 306-377; *Ferraris Chronicle,* pages 147-148; *Fossanova Chronicle/Annales Ceccanenses,* year 1191.

809. Peter of Eboli, chapter 25, lines 724-741.

810. For Constance's release see, amongst other sources, *Ottonis de Sancto Blasio Chronica,* page 56; *The Annals of Roger de Hoveden,* volume 2, page 254. For Tancred's pact with the papacy, see *MGH, Legum Sectio IV, Constitutiones et Acta Publica Imperatorum et Regum,* volume 1 (1893), pages 592-595.

NOTES

811. For an account from the English perspective, see *The Historical Works of Ralph de Diceto,* volume 2, pages 104, 127-128.

812. Richard's misadventure at the hands of Leopold and Henry has been chronicled by Geoffrey of Vinsauf, Richard of Devize, Roger of Howden, Ralph of Diceto and others.

813. Sometimes Roger III. A summary of Tancred's reign and compilation of his decrees and those of his son (William III) appears in Palumbo, Pier Fausto, *Tancredi Conte di Lecce e Re di Sicilia* (1991); see also note 815.

814. Sometimes William III, who may have been crowned by Tancred as *rex filius.* See the *Anonymous Cassino Chronicle,* year 1194. Contrarily, the entry for 1194 in the *Annales Casinenses* states that young William was crowned *after* Tancred's death, implying that his coronation was overseen by Sibylla.

815. *Tancredi et Willelmi III Regum Diplomata,* page 91.

816. A minor Milanese annal mentions that in 1194 (on her way southward) a pregnant Constance stayed at the Meda convent near Milan: *Et eodem anno dicta Constantia venit in Mediolano, et hospitata fuit in monasterio de Meda et tunc erat graveda de Fedricho.* See *Memoriae Mediolanenses* in *MGH, Scriptorum,* volume 18, page 400. Despite some historians' speculation, we cannot not know if this was, in fact, Constance's first pregnancy, just that it was the only one she carried to term.

817. Although most modern historians maintain that Sibylla left her children at Caltabellotta while she defended Palermo, not every record states this explicitly. See *Anonymous Cassino Chronicle,* year 1194; Peter of Eboli, chapter 34, lines 1230-1255; *PCC,* book 214, section 18; *Fossanova Chronicle/Annales Ceccanenses,* years 1194 and 1195.

818. *Anonymous Cassino Chronicle,* loc. cit. supra; *Annales Casinenses,* entries for 1194 and 1195; Richard of San Germano, year 1194. For Eugenio, son of the John mentioned in Chapter 11, see also Jamison, Evelyn, *Admiral Eugenius of Sicily* (1957).

819. Contemporary chroniclers state that young William was castrated and/or blinded. Whether or not this is factual, it is consistent with what was then current practice. See, in particular, *Ottonis de Sancto Blasio Chronica,* pages 65-66 (states he was blinded); *The Annals of Roger de Hoveden,* volume 2, page 341 (states he was blinded and castrated). He probably died in 1198.

820. For Richard of Acerra see Richard of San Germano, year 1197. For the royal tombs see note 25; this detail is not reported by the local chroniclers, and excavations in the church and its vicinity following the extensive destruction of the Second World War revealed no identifiable vestiges of these tombs. For early charters indicating Tancred's patronage of the Magione and its subsequent possession by Henry VI see Mongitore, Antonino, *Monumenta Historica Sacrae Domus Mansionis SS Trinitatis Militaris Ordinis Theutonicorum Urbis Panormi* (1721), pages 1-14.

821. This coronation was important news across Europe; see, in addition to Richard of San Germano, Peter of Eboli and other sources, *The Annals of Roger de Hoveden,* volume 2, pages 340-341. The population of the Kingdom of Sicily was probably slightly over two million; see note 625.

822. The oft-repeated account of Constance giving birth in a public square before witnesses has been questioned because it does not appear in extant contemporary records. The queen depicted in an illumination in manuscript *Codex Chigi L.VIII.296* (in the Vatican Library), from the chronicle of John Villani, giving birth under a tent with ladies-in-waiting present appears not to be Constance Hauteville but Constance of Aragon, the wife of Frederick II; one notes the coat of arms of Aragon depicted in the rendering. Villani (in book 5, chapter 16 of his *Nuova Cronica* begun in 1308), narrates what seems to be the origin of the tradition: *E troviamo quando la 'mperadrice Gostanza era grossa di Federigo, s'avea sospetto in Cicilia e per tutto il reame di Puglia che per la sua grande etade potesse essere grossa; per la qual cosa quando venne a partorire*

fece tendere uno padiglione in su la piazza di Palermo, e mandare bando che qual donna volesse v'andasse a vederla, e molte ve n'andarono e vidono, e però cessò il sospetto. Pietro Grizio, a historian of Jesi, mentions Frederick's "public" birth in his *Ristretto dell'Istorie di Iesi* (1578), pages 22-23, based on some writings of the local chronicler Angelo Bernardo, *floruit* 1315, whose little-known (and perhaps dubious) work is only partially conserved. Tomaso Baldassini's *Notizie Historiche della Reggia Città di Iesi* (1703), pages 24-26, quotes the Neapolitan historian Giovanni Tarcagnota (1490-1566) and even the Spaniard Pedro Mexía (1497-1551), official court chronicler of Emperor Charles V; on page 142 Baldassini cites the chronicle of Angelo Bernardo.

823. Richard of San Germano, year 1194 (last line in that section): *Tunc imperatrix in Aesia in Marchia filium parit nomine Fredericum.* Peter of Eboli, chapter 43, lines 1363-1388, states (in line 1378) the child's name as "Roger Frederick," *Ex hinc Rogerius, hinc Fredericus eris...* The *Anonymous Cassino Chronicle,* year 1195, states the name as "Frederick Roger or Roger Frederick." In Italy, as elsewhere, he is generally known as "Frederick II" for his ordinal as Holy Roman Emperor; he was also King Frederick I of Sicily. It is only later sources that state *Constantine* as one of his baptismal names.

824. *Ferraris Chronicle,* page 148; Richard of San Germano, years 1195-1196; *Anonymous Cassino Chronicle,* year 1195. Conrad was soon dead, succeeded by Markward of Anweiler. For the travels of Henry VI see Baaken, Katrin, and Baaken, Gerhard, *Die Regesten des Kaiserreiches unter Heinrich VI* (2015), in the *Regesta Imperii* series.

825. *Ferraris Chronicle,* loc. cit. supra; Richard of San Germano, years 1196-1197. Richard of Acerra was executed late in 1196 or early in 1197, reportedly in connection with the baronial convocation at Capua.

826. Constance was *queen regnant* as heiress to the throne and then (following her husband's death) *queen regent* as mother of the future king. In general, a queen in her own right might officially cede her duties to her husband, who would act on behalf *jure uxoris*. In Constance's case, whilst this technically occurred, we find a queen acting in her own name; although many of her decrees identify her as empress, some do not even bear the name of her son. From *Sicilian Queenship,* pages 79-80: Pictorially, Constance's seal is not unlike those used by her father, husband and son, or by monarchs across Catholic Europe. She is depicted enthroned, holding, in her right hand a scepter crowned by a lily or fleur-de-lis as a sign of rule by divine right of the Holy Trinity. This is similar to the representation of her in the illuminated chronicle of Peter of Eboli, where a similar scepter or stem is shown. In the seal, Constance is referred to simply as "Roman Empress and Queen of Sicily," without further equivocation as "queen regnant" or "queen regent." The Latin reads *Constantia dei Gratia Romanorum Imperatrix Semper Augusta et Regina Siciliae.* A well-preserved charter (shown in these pages) issued in April 1196 cedes authority over some serfs. This is perhaps the best-known of Constance's charters, distinguished by its dimensions, state of preservation and the fine condition of its seal, mentioned above.

827. No one German monarch, even the ruler of a large dominion like Saxony or Bavaria, became King of the Germans and then, if he were fortunate, emperor, by hereditary right alone; he needed the approval of the elector princes and bishops. Indeed, there was not, in the true sense, a "capital" of the Holy Roman Empire.

828. *Fossanova Chronicle/Annales Ceccanenses,* year 1195.

829. For the papal bull see *RPR* (1851), charter 10526, pages 900-901. For Henry's expenses and preparations, see his letter to the pope in April 1195 in *MGH, Legum Sectio IV, Constitutiones et Acta Publica Imperatorum et Regum,* volume 1 (1893), pages 514-515. For the crusade in the chronicle of Arnold of Lübeck, see *Arnoldi Chronica Slavorum in Usum Scholarum ex Monumentis Germaniae* (1868), book 5, chapters 26-28, pages 196-209. In September 1197, a force led by Henry of Kalden (see note 780) arrived in the Holy Land with some sixteen thousand men. This "German Crusade" was less than successful, but it motivated future efforts. For a general analysis see Loud, Graham, "The German Crusade of 1197-1198," *Crusades,* volume 13 (2014), pages 143-172.

NOTES

830. The earliest identifiable charter currently known to us was issued at Palermo on 25 June 1195 reiterating ecclesiastical jurisdiction of the Benedictine abbey of Monreale as established by William II. See *Constantiae Imperatricis Diplomata,* document 1, page 40; other decrees of Constance appear in the same compilation, the most complete record of her charters published to date.

831. Niketas Choniates, Alexios Angelos section, book 1; *Ferraris Chronicle,* page 149.

832. A good German source for Henry VI and Philip of Swabia is the chronicle of Burchard of Ursperg, published in Holder-Egger, Osvald (editor), *Burchardi Praepositi Uspergensis Chronicon,* in *Scriptores Rerum Germanicarum in Usum Scholarum,* volume 16 (1916), especially pages 70-101, 108-110.

833. Ibid, page 75. Also *Annales Marbacenses qui Dicuntur,* in *Scriptores Rerum Germanicarum in Usum Scholarum,* volume 9 (1907), pages 66-68.

834. Richard of San Germano, year 1197. An idea, parroted by some, that Constance instigated a revolt against her own husband does not seem to have much substance, though it is very old; see *The Annals of Roger de Hoveden,* volume 2, page 406. The *Ferraris Chronicle* (pages 148-149), brings us this colorful, if dubious, account: In 1197, the emperor subjected the entire kingdom to increased taxes. Some of the barons he mistreated and oppressed went into exile. Henry ordered the burning of the head cantor of the church of Palermo. He commanded that a deacon be drowned in the sea with some nobles. It is said that, when the queen reproved him for this, the emperor angrily threatened her at sword-point and would have killed her were it not for the intervention of Markward of Anweiler. Hearing of these incidents, the Latins and Greeks, as well as Arabs, rebelled against the emperor. But when leaders of the army they gathered learned that the queen was safe, the people were placated and submitted to the emperor.

835. The cause of death is not known but it could have been dysentery; see *Annales Marbacenses* (op. cit. at note 833 supra), page 70.

836. *Burchardi Praepositi Uspergensis Chronicon,* pages 75-78.

837. An informative source from this pontificate is the *Gesta Innocenti III,* or "Deeds of Innocent III" composed by a member of the papal curia before 1210; see Baluze, Etienne, in *Epistolarum Innocenti III,* volume 1 (1682), pages 1-88 (144 chapters); also *PCC, Series Secunda,* volume 214 (1855), columns 387-392. For modern biographies: Sayers, Jane, *Innocent III: Leader of Europe 1198-1216* (1994); Powell, James, *Innocent III: Vicar of Christ or Lord of the World?* (1963).

838. See *Constantiae Imperatricis Diplomata,* documents 41-71, pages 127-281.

839. *Gesta Innocenti III,* chapter 21. For the coronation, *HDF,* volume 1, part 1, pages 8-9; *SIS,* volume 1 (1733 edition), pages 400-401.

840. For example, *PCC, Series Secunda,* volume 214 (1855), columns 387-392 (charters 410-413).

841. *Burchardi Praepositi Uspergensis Chronicon,* in *Scriptores Rerum Germanicarum in Usum Scholarum,* volume 16 (1916), pages 75-88; also *Gesta Innocenti III,* chapter 22.

842. For the text of the forged will, see *Gesta Innocenti III,* chapter 27.

843. Ibid, chapters 23-26; also Richard of San Germano, year 1197.

844. For both papal requests see *PCC, Series Secunda,* volume 214 (1855), columns 20-21. The *Gesta Innocenti III,* chapter 22, reads in part: *Sed et Sibilia, relicta regis Tancredi, cum filiabus suis, ergastulum captivitatus evasit, et in regnum Francorum confugiens, porgenitam suam Gualtero, Brenensi comiti, tradidit in uxorem.*

845. *Constantiae Imperatricis Diplomata,* pages 279-281; Richard of San Germano, year 1198.

846. *RPR,* volume 1: page 38, entry 394; page 41, entry 426; page 42 entry 431; also *HDF,* volume 1, part 1, pages 14-21. Whether the acts by Constance were tantamount to a true renunciation of the legateship is debated (q.v. notes 227 and 840 supra); essentially, they revived the so-called "Concordat of Gravina" negotiated by Tancred in June 1192 and repudiated by Henry VI in 1194. For the Aragonese marriage, see *Constantiae Imperatricis Diplomata,* pages 277-278; this was either Sancha, born in 1186, or Dulcia, born in 1192.

847. There may be a genetic basis for the stereotype that plagued Constance and her son. Recent research suggests that certain traits, such as physical sensitivity to pain, may coincide with the presence of red hair via the recessive MC1R gene, and that this affects personality. See Liem, Edwin, and Joiner, Teresa, et al., "Increased Sensitivity to Thermal Pain and Reduced Subcutaneous Lidocaine Efficacy in Redheads," *Anesthesiology,* number 102 (March 2005), pages 509-514; Pincott, Jena, "Why Are Redheads More Sensitive? Yes, redheads feel more pain," *Psychology Today,* 16 April 2011 (online). Increased susceptibility to melanoma is also indicated.

848. Richard of San Germano, year 1199; *Ferraris Chronicle,* page 150; *Gesta Innocenti III,* chapters 34-35. Markward arrived in Palermo with a Genoan army to depose Walter. For further commentary, Van Cleve, Thomas, *Markward of Anweiler and the Sicilian Regency: A Study of Hohenstaufen Policy in Sicily During the Minority of Frederick II* (1937).

849. For papal censure, see *HDF,* volume 1, part 1, pages 34-40. The pope later (in 1206) addressed the rights of some Muslims near Palermo, ibid, pages 118-120; *Gesta Innocenti III,* chapter 40.

850. See note 829. For a general analysis see Loud, Graham, "The German Crusade of 1197-1198," *Crusades,* volume 13 (2014), pages 143-172.

851. Saint Mary of the Germans was erected as part of a commandery to support German knights and pilgrims *en route* to Palestine, though it probably was not completed for the crusade of 1197. The style is essentially Romanesque with Gothic elements. For patronage of the Teutonic Order by Frederick II see *HDF,* volume 1, part 1, pages 95-97.

852. Joanna died in September 1199. For her story see *Queens of Sicily,* pages 313-356.

853. *Gesta Innocenti III,* chapter 25.

854. Walter was killed in 1205. See *RHC, Historiens Occidentaux,* volume 2, pages 234-235 (from the "Continuation" of the history of William of Tyre written in the thirteenth century); also De Sassenay, Fernand, *Les Brienne de Lecce et d'Athènes,* pages 27-28, 30-33, 46-47, 49-52, 56. Walter's invasion of southern Italy is described in some detail by Richard of San Germano under the chapters for the years 1201-1205.

855. John of Brienne, who we shall meet, eventually became King of Jerusalem and then Emperor of Constantinople. His daughter was destined to wed Frederick II.

856. Very little is known about William of Capparone. His Pisan association is suggested by his use of the Pisan calendar in decrees he issued in Frederick's name and what appears to be his favoritism of Pisan merchants (over Genoans and Venetians) in the kingdom.

857. *Gesta Innocenti III,* chapters 35-36; Richard of San Germano, years 1202-1206.

858. Richard of San Germano, year 1202; *Fossanova Chronicle/Annales Ceccanenses,* year 1202; *Annales Casinenses,* entry for 1202.

859. *RPR,* volume 1: page 104, entry 1138; page 130, entry 1462; page 131, entries 1481-1483, page 146, entry 1688; page 176, entry 2020; page 197, entry 2292; page 310, entry 3595.

860. For Markward, see *HDF,* volume 1, part 1, pages 30-33. It has been suggested, however, that this excommunication was politically motivated insofar as it was meant to punish Markward for encroaching upon papal lands on the mainland.

NOTES

861. See Table 17 and Chapter 22. Irene Angelina was the widow of Tancred's son, Roger III. For more about her story, see *Queens of Sicily*, pages 371-380.

862. Niketas Choniates, Alexios Angelos section, book 2.

863. Ibid. For the papal outrage at the atrocities committed, *PCC, Series Secunda*, volume 215 (1855), columns 447-461. Good surveys are Phillips, Jonathan, *The Fourth Crusade and the Sack of Constantinople* (2005); Queller, Donald, and Madden, Thomas, *The Fourth Crusade: The Conquest of Constantinople* (1999); Perry, David, *Sacred Plunder: Venice and the Aftermath of the Fourth Crusade* (2016). See also Angold, Michael, "The Road to 1204: The Byzantine Background to the Fourth Crusade," *Journal of Medieval History*, volume 25, number 3 (1999), pages 257-278.

864. Had he not (with his sister's help) obtained the support of his brother-in-law, Alexios might never have returned to Constantinople with the large Frankish crusading army that caused so much death and destruction; consequently, the Latins ruled until 1261.

865. See *HDF*, volume 1, part 1, pages 105-110.

866. Ibid, pages 112-113.

867. Richard of San Germano, years 1206-1207; *Annales Casinenses*, entries for 1206-1207.

868. *Fossanova Chronicle/Annales Ceccanenses*, year 1208; Richard of San Germano, year 1208; *Annales Casinenses*, entry for 1208; *HDF*, volume 1, part 1, pages 134-135.

869. *Ferraris Chronicle*, page 155. The *Annales Casinenses* states late June.

870. *PCC, Series Secunda*, volume 215 (1855), column 1449; *HDF*, volume 1, part 1, pages 139-140.

871. On 22 June 1208, Philip and his wife were in Bamberg to celebrate the wedding of his niece, Beatrice of Burgundy. For reasons that are still debated, an unarmed Philip was stabbed and killed by the count palatine Otto of Wittelsbach of Bavaria, who was mentally unstable. Otto's violent temper was known in royal circles, and a few years earlier Philip had terminated the betrothal of one of his daughters to the mad count. See *Burchardi Praepositi Uspergensis Chronicon*, page 90.

872. Constance's precise year of birth is unknown, with estimates ranging from 1179 to 1184.

873. For Constance's story before her marriage see *Queens of Sicily*, pages 409-424. For a discussion with reference to correspondence between Innocent III and Peter II, see Smith, Damian, *Innocent III and the Crown of Aragon*, pages 30, 56, 68, 272.

874. An early motivation for Constance's brother, Peter II, to approve her betrothal to Frederick was the papal annulment he was seeking of his marriage to Marie of Montpelier, who in the event died in Rome in April 1213 just as she was about to return to Aragon, having convinced Pope Innocent III to preserve her conjugal union as valid.

875. *HDF*, volume 1, part 1, pages 169-170.

876. Richard of San Germano, year 1209; *Codex Diplomaticus Hungariae Ecclesiasticus ac Civilis*, pages 57-58; *RPR*, volume 1, page 310, entry 3595.

877. *RPR*, volume 1: page 301, entries 3490 and 3493; page 306, entry 3542; page 310, entry 3592; page 311, entry 3609; page 329 (the coronation), cf. *Burchardi Praepositi Uspergensis Chronicon*, in *Scriptores Rerum Germanicarum in Usum Scholarum*, volume 16 (1916), page 98.

878. For a reliable account from a source near the events, see the *Annales Casinenses* entries for 1209-1211. Other descriptions come to us from the *Ferraris Chronicle*, page 156, and from Richard of San Germano, years 1209-1210. For Otto's activities in Germany and also Italy, *Burchardi Praepositi Uspergensis Chronicon*, in *Scriptores Rerum Germanicarum in Usum Scholarum*, volume 16 (1916), pages 96-101.

879. Alfonso died in Palermo; see *HDF*, volume 2, part 2, page 893. His remaining knights were soon needed in Spain. Peter II of Aragon participated in the Battle of Las Navas de

Tolosa in 1212. He was killed at the Battle of Muret the following year whilst defending his brother-in-law, Raymond VI of Toulouse, and the Cathars against an invasion led by Simon IV of Montfort; to Peter, this was more a question of familial loyalty and territory than a fight against the papacy's Albigensian Crusade. See Marvin, Laurence, *The Occitan War* (2008).

880. *HDF,* volume 1, part 1, pages 164-165.

881. Ibid, pages 179-180.

882. Ibid, pages 170-171.

883. Ibid, pages 195-199.

884. The betrothal of Beatrix Hohenstaufen, daughter of the late Philip of Swabia, probably took place in the autumn of 1208, after the death of her widowed mother (Irene) but before Otto of Brunswick was crowned emperor. It was arranged by Walter of Palear, and it may be one of the unspoken reasons why this prelate was subsequently dismissed.

885. *HDF,* volume 1, part 1, pages 201-203. See also note 846.

886. Ibid, volume 1, part 1, pages 232-234, 241-242.

887. Ibid, pages 253-255, 265-266, 282-283.

888. For a competent analysis see France, John, "The Battle of Bouvines 27 July 1214," in *The Medieval Way of War* (2015), pages 251-272.

889. *RPR,* volume 1, page 410, entry 4725.

890. See Morris, Marc, *King John: Treachery and Tyranny in Medieval England, The Road to Magna Carta* (2015); Jones, Dan, *Magna Carta: The Birth of Liberty* (2016); Crouch, David, *William Marshal: Knighthood, War and Chivalry 1147-1219* (2002).

891. Richard of San Germano, year 1215, mentions Archbishop Berardo and William VI, Marquis of Montferrat. For modern commentary about this council see Wayno, Jeffrey, "Rethinking the Fourth Lateran Council of 1215," *Speculum,* volume 93, number 3 (July 2018), pages 611-637.

892. *HDF,* volume 1, part 1, pages .

893. *MGH, Constitutiones et Acta Publica Imperatorum et Regum,* Legum Sectio IV, volume 2 (1896), pages 54-103.

894. Ibid, page 72, entry 58, dated 1 July 1216. Pope Innocent III died on 16 July 1216 in Perugia. See also the following note.

895. *HDF,* volume 1, part 2, page 468. Years earlier, Nicholas, the son of the chancellor Matthew, had supported Sibylla against Constance Hauteville.

896. Ibid, pages 484, 895. Contrarily, and apparently in error, Richard of San Germano reports that Henry sailed from Palermo to Gaeta, traveling thenceforth to Germany to meet his father, with Constance leaving the *Regnum* in 1217 or 1218. Henry was invested with the Duchy of Swabia and would eventually be crowned King of the Germans. This clearly violated Frederick's promise and offended papal sensibilities, but the situation would worsen over the next few years.

897. Richard of San Germano, year 1216.

898. For a biography see Robinson, Paschal (translator), *The Life of Saint Clare by Thomas Celano* (1910). Also Gilliat-Smith, Ernest, *Saint Clare of Assisi: Her Life and Legislation* (1914); Mooney, Catherine, *Clare of Assisi and the Thirteenth-Century Church: Religious Women, Rules, and Resistance* (2016).

899. An essential reference is Robinson, Paschal, *The Writings of Saint Francis of Assisi* (1906). For a current view, Heimann, Mary, "The Secularisation of St Francis of Assisi," *British Catholic History* (2017) volume 33, pages 401-420.

NOTES

900. For an overview of the places and society known to Frederick and Francis, and some general observations about the two men, see Cassady, Richard, *The Emperor and the Saint: Frederick II of Hohenstaufen, Francis of Assisi, and Journeys to Medieval Places* (2011).

901. Richard of San Germano, years 1217-1218, who tells us that some knights from the northern part of the *Regnum* joined the crusade.

902. Peter II of Courtenay died in captivity in 1219, succeeded as emperor by his son, Robert, who died in 1228. Yolanda died in 1219. Honorius took a special interest in the Latin Empire of Constantinople; see Duba, William, and Schabel, Christopher, *Bullarium Hellenicum: Pope Honorius III's Letters to Frankish Greece and Constantinople 1216-1227* (2015).

903. This chapter is merely an introduction with a few essential translations. A great deal has been written about the Sicilian School and the role of Frederick II as its patron. As a starting point, the reader is referred to the following: Jensen, Frede, *The Poetry of the Sicilian School* (1986); Langley, Ernest, *The Poetry of Giacomo da Lentini* (1915); Lansing, Richard, *The Complete Poetry of Giacomo da Lentini* (2018); Mallette, Karla, *The Kingdom of Sicily 1100-1250: A Literary History* (2005); Mangieri, Cono Antonio, *Il Contrasto di Cielo d'Alcamo: Introduzione, testo manoscritto e diplomatico, testo critico-congetturale, traduzione e note* (2005); Panvini, Bruno, *Le Rime della Scuola Siciliana,* volume 1 (1962); Di Girolamo, Costanzo, et al., *Poeti della Corte di Federico II,* volume 2 in the series *I Poeti della Scuola Siciliana* (2008).

904. Siculo-Arabic survives in its modern form as Maltese; see Agius, Dionisius, *Siculo Arabic* (1996), and for literature (poetry) notes 55 and 367 supra. For the development of Norman French, see Jones, Mari, *Variation and Change in Mainland and Insular Norman* (2014); for its use in England, see Ingham, Richard, et al., *The Anglo-Norman Language and its Contexts* (2010).

905. Brandin, Louis (editor), *La Chanson d'Aspremont,* two volumes (1923 edition), based on the Wollaton Hall manuscript; also Newth, Michael (translator), *The Song of Aspremont* (1989). A defining study is van Waard, Roelof, *Ètudes sur l'Origine et la Formation de la Chanson d'Aspremont* (1937). The *Chanson d'Aspremont* should not be confused with the *Aspramonte* later composed in Tuscan. More generally, some observations about the courtly literature of the *Regnum* during the Norman era are advanced in Guzzo, Cristian, "I Normanni e l'Epica Romanza: Etica Cavalleresca e Cavalleria Etica nel Sud Italia," *L'Età Normanna in Puglia: Mito e Ragione* (2015), pages 85-99. For the sword see Khanmohamadi, Shirin, "Durendal, translated: Islamic object genealogies in the chansons de geste," *Postmedieval: A Journal of Medieval Cultural Studies,* volume 8, number 3 (2017), pages 321-333.

906. The idea that Ligurian, Neapolitan and other languages were dialects of Tuscan was advanced with notable zeal after 1860, when unificationists discouraged the use of "Italic" tongues other than Tuscan Italian; later, the Fascist regime even banned the teaching of English in public schools.

907. For Medieval ("Middle") Sicilian see Sottile, Roberto, *L'Atlante Linguistico della Sicilia* (2019); Sucato, Ignazio, *La Lingua Siciliana: Origine e Storia* (1975). For Modern Sicilian: Bellestri, Joseph, *English-Sicilian Dictionary* (1988); Bonner, Kirk, and Cipolla, Gaetano, *Introduction to Sicilian Grammar* (2001); Cipolla, Gaetano, *Learn Sicilian* (2013); Varvaro, Alberto, *Vocabolario Storico-Etimologico del Siciliano* (2014). For its use by recent immigrants see D'Agostino, Mari, and Mocciaro, Egle, "Palermo 2000-2020: Sicilian in Old and New Migrants," *Italo-Romance Dialects in the Linguistic Repertoires of Immigrants in Italy* (2022), pages 19-46.

908. "I know that the land indicated by the boundaries noted here has been held for thirty years by [the abbey of] Saint Benedict." These charters were discovered by Erasmo Gattola early in the eighteenth century and published in *Ad Historiam Abbatiae Cassinensis Accessiones,* part 1 (1734), pages 68-70; this supplemented his *Historia Abbatiae Cassinensis* (1733).

909. "Whence King William's fleet accompanied him to the city of Venice where the pope mentioned earlier wished to go for greater safety so that the Emperor Frederick could not attack him." This refers to the conference that culminated in the Treaty of Venice (see note 737 supra). Identified by various titles, the *Cronaca di Partenope* is conserved in at least sixteen

known manuscripts; here the authors consulted the highly legible copy in the Biblioteca Estense of Modena (ALFA.H.8.14, formerly ITA 281), where this passage appears on folio 38 recto, differing slightly from the texts in the published editions. The *editio princeps* was the *Cronaca di Partenope e Trattato delli Bagni* (1486), followed by such editions as *Croniche de la Inclita Cità de Napole* (1526); the latter was republished in Tuscanized form in 1680 in *Raccolta di Varii Libri overo Opusculi d'Historie del Regno di Napoli,* pages 1-105. A fine modern transcription is Altamura, Antonio, *Cronaca di Partenope* (1974); in English see Kelly, Samantha, *The Cronaca di Partenope* (2011).

910. For a good discussion of Manfred's poetry see Maggiorella, Antonia, *Il Principe Poeta: Manfredi di Svevia* (2005). For more about Nina of Messina, see *Sicilian Queenship,* pages 381-390; whether Dante of Maiano was, in fact, the colleague with whom she corresponded has been debated.

911. The principal source for Frederick's poems, and those of most of the other poets, are the manuscripts *Codex Vaticanus Latinus 3793* and *Codex Urbinas Latinus 697,* housed in the Vatican Apostolic Library. These are the work of copyists working late in the thirteenth century; earlier copies of the poems of the Sicilian School are virtually unknown. Other manuscripts containing poems of the Sicilian School are the *Banco Rari 217,* formerly *Palatino 418*, and the *Laurenziano Rediano 9,* both in Florence; the former may be the oldest of all.

912. The music, in a work compiled shortly before 1400, appears in *Fonds des Nouvelles Acquisitions Françaises,* volume number 6771, now btv1b8449045j (Reina Codex), folio 29 verso, in the Bibliothèque Nationale, Paris. For commentary see Pirrotta, Nino: "Elementi Rapsodici nella Polifonia Italiana del Trecento," *Ricercare,* volume 1 (1989), pages 7-21; "Musica Polifonica per un Testo Attribuito a Federico II," in *L'Ars Nova Italiana del Trecento,* volume 2 (1968), pages 97-112. Several scholars have suggested that this song may have German or even (through Frederick's first wife) Provençal influences. More generally, Favara, Alberto, *Corpus di Musiche Popolari Siciliane* (1957). For the musical instruments depicted in the Palatine Chapel see Gramit, David, "The Music Paintings of the Cappella Palatina in Palermo," *Imago Musicae,* number 2 (1985), pages 9-49. For liturgical music in Latin see Appendix 5, note e.

913. "Hearing these comments about the potentially great battlefield strength of King Charles raised grave doubts in King Peter's mind. Considering that his opponent might be emboldened enough to march on Palermo, Peter sent couriers around the island to keep watch on the situation. That night, a notary arrived who was acting as an emissary on the part of the city of Messina. He told King Peter how that city had victuals enough for eight days and no more, saying that, 'you must help and succor us by sending men and food, for there is no way we can continue to resist against King Charles. Otherwise we'll have no choice but to surrender.'" See Mendola, Louis, *Sicily's Rebellion against King Charles: The Story of the Sicilian Vespers* (2015), pages 128, 205.

914. Giovanni Maria Barbieri, who died in 1574, had a collection of Sicilian poems, his *Libro Siciliano,* from which he copied several works, lost after his death; see *Dell'Origine della Poesia Rimata* (1790), page 186, note 4.

915. A good reference is the *Declarus* of Angelo Senisio, composed during the middle of the fourteenth century as what may be considered the first "dictionary" of the Sicilian language as it existed at that time, marked by Catalan influences; the manuscript (IV.H.14) is conserved in the Sicilian Regional Library in Palermo; see also Marinoni, Augusto, *Dal Declarus di Angelo Senisio: I Vocaboli Siciliani* (1955).

916. For a competent analysis of the poems of Frederick II, citing the contributions of various scholars, see *I Poeti della Scuola Siciliana* (op. cit. supra), volume 2, chapter 14 (by Stefano Rapisarda), pages 439-494. There have been many papers and opinions published on the topic over the last century; see, for example, Thornton, Hermann, "The Poems Ascribed to Frederick II 'Rex Fredericis' and King Enzio," *Speculum,* volume 2, number 4 (October 1927), pages 463-469, and "The Poems Ascribed to Frederick II and Rex Fredericis," *Speculum,* volume 1, number 1 (January 1926), pages 87-100.

NOTES

917. While the *Contrasto* was quite obviously composed by Cielo of Alcamo some years later, probably after 1234, Frederick's poems were likely written at an earlier date, perhaps even as early as 1220.

918. See Dickson, Gary, *The Children's Crusade: Medieval History, Modern Mythistory* (2007); also note 938.

919. There are numerous original sources for the Fifth Crusade, notably the oft-cited Mas Latrie, Louis, *Chronique d'Ernoul et de Bernard le Trésorier* (1871). For a view by Wali al Din ibn Khaldun, see Amari, Michele, *BAS,* volume 1, page 239. For studies see Perry, Guy (editor), *The Fifth Crusade in Context: The Crusading Movement in the Early Thirteenth Century* (2016); Cassidy-Welch, Megan, *War and Memory at the Time of the Fifth Crusade* (2019).

920. Sayf ad-Din, from "Sword of Faith" (see note 801) was a younger brother of Saladin. Meledin's full name was al-Malik al-Kamil Naser al-Din Abu al-Ma' Ali Muhammad.

921. A fine study is Donovan, Joseph, *Pelagius and the Fifth Crusade* (1950).

922. *RPR,* volume 1, page 562, entry 6442.

923. Richard of San Germano, year 1221.

924. Ibid.

925. For the coronation, *HDF,* volume 2, part 1, pages 1-2; with numerous references at *RPR,* volume 1, page 559.

926. For these laws, *HDF,* volume 2, part 1, pages 2-7; *RPR,* loc. cit., entry 6408.

927. Richard of San Germano, year 1220. Thomas of Celano was ultimately suppressed two years later but permitted to keep some lands.

928. Richard of San Germano, year 1121. These movements are attested in *HDF,* volume 2, part 1, pages 106 (Frederick at Sessa in January), 137-156.

929. This statute regarding the attire of Jews does not appear in a later code, the Constitutions of Melfi, of 1231, which superseded the assizes of Capua and Messina. The dating of the code issued at Messina is consistent with Frederick's travels (see the previous note) and Richard of San Germano, year 1221. The gambling houses of Messina were mentioned by Hugh Falcandus; see note 567 supra.

930. *HDF,* volume 2, part 1, pages 178-182.

931. Ibid, pages 196-197.

932. Ibid, pages 204-224 passim.

933. Ibid, page 254.

934. Ibid, volume 2, part 2, pages 800-801, where a charter of July 1220 confirms Caro's claims to numerous territories.

935. See note 849. Caro was consecrated shortly before 1194, when he subscribed the charter establishing a monastery at Palermo's Martorana church by Godfrey Martorano and his wife Aloisia.

936. The most frequently cited contemporary sources are the *At-Tarikh al-Mansuri* of Muhammad al-Hamawi, the chronicle of Richard of San Germano, and the *Annales Siculi.*

937. Frederick's presence at Jato is attested by decrees, e.g. *HDF,* volume 2, part 1, pages 255-257. Michele Amari offers a sober summary; see *Storia dei Musulmani in Sicilia* (1868), volume 3, chapter 8, pages 589-604. See also Maurici, Ferdinando, *L'Emirato sulle Montagne* (1987); Abulafia, David, "The End of Muslim Sicily," in Powell, James (editor), *Muslims Under Latin Rule 1100-1300* (1990), pages 103-134.

938. The chronicler Alberic of Trois-Fontaines states that the merchants, William of Posquiéres and Hugh Fer, both of Marseille, had sold into slavery some participants in the

ill-fated "Children's Crusade" of 1212, q.v. *MGH, Scriptorum,* volume 23 (1874) pages 631-950, specifically pages 893-894. For commentary see Raedts, Peter, "The Children's Crusade of 1212," *Journal of Medieval History,* number 3 (1977), pages 279-323. See also note 918 supra.

939. For another view see De Luca, Maria Amalia, "Bint Muhammad ibn Abbad," *Siciliane: Dizionario Biografico* (2006), pages 79-81.

940. For comparison to Frederick's German dominions, see Dolan, John, "A Note on Emperor Frederick II and Jewish Tolerance," *Jewish Social Studies,* volume 22, number 3 (July 1960), pages 165-174. For some observations about the complexities, Weltecke, Dorothea, "Emperor Frederick II, 'Sultan of Lucera,' Friend of the Muslims: Promoter of Cultural Transfer: Controversies and Suggestions," Feuchter, Jorg (editor), *Cultural Transfers in Dispute* (2011), pages 85-106.

941. Early in his majority, in 1210, and again in 1215, Frederick renewed the authority of the Archbishop of Palermo as "protector" of the city's Jews. See Mongitore, Antonino, *Bullae, Privilegia et Instrumenta Panormitane Metropolitanae Ecclesiae Regni Siciliae Primariae* (1734), pages 82-84, 98-99. See also note 180 supra.

942. Richard of San Germano, year 1222; *Necrologium Liciense,* page 476; *Necrologia Panormitana,* page 472.

943. *Annales Siculi,* year 1224. There are several editions, the best being Pontieri, Ernesto (editor), *Rerum Italicarum Scriptores, Raccolti degli Storici Italiani* (1927 edition), volume 5, pages 115-120.

944. Richard of San Germano, year 1222.

945. *Annales Siculi,* year 1223. For Frederick's later intervention regarding the Jews of Palermo see *Codice Diplomatico dei Giudei di Sicilia* (1884), volume 1, part 1, document 22, pages 19-20.

946. Ibid, year 1222; Richard of San Germano, years 1223, 1226; *HDF,* volume 2, part 1, pages 356-361. Richard also notes Henry discouraging such vices as gambling. For the gold coins, Richard of San Germano, year 1222; nothing like a formal code was issued at Brindisi.

947. The Sicily entry in the *Zhu Fan Zhi,* a guide by Zhao Rukuo (1170-1231) completed around 1225, is quite concise, mentioning little more than Mount Etna and making the comparison to the Rum lands. See Hirth, Friedrich, and Rockhill, William, *Chau Ju-kua: His Work on the Chinese and Arab Trade in the Twelfth and Thirteenth Centuries Entitled Chu-Fan-Chi* (1911), pages 153-154; for commentary see Wyatt, Don, *The Blacks of Premodern China* (2010), pages 35-36.

948. The ancestry of Oberto Fallamonaca is elusive; he may have been the son of a Genoan father and an Arab mother. He seems to have been fluent in Arabic, subscribing a charter at Agrigento in that language and acting as Frederick's ambassador to Morocco. See Winkelmann, Eduard, *Acta Imperi Inedita Seculi XIII Urkunden und Briefe* (1880), pages 561-562 (charter number 707 and notes); *Annales Siculi,* year 1241.

949. To Muslims, archery was almost a meditative, or quasi-religious, activity, a *fard kifayah.* Although the English longbow archers were considered among Europe's finest, the Arabs may have been better. See Paterson, William, "The Archers of Islam," *Journal of the Economic and Social History of the Orient,* volume 9, number 1 (November 1966), pages 69-87.

950. This effort began around 1230, principally on the mainland where Pope Gregory IX was at odds with Frederick. In 1233, the Dominicans were permitted to erect a church in Lucera for the conversions. For the work of Thomas Aquinas see note 965.

951. *Yolande* initially seems to have been preferred by French historians, while *Isabelle,* which some used, derives directly from *Elizabeth.* Some give both forms; see the notes in *RHC, Historiens Occidentaux,* volume 2, pages 311, 320, 343-344.

952. For more about John see Perry, Guy, *John of Brienne.*

953. Richard of San Germano, year 1223; also *HDF,* volume 2, part 1, page 327.

954. *HDF,* volume 2, part 1, pages 394-395, referring to August 1223. The Fourth Lateran Council relaxed diriment impediment to the fourth degree of consanguinity (using the old canonical measurement). The most recent common ancestor of Frederick and Yolanda was Agnes Waiblingen of Germany (see Table 3), who died in 1143. She was a great great grandmother to each spouse.

955. The lengthiest contemporary account of the marriage of Yolanda of Jerusalem is found in the "Chronicle of the Holy Land" in *Gestes des Chiprois,* pages 19-25. See also *RHC, Historiens Occidentaux,* volume 2, pages 356-361; *Chronique d'Ernoul,* pages 449-450.

956. Frederick's actions had symbolic effects in subsequent centuries. Later kings of Sicily and Naples would claim the crown of Jerusalem by pretension long after the city was lost. This is the basis for the use of the title during the modern era by the Hapsburgs, Bourbons, and even the Savoys, who ruled southern Italy at one time or another.

957. *HDF,* volume 2, part 1, pages 398-404.

958. Ibid, pages 461-463. Henry III did eventually invade France, if not successfully, in 1230 during the reign of Louis IX.

959. Ibid, pages 447-453, citing Peter della Vigna and other sources. See also Richard of San Germano, year 1224. For the scholarships awarded to poor students, see Mendola, Louis, *Frederick, Conrad and Manfred of Hohenstaufen, Kings of Sicily 1210-1258: The Chronicle of Nicholas of Jamsilla* (2016), pages 83-84. For commentary: Delle Donne, Fulvio, "L'Organizzazione dello Studium di Napoli e la Nobiltà del Sapere," in *Il Regno di Sicilia in Età Normanna e Sveva* (2021), pages 37-47; Oldfield, Paul, "The Kingdom of Sicily and the Early University Movement," *Viator,* volume 40 (2009), number 2, pages 135-150.

960. Michael Scot probably arrived at the Sicilian court in 1224 or 1225. See Voskoboynikov, Oleg, *Michael Scot: Liber Particularis, Liber Physonomie* (2019). A good biography is Thorndike, Lynn, *Michael Scot* (1965). More generally, for Michael Scot as well as other intellectuals at the Sicilian court, see Haskins, Charles, *Studies in the History of Mediaeval Science* (1924), pages 155-192, 242-298.

961. Of course, Hindu-Arabic numerals were already used in Sicily, thanks to the Fatimids and Kalbids. In Spain, they appear in the *Codex Vigilanus* compiled in 881.

962. See McClenon, Raymond, "Leonardo of Pisa and His Liber Quadratorum," *The American Mathematical Monthly,* volume 26, number 1 (January 1919), pages 1-8. For recent commentary see Stedall, Jacqueline, *A Discourse Concerning Algebra* (2003), pages 19-54.

963. This was completed around 1240. For the illuminated Vatican codex see Manuscript W in Sources, also Walz, Dorothea, and Willemsen, Carl (editors), *Das Falkenbuch Friedrichs II* (2000), which includes commentary in German. For the Latin text of the most complete codices, see Gottlob, Johann, (editor), *Reliqua Friderici II Imperatoris de Arte Venandi cum Avibus* (1788). In English translation, Wood, Casey, and Fyfe, Marjorie, *The Art of Falconry* (1943). For a fine introductory study, Haskins, Charles, "The 'De Arte Venandi cum Avibus' of the Emperor Frederick II," *The English Historical Review,* volume 36 (1921), pages 334-355. For falconry at the court of Roger II see note 363 supra.

964. In translation, see Arvide, Luisa, *Las Cuestiones Sicilianas* (2009); Spallino, Patrizia, *Le Questioni Siciliane, Federico II e l'Universo Filosofico* (2002). Later chroniclers, notably Salimbene, defamed Frederick by inventing bizarre stories about him ordering experiments on living people, even infants.

965. A fair amount has been written about this. One of the better overviews is Abulafia, David, "Ethnic Variety and its Implications: Frederick II's Relations with Jews and Muslims," *Studies in the History of Art,* number 44 (1994), pages 213-224. The most vitriolic ideological and political attacks on Muslims and Jews by people of the *Regnum* were perpetuated after Frederick's reign, not by his sons but by theologians such as Thomas Aquinas, whose treatise *Summa contra Gentiles* criticized fundamental tenets of Islam and Judaism, while his *Contra errores graecorum* targeted the Orthodox and, arguably, even the Byzantine Greeks as a people. See also notes 1039 and 1181.

KINGDOM OF SICILY

966. Sometimes the "Agreement of San Germano." See *HDF,* volume 2, part 1, pages 501-503; Richard of San Germano, year 1225. A thousand enfeoffed knights was an extremely small force for such an enterprise.

967. See note 955; Richard of San Germano, loc. cit; *HDF,* loc. cit, pages 525-527. For Yolanda's story, see *Queens of Sicily,* pages 424-434.

968. The overt antipathy between Frederick and John was generally known to contemporaries in Italy; see the *Ferraris Chronicle,* pages 168-169.

969. Richard of San Germano, year 1225, states that the suppression in Sicily continued. Khaldun mentions this, and the transfer to Lucera, though he seems to confuse the dates; see Amari, Michele, *BAS,* volume 2, chapter 50, pages 212-213. One of the main sources for details about the Lucerans is the collection compiled by Egidi, Pietro (editor), *Codice Diplomatico dei Saraceni di Lucera dall'anno 1285 al 1343* (1917); a good study is his *La Colonia Saracena di Lucera e la Sua Distruzione* (1914). The forced migration is also described by Michele Amari in his *Storia dei Musulmani di Sicilia* (1868), volume 3, pages 597-610. For a recent perspective see Taylor, Julie Anne, *Muslims in Medieval Italy: The Colony at Lucera* (2003). In recent decades, a few historians have suggested that only part of the population of Sicilian Muslims was transferred to the mainland; the genetic record suggests that some likely chose conversion to Christianity over resettlement in Puglia and are the ancestors of today's Sicilians, for which see Mendola, Louis, *What Became of Medieval Sicily's Arabs? Genetic Demographic Evidence* (2015) and Chiarelli, Leonard, *A History of Muslim Sicily* (2018 edition), page 39.

970. See *HDF,* volume 5, part 1, pages 128-131.

971. For al-Kamil see notes 920 and 987. For the Muslim view, Amari, Michele, *BAS,* volume 2: Abulfeda, chapter 47, page 104; Khaldun, chapter 50, page 242; *Kitab as Suluk,* chapter 53, pages 259-261; appendix, pages 57-63. Jean de Joinville imaginatively claimed that Frederick knighted Fakhr al-Din ibn Shaykh al-Shuyukh, later identified as *Scecedin* (who was killed by French crusaders during the Seventh Crusade in 1250), during what may have been a second visit to the *Regnum* in 1227; see Marzials, Frank (translator), *Memoirs of the Crusades by Villehardouin and de Joinville* (1908), pages 184-185.

972. *HDF,* volume 2, part 1, pages 536-538.

973. Ibid, page 541.

974. See Chapter 17, where the Lombard League is mentioned as a papal vehicle established in 1167 to oppose Frederick Barbarossa. A competent analysis is Simeoni, Luigi, "Note sulla Formazione della Seconda Lega Lombarda," *Memorie della Real Accademia delle Scienze dell'Istituto di Bologna,* series 3, number 6 (1932), pages 3-52.

975. Before 1266, Louis IX (see note 31 supra) is more directly relevant to the Holy Roman Empire than the Kingdom of Sicily. His essential contemporary biographies were written by his friends, Jean de Joinville (q.v. note 971 supra) and Geoffroy of Beaulieu.

976. He was at Messina in January and Catania in February; see *HDF,* volume 2, part 2, pages 706, 712.

977. A detailed study of the role of Honorius III in the crusades into the reign of Frederick II lies beyond the scope of this work, but the curious reader is commended to Smith, Thomas, *Curia and Crusade: Pope Honorius III and the Recovery of the Holy Land 1216-1227* (2017).

978. Pope Lucius III issued the papal bull *Ad Abolendam* in 1184 as a response to the "Catharism" that led to the horrific Albigensian Crusade.

979. This occurred in 1231, and we find the Dominicans attempting to convert non-Christians, though not as part of the Inquisition. See note 950 supra.

980. In the Kingdom of Sicily, it was official policy for Jews to be protected by the local bishop; for the Archdiocese of Palermo see notes 180 and 941. Gregory IX certainly knew this when he confirmed the privileges of the Archbishop of Palermo in 1228; see Mongitore, Antonino, *Bullae,*

NOTES

Privilegia et Instrumenta Panormitane Metropolitanae Ecclesiae Regni Siciliae Primariae (1734), page 101. The legend about Gregory hating cats is based on inferences drawn from the papal bull *Vox in Rama* of 1233, addressed to Frederick's son, Henry, regarding the alleged practices of certain heretics; see Mansi, Giovanni Domenico, *Sacrorum Conciliorum,* volume 23 (1779), columns 323-326.

981. Reported by Richard of San Germano, year 1227; attested by other sources.

982. *HDF,* volume 3, page 18. See also note 958 supra.

983. Ibid, pages 24-30. For other sources see *RPR,* volume 1, page 695, entry 8044. For the epidemic and many deaths, Richard of San Germano, year 1227; for the death of Louis of Thuringia, Alberic of Trois-Fontaines in *MGH, Scriptorum,* volume 23 (1874), page 920.

984. *HDF,* volume 3, pages 36-48.

985. Reports of Yolanda's date of death vary by several days; see, for example, *Breve Chronicon de Rebus Siculis,* page 80. See also *RHC, Historiens Occidentaux,* volume 2, page 420.

986. See note 966 for the so-called "Agreement of San Germano." Whether Honorius III would have excommunicated Frederick, especially in view of *force majeure,* is fodder for debate.

987. The main source for the conquest of Cyprus by Frederick II and some details of the subsequent "War of the Lombards" is the account by Philip of Novara, a man from northern Italy, published in Reynaud, Gaston (editor), *Les Gestes des Chiprois* (1887), pages 25-138. See also note 1068 below.

988. One of the most reliable contemporary accounts of the Sixth Crusade is to be found in *RHC, Historiens Occidentaux,* volume 2, pages 369-373. *Breve Chronicon de Rebus Siculis,* pages 80-92, offers what is probably an eyewitness account. Philip of Novara (see the previous note) also considers it. Another useful source is the work of Jacques de Vitry, consisting of his *Historia Orientalis* and letters. For a Muslim Arab view see Amari, Michele, *BAS:* volume 1, pages 501-507 (al-Athir); volume 2, pages 106-107 (Abulfeda); volume 2, pages 242-243 (Khaldun). Perceptions further afield are reflected in works such as the descriptions by Roger of Wendover and especially Matthew Paris (see note 995 below), who were informed by returning Englishmen. For some recent translations of relevant accounts, see Bird, Peters, et al. (editors), *Crusade and Christendom: Annotated Texts in Translation* (2013), pages 237-265; Richards, Donald, *The Chronicle of ibn al-Athir,* volume 3 (2008). A fine compendium of source documents is Golubovich, Girolamo, *Biblioteca Bio-Bibliografica della Terra Santa e dell'Oriente Francescano* (1906). Among the better modern overviews is Van Cleve, Thomas, "The Crusade of Frederick II," in *A History of the Crusades* (1969), volume 2, pages 429-462. An articulate entry is Takayama, Hiroshi, "Frederick II's Crusade: An example of Christian-Muslim diplomacy," *Mediterranean Historical Review,* volume 25, number 2 (2010), pages 169-185. For a concise but insightful analysis see Abu-Munshar, Maher, "Sultan al-Kamil, Emperor Frederick II and the Submission of Jerusalem," *International Journal of Social Science and Humanity,* volume 3, number 5 (September 2013), pages 443-447.

989. Ibn al-Imad al-Hanbali cites a letter of Frederick to al-Kamil expressing disappointment at his change of heart; see Little, Donald, "Jerusalem Under the Ayyubids and Mamluks 1187-1516," in *Jerusalem in History* (1990), page 183.

990. For text of the treaty see *HDF,* volume 3, pages 86-90. Despite numerous contemporaneous references to the Sixth Crusade and the treaty, there is no known evidence to suggest that Frederick and al-Kamil ever actually met; the illumination of them depicted greeting each other together (in the chronicle of John Villani) was painted long after Frederick's death.

991. Ibid, pages 93-99, citing Matthew Paris and other sources, q.v. note 994 below. Frederick reportedly placed the crown on his own head, with Herman of Salza pronouncing him king. Irregular as the form of such a coronation may have been, Frederick was still King of Jerusalem, or at least regent for Conrad, his young son.

992. *MGH, Epistolae Saeculi XIII* (1883), part 1, pages 299-304 (entry 384); pages 315-317 (entry 397).

KINGDOM OF SICILY

993. As King of Sicily, Charles of Anjou, brother of Louis IX of France, was involved in the Eighth Crusade in 1270 but did not lead it.

994. For an exception see Sharon, Moshe, and Schraeger, Ami, "Frederick II's Arabic Inscription at Jaffa," *Crusades,* volume 11 (2012), pages 139-158.

995. Richard of San Germano, year 1229; *Annales Placentini Gibellini,* in *MGH, Scriptorum,* volume 18 (1863), pages 469-470; Matthew Paris, in Luard, Henry (editor), *Matthaei Parisiensis Chronica Majora,* volume 3 (1876), pages 165-166, which includes the letter of Thomas Aquino of Acerra informing Frederick of the invasion by John and the complicity of the pope, and pages 172-186, 192-194, including Frederick's letter to Henry III and the letter of Patriarch Gerold against Frederick, amongst myriad details. Other sources for the War of the Keys are Roger of Wendover, Alberic of Trois-Fontaines, and John Codagnello's *Annales Placentini Guelfi,* also the *Breve Chronicon de Rebus Siculis* (the text of one codex ends in 1250 and the other with the Battle of Benevento in 1266).

996. Although this was not a crusade by any established definition, occasional use of that term served to express Gregory's view of Frederick. For commentary see Abulafia, David, *Frederick II: A Medieval Emperor* (2002), pages 194-201; Loud, Graham, "The Papal 'Crusade' against Frederick II in 1228-1230," *La Papauté et les Croisades* (2011), pages 91-103; Powell, James, "Church and Crusade: Frederick II and Louis IX," *The Catholic Historical Review,* volume 93, number 2 (April 2007), pages 250-264; Whalen, Brett, *The Two Powers: The Papacy, the Empire and the Struggle for Sovereignty in the Thirteenth Century* (2019).

997. *HDF,* volume 3, page 54 (in March 1128); *Matthaei Parisiensis Chronica Majora,* volume 3, page 154 (in August 1228).

998. *MGH, Epistolae Saeculi XIII* (1883), part 1, pages 346-347 (entry 428); pages 356-357 (entry 442). More at *HDF,* volume 3, pages 239-241. For a concise but informative introduction see Guzzo, Cristian, *Templari in Sicilia: La Storia e le sue Fonti tra Federico II e Roberto d'Angio* (2003).

999. Richard of San Germano, year 1229.

1000. Ibid. *Balbano* is *Balvano,* and *Cicala* is now *Castelcicala.* See also the following note.

1001. In the original, *Raonus* of Balbano, *Raynaldus* of Spoleto.

1002. The son of Walter III of Brienne (whom we met in Chapter 22) and Elvira, daughter of Tancred of Lecce. He would later go on the Barons' Crusade. See Table 16.

1003. For the Treaty of San Germano see *HDF,* volume 3, pages 207-214.

1004. Ibid, pages 276-280.

1005. Much has been written about this concept, with scholars advancing various definitions for the term. See Morris, Colin, *The Papal Monarchy: The Western Church from 1050 to 1250* (1989); Schrader, Charles, "The Historical Development of the Papal Monarchy," *The Catholic Historical Review,* volume 22, number 3 (October 1936), pages 259-282. For an emphasis on southern Italy, see Loud, Graham, *The Latin Church in Norman Italy* (2007). More generally, Baldwin, Marshall, *The Mediaeval Church* (1953).

1006. For Frederick as a "Renaissance man," see Kantorowicz, Ernst, *Kaiser Friedrich der Zweite* (1927); for commentary see the paper cited at note 32 supra. More generally, see Haskins, Charles Homer, *The Renaissance of the Twelfth Century* (1927).

1007. The oldest extant Latin manuscripts are *Latinus 4625* in the Bibliothèque Nationale (Paris) and *Ottobonianus Latinus 2945* in the Vatican Apostolic Library. The code was also issued in Greek and Arabic. See also note 1015.

1008. The *editio princeps* is an incunable published by Francesco del Tuppo in Naples in 1475 after the king, Ferrante I of Aragon, decreed in December 1472 that these laws were still in force, having never been abrogated formally in the Kingdom of Naples. However, it would

NOTES

be incorrect to affirm that the Constitutions survived as current law in the kingdoms of Naples and Sicily into the modern age; see *Codice delle Leggi del Regno di Napoli* (1794), a multi-volume compilation by Alessio De Sariis. See also the following note.

1009. One of the early scholars of the Constitutions was the jurist Andrew of Isernia, an expert on feudalism, who was born around 1230 and died in 1316; see Cervone, Antonio, *Constitutionum Regni Siciliarum ad Friderici II* (Naples 1773), which includes Andrew's commentary and the *Novellae,* some clauses added after 1231, such as the "Assizes of Siracusa" in 1233 (and at San Germano in 1232, Messina in 1234, Foggia in 1240, Grosseto in 1244, Barletta in 1246). An excellent edition containing the Latin and Greek texts is Carcani, Gaetano, *Constitutiones Regum Regni Utriusque Siciliae Mandante Friderico II Imperatore* (1786), which also contains Frederick's lost registers for 1239-1240 (see notes 28 and 1141). A reliable entry is to be found in *HDF,* volume 4, part 1, pages 1-177. A good recent edition is Stürner, Wolfgang, *Die Konstitutionen Friedrichs II,* in *MGH, Constitutiones et Acta Publica Imperatorum et Regum,* supplement, volume 2 (1996). For an English translation with useful notes, see Powell, James, *The Liber Augustalis or Constitutions of Melfi* (1971). There are numerous papers, articles and treatises about this. See, for example, Maffei, Domenico (editor), *Un'Epitome in Volgare del Liber Augustalis* (1995), and note 1021 below.

1010. See the pontiff's initial reaction, or warning, while the code was still being drafted, at *MGH, Epistolae Saeculi XIII* (1883), part 1, pages 357-358 (entry 443); also *HDF,* volume 3, page 289, in July 1231. For Gregory's complaint in June 1239 about Frederick's supposedly insufficient belief in Christian principles, see *HDF,* volume 5, part 1, pages 327-340. See also notes 1126 and 1129 below. For a consideration of the general continuity of the kingdom's ecclesiastical politics from the Hauteville era, see Kamp, Norbert, "L'Héritage Normand dans la Politique Ecclésiastique de Frédéric II," *Frédéric II et l'Héritage Normand de Sicile* (2001), pages 63-78.

1011. According to Richard of San Germano, year 1231, the meeting of barons at Melfi was commanded in February and the statutes were being formulated by June. It is therefore unsurprising that the pope would have learned of this work before it was complete (see the preceding and following notes). Indeed, the consultations and early work may well have begun long before 1231.

1012. James was reprimanded by Pope Gregory IX for contributing to the compilation of the code; see *HDF,* volume 3, page 290, in July 1231. Peter's participation is inferred from the distinctive style of writing for which he was known and the fact of his presence at court. Thaddeus of Suessa, a friend of Peter, was a jurist who became grand justiciar of the kingdom.

1013. Here the authors are being reductive. The number of clauses varies considerably depending on the manuscript, the scribal division, and whether the *Novellae* are included.

1014. In the Constitutions several passages from the Assizes are quoted verbatim. The law against rape applied chiefly to assaults against nuns and virgins (maidens); see note 1021. For passing comparisons to the *Magna Carta* see Hill, Mark, "Magna Carta's Legacy: Common Law and Human Rights," *Comparative Law Review,* volume 6, number 2 (2015); Elkins, Zachary, et al., "On the Influence of Magna Carta and Other Cultural Relics," *International Review of Law and Economics,* number 47 (2016), pages 3-9.

1015. Indeed, supplementary statutes were issued as recently as 1247; see note 1009. The oldest complete texts including some *Novellae* are codices *Vaticanus Latinus 6770* and *Reginensis Latinus 1948,* both in the Vatican Apostolic Library. See also notes 1007 and 1166.

1016. This is not intended as a legal treatise, and by intent "generic" legal terminology is used which is not explicitly American, British, Canadian or Australian. Numeration is intended to be generally indicative, based chiefly on Carcani's bilingual edition of 1786, which sometimes differs from that used in *HDF,* q.v. note 1009 supra.

1017. The first part of the *Prooemium* is worth citing for its historical significance. It quotes passages from Genesis 1:26, Psalms 8:6, and I Samuel 8:20. *Imperator Fridericus Semper Augustus, Ytalicus Siculus Ierosolomitanus Arelatensis Felix Pius Victor et Triumphator: Post mundi machinam, providentia divina formatam, et primordialem materiam naturae melioris conditionis officio, in rerum effigies distributam, qui facienda praeviderat, facta considerans et considerata commendans, a globo circuli lunaris inferius hominem creaturarum dignissimam creaturam ad ymaginem propriam, effigiemque formatam, quem paulo minus minuerat ab Angelis, consilio perpenso disposuit praeponere ceteris creaturis, quem de limo terrae transumptum vivificavit in spiritum, ac eidem honoris et gloriae dyademate coronato, uxorem et sociam, partem sui corporis, aggregavit; eosque tantae praerogativae munimine decoravit, ut ambos efficeret primitus immortales; ipsosque verumtamen sub quadam lege praecepti constituit, quam quia servare tenaciter contempserunt, transgressionis eosdem poena damnatos ab ea, quam ipsis ante contulerat, immortalitate proscripsit.*

1018. The Patarines, who took their name from the Pataria district of Milan, were a lay organization opposed to corruption in the church, but the term eventually came to identify the Cathars.

1019. Although these initial statutes were doubtless sincere, they likely reflected an attempt to placate papal protests as Frederick had done very little to suppress heresy (or perceived heresy) and may not have approved of the efforts of the Dominicans in attempting to convert non-Christians.

1020. Both groups are mentioned explicitly.

1021. See Mazzarese Fardella, Enrico, "La Condizione Giuridica della Donna nel Liber Augustalis," *Archivio Storico Siciliano,* Series 4, Volume 21-22 (Palermo 1997); Byrne, Philippa, "Lascivious Crimes and Legitimate Proofs: Women and the Juridical Transformation of Norman and Staufen Sicily," in *Women and Violence in the Late Medieval Mediterranean, ca. 1100-1500* (2021). In subsequent centuries rape, as a violent form of assault, was not always regarded as a serious crime (felony) in what is now Italy. This necessitated revision of the law in the Italian Republic in 1996 (sic) to treat it as more than an offense akin to pornography; see note 1032 below. For further discussion, Van Cleave, Rachel, "Rape and Querela Law in Italy: False Protection of Victim Agency," *Michigan Journal of Gender and Law,* volume 13, January 2007 (Ann Arbor 2007), pages 273-310.

1022. This *collecta,* succeeded by the modern *donativo,* was a tax outside the regular regime of fees, tithes and excises. It was levied occasionally, typically every five or ten years, to cover a shortfall in the crown's budget, sometimes to cover extraordinary expenses such as a war. See note 1085.

1023. This policy reflected an attempt to treat the accused humanely, without unduly humiliating those not granted the right of parole.

1024. This form of defamation is similar to libel; the term *calunnia* is still used in Italy and its definition is nearly identical to that found in the Constitutions.

1025. This statute applied chiefly to commoners, who served as foot men and archers.

1026. This principle was generally abandoned in Italy in later centuries.

1027. "Sicilian Succession" survived until 1861 in the Kingdom of the Two Sicilies, and successively in the Kingdom of Italy; female feudal inheritance also came to be applied in Spain, Scotland, Sardinia and certain other regions of Europe but not generally in other parts of peninsular Italy despite obvious exceptions such as Matilda of Tuscany (died 1115). It doubtless existed in the Kingdom of Sicily in some form long before Frederick's reign, for we find the heiress Clementia of Catanzaro at the court of William I; see notes 503 and 649. For some traditional views see Dragonetti, Giacinto, *Origine dei Feudi nei Regni di Napoli e Sicilia* (1788); Orlando, Diego, *Il Feudalismo in Sicilia: Storia e Dritto Pubblico* (1847). The most recent statute regarding female succession is article 10 of decree number 1489 of 16 August 1926; translation and notes in Mendola, Louis, *Royal Decree by the King of Italy Governing Succession to Titles of Nobility and Nobiliary Ranks* (Los Angeles 1983).

1028. Although the Latin word for *serf* may also refer to a *slave,* this clause appears to identify the former.

1029. An early attempt at environmentalism.

NOTES

1030. The purity of precious metal is regulated.

1031. Specifically, Statute 70 outlaws the sale of love potions, while Statute 71 prohibits their purchase; Statutes 72 and 73 prescribe harsh penalties. Statute 74 mandates, at the very least, public flogging of an adulterous wife. Statute 75 prohibits a man making a case against his wife for adultery if he has watched her flirt with another man and done nothing to stop it, or pimped her. Statute 76 outlaws a wife flirting with men other than her husband. Statute 77 forbids a woman who has prostituted herself to associate with decent women but prohibits violence against her. Statute 79 prohibits the pimping of women by other women ("madams"). Statute 80 prohibits mothers prostituting their daughters, though prostitution itself was legal under most circumstances.

1032. The medieval practice now sometimes called an "honor killing" was effectively tolerated in practice in Italy until it was abolished by Public Law number 442 in 1981 (sic). Until then, it was punished by minimal penalties, viz. article 377 of the "Zanardelli Code" of 1889. Article 587 of the infamous "Rocco Code" of 1930 retained this, mandating a sentence of imprisonment of just 3-7 years while specifying reference to a husband, father or brother killing (respectively) a wife, daughter or sister; it was this code that outlawed rape merely as "a crime against public decency." See notes 20 and 1021 supra.

1033. The statute specifies that jurisdiction should be granted to the diocese or parish where the adultery occurred. The Assizes of Ariano establish adultery as a civil crime but it was likewise outlawed by the church. See also note 704.

1034. This secular law was somewhat unusual for its time. Divorce was eventually outlawed, and illegal in the short-lived Kingdom of Italy (1861-1946), to be reinstituted only in 1970.

1035. See Powell, James, *Medieval Monarchy and Trade: The Economic Policy of Frederick II in the Kingdom of Sicily* (1961); Abulafia, David, *The Two Italies: Economic Relations Between the Norman Kingdom of Sicily and the Northern Communes* (1977); Toomaspoag, Kristjan, "La Politica Fiscale di Federico II," *Federico II nel Regno di Sicilia: Realtà locali e aspirazioni universali* (2008), pages 231-247.

1036. Richard of San Germano, year 1232; *Annales Siculi,* year 1231 (sic). See also note 1009 supra.

1037. In his *Policraticus,* though this idea cannot be said to be completely original. See also the following note.

1038. Exceptionally, see Kantorowicz, Ernst, *The King's Two Bodies: A Study in Mediaeval Political Theology* (1997 edition), pages 97-142.

1039. Ibid, pages 135-137. Thomas Aquinas set forth some of these ideas in his *Summa Theologiae.* More specifically, he identified eternal, natural, human and divine law. See also notes 965 and 1181.

1040. In Frederick's time the *Magna Carta* comes to mind. Henry of Bracton wrote about kingship and the royal exercise of power, though his chief point of reference was England.

1041. Richard of San Germano, year 1233.

1042. It is not the authors' intent to minimize this idea. See Bynum, Caroline, "Fast, Feast and Flesh: The Religious Significance of Food to Medieval Women," *Representations,* number 11 (summer 1985), pages 1-25. Most of Chapter 27 is adapted from *Sicilian Queenship,* pages 151-190.

1043. The problem in the Kingdom of Sicily is that we have very few household accounts from these reigns that indicate exactly what was being served, either at the royal court or at baronial castles. There is some foreign literature that may be consulted for comparison. See, for example, Kjaer, Lars, "Food, Drink and Ritualized Communication in the Household of Eleanor of Montfort, February to August 1265," *Journal of Medieval History,* volume 37, number 1 (2011), pages 75-89; also Mead, William, *The English Medieval Feast* (1931).

KINGDOM OF SICILY

1044. Hieatt, Constance, "How Arabic Traditions Travelled to England," *Food on the Move: Proceedings of the Oxford Symposium on Food and Cookery 1996* (1997), pages 120-126. For some insights see Salloum, Habeeb, "Medieval and Renaissance Italy: Sicily," in *Regional Cuisines of Medieval Europe: A Book of Essays* (2002), pages 113-123.

1045. Broadhurst, Ronald, *The Travels of Ibn Jubayr* (2008 edition), page 340. This also mentions some crops raised, such as pears, apples and hazelnuts.

1046. Zaouali, Lilia, *Medieval Cuisine of the Islamic World: A Concise History with 174 Recipes* (2007); this is the *Kitab al-Tabikh*. Nasrallah, Nawal, *Annals of the Caliph's Kitchens: Ibn Sayyar al-Warraq's Tenth-Century Baghdadi Cookbook* (2007). For some modern adaptations of some of these recipes, see Salloum, Habeeb, *Scheherazade's Feasts: Foods of the Medieval Arab World* (2013).

1047. We find Frederick in Foggia in April 1240 sending for a shipment of cheeses from Sicily via Naples; see *HDF*, volume 5, part 2, page 884.

1048. See Martellotti, Anna, *La Cassata Siciliana: Un Dolce Arabo e la Sua Fortuna in Occidente* (2012).

1049. Usually meatballs with an egg glaze. See Hieatt, Constance, and Jones, Robin, "Two Anglo-Norman Culinary Collections Edited from British Library Manuscripts Additional 32085 and Royal 12,C.xii," *Speculum,* volume 61, number 4 (October 1996), pages 859-882, especially page 862. Another example is Pegge, Samuel, *The Forme of Cury* (1780), page 106; this is a collection of recipes from the court of Richard II of England around 1390.

1050. For some observations see Anderson, Melitta Weiss, *Food in Medieval Times* (2004), pages 130-121. This is an excellent summary but whether certain introductions, such as pistachios, should be attributed to the Arabs, is debatable as some were also cultivated by the Byzantine Greeks.

1051. Hieatt, Constance, "How Arabic Traditions Travelled to England," op. cit. supra, page 123, page 126n31.

1052. Ibid.

1053. For the complete text of the *Liber de Coquina* and the *Meridionale* see Martellotti, Anna (editor), *I Ricettari di Federico II: Dal Meridionale al Liber de Coquina* (2005). For the *Meridionale* see Boström, Ingemar (editor), *Due Libri di Cucina: Anonimo Meridionale* (1985).

1054. Some recipes influenced by these early compilations are included in *De Arte Coquinaria* by Martin of Como, written in the fifteenth century, for which see the translation by Jeremy Parzen, et al., published in 2005 as *The Art of Cooking*.

1055. Scully, Terence, *The Neapolitan Recipe Collection* (2000).

1056. Musso, Pasquale, et al., "Il 'Ricettario di Cucina' di San Martino delle Scale," *Bollettino del Centro di Studi Filologici e Linguistici Siciliani,* volume 21 (2007), pages 243-321.

1057. Over the course of decades, Jacqueline Alio has sampled or prepared the modern variations of recipes such as *maccu,* and some of these dishes are described in her book on this topic written with Francesca Lombardo, *Sicilian Food and Wine: The Cognoscente's Guide* (2015). Another fine work, which includes many historical Sicilian recipes, is Mary Taylor Simeti's *Pomp and Sustenance: Twenty-Five Centuries of Sicilian Food* (1989), later released under another title. More generally, see Scully, Terence, *The Art of Cookery in the Middle Ages* (1995); Montanari, Massimo, *Medieval Tastes: Food, Cooking and the Table* (2012).

1058. *Si uis facere tortam de lassanis, pone lassanas, ova frissa uel lixa uel perduta et raviolos incisos uel integros, caseum pinguem grattatum uel incisum, lardum sufficientem, et hoc compone solaria faciendo, species apponendo. Et forma super istam de pasta unum serpentem preliantem cum columba, uel quecumque alia animalia uolueris. Deinde, accipe intestina implecta de bona impletura et ponatur in circuitu quasi murus. Tunc solaria coloretur pro uoluntate et ponantur in furno. Postea, portetur coram domino cum pompa.* The last sentence expresses the pride with which the lasagna was presented to the pleasure of the diners.

NOTES

1059. Martellotti, Anna, op. cit. See also Möhren, Frankwalt, *Il Libro de la Cocina: Un Ricettario fra Oriente e Occidente* (2016).

1060. The source for this is a charter of Frederick II given at Foggia in March 1240 ordering Richard of Policoro to procure wine and the ingredients for *scapece* for Berardo (sic), the emperor's cook. See *HDF*, volume 5, part 2, pages 861-862. This was not an isolated request, as two months later, Frederick ordered that some Sicilian livestock herds (cows, sheep, goats) be sent to the mainland to supply the meat he preferred; ibid, pages 943-945. See also note 1047 supra.

1061. The incident was reported much later by Peter Damian, who states that Maria's food was cut into pieces by eunuchs before she ate it with this two-pronged golden fork, *fuscinulis aureis atque bidentibus*. This was cited as divine justification for Maria's death from the plague not long after her wedding to John Orseolo, son of the Doge of Venice. See Migne, Jacques (editor), "Opuscula Varia," in *PCC, Series Secunda,* volume 145, column 744. For Maria's marriage and death see the chronicle of John Sagorino the Deacon in Zanetti, Girolamo Francesco (editor), *Chronicon Venetum* (1765), pages 113-119. For more about the history of the fork, see Wilson, Bee, *Consider the Fork: A History of How We Cook and Eat* (2012).

1062. Very few dining forks are known to exist from the Norman-Swabian era. Such forks might well have been fashioned of silver, and their absence should be considered in light of the general lack of survival of gold and silver objects, or even steel swords or knives, of this period.

1063. See *Queens of Sicily,* pages 537-543.

1064. Barber, Richard, *The Prince in Splendour: Court Festivals in Medieval Europe* (2017).

1065. *Matthaei Parisiensis,* Luard, Henry (editor), *Chronica Majora* (1877) volume 2, page 470.

1066. Batman, Stephen (editor), *De Proprietatibus Rerum* (1585), page 81, chapters 23 ("On Dinner and Fasting") and 24 ("On the Supper") of book 6 ("De State Hominis"). This is the translation by John Trevisa and except for a few spellings it is extracted directly. Bartholomew, who later became minister of Austria and Bohemia, may have met Frederick II.

1067. A number of studies are based on chemical analysis. See, for example, Lundy, Jasmine, and colleagues, "New Insights into Early Medieval Islamic Cuisine: Organic residue analysis of pottery from urban and rural Sicily," *PLoS ONE,* volume 16, number 6 (2021).

1068. In August 1239. In connection with this appointment, he instituted a code for the office of admiral, thus formalizing the duties entailed in this rank.

1069. The chief local source is the *Estoire de Eracles Empereur,* in *RHC, Historiens Occidentaux,* volume 2 (1859), chapters 32-36, pages 398-402. See also notes 955, 987-989 supra. For commentary: Bromiley, Geoffrey, "Philip of Novara's Account of the War Between Frederick II of Hohenstaufen and the Ibelins," *Journal of Medieval History,* volume 3, number 4 (December 1977), pages 325-337; Jackson, Peter, "The End of Hohenstaufen Rule in Syria," *Historical Research,* volume 59, number 139 (May 1986), pages 20-36; Jacoby, David, "The Kingdom of Jerusalem and the Collapse of Hohenstaufen Power in the Levant," *Dumberton Oaks Papers,* number 40 (1986), pages 83-101. Cyprus, like Jerusalem, became one of the dominions of pretension of later kings of Naples and Sicily. See also note 1114 below.

1070. For Henry's *Statutum in Favorem Principum* see *MGH, Legum Sectio IV, Constitutiones et Acta Publica Imperatorum et Regum,* volume 2 (1896), pages 418-420 (document 304 for the charter by Henry of 1231), pages 211-213 (document 171 for the charter of Frederick of 1232 issued at Cividale confirming this following the Diet of Aquileia). Although this conformed to the model established by the imperial *Privilegium in Favorem Principum Ecclesiasticorum* of 1220 (ibid, document 73, pages 86-91), Frederick undertook it reluctantly, finding it difficult to undo what his son had done. These laws ceded power to the bishops and princes in many areas, even the minting of coins, that would survive for centuries to come. In the immediate future, however, Henry's application of this policy would not be very efficient.

1071. Ibid, document 174, pages 215-216, in May 1132 (see also note 958 supra).

1072. Ibid, documents 176-185, pages 217-227; also *RPR,* volume 1, page 769, entry 8966.

1073. Folio 18v (upper-right of the page) of *Codex Palatinus Latinus 1071* shows a bird which appears to be a yellow-crested cockatoo (possibly cacatua galerita); see Dalton, Heather, "Frederick II of Hohenstaufen's Australasian Cockatoo: Symbol of Detente between East and West and Evidence of Ayyubids' Global Reach," *Parergon,* number 35, volume 1 (January 2018), pages 35-60.

1074. For eclectic commentary on the myriad complexities see: Powell, James, "Frederick II and the Church: A Revisionist View," *The Catholic Historical Review,* volume 48, number 4 (January 1963), pages 487-497; Weiler, Björn, "Gregory IX, Frederick II and the Liberation of the Holy Land 1230-9," *Studies in Church History,* volume 36 (2000), pages 192-206; Balan, Pietro, *Storia di Gregorio IX e dei Suoi Tempi* (1873); Pybus, Helen, "The Emperor Frederick II and the Sicilian Church," *Cambridge Historical Journal,* volume 3, number 2 (1930), pages 134-163; Kamp, Norbert, *Kirche und Monarchie im Staufischen Königreich Sizilien* (1982); Lanzani, Francesco, *La Questione Italiana ai Tempi di Federico II* (1868).

1075. Richard of San Germano, year 1233. Many details about the construction of Castel del Monte are unknown but it was essentially complete by 1240.

1076. Ibid.

1077. Ibid.

1078. Ibid. This type of public feast was only vaguely comparable to the *cuccagna* described in the previous chapter.

1079. Richard of San Germano, year 1234.

1080. Ibid. Fruit trees are mentioned.

1081. Ibid. Located between the towns of Monte Romano and Tuscania, this *Rocca Vecchia,* of which little remains, was built around 1012; the Rocca Respampani castle standing northeast of the site is of modern construction.

1082. A fine study is Cassidy-Welch, Megan, "The Stedinger Crusade: War, Remembrance and Absence in Thirteenth-Century Germany," *Viator,* volume 44, number 2 (2013), pages 159-174. See also King, Wilson, "The Stedingers: The Story of a Forgotten Crusade," in *Transactions of the Birmingham Historical Society 1883-1884,* pages 1-24.

1083. Ibid, among other sources. The account of Richard of San Germano, though reductive, reflects the southern Italian and papal views. For Henry's decrees relative to Germany from late 1231 to May 1235, see *HDF,* volume 4, part 2, pages 555-726. The true extent to which Henry was intentionally, even maliciously, defiant of his father's authority cannot be known; biographers are divided on this. Many historians have analyzed Henry's motivations and behavior; one of the more pragmatic treatments is by Abulafia, David, *Frederick II: A Medieval Emperor* (2002), chapter 7, pages 226-248.

1084. Frederick likely fathered several children whose names are lost to time. Among those known to us are Enzio (Enzo) of Sardinia, born around 1218 to a certain Adelaide, who was probably of the Swabian Urslingen family, and Constance (later Anna), born around 1230 to Bianca Lancia. For Bianca's story see *Queens of Sicily,* pages 453-460.

1085. By definition, this was a general, occasional "one time" tax, or *aid,* sometimes the *adoha* (sic) or *subventio generalis,* imposed at royal discretion, in contrast to various regularly-levied taxes. Here the authors prefer the term popularized in the Kingdom of Sicily around 1238, when several taxes of this kind were combined into the *collecta.* See also note 1022 supra.

1086. For Isabella's story see *Queens of Sicily,* pages 435-452; *Sicilian Queenship,* pages 128-132.

1087. According to Matthew Paris, Frederick actually offered to begin such a campaign immediately after Henry approved the betrothal of Isabella; this seems unlikely, but see *Matthew Paris's English History,* volume 1, page 11.

NOTES

1088. *Foedera,* pages 120-121, 123-124, 126, 130. Some of these patents are misdated in this compilation; for example the dowry money was withdrawn from the exchequer (page 130) in June 1235, not 1236. For the tax levied in Ireland, see *Close Rolls,* volume 3, pages 510, 571, 573; for debts forgiven, ibid, pages 81 (royal debt to several English Jews) and 241 (debt of Thomas Daniel who wed Isabella's attendant Isolda of Kidderminster).

1089. This facet of Frederick's reign is a gateway to modern debates about whether his character, ethos and politics were more distinctly "Italian" or "German," though neither of those "national" identities existed in the thirteenth century as in modern times, or perhaps even "Norman." For related commentary: Rader, Olaf, *Friedrich II: Der Sizilianer auf dem Kaiserthron* (2019); Houben, Hubert, *Kaiser Friedrich II: Herrscher, Mensch, Mythos* (2007); Stern, Horst, *Mann aus Apulien* (1986); Stürner, Wolfgang, *Friedrich II* (2009) and *Staufisches Mittelalter Ausgewählte Aufsätze zur Herrschaftspraxis und Persönlichkeit Friedrichs II* (2012); Delle Donne, Fulvio, *Federico II: La Condanna della Memoria* (2012); Brando, Marco, *Lo Strano Caso di Federico II: Un Mito Medievale nella Cultura di Massa* (2008). The biography by Ernst Kantorowicz enhanced the image of Frederick as a German nationalist symbol in the public mind; early in July 1943, shortly before the Allied invasion of Sicily, Hermann Göring ordered the emperor to be removed from Palermo's cathedral (viz. Friedrich Ruge, in *Allan Malcolm Morrison Papers 1940-1968,* Schomburg Center for Research in Black Culture, New York Public Library, Sc Micro R-3537, Armed Forces: Evacuation of Sicily, 1948, page 45): "Some days before Palermo was lost, the German admiral received orders from Reichsmarschel Goering through 3KL to evacuate the sarcophagi containing the remains of Frederick II and of members of his family. This order was quietly ignored in the conviction that the dead should rest undisturbed, and that Frederick II, perhaps the greatest of all the Emperors of the Middle Ages, should under no circumstances be separated from Palermo, his famous capital and historic background."

1090. Conrad was crowned King of the Germans at Vienna in February 1237.

1091. Henry died around 1243, Frederick in 1251, the latter inheriting money and lands (but no other rights) from his grandfather; see *Matthaei Parisiensis, Chronica Majora,* volume 5, page 448. Margaret retreated to a convent and later, in 1252, wed the much-younger Ottokar II of Bohemia; she died in 1266.

1092. See, for example, *Foedera,* pages 133-135; *Royal and Other Historical Letters,* volume 2, pages 8-9, 25-29.

1093. This is mentioned by Richard of San Germano. Some historians identify the girl as Agnes, others as Margaret. It is possible that a boy (apocryphally identified as Jordan) was born to Isabella in the spring of 1236 but died in infancy. There is, however, much doubt about this.

1094. By August 1237, Isabella was in Italy. Sadly, she may have suffered from depression, q.v. note 1086 supra.

1095. Richard of San Germano, year 1235.

1096. Ibid, year 1236, also other sources, notably the *Weltchronic* of Jans der Enike in *MGH, Deutsche Chroniken,* volume 3 (1900), pages 1-596. Frederick II of Austria, who succeeded his father, Leopold VI, in 1230, might have been less aggressive if his brother-in-law, Henry, had not been arrested and imprisoned, and his own sister, Margaret, disgraced. Yet his rebellion (and collaboration with Henry) antedated this; he had refused to attend the diet at Aquilea in 1232 and the one at Mainz in 1235. Later, in 1239, he became a staunch imperial supporter and subsequently defended the eastern regions against an invading Mongol army.

1097. Richard of San Germano, year 1236.

1098. Ibid, year 1237.

1099. There are various sources for the Battle of Cortenuova and successive events, including references by Peter della Vigna and of course local chronicles written in that region. For the relevant letters and charters of Frederick II see *HDF,* volume 5, part 1, pages 132-151. For commentary and analysis, a fine monograph is Hadank, Karl, *Die Schlacht bei Cortenuova* (Berlin 1905).

1100. Richard of San Germano, year 1236. Taxes on Muslims and Jews are reported in the royal registers for 1239-1240, q.v. Carcani at note 1009 supra.

1101. Histopathology reported by Gino Fornaciari, Francesco Mallegni and Pietro De Leo in "The Leprosy of Henry VII: Incarceration or Isolation?" published in *The Lancet,* volume 353 (27 February 1999), page 758.

1102. Richard of San Germano, year 1238. Enzio of Sardinia and Frederick of Antioch reappear later in these pages. A fine secondary work is Sperle, Christian, *Koenig Enzo von Sardinien und Friedrich von Antiochia: Zwei Illegitime Soehne Kaiser Friedrich II* (2001).

1103. Richard of San Germano, year 1238; *HDF,* volume 5, part 1, page 228.

1104. Precisely when Elias, a friend of Francis of Assisi and Salimbene di Adam, first arrived at Frederick's court is unclear. See Huber, Raphael, "Elias of Cortona," *The Catholic Historical Review,* volume 22, number 4 (January 1937), pages 395-408.

1105. Richard of San Germano, year 1239

1106. Ibid, where the chronicler paints this as a pledge of fealty even though the abbey (despite its proximity to the Kingdom of Sicily) was a quasi-sovereign institution in papal territory answering only to its abbot and the pope.

1107. See *RPR* (1874), volume 1, entries on page 908. For the text see (amongst other sources cited by Potthast), *HDF,* volume 5, part 1, pages 286-308.

1108. Potthast, op. cit., page 914, entries 10798 and 10806; also *Recueil des Historiens des Gaules et de la France* (1840), volume 20, pages 347-351.

1109. For a letter see *HDF,* volume 5, part 1, pages 346-348.

1110. Ibid, pages 359-362.

1111. Ibid, volume 4, part 2, page 872, etc. Abd al-Aziz had been a guest of the Sicilian court for some time. Except for the papal claim, there is nothing to suggest that he sought conversion, and Frederick himself challenged that notion.

1112. Ibid, volume 5, part 1, pages 571-574. The immigrants were granted their own synagogue in Palermo, as some of their customs may have differed from those of the Sicilian Jews.

1113. Ibid, volume 5, part 1, pages 390-394; Richard of San Germano, year 1240.

1114. Jerusalem and the other territories ultimately fell in 1244, along with what little Sicilian influence remained in the Holy Land. See sources and studies at note 1069 supra; also Lower, Michael, *The Barons' Crusade: A Call to Arms and Its Consequences* (2005).

1115. Accounts about Richard's meetings with Frederick and Isabella vary. In his *Chronica Majora,* volume 4, pages 145-147, Matthew Paris reports that Richard saw Isabella at Palermo and that Frederick was present; that is inaccurate, but historians have often conflated Matthew's account with what little is known of the meeting in Faenza. See also Richard of San Germano. For Frederick's movements see *HDF,* volume 5, part 2, pages 1130-1167.

1116. In his many letters, the chancellor Peter della Vigna, who was often present at court and had negotiated Isabella's marriage, scarcely mentions her. Unlike Richard of San Germano and Matthew Paris, he was at court (when he wasn't traveling on diplomatic missions for Frederick) and actually knew Isabella. See *Petri de Vineis Friderici II Imperatoris Epistolarum,* volume 1, book 3, chapter 21, pages 419-420; volume 1, book 3, chapter 70, pages 502-504; volume 1, book 3, chapter 71, pages 504-506; volume 2, book 4, chapter 2, pages 6-7.

1117 This seems to refer to a recent improvement in her relationship with her husband, as if that were necessary. Matthew's source is not identified, but being farther from imperial circles than Peter della Vigna afforded him the privilege of candor without fear of reprisal. See *Chronica Majora,* volume 4, page 83. See also note 1086 supra.

NOTES

1118. Richard of San Germano, year 1239.

1119. *Annales Siculi,* year 1240; see also note 948. Oberto was back in Sicily early in 1242, q.v. *HDF,* volume 6, part 2, page 20.

1120. Richard of San Germano, year 1239.

1121. Ibid, year 1241.

1122. Ibid.

1123. Ibid. Batu Khan, a grandson of Genghis Khan, fought his last major European battle at Esztergom (Hungary) in January 1242, for which the chief account is that of Roger of Torre Maggiore (in Puglia), later Archbishop of Split; first published in 1488, Roger's *Carmen Miserabile Super Destructione Regni Hungariae per Tartaros Facta* appears in *MGH, Scriptorum,* volume 29 (1892), pages 547-567. Frederick of Austria (see note 1096 supra) fought a few minor engagements against the invaders, and Wenceslaus of Bohemia prepared his country for an attack, but in March, 1242, the Golden Horde ceased its westward march, perhaps because Batu Khan was summoned to Mongolia. Thus ended its threat to the Holy Roman Empire.

1124. This was ordered by the infamous *Disputation.* For sources in translation see Hoff, Jean, *The Trial of the Talmud,* Paris 1240 (2012). More generally, Michael, Robert, *A History of Catholic Antisemitism: The Dark Side of the Church* (2008); Grayzel, Solomon, *The Church and the Jews in the Middle Ages* (1966). See also note 1171.

1125. For a recent perspective see Whalen, Brett, *The Two Powers: The Papacy, the Empire, and the Struggle for Sovereignty in the Thirteenth Century* (2019). See also the monographs by Brian Tierney: *The Crisis of the Church and State 1050-1300* (1988); *Origins of Papal Infallibility 1150-1350* (1972, 1988).

1126. In this context, *hierocracy,* sometimes "papalism," is the medieval doctrine or belief that the power of the pope was temporal as well as spiritual. This issue was addressed over the next few centuries, notably by Pope Boniface VIII with the bull *Unam Sanctam* in 1302 (asserting papal authority over King Philip IV of France), to which the theologian John of Paris famously responded with his *De potestate regia et papali* defending the sovereign rights of kings. It should not be confused with the dogma of *papal infallibility,* the theological concept that the word of the pontiff is unerring in matters regarding faith and morals, an idea expressed by Peter Olivi in his *De perfectione evangelica a quaestio* around 1280; see Brian Tierney's works at the previous note.

1127. Pope Innocent IV deposed Frederick II on 17 July 1245 at the Council of Lyon. Several (slightly varying) texts are known, including that of Matthew Paris, who quotes the pope's accusation of Frederick's sympathy to Islam; see *Matthaei Parisiensis, Chronica Majora,* volume 4, pages 445-456. For the *Historia Anglorum* see Giles, John, *Matthew Paris's English History* (1853) volume 2, pages 77-86. Also: *HDF,* volume 6, part 1, pages 319-327, 391-393 (Frederick's letter in 1246 to fellow monarchs reacting to recent papal actions against him); Mansi, Giovanni Domenico, *Sacrorum Conciliorum,* volume 23 (1779), columns 613-619. The same pontiff deposed Sancho II of Portugal on 24 July 1245. Additional references in *RPR* (1874), volume 2, page 997, entry 11733. For subsequent events see note 1189 below.

1128. See Chapter 8. In February 1076, Henry IV became the first king in recent memory to be deposed by a pope. Frederick I Barbarossa was deposed by Pope Alexander III in April 1160.

1129. A noteworthy medieval precedent is the *Dictatus Papae* (specifically its dictates 9 and 10) of Pope Gregory VII of 1075 applied, in particular, to emperors. See also notes 1126 and 1128.

1130. In Italy, notably, we find Dante's *De Monarchia* some sixty years after Frederick's death; John Quidort of Paris, a Dominican, also questioned papal authority. Advocating for the papal position were Giles of Rome, Agostino of Ancona, James Capocci of Viterbo, Henry of Segusio and Alvaro Pelayo, among others.

1131. *Foedera,* page 140; *Chronica Majora,* volume 4, page 175; Richard of San Germano, year 1241. For Frederick's letter to Henry see also *HDF,* volume 6, part 1, page 26.

1132. *HDF,* volume 6, part 1, pages 68-70, from the letters of Peter della Vigna.

1133. Celestine IV was born around 1180 or slightly afterward. At his death he was probably 55-60 years old.

1134. *RPR,* volume 1, page 853, entries 10032-10033. From 1240, Sinibaldo was in Rome.

1135. *Richeri Gesta Senoniensis Ecclesiae,* in *MGH, Scriptorum,* volume 25 (1947), pages 303-304.

1136. Richard of San Germano, year 1242.

1137. Ibid. It is to be noted that the so-called *Statutum de Reparatione Castrorum* was not the result of a single decree, nor was it a formal statute. It was part of a general policy to repair fortifications around the kingdom using local (rather than royal) resources; for commentary see Fasoli, Gina, "Castelli e Strade nel Regnum Siciliae: L'Itinerario di Federico II," *Federico e l'Arte del Duecento Italiano* (1980), pages 27-52.

1138. Richard of San Germano, year 1242.

1139. Ibid; quoted in *HDF,* volume 6, part 1, pages 28-32. See also notes 1091 and 1101 supra.

1140. Fine biographies are: Huillard-Bréholles, Jean, *Vie et Correspondance de Pierre de la Vigne* (1865); De Blasi, Giuseppe, *Della Vita e delle Opere di Pietro della Vigna* (1860).

1141. A fine exposition regarding the significance of Frederick's chancery registry of this period, and its partial destruction in 1943, is presented in Abulafia, David, *Frederick II: A Medieval Emperor* (2002), pages 320-327 (the first part of chapter 10); see also notes 28 and 1009 supra. In Carcani's *Constitutiones* of 1786 the invaluable registry entries for the Kingdom of Sicily for the years 1239-1240 begin on page 233, but here, for the reader's convenience, the authors usually cite the clearer texts published in the *Historia Diplomatica Friderici Secundi* compilation of Huillard-Bréholles. It is in this register that we find Frederick's request for cheeses whilst in Puglia; see note 1045 supra.

1142. At this time, the *secretus* was the bailiff (governor) of Palermo, what would later be called a *mayor.* For Oberto see note 1119.

1143. Richard of San Germano, year 1242.

1144. Ibid, quoted in *HDF,* volume 6, part 1, pages 59-63.

1145. Richard of San Germano, year 1243.

1146. Ibid; also *HDF,* volume 6, part 1, pages 80-82.

1147. *Annales Siculi,* year 1243.

1148. Ibid, year 1245. Other sources at note 1188.

1149. Born around 1193, Alice was the daughter of Isabella I of Jerusalem by her second husband, Henry II of Champagne (see Table 20). She was therefore an aunt to Yolanda of Jerusalem, Frederick's wife who died in 1228. Alice was married three times: firstly to Hugh I of Cyprus, secondly to Bohemond V of Antioch, thirdly to Raoul of Nesle. Henry I of Cyprus, to whom Frederick lost that island in 1232, was her son (see note 1069). When Alice died in 1246, Henry became titular regent of Jerusalem for Conrad. See also *HDF,* volume 6, part 1, pages 116-118, 147-148; and note 764 supra.

1150. Some informative essays will be found in the collection *Itinerari e Centri Urbani nel Mezzogiorno Normanno-Svevo* (1993) edited by Giosuè Musca; see also Poloni, Alma, *Potere al Popolo: Conflitti Sociali e Lotte Politiche nell'Italia Comunale del Duecento* (2010); Oldfield, Paul, *City and Community in Norman Italy* (2009); Morreale, Laura, "Wealth and Material Goods in Medieval Italian Civic Historiography," *Traditio,* volume 77 (2022), pages 185-233.

NOTES

1151. For some general observations see Matthews, Karen, *Conflict, Commerce and an Aesthetic of Appreciation in the Italian Maritime Cities 1000-1150* (2018).

1152. For Lucera see the works at note 969.

1153. Some recent studies address certain aspects of this topic: Fasoli, Gina, "Organizzazione delle Città ed Economia Urbana," in *Potere, Società e Popoli nell'Età Sveva* (1985), pages 167-190; Martino, Federico, "Federico II e le Autonomie Locali: Considerazioni sulla Formula Consuetudines Approbatae," *Studi Senesi,* number 103 (1991), pages 427-455; Andenna, Giancarlo, "Autonomie Cittadine del Mezzogiorno dai Normanni alla Morte di Federico II," in *Federico II nel Regno di Sicilia* (2008), pages 35-121.

1154. Richard of San Germano, year 1234, refers to the royal *curiae generales* in January, over which Frederick presided, at which participants agreed to meet on their own at least twice annually.

1155. See the preceding note. This was also true of the Norman dukes and kings of the previous century when convening the collective leadership of demesnial cities like Bari and Catania.

1156. See note 306. In Sicilian the term *parlamentu* (from the word for "conversation") referred to any meeting.

1157. The studies that have attempted to ascertain populations in Italy before 1300 are necessarily highly conjectural. See, for example, Malanima, Paolo, *Italian Urban Population 1300-1861* (2015).

1158. Tombs and crypts from this era have not generally been preserved. There were no parochial records of birth, marriage and death until the end of the fifteenth century, when *riveli* records of the *donativo* property tax were begun in Sicily. For an overview see Barbiera, Irene, *Le Dinamiche di Popolazione dell'Italia Medievale* (2007); more generally, Jonker, Marianne, "Estimation of Life Expectancy in the Middle Ages," *Journal of the Royal Statistical Society,* Series A, volume 166, number 1 (2003), pages 105-117. For perceptions see Shahar, Shulamith, *Growing Old in the Middle Ages: Winter clothes us in shadow and pain* (1997); Thane, Pat (editor), *A History of Old Age* (2005).

1159. The Assizes of Ariano mandated the licensing of physicians. The Muslim approach common in Sicily when the Normans arrived is described in Chiarelli, Leonard, "Muslim Sicily and the Beginning of Medical Licensing in Europe," *Journal of the Islamic Medical Association of North America,* volume 31, number 2 (1999), pages 79-82. For a fine introduction and translation of Frederick's legislation see Walsh, James, "The Earliest Modern Law for the Regulation of the Practice of Medicine," *Bulletin of the New York Academy of Medicine,* volume 11, number 8 (August 1935), pages 521-527. The regulations and text of the Salernitan licenses appear in the original Latin in De Renzi, Salvatore, *Storia Documentata della Scuola Medica di Salerno* (second edition, 1857), pages LXXVI-LXXVIII (documents 178-181): *Utilitati speciali prospicimus, cum communi saluti fidelium providemus. Attendentes igitur grave dispendium et irrecuperabile damnum, quod posset contingere ex imperitia medicorum, jubemus in posterum nullum medici titulum praetendentem audere practicari aliter, vel mederi nisi Salerni primitus et in conventu publico magistrorum judicio comprobatus cum testimonialibus litteris de fide et sufficienti scientia, tam magistrorum, quam ordinatorum nostrorum, ad praesentiam nostram, vel nobis a regno absentibus, ad illius praesentiam, qui vice nostra in regno remanserit, ordinatus accedat, et a nobis vel ab eo medendi licentiam consequatur: poena publicationis bonorum et annalis carceris imminente his, qui contra hujusmodi nostrae serenitatis edictum in posterum ausi fuerint practicari. Quia nunquam sciri potest scientia medicinae, nisi de scientia logicali praescribatur, statuimus, quod nullus studeat in medicinali scientia, nisi prius studeat ad minus triennio in scientia logicali: post triennium, si voluerit, ad studium medicinae procedat: ita quod chirurgiam, quae est pars medicinae, infra praedictum tempus addiscat. Post quod, et non ante, concedatur sibi licentia practicandi examinatione, juxta curiae formam, praehabita; et nihilominus recepto pro eo de praedicto tempore studii testimonio magistrali. Iste medicus jurabit servare formam curiae hactenus observatam, eo adjecto, quod si pervenerit ad notitiam suam quod aliquis confectionarius minus bene conficiat, curiae denunciabit, et quod pauperibus consilium gratis dabit. Iste medicas visitabit aegrotos suos ad minus bis in die, ad requisitionem infirmi semel nocte: a quo non recipiet per diem, si pro eo non egrediatur civitatem vel castram, ultra dimidiom tarenum auri. Ab infirmo autem, quem extra civitatem visitat, non recipiet per diem ultra tres tarrenos, com expensis infirmi, vel ultra quatuor tarrenos, cum expensis suis. Non contrahet societatem cum confectionariis, nec recipiet aliquem sub cura sua ad expensas suas pro certa pretii quatitate, nee ipse etiam habebit propriam stationem. Confectionarii vero facient confectionem expensis suis, cum testimonio medicorum, juxta formam constitutionis, nec admittentur ad hoc, ut teneant confectiones nisi praestito juramento, quod omnes confectiones suas secundum praedictam formam facient sine fraude. Lucrabitor autem stationarius de confectionibus suis secundum istum modum de confectionibus et simplicibus medicinis, quae non teneri consueverunt ultra annum a tempore emptionis, pro qualibet uncia poterit et licebit tres tarrenos lucrari. De aliis vero, quae ex natura medicaminum, vel ex alia causa, ultra annum in apotheca tenentur, pro qualibet uncia licebit lucrari sex tarrenos. Nec stationes hujusmodi erunt ubique, sed in certis civitatibus per regnum, ut inferius describitur. Nec tamen post completum quinquennium practicabit, nisi per annum integrum cum consilio experti medici practicetur. Magistri vero infra istud quinquennium libros authenticos, tam Hippocraticos, quam Galeni, in scholis doceant, tam in theoretica, quam in practica medicina. Salubri etiam constitutione sancimus, ut nullus chirurgicus ad practicam admittatur, nisi testimoniales litteras offerat magistrorum, in medicinali facultate legentium, quod per annum saltim in ea medicinae parte studuerit, quae chirurgiae instruit facultatem, et praesertim anatomiam humanorum corporum in scholis didicerit, et sit in ea parte medicinae perfectus, sine qua nec incisiones salubriter fieri poterunt, nec factae curari. In terra qualibet regni nostri nostrae jurisdictioni subjecta duos viros circumspectos et fide dignos volumus ordinari, et corporali per eos praestito sacramento teneri, quorum nomina ad curiam nostram mittentur: sub quorum testificatione electuaria et syrupi ac aliae medicinae legaliter fiant et sic factae vendantur. Salerni maxime per magistros in physica hoc volumus approbari. Praesenti etiam lege statuimus, ut nullus in medicina vel chirurgia nisi apud Salernum vel Neapolim legat in regno, nec magistri nomen assumat, nisi diligenter examinatus in praesentia nostrorum officialium et magistrorum artis ejusdem. Conficientes etiam medicinas sacramento corporaliter praestito volumus obligari, ut ipsas fideliter juxta artes et hominum qualitates in praesentia juratorum conficiant, quod si contra fecerint, publicatione bonorum suorum mobilium sentenionaliter condemnentur. Ordinati vero, quorum fidei praedicta sunt commissa, si fraudem in credito ipsis officio commisisse probentur, ultimo supplicio feriendos esse censemus.* The text of the diplomas awarded to qualified physicians was recorded by Peter della Vigna (in his letters, book 6, chapter 24): *Notum facimus fidelitati vestrae, quod fidelis noster* [name] *ad curiam nostram accedens, examinatus, inventus fidelis, et de genere fidelium ortus, et sufficiens ad artem medicinae exercendam extitit per nostram curiam approbatus. Propter quod de ipsius prudentia et legalitate confisi, recepto ab eo in curia nostra fidelitatis sacramento, et de arte ipsa fideliter exercenda, juxta consuetudinem juramento, dedimus ei licentiam exercendi artem medicinae in partibus ipsis: ut amodo artem ipsam ad honorum et fidelitatem nostram et salutem eorum qui indigent, fideliter ibi debeat exercere. Quo circa fidelitati vestrae praecipiendo mandamus, quatenus nullus sit, qui praedictum* [name] *fidelem nostrum super arte ipsa medicinae in terris ipsis, ut dictum est, fideliter exercendi, impediat de caetero, vel perturbet.* These general principles were followed by the Angevins after 1266; see *Codice Diplomatico del Regno di Carlo I e Carlo II d'Angio 1265-1309* (1863), volume 1, document 72, pages 234-235.

1160. Popularized by Philippe Ariès in his *Centuries of Childhood* (1960), though some of his theories have been legitimately challenged.

1161. Richard of San Germano, year 1243. For other sources *HDF*, volume 6, part 1, pages 98, 104-105; *RPR*, volume 2, page 943-944.

1162. Richard of San Germano, year 1243, states that the delegates were treated cordially, *a quo benigne satis recepti sunt, et benignum ad principem retulerunt responsum.* See also *HDF*, volume 6, part 1, pages 104-105; *Vie et Correspondance de Pierre de la Vigne,* page 309, number 13.

1163. Richard of San Germano, loc. cit.

1164. Ibid. Also *HDF*, volume 6, part 1, pages 124-130, 140-142.

1165. Richard of San Germano, year 1243; also *HDF*, volume 6, part 1, pages 112-116, 140, 146-147; *Chronica Regia Coloniensis*, in *MGH, Scriptores Rerum Germanicarum in Usum Scholarum,* volume 18 (1880), page 285.

1166. *Nichil veterum actoritati detrahitur.* See Richard of San Germano, loc. cit.; *HDF*, volume 6, part 1, pages 156-161. The statutes in the Constitutions addressed were book 1, numbers: 38, 39, 40, 42. For commentary see Caruso, Angelo, "Indagini sulla Legislazione di Federico II di Svevia per il Regno di Sicilia: Le Leggi Pubblicate a Foggia nell'Aprile 1240," in *Il Liber Augustalis di Federico II nella Storiografia* (1987) pages 41-68.

NOTES

1167. See note 1149 supra. Richard's brother and nephew were arrested with him.

1168. *HDF,* volume 6, part 1, pages 169-172.

1169. Ibid, pages 184-187.

1170. For his letter to his brother-in-law, Richard of Cornwall, *Matthaei Parisiensis, Chronica Majora,* volume 4, pages 300-305; other descriptions follow, pages 306-311.

1171. The incipit of an infamous bull of 9 May 1244 referred to the "perfidious Jews," *Impia Judaeorum perfidia,* a phrase used in Catholic liturgy into the middle of the twentieth century as *Oremus et pro perfidis Judaeis.* The same bull formally ordered that the *Talmud* be burned, a process Louis IX had already begun. See *RPR,* volume 2, page 966, entry 11376; also Mansi, Giovanni Domenico, *Sacrorum Conciliorum,* volume 23 (1779), columns 591-592. For apologetic commentary about the meaning of the words, see Oesterreicher, John, "Pro Perfidis Judaeis," *Theological Studies,* volume 8 (February 1947), pages 80-96. See also note 1124 supra.

1172. Mansi, Giovanni Domenico, *Sacrorum Conciliorum,* volume 23 (1779), columns 586-591. Founded by Peter Waldo around 1173, the Waldensians were declared heretical in 1215. For the Patarines see note 1018 supra.

1173. *Matthaei Parisiensis, Chronica Majora,* volume 4, page 299. The marriage of Constance (later Anna) to John III of Nicaea is noted by the chroniclers George Pachymeres and George Acropolites.

1174. *Matthaei Parisiensis,* volume 4, pages 311-316.

1175. Matthew Paris was present, hence the reliability of his account. See note 1127 supra, also Lunt, William, "The Sources for the First Council of Lyon, 1245," *The English Historical Review,* volume 33, number 129 (January 1918), pages 72-78.

1176. Frederick's sympathy toward Islam and its exponents is mentioned in *Sacrorum Conciliorum,* volume 23 (1779), column 635, and in other sources at note 1127, viz. *Matthaei Parisiensis,* volume 4, page 453: *Et quod execrabilius est, olim existens in partibus transmarinis, facta compositione quadam, immo verius collusione, cum Soldano, Machometi nomen in templo Domini diebus ac noctibus publice proclamari permisit. Et nuper nuntios Soldani Babiloniae, postquam idem Soldanus Terrae Sanctae, ac Christianis habitatoribus ejus per se ac suos dampna gravissima et inaestimabiles injurias irrogarat, fecit per Regnum Siciliae cum laudibus ad ejusdem Soldani excellentiam, sicut fertur, honorifice suscipi et magnifice procurari.*

1177. Namely John III of Nicaea; see note 1173.

1178. *Matthaei Parisiensis,* volume 4, page 456: *Haec igitur in medio concilio prolata cunctis audientibus, ad instar choruscantis fulguris, non mediocrem timorem incusserunt. Magistri igitur Thadaeus de Suessa et Walterus de Ocra, et alii procuratores imperatoris, et qui cum ipsis erant, emisso ejulatu flebili, hic femur, hic pectus in indicium doloris percutientes, vix a profluvio lacrimarum sese continuerunt. Et ait Thadaeus memoratus "Dies ista dies irae, calamitatis, et miseriae."* [Zephaniah 1:15] *Dominus igitur Papa, et praelati assidentes concilio, candelis accensis, in dictum imperatorem, qui jam imperator non est nominandus, terribiliter, recedentibus et confusis ejus procuratoribus, fulgurarunt.*

1179. For a detailed, complete text see *Sacrorum Conciliorum,* volume 23 (1779), columns 619-686; also works at note 1127.

1180. *Matthaei Parisiensis,* volume 4, pages 474-478.

1181. See notes 965 and 1039; also Davies, Brian (editor), *The Oxford Handbook of Aquinas* (2012); Hood, John, *Aquinas and the Jews* (1995); Sapir Abulafia, Anna, *Christians and Jews in the Twelfth-Century Renaissance* (1995); Waltz, James, "Muhammad and the Muslims in St Thomas Aquinas," *The Muslim World,* volume 66, number 2 (April 1976), pages 81-95; Plested, Marcus, *Orthodox Readings of Aquinas* (2012). The Orthodox theologian Sergei Bulgakov (1871-1944) was particularly critical of some of the views of Thomas Aquinas. Most of the work authored about Thomas Aquinas by Catholics is fawningly apologetic (comparatively few critiques of his commentary regarding other confessions have been written from Jewish, Muslim or Eastern Orthodox perspectives), and some concepts have found their way into recent jurisprudence, notably in the United States of America; see, for example, George, Robert, "Natural Law, the Constitution, and the Theory and Practice of Judicial Review," *Fordham Law Review,* volume 69, number 6 (2001), pages 2269-2283.

1182. *Historia Anglorum,* British Library Royal Manuscript 14.C.VII, folio 141 recto. The text, in *Matthaei Parisiensis,* volume 4, pages 544-545, 548-549, 610-612, reports that Conrad treated the prisoners, viewed as traitors, harshly. See also *HDF,* volume 6, part 1, pages 414-415, 429-431, 449-452.

1183. *Matthaei Parisiensis,* volume 4, pages 609-610.

1184. Ibid, pages 592-594, 605-607.

1185. Ibid, pages 612-613. The "crusade" against Frederick was not formally declared until 1249.

1186. *HDF,* volume 6, part 1, pages 465-467.

1187. Ibid, volume 6, part 2, pages 875-876, for the text of the betrothal agreement. For Elisabeth's story see *Queens of Sicily,* pages 461-468.

1188. See note 1148; the *Annales Siculi* mentions Nocera, perhaps intending Lucera, though Salimbene di Adam notes Nocera in his chronicle for Frederick's attack on Parma in 1248: *et Saraceni de Nuceria* (see note 1197). See also *HDF,* volume 6, part 1, pages 456-457, 471-472, issued at Lucera. Frederick was at Lucera in November 1246 when he ordered supplies for Louis; see note 1186.

1189. This was in March 1246, *HDF,* volume 6, part 1, pages 395-399, 402-406; volume 6, part 2, page 726. *Matthaei Parisiensis,* volume 4, pages 570-575, and the pope in turn suspected an assassination conspiracy by Frederick, ibid, pages 585, 605-607. See also note 1127 supra.

1190. *HDF,* volume 6, part 1, pages 487-489, for an example.

1191. *Matthaei Parisiensis,* volume 4, pages 566-568.

1192. For the renewal of royal privileges to the archdiocese in July 1247, *HDF,* volume 5, page 553; also Mongitore, Antonino, *Bullae, Privilegia et Instrumenta Panormitane Metropolitanae Ecclesiae Regni Siciliae Primariae,* page 106.

1193. After Berardo of Castagna died in September 1252, the primatial see of the *Regnum* remained vacant until 1257, probably because neither Pope Innocent IV, nor his successor Alexander IV, wanted to risk vesting much power in one prelate so soon after Frederick's death.

1194. For Beatrice's story see *Queens of Sicily,* pages 469-474; also the following note. For the agreements with Thomas of Savoy, uncle of Beatrice (Table 25), also *HDF,* volume 6, part 2, pages 657-665, 674-676, 740-743, etc.

1195. *Matthaei Parisiensis Chronica Majora,* volume 5, pages 571-573. Matthew Paris wrote this around 1256 to explain the paternity, royal status and legitimacy of Bianca's son, Manfred. Scholars often cite the wording of the marriage contract of Manfred (to Beatrice of Savoy) as evidence that the wedding between Bianca and Frederick was not celebrated until 1247 or even 1248, as Frederick's charter of April/May 1247 refers to "Manfred *Lancia,* son of the emperor," q.v. *HDF,* volume 6, part 1, pages 526-528. By December 1248, Frederick was referring to his wife's kinsman, Manfred Lancia, as *dilectus affinis noster,* implying canonical affinity through marriage; ibid, volume 6, part 2, page 672.

1196. Further discussion at *Queens of Sicily,* pages 453-460, and *Sicilian Queenship,* pages 132-136. See Table 23.

1197. The chief narrative account of this battle comes to us from Salimbene di Adam, hardly an unbiased source, and he based his version of events on hearsay. See Bernini, Ferdinando (editor), *Salimbene de Adam: Cronica* (1942), volume 1, pages 281-284.

NOTES

1198. See note 1186. Jean de Joinville's account is that of a participant; see Marzials, Frank (translator), *Memoirs of the Crusades by Villehardouin and de Joinville* (1908). For commentary on Arabic sources see El Merheb, Mohammad, "Louis IX in Medieval Arabic Sources: The Saint, the King, and the Sicilian Connection," *Al-Masaq: Journal of the Medieval Mediterranean*, volume 28, issue 3 (London 2016), pages 282-301.

1199. Beatrix, a daughter of Frederick Barbarossa, was a great-grandmother of Jean de Joinville and an aunt of Frederick II. It was this Beatrix who Barbarossa wished to betroth to King William II of Sicily (see Chapter 18).

1200. *Matthaei Parisiensis Chronica Majora*, volume 4, pages 613-614.

1201. *HDF*, volume 6, part 2, pages 567-568, 701-703.

1202. Ibid, pages 714-716.

1203. Ibid, volume 6, part 1, pages 487-489.

1204. Ibid, volume 6, part 2, pages 708-709.

1205. Ibid, pages 718-721, 743.

1206. Ibid, pages 733 (Naples), 740-743 (Benevento), 750-751 (Melfi), 751-775 (Foggia).

1207. *Chronica Majora*, volume 5, page 196.

1208. Ibid, pages 216-217. See also *HDF*, volume 6, part 2, pages 810-812, and for Frederick's testament (dated 10 December 1250) pages 805-810. The account by "Matthew Spinelli of Giovinazzo" (ibid, pages 812-813) was a hoax.

1209. From Matthew Paris: *Ab alto igitur suspirans pectore, et asserens se malle nunquam fuisse natum vel habenas imperii suscepisse, pro cujus juribus recuperandis et sustinendis tot et tantis fuerat inebriatus amaritudinibus, tale dicitur condidisse testamentum: Ego Fretthericus in primis relinquo pro anima mea 100,000 uncias auri pro Terra Sancta, sanctae Romanae ecclesiae recuperanda, expendenda, et exponenda, ad voluntatem filii mei Conradi. Item volo, quod omnia male ablata restituantur. Item, omnes captivos de imperio et regno relinquo liberos, exceptis proditoribus tantum. Item, relinquo totam terram ecclesiae liberam, et volo quod jura ecclesiae restituantur. Item, meum haeredem relinquo Conradum in imperio Romano et regno Siciliae. Item, relinquo filio meo Henrico regnum Jerosolimitanum et 10,000 uncias, secundum voluntatem Conradi filii mei. Item, nepoti meo filio scilicet filii mei Henrici, relinquo ducatum Austriae et 10 milia unciarum auri. Item, Manfredum filium meum relinquo ballivum Conradi in imperium, a Papia et citra, et regno Siciliae, usque ad XII annos, excepto quando Conradus erit praesens. Item, sepulturam meam eligo apud Panormi, ubi jacuit rex Willelmus II. Haec et alia multa continet dictum testamentum, quorum non recordor, quia minus fuerunt notabilia. Amicis autem suis et aliis filiis suis et ministris multa distribuit in auro praecipue et argento, Et hoc credibile fuit, quia eodem anno venerunt ad eum duodecim cameli onusti auro ed argento de partibus Orientalibus. Erat enim omnibus Soldanis Orientis particeps in mercimoniis institoriis et amicissimus, ita ut usque ad Indos sui currebant ad commodum suum tam per mare quam per terras institores.*

1210. Though chroniclers noted that Frederick II did not seem very pious, the accusation by Pope Gregory IX (in 1239) that the emperor had cynically declared Moses, Jesus and Muhammad to be "impostors" had no basis in fact and was refuted by Frederick himself. It was alleged (without proof) that Peter della Vigna wrote a treatise expounding this view of the Abrahamic faiths, and during the print era such a work was invented; a fine exposition is Minois, Georges, *The Atheist's Bible: The Most Dangerous Book That Never Existed* (2012). See also note 1010 supra.

1211. There are several definitions of "freethought," some more rigid or restrictive than this recent one. Bertrand Russell famously recognized that a freethinker could be a deist/theist.

1212. This is the simplest definition of a "secularist," who is not necessarily an atheist.

1213. As stated in the Introduction, "multiculturalism" (sometimes "ethnic pluralism" or "polyculturalism") is not used here in the recently-coined political sense.

1214. See Appendix 6; also Mendola, Louis, *The Kingdom of the Two Sicilies 1734-1861* (2020).

1215. *RPR,* volume 2, page 1169, entry 14163 (letter to clergy); ibid, page 1170, entry 14164 (letter to Berardo).

1216. Mendola, Louis, *Frederick, Conrad and Manfred of Hohenstaufen, Kings of Sicily 1210-1258: The Chronicle of Nicholas of Jamsilla* (2016), hereinafter *Jamsilla,* page 89, the chief source for Manfred's age.

1217. Ibid, pages 89-90.

1218. Sources such as *Jamsilla* (see the previous note) do not always distinguish very clearly between generic "German knights" and the Teutonic Knights (as knights of the Teutonic Order). For the Teutonic Order in Puglia see, amongst many other examples, *HDF,* volume 6, part 1, page 487; Capasso, Bartolomeo, *Historia Diplomatica Regni Siciliae* (1874), page 85-86, entry 176.

1219. The bull *Ad extirpanda,* issued at Perugia on 15 May 1252, authorized the use of torture by the Inquisition in particular cases. Much has been written about this directive, usually considered the earliest authority for torture to be condoned by the church. See *RPR,* volume 2, page 1203, entry 14592; for the text see *BRP,* volume 3, pages 552-558.

1220. This was encouraged by the bull *Purae fidei claritate* of 13 December 1251. See *RPR,* volume 2, page 1192, entry 14438; for the text see *BRP,* volume 3, pages 544-546.

1221. In 1254, thus after the death of Henry "the Younger," whom he served. See *RPR,* volume 2, page 1279, entry 15551; *Jamsilla,* pages 173-175.

1222. There is no foundation for the claim that Henry was poisoned on Conrad's orders.

1223. *Jamsilla,* pages 101-103; Saba Malaspina, chapter 3; *Annales Siculi,* year 1252 (sic).

1224. Manfred transferred the *Studium* back to Naples in 1258. For confirmation and expansion of its status by Charles I in October 1266 see *Codice Diplomatico del Regno di Carlo I e Carlo II d'Angio 1265-1309* (1863), volume 1, document 82, pages 250-269 (accompanied by numerous citations).

1225. *Annales Siculi,* year 1152 (sic). The tomb was destroyed a few years later in a great fire.

1226. *Jamsilla,* page 105; Saba Malaspina, chapter 4. Conradin was made a ward of the pope in Conrad's will. Although Berthold was nominally responsible for him, in childhood Conradin lived with his mother, Elisabeth, in Swabia and sometimes at the court of his uncle, Louis II, Duke of Bavaria. Only later did Manfred become the boy's regent. Here we must distinguish among four positions: the parenthood of Elisabeth as Conradin's mother, the official (and spiritual) guardianship exercised by the pope, the physical protection ensured by Louis, the political regency of the Kingdom of Sicily held by Berthold on Conradin's behalf.

1227. See Appendix 6 for a discussion of the authorship of *Jamsilla.*

1228. Adapted from *Jamsilla,* pages 105-106.

1229. Saba Malaspina, book 1, chapter 4. See also note 1226 supra.

1230. *Jamsilla,* page 118.

1231. For various sources see *RPR,* volume 2, page 1283.

1232. *Jamsilla,* page 151.

1233. Ibid, pages 155-162; Saba Malaspina, chapters 5-6.

1234. Construction of this church at the site of an earlier structure began around 1255; it is located in Piazza San Francesco d'Assisi, the nave running along what is now Via Merlo.

1235. *Jamsilla,* pages 211-212, 221.

1236. The Guelph and Ghibelline parties were not as formally organized in the Kingdom of Sicily as in other parts of Italy.

NOTES

1237. *Jamsilla,* pages 120-125. This was in 1254.

1238. Ibid, pages 173-193. 203-210.

1239. Ibid, pages 223-225.

1240. Ibid, page 226-227.

1241. The celebrant was William, about whom little is known with certainty; he was Archbishop of Palermo from 1257 until 1260 following a *sede vacante* (1254-1257).

1242. Saba Malaspina, book 2, chapter 2.

1243. *Matthaei Parisiensis Chronica Majora,* volume 5, pages 457-459.

1244. For Helena's story see *Queens of Sicily,* pages 475-484. Whether the nuptials actually took place in Trani at this time has been debated.

1245. Saba Malaspina, book 2, chapter 5. For the text see *BRP,* volume 3, pages 722-726.

1246. Though used for Frederick's dominions collectively, the phrase was coined by Augustine of Hippo.

1247. Saba Malaspina, book 2, chapter 7.

1248. Ibid, book 2, chapter 6. Also *RPR,* volume 2, page 1486, entry 18283; page 1495, entry 18402.

1249. Saba Malaspina, book 2, chapter 7; also *RPR,* volume 2, page 1484, entry 18256a.

1250. See *Il Tabulario della Magione di Palermo, Repertorio* (2011), pages 81-82, entries 115-116, of July 1262.

1251. Learning of the change of dynasty in 1266, Muhammad al-Mustansir ibn Yahya, who had treaties with Frederick II but not the Angevins, renounced his commitments to the Kingdom of Sicily.

1252. Sometimes Peter of Ireland, who may have taught Thomas Aquinas at the *Studium.* For more, see De Leemans, Pieter (editor), *Translating at Court: Bartholomew of Messina and Cultural Life at the Court of Manfred, King of Sicily* (2014).

1253. Saba Malaspina, book 2, chapter 9.

1254. This was mentioned in the *Chronicon Siculum* in 1389, the narrative stating that it had occurred already for a number of years; see De Blasi, Giuseppe, *Chronicon Siculum Incerti Authoris ab Anno 340 ad Annum 1396* (1887), page 85, transcribed from *Codex Ottobonianus Vaticanus,* number 2940.

1255. Sufism is associated more with the Sunni than other sects. During the Fatimid and Kalbid periods most of the Muslims of southern Italy remained Sunni despite the ruling class being Shia.

1256. An example, though it is not mentioned explicitly in the *Trotula* or other sources, survived into the twentieth century. This was a "cure" for male infidelity that called for a wife to sprinkle some of her dried, powdered menstrual blood over some food, such as pasta, to be consumed by her unfaithful husband. The folklorist and philologist Giuseppe Pitrè (1841-1916) collected information on modern witchcraft, of which some practices appear to have originated in medieval times; see his *Esseri Soprannaturali e Meravigliosi,* volume 4 in *Usi e Costumi: Credenze e Pregiudizi del Popolo Siciliano* (1952), pages 153-162; also note 372 supra.

1257. This scrutiny increased in later times, especially with the Holy Office (Spanish Inquisition) in 1478. See, among other works, Messana, Maria, *Inquisitori, Negromanti e Streghe nella Sicilia Moderna 1500-1782* (2007).

1258. For the text see *BRP,* volume 3, pages 744-747.

1259. See Goldstone, Nancy, *Four Queens: The Provencal Sisters Who Ruled Europe* (2007).

1260. Saba Malaspina, book 2, chapters 10-11.

1261. A good overview (in English) of the dynasty during this period is Cox, Eugene, *The Eagles of Savoy: The House of Savoy in Thirteenth-Century Europe* (1974).

1262. Saba Malaspina, book 2, chapters 17-19.

1263. See *RPR,* volume 2, page 1556, entry 19213; page 1577, entry 19515. For the text see *BRP,* volume 3, pages 760-763. A good source for the various papal and Angevin decrees is *Codice Diplomatico del Regno di Carlo I e Carlo II d'Angio 1265-1309* (1863), volume 1, pages 1-250.

1264. *RPR,* volume 2, page 1580, entry 19553.

1265. Here the focus is the Kingdom of Sicily. Fine general expositions of Charles and his activities during this period are provided by Nancy Goldstone (q.v. note 1259 supra) and Steven Runciman (in *The Sicilian Vespers,* chapter 6).

1266. It has been stated elsewhere that the numbers reported in these battles must be considered with caution. For that reason, those indicated here are merely approximate.

1267. See Chapter 12. Many shields of Manfred's knights bore the imperial eagle across the top section; those of the Angevin side were decorated with fleurs-de-lis between a red "label," described in Mendola, Louis, "Italian Chiefs of Allegiance" in *Journal of Heraldic Studies*, number 1 (1985), pages 33-39.

1268. Reported in the account by Andrew of Hungary.

1269. The chief sources are the chronicles of Saba Malaspina (book 3, chapters 6-10), Andrew of Hungary and Bartholomew of Neocastro, supplemented by a codex of the *Breve Chronicon de Rebus Siculis.* A recent edition of Andrew's original text is Tamburrini, Alberto, *Descrizione della Vittoria Riportata da Carlo Conte d'Angio* (2010). Translations appear in Mendola, Louis, *The Battle of Benevento according to Andrew of Hungary and Saba Malaspina* (2021). A good recent entry is Grillo, Paolo, *L'Aquila e il Giglio: La Battaglia di Benevento* (2015), but see also Meomartini, Almerico, *La Battaglia di Benevento* (1895).

1270. See Capasso, Bartolomeo, *Historia Diplomatica Regni Siciliae* (1874), pages 320-323, entry 521. The historicity of this episode (popularized by Dante) is disputed.

1271. *BRP,* volume 3, pages 793-798.

1272. Saba Malaspina, book 4, chapters 1-16; Bartholomew of Neocastro, chapters 8-10.

1273. Peter of Pretio famously condemned this action. A fine recent edition is Caperna, Umberto, *Invettiva contro Carlo d'Angio per l'Uccisione di Corradino di Svevia* (2010).

1274. Much has been written about this. In addition to the contemporary accounts cited at notes 31, 971 and 975 supra, a good recent entry is Lower, Michael, *The Tunis Crusade of 1270: A Mediterranean History* (2018). Steven Runciman considers it in *The Sicilian Vespers* (1958), and see also the following note.

1275. For example, in February of 1267, Charles ordered regular annual convocations of the kingdom's barons and justiciars; see *Codice Diplomatico del Regno di Carlo I e Carlo II d'Angio 1265-1309* (1863), volume 1, document 96, pages 286-289. A good study is Dunbabin, Jean, *Charles I of Anjou: Power, Kingship and State-Making in Thirteenth-Century Europe* (1998). Émile Léonard's *Les Angevins de Naples* (1954) is highly informative; this was published in Italian translation in 1967. A more recent entry is Georges Jehel's *Les Angevins de Naples: Une Dynastie Européenne* (2014). A good biography of Charles I is Michel Grenon's *Charles d'Anjou: Frère conquérant de Saint Louis* (2012).

1276. In English, see Runciman, Steven, *The Sicilian Vespers* (1958), and Mendola, Louis, *Sicily's Rebellion against King Charles* (2015), both containing fine bibliographies. Also Schneidman, Lee, "Aragon and the War of the Sicilian Vespers, *The Historian,* volume 22, number 3 (May 1960), pages 250-263.

1277. There are several traditional biographies of John of Procida, of which a classic entry is Niccolò Buscemi's *La Vita di Giovanni di Procida, Privata e Pubblica* (1836).

NOTES

1278. Archivo de la Corona de Aragón (Barcelona), Cancillería, Cartas Reales, Pedro II [III], Serie general, 10, issued at Trapani 1 May 1283, written in Catalan to Pedro de Aibar, one of the knights in the royal suite.

1279. See note 969; also Abulafia, David, "The Last Muslims in Italy," in *Dante and Islam* (2015); Maier, Christoph, "Crusade and rhetoric against the Muslim colony of Lucera: Eudes of Châteauroux's Sermones de Rebellione Sarracenorum Lucherie in Apulia," *Journal of Medieval History,* volume 21 (1995), pages 343-385.

1280. An early mention of the Hundred Horse Chestnut in print is Filoteo, Antonio, *La Descrittione Latina del Sito di Mongibello* (1611), pages 67-69; another account comes to us from *Il Mongibello Descritto da Don Pietro Carrera in Tre Libri* (1636), pages 15-16, which suggests that thirty horses can be accommodated. In 1745, the *Tribunale del Real Patrimonio del Regno di Sicilia,* an agency charged with protecting royal assets and collecting certain taxes such as the *donativo,* established formal protection for the tree. See also Capozzo, Guglielmo, *Memorie su la Sicilia* (1840), volume 1, pages 249-252. The legend was popularized by, amongst others, the poet Giuseppe Borrello (1820-1894). More generally, see Cusack, Carole, *The Sacred Tree: Ancient and Medieval Manifestations* (2011). Queen Isabella does not seem to have spent much time in Sicily, but neither do the Angevin queens sometimes associated with the legend.

1281. In the middle of the twelfth century, Peter Lombard posited that there were seven Catholic sacraments, but only later, at the Council of Trent (1545) was the number formally established in canon law.

1282. See, for example, Di Franco, Saverio, *Alla Ricerca di un'Identità Politica: Giovanni Antonio Summonte e la Patria Napoletana* (2012).

1283. The "Four Days of Naples" was a civilian revolt against repressive forces, mostly German with a few Fascist Italians, beginning on September twenty-eighth, 1943, before the Allied armies arrived to liberate the city. The civilian leader of the Fascist faction was Domenico Tilena. Two generals, Riccardo Pentimalli and Ettore Deltetto (Italian commissioned officers were Fascist), failed to respond to German action and fled the city dressed as civilians. The essential facts are generally known, but additional details were provided to one of the authors by Marquis Achille Di Lorenzo (1909-2000), an anti-Fascist imprisoned during the riots who served as a liaison officer for Mark Clark, the American general.

1284. Despite substantial investment, a chain of pizza restaurants founded by an Irish-American in the United States failed in Italy after seven years of activity; see Povoledi, Elisabetta, "In Italy, Where Pizza Was Born, Domino's Bows Out," *The New York Times* (9 August 2022). In the academic sphere, similar phenomena usually involve xenocentric (foreign) historians attempting to impose their "outsider's" views upon the "natives" (see note 12 supra), a mentality that sometimes spawns bizarre results (see note 34).

1285. Here *identity politics* may be defined as the promotion of the interests peculiar to a specific social, ethnic or religious group within a larger society over the concerns of the majority. See note 15 for various paradigms and interpretations of the concepts of ethnicity and nationhood.

1286. The Introduction mentions standpoint theory, the UNESCO protection of the Sicilian and Neapolitan languages, xenocentrism and cultural appropriation. A recent exposition is Francioni, Francesco, "Beyond State Sovereignty: The Protection of Cultural Heritage as a Shared Interest of Humanity," *Michigan Journal of International Law,* volume 25, number 4 (2004), pages 1209-1228. See also note 1284 supra.

1287. The biography of Frederick II authored by Ernst Kantorowicz was zealously criticized by his rivals, but there are other (recent) works, some concerning the Hauteville era, that propound dubious theses. This occurs rather frequently in academia, where every thesis, dissertation and published paper is expected to present "new" facts or theories.

1288. In Britain, Denis Mack Smith infamously permitted one of his students to submit a doctoral dissertation, later published as a monograph, advancing the bizarre notion that the Mafia, which originated at the end of the eighteenth century, was an idea but not an organization. Such a theory would never have been promoted by the authors of this book, Sicilians who live in Palermo and know its social culture (see also note 34). More generally, see MacKenzie, Alison (editor), *The Epistemology of Deceit in a Postdigital Era: Dupery by Design* (2021). The notion that female infanticide was practiced in some parts of Italy, such as Tuscany, after 1500 is based on a flawed interpretation of information in baptismal registers that sometimes record more baptisms for males than females; Louis Mendola, who has researched such records since 1991 and wrote a book on Sicilian genealogy, has debunked this hypothesis, which seems to reflect certain biases.

1289. A noteworthy contribution is Patroni Griffi, Filena, and Leone, Alfonso, *Le Origini di Napoli Capitale* (1987), which challenges some theories advanced by the onetime Fascist Benedetto Croce (1866-1952). Croce was not alone in his Italianist zeal; Michele Amari (1806-1889), a unificationist, infamously compared the War of the Vespers of 1282 to the unification effort, or *Risorgimento*, that annexed Sicily (and the entire Kingdom of the Two Sicilies) to the Kingdom of Italy six centuries later.

1290. See Horowitz, Donald, *Ethnic Groups in Conflict* (second edition, 2000); Chandra, Kanchan, "What is Ethnic Identity and Does It Matter?" *Annual Review of Political Science,* volume 9 (2006), pages 397-424.

1291. In a national election in 2018, a new political movement popular among younger voters edged out other parties in the south while older parties won more seats in the north; see Kington, Thomas, "Italy's Political Map is Like a Flashback to 200 Years Ago," *The Times* (UK), 7 March 2018. This occurred again four years later, though the numbers were lower; see Pianigiani, Gaia, "Key Takeaways from Italy's Landmark Election," *The New York Times* (26 September 2022).

1292. In literature, expressionism is closely linked to the work of James Joyce, William Faulkner and Franz Kafka; in cinema it has been utilized by directors such as Steven Spielberg. Historians make use of it in such fields as modern (contemporary) biography; this relates to the forms of historicism mentioned in Appendix 6. See also the following note.

1293. See Mendola, Louis, *Sicily's Rebellion against King Charles: The Story of the Sicilian Vespers* (2015). The journalistic style called "literary journalism" or "creative nonfiction," popularized by the American journalists Gaetano (Gay) Talese and Tom Wolfe, also reflects a form of expressionism.

1294. For observations regarding analogous rights, see Wahlström, Ninni, "Understanding the Universal Right to Education as Jurisgenerative Politics and Democratic Iterations," *European Educational Research Journal,* volume 8, number 4 (2009), pages 520-533.

1295. Sicily affords researchers the world's most complete genealogical records. See Mendola, Louis, *Sicilian Genealogy and Heraldry* (2014).

1296. See Hoffman, Jan, "Race Question in Supreme Court Adoption Case Unnerves Tribes," *The New York Times* (7 November 2022); Berbery, Maria, and O'Brien, Karen, "Predictors of White Adoptive Parents' Cultural and Racial Socialization Behaviors With Their Asian Adopted Children," *Adoption Quarterly,* volume 14, number 4 (2011), pages 284-304; Castner, Jessica, and Foli, Karen, "Racial Identity and Transcultural Adoption," *The Online Journal of Issues in Nursing,* volume 27, number 1 (January 2022). See also note 1302.

1297. Social and economic reasons for this situation are noted in Appendix 7.

1298. An obvious example is the observance of the feast of Saint Louis in August in Monreale, where his heart reposes. See note 31.

1299. The most colorful of these is the liquefaction of the blood of Saint Januarius, who died at Pozzuoli in 305. See note 1254.

1300. The role of the church cannot be understated. In many small towns of the former *Regnum* into the twentieth century, it was not unusual for the principal local parish of the *chiesa madre* to be, or appear to be, more important than the *municipio* (town hall). The archbishops of Naples and Palermo were sometimes viewed as being more important than mayors; at the least, they enjoyed (and still enjoy) greater prestige.

NOTES

1301. See Alessandria, Kathryn, et al., "Italian American Ethnic Identity Persistence: A Qualitative Study," *Identity: An International Journal of Theory and Research,* volume 16 (2016), number 4, pages 282-298.

1302. See Leong, Frederick, and Chou, Elayne, "The Role of Ethnic Identity and Acculturation in the Vocational Behavior of Asian Americans: An Integrative Review," *Journal of Vocational Behavior,* volume 44, number 2 (April 1994), pages 155-172. See also note 1296 supra.

1303. See notes 310 and 1073. The stylized rendering of the Komodo dragon in a painting of the ceiling of the Palatine Chapel was first identified by Antonino Costantino and Marco Masseti. Previously, it was usually thought to be a simple (mythological) dragon, though it is clearly depicted as a carnivore with scales, yet lacks wings, nor is it shown breathing fire or in any way rendered as a fabulous beast, cf. the depictions in the carved cloister capitals of Monreale created a few years later.

1304. In Giuseppe Tomasi di Lampedusa's novel, *The Leopard* (1959), the protagonist makes reference to Sicily's polyglot history in speaking about the island being conquered so many times.

1305. See, most notably, Dyde, Samuel Walters (translator), *Hegel's Philosophy of Right* (1896), page 288. Hegel's essential point of reference was monarchy, and Karl Marx famously disagreed with some of his conclusions while accepting his fundamental methodology as sound.

1306. A wide interpretation of the term "ethnicity" extends to related areas such as caste. See Kaur, Harmeet, "Brown University bans caste discrimination throughout campus in a first for the Ivy League," *CNN* (7 December 2022).

1307. As it is used here, "transethnic" describes those who identify personally with an ethnicity other than one into which they were born and/or raised; this often involves cultural appropriation (see note 13 supra). The perceptions and misperceptions of some foreigners writing about the history of southern Italy and its people were considered in the Introduction (see also Appendix 6). Conversely, a condition inherent in the work of some Italian history professors here in Italy is that, being employees of the Italian state, they are often reluctant to overtly "criticize" movements such as the *Risorgimento* (and the view of the Middle Ages advocated by many of its proponents).

1308. See Takei, Milton, "Collective Memory as the Key to National and Ethnic Identity: The Case of Cambodia," *Nationalism and Ethnic Politics,* volume 4 (1998), number 3, pages 59-78.

1309. See Pac, Teresa, *Common Culture and the Ideology of Difference in Medieval and Contemporary Poland* (2022), page 7; more generally, Boyer, Ernest, "The Scholarship of Engagement," *Journal of Public Service and Outreach,* volume 1, number 1 (1996), pages 11-20. The National Endowment for the Humanities (an agency of the United States government) defines a "public scholar" as an expert in a humanistic field when writing for the broad public, and not specifically for an academic readership.

1310. See Appiah, Kwame Anthony: *The Ethics of Identity* (2005); *The Lies That Bind: Rethinking Identity* (2018).

1311. Fazello, Thomas. *De Rebus Siculus* (1558-1560); *Le Due Deche dell'Historia di Sicilia* (1573).

1312. This has been considered by a number of modernists in recent decades, though rather few medievalists outside Italy have noted the social impact of the Kingdom of Sicily (pre-1266) on life in southern Italy into recent times. The authors suggest that only by living in southern Italy for decades can one truly appreciate the extent of the social differences between the so-called *Mezzogiorno* and regions north of Rome. Moreover, the social culture of Sicily seems even more removed from that of Italy generally than that of mainland parts of the *Regnum* such as Campania. See notes in Appendix 7 and also, for numerous references, the bibliography in Mendola, Louis, *The Kingdom of the Two Sicilies 1734-1861* (2020).

1313. Noted by Anne Olivia Bauso, an American, in "25 Most Beautiful Cities in the World: Beauty Lies in All Corners of the Globe," *Travel and Leisure* (New York, 8 January 2023), where it was sixth in the list after Barcelona, Queenstown, Istanbul, Paris and San Francisco.

F. THOMÆ FAZELLI
SICVLI OR. PRÆDICA-
TORVM

DE REBVS SICVLIS DECADES DVAE, NVNC
PRIMVM IN LVCEM EDITAE.

HIS ACCESSIT TOTIVS OPERIS IN-
DEX LOCVPLETISSIMVS.

CAVTVM EST PHILIPPI ANGLIAE, HISPANIAE,
Siciliæq; Regis, Pauli. IIII. Pont. Max. ac Venetæ Reip. priuilegio, ne
cui has Decades de Siculis rebus ad decennium in eorum ditione vel imprimere, vel alibi impreſſas venales
habere, neue in sermonē Italicū iniuſ-
ſu authoris vertere ſub nul
la liceat.

First published history of Sicily, by Thomas Fazello, in 1558

SOURCES AND BIBLIOGRAPHY

Manuscript Sources

A number of charters and other documents were consulted directly at archives in Italy and elsewhere. For the benefit of scholars wishing to consult these manuscripts, it should be noted that cataloguing systems change over time. For example, the collection at the Palermo Archive of State formerly known as *Pergamene Varie* (sundry manuscripts) has been known since 2007 as *Pergamene di Diversa Provenienza,* literally "manuscripts from various sources," and it is presently housed in the more modernized, more secure Catena division rather than the Gancia off Via Alloro at the opposite end of Piazza Marina. The *Fondo Messina* (Messina Collection) of the Fundación Casa Ducal de Medinaceli, formerly housed in Seville, is now conserved at the archive of the Hospital de Tavera (de San Juan Bautista) in Toledo. The Vatican Apostolic Library has retained many call numbers. Other idiosyncrasies confront the researcher; for example, most Spanish charters and chronicles of the twelfth century are dated with reference to the "Spanish era" dating system that begins with the year 38 BC (BCE), probably based on the infelicitous date that a certain Roman tax was imposed in Iberia. A few charters, letters and chronicles may be consulted online, where some published transcriptions and extracts are also made available. For convenience in identification, the letters A-II correspond to references to each manuscript in this volume's endnotes.

A) Archivio di Stato di Palermo, Tabulario dei Monasteri di San Filippo di Fragalà e di Santa Maria di Maniace: Manuscript 6 (decree issued on parchment before 1113, probably *circa* 1110, by Adelaide in the name of her son Roger II renewing to the monastery privileges granted by her late husband replacing the previous decree written on paper).

B) Archivio di Stato di Palermo, Tabulario dei Monasteri di San Filippo di Fragalà e di Santa Maria di Maniaci: Manuscripts 7, 11, 12 (decrees made into 1112 endowing the monastery on Adelaide's initiative); Manuscript 10 (reissue in 1109 of former decree of Roger I delimiting territory of abbey of Saint Barbarus).

C) Archivio di Stato di Palermo, Tabulario dei Monasteri di San Filippo di Fragalà e di Santa Maria di Maniace: Manuscript 9 (paper letter of March 1109 in Greek on upper half and Arabic on lower half from Adelaide commanding jurats of Kasr'Janni, now Enna, to protect the monastery of Saint Philip of Demenna, in the San Marco Valley, under her personal patronage).

D) Tabulario Cappella Palatina: Manuscript number 13 (royal concession of ecclesiastical property in Palermo by Margaret and young William, in March 1167, bearing signatures of Matthew of Aiello, Caïd Martin and Walter the rector and future archbishop).

E) Tabulario della Cattedrale di Palermo: Manuscript number 21 (royal concession of the feudal rights of the mills on the manor of Brucato, the Arabic *Bur-Ruqqad,* to Walter, the newly-consecrated Archbishop of Palermo, in September 1169).

F) Tabulario della Cattedrale di Palermo: Manuscript number 22 (William grants Archbishop Walter of Palermo rights to judge adulterers except for claims falling under civil jurisdiction, 15 April 1172).

G) Tabulario di Santa Maria Nova, Monreale (in the Biblioteca Centrale della Regione Siciliana, Palermo): Manuscript number 8, 1 March 1174, (Nicholas, Archbishop of Messina, exempts Abbey of Maniace founded by Margaret from taxation).

H) Tabulario di Santa Maria Nova, Monreale (in the Biblioteca Centrale della Regione Siciliana): Manuscript number 20, March 1177, (Theobald, Bishop of Monreale, establishes rights of Abbey of Maniace).

I) Archivio di Stato di Palermo, Pergamene Varie: Manuscript number 3, November 1146 (recorded in Greek, confirms the sale of familial property near the Martorana by the children of Eugenius for a thousand gold tarì, includes epitaph to George of Antioch, founder of the Martorana, dated 1151).

KINGDOM OF SICILY

J) Archivio di Stato di Palermo, Tabulario di Santa Maria Maddalena of Messina: Manuscript number 50 (Margaret and William order nobles to exempt a monastery from taxation based on established policy, in 1168).

K) Archivio di Stato di Palermo, Tabulario dei Monasteri di San Filippo di Fragalà e di Santa Maria di Maniace: Manuscript 17 (TSFF17), 27 November 1171 (unsealed, probably a copy of an original, sealed charter; recorded in Greek and Latin, confirms privileges of Roger II protecting said monasteries, exempting them from the obligation to provide timber and livestock, lodge men-at-arms, and so forth, effectively exempting them from local civic authority).

L) Tabulario della Cattedrale di Palermo: Manuscript number 29 (Queen Constance's assignment of some serfs, formerly under the feudal jurisdiction of the late Archbishop Walter, to the authority of the notary Rainaldo, dated April 1196).

M) Tabulario di Santa Maria Nova, Monreale (in the Biblioteca Centrale della Regione Siciliana): Manuscript number Balsamo 31, 30 December 1174, (Pope Alexander III grants status and privileges of "major abbey" to Monreale's Benedictine monastery).

N) Archivio di Stato di Palermo, Tabulario della Magione: Manuscripts 3 (April 1136) and 4 (January 1145) both copied in February 1291 (King Roger II grants serfs and lands to Adeline, the wet nurse of his late son Henry, near Vicari).

O) Vatican Apostolic Library: Codice Vaticano Latino 3880, "Liber Privilegiorum Sanctae Montis Regalis Ecclesiae" chartulary (transcriptions of royal and papal charters relative to Monreale Abbey, several during the reign of William II).

P) Archivo de la Catedral de Tudela: Cajón 1, D. Manuscript number 20 (marriage charter between García Ramírez and Margaret l'Aigle).

Q) British Library, London: Harley Manuscript 5786, folio 79r (trilingual psalter composed in Sicily in Latin, Greek and Arabic during the reign of Roger II).

R) Archivio di Stato di Palermo: Direzione Centrale Statistiche (maps drawn between 1820 and 1850 showing medieval manors in Sicily).

S) Fundación Casa Ducal de Medinaceli (Toledo), Fondo Messina: Manuscript number 1118, November 1167 (Caïd Martin, acting on orders of Margaret and William II, issues this directive in Greek and Arabic restoring authority to Nicholas, Archbishop of Messina; only the Greek text mentions Margaret).

T) Fundación Casa Ducal de Medinaceli (Toledo), Fondo Messina: Manuscript number 109, March 1168, 1st indiction (William II and Margaret cede the Agrò Woods to the Holy Savior monastery of Messina).

U) Fundación Casa Ducal de Medinaceli (Toledo), Fondo Messina: Manuscript number 528, November 1176, 10th indiction (Margaret renews a donation effected five years earlier of some flat land near Milazzo to the Cistercian monastery of Santa Maria at Novara).

V) Fundación Casa Ducal de Medinaceli (Toledo), Fondo Messina: Manuscript number 522, May 1161, 9th indiction (William I confirms to the eldest sons of feudal vassals their hereditary rights to succeed their fathers killed in the service of the king, while conceding the citizens of Messina certain tax exemptions).

W) Vatican Apostolic Library: Codex Pal. Lat 1071. King Manfred's copy of Frederick's treatise *De Arte Venandi cum Avibus*.

X) Biblioteca Nacional de España (Madrid): Codex number VITR/26/2 (bdh0000022766), the *Historia Bizantina* ("Synopsis of Histories") of Ioannes Skylitzes, copied in Greek in Palermo circa 1130 from an older manuscript, chronicling years 811-1057.

Y) Burgerbibliothek, Berne: Codex number 120.2, *Liber ad Honorem Augusti sive de Rebus Siculis* by Peter of Eboli, written in Latin verse in Palermo around 1197.

SOURCES AND BIBLIOGRAPHY

Z) Vatican Apostolic Library: Codex Vaticanus Latinus 3793 (electronic ID 214430), pages 60, 61, 62. *Contrasto* of Cielo d'Alcamo.

AA) British Library, London: Yates Thompson Manuscript 12, folio 188v (French translation executed and illuminated after 1232 of the *Historie d'Outremer* originally written in Latin by William of Tyre).

BB) British Library, London: Royal Manuscript 14B.VI ("Royal Chronicle" showing genealogy of kings of England, composed around 1300, featuring illumination of a young, blonde Joanna).

CC) British Library, London: Royal Manuscript 20A.II, folios 152v and 154r (copy of a letter attributed to Queen Joanna written to Hugh IV, King of Cyprus).

DD) British National Archives, Kew: Document C47/3/3 (account of fabric issued at Easter 1135 for trousseau of Isabella of England).

EE) Archivio di Stato di Palermo, Tabulario della Magione: Manuscripts 94, 96, charters of July 1262 (Manfred confirms rights of Magione commandery of Teutonic Order in Palermo).

FF) Biblioteca Casanatense, Rome: Codex 614, folios 33-36 (rite of reginal coronation).

GG) Archivio di Stato di Palermo, Tabulario dei Monasteri di San Filippo di Fragalà e di Santa Maria di Maniace: Manuscript 1 (TSFF1), 1091 (copy recorded in Greek and Latin, confirms privileges of Roger II protecting said monasteries).

HH) Biblioteca Comunale di Casa Professa, Palermo: Manuscript QqD3, folios 66-68, 76-79 (folio 76 recto is a near-contemporary copy of charter issued by Lucy of Cammarata in August 1141).

II) Biblioteca Estense Universitaria, Modena: Manuscript ALFA.H.8.14 (ITA 281). Contemporary copy of the *Cronaca di Partenope*.

Primary Sources in Print

This list includes a few works in translation, with others in the next section. In the endnotes, passages in certain chronicles (e.g. Godfrey Malaterra, Hugh Falcandus) are cited by chapter or year, thus facilitating ready consultation in *any* published edition. Some major works in series are referred to generally, with detailed references in the notes.

Acta Imperii Inedita seculi XIII, Urkunden un Briefe. Collection. Edited by Winkelmann, Eduard (1880).

Adémar de Chabannes, Chronique. The *Ademari Chronicon,* edited by Chavanon, Jules (1897).

Albertus Magnus De Animalibus Libri XXVI. Edited by Stadler, Hermann (1920).

Alexiad of Anna Comnena. Translated by Sewter, Edgar Robert Ashton (1969).

The Anglo Saxon Chronicle According to the Several Original Authorities. Translation by Thorpe, Benjamin (1861).

Annales Barenses, in *Monumenta Germaniae Historica,* volume 5. Edited by Pertz, Georg (1844), pages 52-63.

The Annales Barensis and the Annales Lupi Protospatharii: Critical Edition and Commentary. Edited by Churchill, William. (1979).

Annales Beneventani, in *Monumenta Germaniae Historica,* volume 3. Edited by Pertz, Georg (1839).

Annales Casinenses, in *Monumenta Germaniae Historica,* volume 19. Edited by Pertz, Georg Heinrich (1866), pages 303-320.

Annales Cavenses, in *Monumenta Germaniae Historica,* volume 3. Edited by Pertz, Georg (1839).

KINGDOM OF SICILY

Annales Ceccanenses, in *Monumenta Germaniae Historica,* volume 19. Edited by Pertz, Georg Heinrich (1866), pages 275-302.

Annales Ecclesiastici. Compendium. Baronio, Cesare (1746).

Annales Erphesfurdenses Lothariani, in *Monumenta Erphesfurtensia Saec XII, XIII, XIV: Scriptores Rerum Germanicarum in Usum Scholarum,* volume 9. Edited by Holder-Egger, Osvald (1899).

Annales Marbacenses, in *Monumenta Germaniae Historica,* volume 17. Edited by Pertz, Georg (1861), pages 142-180.

Annales Marbacenses qui Dicuntur, in *Scriptores Rerum Germanicarum in Usum Scholarum,* volume 9 (1907).

Annales Patherbrunnenses. Edited by Scheffer-Boichorst, Paul (1870).

Annales Pisani in *Rerum Italicarum Scriptores,* volume 6, part 2 (1936).

Annales Siculi, in *Rerum Italicarum Scriptores,* volume 5. Edited by Muratori, Lodovico (1774, reprint Bologna 1927).

Annalista Saxo, in *Monumenta Germaniae Historica, Scriptorum,* volume 6 (1844).

Anonymous Historia Sicula, in *Bibliotheca Historica Regni Siciliae,* volume 2. Edited by Caruso, Giovanni Battista (1723).

Arnoldi Chronica Slavorum in Usum Scholarum ex Monumentis Germaniae, in the *Scriptores Rerum Germanicarum* series. Edited by Pertz, Georg (1868).

The Art of Courtly Love by Andreas Capellanus. Translated by Parry, John Jay (1969).

The Art of Falconry. Translated by Wood, Casey, and Fyfe, Marjorie (1943).

Biblioteca Arabo-Sicula, 2 volumes. Translation and notes by Amari, Michele (1880): Ali ibn al-Athir al-Jazari, Wali al Din ibn Khaldun, Abulfeda, Abu Abd Allah al Tijani, et al.

Biblioteca Bio-Bibliografica della Terra Santa e dell'Oriente Francescano. Compilation edited and annotated by Golubovich, Girolamo (1906).

Bibliotheca Scriptorum qui Res in Sicilia Gestas, 2 volumes. Edited by Gregorio, Rosario (1791-1792): Bartholomew of Neocastro, Niccolò Speciale, Simon of Lentini, *Anonymous Historia Sicula,* etc.

Book in Honor of Augustus by Pietro da Eboli. Translated and annotated by Hood, Gwenyth (2012).

Book of King Roger by Abdullah al Idrisi: *L'Italia Descritta nel Libro di Re Ruggero Compilato da Edrisi* (1883), Italian translation by Michele Amari and Celestino Schiaparelli, with original Arabic text; *Al-Idrisi's Description of Sicily* (1977), English translation by Leonard Chiarelli; *Il Libro di Ruggero* (2008), Italian translation by Umberto Rizzitano.

Boso's Life of Alexander III. Translated by Ellis, George (1973).

Breve Chronicon de Rebus Siculis, in *Monumenta Germaniae Historica,* volume 72. Edited by Stürner, Wolfgang (2004).

Bullae, Privilegia et Instrumenta Panormitane Metropolitanae Ecclesiae Regni Siciliae Primariae. Mongitore, Antonino (1734).

Bullarium Hellenicum: Pope Honorius III's Letters to Frankish Greece and Constantinople 1216-1227. Translated by Duba, William, and Schabel, Christopher (2015).

Bullarum Diplomatum et Privilegiorum Sanctorum Romanorum Pontificum. Compilation by Gaude, Francesco from the *Bullarium* (Turin 1859).

Burchardi Praepositi Uspergensis Chronicon, in *Scriptores Rerum Germanicarum in Usum Scholarum,* volume 16. Edited by Holder-Egger, Osvald (1916).

SOURCES AND BIBLIOGRAPHY

Calendar of Documents Preserved in France Illustrative of the History of Great Britain and Ireland 918-1206, volume 1. Round, Horace, editor (1899).

Carmen Miserabile Super Destructione Regni Hungariae per Tartaros Facta, by Roger of Torre, in *Monumenta Germaniae Historica, Scriptorum,* volume 29 (1892).

Cartulaire Général de l'Ordre des Hospitaliers de S. Jean de Jérusalem. Edited by Delaville Le Roulx, Joseph (1894).

Catálogo de los Cartularios Reales del Archivo General de Navarra 1007-1384. Idoate, Florencio (1974).

Catalogo Illustrato del Tabulario di Santa Maria Nuova in Monreale. Garufi, Carlo Alberto (1902).

Catalogus Baronum. Jamison, Evelyn (1972). See also Del Re's *Cronisti,* volume 1, below.

La Chanson d'Antioche. Edited by Graindor de Douai (1862).

La Chanson d'Aspremont. Edited by Brandin, Louis (1923 edition).

The Book of Chivalry of Geoffroi de Charney: Text, Context and Translation. Kaeuper, Richard, and Kennedy, Elspeth (1996).

Chronica Adefonsi Imperatoris. Edited by Sánchez Belda, Luis (1950).

Chronica Albrici Monachi Trium Fontium of Alberic of Trois-Fontaines, in *Monumenta Germaniae Historica, Scriptorum,* volume 23. Edited by Pertz, Georg Heinrich (1874), pages 631-950.

Chronica Regia Coloniensis, in *Monumenta Germaniae Historica, Scriptores Rerum Germanicarum in Usum Scholarum,* volume 18 (1880).

The Chronicle of Ibn al-Athir for the Crusading Period from al-Kamil fi'l-Ta'rikh by Ali ibn al-Athir. Part 2, 541-589/1146-1193. Richards, Donald (2007-2008).

Chronica Magistri Rogeri de Houedene (4 volumes). Edited by Stubbs, William (1870).

Chronica Monasterii Casinensis, in *Monumenta Germaniae Historica,* volume 34. Edited by Hoffmann, Hartmut (1980).

Chronicle of Alfonso the Emperor. Translation of the *Chronica Adefonsi Imperatoris* by Lipskey, Glenn Edward (1972).

Chronicles of the Reigns of Stephen, Henry II and Richard I, volume 2. Edited by Howlett, Richard (1885).

The Chronicle of Robert of Torigni. Edited by Howlett, Richard (1889).

Chronicon Budense post Elapsos ab Editione. Edited by Podhradczky, Josef (1838).

Chronicon Hierosolymitanae (1584), chronicle of Albert of Aix (or Aachen).

Chronicon Ignoti Civis Barensis, in *Rerum Italicarum Scriptores,* volume 5. Edited by Peregrino, Camillo (1724). Based on edition of the "Salerno Codex" published in 1643.

Chronicon de Lanercost. Edited by Stevenson, Joseph (1839).

Chronicon Pictum Vindobonense, in *Historiae Hungaricae Fontes Domestici,* part 1 (Scriptores), volume 2, pages 100-315. Edited by Florian, Matyas (1883).

Chronicon Siculum Incerti Authoris ab Anno 340 ad Annum 1396. Edited by De Blasi, Giuseppe (1887).

Chronicon Venetum. Edited by Zanetti, Girolamo Francesco (1765).

Chronicon Vulturnense de Monaco Giovanni, 3 volumes. Edited by Federici, Vincenzo (1925-1938).

Chronique d'Ernoul et de Bernard le Trésorier. Edited by de Mas Latrie, Louis (1871).

Chronique Latine de Guillaume de Nangis, volume 1. Géraud, Hercule, editor. (1843).

KINGDOM OF SICILY

Chronique de Maitre Guillaume de Puylaurens sur la Guerre des Albigeois. Translation, Lagarde, Charles (1864).

Chronaca di Saluzzo, in *Monumenta Historiae Patriae, Scriptores,* volume 3. Edited by Della Chiesa, Goffredo (1848).

O City of Byzantium: Annals of Nicetas Choniates. Translation. Magoulias, Harry (1984).

Close Rolls of the Reign of Henry III Preserved in the Public Record Office (London 1902-1916), volumes: 1 (1227-1231), 2 (1231-1234), 3 (1234-1237), 4 (1237-1242), 5 (1242-1247).

Codex Diplomaticus Cavensis. Compilation. Morcaldi, Michele, et al. (1873-2015).

Codex Diplomaticus Hungariae Ecclesiasticus ac Civilis, series 3, volume 1. Compilation. Fejér, Georg (1829).

Codex Diplomaticus Regni Siciliae, volumes 1-5. Compilation. Various editors (1982).

Codex Diplomaticus Siciliae. Compilation. Di Giovanni, Giovanni (1743).

Codex Legum Longobardorum. Facsimile and compilation. Gasparri, Stefano (2017).

Codice Diplomatico Barese, Volume 5: Le Pergamene di San Nicola di Bari 1075-1194. Compilation. Nitti, Francesco (1902).

Codice Diplomatico Brindisino. Compilation. Volume 1: 492-1200. Monti, Gennaro (1940).

Codice Diplomatico dei Giudei di Sicilia. Compilation. Lagumina, Bartolomeo (1884).

Codice Diplomatico dei Re Aragonesi di Sicilia 1282-1355. Compilation. La Mantia, Giuseppe (1918).

Codice Diplomatico del Regno di Carlo I e Carlo II d'Angio 1265-1309. Compilation. Del Giudice, Giuseppe (1863).

Codice Diplomatico dei Saraceni di Lucera dall'anno 1285 al 1343. Edited by Egidi, Pietro (1917).

Codice Diplomatico di Sicilia sotto il Governo degli Arabi. Compilation. Airoldi, Alfonso (1790).

Codice Diplomatico Verginiano. Compilation. Tropeano, Placido Maria (1977).

Codice delle Leggi del Regno di Napoli. Compilation. De Sariis, Alessio (1794).

Colección Diplomática de Alfonso I de Aragón y Pamplona 1104-1134. Edited by Lema Pueyo, José (1990).

Colección Diplomática de la Catedral de Pamplona, volume 1 (829-1243). Compilation. Edited by Gaztambide, José Goñi (1997).

Colección Diplomática Medieval de la Rioja 923-1225 (2 volumes). Rodríguez de Lama, Ildefonso (1976).

Complete Philosophical and Theological Treatises of Anselm of Canterbury. Richardson, Herbert (2000).

Conciliengeschichte. Compilation. von Hefele, Karl (1886).

La Conquesta di Sichilia Fatta per li Normandi of Simon of Lentini, in *Cronache Siciliane dei Secoli XIII, XIV, XV,* pages 1-111. Compilation. Di Giovanni, Vincenzo (1865).

Constantiae Imperatricis Diplomata, in *Monumenta Germaniae Historica, Diplomata Regum et Imperatorum Germaniae,* volume 11, part 3. Compilation. Koelzer, Theo (1990).

Constantiae Imperatricis et Reginae Siciliae Diplomata, in *Codex Diplomaticus Regni Siciliae,* series 2, part 1. Compilation. Koelzer, Theo (1983).

Constitutiones Regum Regni Utriusque Siciliae Mandante Friderico II Imperatore. Compilation. Carcani, Gaetano. (Royal Press, Naples 1786).

Constitutionum Regni Siciliarum ad Friderici II. Compilation. Cervone, Antonio (Naples 1773).

SOURCES AND BIBLIOGRAPHY

Continuatio Admuntensis, in *Monumenta Germaniae Historica*, volume 9, pages 579-593. Edited by Pertz, Georg (1851).

Continuatio Praemonstratensis (Sigebert of Gembloux), in *Monumenta Germaniae Historica, Scriptores*, volume 6 (1844).

La Continuation de Guillaume de Tyr. Translation. Morgan, Margaret (1982).

Corónicas Navarras. Edited by Ubieto Arteta, Antonio (1989).

Corpus Scriptorum Historiae Byzantinae, volume 35. Edited by Bekker, Immanuel (1839).

Corpus Scriptorum Historiae Byzantinae, Ioannis Cinnami. Edited by Meineke, Augustus, (Bonn 1836).

Cronaca di Sicilia di Anonimo del Trecento. Edited by Colletta, Pietro (2003).

La Cronaca Siculo-Saracena di Cambridge. Edited by Cozza-Luzzi, Giuseppe (1890).

Cronica Fratis Salimbene de Adam Ordinis Minorum, in *Monumenta Germaniae Historica*, volume 32. Edited by Pertz, Georg (1913).

Crónica Nájerense. Edited by Ubieto Arteta, Antonio (1985).

Crónica Nájerense. Translated by Estévez Sola, Juan (2003).

Crónica Navarro-Aragonesa, in *Crónica de los Estados Peninsulares*. Edited by Ubieto Arteta, Antonio (1955).

Crónica de Rey en Pere of Bernat Desclot. Edited by Coroleu, Joseph (1885).

Cronisti e Scrittori Sincroni Napoletani, volume 1 ("Normanni"), edited by Del Re, Giuseppe (Naples 1845); pages 5-71 and 559-563 (Romuald of Salerno); pages 88-156 (Alexander of Telese); pages 160-276 (Falco of Benevento); pages 277-391 (Hugh Falcandus); pages 405-439 (Peter of Eboli); pages 461-480 (Anonymous Cassino Chronicle); pages 571-616 (Catalogus Baronum).

Cronisti e Scrittori Sincroni Napoletani, volume 2 ("Svevi"), edited by Del Re, Giuseppe (Naples 1868); pages 5-100 (Richard of San Germano); pages 101-200 ("Nicholas Jamsilla"); pages 201-408 (Saba Malaspina); pages 409-627 (Bartholomew of Neocastro).

The Deeds of Frederick Barbarossa. Translation of the *Gesti Friderici Imperatoris* of Otto of Freising. Mierow, Charles (1953).

The Deeds of Pope Innocent III: By an Anonymous Author. Translation of the *Gesti Innocenti* from *PCC, Series Secunda*, volume 214. Powell, Joseph (2004).

Descrizione della Vittoria Riportata da Carlo Conte d'Angio. Edited by Tamburrini, Alberto (2010).

De Vita sua Opusculum. Memoir of Michael VIII of Constantinople (1885).

I Diplomi della Cattedrale di Messina. Compilation of the Antonino Amico index. Starrabba, Raffaele (1876-1890).

I Diplomi Greci ed Arabi di Sicilia Pubblicati nel Testo Originale, Tradotti ed Illustrati (2 volumes). Cusa, Salvatore (1868).

I Documenti Inediti dell'Epoca Normanna in Sicilia. Compilation. Garufi, Carlo Alberto (1899).

Documenti Latini e Greci del Conte Ruggero I di Calabria e Sicilia. Compilation. Becker, Julia (2013).

Documentos de Sigena, volume 1. Compilation. Ubieto Arteta, Antonio (1972).

The Ecclesiastical History of England and Normandy, 4 volumes. Translation and notes of the *Historia Ecclesiastica* of Orderic Vitalis. Forester, Thomas (1853-1856).

Edicta Regum Langobardorum, in *Historiae Patriae Monumenta*, volume 8 (Turin 1855).

España Sagrada, volume 20. Edited by Henrique Florez (1765).

KINGDOM OF SICILY

Epistolae Sancti Thomae Cantuariensis, volume 1. Compilation. Giles, John (1845).

De Expugnatione Terrae Sanctae per Saladinum, Libellus in *Radulphi de Coggeshall Chronicon Anglicanum.* Edited by Stevenson, Joseph (1875).

Fagrskinna Nóregs Kononga Tal. Edited by Jónsson, Finnur (1903).

Dancus Rex, Guillelmus Falconarius, Gerardus Falconarius. Edited by Tilander, Gunnar (1963).

Epistolarum Innocenti III, volume 1. Baluze, Etienne (1682), the *Gesta Innocenti III.*

Epistolarum Turcicarum Variorum et Diversorum Authorum. Edited by Reusner, Nicolaus (1598).

Estoire de Eracles Empereur, in *Recueil des Historiens des Croisades, Historiens Occidentaux,* volume 2 (1859).

Das Falkenbuch Friedrichs II. Photography and notes of Vatican codex *Pal. Lat 1071.* Walz, Dorothea, and Willemsen, Carl (2000).

The Ferraris Chronicle: Popes, Emperors, and Deeds in Apulia 1096-1228. Translation and notes. Alio, Jacqueline (2017).

Foedera, Conventiones, Literae et Cujuscunque Generis Acta Publica inter Reges Angliae, third edition, volume 1, parts 1 and 2. Edited by Rymer, Thomas (1869).

Friderici II Diplomata, in *Monumenta Germaniae Historica,* volume 14, parts 1 and 2. Compilation. Koch, Walter (2002, 2007).

Frederick, Conrad and Manfred of Hohenstaufen, Kings of Sicily 1210-1258: The Chronicle of Nicholas of Jamsilla. Translation by Mendola, Louis (2016).

Gesta Francorum et aliorum Hierosolimitanorum. Parallel Latin/English text. Hill, Rosalind (1967).

Anonymi Gesta Francorum et Aliorum Hierosolymytanorum. Hagenmeyer, Heinrich (1890).

Gesta Henrici VI of Godfrey of Viterbo, in *Monumenta Germaniae Historica,* volume 22, pages 334-338. Compilation. Pertz, Georg (1872).

Gesta Hungarorum of Simon of Keza, in *Historiae Hungaricae Fontes Domestici,* part 1 (Scriptores), volume 2, pages 52-99. Edited by Florian, Matyas (1883).

Gesta Hungarorum - The Deeds of the Hungarians. Translated by Vezprémy, Laszlo (1999).

Gesta Regis Henrici Secundi Benedicti Abbatis (formerly attributed to Benedict of Peterborough) in *Rerum Britannicarum Medii Aevi Scriptores* (2 volumes). Stubbs, William (1867).

Gesta Roberti Wiscardi of William of Apulia. Mathieu, Marguerite (1961).

Gesta Tancredi in Expeditione Hierosolymitana, in *Recueil des Historiens des Croisades, Historiens Occidentaux,* volume 3 (Paris 1866).

The Gesta Tancredi of Ralph of Caen: A History of the Normans on the First Crusade. Translation. Bachrach, Bernard (2016).

Gestes des Chiprois of Philip of Navarre and Gerard of Monreal. Raynaud, Gaston (1887).

Giraldus Cambrensis, De Instructione Principum Libri III. Brewer, John (1846).

Gisleberti Chronicon Hanoniense, in the *Scriptores Rerum Germanicarum* series. Edited by Arndt, Wilhelm (1869).

The Heimskringla or the Sagas of the Norse Kings Translation. Sturluson, Snorri (second edition, 1889).

Historia Bizantina ("Synopsis of Histories") of John Skylitzes (PDF file of codex). See Manuscript source X.

Historia Diplomatica Friderici Secundi. Compilation. Huillard-Bréholles, Jean (1852-1857).

SOURCES AND BIBLIOGRAPHY

Historia Diplomatica Regni Siciliae inde ab anno 1250 ad annum 1266. Compilation. Capasso Bartolommeo (1874).

Historia de Hierosolymitano Itinere of Peter Tudebode, in *Recueil des Historiens des Croisades, Historiens Occidentaux,* volume 3 (Paris 1866).

Historia Longobardorum. Facsimile and transcription. Pani, Laura (2015).

Historia Rerum Angicarum Willelmi Parvi de Newburgh. Edited by Hamilton, John (1856).

Historia Roderici, o Gesta Roderici Campi Docti. Edited by Risco, Manuel (1792).

Historia Salonitanorum atque Spalatinorum Pontificum by Thomas of Split. Edited and translated by Sweeney, James, and Karbic, Damir (2006).

The Historical Works of Ralph de Diceto, Dean of London (2 volumes). Stubbs, William (1876).

A History of Deeds Done Beyond the Sea, by William, Archbishop of Tyre. Translation of *Historia Rerum in Partibus Transmarinis Gestarum* with notes. Babcock, Emily, and Krey, August (1943).

History of the Lombards by Paul the Deacon. Translated by Foulke, William (1907), edited by Peters, Edward (1975).

Indices Rerum ab Aragoniae Gestarum, book 3, in *Hispaniae Illustrata,* volume 3, pages 1-231. Compilation. Schott, Andreas (1606).

Die Innsbrucker Briefsammlung: Eine neue Quelle zur Geschichte Kaiser Friedrichs II und König Konrads IV, in *Monumenta Germaniae Historica, Briefe des späteren Mittelalters,* volume 3. Compilation and notes. Riedmann, Josef (2017).

Invettiva contro Carlo d'Angio per l'Uccisione di Corradino di Svevia. Edited by Caperna, Umberto (2010).

Italia Pontificia, volumes 1 (Rome), 2 (Lazio), 3 (Tuscany), 8 (Campania), 9 (Molise, Apulia, Basilicata), 10 (Calabria and islands). Compilation. Kehr, Paul (1906-1975).

Italia Sacra. Compilation by Ughelli, Ferdinando (1721).

Iter Italicum. Compilation by Pflugk-Harttung, Julius (1883).

Itinerarium Peregrinorum et Gesta Regis Ricardi in *Chronicles and Memorials of the Reign of Richard I,* volume 1. Edited by Stubbs, William (1864).

The Itinerary of Benjamin of Tudela (1907). Translation and commentary by Adler, Marcus Nathan; *The Itinerary of Rabbi Benjamin of Tudela* (1840) by Asher, Adolf (with Hebrew text).

John of Salisbury's Memoirs of the Papal Court. Transcription and translation of the *Historia Pontificalis of John of Salisbury* by Chibnall, Marjorie (1956).

Kitab al-masalik w'al-mamalik. Muhammad ibn Hawqal, in *Bibliotheca Geographorum Arabicorum* (Leiden 1873).

Das Kitab surat al-ard des Abu Gafar Muhammad ibn Musa al-Huwarizmi. Translation by von Mzik, Hans (1926).

Die Konstitutionen Friedrichs II, in *Monumenta Germaniae Historica, Constitutiones et Acta Publica Imperatorum et Regum,* supplement, volume 2. Stürner, Wolfgang (1996).

Layettes du Tresor des Chartes in *Inventaires ed Documents,* volume 1. Edited by Teulet, Alexandre (1863).

Lettera a un Tesoriere di Palermo sulla Conquista Sveva di Sicilia. Tramontana, Salvatore (1988).

Lettres de Rois, Reines et Autres Personnages des Cours de France et d'Angleterre, volume 1. Edited by Champollion-Figeac, Jacques-Joseph (1839).

The Liber Augustalis or Constitutions of Melfi. Translation and notes. Powell, James (1971).

KINGDOM OF SICILY

Liber ad Honorem Augusti di Pietro da Eboli. Translated by De Rosa, Francesco (2000).

Liber ad Honorem Augusti di Pietro da Eboli, in *La Historia o Liber de Regno Sicilie e la Epistola ad Petrum Panormitane Ecclesie Thesaurarium di Ugo Falcando.* Edited by Siragusa, Giovanni Battista (1897, 1906).

Liber Iurium Reipubblicae Genuensis, in *Historiae Patriae Monumenta,* volume 7 (1854).

The Life of Saint Anselm, Archbishop of Canterbury, by Eadmer. Southern, Richard William (1962).

The Life of Saint Clare by Thomas Celano. Translation and notes. Robinson, Paschal (1910).

The Life of Saladin by Baha ad-Din Yusuf ibn Rafi ibn Shaddad. Translation. Palestine Pilgrims' Text Society (1897).

The Lombard Laws. Translation and notes. Drew, Katherine (1973).

Mann aus Apulien: Die privaten Papiere del italienischen Staufers. Compilation by Stern, Horst (2015).

Materials for the History of Thomas Becket, Archbishop of Canterbury (7 volumes). Compilation. Robertson, James (1877).

Matthaei Parisiensis, Chronica Majora (5 volumes). Edited by Luard, Henry (1877).

Matthew Paris's English History (2 volumes). Translated by Giles, John (1853).

Memoirs of the Crusades by Villehardouin and de Joinville. Translation by Marzials, Frank (1908).

Memoriae Mediolanenses, in *Monumenta Germaniae Historica, Scriptorum,* volume 18, pages 399-402. Edited by Pertz, Georg (1863).

Michael Scot: Liber Particularis, Liber Physonomie. Edited by Voskoboynikov, Oleg (2019).

Miscellany of Hebrew Literature. Includes writings of Obadja da Bertinoro. Edited by Neubauer, Adolf (1872).

Monumenta Bambergensia, Bibliotheca Rerum Germanicarum, volume 5. Compilation. Jaffé, Phillip (1869).

Monumenta Germaniae Historica, Deutsche Chroniken, volume 3 (1900).

Monumenta Germaniae Historica, Epistolae Saeculi XIII (1883).

Monumenta Germaniae Historica, Legum Sectio IV, Constitutiones et Acta Publica Imperatorum et Regum, volumes 1 (1893) and 2 (1896).

Monumenta Germaniae Historica, User's Guide. Edited by Janssens, Bart (2018).

Monumenta Wormatiensia, Annalen und Chroniken. Edited by Boos, Heinrich (1893).

Monumenti Storici, series 1 ("Cronache"), *Ignoti Monachi Cisterciensis: Sancta Mariae de Ferraria Chronica et Ryccardi de Sancto Germano Chronica Priora.* Edited by Gaudenzi, Augustus (1888).

Necrologia Panormitana, in *Forschungen zur Deutschen Geschichte,* pages 471-475. Edited by Winkelmann, Eduard (1878).

Necrologio del Liber Confratrum di San Matteo di Salerno. Edited by Garufi, Carlo Alberto (1922).

Necrologium Liciense, in *Forschungen zur Deutschen Geschichte,* pages 476-477. Edited by Winkelmann, Eduard (1878).

Necrologium Salernitanum, in *Forschungen zur Deutschen Geschichte,* page 475. Edited by Winkelmann, Eduard (1878).

Nicetae Choniatae Historia. Edited by Bekker, Immanuel (1835).

Opere Storiche Inedite sulla Città di Palermo. Di Marzo, Gioacchino (1873).

Ottonis de Sancto Blasio Chronica, in the *Scriptores Rerum Germanicarum* series. Edited by Hofmeister, Adolf (1912).

SOURCES AND BIBLIOGRAPHY

Cronaca di Partenope. Edited byAltamura, Antonio (1974).

Patent Rolls of the Reign of Henry III, volume 1 (1216-1225), volume 3 (1232-1247). Edited by Lyte, Henry Maxwell (1901, 1906).

Patrologiae Cursus Completus, Patrologiae Latinae, Series Secunda, volume 143. Edited by Migne, Jacques Paul (1882).

Patrologiae Cursus Completus, Patrologiae Latinae, Series Secunda, volume 145. Edited by Migne, Jacques Paul (1882).

Patrologiae Cursus Completus, Patrologiae Latinae, Series Secunda, volume 148. Edited by Migne, Jacques Paul (1853).

Patrologiae Cursus Completus, Patrologiae Latinae, Series Secunda, volume 151. Edited by Migne, Jacques Paul (1853).

Patrologiae Cursus Completus, Patrologiae Latinae, Series Secunda, volume 163. Edited by Migne, Jacques Paul (1893).

Patrologiae Cursus Completus, Patrologiae Latinae, Series Secunda, volume 170. Edited by Migne, Jacques Paul (1894).

Patrologiae Cursus Completus, Patrologiae Latinae, Series Secunda, volume 179. Edited by Migne, Jacques Paul (1855).

Patrologiae Cursus Completus, Patrologiae Latinae, Series Secunda, volume 180. Edited by Migne, Jacques Paul (1855).

Patrologiae Cursus Completus, Patrologiae Latinae, Series Secunda, volume 188. Edited by Migne, Jacques Paul (1855).

Patrologiae Cursus Completus, Patrologiae Latinae, Series Secunda, volume 202. Edited by Migne, Jacques Paul (1855).

Patrologiae Cursus Completus, Patrologiae Latinae, Series Secunda, volume 204. Edited by Migne, Jacques Paul (1855).

Patrologiae Cursus Completus, Patrologiae Latinae, Series Secunda, volume 214. Edited by Migne, Jacques Paul (1855). Includes *Gesta Innocenti III.*

Patrologiae Cursus Completus, Series Graeca, volume 122. Edited by Migne, Jacques Paul (1889).

Patrologiae Cursus Completus, Series Graeca Posterior, volume 132. Edited by Migne, Jacques Paul (1864).

Le Pergamene Greche Esistenti nel Grande Archivio di Palermo Tradotte ed Illustrate. Compilation. Spata, Giuseppe (1862).

Els pergamins de l'Arxiu Comital de Barcelona from Ramon Berenguer II to Ramon Berenguer IV (2010).

Petri Blesensis Opera Omnia (volume 1), Letters of Peter of Blois. Giles, John (1847).

Petri de Vineis Friderici II Imperatoris Epistolarum (2 volumes). Letters of Peter della Vigna. Edited by Iselin, Johann Rudolf (1740).

Policraticus, sive De Nugis Curialium et Vestigiis Philosophorum. John of Salisbury. Edited by Maire, Johann (Leiden, 1639).

I Privilegi di Messina con Documenti Inediti. Compilation. La Mantia, Vito (1897).

Protectione in Orientem de Ludovici VII Regis of Odo of Deuil (1660).

Quarternus de Excadenciis et Revocatis Capitinatae de Mandato Imperialis Maiestatis Federici Secondi. Edited by Amelli, Ambrogio (1903).

The Rare and Excellent History of Saladin. Translation. Richards, Donald (2002).

KINGDOM OF SICILY

De Rebus Gestis Ioannis et Manuelis. Published by Tollius, Cornelius (1652).

De Rebus Gestis Rogerii Calabriae et Siciliae Comitis et Roberti Guiscardi Ducis Fratris Eius of Godfrey Malaterra, *Rerum Italicarum Scriptores,* volume 5, part 1. Pontieri, Ernesto (1928).

Recueil des Historiens des Croisades - Historiens Occidentaux, 5 volumes (1844-1895).

Recueil des Historiens de la France - Obituaires de la Province de Sens (1906).

Recueil des Historiens des Gaul et de la France, 19 volumes. Edited by Brial, Michel Jean (1840-1878).

Regesta Pontificum Romanorun ab Condita Ecclesia ad Annum Post Christum Natum MCXCVIII. Compilation by Jaffé, Philippe (1 volume, 1851).

Regesta Pontificum Romanorum. Compilation by Potthast, Augustus (2 volumes, 1874).

Die Regesten des Kaiserreiches unter Heinrich VI. Edited by Baaken, Katrin, and Baaken, Gerhard (2015).

Regesto dei Marchesi di Saluzzo 1091-1340. Edited by Tallone, Armando (1906).

Registro della Cancelleria 1239-1240. Carcani, Gaetano (1786).

Regii Neopolitani Archivi Monumenta Edita ac Illustrata. Edited by Spinelli, Antonio, et al. (1845).

Regni Siciliae Capitula. Edited by Raimondetta, Raimondo (1573).

Reliqua Friderici II Imperatoris de Arte Venandi cum Avibus. Edited by Gottlob, Johann (1788).

Richeri Gesta Senoniensis Ecclesiae, in *Monumenta Germaniae Historica, Scriptorum,* volume 25 (1947).

Le Rime della Scuola Siciliana, volume 1. Compilation and translations by Panvini, Bruno (1962).

Robert the Monk's History of the First Crusade: Iherosolimitana. Translation. Sweetenham, Carol (2006).

Roger II und die Gründung der Normannische-sicilischen Monarchie. Compilation. Caspar, Erich (1904).

The Annals of Roger de Hoveden. Translation. Riley, Henry (1853).

Roger of Wendover's Flowers of History. Translation. Giles, John (1849).

Rogerii II Regis Diplomata Latina (Codex Diplomaticus Regni Siciliae), Diplomata Regum et Principum e Gente Normannorum (series 1). Brühl, Carlrichard (1987).

Rollus Rubeus: Privilegia Ecclesie Cephaleditane, a Diversis Regis et Imperatoribus Concessa, Recollecta et in hoc Volumine Scripta. Mirto, Corrado (1972).

Royal and Other Historical Letters Illustrative of the Reign of Henry III (2 volumes). Compilation by Shirley, Walter (1862).

Sacrorum Conciliorum. Series edited by Mansi, Giovanni Domenico (1776-1779).

Saggio di Codice Diplomatico Formato sulle Antiche Scritture dell'Archivio di Stato di Napoli. Compilation. Minieri Riccio, Camillo (1882).

Salimbene de Adam: Cronica. Edited by Bernini, Ferdinando (1942).

Sancti Gregorii VII Epistolae et Diplomata Pontificia, volume 1 (Paris 1877).

Scriptores Rerum Brunsvicensium, volume 3. Leibnitz, Gottfreid (1711).

Scriptores Rerum Germanicarum in Uso Scholarum ex Monumentis Germaniae Historicis, volume 38. Holder-Egger, Osvald, (1894).

Scriptores Rerum Langobardicarum et Italicarum, in the *Monumenta Germaniae Historica* series. Bethmann, Ludwig, and Waitz, Georg (Hanover 1878).

Select Charters and Other Illustrations of English Constitutional History (eighth edition). Compilation by Stubbs, William (1905).

SOURCES AND BIBLIOGRAPHY

Sicilia Sacra. Compilation. Pirro, Rocco (1647, 1733).

Sicily's Rebellion against King Charles: The Story of the Sicilian Vespers. Translation and notes of the *Rebellamentu* of John of Procida. Mendola, Louis (2015).

Solwan el Motà, ossiano Conforti Politici, by Ibn Zafar. Translated by Amari, Michele (1851).

The Song of Aspremont. Translated by Newth, Michael (1989).

Suite de la Troisieme Croisade, in *Bibliotheque des Croisades (Chroniques Arabes),* volume 4. Edited by Michaud, Joseph (1829).

Il Tabulario della Magione di Palermo, Repertorio (2011).

Tabulario di San Filippo di Fragalà e Santa Maria di Maniace. Silvestri, Giuseppe (1887).

Tabularium Regiae et Imperialis Cappellae Collegiatae Divi Petri in Regio Palermitano Palatio. Garofalo, Luigi (1835).

Tancredi et Willelmi III Regum Diplomata, in *Codex Diplomaticus Regni Siciliae,* series 1, volume 5. Zielinski, Herbert (1982).

The Life and Letters of Thomas à Becket (2 volumes). Documents in translation. Giles, John (1846).

St Thomas of Canterbury: An Account of His Life and Fame from the Contemporary Biographers and other Chroniclers. Hutton, William (1899).

The Travels of Ibn Jubayr. Broadhurst, Ronald (1952, 2008).

The Trotula: A Medieval Compendium of Women's Medicine. Translated by Green, Monica (2001).

Urkunden und Kanzlei der Kaiserin Konstanze, Königin von Sizilien 1195-1198, in *Monumenta Germaniae Historica,* volume 6, part 3. Compiled by Kölzer, Theo (1983).

Die Urkunden Konrads III und seines Sohnes Heinrich, in *Monumenta Germaniae Historica, Diplomata Regum et Imperatorum Germaniae,* volume 9 (1969).

Vita Sancti Thomae by William Fitzstephen and Herbert of Bosham, in *Materials for the History of Thomas Becket,* volume 3 (see above).

The History of William of Newburgh and the Chronicles of Robert de Monte in *The Church Historians of England: Pre-Reformation Period.* Edited by Stevenson, Joseph (1856).

The Winchester Chronicle, in *Annales Monastici,* volume 2. Edited by Luard, Henry (1865), pages 3-128.

Wiponis Gesta Chuonradi II, Monumenta Germaniae Historica, Scriptores Rerum Germanicarum in Usum Scholarum, volume 7 (Hanover 1878).

The World of El Cid: Chronicles of the Spanish Reconquest (2000); includes the *Chronicon Regum Legionensium,* or *Liber Chronicorum,* of Pelayo of Oviedo. Translation by Barton, Simon, and Fletcher, Richard.

L'Ystoire de li Normant of Amatus of Montecassino. *Storia dei Normanni.* Parallel French/Italian text. Tamburrini, Alberto (1999).

Selected Secondary Literature

Herein are listed works cited in the notes which are closely relevant to the text, and others useful for reference. For the sake of brevity, certain monographs and papers related to peripheral topics, including some of those considered in the Introduction and appendices, are cited in detail in the notes but not listed in this section. A few secondary references cited in the notes for chapters 24 and 27 are not listed here. Some translations of medieval sources into English appear below. Hundreds of works could be added to this list.

KINGDOM OF SICILY

Abbas, Ihsan. *A Biographical Dictionary of Sicilian Learned Men and Poets* (Arabic, 1994).
Abulafia, David. "L'Attività Commerciale Genovese nell'Africa Normanna: La Città di Tripoli," *Atti del Congresso Internazionale di Studi sulla Sicilia Normanna* (Palermo 1974), pages 395-402.
Abulafia, David. *Commerce and Conquest in the Mediterranean 1100-1500* (1993).
Abulafia, David. "The Crown and the Economy under Roger II and his Successors," *Dumbarton Oaks Papers,* number 37 (Washington DC, 1983), pages 1-14.
Abulafia, David. "The End of Muslim Sicily," in *Muslims Under Latin Rule 1100-1300* (1990), pages 103-134.
Abulafia, David. "Ethnic Variety and its Implications: Frederick II's Relations with Jews and Muslims," *Studies in the History of Art,* number 44 (1994), pages 213-224.
Abulafia, David. *Frederick II: A Medieval Emperor* (2002 edition).
Abulafia, David. *Italy, Sicily and the Mediterranean 1100-1400* (1987).
Abulafia, David. "The Jews of Sicily under the Norman and Hohenstaufen Rulers," in *Ebrei in Sicilia* (2002), pages 69-92.
Abulafia, David. "The Jews of Southern Italy and Sicily: Economic Activity," *Wirtschaftsgeschichte der Mittelalterlichen Juden* (2008), pages 49-62.
Abulafia, David. "Kantorowicz and Frederick II," *History,* volume 62, number 205 (June 1977), pages 192-210.
Abulafia, David. "The Last Muslims in Italy," in *Dante and Islam* (2015).
Abulafia, David. *A Mediterranean Emporium: The Catalan Kingdom of Majorca* (1994).
Abulafia, David. "Mediterranean History as Global History," *History and Theory,* volume 50, number 2 (May 2011), pages 220-228.
Abulafia, David. "The Norman Kingdom of Africa," *Anglo-Norman Studies VII: Proceedings of the Battle Conference 1984* (1985), pages 26-49.
Abulafia, David. "The Norman Kingdom of Sicily: From Arab-Norman kingdom to Latin kingdom," in *Crossroads Between Latin Europe and the Near East* (January 2011), pages 15-40.
Abulafia, David. "The Servitude of Jews and Muslims in the Medieval Mediterranean: Origins and Diffusion," *Mélanges de l'École Française de Rome: Moyen Âge,* volume 112, number 2 (2000), pages 687-714.
Abulafia, David. *The Two Italies: Economic Relations Between the Norman Kingdom of Sicily and the Northern Communes* (1977).
Abulafia, David. *The Western Mediterranean Kingdoms: The Struggle for Dominion 1200-1500* (1997).
Abu-Munshar, Maher. "Sultan al-Kamil, Emperor Frederick II and the Submission of Jerusalem," *International Journal of Social Science and Humanity,* volume 3, number 5 (September 2013), pages 443-447.
Abun-Nasr, Jamil. *A History of the Maghrib in the Islamic Period* (1987).
Accascina, Maria. *Oreficeria di Sicilia dal XII al XIX Secolo* (1974).
Agius, Dionisius. *Siculo Arabic* (1996).
Agnello, Giuseppe. *L'Architettura Sveva in Sicilia* (1935).
Ahmad, Aziz. *A History of Islamic Sicily* (1975).
Alessandria, Kathryn, et al. "Italian American Ethnic Identity Persistence: A Qualitative Study," *Identity: An International Journal of Theory and Research,* volume 16 (2016), number 4, pages 282-298.
Alio, Jacqueline. "Italy's Forgotten Queens: How the most powerful women in Europe were ignored," *Rivista,* number 105 (London 2022), pages 28-29.
Alio, Jacqueline. *Margaret, Queen of Sicily* (2016).
Alio, Jacqueline. *Notes on Norman-Swabian Sicily: New Research in Old Sources* (2021).
Alio, Jacqueline. "Palermo's Nobles and Jews in 1492," in *Sicilian Genealogy and Heraldry* (2014), pages 279-282.
Alio, Jacqueline. *Queens of Sicily 1061-1266: The Queens Consort, Regent and Regnant of the Norman-Swabian Era of the Kingdom of Sicily* (2018).
Alio, Jacqueline. *Sicilian Queenship: Power and Identity in the Kingdom of Sicily 1061-1266* (2019).
Alio, Jacqueline. *Women of Sicily: Saints, Queens and Rebels* (2015).
Alio, Jacqueline, and Lombardo, Francesca. *Christians, Muslims and Jews in Medieval Sicily: An Island and Its Faiths* (2018).

SOURCES AND BIBLIOGRAPHY

Alio, Jacqueline, and Mendola, Louis. *Norman-Arab-Byzantine Palermo, Monreale and Cefalù: The Time Traveler's Guide* (2017).
Alio, Jacqueline, and Mendola, Louis. *Sicilian Court Culture 1061-1266: The Time Traveler's Guide* (2020).
Alio, Jacqueline, and Mendola, Louis. *Sicilian Studies: A Guide and Syllabus for Educators* (2018).
Alio, Jacqueline, and Mendola, Louis. *Sicily: The Time Traveler's Guide* (2020).
Amari, Michele. *Carte Comparèe de la Sicile* (1859).
Amari, Michele. *Le Epigrafi Arabiche di Sicilia* (1875).
Amari, Michele. *La Guerra del Vespro Siciliano* (1876).
Amari, Michele. *Un Periodo delle Istorie Siciliane del Secolo XIII* (1842).
Amari, Michele. *Storia dei Musulmani di Sicilia* (1854, 1868, 1872).
Amico, Vito. *Dizionario Topografico della Sicilia* (1859).
Amundsen, Darrel, and Diers, Carol Jean. "The Age of Menarche in Medieval Europe," *Human Biology,* number 45, volume 3 (Detroit 1973), pages 363-369.
Amundsen, Darrel, and Diers, Carol Jean. "The Age of Menopause in Medieval Europe," *Human Biology,* volume 45, number 4 (Detroit 1973), pages 605-612.
Andenna, Giancarlo. "Autonomie Cittadine del Mezzogiorno dai Normanni alla Morte di Federico II," in *Federico II nel Regno di Sicilia* (2008), pages 35-121.
Anderson, Melitta Weiss. *Food in Medieval Times* (2004).
Anderson, Rasmus. *America Not Discovered by Columbus* (1891).
Andrieu, Michel. *Les Ordines Romani du Haute Moyen-Age* (1931).
Andrieu, Michel. *Le Pontifical Romain au Moyen-Age* (1938).
Angeli Murzaku, Ines, and Crostini, Barbara. *Greek Monasticism in Southern Italy: The Life of Neilos in Context* (2017).
Angold, Michael. *The Byzantine Empire 1025-1204: A Political History* (1997 edition).
Angold, Michael. "The Norman Sicilian Court as a Centre for the Translation of Classical Texts," *Mediterranean Historical Review,* volume 35, number 2 (July 2020), pages 147-167.
Angold, Michael. "The Road to 1204: The Byzantine Background to the Fourth Crusade," *Journal of Medieval History,* volume 25, number 3 (1999), pages 257-278.
Antonopoulos, Panagiotis. "Emperor Constans II's Intervention in Italy and its Ideological Significance," *Byzantine War Ideology between Roman Imperial Concept and Christian Religion* (Vienna 2013), pages 27-32.
Anzelmo, Francesca. "Dress and Textiles in the 12th-Century Painted Ceilings of the Cappella Palatina of Palermo," *Romanesque and the Mediterranean* (2015), pages 91-127.
Appiah, Kwame Anthony. *The Ethics of Identity* (2005).
Appiah, Kwame Anthony. *The Lies That Bind: Rethinking Identity* (2018).
Arbel, Benjamin, et al. *Latins and Greeks in the Eastern Mediterranean after 1204* (1989).
Arblaster, Paul. *A History of the Low Countries,* second edition (2012).
Arcifa, Lucia, and Nef, Annliese, with Prigent, Vivien. "Sicily in a Mediterranean Context: Imperiality, Mediterranean Policentrism and Internal Diversity, 6th-10th Century," *Mélanges de l'École Française de Rome: Moyen Âge,* volume 133, number 2 (2021), pages 339-374.
Ardizzone, Maria Luisa, et al. *Dante as Political Theorist: Reading Monarchia* (2018).
Arlotta, Giuseppe. "Vie Francigene, Hospitalia e Toponimi Carolingi nella Sicilia Medievale," in *Tra Roma e Gerusalemme nel Medioevo* (2005), volume 3, pages 815-886.
Armstrong-Partida, Michelle. "Concubinage, Illegitimacy and Fatherhood: Urban Masculinity in Late-Medieval Barcelona," *Gender and History,* volume 31, number 1 (March 2019), pages 195-219.
Armstrong-Partida, Michelle, et al. *Women and Community in Medieval and Early Modern Iberia* (2020).
Arvide, Luisa. *Las Cuestiones Sicilianas* (2009).
Avery, Myrtilla. *The Exultet Rolls of South Italy* (1936).
Backman, Clifford. *The Decline and Fall of Medieval Sicily: Politics, Religion and Economy in the Reign of Frederick III, 1296-1337* (1995).
Bagehot, Walter. *The English Constitution* (second edition, 1872).
Balan, Pietro. *Storia di Gregorio IX e dei Suoi Tempi* (1873).
Baldwin, Marshall. *The Mediaeval Church* (1953).

Barber, Malcolm. *The Crusader States* (2012).
Barber, Richard. *Henry Plantagenet* (1964).
Barber, Richard. *The Knight and Chivalry* (2000 edition).
Barber, Richard. *Magnificence: Princely Splendour in the Middle Ages* (2020).
Barber, Richard. *The Prince in Splendour: Court Festivals in Medieval Europe* (2017).
Barber, Richard, and Barker, Juliet. *Tournaments: Jousts, Chivalry and Pageants in the Middle Ages* (2000 edition).
Barbiera, Irene. *Le Dinamiche di Popolazione dell'Italia Medievale* (2007).
Barbieri, Giovanni. *Dell'Origine della Poesia Rimata* (1790).
Barlow, Frank. "Roger of Howden," *The English Historical Review*, volume 65, number 256 (July 1950), pages 352-360.
Barlow, Frank. *William Rufus* (1983).
Barth, Fredrik. *Ethnic Groups and Boundaries: The Social Organization of Culture Difference* (1969).
Basile, Giovan Battista. *Lo Cunto de li Cunti*, as Gian Alesio Abbattutis (1644-1645).
Basile, Giovan Battista. *Il Pentamerone or the Tale of Tales*, English translation by Richard Burton (1835).
Baskin, Judith. "Some Parallels in the Education of Medieval Jewish and Christian Women," *Jewish History*, volume 5, number 1 (1991), pages 41-51.
Bates, David. "The Character and Career of Odo, Bishop of Bayeux," *Speculum*, volume 50, number 1 (January 1975), pages 1-20.
Bates, David. *Normandy Before 1066* (1982).
Bates, David, et al. *People, Texts and Artefacts: Cultural Transmission in the Medieval Norman Worlds* (2017).
Bates, David. "The Representation of Queens and Queenship in Anglo-Norman Royal Charters," *Frankland: The Franks and the World of the Early Middle Ages* (2008).
Bates, David, and Crick, Julia (editors). *Writing Medieval Biography 750-1250: Essays in Honour of Professor Frank Barlow* (2006).
Batman, Stephen (editor). *De Proprietatibus Rerum* (1585).
Bäuml, Franz. "Varieties and Consequences of Medieval Literacy and Illiteracy," *Speculum*, volume 55, number 2 (April 1980), pages 237-265.
Beckmann, Johann. *Noticia Dignitatum Illustrium Civilium, Sacrarium Equestrium* (1677 edition).
Beckwith, John. *Early Christian and Byzantine Art* (1979).
Beihammer, Alexander. "Defection across the Border of Islam and Christianity: Apostasy and Cross-Cultural Interaction in Byzantine-Seljuk Relations," *Speculum*, volume 86, number 3 (July 2011), pages 597-651.
Bellafiore, Giuseppe. *La Zisa di Palermo* (1994).
Benjamin, Sandra. *The World of Benjamin of Tudela* (1995).
Bennett, Judith. "Medievalism and Feminism," *Speculum*, volume 68, number 2 (Spring 1993), pages 309-331.
Bennett, Judith, and Karras, Ruth (editors). *The Oxford Handbook of Women and Gender in Medieval Europe* (2013).
Berg, Beverly. "Manfred of Sicily and Urban IV: Negotiations of 1262," *Mediaeval Studies* (Pontifical Institute of Mediaeval Studies, Toronto), volume 55 (1993), pages 111-136.
Bernhardi, Wilhelm. *Lothar von Supplinburg* (1879).
Berto, Luigi. *Ethnic Identity, Memory and the Use of the Past in Italy's Dark Ages* (2022).
Berto, Luigi. "The Image of the Byzantines in Early Medieval South Italy: The Viewpoint of the Chroniclers of the Lombards and Normans," *Mediterranean Studies*, volume 22, number 1 (2014), pages 1-37.
Betancourt, Roland. *Byzantine Intersectionality: Sexuality, Gender and Race in the Middle Ages* (2020).
Bibicou, Hélène. "Une Page d'Histoire Diplomatique de Byzance au XI Siècle: Michel VII Doukas, Robert Guiscard et la Pension des Dignitaires," *Byzantion*, number 29/30 (1960), pages 45-73.
Birk, Joshua. *Norman Kings of Sicily and the Rise of the Anti-Islamic Critique: Baptized Sultans* (2017).
Blud, Victoria. *The Unspeakable, Gender and Sexuality in Medieval Literature 1000-1400* (2017).
Bolton, Brenda, and Duggan, Anne (editors). *Adrian IV The English Pope: Studies and Texts* (2003).

SOURCES AND BIBLIOGRAPHY

Bordone, Renata. "Il 'Famosissimo Marchese Bonifacio,' Spunti per una storia degli Aleramici detti del Vasto," *Bollettino Storico-bibliografico Subalpino*, volume 81 (1983), pages 586-602.
Borella, Andrea. *Annuario della Nobiltà Italiana* (2006-2023).
Borsook, Eve. *Messages in Mosaic: The Royal Programmes of Norman Sicily 1130-1187* (1990).
Boström, Ingemar (editor). *Due Libri di Cucina: Anonimo Meridionale* (1985).
Boulton, D'Arcy Jonathan. "Classic Knighthood as Nobiliary Dignity: The Knighting of Counts and Kings' Sons in England 1066-1272," *Medieval Knighthood V: Papers from the Sixth Strawberry Hill Conference 1994* (1995), pages 41-100.
Bouras-Vallianatos, Petros. "Cross-cultural Transfer of Medical Knowledge in the Medieval Mediterranean: The Introduction and Dissemination of Sugar-based Potions from the Islamic World to Byzantium," *Speculum*, volume 96, number 4 (October 2021), pages 963-1008.
Bowie, Colette. *The Daughters of Henry II and Eleanor of Aquitaine: A Comparative Study of Twelfth-century Women* (2014).
Bowie, Colette. "To Have and Have Not: The Dower of Joanna Plantagenet, Queen of Sicily," *Queenship in the Mediterranean: Negotiating the Role of the Queen in the Medieval and Early Modern Eras* (2013), pages 27-50.
Bozzarello, Luca. "Napoli e Bisanzio," *Bizantinistica: Rivista di Studi Bizantini e Slavi*, volume 21 (2020), pages 37-76.
Bradbury, Jim. *The Routledge Companion to Medieval Warfare* (2004).
Brand, Charles. "The Byzantines and Saladin 1185-1192: Opponents of the Third Crusade," *Speculum*, volume 37, number 2 (April 1962), pages 167-181.
Brandileone, Francesco. *Il Diritto Romano nelle Leggi Normanne e Sveve del Regno di Sicilia* (1884).
Brando, Marco. *Lo Strano Caso di Federico II: Un Mito Medievale nella Cultura di Massa* (2008).
Brantl, Markus. "Itinerar und Regesten Manfreds 1250-1266," in *Studien zum Urkunden und Kanzleiwesen König Manfreds von Sizilien*, pages 226-448 (2005).
Brenk, Beat. *La Cappella Palatina a Palermo* (2010).
Brenk, Beat. "The Mosaics of Cefalù Revisited," *Codex Aquilarensis*, number 34 (2018), pages 13-34.
Bresc, Henri. "Féodalité Coloniale en Terre de Islam: La Sicile," *Structures Foédales et Foédisme dans l'Occident Meditérranéen* (1978), pages 631-647.
Bresc, Henri. "Frédéric et l'Islam," *Frédéric II et l'Héritage Normand de Sicile* (2001), pages 79-92.
Bresc, Henri. *Palermo al Tempo dei Normanni* (2012).
Bresc, Henri. "Spazio e Potere nella Palermo Medievale," *Palermo Medievale: Testi dell'VIII Colloquio Medievale* (1996), pages 7-18.
Brett, Michael. *The Rise of the Fatimids* (2001).
Briggs, Charles. "Literacy, Reading and Writing in the Medieval West," *Journal of Medieval History*, volume 26, number 4 (2000), pages 397-420.
Britt, Karen. "Roger II of Sicily: Rex, Basileus, and Khalif? Identity, Politics, and Propaganda in the Cappella Palatina," *Mediterranean Studies*, volume 16 (2007), pages 21-45.
Bromiley, Geoffrey. "Philip of Novara's Account of the War Between Frederick II of Hohenstaufen and the Ibelins," *Journal of Medieval History*, volume 3, number 4 (December 1977), pages 325-337.
Brown, Virginia. *Giovanni Boccaccio: Famous Women* (2003).
Brühl, Carlrichard. *Urkunden und Kanzlei König Rogers II von Sizilien* (1978).
Bucaria, Nicolò. *Sicilia Judaica: Guida alle Antichità Giudaiche della Sicilia* (1996).
Bucaria, Nicolò, and Cassuto, David. "La Sinagoga e il Miqweh di Palermo alla Luce dei Documenti e delle Scoperte Archeologiche," *Archivio Storico Siciliano*, Series 4, Volume 31 (Palermo 2005), pages 171-209.
Buchtal, Hugo. "The Beginnings of Manuscript Illumination in Norman Sicily," *Papers of the British School at Rome*, volume 24 (London, November 1956), pages 78-85.
Bucossi, Alessandra, et al. *John Komnenos, Emperor of Byzantium: In the Shadow of Father and Son* (2016).
Buonanno, Michael. *Sicilian Epic and the Marionette Theater* (2014).
Burgarella, Filippo. "Greci e Arabi nella Calabria Medievale," *La Calabria nel Mediterraneo: Flussi di persone, idee e risorse* (2013), pages 179-187.

Burkhardt, Stefan, et al. *Norman Tradition and Transcultural Heritage: Exchange of Cultures in the "Norman" Peripheries of Medieval Europe* (2013).
Burnett, Charles. *Adelard of Bath: Conversations with His Nephew* (1998).
Burnett, Charles. "The Use of Arabic Numerals Among the Three Language Cultures of Norman Sicily," *Römisches Jahrbuch der Bibliotheca Hertziana*, number 35 (2003), pages 39-48.
Buscemi, Niccolò. *La Vita di Giovanni di Procida, Privata e Pubblica* (1836).
Bynum, Caroline. "Fast, Feast and Flesh: The Religious Significance of Food to Medieval Women," *Representations*, number 11 (summer 1985), pages 1-25.
Byrne, Philippa. "Lascivious Crimes and Legitimate Proofs: Women and the Juridical Transformation of Norman and Staufen Sicily," *Women and Violence in the Late Medieval Mediterranean, ca. 1100-1500* (2021).
Cahen, Claude. *Le Régime Féodal de l'Italie Normande* (1940).
Calisse, Carlo. *Storia del Parlamento in Sicilia dalla Fondazione alla Caduta della Monarchia* (1887).
Campagna, Giuseppe. "Note sulla Schiavitù in Sicilia tra Tardo Medioevo e Prima Età Moderna," *Rivista dell'Istituto di Storia dell'Europa Mediterranea*, volume 4, number 2 (June 2019), pages 99-123.
Canning, Joseph. *A History of Medieval Political Thought 300-1450* (1996).
Cantarella, Glauco. *Ruggero II: Il conquistatore normanno che fondò il Regno di Sicilia* (2020).
Caperna, Umberto. *Cronaca di Santa Maria della Ferraria* (2008).
Capozzo, Guglielmo. *Memorie su la Sicilia* (1840).
Caravale, Mario. "La Feudalità nella Sicilia Normanna," *Atti del Congresso Internazionale di Studi sulla Sicilia Normanna* (Palermo 1974), pages 21-50.
Carbonaro, Francesco. *The Norman Admiralty: History of an Office Between Two Worlds* (2021).
Carey, Hilary. *Courting Disaster: Astrology at the English Court and University in the Later Middle Ages* (1992).
Carini, Isidoro. "Una Pergamena sulla Fondazione del Duomo di Cefalù," *Archivio Storico Siciliano*, new series, year 7, numbers 1-4 (1883), pages 136-138.
Carpenter, David. *Henry III: The Rise to Power and Personal Rule 1207-1258* (2020).
Carpentieri, Nicola. "Adab as Social Currency: The Survival of the Qasida in Medieval Sicily," *Mediterranea*, volume 3 (Córdoba 2018), pages 1-18.
Carini, Isidoro. "Una Pergamena sulla Fondazione del Duomo di Cefalù," *Archivio Storico Siciliano*, new series, year 7, numbers 1-4 (1883), pages 136-138.
Caruso, Angelo. "Indagini sulla Legislazione di Federico II di Svevia per il Regno di Sicilia: Le Leggi Pubblicate a Foggia nell'Aprile 1240," in *Il Liber Augustalis di Federico II nella Storiografia* (1987) pages 41-68.
Caruso, Stefano. "Echi della Polemica Bizantina Antilatina dell' XI-XII Secoli nel *De Oeconomia Dei* di Nilo Doxapatres," *Atti del Congresso Internazionale di Studi sulla Sicilia Normanna* (Palermo 1974), pages 403-432.
Casano, Alessandro. *Del Sotterraneo della Chiesa Cattedrale di Palermo* (1849).
Caspar, Erich. "Die Legatengewalt der Normannisch-Sicilischen Herrscher," *Quellen und Forschungen aus Italienischen Archiven und Bibliotheken*, volume 7 (Rome 1904), pages 189-219.
Cassady, Richard. *The Emperor and the Saint: Frederick II of Hohenstaufen, Francis of Assisi, and Journeys to Medieval Places* (2011).
Cassidy-Welch, Megan. "The Stedinger Crusade: War, Remembrance and Absence in Thirteenth-Century Germany," *Viator*, volume 44, number 2 (2013), pages 159-174.
Cassidy-Welch, Megan. *War and Memory at the Time of the Fifth Crusade* (2019).
Catel Guillaume. *Histoire des Comtes de Tolose* (1623).
Catlos, Brian. *Muslims of Medieval Latin Christendom c. 1050-1614* (2014).
Catlos, Brian. "Who Was Philip of Mahdia and Why Did He Have to Die?" *Mediterranean Chronicle*, volume 1 (2011), pages 73-103.
Ceruti, Antonio. "Trattato di Falconeria, Testo di Lingua Inedito del Secolo XIV," *Il Pugnatore*, volume 2, part 2 (1869), pages 221-230.
Cesaretti, Paolo. *Theodora, Empress of Byzantium* (2004).
Chalandon, Ferdinand. *Les Comnène: Essai sur le Règne d'Alexis I Comnène* (1900, 1960).
Chalandon, Ferdinand. *Histoire de la Domination Normande en Italie et en Sicile* (1907).
Chappuys, Gabriel. *L'Historie du Royaume de Navarre* (1616).

SOURCES AND BIBLIOGRAPHY

Chaytor, Henry. *A History of Aragon and Catalonia* (1933).
Chiarelli, Leonard. *A History of Muslim Sicily* (second edition, 2018).
Chiarelli, Leonard. "The Ibadi Communities in Muslim Sicily," *Ibadi Jurisprudence: Origins, Development and Cases*, in the series *Studies on Ibadism and Oman*, volume 6 (2015), pages 159-166.
Chiarelli, Leonard. "Al-Idrisi's Description of Sicily: A Critical Survey," *Scripta Mediterranea*, number 1 (1980), pages 34-38.
Chiarelli, Leonard. "Immigration and Settlement in Islamic Sicily," *Qantara*, number 72 (2009), pages 37-40.
Chiarelli, Leonard. "Muslim Sicily and the Beginning of Medical Licensing in Europe," *Journal of the Islamic Medical Association of North America*, volume 31, number 2 (1999), pages 79-82.
Chiarelli, Leonard. *Sicily during the Fatimid Age* (1991 edition).
Charanis, Peter. "The Origin of the First Crusade," *Byzantion*, number 19 (1949), pages 17-36.
Charlier, Philippe, et al. "Schistosomiasis in the Mummified Viscera of Saint Louis (1270 AD)," *Forensic Science, Medicine and Pathology*, volume 12, number 1 (March 2016), pages 113-114.
Chibnall, Marjorie. *The Empress Matilda: Queen Consort, Queen Mother, and Lady of the English* (1991).
Chibnall, Marjorie. *Piety, Power and History in Medieval England and Normandy* (2000).
Christie, Neil. *The Lombards: The Ancient Longobards* (1999).
Christys, Ann. *Vikings in the South* (2015).
Churchill, William. *The Annales Barenses and the Annales Lupi Protospatharii* (1979).
Cilento, Adele and Routt, David. "Foundation of a Monastery in Byzantine Calabria 1053/54" *Medieval Italy: Texts in Translation* (2009), pages 506-507.
Cipolla, Gaetano. *The Sounds of Sicilian: A Pronunciation Guide* (2005).
Clarke, Peter, and Duggan, Anne (editors). *Pope Alexander III 1159-1181: The Art of Survival* (2012).
Cobb, Paul. *The Race for Paradise: An Islamic History of the Crusades* (2014).
Cochrane, Louise. *Adelard of Bath: The First English Scientist* (1994).
Collins, Roger. *The Basques* (1990).
Collura, Paolo. "Appendice al Regesto dei Diplomi di Re Ruggero Compilato da Erich Caspar," *Atti del Convegno Internazionale di Studi Ruggeriani* (Palermo 1955), pages 545-625.
Collura, Paolo. *Le Più Antiche Carte dell'Archivio Capitolare di Agrigento 1092-1282* (1961).
Columba, Gaetano. "Note di Topografia Medievale Palermitana," *Archivio Storico Siciliano* (Palermo 1910), pages 325-350.
Constable, Giles. "The Second Crusade as Seen by Contemporaries," *Traditio*, volume 9 (1953), pages 213-279.
Constable, Olivia Remie. "Cross-Cultural Contracts: Sales of Land between Christians and Muslims in 12th-Century Palermo," *Studia Islamica*, number 85 (1997), pages 67-84.
Conti, Emanuele. "L'Abbazia della Matina," *Archivio Storico per la Calabria*, volume 35 (Rome 1967), pages 11-30.
Corrao, Pietro. "Fiere e Mercati," *Strumenti, Tempi e Luoghi di Comunicazione nel Mezzogiorno Normanno-Svevo* (1995), pages 345-361.
Corrao, Pietro. *Governare un Regno: Potere, Società e Istituzioni in Sicilia fra Trecento e Quattrocento* (1991).
Correnti, Santi. *Storia di Sicilia come Storia del Popolo Siciliano* (1995 edition).
Cortese, Delia. *Women and the Fatimids in the World of Islam* (2006).
Cortonesi, Alfio, and Passigli, Susanna. *Agricoltura e Allevamento nell'Italia Medievale: Contributo Bibliografico 1950-2010* (2016).
Cosentino, Salvatore, and Zanini, Enrico (editors). *A Companion to Byzantine Italy* (2021).
Costantino, Antonino. *La Cappella Palatina di Palermo: Essenza di un Regno* (2021).
Coulton, George. *From St Francis to Dante: Translations from the Chronicle of the Franciscan Salimbene 1221-1288* (1907).
Cox, Eugene. *The Eagles of Savoy: The House of Savoy in Thirteenth-Century Europe* (1974).

Croce, Orazio. *Influssi del "De Amore" di Andrea Cappellano nella Scuola Poetica Siciliana: Una Revisione Critica* (2010).
Crofts, Thomas. "Geoffrey of Monmouth's Byzantine Reception," in *A Companion to Geoffrey of Monmouth* (2020), pages 427-431.
Crook, David, et al. *The Growth of Royal Government Under Henry III* (2015).
Crouch, David. *The Birth of Nobility: Constructing the Aristocracy in England and France 900-1300* (2005).
Crouch, David. *The Chivalric Turn: Conduct and Hegemony in Europe before 1300* (2019).
Crouch, David. *William Marshal: Knighthood, War and Chivalry 1147-1219* (2002).
Croutier, Alev. *Harem: The World Behind the Veil* (1989).
Cuozzo, Errico. *Catalogus Baronum: Commentario* (1984).
Cuozzo, Errico. "Intorno alla prima contea normanna nell'Italia meridionale," *Cavalieri alla Conquista del Sud: Studi sull'Italia Normanna in Memoria di Lèon-Robert Ménager* (1998), pages 171-193.
Cuozzo, Errico. "Ruggiero, Conte d'Andria: Ricerche sulla nozione di regalità al tramonto della monarchia normanna," *Archivio Storico per le Province Napoletane,* number 20 (1981), pages 129-168.
Daftary, Farhad. *The Isma'ilis: Their History and Doctrines* (second edition, 2007).
Dalli, Charles. "Bridging Europe and Africa: Norman Sicily's Other Kingdom," *Bridging the Gaps: Sources, Methodology and Approaches to Religion in History* (2008), pages 77-93.
Dalli, Charles. "Contriving Coexistence: Muslims and Christians in the Unmaking of Norman Sicily," *Routines of Existence* (2009), pages 31-43.
Dalton, Heather. "Frederick II of Hohenstaufen's Australasian Cockatoo: Symbol of Detente between East and West and Evidence of Ayyubids' Global Reach," *Parergon,* number 35, volume 1 (January 2018), pages 35-60.
D'Andrea, David, and Marino, Salvatore (editors). *Confraternities in Southern Italy: Art, Politics, and Religion 1100-1800* (2022).
D'Angelo, Edoardo. *Pseudo Ugo Falcando: De Rebus circa Regni Siciliae Curiam Gestis* (2014).
D'Angelo, Edoardo. *Storiografi e Cronologi Latini nel Mezzogiorno Normanno-Svevo* (2003).
D'Angelo, Franco. "La Ceramica Normanna in Sicilia," *Atti del Congresso Internazionale di Studi sulla Sicilia Normanna* (Palermo 1974), pages 433-437.
Davanzati, Domenico Forges. *Dissertazione sulla Seconda Moglie del Re Manfredi e sù Loro Figliuoli* (1791).
Davies, Brian (editor). *The Oxford Handbook of Aquinas* (2012).
Davies, Norman. *Vanished Kingdoms* (2012).
Davies, Rees. "Nations and National Identities in the Medieval World: An Apologia," *Belgisch Tijdschrift voor Nieuwste Geschiedenis: Revue belge d'historie contemporaine,* volume 34, number 4 (2004), pages 567-577.
Davis-Secord, Sarah. "Muslims in Norman Sicily: The Evidence of Imam al-Mazari's Fatwas," *Mediterranean Studies,* volume 16 (2007), pages 46-66.
Davis-Secord, Sarah. *Where Three Worlds Met: Sicily in the Early Medieval Mediterranean* (2017).
De Blasi, Giuseppe. *La Insurrezione Pugliese e la Conquista Normanna nel Secolo XI* (1864).
De Blasi, Giuseppe. *Della Vita e delle Opere di Pietro della Vigna* (1860).
D'Erme, Giovanni. "The Cappella Palatina in Palermo: An Iconographical Source to be Read En Lieu of Lacking Texts," *Oriente Moderno,* volume 84, number 2 (2004), 401-416.
De Falco, Fabrizio. "The Reception of the Work of Geoffrey of Monmouth in Italy," in *A Companion to Geoffrey of Monmouth* (2020), pages 477-481.
De Leemans, Pieter, et al. *Translating at Court: Bartholomew of Messina and Cultural Life at the Court of Manfred, King of Sicily* (2014).
De Luca, Maria Amalia. "Bint Muhammad ibn Abbad," *Siciliane: Dizionario Biografico* (2006), pages 79-81.
De Luca, Maria Amalia. *Giudici e Giuristi nella Sicilia Musulmana* (1989).
De Renzi, Salvatore. *Storia Documentata della Scuola Medica di Salerno* (1857 edition).
De Sassenay, Fernand. *Les Brienne de Lecce et d'Athènes* (1869).
De Stefano, Antonino. *La Cultura alla Corte di Federico II Imperatore* (1938).
De Stefano, Antonino. *La Cultura in Sicilia nel Periodo Normanno* (1956 edition).

SOURCES AND BIBLIOGRAPHY

De Wailly, Natalis. "Examen Critique de la *Vie de Saint Louis* par Geoffroi de Beaulieu," *Bibliothèque de l'École des Chartes* (1844), volume 5, pages 205-231.
Deér, Josef. *The Dynastic Porphyry Tombs of the Norman Period in Sicily* (1959).
Delisle, Leopold. "Un Livre de Choeur Normano-Sicilien Conservé en Espagne," *Journal des Savants*, year 6 (January 1908), pages 42-49.
Delle Donne, Fulvio. *Federico II: La Condanna della Memoria* (2012).
Delle Donne, Fulvio. "L'Organizzazione dello Studium di Napoli e la Nobiltà del Sapere," in *Il Regno di Sicilia in Età Normanna e Sveva* (2021), pages 37-47.
Del Giudice, Giuseppe. *La Famiglia di Re Manfredi* (1896).
Delogu, Paolo. "L'Evoluzione Politica dei Normanni d'Italia fra Poteri Locali e Potestà Universale," *Atti del Congresso Internazionale di Studi sulla Sicilia Normanna* (Palermo 1974), pages 51-104.
Delogu, Paolo. *I Normanni in Italia: Cronache della Conquista e del Regno* (1984).
Del Vecchio, Alberto. *La Legislazione di Federico II Imperatore* (1874).
Demus, Otto. *The Mosaics of Norman Sicily* (1950, 1988).
Dewing, Henry. *Procopius: Volume 7, The Anecdota or Secret History* (1935).
Di Cesare, Giuseppe. *Storia di Manfredi Re di Sicilia e di Puglia* (1837).
Geanakoplos, Deno John. *Emperor Michael Palaeologus and the West 1258-1282: A Study in Byzantine-Latin Relations* (1959).
Dickinson, John. "The Mediaeval Conception of Kingship and Some of Its Limitations, as Developed in the Policraticus of John of Salisbury," *Speculum*, volume 1, number 3 (July 1926), pages 308-337.
Dickson, Gary. *The Children's Crusade: Medieval History, Modern Mythistory* (2007).
Di Cosmo, Antonio. "Immaginare e visualizzare la monarchia in Sicilia," *Territorio, Sociedad y Poder*, number 16 (2021), pages 23-41.
Di Costanzo, Angelo. *Le Istorie del Regno di Napoli dal 1250 fino al 1498* (1572).
Di Franco, Saverio. *Alla Ricerca di un'Identità Politica: Giovanni Antonio Summonte e la Patria Napoletana* (2012).
Di Giovanni, Giovanni. *L'Ebraismo della Sicilia* (1748).
Di Giovanni, Giovanni. *Sanctae Panormitanae Ecclesiae Canonici de Divinis Siculorum Oficiis Tractatis* (1736).
Di Giovanni, Giovanni. *Storia Ecclesiastica di Sicilia* (1847).
Di Giovanni, Vincenzo. "Appendice alla Topografia Antica di Palermo," *Archivio Storico Siciliano* (Palermo 1899), pages 379-396.
Di Giovanni, Vincenzo. "Il Quartiere degli Schiavoni nel Secolo X," *Archivio Storico Siciliano* (Palermo 1887), pages 40-64.
Di Giovanni, Vincenzo. *La Topografia Antica di Palermo dal Secolo X al XV* (1890).
Di Girolamo, Costanzo, et al. *Poeti della Corte di Federico II*, in *I Poeti della Scuola Siciliana* (2008), volume 2.
Di Matteo, Ignazio, "Antologia di Poeti Arabi Siciliani," *Archivio Storico per la Sicilia*, number 1 (1935), pages 95-133.
Di Meo, Alessandro. *Annali Critico-Diplomatici del Regno di Napoli* (1805).
Dolan, John. "A Note on Emperor Frederick II and Jewish Tolerance," *Jewish Social Studies*, volume 22, number 3 (July 1960), pages 165-174.
Dolezalek, Isabelle. *Arabic Script on Christian Kings: Textile Inscriptions on Royal Garments from Norman Sicily* (2017).
Domínguez Fernandez, Enrique, and Larrambebere Zabal, Miguel. *García Ramírez el Restaurador 1134-1150* (1986).
Donald, Alexander (translator). *Melusine by Jean d'Arras* (1895).
Donovan, Joseph. *Pelagius and the Fifth Crusade* (1950).
Doran, John, and Smith, Damian (editors). *Pope Innocent II (1130-43): The World vs the City* (2016).
Dorveaux, Paul. *L'Antidotaire Nicolas* (1896).
Dragonetti, Giacinto. *Origine dei Feudi nei Regni di Napoli e Sicilia* (1788).
Drell, Joanna. *Kinship and Conquest: Family Strategies in the Principality of Salerno during the Norman Period 1077-1194* (2002).

Duggan, Anne. *Queens and Queenship in Medieval Europe: Proceedings of a Conference Held at King's College, London, April 1995* (1997).
Duggan, Anne. *Thomas Becket* (2004).
Dujcev, Ivan. "I Normanni e l'Oriente Bizantino," *Atti del Congresso Internazionale di Studi sulla Sicilia Normanna* (Palermo 1974), pages 105-131.
Dunbabin, Jean. *Charles I of Anjou: Power, Kingship and State-Making in Thirteenth-Century Europe* (1998).
Dunbabin, Jean. *The French in the Kingdom of Sicily 1266-1305* (2011).
Dunbar, Prescott. *The History of the Normans by Amatus of Montecassino* (2004).
Eads, Valerie. "Sichelgaita of Salerno: Amazon or Trophy Wife?" *Journal of Medieval Military History*, volume 3 (2005), pages 72-87.
Earenfight, Theresa. "Highly Visible, Often Obscured: The Difficulty of Seeing Queens and Noble Women," *Medieval Feminist Forum*, volume 44, issue 1 (2008), pages 86-90.
Earenfight, Theresa. *Queenship in Medieval Europe* (2013).
Earenfight, Theresa. "Without the Persona of the Prince: Kings, Queens and the Idea of Monarchy in Late Medieval Europe," *Gender and History*, volume 19, number 1 (2007), pages 1-21.
Edbury, Peter. *The Conquest of Jerusalem and the Third Crusade: Sources in Translation* (1998).
Egidi, Pietro. *La Colonia Saracena di Lucera e la Sua Distruzione* (1912).
Eisenberg, Robert. "The Battle of Adrianople: A Reappraisal," *Hirundo*, volume 8 (2009-2010), pages 108-120.
El-Azhari, Taef. *Queens, Eunuchs and Concubines in Islamic History 661-1257* (2019).
Elkins, Zachary, et al. "On the Influence of Magna Carta and Other Cultural Relics," *International Review of Law and Economics*, number 47 (2016), pages 3-9.
Ellis, George (translator). *Boso's Life of Alexander III* (1973).
El Merheb, Mohammad. "Louis IX in Medieval Arabic Sources: The Saint, the King, and the Sicilian Connection," *Al-Masaq: Journal of the Medieval Mediterranean*, volume 28, issue 3 (London 2016), pages 282-301.
Elze, Reinhard. "Tre Ordines per l'Incoronazione di un Re e di una Regina del Regno Normanno in Sicilia," *Atti del Congresso Internazionale di Studi sulla Sicilia Normanna* (Palermo 1974), pages 438-459.
Elze, Reinhard. "The Ordo for the Coronation of King Roger II of Sicily: An Example of Dating from Internal Evidence," *Coronations: Medieval and Early Modern Monarchic Ritual* (1990), pages 165-178.
Enzensberger, Horst. "Chanceries, Charters and Administration in Norman Sicily," *The Society of Norman Italy* (Leiden 2002), pages 117-150.
Enzensberger, Horst. "Il Documento Regio come Strumento del Potere," *Potere, Società e Popolo nell'Età dei Due Guglielmi* (Bari 1981), pages 104-138.
Enzensberger, Horst. "Fondazione o 'rifondazione'? Alcune osservazioni sulla politica ecclesiastica del Conte Ruggero," *Chiesa e Società in Sicilia: L'Età Normanna* (1995), pages 22-49.
Epifanio, Vincenzo. "Ruggero II e Filippo di Al Mahdiah," *Archivio Storico Siciliano* (Palermo 1905), pages 471-501.
Epstein, Stephan. *An Island for Itself: Economic Development and Social Change in Late Medieval Sicily* (2003).
Epstein, Steven. *Genoa and the Genoese 958-1528* (1996).
Erler, Mary, and Kowaleski, Maryanne (editors). *Gendering the Master Narrative: Women and Gender in the Middle Ages* (2003).
Evans, Michael. *Inventing Eleanor: The Medieval and Post-Medieval Image of Eleanor of Aquitaine* (2014).
Eyton, Robert William. *Court, Household and Itinerary of King Henry II, Instancing also the Chief Agents and Adversaries of the King in his Government, Diplomacy and Strategy* (1878).
von Falkenhausen, Vera. *La Dominazione Bizantina nell'Italia Meridionale dal IX al XI Secolo* (1978).
von Falkenhausen, Vera. "Zur Regentschaft der Gräfin Adelasia del Vasto in Kalabrien und Sizilien 1101-1112," *AETOS: Studies in Honor of Cyril Mango Presented to Him on April 14, 1998* (Stuttgart 1998), pages 87-115.
Fasoli, Gina. "Castelli e Strade nel Regnum Siciliae: L'Itinerario di Federico II," *Federico e l'Arte del Duecento Italiano* (1980), pages 27-52.
Fasoli, Gina. "Le Città Siciliane dall'Istituzione del Tema Bizantino alla Conquista Normanna," *Archivio Storico Siracusano*, number 2 (1956), pages 65-81.

SOURCES AND BIBLIOGRAPHY

Fasoli, Gina. "Organizzazione delle Città ed Economia Urbana," in *Potere, Società e Popoli nell'Età Sveva* (1985), pages 167-190.
Favara, Alberto. *Canti della Terra e del Mare di Sicilia* (1921).
Favara, Alberto. *Corpus di Musiche Popolari Siciliane* (1957).
Fazello, Thomas. *De Rebus Siculus* (1558-1560).
Fazello, Thomas. *Le Due Deche dell'Historia di Sicilia* (1573).
Fernandez Perez, Gregorio. *Historia de la Iglesia y Obispos de Pamplona* (1820).
Filoteo, Antonio. *La Descrittione Latina del Sito di Mongibello* (1611).
Flambard Héricher, Anne-Marie (editor). *Frédéric II et l'Héritage Normand de Sicile* (2001).
Fletcher, Richard. *The Quest for El Cid* (1991).
Fletcher, Richard. "Reconquest and Crusade in Spain c. 1050-1150," *Transactions of the Royal Historical Society*, volume 37 (1987), pages 31-47.
Florez, Enrique. *Memorias de las Reynas Catholicas de Castilla e de Leon*, volume 1 (1761).
Flori, Jean. *Bohémond d'Antioche: Chevalier d'Adventure* (2007).
Flori, Jean. *Eleanor of Aquitaine: Queen and Rebel* (English edition, 2007).
Fodale, Salvatore. *Comes et Legatus Siciliae: Sul privilegio di Urbano II e la pretesa Apostolica Legazia dei Normanni in Sicilia* (1970).
Fonnesberg-Schmidt, Iben, and Jotischky, Andrew (editors). *Pope Eugenius III (1145-1153): The First Cistercian Pope* (2018).
Fonseca, Cosimo Damiano (editor). *L'Esperienza Monastica Benedettina e la Puglia* (1983).
Fornaciari, Gino, et al. "The Leprosy of Henry VII: Incarceration or Isolation?" *The Lancet*, volume 353 (27 February 1999), page 758.
Foulke, William Dudley. *History of the Langobards by Paul the Deacon* (1907).
France, John. *The Medieval Way of War* (2015).
Franceschini, Ezio. "I Due Assalti dei Saraceni a San Damiano e ad Assisi," *Aevum*, year 27, number 4 (July-August 1953), pages 289-306.
Franchi, Antonino. *I Vespri Siciliani e le Relazioni tra Roma e Bisanzio* (1984).
Francovich Onesti, Nicoletta. *Goti e Vandali: Dieci saggi di lingua e cultura medievali* (2013).
Francovich Onesti, Nicoletta. *Le Regine dei Longobardi e Altri Saggi* (2013).
Francovich Onesti, Nicoletta. *I Longobardi nel Sud: Culture Scritte e Tracce Linguistiche* (2016).
Frankopan, Peter. *The First Crusade: The Call from the East* (2012).
Frascadore, Angela. "Le Badesse del Monastero di San Giovanni Evangelista di Lecce," *Tancredi Conte di Lecce Re di Sicilia* (2004), pages 233-286.
Freed, John. *Frederick Barbarossa: The Prince and the Myth* (2016).
Fried, Johannes. *Charlemagne* (2016).
Fröhlich, Walter. "The Marriage of Henry VI and Constance of Sicily: Prelude and Consequences," *Anglo Norman Studies 15* (1993), pages 99-125.
Frugoni, Arsenio. *Scritti su Manfredi* (2006).
Fuhrmann, Horst. *Germany in the High Middle Ages c. 1050-1200* (1986).
Fuiano, Michele. "La Fondazione del *Regnum Siciliae* nella Versione di Alessandro di Telese," *Papers of the British School at Rome*, volume 24 (London, November 1956), pages 65-77.
Gabriele, Matthew, and Palmer, James (editors). *Apocalypse and Reform from Late Antiquity to the Middle Ages* (2018).
Gabrieli, Francesco. "Ibn Hawqal e gli Arabi in Sicilia," *L'Islam nella Storia: Saggi di storia e storiografia musulmana* (1966), pages 57-67.
Galasso, Giuseppe. "Due Italie nel Medioevo?" *Mediterranea: Ricerche Storiche*, number 22 (August 2011), pages 217-236.
García-Ballester, Luis (editor). *Practical Medicine from Salerno to the Black Death* (1994).
Garofalo, Vincenza. "A Methodology for Studying Muqarnas: The Extant Examples in Palermo," *Muqarnas*, number 27 (2011), pages 357-406.
Garufi, Carlo Alberto. "I Diplomi Purpurei della Cancelleria Normanna ed Elvira Prima Moglie di Re Ruggero," *Atti della Reale Accademia di Scienze, Lettere e Belle Arti di Palermo*, series 3, volume 7 (1904).
Garufi, Carlo Alberto. "Monete e Conii nella Storia del Diritto Siculo dagli Arabi ai Martini," *Archivio Storico Siciliano* (Palermo 1898), pages 11-171.

Garufi, Carlo Alberto. "Sull'Ordinamento Amministrativo Normanno in Sicilia: Exhiquier o Diwan?" *Archivio Storico Italiano,* series 5, volume 27 (1901).
Garufi, Carlo Alberto. "Per la Storia dei Secoli XI e XII," *Archivio Storico per la Sicilia Orientale,* volume 9 (1912), number 2, pages 342-343, 353-365.
Gattola, Erasmo. *Historia Abbatiae Cassinensis* (1733).
Gattola, Erasmo. *Ad Historiam Abbatiae Cassinensis: Accessiones* (1734).
Gaudioso, Matteo. *La Schiavitù Domestica in Sicilia Dopo i Normanni* (1926).
Geary, Patrick. *The Myth of Nations: The Medieval Origins of Europe* (2002).
Gelfer-Jorgensen, Mirjam. *Medieval Islamic Symbolism and the Paintings in the Cefalù Cathedral* (1986).
Gelin, Marie-Pierre, et al. *The Cult of Saint Thomas Becket in the Plantagenet World c. 1170-c.1220* (2016).
George, Robert. "Natural Law, the Constitution, and the Theory and Practice of Judicial Review," *Fordham Law Review,* volume 69, number 6 (2001), pages 2269-2283.
Ghignoli, Antonella, and Bougard, François. "Elementi Romani nei Documenti Longobardi?" *L'Héritage Byzantin en Italie VIIIe-XIIe Siècle: La fabrique documentaire* (Rome 2011), pages 241-301.
Gibbon, Edward. *Decline and Fall of the Roman Empire* (1826 edition), volume 5.
Gies, Frances and Joseph. *Life in a Medieval Village* (1975, 1991).
Gilliat-Smith, Ernest. *Saint Clare of Assisi: Her Life and Legislation* (1914).
Giordano, Nicola. "Nuovo Contributo alla Determinazione dei Rapporti tra Stato e Chiesa in Sicilia al Tempo dei Normanni," *Archivio Storico Siciliano* (Palermo 1916), pages 25-48.
Giunta, Francesco. *Bizanti e Bizantinismo nella Sicilia Normanna* (1950).
Giunta, Francesco. "Federico II e Ferdinando III di Castiglia," *Papers of the British School at Rome,* volume 24 (London, November 1956), pages 137-141.
Goldstone, Nancy. *Four Queens: The Provencal Sisters Who Ruled Europe* (2007).
Goldstone, Nancy. *Joanna: The Notorious Queen of Naples, Jerusalem and Sicily* (2011).
Goodman, Jennifer. *Medieval England and Iberia: A Chivalric Relationship* (2007).
Goskar, Tehmina. "Material Worlds: The Shared Cultures of Southern Italy and Its Mediterranean Neighbours in the Tenth to Twelfth Centuries," *Al-Masaq: Journal of the Medieval Mediterranean,* volume 23, issue 3 (London 2011), pages 189-204.
Gramit, David. "The Music Paintings of the Cappella Palatina in Palermo," *Imago Musicae,* number 2 (1985), pages 9-49.
Granara, William. *Ibn Hamdis the Sicilian: Eulogist for a Falling Homeland* (2021).
Granara, William. "Ibn Hawqal in Sicily," *Alif: Journal of Comparative Poetics,* number 3, (Cairo 1983), pages 94-99.
Granara, William. *Narrating Muslim Sicily: War and Peace in the Medieval Mediterranean World* (2019).
Grant, Lindy. *Blanche of Castile, Queen of France* (2016).
Grassotti, Hilda. "Homenaje de García Ramírez a Alfonso VII dos Documentos Ineditos," *Principe de Viana,* volume 25 (number 94-95), 1964, pages 57-66.
Grayzel, Solomon. *The Church and the Jews in the Middle Ages* (1966).
Green, Judith. *The Normans: Power, Conquest and Culture in 11th-Century Europe* (2022).
Green, Mary Anne Everett. *Lives of the Princesses of England from the Norman Conquest,* volumes 1 and 2 (1850).
Green, Monica. "Medicine in Southern Italy, Twelfth-Fourteenth Centuries: Six Texts," *Medieval Italy: Texts in Translation* (2009), pages 311-327.
Grenon, Michel. *Charles d'Anjou: Frère conquérant de Saint Louis* (2012).
Grillo, Paolo. *L'Aquila e il Giglio: La Battaglia di Benevento* (2015).
Grizio, Pietro. *Ristretto dell'Istorie di Iesi* (1578).
Gross, Thomas. *Lothar III und die Mathildischen Güter* (1990).
Grossi, Giovanni Battista. *Catana Sacra* (1654).
Guillou, André. *Aspetti della Civiltà Bizantina in Italia: Società e Cultura* (1976).
Guzzo, Cristian. "I Normanni e l'Epica Romanza: Etica Cavalleresca e Cavalleria Etica nel Sud Italia," *L'Età Normanna in Puglia: Mito e Ragione* (2015), pages 85-99.
Guzzo, Cristian. *Templari in Sicilia: La Storia e le sue Fonti tra Federico II e Roberto d'Angio* (2003).
Hadank, Karl. *Die Schlacht bei Cortenuova* (Berlin 1905).

SOURCES AND BIBLIOGRAPHY

Hailstone, Paula. *Recalcitrant Crusaders? The Relationship Between Southern Italy and Sicily, Crusading and the Crusader States, c. 1060-1198* (2020).
Haller, Dieter. "The Cosmopolitan Mediterranean: Myth and Reality," *Zeitschrift für Ethnologie*, volume 29, number 1 (2004), pages 29-47
Halm, Heinz (editor). *The Fatimids and Their Traditions of Learning* (1997).
Hamilton, Bernard. "Women in the Crusader States: The Queens of Jerusalem 1100-1190," *Studies in Church History: Medieval Women* (Oxford 1978), pages 143-174.
Hanley, Catherine. *Louis: The French Prince Who Invaded England* (2016).
Hanley, Catherine. *Matilda: Empress, Queen, Warrior* (2019).
Harris, Carolyn. *1000 Years of Royal Parenting* (2017).
Haskins, Charles Homer. "Adelard of Bath," *The English Historical Review*, volume 26, number 103 (July 1911), pages 491-498.
Haskins, Charles Homer. "The 'De Arte Venandi cum Avibus' of the Emperor Frederick II," *The English Historical Review*, volume 36 (1921), pages 334-355.
Haskins, Charles Homer. "Some Early Treatises on Falconry," *The Romanic Review*, volume 13 (1922), pages 18-27.
Haskins, Charles Homer. "England and Sicily in the Twelfth Century," *The English Historical Review*, volume 26, number 103 (July 1911), pages 432-447, 641-665.
Haskins, Charles Homer. "Michael Scot and Frederick II," *Isis*, volume 4, number 2 (1921), pages 250-275.
Haskins, Charles Homer. *The Normans in European History* (1915).
Haskins, Charles Homer. *The Renaissance of the Twelfth Century* (1927).
Haskins, Charles Homer. "Science at the Court of Frederick II," *American Historical Review*, volume 27, number 4 (July 1922), pages 669-694.
Haskins, Charles Homer. "The Sicilian Translators of the Twelfth Century and the First Latin Version of Ptolemy's Almagest," *Harvard Studies in Classical Philology*, volume 21 (1910), pages 75-102.
Haskins, Charles Homer. *Studies in the History of Mediaeval Science* (1924).
Hastings, Adrian. *The Construction of Nationhood: Ethnicity, Religion and Nationalism* (1997).
Haverkamp, Alfred. *Medieval Germany 1056-1273*. Translation (1992).
Hayes, Dawn Marie. "The Cult of St Nicholas of Myra in Norman Bari, c1071-c1111," *The Journal of Ecclesiastical History*, volume 67, number 3 (2016), pages 492-512.
Heimann, Mary. "The Secularisation of St Francis of Assisi," *British Catholic History* (2017) volume 33, pages 401-420.
Heneveld, Amy. "The Falcon and the Glove or How the Courtly Exemplum Teaches Love in Andreas Capellanus' Tractatus de Amore," *Cahiers de Recherches Médiévales et Humanistes*, number 23 (2012), pages 49-60.
Herrin, Judith. *Byzantium: The Surprising Life of a Medieval Empire* (2009).
Herrin, Judith. *Unrivalled Influence: Women and Empire in Byzantium* (2013).
Herzfeld, Michael. "The Horns of the Mediterraneanist Dilemma," *American Ethnologist*, volume 11, number 3 (August 1984), pages 439-454.
Hiatt, Alfred (editor). *Cartography between Christian Europe and the Arabic-Islamic World 1100-1500* (2021).
Hieatt, Constance. "How Arabic Traditions Travelled to England," *Food on the Move: Proceedings of the Oxford Symposium on Food and Cookery 1996* (1997), pages 120-126.
Hildt, John. "The Ministry of Stephen of Perche During the Minority of William II of Sicily," *Smith College Studies in History*, number 3 (April 1918).
Hiley, David, and Manfredi, Agnes. "Quanto c'è di Normanno nei Tropari Siculo-Normanni?" *Rivista Italiana di Musicologia*, volume 18, number 1 (1983), pages 3-28.
Hill, Barbara. *Imperial Women in Byzantium 1025-1204: Power, Patronage and Idealogy* (1999).
Hill, Mark. "Magna Carta's Legacy: Common Law and Human Rights," *Comparative Law Review*, volume 6, number 2 (2015).
Hilton, Lisa. *England's Medieval Queens* (2010).
Hines, Melissa. *Brain Gender* (2005).
Hirth, Friedrich, and Rockhill, William. *Chau Ju-kua: His Work on the Chinese and Arab Trade in the Twelfth and Thirteenth Centuries Entitled Chu-Fan-Chi* (1911), pages 153-154.

Hodgson, Natasha. "Nobility, Women and Historical Narratives of the Crusades and the Latin East," *Al-Masaq: Journal of the Medieval Mediterranean,* volume 17, issue 1 (London 2005), pages 61-85.

Hoff, Jean. *The Trial of the Talmud,* Paris 1240 (2012).

Hoffmann, Hartmut. "Die Anfänge der Normannen in Süditalien" *Quellen und Forschungen aus Italienischen Arxhiven un Bibliotheken,* number 49 (Tübingen 1969), pages 95-144.

Hollway, Don. *The Last Viking: The True Story of King Harald Hardrada* (2021).

Holmes, Catherine. *Basil II and the Governance of Empire 976-1025* (2005).

Holmes, Catherine. "Political Literacy," *The Byzantine World* (2010), pages 137-148.

Holmes, George. *The Oxford History of Medieval Europe* (1988).

Hood, Gwenyth. "Falcandus and Fulcaudus Epistola ad Petrum liber de Regno Sicilie: Literary Form and Author's Identity," *Studi Medievali* (June 1999), 3rd Series, XL, pages 1-41.

Hood, John. *Aquinas and the Jews* (1995).

Horn, Walter. "On the Origins of the Medieval Cloister," *Gesta,* volume 12, number 1 (1973), pages 13-52.

Houben, Hubert. "Adelaide 'del Vasto' nella Storia del Regno di Sicilia," *Itinerari di Ricerca Storica,* number 4 (Lecce 1990), pages 9-40.

Houben, Hubert. *Kaiser Friedrich II: Herrscher, Mensch, Mythos* (2007).

Houben, Hubert. *Roger II von Sizilien* (1997).

Houben, Hubert, and Vetere, Benedetto. *Tancredi Conte di Lecce Re di Sicilia* (2004).

Hoving, Thomas. "A Newly Discovered Reliquary of St Thomas Becket," *Gesta,* volume 4, spring 1965 (New York 1965), pages 28-30.

Howard-Johnston, James. "The Chronicle and Other Forms of Historical Writing in Byzantium," *The Medieval Chronicle,* number 10 (Leiden 2015), pages 1-22.

Howe, John. *Church Reform and Social Change in Eleventh-Century Italy* (1997).

Howell, Margaret. *Eleanor of Provence: Queenship in Thirteenth-Century England* (1998).

Huber, Raphael. "Elias of Cortona," *The Catholic Historical Review,* volume 22, number 4 (January 1937), pages 395-408.

Hudson, Richard. "The Judicial Reforms of the Reign of Henry II," *Michigan Law Review,* volume 9, number 5 (Ann Arbor 1911), pages 385-395.

de Huesca, Ramon. *Teatro Historico de las Iglesias del Reyno de Aragón* (1785).

Huillard-Bréholles, Jean. *Vie et Correspondance de Pierre de la Vigne* (1865).

Hurlburt, Holly. "Women, Gender and Rulership in Medieval Italy," *History Compass,* volume 4, number 3 (2006), pages 528-535.

Hurlock, Kathryn, and Oldfield, Paul, et al. *Crusading and Pilgrimage in the Norman World* (2015).

Huston, Emmaleigh. *Power Through Patronage: Examining Margaret of Navarre's Political Influence Through Sicily's Cathedral of Monreale* (May 2021).

Hysell, Jesse. *Videbantur Gens Effera: Defining and Perceiving Peoples in the Chronicles of Norman Sicily* (2011).

Ingraiti, Gaetano. "Sulla Legittimità della Legazia Apostolica in Sicilia," *Atti del Congresso Internazionale di Studi sulla Sicilia Normanna* (Palermo 1974), pages 460-466.

Jäckh, Theresa, and Kirsch, Mona (editors). *Urban Dynamics and Transcultural Communication in Medieval Sicily* (2017).

Jackson, Peter. "The End of Hohenstaufen Rule in Syria," *Historical Research,* volume 59, number 139 (May 1986), pages 20-36.

Jacoby, David. "The Kingdom of Jerusalem and the Collapse of Hohenstaufen Power in the Levant," *Dumberton Oaks Papers,* number 40 (1986), pages 83-101.

Jaeger, Pier Giusto. *L'Ultimo Re di Napoli* (1982).

Jakobsson, Armann. "Image is Everything: The Morkinskinna Account of King Siguror of Norway's Journey to the Holy Land," *Parergon,* volume 30, number 1 (2013), pages 121-140.

Jamison, Evelyn. *Catalogus Baronum* (1972).

Jamison, Evelyn. A*dmiral Eugenius of Sicily: His Life and Work and Authorship of the Epistola ad Petrum and the Historia Hugonis Falcandi Siculi* (London 1957).

Jamison, Evelyn. "Alliance of England and Sicily in the Second Half of the Twelfth Century," *Journal of the Warburg and Courtauld Institutes,* volume 6 (London 1943), pages 20-32.

SOURCES AND BIBLIOGRAPHY

Jamison, Evelyn. "Judex Tarentinus: The Career of Judex Tarentinus *Magne Curie Justiciarius* and the Emergence of the Sicilian *Regalis Magna Curia* under William I and the Regency of Margaret of Navarre, 1156-72," *Proceedings of the British Academy,* volume I, iii (London 1968), pages 289-344.
Jamison, Evelyn. "The Norman Administration of Apulia and Capua, More especially under Roger II and William I, 1127-1166," *Papers of the British School at Rome,* volume 6, number 6 (January 1913), pages 211-481.
Jehel, Georges. *Les Angevins de Naples: Une Dynastie Européenne* (2014).
Jensen, Frede. *The Poetry of the Sicilian School* (1986).
Jimeno Jurío, José María. *¿Dónde fue la batalla de Roncesvalles?* (1974).
Jimeno Jurío, José María. *Historia de Pamplona: Síntesis de una Evolución* (1974).
Jiwa, Shainool. *The Fatimids: The Rise of a Muslim Empire* (2018).
Johns, Jeremy. *Arabic Administration in Norman Sicily: The Royal Diwan* (2002).
Johns, Jeremy. "Malik Ifriqiya: The Norman Kingdom of Africa and the Fatimids," *Libyan Studies,* number 18 (1997), pages 89-101.
Johns, Jeremy. "Muslim Artists and Christian Models in the Painted Ceilings of the Cappella Palatina," in *Romanesque and the Mediterranean* (2015).
Johns, Jeremy. "The Norman Kings of Sicily and the Fatimid Caliphate," *Anglo-Norman Studies XV* (1995), pages 133-159.
Johns, Jeremy. "Parchment versus Paper: Countess Adelaide's Bilingual Mandate of 1109," *Documenting Multiculturalism* (Oxford, November 2018).
Johns, Susan. *Noblewomen, Aristocracy and Power in the Twelfth-Century Anglo-Norman Realm* (2003).
Johnson, Ewan. "The Process of Norman Exile into Southern Italy," *Exile in the Middle Ages: Selected Proceedings* (2004), pages 29-38.
Jones, Dan. *Magna Carta: The Birth of Liberty* (2016).
Jones, Mari. *Variation and Change in Mainland and Insular Norman* (2014).
Jonker, Marianne. "Estimation of Life Expectancy in the Middle Ages," *Journal of the Royal Statistical Society,* Series A, volume 166, number 1 (2003), pages 105-117.
Joranson, Einar. "The Inception of the Career of the Normans in Italy: Legend and History," *Speculum,* number 23, number 3 (July 1948), pages 353-396.
Jordan, Edouard. "La Politique Ecclésiastique de Roger I et les Origines de la Légation Sicilienne," *Le Moyen Age* (1922), volume 2, pages 237-273.
Jordan, Erin. *Women, Power and Religious Patronage in the Middle Ages* (2006).
Jordan, William, et al. *The Capetian Century 1214-1314* (2017).
Kaeuper, Richard. *Medieval Chivalry* (2016).
Kahf, Mohja. *Western Representations of the Muslim Woman: From Termagant to Odalisque* (1999).
Kamp, Norbert. "L'Héritage Normand dans la Politique Ecclésiastique de Frédéric II," *Frédéric II et l'Héritage Normand de Sicile* (2001), pages 63-78.
Kamp, Norbert. *Kirche und Monarchie im Staufischen Königreich Sizilien* (1982).
Kamp, Norbert. *Vescovi e Diocesi nell'Italia Meridionale nel Passaggio dalla Denominazione Bizantina allo Stato Normanno* (1977).
Kantorowicz, Ernst. *Kaiser Friedrich der Zweite* (1927).
Kantorowicz, Ernst. *Kaiser Friedrich der Zweite: Ergänzungsband* (1930).
Kantorowicz, Ernst. *The King's Two Bodies: A Study in Mediaeval Political Theology* (1957, 1997).
Kantorowicz, Ernst. *Laudes Regiae: A Study in Liturgical Acclamations and Mediaeval Ruler Worship* (1958).
Kantorowicz, Ernst. "A Norman Finale of the Exultet and the Rite of Sarum," *Harvard Theological Review,* volume 34, number 2 (April 1941), pages 129-143.
Kapitaikin, Lev. "The Daughter of al-Andalus: Interrelations between Norman Sicily and the Muslim West," *Al-Masaq: Islam and the Medieval Mediterranean,* volume 25, number 1 (2013), pages 113-134.
Kapitaikin, Lev. *The Twelfth-century Painted Ceilings of the Cappella Palatina, Palermo* (2011).
Karras, Ruth. "The Regulation of 'Sodomy' in the Latin East and West," *Speculum,* volume 95, number 4 (October 2020), pages 969-986.
Karras, Ruth. *Sexuality in Medieval Europe: Doing Unto Others* (2005).
Karst, August. *Geschichte Manfreds vom Tode Friedrichs II bis ze seiner Krönung 1250-1258* (1897).

Keen, Maurice. *Chivalry* (1984).
Kehr, Karl Andreas. "Ergänzungen zu Falco von Benevent," *Neues Archiv der Gesellschaft für ältere deutsche Geschichtskunde,* number 27 (Hannover and Leipzig, 1902), pages 445-472.
Kehr, Paul. "Diploma Purpureo di Re Roggero II per la Casa Pierleone," *Archivio della Reale Società Romana di Storia Patria,* number 24 (1901), pages 253-259.
Kelly, Amy. "Eleanor of Aquitaine and Her Courts of Love," *Speculum,* volume 12, number 1 (January 1937), pages 3-17.
Kelly, Samantha. *The Cronaca di Partenope* (2011).
Kelly, Samantha. "Medieval Influence in Early Modern Neapolitan Historiography: The Fortunes of the Cronaca di Partenope, 1350-1680," *California Italian Studies,* volume 3, number 1 (2012), pages 1-27.
Kelly, Thomas. *The Exultet in Southern Italy* (1996).
Kelly-Gadol, Joan. "Did Women Have a Renaissance?" in *Becoming Visible: Women in European History* (1977 edition), pages 137-164.
Khanmohamadi, Shirin. "Durendal, translated: Islamic object genealogies in the chansons de geste," *Postmedieval: A Journal of Medieval Cultural Studies,* volume 8, number 3 (2017), pages 321-333.
Khanmohamadi, Shirin. *In Light of Another's Word: European Ethnography in the Middle Ages* (2013).
Khanmohamadi, Shirin. *Splendorous Saracens: Appropriating Islamicate Prestige in Medieval European Literature* (2023).
Kharanbe, Saleh, and Asaqli, Eisam. "Intellectual Life During the Reign of the Two Fatimid Caliphs: al-Amir bi-Ahkam Allah and al-Hafiz li-Din Allah," *International Journal of Humanities and Social Science,* volume 6, number 3 (March 2016), pages 222-233.
King, Edmund, et al. *The Anarchy of King Stephen's Reign* (1994).
King, Matthew. *Dynasties Intertwined: The Zirids of Ifriqiya and the Normans of Sicily* (2022).
King, Matthew. *Perceptions of Islam in the Carmen in Victoriam Pisanorum* (2015).
King, Wilson. "The Stedingers: The Story of a Forgotten Crusade," in *Transactions of the Birmingham Historical Society 1883-1884,* pages 1-24.
Kington, Thomas. *History of Frederick II* (1862).
Kitzinger, Ernst. *I Mosaici di Monreale* (1960).
Kitzinger, Ernst. "The Mosaics of the Cappella Palatina in Palermo," *Art Bulletin,* number 31 (New York 1949), pages 290-319.
Kitzinger, Ernst, and Curcic, Slobodan. *The Mosaics of St Mary's of the Admiral in Palermo* (1990).
Kjaer, Lars. "Food, Drink and Ritualized Communication in the Household of Eleanor of Montfort, February to August 1265," *Journal of Medieval History,* volume 37, number 1 (2011), pages 75-89.
Knight, Gareth. *The Book of Melusine of Lusignan in History, Legend and Romance* (2013).
Kölzer, Theo. *Die Staufer im Süden: Sizilien und das Reich* (1996).
Kostick, Conor (editor). *The Social Structure of the First Crusade* (2008).
Kraye, Jill (editor). *Adelard of Bath* (1987).
Kreutz, Barbara. *Before the Normans: Southern Italy in the Ninth and Tenth Centuries* (1996).
Kristeller, Paul. "The School of Salerno," *Bulletin of the History of Medicine,* volume 17, number 2 (1945), pages 138-194.
Krönig, Wolfgang. "Sul Significato Storico dell'Arte sotto i Due Guglielmi," *Potere, Società e Popolo nell'Età dei Due Guglielmi* (Bari 1981), pages 292-310.
Kunz, Keneva, and Sigurdsson, Gisli (translators). *The Vinland Sagas* (2008).
Lachmann, Karl. *Die Gedichte Walthers von der Vogelweide, Herausgegeben* (1827).
La Corte, Giorgio. "Appunti di Toponomastica sul Territorio della Chiesa di Monreale nel Secolo XII," *Archivio Storico Siciliano* (Palermo 1902), pages 336-345.
La Grua, Gregorio. *La Corona di Costanza di Aragona Regina di Sicilia* (1988).
La Lumia, Isidoro. *Storia della Sicilia sotto Guglielmo II il Buono* (1867)
La Mantia, Giuseppe. "Sul Commercio Marittimo tra Sicilia, Calabria e Principato di Salerno nell'Epoca dei Re Normanni," *Archivio Storico per la Provincia di Salerno,* new series, volume 3 (1935), pages 5-11.
La Mantia, Giuseppe. "Su l'Uso della Registrazione nella Cancelleria del Regno di Sicilia dai Normanni a Federico III d'Aragona 1130-1377," *Archivio Storico Siciliano* (Palermo 1908), pages 197-209.

La Mantia, Giuseppe. "La Sicilia ed il suo Dominio nell'Africa Settentrionale," *Archivio Storico Siciliano,* new series, year 44 (1922), pages 154-265.
La Mantia, Giuseppe. *Il Primo Documento in Carta (Contessa Adelaide, 1109) Esistente in Sicilia e Rimasto Sinora Sconosciuto* (Palermo 1908).
La Mantia, Giuseppe. "Su gli Studi di Topografia Palermitana del Medio Evo e su la Fonte detta dagli Arabi Ayb-Rum," *Archivio Storico Siciliano* (Palermo 1917), pages 317-357.
Lancia, Domenico. *Storia della Chiesa in Sicilia* (1884).
Landon, Lionel. *The Itinerary of King Richard I, with Studies on Certain Matters of Interest Connected with his Reign* (1935).
Langley, Ernest. *The Poetry of Giacomo da Lentino, Sicilian Poet of the Thirteenth Century* (1915).
Lansing, Richard. *The Complete Poetry of Giacomo da Lentini* (2018).
Lanzani, Francesco. *La Questione Italiana ai Tempi di Federico II* (1868).
Larner, John. *Italy in the Age of Dante and Petrarch 1216-1380* (1983).
Lavermicocca, Nino. *Puglia Bizantina: Storia e cultura di una regione Mediterranea 876-1071* (2012 edition).
La Via, Mariano. "Le Così Dette 'Colonie Lombarde' in Sicilia," *Archivio Storico Siciliano* (Palermo 1899), pages 1-35.
Lawn, Brian. *The Prose Salernitan Questions, Edited from a Bodleian Manuscript* (1979).
Lello, Giovanni Luigi. *Descrizione del Real Tempio, e Monasterio di Santa Maria Nuova di Morreale* (1702).
Léonard, Emile. *Les Angevins de Naples* (1954).
Letronne, Antoine. *Examen Critique de la Découverte du Prétendu Coeur de Saint Louis* (1844).
Levtzion, Nehemia. "Ibn-Hawqal, the Cheque, and Awdaghost," *Journal of African History,* volume 9, number 2 (Cambridge 1968), pages 223-233.
Lewis, Matthew. *Henry III: The Son of Magna Carta* (2016).
Licinio, Raffaele. *Castelli Medievali: Puglia e Basilicata dai Normanni a Federico II e Carlo d'Angio* (1994).
Lieberman, Max. "A New Approach to the Knighting Ritual," *Speculum,* volume 90, number 2 (April 2015), pages 391-423.
Ligresti, Domenico. *Dinamiche Demografiche nella Sicilia Moderna 1505-1806* (2002).
Lipinsky, Angelo. "Le Insegne Regali dei Sovrani di Sicilia e la Scuola Orafa Palermitana," *Atti del Congresso Internazionale di Studi sulla Sicilia Normanna* (Palermo 1974), pages 162-194.
Lipinsky, Angelo. "Sicaniae Regni Corona: Il Kamelaukion detta Cuffia di Costanza nel Tesoro del Duomo di Palermo," *Bizantino-Sicula II: Miscellanea di Scritti in Memoria di Giuseppe Rossi Taibbi* (Palermo 1975), pages 347-370.
Little, Donald. "Jerusalem Under the Ayyubids and Mamluks 1187-1516," in *Jerusalem in History* (1990).
Loewenthal, Leonard Joseph Alphonse. "For the Biography of Walter Ophamil Archbishop of Palermo," *The English Historical Review,* volume 87, number 342 (January 1972), pages 75-82.
Lombardo, Francesca, and Alio, Jacqueline. *Sicilian Food and Wine: The Cognoscente's Guide* (2015).
Lopez-Santos Kornberger, Francisco. "Byzantine Perceptions of the West in John Kinnamos' Account of the Reign of Manuel Komnenos," *Bisanzio e l'Occidente,* number 3 (2021), pages 1-10.
Loud, Graham. *The Age of Robert Guiscard: Southern Italy and the Norman Conquest* (2000).
Loud, Graham. "The Chancery and Charters of the Kings of Sicily 1130-1212, *The English Historical Review,* volume 124, number 509 (August 2009), pages 779-810.
Loud, Graham. "The Image of the Tyrant in the Work of 'Hugo Falcandus,'" *Nottingham Medieval Studies,* Number 57 (January 2013), pages 1-20.
Loud, Graham. "The Genesis and Context of the Chronicle of Falco of Benevento," *Anglo-Norman Studies IV: Proceedings of the Battle Conference 1992* (1993).
Loud, Graham. "History Writing in the Twelfth-Century Kingdom of Sicily," *Chronicling History: Chroniclers and Historians in Medieval and Renaissance Italy* (2007).
Loud, Graham. "The German Crusade of 1197-1198," *Crusades,* volume 13 (2014), pages 143-172.
Loud, Graham. "How 'Norman' was the Norman conquest of southern Italy?" *Nottingham Medieval Studies,* volume 25 (1981), pages 13-34.

Loud, Graham. *The Latin Church in Norman Italy* (2007).
Loud, Graham. "The Papal 'Crusade' against Frederick II in 1228-1230," *La Papauté et les Croisades* (2011), pages 91-103.
Loud, Graham. *Roger II and the Creation of the Kingdom of Sicily* (2012).
Louda, Jiri, and Maclagan, Michael. *Heraldry of the Royal Families of Europe* (1988). Also published as *Lines of Succession*.
Lourie, Elena. "The Will of Alfonso I 'El Batallador,' King of Aragon and Navarre: A Reassessment," *Speculum*, volume 50, number 4 (October 1975), pages 635-651.
Lower, Michael. *The Barons' Crusade: A Call to Arms and Its Consequences* (2005).
Lower, Michael. *The Tunis Crusade of 1270: A Mediterranean History* (2018).
Lucas-Avenel, Marie-Agnés. "Le récit de Geoffroi Malaterra ou la légitimation de Roger, grand comte de Sicile," *Anglo-Norman Studies 34: Proceedings of the Battle Conference* (2012), pages 169-192.
Lundy, Jasmine, et al. "New Insights into Early Medieval Islamic Cuisine: Organic residue analysis of pottery from urban and rural Sicily," *PLoS ONE*, volume 16, number 6 (2021).
Lunt, William. "The Sources for the First Council of Lyon, 1245," *The English Historical Review*, volume 33, number 129 (January 1918), pages 72-78.
Lupo, Carmelina. "I Normanni di Sicilia di Fronte al Papato," *Archivio Storico Siciliano per la Sicilia Orientale*, volume 20 (Catania 1924), pages 1-74.
Mack Smith, Denis. "Documentary Falsification and Italian Biography" in *History and Biography: Essays in Honour of Derek Beales* (Cambridge 1996), pages 173-187.
Madden, Thomas. "The Venetian Version of the Fourth Crusade: Memory and the Conquest of Constantinople in Medieval Venice," *Speculum*, volume 87, number 2 (April 2012), pages 311-344.
Maffei, Domenico (editor). *Un'Epitome in Volgare del Liber Augustalis* (1995).
Magdalino, Paul. *The Empire of Manuel I Komnenos 1143-1180* (1993).
Maggiorella, Antonia. *Il Principe Poeta: Manfredi di Svevia* (2005).
Maier, Christoph. "Crusade and rhetoric against the Muslim colony of Lucera: Eudes of Châteauroux's Sermones de Rebellione Sarracenorum Lucherie in Apulia," *Journal of Medieval History*, volume 21 (1995), pages 343-385.
Mainoni, Patrizia (editor). *Comparing Two Italies: Civic Tradition, Trade Networks, Family Relationships between the Italy of Communes and the Kingdom of Sicily* (2020).
Makdisi, John. "The Islamic Origins of the Common Law," *North Carolina Law Review*, volume 77, number 5, June 1999, pages 1635-1737.
Makk, Ferenc. *The Arpáds and the Comneni: Political Relations Between Hungary and Byzantium in the 12th Century* (1989).
Malanima, Paolo. *Italian Urban Population 1300-1861* (2015).
Mallette, Karla. *The Kingdom of Sicily 1100-1250: A Literary History* (2005).
Mallette, Karla. *Lives of the Great Languages: Arabic and Latin in the Medieval Mediterranean* (2021).
Maltempi, Anne. "Writing History in Renaissance Sicily: The Formation of Sicilian National Identity in the Work of Tommaso Fazello," *Mediterranean Studies*, volume 29, number 1 (2021), pages 4-31.
Mangieri, Cono Antonio. *Il Contrasto di Cielo d'Alcamo: Introduzione, testo manoscritto e diplomatico, testo critico-congetturale, traduzione e note* (2005).
Mansouri, Tahar. "Produits Agricoles et Commerce Maritime en Ifriqiya aux XII-XV Siècles," *Médiévales*, volume 33 (autumn 1997), pages 125-139.
Marazzi, Federico. "Byzantines and Lombards," *A Companion to Byzantine Italy* (2021), chapter 5, pages 169-199.
Marinoni, Augusto. *Dal Declarus di Angelo Senisio: I Vocaboli Siciliani* (1955).
Marongiù, Antonio. "Concezione della Sovranità di Ruggero II," *Atti del Convegno Internazionale di Studi Ruggeriani* (Palermo 1955), pages 195-212.
Marongiù, Antonio. "La Legislazione Normanna," *Atti del Congresso Internazionale di Studi sulla Sicilia Normanna* (Palermo 1974), pages 195-212.
Marongiù, Antonio. "A Model State in the Middle Ages: The Norman and Swabian Kingdom of Sicily," *Comparative Studies in Society and History*, number 6 (1964), pages 307-320.
Martellotti, Anna. *La Cassata Siciliana: Un Dolce Arabo e la Sua Fortuna in Occidente* (2012).

SOURCES AND BIBLIOGRAPHY

Martellotti, Anna (editor). *I Ricettari di Federico II: Dal Meridionale al Liber de Coquina* (2005).
Martin, Edward. *A History of the Iconoclastic Controversy* (1930).
Martino, Federico. "Federico II e le Autonomie Locali: Considerazioni sulla Formula Consuetudines Approbatae," *Studi Senesi,* number 103 (1991), pages 427-455.
Martorana, Pierluigi. *La Monetazione Aurea in Sicilia* (2007).
Marvin, Laurence. *The Occitan War: A Military and Political History of the Albigensian Crusade 1209-1218* (2008).
Mason, Emma. *King Rufus: The Life and Murder of William II of England* (2008).
Masseti, Marco. *Zoologia della Sicilia Araba e Normanna 827-1194* (2016).
Mathews, Karen. *Conflict, Commerce, and an Aesthetic of Appropriation in the Italian Maritime Cities, 1100-1150* (2018).
Matthew, Donald. "The Chronicle of Romuald of Salerno" in *The Writing of History in the Middle Ages: Essays Presented to Richard William Southern* (Oxford 1981), pages 239-274.
Matthew, Donald. "Modern Study of the Norman Kingdom of Sicily," *Reading Medieval Studies,* volume 18 (1992), pages 34-56.
Matthew, Donald. *The Norman Kingdom of Sicily* (1992).
Matthews, Helen. *The Legitimacy of Bastards: The Place of Illegitimate Children in Later Medieval England* (2019).
Matthews, Karen. *Conflict, Commerce and an Aesthetic of Appreciation in the Italian Maritime Cities 1000-1150* (2018).
Maurici, Ferdinando. *Castelli Medievali in Sicilia: Dai Bizantini ai Normanni* (1992).
Maurici, Ferdinando. *L'Emirato sulle Montagne* (1987).
Maurici, Ferdinando. *Palermo Araba: Una sintesi dell'evoluzione urbanistica 831-1072* (2015).
Maurolico, Francesco. *Sicanicarum Rerum Compendium* (1562).
Mazzarese Fardella, Enrico. *Aspetti dell'Organizzazione Amministrativa nello Stato Normanno e Svevo* (1966).
Mazzarese Fardella, Enrico. "La Condizione Giuridica della Donna nel Liber Augustalis," *Archivio Storico Siciliano,* Series 4, Volume 21-22 (Palermo 1997).
Mazzarese Fardella, Enrico. "La Struttura Amministrativa del Regno Normanno," *Atti del Congresso Internazionale di Studi sulla Sicilia Normanna* (Palermo 1974), pages 213-224.
McClenon, Raymond. "Leonardo of Pisa and His Liber Quadratorum," *The American Mathematical Monthly,* volume 26, number 1 (January 1919), pages 1-8.
McCracken, Peggy. *The Romance of Adultery: Queenship and Sexual Transgression in Old French Literature* (1998).
McDougall, Sara. *Royal Bastards: The Birth of Illegitimacy 800-1230* (2016).
McKenna, Thomas. "Greek and Latin Gods: Anselm's Defense of the Filioque," *Saint Anselm Journal,* volume 14, number 1 (2018), pages 111-131.
Memoli Apicella, Dorotea. *Sichelgaita tra Longobardi e Normanni* (1996).
Mendola, Louis. *The Battle of Benevento according to Andrew of Hungary and Saba Malaspina* (2021).
Mendola, Louis. "Distinguishing Characteristics of Early Italian Heraldry," *The New Zealand Armiger,* number 27 (June 1995), pages 14-19.
Mendola, Louis. "The Distinguished Royal Order of Saint Januarius," *The Journal of the Orders and Medals Research Society,* volume 29, number 3 (London 1990), pages 194-199.
Mendola, Louis. "English and Italian Legacy of the Norman Knight Figures of Monreale," *The Coat of Arms,* journal of The Heraldry Society, NS Volume X, Number 166 (London 1994), pages 245-254 (a correction to a typesetting error appears in the next issue).
Mendola, Louis. "Italian Chiefs of Allegiance," *Journal of Heraldic Studies,* number 1 (1985), pages 33-39.
Mendola, Louis. *The Kingdom of Sicily 1130-1860* (2015).
Mendola, Louis. *The Kingdom of the Two Sicilies 1734-1861* (2020).
Mendola, Louis. "The Norman Origins of Heraldry," *The Coat of Arms,* journal of The Heraldry Society, NS Volume VIII, Number 148 (London 1989), pages 128-129.
Mendola, Louis. "Pre-Armorial Use of the Lion Passant Guardant and the Fleur-de-lis as Heraldic Badges in Norman Sicily," *The Coat of Arms,* journal of The Heraldry Society, NS Volume X, Number 165 (London 1994), pages 210-212.
Mendola, Louis. *Royal Decree by the King of Italy Governing Succession to Titles of Nobility and Nobiliary Ranks* (Los Angeles 1983).

Mendola, Louis. *Sicilian Genealogy and Heraldry* (2014).
Mendola, Louis. *What Became of Medieval Sicily's Arabs: Genetic Demographic Evidence* (2015).
Mendola, Louis, and Alio, Jacqueline. *The Peoples of Sicily: A Multicultural Legacy* (2013).
Menéndez Pidal, Ramón. *Cantar de Mio Cid: Texto, Gramática y Vocabulario* (1908).
Meomartini, Almerico. *La Battaglia di Benevento* (1895).
Messana, Maria. *Inquisitori, Negromanti e Streghe nella Sicilia Moderna 1500-1782* (2007).
Metcalfe, Alexander. *Muslims and Christians in Norman Sicily: Arabic Speakers and the End of Islam* (2011).
Metcalfe, Alexander. *The Muslims of Medieval Italy* (2009).
Meyendorff, John. *Orthodoxy and Catholicity* (1966).
Michael, Robert. *A History of Catholic Antisemitism: The Dark Side of the Church* (2008).
Mielke, Christopher. "From Her Head to Her Toes: Gender-Bending Regalia in the Tomb of Constance of Aragon, Queen of Hungary and Sicily," *Royal Studies Journal,* volume 5, number 2 (2018), pages 49-62.
Miller, Nathaniel. "Muslim Poets under a Christian King: An Intertextual Reevaluation of Sicilian Arabic Literature under Roger II," *Mediterranean Studies,* volume 28, number 1 (2020), pages 51-87.
Millunzi, Gaetano. "Il Mosaicista Mastro Pietro Oddo ossia Restauri e Restauratori del Duomo di Monreale nel Secolo XVI," *Archivio Storico Siciliano* (Palermo 1890), pages 195-251.
Millunzi, Gaetano. *Il Tesoro, la Biblioteca ed il Tabulario della Chiesa di Santa Maria Nuova in Monreale: Studi e Documenti* (1904).
Minois, Georges. *The Atheist's Bible: The Most Dangerous Book That Never Existed* (2012).
Möhren, Frankwalt. *Il Libro de la Cocina: Un Ricettario fra Oriente e Occidente* (2016).
Mongitore, Antonino. *Monumenta Historica Sacrae Domus Mansionis SS Trinitatis Militaris Ordinis Theutonicorum Urbis Panormi* (1721).
Montanari, Massimo. *Medieval Tastes: Food, Cooking and the Table* (2012).
Montaner Frutos, Alberto. "La Mora Zaida, entre Historia y Leyenda," *Historicist Essays on Hispano-Medieval Narrative* (2005), pages 272-352.
Mooney, Catherine. *Clare of Assisi and the Thirteenth-Century Church: Religious Women, Rules, and Resistance* (2016).
Mor, Carlo. "Le Assise Ruggeriane Non Accolte nel Liber Augustalis," *Atti del Convegno Internazionale di Studi Ruggeriani* (Palermo 1955), pages 236-246.
Morreale, Laura. "Wealth and Material Goods in Medieval Italian Civic Historiography," *Traditio,* volume 77 (2022), pages 185-233.
Morreale, Laura, and Gilsdorf, Sean. *Digital Medieval Studies: Practice and Preservation* (2022).
Morreale, Laura, and Paul, Nicholas (editors). *The French of Outremer: Communities and Communications in the Medieval Mediterranean* (2018).
Morris, Colin. *The Discovery of the Individual 1050-1200* (1974).
Morris, Colin. *The Papal Monarchy: The Western Church from 1050 to 1250* (1989).
Morris, Marc. *King John: Treachery and Tyranny in Medieval England, The Road to Magna Carta* (2015).
Morrison, James Cotter. *The Life and Times of Saint Bernard, Abbot of Clairvaux* (1877).
Morrison, Susan Signe. *A Medieval Woman's Companion: Women's Lives in the European Middle Ages* (2016).
Morso, Salvadore. *Descrizione di Palermo Antico* (1827).
Mortimer, Ian. *The Time Traveller's Guide to Medieval England* (2008).
Morton, James. "A Byzantine Canon Law Scholar in Norman Sicily: Revisting Neilos Doxapatre's 'Order of the Patriarchal Thrones,'" *Speculum,* volume 92, number 3 (July 2017), pages 724-754.
Morton, James. *Byzantine Religious Law in Medieval Italy* (2021).
Moshe, Gil. "The Jews in Sicily under Muslim Rule in the Light of Geniza Documents," *Italia Judaica 1* (1983), pages 87-134.
Moshe, Gil. "Sicily 827-1072 in Light of the Geniza Documents and Parallel Sources," *Italia Judaica 5* (1995), pages 96-171.
Mullett, Margaret. *Letters, Literacy and Literature in Byzantium* (2007).
Mumelter, Maria Luise. *Irene von Byzanz,* University of Innsbruck (1936); Universitäts und Landesbibliothek Tirol, C87782809.

SOURCES AND BIBLIOGRAPHY

Murray, Jacqueline. "Twice Marginal and Twice Invisible: Lesbians in the Middle Ages," *Handbook of Medieval Sexuality* (1996), pages 191-222.

Murrell, Stacey. "Concubinage in New Contexts: Interfaith Borrowings and the Rulers of Castile-León in the High Middle Ages," *Authorship, Worldview, and Identity in Medieval Europe* (2022), chapter 4.

Musca, Giosuè (editor). *Itinerari e Centri Urbani nel Mezzogiorno Normanno-Svevo* (1993).

Musso, Pasquale, et al. "Il 'Ricettario di Cucina' di San Martino delle Scale," *Bollettino del Centro di Studi Filologici e Linguistici Siciliani*, volume 21 (2007), pages 243-321.

Musto, Ronald (editor). *Medieval Naples: A Documentary History, 400-1400* (2013).

Musto, Ronald. *Writing Southern Italy Before the Renaissance: Trecento Historians of the Mezzogiorno* (2018).

Nancarrow, Jane-Heloise. "Normanitas and Memorial Traditions in the Apulian Architecture of Emperor Frederick II," *Mediterranean Studies*, volume 27, number 1 (2019), pages 36-62.

Narducci, Enrico. *Saggio di Voci Italiane Derivate dall'Arabo* (1858).

Naro, Massimo, and Abulafia, David. *Il Duomo di Monreale: Lo Splendore dei Mosaici* (2009).

Naro, Massimo. *Gloria di Cristo: I Mosaici del Duomo di Monreale* (2006).

Nasrallah, Nawal. *Annals of the Caliph's Kitchens: Ibn Sayyar al-Warraq's Tenth-Century Baghdadi Cookbook* (2007).

Nef, Annliese (editor). *A Companion to Medieval Palermo* (2013).

Nef, Annliese. *Conquérir et Gouverner: La Sicile Islamique aux XIe et XIIe Siècles* (2011).

Nef, Annliese, and Bagnera, Alessandra (editors). *Les Bains de Cefalà: Pratiques thermales d'origine islamique dans le Sicile médiévale* (2018).

Nef, Annliese, and Cressier, Patrice. "Les Fatimides et la Méditerranée Centrale," *Revue des Mondes Musulmans et de la Méditerranée*, number 139 (2016), pages 12-28.

Nef, Annliese, and Prigent, Vivien. "Contrôle et exploitation des campagnes en Sicile," *Authority and Control in the Countryside: From Antiquity to Islam in the Mediterranean and Near East* (2018), pages 313-366.

Nelson, Lynn. "Rotrou of Perche and the Aragonese Reconquest," *Traditio*, number 26 (New York 1970), pages 113-133.

Neocleous, Savvas. "Byzantine-Muslim Conspiracies Against the Crusades: History and Myth," *Journal of Medieval History*, volume 36, number 3 (2010), pages 253-274.

Neocleous, Savvas. *Heretics, Schismatics or Catholics? Latin Attitudes to the Greeks in the Long Twelfth Century* (2019).

Neville, Leonora. *Anna Komnene: The Life and Work of a Medieval Historian* (2016).

Niccolini, Giovanni Battista. *Storia della Casa di Svevia in Italia* (1873).

Nichols, Aidan. *Rome and the Eastern Churches: A Study in Schism* (2010 edition).

Nicholson, Helen. *The Knights Hospitaller* (2001).

Nicholson, Robert. *Tancred: A Study of His Career and Work* (1978).

Nicol, Donald. *Byzantium and Venice: A Study in Diplomatic and Cultural Relations* (1988).

Noble, Thomas. *Images, Iconoclasm and the Carolingians* (2013).

Noble, Thomas. *The Republic of Saint Peter: The Birth of the Papal State 680-825* (1986).

Norwich, John Julius. *Byzantium* (1988).

Norwich, John Julius. *The Kingdom in the Sun 1130-1194* (1970).

Norwich, John Julius. *The Normans in the South 1016-1130* (1967).

Norwich, John Julius. *Sicily: A Short History, from the Greeks to Cosa Nostra* (2015), published in North America as *Sicily: An Island at the Crossroads of History*.

Oeillet des Murs, Marc-Athanase. *Historie des Comtes du Perche de la Famille des Rotrou de 943 a 1234* (1856).

Oldfield, Paul. *City and Community in Norman Italy* (2009).

Oldfield, Paul. "The Kingdom of Sicily and the Early University Movement," *Viator*, volume 40 (2009), number 2, pages 135-150.

Oldfield, Paul. *Sanctity and Pilgrimage in Medieval Southern Italy 1000-1200* (2014).

Omodei, Filoteo. "La Versione Italiana della Historia di Ugo Falcando," *Archivio Storico Siciliano* (Palermo 1898), pages 465-477.

Orlando, Diego. *Il Feudalismo in Sicilia: Storia e Dritto Pubblico* (1847).

Ostrogorsky, George. *History of the Byzantine State* (1956).

Pakenham, Frank. *A History of the House of Lords* (1988).
Palermo, Gaspare. *Guida Istruttiva per Potersi Conoscere Tutte le Magnificenze della Città di Palermo* (1816).
Palmarocchi, Roberto. "Sul Feudo Normanno," *Studi Storici* (Pavia 1912), pages 349-376.
Palumbo, Pier Fausto. "Gli Atti di Tancredi e Guglielmo III in Sicilia," *Atti del Convegno Internazionale di Studi Ruggeriani* (Palermo 1955), pages 465-525.
Palumbo, Pier Fausto. *I Precedenti, la Vicenda Romana e le Ripercussioni Europee dello Scismo di Anacleto II* (1995).
Palumbo, Pier Fausto. *Tancredi Conte di Lecce e Re di Sicilia* (1991).
Panvini, Bruno. *Le Rime della Scuola Siciliana,* volume 1 (1962).
Paoli, Sebastiano. *Codice Diplomatico del Sacro Militare Ordine Gerosolimitano, oggi di Malta* (1733).
Paratore, Ettore. "Esame delle Varianti dei Codici Vaticano e Cassinense delle Leggi," *Atti del Congresso Internazionale di Studi sulla Sicilia Normanna* (Palermo 1974), pages 477-479.
Parker, John, "The Attempted Byzantine Alliance with the Sicilian Norman Kingdom 1166-1167," *Papers of the British School at Rome,* volume 24 (London, November 1956), pages 86-93.
Parsons, John Carmi, et al. *Medieval Queenship* (1993).
Pasca, Cesare. "Cenno Storico e Statistico del Comune di San Giovanni e Camerata," *Giornale di Scienze Lettere e Arti per la Sicilia,* volume 60, number 178 (October 1837), pages 41-46.
Pasciuta, Beatrice. "From Ethnic Law to Town Law: The Customs of the Kingdom of Sicily from the Twelfth to the Fifteenth Century," *Rechtsgeschichte Legal History,* number 24 (2016), pages 276-287.
Paterson, William. "The Archers of Islam," *Journal of the Economic and Social History of the Orient,* volume 9, number 1 (November 1966), pages 69-87.
Patroni Griffi, Filena, and Leone, Alfonso. *Le Origini di Napoli Capitale* (1987).
Pavillon, Balthazar. *La Vie du Bienheureux Robert d'Arbrissel, Patriarche des Solitaires de la France et Institueur de l'Ordre de Font-Evraud* (1666).
Pegge, Samuel. *The Forme of Cury* (1780).
Pennington, Kenneth. "The Birth of the Ius Commune: King Roger II's Legislation," *Rivista Internazionale del Diritto Comune,* number 17 (Enna 2006).
Perla, Raffaele. *Le Assise de' Re di Sicilia: Osservazioni Storico-Giuridiche* (1881).
Perrino, Pietro, and Hammer, Karl. "Sizilianische Weizensorten," *Die Kulturpflanz,* volume 31 (1983), pages 227-279.
Perry, Charles. *A Baghdad Cookery Book.* Translation of the *Kitab al-Tabikh* of Muhammad al Baghdadi (2009).
Perry, David. *Sacred Plunder: Venice and the Aftermath of the Fourth Crusade* (2016).
Perry, Guy (editor). *The Fifth Crusade in Context: The Crusading Movement in the Early Thirteenth Century* (2016).
Perry, Guy. *John of Brienne: King of Jerusalem, Emperor of Constantinople* (2013).
Petacco, Arrigo. *La Regina del Sud* (1992).
Pezzini, Elena. "Un tratto della cinta muraria della città di Palermo," *Mélanges de l'école française de Rome,* volume 110, number 2 (1998), pages 719-771.
Phillips, Jonathan. *The Fourth Crusade and the Sack of Constantinople* (2005).
Phillips, Jonathan. *The Second Crusade: Extending the Frontiers of Christianity* (2010).
Piaggia, Giuseppe. *Illustrazione di Milazzo* (1853).
Pick, Lucy. *Her Father's Daughter: Gender, Power and Religion in the Early Spanish Kingdoms* (2017).
Pieri, Piero. "I Saraceni di Lucera nella Storia Militare Medievale" *Atti del Terzo Congresso Storico Pugliese,* number 6 (1953), pages 94-101.
Pirri (Pirro), Rocco. *Chronologia Regum Penes Quos Siciliae* (1643).
Pirri (Pirro), Rocco, et al. *Sicilia Sacra Disquisitionibus et Notitiis Illustrata,* 4 volumes (1647).
Pirrotta, Nino. "Elementi Rapsodici nella Polifonia Italiana del Trecento," *Ricercare,* volume 1 (1989), pages 7-21.
Pispisa, Enrico. *Il Regno di Manfredi: Proposte di Interpretazioni* (1991).
Pistarino, Geo. "I Normanni e le Repubbliche Marinare Italiane," *Atti del Congresso Internazionale di Studi sulla Sicilia Normanna* (Palermo 1974), pages 241-262.
Pitrè, Giuseppe. *Esseri Soprannaturali e Meravigliosi* (1952).

SOURCES AND BIBLIOGRAPHY

Pitrè, Giuseppe. *Medicina Popolare Siciliana* (1896).
Plastino, Goffredo. *La Musica Folk: Storie, Protagonisti e Documenti del Revival in Italia* (2016).
Plested, Marcus. *Orthodox Readings of Aquinas* (2012).
Poloni, Alma. *Potere al Popolo: Conflitti Sociali e Lotte Politiche nell'Italia Comunale del Duecento* (2010).
Pontieri, Ernesto. "La madre di re Ruggero: Adelasia del Vasto, contessa di Sicilia, regina di Gerusalemme," *Atti del Covegno Internazionale di Studi Ruggeriani,* volume 1 (Palermo 1955), pages 327-432.
Poole, Reginald. *Medieval Reckonings of Time* (1918).
Powell, James. "Church and Crusade: Frederick II and Louis IX," *The Catholic Historical Review,* volume 93, number 2 (April 2007), pages 250-264.
Powell, James. *The Crusades, the Kingdom of Sicily and the Mediterranean* (2007).
Powell, James. "Frederick II and the Church: A Revisionist View," *The Catholic Historical Review,* volume 48, number 4 (January 1963), pages 487-497.
Powell, James. *Innocent III: Vicar of Christ or Lord of the World?* (1963).
Powell, James. *Medieval Monarchy and Trade: The Economic Policy of Frederick II in the Kingdom of Sicily* (1961).
Powell, James. *The Papacy, Frederick II, and Communal Devotion in Medieval Italy* (2014).
Prawer, Joshua. *The Crusaders' Kingdom: European Colonialism in the Middle Ages* (1972).
Prioreschi, Plinio. *A History of Medicine,* volume 5 (2003), pages 229-243.
Pybus, Helen. "The Emperor Frederick II and the Sicilian Church," *Cambridge Historical Journal,* volume 3, number 2 (1930), pages 134-163.
Queller, Donald, and Madden, Thomas. *The Fourth Crusade: The Conquest of Constantinople* (1999).
Quintana Prieto, Augusto. *La Documentation Pontificia de Innocencio IV 1243-1254* (1987).
Rader, Olaf. *Friedrich II: Der Sizilianer auf dem Kaiserthron* (2019).
Radici, Benedetto. "Il Casale e l'Abbazia di Santa Maria di Maniace," *Archivio Storico Siciliano* (Palermo 1909), pages 1-104.
Raedts, Peter. "The Children's Crusade of 1212," *Journal of Medieval History,* number 3 (1977), pages 279-323.
Ramseyer, Valerie. *The Transformation of a Religious Landscape: Medieval Southern Italy 850-1150* (2006).
Re, Edward. "The Roman Contribution to the Common Law," *Fordham Law Review,* number 447 (New York 1961), pages 447-494.
Reilly, Bernard. *The Kingdom of León-Castilla under King Alfonso VI 1065-1109* (1988).
Reilly, Bernard. *The Kingdom of León-Castilla under King Alfonso VII 1126-1157* (1998).
Reilly, Bernard. *The Kingdom of León-Castilla under Queen Urraca 1109-1126* (1982).
Reilly, Lisa. *The Invention of Norman Visual Culture: Art, Politics and Dynastic Ambition* (2020).
Resta, Gianvito. "La Cultura Siciliana dell'Età Normanna." *Atti del Congresso Internazionale di Studi sulla Sicilia Normanna* (Palermo 1974), pages 263-278.
Reston, James. *Warriors of God: Richard the Lionheart and Saladin in the Third Crusade* (2002).
Richardson, Henry Gerald. "The Letters and Charters of Eleanor of Aquitaine," *The English Historical Review,* volume 74, number 291 (April 1959), pages 193-213.
Riley-Smith, Jonathan. *The First Crusade and the Idea of Crusading* (1986).
Rinaldi, Luigi. *Le Parole Italiane Derivate dall'Arabo* (1906).
Rios Saloma, Martin. "La Reconquista: Génesis de un Mito Historiográfico," *Historia y Grafía,* number 30 (2008), pages 191-216.
Rizzitano, Umberto. *La Cultura Araba nella Sicilia Normanna* (1962).
Rizzitano, Umberto. "La Cultura Araba nella Sicilia Normanna," *Atti del Congresso Internazionale di Studi sulla Sicilia Normanna* (Palermo 1974), pages 279-297.
Rizzitano, Umberto. *La Sicilia Islamica nelle Cronache del Medioevo* (2004).
Rizzitano, Umberto. "La Sicilia nella Cultura Araba," *Studi arabo-islamici in memoria di Umberto Rizzitano* (1991).
Rizzitano, Umberto. *Storia e Cultura nella Sicilia Saracena* (1965).
Rizzitano, Umberto, and Giunta, Francesco. *Terra Senza Crociati: Popoli e Culture nella Sicilia del Medioevo* (1967).
Robinson, Paschal. *The Writings of Saint Francis of Assisi* (1906).

Roche, Jason. *The Crusade of King Conrad III of Germany* (2021).
Rohlfs, Gerhard. *La Sicilia nei Secoli: Profilo Storico Etnico Linguistico* (1984).
Rouighi, Ramzi. *Inventing the Berbers: History and Ideology in the Maghrib* (2019).
Rowley, Trevor. *The Normans: A History of Conquest* (2021).
Runciman, Steven. *Byzantine Civilisation* (1933, 1969).
Runciman, Steven. *The Eastern Schism: A Study of the Papacy and the Eastern Churches during the XIth and XIIth Centuries* (1955).
Runciman, Steven. *A History of the Crusades* (1951).
Runciman, Steven. *The Sicilian Vespers: A History of the Mediterranean World in the Later Thirteenth Century* (1958).
Runde, Ingo. "Konstanze von Aragon," *Die Kaiserinnen des Mittelalters* (2011), pages 232-248.
Ruffino, Giovanni, et al. *Lingue e Culture in Sicilia* (2013).
Russo, Luigi. *Boemondo: Figlio del Guiscardo e Principe di Antiochia* (2009).
Russo, Rocco. *La Magione di Palermo negli Otto Secoli della Sua Storia* (1975).
Rustow, Marina. "Jews and the Fatimid Caliphate," *Al-Masaq: Journal of the Medieval Mediterranean*, volume 33, issue 2 (London 2021), pages 169-187.
Salloum, Habeeb. "Medieval and Renaissance Italy: Sicily," in *Regional Cuisines of Medieval Europe: A Book of Essays* (2002), pages 113-123.
Salloum, Habeeb. *Scheherazade's Feasts: Foods of the Medieval Arab World* (2013).
San Martino de Spucches, Francesco. *Storia dei Feudi e dei Titoli Nobiliari di Sicilia,* 10 volumes (1927).
Santagati, Luigi. *La Sicilia di al-Idrisi ne Il Libro di Ruggero* (2010).
Santoro Rodolfo. "Architettura Castellana della Feudalità Siciliana," *Archivio Storico Siciliano,* Series 4, Volume 7 (Palermo 1981), pages 59-113.
Sapio Vitrano, Francesco. *Il Nummarium Islamico e Normanno della Biblioteca Comunale di Palermo* (1975).
Sapir Abulafia, Anna. *Christian-Jewish Relations 1100-1300: Jews in the Medieval Service of Medieval Christendom* (2011).
Sapir Abulafia, Anna. *Christians and Jews in the Twelfth-Century Renaissance* (1995).
Sauer, Michelle. *Gender in Medieval Culture* (2015).
Savagnone, Guglielmo. "Il Diploma di Fondazione della Cappella Palatina di Palermo 1140," *Archivio Storico Siciliano* (Palermo 1901), pages 66-83.
Savvides, Alexios. *Byzanto-Norrmmanica: The Norman Capture of Italy and the First Two Invasions in Byzantium* (2007).
Sayers, Jane. *Innocent III: Leader of Europe 1198-1216* (1994).
Scaduto, Mario. *Il Monachesimo Basiliano nella Sicilia Medievale* (1947).
Scandaliato, Angela, and Mulè, Nuccio. *La Sinagoga e il Bagno Rituale degli Ebrei di Siracusa* (2002).
Scarlata, Marina. "Sul Declino del Regno Normanno e l'Assunzione al Trono di Tancredi," *Atti del Congresso Internazionale di Studi sulla Sicilia Normanna* (Palermo 1974), pages 480-499.
von Schack, Adolf. *Poesie und Kunst der Araber in Spanien und Sicilien* (1865).
Schiaparelli, Celestino. *Il Canzoniere di Ibn Hamdis, Poeta Arabo di Siracusa* (1897).
Schippers, Arie. "Arabic and Hebrew Love Poetry in Sicily in the Middle Ages and Their Contacts with Early Romance and German Poets in Sicily," *Quaderni di Studi Arabi,* volume 10 (2015), pages 87-102.
Schlunz, Thomas Paul. *Archbishop Rotrou of Rouen 1164-1183: A Career Churchman in the Twelfth Century* (1984).
Schmandt, Raymond. "The Election and Assassination of Albert of Louvain, Bishop of Liège 1191-1192," *Speculum,* volume 42, number 4 (October 1967), pages 639-660.
Schneidman, Lee. "Aragon and the War of the Sicilian Vespers, *The Historian,* volume 22, number 3 (May 1960), pages 250-263.
Scholz, Piotr. *Eunuchs and Castrati: A Cultural History* (1999).
Schrader, Charles. "The Historical Development of the Papal Monarchy," *The Catholic Historical Review,* volume 22, number 3 (October 1936), pages 259-282.
Schwalm, Jacob. "Reise nach Italien im Herbst 1894," *Neues Archiv der Gesellschaft für ältere Deutsche Geschichtskunde,* number 23 (1898), pages 21-22.
Scully, Terence. *The Art of Cookery in the Middle Ages* (1995).

SOURCES AND BIBLIOGRAPHY

Scully, Terence. *The Neapolitan Recipe Collection* (2000).
Selden, John. *Titles of Honor* (1614 edition).
Sentis, Franz Jacob. *Die Monarchia Sicula* (1869).
Setton, Kenneth. *The Papacy and the Levant 1204-1571* (1976).
Severini Giordano, Franco. *I Castelli Normanno-Svevi di Calabria nelle Fonti Scritte* (2014).
Seward, Desmond. *The Monks of War: The Military Religious Orders* (1972, 1996).
Shadis, Miriam. *Berenguela of Castile and Political Women in the High Middle Ages* (2009).
Shahar, Shulamith. *Growing Old in the Middle Ages: Winter clothes us in shadow and pain* (1997).
Sharon, Moshe, and Schraeger, Ami. "Frederick II's Arabic Inscription at Jaffa," *Crusades,* volume 11 (2012), pages 139-158.
Shepard, Mary, et al. *The Cloisters: Studies in Honor of the Fiftieth Anniversary* (1992), page 226.
Siecienski, Edward. *The Papacy and the Orthodox: Sources and History of a Debate* (2017).
Simeoni, Luigi. "Note sulla Formazione della Seconda Lega Lombarda," *Memorie della Real Accademia delle Scienze dell'Istituto di Bologna,* series 3, number 6 (1932), pages 3-52.
Simeti, Mary Taylor. *Travels With a Medieval Queen: The Journey of a Sicilian Princess to Reclaim Her Father's Crown* (2001).
Simonsohn, Shlomo. *Between Scylla and Charybdis: The Jews in Sicily* (2011).
Simpson, Alicia. *Niketas Choniates: A Historiographical Study* (2013).
Siragusa, Giovanni Battista. *Il Regno di Guglielmo I in Sicilia* (1885, 1929).
Skinner, Patricia. *Family Power in Southern Italy: The Duchy of Gaeta and Its Neighbors 850-1139* (1995).
Skinner, Patricia. "Halt, Be Men! Sikelgaita of Salerno, Gender and the Norman Conquest of Southern Italy," *Gender and History,* volume 12, issue 3 (2000), pages 622-641.
Skinner, Patricia. "The Light of My Eyes: Medieval Motherhood in the Mediterranean," *Women's History Review,* volume 6, number 3 (1997), pages 391-410.
Skinner, Patricia. *Studying Gender in Medieval Europe: Historical Approaches* (2018).
Skinner, Patricia. "Women, Literacy and Invisibility in Southern Italy 900-1200," *Women, the Book and the Godly: Selected Proceedings of the St Hilda's Conference 1993* (1995), pages 1-11.
Skinner, Patricia. *Women in Medieval Italian Society 500-1200* (2001).
Smith, Anthony. *The Ethnic Origins of Nations* (1991).
Smith, Anthony. *Nationalism: Theory, Ideology, History* (2010 edition).
Smith, Damian. *Innocent III and the Crown of Aragon: The Limits of Papal Authority* (2004).
Smith, Jennifer. "Women, Land and Law in Occitania 1130-1250," *Medieval Women and the Law* (2000), pages 19-40.
Smith, Romney. "The Business of Human Trafficking: Slaves and Money between Western Italy and the House of Islam before the Crusades," *Journal of Medieval History,* volume 45, number 5 (2019), pages 523-552.
Smith, Thomas. *Curia and Crusade: Pope Honorius III and the Recovery of the Holy Land 1216-1227* (2017).
Sortino Trono, Eugenio. "Il Conte Goffredo di Ragusa 1093-1120," *Archivio Storico per la Sicilia Orientale,* volume 12 (1915), pages 181-185.
Sottile, Roberto. *L'Atlante Linguistico della Sicilia* (2019).
Spagnuolo, Edoardo. *La Contea di Puglia dalle Origini alla Battaglia di Civitate 1042-1053* (2017).
Spallino, Patrizia. *Le Questioni Siciliane, Federico II e l'Universo Filosofico* (2002).
Spahr, Rodolfo. *Le Monete Siciliane dai Bizantini a Carlo I d'Angio 582-1282* and *Le Monete Siciliane dagli Aragonesi ai Borboni 1282-1836* (1959).
Spampinato Beretta, Margherita. *Poeti della Corte di Federico II,* volume 2 in the series *I Poeti della Scuola Siciliana* (2008).
Spencer, Charles. *The White Ship: Conquest, Anarchy and the Wrecking of Henry I's Dream* (2021).
Sperle, Christian. *Koenig Enzo von Sardinien und Friedrich von Antiochia: Zwei Illegitime Soehne Kaiser Friedrich II* (2001).
Spiegel, Gabrielle. *The Past as Text: The Theory and Practice of Medieval Historiography* (1999).
Spike, Michèle. *Tuscan Countess: The Life and Extraordinary Times of Matilda of Canossa* (2004).
Stafford, Pauline (editor). *Gendering the Middle Ages* (2001).
Stafford, Pauline. *Queens, Concubines and Dowagers: The King's Wife in the Early Middle Ages* (1983).
Stafford, Pauline. "Writing the Biography of 11th-century Queens," *Writing Medieval Biography 750-1250: Essays in Honour of Professor Frank Barlow* (2006), pages 99-109.

Stalls, Clay. *Possessing the Land: Aragon's Expansion into Islam's Ebro Frontier under Alfonso the Battler 1104-1134* (1995).
Stanton, Charles. *Norman Naval Operations in the Mediterranean* (2011).
Stanton, Charles. "Roger de Hauteville, Emir of Sicily," *Mediterranean Historical Review*, volume 25, number 2 (2010), pages 113-132.
Stanton, Charles. *Roger of Lauria: Admiral of Admirals* (2019).
Starrabba, Raffaele. "Del Dotario delle Regine di Sicilia," *Archivio Storico Siciliano* (Palermo 1874), pages 7-25.
Staub, Martial, et al. *The Making of Medieval History* (2017).
Stedall, Jacqueline. *A Discourse Concerning Algebra* (2003), pages 19-54.
Stenton, Doris Mary. "Roger of Howden and Benedict," *The English Historical Review*, volume 68 (October 1953), pages 574-582.
Stephenson, Carl. *Mediaeval Feudalism* (1942).
Stern, Horst. *Mann aus Apulien: Die privaten Papiere del italienischen Staufers* (1986).
Stevenson, Joseph. *The Chronicles of Robert de Monte* (1991 edition).
Stevenson, Joseph. *The Church Historians of England* (1858).
Stopani, Renato. *La Via Francigena: Una Strada Europea nell'Italia del Medioevo* (2003 edition).
Storey, Gabrielle. *Berengaria of Navarre: Queen of England, Lord of Le Mans* (2022).
Strauss, Raphael. *Die Juden im Königreich Sizilien unter Normannen und Staufen* (1910).
Stringer, Keith, and Jotischky, Andrew (editors). *The Normans and the Norman Edge: Peoples, Polities and Identities on the Frontiers of Medieval Europe* (2019).
Stürner, Wolfgang. *Friedrich II* (2009).
Stürner, Wolfgang. *Staufisches Mittelalter Ausgewählte Aufsätze zur Herrschaftspraxis und Persönlichkeit Friedrichs II* (2012).
Sucato, Ignazio. *La Lingua Siciliana: Origine e Storia* (1975).
Summerlin, Danica. *The Canons of the Third Lateran Council of 1179: Their Origins and Reception* (2019).
Summonte, Giovanni Antonio. *Historia della Città e Regno di Napoli* (1601).
Sunderland, Luke. *Rebel Barons Resisting Power in Medieval Culture* (2017).
Symes, Carol, et al. *Sicily, al-Andalus and the Maghreb: Writing in Times of Turmoil*, special issue of *The Medieval Globe*, volume 5, number 1 (2019).
Szabados, György. "Aragóniai Konstancia Magyar Királyné," *Királylányok Messzi Földrol: Magyarország és Katalónia a Középkorban* (2009), pages 163-175.
Takayama, Hiroshi. *The Administration of the Norman Kingdom of Sicily* (1993).
Takayama, Hiroshi. "The Administrative Organization of the Norman Kingdom of Sicily," *Studi in Onore di Salvatore Tramontana* (2003), pages 415-429.
Takayama, Hiroshi. "Familiares Regis and the Royal Inner Council in Twelfth-Century Sicily," *The English Historical Review*, volume 104, number 411 (April 1989), pages 357-372.
Takayama, Hiroshi. "Frederick II's Crusade: An example of Christian-Muslim diplomacy," *Mediterranean Historical Review*, volume 25, number 2 (2010), pages 169-185.
Takayama, Hiroshi. *Sicily and the Mediterranean in the Middle Ages: Collected Studies* (2019).
Tarallo, Giovanni. "Sopra i Reali Sepolcri del Duomo di Monreale: Memoria del Padre Don Giovan Battista Tarallo," *Giornale di Scienza, Letteratura ed Arti per la Sicilia* (Palermo), July-September 1826, page 166.
Taviani-Carozzi, Huguette. *La Principauté Lombarde de Salerne* (1991).
Taylor, Julie Anne. *Muslims in Medieval Italy: The Colony at Lucera* (2003).
Tedeschi, Nicola Maria. *Istoria della Pretesa Monarchia di Sicilia* (1715).
Testa, Francesco. *De Vita, et Rebus Gesti Guilelmi II, Siciliae Regis, Monregalensis Ecclesii Fundatoris*, 4 volumes (1705-1773).
Theotokis, Georgios. *Bohemond of Taranto: Crusader and Conqueror* (2020).
Theotokis, Georgios. "The Norman Invasion of Sicily, 1061-1072: Numbers and Military Tactics," *War in History*, volume 17, number 4 (November 2010), pages 381-402.
Thompson, Kathleen. "The Lords of Laigle: Ambition and Insecurity on the Borders of Normandy," *Anglo-Norman Studies XVIII* (1996), pages 177-180.
Thompson, Kathleen. *Power and Border Leadership in Medieval France: The County of the Perche 1000-1226* (2002).

SOURCES AND BIBLIOGRAPHY

Thompson, James. *The Literacy of the Laity in the Middle Ages* (1960 edition).
Thorndike, Lynn. *Michael Scot* (1965).
Thorndike, Lynn. *The Place of Magic in the Intellectual History of Europe* (1905).
Thornton, Hermann. "The Poems Ascribed to Frederick II and Rex Fredericus," *Speculum*, volume 1, number 1 (January 1926), pages 87-100.
Thumser, Matthias. "Der König un sein Chronist: Manfred von Sizilien in der Cronik des sogenannten Nikolaus von Jamsilla" *Die Reichskleinodien: Herrschaftszeichen des Heiligen Römischen Reiches*, pages 222-242 (1997).
Tierney, Brian. *The Crisis of the Church and State 1050-1300* (1988).
Tierney, Brian. *Origins of Papal Infallibility 1150-1350* (1972, 1988).
Toomaspoag, Kristjan. "La Politica Fiscale di Federico II," *Federico II nel Regno di Sicilia: Realtà locali e aspirazioni universali* (2008), pages 231-247.
Toomaspoeg, Kristjan. *Les Teutoniques en Sicile 1197-1492* (2003).
Tounta, Eleni. "The Italo-Greek Courtiers and their Saint: Constructing the Italo-Greek Elite's Collective Identity in the Twelfth-Century Norman Kingdom of Sicily," *Mediterranean Studies*, volume 28, number 1 (2020), pages 88-129.
Tramontana, Salvatore. "Aspetti e Problemi dell'Insediamento Normanno in Sicilia," *Atti del Congresso Internazionale di Studi sulla Sicilia Normanna* (Palermo 1974), pages 310-359.
Tramontana, Salvatore. "Gestione del Potere, Rivolte e Ceti al Tempo di Stefano di Perche," *Potere, Società e Popolo nell'Età dei Due Guglielmi* (Bari 1981), pages 79-101.
Tramontana, Salvatore. *L'Isola di Allah* (2014).
Tramontana, Salvatore. *La Monarchia Normanna e Sveva* (1986).
Travagliato, Giovanni, and Sebastianelli, Mauro. *Il Restauro della Tavola Antiquissima di Santa Rosalia del Museo Diocesano di Palermo* (2012).
Travaini, Lucia. "La Monetazione del Regno di Sicilia al Tempo di Tancredi" *Tancredi, Conte di Lecce Re di Sicilia* (2004), pages 193-206.
Travaini, Lucia. *La Monetazione nell'Italia Normanna* (second edition 2016).
Travaini, Lucia. "The Normans Between Byzantium and the Islamic World," *Dumbarton Oaks Papers*, volume 55 (2001), pages 179-196.
Treviño, Gloria. *Santa María la Real de Nájera* (2012).
Trindade, Ann. *Berengaria: In Search of Richard the Lionheart's Queen* (1999).
Tronzo, William. *The Cultures of His Kingdom: Roger II and the Cappella Palatina of Palermo* (1997).
Tronzo, William. *Intellectual Life at the Court of Frederick II* (1994).
Tropea, Giovanni. "Effetti della simbiosi linguistica nella parlata gallo-italica di Aidone, Nicosia e Novara di Sicilia," *Bollettino dell'Atlante Linguistico Italiano*, New Series number 13-14 (1966), pages 3-50.
Tuchman, Barbara Wertheim. *Practicing History: Selected Essays* (1982).
Turner, Ralph. *Eleanor of Aquitaine: Queen of France, Queen of England* (2009).
Turner, Ralph. "Eleanor of Aquitaine and Her Children: An inquiry into medieval family attachment," *Journal of Medieval History*, volume 14, issue 4 (1988), pages 321-335.
Turner, Ralph. *King John* (1992, 2009).
Tyerman, Christopher. *The Debate on the Crusades* (2011).
Upsher Smith, Richard. "'Nobilissimus' and Warleader: The Opportunity and the Necessity Behind Robert Guiscard's Balkan Expeditions," *Byzantion*, volume 17, number 2 (2000), pages 507-526.
Vagnoni, Mirko. *Dei Gratia Rex Siciliae: Scene di Incoronazione Divina nell'Iconografia Regia Normanna* (2017).
Vaissete, Joseph. *Abregé de l'Histoire Générale de Languedoc*, volume 3 (1749).
Valenziano, Maria Giovanna "Tancredi e il Monastero di San Giovanni Evangelista in Lecce," *Tancredi Conte di Lecce Re di Sicilia* (2004), pages 217-232.
Van Cleave, Rachel. "Rape and Querela Law in Italy: False Protection of Victim Agency," *Michigan Journal of Gender and Law*, volume 13, number 273, January 2007 (Ann Arbor 2007).
Van Cleve, Thomas Curtis. "The Crusade of Frederick II," *A History of the Crusades* (1969), volume 2, pages 429-462.
Van Cleve, Thomas Curtis. *The Emperor Frederick II of Hohenstaufen, Immutator Mundi* (1972).
Van Cleve, Thomas Curtis. *Markward of Anweiler and the Sicilian Regency* (1937).

Van Waard, Roelof. *Ètudes sur l'Origine et la Formation de la Chanson d'Aspremont* (1937).
Vargas Macciucca, Francesco. *Esame delle Vantate Carte e Diplomi di Santo Stefano del Bosco in Calabria* (1765), pages 250-256.
Varvaro, Alberto. *Lingua e Storia in Sicilia* (2000).
Varvaro, Alberto, et al. *Vocabolario Storico-Etimologico del Siciliano* (2014).
Venuti, Antonino. *De Agricultura Opusculum* (1516).
Verlinden, Charles. "Markets and Fairs," *Cambridge Economic History of Europe* (1963), volume 3, pages 119-154.
Vetere, Benedetto. "Tancredi di Lecce nella Storiografia Medievale," *Tancredi, Conte di Lecce Re di Sicilia* (2004), pages 1-32.
Visioli, Giovanna, et al. "Traceability of Sicilian Durum Wheat Landraces and Historical Varieties by High Molecular Weight Glutenins Footprint," *Agronomy* 2021, volume 11, number 143.
Vitrano, Francesco Sapio. "La Zecca di Palermo dai Primi Insediamenti Fenici al 1836," *Archivio Storico Siciliano,* Series 3, Volume 20 (Palermo 1970), pages 107-202.
Vivanco, Miguel. "Liber Misticus," *Hispania Vetus: Musical-Liturgical Manuscripts from Visigothic Origins to the Franco-Roman Transition* (2007), pages 290-291.
Vodola, Elizabeth. *Excommunication in the Middle Ages* (1986).
Volpi, Giuseppe. *Cronologia de' Vescovi Pestani ora detti Capaccio* (1752).
Vones, Ludwig. "The Substitution of the Hispanic Liturgy by the Roman Rite in the Kingdoms of the Iberian Peninsula," *Hispania Vetus: Musical-Liturgical Manuscripts from Visigothic Origins to the Franco-Roman Transition* (2007), pages 43-59.
Waern, Cecilia. *Mediaeval Sicily: Aspects of Life and Art in the Middle Ages* (1910).
Waley, Daniel. "'Combined Operations' in Sicily AD 1060-1078," *Papers of the British School at Rome,* volume 22 (London, November 1954), pages 118-125.
Wallis, Peter (editor). *Adelard of Bath: The First English Scientist* (2013).
Walsh, James. "The Earliest Modern Law for the Regulation of the Practice of Medicine," *Bulletin of the New York Academy of Medicine,* volume 11, number 8 (August 1935), pages 521-527.
Waltz, James. "Muhammad and the Muslims in St Thomas Aquinas," *The Muslim World,* volume 66, number 2 (April 1976), pages 81-95.
Wansbrough, John. "A Judaeo-Arabic Document from Sicily," *Bulletin of the School of Oriental and African Studies, University of London,* volume 30, number 2 (1967), pages 305-313.
Ward, Paul. "The Coronation Ceremony in Medieval England," *Speculum,* volume 14, number 2 (April 1939), pages 160-178.
Ware, Timothy. *The Orthodox Church* (1964).
Wayno, Jeffrey. "Rethinking the Fourth Lateran Council of 1215," *Speculum,* volume 93, number 3 (July 2018), pages 611-637.
Webb, Simon. *The Life and Times of Adelard of Bath* (2019).
Webber, Nick. *The Evolution of Norman Identity 911-1154* (2005).
Weber, Hans. *Der Kampf Zwischen Papst Innocenz IV und Kaiser Friedrich II, bis zur Flucht des Papstes nach Lyon* (1900).
Weikert, Katherine, and Woodacre, Elena, "Gender and Status in the Medieval World," *Historical Reflections,* volume 2, issue 1, spring 2016 (Oxford 2016), pages 1-7.
Weiler, Björn. "Gregory IX, Frederick II and the Liberation of the Holy Land 1230-9," *Studies in Church History,* volume 36 (2000), pages 192-206.
Weiler, Björn. *Henry III of England and the Staufen Empire 1216-1272* (2006).
Weir, Alison. *Eleanor of Aquitaine: By the Wrath of God, Queen of England* (1999).
Weir, Alison. *Queens of the Conquest: England's Medieval Queens* (2017).
Wellas, Michael. *Griechisches aus dem Umkreis Kaiser Friedrichs II* (1983).
Wells, Spencer. *The Journey of Man: A Genetic Odyssey* (2004).
Weltecke, Dorothea. "Emperor Frederick II, 'Sultan of Lucera,' Friend of the Muslims: Promoter of Cultural Transfer: Controversies and Suggestions," Feuchter, Jorg (editor), *Cultural Transfers in Dispute* (2011), pages 85-106.
Whalen, Brett. *The Two Powers: The Papacy, the Empire and the Struggle for Sovereignty in the Thirteenth Century* (2019).

White, Lynn Townsend. "The Byzantinization of Sicily," *American Historical Review*, volume 41, number 1 (October 1936), pages 1-21.
White, Lynn Townsend. *Latin Monasticism in Norman Sicily* (1938).
Wickham, Chris. *The Inheritance of Rome: A History of Europe from 400 to 1000* (2009).
Wickham, Chris. *Medieval Rome: Stability and Crisis of a City 900-1150* (2015).
Wickham Legg, Leopold. *English Coronation Records* (1901).
Wieruszowski, Helene. "The Norman Kingdom of Sicily and the Crusades," *Politics and Culture in Medieval Spain and Sicily* (1971), pages 1-50.
Wieruszowski, Helene. "Roger II of Sicily, *Rex-Tyrannus,* in Twelfth-century Political Thought," *Speculum,* volume 38, number 1 (January 1963), pages 46-78.
Wilson, Bee. *Consider the Fork: A History of How We Cook and Eat* (2012).
Wilson, Henry Austin. *The Pontifical of Magdalen College with an Appendix of Extracts from Other English Manuscripts of the Twelfth Century* (1910).
Winkelmann, Eduard. *Kaiser Friedrich II* (1889).
Wolf, Kenneth. *Making History: The Normans and their Historians in Eleventh-century Italy* (1995).
Woodacre, Elena (editor). *Queenship in the Mediterranean: Negotiating the Role of the Queen in the Medieval and Early Modern Eras* (2013).
Woodacre, Elena, and Fleiner, Carey (editors). *Royal Mothers and Their Ruling Children: Wielding Political Authority from Antiquity to the Early Modern Era* (2015).
Yewdale, Ralph. *Bohemond I, Prince of Antioch* (1924).
Zaouali, Lilia. *Medieval Cuisine of the Islamic World: A Concise History with 174 Recipes* (2007).
Zappata, Pietro Giuseppe. *Difesa Storica della Monarchia Siciliana* (1716).
Zchomelidse, Nino. *Art, Ritual and Civic Identity in Medieval Southern Italy* (2014).
Zecchino, Ortensio. *Le Assise di Ariano: Testo Critico, Traduzione e Note* (1984).
Zepeda, Henry. *The First Latin Treatise of Ptolemy's Astronomy: The Almagesti Minor* (2019).
Ziegler, Wolfram. *König Konrad III* (2008).

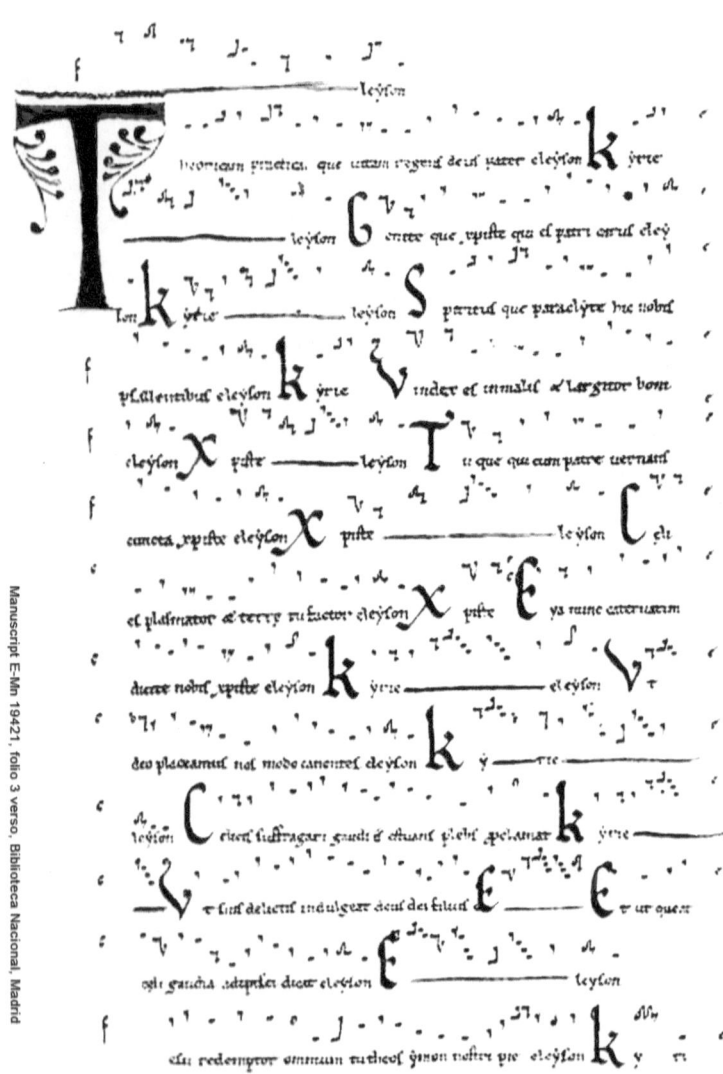

Liturgical chants in troparium of Saint Agatha Cathedral, Catania, of circa 1160, similar to those used at coronations and other ecclesiastical rites

INDEX

The focus of these entries is the period from 1000 to 1300. Personal names are listed according to common usage, e.g. *Michael Scot* and *Dante Alighieri* but *Boccaccio, Giovanni*. Most individuals are listed by given name rather than surname or toponym. Some personal names, particularly those in Arabic, are shortened based on popular usage as mononyms, e.g. *Saladin*. Certain Arabic names are listed as if the last part, sometimes part of a patronym or toponym, were a surname, but Muhammad al-Maziri appears after the entry for Mazara, his *nisbah* (presumed birthplace); names beginning with a *nasab* such as *ibn* or *bin* are listed by the main name, e.g. *Abbad* or *Jubayr*. Spellings should be noted, namely *Koran* rather than *Quran* and *Comnena* instead of *Komnena,* and *Muhammad* in preference to its variants. Places named for saints vary as well, so the town of Saint-Gilles is listed under the letter G and the abbey of Saint Euphemia under E but the castle of San Marco d'Alunzio under S. Minor variations in the spelling of a few entries depend upon which author drafted a passage, hence *Sicanian* but also *Sikanian,* with medieval spellings preferred for some proper nouns.

Aachen, 226, 424
aaneth, 484
Abbad III of Seville, 708n262
ibn Abbad, Muhammad (Bernavert, Morabit), 446-447
Abbasids, 148, 214, 361
abbeys, 34, 39, 78, 95, 102, 110, 123, 133, 141, 146, 158, 176, 182, 184, 192, 206, 236, 246, 247, 272, 279, 350, 370, 369, 518, 639. *See also* Cassino, Cava, monasticism, Monreale, Venosa, *etc*
abortion, 110-111, 251
Abruzzi (Abruzzo) region, 51, 71-72, 161, 203, 207, 212, 236, 293, 422, 445, 452, 469, 516
Abu I-Daw, 280
Abulafia, David, viii, x, 8
Abul Kasim, 249, 322
accolade. *See* investiture
accommodation, social, 21
acculturation, 21, 666
Acerenza, 452
Acerra, 391, 396
Achard II of Lecce, 297
Acre, 392, 400, 403, 444, 451, 454, 456, 457, 498

Acton, Harold, 45
Adelaide Hauteville (daughter of Roger I), 170, 589
Adelaide (Adelisa) Hauteville (daughter of Roger II), 203, 592
Adelaide del Vasto, v, 16, 32, 34, 80, 135, 171, 172, 179-193 passim, 194, 591
Adelard of Bath, 340
Adelasia of Torres, 504
Adele of Flanders, 172, 185
Adeline, nurse, 790 (N)
Adelisa of Adernò, 288
Ademar of Chabannes, 688n71
Adenolf (chamberlain), 299
Adenolfo of Pontecorvo, 388, 568
al-Adil (Saphadin), 400, 444
admiral, 39, 242, 273, 353, 391, 409, 423, 497, 708n255. *See also* amiratus
Admiral's Bridge, 215
Adrano, 86
Adrian IV, Pope, 132, 288-293 passim, 296
Adrianople (Edirne): Battle of 378, 75; Battle of 1205, 132
adultery, 107, 218, 238, 320, 363, 466, 469, 623, 628

affinity *defined,* 721n405
Africa. *See* Cairo, Ifriqiya, Mahdia, Tunisia, *etc*
St Agatha, 72, 557, 559-560
St Agatha church (Palermo), 56, 156
St Agatha's Gate (Palermo), 56, 156, 476
Aghlabids, 84-85, 134-135, 156, 169, 214, 446, 475, 477
Agira, 186
agriculture, 72, 105, 257, 475, 481-482, 520, 720n391. *See also* almonds, manorialism, olives, *etc*
Agridi, Battle of, 497
Agrigento (Girgenti), 49, 50, 52, 85, 150, 153, 170, 176, 211, 334-335, 352, 517, 573
Agrò forest, 332
Ahimaaz, Chronicle of, 685n49
Ahmed es-Sikeli. *See* Caïd Peter
Aix-la-Chapelle. *See* Aachen
Aidone, 750n639
Alaimo of Lentini, 688n75
Al-Andalus. *See* Andalusia
Albania, 21, 167, 183
Alberarda of Buonalbergo, 708n256
Alberic Hauteville, 690n85
Alberic of Trois-Fontaines, 761n938
Albert of Cologne, 716n363
Albert of Louvain, 501
Albert Magnus, 525
Albert of Rethel, 594
Albigensian Crusades, 427, 443, 452
Albigensians. *See* Cathars
Al-Bitruji (Alpetragius), 450
Alcamo, 31
Alcherio, bishop, 134-135, 156-157, 188
Aleramid dynasty, 171, 448, 513, 591, 601, 604
Alexander II, Pope, 149, 162
Alexander III, Pope, 132, 292, 296, 298, 321, 359, 385-386
Alexander III of Scotland, 494
Alexander IV, Pope, 544, 547, 548
Alexander of Conversano, 205-208 passim

Alexander of Telese, 31, 182, 217
Alexiad, 655, 695n145
Alexios I Comnenus, Emperor, 167, 172, 183, 185, 587, 608
Alexios II Comnenus, Emperor, 203, 388, 608
Alexios III Comnenus, Emperor, 419, 587
Alexios IV Angelus, Emperor, 587
Alfano II of Salerno, archbishop, 176
Alexios Branas, 391, 393
Alfano of Capaccio, bishop, 207
Alfano of Capua, archbishop, 383
St Alfonso. *See* Liguori, Alfonso
Alfonso I of Aragon, 217, 588, 600
Alfonso I of Portugal, 275
Alfonso II of Aragon, 421, 600
Alfonso VI of Castile, 192, 588
Alfonso VIII of Castile, 353, 355, 366
Alfonso X of Castile, 554, 689n75
Alfonso of Aragon (brother of Constance), 757n879
Alfonso of Capua (son of Roger II), 203, 222, 228, 236, 274, 592
algebra, 87, 450
Alhambra (Granada), 496, 686n53
Alice of Champagne, 776n1149
Alife, 191, 217
Almagest, 257
Almohads, 279-280, 289, 294-295, 353, 386, 669
almonds, 474, 475, 478-479, 484, 488-491 passim
Almoravids, 192, 197, 198, 204, 205, 226, 279, 476
Aloisia Martorano, 761n935
Alpetragius. *See* Al-Bitruji
Alps, 78, 125, 268, 423, 501-503 passim
Altofonte, 374
Alys of France, 399
Amalfi, 111, 165-166, 171, 173, 175, 189, 201, 215, 217, 222, 225, 243, 447, 517
amalgamation, social, 21
Amari, Michele, 7, 28, 34, 43, 655, 658

INDEX

Amato of Montecassino, 32, 93, 94, 123, 476, 654

Amazigh. *See* Berbers

Amico, William, 689n75

amir. *See* emir

amiratus, 39, 181, 191, 198, 222, 242, 273, 280, 289, 298, 408, 669, 708n255

Anacletus II, Pope, 209, 211-212, 215-227 passim

Anagni, 296, 354, 446, 454, 514, 520, 543, 565, 703n226

Anarchy (in England), 18, 223, 227, 270, 273, 275, 280, 289, 357, 721n409

Anastasius IV, Pope, 280, 288

Anatolia, 165, 172-173, 274, 275

Ancona, 224, 408, 422, 508, 514, 530, 734n559

Andalusia (Al-Andalus), 205, 279, 451, 479, 496

André the Chaplain, 688n74

Andrew II of Hungary, 444

Andrew of Cicala, 516

Andrew of Hungary (chronicler), 33, 657

Andrew of Isernia, 471, 767n1009

Andrew, governor of Messina, 335-336

Andrew of Rupecanina, 291, 585

Andria, 19, 291, 384, 453, 454, 499, 504, 513, 541, 652

Angers, 64

Angevin dynasty (in Italy), 6, 28, 462, 549, 552, 565

Angevin Empire. *See* Plantagenet Empire

Anglo-French War, 424

animal rights, 425-426

Anjou, House of. *See* Angevin, Louis IX, *etc*

Anjou region, 64, 424

Annaba, 276, 280-281

Anna Comnena, historian, 31, 167, 557, 655

annal *defined,* 653. *See* charters

anointings, royal, 113, 211, 282, 286, 384. *See also* coronations

Anonymous Historia Sicula, 690n84

Ansaldo of Arri, 699n188

Ansaldo, castellan, 342-343

Anselm of Canterbury, archbishop, 173, 175

Antidotarium Magnum, 251

Antidotarium Nicolai, 251, 718n375

Antioch, 131, 173, 174, 182, 185, 191, 206, 209, 224, 269, 300-301, 391, 456

Apicius, 474, 485

apostolic (papal) legateship, 175-176, 186-188, 240, 292, 412, 703n225, 704n227, 756n846

apprenticeship, 104-105

Apulia (Puglia), 20, 40, 78, 79, 81, 112, 117, 121-123, 124, 131, 139-142 passim, 180, 226-229 passim, 312, 324, 325, 362, 364, 371, 399, 445, 446, 452, 531. *See also* Bari, Brindisi, *etc*

Aquileia, Diet of, 500, 771n1070

Arabia (Saudi Arabia), 77, 84

Arabian horse, 100, 120

Arabic, xvi, xvii, 16, 23, 34, 39, 40, 43, 82-88 passim, 128-129, 135, 145, 155, 176, 177, 191, 194-196, 198, 235, 243, 244, 245, 246, 250, 256, 267, 306, 389, 418, 429, 429-433 passim, 478

Arabic numerals. *See* Hindu-Arabic

Arabs: *defined,* xvi, 40; collectively, xv, 22, 32, 39, 80, 82, 83-88, 94, 115, 120, 135, 145, 149, 153, 156, 161, 177, 371, 447, 516. *See also* Aghlabids, Fatimids, Kalbids, *etc*

Aragon: xv, 13, 23, 193, 270, 421, 477, 565; Crown of, 757n873

Aragonese Crusade, 565

arancina (rice ball), 480

archers (and arbalists), 100, 125, 153, 163, 167, 174, 221, 247, 276, 284, 291, 325, 344, 481, 524, 554-555, 762n949

archimandrite (title), 40
Archimandrite of Messina, 729n490
architecture: Classical, 74, 573; Gothic, 23, 102, 270, 370, 512, 756n851; Norman-Arab, 22, 129, 137, 138, 183, 214, 220, 229, 231-232, 349, 369-380, 393, 405, 415, 580; Romanesque, 129, 183, 220, 427
Archivio Storico Siciliano, 659
archon. *See* familiare
Arda of Edessa, 188
Ardennes, 280
Arduin of Melfi, 119-121 passim, 690n88
Arechi Castle, 198, 493
Arechisi of Capua, 432
arengo *defined,* 517
Arenula, Battle of, 95
Argiro, rebel, 200
Argyros, 125, 127
Arianism, 76
Ariano, Assizes of, 33, 72, 111, 237-238, 261, 619-631
Aristotle, xiv, 257
Armenia, 130, 151, 274
Armenia, Lesser, 174, 209
armor, 96-97, 100, 465, 554
Arnold the Catalan, 450
Arnold of Lübeck, 754n829
Arnolf of Capaccio, bishop, 382-383
Arnulf of Chocques, patriarch, 188
Artemis (Diana), 220, 551, 557
Arthurian legend, 717n366
Arthur of Brittany, 399
artichokes, 257, 475, 484
Artuqid dynasty, 173, 274
Ascalon, 204, 392, 401, 707n250
Asclettin, general, 289-291
Ascoli, 121, 516
Aspremont, Song of, 80, 429, 568, 739n905
Aspromonte region, 112
Assassin sect, 524, 669
assimilation, social, 21, 22
astrology, 340, 343, 346, 450, 551

astronomy, 87, 340, 450, 451, 551
Atenulf of Benevento, 121
Athena (Minerva), 557, 568
al-Athir al-Jazari (historian), 32, 185, 654
Attila, 76
attire. *See* clothing
aubergine. *See* eggplant
Audita tremendi, 392
augustale (augustalis) coin, 40, 244, 263, 445, 498, 505, 638
Augustine of Hippo, 76, 131, 280, 783n1246
Aurora, Princess. *See* Sleeping Beauty
autoethnography, 12, 679n12
autohistory, 12, 679n12
Avellino, 51, 217, 348
Avengers. *See* Vendicosi
Aversa, 79, 118, 139, 175, 222, 401
Avicenna (Ibn Sina), 111
Ayyubids, 295, 354, 361, 366, 400, 401, 408, 444, 449, 452, 456, 522-523, 528, 530
al-Aziz, 506
ibn al-Ba'ba (emir), 153, 154, 697n165
Badiazza. *See* St Maria delle Scale
baccalà, 474
Baghdad, 87, 148, 214, 361, 387, 477
baglio (bailey), 99, 101
Bagnara, 399
bagpipies, 434
Baha ad-Din, 400
Bahlara, 84
Baida, 57, 496, 746n727
bailey. *See* baglio
bailiffs (governors), 184, 241-242, 264, 310, 318, 334, 453, 465, 469, 499, 503, 515, 517, 540
Balat, 84, 258
Baldwin I of Jerusalem, 174, 188, 189, 193
Baldwin II of Constantinople, 523, 552, 563
Baldwin II of Jerusalem, 207, 280
Balearic Islands, xxi, 63, 64, 387. *See also* Majorca

Balharm. *See* Palermo
Balkan region, 41, 61, 77, 130, 167, 257, 522, 564
Ballarò souk, 56, 62, 84, 116, 156, 253, 258, 476, 477
Baltic Crusades, 521, 533
Bamberg, 117
Bañuelo (Granada), 686n53
Banu Bakr tribe (Turkey), 654
Banu Raja family (Palermo), 242, 280
baptism, 92, 111, 133, 135, 215, 506, 559
Barasht, 272
St Barbara church (Palermo), 56, 73, 156
Barber, Richard, 5
Barcelona, 23, 192, 208, 362, 477
Bari, xv, 51, 78, 84, 94, 95, 117, 122, 125, 145, 151-153, 166, 171, 200-205 passim, 220, 224, 241, 276, 290, 292, 326, 499, 514
Bari, Council of, 131, 176
Barletta, 51, 95, 364, 454, 545
baron (and barony) *defined*, 39, 97, 140
baronage, 99, 144, 156, 161, 163, 180, 182, 186, 191, 201, 205, 209, 227, 297, 302, 321, 395
Barons' Crusade, 507
Bartholomew the Englishman, 495
Bartholomew of Lusci, 738n612
Bartholomew of Messina, 550
Bartholomew of Neocastro (Nicastro), 657, 689n75
Bartholomew of Parisio, 329, 332
Bartholomew, familiare, 354
St Basil, 133
Basil Mesardonites, 94, 95
Basile, Giovan Battista, 432
Basilian. *See* Orthodox
Basilian Rule, 133, 569
Basilicata. *See* Lucania
Basque region. *See* Navarre
bastardy. *See* illegitimacy
baths. *See* hammams, mikvehs
Batu Khan, 508, 522
Bavaria, 113, 223, 525, 544

Bayeux Tapestry, 97, 720n399
bazaars. *See* souks
bears, 73, 98
Beati Paoli, 562
Beatrice of Namur, 280
Beatrice of Provence, 553
Beatrice of Rethel, 280, 365, 390, 556, 594
Beatrice of Savoy, 529, 548, 606
Beatrix Hohenstaufen (daughter of Frederick I), 365, 781n1199
Beatrix Hohenstaufen (daughter of Philip of Swabia), 758n884
Becket home (Palermo), 34, 56, 316
Becket, Thomas. *See* Thomas Becket
Bedouins, 84, 271, 294
Befana, 249, 666
Bejaia (Bougie), 271
Béla III of Hungary, 734n565
Belisarius, 77
Belprand of Cosenza, archbishop, 657
Benedict VIII, Pope, 96, 117
Benedict X, antipope. *See* John Mincio
Benedictine order, 79, 98, 102, 129, 135, 140, 141, 189, 246, 371, 388, 426
Beneventan script, 644
Benevento: xv, 16, 79, 94, 124, 162, 206, 208, 220, 224, 227, 274, 290, 354, 531; Battle of, 483, 553-554; Treaty of, 43, 292-294, 727-729
Benjamin of Tudela, 362-363, 656
Berardo of Castagna, archbishop, 423-424, 454, 463, 505, 515, 529
Berbers (Amazigh), xvi, 12, 40, 84, 85, 135, 148-149, 164, 198, 271, 285-287, 476, 477, 560
Berengaria of Navarre, 397, 400
Bergamo, 503
Bernard of Clairvaux, 209, 216, 226, 246, 259, 274, 281
Bernard of Gaeta, bishop, 127
Bernard of Ventadour, 108
Bernardo, Angelo, 754n822

Bernavert. *See* al Wardi
Bertha of Sulzbach, 269, 272, 313
Berthold of Hohenberg, 531, 541, 542-545 passim
betrothals. *See* marriages
Bianca Lancia, 468, 501, 513, 523, 529, 604
biancomangiare, 491
bidì wheat, 252, 257, 478
Bint Muhammad ibn Abbad, 447, 762n939
births. *See* childbirth
Black Death, 104, 566
Blanca of Navarre, 353, 588, 595
blazon, 260
Blois, 361
boar, 73, 98, 251, 374, 475, 479, 500
Boccaccio, Giovanni, 37, 386, 432, 659, 682n26
Bohemond II, 185, 200, 205-209 passim, 220, 706n248
Bohemond of Manopello (Tarsia), 324, 33, 737n595
Bohemond of Taranto (and Antioch), 172, 173, 182
bohort, 259
Boiannes, Basil, 95
Bologna, 75, 282, 356, 425, 463, 539-540, 656
Bonatti, Guido, 450
St Bonaventure (John of Fidanza), 561, 562
Boniface VIII, Pope, 775n1126
Boniface Lancia, 546
Book of Roger, 250, 268
Borrello, William, 100, 545
Boson of Gorron, bishop, 332
Bradano river, 208
bread: 123, 486, 490, 495; black, 257; votive, 561
Breakspear, Nicholas. *See* Adrian IV
Breitenwang, 225
bribery outlawed, 238, 319
bridges, 86, 215, 554
Brindisi, 94, 140, 152, 207, 208, 220, 243, 291, 366, 428, 448, 451, 453, 456, 505, 542
broccoli, 257, 475, 477, 483, 486, 488
Brucato, 354
Bruno of Cologne, 176, 184
bubonic plague, 78, 104, 566. *See also* Black Death
buckwheat, 478
Buonalbergo family, 191, 192, 197, 207
burgenses. *See* jurats
Burgundio, justiciar, 335
Burgundy, 140, 278, 292, 532
Butera, 171, 172, 291, 303, 740n639
Byzantine Christians. *See* Orthodox Church
Byzantine (Eastern Roman) Empire, xiv, 61, 77, 78, 81, 84, 95, 100, 118, 122, 123, 131, 151, 162, 166, 173, 203, 224, 269, 272, 276, 290, 354, 364, 381, 388, 393, 400, 419, 564. *See also* Michael IV, *et al*
Byzantine Greeks (in Italy), 53, 81-82, 87, 117, 119, 121, 127-129, 145, 177, 251, 446, 477
Byzantium. *See* Constantinople
Caccamo, 101, 297, 298, 303
caciocavallo, 478
cafiso, 245
caïd (title) *defined*, 39, 143
Cairo (al-Qahira), xv, 87, 101, 143, 148, 204, 256, 361
Calabria, 41, 71-72, 76-83 passim, 94, 95, 120, 122, 128, 139-142, 144, 146, 148-188 passim, 198, 203, 226, 246, 332, 385, 429, 479, 545. *See also* Cosenza, Mileto, *etc*
Mt Calanna, 742n675
Calascibetta, 86, 148, 184, 517
Calatrasi, 371, 446, 746n721
Calixtus. *See* Callixtus
Callixtus II, Pope, 199-200, 206, 704n228
St Calogero, 559
Calomeno, John of, 337
Calore River, 554
Caltabellotta: 86, 433; Peace of, 565

INDEX

Caltagirone, 164, 445
Caltanissetta, 184, 314
Cambridge Chronicle, 658
camels, 149, 163, 498
Camera Reginale, 40, 720n404
Camino de Santiago, 561
Campania, 40, 71, 79, 94, 118, 125, 176, 203, 220, 226, 245, 291, 469, 541. *See also* Capua, Naples, Salerno, *etc*
Campanian Placets, 431
campanilismo, 240, 570
Cannae, 95, 121
cannolo, 478
canonization, 130, 133, 427, 434, 454, 474, 558, 560
Canossa, 163
cantaro, 245
Canterbury: 130, 175; archbishops (see) of, 113, 176; artisans, 632-634; cathedral, 29, 316
Cantuese, Alduin, 741n649
Capetians, 15, 213, 278. *See also* Angevin dynasty, Charles I, Louis IX, *et al*
Capitanata, 124. *See also* Apulia
Capizzi, 740n639
caponata, 479, 481, 486
Capua: 36, 79, 94, 96, 118, 119, 172, 175, 191, 207, 211, 221, 222, 227, 445; Assizes of, 238, 445; Placet of, 26, 142, 431
Mt Caputo (Monreale), 370
cardinal, rank of, 140, 693n121
cardinals collectively, 168, 321, 508, 521
cardoon (carduna), 257, 474-475
Caro of Monreale, archbishop, 446
Carpineto, 552
Carr, Edward, 12, 660
carroccio, 504
Carthaginians, 71-72, 77, 83
Carthusian order, 176, 184
Caruso, Giovanni Battista, 650
Casauria, 236
cassata, 478

Cassino abbey (Mount Cassino), 50, 78, 79, 93, 95, 119, 171, 206, 223, 224, 236, 251, 371, 401, 431, 499, 504, 505, 654
Cassodoren, 746n723
Castelbuono, 481
Castel dell'Ovo (Naples), 460
Castel del Monte, 102, 376, 453, 493, 499, 504
Castel Fiorentino, 531
Castellaccio (St Benedict Castle), 370
Castel Sant'Angelo (Rome), 168, 209
Castile, 55, 61, 192
castles, 19, 42, 60, 73, 74, 98, 101-102, 105, 120, 147, 154, 177, 178, 184, 190, 220, 227, 232, 242, 287, 298, 301, 305, 330, 337, 339, 349, 352, 374, 403, 456, 460, 732n541. *See also* Arechi, Castel del Monte, Norman Palace, Trifels, Ursino, *etc*
Castrogiovanni (Enna). *See* Kasr'Janni
Catalan language, 430, 660
St Cataldo chruch, 128-129, 137, 362
Catalogus Baronum, 34, 243, 247, 302, 716n362
Catalonia, 15, 23, 166, 422, 570. *See also* Barcelona, *etc*
Catalonian Gothic, xvi, 23
Catania, 50, 52, 72, 120, 144, 153, 164, 184, 340, 352, 354, 390, 399, 445, 447, 560
Catanzaro, 51, 140, 169, 288
catepan (title), 81, 94, 95, 96, 121, 122, 124, 125, 127, 151, 152, 158, 183, 201
Cathars (Albigensians), 386, 427, 443, 452, 453, 500, 523, 549
Catholicism, 29, 41, 103, 109, 110, 115, 127-136, 145, 157-159 passim, 166, 175, 180, 184, 187, 199, 202, 206, 223, 237, 247, 256, 273, 310, 320, 372, 400, 424. *See also* abbeys, papacy, *etc*
cats, 73, 426
Cattan, Henry, 715n356
Caudine Valley, 217

cauliflower, 257, 475, 483
Cava abbey, 7, 51, 78, 80, 95, 192, 261, 279, 371, 518
Ceccano, 42, 206-207
Cecile of France, 174
Cefala Diana, 86, 686n53
Cefalù, 149, 166, 215, 220, 273, 281, 332, 370, 557, 565, 712n310
Celestine II, Pope, 272-273
Celestine III, Pope, 401, 751n774
Celestine IV, Pope, 508, 510, 513
celiac disease, 252
Celts (in France), 76, 92
Cenci, Francesca, 717n368
Cephalonia, 168, 391
Ceprano, 51, 273, 279, 403, 458, 544, 554
Ceprano, Treaty of, 164-165, 700n201
Cerami, Battle of, 148-149
Chalandon, Ferdinand, 8, 658
chancellor (office), 191, 211, 222, 242-243, 273, 280, 289, 314-331 passim, 333, 335, 340, 351, 396, 410, 443, 565. *See also* amiratus, logothete
Chanson d'Aspremont. *See* Aspremont, Song of
chant, 434, 576, 644, 830
Charlemagne, 77, 89, 91, 98
Charlemagne Cycle, 80
Charles I (Anjou) of Naples, 549, 555, 563
Charles II (Anjou) of Naples, 565, 657
Charles III (Bourbon) of Spain, 665
Charles the Bald, 92
Charles Martel, 84, 89, 97
Charles the Simple, 92
charters (writs and decrees), xxiii, 31-38 passim, 45, 73, 653
cheese, 474, 478, 485, 491, 770n1047
chess, 86, 105, 214, 688n75
chicken, 474, 477, 481, 483-488 passim
chickpeas, 479, 481, 488, 564
childbirth, 110, 133, 279, 448, 513, 520
childhood, 103, 573, 778n1160
Children's Crusade, 443, 541, 761n938
China, xv, 87, 448, 573, 762n947
chivalry. *See* courtliness, knighthood, minstrels, poetry, tournaments, troubadours
chrism, 643, 646
chrismation (sacrament), 133
Christ. *See* Jesus Christ
Christendom *defined,* 83, 128, 511
Cristianity and Christians. *See* baptism, Catholicism, Orthodoxy, *etc*
Christmas witch. *See* Befana
Christodoulos, amiratus, 181, 185, 191, 197, 204-206 passim, 705n237
chronicles *defined,* 6, 11, 29, 32, 653
chronocentrism, 75
ciaramella (shawm), 434
Cicero, xiii, 101, 181
ciciri, 564
Cielo of Alcamo, 18, 31, 432-433, 637
Cinderella, 432
Cingoli, 530
Cinisi, 446
circumcision, 252, 718n376
cirneco (Sicilian hound), 73
Cistercians, 246, 274, 461, 375, 392
citizenship *defined,* 689n77
citron, 475, 489-490
citrus fruits. *See* lemons, oranges
city life. *See* urban
city-states. *See* communes
Ciullo. *See* Cielo of Alcamo
Cividale, 500, 685n40
Civitate, Battle of, 95, 124-126, 148
Clare Offreduccio of Assisi, 426, 506, 566
Clarendon: Assize, 347, 359; Constitutions, 358, 360
Clement III, Pope, 393
Clement IV, Pope, 553
Clementia of Catanzaro, 288, 347
clergy, 99, 134, 255, 286, 358, 429, 464, 471, 561. *See also* abbeys, car-

dinals
Clermont, Council of, 258, 172
climate (and climate change), 480, 486, 651
cloisters, 215, 370-374, 667
clothing, 97, 109 129, 163, 633, 642
cloves, 484, 487, 642
Cluniacs, 736n573
coats of arms. *See* heraldry
cockatoo, 498, 573
co-culturalism, 283, 670
cod, 11, 474
coinage, 40, 41, 105, 213, 238, 243-245, 260, 263, 271, 397, 406, 431, 447, 467, 468, 498, 642
Colapesce, 552
colascione, 434
collecta tax, 104, 501, 504, 505, 507, 514, 516, 519, 529, 530, 549
Colocci, Angelo, 637
Cologne, 176, 502
Coloman of Hungary, 279
combat, trial by, 159, 311, 331, 332
Comino cheese, 490
commare *defined*, 724n445
commonalty, 24, 99, 104, 159, 286, 428, 464, 465, 467, 535, 559. *See also* peasants
common law, 85, 237, 239, 286, 347, 360, 463, 464, 741n656
communes (in northern Italy), 25, 201, 202, 241, 247, 270, 282, 290, 384, 385, 425, 452, 465, 498, 501, 503, 518. *See also* Milan, *etc*
Comnenus dynasty, 167, 172, 203, 223, 386, 387, 391, 419, 557, 587, 608. *See also* Anna Comnena, Isaac II, Manuel I, *et al*
concubines, 107, 252-254, 301. *See also* harems
confetti, 478
confraternities, 241, 246, 562, 667
Conrad I of Sicily (Conrad IV of Germany), 518, 542-542, 605
Conrad II of Sicily (Conradin), 542-546 passim, 548, 549, 555, 605

Conrad II of Germany, 79, 118
Conrad II of Italy, 172
Conrad III of Germany, 206, 223, 226, 269, 280
Conrad Lutzelinhart (Lützelhardt), 408
Conrad of Marburg, bishop, 500-501
Conrad of Montferrat, King of Jerusalem, 393, 403, 404
Conrad of Urslingen, 516
constables, 241, 242, 264, 311, 344, 388, 721n405
Constance (Konstanz), Treaty of, 280, 290
Constance of Aragon, xviii, 262, 421, 557, 600
Constance of France, 185, 200, 205, 206, 706n248
Constance Hautevilleof Sicily, daughter of Roger II, 40, 108, 110, 175, 326, 390, 391, 397, 398, 401-413 passim
Constance (Anna) Hohenstaufen of Sicily, daughter of Bianca, 468, 523, 604
Constance Hohenstaufen of Sicily, daughter of Manfred, 549, 565, 606
Constans II, Emperor, 29, 81
Constantine IX, Emperor, 122
Constantine the African (monk), 251
Constantine the Great, Emperor, 78, 130
Constantinople (Byzantium), 75, 77, 81, 82, 94, 118, 127, 131, 132, 151, 162, 165, 167, 170, 183, 215, 269, 277, 361, 363, 445, 548
constitutions, development of, 237, 358, 462, 465
consuocera *defined*, 724n445
contraception, 111, 251
Contrasto, 44, 106, 432-433, 637-642
convents (nunneries), 103, 105, 133, 162, 188, 192, 303, 332, 370, 411, 426, 551
Conversano family, 112, 205, 207, 208
convivencia, 193, 284, 285

Conza, 691n99
Cordoba, 156, 249, 390, 479, 481, 686n53
Corfu, 167-168, 276, 354
Corinth, 276
Corleone, 86, 371, 451
Corno Grande (mountain), 72
coronations, 113, 122, 167, 187, 209, 211, 212, 216, 226, 233, 272, 279, 281, 373, 384, 391, 408, 411, 423, 456, 503, 546, 553, 643-650
Correnti, Santi, 32, 665
Cortenuova, Battle of, 503, 505
Cosenza, 50, 51, 76, 122, 149, 169, 172, 389, 499, 515
Cosmas of Mahdia, 38, 135, 295, 721n411
cosmetics (make-up), 108, 251
Cotentin Peninsula, 92
cottage cheese. *See* ricotta
cotton, 86, 109, 163, 469
councils, urban. *See* demesnial, jurats
counsellors. *See* familiares
count (and county) *defined*, 39
courtliness ("chivalry"), 106, 247, 259, 430
Crati Valley, 51
Cremona, 425, 452, 503-504
crespelle, 486, 491
Croce, Benedetto, 659
Cronaca di Partenope, 432, 442
crossbow, 497, 510, 514, 554, 714n349
crossbowmen (arbalists). *See* archers
crowns, 19, 114, 213, 233, 635-636
crusades. *See* First, Second, *etc*
Cuba palace, 386, 496
Cubola, 580
cuccagna, 482
Mt Cuccio. *See* Kuz
cuisine, 473-496
cultural appropriation, 22
cultural transmission, 578
curia, royal, 240-242, 264
curiae generales, 209, 321, 519, 541, 545

Cusa, Salvatore, 7
cuttlefish, 474-475, 485, 489
cuzzupa. *See* bread
Cyprus, 115, 134, 391, 400, 455, 497, 530
cystitis, 718n376
daggers, 301, 331, 342, 514
Damascus, 276, 444, 456
Damietta, 354, 362, 444
damsels, 261, 637-642
Dancus, 716n363
danegeld, 92
Dante Alighieri, 37, 427, 429, 509, 536
Dante of Maiano, 760n910
dar al-hikma, 256, 340
Dar al-Islam, xiv, 83
Dar al-Kufr, 83
Dark Ages *defined*, 77
Dattus, 117
Davanzati, Chiaro, 434
Decameron. *See* Boccaccio
deconstructionism (post-structuralism), 660, 661
decrees. *See* charters
Decretals of Gregory IX, 502, 504
deer, 73, 98, 475, 483, 500
deerhound, 73, 670
Delta Aquariids, 521
demesnial (royal) lands/localities, 39, 98, 102, 180, 184, 208, 236, 238, 241-243, 261, 317, 451, 464-471 passim, 499, 503, 516-519, 530, 544, 667
Demetritzes, 391
val Demone (Sicily), 52, 184
Demus, Otto, 712n310
depilation, cosmetic, 108, 251
Desclot, Bernat, 689n75
Desiderio of Benevento, abbot, 141
destriers (war horses), 100, 671
diaspora, Jewish, xiv
diaspora, Siculo-Neapolitan, 570, 578
Diceto, Ralph of, 743n685
Di Costanzo, Angelo, xiii, xxi, 569, 573

Dictatus Papae, 700n201, 775n1129
Diego Gelmírez, archbishop, 205
Dietpold of Schweinspünt, 418, 420
Digest of Justinian, 111, 222
digital humanities, 653
Di Lorenzo, Achille, 785n1283
al-Dimas, 205
dinar coin, 244, 468
ad-Din, Baha, 752n800
dining, 492-495
Diocletian, Emperor, 78, 97
Diodorus Siculus, 71
Diophantus of Alexandria, 87, 450
distillation process, 86
diversity. *See* multiculturalism
divorce, xiv, 107, 111, 132, 260, 329, 467, 665, 721n405
diwan (treasury), 22, 31, 87, 157, 170, 181, 198, 242-243, 273, 301, 309, 354, 465
diwan al-mazalim (grievance board), 242
Djerba, 222, 224, 226, 270-272, 295, 447, 458, 507
Djidjelli, 272
DNA. *See* genetics
Docibilian dynasty, 127, 211
dog breeds, 73
Dokeianos family, 121
dolmens, 71
Dominican order, 448, 453, 454, 461, 509, 522, 533, 544, 563, 566
Donation of Constantine, 692n109
donativo. *See* collecta
Dorylaeum, 275
Douglass, Frederick, 11
dowers and dowries, 40, 100, 188, 217, 219, 221, 261, 315, 382, 391, 396, 398-399, 421, 501, 529, 540, 545, 548
Dragonetti, Giacinto, 658
dragons, 551-552, 635
Drengot family, 95, 98, 100, 106, 117-122 passim, 125, 132, 139-141 passim, 152, 162, 175, 208, 217, 219, 585

dress. *See* clothing
Drogo Hauteville, 119, 122, 124, 125, 583
droit du seigneur (wedding tax), 261
dubbing, knightly. *See* investiture
Du Bois, W.E.B., 11
ducat coin, 19, 33, 40, 213, 236, 237, 243, 244, 263
duels, 159, 236, 332, 359, 466, 565
Durendal, 430, 759n905
Dürnstein Castle, 404
Durrës (Durazzo), 167, 183, 391, 655
dysentery, 306, 519, 531
Eadmer of Canterbury, 177, 702n220
earthquakes, 182, 206, 352-353, 372, 389, 493
Eastern Christians. *See* Orthodox church
Eberhard II, bishop, 549
Eboli, Peter of. *See* Peter of Eboli
Edessa (Urfa), 119, 174, 269, 274
Edmund of England, 547, 549
Edrisi. *See* Idrisi
education. *See* literacy
Edward I of England, 726n464
eel, 474, 481
eggplant (aubergine), 86, 479, 485
Eighth Crusade. *See* Tunisian Crusade
El Cid. *See* Rodrigo Diaz
Eleanor of Aquitaine, 106, 108, 276, 278, 280, 307, 374, 382, 397, 633
Eleanor of England (daughter of Henry II). *See* Leonor
Eleanor of Provence, 553
Eleazar of Argirò, 706n246
elephants, 498
St Elias, 247
Elias of Bari, archbishop, 183
Elias of Cortona, 505
Elias of Gesualdo, 402
Elias of Troia, bishop, 382-383
Elisabeth of Bavaria, 524, 528, 605
Elizabeth of Blois, 724n444
Elizabeth of Champagne, 246
Elizabeth of England. *See* Isabella
elopements, 261. *See also* fuitina.

Elvira of Castile, 116, 192, 197-199 passim, 203, 209-211, 217-218, 221-222, 262, 277, 476, 588, 592
Elvira of Lecce, 399, 418
Elymians. *See* Segesta
Emeric (Imre) of Hungary, 421
emir *defined*, xv, 39, 85, 177
emirs (and emirates), Muslim, 30, 84, 85, 87, 143, 144, 145, 149, 153, 158, 163, 164, 170, 202, 243, 249, 370, 518, 574. *See also* Hassan al-Kalbi, *et al*
Emma Hauteville, 205-206, 288, 589
Emma of Lecce, 297
endotaph, 617, 635
England, xviii, 93, 206, 210, 211, 215, 285, 360, 358, 374, 382, 400, 430, 521. *See also* Canterbury, London, *etc*
Enna. *See* Kasr'Janni
ensoulment, 110
Entella, 446
environmentalism, 426, 467
Enzio (Enzo) of Sardinia, 432, 506, 508, 531, 539
Epicharmus of Kos, 485
epidemics, 78, 104, 321, 364, 401, 422, 454
Epirus, 419, 428, 511, 548
epistemology, 4, 7
Eremburga of Mortain, 164, 166, 171, 172, 590
Eribert of Buonalbergo, 191
Erice (Eryx), 52, 74, 101, 164, 249, 548
Ernoul Chronicle, 725n446, 749n761
Erveo of Tropea, bishop, 730n510
esquire rank, 99, 100, 105, 125, 145, 181, 315, 357, 422, 494, 519
ethnicity (ethnic identity), modern, xvi, xxi, 3, 11, 12, 13-18, 91, 572-574
ethnogenesis, xvi, 3, 14, 21, 81, 89, 91-92, 462, 532, 567, 573, 578, 661
Mt Etna, 52, 72, 352, 474, 552
Etruscans, 20
eucabam, 484

Eucharist, 131, 133, 163, 426, 525
Euclid, 82
Eugene III, Pope, 274, 280
Eugene IV, Pope, 718n376
Eugene of Palermo, amiratus, 408
eunuchs, 109, 242, 247, 253-254, 299
St Euphemia abbey (Calabria), 163
Euphemius (general), 84
Eurocentrism, 6, 27
European, concept of, 89, 680n15
Eustathios Palatinos, 122
Exaugustus Boiannes, 121
Excalibur, 248, 399
excommunication, 131, 162, 163, 168, 186, 206, 207, 222, 227, 291, 359, 454, 501, 505, 524, 525, 549
Exultet (Exsultet) rolls, 246, 648
eye color, 26, 77
Faenza, 507
fairs, 116, 257-258. *See also* souks
fairy tales, 432
Falco of Benevento, 32, 217, 237, 282, 656
falconry, 716n363, 763n963
familiare *defined*, 39, 242
familiares (counsellors), 240, 264, 305, 306, 309, 312, 346, 447
fard kifayah *defined*, 762n949
Faro, Cape, 145
Fascism, 19, 660
fastùka, 481
Fatimids, xv, 40, 85, 87, 104, 134, 157, 165, 174, 189, 204, 215, 244, 254, 270, 295, 354
fava beans, 484-486
Favara palace, 56, 153, 188, 306
Fazello, Thomas, xiii, 13, 17, 30, 34, 35, 788
feasts and festivals, 72, 116, 187, 298, 363, 399, 482, 493-494, 499, 561. *See also* sagra
Felicia Hauteville, 279, 590
feminine estates, 287-288, 666, 768n1027
feminism, 27, 29-31
fennel, 484-488 passim

INDEX

Ferentino, 274, 449
Ferrante I of Naples, 569
Ferraris Chronicle, 6, 32, 44, 94, 657
feudalism, xiv, 5, 82, 96-102 passim, 111-113, 115, 122-123, 125, 140, 157-159, 163, 170, 180, 181, 190, 207, 236, 242, 255, 261, 312, 455. *See also* manorialism
feudal system *defined,* 39, 78, 82, 98
Fibonacci (Leonardo Pisano Bigollo), 245, 450
Fiera Vecchia, 258
Fifth Crusade, 424, 426, 443-444
figs, 475, 491
filioque (in creed), 131, 173
San Filippo di Fragalà, 158, 180
Fiore abbey, 423, 745n713
First Barons' War, 424
First Crusade, 131, 172-174, 189, 191, 206
fitra, 718n374
Flandina Hauteville, 590, 591
flax, 467
fleur-de-lis (heraldry), 213
Florence, 240, 549
Florio of Camerota, 382-383, 411-412
flute, 434
Focerò, 177
Foggia: Battle of, 544
folk tales, 432, 552
follaris (follis) coin, 40, 244, 263, 406
Fontevrault, 34, 745n713
food. *See* cuisine, rice, *etc*
forests (woods), 76, 98, 101, 257, 332, 467, 520
forgeries (of charters), 32, 238, 312, 660, 692n109
fork, 492
Fortore River, 95, 124, 126
fortress *defined,* 102. *See* castles
Fourth Crusade, 132, 418, 419-420, 548
foxes, 655
Fragneto, 169, 227
France, 13, 81, 91, 107, 189, 213, 215, 262, 273, 278, 318, 365, 402, 424, 457, 494, 522, 541. *See also* Aquitaine, Burgundy, Capetians, Normandy, *etc*
Francesco II, 485, 666
Francis of Assisi, 425-428
Franciscan order, 246, 426, 428, 453, 506, 512, 544
Frangipani family, 199, 503, 555
Frankish feudal law, 36, 93, 100, 190
Franks (of France), 79, 89, 91, 95
Franks (Catholic Europeans), 174, 401, 419
Frazzanò, 135, 180
Frederican Canon, 436-440
Frederick I Barbarossa, Emperor, xiv, 280, 288-293 passim, 312, 365, 385, 393, 397, 584
Frederick II: 422-537 passim, 582, 584; defamation of, 781n1210; legislation, 445, 462-467; minority, 408, 410-419 passim, 421; poetry of, 436; quoted incorrectly, 682n24
Frederick II of Austria, 503
Frederick III of Sicily, 582, 711n306
Frederick of Antioch, 504, 539, 543
Frederick of Castile, 554, 555
Frederick Lancia, 544, 545, 548
Fressenda, 583, 690n85
fritella (fritedda), 11, 484
Fucino (lake), 452
fuitina, 261
Fulda, 504
funerary practices, 388, 666
al-Furat, Asad, 84
furusiyya, 187
Gabés, 198, 204, 222, 271, 272, 276
Gaeta, 127, 199, 352, 354, 423, 425, 457-458, 499-500, 666
Gaiseric (Genseric), 76, 77
Gaitelgrima (wife of Atenulf I), 29
Galera Antica, 141
Gallican rite, 131, 246
Gallo-Italic, 684n42
Galluccio, 228, 457
Galvano Lancia, 545

gaming (gambling), 314, 335
García Ramírez of Navarre, 588
Mt Gargano, 94, 124, 364
Gargano tradition (Normans in Italy), 688n71
Garigliano, 85, 128
Garufi, Carlo Alberto, 7
gastald (title), 39, 99, 432
Gattola, Erasmo, 759n908
gebbia, 666
Gelasius II, Pope, 199
gender identity, 107, 109-110, 253
genealogy (family history), 105, 572
genetics (DNA), 21, 25-26, 44, 53, 88, 651
Genghis Khan, 410, 775n1123
San Gennaro. *See* St Januarius
Genoa, 165, 198, 293, 362
Genoans, 171, 218, 221, 224, 275, 391, 497
Genoard park, 56-57, 304, 306, 343, 384
Genseric (Gaiseric), 76, 77
Gens Siculorum, 262
Gentile Tuscus, bishop, 293, 309, 310, 333-336, 341, 352, 361
Geoffrey of Ely, 383
Geoffrey Hauteville, 140
Geoffrey Malaterra. *See* Godfrey Malaterra
Geoffrey of Monmouth, 286, 717n366
Geoffrey of Perche, 586, 735n569
Geoffrey Ridel, 144
Geoffroy of Beaulieu, 683n31
geography (topography), 72-73, 85, 95, 101
St George, 220, 552, 559, 667
George of Antioch, 134, 215, 271, 273-276 passim, 280
George Maniakes, 38, 119-122 passim, 128, 150
Gerace (Calabria), 146
Gerald of Wales, 746n723
Gerard of Amalfi (Martigues), 189
Gerard of Cremona, 479

Gerard of Buonalbergo, 708n256
Gerard of Lorraine, 125, 126
Gerhard of Bremen, archbishop, 501
Gerhard of Malberg, 515
Gerland of Besançon, bishop, 560
German Crusade, 418
Germans: 5, 125, 270, 275, 393; *defined*, 40; elector princes, 410, 411, 424, 527, 754n827
Germany, 48, 53, 54, 60 91, 118, 165, 186, 206, 221, 403, 409, 422, 443, 501, 532. *See also* Holy Roman Empire, Swabia, *etc*
Gertrude of Austria, 525
Gertrude of Sulzbach, 269-270
Gervase of Tilbury, 552, 653, 717n366
Gesta Francorum, 699n187
Gesta Innocenti III, 755n837
Getica, 76, 77
Ghibellines: 240, 435, 509, 514, 523, 553, 555; *defined*, 227; in historiography, 659
ghironda, 434
Giacomo of Lentini, 18, 432, 637
Giglio, Battle of, 508, 510, 513
Gilbert Becket, 356
Gilbert Drengot, 95
Gilbert (Perche) of Gravina, 297, 300, 303, 310-312, 324, 329-333, 347
Giles of Anagni, 403
Giles of Evreux, bishop, 383
St Gilles (town), 64, 383
Giovinazzo, 291
giraffes, 498
Girgentan goat, 86, 477
Girgenti. *See* Agrigento
Girifalco, 452
Gisulf II of Salerno, 162, 171, 607
Global Siculo-Neapolitan, 577-578
Gloucester, 227
gluten intolerance, 252
gnocchi, 490
goats, 86, 98, 474, 477, 562
Göbekli Tepe, 274
Godfrey of Bouillon, 173-174

INDEX

Godfrey Busardo, 469
Godfrey of Cosenza, 657
Godfrey Hauteville, 172, 700n198, 704n232
Godfrey Malaterra, 10, 32, 147, 161, 185, 435, 479, 654
Godfrey Martorano, 761n935
gold, 92, 163, 212, 244, 271, 343-344, 352, 384, 399, 468
Golden Chain, knights of, 17, 248, 286
Golden Horde, 508, 522, 525
Golden Legend, 552
Göring, Hermann, 773n1089
Gothic movements. *See* architecture
Gothic War, 77-78
Goths. *See also* Ostrogoths, Visigoths
government, 113, 130, 140, 170, 210, 239-243, 264, 304, 346, 448, 517
Gozo. *See* Malta
Granada, 656, 686n53. *See also* Alhambra
Gran Sasso Mountains, 72
grapes, 101, 374, 431, 479. *See also* Nero d'Avola, *etc*
Gravina, 221, 297
Gravina, Concordat of, 408, 755n845
Greco wine, 486
Greeks, ancient, xiv, 13, 14, 71-72, 75, 77
Greeks, medieval. *See* Byzantine Greeks
Gregory I, Pope, 78, 79
Gregory II, Pope, 79
Gregory VII, Pope, 134, 162, 164
Gregory IX, Pope, 110, 453, 457, 461, 464, 498, 511, 513, 524, 562. *See also* Decretals
Gregory X, Pope, 710n287
Gregory of Nazianzus, 257
Gregory of Nissa, 215
Gregory the Theologian, 215
greyhound, 73
grey tabby, 73
Gromoald Alferanites, 192, 200, 202, 207-208, 219, 220

Grosseto, 521, 528, 767n1009
Grottaferrata, 134, 373, 516
Guaimar III of Salerno, 93-95 passim, 118, 607
Guaimar IV of Salerno, 119, 121-122, 141, 170, 607
Guaranca, 192
Guarino (Warren), counsellor, 211, 221-223 passim
Guelphs (Guelfs), 227, 240, 424, 452, 518, 529, 553
Guibert of Ravenna, bishop, 168
Guida of Sorrento, 122
guilds, 105, 241, 246, 667
Guiscard. *See* Robert
guitar, 460
Guitier of Rethel, 280, 594
Guittone of Arezzo, 434
Guy of Sorrento, 122
gynecology, 111, 250. *See also* obstetrics

hadiths, 83, 110, 426, 695n148
Hafsid dynasty, 458, 463, 468, 506, 507, 550, 563
hairstyles, 108
Halakah law, 83
halal observance, 86, 474, 493
Halkah district (Palermo), 56, 155, 156, 177, 187
Halykos. *See* Platani
ibn Hamdis, Abd al Gabbar ibn Muhammad (poet), 155, 198, 654
Hamelin of Warenne, 383
Hammadids, 198, 271, 279
hammams, 86, 686n53
ibn Hammud (emir), 171
ibn Hammud ibn al-Hajar, Abul Kasim, 249
Hammudi family (Palermo), 242, 249
Hanafi (Sunni) Islam, 85
haplogroups, 21, 25-26, 53, 652, 681n17
Harald Hardrada Sigurdsson, 81, 120, 150
hare (and rabbit), 98, 474, 475, 483, 494

845

harems, 107, 192, 252-254, 301, 303, 524
harp, 434, 493, 495
al-Hasan ibn Ali, Abul-Hasan, 204, 270, 271
Hasan as-Samsam al-Dawla, 143, 144
Haskins, Charles, vii, 5, 8, 35
Hassan al-Kalbi, 87
Hauteville dynasty, 17, 28, 44, 88, 101, 118-119. *See also* Roger I, Roger II, *et al*
ibn al-Hawas (emir), 148-150
Hawisa of Echauffour, 589
hawking. *See* falconry
ibn Hawqal, Abdullah (emir), 610
ibn Hawqal, Muhammad (traveler), 87, 387, 390, 654
Hector of Montefusculo, 499
Hegel, Friedrich, 10, 573
Helena Angelina of Epirus, 548, 602
hemp, 467
henna, 108, 507
Henry I of Cyprus, 497, 776n1149
Henry I of England, 183, 187
Henry II of England, 294, 316, 340, 353, 354, 356, 366, 381-383
Henry II, Emperor, 117
Henry III of England, 449, 494, 501, 507, 521, 525
Henry III, Emperor, 124, 139
Henry IV, Emperor, 162, 163-165 passim, 168, 172, 175, 183, 510
Henry V, Emperor, 183, 186, 199, 202, 206, 223
Henry VI, Emperor, King of Sicily, 248, 395, 403, 407, 417, 422, 584
Henry X "the Proud" of Bavaria, 223-227 passim
Henry Aristippo, deacon, 280, 300-301, 303-304
Henry of Burgundy, 593
Henry of Castile, 555
Henry of England, the Young King, 359, 383
Henry Hauteville (Prince of Capua), 363, 364-365
Henry of Kalden, 397, 751n780
Henry the Lion (of Saxony and Bavaria), 260, 270, 278, 397, 422
Henry of Malta, 423, 444, 451
Henry of Montescaglioso. *See* Rodrigo of Navarre
Henry of Mount Sant'Angelo, 170
Henry Raspe IV of Thuringia, 527-528
Henry of Sicily (son of Constance of Aragon), 423-425, 446, 451, 452, 470, 498, 500-501, 515
Henry del Vasto (brother of Adelaide), 179, 188, 591
Henry the Younger of Sicily (son of Isabella of England), 504, 530, 539, 540, 542
heraldry (coats of arms), xii, 213, 258-260, 265-266, 554
Hercules, Temple of, 178, 181
Herman of Salza, 423, 444, 453, 454, 463, 503
herring (sardines), 485, 489
Hervé the Florid, 343
heteronormativity, 109-110
hierocracy, 115, 462, 508-511, 533
high notary (protonotaro), 241, 264, 306, 334, 354
Hildegard of Bingen, 109, 274
Himera (Hymera), 324
Hindu-Arabic numerals, xv, 87, 450, 573
Hippo Regius, 76, 131, 280
Historia Bizantina, 656
historicism, 2, 10, 651, 660
historiography, 27, 45, 536, 651-663
Hohenems Castle, 408
Hohenstaufen dynasty, 37, 206, 216, 255, 278, 390, 409, 584. *See also* Frederick I, Frederick II, Manfred, *et al*
holy days. *See* feasts
Holy Land. *See* Jerusalem, Palestine
Holy Roman Empire, 5, 40, 79, 139, 163, 165, 221, 270, 296, 390, 422, 447, 522, 532. *See also* Germany

Holy Savior Convent (Patti), 192, 193
homosexuality, 109
Honorius II, Pope, 206, 209
Honorius III, Pope, 417, 425, 443, 551
honor killing, 467
horse breeds, 100, 120
Hospitallers (knights), 102, 189, 190, 209, 392, 457, 557
Howden (Hoveden), Roger of, 248, 399, 633, 653
Hrolf (Rollo), 92
Hugh II of Burgundy, 278, 593
Hugh III of Burgundy, 424
Hugh III of Cyprus, 115
Hugh (Lupino) of Catanzaro, 741n649
Hugh Falcandus, 10, 13, 30, 72, 80, 107, 135, 254, 281, 289, 306, 309, 347, 389
Hugh Fer, 761n938
Hugh of Palermo, archbishop, 292, 293
Huillard-Bréholles, Jean Louis, 34, 776n1140
Humbert of Silva Candida, 124, 131, 140
Humphrey (Onofrio) Hauteville, 119, 122, 124-126 passim, 140
Hundred Horse Chestnut, 552
Hungary (and Hungarians), 54, 61, 278, 421, 443-444
Huns, 75-76
Hymera. *See* Himera
Iato. *See* Jato
Ibadi Islam, 87, 236
Iconoclast Controversy, 82, 129
icons (holy images), 128, 129-130, 138, 214-214, 220, 231, 233, 360, 367, 372-373, 380, 559, 644
identity politics, 571
al Idrisi, Abdullah (Muhammad), geographer, 73, 86, 249-250, 268, 287, 289, 477, 656
Iesi. *See* Jesi.
Ifriqiya, 54, 83, 135, 165, 174, 185, 191, 198, 204-205, 222, 270-272, 276, 281, 294-296, 458, 550, 654. *See also* Tunisia
illegitimacy (bastardy), 99, 103, 107, 113, 396, 412
Imad al-Din Zengi, 274
identity fraud, 679n13
indigo, 507
individual, concept of, 283
infanticide, 111
Innocent II, Pope, 209, 212, 215, 221, 227, 258, 270, 272
Innocent III, Pope, 410, 411, 421, 425
Innocent IV, Pope, 521, 533, 539, 540, 547
Inquisition, 453, 502, 509, 566
integration, social, 21
interdict, 273, 360, 411, 456, 457, 510
investiture, knightly, 98, 99, 115, 187, 188, 190, 238, 259, 643
Investiture Controversy, 199, 206, 221, 224
Ioaria (Joaria) Tower, 715n352
Ireland, 77, 82, 129, 361, 450, 704n228
Irene Angelina of Constantinople, 408, 419, 420, 598
Iron Arm. *See* William
irrigation. *See* kanats
Iruña. *See* Pamplona
Isaac II Angelus Comnenus, Emperor, 391, 419, 587, 608
Isaac Comnenus of Cyprus, 391
Isabella I of Jerusalem, 448, 455, 601, 776n1149
Isabella of Brienne. *See* Yolanda of Jerusalem
Isabella of England, 494, 501, 502, 504, 507, 513, 603
Isabella of Jerusalem, Queen of Sicily. *See* Yolanda of Jerusalem
Islam, 78, 84, 85, 86, 132, 159, 250, 281, 304. *See also* Muslims
Ismailis, 719n387
Israel, 174, 649, 661
Istanbul. *See* Constantinople

Italianism, 572, 577
Italian language. *See* Tuscan
Italy (modern nation state), xv, 435, 483, 577, 578
itria/itriya (spaghetti), 250, 477, 486, 492
Jacob de Voragine, 552
Jacqueline of Settesoli, 474
Jacques de Vitry, 765n988
Jafar al-Kalbi II, 697n166
Jaffa, 392, 455
Jaffa, Treaty of, 401, 456
St James of Campostela. *See* Camino de Santiago
James of Morra, 447, 452, 457, 499, 503, 504, 516
James of Molino, 503
James of Trani, archbishop, 542
Jamison, Evelyn, vii, 8, 9, 655
Jamsilla Chronicle, 44, 100, 475, 543, 653, 657
Janara, 551
St Januarius (San Gennaro), 72, 550, 560, 570, 664, 665
Jaquinto of Bari, 228
Jato (Iato), 20, 371, 446, 447, 451, 516
Jean de Joinville, 530, 764n971
Jerba. *See* Djerba
Jerusalem: city, 101, 131, 174, 188, 209, 276, 346, 353, 361, 391-392, 401; kingdom, xv, 16, 115, 173, 189, 193, 280, 392, 444, 448-449
Jesi (Iesi), 408, 530, 754n822
Jesus Christ, vi, 19, 130, 138, 176, 210, 214, 231, 233, 373, 374, 380, 427
Jews (and Judaism), xvi, xxi, 21, 82-83, 86, 107, 156, 159, 160, 170, 193, 202, 206, 238, 253, 256, 260, 347, 361-363 passim, 424, 448, 453, 502, 504, 509, 534
jihads, 185, 193, 295
Jiménez dynasty, 116, 192-193, 199, 262, 277, 478, 588, 592, 595. *See also* Elvira of Castile, Margaret of Navarre, *et al*
Joachim of Fiore, 509

Joanna I Anjou of Naples, 11, 31
Joanna of England, 34, 64, 108, 115, 307, 354, 355, 381-384, 386, 388, 389, 397-401 passim, 418
Joaria. *See* Ioaria
Jocelin de Bohun, 359, 633
John II Comnenus, Emperor, 203, 223, 269, 270, 272, 587, 608
John II of Trani, bishop, 131, 141
John III Doukas Vatatzes, Emperor, 523, 779n1173
John of Aiello, bishop, 352, 353
John of Brienne (of Jerusalem), 418, 432, 444, 448, 454, 456-458 passim
John of Calomeno, 337
John Chrysostom, 215
John Cinnamus (Kinnamos), 655, 724n442
John Colonna, 458, 507
John Curopalates, 699n192
John of England, 424, 548
John of Fécamp, 691n102
St John of the Hermits church (Palermo), 130, 183, 232, 246, 326
John Kinnamos. *See* John Cinnamus
St John, Knights of. *See* Hospitallers
John of Lavardin, 333, 342
St John of the Lepers church (Palermo), 156, 183, 189, 697n169
John of Malta, 346
John Mincio, 140, 141
John of Naples, cardinal, 721n405
John of Ocrea, 531
John of Palermo, amiratus, 222
John of Palermo, philosopher, 450
John of Paris, 775n1126
John of Procida, 31, 386, 435, 441, 516, 520, 531, 540, 548, 564, 657
John of Saint Rémy, 564
John of Salisbury, 115, 259, 273, 293
John Skylitzes, 656
Jordan I of Capua, 169, 585
Jordan of Buonalbergo, 191, 192, 197, 200, 207
Jordan Drengot of Capua, diplomat, 132

Jordan Hauteville (son of Roger I), 169, 171-172, 694n129
Jordanes the Goth, 76
Joscelin II of Odessa, 272, 300
Joscelin of Molfetta, 152
jousting grounds, 258
jousts, 259, 374, 510
ibn Jubayr, 86, 87, 249, 252, 253, 389-390, 656
Judaism, 85, 105, 110, 236, 237, 525, 666. *See also* Jews
Judeo-Arabic (Judeo-Siculo-Arabic), xvi, 83, 196, 256
Judeo-Tripolitanian. *See* Judeo-Arabic
judicium dei, 236. *See also* trial by ordeal, *etc*
Judith of Evreux, 106, 146-148 passim, 155, 163, 169, 589
jurats (burgenses), 135, 228, 304, 464, 471, 517, 518, 667
jure uxoris *defined*, 113, 248, 673
jury, trial by, 347, 359
justiciars, 186, 238, 241-243 passim, 264, 286, 305, 309, 317-320 passim, 323, 328, 332, 338, 385, 386, 447, 464, 465, 466, 469, 507
Justinian I, Emperor, 72, 81, 111, 222
Justus (apothecary), 323
Kairouan (Qayrawan), 83, 163, 654
Kala harbor (Palermo), 56, 58-59, 154, 293, 301, 344
Kalamata olive, 44, 257
Kalbids, 81, 85, 87, 104, 120, 143, 158, 163, 166, 170, 183, 184, 198, 654. *See also* Jafar al-Kalbi, Hassan al-Kalbi, *et al*
Kalsa district (Palermo). *See* Khalesa
al-Kamil (Meledin), 444, 452-457 passim
kanats, 56-57, 86, 257, 298, 475, 496
Kantorowicz, Ernst, 37, 659
Kara Aslan, 274
Kasr district (Palermo), 56, 153-156 passim, 177, 187, 342, 344
Kasr'Janni (Enna), 52, 87, 101, 135, 146, 148, 161, 184

Kelheim, 524
Kemonia River, 56-57, 386, 496, 686n53
al-Kenani. *See* bin Jubayr
Kerkennah, 272
Kerkent. *See* Agrigento
Keys, War of (1229), 457-458, 499, 503, 507, 524
ibn Khaldun, Wali al Din (historian), 33, 654
Khalesa district (Palermo), 56, 153, 154, 157, 170, 248, 258, 362, 392
kharruba coin, 244
Khorasan wheat, 257, 478
al Khwarizmi, Abdallah Muhammad, 87
kidnapping, 200, 205, 238, 261, 431, 524, 708n260
kingship (as concept), 39, 76, 97, 115
Kirimbi, 715n352
Kitzinger, Ernst, 712n310
knighthood, 96-101, 135, 186, 187, 238. *See also* investiture
knightly orders. *See* Hospitallers, Templars, Teutonic Order
Knot, Order of the, 562, 568
Koloman. *See* Coloman
Komnenus. *See* Comnenus
Komodo dragon, 573, 712n310, 787n1303
Konstanz (Constance), Treaty of, 280, 290
Kontoleon Tornikios, 95
Koran, xvii, 83, 214, 220, 254, 385
kosher observance, 86, 474, 493
Kuba. *See* Cuba palace
Kurds, 190, 361, 654, 661
Mt Kuz (Cuccio), 298, 345, 652
Kyriaca (Kyriaka) church, 134, 153, 158
Ladislas III of Hungary, 421, 600
Lagopesole, 225
La Guardia, Navarra (now Laguardia, Rioja), 55
La Lumia, Isidoro, 35, 683n33
Lambert of Hersfeld, 700n196

Lancia (Lanza) family, 468, 540, 542, 544, 545, 546, 553, 604
Lando IV of Capua, 80, 175
Landolf of Garderisio, archbishop, 220
Landulf of Graeca, 708n257
lasagna, 485, 490
Lateran Councils: First, 199; Second, 253, 259; Third, 386; Fourth, 424
latifondi, 5
Latin Empire, 419
Latinization: ecclesiastical, 21, 81, 96, 125, 127-128, 132, 134, 140, 141, 146, 166, 201, 559; social, xiv, 23, 80, 88, 96, 176, 429
Latin language, 13, 77, 80, 82, 87, 92, 105, 123, 130, 134
Latins (Catholic Europeans), 132, 181, 255, 336, 433. *See also* Franks
laudo, 484
Lavello, 543
law and legal codes. *See* Assizes, Constitutions, justiciars, *etc*
St Lazarus, Order of, 189, 664
Lecce, 50, 51, 297, 396, 402, 407, 418, 458
legateship. *See* apostolic legateship
lemons, 475, 487, 489
lentils, 474, 490
Leo III, Pope, 95
Leo IX, Pope, 123, 124, 127, 128, 131, 139
Leo Marsicano, 42, 654
León, 61, 192, 205
Leonardo Pisano Bigollo. *See* Fibonacci
Leonine City (Rome), 209, 216
Leonor (Eleanor) of England, 353, 355, 384
Leopold VI of Austria, 451
Leo Tornikios Kontoleon, 95
leprosy, 189, 504, 700n198, 704n232
lesbianism. *See* homosexuality
Lesina, 545
Levanzo, 71
LGBTQ. *See* homosexuality

libbra, 245
Liber Augustalis. *See* Melfi, Constitutions of
Licata, 346, 516
life expectancy, 104, 519
Liguori, Alfonso, 434
Liguria, 486, 514, 684n42. *See also* Genoa
linen, 109, 492
lions, 19, 214, 220, 230, 260, 373
Lisbon, 275
literacy, xv, 82, 87, 104, 255-256, 666
Littera Florentina, 111
liturgical scrolls. *See* exultet rolls
liturgy, 81, 95, 96, 131, 134, 135, 157, 267, 361, 372, 433
Liutprand, 78-79
Llywelyn ap Gruffudd, 14
logothete (chancellor), 530
Loire river, 361, 740n643
Lombard feudal law, 93, 99, 100, 190, 687n64
Lombardic language, 80, 112, 171
Lombard League, 321, 452, 498, 500
Lombards (and Longobards), 78-81, 85, 88, 95, 118-128 passim, 142, 254, 560
Lombardy. *See* Milan, *etc*
London: 85, 356, 382; Council of, 187
longbowmen. *See* archers
Longobardia (southern Italy), 41, 81, 122, 142
lord, manorial, 39, 85, 97, 99, 187
Loritello (Rotello), 289, 332
Lothar of Segni. *See* Innocent III
Lothair III (II), Emperor, 206, 215-228 passim
Louis II of Bavaria, 782n1226
Louis (Ludwig) III of Thuringia, 397
Louis VII of France, 270, 273, 275-282 passim, 307
Louis VIII of France, 449, 452
Louis IX of France (St Louis), 17, 37, 375, 452, 453, 498, 501, 506, 511, 513, 527, 530
Lucania (Basilicata), 79, 81, 141, 203,

220, 469. *See also* Melfi, Venosa, *etc*
Lucera, 252, 447, 448, 451, 452, 497, 499, 503, 506, 516, 518, 555, 574
Lucius II, Pope, 273
Lucius III, Pope, 386, 388, 391
St Lucy, 72, 120, 559
Lucy of Cammarata, 73, 287-288, 557
Ludwig Kelheimer of Bavaria, 524
Lupus Protospatharius, 690n93
Lyon: First Council of, 523; Second Council of, 564
Mabel Hauteville, 589, 607
Macalda of Scaletta, 658, 688n75
maccu, 484
al-Madinah, 84, 155-157
Madonian Mountains, 52, 72, 149, 539, 652
madrasa, 256
Mafia, 663, 683n34, 785n1288
Magdalen chapel (Palermo), 249, 375, 387
magic, 550-552. *See also* mysticism, witchcraft
Magione church, 32, 102, 258, 362, 376, 404, 415, 416
Magna Carta, 346, 424, 471, 548
Magna Graecia (Megale Hellas), 71-72
Mahdia, 87, 135, 163, 171, 198, 204, 271-272, 276, 295, 386
Maifreda of Pirovano, 551
Mainz, 411, 423, 502
Maio of Bari, 273, 280, 284, 289, 291, 292, 295-299 passim, 362
Majorca (Mallorca), xxi, 387, 748n747
majority, age of, 103, 180-183 passim, 187, 322, 363, 421
Makkah. *See* Mecca
Malaga, 37
malaria, 76, 290, 519, 543, 565
Malaterra, Godfrey (Geoffrey), 32, 42, 147, 161, 172, 479, 654
Malgerio. *See* Mauger
malik, title, 177, 198
malikah, title, 177, 188, 220-221
Malik ibn Anas, vii, 673

Maliki law, vii, 83, 85, 110, 159, 205, 236, 239, 685n51
Mallorca. *See* Majorca
Malta (and Gozo), 71, 84, 172, 295, 373, 409, 665
mandolin, 434
Manfred III of Saluzzo, 606
Manfred of Sicily, 16, 100, 248, 432, 529, 540-550 passim, 553-555, 563
Manfredonia, 550
Maniace monastery, 365-366, 370, 371, 374, 388
Maniakes. *See* George
Maniero of Manopello, 417
manorialism, 39, 78, 82, 93, 97-102 passim, 104, 106, 123, 170, 254, 565. *See also* feudalism
Abu Ali Mansur, caliph, 189
Manuel I Comnenus, Emperor, 272, 272-279 passim, 288, 290-292, 313, 353, 361, 587
Manzikert, Battle of, 165
Marco Polo, 250
maremmano (sheepdog), 73
Margam bin Sebir, 689n75
Margana Castle, 102
Margaret of l'Aigle, 698n186
St Margaret of Antioch, 559
Margaret of Austria, 451
Margaret of Navarre, Queen of Sicily, 27, 262, 277-281 passim, 287-288, 297-381 passim, 387-389, 407, 468, 588, 595, 632-634
Margaret of Poli, 504
Margaritus of Brindisi, 391, 392, 398, 407-409
margherito wheat, 257, 478
Maria of Montferrat, Queen of Jerusalem, 448
Maria Porphyrogenita, 313, 363-364, 388, 393, 587
Maria Sophia of Bavaria, Queen of the Two Sicilies, 634
St María la Real (Nájera), 700n195
St Maria delle Scale, 332, 350
Marino II of Gaeta, 127

Marino Filangieri, archbishop, 515
marionettes, 29, 570
mark (coin), 404, 501
St Mark of the Venetians (Bari), 151
markets. *See* fairs, souks
markhor, 86, 477
Markward of Anweiler, 411, 417, 446
marriages (betrothals), 103, 115, 167, 260-261, 382
Marsia, 293
Marsican bear, 73, 98
St Martin, 298, 561
Martin IV, Pope, 564, 565
Caïd Martin, 254, 304, 305, 354
Martirano, 515
Martorana church, 70, 128, 130, 134, 137, 138, 212, 233, 273
Marx, Karl, 787n1305
Mary (Mother of God). *See* Theotokos
St Mary of the Germans (Messina), 756n851
St Mary of the Latins (Palermo), 362, 742n674
Mary Magdalene. *See* Magdalen
mastiff, 73
Mategriffon castle, 399, 400, 689n75
Matera, 71, 208
Matilda (Maud) of England, Empress, 183, 202, 260, 270, 280
Matilda of England, 353, 397
Matilda Hauteville, eldest daughter of Roger I (wed Raymond IV of Toulouse), 166
Matilda Hauteville, daughter of Roger I (wed Ranulf of Alife), 217-219, 585
Matilda of Tuscany, 168, 221, 768n1027
mattanza, 88, 478
Matthew of Aiello, 292, 298, 303, 305, 306-314 passim, 317, 322-324, 331, 333, 334, 336, 341, 342, 346
Matthew Bonello, 116, 297-303 passim
Matthew Paris, 494, 507, 531, 657

Matthew of Salerno. *See* Matthew of Aiello
Mauger (Malgerio) Hauteville, 166, 590
Maximilla Hauteville, 170, 181, 590, 591
Mazara, 84, 153, 162, 163, 204, 205
val di Mazara, 184, 564
al-Maziri, Muḥammad, 205
mazzeratura, 117
meatballs, 480
Mecca, 78, 656
Meda (San Vittore) convent, 753n816
medicine, 111, 171, 250-252, 479, 519-520, 551. *See also* gynecology, Trota, *etc*
Mediterraneocentricism, 6
Megale Hellas. *See* Magna Graecia
Meinhard of Gorizia, 605
Meledin. *See* al-Kamil
Melfi, 121-125, 141, 208, 462, 493, 497, 531
Melfi, Constitutions of, 462-468, 472, 523
Melfi, Treaty of, 141
Melisende of Jerusalem, 733n550, 745n713
Melus (Melo), 94, 95, 117, 125
Melusina (Melusine), 108, 374, 552
menarche, 748n743
menopause, 720n402
mercatino, 258
mermaids. *See* Melusina
mermen, 552
Merovingians, 91
Messina: 143, 153, 166, 181, 184, 203, 254, 314, 326, 335-337, 397, 402, 422, 499, 545; Assizes of, 445; Battle of (1061), 144-145; earthquake (1184), 352
Mezzogiorno, 536, 787n1312
St Michael, 94, 304, 364, 559, 569
St Michael chapel (Altofonte), 304, 374
Michael I Cerularius, Patriarch, 131
Michael II, Emperor, 84

Michael II Comenus Doukas, 548
Michael II, Patriarch, 272
Michael IV the Paphlagonian, Emperor, 119, 121
Michael VII, Emperor, 162, 165
Michael VIII of Nicaea, 548, 552
Michael Dokeianos, 121
Michael Scot, 450, 451
microhistory, 36
Middle Sicilian. *See* Sicilian language
midwifery, 111, 520, 556
Mignano, 228
Mikalis (sword), xii, 17, 248
mikvehs, 56, 62, 83, 206, 496
Milan: 216, 391, 503-504, 519, 527, 551; Edict of, 130
Milazzo, 177, 332
Mileto, 50-51, 102, 123, 143, 146, 179, 657
minstrels, 260, 429, 493
Minturno, 85
mirror for princes, 115
Misilmeri, 150
Mistretta, 302
Mohammad. *See* Muhammad
Monarchia Sicula. *See* apostolic legateship
monarchy (as concept), 14, 112-116
Monastir, 205
monasteries. *See* abbeys
monasticism, 133, 428, 509, 566. *See also* abbeys, Benedictines, Dominicans, *etc*
moneylending. *See* usury
monks. *See* abbeys, monasticism
Mongolia, 775n1123
Mongols, 410, 508. *See also* Golden Horde
Monreale abbey, 66-69, 84, 367, 369-380
Monte Ilaro, 691n103
Montemaggiore, Battle of, 121
Montepeloso, Battle of, 121
Monte San Giuliano. *See* Erice
Montferrat, 448
Moor's Head. *See* Saracen's Head

Moors (in Iberia), 193, 481
Morabit. *See* ibn Abbad
Morris, Colin, 3, 726n468
Morso, Salvadore, 7, 685n50
mortality, infant, 103
mosaics, 65, 68, 70, 128, 130, 138, 210, 213, 214, 231, 233, 367, 372-373, 380, 559
Moscencervello, Corrado. *See* Conrad Lutzelinhart
mosques, xvi-xvii, 85, 90, 153, 157, 387, 390
Mount Cassino. *See* Cassino
Mount Sant'Angelo, 51, 94, 261, 382, 421
Mount Saint Julian. *See* Erice
Mozarabic Rite, 131, 700n195
Mudéjar architecture, 686n53
Muhammad, Prophet, 78, 656
multiculturalism (diversity), 155, 184, 283, 532
multiple sclerosis, 26
Mumelter, Maria, 661
Abd al-Mumin, 295
muqarnas, 90, 214, 306, 349, 372, 377, 387, 733n544
Muriella, 690n85, 583
muscat grape. *See* Zibibbo
mushrooms, 485, 490
music, 434, 576, 643-644, 830
Muslims, xiv, 83, 85-89, 145, 156, 159, 171, 242, 249, 256, 260, 284, 322, 446-448. *See also* Ibadi, Lucera, mosques, Shia, Sunni, *etc*
Mussomeli, 288
al-Mustansir, Muhammad, 550, 555, 563
Myra, 171, 183, 248, 560
mysticism, 99, 550-552. *See also* magic, witchcraft
Naples, 51, 72, 84, 127, 175, 211, 225, 227, 384, 407, 420, 426, 446, 460, 499, 503, 516, 541, 542, 555. *See also* Charles I, St Januarius, Joanna I, Sergio I, Studium, *et al*
Naples, Kingdom of (post-1282), 40,

432, 665
Naples, University of. *See* Studium
Napoletanità, 12, 567, 674
Nasrid architecture, 686n53
nationhood (and nation-building), 14, 262
natural law, 109, 470, 769n1039, 780n1181
Navarre (Navarra), 55, 61, 193, 210, 314, 362. *See also* Pamplona, Tudela, *etc*
Neapolitan language, 15, 24, 26, 80, 112, 135, 431-434, 483
Neapolitan Nation, 16, 665
Nebrodian fir, 73, 214, 375
Nebrodian Mountains, 52, 120, 146, 177, 192, 201, 479
Neilos. *See* Nilos
neolithic sites, 71
Nerello Mascalese, 479
Nero d'Avola, 479
Neustria, 92
Nicaea: 523, 541, 548; Council of, 156
Nicastro (Neocastro), 657
Nicea. *See* Nicaea
Nicetas Choniates, 653, 656
St Nicholas (of Myra), 171, 183
Nicholas II, Pope, 140, 141, 145, 148
Nicholas III, Pope, 23
Nicholas of Aiello, 386, 401, 402, 425
Nicholas of Aversa, 251
Nicholas of Brindisi, 531, 657
Nicholas of Cicala, 457
Nicholas the Fish. *See* Colapesce
Nicholas of Rocca, 657
Nicodemus of Palermo, 35, 134-135, 153-154, 156, 158
Nicosia (Sicily), 147, 187
Nicotera, 162, 169
Nietzsche, Friedrich, 45
Nijmegen, Diet of, 117
Nikephoros III, Emperor, 165, 167
Nikephoros Dokeianos, 121
Niketas Stethatos, 692n111
Nilo of Rossano, 134
Nilos Doxopatrios, 132, 134, 234, 246, 273, 280
Nina of Messina, 256, 433
St Ninfa, 17, 560
nobility. *See* baronage
Nocera, 220, 454, 455
Nola, 541
Norman-Arab architecture. *See* architecture
Normandy, 92, 93, 102, 115, 122, 124, 146, 155, 220, 235, 262, 280, 360, 383
Norman French language, 18, 31, 41, 80, 93, 135, 142, 155, 177, 182, 256, 308, 393, 431, 480
Normanitas, 93, 262, 376
Normanization, 235-239. *See also* Latinization
Norman Palace (Palermo), 102, 373, 476, 548, 715n352
Normans. *See* Normandy
Norsemen (Vikings), xv, 48, 80-81, 92, 93, 144
Norwich (Cooper), John Julius, 7, 12, 35
notaries, 31, 292, 303, 317, 318, 323, 337, 432, 637, 656, 657. *See also* high notary
Noto, 52, 164, 169, 171, 314
val di Noto, 52, 184
Novellae laws, 464, 470, 521, 767n1009
Novgorod, 132
nunneries. *See* convents
nursing, 189
Nusco, 200
Obadiah of Bertinoro, 363
Oberto Fallamonaca, 507, 516
obstetrics, 111. *See also* gynecology
Occitan language group, 92, 384
Ockham, William of, 36
octopus, 489
Oderisio of Sangro, abbot, 207
Odo II of Burgundy, 593
Odo of Bayeux, 174, 187
Odo of Deuil, 723n436
Odo Quarrel, 315-316, 332-338 passim

Odoacer, 77
Oenotrians, 71
Ofanto river, 95, 121
St Oliva, 17, 247, 560
olives (and olive oil), 44, 257, 425, 474, 477, 486
Olympia (Helena) Hauteville, 162, 167
oncia (onza), 245, 642
onions, 477-479, 487
Onofrio Hauteville. *See* Humphrey
oranges, 86, 431, 475
orb, 643-649 passim
ordeal, trial by, 159, 236, 360, 468
Orderic Vitalis, 31, 653
Oreto river, 56, 149, 153, 154, 215, 375
organistrum, 434
Oria, 169, 546
Orthodox church, xv, 41, 70, 127-138, 140, 145, 164, 173, 181, 215, 283, 424, 561
Osmond Drengot, 95, 118
Osterio Magno (Cefalù), 220
Ostrogoths, xv, 77-78, 560
Otranto, 152, 153, 167, 169, 189, 207, 453, 546
Ottaviano degli Ubaldini, 491, 529, 544
Otto II, Emperor, 687n68
Otto III of Germany, 94
Otto (Welf) of Brunswick, 422
Otto of Freising, 276
Ottokar II of Bohemia, 773n1091
paella, 480
Paestum, 557, 573
Paglia, Camille, 662
Paine, Thomas, 658
Palatine Chapel (Palermo), 10, 65, 177, 214, 236, 246, 249, 253, 260, 373, 377, 434, 493
Palermo: 84, 116, 128, 134, 155-157, 161, 171, 184, 198, 211, 225, 278, 281, 302, 314, 322, 332-334, 386, 390, 409, 418, 445, 481; Battle of, 150, 153-154; origin of, 40, 72. *See also* Norman Palace, Khalesa, *etc*
Palestine, 102, 173, 189, 275, 366, 399, 418, 454-457. *See also* Jerusalem
palio, 570
palmento, 101
Pamplona, 193, 278, 332, 396
pancakes, 491
St Pancras church (Palermo), 56, 156
pandemics. *See* epidemics
Pandulf IV of Capua, 36, 117-118, 121
Pandulf of Fassanella, 506
panella, 481
Panormus. *See* Palermo
Pantelleria, 52, 84, 205, 270, 295, 458, 479, 697n171
Pantocrator, 214, 220, 231, 373, 380, 384
papacy (as institution), 79, 85, 88, 95, 131, 141, 184, 199, 279, 293
papal infallibility, 775n1126
papalism. *See* hierocracy
papal monarchy (as concept), 115, 212, 272, 285, 461, 464, 509, 533, 766n1005
Papal State, 51, 78-79, 165, 202, 222, 508, 522, 524
paper making, 194, 573
Papyrus (Papireto) River, 56-57, 298, 302, 476
Paris, 356, 540
parliaments, 321, 346, 445, 471, 519, 711n306
Partenope chronicle, 432, 759n909
Paschal II, Pope, 175-176, 184, 186, 189, 199
Paschal III, antipope, 305
pasta. *See* itria
Patarines, 465, 523
Patti, 16, 192, 193, 493
Paul of Tarsus (St Paul), 71, 313, 559, 568
Paul the Deacon, 79, 653
Pavia, 78, 79, 166, 316
Peace of God, 199

peasants, 98, 103, 107, 158, 246, 255, 304, 385, 463, 466, 467. *See also* commonalty, *etc*
Pelagio of Albano, 458
Pelagio Galvani, 444
Pelayo of Oviedo, 708n263
Mt Pellegrino, 248
penitentials, 109
Pentamerone, 432
Pepin the Short, 91
perciasacchi wheat, 252, 257
perjury, 320, 466, 524, 721n405
Persephone, 474
Perugia, 553
St Peter, apostle, 249, 559
Caïd Peter (Ahmed), 254, 309-312, 320, 331-332, 353
Peter II of Aragon, 412, 420, 600
Peter II of Courtenay, 428
Peter II of Sicily, 582, 720n396
Peter III of Aragon, 549, 564, 565, 582
St Peter of the Bagnara church (Palermo), 156
Peter of Blois, 315, 340, 346, 348, 352, 353, 656
Peter of Caesarea, archbishop, 456
Peter Cantor, 109
Peter the Deacon, 654
Peter of Eboli, 10, 31, 46, 402, 412, 575, 656
Peter Frangipane, 503
Peter of Gaeta, 352
Peter of Ibernia, 550
Peter of Ireland, 450
Peter Lombard, 785n1281
Peter Olivi, 775n1126
Peter of Palermo, archbishop, 211
Peter of Trani, 692n107
Peter of Vico, 553
Peter della Vigna, 432, 445, 463, 501, 503, 505, 515, 521, 530, 533, 538, 657
Peter, notary, 317-318
Petralia, 149
Petronella of Aragon, 588

Petrosinella, 432
Phaedo, 550, 731n518
St Philip monastery. *See* San Filippo
Philip I of France, 174
Philip II of France, 397, 424
Philip III of France, 565
Philip of Aquino, 469
Philip of Mahdia, 254, 280, 281, 289
Philip of Novara, 765n987
Philip of Swabia, 408, 410, 417-419 passim, 421, 584, 598
Philip of Zuncolo, 469
philology, 23, 684n42
Phoenicians, 71-72, 77, 474, 681n17
phylloxera, 479
phylogeography, 25-26, 53, 681n17
physicians, licensing of, 238, 252, 467
Piacenza, Council of, 172
Piazza Armerina, 499, 517, 570
Piedmont, 172, 467, 480, 483, 529
Pierleoni (Pierleone) family, 209, 382, 711n304, 713n327
Pierre de Chatre, archbishop, 270, 721n409
Pignatelli, Bartholomew, archbishop, 554
pilgrimage, 93, 173, 189-190, 246, 314, 360, 362, 400-401, 401, 561, 656
Pipe Rolls (England), 633-634
pipita. *See* ciaramella
piracy, 80, 93-94, 119-120, 144, 163, 222, 271, 314, 391, 447
Pirro/Pirri, Rocco, 658
Pisa and Pisans, 149, 154, 166, 171, 172, 174, 189, 192, 215, 218, 221, 225, 275, 364, 387, 507, 508, 639
Pisan Tower, 232, 300-301, 344, 715n352
pistachios, 477, 481, 770n1050
pizza, 785n1284
Pizzo Carbonara (mountain), 72
Plantagenet dynasty. *See* Henry II, Joanna, *et al*
Plantagenet Empire, 285, 294
Platani (town), 73

Platani (Halykos) river, 73, 287
Plato, x, 257, 474, 550
plenitudo protestatis, 511
poena cullei (mazzeratura), 117
poetry and poets, 88, 106, 108, 144, 280, 429-440, 568. *See also* Sicilian School, qasida, *etc*
Poggiodiana, 480
Poitiers, 270, 383
Poitou, 64, 108
Poland, 64, 521, 532-533
Policraticus, 115
polycentrism, 285
polyculturalism. *See* multiculturalism
polygyny, 157, 253, 260
Poor Clares, 426, 557
popes. *See* papacy, Nicholas II, *et al*
pork, 86, 474, 483, 485, 489
Porta Felice gate, 370
Portugal, 275, 275, 457, 525
positionality, 3
postmodernism, 30, 661
post-traumatic stress (PTSD), 692n106
Potenza, 278, 709n275, 713n327
prawns. *See* shrimp
precipitation. *See* rainfall, snowfall
pregnancy. *See* childbirth, obstetrics
priests. *See* clergy
Primate of Sicily, 113, 282, 293, 296, 314, 316, 351-352
Princes' Crusade, 173
princess (as title), 13, 203, 557
Principate (Principato), 40, 348, 469
Prizzi, 102, 297
Procopius of Caesarea, 737n589
prosopography, 31, 36
protonotaro. *See* high notary
Protospatharius, Lupus, 690n93
Provençal culture, 215, 369, 374, 430, 431
Provence, 553
Ptolemy, 257
PTSD. *See* post-traumatic stress
Puglia. *See* Apulia
Puglian language, 432

Punics. *See* Carthaginians, Phoenicians
Putignano, 482
al-Qahira. *See* Cairo
qasida poems (odes), 144, 429
Qayrawan. *See* Kairouan
Quarrel (town), 688n72
Quarrel, Odo. *See* Odo Quarrel
queenship, 39, 346-348
Quran. *See* Koran
Quaternus Excadeniciarum Capitinate, 245
rabbit. *See* hare
race memory, 12, 14
Rafi ibn Makken al Dahmani, 198, 204
Rainald of Avenella, 288
Rainald of Spoleto, 455
rainfall, 37
rais (title), 88
Ralph Diceto, 743n685
Ralph of Vermandois, 260
Randazzo, 740n639
Ranier of Montferrat, 734n565
Ranieri Capocci, 521, 523
von Ranke, Leopold, 660
Ranulf II of Alife, 200, 207, 216-218, 221, 225, 227, 228, 585
Ranulf I Drengot of Aversa, 118, 585
Ranulf of Glanville, 357, 715n356
Raoul of Fragneto, 227
rape, 106, 119, 145, 238, 252, 261, 301, 464, 621, 626
rapini, 475
Rapunzel, 432
Ravenna: 75, 77, 133, 168, 504; Diet of, 498
Raymond IV of Toulouse, 166, 174
Raymond VI of Toulouse, 418, 596
Raymond VII of Toulouse, 521, 523
Raymond Berenguer II of Barcelona, 607, 701n203
Raymond Berenguer III of Barcelona, 192, 208, 421, 607
rebec, 434
Rebecca Guarna, 252

Rebellamentu, 435
Reconquista, 173, 189-190, 205, 275, 289
redemption tax, 309, 734n554
regalia, 19, 185, 230, 233, 298, 301, 311, 529, 633, 635
Reggio Calabria, 143, 169, 332, 337, 499
Reginald of Bath, bishop, 384, 633
Reginald of Spoleto, 457
De Regno ad Regem Cypri, 115
Regnum Siciliae *defined*, xiv, 4, 40
religions. *See* Catholicism, Islam, Judaism, Orthodox church
Renaissance, xv, 3, 75, 462, 519, 572, 658, 659
Res Publica Christiana, 549
revisionism, historical, 7, 26-27, 571
rex filius, 279, 281, 282, 359
Rhodes, 400
Rhum. *See* Rum
Ribera, 480
rice, 24, 86, 252, 257, 475
rice balls, 480
Richard I Lionheart of England, 248, 373, 397, 399, 404, 422, 430, 596
Richard I of Normandy, 596
Richard II of Capua, 585
Caïd Richard, 254, 314, 325-326, 333-346 passim, 354
Richard of Acerra, 391, 397, 408, 597
Richard of Aigle, 316, 356
Richard of Avella, 545
Richard of Aversa, 327-329, 335
Richard of Balbano, 737n595
Richard of Canterbury, archbishop, 383
Richard of Caserta, 516, 531
Richard of Cornwall, 507
Richard Filangieri, 454-455
Richard of Mandra/Molise, 112, 311-314 passim, 324, 331-333, 339-341, 346, 347
Richard of Montenegro, 469, 499, 507, 531
Richard Palmer, bishop, 305, 309-318 passim, 346, 348, 353, 354, 355, 383
Richard of Policoro, 771n1060
Richard of Sai (Say), 329, 721n405
ricotta, 468, 478, 485
Rieti, 499, 500, 516
Rignano, Battle of, 226
Riso (Risus), 691n103
Risone of Bari, archbishop, 200
Risorgimento (Italian unification movement), 536, 659, 666
riveli, 104, 111, 435
rivers and streams, 56-57, 73, 390, 467, 496
robbery, 238, 320, 327, 388, 709n272
Robert I of Capua, 186
Robert II of Capua, 132, 207, 208, 291, 585
Robert II of Flanders, 174
Robert of Alife, 191, 192, 585
Robert of Aquino, 469
Robert Avenel, 186
Robert of Bassonville. *See* Robert of Loritello
Robert of Bellisina, 323
Robert of Burgundy, 181
Robert of Calatabiano, 305, 319-322 passim
Robert of Caserta, 326, 327, 383
Robert of Conversano, 205
Robert of Grandmesnil (abbot), 146
Robert Guiscard Hauteville, 112, 122, 125, 140-145 passim, 150, 156, 157, 162, 165-176 passim, 185, 583
Robert of Loritello (Bassonville), 281
Robert of Meulan, 343-344
Robert of Neubourg, 315
Robert of Normandy (brother of William I of England), 589
Robert of Palermo, 531
Robert of Sablé, 398
Robert of Selby, 211, 223, 225, 273-274, 279, 280
Robert of Sicily (romance), 566
Robert of Torigni, 32, 386, 653
Robin Hood, 388, 568
Roccamena, 86

Rocca Vecchia (Tuscania), 772n1081
Rodelgrimo of Aquino, 431
Rodrigo Diaz of Vivar (El Cid), 314
Rodrigo (Henry) of Navarre of Montescaglioso, 107, 112, 314, 324, 588
Roffred of Liri, abbot, 403
Roger I, 34, 140, 146-177 passim, 179, 583. *See also* Judith, Adelaide, Guiscard, Mileto, Palermo, *etc*
Roger II: 171, 175-282 passim, 583; coronation, 211-213; death of, 281-282; knighting of, 188; legacy of, 282-286; symbolism of, 130. *See also* Assizes of Ariano, *etc*
Roger III, 404, 597, 598
Roger of Acerenza, 730n504
Roger of Acerra, 597
Roger de Amicis, 507
Roger of Andria, 384, 396, 397, 408
Roger of Apulia (son of Roger II), 222, 228, 582, 583
Roger of Avellino, 342-344 passim
Roger Borsa, 157, 169-191 passim, 202, 607
Roger of Gerace, 341, 346
Roger Hauteville (son of William I), 302-303
Roger of Howden (Hoveden), 248, 399, 633, 653
Roger of Lauria, 565
Roger of Martorano, 297
Roger of Porcastrello, 515
Roger Sclavo, 303
Roger Sorello, 331
Roger of Tiron, 344
Roger of Torre Maggiore, 775n1123
Roger of Wendover, 765n998
Rogerian Legend, xii, 286, 675, 717n366
Roland, 570
Roland of Siena. *See* Alexander III
Rollo. *See* Hrolf
Roman Empire, 40, 71, 75-77
Romanesque. *See* architecture
Roman law. *See* Justinian
Romani, Peter, 553

Romanos IV, Emperor, 151, 152
Roman villa system and economy, 78, 97, 254
Rome, 71, 79, 82, 104, 126, 169, 199, 206, 216, 221, 273, 290, 420, 422, 502, 509, 540, 553, 562
Rometta, 87, 339
Rometta, Battle of, 87
Romuald I of Salermo, archbishop, 207,
Romuald II of Salerno, archbishop and chronicler, 180, 185, 214, 238, 242, 250, 292, 306, 309, 316, 323, 346, 384, 386
Romulus Augustulus, 77
rosacea, 26
St Rosalie, 45, 247-248
Rosendorn, 108
Rothari, Edict of, 78
Rotrou of Perche, 159, 362, 586
Rotrou of Rouen, bishop, 315, 351, 382, 586
Rouen, 92
royal woman *defined*, 389, 722n424
Rudolf of Benevento, 125
Rudolf Maccabeo of Montescaglioso, 205, 288
Rudolph of Catanzaro, 169
Ruffo, Fulco, 531
Ruffo, Peter, 531, 542, 544, 545
Rufino, 545
Rum Sultanate, 165
Runciman, Steven, 8, 276, 659
ruotolo, 245
russello wheat, 252, 257, 478
Russia (Rus), 61, 81, 92, 132, 210, 268, 476
Saba Malaspina, 550, 657
Mt Sableta (Saglieta), 708n257
Sabtah (Ceuta), 249, 289, 656
sacrality, royal, 114
sacraments, 115, 133, 283, 569, 643, 785n1281
saffron, 479, 480, 484-491 passim
sagra, 481-482. *See also* feasts
Sahara, 88, 163, 268, 271, 468

Saintonge War, 521
Saladin (An-Nasir Salah ad-Din Yusuf ibn Ayyub), 354, 361, 366, 392, 393, 400, 401
Salerno: 78, 78-83 passim, 95, 112, 123, 139, 162, 164, 197, 207, 217, 384, 388, 401, 499, 545; Edict of, 519; medical school, 79, 111, 250-252, 364, 401, 450, 516, 519, 657
Salerno tradition (Normans in Italy), 688n71
Salernus, physician, 323-324
Salian dynasty, 183, 206, 227, 584
Salic Law, 113, 207, 365, 395
Salih Najim al-Din, Al-Malik, 528
Salimbene de Adam, 427, 552, 658
salma, 245, 642
salt mining/extraction, 135, 493
Samnites, 71, 82
Sancho II of Portugal, 525
Sancho VI of Navarre, 332, 355-356, 588
San Damiano, 506
San Filippo of Fragalà, 158, 180
Sanfratellan horse, 100
San Fratello, 171, 740n639
San Gennaro. *See* St Januarius
San Germano, 227, 371, 385, 402, 421, 458, 469, 500, 508, 553, 656. *See also* Cassino
San Germano, Agreement of (1225), 451, 764n966
San Marco d'Alunzio, 101, 146, 155, 171, 177, 178, 180, 183, 303, 335, 366
San Marco Argentano, 200, 201
Sansone of Bari, 469
Sant'Agata de' Goti, 36, 689n83
Sant'Alfio, 552
Santa Maria della Ferraria, 217, 657. *See also* Ferraris Chronicle
Santiago (St James), Order of, 190
Saphadin. *See* al-Adil.
Saqaliba district (Palermo), 56, 362
saqq (cheque), 189
Saracens. *See* Arabs, Berbers, *etc*

Saracen's Head legend, 248
Saragossa. *See* Zaragoza
Sari al Kadi district (Palermo), 56, 156, 258, 302, 476
Sarum Rite, 131
Savona, 171
Savoy, 30, 529, 553
scapece, 485-486, 494
Scarlata, Marina, 9
scarves. *See* veils
Scecedin, 764n971
sceptre, 643, 644, 646
schifatus coin, 212, 244, 293
Schism of 1054, 129, 132, 134, 139, 173
scholasticism, 109, 132, 463, 511, 525, 561
Sciacca, 84, 85, 555
Scibene (Uscibene) palace, 57, 306, 496, 715n352
Scot, Michael. *See* Michael Scot
seals, 194, 260, 293, 317-318, 385, 410, 414
Second Barons' War, 548
Second Crusade, 132, 274-276, 292, 391-393 passim
Second World War, 34, 574, 660
Segesta (Egesta), 74, 573
Seine river, 92
Seljuk Turks, 151, 162, 165, 167, 171-174 passim, 204, 274
semiotics, 36
Serbia (and Serbs), 279
serfdom, 39, 96-99, 157, 158, 163, 164, 170, 180, 237, 238, 242, 254, 255, 385, 466, 565. *See also* manorialism
Sergio I of Naples, 84
Sergio II of Naples, 85
Sergio IV of Naples, 118
Sergio VI of Naples, 162
Sergio VII of Naples, 208
Serlo Hauteville, 149, 161
servitude. *See* slavery
Sessa Arunca, 542
Seventh Crusade, 524, 530, 540, 553

Seville, 192, 686n53
sexuality, 107-110 passim, 253, 322
sexual orientation. *See* heteronormativity
Sfax, 276, 294
sfincia, 478, 561
sfogliatella, 479
ibn Shaddad, Abd al-Aziz (historian), 32, 33, 185, 654
Shakespeare, William, 45, 435
shawm (ciaramella), 434
sheep, 73, 98, 105, 258, 426, 475, 771n1060
Shepherds' Crusade, 541
Shia Islam, 83, 85, 87, 174, 236, 361
shields, 98, 259, 331, 374, 399, 554
Ship, Order of the, 568
shrimp, 474, 489
Sibylla of Acerra, 396, 597
Sibylla of Burgundy, 278, 279, 593
Sicanian Mountains, xxi, 287
Sicanians (Sikanians), 71, 82
Sichelgaita of Salerno, 28, 106, 141, 142, 146, 156-163 passim, 167-171 passim, 179, 250, 252
Sicignano degli Alburni, 101
Sicilian language, 429-441, 637-642
Sicilian Questions, 451
Sicilian School, 44, 106, 108, 429-434
Sicilian Succession, 288
Sicilianistics, xvii, 11, 653
Sicilianità, 12, 658
Sicily. *See* Palermo, *etc*
Sicily, Kingdom of, *defined*, xiv, 4, 40
Sicily, Primate of. *See* Primate
Siculo-Arabic, 702n218
Siculo-Neapolitan, xvii, xxi, 88, 462, 532, 573, 575, 577
Siculo-Tuscan School, 434
Sicut Judaeis, 206
Caïd Siddiq, 322
sieges (generally), 149, 152, 507, 514, 524, 700n197
Sigena, 557, 745
Sigurd I Magnusson, 184, 198
Sikanians. *See* Sicanians

Sikelgaita. *See* Sichelgaita
Sikels, 148, 431
Sila Mountains, 72, 331, 423
silk making, 86, 116, 181, 252, 276, 475
Silos, Missal of, 700n195
Silva Marca, assize of, 715n355
silver, 92, 214, 236, 244, 263, 271, 293, 301, 383, 468, 635
Simon, King of Sicily, 179-182, 187
Simon of Lentini, 435
Simon of Taranto, 241, 277, 290, 297-303 passim
simony, 139, 199, 238, 299
Sinibaldo de' Fieschi. *See* Innocent IV
Siponto, 224, 541, 550
al-Siqilli, Jawhar, 87
Siqilliyyat, 155
Siracusa. *See* Syracuse
Siragusa, Giovanni Battista, 7, 44
sirens. *See* mermaids
sisterhood, 556-558
Sixth Crusade, 455-457, 498
slavery, 99, 149, 253, 254-255, 271, 304
Sleeping Beauty, 432
slut shaming, 322, 721n405
snowfall, 147, 154, 182, 352, 499, 652
sodomy, 109
Solunto, 389, 656
Song of Aspremont. *See* Aspremont
St Sophia basilica, 78, 693n113
Sorello, Roger, 331
souks, 84, 116, 156, 253, 258, 476, 496, 499. *See also* fairs
soups, 484, 488-490 passim
Sousse, 276
sovereignty, 79, 141, 165, 176, 197, 203, 210, 227, 270, 292, 525, 571. *See also* heirocracy, papal monarchy
spaghetti. *See* itria
Sperlinga, 740n639
Speyer, 404, 423
Spinola, Nicholas, 497
Split, 775n1123
Spoleto, 79, 96, 292, 422, 455, 506

springs, 153, 371, 390, 496. *See also* kanats
squid, 474, 489
Squillace, 184, 544, 704n231
squire. *See* esquire
Stamford Bridge, Battle of, 150
standpoint theory, 12
Statutum de Reparatione Castrorum, 776n1137
Staufen, Staufer. *See* Hohenstaufen
Stedinger Crusade, 501
stemperata, 479, 486
St Stephen, 482, 499, 559
Stephen IX, Pope, 140
Stephen of Blois (crusader), 173-174
Stephen of Blois (theologian), 315
Stephen of England, 223, 227, 277, 280
Stephen of Messina, 550
Stephen Pateran, 152
Stephen of Perche, 315, 321-348 passim, 352, 586
Steri (Palermo), 637
Stilo, xvi, 80, 245, 475, 687n68
stirrup, 76, 96-97
Stornara, 451
storks, 73, 475, 487
stratigotus *defined*, 737n581
streams. *See* rivers
Studium (University of Naples), 450, 500, 519, 534, 542, 550
Stupor Mundi. *See* Frederick II
sugar cane, 86, 251, 475
Suger of Saint-Denis, 724n446
suks. *See* souks
Sulmona, 499
Sulwan, 655
Summa Theologiae, 718n376, 769n1039
Summonte, Giovanni, xii, xiii, 569, 571, 573, 658
Sunni Islam, 83, 85, 174, 185, 236, 361, 390
surnames, origin of, 98, 112, 247
Sutri, Donation of, 78
Swabia, 40, 60, 124, 125, 139

swords, xii, 17, 96, 97, 98, 120, 187, 248, 286, 298, 311, 399
Syene (Aswan), 372
synagogues, xxi, 62, 77, 86, 206, 288, 363, 481, 496, 744n703
Syracuse (Siracusa): 29, 71, 76, 77, 84, 120, 131, 169, 310, 470; Assize of, 767n1009; Cathedral, 72; mikveh, 62, 83, 496
tabby cat. *See* grey tabby
Tabula Rogeriana, 250, 268
Tacitus, 76, 98, 113
Taginae, Battle of, 78
Tagliacozzo, Battle of, 555-556
taifas, 143, 145
Takayama, Hiroshi, 705n235
Tamim ibn al-Mu'izz, 162, 191
Tancred of Bari (son of Roger II), 203, 222, 241, 583
Tancred of Bologna, 282n467
Tancred of Conversano, 208, 219, 220
Tancred of Galilee, 173-174, 607
Tancred of Hauteville (dynastic progenitor), 119, 583, 690n85
Tancred of Lecce, King of Sicily, 297, 300-303, 366, 386, 391, 396-404 passim, 407, 408, 583, 597
Taormina, 120, 164, 169, 332, 339-340, 352, 421, 566
Taranto, 122, 129, 140, 169, 172, 174, 189, 200, 209, 241, 289-291 passim, 330, 363, 540, 560
tarì coin, 40, 244, 245, 263, 301, 311, 411, 431
tarot, 551
Tatars (Tartars), 508
taxation. *See* collecta, droit du seigneur, *etc*
Taylor, Charles, 3, 11
Telese, 182, 655
Templars (knights), 102, 136, 189-190, 209, 244, 248, 259, 353, 392, 449, 454-458 passim, 528
temples, ancient, 71, 72, 74, 101, 178, 181, 220, 274, 334, 372, 557, 568,

573
Termini Imerese, 288, 324, 389, 656
Terra di Lavoro, 40, 421, 469, 734n554
Teutonic Order, 102, 132, 189, 248, 258, 409, 416, 418, 423, 425, 427, 449, 452, 457, 530
Thaddeus of Suessa (Sessa), 423, 463, 515, 521, 523, 529
thalassemia, 26
thalassocracies, 168
Thebes, 276
Theobald of Bec, 356
Theobald of Monreale (abbot), 386, 744n708
Theodora I, Empress, 111, 737n589
Theodora of Sai (Say), 721n405
Theodore of Antioch, 450
Theodore Comnenus of Epirus, 428
St Theodore church (Palermo), 56
Theodoric the Great, 77, 91
Theodosius II of Constantinople, 643
Theophanes Kerameus, 134, 201
Theotokos, xvii, 129, 373, 568
Thibauld of Saint-Arnoult, 735n573
Third Crusade, 392, 395, 397, 399-401, 403, 430
Thomas of Acco, 717n364
Thomas Aquinas, 109, 110, 115, 450, 470, 509, 525
Thomas Aquino of Acerra, 445, 453-457 passim, 469, 503, 505
Thomas Becket, 130, 348, 356-360
Thomas Berardi of Celano, 445, 447
Thomas Brown. *See* Thomas le Brun
Thomas le Brun, 211, 273, 284, 289
Thomas of Saluzzo, 606
three estates, 99, 428
al-Thumna (Timnah), Muhammad (emir), 144, 148, 153, 481
al Tijani, Abu Abd Allah (historian), 33, 654
timbale (timballo), 481
timber, 73, 98, 103, 372, 375, 400
ibn Timnah. *See* al-Thumna
Tinnis, 294

tiraz (workshop), 22, 635
tirocinio, 259
de Tocqueville, Alexis Clérel, 470-471
Toledo, 192, 193, 384
tomolo, 245
Torah, xxi
Torriani family, 553
torrone, 479
Tortona, 290
torture, 255, 319, 391, 453, 529
Totila, 78
Toulouse, 166, 174
tournaments, 258-260, 374, 473, 525
Tours, Battle of, 84, 89, 91, 97
Trani, 131, 291, 541
transethnic *defined,* 787n1307
transubstantiation, 525
Trapani, 52, 164, 212, 363, 390, 478, 493
trappeso, 245
treason, 238, 308, 321, 333, 336, 341, 657
trial by combat, 159, 311, 331, 332
trial by jury, 347, 359
trial by ordeal, 159, 236, 360
Trifels Castle, 403, 404, 502
Tripoli (Lebanon), 174, 269, 275
Tripoli (Libya), 271, 272
Trocta. *See* Trota
Troia, 95, 117, 122, 144, 200, 227, 331, 499
Troina, 120, 146-148, 158, 166, 171, 479
Tronto River, 236
troparia, 576, 647-648, 830
Tropea, 146
Trota (Trocta) of Salerno, 250-252, 256, 557. *See also* Trotula
Trotula, 108, 111
troubadours, 107-108, 260, 384, 429, 458, 637
Troyes, Council of, 209
Truce of God, 199, 200
trullo, 103
Tuchman, Barbara, 2, 36, 662
Tudela, 55, 362

tummàla, 481
tumminìa, 252, 257, 478
Tunis, 295, 555, 564
Tunisia, 77, 83, 84, 135, 148, 154, 161, 198, 205, 252, 270, 279, 306, 375, 386, 509. *See also* Ifriqiya
Tunisian Crusade (Eighth Crusade), 564
Turgisio of Troia, 331
Turkey (Asia Minor), 75, 132, 274, 654. *See also* Rum, Seljuk Turks
Turks. *See* Seljuk Turks
Turk's Head (pastry), 481
Tuscan language, 23, 426, 429, 433, 434
Tuscany, 168, 221, 439, 506. *See also* Florence
Tustin of Mazara, bishop, 732n531
twin kingdoms, 23, 462, 568, 665
Two Sicilies, Kingdom of, 485, 536, 565, 577, 634, 659
tryants, Greek, 14
Tyre, 392-393, 653
Ubaldo of Ostia, cardinal, 721n405
unction. *See* anointing, chrism
UNESCO, 15
universities: 37; Bologna, 356, 463; Naples, 450, 500; Salerno, 79, 111, 251. *See also* Studium
Urban II, Pope, 131, 169-176 passim
Urban IV, Pope, 548, 553
urban (civic) society. *See* communes, jurats, *etc*
Urfa. *See* Edessa
Urraca of Castile (daughter of Alfonso VI), 192, 199
Urso of Bari, archbishop, 183
usury, 465
Vaccarizza, Battle of, 95
Val Demone, 52, 184
Vandals, 76-78, 83, 560, 651
Varangian Guard, 95-96, 120-121, 150, 167
vegetarianism, 425-427
veils, 86, 108, 253, 390
veneficium, 551

St Venera, 247
Venetians, 151, 166, 167, 200, 364, 381, 391, 419, 507, 508
Venice: 129, 271, 373; Treaty of, 384
Vendicosi (Avengers), 388, 562
Venosa, 121, 141, 168, 540
Verdura river, 480
vermicelli. *See* itria
Verona, 555
Vespers war (1282), 552, 564
Mt Vesuvius, 72, 227
Via Francigena, 189, 561, 707n252
Via Micaelica, 561
Vicari, 740n639
vice chancellor. *See* chancellor
Victor II, Pope, 139, 140
Victor III, Pope, 171, 694n125
Victor IV, antipopes: Gregory of Ceccano, 227; Octavian di Monticella, 296, 305
Vienna, 19, 503, 659
Vikings. *See* Norsemen
Villani, John (Giovanni), 753n822, 765n990
violets, 491
violin (rebec), 434
Virdimura of Catania, 717n368
Visigoths, 76, 78, 643, 700n195
Vitale of Aversa, 506
Viterbo, 500, 521
Viterbo, Treaty of, 563
Vlore, 548
Waldensians, 453, 523, 549
Waldo, Peter, 779n1172
Wales, 14
Walter III of Brienne, 411, 597
Walter, archbishop, 188
Walter "of the Mill" (archbishop and familiare), 302, 314-316 passim, 346, 352, 354, 361, 363, 370, 376, 393, 396
Walter of Bibbesworth, 688n75
Walter of Manopello, 506
Walter of Moac (Modica), 332
Walter of Palear, 410, 417-423 passim, 443-445

ibn al Wardi (Bernavert), 164, 169, 171
Warren. *See* Guarino
watermelon, 478
weddings. *See* marriages
wedding tax. *See* droit du seigneur
Weinsberg, 270
Welf VI of Bavaria, 270, 278
Welf dynasty, 227, 410, 411, 420, 424
Weltchronic, 773n1096
Wenceslaus of Bohemia, 775n1123
wheat, 163, 204, 205, 257, 340, 425, 463, 478
White Ship, 202
Wilhelmina of Bohemia, 551
William I of England (Duke of Normandy), 149, 174, 187, 396, 589
William I of Sicily, 243, 244, 250, 254, 262, 288-306 passim
William II of Apulia, 185, 186, 191, 197, 202, 207
William II of England, 173, 175
William II of Holland, 528
William II of Sicily, 306, 307, 327, 330, 355, 359-391 passim
William III of Sicily, 407, 753n814
William of Apulia (chronicler), 32, 654, 687n69
William of Blois, 375
William of Burgundy, 699n191
William of Capparone, 418, 420
William the Falconer, 243
William of Gesualdo, 172
William "Iron Arm" Hauteville, 119-122
William of Leluce, 739n626
William Marshal, 259
William of Monreale, archbishop, 388
William of Mortain, 590
William of Pavia, 316
William of Posquiéres, 761n938
William Repostel, 106
William of San Severino, 326, 327, 741n649
William of Spinosa, 469
William of Tyre, 653

Winchester, 64, 382, 633
wine, 86, 101, 147, 245, 469, 474, 477, 479, 486, 504
witchcraft (and witches), 107, 249, 251, 550-551. *See also* Befana, magic
Wittelsbach dynasty, 528, 605, 634, 668
women's movements. *See* feminism
Women's Studies. *See* feminism
woods. *See* forests
World War II. *See* Second World War
Worms, Concordat of, 199
wren pie, 491
xenocentrism, 11, 13
Ximenez. *See* Jiménez
Yaha ibn Abd al-Aziz, 271-272, 297
Yahya ibn Tamim, Abu Ali, 191, 198, 654
Yahya, Abu Zakariya, 458, 506, 550
Yewdale, Ralph, 661
Yolanda of Flanders, 428
Yolanda (Isabella) of Jerusalem, 448-449, 451-455 passim, 601
York, 359, 495
ibn Zafar al Siqilli, 87, 214, 242, 655
Zaida (Isabel) of Seville, 192
zampogna (bagpipes), 434
Zaragoza, 193, 362
Zawila, 295
Zengid dynasty, 274, 276
Zhao Rukuo, 762n947
Zhu Fan Zhi, 762n947
Zibibbo grape, 479
Zirid dynasty, 148-157 passim, 161-165, 171, 172, 174, 180, 191, 204, 205, 270-275, 279
Zisa palace, 102, 305-306, 349, 384, 386, 396, 493
Ziyadat Allah I, 84
Zoë Porphyrogenita, 121

KINGDOM OF SICILY

Frederick II and Isabella of England
in the chronicle of Matthew Paris

Completed in September 2021, this book was first printed in its softcover edition in Italy and in the United States of America in March 2023 with the text in Garamond.

Royal crown as depicted in the chronicle of Peter of Eboli

www.ingramcontent.com/pod-product-compliance
Lightning Source LLC
Chambersburg PA
CBHW022006120526
44592CB00032B/95